D0899094

Dictionary for Library and Information Science

Dictionary for Library and Information Science

Joan M. Reitz

LIBRARIES UNLIMITED

A Member of the Greenwood Publishing Group

Westport, Connecticut • London

Library of Congress Cataloging-in-Publication Data

Reitz, Joan M.
    Dictionary for library and information science / Joan M. Reitz.
      p. cm.
    Includes bibliographical references.
    ISBN 1–56308–962–9 (alk. paper)—ISBN 1–59158–075–7 (pbk. : alk paper)
    1. Library science—Dictionaries.   2. Information science—Dictionaries.   I. Title.
Z1006.R45   2004
020'.3—dc22   2003065653

British Library Cataloguing in Publication Data is available.

Library of Congress Catalog Card Number: 2003065653
ISBN: 1–56308–962–9
     1–59158–075–7 (pbk)

First published in 2004

Libraries Unlimited, 88 Post Road West, Westport, CT 06881
A Member of the Greenwood Publishing Group, Inc.
www.lu.com

Printed in the United States of America

The paper used in this book complies with the
Permanent Paper Standard issued by the National
Information Standards Organization (Z39.48–1984).

10 9 8 7 6 5 4 3 2 1

To Grant Skelley, Peter Hiatt, and Jerold Nelson
of the University of Washington, in gratitude.

Contents

Preface

Work on this *Dictionary for Library and Information Science* began in 1994 when, in the course of the author's work as instruction librarian at Western Connecticut State University (WCSU), a four-page printed handout on *Library Lingo* was developed for undergraduates lacking fluency in English and for English-speaking students unfamiliar with basic library terminology. In 1996, the text was converted to HTML format for installation on the Web site maintained by WCSU Libraries, under the title *Hypertext Library Lingo: A Glossary of Library Terminology*. Over the next seven years, many more terms were added and the definitions extensively revised and interlinked. The present print version of the dictionary contains approximately 4,000 terms with definitions.

The purpose of the dictionary is to define terms encountered and used by library and information professionals, library technicians, and students of library and information science to assist them in expanding their knowledge. The primary criterion for including a term is whether a librarian or other information provider might be expected to understand its meaning(s) in the course of executing his or her professional duties and responsibilities. A newly coined term is added when, in the author's judgment, it seems likely to become a permanent addition to the lexicon of library and information science.

Since the author's professional training occurred in the United States, the dictionary reflects North American practice; however, because the dictionary was first developed as an online resource available worldwide, with an e-mail contact address for feedback, users from many countries have contributed to its growth, often suggesting additional terms and commenting on existing definitions. Expansion of the dictionary is an ongoing process, making it a "work in progress."

Broad in scope, the dictionary includes not only the terminology of the various specializations within library science and information studies but also the vocabulary of publishing, printing, the book trade, graphic arts, book history, literature, bibliography, telecommunications, and computer science when, in the author's judgment, a definition might prove helpful to librarians and information specialists in their work. Entries are descriptive, with examples provided in boldface when appropriate. The definitions of terms used in *Anglo-American Cataloging Rules* follow *AACR2* closely and are therefore intended to be prescriptive. The dictionary includes some slang terms and idioms, and a few obsolete terms, often as *See* references to the current term. When the meaning of a term varies according to the field in which it is used, priority is given to the definition that applies within the field with which it is most closely associated. Definitions unrelated to library and information science are generally omitted. As a rule, definition is given under an acronym only when the full term is rarely used. Alphabetization is letter-by-letter. The authority for spelling and hyphenation is *Webster's New World Dictionary of the American Language* (College Edition). URLs are current as of date of publication.

The author would like to thank Edward Kurdyla, for providing the means of publishing the dictionary in print, Dr. Martin Dillon of Libraries Unlimited and Emma Bailey of the Greenwood Publishing Group, and John Donohue of Westchester Book Services, for their assistance in preparing the print version for publication. Priscilla Kaplan deserves special appreciation for her careful reading of the manuscript and for contributing several dozen terms and definitions related to library systems, networking, and cataloging. Special thanks are extended to Brian Hickam, Head of Reference at the Bromfield Library, Ohio State University at Mansfield, for suggesting a significant number of terms for inclusion in the dictionary. His ongoing interest in the project is appreciated. The author is also indebted to Dr. John V. Richardson, Jr., and Brad Eden for their critical reading of the manuscript.

The author would also like to acknowledge the contributions of her colleagues at Western Connecticut State University in their areas of specialization: Russell Gladstone in access services; Deborah Barrett, Teresa Saunders, and XiaoHua Yang in acquisitions; Meg Moughan in archives and special collections; Alesia Szabo in technical services; Jenny Innes in public services; Joanne Elpern in interlibrary loan; Vijay Nair in reference; Lorraine Furtick and Barbara Heuer in serials; Veronica Kenausis and Brian Kennison in systems; and Mary Kay Loomis and Jane Fowler of the Robert S. Young Business Library. The author is especially indebted to Brian Kennison for his advice and assistance in overcoming problems related to file size and other technical issues.

A

A&I   *See*: abstracting and indexing.

AACR   *See*: *Anglo-American Cataloging Rules*.

AACR2   *See*: *Anglo-American Cataloging Rules*.

AACR2 2002   *See*: *Anglo-American Cataloging Rules*.

AACR2-e   *See*: *Anglo-American Cataloging Rules*.

AACR2R   *See*: *Anglo-American Cataloging Rules*.

AAHSL   *See*: Association of Academic Health Sciences Libraries.

AALL   *See*: American Association of Law Libraries.

AAP   *See*: Association of American Publishers.

AAS   *See*: American Antiquarian Society.

AASL   *See*: American Association of School Librarians.

AAT   *See*: *Art & Architecture Thesaurus*.

AAUP   *See*: American Association of University Professors *and* Association of American University Presses.

ABA   *See*: American Booksellers Association.

ABAA   *See*: Antiquarian Booksellers Association of America.

AB Bookman's Weekly   A trade publication used mainly by antiquarian booksellers to locate rare, out of print, and difficult to find titles, *AB Bookman's Weekly* began as a section of *Publisher's Weekly* under the title *Antiquarian Bookman*. In 1948 it became an independent weekly of the same title published by R.R. Bowker. Publication under the current title began in 1967.

abbreviation   A shortened form of a word or phrase used for brevity in place of the whole, consisting of the first letter, or the first few letters, followed by a period (full stop), for example, **assoc.** for *association* or **P.O.** for *post office*. Some terms have more than one abbreviation (**v.** or **vol.** for *volume*). Also used as an umbrella term for any shortened form of a word or phrase not an *acronym*, *initialism*, or *contraction*, for example, the postal code **CT** for Connecticut. The rules governing the use of abbreviations in library catalog entries are given in *Appendix B* of *AACR2*. Abbreviated *abbr.*

In medieval manuscripts, abbreviations were often used to save time and space, and readers of the time would have been familiar with them. Michelle Brown notes in *Understanding Illuminated Manuscripts* (Getty Museum/British Library, 1994) that Irish scribes relied on them extensively in copying pocket-size Gospel books used for study.

ABC book   *See*: abecedary *and* alphabet book.

Abebooks   A leading online market place for used, rare, and out of print books, Abebooks provides a list of over 40 million titles available from a network of over 10,000 booksellers. Abelibrary.com provides additional services to librarians, such as consolidated billing and purchase orders. URL: www.abebooks.com. *See also*: *Alibris*.

abecedarium   *See*: abecedary.

abecedarius   *See*: acrostic.

abecedary   A book containing the letters of the alphabet and basic rules of spelling and grammar, used in Europe as a primer before the invention of the printing press. Early printed examples (sometimes in the form of a broadsheet) displayed the alphabet in uppercase and lowercase letters in both roman and gothic type, with separate lists of vowels, dipthongs, and consonants. By 1700, some ABC books included children's rhymes. Synonymous with *abecedarium* (plural: *abecedarii*). *See also*: *horn book*.

aberrant copy   A copy of a book containing obvious printing and/or binding errors that are more serious than minor defects.

ABF   *See*: Association des Bibliothécaires Français.

aboutness   The totality of subjects explicitly or implicitly addressed in the text of a document, including but not limited to the meaning(s) of the title, the stated and unstated intentions of the author, and the ways in which the information may be used by readers. Levels of specificity must be considered in ascertaining the subject(s) of a work. In the case of the hypothetical title ***The Japanese Teamwork Approach to Improving High School Effectiveness***, is the work about:

1. education?
2. educational effectiveness?
3. high school effectiveness?
4. teamwork?
5. a Japanese approach to teamwork?

As a general rule, catalogers and indexers assign the most specific subject headings that describe the significant content of the item. In a post-coordinate indexing system such as the one used in *ERIC*, the descriptors "Educational effectiveness," "High schools," "Japan," and "Teamwork" would probably be assigned to the example given above, but in a pre-coordinate system, such as the *Library of Congress Subject Head-*

ings list, the appropriate headings might be "High schools—Japan," "Teacher effect-iveness—Japan," and "Teaching teams—Japan." *See also*: *summarization*.

above the fold   The half of a broadsheet newspaper that appears above the horizontal fold. Articles printed near the top have greater prominence because most languages are read from top to bottom of page.

abridged   *See*: abridgment.

Abridged Decimal Classification (ADC)   A logical truncation of the notational and structural hierarchy of the *full edition* of Dewey Decimal Classification, developed for general collections of 20,000 titles or less.

abridgment   A shortened version or edition of a written work that preserves the overall meaning and manner of presentation of the original but omits the less important pas-sages of text and usually the illustrations, notes, and appendices. Often prepared by a person other than the original author or editor, an *abridged edition* is generally in-tended for readers unlikely to purchase the unabridged version because of its length, complexity, or price (*example*: **The New Shorter Oxford English Dictionary**). Also spelled *abridgement*. Abbreviated *abr*. Synonymous with *condensation*. Compare with *simplified edition*. *See also*: *abstract*, *brief*, *digest*, *epitome*, *summary*, and *synopsis*.

absenteeism   The failure of an employee to report for work, usually due to illness, accident, family responsibilities, or personal business. A persistently high rate of ab-senteeism may be a sign of low morale among the staff of a library or library system. *See also*: *burnout*.

absolute humidity   *See*: humidity.

absorbed title   *See*: absorption.

absorbency   The capacity of paper to absorb and retain moisture, which varies with type of paper and is of particular importance in printing processes that use liquid ink. *See also*: *water-damaged*.

absorption   The incorporation of one serial by another. The note *Absorbed*: followed by the title of the assimilated serial is added to the bibliographic record representing the assimilating publication, and the corresponding note *Absorbed by*: followed by the title of the assimilating serial is added to the record for the assimilated publication. The absorbed title usually assumes the title and numbering of the assimilating pub-lication. Compare with *merger*.

abstract   A brief, objective summary of the essential content of a book, article, speech, report, dissertation, or other work that presents the main points in the same order as the original but has no independent literary value. An abstract can be indicative, informative, critical, or written from a particular point of view (slanted). In a scholarly journal article, the abstract follows the title and the name(s) of the author(s) and precedes the text. In an entry in a printed indexing and abstracting service or biblio-graphic database, the abstract accompanies the citation. Compare with *summary*. *See also*: *abstracting journal* and *author abstract*.

abstracting   The preparation of a brief, objective statement (abstract) of the content of a written work to enable the researcher to quickly determine whether reading the entire text might satisfy the specific information need. Abstracting is usually limited to the literature of a specific discipline or group of related disciplines and is performed by an individual or commercial entity, such as an indexing and abstracting service, that provides abstracts regularly to a list of subscribers.

abstracting and indexing (A&I)   A category of database that provides bibliographic citations and/or abstracts for the literature of a discipline or broad subject area, as distinct from a retrieval service that provides information sources in full-text.

abstracting journal   A journal that specializes in providing summaries (called *abstracts*) of articles and other documents published within the scope of a specific academic discipline or field of study (*example*: ***Peace Research Abstracts Journal***). Synonymous with *abstract journal*. Compare with *abstracting service*.

abstracting service   A commercial indexing service that provides both a citation and a brief summary or *abstract* of the content of each document indexed (*example*: ***Information Science & Technology Abstracts***). Numbered consecutively in order of addition, entries are issued serially in print, usually in monthly or quarterly supplements, or in a regularly updated bibliographic database available by subscription. Abstracting services can be comprehensive or selective within a specific academic discipline or subdiscipline. Compare with *abstracting journal*.

abstract journal   *See*: abstracting journal.

ACA   *See*: Association of Canadian Archivists.

academic freedom   The principle that faculty members employed at institutions of higher education (including librarians with faculty status) should remain free to express their views and teach in the manner of their own choosing, without pressure or interference from administration, government, or any outside organization.

academic library   A library that is an integral part of a college, university, or other institution of postsecondary education, administered to meet the information and research needs of its students, faculty, and staff. In the United States, the professional association for academic libraries and librarians is the Association of College and Research Libraries (ACRL). Compare with *research library*. ***See also***: *college library*, *departmental library*, *graduate library*, *undergraduate library*, and *university library*.

academic press   *See*: university press.

academic status   Recognition given by an institution of higher education that the librarians in its employ are considered members of the teaching or research staff but are *not* entitled to ranks, titles, rights, and benefits equivalent to those of faculty. Compare with *faculty status*.

acanthus   A stylized representation of the elegantly scalloped leaf-form of *Acanthus spinosus*, a species of Mediterranean herbaceous plant with thick, fleshy leaves, used in Antiquity to ornament Corinthian capitals and later as a decorative motif in medieval art, especially in the borders and initial letters of illuminated manuscripts where it usually appears painted in unrealistic colors (red, yellow, blue, purple), often in combination with small images of flowers, birds, insects, and animals. Compare with rinceaux.

acceptable use policy (AUP) Guidelines established by a library or library system concerning the manner in which its computer systems and equipment may be used by patrons and staff; for example, most public and academic libraries prohibit the use of library computers for private commercial or unlawful activities. In most libraries, a printed copy of acceptable use policy is posted near the workstations to which restrictions apply. Some libraries make their policy statement available electronically, and users may be required to assent to it by clicking on a small box or icon before access is granted. Synonymous with *Internet use policy*.

access The right of entry to a library or its collections. All public libraries and most academic libraries in the United States are open to the general public, but access to certain areas such as closed stacks, rare books, and special collections may be restricted. In a more general sense, the right or opportunity to use a resource that may not be openly and freely available to everyone. *See also*: *accessibility*.

In computing, the privilege of using a computer system or online resource, usually controlled by the issuance of access codes to authorized users. In a more general sense, the ability of a user to reach data stored on a computer or computer system. *See also*: *open access*.

access code An identification code, such as a username, password, or PIN, which a user must enter correctly to gain access to a computer system or network. In most proprietary systems, access codes are tightly controlled to exclude unauthorized users. Synonymous with *authorization code*.

accessibility The ease with which a person may enter a library, gain access to its online systems, use its resources, and obtain needed information regardless of format. In a more general sense, the quality of being able to be located and used by a person. In the Web environment, the quality of being usable by everyone regardless of disability.

In information storage and retrieval, the manner in which a computer system retrieves records from a file, which usually depends on the method of their arrangement in or on the storage medium.

accession To record in an *accession list* the addition of a bibliographic item to a library collection, whether acquired by purchase or exchange or as a gift. Also refers to the material added. In automated libraries, the addition is usually recorded by enhancing a brief order record that is expanded in cataloging to become the full bibliographic record entered permanently in the catalog. The process of making additions to a collection is known as *accessions*. The opposite of *deaccession*. Compare with *acquisitions*. *See also*: *accession number* and *accession record*.

In archives, the formal act of accepting and documenting the receipt of records taken into custody, part of the process of establishing physical and intellectual control over them. In the case of donated items, a deed of gift may be required to transfer legal title.

accession list   *See*: accession record.

accession number   A unique number assigned to a bibliographic item in the order in which it is added to a library collection, recorded in an *accession record* maintained by the technical services department. Most libraries assign accession numbers in continuous numerical sequence, but some use a code system to indicate type of material and/or year of accession in addition to order of accession. *See also*: *Library of Congress Control Number* and *OCLC control number*.

accession order   The arrangement of books or other documents on shelves in the chronological and numerical order of their *addition* to a specific category or class, as opposed to an arrangement based entirely on a classification system.

accession record   A list of the bibliographic items added to a library collection in the order of their addition. Normally such a list includes the accession number, brief bibliographic identification, source, and price paid for each item. Synonymous with *accession catalog*, *accession list*, and *accession register*.

accessions   *See*: accession.

access point   A unit of information in a bibliographic record under which a person may search for and identify items listed in the library catalog or bibliographic database. Access points have traditionally included the main entry, added entries, subject headings, classification or call number, and codes such as the standard number; but with machine-readable cataloging, almost any portion of the catalog record (name of publisher, type of material, etc.) can serve an access point. In the MARC record, most access points are found in the following fields (with XX in the range of 00–99):

1XX—Main entries
4XX—Series statements
6XX—Subject headings
7XX—Added entries other than subject or series
8XX—Series added entries

In a more general sense, any unique data element that serves as a point of entry to an organized file of information. In files indexed with controlled vocabulary, an access point may be a preferred or nonpreferred term.

access policy   A formal written statement issued by the person(s) or body responsible for managing archives or special collections, specifying which materials are available for access and by whom, including any conditions or restrictions on use, usually posted or distributed in some manner to users.

access services   The provision of access to a library's resources and collections, which includes the circulation of materials (general circulation, reserves, interlibrary loan, document delivery), reshelving, stack maintenance, and security. Large libraries employ an *access services librarian* to manage these activities.

access time   The amount of time it takes a computer system to provide stored data to a person who logs on and follows correct procedures for retrieval. Access time may be slower during periods of peak use.

accompanying material   Related material issued with an item, for example, a floppy disk, CD-ROM, slide set, answer book, teacher's manual, atlas, or portfolio of prints or plates, intended by the publisher to be used and stored with it, often in a pocket inside the cover or loose inside the container. In *AACR2*, the presence of accompanying material is indicated in the physical description area of the bibliographic record. *See also*: *dashed-on entry*.

accordion fold   A method of folding a piece of paper (or several pieces pasted together edge to edge) in which each successive fold is parallel with, but in the opposite direction to, the preceding one. Asian manuscript books were often produced in this format. Synonymous with *fan fold* and *z-fold*. *See also*: *Chinese style* and *concertina*.

accountability   The extent to which persons in government and the workplace are held answerable for their conduct in office and for the quality of their performance of assigned duties, particularly when incompetence, dereliction, or malfeasance is at issue. *See also*: *performance evaluation*.

accreditation   The voluntary evaluation process by which an educational or service organization regularly establishes that its programs, or the institution as a whole (or one of its schools or units), meets pre-established standards of quality and integrity. In higher education, accreditation is a collegial process based on self-assessment and peer evaluation for the improvement of academic quality and public accountability. In the United States, institutions of higher learning are evaluated by regional accrediting bodies. Evaluation of academic libraries is included in the institutional process. Graduate programs of library and information science are evaluated by the Committee on Accreditation (COA) of the American Library Association (ALA). Formal evaluation of individual competence is called *certification*. *See also*: *accredited library school* and *credential*.

accredited library school   In the United States, a school of library and information science offering a professional degree program regularly evaluated by the Committee on Accreditation (COA) of the American Library Association (ALA), and found to meet or exceed pre-established standards of quality, as distinct from an *approved library school* offering a program recognized or certified by a state board or educational agency as meeting its standards. Some approved library schools are also ALA-accredited.

accuracy   The quality of correctness as to fact and precision as to detail in information resources and in the delivery of information services. In libraries, it is essential that the resources used by librarians to provide reference service be free of error. Accuracy is also an important criterion in judging the reliability of information provided on the Internet. The accuracy of a statement can be verified by checking other sources that provide the same information. The opposite of *inaccuracy* (the quality of being incorrect or mistaken).

acid barrier   A sheet of acid-free or buffered paper, or polyester film, placed loose between an acidic component of a book, such as a bookplate, and the adjacent leaf or board to prevent acid migration.

acid-free   Materials with a pH value of 7.0 (neutral) or higher (alkaline), preferred in printing and binding to prevent deterioration caused by acid over time. Acid-free papers are often buffered to counteract acids that may develop with age as a result of bleaching and sizing or be introduced through acid migration or atmospheric pollution. Synonymous with *nonacidic*.

acidic   Substances that have a pH value less than 7.0 (neutral). The main source of acid in paper products is lignin contained in wood used for pulp. Because acid causes the paper and board used in printing and binding to deteriorate over time, lignin is removed in all but the lowest-grade papers. A buffer such as calcium carbonate or magnesium carbonate may be added in papermaking to neutralize acids that develop or are introduced in paper after its manufacture. The opposite of *alkaline*. Compare with *acid-free*.

acid migration   The movement of acid from a material containing acid to one that is less acidic, pH neutral, or alkaline. The process can occur through direct contact or vapor transfer. One of the most common problems in document preservation is the migration of acid from the boards, endpapers, or paper covers of a book to the less acidic paper of the text block (or vice versa). Acid can also migrate from bookplates, inserts, tissues used in interleaving, and labels that are not acid-free. The result may be discoloration and eventual embrittlement. The process can be arrested by removing the contaminating material and subjecting the sheet(s) or volume to deacidification. Synonymous with *acid transfer*. *See also*: *buffered paper*.

acid paper   Paper that has a pH value less than 7.0 (neutral). The primary source of acid in paper is lignin, an organic substance contained in untreated wood pulp, but acid can also develop from the addition of certain types of sizing or from residual chlorine used in bleaching. It can also be introduced by acid migration or atmospheric pollution (sulfur dioxide). Because acidity weakens the cellulose in plant fiber, it can cause paper, board, and cloth to yellow and become brittle over time, making it an important factor in the preservation of printed materials. To ensure durability, publishers are encouraged to use acid-free permanent paper in printing trade books. Buffering helps neutralize acids that develop after manufacture. Acid can be removed from fiber-based materials by means of an expensive process called *deacidification*.

acid transfer   *See*: acid migration.

acknowledgments   The section of the front matter of a book in which the author gives formal recognition to the contributions others have made to the work. The acknowledgments usually follow the preface or foreword and precede the introduction. Some authors include their acknowledgments in the preface. Also spelled *acknowledgements*. Compare with *dedication*.

ACL   *See*: Association of Christian Librarians.

ACP   *See*: Association of Canadian Publishers.

acquisition number   A unique number used by the acquisitions department of a library to identify a specific bibliographic item on a purchase order. Some libraries use a standard number such as the ISBN (International Standard Book Number) or ISSN (International Standard Serial Number) as the acquisition number.

acquisitions   The process of selecting, ordering, and receiving materials for library or archival collections by purchase, exchange, or gift, which may include budgeting and negotiating with outside agencies, such as publishers, dealers, and vendors, to obtain resources to meet the needs of the institution's clientele, in the most economical and expeditious manner.

Also refers to the department within a library responsible for selecting, ordering, and receiving new materials and for maintaining accurate records of such transactions, usually managed by an *acquisitions librarian*. In small libraries, the acquisitions librarian may also be responsible for collection development, but in most public and academic libraries, this responsibility is shared by all the librarians who have an interest in collection building, usually on the basis of their expertise and subject specializations. For a more detailed description of the responsibilities entailed in acquisitions, please see the entry by Liz Chapman in the *International Encyclopedia of Information and Library Science* (Routledge, 2003). Compare with *accession*. *See also*: *Association for Library Collections and Technical Services*.

ACRL   *See*: Association of College and Research Libraries.

Acrobat   *See*: *Adobe Acrobat*.

acronym   A new name or word (neologism) that is pronounceable and hence memorable, coined from the first or first few letters or parts of a phrase or compound term (*example*: **ERIC** for **E**ducational **R**esources **I**nformation **C**enter). Compare with *abbreviation* and *initialism*.

acrostic   A verse or list of words composed in such a way that certain letters of each line (usually the first and/or last), when read in order of appearance, spell a word, phrase, or sentence. An acrostic can be *single*, *double*, or *triple*, depending on how many words in each line are composed in this way. As a matter of policy, newspaper and magazine editors routinely check verses for acrostics prior to publication to avoid embarrassment. The following well-known example is an *all-around* acrostic in Latin:

R O T A S
O P E R A
T E N E T
A R E P O
S A T O R

act   One of the major divisions in the action of a play, usually marked by the dropping of the curtain, followed by an intermission. In modern drama, most plays are divided into three acts, which may be further subdivided into *scenes*. *See also*: *one-act play*.

Also refers to a piece of legislation (a bill) after it has been passed into law (*example*: ***Digital Millennium Copyright Act of 1998***).

Acta Diurna   A daily gazette published in ancient Rome from the period of the late Republic onward, devoted primarily to matters of state (official events, public speeches, legal proceedings, public building projects, major military actions) and announcements of births, marriages, and deaths. It also contained news of unusual occurrences (earthquakes, strange accidents, portents) and information about the private lives of prominent persons (scandals, divorces, lawsuits).

The text was posted on public buildings, and copies were made for wealthy Romans living in the city and provinces or away temporarily on public business. The *actuarii* responsible for gathering the news were sometimes misled by persons intent on manipulating commodity markets and political events for personal gain. Surviving fragments, preserved in the writings of Petronius, read very much like a modern newspaper.

acting edition   An edition of a play intended for the use of actors and others directly involved in theater production, which includes fuller stage directions (entrances, exits, stage properties, etc.) than one intended for reading, usually published in limp paper covers and priced lower than other editions of the same work. Compare with *script*.

active records   Records required by an agency or individual to function effectively on a daily basis, usually kept close at hand, organized in a manner that renders them readily accessible. Synonymous with *current records*. The opposite of *inactive records*. **See also**: *intermediate records*.

active relation   *See*: semantic relation.

activity book   A book designed to engage the user in a pursuit other than (or in addition to) reading, for example, an instruction manual for science or craft projects, or a volume containing puzzles or word games. Some children's activity books are oversize. Libraries select judiciously, avoiding formats that require the reader to fill in the blanks or otherwise alter the physical state of the item. When an activity book is part of a kit, its presence is indicated in the physical description area of the bibliographic record.

activity card   A card or set of cards printed with symbols, words, numerals, and/or pictures intended for use by an individual or group in performing a specific action (or set of actions) or in following a pursuit. Compare with *flash card*. **See also**: *game* and *kit*.

ADA   *See*: *Americans with Disabilities Act*.

adaptation   A work that has been edited or rewritten, in part or in its entirety, for a new use, audience, or purpose. Also, a work converted to another literary form or artistic medium to serve a different or related purpose, while retaining as much of the action, characters, language, and tone of the original as possible, for example, a novel adapted for performance on the stage, a play adapted for the motion picture screen, or an engraving based on a painting. In *AACR2*, adaptations of texts are cataloged under the name of the *adapter*, or under the title if the adapter is unknown, with a name-title added entry for the original work.

In music, a work that is a distinct alteration of another musical work (for example, a free transcription), or that paraphrases parts of various works or imitates the style of another composer, or that is somehow based on another musical work (*AACR2*). Cataloging follows the practice used for texts. **See also**: *arrangement*.

adaptive technology   Devices and software specifically designed to make library materials and services more accessible to people with physical and/or cognitive disabilities, including large print books, closed captioned videorecordings, Braille signage, voice amplification devices, screen magnification and screen reading software, voice recognition software, etc. Some libraries have found focus groups helpful in selecting adaptive technologies.

ADC   *See*: Abridged Decimal Classification.

added charge   A further charge made by a publisher or vendor against a subscriber's account after initial payment has been received, usually to cover (1) an increase in the subscription price that occurs after billing, before the order is processed; (2) publication of additional volumes; or (3) fluctuations in currency exchange rates. The charge is made in the form of a supplemental invoice.

added copy   A copy of an item already owned by a library, added to the collection usually when demand warrants. Compare with *duplicate*.

added edition   An edition of a work added to a library collection, which is not the same as editions of the same title already owned by the library.

added entry   A secondary entry, additional to the main entry, usually under a heading for a joint author, illustrator, translator, series, or subject, by which an item is represented in a library catalog (*AACR2*). *See also*: *name-title added entry* and *tracing*.

added title page   A title page preceding or following the one used by the cataloger as the chief source of information in creating the bibliographic description of an item. It may be more general, as in a series title page, or of equivalent generality, as in a title page in another language (*AACR2*).

addendum   Brief printed matter, less extensive than a supplement or appendix, included in a book or other publication after the work has been typeset because it is considered essential to the meaning or completeness of the text, usually printed separately on a slip of paper tipped in at the beginning or end of the text. Plural: *addenda*. Compare with *errata*.

additional volume   An extra volume issued by the publisher of a serial, not included in the original publication schedule for the title, for which an added charge may be made against the customer's account, on a supplemental invoice.

add note   A brief note in the Dewey Decimal Classification schedules instructing the cataloger to append to a given base number one or more numerals found elsewhere in the classification in order to build a class number. For example, the instruction to "add to base number **027.1** (private and family libraries) notation from 1–9 from Table 2, e.g., family libraries in the United Kingdom **027.141**."

address   In computing, a character or set of characters used to identify a specific location in main memory or peripheral storage, usually for the purpose of accessing stored data. *See also*: *Internet address*.

adhesive   A substance applied to a material to make it stick to another surface by chemical or mechanical action. Gummed adhesives require moisture to be effective.

Solid at room temperatures, hot-melt adhesives liquefy when heated and set up quickly as they cool. Some types of adhesive are pressure-sensitive. Adhesives of various kinds are used extensively in binding and technical processing in libraries. In document conservation, adhesives are often selected for their reversibility. *See also*: *adhesive binding*, *glair*, *glue*, *paste*, and *polyvinyl acetate*.

adhesive binding   A generic term for binding methods in which the leaves are held together by a strong adhesive applied directly to the back of the text block, usually done after the binding edge is milled but sometimes after the sections are sewn. The most commonly used adhesives are animal glues, hot-melts, and polyvinyl acetate (PVA). Synonymous with *threadless binding* and *unsewn binding*. Compare with *nonadhesive binding*. *See also*: *caoutchouc binding*, *double-fan adhesive binding*, *notched binding*, *Otabind*, and *perfect binding*.

ad hoc   Latin for "to this," used to indicate that something was created or exists for the particular purpose in view at the moment. Also refers to something organized for a specific purpose, for example, an *ad hoc committee* elected or appointed to address a specific issue or handle an unanticipated contingency, usually dissolved once the need has been met.

adjacency   *See*: proximity.

adjunct   A librarian employed part-time in an academic library at an institution that grants librarians faculty status. Synonymous with *part-time faculty*.

adjustable shelving   *See*: fixed shelving.

ad loc.   An abbreviation of the Latin phrase *ad locum*, meaning "at the place [cited]."

administration   The range of activities normally associated with the management of a government agency, organization, or institution, such as a library or library system. Also refers collectively to the persons responsible for such activity, from director to secretary. *See also*: *library administration*.

administrative history   In archives, the part of a finding aid that provides pertinent information concerning the records it lists and describes, such as the history and organizational structure of the agency (or group of related agencies) that generated them, or significant details in the life and career of the individual or family with which they are associated, usually in the form of a biographical note.

administrative value   *See*: archival value.

Adobe Acrobat   A document exchange program created by Adobe Systems that allows data files created on one software platform (DOS, Windows, Macintosh, etc.) to be displayed and printed on another without loss of text formatting. This capability is particularly important in communication over the Internet, which interconnects computers of all types and sizes. Adobe Systems sells the software required to create or convert documents to its Portable Document Format (PDF) but does not charge users for the software needed to read PDF documents. The *Acrobat Reader* program can be downloaded directly from the company Web site at: www.adobe.com. *See also*: *plug-in*.

adult   A fully grown, mentally competent person of sufficient age to be considered capable of making mature decisions and held legally accountable for the consequences of his (or her) actions. Libraries operate on the assumption that adult patrons are capable of deciding independently what they wish to read and borrow. Although the parent is responsible for supervising the actions of his or her child, it is appropriate for a librarian to provide guidance to users of all ages in the selection of materials suitable to their age level and interests, if asked to do so. Older adults often have special needs that can be met through outreach. *See also*: *readers' advisory*.

adult content filter   Software designed to block retrieval over the Internet of material available considered unsuitable for children (violence, sexually explicit text and images, etc.). The constitutionality of laws requiring the use of such filters in libraries is a subject of debate in the United States. Most image search engines include a default adult content filter that the user can turn off. Synonymous with *mature content filter*.

adult education   Courses designed specifically for adults who have spent their lives outside the system of formal higher education. Because nontraditional students often lack the library skills of students who follow a traditional course of study, they may require more assistance at the reference desk and a more basic level of bibliographic instruction.

adult learner   A person older than traditional college age who pursues an independent, organized course of study, usually without the benefit of formal instruction at an established educational institution. When enrolled as a nontraditional student at a college or university, such a person may require reference services and bibliographic instruction at a more basic level than traditional students.

adult literacy   *See*: literacy.

adult services   Materials, services, and programs intended to meet the needs of the adult users of a public library, as opposed to those designed for children and young adults. *See also*: *readers' advisory*.

advance copy   A copy of a book or other publication bound in advance of the normal press run to enable the publisher to check that all is in order before binding of the edition proceeds. Advance copies are also sent to booksellers, book club selection committees, and reviewers before the announced publication date, sometimes unbound or in a binding other than the publisher's binding, often with a review slip laid in. Copies sent unbound are known as *advance sheets*. Synonymous with *early copy*. Compare with *reading copy* and *review copy*.

advanced search   *See*: search mode.

advance on royalty   An amount paid to the author(s) of a new book prior to its publication against the royalties it is expected to earn, usually offered as an inducement to sign a book contract with the publisher. Synonymous with *author's advance*. *See also*: *publisher's agreement*.

advance order   An order placed for a new book prior to its date of publication, usually in response to prepublication promotion. The number of copies ordered in advance may assist the publisher in determining the size of the first printing, the price, and how much to spend on advertising.

advance sheet   *See*: advance copy.

adventure   A fiction genre in which the hero undertakes a difficult venture of uncertain issue, usually in an exotic setting, often culminating in a hazardous chase or decisive struggle. Adventure appeals to a predominantly male audience. Subgenres include the spy/espionage novel, tale of political intrigue and/or terrorism, technothriller, survival story, and male romance (*example*: **Kim** by Rudyard Kipling). Adventure stories are often published in series featuring a series hero (*example*: the **Horatio Hornblower** novels of C.S. Forester). If the hero is a swaggering ruffian, the tale is often called a *swashbuckler*. *See also*: *romance* and *western*.

advertorial   Advertising text written in editorial style and format. To avoid confusion, most magazine publishers add the word "Advertisement" to the running head.

adverts   Advertisements bound into a book, usually at the end of the back matter. Abbreviated *ads* or *advrts*.

advisory service   A periodical publication, usually issued weekly, biweekly, or monthly in print or online, providing research, statistical analysis, and guidance on financial investments (stocks, bonds, options, mutual funds, etc.), for example, *The Value Line Investment Survey*, published weekly since 1936 by Value Line, Inc. Libraries often store current issues of a print advisory service in loose-leaf bindings to facilitate updating.

advocacy   *See*: library advocate.

aerial map   A map of the earth, or of another planetary body, composed of one or more photographs taken from a position above its surface, usually from a passing aircraft, satellite, or space vehicle. *See also*: *photomosaic*.

aerial photograph   A detailed photographic image taken of the earth or another celestial body from a position above its surface, usually from an aircraft or satellite for use in mapping, reconnaissance, exploration, etc. Libraries catalog aerial photographs as cartographic materials. *See also*: *aerial map* and *remote sensing image*.

affiliate   A separately administered organization closely connected with another by formal agreement, for example, the various organizations affiliated with the American Library Association (AALL, ASIST, ALISE, ARL, CLA, FOLUSA, etc.). Also refers to the process of forming such a link. *See also*: *affiliated library*.

affiliated library   A library that is, by formal agreement, part of a larger library system but administered independently by its own board or management structure. Medical and law libraries at large universities often fall into this category. Compare with *branch library*.

affirmative action   An active effort, begun in the late 1960s, to enhance opportunities in the United States for minority groups and women, through federal regulations and programs intended to counteract bias and discrimination in government employment and contracting and in admissions to state-supported educational institutions. Most publicly supported libraries in the United States are affirmative action employers. The legality of affirmative action has been called into question by individuals and political groups who believe that legislating equality discourages initiative and causes reverse discrimination. *See also*: *diversity*.

afterword   A brief passage or essay, usually written by the author, appearing at the end of a work as explanation or, in a special edition, as commentary on the work's reception. In a collection, the editor(s) may include an afterword to tie together or sum up the main themes developed in the selected works. Compare with *epilogue*.

against the grain   A popular expression meaning "contrary to natural inclination" originally used in the printing trade to refer to machine-made paper folded across the grain of its fibers. In book production, sheets are printed with the grain running from top to bottom of the leaves, allowing them to flex easily lengthwise after they are bound. When folded *with* the grain, paper tears easily and cleanly along the fold. When folded *across* the grain, it cracks and leaves a ragged edge when torn.

Against the Grain (ATG)   A bimonthly journal providing news about libraries, publishers, book jobbers, and subscription agents, with reports on the issues, literature, and people affecting books and journals. ISSN: 1043–2094. URL: www.against-the-grain.com.

agency   For archival purposes, any commercial enterprise, organization, institution, or other corporate body that creates and manages records of its business, activities, or affairs. In very large organizations, subordinate units (sections, departments, offices) may function as separate agencies. In a more general sense, any person (agent) or organization that has the authority to perform a specific function, for example, the National Endowment for the Humanities (NEH). *See also*: *government agency*.

agenda   A list of topics or issues to be discussed at a meeting, sometimes solicited from prospective attendees in advance by the person who calls or chairs the meeting. It is customary to distribute the agenda before the meeting begins, to allow attendees time to prepare. A *hidden agenda* is a goal or intention consciously or unconsciously concealed, usually to gain the advantage of surprise, a tactic that often backfires when unsuspecting persons discover that they are being manipulated.

agent   An individual or company that acts as middleman between a library or library system and a publisher in the purchase of materials, for example, a subscription service such as EBSCO that manages periodical subscriptions for client libraries. *See also*: *literary agent*.

aggregator   A bibliographic service that provides online access to the digital full-text of periodicals published by different publishers. Because aggregator databases can be very large, tracking their coverage is not an easy task for serials librarians. A task group of the Program for Cooperative Cataloging (PCC) is working on standards for analytic catalog records for serials titles available electronically from aggregator services. Currently, the top three journal aggregators in the United States are EBSCO, Gale Group, and ProQuest. Recently, EBSCO has been building market share by offering higher up-front payments to secure exclusivity from the publishers of certain journals. The effects of this competitive practice on libraries and the end-user are as yet unclear.

AI *See*: artificial intelligence.

AIGA *See*: American Institute of Graphic Arts.

AIIP *See*: Association of Independent Information Professionals.

AILA *See*: American Indian Library Association.

air pollution Particulate and gaseous air contaminants (sulfur dioxide, ozone, nitrogen dioxide, and chlorides) are ubiquitous, especially in urban areas where industry and transportation are heaviest. Difficult and expensive to control, air pollutants affect the condition of books by interacting with impurities in paper and with unfavorable climatic conditions to further degrade a book's components. One obvious symptom is discoloration around the edges of the leaves.

According to former Yale University conservator Jane Greenfield, levels inside a building are roughly half those found outside (*The Care of Fine Books*, Nick Lyons Books, 1988). Complete removal requires a ducted air-conditioning system. Room air cleaners with synthetic and fiberglass filters remove particulates; activated carbon filters eliminate gaseous pollutants. Electrostatic precipitators are not recommended because they release damaging ozone and facilitate the conversion of sulfur dioxide to sulfuric acid. Storing rare and valuable items in boxes or other protective covering can help minimize the effects of air pollution. Smoking should not be allowed near books because it introduces pollutants into the air. Synonymous with *atmospheric pollution*.

aisle The space left unoccupied between two parallel bookcases or shelf ranges, or at right angles to a bank of ranges, to allow library patrons and staff to access the stacks. Minimum aisle width is 36 inches for fixed shelving in libraries open to the public in the United States. Some types of compact shelving allow staff or users to shift movable ranges, usually along tracks in the floor, opening aisles as needed. *See also*: *cross aisle* and *range aisle*.

AJL *See*: Association of Jewish Libraries.

a.k.a. An abbreviation of *also known as*. *See*: allonym, eponym, pen name, *and* pseudonym.

AL *See*: *American Libraries*.

ALA *See*: American Library Association.

ALA Allied Professional Association (ALA-APA) A separate adjunct organization operating under bylaws approved by the governing Council of the American Library Association at the 2002 Midwinter Meeting, which allows the ALA to conduct activities prohibited under its current 501(c)(3) tax status. In the planning stages since 1996, the ALA-APA is a 501(c)(6) entity focused on postgraduate specialty certification, pay equity, and other activities aimed at improving the status of librarians and other library employees. URL: www.ala-apa.org.

ALA-APA *See*: ALA Allied Professional Association.

ALA character set   An informal name for the set of characters specified in MARC documentation for use in the MARC record, including the Latin alphabet, special characters, diacritics, 14 superscript characters, 14 subscript characters, and three Greek letters. Synonymous with *USMARC character set*. *See also*: *ANSEL*.

ALA Code of Ethics   *See*: code of ethics.

ALA Editions   Established in 1886, the Publishing Section of the American Library Association first evolved into ALA Books and Pamphlets, then into ALA Editions in 1993. Its roster of first editions includes *Reference Books for Libraries* (1902), *Books for College Libraries* (1967), *Anglo-American Cataloging Rules* (1967), and the *Intellectual Freedom Manual* (1974). Income from annual sales of over 100,000 copies of titles published by ALA Editions supports ALA's other programs. Publications currently available from ALA Editions are listed in its trade catalog. URL: www. ala.org.

ALA Filing Rules   A set of guidelines for determining the order in which entries are to be filed in a library catalog, originally published by the American Library Association in 1942 under the title *A.L.A. Rules for Filing Catalog Cards*. Revised in 1967 to correspond with *Anglo-American Cataloguing Rules*, the filing rules were expanded and published under the current title in 1980 to cover any form of bibliographic display (print, microform, digital, etc.) and any catalog code.

ALA Graphics   A marketing section of the American Library Association that sells posters, bookplates, bookmarks, T-shirts, and other graphic materials designed to promote libraries, literacy, and reading. ALA graphics can be ordered from a printed catalog or electronically from the ALA Online Store (www.alastore.ala.org).

album   A bound or loose-leaf book containing blank pages for mounting stamps, photographs, poems, quotations, newspaper clippings, or other memorabilia or for collecting autographs. Also, a book containing a collection of pictures, with or without accompanying text. *See also*: album amicorum and *record album*.

album amicorum   Latin for "book of friends." A personal album containing memorabilia contributed by the owner's family and close friends (inscriptions, original poems and songs, allegorical emblems, heraldic devices, sketches of contemporary scenes, etc.). Precursor of the modern autograph book, this type of volume originated in Germany in the 16th century and was fashionable among university students and scholars who traveled from place to place in the course of their careers. Some contain illustrations contributed by the signatories and occasionally more professional artwork commissioned in a manner similar to the illumination of preceding centuries. Synonymous with liber amicorum.

alcove   A semiprivate recessed area within a library formed when two free-standing shelving units are placed at right angles to one or more units of wall shelving, usually large enough to provide access to materials on the shelves and to accommodate a small number of readers, seated at desks or around a study table. The architect Sir Christopher Wren is credited with originating this style of seating in his design of the library at Trinity College, Cambridge, in 1676. Synonymous with *cell*. *See also*: *carrel*.

ALCTS   *See*: Association for Library Collections and Technical Services.

Alcuin of York (c. 735–804)   Educator, scholar, and liturgist, Alcuin was born of noble parentage in Northumbria in about A.D. 735. At the cathedral school in York, his abilities attracted the attention of its master Aelbert and of the Archbishop. He made several trips to the continent with his master, whom he succeeded in 767 when Aelbert became Archbishop. For the next 15 years, his efforts were devoted to instruction and enhancing the library at York. In 781, on a return trip from Rome, he met Charlemagne and was persuaded to head the Palace School at Aachen (Aix-la-Chapelle), where he instructed royalty and members of the Frankish nobility and was responsible for organizing an educational system to revive and diffuse learning throughout the new realm. He also undertook a complete revision of the Latin Vulgate to return the Bible as closely as possible to the 4th-century text of St. Jerome.

To achieve Charlemagne's goal of replacing the Gallican with the Roman rite, Alcuin compiled liturgical works, most notably a missal that was widely adopted, establishing uniformity in the liturgy of the Mass throughout the Western Church. In 796, he was appointed Abbot of St. Martin at Tours, where he focused on building a model monastic school and library, while supervising production of a series of bibles for circulation among European monastic establishments. To facilitate copying, a new script known today as Carolingian minuscule was adopted, eventually becoming the basis of modern roman type. Practical reforms, such as beginning a written sentence with a capital letter and ending it with a period, were also introduced. Whether Alcuin was a monk or a member of the secular clergy remains uncertain, but in any case, he died in 804 at the end of a long and fruitful career.

Alexandrian Library   Founded by Ptolemy I in about 300 B.C., the great library at Alexandria in Egypt became the most important center of Hellenistic culture in Antiquity. At its peak, it contained over 500,000 manuscripts, mostly papyrus scrolls, some of which were translated into Greek from other languages. The collection was cataloged in the "Pinakes" of Callimachus, which included the author's name and a summary of the content of each item. The main library was part of a museum that functioned as an academy, attracting scholars from all parts of the Mediterranean world. A smaller library was established in the Temple of Serapis by Ptolemy III in about 235 B.C.

Although the main library was damaged in 47 B.C. during the siege by Julius Caesar, both libraries flourished under the Romans until the civil war that occurred in the late 3rd century A.D. under Emperor Aurelian. The smaller library was destroyed in A.D. 391 by edict of Byzantine Emperor Theodosius. In 1987, UNESCO embarked on a project in cooperation with the government of Egypt to revive the Bibliotheca Alexandrina as a center of culture, science, and academic research. URL: www.bibalex. org. *See also*: *Pergamum*.

algorithm   A *finite* sequence of unambiguous steps or instructions designed to solve a complex problem or accomplish a specific task in a way that produces at least one output, for example, a formula used to encrypt data. Algorithms can be expressed in natural language (for example, a culinary recipe or the instructions for assembling an item shipped in pieces), in a symbolic language such as that used in mathematical logic, or in a computer programming language. One measure of proficiency in programming is the ability to create *elegant* algorithms that achieve the desired result in a minimum number of ingenious steps. *See also*: *automatic indexing*.

ALHHS   *See*: Archivists and Librarians in the History of the Health Sciences.

ALIA   *See*: Australian Library and Information Association.

alias   A shortened form of an e-mail address that allows a computer user to type a brief identifier (*example*: **susan**) to send a message to a person whose full e-mail address is much longer (**susanmiller@library.myuniversity.edu**). Compare with *macro*.

Also, an assumed name, especially one adopted by a person engaged in illegal activity to avoid detection and possible prosecution. Compare with *pseudonym*.

Alibris   A commercial company that specializes in supplying rare, out of print, and hard-to-find books to bookstores, libraries, and retail customers through a worldwide network of booksellers and distribution capabilities. URL: www.alibris.com. *See also*: *Abebooks*.

alignment   In typography, the arrangement of characters in a line of type in such a way that the tops and bottoms form a straight line across the page, parallel with other lines. Also, the setting of type in lines that are even at both right and left margins. Compare in this sense with *justification*.

In a more general sense, the lining up of type or graphic matter in relation to any common horizontal or vertical line for printing on a page.

ALISE   *See*: Association for Library and Information Science Education.

alkaline   Substances with a pH exceeding 7.0 (neutral), for example, calcium carbonate or magnesium carbonate added to paper in manufacture as a reserve or buffer to neutralize any acids that might develop with age. Alkaline substances are also used in the deacidification of materials made from acid paper or board. The opposite of *acidic*.

all across   *See*: all along.

all along   A sewing method used in hand-binding in which each section of the text block is sewn separately to cords or tapes, from kettle stitch to kettle stitch inside the fold. For the sake of economy or to reduce swell, sections may be hand sewn two on. Synonymous with *all across* and *all on*.

alla rustica   Binding a book in a plain but sturdy paper case, a technique used from the 17th to the 19th century in Italy and Spain on remaindered books. According to former Yale University conservator Jane Greenfield, the sections were sewn on supports laced into paper covers with wide turn-ins (*ABC of Bookbinding*, Oak Knoll/ Lyons Press, 1998). In modern conservation binding, vellum or paper cases are sometimes used without adhesive.

allegory   A narrative that can be interpreted literally but that also has at least one symbolic meaning, usually expressing or elucidating an abstract idea or moral principle. Also, a form of extended metaphor used primarily in works of fiction and poetry in which an event, idea, thing, or person stands for itself and simultaneously for something else. A *dream allegory* is a medieval poem or story about a dream that has allegorical significance, for example, King René's ***Book of Love*** (*Le Cueur d'Amours Espris*). Allegory is a common theme in medieval manuscript illumination. ***See also***: *beast epic*, *fable*, *morality play*, and *parable*.

all firsts   An expression used in the antiquarian book trade and in library cataloging to indicate that all the items in a group of publications are known to be first editions.

Allied Professional Association   *See*: ALA Allied Professional Association.

alligator   Leather made from the skin of a reptile, not as widely used in bookbinding as it once was for shoes and fashion accessories. In England, the material is known in the binding trade as *crocodile*.

allocation   A quantity of time, money, materials, or other resources reserved by an organization for a specific purpose, usually to meet a need essential to realizing its goals and objectives. In most libraries and library systems, funds are *allocated* in accordance with an annual or biennial budget determined by the availability of funds.

all on   *See*: all along.

allonym   The name of a person known to have existed, assumed as a pen name by another writer, as opposed to a fictional *pseudonym*. For example, the name "Publius" for the Roman tribune Publius Clodius Pulcher, used by Alexander Hamilton, John Jay, and James Madison in writing *The Federalist*.

all over   A style of binding in which the entire surface of both covers is decorated, as opposed to design appearing on the front or back cover only, in the centers and/or corners, or around the edges.

all published   A note in the bibliographic record describing a publication originally proposed in more than one part or volume but never completed, usually because it was discontinued by the publisher. Similarly, a note describing all the issues of a periodical for which publication ceased.

all-rag   *See*: rag paper.

all rights reserved   A phrase printed in or on a published work, usually on the verso of the title page of a book, giving formal notice that all rights granted under existing copyright law are retained by the copyright holder and that legal action may be taken against infringement.

all through   *See*: letter-by-letter.

allusion   A brief figurative or symbolic reference in a literary text usually made indirectly to a familiar person, place, thing, or event outside the text or to another literary work or passage in it. Allusions are sometimes indexed and published in collections (*example*: ***Allusions—Cultural, Literary, Biblical, and Historical: A Thematic Dictionary*** by Laurence Urdang and Frederick Ruffner). In a more general sense, any implied indication, indirect reference, or casual mention, as opposed to an explicit reference.

almanac Originally, a book introduced by the Moors to Spain, listing the days, weeks, and months of the year and providing information about festivals, holidays, astronomical phenomena, etc. In modern usage, an annual compendium of practical dates, facts, and statistics, current and/or retrospective, often arranged in tables to facilitate comparison. Almanacs can be general (*example*: *World Almanac and Book of Facts*) or related to a specific subject or academic discipline (*Almanac of American Politics*). Some are available online (*Information Please* at www.infoplease.com). Almanacs also occupy an important place in early Americana.

alphabet The complete set of characters used to write or indicate the speech sounds of a language, usually arranged in traditional order. The roman alphabet used in writing the English language contains 26 letters (5 vowels and 21 consonants), each with an uppercase and lowercase form. The roman alphabets used for other languages may contain fewer or additional letters, with diacritical marks used to indicate specific sounds. Compare with *syllabary*. *See also*: *alphabetical* and *exotics*.

alphabet book A picture book for preschool children with illustrations designed to teach the letters and sequence of the alphabet by showing on each page, or double spread, one or more objects, animals, etc., belonging to a class whose name begins with the letter displayed (**a** for **apple**, etc.). Compare with *counting book*. *See also*: *abecedary* and *horn book*.

alphabetical In the customary order of the letters of the alphabet of a language. Alphabetizing can be letter-by-letter, ignoring punctuation and divisions between words, or word-by-word, with entries beginning with the same word alphabetized by the next word, and so on. The terms in this dictionary are listed alphabetically letter-by-letter.

alphabetization Arranging items or entries in the conventional order of the letters of the alphabet of a language, usually by author, title, subject, or other heading. The most frequently used methods are letter-by-letter and word-by-word, as illustrated in the following examples.

Letter-by-Letter	Word-by-Word
New	New
Newel	New Haven
Newfoundland	New moon
New Haven	New York
New moon	Newel
Newport	Newfoundland
Newt	Newport
New York	Newt

For a brief discussion of the history of alphabetization, please see the entry on "Alphabetization Rules" by Geoffrey Martin in the *International Encyclopedia of Information and Library Science* (Routledge, 2003).

alphameric   *See*: alphanumeric.

alphanumeric   A contraction of *alphabetic-numeric*, referring to a character set containing letters of the alphabet, numerals, and/or special characters. The access codes used in computer systems are often alphanumeric (*example*: the username **smith003**). Synonymous with *alphameric*.

Alpha-Numeric System for Classification of Recordings (ANSCR)   A scheme for classifying sound recordings of all types, based on a set of 23 major subject categories represented by letters of the Latin alphabet (*example*: **M** for popular music), with some categories subdivided and represented by double letters (**MJ** for jazz). To the alphabetic category is added a three- or four-letter code representing type of subarrangement (by title of work; name of composer, performer, or author; name of skill, language, or sound; etc.). The third part of the classification number is composed of the first letter of each of the first three keywords in the title of the work or album, or a number if the work is known by form and numbered. The fourth part is composed of a letter representing the name of an individual closely associated with the performance on the recording, followed by the last two digits of the commercial recording number.

Example: **ES**
    BEET
    5
    O 98

In the preceding example, **ES** indicates that the recorded work is orchestral and of symphonic form, **BEET** that it was composed by Ludwig Van Beethoven, **5** that it is his fifth symphony, and **O 98** that the performance was conducted by Eugene Ormandy and that the last two digits of the Columbia record number are 98.

   ANSCR is used mainly by libraries holding large numbers of sound recordings. Libraries with smaller collections generally use accession number or some other "home-grown" classification system to organize sound recordings. Pronounced "answer."

alpha test   The first full-scale test of a newly designed computer software system or hardware device, or of existing software or hardware that has undergone a major upgrade, usually conducted by the designer in a laboratory environment. Compare with *beta test*.

ALSC   *See*: **A**ssociation for **L**ibrary **S**ervice to **C**hildren.

ALTA   *See*: **A**ssociation for **L**ibrary **T**rustees and **A**dvocates.

alternate delivery   Shipment by a publisher or vendor of materials ordered by a library via a commercial delivery service rather than the U.S. Postal Service.

alternate title   A title, found in or on a bibliographic item, that varies from the one given in or on the chief source of information, for example, a title appearing on the label or container of a videocassette that differs from the one given in the videorecording itself. In library cataloging, any alternate titles are recorded in the note area of the bibliographic record. Compare with *alternative title*.

alternative press   A small, politically progressive publisher not controlled by the handful of giant multinational corporations that dominate the publishing industry worldwide. Alternative press publications often address important social issues and publish innovative and experimental works largely ignored or covered superficially in the mainstream press. For the past 30 years, the Alternative Press Center (APC), an affiliate of the Social Responsibilities Round Table (SRRT) of the American Library Association, has provided access to such publications through the *Alternative Press Index*, available in the reference section of large academic and public libraries.

alternative title   The second part of a title proper consisting of two parts, each a title in itself, connected by the word "or" or its equivalent in another language (*example*: **The Female Quixote, or, The Adventures of Arabella**), not to be confused with *alternate title*. Compare with *subtitle*.

alum-tawed   *See*: tawing.

ambient conditions   The prevailing characteristics of the environment within the room or building in which library or archival materials are stored or used, including temperature, humidity, natural and artificial light, air pollution, dust, etc., important considerations for long-term preservation. *See also*: *microclimate*.

ambient light   The level of illumination in an enclosed space, from both natural and artificial sources, an important consideration in the preservation of materials that deteriorate when exposed to light, especially the ultraviolet radiation (UV) in direct sunlight. Former Yale University conservator Jane Greenfield recommends that in libraries and archives visible radiation be kept below 200 lux, and UV radiation below 75 lux because the damage it causes continues to a lesser extent even after the source is removed (*The Care of Fine Books*, Nick Lyons Books, 1988). Incandescent light is the least damaging, but it emits more heat and is more costly than fluorescent light, which is higher in UV radiation. UV filters are available for fluorescent fixtures. As a general rule, the lights in a library should be turned off when not needed. *See also*: *blue scale*.

Amelia Frances Howard-Gibbon Illustrator's Award   A literary award established in 1971, presented annually for the best illustrated children's book published in Canada during the preceding year. The illustrator must be a citizen or permanent resident of Canada, and the text must be worthy of the illustrations. The award is sponsored by the National Book Service and administered by the Canadian Association of Children's Librarians. Compare with *CLA Book of the Year for Children*. *See also*: *Caldecott Medal* and *Greenaway Medal*.

Americana   A term used in the book trade and by collectors to refer to books and other materials written about the Americas (North, South, and Central America), not necessarily published in the Americas or written by authors from the Americas. Libraries that own extensive or valuable collections of Americana often store them in special collections. *See also*: *American Antiquarian Society*.

American Antiquarian Society (AAS)   An independent national research library founded in 1812 in Worcester, Massachusetts, to document the history of the American people from the colonial period through the Civil War and Reconstruction. The collections of the AAS include books, pamphlets, newspapers, periodicals, manuscripts, broadsides, juvenile literature, music, graphic arts, genealogy, and local history. URL: www.americanantiquarian.org.

American Association of Law Libraries (AALL)   Founded in 1906, AALL has a membership of librarians and related information professionals who serve the legal profession in bar associations, courts, law schools, law societies, private law firms, businesses, and government. AALL seeks to promote and enhance the value of law libraries to the legal community and general public, fosters the profession of law librarianship, and provides leadership in the field of legal information. An affiliate of the American Library Association, AALL has published the quarterly *Law Library Journal* since 1908. URL: www.aallnet.org.

American Association of School Librarians (AASL)   Founded in 1951, AASL is a division of the American Library Association with a membership of elementary and secondary school library media specialists and others interested in the improvement and extension of services for children and young adults. AASL publishes the quarterly journal *School Library Media Research* and its bimonthly companion *Knowledge Quest*. URL: www.ala.org.

American Association of University Professors (AAUP)   A professional association founded in 1915 to represent college and university faculty, the AAUP is also open to administrators, graduate students, and the general public. The organization is dedicated to defending academic freedom and tenure, advocating collegial governance, developing policies to ensure due process in the workplace, lobbying government in the interests of higher education, and providing statistics and analysis of trends in academic employment. Library faculty members at colleges and universities in the United States who are members of the AAUP may be covered by a collective bargaining agreement negotiated by their chapter. URL: www.aaup.org.

American Booksellers Association (ABA)   Founded in 1900, the ABA is the oldest trade association of independent bookstores with store front locations in the United States. Its mission is to meet the needs of its members through advocacy, education, research, and the dissemination of information. The ABA actively supports fee speech, literacy, and programs that encourage children to read. The organization also publishes an annual handbook for book buyers and maintains the *BookWeb.org* site on the World Wide Web (www.bookweb.org).

American Book Trade Directory (ABTD)   Published annually by R.R. Bowker, *ABTD* provides basic directory information on booksellers, jobbers, dealers, and antiquarians in the United States and Canada, listed geographically by state/province and indexed by name and type of store, as well as information about auctioneers of literary property, appraisers of library collections, book exporters and importers, and national and regional associations involved in the book trade.

American Folklife Center　　Created by Congress in 1976, the American Folklife Center is an agency within the Library of Congress dedicated to preserving and presenting the American folk tradition. It incorporates the Archive of Folk Culture, established in 1928 as a repository of American folk music. URL: lcweb.loc.gov/folklife.

American Indian Library Association (AILA)　　Founded in 1979, AILA is an affiliate of the American Library Association with a membership of individuals and institutions committed to promoting the development, maintenance, and improvement of library services and collections for Native Americans, particularly cultural and information resources needed on reservations and in communities of Native Americans and Native Alaskans. AILA publishes the quarterly *AILA Newsletter*. URL: www.nativeculture.com/lisamitten/aila.html.

American Institute of Graphic Arts (AIGA)　　Founded in 1914 in New York, AIGA is a nonprofit organization that fosters excellence in graphic design as an academic discipline, communication medium, business tool, and cultural force by providing a forum for graphic designers, art directors, illustrators, and craftsmen involved in printing and allied graphic arts to exchange ideas and information, participate in research and critical analysis, and enhance education and ethical practice. AIGA publishes *Trace: AIGA Journal of Design* in three issues per year. URL: www.aiga.org.

americanize　　To convert to American English the style and spelling of a work written in (or translated into) British English. Compare with *briticize*.

American Libraries (AL)　　A professional magazine for librarians published since 1907 by the American Library Association, *AL* provides news and announcements, analysis of trends, feature articles, job postings, and advertising by library-related businesses in 11 issues per year (ISSN: 0002–9769). *AL* is available online at: www.ala.org. For reviews of books and other categories of materials collected by libraries, see *Booklist*, also published by the ALA.

American Library Association (ALA)　　The leading professional association of public and academic libraries and librarians in the United States, the ALA was founded in Philadelphia in October 1876 by a group of library leaders (90 men and 13 women) that included Melvil Dewey. An "association of associations," the ALA is organized in divisions, each with its own officers, budget, and programs, and is closely tied to over 50 state and regional chapters. The Association also sponsors round tables on specific issues and topics and is affiliated with other independent library–related organizations. Its imprint is ALA Editions. The most widely read periodicals published by the ALA are the trade journal *American Libraries* and the review publication *Booklist*. URL: www.ala.org. ***See also***: *ALA Allied Professional Association, Association des Bibliothécaires Français, Australian Library and Information Association, Canadian Library Association, Chartered Institute of Library and Information Professionals*, and *Deutscher Bibliogtheksverband e.V.*

　　ALA divisions:

American Association of School Librarians (AASL)
Association for Library Collections and Technical Services (ALCTS)

Association for Library Service to Children (ALSC)
Association for Library Trustees and Advocates (ALTA)
Association of College and Research Libraries (ACRL)
Association of Specialized and Cooperative Library Agencies (ASCLA)
Library Administration and Management Association (LAMA)
Library and Information Technology Association (LITA)
Public Library Association (PLA)
Reference and User Services Association (RUSA)
Young Adult Library Services Association (YALSA)

American Library Directory (ALD)   A serial published annually by R.R. Bowker since 1923, available in the reference sections of most libraries, providing directory information (name, location, phone and fax number[s], department heads, budget, collection size, special collections, electronic resources, network participation, etc.) for over 30,000 academic, public, research, county, provincial, regional, medical, law, and other special libraries in the United States, Canada, and Mexico. *ALD* also includes separate sections listing library networks and consortia, library systems, libraries for persons with special needs, and state and federal library agencies. It also contains an alphabetically arranged *Personnel Index* of all the individuals named in the entries for libraries, library systems, and library consortia, with contact information. ISSN: 0065–910X.

American National Standards Institute (ANSI)   A nonprofit national clearinghouse founded in 1918 to facilitate standardization by voluntary consensus in the United States in both the public and private sectors and to coordinate and administer standards of all types. ANSI membership includes over 1,400 companies, organizations, government agencies, and other institutions. The United States is represented by ANSI in the International Organization for Standardization (ISO). Standards for library and information science are developed by the National Information Standards Organization (NISO), a nonprofit association accredited by ANSI. URL: www.ansi.org.

American Printing History Association (APHA)   Founded in 1974, APHA encourages study and research in printing history and related arts and skills, including calligraphy, type founding, papermaking, bookbinding, illustration, and publishing. From its headquarters in New York City, APHA publishes the *APHA Newsletter* and the biannual journal *Printing History*. URL: www.printinghistory.org.

American Reference Books Annual (ARBA)   A reference serial published annually by Libraries Unlimited since 1970, *ARBA* provides comprehensive coverage of English-language reference books and electronic reference works published in the United States and Canada during the previous year, listing reviews in a classified arrangement, indexed by author/title and subject. The reviews are usually 100 to 300 words long, written by scholars, librarians, and library educators who are asked to examine new works as they are published and provide well-documented critical comments, both positive and negative. All reviews are signed. *ARBA* is usually shelved in the reference section of large academic and public libraries. In *ARBAonline*, reviews are provided in a searchable database that is available on subscription. ISSN: 0065–9959.

American Society for Information Science and Technology (ASIST)   An affiliate of the American Library Association, ASIST is a nonprofit association established in 1937 to provide opportunities for professionals in the information science field to communicate across the disciplines of library science, computer science, linguistics, mathematics, and the physical sciences. Formerly the American Society for Information Science (ASIS). URL: www.asis.org. ASIST publications:

ARIST: Annual Review of Information Science and Technology
Bulletin of the American Society of Information Science and Technology
Journal of the American Society for Information Science and Technology

American Society of Composers, Authors and Publishers (ASCAP)   Established in 1914, ASCAP is a membership association of over 160,000 American composers, songwriters, lyricists, and music publishers of every kind of music, dedicated to protecting the rights of its members by licensing and distributing royalties for nondramatic public performances of their copyrighted works. Through agreements with international affiliates, ASCAP also represents hundreds of thousands of music creators worldwide. URL: www.ascap.org/index.html.

American Society of Indexers (ASI)   Founded in 1968, ASI is an affiliate of the American Library Association that seeks to promote indexing, abstracting, and database construction. Its members are professional indexers, librarians, editors, publishers, and organizations that employ indexers. ASI publishes the semiannual journal *The Indexer* and the bimonthly bulletin *Key Words*. URL: www.asindexing.org.

American Standard Code for Information Interchange   *See*: ASCII.

Americans with Disabilities Act (ADA)   Legislation passed by Congress in 1990 guaranteeing right of access to public facilities and resources to persons with physical disabilities and prohibiting discrimination against them in employment. The *ADA* has had a profound effect on the delivery of library services in the United States, from architectural planning (ramps, elevators, automatic door-openers, signage in Braille, etc.) to the design and placement of furniture, equipment, and shelving and even the design of computer interfaces. For more information, please see *How Libraries Must Comply with the Americans with Disabilities Act (ADA)* by Donald Foos and Nancy Pack (Oryx, 1992). *See also*: *adaptive technology*.

American Theological Library Association (ATLA)   Founded in 1947, ATLA is an affiliate of the American Library Association with an ecumenical membership that includes theological librarians, persons interested in theological librarianship, and theological institutions dedicated to providing programs, products, and services in support of theological and religious studies libraries and librarians. ATLA publishes the quarterly *ATLA Newsletter*. URL: www.atla.com.

AMIA   *See*: Association of Moving Image Archivists.

amicus curiae   A Latin term meaning "friend of the court." An individual, group, or organization seeking to advise the court on a point of law or fact in a legal case to which the amicus is neither party nor counsel but that may set a legal precedent affecting its interests. Although it is not required, the amicus is usually an attorney.

Permission must be obtained from the court but is usually given if the parties consent. Such appearances occur most frequently at the appellate level in cases involving civil rights and issues of public interest, by formal brief or, in rare cases, oral argument. The American Library Association sometimes files an amicus curiae brief, as in the case of *New York Times Co. v. Tasini*. Plural: *amici curiae*.

amnesty   *See*: grace period.

ampersand   The symbol & derived from a fusion of the letters of the Latin word *et*, meaning "and." Under *AACR2*, when the title proper contains an ampersand (*example*: *Notes & Queries*), it is transcribed in the title and statement of responsibility area of the bibliographic description exactly as it appears on the chief source of information, and an added entry is made under the title with "and" spelled out.

-ana, -iana   A suffix added to the name of a person, place, or institution to signify the body of related literature, information, memorabilia, etc., that has accumulated over time (*examples*: **Conradiana**, **Americana**, **librariana**). In libraries, such materials are usually housed in special collections. *See also*: *local collection* and *regional book*.

anaglyph   A composite stereographic image produced by printing the same image twice, in complementary colors slightly displaced laterally, rather than superimposed exactly. In cartography, red is normally used for the right component and green or blue for the left. Although the image appears to be out of register when seen with the naked eye, a three-dimensional effect is produced by viewing it through a pair of eyeglasses equipped with filters of corresponding colors.

analects   From the Greek *analekta*, meaning "things gathered up." A collection or "gleaning" of miscellaneous literary excerpts or fragments, for example, the teachings of the Chinese philosopher Confucius.

analog   A representation of an object, physical condition, or process that closely replicates the original, reflecting any variations in its state. In technology, analog devices are designed to monitor conditions such as sound, movement, or temperature and convert the resulting measurements into electrical signals or mechanical patterns representing the fluctuations of the actual phenomenon, for example, sounds recorded on a phonograph record. Analog data is encoded in signals that are continuous over a range or interval of values, for example, data transmitted over a telephone line that must be converted by a modem into the discrete values of digital code in order to be processed by a digital computer.

analytical bibliography   The comparative and historical study of books as physical objects, including the methods and techniques of book production and their influence on texts. Synonymous with *critical bibliography*. Analytical bibliography has three main branches:

Historical bibliography—the history of books and their methods of production
Textual bibliography—the relationship between the text as conceived by the author and the text in published form
Descriptive bibliography—detailed account of the physical characteristics of books

analytical entry   An entry in a library catalog for a part of a work (chapter in a book) or an entire work (story, play, essay, or poem) contained in an item, such as an anthology or collection, for which a comprehensive entry is also made. Analytical entries are made under the author, title, and subject of the part and include a reference to the title of the work containing the part. Because preparation of analytical entries is time-consuming, the level of bibliographic description provided in a catalog depends on the administrative policy of the library and its assessment of local needs. Synonymous with *analytics*. *See also*: *analytical note*.

analytical note   The statement in an analytical entry indicating the relationship of the work, or part of a work, to the more comprehensive work of which it is a part, for example, giving the title of an anthology containing a short story, play, essay, or poem.

analytic classification   *See*: hierarchical classification.

analytics   *See*: analytical entry.

ancillary map   *See*: inset map.

AND   *See*: logical product.

Anglo-American Cataloging Rules (AACR)   A detailed set of standardized rules for cataloging various types of library materials that had its origin in *Catalog Rules: Author and Title Entries*, published in 1908 under the auspices of the American Library Association and the Library Association (UK), and the *A.L.A. Cataloging Rules for Author and Title Entries* (1949), with its companion volume *Rules for Descriptive Cataloging in the Library of Congress*. Cooperation between the ALA, the Library Association, and the Canadian Library Association resumed with the joint publication in 1967 of *Anglo-American Cataloging Rules*, which is divided into two parts: rules for creating the bibliographic description of an item of any type, and rules governing the choice and form of entry of headings (access points) in the catalog.

A second edition (*AACR2*) was published in 1978 and revised in 1988 (*AACR2R*) to reflect changes in information formats. The 1998 revision includes changes and corrections authorized by the Joint Steering Committee (JSC) for revision of *AACR* since 1988, including amendments authorized through 1997. Additional amendments were issued in 1999 and 2001. The current version, *Anglo-American Cataloguing Rules, Second edition, 2002 Revision* (*AACR2 2002*), includes extensive revisions to chapter 12 on continuing resources (formerly known as serials). *AACR2-e* is a hypertext version published by ALA Editions that includes all amendments through 2001. *See also*: *catalog code* and Paris Principles.

Anglo-Saxon minuscule   A distinctive minuscule script that developed in England beginning in the 8th century, under the influence of Insular scripts and Carolingian minuscule.

animated graphics   A graphic design technique in which a sequence of related still images, such as cartoon drawings or diagrams, is displayed in such rapid succession that the illusion of continuous motion is created on a computer screen. Animated graphics require less bandwidth than full-motion video when transmitted over the

Internet (and also less memory), so they can be downloaded more quickly when a Web site containing them is selected by the viewer.

animation   The optical illusion of continuous motion created on film by photographing a sequence of drawings, cartoon cels, or still images, each representing a slight change from the preceding one, then viewing them in rapid succession. Animation is also done by applying paint (or some other medium) directly to the surface of the film or by photographing three-dimensional objects (models, puppets, clay figures, etc.) one frame at a time. Developed into an art form by *animators* in the studios of Walt Disney, animation techniques have provided pleasure to audiences since the early 20th century. Compare with *live action*. *See also*: *animated graphics*.

annals   A periodical in which the transactions of a society or organization, or events and developments in a specific discipline or field of study, are recorded (*example*: ***Annals of the American Academy of Political and Social Science***, published since 1890). In a more general sense, a list of events recorded in chronological order. *See also*: *chronicle*.

annex   An addition to an existing library or archive, or a nearby facility used as an addition to the main building, usually of smaller size. A library annex is sometimes used to store low-use materials in closed stacks.

anniversary edition   A special edition of a previously published work of fiction or nonfiction, often containing revisions and/or additional material, such as a new introduction or preface (or an afterword), issued to commemorate the publication date of the first edition or (less often) the date of the event that is its subject. Cover design, format, and/or illustrations may also be altered. Most anniversary editions are of classic or standard works, reissued 20 or more years after the original edition.

annotate   To add notes to a written document to explain, comment on, or evaluate its content, as in an *annotated edition*. Also, to add brief notes (called *annotations*) to the entries in a bibliography or catalog to describe, explain, or evaluate the sources listed.

annotated bibliography   A bibliography in which a brief explanatory or evaluative note is added to each reference or citation. An annotation can be helpful to the researcher in evaluating whether the source is relevant to a given topic or line of inquiry.

annotated edition   An edition that includes comments written by the author or another *annotator*, which are explanatory or supplemental rather than evaluative. Compare with *critical edition*.

annotation   A brief note, usually no longer than two or three sentences, added after a citation in a bibliography to describe or explain the content or message of the work cited or to comment on it.

Example:
Bradbury, Malcolm, ed. *The Atlas of Literature*. London: De Agostini Editions, 1997.
A heavily-illustrated international thematic history of the relationship between

geography and literature, from the Middle Ages and Renaissance to the post–Cold War era. Includes references for further reading and a list of places to visit by country.

In a more general sense, any brief explanatory or descriptive comment added to a document, text, catalog entry, etc. In a critical annotation, the commentary is evaluative. Also refers to the process of annotating a document or entry in a bibliography or catalog.

annual Issued once a year, every year, as in an *annual report* or *annual review*. Also refers to a form of literary anthology popular during the 19th century, usually illustrated with engravings. According to Geoffrey Glaister (*Encyclopedia of the Book*, Oak Knoll, 1996), this type of book was intended mainly for female readers.

In modern usage, a serial publication in any format, issued once a year. Compare with *yearbook*. *See also*: *biennial*, *triennial*, *quadrennial*, *quinquennial*, *sexennial*, *septennial*, and *decennial*.

annual invoice The consolidated billing for a library's subscriptions, sent once a year by the publisher or vendor, usually in late summer or fall. The invoice is based on the titles selected by the library for renewal from an annual *renewal list* sent by the publisher or vendor, usually in the spring. *See also*: *supplemental invoice*.

annual report A printed publication, usually less than 100 pages in length, submitted each year by the officers of a publicly held company to its board of directors (or other governing body) and issued in softcover for distribution to current and prospective shareholders, describing the firm's activities during the preceding fiscal year and its current financial position. Some corporations make their annual reports available online. In business libraries, annual reports are usually retained in a company file for a fixed number of years and subsequently discarded.

annual review A serial publication that surveys the most important works of original research and creative thought published in a specific discipline or subdiscipline during a given calendar year (*example*: ***Annual Review of Information Science and Technology***). In most academic libraries, annual reviews are placed on continuation order. *See also*: *review journal*.

In the workplace, an inspection or personnel evaluation conducted once a year.

Annual Review of Information Science and Technology (ARIST) Issued once a year by the American Society for Information Science and Technology (ASIST) and Information Today, *ARIST* provides scholarly reviews of current topics in information science and technology, as substantiated by the published literature of the field. Publication of *ARIST* began in 1966 with the financial support of the National Science Foundation. Because the field is broad and dynamic, no single topic is treated on an annual basis. The reviews are critical in the sense of presenting the contributor's opinion concerning activities, developments, and trends within the subject area reviewed. Each volume includes a cumulative keyword and author index to the entire series. Indexing and abstracting of *ARIST* is provided in *Library and Information*

Science Abstracts, *Library Literature & Information Science*, and *ERIC*. ISSN: 0066–4200.

anonymous   A work in which the author's name does not appear and cannot be traced with certainty in catalogs, bibliographies, or any other reliable source, hence a work of *unknown authorship*. For an entertaining introduction to the methods used to detect the identities of writers of anonymous works, please see *Author Unknown: On the Trail of Anonymous* by Don Foster (Henry Holt, 2000). Abbreviated *anon*. Compare with *apocryphal* and *spurious work*.

anonymous FTP   *See*: FTP.

ANSCR   *See*: Alpha-Numeric System for Classification of Recordings.

ANSEL   A character set for use in bibliographic records, formally defined in ANSI/NISO standard Z39.47 (*Extended Latin Alphabet Coded Character Set for Bibliographic Use*). It is nearly identical to, and sometimes used synonymously with, the extended character set defined in MARC documentation for use in the MARC record, informally known as the *ALA character set*.

ANSI   *See*: American National Standards Institute.

anthology   A collection of extracts or complete works by various authors, selected by an editor for publication in a single volume or multivolume set. Anthologies are often limited to a specific literary form or genre (short stories, poetry, plays) or to a national literature, theme, time period, or category of author. The works *anthologized* are listed in the table of contents by title in order of appearance in the text. In the card catalog, analytical entries are prepared for works published in anthologies. In the online catalog, the individual works contained in an anthology are listed in the bibliographic record in a contents note searchable by keyword(s) in most catalog software. Compare with *compilation*. *See also*: *garland* and *miscellany*.

anthropomorphic initial   A figure initial in a medieval manuscript or early printed book, composed wholly or in part of one or more human figures (or parts of figures), used as decoration rather than as elements of a picture or narrative scene. Anthropomorphic motifs are also used in ornamental borders and as line fillers. Compare with *historiated initial* and *inhabited initial*. *See also*: *zoo-anthropomorphic initial* and *zoomorphic initial*.

antiphonal   A liturgical work containing hymns, psalms, or verses chanted or sung responsively by the choir in a worship service. Also, the book containing the choral parts (antiphons) of the Divine Office (canonical hours) of the Catholic Church, sung alternately by two halves of the choir before and after a psalm or canticle. Because the antiphonal had to be visible to a group of singers, it was typically of large size, with text and notation written in large script. Many included decorated and historiated initials. Synonymous with *antiphonary* and *antiphoner*. Compare with *hymnal*.

antiphonary   *See*: antiphonal.

antiphoner   *See*: antiphonal.

antiquarian book   An old, used, out-of-print book, more valuable than most second-hand books because of its rarity and/or condition, usually sold by an antiquarian bookseller. Very rare and valuable old books are sold at auction. Price guides are available for appraising old books. *See also*: AB Bookman's Weekly and *first edition*.

antiquarian bookseller   A bookseller who deals in old, rare, fine, out of print, and/or secondhand books. *See also*: AB Bookman's Weekly, *Abebooks, Alibris, Antiquarian Booksellers Association of America*, and *Oak Knoll*.

Antiquarian Booksellers Association of America (ABAA)   Founded in 1949, the ABAA encourages interest in fine and antiquarian books and manuscripts (and other rare or valuable printed materials), promotes ethical standards and professionalism in the antiquarian book trade, encourages collecting and preservation, advances technical and general knowledge useful to the trade, sponsors book fairs, and facilitates collegial relations among booksellers, librarians, scholars, and collectors. URL: www.abaa. org. *See also*: *International League of Antiquarian Booksellers*.

antique   In papermaking, the unpolished matte finish produced when uncoated paper is *not* processed through a calendering machine. Eggshell is a smooth, slightly pitted antique finish. Also refers to a contemporary calf binding designed to imitate an older binding and to gilding that has been left unburnished.

antique binding   A modern binding done in the style of an earlier period, with no intent to mislead prospective buyers as to its actual age.

anti-virus software   A computer program designed to periodically check the hard drive of a computer (or all the computers attached to a network) for the presence of man-made computer viruses and eliminate them if found. The anti-virus software used on computer networks usually includes an update feature that automatically downloads profiles of newly created viruses soon after they are detected.

antonym   A word or phrase that is the *opposite* in meaning of another term. Dictionaries of antonyms are available in the reference section of larger libraries. In some indexing languages, one of the terms in a pair of opposites may be selected to represent both, with a cross-reference made from the other. The opposite of *synonym*.

APA   *See*: ALA Allied Professional Association.

APALA   *See*: Asian/Pacific American Librarians Association.

APA style   A guide for typing research papers in the social sciences, developed by the American Psychological Association, which includes the proper format for typing notes and bibliographic citations. APA style is described fully in the most recent edition of the *Publication Manual of the American Psychological Association*, available in the reference section of most academic libraries. Compare with *MLA style*. *See also*: *electronic style*.

aperture card   A card containing one or more small windows in which individual frames cut from a strip of microfilm are mounted. This format allows microfilm images to be used independently and provides a convenient surface for recording pertinent information about each frame. Synonymous with *image card*.

APHA   *See*: American Printing History Association.

aphorism   A very concise sentence or statement ("nugget") that expresses, in a memorable and pointed way, a universally recognized truth or principle, for example, "Well begun is half done." Aphorisms published in collections are usually shelved in the reference section of a library (*example*: **Oxford Book of Aphorisms**). Synonymous with *maxim*.

Apocalypse   A medieval manuscript devoted to the second coming of Christ and the events preceding it, as described in the Book of Revelation of the New Testament. In *Understanding Illuminated Manuscripts* (Getty Museum/British Library, 1994), Michelle Brown notes that although *Apocalypse* manuscripts existed in the early Middle Ages, they were especially popular in 10th- and 11th-century Spain, where the text was often integrated with commentary and lavish illustration, and also in England from about 1250–1275. *See also*: *beatus manuscript*.

apocryphal   Writings that scholars consider to be of dubious authorship or authenticity (not genuine), for example, the 14 to 15 books of the Greek translations of the Old Testament (Septuagint), known as the *Apocrypha*, accepted as authoritative by the Roman Catholic and Greek Orthodox churches but rejected in Judaism and not considered canonical in Protestantism. Compare with *anonymous*. *See also*: *spurious work*.

apograph   A text that is an exact copy made from an exemplar.

apostil   A marginal note or annotation in a book or manuscript. Also spelled *apostille*.

appendix   A part of a written work, not essential to the completeness of the text, containing complementary information such as statistical tables or explanatory material too long to be included in the text or in footnotes or endnotes. An appendix differs from an addendum in having been planned in advance as an integral part of the publication, rather than conceived after typesetting occurs. *Appendices* usually appear in the back matter, following the text and preceding the notes, glossary, bibliography, and index. Abbreviated *app*.

applet   A small application program written in the Java programming language developed by Sun Microsystems for distribution over the Internet. Applets run on any Java-enabled Web browser independent of platform (Windows, Macintosh, UNIX, etc.).

applicant   A person who has made a formal request to be considered for employment, usually by filling out an application form or by sending a resume or curriculum vitae with cover letter to a prospective employer in response to a job posting. Compare with *candidate*.

application   Computer software that allows the user to process data or perform calculations necessary to achieve a desired result, as opposed to the operating system designed to control the computer's hardware and run all other programs. Common microcomputer applications include word processing, spreadsheet, e-mail, presentation graphics, desktop publishing, database management systems, and Web browsers. *See also*: *multitasking*.

Also refers to a formal request to be considered for employment, usually made by filling out a form or by submitting a resume or curriculum vitae with cover letter in response to a job posting. Each library develops its own application procedure, unless it is part of a larger organization that uses a standardized procedure.

applied cover   A thin, decorative plaque, usually made of carved ivory or fine enamel or metalwork, set into or onto one of the boards of a medieval manuscript book (usually the upper board). This form of decoration was used on bookbindings from the early Christian period on. Although many survive the binding (and in some cases, the book) for which they were made, their use can be inferred from their size and rectangular or oval shape and from small holes in the corners and along the sides, points of attachment to the cover.

APPM   Archives, Personal Papers, and Manuscripts, a standard for the description of archival materials based on *AACR2*, accepted by most archives in the United States.

appraisal   The monetary valuation of a gift, usually determined at the request of a library, museum, or archives by a professional *appraiser* familiar with the market for the type of item. Knowing the value of an item may be necessary in case of theft, for insurance purposes, or in deciding whether the expense of restoration is justified. Appraisal can be an expensive undertaking because the appraiser's specialized knowledge of books, bibliography, and reference sources must be extensive.

Also refers to the process of evaluating records to determine whether they are to be archived indefinitely, retained for a shorter period, or disposed of in some other way (sold, donated, destroyed, etc.).

approval plan   A formal arrangement in which a publisher or wholesaler agrees to select and supply, subject to return privileges specified in advance, publications exactly as issued that fit a library's pre-established collection development profile. Approval profiles usually specify subject areas, levels of specialization or reading difficulty, series, formats, price ranges, languages, etc. In a *slip plan*, the vendor provides advance notification slips instead of sending the actual item. Compare with *blanket order* and *book lease plan*. *See also*: *continuation order*.

approvals   New books sent automatically by a publisher or wholesaler in accordance with a pre-established profile of the library's needs, rather than ordered title by title by the selectors responsible for collection development. Approvals not returned within an agreed-upon time are understood to have been accepted by the library.

approval shelf   A shelf or shelves, usually located in or near the acquisitions department of a library, where new books ordered on approval are stored pending timely examination by the selectors responsible for deciding whether they are to be added to the collection or returned to the publisher or wholesaler.

approved library school   In the United States, a school of library and information science that offers a postgraduate program recognized or certified by a state board or educational agency as meeting its standards of quality and professionalism. Some approved library schools are also ALA-accredited.

approximate the whole   Said of a work that is nearly coextensive with the subject(s) represented by a class in Dewey Decimal Classification (DDC), or that covers more than half the content of the heading, or that covers representative examples from three or more subdivisions of the class. The cataloger is permitted to add standard subdivisions to a work that approximates the whole of a subject (adapted from *DDC*). Compare with *standing room*.

arabesque   An elaborate Islamic-style design consisting of intricately interlaced lines that may include flowers and foliage, or form geometric patterns, tooled or stamped as decoration on the covers of a book, or used by a printer to ornament a text.

arabic numeral   One of the 10 digits (**0 1 2 3 4 5 6 7 8 9**) developed in India in the 6th century to indicate number in a system of place value based on 10. Arabic numerals were adopted by the Arabs around A.D. 900, who introduced them in Europe via Spain about 100 years later, replacing roman numerals. Colonization introduced them to the rest of the world.

   The notation used in Dewey Decimal Classification is composed entirely of arabic numerals. They are also used in Library of Congress Classification notation to indicate subclasses, following letters of the alphabet used to represent main classes and divisions. In printing, pagination is in arabic numerals, except for the front matter in books, usually paginated in roman numerals. Arabic numerals are also used to indicate the sequence of footnotes and endnotes. Under *ALA Filing Rules*, headings and titles that begin with arabic numerals (including dates) precede those beginning with letters of the alphabet, arranged from lowest to highest value.

ARBA   *See*: *American Reference Books Annual*.

archetypal novel   Early fictional tales and romances considered to be precursors of the novel in its modern form (*example*: ***The Tale of Genji*** by Lady Murasaki Shikibu).

architectural binding   A form of ornamental bookbinding popular during the 16th century in which the front cover was decorated with architectural columns on either side, supporting an arch or lintel across the top, beneath which the title is displayed on a panel, the style of the cover bearing no relation to the content of the work. *See also*: *cathedral binding*.

architectural drawing   A technical drawing or sketch of a proposed construction project done by an architect or architectural firm. A full set of drawings, showing all phases of the construction process, includes the specifications used by contractors for bidding, purchase of materials and equipment, etc. Synonymous with *blueprint*, a term derived from the process used in duplication, producing a white image on a blue ground. Compare with *architectural rendering*.

architectural initial   An embellished initial letter in a medieval manuscript or early printed book composed wholly or in part of architectural motifs. This type of decorated initial is comparatively rare, foliate and figure initials being much more common.

architectural rendering   A pictorial representation of a building or other structure, usually from an angle showing the front or main entrance, created by the architect or an architectural firm to give an accurate, if somewhat idealized, impression of how the structure will appear after it is constructed. Sometimes used in fund-raising to promote capital projects, such as the construction of a new library facility or the renovation and/or expansion of an existing one. Compare with *architectural drawing*.

architecture library   A specialized library associated with a graduate school of architecture or a large architectural firm, containing books and periodicals on architecture and architectural engineering, building codes and standards, architectural drawings and renderings, abstracting and indexing services, databases, and other reference materials for research in architecture and related fields.

archival box   A strong cardboard container specifically designed for the long-term storage of archival materials (manuscripts, papers, letters, periodicals, maps, prints, mounted photographs, etc.), made from strong acid- and lignin-free board, usually lined with buffered paper and fastened on the exterior with metal-edged corners, without the use of adhesive or staples. Containers made of inert polypropylene plastic are also used for this purpose. Archival boxes are available from library suppliers in a variety of sizes and designs (clamshell-hinged, drop-fronted, with telescoping lids, etc.), shipped flat or pre-assembled. They are usually neutral in color. Synonymous with *archives box*. *See also*: *box list*.

archival copy   A copy of a document specifically created or designated for archival storage by the company, government, organization, or institution that wishes to preserve it, usually for legal, evidential, or historical purposes. *See also*: *archival quality* and *preservation photocopy*.

archival database   An organized collection of records in digital format, containing information to be retained for an indefinite period of time, usually for future reference, for example, the messages received and distributed by an e-mail discussion list or the reference questions received by a digital reference service, including the answers provided.

archival journal   A journal published mainly for archival purposes, as opposed to one intended for distribution to retailers and individual subscribers, usually priced for the library market with little or no attempt to market it to a wider audience.

archival paper   A grade of paper that is permanent and highly durable, particularly with respect to fading and physical deterioration caused by acidity, used for printing materials of archival quality. *See also*: *rag paper*.

archival quality   The physical properties of records in all media (paper, microform, magnetic tape or disk, optical disk, etc.) that make them suitable for permanent storage in archives. Items printed on paper must have a pH of 7 or higher and be free of other contaminates (chemicals, mildew, etc.). Synonymous with *archival standard*. *See also*: *archival paper*.

archival value   The decision, following appraisal by a knowledgeable expert (or experts), that a document, record, or group of records is worth preserving, permanently or for an indefinite period. Records are retained for their:

Administrative value—utility in the conduct of current or future administrative affairs

Evidential value—capacity of records to furnish proof of facts concerning their creator or the events/activities to which they pertain

Fiscal value—utility in the conduct of financial business or fiscal accounting

Historical value—capacity to document past events, providing information about the lives and activities of persons involved in them

Informational value—usefulness for reference and research

Intrinsic value—inherent worth of a document based on its content, cultural significance, antiquity, past uses, etc.

Legal value—utility in the conduct of future legal proceedings, or as evidence of past legal decisions

Monetary value—worth in the market place, based on appraisal by a person experienced in making such judgments

Compare with *artifactual value*. *See also*: *primary values* and *secondary values*.

archive   The building, facility, or area that houses an archival collection (the term *repository* is preferred by most archivists). Also, to place documents in storage, usually to preserve them as a historical, informational, legal, or evidential record, permanently or for a finite or indefinite period of time. *See also*: *digital archive*.

archives   An organized collection of the noncurrent records of the activities of a business, government, organization, institution, or other corporate body, or the personal papers of one or more individuals, families, or groups, retained permanently (or for a designated or indeterminate period of time) by their originator or a successor for their permanent historical, informational, evidential, legal, administrative, or monetary value, usually in a repository managed and maintained by a trained archivist. Also refers to the office or organization responsible for appraising, selecting, preserving, and providing access to archival materials.

Archives can be classified in three broad categories: government archives (*example*: **National Archives and Records Administration**), in-house archives maintained by a parent institution, and collecting archives (manuscript libraries, film archives, genealogical archives, sound archives, personal archives, etc.). Compare with *archive*. *See also*: *archival copy*, *archival database*, *archival paper*, *archival quality*, *archival value*, *digital archives*, and *Society of American Archivists*.

The term is also used in academia to refer to a repository of electronic preprints, working papers, and similar documents, commonly called *e-print archives*. Used in this sense, there is no implication of archival management, which has caused some confusion, for example, around the purpose of the Open Archives Initiative (OAI).

archives policy   A formal written statement defining the authority under which an archives operates, the scope of its activities (mission, objectives, conditions/restrictions, etc.), and the range of services it provides. Compare with *access policy*.

archivist   The person responsible for managing and maintaining an archival collection, usually a librarian with special training in archival practices and methods, including the identification and appraisal of records of archival value, authentication, accessioning, description/documentation, facilitation of access and use, preservation and conservation, and exhibition and publication to benefit scholarship and satisfy public interest. Archivists are organized in the Society of American Archivists (SAA).

Archivists and Librarians in the History of the Health Sciences (ALHHS)   An association of librarians, archivists, and other specialists actively engaged in the librarianship of the history of the health sciences, dedicated to the exchange of information and to improving standards of service. URL: www.alhhs.org.

area   One of the major sections of description comprising the bibliographic record created to represent an item in a library catalog or bibliographic database, reserved for data elements of a specific category (or categories). In *AACR2*, the standard areas of a bibliographic description are:

Title and statement of responsibility (MARC field 245)
Edition (MARC field 250)
Material specific details (MARC field 254 for music, 255 for cartographic materials, and 362 for serials)
Publication, distribution, etc. (MARC field 260)
Physical description (MARC field 300)
Series (MARC fields 4XX)
Note (MARC fields 5XX)
Standard number and terms of availability (MARC field 020 or 022)

area study   A publication that provides factual information about a specific region of the world (Africa, Asia, Europe, Latin America, the Middle East, etc.), including a description of its physical and social geography, economy, history, governments, and cultures, and that may also contain pertinent statistical and directory information. Area studies are often published serially (*example*: *The Far East and Australia* in the *Regional Surveys of the World* series, published annually by Europa). Compare with *country study*.

argot   The idiomatic vocabulary of a group or class of people, or of the members of a specific occupation or profession, particularly those who are on the margins of conventional society (*example*: *A Dictionary of the Underworld* by Eric Partridge). Dictionaries of argot are available in the reference section of larger libraries. Compare with *slang*. *See also*: *jargon*.

Ariel   A document transmission system developed by the Research Libraries Group (RLG) that provides rapid, inexpensive, high-quality document delivery over the Internet by integrating scanning, sending, receiving, and printing functions. The user can send text and gray-scale images (illustrations, photographs, etc.) in letter, legal, and other sizes to another *Ariel* workstation, to an e-mail account used by an *Ariel* machine, or to anyone who uses MIME-compliant e-mail software and a multipage TIFF viewer. The system is used in libraries to facilitate interlibrary loan and document delivery service. For more information, please see the RLG Web page for *Ariel* at: www.infotrieve.com/ariel/index.html.

ARIST   *See*: *Annual Review of Information Science and Technology*.

aristonym   A surname used as, or derived from, a formal title of nobility (*example*: **Louis Aimé Augustin Le Prince**).

ARL   *See*: **A**ssociation of **R**esearch **L**ibraries.

ARLIS/NA   *See*: **A**rt **L**ibraries **S**ociety/**N**orth **A**merica.

ARMA   *See*: Association for Information Management Professionals.

armarian   The person charged with keeping the manuscripts and books owned by a medieval monastery in good order and repair, also responsible for maintaining an accurate catalog of the library's contents. It was also the armarian's duty to keep the scribes and illuminators in the scriptorium well supplied with parchment, vellum, pens, ink, pigments, gold and silver leaf, and other materials needed to copy, illustrate, and bind books by hand. Synonymous with *armarius*. Compare with *armarium*.

armarium   A wooden cupboard or free-standing piece of furniture with shelves and doors, first used to store scrolls and eventually manuscripts and books. Known to have existed during the Roman Empire, armaria were used in medieval monasteries until the end of the Renaissance. Compare with *armarian*. *See also*: *capsa* and *scriptorium*.

armorial   A book containing illustrations of coats of arms, and sometimes other heraldic devices, usually accompanied by explanatory text.

armorial binding   A binding, usually in leather, decorated with a coat of arms or other heraldic device to signify the royal or noble lineage of its original owner. *See also*: *royal binding*.

armorial initial   An illuminated initial letter in a medieval manuscript or early printed book, decorated with a coat of arms, sometimes that of the person or family for whom the book was made.

ARPAnet   **A**dvanced **R**esearch **P**rojects **A**gency **net**work, the first computer network to use packet switching. Funded by the U.S. Advanced Research Projects Agency in 1969, ARPAnet linked research computers on two University of California campuses with the Stanford Research Institute and the University of Utah. In 1983, with more than 300 computers connected, its protocols were changed to TCP/IP, and it became known as the Internet. In 1987, when the National Science Foundation (NSF) began to develop a high-speed fiber-optic backbone to connect supercomputer centers, intermediate networks of regional ARPAnet sites began connecting to the backbone. In 1995, commercial Internet service providers assumed control of the major backbones in the United States. Traffic over the "net" continues to expand.

arrangement   A portion of a musical work, or an entire work, rewritten for a medium of performance or market other than the one for which the original was intended (synonymous in this sense with *transcription*); or a simplified or amplified version of a musical composition, written for the same medium. In *AACR2*, an arrangement is, as a general rule, cataloged under the name of the composer, with an added entry under the name of the arranger. *See also*: *adaptation*.

In archives, the process of putting records into order, following accepted archival principles, with special attention to their provenance and original order. If, upon careful scrutiny, the original order is found to be completely random, the archivist may, after carefully documenting the original sequence, substitute an impartial arrangement that is more convenient to use.

In indexing, the process of putting in systematic and consistent order the headings under which entries are listed. The sequence can be alphabetical, numerical, or classified in some manner.

arranger   A person who transforms an entire musical work, or a major portion of such a work, to a medium of performance other than the one intended by the original composer, or who extends or simplifies a work in the same medium, retaining a substantial amount of the original musical structure. Under *AACR2*, an arrangement is, as a general rule, cataloged under the name of the composer, with an added entry under the name of the arranger.

array   From the Latin *arredare*, meaning "to arrange in order." In an index or thesaurus of indexing terms, a display of entries, headings, descriptors, etc., in an orderly sequence. In classification, a set of mutually exclusive and exhaustive coordinate subclasses dividing a class by a single characteristic, for example, the array "magazine" and "journal" dividing the class "periodical" by form.

arrears   Library materials in need of cataloging, which have accumulated to the point of requiring a special effort to process, usually the result of heavy ordering, receipt of a large gift, or insufficient personnel to maintain normal workflow. Synonymous in this sense with *backlog*. Also refers to the state of being behind in the payment of salaries, wages, invoices, etc.

ARSC   *See*: **A**ssociation for **R**ecorded **S**ound **C**ollections.

art   A general term used in publishing and printing to refer to the illustrative matter in a book or other publication for which no setting of type is required, including any hand lettering, photographs, reproductions of drawings, prints, and paintings, etc. Compare with *artwork*.

Art & Architecture Thesaurus (AAT)   A structured vocabulary for describing and indexing works of visual art and architecture. Initially developed by the Getty Information Institute, the *AAT* is made available through the Getty Research Institute. URL: www.getty.edu/research/conducting_research/vocabularies/aat.

art book   A volume, usually of relatively large size, containing high-quality reproductions of works of visual art (paintings, drawings, prints, etc.) or photographs of sculpture, architecture, or other three-dimensional works of art, usually with accompanying text. In an exhibition catalog, the text may be minimal. Because art books are expensive to produce, they are sometimes co-published to achieve economies of scale. Compare with *artist's book*. ***See also***: *coffee table book*.

article   A self-contained nonfiction prose composition on a fairly narrow topic or subject, written by one or more authors and published under a separate title in a collection or periodical containing other works of the same form. The length of a periodical article is often an indication of the type of publication—magazine articles are usually less than five pages long; articles published in scholarly journals are longer than five pages. Periodical articles are indexed, usually by author and subject, in periodical indexes and abstracting services, known as *bibliographic databases* when available electronically. Compare with *column, editorial*, and *essay*. ***See also***: *cover story* and *feature*.

Also refers to the words *a, an*, or *the*, or their equivalent in another language, used as adjectives preceding a noun, *the* being the definite article, and *a* and *an* indefinite articles. In library filing, an initial article is ignored at the beginning of a heading. An initial article is also ignored in a title search of an online catalog or bibliographic database.

artifact   An object made or modified by the work of one or more persons (replicas excluded), as distinct from a natural object, which is called a *specimen* when collected. Objects created for their aesthetic value are considered works of art. The value to collectors of an item as a physical object is usually reduced by any modification. Artifacts are studied for their historical value. Also spelled *artefact*. ***See also***: *realia*.

artifactual value   The worth of a thing as a physical object, for example, a copy of a book that has little value in the antiquarian market but is important to textual scholars because of its typographical characteristics, or to book historians because of its unusual binding. Normally, any modification of such an object reduces its value. Compare with *archival value*.

artificial digit   In Dewey Decimal Classification (DDC), a letter or symbol used optionally as a substitute for the numerals 0–9 to give various languages, literatures, religions, cultures, and ethnic groups a more prominent location or shorter notation (adapted from *DDC*). For example, under classes 810–890 (Literature of specific languages), option B to "give preferred treatment by placing before **810** through use of a letter or other symbol, e.g., literature of Arabic language **8A0**, for which the base number is **8A**."

artificial intelligence (AI)   Mechanical and electronic devices and applications designed to closely mimic the human ability to learn, reason, and make decisions. AI is used in voice recognition technology, expert systems, natural language and foreign language processing, and robotics.

artificial language   A language constructed from a pre-established set of rules. Its vocabulary can be a subset of a natural language, as in a classification system, or composed of symbols, as in a language used in programming computers. Synonymous with *synthetic language*.

artificial leather   *See*: imitation leather.

artist's book   A book created as a form of visual and/or tactile artistic expression, often of unusual shape or form and incorporating materials not normally used in printing and binding. Artist's books created for exhibition may be one-of-a-kind. For more information, see *Structure of the Visual Book* (1994) by Keith A. Smith. Compare with *art book*. *See also*: *book art* and *novelty binding*.

Art Libraries Society/North America (ARLIS/NA)   Founded in 1972, ARLIS is an organization of librarians, institutions, and individuals with an interest in art librarianship and the curatorship of visual art resources in public and academic libraries, museums, galleries, art institutes, and publishing houses. An affiliate of the American Library Association, ARLIS publishes the newsletter *ARLIS/NA Update* five times a year. URL: www.arlisna.org. *See also*: *art library*.

art library   A library charged with acquiring, organizing, preserving, and providing access to information and resources in the diverse fields constituting the visual arts (architecture, drawing, graphic design, painting, photography, sculpture, etc.). An art library usually functions as a unit within a larger academic or public library, or as a special library maintained by a host organization such as a gallery, museum, art institute, or publishing house. The first modern art library in the United States was founded in 1871 by the San Francisco Art Association (now the San Francisco Art Institute). *See also*: *art book* and *Art Libraries Society/North America*.

art original   An original work of art created in two or three dimensions by an artist, as distinct from a reproduction of such a work. The term includes drawings, paintings, collages, sculpture, etc., but is not applied to photographs and art prints, which can be produced in multiple copies by a person other than the artist.

art print   *See*: print.

art reproduction   *See*: reproduction.

artwork   A general term used in publishing and printing to refer to illustration originals in any medium, as opposed to reproductions of art originals. Such works may have artistic and monetary value independent of the publication for which they were created. Compare with *art*.

ASCAP   Pronounced "as cap." *See*: American Society of Composers, Authors and Publishers.

ascender   In typography and calligraphy, the stroke of a lowercase letter that extends above the highest point of an x-height letter. The letters of the Latin alphabet with ascenders are: **b**, **d**, **f**, **h**, **k**, **l**, and **t**. The *ascender line* is an imaginary horizontal line connecting the tops of ascender letters, often, but not necessarily, the same as the *cap line*. Compare with *descender*. *See also*: *primary letter*.

ASCII   An acronym for **A**merican **S**tandard **C**ode for **I**nformation **I**nterchange (pronounced "askee"), the binary code built into most minicomputers and all personal computers to represent uppercase and lowercase letters of the Latin script, numerals, and special characters in digital format. Each ASCII character consists of seven information bits and one parity bit for error checking.

Designed to facilitate information exchange between nonstandard data processing and communications equipment, ASCII is recognized by the American National Standards Institute (ANSI). Also refers to text that has been converted to ASCII code.

Unlike text containing special formatting, ASCII can be imported and exported by most application programs without conversion and requires no special software for display and printing. *ASCII text* is also called *vanilla text*.

ASCLA *See*: Association of Specialized and Cooperative Library Agencies.

ASI *See*: American Society of Indexers.

Asian/Pacific American Librarians Association (APALA) Founded in 1980, APALA is an affiliate of the American Library Association with a membership consisting of librarians and information specialists of Asian Pacific (APA) descent employed in the Unites States and other interested persons. APALA provides a forum for the discussion of issues and ideas of interest to APA librarians, supports and encourages library services to APA communities, establishes scholarships for APA library school students, recruits and mentors APA library and information science professionals, and fosters cooperation with other organizations with similar interests. APALA publishes the quarterly *APALA Newsletter*. URL: www.apalaweb.org.

ASIS An acronym for **American Society for Information Science**. *See*: American Society for Information Science and Technology.

as issued A term used in the antiquarian book trade to indicate the condition of an item that exists in the same unaltered form as when it was first published, as opposed to one that has been rebound, processed by a library, damaged, etc. Compare with *doctored*.

ASIST *See*: American Society for Information Science and Technology.

Aslib *See*: Association for Information Management.

as new *See*: mint.

aspect In Dewey Decimal Classification, an approach to a subject from a discipline other than the one in which the subject is classified, for example, the economic or sociological aspects of health care delivery.

Also refers to the overall visual impact and appearance of a calligraphic script, as opposed to its *ductus* (the manner in which it is written). Compare the clarity and grace of 9th-century Carolingian minuscule with the dark weight of gothic textura used during the late Middle Ages.

assessment Quantitative and qualitative measurement of the degree to which a library's collections, services, and programs meet the needs of its users, usually undertaken with the aim of improving performance. Assessment is accomplished by various methods, including direct observation, analysis of feedback obtained through interviews, user surveys, testing, etc. When conducted by the library, rather than an outside agency, the process is known as *self-assessment*. *See also*: *quality of service*.

assigned indexing *See*: assignment indexing.

assignment indexing A method of indexing in which a human indexer selects one or more subject headings or descriptors from a list of controlled vocabulary to represent the subject(s) of a work. The indexing terms need not appear in the title or text of the document indexed. Synonymous with *assigned indexing*. Compare with *derivative indexing*.

association   The group of persons who have joined a formal organization devoted to pursuing a common interest or purpose, usually by paying an annual membership fee. Professional associations, such as the American Library Association, are dedicated to promoting the interests of a specific profession and its practitioners. The most comprehensive directory of such organizations is the *Encyclopedia of Associations* published by Gale Group, available in the reference section of most libraries in the United States. The University of Waterloo Library maintains an online directory of scholarly societies in North America at: www.lib.uwaterloo.ca/society/subjects_soc.html. Abbreviated *ass.*, *assn.*, and *assoc.* **See also**: *library association* and *trade association.*

association copy   A copy of a book that has a special association with the author, with a person closely connected to the author or its content, with a well-known individual other than the author, or with a particular library or collection, as indicated by an autograph, bookplate, dedication, inscription, marginalia, special binding, or other physical characteristic.

Association des Bibliothécaires Français (ABF)   Founded in 1906, l'ABF is the oldest and largest association of librarians in France, with approximately 3,500 members. L'ABF publishes the quarterly *Bulletin d'informations*. URL: www.abf.asso.fr.

Association for Information Management (Aslib)   Founded in 1924, Aslib is a nonprofit organization with an international membership consisting of over 2,000 private and public companies and organizations in 70 countries, which have an interest in the efficient management of information resources. Divided into 14 special interest groups covering approximately 60 SIC areas, Aslib specializes in advising organizations, from small companies to large corporations and government agencies, on issues and problems related to information management. URL: www.aslib.co.uk.

Aslib publications:

Journal of Documentation (bimonthly)
Managing Information (10 issues per year)
Online and CD Notes (10 issues per year)
Performance Measurement and Metrics (3 issues per year)
Program: Electronic Library and Information Systems (quarterly)
Records Management Journal (3 issues per year)

Association for Information Management Professionals (ARMA)   A nonprofit international association serving over 10,000 information management professionals in the United States, Canada, and over 30 other countries, including records managers, MIS and ADP professionals, imaging specialists, archivists, hospital and legal administrators, librarians, and educators, ARMA provides education, research, and networking opportunities enabling its members to maximize the value of records, information, and knowledge as corporate assets. Formerly known as the Association of Records Managers and Administrators, ARMA publishes the bimonthly *Information Management Journal* and the monthly newsletter *InfoPro Online*. URL: www.arma.org.

Association for Library and Information Science Education (ALISE)   Founded in 1915, ALISE is an affiliate of the American Library Association, dedicated to promoting excellence in research, teaching, and service in library and information science education. Its members are graduate schools offering degree programs in library and information science and their faculties. ALISE publishes the quarterly *Journal of Education for Library and Information Science (JELIS)*. URL: www.alise.org.

Association for Library Collections and Technical Services (ALCTS)   A division of the American Library Association since 1957, ALCTS has a membership consisting of librarians and other persons interested in the acquisition, identification, cataloging, classification, reproduction, and preservation of library materials. ALCTS publishes the quarterly journal *Library Resources & Technical Services* and *ALCTS Newsletter Online*. URL: www.ala.org.

Association for Library Service to Children (ALSC)   A division of the American Library Association since 1900, ALSC has a membership consisting of librarians and persons interested in improving the quality of services for children in all types of libraries. ALSC publishes the journal *Children and Libraries*. URL: www.ala.org.

Association for Library Trustees and Advocates (ALTA)   A recently formed division of the American Library Association, ALTA has a membership consisting of library trustees and persons interested in promoting outstanding library service through educational programs that develop excellence in trusteeship and actions that advocate access to information for all. URL: www.ala.org. *See also*: *Friends of Libraries USA*.

Association for Recorded Sound Collections (ARSC)   Founded in 1966, with headquarters in Annapolis, Maryland, ARSC has a membership consisting of persons in the broadcasting and recording industry, librarians, archivists, curators, private collectors, and institutions such as museums, national libraries, and foundations. ARSC publishes the semiannual *ARSC Journal* and the quarterly *ARSC Newsletter*. URL: www.arsc-audio.org.

Association of Academic Health Sciences Libraries (AAHSL)   Founded in 1977, AAHSL is an organization of the directors of medical libraries at over 140 accredited medical schools in the United States and Canada belonging to the Association of American Medical Colleges. Its goal is to promote excellence in academic health science libraries and assure that health practitioners acquire the information skills necessary for quality health care delivery, education, and research. URL: www. aahsl.org/new/index.htm.

Association of American Publishers (AAP)   The principal trade association of the book publishing industry in the United States, AAP was created in 1970 by the merger of the American Book Publishers Council (ABPC) and the American Educational Publishers Institute (AEPI). Directed by standing committees, AAP is currently focused on a variety of core issues, such as intellectual property; new technology and telecommunications; First Amendment rights, censorship, and libel; international freedom to publish; funding for education and libraries; postal rates and regulations;

and tax and trade policy. URL: www.publishers.org. *See also*: *Association of American University Presses*.

Association of American University Presses (AAUP)   Established in 1937, AAUP is a trade association representing over 120 scholarly presses, large and small, associated for the most part with colleges and universities in the United States and Canada. Its members publish in a wide range of disciplines, including the arts and humanities, social sciences, and science and technology. Some also publish books of regional interest; others include fiction and poetry in their lists. Through its programs, AAUP seeks to further the interests of scholarly publishing by monitoring legislation affecting university presses, fund-raising for projects beneficial to scholarly publishers, and helping its members market their publications and train personnel effectively. URL: aaupnet.org. *See also*: *Association of American Publishers*.

Association of Canadian Archivists (ACA)   A professional association that originated in the Archives Section of the Canadian Historical Society, ACA is devoted to providing leadership in the preservation of Canada's documentary heritage, encouraging awareness of the importance of archives, advocating the interests of archivists with government and regulatory agencies, and fostering communication within the Canadian archival community. ACA publishes the journal *Archivaria* and the bimonthly newsletter *ACA Bulletin*. URL: archivists.ca/home.

Association of Canadian Publishers (ACP)   Formerly known as the Independent Publishers' Association, ACP is a member-driven professional association representing over 140 Canadian book publishers, including the literary, general trade, scholarly, and education sectors of the publishing industry, devoted to encouraging the writing, publishing, distribution, and promotion of Canadian books. URL: www.publishers. ca. *See also*: *Canadian Publishers' Council*.

Association of Christian Librarians (ACL)   Established in 1957 at Nyack College in New York State, ACL is an international association dedicated to empowering evangelical Christian librarians through professional development, scholarship, and spiritual encouragement for service in higher education. Membership is open to Christians of all denominations who agree with the organization's purposes and doctrinal *Statement of Faith* and who are involved in the practice or support of librarianship. ACL publications include *The Christian Librarian*, a journal issued three times a year, and *Christian Periodical Index*. The organization also sponsors an annual conference. URL: www.acl.org.

Association of College and Research Libraries (ACRL)   A division of the American Library Association since 1889, ACRL has a membership of academic and research librarians committed to improving quality of service in academic libraries, promoting the career and professional development of academic and research librarians, and supporting the programs of academic and research libraries. URL: www.ala.org.

ACRL publications:

CHOICE: Current Reviews for Academic Libraries
College & Research Libraries (C&RL)

College & Research Libraries News (C&RL News)
RBM: A Journal of Rare Books, Manuscripts, and Cultural Heritage

Association of Independent Information Professionals (AIIP)   Founded in 1987, AIIP is an organization of entrepreneurs owning professional firms that provide information-related services, including online and manual information retrieval and research, document delivery, database design, library support, consulting, writing, and publishing. URL: www.aiip.org. *See also*: *information broker*.

Association of Jewish Libraries (AJL)   Founded in 1965 with headquarters in New York City, AJL is dedicated to supporting the production, collection, organization, and dissemination of Judaic resources and library/media/information services in the United States, Canada, and over 23 other countries. AJL publishes the semiannual journal *Judaica Librarianship* and the quarterly *AJL Newsletter*. URL: aleph.lib. ohio-state.edu/www/ajl.html.

Association of Moving Image Archivists (AMIA)   A nonprofit professional association devoted to advancing the field of moving image archiving by encouraging cooperation among the individuals and organizations concerned with the collection, preservation, exhibition, and use of moving image materials, AMIA publishes the quarterly *AMIA Newsletter*. URL: www.amianet.org.

Association of Records Managers and Administrators (ARMA)   *See*: Association for Information Management Professionals.

Association of Research Libraries (ARL)   Founded in 1932, ARL is an organization of large research libraries dedicated to influencing major decisions affecting the future of research libraries and their ability to serve effectively the needs of students, faculty, and the research community, by articulating concerns, forming coalitions, suggesting policy, and supporting innovations and improvements in operations. An affiliate of the American Library Association, ARL provides access to proprietary databases, training and consultation in management and program development, directories, and statistics on its membership. URL: arl.cni.org.

Association of Specialized and Cooperative Library Agencies (ASCLA)   A division of the American Library Association representing state library agencies, specialized library agencies, independent libraries, and multi-type library cooperatives. ASCLA publishes the quarterly newsletter *Interface*. URL: www.ala.org.

Association of Vision Science Librarians (AVSL)   An international association of information professionals employed at educational institutions, eye clinics and hospitals, and private companies whose library collections and services include the literature of vision, AVSL is a special interest group of both the Association of Schools and Colleges of Optometry and the Medical Library Association. The organization publishes standards and guideliness for vision science libraries, a union list of vision-related serials, and a core list for audiovisual collection. URL: spectacle.berkeley.edu/~library/AVSL.HTM.

associative relation   A semantic relation in which two words or phrases are conceptually connected, sometimes within a specific context, but are not related hierarchically, for example, the terms "library extension" and "library outreach." *See also*: *related term*.

asterisk A special character in the shape of a star (*) produced on a standard keyboard by pressing the Shift+8 keys. The asterisk is used as a reference mark in printing to indicate a footnote or other reference on the same page. A series of asterisks is sometimes used in text to indicate ellipsis, for example, to suggest an unprintable word (D***). In most bibliographic databases, the asterisk is used as the end truncation symbol in keywords search.

astronomical map A map of the planets, stars, galaxies, or other heavenly bodies, usually printed against a dark ground. Synonymous with *star map*.

asynchronous Occurring at different times. In communications, a response that is delayed due to the nature of the transmission medium. The opposite of *synchronous*. *See also*: *real time*.

asyndetic Lacking cross-references. Compare with *syndetic structure*.

ATG *See*: *Against the Grain*.

athenaeum The temple of Athena, goddess of knowledge and learning, where scholars and writers met in the city of Athens in ancient Greece to exchange ideas. In early 19th-century New England, the name was applied to certain proprietary libraries, reading rooms, and buildings containing libraries. The Redwood Library & Athenaeum in Newport, Rhode Island, is the oldest surviving library of this kind in the United States. URL: www.redwoodlibrary.org.

ATLA *See*: American Theological Library Association.

Atlantic bible During the 11th and 12th centuries, scribes in Italy produced enormous Bibles, as massive and immovable as pieces of furniture, to serve as permanent fittings in churches and refectories. The term is derived from Atlas, name of the mythical giant whose task was to support the heavens on his shoulders.

atlas A bound or boxed collection of maps, usually related in subject or theme, with an index of place names (gazetteer) usually printed at the end. The first bound collection of maps is known to have been issued in Europe in the mid-16th century. In most modern atlases, the maps are printed in uniform style and format, on a fairly consistent scale. An atlas may be issued as an independent publication or as accompanying material, with or without descriptive text, plates, charts, etc. Some have a special focus (*example*: *The Times Atlas of World Exploration*); others are intended for a specific use (road atlases). In a library, large atlases may be stored in a specially designed atlas case. Atlases are also available online (see the *National Atlas of the United States* at: www.nationalatlas.gov). *See also*: *historical atlas*, *thematic atlas*, and *world atlas*.

The term is also used for a type of medical book containing detailed illustrations of human anatomy.

atlas case A free-standing piece of display furniture used mainly in libraries, usually about waist-high with a sloping top and a book stop along the front edge for displaying an open atlas. Most atlas cases are made of wood, with several deep, wide, closely spaced shelves for storing oversize reference works. Some designs have sliding shelves to facilitate use. Compare with *dictionary stand.*

atlas folio   The largest widely used folio, usually about 16 × 25 inches in size, used mainly for large atlases. Compare with *elephant folio.*

attachment   A computer file of any type linked to an e-mail message in such a way that the two are transmitted together to the designated address. Nontext attachments, such as graphics and database files, may require special encoding and decoding software. Particular care should be taken when opening attachments, as they are sometimes used to transmit computer viruses.

attribute   In classification, one of the distinguishing characteristics of a class, identified as a means of differentiating it from other classes. As defined in *FRBR* (*Functional Requirements for Bibliographic Records*), one of a set of characteristics enabling users of information to formulate queries and evaluate responses when searching for information about a specific entity. Attributes can be inherent in the entity (physical characteristics, labeling information, etc.) or imputed by an external agent (assigned identifiers, contextual information, etc.).

For example, the logical attributes of a creative work include its title, form, date of creation, intended audience, etc. As a general rule, a given instance of an entity exhibits a single value for each attribute, but multiple values are possible (a work may be published under more than one title or in more than one form), or a value may change over time (date of publication for serials). Nor is it necessary for every instance of an entity to exhibit *all* its attributes—some may be appropriate to a specific subtype of the entity, for example, the attribute "coordinates" applicable only to cartographic materials.

In markup languages such as SGML and XML, a named value used to further specify the meaning of an element. For example, in the string **<title type="proper">The Omen</title>** the attribute *type* has the value *proper*, which further specifies the meaning of the element *title*.

attributed   A creative work ascribed to a known person or corporate body, usually on the basis of reliable supporting evidence. Degree of certainty concerning authorship depends on the strength of the existing evidence; for example, some scholars believe the plays and sonnets of William Shakespeare to be the work of another Elizabethan writer, but the available evidence is insufficient to resolve this dispute. When evidence of authorship is inconclusive, a work is said to be of *unknown authorship.*

attributed author   A person believed to have written or created a work published anonymously or that is of doubtful authorship (*example*: ***The Second Maiden's Tragedy*** attributed to the 17th-century writer Thomas Middleton). Attribution is usually based on supporting evidence, but uncertainty may arise when the evidence is meager or conflicting (***The Two Noble Kinsmen*** ascribed to John Fletcher but sometimes erroneously attributed to William Shakespeare). In library cataloging, attributed authorship is indicated in the note area of the bibliographic description. Synonymous with *supposed author*. Compare with *suppositious author*.

auction gallery   *See*: book auction.

audience   The people who actually read a literary work or attend an artistic performance or exhibition, not necessarily the same as the target audience for whom the work is intended by the author or creator, or by the publisher or producer.

audiobook   A book read aloud and recorded on audiotape, usually by a professional actor or reader or, in some cases, by the author. Originally, books were produced on tape for the visually impaired, but the market has expanded to include joggers and walkers who like to listen as they exercise, individuals who must spend long hours traveling, persons who are illiterate or dyslexic, and others who would rather listen than read. Synonymous with *book-on-tape*, *recorded book*, and *talking book*. *See also*: AudioFile Magazine.

audiocassette   An audiotape permanently enclosed in a hard plastic case containing two take-up reels to which the ends of the tape are attached for playback and rewinding. Libraries that allow audiocassettes to circulate usually place them in a section reserved for sound recordings, arranged by composer, performer, genre, or some other means of classification. In *AACR2*, the term "sound cassette" is used in the physical description area of the bibliographic record representing an audiocassette, with "analog" given as type of recording. *See also*: *compact disc*.

audiodisc   *See*: phonograph record.

AudioFile Magazine   Published bimonthly since 1992, *AudioFile* reviews over 100 audiobooks in each issue. Available in print and online, the publication also includes feature articles, announcements, new releases, interviews with authors and narrators, and resources for locating and purchasing audiobooks. A subscription to *AudioFile PLUS* includes access to archives of audiobook reviews, searchable by title, author, narrator, ISBN, subject, or keywords. ISSN: 1063–0244. URL: www.audiofile magazine.com.

audiorecording   A generic term for any medium on which sounds are recorded for mechanical or electronic playback, including phonograph records (vinyl), audiotape, and compact disc. Synonymous with *sound recording*.

audiotape   A continuous strip of thin magnetic tape on which sounds can be recorded as electrical signals and converted back into sound with the proper playback equipment. The most common size in libraries is one-fourth-inch wide, stored on audiocassette. Synonymous with *tape recording*. *See also*: *audiorecording*.

audiovisual (AV)   A work in a medium that combines sound and visual images, for example, a motion picture or videorecording with a sound track, or a slide presentation synchronized with audiotape. Directory information for products and services provided by the audiovisual industry is available in *AV Market Place* (*AVMP*), published annually by R.R. Bowker. Also spelled *audio-visual* and abbreviated *a-v*. *See also*: *media*.

audit   An official examination of the accounts or records of an individual, company, organization, or institution to determine if they are correct. Also, to conduct such an examination, usually on a regular basis. *See also*: *security audit*.

AUP   *See*: acceptable use policy.

Australian Library and Information Association (ALIA)   The professional association for the Australian library and information services sector, ALIA seeks to empower the library profession in the development, promotion, and delivery of quality services to all Australians, through leadership, advocacy, and mutual support. Membership is open to individuals and organizations. ALIA sponsors a biennial national conference, presents national and regional awards, and publishes *Australian Library Journal (ALJ)*. URL: www.alia.org.au/home.html.

authentication   In online systems, the procedure for verifying the integrity of a transmitted message. Also, a security procedure designed to verify that the authorization code entered by a user to gain access to a network or system is valid. *See also*: *password*, *PIN*, and *username*.

In archives, the process of verifying, usually through careful investigation and research, whether a document or its reproduction is what it appears or claims to be. Compare with *certification*.

authenticity   The quality in a thing of being what it is claimed to be (valid, real, genuine, etc.), verified in archives and special collections through an investigative process known as *authentication*, essential in appraising the value of an item. *See also*: *forgery*.

author   The person or corporate entity responsible for producing a written work (essay, monograph, novel, poem, play, screenplay, short story, etc.) whose name is printed on the title page of a book or given elsewhere in or on a manuscript or other item and in whose name the work is copyrighted. A work may have two or more joint authors. In library cataloging, the term is used in its broadest sense to include editor, compiler, composer, creator, etc. *See also*: *attributed author*, *authorship*, *corporate author*, *personal author*, and *suppositious author*.

Under U.S. copyright law (*Title 17 § 201*), the original owner (or owners) of copyright in a work. In the case of works for hire, the employer or other person for whom the work was prepared is considered the author and copyright owner, unless other arrangements are made by the parties in a signed written agreement.

author abstract   A brief summary, called an *abstract*, written by the person responsible for creating the work summarized, as opposed to one written by someone other than the author, usually a professional abstractor or indexer.

author affiliation   The name of the organization with which the author of a publication is formally connected, usually given in books on the back flap of the dust jacket or on the title page, and in journal articles in a note at the foot of the first page, sometimes with the writer's position title and contact information.

author bibliography   A bibliography of works written by or about a specific author, which can vary in detail and extent from an unannotated list of selected titles to a comprehensive, in-depth descriptive bibliography.

author entry   The entry in a catalog, index, or bibliography under the authorized heading for the first-named author of a work, whether it be a person or corporate body. In most library catalogs, the author entry is the main entry.

author index   An alphabetically arranged index in which the headings are the names of the individuals and corporate bodies responsible for creating the works indexed. Author entries may be combined with the subject index or title index, rather than listed separately. Compare with *name index.*

author interview   A conversation in which a writer is questioned about his/her life and work by an *interviewer* who intends to publish the results verbatim in a book or periodical or incorporate them into a radio or television broadcast, in their entirety or excerpted. Also refers to the article or program based on such an interview.

authoritative   A source that is official. Also, a work known to be reliable because its authority or authenticity has been widely recognized by experts in the field.

authority   The knowledge and experience qualifying a person to write or speak as an expert on a given subject. In the academic community, authority is based on credentials, previously published works on the subject, institutional affiliation, awards, imprint, reviews, patterns of citation, etc.

authority control   The procedures by which consistency of form is maintained in the headings (names, uniform titles, series titles, and subjects) used in a library catalog or file of bibliographic records through the application of an authoritative list called an *authority file* to new items as they are added to the collection. Authority control is available from commercial service providers.

authority file   A list of the authoritative forms of the headings used in a library catalog or file of bibliographic records, maintained to ensure that headings are applied consistently as new items are added to the collection. Separate authority files are usually maintained for names, uniform titles, series titles, and subjects. All the references made to and from a given heading are also included in the file. *See also*: *authority control.*

authority record   A printed or machine-readable record of the decision made concerning the authoritative form of a name (personal or corporate), uniform title, series title, or subject used as a heading in a library catalog or file of bibliographic records, listed in an *authority file* governing the application of headings to new items as they are added to the library collection. An authority record may also contain *See from* and *See also from* records, as well as notes concerning the application of the authorized form. *Library of Congress Authorities* are available online at: authorities.loc.gov.

authority work   The process of deciding which form of a name, title, series title, or subject will be used as the authorized heading in a library catalog or file of bibliographic records, including the establishment of appropriate references to the heading, and its relationship to other headings in the authority file.

Example:

Shaw Bernard, with references from **Shaw G.B.** and **Shaw George Bernard**.

authorization   In computing, a username, password, PIN, or other access code issued to a person who is permitted to access a specific electronic resource, application program, network, or other computer system that the user must enter correctly in order to log on. Authorization codes are usually subject to periodic renewal. A single authentication may have multiple authorizations.

authorized biography   A biography written with the explicit consent and sometimes the cooperation of its subject or the subject's family if the *biographee* is deceased. Authorized biographies are more likely to be scrutinized by reviewers for bias because the *biographer* may have been expected to overlook or downplay embarrassing events or unflattering qualities in exchange for access to firsthand information and confidential sources. Compare with *unauthorized biography*.

authorized edition   An edition issued with the explicit sanction of the author or holder of rights in the work or, in the case of a biography, by the person who is its subject or the subject's family if the *biographee* is deceased. The opposite of *unauthorized edition*. Compare with *definitive edition*.

authorized use   A purpose for which the vendor of an electronic database or other online resource allows its content to be used, usually stated explicitly in the licensing agreement signed by the library or information service that provides access. Most licensing agreements allow authorized users to search, retrieve, display, download, and print content solely for educational, research, scholarly, or personal uses. For-profit uses are generally prohibited, with responsibility for recognizing and preventing unauthorized use borne by the licensee.

authorized user   A person permitted to use an electronic database or other online resource under the provisions of the vendor's licensing agreement signed by the library or information service providing access. In academic libraries, authorized users generally include the faculty, staff, and students enrolled at the institution served by the licensee. In public libraries, authorized users include members of the public accessing the resource from computer equipment located on library premises or remotely via a system that requires authentication. *See also*: *authorized use*.

author mark   Letters, numerals, or other symbols representing the last name of an author, added by the cataloger to the call number to distinguish an item from others of the same classification (*example*: the Cutter number **D548** to identify works by Charles Dickens). When a work mark is added to the author mark, the result is known as the *book number* (**D548d** for *David Copperfield*). Synonymous with *author number*.

author portrait   A plate in a book bearing a full-page image of the author, usually a photograph or a reproduction of a painting, drawing, or engraving, printed on the verso of the leaf preceding the title page. Common in books published in the 19th and early 20th centuries, most show just the head and shoulders, with the author's name and the source of the portrait given in a caption. In modern book production, a small portrait photograph of the author is usually printed on the back flap of the dust jacket in hardcover editions.

In medieval manuscripts, the authors of the Gospels were sometimes depicted in a drawing or miniature preceding the text of their work, probably to aid the reader in identifying the text. In 13th-century Bibles, it was common practice to open each book with a picture of the author contained in the initial letter (David for Psalms, Solomon for Proverbs, St. Paul for Epistles, etc.).

author-publisher A writer, photographer, composer, etc., who self-publishes his or her own works. *See also*: *privately printed*.

author's advance An amount paid by the publisher to the author of a work before the completed manuscript is submitted for publication, established by contractual agreement between the two parties, usually refundable if the work is not completed. Synonymous with *advance on royalty*. *See also*: *royalties*.

author's contract *See*: publisher's agreement.

author's copy One of six or more complimentary copies of a published work normally provided to the author free of charge by the publisher at the time of first publication. Faculty members sometimes donate complimentary copies of their works to the academic library at the college or university with which they are affiliated.

author's edition An edition of all the unpublished and previously published works of an author, issued in one or more uniform volumes, usually bearing a collective title or some other indication on the title page that all known works are included. Synonymous with *complete works* and *uniform edition*. Compare with *collected edition*. *See also*: *definitive edition*.

Also refers to an edition published with the author's consent (*authorized edition*).

author's editor An editor familiar with the publishing industry employed by a university or research institution to assist faculty and researchers in preparing their work for publication and to help them negotiate the intricacies of the publishing process, as distinct from an editor employed by a publishing company who helps to prepare a manuscript for printing once it has been accepted for publication.

authorship The origin of a manuscript, book, or other written work, with reference to its author(s). In a more general sense, the source of an idea or creative work in any form, with reference to its creator or originator, for example, the composer of a musical work. When authorship of an anonymous work cannot be determined with a reasonable degree of certainty, it is said to be of *unknown authorship*. *See also*: *diffuse authorship*, *doubtful authorship*, *mixed responsibility*, *shared responsibility*, and *spurious work*.

author-title added entry *See*: name-title added entry.

author tour A tightly scheduled trip, usually arranged by the publisher of a new trade book, in which the author (or a well-known illustrator) agrees to help promote sales by participating in book signings, author interviews, book talks, etc., usually at trade bookstores and through the mass media. Travel expenses are paid by the publisher, but the writer is usually not compensated for his or her time. Author tours are announced in the trade journal *Publishers Weekly*.

authorware   *See*: courseware.

autobiography   An account of a person's life written by its subject, usually in the form of a continuous narrative of events considered by the author to be the most important or interesting, selected from those he or she is willing to reveal. The first fully developed autobiography, the *Confessions* of Saint Augustine, was written in the 4th century A.D. Some autobiographies are largely fictional, for example, the *Confessions* of Jean-Jacques Rousseau. Contemporary autobiographies of famous people are often written with the assistance of a ghost writer. An autobiography differs from a diary or journal in being written for others rather than for purely private reasons. Compare with *biography*.

autograph   An original manuscript written entirely in the hand of the author (or composer) or dictated by the author, often highly prized by rare book collectors. Also refers to a person's own signature. Compare with *holograph*. *See also*: *autograph book*, *autographed copy*, and *autographed edition*.

autograph book   A book with blank pages intended for the collection of signatures of friends and/or famous people, with or without accompanying inscriptions. The value of an autograph book in the collectors' market depends on the rarity of the signatures it contains.

autographed copy   A copy of a book or other published work signed by the author. Autographed copies may be of considerable value to collectors if the author is very well known and signed copies rare, as in the case of a small limited edition. Compare with *inscribed copy*.

autographed edition   An edition of a work in which all the copies are personally signed by the author, possible only in relatively small editions.

automatic indexing   A method of indexing in which an algorithm is applied by a computer to the title and/or text of a work to identify and extract words and phrases representing subjects, for use as headings under which entries are made in the index. Compare with *machine-aided indexing*. *See also*: *derivative indexing*.

automatic renewal   An agreement between a library and a serials vendor authorizing the vendor to renew subscriptions indefinitely without an annual review of the current subscription list by the library.

Automation Vendors Information Advisory Committee (AVIAC)   An informal group of vendors of library automation systems and other information products to libraries, and other interested parties, that meets at ALA annual and midwinter meetings to exchange information related to standards and other topics of mutual interest.

autonym   A person's own name. Also refers to a work published under the real name of its author rather than under a *pseudonym* or *allonym*.

auxiliary schedule   In library classification, a separate list of classes (with their notations) that serves only to subdivide the classes listed in the main schedules, for example, the standard subdivisions listed in Table 1 of Dewey Decimal Classification.

AV   *See*: audiovisual.

availability   The circulation status of a specific item or category of items in a library
collection. For example, a reference work marked "library use only" may not be
checked out except by special permission. Under normal circumstances, an item
marked "available" in an online catalog can be found on the shelf ready to be checked
out. In a more general sense, the capacity of an item to be seen, used, or obtained by
a library patron, including reference materials and items in special collections for
which access may be subject to certain restrictions. Compare with *out of circulation*.
    The term is also used in the book trade and in library acquisitions to indicate that
copies of an edition can be obtained by purchase from the publisher or a jobber.

avant-garde   A period of experimentalism that occurred in the fine arts in Europe from
about 1910 until the beginning of World War II, also influencing the book arts. The
artist was concerned with analyzing and extending the possibilities of the medium
itself as a means of expressing new aesthetic ideas.

average price   The sum of the list prices of all the publications of a specific category
issued over a given period of time, or of a representative sample, divided by the
number of titles in the category selected for the purpose of calculation. In library
acquisitions, average price per title is used to compute the annual rate of inflation in
the cost of various types of materials, important in budgeting and allocating funds.
See also: *price index*.

AVIAC   *See*: Automation Vendors Information Advisory Committee.

Avram, Henriette D. (1919–   )   A leader in library automation and bibliographic control, Henriette Avram began her career in the 1950s as a systems analyst at the National Security Agency (NSA) in Arlington, Virginia, before joining the Library of
Congress in 1965, where she began work on the MARC Pilot Project sponsored by
the Council on Library Resources. With no formal education or training in library
science, Avram mastered on her own the principles of bibliographic control and in
eight months designed a bibliographic record format that could be successfully read
and processed by computer. In 1970, she was appointed chief of the MARC Development Office at the Library of Congress, and from 1969 to 1971 she directed the
RECON Pilot Project to test the use of a centralized source for retrospective conversion of paper records. In 1971, the MARC format was accepted by the American
National Standards Institute (ANSI) as the national standard for the dissemination of
cataloging data in automated form, and in 1973 by the International Standards Organization (ISO) as an international standard.
    As chair of the IFLA Working Group on Content Designators, Avram contributed
to the creation of UNIMARC, the international MARC record. During her long tenure
at the Library of Congress, she continued to advocate standardization of records to
facilitate resource sharing, served as the chair of the Network Advisory Committee

from its inception in 1976, founded the National Cooperative Cataloging Project (NCCP), and helped create the Linked Systems Project (LSP) to connect the Library of Congress with RLIN, OCLC, and WLN (now part of OCLC). She has received many awards, including the ALA Joseph W. Lippincott Award for distinguished service to the profession, and was elected an honorary fellow of IFLA in 1987. She retired from the Library of Congress in 1992.

AVSL   *See*: Association of Vision Science Librarians.

award   *See*: library award *and* literary award.

axonometric map   A detailed, large-scale map of a city or smaller area, such as a campus, showing the buildings and other structures in perspective, usually on an incline, for the use of planners and architects.

B

---

b&w   *See*: black and white.

back   The sewn or binding edge of the gathered sections of a book to which the lining is applied. The back may be flat, but more often it is given a convex curve in a binding procedure called *rounding*. A flexible or hollow back is preferable because it allows a volume to open flat. Compare with *backstrip* and *spine*. ***See also***: *tight back*.

backbone   In telecommunication, the portion of a physical network that covers the longest distance and handles the heaviest traffic. To operate at the highest possible transmission speed, it must be constructed of cable that provides maximum bandwidth. On the Internet, regional networks are connected to the fiber-optic backbone, smaller networks are connected to regional networks, and so on, down the line.
  Synonymous in bookbinding with *spine*.

backdate   To make a document or transaction effective from a date earlier than its actual date, for example, a book order given a prior date with the publisher's permission, to allow the purchaser to qualify for an expired discount.

back file   All the issues of a periodical that precede the current issue, usually bound in annual volumes or converted to microfilm or microfiche to conserve space. In the catalog record, the extent of the back file is indicated in the holdings statement. ***See also***: *holdings*.

back fold   The fold along which a signature is gathered to form the binding edge of a book, left uncut in sewn bindings but trimmed in perfect binding to allow the adhesive to bond more securely. Synonymous with *spine fold*.

background   In pictorial art, the parts of a scene that lie in the distance, behind figures and objects in the foreground. In illuminated manuscripts, the background in a miniature can be undecorated, diapered, or foliate, with or without gilding. In the late Middle Ages, miniatures were often painted against a naturalistic background.

backing   In bookbinding, the process of shaping a shoulder on each side of the binding edge of the text block after rounding, before lining is applied to the back. In hand-binding, a backing hammer is used to bend the backs of the sewn sections from the center of the text block toward the front and back, forming ridges against which the boards of the cover rest. By folding the leaves over each other close to the binding edge, the process also helps maintain the rounded shape of the spine, preventing the leaves from working their way forward. Used since the 16th century, backing also enhances the openability of a volume by creating a slight crease in each leaf near the spine. In edition binding and library binding, backing is done by machine.

Also, a conservation treatment in which an additional layer is applied to a flat item to provide support, usually on the reverse side of a weakened sheet. Also refers to the material added as reinforcement.

back issue   Any issue of a periodical that precedes the current issue. Back issues are usually retained in a *back file*, which may be stored in a different location in the periodicals section of a library, sometimes converted to a more compact format, such as microfilm or microfiche. In the catalog record, the extent of the back file is indicated in the holdings statement. Synonymous with *back number*.

back-lining   *See*: lining.

backlist   All the publications on a publisher's active list that are no longer new, having been published prior to the current season. Kept in stock to meet future demand, backlist titles are often the most profitable part of a publisher's list. Also spelled *back-list*. Compare with *frontlist*. ***See also***: *in print*, *out of print*, and *out of stock*.

backlog   An accumulation of work that remains to be done, often the cause of delays and bottlenecks in workflow. A *cataloging backlog* may result when staffing is insufficient to meet the demands of acquisitions; for example, when a substantial gift is received within a short period of time. Synonymous in this sense with *arrears*.

back matter   The pages following the text at the end of a book on which the appendices, notes, bibliographies, list of contributors, indices, imprint, and any advertising normally appear. In scholarly works, the back matter may be considerable. Back matter is paginated in arabic numerals continuously with the text. Blank leaves may be included at the end to make up a full section. Synonymous with *end matter*, *postliminary matter*, *reference matter*, and *subsidiaries*. Compare with *front matter*. ***See also***: *parts of a book*.

back number   *See*: back issue.

back order (BO)   An order for library materials that could not be filled when originally placed because at least one of the items requested was not in stock or was as yet unpublished. Back orders are held open for future delivery, usually for a designated period of time, after which they are canceled. Synonymous in the UK with *dues*. ***See also***: *reorder* and *short shipment*.

back page   The last page of an issue of a periodical (verso of the last leaf), facing the inside of the back cover. In some publications (*example*: ***Booklist***), the back page is reserved for a regular column or editorial. ***See also***: *front page*.

backslanted   A typeface or handwriting that inclines to the left of center.

backslash A character consisting of a straight line slanting diagonally from upper left to lower right, used mainly in computer programming notation and to separate directory and filenames in DOS and Windows (*example*: **c:\bib\bib.txt** referring to the **bib.txt** file in the **bib** folder stored on the **c:** disk drive). Also spelled *back slash*. Synonymous with *reverse solidus*. Compare with *slash*.

backstrip In bookbinding, the central portion of the covering material, extending from the front joint to the back joint over the inlay separating the boards, stamped with the title and author's name in most editions. Sometimes used synonymously with *spine*. Compare with *back*. *See also*: *lining*.

back title *See*: spine title.

backup In data processing, to make a second copy of an important data file in case the original is lost, damaged, or destroyed. Also refers to computer files, equipment, and procedures created and maintained specifically for use in the event of loss or failure of normal systems. In a more general sense, any strategy designed to be implemented if a preferred method or system fails.

Also, to print the reverse side of a sheet that has already been printed on one side. Also spelled *back up*.

Baker & Taylor A jobber in the business of supplying books, videocassettes, and music materials to retailers and libraries, usually at a discount, and of providing value-added and customized services to meet the needs of libraries of all types. B&T products and services are listed and described in its trade catalogs. URL: www.btol.com.

balance In budgeting, to keep expenditures in line with income, usually for the duration of a fixed accounting period. In printing and Web page design, to arrange text and graphics on a page in a configuration that is aesthetically pleasing.

balanced A library collection containing materials that present the full range of opinion on controversial issues and sensitive topics, for example, the "for" and "against" positions on legalized abortion, or religious books representing various faiths. Although it is an elusive goal, balance is particularly important in developing public library collections that must meet the information needs and reflect the reading tastes of a wide range of patrons. *See also*: *collection development bias*.

ballad Originally, an orally transmitted narrative song composed in an impersonal style for public performance, often sung to a traditional tune that served as a musical accompaniment to a dance. Most ballads tell a popular story of tragic romance or personal catastrophe in short stanzas with a refrain, usually in the form of a dialogue with action. Repetition over an extended period of time tends to produce variants. Synonymous in this sense with *folk ballad*. *See also*: *saga*.

Beginning in 16th-century Britain, broadside ballads about contemporary issues and events were printed on a single sheet of paper and sold in the streets to be sung to well-known popular tunes. In the late 18th century, a new literary form developed in which long narrative poems were written in deliberate imitation of earlier popular ballads (*example*: Coleridge's **Rime of the Ancient Mariner**).

balloon   In cartoons, comic books, and graphic novels, a space encircled by a line drawn from the mouth of one of the characters, containing dialogue or the character's unspoken thoughts.

bands   *See*: sewing supports.

bandwidth   The maximum carrying capacity of a line in an electronic communications network. For digital devices, bandwidth is measured in bits or bytes per second (bps); for analog devices, in Hertz (cycles per second). Bandwidth determines the amount of data that can be transmitted in a fixed amount of time and is often described as narrow or broad, with *broadband* having greater capacity. During periods of peak use, it may also determine speed of transmission, particularly for large data files (graphics, audio, video, etc.) known as *bandwidth hogs*. On the Internet, the fiber-optic backbone has highest bandwidth. *See also*: *T1* and *T3*.

In broadcasting, the width of the band of frequencies or wave lengths assigned (usually by licensing agreement) to a radio or television station for its exclusive use.

banned book   A book, the publication and/or sale of which has been prohibited or suppressed by ecclesiastical or secular authority because its content is considered objectionable or dangerous, usually for political reasons (*example*: ***The Grapes of Wrath***) or social reasons (***Leaves of Grass***). Banned Books Week has been celebrated annually in the United States since 1981. Lists of banned books are available in the reference section of most large libraries. For more information, please see *Banned Books Online* at: digital.library.upenn.edu/books/banned-books.html. Compare with *expurgated*. *See also*: *censorship*, *challenge*, Index Librorum Prohibitorum, and *intellectual freedom*.

Banned Books Week   An annual event observed in the United States since 1981 during the last week of September, Banned Books Week is sponsored by the American Booksellers Association, American Booksellers Foundation for Free Expression, American Library Association, Association of American Publishers, American Society of Journalists and Authors, and National Association of College Stores and endorsed by the Center for the Book at the Library of Congress. Libraries and bookstores throughout the country celebrate the freedom to read by displaying recently banned books and books that have been banned throughout history.

banner   A narrow band of graphic promotional material displayed on a Web site that has leased or sold space on its page(s) to a commercial advertiser. Also, a narrow strip logo across the top or bottom of a Web page, identifying the host organization or suggesting the content of the site.

Also refers to a newspaper headline of one or two lines, large enough to extend across an entire page or most of a page. Compare with *skyline*.

bar border   A decorative band running the length of one of the margins of a page in a medieval manuscript, usually along the left-hand side of the text but sometimes along the right-hand side on the recto. A bar border may begin as an extension of a large initial letter and is often embellished, sometimes in gilt. Bar borders may be used to separate columns of text and in some manuscripts extend across the foot of the page to support bas-de-page scenes.

barcode A printed label containing machine-readable data encoded in vertical lines of equal length but variable thickness, which can be read into an attached computer by an optical scanner. In libraries barcodes are used to identify books and other materials for circulation and inventory and to link the borrower's library card to the appropriate patron record in automated circulation systems. Also spelled *bar code*.

bar graph *See*: histogram.

bark cloth A flexible material used as a writing surface in the Himalayas, South Pacific, and Americas, consisting of pieces of tree bark beaten smooth, then joined with a vegetable adhesive to form large sheets. In the South Pacific, the inner bark of the paper mulberry or breadfruit tree is used. Also spelled *barkcloth*.

bas-de-page French for "bottom of the page." In medieval manuscripts, an unframed scene drawn or painted across the lower margin of a page, sometimes outside the overall border but more often resting on it, with or without reference to the text or other images on the same page. Michelle Brown notes in *Understanding Illuminated Manuscripts* (Getty Museum/British Library, 1994) that this form of decoration is found in gothic illumination beginning in the 13th century.

base line In typography, the imaginary horizontal line connecting the bottoms of lowercase letters lacking descenders, used to measure the intervals between lines of type. The line connecting the tops of letters lacking ascenders is called the *mean line*. Also spelled *baseline*.

base map A topographic map, usually on a scale of 1:10,000 to 1:50,000, used as the basis for other maps. In the United States, the base map is the 1:24,000 7.5-minute topographic quadrangle published in series by the U.S. Geological Survey, popularly known as the *quad*. Synonymous with *mother map*.

base number A class number in Dewey Decimal Classification schedules to which other numbers are appended, for example, **020** representing the library and information sciences, to which a decimal fraction may be added to indicate a subclass, as in **020.5** library and information science periodicals. Compare with *base of notation*. **See also**: *add note*.

base of notation The set of characters or symbols used in the notation of a given classification system. In Dewey Decimal Classification, the arabic numerals 0–9 are used (decimal notation). In Library of Congress Classification, the letters of the English alphabet are used (alphabetic notation), minus the letters O and I, which are easily mistaken for the numerals zero and one. As a general rule, the shorter the base, the longer the notation representing a given class is likely to be. Compare with *base number*.

basic search *See*: search mode.

bastarda A script used for speed in various parts of Europe from the late 13th to the 15th century, combining elements of formal textura (slow to write) with gothic cursive in letterforms that are spiky, with ascenders elongated and bent. Known as *bâtarde* in France and "secretary" in England, bastard hands were written with varying degrees of deliberation and individual style, depending on the amount of speed, elegance, and formality desired. In 15th-century French and Belgian Books of Hours, *littera bastarda* became a formal book hand in its own right.

bastard title   *See*: half title.

batch processing   A group of records accumulated so that they can be processed together, rather than one by one, used mainly in automated cataloging and interlibrary loan to increase efficiency and reduce costs. Synonymous with *batchload processing*.

bathymetric map   A topographic map showing the depth and features of the sea floor, including coastal zones (bays and estuaries), usually by means of contour lines called *isobaths*.

battledore   A type of school primer used in the late 18th century, made of folded paper varnished on the inside, resembling a horn book when opened but sometimes lacking a handle.

baud   Originally, a unit of telegraph signaling speed (one Morse code dot per second) proposed in 1927 at the International Telegraph Conference and named after the French engineer Jean-Maurice-Emile Baudot (1845–1903), who designed the first teleprinter.

In telecommunications, a unit of measurement indicating the number of *signaling elements* (changes of voltage or frequency) transmitted per second over a communication channel, at slower speeds synonymous with *bits per second (bps)*. At higher speeds, more than one bit may be encoded per second; for example, a speed of 4,800 baud may transmit 9,600 bits per second. For this reason, *bps* has replaced the term *baud* as a measure of data transmission speed. The *baud rate* of a modem is one of the factors determining the speed of an Internet connection in dial-up access. Pronounced *bawd*. Plural: *baud*.

Bay Psalm Book   Early in the history of the Massachusetts Bay Colony, Richard Mather and a group of fellow clergy transcribed biblical psalms into metrical verse to be sung in worship by members of the Puritan congregation. In 1640, 20 years after the *Mayflower* landed at Plymouth Rock, 17 copies of *The Whole Booke of Psalmes Faithfully Translated into English Metre* were printed by Stephen Daye at Cambridge, Massachusetts, on the first printing press in New England, purchased and imported specifically to print the hymnal. Issued in several editions over more than 100 years, the work was known at various times as the *New England Book of Psalms* and the *New England Version of the Psalms*. The earliest extant book of size written and printed in the United States, examples of the first edition are extremely rare, but the work is available in facsimile reprint.

BBC   *See*: British Broadcasting Corporation.

BBS   *See*: bulletin board system.

BCALA   *See*: Black Caucus of the American Library Association.

BCCB   *See*: Bulletin of the Center for Children's Books.

BEA   *See*: BookExpo America.

beast epic   A series of stories popular during the Middle Ages in which the characters are animals with human qualities, usually written in the form of an allegory satirizing the Catholic Church, the royal court, or some other powerful person, group, or institution (*example*: Pierre de Saint-Cloud's 12th-century **Roman de Renart**). A more recent example is George Orwell's **Animal Farm** (1945), written in the same tradition. Compare with *bestiary*.

beatus manuscript   A medieval manuscript consisting of an illustrated compilation of allegorical commentaries on passages from the *Apocalypse*, the revelation of the second coming of Christ experienced by St. John the Evangelist. Beatus manuscripts were often beautifully illuminated.

beginning reader   A heavily illustrated work of fiction or nonfiction designed specifically for young children learning to read in which the text is brief, the vocabulary and grammar simplified, and the type size large, shelved in the juvenile collection in public libraries (*example*: **Harry and the Lady Next Door** by Gene Zion).

belles lettres   A French phrase meaning "beautiful letters," referring to polite, refined literature (poetry, essays, drama, orations, letters, literary criticism, etc.) and to the aesthetics of literary studies.

benchmark   A term borrowed from surveying to indicate the superior quality of a product or service recognized as a standard or point of reference in comparisons made by other producers or providers intent on improving their performance. In computing, a measure of the performance of a hardware or software component. Also spelled *bench mark*.

benedictional   From the Latin *benedictus*, meaning "blessed." A liturgical book containing a collection of blessings recited for the benefit of congregants after the consecration and before the giving of communion in the Catholic Mass. In early Church history, when blessings were said only by the bishop, a lavishly illuminated benedictional might be made for a specific bishop. In the later Middle Ages, when any priest holding a Mass could give blessings, benedictionals became more common.

benefits   Compensation to which an employee is entitled in addition to salary or wages, such as health and dental insurance, pension or retirement contributions, free tuition, etc., usually specified in the contract or collective bargaining agreement governing terms of employment. Persons employed part-time are usually not entitled to full benefits. Synonymous with *fringes*. Compare with *perk*.

Berne Convention   An international copyright agreement creating an *International Union for the Protection of Literary and Artistic Works* signed in Berne, Switzerland, in 1886, ratified in 1887 by several European countries and their colonies, and revised periodically. By 1974, there were 64 signatories. The United States joined in 1988. To receive copyright protection under the *Berne Convention*, first publication of a work must occur in a member country. Works published in nonsignatory nations receive protection if published simultaneously in a signatory nation. Protection is for the author's lifetime plus 50 years. *See also*: Universal Copyright Convention.

Berners-Lee, Tim (1955–   )   The inventor of the World Wide Web, Tim Berners-Lee graduated from Oxford University in physics and worked in the telecommunications industry in England before he was granted a fellowship in 1984 at CERN, a high-energy physics lab in Geneva. In 1989, he proposed that CERN fund the development of a hypertext data system and spent the next five years facilitating the design of what quickly became a global electronic communications system. In 1994, Berners-Lee moved to the Laboratory for Computer Science at MIT, where he continued to develop Web tools and standards. Although he has received awards for his work, Berners-Lee elected *not* to copyright or profit from his invention because he wanted the Web to remain widely accessible. He has been quoted as saying, "[Y]ou can have an idea . . . and it can happen. It means that dreamers all over the world should take note and not stop."

best books   A selection of recently published books considered by reviewers to be superior in the field or the type of publication they represent. Most library review publications publish annual lists of highly recommended titles in the various categories reviewed (reference, fiction, nonfiction, young adult, children's books, etc.). Recommended lists are also published in book form (*example*: ***Best Books for Beginning Readers*** by Thomas G. Gunning) for use in collection development. Compare with *bestseller*.

bestiary   A type of medieval literature containing descriptions, folklore, and myths about exotic animals (real or imaginary), with text and illustrations intended to teach both natural history and Christian morals through allegory, for example, the rise of the phoenix symbolizing Christ's resurrection. Based primarily on the *Physiologus* ("The Natural Philosopher"), a Greek text believed to have been written in Alexandria in the 2nd century, bestiaries were particularly popular in 12th- and 13th-century England in versions that incorporated other medieval sources such as the 7th-century encyclopedia of Bishop Isidore of Seville. Michelle Brown notes in *Understanding Illuminated Manuscripts* (Getty Museum/British Library, 1994) that bestiaries were illustrated in a wide variety of styles, and their motifs were often used in other decorative contexts (borders, bas-de-page scenes, *mappae mundi*, etc.). Synonymous with *Bestiarius*, *De Bestiis*, and *Book of Beasts*. Compare with *beast epic*.

best practices   In the application of theory to real-life situations, procedures that, when properly applied, consistently yield superior results and are therefore used as reference points in evaluating the effectiveness of alternative methods of accomplishing the same task. Best practices are identified by examining the empirical evidence of success. Compare with *guidelines* and *standards*.

bestseller   A highly publicized trade book currently in such high demand in bookstores and libraries that large numbers of copies are sold and circulated. Major newspapers and review publications often publish ranked lists of bestsellers in adult fiction and nonfiction (and sometimes in children's literature) based on sales volume over a given period of time. *The Bowker Annual Library and Book Trade Almanac* usually includes an essay analyzing the previous year's bestsellers. Online bestseller lists are indexed in *Yahoo!* (www.yahoo.com). Also spelled *best-seller*. Compare with *classic*.

best-seller   *See*: bestseller.

Beta Phi Mu (BΦM)   Founded at the University of Illinois in 1948, Beta Phi Mu is an international library and information science honor society established to recognize outstanding scholarship and to sponsor professional and scholarly projects in librarianship. Membership is open to graduates of ALA-accredited library schools who have completed the requirements leading to a fifth year or advanced degree (M.L.S. or M.L.I.S.) with a scholastic average of at least 3.75 and in the top 25 percent of their class. An affiliate of the American Library Association, Beta Phi Mu publishes a semiannual national newsletter. URL: www.beta-phi-mu.org.

beta test   A full-scale test of a new software or hardware system involving actual users under normal operating conditions in the field, usually preceded by alpha testing in a laboratory environment.

beveled boards   A technique used in hand-binding in which the upper surface of the edges of heavy boards is cut at a sloping angle, instead of the usual 90 degrees, to give the cover a more elegant appearance or in conscious imitation of an earlier style. Also spelled *bevelled boards*. *See also*: *beveled edge*.

beveled edge   Any edge tapered at less than a 90-degree angle to make the transition from upper to lower surface more gradual than in a right-angle cut. Beveled boards are sometimes used in hand bookbinding. The edges of mats used in framing are normally beveled at a 60-degree angle. Also spelled *bevelled edge*.

BI   *See*: bibliographic instruction.

biannual   Issued twice each year. Also refers to a publication issued twice a year.

bias   Judgment unfairly influenced by subjective opinion when the situation calls for reliance on objective fact. Bias exists even in reference books (compare the entries for "Holocaust" and "Inquisition" in the *Encyclopedia Judaica*, *Encyclopedia of Religion*, and *New Catholic Encyclopedia*). In publicly supported libraries in the United States, bias in employment practices is prohibited by law. *See also*: *affirmative action* and *collection development bias*.

BIBCO   *See*: Program for Cooperative Cataloging (PCC).

bibelot   A French term for a small decorative object of exceptional beauty, rarity, or curiosity. In literature, a book of unusually small size, elegantly designed, and crafted from the finest materials. Also known as a *thumb book*.

bible   Any book or reference work widely accepted as an authoritative and reliable source of information, often a work updated in successive editions. In television series production, a general outline of story and character development for all the episodes of a program, at least for the first broadcast season. *See also*: *Bible*.

Bible   The sacred scripture of the Christian faith, consisting of the Hebrew Old Testament and the New Testament of the followers of Jesus of Nazareth. In the early Christian period, various Latin translations of Greek and Hebrew versions were used.

In the early 5th century, at the behest of Pope Damasus I, St. Jerome completed a new translation, known as the *Vulgata*, which became the authorized text for the Roman Church. The history of the Bible as a book began in the 4th century when large codices were produced on parchment. The earliest surviving examples include the *Codex Sinaiticus* and *Codex Alexandrinus*, both in The British Library, and the *Codex Vaticanus* in the Vatican Library. During the early Middle Ages, corruption of the Vulgate generated attempts to standardize the text, including production in the 9th century of a series of bibles at the scriptorium of Alcuin of York at Tours for circulation among monastic establishments in Europe.

Throughout the Middle Ages, certain books of the Bible were produced separately, especially the Gospels, Pentateuch, Hexateuch, Octateuch, *Psalms*, and *Apocalypse*. Prior to the 12th century, most scriptural texts were produced as beautifully illuminated manuscripts, in large format for liturgical use, but with the growth of universities, a market developed for smaller, less costly bibles written in condensed script. Although biblical texts were translated into the vernacular as early as the 8th century (usually as glosses), vernacular translation did not get fully under way until the mid-13th century. The Latin 42-line *Gutenberg Bible* was the first book printed in Europe. *See also*: *Atlantic bible*, Bible historiale, Bible moralisée, Biblia Pauperum, *picture bible*, and *pocket bible*.

Bible historiale   Available for centuries in Latin, the Bible did not become accessible in the vernacular until the 14th century. In France it appeared in a prose narrative version compiled by the cleric Guiart des Moulins, who based his translation on Peter Comestor's earlier text *Historia scholastica*, a commentary on Bible excerpts, with emphasis on the role of scripture as a record of historical events. Guiart added further commentary to translation of entire books of the Bible, also emphasizing historical narrative. Even before his death, Guiart's work was expanded by others to all the books of the Bible, including some apocrypha he had not translated. Michelle Brown notes in *Understanding Illuminated Manuscripts* (Getty Museum/British Library, 1994) that the illuminated miniatures in *Bibles historiales* often depict biblical images not found in Latin translations. Synonymous with *historical bible*.

Bible moralisée   A type of Latin picture bible made during the 13th century in which short passages or episodes from the Bible are accompanied by commentary providing moral, allegorical, or symbolic interpretation of the text, often drawing parallels between events in the Old and New Testaments (typology). Both text and commentary are illustrated, sometimes with long sequences of miniatures. Synonymous with *Bible allegorisée* and *moralized bible*.

bible paper   A strong, thin, opaque printing paper made from new cotton or linen rags, or from flax fiber, used to reduce the bulk of large volumes such as dictionaries, encyclopedias, bibles, and prayer books that would otherwise be too thick to be easily handled. Sometimes used synonymously with *India paper*.

bible style   A general term for any flexible leather binding that has rounded corners, especially one of dark color.

Biblia Pauperum   A blockbook issued in large numbers beginning in about 1450, consisting mainly of pictures illustrating parallels between the Old and New Testaments (typology), with captions in Latin or German providing lessons from the Scriptures. Jean Peters notes in *The Bookman's Glossary* (R.R. Bowker, 1983) that this form of book was not superseded by the invention of movable type but continued to be produced into the early part of the 16th century. Extremely rare, fewer than two dozen examples are known to survive. Latin for "Bible of the Poor," the name was applied by German scholars in the 1930s who assumed that the purpose of the format was to educate the illiterate. However, since even blockbooks were costly to produce in the late Middle Ages, their real purpose may have been to entertain people of moderate means.

biblio-   From the Greek word *biblion*, meaning "book," used in combination to form a host of terms pertaining to books and libraries (*bibliography*, *bibliomania*, *bibliophile*, *bibliophobia*, *bibliotherapy*, etc.). In interactions with patrons, most public services librarians avoid the "B-words" because the general public is not familiar with the technical terminology of librarianship.

bibliocaper   A term coined by George Eberhart in *The Whole Library Handbook 3* (ALA, 2000) to refer to an odd or wacky event, harebrained prank, or bizarre petty crime involving libraries, librarians, library patrons, or books.

biblioclast   A person who destroys or mutilates books, for one reason or another. Fortunately for bibliophiles, this form of aberrant behavior occurs infrequently. *See also*: *libricide*.

bibliognost   A person with a profound knowledge of books and bibliography.

bibliogony   Of or relating to the production of books in all their forms. Synonymous with *bibliogenesis*.

bibliographee   A person concerning whom a bibliography is compiled, as in a list of references at the end of a biographical essay or book-length biography. *See also*: *biobibliography*.

bibliographer   A person who describes and lists books and other publications, with particular attention to such characteristics as authorship, publication date, edition, typography, etc. The result of this endeavor is a *bibliography*. A person who limits such efforts to a specific field or discipline is a *subject bibliographer*. *See also*: *Bibliographical Society of America*.

Bibliographical Society of America (BSA)   Organized in 1904, the BSA promotes bibliographical research and issues publications on bibliographical topics. Membership is open to all who have an interest in bibliographical problems and projects, including libraries and librarians. The BSA publishes the quarterly journal *Papers of the Bibliographical Society of America*. URL: www.bibsocamer.org.

bibliographic control   A broad term encompassing all the activities involved in creating, organizing, managing, and maintaining the file of bibliographic records representing the items held in a library or archival collection, or the sources listed in an index or database, to facilitate access to the information contained in them. Bibliographic control includes the standardization of bibliographic description and subject access by means of uniform catalog code, classification systems, name authorities, and preferred headings; the creation and maintenance of catalogs, union lists, and finding aids; and the provision of physical access to the items in the collection. *See also*: *authority control*.

bibliographic coupling   The idea that two scientific papers containing a citation in common are bibliographically related in a way that is likely to be of interest to researchers. A similar relationship is established between two or more documents when they are cited in a third. *Citation indexing* is based on this principle. Synonymous with *citation coupling*.

bibliographic database   A computer file consisting of electronic entries called *records*, each containing a uniform description of a specific document or bibliographic item, usually retrievable by author, title, subject heading (descriptor), or keyword(s). Some bibliographic databases are general in scope and coverage; others provide access to the literature of a specific discipline or group of disciplines. An increasing number of bibliographic databases provide the full-text of at least a portion of the sources indexed. Most bibliographic databases are proprietary, available by licensing agreement from vendors, or directly from the abstracting and indexing services that create them.

bibliographic description   In a general sense, all the elements of data necessary to conclusively identify a specific document, presented in some form of record.

In library cataloging, the detailed description of a copy of a specific edition of a work intended to identify and distinguish it from other works by the same author, of the same title, or on the same subject. In *AACR2*, the bibliographic record representing an item in the catalog includes the following standard areas of description: title and statement of responsibility (author, editor, composer, etc.), edition, material specific details, details of publication and distribution, physical description, series, notes, and standard number and terms of availability (ISBN, ISSN, price). *See also*: *chief source of information* and *level of description*.

bibliographic essay   A critical essay in which the bibliographer identifies and evaluates the core literature of a subdiscipline or field of study, providing guidance to students, researchers, and collection development librarians, for example, the bibliographic essay published at the beginning of each issue of the review journal *CHOICE*. Compare with *literature review*.

bibliographic format   The standardized sequence and manner of presentation of the data elements constituting the full description of an item in a specific cataloging or indexing system. The machine-readable MARC record format has become the standard for library catalogs in many countries of the world.

bibliographic hermaphrodite   A term coined by Crystal Graham, serials librarian at the University of California, San Diego, to refer to a publication in any medium that has characteristics of both *monographs* and *serials*. Most are complete in one part but have the potential to continue. Their defining characteristic is "updatability." Examples include loose-leaf services, databases, Web sites, and some electronic journals. Beginning in 1995, reconsideration of issues related to seriality resulted in a new model, dividing the bibliographic universe into *finite resources* and *continuing resources*, a more accurate reflection of changing patterns in publishing. This new distinction has been adopted in *AACR2 2002*.

bibliographic instruction (BI)   Instructional programs designed to teach library users how to locate the information they need quickly and effectively. BI usually covers the library's system of organizing materials, the structure of the literature of the field, research methodologies appropriate to the discipline, and specific resources and finding tools (catalogs, indexes and abstracting services, bibliographic databases, etc.).

In academic libraries, bibliographic instruction is usually course-related or course-integrated. Libraries that have a computer-equipped instruction lab are in a position to include hands-on practice in the use of online catalogs, bibliographic databases, and Internet resources. Instruction sessions are usually taught by an *instructional services librarian* who has specialized training and experience in pedagogical methods. Synonymous with *library instruction* and *library orientation*. Compare with *user education*. **See also**: *information literacy*, *Library Instruction Round Table*, *lifelong learning*, *LOEX*, and *one-shot*.

bibliographic item   In *AACR2*, a document or set of documents in any physical format (print or nonprint) given a single bibliographic description in cataloging, by virtue of having been published, issued, released, or otherwise treated as a single entity. As defined in *FRBR* (*Functional Requirements for Bibliographic Records*), a single concrete exemplar of a manifestation of an expression of an intellectual or artistic work, in most cases a single physical object, such as a copy of an edition of a single-volume monograph. All the items constituting a manifestation normally contain the same intellectual/artistic content and are identical in physical form, but variations can occur subsequent to production, as in the case of a monograph rebound by a library. In some cases an item consists of more than one physical object, for example, a videorecording released on more than one cassette or a multivolume set of reference books. *See also*: *bibliographic record*.

bibliographic record   An entry representing a specific item in a library catalog or bibliographic database, containing all the data elements necessary for a full description, presented in a specific bibliographic format. In modern cataloging, the standard format is machine-readable (*example*: the **MARC record**), but prior to the use of computers, the traditional format was the catalog card. Compare with *catalog record*, *check-in record*, *item record*, and *order record*. **See also**: *brief record*, *encoding level*, *full record*, and *record structure*.

bibliographic resource   In functional terms, an expression or manifestation of a work, or a specific item, that is the basis for bibliographic description in library cataloging (*AACR2*). Such a resource may be tangible (a printed publication) or intangible (an electronic text).

bibliographic retrieval   The process in which a user queries a library catalog or bibliographic database, usually by author, title, subject heading (descriptor), or keyword(s), and receives a list of records representing items that satisfy the parameters of the search. Most commercial databases allow the searcher to use techniques such as Boolean logic, truncation, and proximity to refine search statements. *See also*: *precision*, *recall*, and *search strategy*.

bibliographic service center   A regional broker in the business of handling access, communication, training, billing, and other services for libraries located within a specific geographic area that are connected to an online bibliographic network, for example, Nelinet, which provides access to and support for OCLC and a variety of bibliographic databases to libraries in the northeastern United States. Compare with *bibliographic utility*.

bibliographic utility   An organization that provides access to and support for machine-readable bibliographic databases directly to member libraries or through a network of regional bibliographic service centers, usually via a proprietary interface. The largest bibliographic utility in the world is OCLC.

bibliography   Strictly speaking, a systematic list or enumeration of written works by a specific author or on a given subject, or that share one or more common characteristics (language, form, period, place of publication, etc.). When a bibliography is about a person, the subject is called the *bibliographee*. A bibliography may be comprehensive or selective. Long bibliographies may be published serially or in book form. The person responsible for compiling a bibliography is the *bibliographer*. Bibliographies are indexed by subject in *Bibliographic Index: A Cumulative Bibliography of Bibliographies*, published by H.W. Wilson. Abbreviated *bibl*. Compare with *catalog*. *See also*: *Bibliographical Society of America*, *discography*, and *filmography*.

In the context of scholarly publication, a list of references to sources cited in the text of an article or book, or suggested by the author for further reading, usually given at the end of the work. Style manuals describing citation format for the various disciplines (APA, MLA, etc.) are available in the reference section of most academic libraries and online via the World Wide Web.

Also refers to the art and practice of describing books, with particular reference to their authorship, publication, physical form, and literary content. *See also*: *analytical bibliography*, *annotated bibliography*, *biobibliography*, *current bibliography*, *national bibliography*, *period bibliography*, *retrospective bibliography*, and *selective bibliography*.

biblioholism   An addiction to books and book collecting, a lesser affliction than bibliomania but more intense than bibliophily. A term coined by Tom Raabe that appears in the title of his book *Biblioholism: The Literary Addiction* (Fulcrum, 1991, rev. 2001). Raabe provides a 25-point quiz for self-diagnosis. Compare with *bibliolatry*.

biblioklept   A thief who steals books. A *bibliokleptomaniac* is a person suffering from a compulsion to steal books. When library collections are targeted, biblioklepts are considered problem patrons. *See also*: *bibliomania*.

bibliolatry Excessive reverence for books, carried to the point of emotional dependence on them. A person who is a habitual bookworm may be at risk of becoming a *bibliolater*. Compare with *biblioholism* and *bibliophile*.

Also refers to excessive devotion to a literal interpretation of the Bible.

bibliology The historical and scientific study and description of books as physical objects, from their origins in human society to the present, including knowledge of the processes and materials (booklore) involved in making them. Compare with *codicology*.

bibliomancy The art of divination through the use of books or verses of the Bible or some other sacred text. Also, the practice of opening the Bible, or a book of verses or aphorisms such as the *I Ching*, without previously marking the page, to discover meaning or significance in the passage found.

bibliomania An obsession or mania for collecting and possessing books, especially rare books and editions. In the *International Encyclopedia of Information and Library Science* (Routledge, 2003), the origin of the term is attributed to Thomas Frognall Dibdin (1776–1845), a writer and bibliographer who helped establish book collecting as a popular pursuit among English aristocracy of the 19th century.

Some *bibliomaniacs* are driven by apparent obsession to become *biblioklepts*. In a recent case, Stephen C. Blumberg was convicted on four felony counts, sentenced to five years and 11 months in prison, and fined $200,000 after a collection of 21,000 rare books was found in his home in Iowa, stolen over a period of years from approximately 140 libraries in the United States and Canada. The fact that Mr. Blumberg had a very comfortable independent income from family trusts suggests that his larceny was motivated by the desire to possess rather than profit from his illegal activities. Compare with *biblioholism* and *bibliophile*.

bibliometrics The use of mathematical and statistical methods to study and identify patterns in the usage of materials and services within a library or to analyze the historical development of a specific body of literature, especially its authorship, publication, and use. Prior to the mid-20th century, the quantitative study of bibliographic data and usage was known as *statistical bibliography*. *See also*: *citation analysis* and *informetrics*.

bibliomining The use of statistical methods in the analysis of library records to detect patterns of behavior in groups of patrons and/or staff, which might be of assistance to library administration in making more informed management decisions and in marketing library services effectively. Protection of patron privacy is an important consideration in the use of such data. *See also*: *bibliometrics*.

bibliomystery A work of fiction in the mystery genre in which plot, setting, and/or characters are closely associated with the world of books, manuscripts, libraries, archives, etc. (*example*: ***The Name of the Rose*** by Umberto Eco). A bibliography of bibliomysteries is available at: www.bibliomysteries.com. Also spelled *biblio-mystery*.

biblionarcissism   The art of convincing others that one is more knowledgeable about books or bookish than one really is, a term attributed to Tom Raabe, author of *Biblioholism: The Literary Addiction* (Fulcrum, 1991, rev. 2001).

bibliopegy   The fine art of binding books by hand, performed by a *bibliopegist* (bookbinder).

bibliophilately   The collection and study of library-related postage stamps, usually as a hobby (see "Bibliophilately Revisited" by Larry Nix in the February 2000 issue of *American Libraries*).

bibliophile   A person who loves and treasures books (especially their physical form) and is sufficiently knowledgeable to be able to distinguish editions by their characteristics and qualities. Most bibliophiles are book collectors. The opposite of *bibliophobe*. Synonymous with *booklover* and *bibliophilist*. Compare with *biblioholism* and *bibliomania*.

bibliophilist   *See*: bibliophile.

bibliophobia   An irrational fear or dread of books so intense that the afflicted person, known as a *bibliophobe*, avoids them whenever possible. The opposite of *bibliophily*.

bibliopole   A bookseller, especially one who deals in rare books and editions. *See also*: *antiquarian bookseller*.

bibliopsychology   The psychological study of the interrelationships between authors, books, and readers. *See also*: *bibliotherapy*.

bibliotaph   A person who hoards books and hides them from others, even to the extent of keeping them under lock and key.

bibliotheca   From the Greek *biblion* ("book") and *theke* ("to place"). A library or collection of books. Also refers to a list or catalog of books, especially one prepared by a bibliographer.

Bibliothèque Nationale de France (BNF)   The national library of France, located in Paris. The history of the BNF spans five centuries. King Charles V ("The Wise") made the initial gift of his private library in 1368, but continuity in collection development did not begin until the reign of Louis XI (1461–1483). Francis I established the legal depository in 1537, and the collection was first classified in 1670 by Nicolas Clément. During the French Revolution, the royal library was proclaimed a national library. After the rise of Napoleon Bonaparte in 1799, it became an imperial library until the Republic was re-established in 1870. The creation of a Master Catalog of Printed Books was initiated in 1874 by Léopold Délisle, a medievalist who served as administrator general of the library from 1874 until 1905.

In 1994, the Bibliothèque Nationale (BN) and the newly built Bibliothèque de France (BDF) merged to form a single entity, the Bibliothèque Nationale de France, one of the leading libraries in the world. The collections have been brought together in two locations, the "Site Richelieu" and the "Site François Mitterrand." The latter welcomes both scholars (2,000 seats) and the general public (1,700 seats). URL: www.bnf.fr. The Library of Congress hosts the online exhibit *Creating French Culture:*

Treasures from the Bibliothèque Nationale de France at: http://lcweb.loc.gov/ exhibits/bnf/bnf0001.html.

bibliotherapy   The use of books selected on the basis of content in a planned reading program designed to facilitate the recovery of patients suffering from mental illness or emotional disturbance. Ideally, the process occurs in three phases: personal identification of the reader with a particular character in the recommended work, resulting in psychological catharsis, which leads to rational insight concerning the relevance of the solution suggested in the text to the reader's own experience. Assistance of a trained psychotherapist is advised. *See also*: *readers' advisory*.

biennial   Issued every two years. Also refers to a serial publication issued every two years. Compare with *semiannual*. *See also*: *annual, triennial, quadrennial, quinquennial, sexennial, septennial*, and *decennial*.

bifolium   In modern bookbinding, a pair of conjoint leaves, as opposed to a single leaf, one on each side of the fold down the center of a sheet. In medieval book production, a sheet of writing material (papyrus, parchment, or vellum) was folded in half to produce two leaves or four pages. A number of *bifolia*, nested one inside the other, usually in groups of four (eight leaves or 16 pages), formed a *quire*. A manuscript was assembled as a sequence of quires or gatherings, each sewn through the centerfold and to cords (sewing supports) running perpendicular to the spine. Synonymous with *bifolio*. Compare with *singleton*.

big book   A special edition of a children's picture book, published in very large format to facilitate display of the illustrations to a group in storytelling, usually bound in colorfully illustrated, flexible covers. Library suppliers offer furnishings specially designed for storing big books and other large, flat items.

big red books   A colloquial expression used by reference librarians in directing library users to the *Library of Congress Subject Headings* list, a multivolume set of large, thick reference books traditionally bound in red covers, usually shelved near the reference desk.

Bildungsroman   From the German word *Bildung* ("education" or "culture") and the French word *roman* ("novel"). A novel in which the author traces the maturation of the hero or heroine, from the subjectivity of childhood and early adolescence through the development of objective self-awareness (*examples*: **The Magic Mountain** by Thomas Mann and **The Tin Drum** by Günter Grass). Compare with *Kuntslerroman*.

bilinear script   *See*: majuscule.

bilingual edition   A book or periodical published in two languages, usually because both languages are spoken in the country in which the work was published (for example, English and French in Canada) or because the work was co-published in countries with different national languages.

bill   A law proposed during a formal session of a legislative body. In *AACR2*, bills and drafts of legislation are cataloged under the heading for the appropriate legislative body. Bills proposed in the U.S. Congress are searchable by keyword(s) or bill number in the *THOMAS* database, available online at: thomas.loc.gov.

Example:

A bill to give the consent of Congress to the removal by the legislature of the State of Washington of the restrictions upon the power of alienation of their lands by the Puyallup Indians : 52d Congress, 1st session, S.2306
(Main entry is under the heading for the Senate of the United States)

Also refers to a written statement of the amount owed for goods or services rendered, sent by the seller to the purchaser in expectation of prompt payment. In library acquisitions, the term *invoice* is preferred.

billed   A code used in library catalogs and circulation systems to indicate the circulation status of an item unavailable due to loss or damage, for which a previous borrower has been charged an amount usually based on the cost of replacement. Most libraries make an effort to replace lost and damaged items, even if the patron fails to pay the bill, provided demand exists and a reasonably priced edition is still in print.

bimonthly   Issued in alternate months (six times per year). Also refers to a serial issued every other month. Compare with *semimonthly*.

binary   Literally, *two*. Data used as input in a digital computer must be converted into code made up of the digits 0 and 1, called bits. *Binary code* is transmitted as a series of electrical pulses (0 bits at low voltage and 1 bits at higher voltage), stored as memory cells. When data files in digital format are displayed as output, the binary signals are translated back into characters or images. In *binary notation*, value is indicated by the position of the two digits:

0 0 0 0 position
8 4 2 1 value

Thus the decimal number **15** is expressed in binary as **1111**. *See also*: *ASCII*.

bind   To fasten the leaves of a book together and enclose them in a protective cover, a process known as *binding*, originally done by hand but in modern book production almost entirely by machine.

binder   A removable cover used for filing and storing loose sheets, pamphlets, and issues of periodicals. Commercially made binders used in libraries to protect current issues of magazines usually have a transparent front cover to facilitate browsing. *See also*: *loose-leaf*.

Also refers to a person trained in the art and craft of binding books and other publications, usually employed in a bindery. Also used synonymously with *bindery*. *See also*: *library binder*.

binder's board   A stiff, sturdy board made from pulped fiber derived from rope, wood, or recycled paper, used since the early 18th century to give rigidity to the covers of books published in hardcover, and preferred in hand-binding. Modern high-quality binder's board is single-ply, made by pressing pulp between heavy rollers to achieve the desired thickness and smoothness. Synonymous in the UK with *millboard*. Compare with *pasteboard*.

binder's title   The title stamped or lettered on the spine of a bound volume by the binder, as distinct from the *cover title* on the publisher's edition and the title printed on the title page. *See also*: *spine title*.

bindery   An establishment that performs one or more of the various types of binding. Some large libraries and library systems have an in-house bindery usually associated with centralized technical processing. In smaller libraries, materials in need of binding or rebinding (back issues of periodicals, paperback editions, etc.) are sent to a commercial bindery. *See also*: *library binder*.

In the early Middle Ages, most binding was done in the Catholic monasteries that produced manuscript books. Secular binderies were established in Europe as early as the 12th century near primary markets (towns and cities with universities and government offices), usually in the vicinity of shops owned by booksellers and stationers since most books were bound to the customer's order. Early binderies were often family businesses.

bindery record   The systematic account maintained by a library of materials sent to the bindery and the specific treatment given them. Most bindery records include title of publication, call number (if applicable), style and color of binding, format and placement of spine lettering, description of binding unit, and any special instructions. In some automated serials control systems, bindery information is included in the *check-in record*.

binding   The sewing and outside covering on a volume of printed or blank leaves. Books published in hardcover are bound in boards covered in cloth or some other durable material. Leather was used to bind manuscripts and incunabula but is now used mainly in hand-binding. Books bound in paper covers are called *paperbacks*. Also refers to the process of fastening the leaves or sections of a publication together by sewing or stitching, or by applying adhesive to the back, and then attaching a cover by hand or by machine under the supervision of a skilled *binder*. In large libraries, binding may be done in-house. Smaller libraries usually send materials to a commercial bindery. In any case, most libraries follow an established *binding policy*. Abbreviated *bdg*. *See also*: *finishing* and *forwarding*.

In medieval manuscript books, the collated quires were sewn to leather or hemp cords, and the loose ends of the cords threaded into grooves cut in the inner surface of the wooden boards, then secured with pegs or nails. The spine and outside surface of the boards were covered in damp leather or parchment and the grooves concealed by gluing a leaf, called the *paste-down*, to the inside of each cover. The cover might then be decorated, usually by blocking or tooling, and metal bosses and cornerpieces added to protect the binding from wear, with one or more clasps attached to the edges to keep the volume firmly closed when not in use. During the early Middle Ages, binding was done in monastic scriptoria, but by the late Middle Ages, this stage of book production was done by the stationer or bookseller. The tooled goatskin binding on the pocket-sized *Stonyhurst Gospel of Saint John*, found in the tomb of Saint Cuthbert (died A.D. 687), is believed to be the earliest surviving in Europe.

See also: *adhesive binding, antique binding, architectural binding, armorial binding, case binding, cathedral binding, chemise binding, cloisonné, conservation binding, Coptic binding, cottage binding, custom binding, deluxe binding, dentelle binding, designer binding, desktop binding, easel binding, embroidered binding, Etruscan binding, extended binding, fan binding, fanfare binding, flap binding, flexible binding, flush binding, Greek style, Grolier binding, herringbone, imitation binding,* in quaternis, *jeweled binding, landscape binding, library binding, limp binding, mechanical binding, metal binding, novelty binding, padded binding, painted binding, papier mâché binding, peasant binding, prelibrary binding, presentation binding, publisher's binding, rebinding, reinforced binding, relievo binding, retrospective binding, shaped binding, stationery binding, suede binding, treasure binding,* and *wheel binding.*

Also refers to the association of a particular syntax with the data dictionary of a metadata element set. Because of the popularity of XML, many metadata initiatives have developed XML bindings for their metadata standards.

binding copy   A worn book in such poor condition that it needs to be rebound and is worth the expense of rebinding.

binding edge   The edge at which the leaves of a book are attached to one another, usually by sewing the folded and gathered sections together and gluing them to a lining or by trimming away the back fold and applying strong adhesive to the loose leaves. The three outer edges of a book are the *head, foot* or *tail,* and *fore-edge.* Compare with *spine.*

binding error   A mistake made in binding a publication. Common errors include the incorrect folding of signatures; leaves or an entire section omitted, gathered in incorrect sequence, or bound in upside down; and application of the wrong cover to the body of the book. Under most circumstances, the publisher will replace such copies at no charge. *See also*: *aberrant copy.*

binding margin   The unprinted space between the binding edge of a printed page and the area that bears print. The width of the inner margin often determines whether rebinding is possible. Synonymous with *back, gutter,* and *inside margin.*

binding medium   In the production of medieval manuscripts, an ingredient added to ink or paint to hold the pigment together and make it adhere to the writing surface (parchment or vellum). Gum arabic, made from the sap of the acacia tree, was used to bind ink. For paint, illuminators used glair (clarified egg white), tempera (egg yolk), fish glue, or size made from parchment or gelatin. Type of binding medium could determine finish. *See also*: *gesso.*

binding policy   Guidelines established by a library or library system concerning the manner in which materials not purchased in permanent binding are to be bound. Cataloged monographs are usually bound (except for loose-leaf and spiral bound materials), pamphlets may be placed in pamphlet covers, and serials permanently retained are usually bound unless converted to microform. Large library systems sometimes have an in-house bindery, but most small and medium-size libraries use a commercial bindery.

binding slip A set of written instructions sent by a library to the bindery with each volume or set of volumes, giving the specifications by which the item is to be bound. A form in multiple copies allows the library to maintain a record of the instructions given.

binding unit Two or more consecutive periodical issues bound together to form a volume of optimum size. For most journals published on a quarterly basis, the binding unit is composed of four issues, but for periodicals issued weekly or monthly, it usually consists of less than the total number of issues published in a year.

biobibliography A list of works written about an author, including biographical and critical sources examining the author's life and work. Compare with *author bibliography*.

biographical dictionary A single-volume reference work or set of reference books containing biographical essays about the lives of actual people, sometimes limited to *biographees* who are deceased. Biographical dictionaries may be general (*example*: **Webster's Biographical Dictionary**), subject-specific (**Biographical Dictionary of the History of Technology**), or limited to persons of a specific nationality (**American National Biography**), race (**Contemporary Black Biography**), field or profession (**International Dictionary of Anthropologists**), or period or gender (**Biographical Dictionary of Ancient Greek and Roman Women**). Some are published serially (**Current Biography Yearbook**). Compare with *collective biography*.

biography A carefully researched, relatively full narrative account of the life of a specific person or closely related group of people written by another. The biographer selects the most interesting and important events with the intention of elucidating the character and personality of the *biographee* and placing the subject's life in social, cultural, and historical context. An *authorized biography*, written with the consent and sometimes the cooperation of its subject, may be less critical than an *unauthorized biography*.

The literary form was pioneered by the Roman historians Plutarch, Tacitus, and Suetonius. English literary biography began with James Boswell's *Life of Samuel Johnson*, published in 1791. Modern biographers tend to be objective in approach, but classical and medieval biographers often wrote to confirm a thesis or illustrate a moral principle. Also refers to the branch of literature and history in which the lives of actual people are described and analyzed.

Biographical works are indexed annually in *Biography Index*, published by H.W. Wilson, and in *Biography and Genealogy Master Index*, published by the Gale Group. Biographical information is also available online via the World Wide Web. Abbreviated *bio* and *biog*. Compare with *autobiography* and *memoirs*. **See also**: *biobibliography*, *biographical dictionary*, *collective biography*, and *hagiography*.

biological attack In preservation, damage or deterioration caused by biological organisms. In libraries the worst damage is caused by mold and insects (bookworms, book lice, cockroaches, etc.), but rodents, dogs, cats, and babies may also inflict damage.

Mold weakens the fibers of which paper and binder's board are composed, causing discoloration and in some cases fusing the leaves. Insects feed on paper, adhesives, and bindings, often leaving excretions that cause further damage and can be difficult to remove. Remedies are generally species-specific.

BIP   *See*: **Books in Print**.

birth and death dates   The dates on which a person was born and died. In library cataloging, a person's dates (birth, death, etc.) are added, in prescribed form, as the last element of a heading if the heading is otherwise identical to another (*example*: **Lang, Andrew, 1844–1912**). If the person is still living, the birth date is given, followed by a hyphen, and the death date is added later (*example*: **King, Stephen, 1947–**). If the birth and/or death dates are unknown, the abbreviation *ca.* (*circa*) is used before the estimated date(s) to mean "approximately." Birth and death dates are also included in the entries in biographical reference works. *See also*: *false date*.

birthday book   A type of book popular during the Victorian period in which a quotation from a work by a well-known writer (usually a poet) is given for each day of the year, with blank space for autographs.

BISG   *See*: **Book Industry Study Group**.

bit   A contraction of *binary digit*, either of the two values (0 and 1) used in the binary number system and as the smallest unit of storage in digital computers. In personal computers, data is stored and processed in 8-bit units called *bytes*. In ASCII code, each alphanumeric character is represented by a unique sequence of 7 bits. Although bits are used to measure digital transmission speed (*bit rate*), the capacity of storage (disks, files, databases, etc.) is measured in bytes. *See also*: *bit depth*.

bit depth   In computing, the number of bits used to represent a discrete item, using a coding system based on numeric values. In digital imaging, the number of bits used to represent a pixel (at least 15 bits for digital video and 24 bits to produce full color in RGB). In digital audio, bit depth is a measure of the hardware or software processing the audio file.

bitmap   A digital representation composed of dots arranged in rows and columns, each represented by a single bit of data that determines the value of a pixel in a monochrome image on a computer screen. In a gray scale or color image, each dot is composed of a set of bits that determine the individual values of a group of pixels that *in combination* create the visual impression of a specific shade or hue. The greater the number of bits per dot, the wider the range of possible shades or hues.

   The number of dots per square inch (density) determines the resolution of a bit-mapped image. Resolution may also be expressed as the number of rows multiplied by the number of columns in the map. When documents are scanned into a computer, the image on the page is automatically converted into a bitmapped image that can be viewed on a monitor. Also spelled *bit map*. *See also*: *digital imaging*.

biweekly   Issued every two weeks. Also refers to a serial issued at two-week intervals. Used synonymously with *semimonthly*. Compare with *semiweekly*.

black and white   A still or moving image, such as a photograph, photocopy, or motion picture, produced in black, white, and intermediate shades of gray, without the use of color. Also refers to the process used to produce such an image. In bibliographic description, the abbreviation *b&w* is often used. Also abbreviated *b-w*. Compare with *duotone* and *full-color printing*.

Black Caucus of the American Library Association (BCALA)   Founded in 1970, BCALA has a membership of black librarians and black persons interested in promoting librarianship and encouraging active participation by African Americans in library associations and at all levels of the profession. BCALA publishes the bi-monthly *BCALA Newsletter*. URL: www.bcala.org.

black face   *See*: boldface.

black letter   *See*: gothic.

blank   A leaf intentionally left unprinted in a book, usually preceding the half title and/ or following the back matter. Also refers to any page or sheet of paper (or other writing surface) that does not bear written or printed matter. Compare with *white space*. In a more general sense, any recording medium, such as an audiocassette or videocassette, on which nothing is recorded.

blankbook   A book consisting of clean or ruled leaves for writing or making entries, with printing limited to page headings and/or divisions. Examples include diaries, albums, scrapbooks, account books, exercise books, etc. Because the information recorded in official blankbooks may be of permanent value, good-quality paper and durable bindings are generally used. A blankbook should open flat for ease of use.

blanket order   An agreement in which a publisher or dealer supplies to a library or library system one copy of each title as issued, on the basis of a profile established in advance by the purchaser. Blanket order plans are used mainly by large academic and public libraries to reduce the amount of time required for selection and acquisition and to speed the process of getting new titles into circulation. Unlike approval plans, most blanket order plans do not allow returns. One of the best-known examples in the United States is the Greenaway Plan. Synonymous with *gathering plan*. *See also*: *book lease plan*.

blanking   In binding, the application of a heated brass stamp to the cloth cover of a book to create a glossy impression to serve as a base for lettering or for a stamped decoration.

bleed   In printing, to run an illustration off the trimmed edge of the page without leaving space for a margin. A page can bleed in more than one direction, depending on how many edges are touched by the image printed on it. Also refers to text cropped too closely in binding.

blind   In bookbinding, a procedure done without further embellishment, for example, tooling or blocking applied to a leather binding without the addition of ink or gold leaf to bring out the design.

Also refers to a person whose vision is severely impaired, eligible to receive library services through the National Library Service for the Blind and Physically Handicapped (NLS).

blind folio   A leaf in a manuscript or book included in the foliation but not given a folio number. Compare with *blind page*.

blind page   A page in a book, usually the half title, title page, dedication, or a blank page, included in the pagination but not given a page number. Compare with *blind folio*.

blind reference   A cross-reference in an index or catalog directing the reader to a heading that does *not* exist in the same index or catalog.

blockbook   A form of book containing text alone or text with pictures, printed on only one side of each leaf entirely from woodcuts. Blockbooks originated in Europe during the 15th century at the same time as printing from movable type and may have been an inexpensive alternative to books printed on a press. A well-known example is the *Biblia Pauperum* (Bible of the Poor) printed in large quantities during the second half of the 15th century. Fewer than two dozen copies are known to have survived. Also spelled *block book*. ***See also***: *xylography*.

blockbuster   A slang term for a new book for which the sale of a very large number of copies is virtually guaranteed, usually due to the reputation or popularity of the author (Mary Higgins Clark, Stephen King, Danielle Steel, etc.). Public libraries often order such titles in multiple copies to satisfy initial demand. Also used in reference to the willingness of publishers to repeatedly sign such authors and promote their works, sometimes to the neglect of writers of lesser fame whose works deserve to be read. Synonymous with *megabook*. Compare with *bestseller*.

In the motion picture industry, a newly released feature film that is expected to attract large audiences and sell well on videocassette and DVD, usually because it has won a major award or because its cast includes actors and/or actresses who are stars.

blocked   The status of the borrower account of a patron who is barred from checking out materials from the library, usually because fines for overdue items remain unpaid. Most electronic circulation systems are designed to automatically block a patron record under conditions prescribed by the library.

blocking   The process of impressing a decorative design or lettering on the cover of a book by machine in blind, ink, or metallic leaf, using an engraved plate called a *binder's brass* (die) mounted on a *blocking press*. Michelle Brown notes in *Understanding Illuminated Manuscripts* (Getty Museum/British Library, 1994) that metal blocks were first used on leather bindings in Flanders in the early 13th century, and large wooden blocks were used in the Netherlands during the 16th century. Requiring far less time and labor than hand tooling, blocking was the precursor of modern stamping used in case binding. Synonymous with *stamping*.

Also refers to the tendency of the leaves of a book or other bound publication to stick together, forming a solid block after they have been exposed to water, a problem that can be mitigated by standing the wet item on end with the leaves fanned open to allow them to air dry. Leaves of coated paper can be difficult to separate without damaging the printed surface, especially after drying has commenced.

block letter   A letter printed in a typeface that has strokes of equal width and boldness, straight and without serifs, a style used for legibility in headlines but considered less legible for printing text matter. Used synonymously with *sans-serif*. Compare with *monoline*.

block quotation   *See*: quotation.

blog   *See*: Weblog.

blowback   A hard copy enlargement of an image on microform. Most libraries provide reader-printer machines for enlarging and making copies of documents available on microfilm or microfiche. Also spelled *blow back*. Compare with *blowup*.

blowup   In photography, an enlargement usually made from a copy negative taken of a smaller print (the procedure is demonstrated in the 1966 feature film *Blowup* directed by Michelangelo Antonioni). In document reproduction, any copy made on a scale larger than the original. In the book trade, a greatly enlarged image of a dust jacket, illustration, or specimen page, used in marketing. Also spelled *blow up*. Compare with *blowback*.

blue book   In the United States, the popular name for a manual published by a state government listing the names of elected and appointed officials and providing information about government structure, agencies, voting districts, elections, etc., usually bound in blue covers. Compare with *red book*.

blue pencil   To mark corrections in a manuscript or typescript during the editing process, derived from the color of pencil traditionally used by editors. The term has also been applied to the editing of text by a censor.

blueprint   A photographic copy of the detailed plans for constructing a building or other structure, originally printed in white against a blue ground. Blueprints are usually produced in sets, one for each floor for each phase of construction (plumbing, electrical, HVAC, etc.). They are collected by architecture libraries and by archives and special collections for construction projects of historical significance. Blueprints are used by libraries in planning and overseeing the renovation, expansion, and new construction of facilities. *See also*: *architectural drawing*.

blue scale   A method used in preservation to determine whether a light source is affecting a book or other object. Strips of blue woolen cloth known to fade at different rates are pasted parallel to each other across one side of a card backed with a piece of stiff cardboard. A strip of black paper (or other opaque material), cut to the length of the card, is taped over one-half of the strips, so tightly that light cannot seep under the edges of the shield. The card is positioned beside the object, facing the light source, and checked regularly for evidence of fading. Date of installation should be noted on the back of the card for future reference.

blurb   The publisher's description and recommendation of a new book, usually printed on the front flap of the dust jacket, portions of which may be used in advertisements published in book trade journals and review publications and in the publisher's catalog. Brief excerpts from favorable reviews are usually printed on the back of the dust jacket. *See also*: *puff* and *teaser*.

BNB   *See*: **British National Bibliography**.

BNF   *See*: **B**ibliothèque **N**ationale de **F**rance.

BO   *See*: **b**ack **o**rder.

board   A general term for the sheet of rigid material forming one side of the cover of a book bound in hardcover, the *upper board* preceding the book block and the *lower board* following it. Up to the 16th century, wooden boards were used (seasoned oak or hardwood in England and France to resist worming, beech in Germany and Italy), sometimes beveled or shaped to accommodate clasps. The thickness and weight of wooden boards helped keep leaves made of parchment or vellum pressed flat. With the widespread use of paper following the invention of printing, heavy boards were no longer needed. *Pasteboard* made from sheets of paper stuck together was introduced in the 15th century, and by the late 17th century *millboards* made from rope-fiber were being used. *Strawboard* did not come into use in bookbinding until the 18th century. The boards were attached to the sewn quires by threading the cords through *channels* cut into the boards, then secured with pegs or nails before the spine and sides were covered in leather or parchment. Until about the 15th century, boards were often cut flush with the sections, but after that time they extended beyond the edges of the book block, forming squares.

In modern bookbinding, the cover is usually made of binder's board manufactured from various fibrous materials pulped or laminated and pressed into large, flat sheets cut to size in binding. In less expensive editions, strawboard, chip board, or pasteboard is used. *See also*: *fiberboard* and *pressboard*.

In computers, the flat piece of plastic or fiberglass designed to hold microchips and other computer hardware. The main circuit board in most systems is called the *motherboard*, and all the component chips that plug into the main board are called *cards* or *boards*.

Also refers to a group of prominent persons elected or appointed to serve as trustees responsible for overseeing the policies and major management decisions of an organization or institution, such as a library or library system. *See also*: *editorial board*.

board book   A durable book of small size designed for very young children, consisting of a few unnumbered pages made of pasteboard covered in glossy paper printed with colorful illustrations and little, if any, text. Board books are often alphabet books or counting books.

Bodleian Library   The library of the University of Oxford in England. The original medieval library was severely damaged in 1542, then refounded in 1598 by Sir Thomas Bodley, a former diplomat. Its combination of buildings, constructed between 1490 and 1970, and its vast holdings make it unique among the world's great libraries. Its collections are particularly strong in English literature, history, and typography.

The Bodleian has been a copyright depository library since 1662. Nickname: *The Bodley*. URL: www.bodley.ox.ac.uk. *See also*: *British Library, The*.

body In printing, the main portion of a book, beginning with the first page of the text and including any footnotes and illustrations but excluding the front matter and back matter. In bookbinding, the block of sections sewn or glued together in preparation for attachment to the case or cover.

In an e-mail message, the text of the message, as opposed to the header (e-mail address of sender, address[es] of recipient[s], and subject of message) and any footer.

In typesetting, the small rectangular unit of cast metal bearing a single raised character on one end (the *face*) from which an impression is taken in letterpress printing. Synonymous in this sense with *shank*.

Also refers to a group of people with an official function. Library catalogers recognize: corporate body, related body, and subordinate body.

body matter The text of a work to be printed, as distinct from any display matter (headings, ornaments, illustrations, etc.).

body type *See*: text type.

bold *See*: boldface.

boldface A typeface conspicuous for being **thicker** and **darker** but not larger than the medium weight type of the same font, used mainly for contrast or emphasis and for headings. The words *thicker* and *darker* in the preceding sentence are in boldface. Variations include *semi-bold*, *extra-bold*, and *ultra-bold*. Also spelled *bold face*. Synonymous with *bold* and *black face*. Compare with *lightface*.

bolt The folded edge of a single sheet of paper at the head, tail, or fore-edge of the block in an uncut or unopened book, known, respectively, as the *head-bolt*, *tail-bolt*, or *fore-edge bolt*. In binding, the fourth edge, called the *back fold*, is sewn and glued to the other folded and gathered sections to form the back of a book.

bond measure *See*: library bond.

book A collection of leaves of paper, parchment, vellum, cloth, or other material (written, printed, or blank) fastened together along one edge, with or without a protective case or cover. The origin of the word is uncertain. It may be derived from the Anglo-Saxon *boc* (plural *bec*) or from the Norse *bok*, meaning "book" or "beech tree," possibly in reference to the wooden boards originally used in binding. Also refers to a literary work or one of its volumes. Compare with *monograph*.

To qualify for the special parcel post rate classified by the U.S. Postal Service as "media mail," a publication must consist of 24 or more pages, at least 22 of which bear printing consisting primarily of reading material or scholarly bibliography, with advertising limited to book announcements. UNESCO defines a book as a nonperiodical literary publication consisting of 49 or more pages, covers excluded. The ANSI standard includes publications of less than 49 pages that have hard covers. Abbreviated *bk*. *See also*: *art book, artist's book, board book, children's book, coffee table book, gift book, licensed book, managed book, new book, packaged book, picture book*, *premium book, professional book, promotional book, rare book, reference book, religious book*, and *reprint book*.

Also, a major division of a longer work (usually of fiction) that is further subdivided into chapters. Usually numbered, such a division may or may not have its own title. Also refers to one of the divisions of the Christian Bible, the first being *Genesis*.

book announcement   A brief statement by the publisher announcing the availability of a new book or backlisted title, published as an advertisement in a book trade journal or review publication or in an advertising section included in another book published under the same imprint. A book announcement usually includes the title of the work, the name of the author(s) or editor(s), ISBN, projected date of publication, list price, and prepublication price, if offered. It may also include a blurb or brief excerpts from favorable reviews and a picture of the front cover.

book art   The form of art expressed through the medium of the book. The artist's input extends beyond authorship and illustration, making the physical appearance of the book as object a manifestation of creativity in and of itself. In some artist's books, the traditional format of the book is not altered (*example*: an illustrated collection of poems in which the words and images are embossed, rather than printed, on paper). In other works, the artist experiments with format, even to the extent of challenging the concept of reading (*example*: a book with the covers and leaves consisting entirely of double-sided mirrors). Some publishers specialize in this art form (Ron King's Circle Press). The National Art Library (www.nal.vam.ac.uk) at the Victoria and Albert Museum of decorative and applied arts in London holds an extensive collection of books on the history of this form of artistic experimentation.

book arts   The skills and techniques used in creating fine books and manuscripts, including papermaking, calligraphy, illumination and rubrication, typography, illustration, printing, and bookbinding. *See also*: *Center for Book Arts, Grolier Club*, and *Morris, William*.

book auction   A public or private sale at which rare books and used books are sold to the highest bidder, usually on commission. A firm specializing in such sales is known as a *book auction house*. Extremely rare and valuable books and manuscripts are usually sold by international auction houses such as Christie's and Sotheby's. *See also*: *antiquarian bookseller*.

book award   *See*: literary award.

book band   A strip of printed paper (usually colored) placed around the jacketed cover of a book to call attention to a special characteristic, such as availability at a reduced price, receipt of an award, or special loan status (reserve or interlibrary loan).

bookbin   A wheeled box for transporting books, sometimes with a bottom equipped with a spring mechanism to allow the space inside to fill gradually as books and other materials are returned to a book drop built into the circulation desk or wall of a library.

bookbinding   The process of fastening the leaves of a manuscript or book together in a particular order and enclosing them in a protective cover (forwarding), then applying lettering and decoration to the cover (finishing), formerly done by hand by a tradesman called a *binder* but now largely mechanized (see *case binding*). Prior to the 19th century most books were sold in sheets to be bound to the customer's order. Only titles for which demand was steady would have been sold ready-bound. *See also*: *conservation binding*, *custom binding*, *hand-binding*, *publisher's binding*, and *signed binding*.

book block   All the sections of a book sewn or glued together, plus the endpapers and any other leaves added by the binder, before the cover is applied. Compare with *text block*.

book box   A container made of rigid, solid material, usually rectangular in shape, designed to hold a book and keep it tightly covered on all sides. Categories of books requiring the protection of a box are those in fragile condition, of considerable rarity or value, in significant bindings, or with protrusions that could damage adjacent items, and miniature books and unbound manuscripts. Commercially manufactured boxes of archival quality are available from suppliers in a wide range of shapes and sizes. Custom-made boxes can be ordered from book binders. A box designed for a very small book should be comparable in size to other books on the same shelf, filled in on the inside to the dimensions of the book. Compare with *slipcase*. *See also*: *pull-case* and *solander*.

book burning   The intentional destruction by fire of books considered objectionable or dangerous, usually by a religious or secular authority, as in the mass burning of books considered politically incorrect by the Nazi Party in pre–World War II Germany, or by a mob, usually in the frenzy of political revolt. *See also*: *censorship*, *intellectual freedom*, and *libricide*.

book caddy   A high two-wheeled metal cart with a protruding handle or bar across the top, designed for maximum maneuverability when transporting books to and from locations and across surfaces difficult to manage with a wider four-wheeled *book truck*. Single-stack and multiple-shelf models are available from library suppliers.

book card   A piece of stiff card stock of standard size (three inches wide and five inches high), with space at the top for the call number, name of author, and title of item, and blank lines below for recording the due date and the library card number or name of the borrower, used in manual circulation systems to maintain a card file of items currently checked out. The book card is reinserted in the book pocket inside each item at check-in. Some libraries use color-coded book cards to indicate type of material or applicable loan rule. *See also*: *date due slip*.

bookcase   A set of two or more single- or double-sided shelves in a rigid frame, used to store books, periodicals, videocassettes, and other materials. In libraries, bookcases are usually made of wood or metal with fixed or adjustable shelves.

book catalog   A library catalog in the form of a bound or loose-leaf book, whether handwritten, printed, or computer-generated, practical only for small collections.

book cloth   *See*: cloth.

book club   A commercial company that sells new books and backlisted titles by mail to subscribers who agree to purchase a minimum number of titles per year at discount prices, usually from main, alternate, or special selections offered on a monthly basis that may be rejected or returned by the subscriber. To attract new subscribers, an introductory offer of free or heavily discounted titles may be offered in exchange for a minimum purchase commitment. Some book clubs offer books of general interest (*example*: **Book-of-the-Month Club**); others specialize by genre (mystery, science fiction, etc.), subject (gardening), or academic field or discipline (history). Directory information for book clubs is available in *Literary Market Place*, a reference serial available in most libraries. *See also*: *book club edition*.

Also refers to an informal group of readers who purchase books for circulation and, in some cases, discussion among themselves. Synonymous in this sense with *reading circle*.

book club edition   An edition of a book offered for sale mail-order by a book club. Copies may be purchased by the club from the publisher's stock (usually at a discount) or specially reprinted for club distribution. An edition produced solely for distribution to book club subscribers can usually be distinguished from the trade edition of the same title by the inferior quality of its paper and binding, and by the absence of a price on the dust jacket. Abbreviated *bc* or *bce*.

book collecting   The process of acquiring a collection of books based on their content, history, antiquity, rarity, beauty, monetary value, or other characteristics. A person who systematically acquires books for the pleasure of owning them, as an investment, or with the intention of bequeathing them to a library or other institution is known as a *book collector*. For a brief but fascinating essay on the "history of book collecting," please see the entry under the term in *A Dictionary of Book History* by John Feather (Oxford University Press, 1986).

book contract   A legally binding written agreement between a writer and publisher in which the author grants the publisher the rights to a specific work in exchange for compensation (usually royalties as a percentage of net sales on copies sold) and a commitment to publish the work in specified form within a designated period of time. Synonymous with *publisher's agreement*.

book cradle   A low stand or rack, usually made of wood, metal, or plastic, designed to display a book open at an angle, rather than flat, to minimize strain on the spine. Wedge-shaped props can also be used for this purpose.

book culture   The habits, skills, institutions, etc., of a given people concerning books in all forms, including their manufacture (publishing, printing, and binding), marketing and promotion, bookselling and collecting, book clubs and reading groups, bibliography and conservation, activities of libraries and archives, and the writing, illustrating, reviewing, and reading of books. In the United States, the persistence of book culture is evident in the presence of small cafes intended for readers on the premises of large bookstores and in the success of companies that manufacture and sell giftware, decorative items, and accessories for readers.

book curse   A brief passage written in a book usually by the owner or a scribe invoking misfortune to anyone who steals or harms it, a form of security used in periods when books were very rare and therefore valuable. The oldest known book curse, traced to the Assyrian king Ashurbanipal (7th century B.C.), is inscribed on a clay tablet now in the collections of The British Library. Medieval book curses sometimes specified excommunication and were often highly imaginative, as in the following example in a volume from the library of the Monastery of San Pedro of Barcelona:

> For him that stealeth, or borroweth and returneth not, this book from its owner, let it change into a serpent in his hand & rend him. Let him be struck with palsy, & all his members blasted. Let him languish in pain crying aloud for mercy, & let there be no surcease to his agony till he sing in dissolution. Let bookworms gnaw his entrails in token of the Worm that dieth not, & when at last he goeth to his final punishment, let the flames of Hell consume him forever.

For more on book curses, see Marc Drogin's *Anathema! Medieval Scribes and the History of Book Curses* (Allanheld & Schram, 1983).

book detection system   *See*: security gate.

book drop   A slot, chute, bin, or box to which books and other items borrowed from a library may be returned, especially during hours when the facility is closed. Book drops may be free-standing (usually outside the walls of the library) or built into the circulation desk or an exterior wall. Security is an important consideration in the design of an after-hours book drop. Libraries have suffered damage from hazardous materials deposited in book drops by malicious persons.

bookend   A rigid barrier placed at the end of a row of books, periodicals, videocassettes, etc., to keep them upright on the shelf, usually a T- or L-shaped movable piece of metal, wood, or strong plastic. Libraries sometimes use hanging bookends made of metal tubing inserted in tracks beneath the front and back edges of the shelving. Bookends manufactured as gift items may be covered in leather, carved in fine stone, or cast in metal and given a decorative finish.

BookExpo America (BEA)   The largest book fair in the United States, BEA is an exhibition of books in all formats (plus retail multimedia), a forum for educating persons involved in the book trade, and a center for negotiating rights to intellectual property. Formerly known as the *ABA Convention and Trade Exhibit*, BEA is held in a different city in the United States each year. URL: www.bookexpoamerica.com.

book fair   A trade exhibition, usually held annually, at which book publishers and distributors display their products in spaces called *booths* leased for that purpose. The first international book fair was held in France at Lyon during the late medieval period. The Frankfurt Book Fair began in the 1490s and is still the chief market place for publishers who wish to buy and sell intellectual property rights, translation rights, and other privileges to overseas buyers. Also refers to a non-trade exhibition of books and the book arts open to the general public, which may include presentations by authors, illustrators, publishers, binders, etc. A list of links to book fair/festival homepages is maintained by Peter Scott of the University of Saskatchewan Library at: www. lights.com/publisher/bookfairs.html. *See also*: *BookExpo America*.

book format   *See*: book size.

book hand   A style of handwriting used by scribes to produce books before the invention of the printing press, less formal than the lapidary script used on permanent monuments but more formal than the cursive hand used for writing letters and other informal documents. A book hand must be easy to read en masse (entire paragraphs or pages of text) but capable of being written with reasonable speed. Compare with *court hand*.

book history   The study of the origins and development of written works, from the cuneiform clay tablets and papyrus scrolls of Antiquity, through the manuscripts and incunabula of the Middle Ages, to modern printing and publishing. For an online chronology of book history, see: www.xs4all.nl/~knops/timetab.html. Synonymous with *history of the book*. *See also*: *American Printing History Association*, *Bibliographical Society of America*, and *Grolier Club*.

book holder   A piece of equipment, usually made of metal or plastic, designed to hold a book open and upright, usually at about a 60- to 70-degree angle from the surface of a desk, leaving the hands of the reader free for writing or typing. Collapsible models are available from library suppliers.

Book Industry Study Group (BISG)   Established in November 1975 at the annual conference of the Book Manufacturers Institute, BISG published a *Report on Book Industry Information Needs* in April 1976 confirming the feasibility of a program of major research studies by and about the book industry. Since then, the nonprofit organization has been a leader in setting industry standards and conducting research on behalf of publishers, booksellers, libraries, vendors, and manufacturers. Actively engaged in promoting standardization of e-content, BISG helps manage the Online Information Exchange (ONIX) standard for improved dissemination of electronic materials. URL: www.bisg.org.

bookish   Pertaining to a book, or to books and reading in general, usually in the literary sense. Also refers to a person who is fond of reading books or excessively studious. As a term of disparagement, any person whose knowledge of life is acquired largely by reading books rather than from actual experience.

book jacket   *See*: dust jacket.

book label   A card, strip, etc., smaller than a bookplate, usually made of paper, affixed to the inside of a book, in most cases to indicate ownership.

book lease plan   An acquisitions plan offered by some book jobbers that allows a library or library system to lease an agreed-upon number of popular fiction and non-fiction titles, usually for a fixed monthly fee. After a prescribed period of time, or a decline in demand, titles are returned for credit toward new books usually selected from a monthly list provided by the jobber (*example*: **McNaughton Plan**). Because leased books arrive fully cataloged and processed for circulation, some public libraries rely on leasing plans for high-demand items. Leasing is also used in academic libraries with limited space for a permanent collection of popular fiction and nonfiction. Synonymous with *rental plan*. Compare with *approval plan* and *blanket order*.

booklet   A book of small size or containing little text. Also used synonymously with *pamphlet*.

book lice   A species of minute (one-sixteenth-inch) soft-bodied, wingless insects of worldwide distribution (*Liposcelis divinatorius*) that damages old books by feeding on the glue and paste in bindings. Usually gray, white, or translucent in color, book lice also consume mold, cereal products, and the bodies of dead insects, which makes them a menace to botanical and zoological specimens. Keeping relative humidity low helps to control them in libraries and exhibit spaces. Book lice are prey to book scorpions. They can be exterminated by freezing the infested item. Synonymous with *book mites*. ***See also***: *bookworm*.

book lift   A fixed mechanical device similar to a dumb waiter, designed for transporting books from one floor or stack level to another in a library, without having to use a stairway or full-size elevator.

book light   A very small electric light designed to attach, usually by means of a clip, to the cover of a book for reading in a dark place (airplane seat, bed, tent, etc.) without disturbing others.

book list   A selected list of books, usually on a specific topic or in a particular genre, arranged in some kind of order (by author, title, subject, theme, etc.), that may include brief descriptive annotations, used mainly in readers' advisory.

Booklist   A trade journal for librarians published since 1905 by the American Library Association, *Booklist* reviews nearly 4,000 books for adults in 22 issues per year, plus 2,500 titles for children and young adults, 1,000 nonprint titles, and approximately 500 reference books and electronic resources in *Reference Books Bulletin*, a separate section at the end of each issue. *Booklist* also includes feature articles, author interviews, bibliographies, and regular columns. ISSN: 0006–7385. URL: www.ala.org. ***See also***: CHOICE *and* Library Journal.

book louse   *See*: book lice.

booklover   *See*: bibliophile.

bookman   A man in the business of publishing, making, or selling books. Also, a man of literary or scholarly inclination who is familiar with books.

book mark   *See*: book number.

bookmark   A narrow strip of paper, leather, ribbon, or other thin, flexible material placed between the pages of a book to mark a place. Hand-crafted decorative bookmarks are sometimes given as gifts. In older and more expensive editions, a piece of narrow ribbon longer than the length of the pages, called a *register*, is sometimes glued to the top of the spine to serve as a bookmark.

When and where the use of bookmarkers originated has not been established, but a variety of devices are known to have been in use from the 12th century on. Some medieval manuscripts have small finger tabs or knotted strips of parchment (sometimes marked with pigment) attached to the fore-edge. In other volumes linen or silk ribbons, or long strips of parchment, were attached to the headband, sometimes with an ornament or reading device suspended from the free end.

In computing, to mark a document or a specific location in a document for subsequent retrieval. Most Web browser software includes a "bookmark" option that allows an Internet address (URL) to be archived, enabling the user to revisit the site without having to retype the address or repeat the original search from scratch.

bookmarker   *See*: bookmark.

book mite   *See*: book lice.

bookmobile   A large motorized van equipped with shelves to accommodate a small library collection and a desk for a librarian or paraprofessional member of the library staff, serving as a traveling branch library in neighborhoods and communities too remote to be easily served by the nearest public library. Synonymous in the UK with *mobile library* and in France with *bibliobus*. *See also*: *rural library*.

book number   The portion of the call number following the class notation, added to distinguish a specific item within its class. A book number is composed of an *author mark* appended by the cataloger to subarrange works of the same class by name of author, followed by a *work mark* added to subarrange works of the same author by title or edition (*example*: **H5371m** in the Dewey Decimal call number **993.101 H5371m** assigned to the book *The Maoris* by Charles Higham). Synonymous with *book mark*.

Book of Hours   A book of common prayers for the Catholic laity, said at the eight canonical hours of the day and night, introduced in France in the 10th century. Originally intended for ecclesiastical use, its main text, the Little Office of the Virgin, is a shorter version of the Divine Office contained in the breviary. By the 12th century, the Book of Hours was being used in private devotion, usually in conjunction with the psalter. By the time its contents became standardized in the 13th century, other sections had been added. Especially popular in Flanders and France through the end of the 16th century, many fine examples survive, some magnificently illuminated, usually with depictions of important events in the life of the Virgin, Christ, King David (author of the *Psalms*), and various saints. Synonymous with *horae* (Latin), *Livre d'Heures*, and *primer*.

Book of Kells   Considered by many to be the most beautiful illuminated manuscript produced in medieval Europe, the *Book of Kells* was copied by hand and decorated by Celtic monks, probably around A.D. 800. The Latin text of the four Gospels is written in Insular majuscule script, lavishly decorated in Celtic style. Unlike the *Lindisfarne Gospels*, there is no record of the identity of the monks who created the *Book of Kells*, and their work remained unfinished, some of the ornamentation appearing only in outline.

Although it may have been brought to Ireland from a monastery founded by St. Columba on Iona, an island between Ireland and Scotland, the 680-page manuscript is named after the Abbey of Kells, located in the Irish Midlands, where it remained from the 9th century until 1541. Since 1661, it has been in the possession of the Library of Trinity College in Dublin. During a major restoration in 1953, it was rebound in four volumes, two of which are on permanent public display under controlled conditions, the pages turned at regular intervals to allow visitors to see and appreciate its beauties. In 1986, the Swiss publisher Urs Duggelin of Faksimile Verlag was allowed to reproduce from photographs a limited edition of 1,480 high-quality facsimile copies.

book-on-tape *See*: audiobook.

book paper A grade of paper suitable for printing books, pamphlets, periodicals, catalogs, etc., as opposed to various other grades (newsprint, tissue paper, wallpaper, wrapping paper, etc.). Book papers vary in content, color, finish, opacity, weight, and permanence. For books that are to be retained indefinitely in the collection, librarians prefer permanent papers, acid-free and of high rag content.

bookplate A small paper label or similar device affixed to a book, usually on the inside of the front cover or on the front endpaper, providing a space to record the name of the owner or some other identification. Bookplates can be printed, engraved, typographical, calligraphic, or illustrated. They should be acid-free and pasted on or tipped in, with the grain of the paper running parallel with the spine of the volume. Former Yale University conservator Jane Greenfield recommends that gummed or pressure-sensitive bookplates be avoided (*The Care of Fine Books*, Nick Lyons Books, 1988).

Decorative bookplates are a category of gift item sold blank or with name of the recipient custom-printed in space allowed for the name, sometimes following the Latin phrase *ex libris*. The earliest known examples appeared in Germany a few years after the invention of movable type. They often expressed gratitude to the donor from the person receiving the book as a gift, a practice still followed in some libraries that receive books as gifts. The presence of a bookplate usually does not affect the value of a book (probably because they are easily removed) and may be useful in establishing provenance.

Bookplate design as an art form began with Albrecht Dürer in the early 16th century. Heraldic bookplates usually bore a coat of arms and/or family motto. Professional mottos and designs commemorating important historical events were also popular, but the mottos on modern bookplates usually praise books or scholarly pursuits. The New York Public Library and the Yale University Library own substantial collections of historically significant bookplates. Compare with *book label*.

book pocket A three-inch-wide strip of stiff paper with a small pocket folded and glued across the bottom third of its height to hold a book card, affixed to items held by a library that does not have an automated circulation system. Available ungummed or with a self-adhesive back, plain or with a date due slip printed at the top, pockets are affixed to the inside cover or endpaper in books, or to some other part in nonbook items. To enable circulation staff to match card to item at check-in, the front of the pocket and the top of the corresponding card are marked with the call number, name of author, and title of item.

book press   A mechanical device consisting of two thick composite boards with a long screw at each of the four corners, used like a sandwich to apply pressure to a book, to ensure that glued or pasted surfaces adhere properly in binding, rebinding, and repairing. In heavy-duty models, the boards are positioned on a base between two sturdy metal uprights to which a horizontal bar is attached, with a single large screw for increasing the downward pressure of the bar.

book prize   *See*: literary award.

book proposal   A plan for a prospective book submitted by the author (or the author's literary agent) to a publisher for consideration, sometimes at the publisher's invitation. A book proposal usually includes: tentative title, brief discussion of scope and purpose of work, intended audience and market, outline or summary of content, list of proposed chapters or entries, analysis of competing works, approximate length, form of illustration, proposed schedule, and sometimes a sample of the text, accompanied by a cover letter. Book proposals are also used by academic faculty in applying for sabbatic leave. *See also*: *book contract* and *over the transom*.

book rate   *See*: media mail.

book repair   *See*: repairing.

bookrest   A portable device similar to the music rest on a piano, designed to be placed on a desk or table to hold a book at an angle convenient for reading. Bookrests are also available in metal for attachment to indoor exercise machines and in the form of a soft cushion for laptop use or bedtime reading.

book return   *See*: book drop.

book review   *See*: review.

book sale   Libraries often dispose of discarded materials and unused gifts at an annual or ongoing public sale, sometimes organized by a Friends of the Library group, which uses the proceeds to benefit the library. Library book sales are a good place to find out of print editions and bargains.

books-by-mail   Circulation of library materials via the postal system to registered borrowers who request items by telephone or post, usually from a mail-order catalog, a service provided by public libraries serving rural areas and homebound patrons. *See also*: *bookmobile* and *direct delivery*.

book scorpion   A species of small (one-eighth- to one-quarter-inch) stingless arachnid (*Chelifer cancroides*), also known as the *false scorpion*, that diets on tiny insects such as book lice that damage books by feeding on paper and bindings.

book scout   A person in the business of scouring obscure or remote bookshops, secondhand stores, and book sales in search of books and editions desired by librarians, private collectors, and antiquarian booksellers. *See also*: *scout*.

bookseller   A person in the business of selling books and related materials to the retail trade at the full net published price, especially one who owns a bookstore. Also refers to anyone in the business of selling used books. In the United States, the trade association of the bookselling industry is the American Booksellers Association whose homepage *BookWeb* (www.bookweb.org) includes a searchable Bookstore Directory. Information about book retailers in the United States and Canada is also available in the *American Book Trade Directory*, published annually by R.R. Bowker. Compare with *dealer* and *jobber*.

bookshelves   A set of thin, flat pieces of rigid material set horizontally at right angles into a frame or wall, to hold books and similar items. To take the weight of a full row of books without sagging, a bookshelf usually requires upright supports at least every 36 inches. Shelving used in libraries and archives should be adjustable and easy to clean, with at least 1 inch of airspace above the tallest book and no rough edges or protrusions that might damage bindings. In unpolluted areas, bookshelves should be open, except at the ends, to allow maximum air circulation. In heavily polluted areas, shelves with closed backs and glass fronts are preferable and may provide some protection against fire. The bottom shelf should be at least 6 inches above the floor to facilitate cleaning and prevent water damage in the event of flooding.

Bookshelves should be located away from heat sources such as radiators. To avoid damp and condensation, shelving should not be positioned against an exterior wall or beneath water or steam pipes. To avoid exposing books to ultraviolet radiation, shelves should not receive direct sunlight. Many libraries use free-standing adjustable steel shelving with a baked-on finish, available from suppliers in 36-inch widths by height and shelf depth, in a variety of colors. Sloping shelving is available for displaying current periodicals face out. *See also*: *compact shelving*.

bookshop   *See*: bookstore.

book signing   An event scheduled at a retail bookstore or library at which the author and/or illustrator of a new book is available to autograph copies of his or her work(s), sometimes scheduled in conjunction with a book talk or a reading from the text. *See also*: *autographed copy*.

Books in Print (BIP)   A multivolume reference set that lists books currently published or distributed in the United States, by author, title, and subject (ISSN: 0068–0214). Entries include information useful to acquisitions librarians such as publisher, price, edition, binding type, and ISBN. Published annually by R.R. Bowker, *BIP* includes a directory of publishers in a separate volume. It is supplemented by *Forthcoming Books*. Bowker also publishes *Children's Books in Print* and *El-Hi Textbooks & Serials in Print* annually. *BIP* is also available online. *International Books in Print* is published by K.G. Saur and distributed in the United States by the Gale Group.

book size   The height and width of a book, usually measured in inches or centimeters from head to tail and from spine to fore-edge of the cover. Historically, the size of a printed book was determined by the number of times a full sheet of printing paper measuring approximately 19 × 25 inches was folded, once to form signatures of 2 leaves (4 pages) known as *folio*, twice to form 4 leaves (8 pages) known as *quarto*, three times to form 8 leaves (16 pages) known as *octavo* or to form 12 leaves (24 pages) known as *duodecimo*, four times to form 16 leaves (32 pages) known as *sextodecimo*, etc.

In modern book production, the size of an edition depends on the size of the unfolded sheet used in printing. In the bibliographic description of rare books, the historical dimensions are still used, but in modern book production, size is based on the height and width of the binding. Slight differences exist between American and British practice in the standardization of book sizes. American sizes are given below. Synonymous with *book format*. **See also**: *exact size*.

Name	Height & Width
Thirty-sixmo	4 × 3⅓ inches
Medium Thirty-twomo	4¾ × 3 inches
Medium Twenty-fourmo	5½ × 3⅝ inches
Medium Eighteenmo	6⅔ × 4 inches
Medium sixteenmo	6¾ × 4½ inches
Cap Octavo	7 × 7¼ inches
Duodecimo	7½ × 4½ inches
Crown Octavo	7½ × 5 inches
Post Octavo	7½ × 5½ inches
Medium Duodecimo	7⅔ × 5⅛ inches
Demy Octavo	8 × 5½ inches
Small Quarto (usually less)	8½ × 7 inches
Broad Quarto (varies up to 13 × 10)	8½ × 7 inches
Medium Octavo	9½ × 6 inches
Royal Octavo	10 × 6½ inches
Super Royal Octavo	10½ × 7 inches
Imperial Quarto	11 × 15 inches
Imperial Octavo	11½ × 8¼ inches

bookstall   A small open-air retail book outlet, usually found in airports and railway stations and at fairs and markets. In France, quay-side bookstalls have been an important part of Parisian culture for centuries. Compare with *bookstore*.

book stamp   A wood, metal, or rubber stamp used to make an inked impression on the cover, edge, endpaper, or title page of a book as a mark of ownership.

book stock   The total number of books in a library's collections, subject to growth through acquisition and to diminution through loss, damage, theft, weeding, etc. Synonymous with *book collection*. **See also**: *inventory*.

book stop   A narrow ridge or ledge along the lower edge of the sloping top of a dictionary stand, atlas case, or lectern allowing an open book or sheaf of papers to rest at an angle convenient for reading without sliding off.

bookstore   An enclosed store devoted to the retail sale of books, usually in both hardcover and softcover. Some bookstores specialize in used books, rare books, children's books, or materials on a specific subject or in a particular genre (science fiction, comics, etc.). Large trade bookstores may also sell magazines and newspapers, maps, calendars, greeting cards, nonprint media (videocassettes, DVDs, audiocassettes, CDs, CD-ROMs), and reading paraphernalia. Bookstore chains have outlets in most large cities in the United States, offering nearly identical stock (*examples*: **Barnes & Noble** and **Borders Books & Music**). College bookstores sell mainly textbooks and trade editions for the use of students. Information on book retailers in the United States and Canada is available in the annual *American Book Trade Directory*, published by R.R. Bowker. Synonymous with *bookshop*. Compare with *bookstall*. *See also*: *bookseller*.

book talk   An event, usually scheduled in a library, bookstore, or educational institution, at which the author, a librarian, or other interested person discusses a book and reads excerpts from it to encourage readership and promote reading in general. Also spelled *booktalk*. *See also*: *book signing*.

book trade   The operations and arrangements that exist in a specific country for the manufacture, distribution, and sale of books to the public, including publishers and their associations, printers and binders, retail booksellers and their trade associations, jobbers and dealers, and the generally accepted practices, standards, and codes governing their activities. Statistics on the U.S. book trade can be found in *The Bowker Annual Library and Book Trade Almanac*, available in the reference section of most larger libraries. Directory information can be found in the annual *American Book Trade Directory*, also published by R.R. Bowker.

book trade journal   A periodical issued by publishers, booksellers, and others engaged in the book trade for the purpose of announcing and promoting newly published titles. Book trade journals also include trade news, bestseller lists, author interviews, book reviews, feature articles, regular columns, analysis of current trends and issues, and information about book production/distribution, book fairs, and book signings. In the United States, the leading book trade journals are *Publisher's Weekly* and BookWeb.org's *Industry Newsroom* from the American Booksellers Association.

book truck   A wheeled metal or wooden cart with two or three shelves, used by a page or other library staff member for transporting books and other materials from one area of the library to another. Book trucks are available from library suppliers. Compare with *book caddy*. *See also*: *reshelving cart*.

Book Week   *See*: Children's Book Week.

bookworm   The larval form of a variety of flying beetles that damages books and other printed materials by feeding on digestible materials in paper, paste, glue, sewing thread, boards, and leather, leaving small holes in leaves and bindings, a highly undesirable condition known as *worming*. Their presence is indicated by small piles of cream-colored dust (excreta).

Former Yale University conservator Jane Greenfield recommends an ingenious method of trapping the adult beetles in her book *The Care of Fine Books* (Nick Lyons Books, 1988): apply a coat of flour paste to the outside of several glass evaporating dishes no more than three inches in diameter to enable the insects to climb up the slippery sides; then deposit a teaspoon of wheat flour in the center of each dish and place the dishes on low bookshelves in the room containing signs of their presence. Attracted to the flour, the adult beetles will be unable to fly away because the take-off area inside the dish is too small. Bookworms can also be exterminated by freezing the infested item. Also spelled *book-worm*. Compare with *book lice*. *See also*: *fumigation*.

Also, a slang expression used as a term of disparagement for someone who prefers reading over most other activities and can usually be found with his or her nose in a book.

Boolean   A system of logic developed by the English mathematician George Boole (1815–64) that allows the user to combine words or phrases representing significant concepts in a keywords search of an online catalog or bibliographic database. Three logical commands (sometimes called "operators") are available in most search software:

The **OR** command is used to *expand* retrieval by including synonyms and related terms in the query. *See also*: *logical sum*.

Search statement: **violence or conflict or aggression**

The **AND** command is used to *narrow* search results. Each time another concept is added using "and," the search becomes more specific. In some online catalogs and databases, the "and" command is *implicit* (no need to type it between terms). In other interfaces, keywords will be searched as a phrase if not separated by "and." *See also*: *logical product*.

Search statement: **violence and television and children**

The **NOT** command is used to *exclude* unwanted records from search results. *See also*: *logical difference*.

Search statement: **television not news**

When two *different* Boolean commands are used in the same search statement, parentheses must be included to indicate the sequence in which they are to be executed (syntax). This technique is called *nesting*.

Search statement: **television and (violence or aggression) and children**

For a detailed discussion of Boolean logic, please see the entry by Gwyneth Tseng in the *International Encyclopedia of Information and Library Science* (Routledge, 2003). *See also*: *proximity*, *truncation*, and *Venn diagram*.

boot   In computing, a slang term borrowed from the expression "to pull oneself up by one's bootstraps," meaning to start a computer, causing the files in its operating system to automatically begin executing. Application programs are "loaded" rather than "booted." Synonymous with *boot up*. *See also*: *cold boot* and *reboot*.

bootleg   A product illegally imported or sold. In the case of commercially published CDs, computer software, videocassettes, books, and other intellectual property, a copy made for sale in violation of existing copyright law. *See also*: *pirated edition*.

bootstrap   A program that causes the first piece of software installed on a computer (usually the operating system) to load when the power is switched on, enabling the CPU to begin executing instructions. The word *bootstrap* originally referred to a leather strap or tab attached to the back of a boot to help the wearer pull it on—hence the expression "to pull oneself up by one's bootstraps." In computing, it has spawned *boot, cold boot, reboot,* etc.

border   Continuous ornamentation running parallel with the edges of a page or cover of a book or other printed publication, or around a block of text or illustration. A border can consist of one or more unbroken rules, plain or embellished, or units of geometric or organic design arranged in an unbroken repeating pattern.

In medieval manuscripts, decorative borders evolved from pen-flourishes and ex-tenders on decorated initial letters into elaborate foliate, zoomorphic, anthropomor-phic, and/or zoo-anthropomorphic designs occupying the margins and sometimes the space between columns of text. A *full border* surrounds text and miniatures on all four sides. In especially ornate manuscripts, borders may be historiated and/or gilded. Compare with *frame*. **See also**: *acanthus*, *bar border*, and rinceaux.

born digital   An informal term for a work created from scratch in electronic form, for example, a hypermedia thesis or dissertation, or an electronic journal that has no print counterpart. Preservation dilemmas are posed by the rapid obsolescence of digital equipment and formats.

borrower   A person who checks out books and other materials from a library. Most libraries require users to register to receive the borrowing privileges associated with a library card. Some form of identification is usually required of new applicants. Not all library patrons are registered borrowers—in most public libraries and publicly supported academic libraries in the United States, unregistered persons may use ref-erence materials and items in the circulating collection without removing them from library premises. The library privileges to which a borrower is entitled are indicated by the individual's borrower status.

borrower account   A patron's ongoing transactions with a library, including items currently checked out, overdues, unpaid fines, holds, etc. Library staff can check the status of an individual's account by examining the patron record. Most automated circulation systems are designed to protect the borrower's confidentiality by deleting transaction history as soon as items are returned and fines paid.

borrower status   The borrowing privileges to which a registered borrower is entitled, determined by *borrower type* as indicated in the patron record. Each library establishes its own list of borrower categories to reflect local conditions. In public libraries, all registered users generally enjoy the same privileges, but in academic libraries, certain privileges, such as length of loan period, may not be the same for faculty and students. In special libraries, privileges may depend on a person's rank in the parent organi-zation.

borrowing library   A library or institution that requests and receives materials from another library, usually on interlibrary loan. Compare with *lending library*. **See also**: *net borrower*.

borrowing period   *See*: loan period.

borrowing privileges   The rights to which a library borrower is entitled, usually established by registering to receive a library card. Such privileges normally include the right to check out books and other materials from the circulating collection for a designated period of time, interlibrary loan, use of special collections, etc. They may be suspended if fines remain unpaid. In most public libraries, all registered users enjoy the same privileges, but in academic libraries, certain privileges, such as length of loan period, may be different for faculty than for students. In special libraries, borrowing privileges may depend on a person's rank in the parent organization.

boss   A plain or embellished metal knob or raised cleat firmly attached to the outside of a book cover, usually at the center and/or corners. Bosses were used on medieval bookbindings from the 13th to the 15th century, as decoration and to protect the sides from abrasion, as books were usually stored flat instead of on end. Compare with *shoe*.

bounced   An undeliverable e-mail message returned to the sender's mailbox, usually because the recipient's e-mail address was incorrectly typed, the user unknown to the mail server, or the e-mail box full. Incoming messages incorrectly identified as junk mail may be bounced by an e-mail filter.

bound as is   An incomplete or defective volume bound in the condition in which it is received by the binder, usually in compliance with specific instructions from the library as indicated on the binding slip.

Bound to Stay Bound (BTSB)   Established in 1920 as a family-owned business, BTSB is the leading vendor of prelibrary bound children's books to school and public libraries in the United States, providing a list of 18,000 books and media items. For heavily used titles, libraries rely on BTSB because the bindings are so sturdy that the pages usually wear out first. URL: www.btsb.com.

bowdlerize   To change the text of a literary work by altering or deleting words or entire passages considered objectionable. Derived from the name of the Reverend Thomas Bowdler (1754–1825), who published an edition of the works of Shakespeare in the early 19th century from which passages considered "unfit to be read by a gentleman in the presence of ladies" were omitted. He produced a similar edition of the *Old Testament*. Chaucer's *The Canterbury Tales* and Jonathan Swift's *Gulliver's Travels* have received the same kind of treatment. Synonymous with *expurgate*. *See also*: *censorship* and *unexpurgated*.

bowed   The condition of a book bound in boards that have warped away from the book block or toward it, usually as a result of changes in humidity or differences in the expansion/contraction of the covering material and the paste-down. The solution is rebinding.

Bowker   *See*: Bowker, Richard Rogers *and* R.R. Bowker.

Bowker, Richard Rogers (1848–1933)   A literary editor who in 1876 founded, with Frederick Leypoldt and Melvil Dewey, the publication *Library Journal*. In the same year, he helped found the American Library Association and with Leypoldt began publication of *American Catalogue*, a comprehensive index of books published in the United States. In 1879, he purchased *Publishers Weekly*, which Leypoldt had created in 1873, assuming editorial control of the trade journal after Leypoldt's death in 1884. During this period, Bowker also helped found a liberal movement within the Republican Party known as the "Mugwumps" that was instrumental in preventing the nomination of Ulysess S. Grant for a third term. In 1880, he traveled to England to start the British edition of *Harper's Magazine*.

Bowker is also known for his interest in international copyright law and his success as a businessman. In 1911, he consolidated his business and publishing interests in the R.R. Bowker Co., which continues to be a leading publisher of reference books on libraries and the publishing industry. Bowker remained an active member of the ALA throughout his life but refused its presidency three times because he felt the position should be held by a librarian. He finally accepted the title Honorary President when he was in his seventies. Although he eventually lost his sight, he published a book of essays titled *The Arts of Life* and two volumes of verse in his later years.

Bowker Annual Library and Book Trade Almanac, The   A reference serial published annually by R.R. Bowker since 1955, *The Bowker Annual* is a compilation of practical information and informed analysis of topics and issues of interest to the library, information, and book trade community. It includes news of the year; reports from federal agencies, national libraries, and national associations/organizations; developments in library legislation, funding, and grants; library research and statistics; information on library and information science education, placement, and salaries; a directory of organizations; and a reference section that includes lists of distinguished books and literary award winners. Many libraries receive *The Bowker Annual* on continuation order. ISSN: 0068–0540.

box   In printing, a square or oblong area within a larger area of type, or between two columns, delineated by rules or white spaces that set apart the text and/or illustration contained in it. Also refers to a square or rectangular border of one or more parallel rules, printed around a block of type, sometimes with embellishment at the corners. Type matter set apart in this manner is said to be *boxed-in*.

boxed   A set of books or other documents stored in a close-fitting box-shaped container, usually to keep the volumes together and provide protection but sometimes for decorative effect. *See also*: *slipcase*.

boxed-in   *See*: box.

box list   An initial list of the contents of an archival box, usually made at the time the materials are packed for transfer, identifying the contents and giving a date range if applicable, used for control and access until a more complete inventory can be undertaken. Synonymous with *consignment list* and *container list*.

bracing   Heavy metal rods attached in the form of a large X to the uprights across the back of a section of single-sided shelving, or down the middle of a double-sided section of free-standing shelving, for the purpose of reducing lengthwise sway. Metal braces are also attached to sections in parallel ranges, over the aisles, to reduce side-to-side sway, particularly in geographic areas prone to earthquake.

bracketed interpolation   Description added to a bibliographic record inside square brackets [ ] to indicate information that has been provided by the cataloger, usually because it is not available in or on the item itself, for example, **[15] p**. to indicate that an unpaginated work is 15 pages long.

Braille   A tactile system of embossed print invented in 1829 by blind Parisian Louis Braille in which the letters of the alphabet are represented by combinations of six raised dots arranged in columns three dots high and two dots wide to enable visually impaired persons to read by touch. The most widely used tactile medium in the world, Braille is employed by libraries in the United States for signage and materials for readers with visual impairments that prevent them from reading conventional print. The form of Braille used in mathematics is called *Nemeth code*. The *Braille Book Review* is available online (www.loc.gov/nls/bbr/index.html), courtesy of the National Library Service for the Blind and Physically Handicapped.

branch library   An auxiliary service outlet in a library system, housed in a facility separate from the central library, which has at least a basic collection of materials, a regular staff, and established hours, with a budget and policies determined by the central library. A branch library is usually managed by a *branch librarian* who may have responsibility for more than one branch. In a public library system, new branches may be sited on the basis of a comprehensive plan for the entire city, county, region, or library district served by the system. Compare with *affiliated library*. **See also**: *bookmobile* and *books-by-mail*.

brand name   The part of the name or logo associated with a specific product or service, which can be vocalized, usually letters, words, and/or numerals identifying and distinguishing it from varieties of the same product or service marketed by competing companies (*example*: **Coca-Cola** versus **Pepsi-Cola**). When registered with the U.S. Patent and Trademark Office, a brand or part of a brand is known as a *trademark*.

brass   *See*: blocking.

breach of contract   Failure to keep the terms of an agreement or contract. Some employment contracts include penalties for breach of certain provisions, such as length of notice required at time of resignation, but enforcement is usually at the discretion of the employer. **See also**: *book contract*.

break   *See*: gap *and* nongap break.

breviary   A liturgical book containing the Divine Office, the prayers said by the clergy of the Roman Catholic and the Eastern Orthodox Church at the canonical hours of the day and night. The breviary was created in the 11th century by combining several formerly separate volumes (antiphonal, psalter, lectionary, etc.). Its purpose may have been to provide poorer communities of clerics with the texts required to conduct services. Because of its size, it was originally used only by the members of monastic establishments, but the Franciscans and Dominicans produced a portable breviary that could be used for private devotion. Although its contents vary slightly with the use of a particular region, it is divided into the calendar, temporale (Proper of Time), sanctorale (Proper of Saints), and Common of Saints. Hand-copied medieval breviaries were often beautifully illuminated. The lay counterpart of the breviary is the Book of Hours, used in personal devotion.

bricks-and-mortar The traditional library, functioning for millennia as a physical repository ("warehouse") for the permanent storage of tangible items, as opposed to the modern concept of the library as an institution dedicated to providing access to information maintained onsite or remotely, in print or nonprint formats. The opposite of *library without walls*.

brief An outline of the evidence and arguments supporting one side of an argument. In a more general sense, any concise statement in written form. In law, a summary statement of the main points of an oral or written argument presented in court. Also refers to a letter of authority, especially one sent by the pope to the members of a Roman Catholic religious community.

brief record An abbreviated display of a bibliographic record in an online catalog or database, omitting data elements contained in some of the less essential fields and subfields, in contrast to the full record providing a complete bibliographic description of the item. In most catalogs and bibliographic databases, search results can be displayed in both formats.

bright copy A copy of an older book that is as fresh and new as the day it was published, a condition likely to command a higher price in the market for antiquarian and used books than a copy of the same edition showing signs of wear. *See also*: *mint*.

briticize To convert to British English the style and spelling of a work written in (or translated into) American English. Compare with *americanize*.

British Broadcasting Corporation (BBC) An independent broadcasting service that began daily "wireless" transmission in 1922, supported by individual licenses sold at 10 shillings apiece. By the end of the 1930s, the number of licenses had increased to nearly 9 million, and the BBC had become a major patron of the arts. In 1936, the BBC Television Service was launched, only be to be closed down during World War II, but the BBC emerged from the war with an enhanced reputation for the quality of its news broadcasts.

Today, individuals and businesses in Britain that use or install equipment to receive or record television programming are required to pay an annual license fee in support of the BBC, which is run by a 12-member board of directors appointed by the queen in council to monitor performance standards and appoint a director-general and upper-level management. Many of the television programs and series shown on PBS in the United States are co-produced with or acquired from the BBC. URL: www.bbc.co. uk. *See also*: *public television*.

British Library, The Located mainly in London, The British Library is the national library of the United Kingdom (UK), created in 1973 by an act of Parliament that merged the British Museum Library, the National Central Library, and the National

Lending Library for Science and Technology (Patent Office Library). In later years, the *British National Bibliography*, the National Sound Archive, and the India Office Library and Records were added to the institution. In 1997, its constituent parts were brought together in a new building at St. Pancras, with the exception of the Newspaper Library which remains at Colindale. Covering all known languages and periods of history, its collections are a resource for scholars worldwide. The British Library is also the legal depository for UK publications. URL: www.bl.uk. *See also*: *Bodleian Library*.

British National Bibliography (BNB)   The most comprehensive record of books and first issues of serials published since 1950 in the United Kingdom (UK) and Ireland, the *BNB* has been the responsibility of The British Library since the library's inception in 1973. Since 1990, bibliographic records created in accordance with international cataloging standards have been contributed by all the legal depository libraries in the UK, with CIP data on forthcoming titles provided by the Bibliographic Data Services. Coverage is selective, with emphasis on mainstream monographs available through regular book-buying channels. Research reports and non-trade monographs are recorded separately in the *British National Bibliography for Report Literature*. The *BNB* is available weekly in print, monthly on CD-ROM, and online. URL: www.bl.uk/ services/bibliographic/natbib.html.

brittle   The condition of being easily broken or shattered. In time, acid papers turn yellow and become brittle, tearing easily and even crumbling under normal use. For paper, the standard test of brittleness is whether the corner of a page can withstand folding in each direction twice. Encapsulation is used to preserve individual sheets but is not practical for entire volumes. Digital reformatting is replacing conversion to microforms in the preservation of *embrittled* books.

broadcast   Simultaneous transmission to all who own the equipment required to receive a signal communicating information content (radio and television) or to those who have paid for a specific type of communication service (cable television). The opposite of *narrowcast*. Compare with *multicast*.

   Also refers to a radio or television program or announcement once it has been transmitted to its audience. In the most general sense, to make any message widely known.

broad classification   A classification system in which the main classes are not extensively subdivided, for use in small libraries that do not require *close classification* to organize their collections effectively.

   In Dewey Decimal Classification, the classification of works in general categories by logical abridgment, even when more specific class numbers are available, for example, use of the class **641.5 Cooking** instead of the subclass **641.5945 Italian cooking** for a cookbook consisting of Italian recipes.

broader term (BT)   In a hierarchical classification system, a subject heading or descriptor that includes another term as a subclass, for example, "Libraries" listed as a broader term under "School libraries." In some indexing systems, a subject heading or descriptor may have more than one broader term, for example, "Documentation" and "Library science" under "Cataloging." Also abbreviated *B*. Compare with *narrower term* and *related term*.

broadsheet   A long, narrow unfolded sheet of paper printed on one or both sides, used mainly for advertising purposes and formerly to disseminate religious or political views. Sometimes used synonymously with *broadside*. Also refers to a full-size newspaper, as opposed to a *tabloid*.

broadside   Originally, a large sheet of paper printed across one side only, intended to be read unfolded or posted, bearing a royal proclamation or official notice, but later used to disseminate news or political views. Also used in 16th-century England to distribute ballads and other poems. Sometimes used synonymously with *broadsheet*. An archival collection of broadsides is available online, courtesy of the *American Memory* project, at: memory.loc.gov/ammem/rbpehtml/pehome.html. *See also*: *handbill*.

In modern usage, a separately published item consisting of a large sheet printed on one or both sides, folded down the center for mailing and meant to be read unfolded. Sometimes restricted to a sheet on which the text is printed from side to side across the fold. Also refers to the substance of the matter printed in such a format.

brochure   From the French word *brocher* ("to stitch"). An independent nonserial publication consisting of a few leaves of printed material stitched together but not bound, usually issued in paper covers. Considered ephemera in most libraries, brochures are not cataloged separately unless they are of historical interest or issued by a government agency and selected for inclusion in a government documents collection. Used synonymously with *pamphlet*.

Brodart   A commercial company that supplies books, furniture, equipment, supplies, and automation services to libraries of all kinds, largely through its printed trade catalog. URL: www.brodart.com.

broken link   A link in an HTML document that is not functioning properly, usually because the link address is incorrect or the Web site is no longer available or has been moved to another server with no forwarding address provided. When a broken link is selected in a Web document, an error message appears on the screen. The tendency of links in a hypertext document to become nonfunctional over time is known colloquially as *link rot*.

broken up   A book disassembled to enable its parts (usually plates or other illustrations) to be sold separately. Copies of the *Gutenberg Bible* have been broken up, and the leaves sold separately.

browsability   The ease with which a library catalog, index, bibliographic database, or other list of resources can be searched in a casual, unsystematic manner. A printed index is often more *browsable* than its online counterpart because the page format makes it easy for the user to scan a list of headings to find related information. *See also*: *serendipity*.

browse   To look through a library collection, catalog, bibliography, index, bibliographic database, or other finding tool in a casual search for items of interest, without clearly defined intentions. To facilitate browsing, libraries assign similar call numbers to items on the same subject, which groups them together on the shelf.

In information retrieval, a search directed by the user in a dynamic but casual way. A clearly formulated query may determine the initial point of entry into an index or database, but searches that begin systematically often give way to an exploratory approach as new terminology is revealed in the results retrieved. Some researchers consider print indexes to be more *browsable* than electronic databases because page format allows the user to scan with ease the headings and entries that precede and follow the initial point of access.

Also, to search for information available on the World Wide Web in a casual, serendipitous manner. Hypertext is designed to facilitate online browsing by providing embedded links to related documents and electronic resources. Compare with *surf*. *See also*: *Web browser*.

browser   A person who searches a library collection, catalog, index, bibliography, bibliographic database, or other list of resources in a casual, unsystematic manner. *See also*: *serendipity*.

Also refers to a type of application software called a Web browser, designed to facilitate searching for information available on the Internet.

browser cache   The portion of microcomputer memory reserved by Web browser software for storing the contents of Web pages previously visited by the user, reducing the amount of time required to revisit a page using the same machine. Clicking on "Reload" or "Refresh" in the toolbar of a browser will cause the Web page displayed on the screen to be retrieved from its original remote address, rather than from the cache. Most browsers allow the user to specify the length of time search history will be retained before it is automatically deleted.

BSA   *See*: **B**ibliographical **S**ociety of **A**merica.

BT (or B)   *See*: **b**roader **t**erm.

BTSB   *See*: **B**ound **t**o **S**tay **B**ound.

buckram   A strong, durable book cloth consisting of a heavy woven base in cotton, linen, or jute filled with starch or impregnated with pyroxylin, used to cover volumes for which heavy use is anticipated (bound periodicals, periodical indexes, children's picture books, etc.).

budget   The total amount of funds available to meet a library's expenditures over a fixed period of time (usually one or two years). In most budgets, funds are allocated by category of expenditure, called *lines*. In chronically underfunded libraries and library systems, *budgeting* can be a major source of frustration for librarians and library administration. *See also*: *line-item budget*, *operating budget*, and *zero-base budget*.

buffer   In computing, temporary storage (usually RAM) used for data while it is being processed or for special purposes such as the transfer of data between two system components that have different operating speeds, for example, a printer and a CPU capable of processing data more quickly than output can be printed. A buffer may be a section of memory reserved for a specific processing function or a portion of general memory allocated and deallocated as needed.

In papermaking, a substance or mixture of substances added to paper stock during manufacture to control the acidity or alkalinity of the product. In document preservation, a substance or mixture used to maintain the acidity or alkalinity of paper (or of a solution) at an optimum level.

buffered paper   Printing paper to which an alkaline substance, such as calcium carbonate or magnesium carbonate, is added in manufacture to neutralize any acid produced internally as a result of aging or introduced by acid migration or exposure to atmospheric pollution. *Non-buffered* paper is required for certain types of photographic prints.

buffering   In papermaking, the addition of an alkaline substance such as calcium carbonate or magnesium carbonate to the pulped fiber to neutralize any acid that may develop as paper ages or that is introduced through acid migration or exposure to atmospheric pollution. Extent of buffering is indicated as a percentage of the paper weight, usually no more than 2 to 3 percent.

bug   In computing, a slang term for a persistent error in software or hardware. Once it has been located, a software bug can be corrected by altering the program, a process known as *debugging*. To correct a hardware bug, it is usually necessary to reconfigure circuitry. Compare with *glitch*.

Also refers to an electronic eavesdropping device installed in a telephone receiver, or in some other hidden location, usually for the purpose of espionage.

built number   In Dewey Decimal Classification, a class number constructed according to add instructions stated or implied in the schedules or tables. Number building is employed only when there is no existing class in the schedules that precisely represents the subject of the work.

bulk   The thickness of a book without its cover, normally less after binding than in its unbound state. Also, the thickness of a sheet of paper in relation to its weight, as measured in thousandths of an inch. The thickness of printing papers is also measured in pages per inch. Publishers sometimes "bulk" a short text by printing it on thick, low-density paper. India paper and bible paper are used to *reduce* the bulk of a large volume.

bulk lending   The lending of a large volume of materials by one library to another, usually for a period of time longer than the normal borrowing period. Books published in large print and audiobooks are sometimes loaned in bulk to the branch libraries within a public library system, or even outside the system.

bulk subscription   A subscription for a substantial number of copies (usually 10 or more) of the same serial title, sent to a single address for subsequent distribution (ALCTS *Serials Acquisitions Glossary*, Chicago, 1993).

bull   Narrowly speaking, a document, letter, edict, or decree issued by the pope, to which his official seal (*Bulla*) is affixed. Also refers to any statement of belief or doctrine, whether ecclesiastical or not.

bullet   In printing, word processing, and Web page design, a small graphical element, usually in the shape of a:

○ small circle,

● large dot,

■ square,

◆ diamond, or

★ other shape.

Used to emphasize a part of a text or to itemize an unnumbered list. Such a list is said to be *bulleted*.

bulletin   A periodical, usually in the form of a pamphlet, issued by a government agency, society, or other institution, containing announcements, news, and information of current interest, usually more substantial than a newsletter. In a more general sense, any brief report on the latest developments in an ongoing process or situation, issued in print or nonprint format. Abbreviated *bull*. *See also*: *bulletin board*.

bulletin board   A flat notice board, usually attached to a wall near the entrance to a library, used to display announcements of forthcoming events, dust jackets removed from new books recently added to the collection, reading lists, comments and suggestions from library users (sometimes with responses from the library administration), and other information pertinent to library operations. Some libraries use a kiosk for this purpose. *See also*: *bulletin board system*.

bulletin board system (BBS)   An online messaging system and discussion forum that allows users to post notices and comments to members of an interest group connected to the same network. A BBS is similar in function to a Web site but lacks graphics and has its own telephone number that the user must dial with the aid of a communications program. Bulletin board systems have been largely superseded in the United States by the World Wide Web but are still used in parts of the world that lack direct access to the Internet. Compare with *mailing list*.

Bulletin of the Center for Children's Books (BCCB)   Published since 1945, *BCCB* provides concise summaries and critical evaluations of current books for children, written mostly from galley proofs. Each review provides information on content, reading level, strengths and weaknesses, and quality of format, as well as suggested use in curriculum. Published monthly (except August), each issue also includes a front page editorial and a section featuring bibliographies, reviews of new professional books, and abstracts of research articles. *BCCB* also publishes an annual selection of the year's most distinguished children's titles. ISSN: 0008–9036. URL: www.lis. uiuc.edu/puboff/bccb.

bumped   The condition of a binding that has at least one corner bent, compressed, or rounded by forceful contact with a hard surface, such as the floor in a fall from a bookshelf.

bureau   An office or department within an organization or government agency, responsible for collecting and disseminating information, usually on a specific topic, in a particular field, or of a certain type, for example, demographic information in the case of the U.S. Census Bureau.

burlesque   From the Italian word *burla*, meaning "mockery." A crude form of satire in which the style of a work, or of an entire genre, is ridiculed by trivializing a serious subject or dignifying a trivial one, usually in the form of a stage performance. The purpose is to amuse and entertain, rather than to inform. Compare with *parody*.

burnish   In bookbinding, to polish the colored or gilt edges of a volume with a smooth hard tool, such as an agate, until the surface gleams elegantly in the light. Left unburnished, a gilt edge is *antique*.

burnisher   *See*: burnish.

burnout   Physical and mental exhaustion caused by working hard for too long, sometimes out of excessive devotion to a demanding project. When overwork is chronic in a workplace, the effect on staff morale may be felt in higher rates of absenteeism and turnover and in deterioration of quality of service. Also spelled *burn-out*.

business library   A branch of a metropolitan public library system that serves the specialized information needs of persons engaged in business, usually located in or near the commercial or financial district. Also, a separately administered library associated with the business department of a college or university, administered to serve the curriculum needs of the business faculty and the information needs of students enrolled in courses in business, management, accounting, and related fields. The collection usually includes books, periodicals, and reference materials on business, as well as company reports, economic and business statistics, business-related periodical indexes and databases, etc., managed by a *business librarian*. Compare with *corporation library*.

buying guide   A publication intended for professional librarians, providing authoritative guidance on the purchase of a specific type of resource (*example*: **Purchasing an Encyclopedia: Twelve Points to Consider** published by the American Library Association in 1996). Buying guides usually begin with a discussion of evaluation techniques, then provide detailed analysis of possible selections, usually broken down by type of work. The relative strengths/weaknesses of available alternatives may be presented in tabular format to facilitate comparison. Also used synonymously with *consumer guide*.

B-word   *See*: biblio-.

byline   A line of type usually printed at the beginning or end of a newspaper or magazine article to indicate its authorship. *See also*: *date line*.

byte   The common unit of computer storage used in digital computers of all types and sizes, composed of eight binary digits called bits. Hardware specifications for computers (microcomputers to mainframes) are indicated in bytes. Each unique sequence of 8 bits can encode a single character, for a total of 256 possible characters. In ASCII text, the characters are alphanumeric. Disagreement exists about the origin of the term. It may be an abbreviation of *binary table* or *binary term* or derived from the expression "by eights."

1 byte = 8 bits
1 kilobyte (K) = 1,024 bytes
1 megabyte (MB) = 1,024 kilobytes or approximately 1 million bytes
1 gigabyte (GB) = 1,024 megabytes or approximately 1 billion bytes

Text and image files are usually measured in kilobytes, portable storage and program files in megabytes, and hard disk capacity in gigabytes.

C

cache   A small section of dedicated high-speed memory built into a microcomputer to improve system performance by providing temporary storage for blocks of data and instructions that would otherwise be retrieved from slower memory. As a general rule, the larger the cache, the greater the enhancement of performance and speed. Pronounced "cash." *See also*: *browser cache*.

CACUL   *See*: Canadian Association of College and University Libraries.

cadastral map   From the Latin word *capitastrum*, meaning "register of the poll tax." A map showing boundaries and subdivisions, made to record ownership and rights in land and to describe and establish the value of property, usually for the purpose of tax assessment.

cadel   A large, highly creative capital letter composed of sweeping pen strokes embellished with patterned calligraphic flourishes, giving the letterform the appearance of a versal. Cadels were an exaggerated form of gothic *littera bastarda*, used in medieval manuscripts from the 13th to the 15th century. Also spelled *cadelle*.

CALA   *See*: Chinese American Librarians Association.

calamus   The pen made from a dried reed, used from about 200 B.C. for writing in ink on papyrus, as distinct from the stylus used during the same period for writing on wax tablets and the quill pen used from the 6th century for writing on parchment and vellum. Marc Drogin notes in *Medieval Calligraphy: Its History and Technique* (Allanheld & Schram, 1980) that a sharp point was used at first, producing monoline script. After about 100 B.C., a broad-nibbed reed was used, allowing the scribe to vary the width of pen strokes, giving the letterforms a more calligraphic appearance.

Caldecott Medal   A literary award given annually since 1938 under the auspices of the American Library Association to the illustrator of the most distinguished children's picture book published in the United States during the preceding year. The medal is donated by the family of Frederic G. Melcher. Compare with *Newbery Medal*. *See also*: *Amelia Frances Howard-Gibbon Illustrator's Award* and *Greenaway Medal*.

calendar   A list of the days in a year, usually arranged by month and within each month by week, sometimes indicating the dates of important events such as national and religious holidays. Also, an almanac listing days of the year that are significant to a particular culture or political entity. The calendar of forthcoming library events, provided in *The Bowker Annual Library and Book Trade Almanac*, includes state, regional, national, and international association meetings. Compare with *chronology*. *See also*: *calendar year*.

In medieval manuscripts used in Church services and private devotion, a calendar section often preceded the text, identifying the feast days celebrated in the region. The most important were highlighted in red ink ("red letter days") with other colors used to indicate degrees of importance. The Julian calendar (365 days with an extra day every four years) was adopted from the Romans, but the Roman civil year (beginning on January 1) was replaced by the Christian year in the 7th century. The illumination of medieval calendars often depicted the labors of the month (largely agrarian) and the signs of the zodiac.

Also refers to a list of the documents included in an archival collection (rolls, charters, state papers, etc.), usually annotated to indicate the date, contents, and other characteristics of each item.

calendar year   The one-year period beginning on January 1 and ending on December 31 (following the civil year of the ancient Romans). Most journal subscriptions run for a single calendar year, although some publishers offer a financial incentive to subscribe or renew for multiple years. Compare with *publication year*. *See also*: *subscription period*.

calender   The part of a papermaking machine consisting of a series of rollers designed to smooth paper after drying, reducing its permeability to moisture by closing the pores in its surface. In *calendering*, the degree of smoothness depends on the amount of pressure applied by the rollers. *Supercalendering* produces the glossiest finish that can be applied to paper without coating it.

calf   A leather binding made from the skin of a calf usually no more than a few weeks old. Its soft, smooth, unblemished surface made it the preferred material in England for hand-binding trade editions but not on the Continent, where printed books were usually sold in paper covers to be custom-bound at the discretion of the purchaser. Calfskin bindings can be dyed any color and decorated in various ways (marbled, mottled, speckled, stained, tree, etc.). Although it is sturdy and provides a good base for tooling or blocking, the smooth surface of calfskin makes it susceptible to scratching and scuffing. *See also*: *ooze leather*, *rough*, *russia*, and *Spanish calf*.

calligraphy   The art of elegantly beautiful handwriting. A highly skilled penman is a *calligrapher*. The term also refers to handwritten characters, words, pages, and entire documents that meet the aesthetic requirements of highly skilled penmanship. In Far Eastern cultures, calligraphy is done with a pointed brush held in a vertical position. In Western and Islamic cultures, it is done with a reed, quill, or nib pen held at an angle to the writing surface. During the Middle Ages, certain scribes were known for the beauty of their script. Some became writing masters and wrote model books. In the Islamic world, the proscription on religious imagery facilitated the development of Arabic calligraphy into a sophisticated art form.

call number   A unique code printed on a label affixed to the outside of an item in a library collection, usually the lower spine of a book or videocassette, also handwritten or printed on a label inside the item. Assigned by the cataloger, the call number is also displayed in the bibliographic record representing the item in the library catalog, to identify the specific copy of the work and give its relative location on the shelf.

In most collections, a call number is composed of a classification number followed by additional notation to make the call number unique. This gives a classified arrangement to the library shelves, facilitating browsing. Generally, the class number is followed by an *author mark* to distinguish the work from others of the same class, followed by a *work mark* to distinguish the title from other works of the same class by the same author, and sometimes other information such as publication date, volume number, copy number, and location symbol.

In Library of Congress Classification (LCC), used by most academic and research libraries in the United States, class notation begins with letters of the English alphabet (*example*: **PN 2035.H336 1991**). In Dewey Decimal Classification (DDC), used by most public and school libraries in the United States, class notation consists of arabic numerals (*example*: **480.0924 W3**). U.S. federal government documents are assigned SuDocs numbers (*example*: **L 2.2:M 76**).

call slip   A brief form that must be filled out by a registered borrower to request an item from the closed stacks of a library, usually retrieved by hand by a staff member called a *page*, although automated and semi-automated systems are used in some large libraries.

cameo   A typeface used for special effect in which the normal method of printing is reversed, the characters appearing in white against a solid or shaded background, instead of in black against a light background. Compare with *outline letter*.

cameo binding   A style of bookbinding popular in Italy from about 1500–1560 in which the centers of the boards forming the cover are stamped in relief in imitation of a coin or medallion. The decoration may be left blind or embellished with ink, silver, or gold leaf. Synonymous with *plaquette binding*. Compare with *centerpiece*.

cameo stamp   In binding, a metal tool of oval shape engraved with a design, usually in the form of a picture, used from the 11th to 16th century in blind tooling to make an impression resembling cameo jewelry on the side of a leather-bound book. *See also*: *cameo binding*.

camera microfilm   In reprography, an image of an original source document, made with a camera on high-quality film, usually retained by the producer for the purpose of making archival or distribution copies. Synonymous with *first generation* and *master negative*.

camera-ready copy (CRC)   In printing, copy typed using word processing software, or produced by some other means, that has been fully edited and is ready to be photographed for platemaking without having to be typeset. Synonymous with *camera copy*.

Canadiana   The national bibliography of Canada, produced since 1950 by the National Library of Canada for use in reference and research as a selection aid, to provide bibliographic information for cataloging, and as a record of the nation's published heritage. Available online, on CD-ROM, and via FTP, *Canadiana* is a comprehensive list of titles published in Canada, including books, periodicals, sound recordings, microforms, music scores, pamphlets, government documents, theses, educational kits, videorecordings, and electronic documents. It also provides information about forthcoming titles to facilitate advance ordering. The printed edition of *Canadiana* was discontinued after the December 1991 issue and the microfiche edition after December 2000. URL: www.nlc-bnc.ca/canadiana/index-e.html.

Canadian Association of College and University Libraries (CACUL)   A division of the Canadian Library Association, CACUL seeks to develop and promote high standards of librarianship in institutions of postsecondary education. The organization gives awards, publishes *CACUL Divisional Notes*, and sponsors the *CACUL List-Serv*. URL: www.cla.ca/divisions/cacul/cacul.htm.

Canadian Booksellers Association (CBA)   A nonprofit national trade association devoted to promoting the current and future interests of the bookselling industry in Canada and to meeting the needs of Canadian booksellers. Its members include over 1,200 bookstores and over 350 publishers across Canada. CBA publishes the trade journal *Canadian Bookseller* in nine issues per year. URL: www.cbabook.org.

Canadian Library Association (CLA)   Founded in 1946, CLA has a membership of librarians and other persons involved or interested in libraries, librarianship, and information science in Canada. An affiliate of the American Library Association, CLA sponsors a national conference held at a different location in Canada each year. CLA is also co-publisher with the ALA and the Library Association (UK) of *Anglo-American Cataloguing Rules*. URL: www.cla.ca.

Canadian Publishers' Council (CPC)   Founded in 1910, CPC is a trade association representing the interests of Canadian publishers of English-language books and media for schools, colleges and universities, professional and reference markets, and the retail and library sectors. Located in Toronto, CPC also represents the Canadian publishing industry internationally and maintains a liaison with the Association of American Publishers. URL: www.pubcouncil.ca/home.htm. ***See also***: *Association of Canadian Publishers*.

Canadian-U.S. Task Force on Archival Description (CUSTARD)   An international group of archivists working to reconcile the three existing descriptive content standards used by archivists—APPM (Archives, Personal Papers, and Manuscripts); the Canadian Rules for Archival Description (RAD); and the General International Standard Archival Description (ISAD[G])—into a single descriptive standard. The product is expected to be the foundation of a truly international content standard.

cancel   A new leaf or leaves printed to replace part of a book or other publication when changes are required in the text or illustrations, usually before binding but after the work has gone to press, more common in the 17th and 18th centuries than today because as printing developed, the frequency of printing errors declined.

canceled   Said of a regular order, continuation order, or periodical subscription terminated for some reason by the library or the seller. A nonserial item may be reordered if it is still available. Library holdings of a canceled serial title are noted in the catalog record in a closed entry. Serial cancellations have increased in recent years, particularly in academic libraries, due to the rising cost of print subscriptions and the availability of full-text in bibliographic databases. Compare with *discontinued*. *See also*: *noncancellable*.

cancellation   In the context of medieval manuscripts, a superimposed "x" used to indicate a correction by crossing out one or more letters; a form of deletion. *See also*: *expunction*.

cancellation period   The period of time a library allows a publisher, jobber, or other vendor for shipment of a book or item before the order is automatically canceled, usually 90 to 180 days. The item may subsequently be reordered from the same vendor or a different source.

candidate   A person whose application for employment has been accepted and who is being seriously considered for a position. Also refers to a person taking an examination, running for an elected office, considered for an award or degree, or destined for a particular purpose or fate. *See also*: *short list*.

canon   In literature, the accepted list of works by a given author considered by scholars to be authentic, for example, the 37 plays of William Shakespeare. Also refers to the approved list of works included in the Bible. In the most general sense, a criterion or standard of judgment applied for the purpose of evaluation. Compare with *apocryphal*. *See also*: *canonical order*.

canonical order   The arrangement of headings, parts, divisions, or items in an order established by law or tradition, the classic example being the sequence of the books of the Bible.

canon tables   A system of indexing the canonical Gospels devised in the 4th century by Eusebius of Caesarea, in which the concordance of passages numbered in the text is displayed in four parallel columns, usually placed at the beginning of a Gospel book, Bible, or New Testament. Popular during the early Middle Ages, canon tables were usually given architectural treatment in manuscript decoration. Some designs include the symbols of the four evangelists, Matthew, Mark, Luke, and John.

canto   A major subdivision of a long narrative or epic poem serving the same function as a chapter in a novel. Cantos are traditionally numbered in roman numerals. Examples of works divided in this way are Dante's ***Divina Commedia***, Spenser's ***Faerie Queene***, and Byron's ***Don Juan***.

caoutchouc binding   The precursor of modern *perfect binding*. In 1836, William Hancock was granted a patent for a binding method in which single leaves, produced by trimming away the back folds of the sections, were attached directly to the cover without the use of thread by applying to the binding edge a layer of rubber solution made from the latex of various plants. This form of adhesive binding did not wear well—spines cracked and pages fell out. Also called *gutta percha* and *rubberback*.

capital expenditure   In budgeting, an allocation made on a one-time basis, usually for the construction of new facilities, the renovation or expansion of existing facilities, or a major upgrade of automation equipment or systems, as opposed to the operating budget allocated annually or biennially to meet ongoing expenses incurred in running a library or library system.

capital improvement   The acquisition of a long-term asset, such as a new or renovated facility, initial book stock, or new equipment, furnishings, or vehicle(s), funded on a one-time basis from a budget for capital expenditures, as distinct from the ongoing purchase of library materials, payment of salaries and wages, routine repair and replacement of existing equipment and furnishings, and regular maintenance of facilities, funded from the operating budget.

capitalization   The writing or printing of a letter, word, or words in uppercase rather than lowercase. Also refers to the conventions in a language with respect to words written or printed with certain letters in uppercase. For example, in English the first letter of the first word of a paragraph, and of each of the parts of a proper name, is normally *capitalized* (unless you are a cockroach and not heavy enough to depress the "Caps" key). The general rules governing capitalization in library catalog entries can be found in *Appendix A* of *AACR2*.

capital letter   A large letter of the roman alphabet (**A**, **B**, **C**, etc.) that prior to the 4th century A.D. consisted of capitals only. The name is derived from the lapidary Roman letterforms incised with a chisel at the top (*capital*) of architectural columns and on other stone monuments. Also, any letter written or printed in a form larger and usually different from that of the corresponding small letter. Abbreviated *cap*. Synonymous with *uppercase*. Compare with *majuscule*. *See also*: *capitalization, cap line, rustic capital, small capital*, and *square capital*.

cap line   In typography, the imaginary horizontal line connecting the tops of the uppercase letters of a type font, often, but not necessarily, the same as the *ascender line*. Compare with *mean line*. *See also*: *base line*.

caps   *See*: capital letter.

capsa   A box of cylindrical shape used in libraries of antiquity for storing scrolls in an upright position. *See also*: *scrinium*.

caption   From the Latin word for "capture" or "seizure." A brief title, explanation, or description appearing immediately above, beneath, or adjacent to an illustration or photograph on a page, sometimes indicating the source of the image. Synonymous in this sense with *cut line* or *legend*. *See also*: *overleaf*.

    Also refers to a heading printed at the beginning of a chapter or other section of a book and to the headline at the beginning of the text of a periodical article or section of it.

In microforms, a title or brief line of description in a type size large enough to enable the viewer to identify the photographed document without the aid of magnification. In films and filmstrips, a line of text at the bottom of a frame or sequence of frames identifying or explaining the content. A continuously moving line of text at the bottom of television screen is called a *crawl*. Compare with *subtitle*. *See also*: *closed caption*.

caption title   A title printed at the beginning of a chapter, section, or other major division of a book, or at the beginning of the first page of the text, which, in the absence of a title page, is sometimes used as the title of the whole in creating the bibliographic description. The cataloger usually adds *Caption title*: as a note in the bibliographic record to indicate its source. In a musical score, the title that appears immediately above the opening bars may be used as the caption title. Synonymous with *head title*. Compare with *drop-down title*.

card catalog   A list of the holdings of a library, printed, typed, or handwritten on catalog cards, each representing a single bibliographic item in the collection. The cards are normally filed in a single alphabetical sequence (dictionary catalog), or in separate sections by author, title, and subject (divided catalog), in the long narrow drawers of a specially designed filing cabinet, usually constructed of wood. Most large- and medium-sized libraries in the United States have converted their card catalogs to machine-readable format. Also spelled *card catalogue*. Compare with *online catalog*.

caricature   A deliberately distorted picture of a person, or imitation of a performance or literary style, achieved by grossly exaggerating certain features or mannerisms peculiar to the object of satire. *See also*: *cartoon* and *lampoon*.

Carnegie library   A library facility constructed wholly or in part with grant funds provided by the American steel magnate and philanthropist Andrew Carnegie (1835–1919), who, in his later years, devoted his considerable wealth to the promotion of libraries and world peace. Between 1881 and 1917, over 2,500 Carnegie libraries were built around the world, the majority in the United States, United Kingdom, and Canada. The libraries of many small towns in the United States still occupy facilities built with Carnegie funds. *See also*: *Carnegie Medal*.

Carnegie Medal   A literary award presented annually since 1936 by the Library Association of the United Kingdom to the author of the most outstanding English-language children's book published in the UK during the preceding year. The prize is named after the American steel magnate and philanthropist Andrew Carnegie (1835–1919) who devoted the last years of his life to the advancement of libraries and world peace. Compare with *Greenaway Medal*. *See also*: *CLA Book of the Year for Children* and *Newbery Medal*.

Caroline minuscule   *See*: Carolingian minuscule.

Carolingian minuscule   The first script to introduce small letters, Carolingian minuscule may have evolved from *Luxeuil minuscule*, a script developed at the monastery in Corbie. It was adopted in the late 8th century by Alcuin of York, Abbot of St. Martin at Tours, in response to Charlemagne's desire for a standard alphabet in which books of the Catholic Church could be copied throughout his realm. Also influenced by English half uncials, the script Alcuin learned in his youth at the cathedral school in York, Carolingian minuscule quickly became the dominant book hand in Europe, where it was used through the 11th century and adopted in England following the Norman Conquest, replacing Insular and Anglo-Saxon scripts.

Its letterforms are wide and curved, with ligatures sparingly used, each letter written separately. Carolingian style systematized punctuation and the division of text formerly written in *scriptio continuo* into words and sentences. The practice of beginning each sentence with a single majuscule and completing it in minuscules was also standardized. Marc Drogin notes in *Medieval Calligraphy: Its History and Technique* (Allanheld & Schram, 1980) that Carolingian minuscule made possible the copying of thousands of early manuscripts that would otherwise have been lost to history. Interest in Carolingian minuscule revived in the late 14th century in Italy, resulting in a new *humanistic script* that became the basis for the lowercase letters of many modern typefaces. Synonymous with *Caroline minuscule.*

carousel   A detachable, circular slotted container, usually made of plastic, in which dozens of slides can be queued for sequential viewing on a specially designed slide projector. Although carousels are bulky, they can also be used to store slides when not in use. Compare with *magazine.*

carpet page   A page in a medieval manuscript or early printed book covered with elaborate decoration and bearing no text, sometimes with the Christian cross incorporated into the overall design. The term is derived from its resemblance to hand-knotted carpets imported from the East. Michelle Brown notes in *Understanding Illuminated Manuscripts* (Getty Museum/British Library, 1994) that this style of ornamentation, popular with the scribes of Ireland and Britain from about A.D. 550 to 900, was used to separate the major divisions of Gospel books and Bibles and may have been of Coptic origin. Examples can be seen in the *Book of Kells* and *Lindisfarne Gospels.*

carrel   Originally a small stall or pew in a medieval cloister containing a desk for reading, writing, and semiprivate study. In modern libraries, a small room or alcove in the stacks designed for individual study. Also refers to a free-standing desk (or two desks face-to-face) with low partitions at back and sides to provide some degree of privacy, with a shelf across the back facing the reader. Newer study carrels have built-in illumination and may be wired to provide network access for patrons using laptops.

carrier   *See*: physical carrier.

carta lustra   A form of tracing paper, probably made from kid parchment, that may have been used in medieval book production to transfer designs from a finished exemplar to a manuscript in process (Christopher de Hamel, *The British Library Guide to Manuscript Illumination*, University of Toronto Press, 2001).

cartobibliography   A list of references to maps and/or works about maps arranged in some kind of order, with or without annotations. Also, the branch of bibliography pertaining to maps and mapping. *See also*: *cartographic materials*.

cartogram   A simplified map in which the size, outline, or location of geographic features is altered or exaggerated to illustrate diagrammatically a principal concept or set of statistical data.

cartographic materials   Any representation of part or all of the surface of the earth or another celestial body (real or imaginary) on any scale, including two- and three-dimensional maps, atlases, globes, aeronautical and navigational charts, remote sensing images (including aerial photographs), profiles, sections, cartograms, views, etc. (*AACR2*). In the bibliographic record representing a cartographic item, the nature of the material is described in the material specific details area (MSD). *See also*: *cartography*, *map library*, and *spatial data*.

cartography   The art and craft of making maps and other cartographic materials. A person who makes or produces maps is a *cartographer*. Synonymous with *mapmaking*. *See also*: *cartobibliography*.

cartonnage   Pieces of papyrus glued and tightly pressed together to form rigid sheets, used as boards in early bookbinding (see *Coptic binding*). The same process was used in ancient Egypt for making mummy cases.

cartoon   A symbolic or representational drawing in one or more panels intended to caricature a person or institution or satirize in a witty and imaginative way an action or situation of current popular interest. Usually published in a newspaper or magazine, cartoons may be captioned or use balloons to convey monologue or dialogue. Political cartoons usually appear on or near the editorial page of a newspaper. Successful *cartoonists* are often syndicated. *See also*: *comic book* and *lampoon*.

   Also refers to an animated film created by photographing a series of drawings done as individual cels, then editing the images into a sequence of frames which, when viewed in rapid succession, create the illusion of continuous motion.

   In art, a full-sized drawing done on paper as a preliminary draft, to be transferred to a large working surface, sometimes in sections, a technique used in creating large frescoes, tapestries, and stained glass windows.

cartouche   An ornamental frame in the form of a scroll with the ends rolled up, drawn or printed on a map around the inscription, giving the map's title or subject, name of cartographer, scale, and other descriptive information. In older maps, the cartouche often includes decorative elements. Also found on engravings and older bookbindings. In a more general sense, a decorative element in the form of a scroll, often used in the Islamic decorative arts.

   In Egyptian hieroglyphic inscriptions, a group of characters representing a divine or royal name or title, enclosed in an oval or oblong frame, often identifying a figure in a painting or sculpture.

cartulary   The room or place where the official papers or records of a medieval monastery, landowner, or corporation were kept. Also refers to the register in which they were listed, synonymous in the latter sense with *chartulary*.

cascading style sheets (CSS)   A feature added to HTML code that allows Web site developers to automatically apply the same layout to multiple documents. The appearance of design elements (logos, headers, footers, fonts, links, margins, etc.) is determined by one or more templates called *style sheets* linked to or embedded in the HTML document, rather than specified in the source code of each document. By governing style externally, CSS enables the site developer to give the pages of a Web site a uniform look and alter style of presentation as desired without having to rewrite source code. The HTML Writers Guild provides *CSS Frequently Asked Questions* at: www.hwg.org/resources/faqs/cssFAQ.html.

case   In machine binding, a cover made completely before it is attached to the body of a book, consisting of two boards and a paper inlay covered in book cloth or some other protective material. The edition binder submits a *specimen case* to the publisher for approval showing the size, boards, covering, lettering, and squares. The process of attaching the case to the text block by pasting down the endpapers is called *casing-in*. *See also*: *case binding* and *recased*.

Also refers to a container used by a typesetter to hold movable type. The words *uppercase* and *lowercase* are derived from the relative positions of the compartments used to store the two kinds of type.

case binding   A form of mechanized bookbinding in which a hard cover (called a *case*), consisting of two boards and an inlay covered in cloth, leather, or paper, is assembled separately from the book block and attached to it after forwarding by gluing the hinges, sewing supports, and paste-downs to the boards in a process called *casing-in* or *hanging-in*. The spine of the case is not adhered to the binding edge of the sections in case binding. When the method was first introduced in 1823, plain cloth was used to cover the boards, but by the 1830s a variety of finishes had been developed and embossing was often added. *See also*: *recased*.

casebook   A book containing records or descriptions of actual cases that have occurred in a professional discipline (law, medicine, psychology, sociology, social work, counseling, etc.), selected to illustrate important principles and concepts, for the use of students as a textbook and practitioners for reference. Compare with *case study*.

cased   *See*: case binding.

case-sensitive   A computer system or software program in which uppercase letters (**A, B, C** . . .) and lowercase letters (**a, b, c** . . .) are *not* interchangeable as input (**FAQ** versus **faq**). On the Internet, Web addresses (URLs) are case-sensitive, but e-mail addresses and filenames usually are not.

case study   In the social and medical sciences, analysis of the behavior of one individual in a population, or a single event in a series, based on close observation over a period of time, often to reveal principles underlying individual behavior or events in general. A case study may be published as an article in a journal, as an essay in a collection, or in book form. In bibliographic databases that permit the user to limit retrieval by type of publication, case studies may be one of the options (*example*: *PsycINFO*). Compare with *case book*.

casing-in *See*: case binding.

catalog A comprehensive list of the books, periodicals, maps, and other materials in a given collection, arranged in systematic order to facilitate retrieval (usually alphabetically by author, title, and/or subject). In most modern libraries, the card catalog has been converted to machine-readable bibliographic records and is available online. The purpose of a library catalog, as stated by Charles C. Cutter in *Rules for a Dictionary Catalog* (1904), later modified by Bohdan S. Wynar in *Introduction to Cataloging and Classification* (8th ed., 1992), is to offer the user a variety of approaches or access points to the information contained in the collection:

Objects:
1. To enable a person to find any work, whether issued in print or in nonprint format, when one of the following is known:
   a. The author
   b. The title
   c. The subject
2. To show what the library has
   d. By a given author
   e. On a given and related subjects
   f. In a given kind of literature
3. To assist in the choice of a work
   g. As to the bibliographic edition
   h. As to its character (literary or topical)

The preparation of entries for a library catalog (called *cataloging*) is performed by a librarian known as a *cataloger*. British spelling is *catalogue*. Abbreviated *cat*. Compare with *bibliography* and *index*. *See also*: *classified catalog*, *dictionary catalog*, *divided catalog*, and *online catalog*.

In a more general sense, a list of materials systematically arranged for a specific purpose, usually with brief descriptive information included in each entry, for example, a publisher's catalog, exhibition catalog, or film rental catalog. Sales catalogs are often heavily illustrated.

catalog card In manual cataloging systems, a paper card used to make a handwritten, typed, or printed entry in a card catalog, usually of standard size (7.5 centimeters high and 12.5 centimeters wide), plain or ruled. With the conversion of paper records to machine-readable format and the use of online catalogs, catalog cards have fallen into disuse. British spelling is *catalogue card*.

catalog code A detailed set of rules for preparing bibliographic records to represent items added to a library collection, established to maintain consistency within the catalog and between the catalogs of libraries using the same code. In the United States, Great Britain, and Canada, libraries use the *Anglo-American Cataloguing Rules* developed jointly by the American Library Association, Library Association (UK), and Canadian Library Association.

cataloger A librarian primarily responsible for preparing bibliographic records to represent the items acquired by a library, including bibliographic description, subject analysis, and classification. Also refers to the librarian responsible for supervising a cataloging department. British spelling is *cataloguer*. Synonymous with *catalog librarian*. *See also*: *Association for Library Collections and Technical Services* and Cataloger's Desktop.

Cataloger's Desktop Published on a single CD-ROM, *Cataloger's Desktop* is a product of the Library of Congress that provides basic cataloging documentation (including MARC formats), the *Library of Congress Subject Headings* list, Cutter Tables, and much more, based on *Anglo-American Cataloguing Rules* (*AACR2*), Second edition (2002 revision with 2003 update). URL: lcweb.loc.gov/cds/cdroms1.html.

cataloging The process of creating entries for a catalog. In libraries, this usually includes bibliographic description, subject analysis, assignment of classification notation, and all the activities involved in physically preparing the item for the shelf, tasks usually performed under the supervision of a librarian trained as a cataloger. British spelling is *cataloguing*. *See also*: *cataloging agency*, *cataloging-in-publication*, *centralized cataloging*, *cooperative cataloging*, *copy cataloging*, *descriptive cataloging*, *encoding level*, and *recataloging*.

cataloging agency A library or other institution that provides authoritative cataloging data in the form of new bibliographic records and modifications of existing records, for the use of other libraries. In the United States, the leading source of cataloging data is the Library of Congress. In the MARC record, the identity of the cataloging agency is indicated by its three-letter OCLC symbol in the cataloging source field (*example*: **DLC** for Library of Congress).

Cataloging Distribution Service (CDS) An agency within the Library of Congress that develops and markets, on a cost-recovery basis, bibliographic products and services that provide access to its resources for libraries in the United States, the American public, and the international information community. To accomplish its goals, the CDS employs librarians, product developers, systems analysts, programmers, operators, marketers, shippers, customer service representatives, accountants, and production staff. URL: lcweb.loc.gov/cds/cdsintro.html.

cataloging-in-publication (CIP) A prepublication cataloging program in which participating publishers complete a standardized data sheet and submit it with the front matter or entire text of a new book (usually still in galleys) to the Library of Congress for use in assigning an LCCN and preparing a bibliographic record, which is sent back to the publisher within 10 days to be printed on the verso of the title page. The Library of Congress distributes CIP records to large libraries, bibliographic utilities, and book vendors on a weekly basis to facilitate book processing. If incomplete, the initial record may be amended by the Library of Congress after the U.S. Copyright Office receives the deposit copy of the published work. The CIP Program began at the Library of Congress in 1971 and is used throughout the world. British spelling is *cataloguing-in-publication*. URL: cip.loc.gov/cip.

cataloging level   *See*: encoding level.

cataloging source   Field (040) of the MARC record, reserved for the three-letter OCLC symbol representing the cataloging agency that created, transcribed, or modified the bibliographic record (*example*: **DLC** for Library of Congress). If English is not the language of the cataloging agency, the 040 field may also contain information about the language in which the item is cataloged.

catalog record   In the manual card catalog, all the information given on a library catalog card, including a description of the item, the main entry, any added entries and subject headings, notes, and the call number. In the online catalog, the screen display that represents most fully a specific edition of a work, including elements of description and access points taken from the complete machine-readable bibliographic record, as well as information about the holdings of the local library or library system (copies, location, call number, status, etc.) taken from the item records attached to the bibliographic record. British spelling is *catalogue record*. Compare with *entry*.

catch letters   A sequence of letters (usually three) printed at the top of a page in a dictionary, gazetteer, or similar work that duplicates the first few letters of the first or last word on the page. Those printed on the verso indicate the first letters of the *first* word on the page; those on the recto, the first letters of the *last* word on the page. In some works, the letters appear in two groups separated by a hyphen, representing the first *and* last words on the page. Compare with *catchword*.

catch stitch   *See*: kettle stitch.

catch title   *See*: catchword title.

catchword   A word or part of a word printed in boldface or uppercase at the top of a column or page in a dictionary or encyclopedia that repeats the first and/or last heading appearing in the column or on the page. Synonymous with *guideword*. Compare in this sense with *catch letters*.

In medieval manuscripts and early printed books, a word or part of a word appearing in the lower margin of the last page of a quire that duplicates the first word on the first page of the following quire, enabling the binder to assemble the gatherings in correct sequence. In hand-copied books, the sequence of catchwords is unique to a specific copy. Michelle Brown notes in *Understanding Medieval Manuscripts* (Getty Museum/British Library, 1994) that the practice was probably introduced into Europe by the Moors.

Also refers to a word or phrase repeated so frequently that it has become a motto or slogan. Compare in this sense with *cliché*.

catchword title   A partial title composed of an easily remembered word or phrase likely to be used as a heading or keyword in a search of the library catalog, sometimes the same as a subtitle or the alternative title. Synonymous with *catch title*.

Categories for the Description of Works of Art (CDWA)   A specification developed by the Art Information Task Force (AITF) defining metadata elements to be used in describing works of art and architecture and surrogates of these works (*example*: **digital images**), from an art-historical perspective. URL: www.getty.edu/research/conducting_research/standards/cdwa.

cathedral binding   A cloth or leather binding decorated with architectural motifs of the gothic period blocked in gold, ink, or blind, sometimes including a rose window, popular in France and England from about 1815 to 1840 when interest in gothic art underwent a revival.

Catholic Library Association (CLA)   Established in 1921, CLA has a membership of librarians, teachers, and booksellers involved with Catholic libraries and the writing, publication, and distribution of Catholic literature. CLA publishes the quarterly *Catholic Library World*. URL: www.cathla.org.

CatME   OCLC's *Cataloging Micro Enhancer*, software that enables catalogers to search the *WorldCat* database and *OCLC Authority File* interactively online, edit bibliographic and authority records offline, and send updates to OCLC in batches to increase cataloging efficiency and reduce costs. URL: www.oclc.org/catme.

caucus   An interest group within a political faction or party, legislative body, or organization formed (sometimes spontaneously) to address an immediate need for action on a given issue or series of related issues, usually by formulating policy, supporting candidates for political office, drafting campaign strategy, lobbying, etc. (*example*: **Black Caucus** of the ALA). Compare with *task force*.

causal relation   *See*: semantic relation.

Caxton, William (c. 1422?–1491)   England's first printer, Caxton learned the trade relatively late in life while living in Cologne and Bruges. He brought the first printing press to England and installed it in the Chapter House at Westminster Abbey, issuing the first dated book known to have been printed in England (probably his *The Dictes and Sayings of the Philosophers*) in 1477. By the time he died in 1491, his press had issued approximately 100 works, including folio editions of Chaucer's *The Canterbury Tales* (1478) and Mallory's *Morte D'Arthur* (1485), which he sold to English readers in bound copies. He was an expert editor and translated into English many of the works he printed. For a succinct, informative essay on his life and work, please see the entry under his name in Geoffrey Glaister's *Encyclopedia of the Book* (Oak Knoll/British Library, 1996). *See also*: *Gutenberg, Johann*.

CBA   *See*: Canadian Booksellers Association *and* Center for Book Arts.

CBC   *See*: Children's Book Council.

CBIP   See: *Children's Books in Print*.

CC   *See*: closed caption *and* common carrier.

CCC   *See*: Copyright Clearance Center, Inc.

CCTV   *See*: closed circuit television.

CD   *See*: compact disc.

CDA   *See*: *Communications Decency Act.*

CD-I   Compact Disc–Interactive, a software and hardware standard developed in 1986 by Philips International and Sony Corporation for storing video, audio, and binary data on compact optical disk. A special stand-alone player that includes a CPU, memory, and an integrated operating system is required, capable of connecting to a television receiver for displaying images and sound or to a stereo system for sound only. CD-I technology allows the user to interact with the system by positioning a cursor to select options via a remote control device. Not widely accepted, CD-I applications are used in education, recreation (music and computer games), etc. Sometimes referred to as the *Green Book* standard. Also spelled *CD-i.*

CDP   *See*: collection development policy.

CD-ROM   Compact Disc–Read Only Memory (pronounced "see dee rom"), a small plastic optical disk similar to an audio compact disc, measuring 4.72 inches (12 centimeters) in diameter, used as a publishing medium and for storing information in digital format. Stamped by the producer on the metallic surface, the data encoded on a CD-ROM can be searched and displayed on a computer screen but not changed or erased. The disc is read by a small laser beam inside a device called a *CD-ROM drive.*

   Each disc has the capacity to store 650 megabytes of data, the equivalent of 250,000 to 300,000 pages of text or approximately 1,000 books of average length. CD-ROMs can be used to store sound tracks, still or moving images, and computer files, as well as text. In libraries, CD-ROMs are used primarily as a storage medium for bibliographic databases and full-text resources, mostly dictionaries, encyclopedias, and other reference works. Compare with *WORM. See also*: *CD-ROM drive, CD-ROM network,* and *CD-ROM tower.*

CD-ROM changer   A computer hardware device designed to store a small number of CD-ROMs or disc modules, with carousels and robot arms to move one disc at a time to an optical or magnetic reader and back to its storage location. Colloquially known as a *jukebox.* Compare with *CD-ROM drive* and *CD-ROM tower.*

CD-ROM drive   A hardware component designed to read data recorded on a CD-ROM disc, originally an external device but built into most newer microcomputers. CD-ROM drives can also be used to play audio compact discs when attached to a sound card via cable. Compare with *CD-ROM changer* and *CD-ROM tower.*

CD-ROM LAN   *See*: CD-ROM network.

CD-ROM network   A client-server system that makes multiple CD-ROM discs stored in a CD-ROM tower accessible to users authorized to log on to a computer network. Most bibliographic databases available on CD-ROM require special licensing for network access. Synonymous with *CD-ROM LAN.*

CD-ROM tower   A computer hardware device designed to store a large number of CD-ROM discs, usually connected to a server programmed to handle network access. Compare with *CD-ROM changer* and *CD-ROM drive.*

CDS   *See*: Cataloging Distribution Service.

CDWA   See: *Categories for the Description of Works of Art.*

ceased publication   Said of a periodical or newspaper no longer published. Publication may eventually resume under the same title or an altered title. Also said of a work published in more than one volume, which was never completed. Library holdings are indicated in a closed entry. Compare with *canceled* and *discontinued*. *See also*: *cessation*.

cel   A thin sheet of transparent material of standard size (usually acetate) having the same proportions as a frame of motion picture film, on which is drawn or painted a single image in a sequence of animation. Original cels from early animated films may have independent value as works of art. Also refers to a transparent sheet used as an overlay against an opaque background, as in textbooks on anatomy to show in layers the various systems of the human body.

cell   *See*: alcove.

cellulose   The fibrous vegetable material used in papermaking, derived primarily from wood pulp but formerly from cotton or linen rags. The cellulose in paper and board made from wood pulp is weakened over time by the presence of acid unless lignin is removed in manufacture and an alkaline buffer added.

cellulose nitrate film   *See*: nitrate film.

censorship   Prohibition of the production, distribution, circulation, or display of a work by a governing authority on grounds that it contains objectionable or dangerous material. The person who decides what is to be prohibited is called a *censor*. Commonly used methods include decree and confiscation, legislation, repressive taxation, and licensing to grant or restrict the right to publish.

The *ALA Code of Ethics* places an ethical responsibility on its members to resist censorship of library materials and programs in any form and to support librarians and other staff who put their careers at risk by defending library policies against censorship. Compare with *suppressed*. *See also*: *banned book*; *book burning*; *challenge*; *Comstock, Anthony*; *expurgated*; *filtering*; Index Librorum Prohibitorum; *intellectual freedom*; and *precensorship*.

census   An official count and statistical analysis of the population of a given geographic entity (city, county, state, province, country, etc.) taken at a particular point in time. The earliest known census of taxpaying households was recorded in China in the 3rd century B.C. More complete enumerations were conducted for military and tax purposes in ancient Rome by special magistrates called *censors*. The development of the modern census began in Europe in the 17th century and today includes questions concerning age, gender, ethnicity, income, housing, etc., formulated to generate data used in social planning, political redistricting, business marketing, etc. In most countries, participation in the census is compulsory, and the information collected on individual households and businesses is confidential.

In the United States, the national census is conducted every tenth year by the U.S. Census Bureau, which reports the detailed results in statistical form by state. Census data is available in the government documents collections of larger libraries and online at: www.census.gov. Summary tables are published in the *Statistical Abstract of the United States*, prepared annually since 1879 by the Bureau of Statistics (Department of U.S. Treasury), available in the reference section of most libraries in the United States. *See also*: *census tract*.

census tract   One of many small geographic areas into which a state or country is divided for the purpose of gathering and reporting census data. In the United States, the average tract contains 4,000 residents or approximately 1,200 households. Census tract outline maps are available from the U.S. Census Bureau.

center fold   The two innermost facing pages of a section in a book or other bound publication (the verso and recto of conjoint leaves). In sewn bindings, the threads can be seen along the fold. In a saddle-stitched periodical or pamphlet, wire staples can be seen in the fold. Synonymous with *center spread*.

Center for Book Arts (CBA)   Founded in 1974, CBA is a nonprofit organization with headquarters in New York City, dedicated to preserving the traditional craft of bookmaking and encouraging contemporary interpretations of the book as an art object through exhibitions, lectures, publications, and services to artists, including courses, workshops, and seminars on all aspects of the book arts. URL: www.centerforbook arts.org.

Center for Research Libraries (CRL)   Founded in 1949, CRL's members are large research libraries that seek to improve access to scholarly collections. CRL publishes a bimonthly newsletter and serves as a depository for infrequently used research materials that its members may use cooperatively. URL: www.crl.uchicago.edu.

Center for the Book   An educational outreach program established in 1977 by the Library of Congress to stimulate public interest in and awareness of books, reading, and libraries and to encourage the study of books and the printed word. The Center is a public-private partnership between the Library of Congress, 35 affiliated state centers, and over 50 national and civic groups. URL: lcweb.loc.gov/loc/cfbook.

centerpiece   In bookbinding of the late 16th and early 17th centuries, an ornamental design such as a diamond tooled or stamped in the center of the front and/or back cover, sometimes accompanied by matching *cornerpieces*. Also refers to an embossed or engraved metal ornament attached to the center of the front cover of a book. Also spelled *centrepiece*. *See also*: *cameo binding*, *diamond*, and *mandorla*.

centralized cataloging   The preparation of bibliographic records for books and other library materials by a central cataloging agency that distributes them in printed and/or machine-readable form to participating libraries, usually for a modest fee. Also refers to the cataloging of materials for an entire library system at one of its facilities, usually the central library, to achieve uniformity and economies of scale. Also spelled *centralized cataloguing*.

centralized processing   The practice of concentrating in a single location all the functions involved in preparing materials for library use, as opposed to technical processing carried out at multiple locations within a library or library system. Centralization allows processing methods to be standardized, but increased efficiency may be offset by the cost of distributing materials to the units where they will be used.

central library The administrative center of a library system where system-wide management decisions are made, centralized technical processing is conducted, and principal collections are located. Synonymous with *main library*. *See also*: *branch library*.

central processing unit (CPU) The hardware component of a computer that houses the circuitry for storing and processing data according to instructions contained in the programs installed on it, including the operating system, utilities to run peripheral devices, and application software. Generally speaking, the more memory and disk storage a CPU has, the more processing it can handle within a given amount of time, and the faster it can accomplish a task.

cerf *See*: kerf.

certificate of issue In a limited edition, the statement in each copy giving the total number of copies printed and the copy number. In an autographed edition, the certificate may also bear the signature of the author, editor, or illustrator.

certification In archives, the formal act of attesting to the official identity and nature of an original document or its reproduction. Compare with *authentication*.

Also, the process by which a state agency, or a nongovernmental agency or organization authorized by a state government, evaluates the qualifications of an individual, organization, or institution to perform a specific service or function for the purpose of granting a credential. Compare with *accreditation*. *See also*: *approved library school*.

cessation A serial or annual for which publication has ceased. Cessations are listed alphabetically by title in a separate section of *Ulrich's International Periodicals Directory* published annually by R.R. Bowker and in *The Serials Directory* published by EBSCO. In library cataloging, the holdings of a serial that has ceased publication are indicated in a closed entry (*example*: **v. 1–26, 1950–76**).

cf. An abbreviation of the Latin *confer*, meaning "compare."

CGI *See*: Common Gateway Interface.

chained book A book with a strong metal chain firmly attached to the binding, usually at its head, to secure the volume to the shelf on which it is stored, or to the desk or lectern where it is to be read, as a means of preventing unauthorized removal. In medieval Europe, the practice was common in ecclesiastical and educational institutions because the amount of labor required to produce manuscript books made them valuable. The chain could be up to five feet long, often fitted with a swivel to prevent twisting. A chained library survives in England at Hereford Cathedral. Synonymous with *catenati*.

chain stitch In bookbinding, a sewing stitch linked to previous sewing threads but not sewn to a support (tape, cord, thong, etc.). In Islamic binding, chain stitching was in multiples of two or four chains. Jane Greenfield notes in *ABC of Bookbinding* (Oak Knoll/Lyons Press, 1998) that it was also used in Coptic binding and in France during the 16th century and that modern machine stitching is a form of chain stitch. Synonymous with *unsupported sewing*.

challenge   A complaint lodged by a library user acting as an individual or representing a group concerning the inclusion of a specific item (or items) in a library collection, usually followed by a demand that the material be removed. Library programs may also be targeted. Public libraries are challenged far more frequently than other types of libraries because they are supported by public funds and must provide resources and services for a highly diverse clientele ("This library has something to offend everyone"). An unambiguously worded collection development policy is a library's best defense against such objections. *See also*: *banned book*, *censorship*, and *intellectual freedom*.

chancery script   A cursive script used from the 14th to the 16th century in the offices (chanceries) of royal, noble, and ecclesiastical houses for writing letters and less formal documents, adapted in 1501 as the basis of a typeface commissioned by the publisher Aldus Manutius, executed by the lettercutter Francesco Griffo.

changed title   *See*: title change.

channel   A pathway along which data is transmitted electronically from one computer, terminal, or device to another. The term also refers to the physical medium carrying the signal (optical fiber, coaxial cable, etc.) and to the properties that distinguish a specific channel from others. In data storage, a track on a specific storage medium (magnetic tape, magnetic disk, CD-ROM, DVD, etc.) on which electrical signals are recorded.

In communications, a band of frequencies assigned by the Federal Communications Commission (FCC) to a radio or television transmitting station for its exclusive use. In a more general sense, a one-way communications link.

Also refers to the blank space dividing columns of text written or printed on a page.

chanson de geste   French for "songs of deeds." A group of approximately 80 Old French epic poems produced from the 11th to 14th century relating historical and legendary events that occurred in the 8th and 9th centuries during the reigns of the Frankish King Charlemagne and his successors (*example*: ***Le Chanson de Roland***). Largely anonymous, they typically recount deeds of valor in struggles of the nobility among themselves and against Muslim invaders, emphasizing the heroic ideals of knighthood and chivalry and affirming the triumph of Christianity. Whether they evolved from a continuous oral tradition sustained by wandering *trouvères* (minstrels) or are the work of individual poets remains a subject of debate, but in any case, they are not historically accurate.

chapbook   From the Anglo-Saxon root *ceap*. A pamphlet containing a popular legend, tale, poem, or ballad, or a collection of prose or verse, hawked for about a penny a copy in the streets of England from the late 17th through the 19th century, and in the United States, by traveling peddlers called *chapmen* or *colporteurs*. The content was usually sensational (abduction, murder, witchcraft, etc.), educational (travel), or moral. Chapbooks were typically of small size (6 × 4 inches), containing up to 24 pages illustrated with woodcuts, bound in paper or canvas, usually with a decorated cover title. Also refers to a modern pamphlet of the same type. Also spelled *chap-book*.

chapter   One of two or more major divisions of a book or other work, each complete in itself but related in theme or plot to the division preceding and/or following it. In works of nonfiction, chapters are usually given a chapter title, but in works of fiction they may simply be numbered, usually in roman numerals. Chapters are listed in order of appearance by title and/or number in the *table of contents* in the front matter of a book. Abbreviated *ch.* Compare with *canto*. *See also*: *chapter drop*, *chapter heading*, and *run-on chapter*.

Also, a local division of an organization. Over 50 independent state and regional library associations are closely affiliated with the American Library Association. Each has a separate budget and dues structure, elects its own officers, and sponsors an annual conference. Each of the state chapters is represented in the ALA's governing assembly by an elected chapter councilor. The ALA also has student chapters in over 25 states. Within the ALA, chapter interests are represented by the Chapter Relations Committee and the Chapter Relations Office (www.ala.org).

chapter drop   The position below the chapter heading at which the text of a chapter begins—lower than on succeeding pages of the text and, in most books, the same for all chapters.

chapter heading   A display heading in a book or manuscript usually consisting of a roman numeral indicating the chapter number, followed by the chapter title, written or printed on the first page of the chapter in uniform style and position above the first paragraph of the text. Set in a type size larger than the text and running heads, chapter headings are sometimes embellished with an illustration or head-piece in older editions. *See also*: *chapter drop*.

chapter title   The title that appears at the beginning of a chapter in a book, usually bearing some relation to the content of the division of the work. Chapters may simply be numbered (usually in roman numerals) or given a number and a title. They are listed in order of appearance by number and/or title in the *table of contents* in the front matter. *See also*: *chapter heading*.

character   Any mark, sign, or symbol conventionally used in writing or printing, including letters of the alphabet, numerals, punctuation marks, and reference marks. In indexing, the smallest unit used in the arrangement of headings. *See also*: *loan character* and *nonfiling character*.

In data processing, a sequence of eight binary digits (one byte) representing a letter of the alphabet, numeral, punctuation mark, or other symbol. *See also*: *character set*.

Also, a fictional person in a novel, play, short story, or other literary work. A *character study* is a work in which the primary theme is the inner development of a person or group of persons (*example*: **Hamlet**). In Library of Congress subject headings, "Characters" is a standard subdivision used in personal name headings for writers of fiction, particularly playwrights (*example*: **Shakespeare, William, 1546–1616—**

Characters—Falstaff). Well-known characters may be given a separate heading, followed by a parenthetical qualifier, as in **Jeeves (Fictitious character)**.

characteristic   An attribute, property, or quality that forms the basis for dividing a class into clearly differentiated subclasses, for example, the characteristic "period" dividing the class "European literature" into the subclasses "classical," "medieval," "renaissance," "modern," and "contemporary," as opposed to the characteristic "form" dividing the same class into "drama," "essay," "novel," "poetry," "short story," etc.

character masking   *See*: truncation.

character set   A group of symbols used in computing to print and display text electronically. In alphabetic writing systems, character sets include letters, numerals, punctuation marks, signs and symbols, and control codes. The character sets of languages written in the Latin alphabet normally contain 256 symbols, the maximum number of combinations that can be contained in a single byte of data, the first 128 of which are the same for all fonts. Each character is associated with a unique binary number recognized by the computer as representing the symbol. The original IBM PC used the ASCII character set. A *double-byte character set*, such as the Unicode Standard, uses 16-bit (two-byte) codes, expanding the maximum number of combinations from 256 to 65,536 (or 256 $\times$ 256), necessary for Chinese, Japanese, and Korean languages in which thousands of characters are used. *See also*: *ALA character set* and *ANSEL*.

charge   To record the loan of a book or other item from the circulating collection of a library to a borrower. In modern libraries, this task involves the use of a computer. Also refers to the library's record of such a transaction, including the identity of the borrower, the title and call number of the item, and its due date. Compare with *discharge*. *See also*: *item record* and *patron record*.

Also refers to a fee or payment required of a library patron, usually for the use of nontraditional services, such as rental collections and certain methods of document delivery.

charge slip   *See*: date due slip.

Charleston Conference   An informal, collegial gathering of librarians and library administrators, publishers and vendors of library materials, and other interested persons held annually since 1980 (usually in November) in Charleston, South Carolina, to discuss issues of mutual interest. Conceived by Katina Strauch, head of collection development at the College of Charleston Libraries and editor of the journal *Against the Grain*, the Charleston Conference does not include exhibits and is not associated with any professional organization.

Discussions at past Conferences have focused on the escalating cost of materials (particularly serials subscriptions), the effects of electronic publishing on libraries and vendors, licensing and access to digital content, the impact of journal aggregators on institutional subscriptions, e-journal archiving, the need for reliable and consistent usage statistics for digital resources, and the impact of market forces on scholarly communication. Attendance has grown to over 500, with librarians accounting for about one-half of the attendees. Most of the librarians represent academic libraries, many from large research institutions. URL: www.katina.info/conference.

chart   In cartography, a map designed to meet the requirements of navigation or one showing meteorological phenomena or heavenly bodies. A *nautical chart* indicates soundings, currents, coastlines, and other important maritime features. An *aeronautical chart* shows features of interest to aircraft pilots. A *celestial chart* shows celestial bodies and systems of interest to astronomers and amateur stargazers.

Also, an opaque sheet on which data are displayed in graphic or tabular form, for example, a calendar. *See also*: *flip chart*.

charter   A legal document recording the franchise or granting of specific rights to an individual or corporate body by a governmental authority such as a legislature or sovereign, for example, the Charter of the United Nations. The texts of important charters are usually available in the government documents or reference section of large libraries. The originals are preserved by the institutions and individuals that own them, usually in archives. *See also*: *chartulary*.

Chartered Institute of Library and Information Professionals (CILIP)   A new professional association formed in April 2002 by the unification of the Institute of Information Scientists (IIS) and the Library Association (UK). The CILIP homepage (www.cilip.org.uk) provides information about the mission, goals, and action plan of this new organization.

chartulary   A list or register of charters. Also, a collection or set of charters or copies of charters, especially when bound into one or more volumes for the use of the monastery, landowner, corporation, etc., to which they belong. Sometimes used synonymously with *cartulary*.

chase   In letterpress, the portable rectangular metal frame in which assembled type and display matter, composed into pages, is firmly locked into position. The resulting *forme* is then ready to be transferred to the bed of the press for printing. The expression *in chase* means "ready for printing."

chased edges   *See*: gauffered edges.

chat   A real time computer conferencing capability between two or more users of a network (LAN, WAN, Internet) by means of a keyboard rather than voice transmission. Most Internet service providers offer a *chat room* to their subscribers. *See also*: *instant messaging*.

chat reference   *See*: digital reference.

check digit   A character added to a sequence of digits, related arithmetically to the sequence in such a way that input errors can be automatically detected whenever the sequence is entered as data into a computer, for example, the last character of the ISBN. When a calculated check digit is the number 10, it is represented as the character *X*.

checked out   The circulation status of an item that has been charged to a borrower account and is not due back in the library until the end of the loan period. In the online catalog, the due date is usually displayed as a status code in the catalog record to indicate that the item is currently not available for circulation. *See also*: *overdue*, *recall*, and *renew*.

check-in   The ongoing process of recording the receipt of each issue of a newspaper or periodical, a routine task accomplished by the serials department of a library, manually or with the aid of an automated serials control system. Some automated systems allow the patron to view the *check-in record*. *See also*: *claim*.

check-in record   A separate record attached to the bibliographic record for a serial title in which the receipt of individual issues or parts is entered on an ongoing basis, usually by an assistant working in the serials department. Most online catalogs allow users to view the check-in record to determine if a specific issue or part has been received. The check-in record may also indicate whether an issue is missing, claimed, or at the bindery. In most libraries, the check-in record is separate from the *holdings record*.

checklist   A comprehensive list of books, periodicals, or other documents that provides the minimum amount of description or annotation necessary to identify each work— briefer than a bibliography. Also, the log kept by a library to record the receipt of each number of a serial publication or part of a work in progress. Also refers to a list of items required, or procedures to be followed, such as the steps in a library's opening or closing routine. Also spelled *check-list*.

checkout period   *See*: loan period.

chef-d'oeuvre   *See*: magnum opus *and* masterpiece.

chemise binding   A slip-on cover of soft leather or cloth designed with pockets to fit over the boards of a hand-bound book, sometimes secured to the boards with bosses, used in Europe from the 12th to the 15th century as a substitute for full binding or to protect a permanent leather binding from wear. Velvet was often used for devotional books.

chief information officer (CIO)   The title of the person in a commercial company or nonprofit organization who is responsible for managing the flow of official information, including computing and any library services—a relatively new position in companies and organizations that recognize the need for such a management function.

Chief Officers of State Library Agencies (COSLA)   An independent organization of the chief officers of state and territorial agencies designated as the state library administrative agency and responsible for statewide library development. COSLA is dedicated to identifying and addressing issues of common concern and national interest, furthering state library agency relationships with federal government and national organizations, and initiating cooperative action for the improvement of library services to the people of the United States. URL: www.cosla.org.

chief source of information   The source of bibliographic data prescribed by *AACR2* as having precedence over all others in the preparation of the bibliographic description of an item, usually the title page or a substitute, for example, the title frame at the beginning of a filmstrip or motion picture, or the title screen of a Web page. *See also*: *supplied title*.

chiffon silk   Extra-thin but strong silk tissue used to mend or strengthen a leaf in a book or other document printed on paper.

Child Online Protection Act (COPA)   Federal legislation passed in 1998 imposing civil and criminal penalties on commercial Web publishers who allow persons under the age of 18 to access material deemed "harmful to minors" under prevailing community standards. An injunction won by free speech advocates prevented enforcement of *COPA*. In September 1999, the Freedom to Read Foundation of the American Library Association filed an amicus curiae brief in support of 17 online content providers, plaintiffs in a successful challenge (*ACLU v. Ashcroft*) in which the Third U.S. Circuit Court of Appeals found the community standards clause in the law overly broad.

In May 2002, the U.S. Supreme Court upheld the application of community standards to the Internet but remanded the case to the lower court for examination of unresolved free speech issues. On March 6, 2003, the federal appeals court in Philadelphia again ruled *COPA* unconstitutional on grounds that the law deters adults from accessing materials protected under the First Amendment. On August 11, 2003, on the heels of the U.S. Supreme Court decision upholding the *Children's Internet Protection Act*, the Bush administration filed a new appeal asking the Supreme Court to reconsider *COPA* on grounds that other methods of protecting children from exposure to sexually explicit materials, such as filtering software, are inadequate. *See also*: Communications Decency Act.

children's book   A book written and illustrated specifically for children up to the age of 12–13. Included in this category are juvenile fiction and nonfiction, board books, nursery rhymes, alphabet books, counting books, picture books, easy books, beginning readers, picture storybooks, and storybooks. Children's books are shelved in the juvenile collection of most public libraries and in the curriculum room in most academic libraries. Currently available children's titles are indexed in *Children's Books in Print* published by R.R. Bowker. *See also*: *children's book award*, *Children's Book Council*, and *children's literature*.

children's book award   A literary award or prize given to the author or illustrator of a book published specifically for children. In the United States, the two best-known awards are the Caldecott Medal and the Newbery Medal. *See also*: *Amelia Frances Howard-Gibbon Illustrator's Award*, *Carnegie Medal*, *CLA Book of the Year for Children*, and *Greenaway Medal*.

Children's Book Council (CBC)   Established in 1945, the CBC is a nonprofit trade association dedicated to encouraging literacy and the use and enjoyment of children's books. Its membership includes publishers and packagers of children's trade books and producers of book-related multimedia for children. The CBC sponsors Children's Book Week, celebrated in schools, libraries, and bookstores throughout the United States each November, and Young People's Poetry Week, celebrated in April in conjunction with National Poetry Month. URL: www.cbcbooks.org.

Children's Books in Print (CBIP)   An author, title, and illustrator index of currently available books for children and young adults, published annually by R.R. Bowker since 1962 (ISSN: 0069–3480). Each volume includes an index of major book awards for the past 10 years. The separately published *Subject Guide to Children's Books in Print* (ISSN: 0000–0167) includes indexes by publisher, wholesaler, and distributor. Former title: *Children's Books for Schools and Libraries*. *See also*: El-Hi Textbooks & Serials in Print.

Children's Book Week   Sponsored since 1919 by the Children's Book Council, Children's Book Week is a local and national celebration held each November in which librarians, booksellers, publishers, and educators schedule book exhibits, read-a-thons, story hours, swap sessions, contests, book raffles, and other activities to stimulate interest in books and reading among young people. Synonymous with *Book Week*. URL: www.cbcbooks.org/html/book_week.html.

children's collection   *See*: juvenile collection.

Children's Internet Protection Act (CIPA)   Legislation passed by Congress in 2000 that makes the E-rate discount on Internet access and internal connection services provided to schools and libraries under the *Telecommunications Reform Act of 1996* and eligibility for *Library Services and Technology Act* funds contingent on certification that certain "Internet safety policies" have been put in place, most notably technology designed to block all users from accessing visual materials that depict child pornography or are considered obscene or harmful to minors. Filtering of text is not required. In March 2001, the American Library Association (ALA) and the American Civil Liberties Union (ACLU) filed separate suits challenging *CIPA* on grounds that filtering restricts access to constitutionally protected information.

In May 2002, a three-judge panel in federal district court unanimously ruled *CIPA* unconstitutional, agreeing that current Internet filtering software blocks speech protected under the First Amendment. In June 2002, the U.S. Department of Justice appealed the decision to the U.S. Supreme Court and on June 23, 2003, by a 6–3 vote, the Supreme Court reversed the lower court decision, ruling that First Amendment protections are met by the law's provision that filtering software is to be disabled by the library without significant delay at the request of an adult user. The Federal Communications Commission (FCC) announced that public libraries and schools wishing to retain federal technology funding must certify by July 1, 2004 that filtering software is installed and in use on all computers providing Internet access, including those for staff use only. *CIPA* provides no funds for libraries to implement filtering. Some libraries and library systems have decided to forgo federal library funds in order to maintain local control over Internet access.

In a statement of objectives regarding *CIPA* issued on July 25, 2003 by ALA president Carla Hayden and the ALA executive board, the ALA pledged to identify technological options that minimize the burden on libraries, continue to develop and promote viable alternatives to filtering, and gather and disseminate authoritative information and research on the effects of *CIPA* and filtering on libraries and library users, including evaluative information for use in selecting filtering software. The ALA maintains a Web site on *CIPA* at: www.ala.org. *See also*: Child Online Protection Act *and* Communications Decency Act.

children's librarian   A librarian who specializes in services and collections for children up to the age of 12–13. Most children's librarians have extensive knowledge of children's literature and are trained in the art of storytelling. *See also*: *children's room.*

children's literature   Literary works created specifically for children, as distinct from works written for adults and young adults, including poetry and prose, fiction and nonfiction. Children's literature began with the oral transmission of nursery rhymes, songs, poems, fairy tales, and stories. During the early 17th century, the horn book came into widespread use in Britain and the American colonies, but it was not until the late 17th century with the publication of the popular *Tales of Mother Goose* by Charles Perrault (1628–1703) that written literature for children emerged as a separate genre.

By the mid-18th century, the British writer, printer, and publisher John Newbery (1713–67) perceived that a market existed for children's books and began publishing illustrated works intended to be morally instructional (*Little Goody Two-Shoes*). Not until the 19th century did children's literature break away from didacticism, first with the publication of the fairy tales of Hans Christian Anderson (1805–75) and the brothers Grimm, and later with Edward Lear's *Book of Nonsense* (1846) and Lewis Carroll's *Alice's Adventures in Wonderland* (1865) and the sequel *Through the Looking Glass* (1871).

The illustrations in most early children's books were printed in black and white, but by the 1860s the English printer Edmund Evans (1826–1905) began issuing picture books in color, illustrated by artists such as Walter Crane (1845–1915), Kate Greenaway (1846–1901), and Randolph Caldecott (1846–86). The publication of the children's classics *Little Women* by Louisa May Alcott in 1868 and *The Adventures of Tom Sawyer* by Mark Twain in 1876 marked the beginning of realism in juvenile fiction. Today, children's literature has earned a place in the hearts of millions of readers, and a worldwide market exists for books and periodicals for children of all ages.

Recently published children's books are reviewed in *Booklist*, *The Bulletin of the Center for Children's Books*, *Horn Book Magazine*, *The Lion and the Unicorn*, and *School Library Journal*, and reviews are excerpted in *Children's Literature Review*, a reference serial published by the Gale Group. Synonymous with *juvenile literature*. *See also*: *children's book award* and *juvenile collection.*

Children's Literature Review (CLR)   An annual reference serial published since 1976 by the Gale Group, providing excerpts from reviews, criticism, and commentary on books for children and young adults, arranged alphabetically by name of author, with cumulative author and title indexes at the end of each volume. ISSN: 0362–4145.

children's magazine   A periodical published specifically for young people, usually geared to a specific reading level. Some children's magazines focus on a particular subject or interest. Examples include *Your Big Backyard* for preschoolers (ages 3–5) and *Ranger Rick* (ages 6–12) in natural history. A selection of magazines for children is provided in the reference serial *Magazines for Libraries*.

children's room   The area in a public library, or one of its branches, reserved for collections and services intended specifically for children up to the age of 12–13, usually staffed by at least one children's librarian and furnished to accommodate persons of small stature. Some children's rooms include a comfortable corner or alcove designed for group storytelling, puppetry, etc.

children's services   Library services intended for children up to the age of 12–13, including juvenile collection development, lapsit services, storytelling, assistance with homework assignments, and summer reading programs, usually provided by a children's librarian in the children's room of a public library. Compare with *adult services* and *young adult services*. *See also*: *Association for Library Service to Children*.

Chinese American Librarians Association (CALA)   Established in 1983, CALA seeks to promote better communication between Chinese American librarians employed in the United States and serves as a forum for discussion of the problems of its members. An affiliate of the American Library Association, CALA publishes the semiannual *Journal of Library and Information Science* in English and Chinese, the *CALA Newsletter* in three issues per year, and the semiannual *CALA E-Journal*. URL: www.cala-web.org.

Chinese style   In China and Japan, the evolution of the book proceeded as in the West, from scroll to leaves enclosed in a cover, but by a different route. Instead of binding separately cut leaves in codex form, a continuous roll of writing material was accordion-pleated, creating a series of folded leaves left uncut at the fore-edge with writing (and later printing) on one side only. Also known as *Japanese style*. *See also*: *double leaf*.

chip   A shortened form of *microchip*, a high-speed miniaturized integrated circuit, etched in a semiconducting material (usually silicon) on the surface of a tiny, wafer-thin piece of metal, for use as microprocessor and memory in computers and other electronic equipment. The design of increasingly powerful microchips has been the driving force behind the information technology revolution that began in the second half of the 20th century. *See also*: *random access memory* and *read-only memory*.

chip board   A thin, cheap, low-density board manufactured from recycled paper and other cellulose fibers. Although chip board is sometimes used in case binding, binder's board is preferred in hardcover trade editions. Also spelled *chipboard*.

chipped   The condition of a book that has small pieces missing from the edges of its cover, dust jacket, or pages, not as prized in the market for antiquarian books as a copy in mint condition.

chiro-xylographic   A type of blockbook produced during the 15th and 16th centuries, combining woodcut illustrations with manuscript text, an early method of producing multiple copies of illustrated books. *See also*: *xylography*.

CHOICE: Current Reviews for Academic Libraries   A review publication founded in 1964 by the Association of College and Research Libraries (ACRL) and published in 11 issues/year, *CHOICE* provides reviews of 6,000 to 7,000 English-language books, Web sites, and other resources per year, focusing on titles of interest to the librarians and teaching faculty responsible for collection development in college and university libraries (ISSN: 0009–4978). Arranged by discipline, *CHOICE* reviews are prepared by academic reviewers from completed books, not galley proofs. Each issue also includes an editorial, a bibliographic essay, and at least one feature article, with separate author, title, and topic indexes at the end. *Reviews on Cards (ROC)* contains the same set of reviews as the printed magazine, each printed on heavy-duty 4¼ inch × 5½ inch paper stock to facilitate routing to individual selectors. *CHOICE* is also available online by subscription under the title *Choice Reviews.online*. URL: www. ala.org.

choir book   A book containing music sung or chanted by the choir in religious services. Medieval choir books used in services of the Catholic Church were of large size in order to be visible to the entire choir, often beautifully illuminated for display on a lectern in the sanctuary. The category includes the *antiphonal*, *gradual*, and *missal*. Compare with *hymnal*.

choropleth map   A map on which color, shading, or some other graphic technique is used to show the density or frequency of a variable (e.g., mortality, population, precipitation) in each of several areas, based on the average number of occurrences per unit of area. *See also*: *isogram*.

chorus score   The score of a musical work originally written for solo voice and chorus, which shows only the choral parts and any accompaniment arranged for keyboard instrument. *See also*: *vocal score*.

chrestomathy   A collection of choice passages from the literary works of an author (or authors), especially one compiled as a sample of literary specimens or as an aid in the study of a language.

Christian fiction   Novels and stories in which Christian religious belief is a major (sometimes predominant) element in the development of plot, theme, and character. The market for Christian fiction has expanded considerably in the United States in recent years. New titles are regularly reviewed in *Booklist* and *Library Journal*. *See also*: *religious book*.

chromolithography   *See*: lithography.

chronicle   Originally, a detailed chronological record of contemporary events, usually recorded by year over an extended period of time, with little or no interpretation or analysis and no pretense of literary style. The first examples, world histories beginning with Creation, relied largely on the biblical sources. Local chronicles began in the 9th century during the reign of King Alfred with the *Anglo-Saxon Chronicle*, eventually covering the history of England from 60 B.C. to the 12th century. In the 13th century vernacular chronicles began to emerge, such as the *Grandes Chroniques de France*

(14th century) and Jean Froissart's *Chroniques* (15th century), the latter representing a fusion of the traditional chronicle with the medieval romance.

In modern usage, a list of events described and recorded in the order in which they occurred. The treatment is fuller and more connected than *annals*.

chronicle play A drama based on material from the chronicle histories of England, for example, those written by Hall and Holinshead. Popular during the Elizabethan period, chronicle plays were at first loosely structured but evolved into sophisticated character studies, exemplified by the *history plays* of William Shakespeare. A more recent example of a history play is *A Man for All Seasons* by Robert Bolt (1960).

chronological The arrangement of data, records, items, headings, entries, etc., according to their relation in time, from earliest to latest. In library classification systems, the period subdivisions added to subject headings are listed in chronological order (*example*: —**Antiquity**, —**Medieval**, —**Renaissance**, then by century from the 15th to 20th). The opposite of *reverse chronological*.

chronological subdivision In library cataloging, a subdivision added to a class or subject heading to indicate the period of time covered by the work. Generally associated with historical treatment of a topic, chronological subdivisions are often used after the subdivision —**History**, as in **France—History—1789–1815**. They are also used under artistic, literary, and music form/genre headings to modify the main heading, as in **American poetry—20th century**. Synonymous with *period subdivision*.

chronology A book or section of a book that lists events and their dates in the order of their occurrence. Most chronologies are limited to a specific period (*example*: **Roman Empire**), event (**World War II**), or theme (**women's history**). Book-length chronologies are usually shelved in the reference section of a library (*example*: ***Day by Day: The Sixties***, Facts on File, 1983). Compare with *calendar*.

In serials control, the date of publication associated with the volume enumeration.

chrysography From the Greek *chrys* ("gold") and *graphia* ("writing"). The art and craft of writing in ink made from powdered gold, as practiced by the medieval scribes who produced illuminated manuscripts from the early Christian period on. Beginning in the 6th century, the vellum leaves of some Byzantine books were dyed or painted purple to provide a luxurious, high-contrast background for text written in gold. Also refers to writing done in gold letters. *See also*: *gilding*.

Church and Synagogue Library Association (CSLA) Founded in 1967, CSLA provides a forum for church and synagogue libraries to share practices and find solutions to common problems, inspire a sense of purpose among church and synagogue librarians, and guide the development of church and synagogue librarianship toward recognition as a formal branch of the profession. CSLA publishes the bimonthly *Church & Synagogue Libraries*. URL: www.worldaccessnet.com/~csla. *See also*: *Association of Christian Librarians*, *Association of Jewish Libraries*, and *Catholic Library Association*.

church library A library maintained on the premises of a house of worship, containing books, pamphlets, and other materials related to its faith and to the history of the institution. Very old church libraries often have rare books and manuscripts in their collections, for example, the Hereford Cathedral Library in England which owns a historical collection of chained books. Cathedral libraries may restrict the use of all or a portion of their holdings to readers with a research interest in their collections. Most synagogues also have a library, with some materials in Hebrew. *See also*: *Association of Jewish Libraries* and *Church and Synagogue Library Association.*

CILIP   *See*: Chartered Institute of Library and Information Professionals.

cinefilm   *See*: motion picture.

cinema   A broad term encompassing the motion picture industry and distribution system, the films produced, and the art form they represent. It is also used in Europe and the UK to refer to the theater in which motion pictures are publicly shown.

CIO   *See*: chief information officer.

CIP   *See*: cataloging-in-publication.

CIPA   *See*: *Children's Internet Protection Act.*

cipher   The initials of a personal name, written or arranged in ornamental form of such complexity and/or artistry as to form a private mark or symbol. Compare with *cryptonym.*

In a more general sense, secret writing or code intended to be understood (*deciphered*) only by those who know the key to it. In data processing, an encrypted character that can only be decrypted with a key.

circa   A Latin word meaning "about," used to indicate lack of certainty but reasonable probability concerning a date, for example, the approximate birth and/or death date(s) of a person for whom official records are lacking. Abbreviated *c.* or *ca.*

Example: *c.* **1922** (*about 1922*)

circuit edges   A style of flexible leather binding with projecting covers that fold over at the head, tail, and fore-edge, completely covering the edges of the sections like a box, used mainly on Bibles and prayer books carried by clergymen who traveled a regular circuit of rural parishes, presumably to protect the text from exposure to the elements. Synonymous with *divinity circuit* and *divinity edges*. Compare with *Yapp binding.*

circular   An advertisement, announcement, or directive, usually in the form of a printed letter or leaflet, distributed to a large circle of people at the same time and intended to be passed on to others to whom its content might be of interest.

circulating book   A book that can be charged to a borrower account for use inside or outside the library facility, as opposed to one restricted to library use only. Compare with *noncirculating.*

circulating collection   Books and other materials that may be checked out by registered borrowers for use inside or outside the library. In most academic and public libraries in the United States, circulating materials are shelved in open stacks to facilitate browsing. Compare with *noncirculating.*

circulating library   A library containing materials that can be borrowed by persons authorized to do so, usually for a fixed period of time, after which prompt return is expected. The idea of a subscription library to circulate fiction and other books of general interest was first conceived and implemented by London booksellers in the 17th century. By the Victorian period, this type of library was sufficiently widespread to provide a market for the publication of quality fiction in Britain.

circulation   The process of checking books and other materials in and out of a library. Also refers to the total number of items checked out by library borrowers over a designated period of time and to the number of times a given item is checked out during a fixed period of time, usually one year. In public libraries, low circulation is an important criterion for weeding items from the collection. Books for which circulation is anticipated to be high may be ordered in multiple copies to satisfy demand or given a more durable binding to withstand heavy use. Some online circulation systems provide circulation statistics by classification and material type for use in collection development. Circulation is a fundamental to *access services*. Abbreviated *circ*.

In publishing, the number of copies distributed of each issue of a serial publication, including complimentary copies, single-copy retail sales, and copies sent to paid subscribers. Compare with *total circulation*.

circulation analysis   Close examination of statistics compiled on the circulation of library materials, usually broken down by classification, material type, category of borrower, time of year, etc., to determine patterns of usage, an important tool in budgeting, collection development, staffing, etc.

circulation desk   The service point at which books and other materials are checked in and out of a library, usually a long counter located near the entrance or exit, which may include a built-in book drop for returning borrowed materials. In small and medium-sized libraries, items on hold or reserve are usually available at the circulation desk, which is normally staffed by one or more persons trained to operate the circulation system and handle patron accounts. Synonymous with *loan desk*. Compare with *reference desk*.

circulation history   A record that a patron borrowed a specific item, retained (with or without the borrower's consent) for a significant length of time after the item is returned to the library. Most online circulation systems are designed to automatically delete all indication that a lending transaction has occurred, once the item has been checked in, and in the United States retaining such records may be a violation of state law. Although it has been argued that circulation histories are useful in demographic studies, and would enable libraries to offer patron-friendly services, retention of such information raises serious concerns about privacy, especially in the light of recent federal legislation intended to facilitate investigation of terrorist activities (see *USA Patriot Act*).

circulation record   *See*: patron record.

circulation statistics   A count maintained of the number of items checked out from a library during a given period (usually a year), or the number of times a specific item is checked out during a given period, usually broken down by type of material and/ or classification. Circulation statistics can be kept by hand, but most automated circulation systems provide detailed statistical reports by day, week, month, and year, which can be analyzed to determine usage patterns, an important aid in budgeting, collection development, staffing, etc. Compare with *circulation history*. *See also*: *in-house use*.

circulation status   The conditions under which a specific item in a library collection is available for use. An item may be on order, in process, at the bindery, for library use only, available to be checked out, on loan until a certain due date, recently returned, missing, lost, or billed. Compare with *loan status*.

circulation system   The methods used to record the loan of items from a library collection by linking data in the patron record to the item record for each item loaned. An effective circulation system provides the means of identifying items on loan to a specific patron (including those that are overdue) and enables circulation staff to place holds, recall items needed before the due date, and notify borrowers when items are overdue. An *automated* circulation system is capable of generating circulation statistics for planning and reporting purposes. Abbreviated *circ system*. Synonymous with *charging system*. *See also*: *barcode*, *library card*, and *self-checkout*.

citation   In the literary sense, any written or spoken reference to an authority or precedent or to the verbatim words of another speaker or writer. In library usage, a written reference to a specific work or portion of a work (book, article, dissertation, report, musical composition, etc.) by a particular author, editor, composer, etc., that clearly identifies the document in which the work is to be found. The frequency with which a work is cited is sometimes considered a measure of its importance in the literature of the field. Citation format varies from one field of study to another but includes at a minimum author, title, and publication date. An *incomplete* citation can make a source difficult, if not impossible, to locate. Abbreviated *cite*. *See also*: *citation index* and *self-citation*.

Examples:
  Book:
    Chappell, Warren. *A Short History of the Printed Word*. **Boston: Nonpareil Books, 1970.**
  Periodical article:
    Dow, Ronald F. "Editorial Gatekeepers Confronted by the Electronic Journal." *College & Research Libraries* **61 (2000): 146–154.**

Citation style manuals are available in the reference section of most academic libraries. *See also*: *APA style*, *electronic style*, and *MLA style*.

citation analysis   A bibliometric technique in which works cited in publications are examined to determine patterns of scholarly communication, for example, the comparative importance of books versus journals, or of current versus retrospective sources, in one or more academic disciplines.

citation chasing A legitimate research technique in which the bibliographies of works already located in a literature search are examined ("mined") for additional sources containing further information on the topic. The process can be facilitated by using a *citation index*.

citation index A three-part index in which works cited during a specific year are listed alphabetically by name of author cited, followed by the names of the citing authors (sources) in a "Citation Index." Full bibliographic information for the citing author is given in a "Source Index." Also provided is a "Subject Index," usually listing articles by significant words in the title. Researchers can use this tool to trace interconnections among authors citing papers on the same topic and to determine the frequency with which a specific work is cited by others, an indication of its importance in the literature of the field.

Citation indexing originated in 1961 when Eugene Garfield, Columbia University graduate in chemistry and library science, and founder of the fledgling Institute for Scientific Information (ISI), received an NIH grant to produce the experimental *Genetics Citation Index*, which evolved into the reference serial *Science Citation Index*. ISI subsequently published *Social Sciences Citation Index* beginning in 1972 and *Arts & Humanities Citation Index* from 1978. *See also*: *bibliographic coupling* and *citation chasing*.

citation order In Dewey Decimal Classification (DDC), the order in which the facets or characteristics of a class are to be combined in number building. For example, the subject "juvenile court procedure in the United States" is expressed in a notation built or synthesized from four facets: **345/.73/081/0269**. The citation order for the discipline of law (**34**) is: branch of the law (criminal **5**), jurisdiction (United States **73**), topic in branch of law (juvenile court **081**), and standard subdivision (procedure **0269**). Instructions for citation order are provided in the Schedules. When number building is not permitted or possible, instructions are provided with respect to preference order in the choice of facets (DDC).

citation style *See*: citation.

cite To quote or refer to an authority outside oneself, usually in support of a point or conclusion or by way of explanation or example. In scholarly publication, the source of such a reference is indicated in a footnote or endnote. Also used as a shortened form of the term *citation*.

city directory A three-way directory that lists the residents and businesses located in a specific town or city alphabetically by name, with street address and telephone number included in each entry. In a second section, name(s) and addresses are listed by phone number, and in a third section, names and phone numbers are listed by street address. Published annually and sold by subscription, current city directories often include zip code and census tract locators for use in marketing. In libraries, they are usually shelved in ready reference or in the reference stacks. Synonymous with *cross-reference directory*.

city map   A map, larger in scale than a road map, showing in considerable detail the streets, public transportation lines, hospitals, schools, libraries, museums, parks, and other major institutions and landmarks within the boundaries of a city.

CJK   An abbreviation that stands for materials published in the Chinese, Japanese, and Korean languages and for the Chinese, Japanese, and Korean character sets.

CLA   *See*: Canadian Library Association *and* Catholic Library Association.

CLA Book of the Year for Children   A literary award established in 1947 and presented annually under the auspices of the Canadian Library Association to the author of the most outstanding children's book of creative writing (fiction, poetry, retelling of traditional literature, etc.) published in Canada during the preceding year. The author must be a citizen or permanent resident of Canada. Compare with *Amelia Frances Howard-Gibbon Illustrator's Award*. *See also*: *Carnegie Medal* and *Newbery Medal*.

claim   A notice from a library informing the publisher or subscription agent that a specific issue of a newspaper or periodical on subscription, or item on continuation order, has not been received within a reasonable time, with a request that a replacement copy be sent. Claimed items are noted in the check-in record attached to the bibliographic record created to represent the publication in the library catalog. *See also*: *claim report*.

claim report   The publisher's or vendor's response regarding the status of a claim made by a library for material not received as expected on subscription or continuation order. Synonymous with *claim check*.

clasp   A hinged fitting made of ornamented metal, ivory, or bone attached to the fore-edge of the boards of a book, used from the 14th to the early 17th century to keep the leaves pressed firmly together and prevent the covers from warping. Prior to 1200, leather strap fastenings were used for this purpose. Greek-style bindings sometimes had a clasp at the head and tail and two on the fore-edge. Michelle Brown notes in *Understanding Illuminated Manuscripts* (Getty Museum/British Library, 1994) that in English bindings the catch or pin was attached to the lower board, and in most Continental bindings to the upper board. On luxury bindings, clasps of precious metal were sometimes engraved with a name, motto, or religious phrase. Today, clasps are used mainly on personal diaries and albums, sometimes with lock and key.

class   A grouping of objects or concepts based on one or more characteristics, attributes, properties, qualities, etc., that they have in common, for the purpose of classifying them according to an established system, represented in library classification systems by a symbolic notation. In hierarchical classification systems, the members of a class (*example*: **books**) are divided into *subclasses* (**children's books**), which are in turn subdivided into more specific subclasses (**picture books**), and so on.

In Dewey Decimal Classification, a subdivision of any degree of specificity, for example, the class "Library and information sciences" represented by the notation

020. The 10 highest-level divisions of the DDC (numbered 0–9 in the first-digit position) are its *main classes*.

In human resources management, a group of positions within an organization for which the qualifications, duties, responsibilities, evaluation procedures, etc., are comparable and which share the same scale of rank and pay. In library employment, positions are typically classified as follows: library director, librarian, library technician, library technical assistant, and clerical assistant.

classic A widely read work recognized as outstanding in its field. Such a work remains in print long after initial publication; is translated, adapted, and issued in multiple editions; and continues to be the subject of criticism, commentary, study, and analysis (*example*: ***The Adventures of Huckleberry Finn*** by Mark Twain). Also refers to a feature film (Chaplin's ***The Gold Rush***) or documentary (Robert Flaherty's ***Nanook of the North***) that has withstood the test of time. Compare with *classics*.

classics All the non-Christian works written in the Greek and Latin languages prior to A.D. 600 (*example*: ***The Republic*** of Plato). In a broader sense, outstanding books on any subject, fiction or nonfiction, written for adults or children. Compare with *classic*.

classification The process of dividing objects or concepts into logically hierarchical classes, subclasses, and sub-subclasses based on the characteristics they have in common and those that distinguish them. Also used as a shortened form of the term *classification system* or *classification scheme*. *See also*: *cross-classification*.

classification schedule The names assigned to the classes and subdivisions of a classification system, listed in the order of their symbolic notation. In a hierarchical classification system, the arrangement of the schedule(s) indicates logical subordination. For example, in Dewey Decimal Classification the schedules consist of the class numbers 000–999, the associated headings, and notes concerning use, with logical hierarchy indicated by indention and length of notation. *See also*: *auxiliary schedule*, *main schedule*, *relative index*, and *schedule reduction*.

classification scheme *See*: classification system.

Classification Society of North America (CSNA) A nonprofit interdisciplinary organization devoted to promoting the scientific study of classification and clustering and to the dissemination of scientific and educational information related to its fields of interest. The CSNA publishes the biannual *Journal of Classification* and the *CSNA Newsletter*. URL: www.pitt.edu/~csna. *See also*: *International Federation of Classification Societies*.

classification system A list of classes arranged according to a set of pre-established principles for the purpose of organizing items in a collection, or entries in an index, bibliography, or catalog, into groups based on their similarities and differences, to facilitate access and retrieval. In the United States, most library collections are classified by subject. Classification systems can be enumerative or hierarchical, broad or close. In the United States, most public libraries use Dewey Decimal Classification, but academic and research libraries prefer Library of Congress Classification. *See also*: *Classification Society of North America*, *Colon Classification*, and *notation*.

Classification Web   A Web-based cataloging and reference product released in 2002 by the Cataloging Distribution Service of the Library of Congress that enables users to search and browse the complete LC Classification Schedules and LC Subject Headings. Correlations are provided between LC class numbers and subject headings. Updated weekly, the product also provides automatic calculation of classification table numbers, a permanent institutional or personal notes file, and the ability to link to local Web-based online catalogs for most of the major vendors. URL: lcweb.loc. gov/cds/classweb.html.

classified   The status of a document to which access is restricted to a few authorized individuals within a military or government agency, research institution, private corporation, or other organization, usually because it contains highly sensitive information that might be misused by unauthorized persons. When secrecy is no longer required, the document may be *declassified*. ***See also***: Freedom of Information Act (FOIA), *intelligence*, and *need to know*.

Also refers to a reference tool (catalog, index, dictionary, encyclopedia, etc.) organized according to a classification system, usually by subject or some other arrangement based on content, as opposed to a strictly alphabetical or numerical listing of entries.

classified catalog   A subject catalog in which entries are filed in the notational order of a pre-established classification system, with bibliographic records under as many subject headings as apply to the content of each item. An alphabetical subject index facilitates the use of a classified catalog, which is usually maintained alongside an author and/or title catalog. Synonymous with *classed catalog* and *class catalog*. Compare with *dictionary catalog* and *divided catalog*.

classified index   An index in which entries are arranged under headings and subheadings indicating hierarchical divisions and subdivisions within classes based on the subject matter indexed, rather than in alphabetical or numerical sequence. To use such an index effectively, a subject index is required.

classify   To arrange a collection of items (books, pamphlets, maps, videocassettes, sound recordings, etc.) according to a system of classification, based on the characteristics (facets) of each item. Also, to assign a class number to an individual item in a collection, based on its characteristics.

class number   The specific notation used in Dewey Decimal Classification to designate a class, for example, **943.085** assigned to works on the history of the Weimar Republic in Germany. In Library of Congress Classification, the corresponding notation is **DD237**. ***See also***: *base number*, *discontinued number*, *interdisciplinary number*, and *number building*.

classroom collection   A small semi-permanent collection of library materials selected by a school library or academic library for the general classroom use of an instructor and the students enrolled in a course (or courses). Compare with *classroom library* and *classroom loan*.

classroom library A small collection of library materials located permanently in a school classroom for the use of instructor and students in support of the general curriculum. Such a collection may include reference materials such as a dictionary, thesaurus, atlas, general encyclopedia, etc. Compare with *classroom collection* and *classroom loan*.

classroom loan A small collection of library materials on temporary loan from a school library or academic library to a classroom, for the use of instructor and students, usually in support of a specific project or curriculum unit. Compare with *classroom collection* and *classroom library*.

clay tablet The earliest known books were inscribed on small, thin, wet slabs of clay, using a thin, sharp instrument called a *stylus* to incise the wedge-shaped cuneiform characters of the written languages of ancient Mesopotamia. The finished tablets were sun-dried or kiln-fired, then enclosed in a protective outer shell of dried or fired clay inscribed with a title or abstract of the contents. Although clay tablets were too heavy to be portable in large numbers and too small to record long texts effectively, they were much more durable than the papyrus scrolls that superseded them.

clearinghouse An organization or unit within an organization that functions as a central agency for collecting, organizing, storing, and disseminating documents, usually within a specific academic discipline or field. A clearinghouse may also assist the research process by maintaining records of information resources for referral (*examples*: **ERIC** and **LOEX**). Also spelled *clearing house*.

cliché From the French word *clicher*, meaning "to stereotype." A word, phrase, or expression so overused that it has lost its impact and, to some degree, its original meaning. Considered unimaginative, clichés are avoided by serious writers and speakers, except in dialogue when the author wishes to make a point about the mentality of the speaker. Dictionaries of clichés are available in the reference section of larger libraries.

In literature, an overused plot element or character type whose lack of originality detracts from the quality of the work.

click-and-drag To change the position of an icon, filename, window, or other movable element on a computer screen by clicking on it with a pointing device, such as a mouse, and then holding down the button to shift the element to another location on the screen. The technique can be used to reposition windows on a microcomputer desktop, move computer files from one directory or subdirectory to another in storage, and organize bookmarked Web sites in folders in most Web browsers.

click-on license Licensing terms stated in a notice appearing on the installation or opening screen of a software or electronic information product, which the manufacturer considers the user to have accepted by the act of selecting an icon or link to continue. Such agreements often include provisions and restrictions that have not been uniformly enforced in the courts, because they give software publishers more rights than are permitted under federal copyright or patent law. The controversial *Uniform Computer Information Transactions Act (UCITA)* would allow software publishers to embed non-negotiable, enforceable contract terms in this type of mass-market license. Synonymous with *click-through license* and *click-wrap license*. *See also*: *shrink-wrap license*.

client   A person who uses the services of a professionally trained expert, or of a professional organization or institution, usually in exchange for payment of a fee. Librarians employed in academic and public libraries usually refer to the people they serve as users or patrons because libraries have traditionally provided most services without charge. Information brokers who operate on a fee-for-service basis can be more appropriately said to serve "clients."

Also refers to a computer connected to a network, such as the Internet, equipped with software enabling the user to access resources available on another computer, called a *server*, connected to the same network. *See also*: *client-server*.

clientele   All the persons who use a library's services and collections on a regular or irregular basis, usually those who live in the district that funds its operations or are members of the institution it serves. Successful collection development depends on the librarian's knowledge of the information needs and preferences of the library's clientele. *See also*: *user survey*.

client-server   Wide area (WAN) or local area network (LAN) architecture that makes it possible for a client computer (usually a PC workstation) to download information or processing from a server machine, as opposed to a system that uses dedicated terminals connected to a minicomputer or mainframe. The size and speed of computer required as a server (microcomputer, minicomputer, or mainframe) depend on the nature of the applications to be installed and the amount of anticipated use. Also refers to the software used to establish the connection between a client and server. *See also*: *Open Systems Interconnection*.

clipboard   A small amount of computer memory reserved as a temporary storage place in the exchange of data between software applications. In word processing, this is normally accomplished by selecting the option to "cut" or "copy" from one document and "paste" into another. Data transferred to the clipboard is lost when another cut/copy operation commences, unless saved as a separate file.

clipping   A page, piece of a page, or pages cut or torn from a printed publication, usually from a newspaper or magazine, by a person who wishes to save an article, editorial, letter to the editor, photograph, cartoon, etc. Large collections of clippings are usually stored in a *clipping file*, arranged by subject or some other method of classification. Compare with *cutting* and *tear sheet*. *See also*: *clipping service*.

clipping service   A service, usually performed in a special library, in which news announcements, articles, photographs, and other items of interest to the host organization are clipped from current periodicals and news services on a daily or weekly basis to be forwarded to appropriate personnel within the organization, based on pre-established interest profiles. Directory information for clipping services is available in the reference serial *Literary Market Place*. Synonymous with *clipping bureau*.

CLIR   *See*: Council on Library and Information Resources.

cloisonné   An elegant style of book cover produced by Italian and Greek craftsmen of the 11th century in which an ornamental design in narrow metal strips was soldered onto a metal plate, and the open spaces between the strips filled with enamel in various colors, to form the outer surface of the cover. Books bound in this style are usually very valuable, especially if they are in good condition. *See also*: *rare book*.

close classification   A classification system in which the main classes and divisions are minutely subdivided, allowing very specific characteristics of each subject to be differentiated. Also, the classification of works to the fullest extent permitted by the notation of a classification system (DDC). The opposite of *broad classification*.

closed caption (CC)   A continuous moving line of text (called a *crawl*) along the bottom of the screen in a television broadcast giving the narration or dialogue and noting any non-speech vocalizations (laughter, screams, dogs barking, etc.) or sound effects (music, applause, doorbells, etc.). Used mainly for the hearing-impaired and in bilingual programming, *closed captioning* is visible only with the aid of a special decoder. In library cataloging, the phrase *closed captioned* is entered in the note area of the bibliographic description to identify an item that includes the feature.

closed catalog   A library catalog to which new bibliographic records are no longer added or in which additions are restricted to certain categories, although existing records continue to be removed as they are revised, corrected, and/or converted to machine-readable format. After retrospective conversion is completed, a closed catalog is usually removed from public access and eventually discarded. Compare with *frozen catalog* and *open catalog*.

closed circuit television (CCTV)   A video system used internally in some large libraries for conferencing and to monitor traffic for security purposes.

closed-end index   An index covering one or more documents or publications compiled all at one time (*example*: *Canadian Feature Film Index, 1913–1985*). Compare with *open-end index*. *See also*: *single index*.

closed entry   A note in the bibliographic record for a serial or continuation giving the complete information for all the parts or volumes published, or in the holdings statement in the catalog record for such a title, indicating all the parts or volumes held by the library (*example*: **v. 1–10, 1936–46**), as distinct from the open entry for an *ongoing* serial subscription or continuation order (*example*: **v. 1–   , 1936–   **). For newspapers and periodicals, a closed entry usually indicates that the subscription was canceled or the publication ceased.

closed file   In archives, a collection of documents in which additions or changes are unlikely to occur or a file of records to which access is restricted or denied, except under special circumstances.

closed reserve   An item on reserve that may be checked out by a registered borrower but may not be removed from library premises. Also, a reserve collection shelved in a closed stack from which requested items must be retrieved by a member of the library staff. Compare with *open reserve*.

closed stacks   A shelving area in a library to which only members of the library staff have access, established to protect the collection or conserve space by using aisles narrower than the standard width in open stacks. Materials are retrieved from closed stacks by staff members upon request. *See also*: *call slip*.

closeout   A book title offered for retail sale at a significantly reduced price because the publisher is allowing it to go out of print. A rebate may be offered by the publisher to the bookseller for copies that do not sell.

close score   A vocal music score in which all the parts are given on a minimum number of staves, usually two, as in a hymn (*AACR2*).

closet drama   A play written to be read rather than performed on the stage, for example, the dramatic works of the French poet Alfred de Musset. Also refers to a drama originally intended for performance, which survives as a work of literature but is rarely if ever performed (*example*: Byron's **Manfred**).

closing   All the procedures followed by the staff of a library when the facility closes at the end of a day, such as informing patrons that it is time to leave, checking the premises to be certain all users have vacated, logging off computer systems, turning off lights and equipment, locking doors, switching on pre-recorded phone messages, activating security alarms, etc. Size and design of facility determine the length of time and number of staff required to close. In very large facilities, a checklist may be followed for each floor, and one or more security guards may assist in clearing the building. Compare with *opening*. *See also*: *library closure*.

cloth   A generic term for any woven material used since the early 19th century to cover the boards of a book, as opposed to the leather, parchment, or vellum used in earlier bookbinding or the paper covers used today. Dyed book cloth used in edition binding is woven from cotton or linen, filled with starch sizing, or coated or impregnated with some other compound to prevent adhesives from penetrating, then pressed under heat. Because the covers of cloth-bound trade editions are not designed to withstand heavy use, publishers add an attractively designed paper dust jacket for protection (and marketing purposes). Volumes that must withstand heavy use are often given a library binding in a heavier, more durable material such as buckram. The term is also used in publishers' catalogs to distinguish the hardcover from the softcover edition of a work. Synonymous with *cloth-bound*. *See also*: *half cloth*.

   Cloth was also used as a covering material in luxury hand-binding of the 16th and 17th centuries. Bindings in canvas, satin, or velvet were often embroidered in silk and/or metallic thread. *See also*: *textile binding*.

cloth board   *See*: flannel board.

cloth book   A small, illustrated children's book printed entirely on sturdy woven fabric and given a flexible binding for toddlers who have not yet developed sufficient manual dexterity to turn paper pages without tearing them. To withstand drooling, the cloth pages may be treated with a moisture-resistant substance. In the 19th century, this type of toy book was called a *rag book*.

cloth-bound   *See*: cloth.

cloth joint A strip of cloth used to reinforce the inside of the front and back joints in some library bindings and in very large, thick, or heavy books. In volumes of normal size and thickness, the unreinforced joints are usually formed on the inside by the fold in each endpaper.

CLR *See: Children's Literature Review.*

CLR *See*: Council on Library and Information Resources.

club line A single indented line at the beginning of a paragraph when it appears at the foot of a printed column or page of text, considered awkward by skilled typesetters and avoided whenever possible. Compare with *orphan*.

CNI *See*: Coalition for Networked Information.

COA *See*: Committee on Accreditation.

Coalition for Networked Information (CNI) Founded in 1990, CNI is a nonprofit organization with headquarters in Washington, D.C., dedicated to supporting the future of networked information technology for the advancement of scholarly communication and the enhancement of intellectual productivity. Sponsored by the Association of Research Libraries (ARL) and EDUCAUSE, CNI's membership includes 200 institutions representing higher education, publishing, telecommunication, information technology, libraries, and library-related activities. URL: www.cni.org.

coated The smooth surface of papers to which a thin layer of mineral, wax, resin, plastic, or emulsion has been applied, either in the papermaking machine prior to drying and finishing or by a separate coating machine after manufacture (some papers are double-coated using both methods). Coated papers are used to print posters, wall calendars, dust jackets, magazine and catalog covers, and other materials in which detailed visual elements predominate (art books, exhibit catalogs, coffee table books, etc.). The finish can be glossy or dull. Also known as *art papers*.

coauthor *See*: joint author.

coaxial cable A high-capacity metal cable consisting of four layers: a solid or stranded wire encased in insulation, shielded by braided wire covered in plastic insulation. Various types of coaxial cable are used extensively in cable television transmission and computer networks because "coax" can carry more data and is less susceptible to interference than the twisted pair wire used in older telephone systems. Compare with *optical fiber*.

cocked A serious binding defect in which the spine of a book is angled or twisted in a way that prevents the boards from lining up evenly with each other. *See also*: *shelf-cocked*.

cocked-up initial *See*: raised capital.

cockle A slightly puckered finish produced naturally or artificially when paper shrinks unevenly as it is dried under little or no tension, as in the production of onionskin. The boards and paper in a finished book may cockle if heat is applied following exposure to excessive moisture. The condition can be prevented by controlling temperature and relative humidity in storage. The parchment and vellum used as a writing surface in medieval manuscripts is also susceptible to cockling because it is made from membrane.

cockled The condition of a book in which the leaves or boards appear puckered, wavy, wrinkled, or curled, usually due to excessive heat and/or humidity in drying. In a book cover, the condition can result from the incorrect use of adhesive (too much or the wrong kind).

cockroach A very common nocturnal beetle-like insect of the genus *Blatta*, dark brown in color and of comparatively large size, known for its voraciousness and affinity for human habitations. It prefers kitchens where it multiplies rapidly if sufficient food is available. Cockroaches also feed on paste and glue and will chew through the binding of a book to get to it. They also excrete a dark-staining liquid that can be difficult to remove. The best way to prevent infestation is to prohibit food and drink near the library's collections. According to Jane Greenfield (*The Care of Fine Books*, Nick Lyons Books, 1988), boric acid powder sprinkled lightly on the shelves around books also discourages cockroaches.

coda From the Latin word *cauda*, meaning "tail." An independent passage added at the end of a musical work or literary composition to bring the piece to a graceful conclusion by drawing preceding motifs and themes together in a satisfying resolution. The last chapter of a biography, the last essay in a collection of essays, or the last story in a book of short stories is sometimes written as a coda to tie the other parts together.

codebook The metadata that describes a social science data set. Although codebooks have been digitized since the 1970s, social scientists continue to refer to them as "books" because they originally existed in the form of bound manuals. A codebook contains bibliographic information about a scientific study, describes the composition and format of data files, and documents methodology and study variables. *See also*: *Data Documentation Initiative*.

CODEN A system of alphanumeric codes developed by the American Society for Testing and Materials (ASTM) to uniquely and permanently identify sci-tech serial and monographic publications. Responsibility for administering the system was transferred to Chemical Abstracts Service (CAS) in 1975. The CODEN is used in electronic information systems to process bibliographic data because it is more concise than the full title and less ambiguous than an abbreviated title.

code of ethics A set of standards governing the conduct and judgment of librarians, library staff, and other information professionals in their work. The *ALA Code of Ethics* sets standards for equitable access, intellectual freedom, confidentiality, respect for intellectual property rights, excellence, accuracy, integrity, impartiality, courtesy, and respect for colleagues and library patrons.

codex From the Latin *caudex*, meaning "tree bark." Originally an ancient manuscript written with a stylus on hinged wax-covered tablets made of wood, metal, or ivory, called codices. From the 1st century on, a manuscript written on sheets of papyrus, fastened at one side to allow the leaves to open and close like a book, a format used for law books in ancient Rome, also popular among the Christians because of its portability (scrolls were difficult to carry and had to be unrolled to locate a specific portion of text). Parchment replaced papyrus in about the 3rd century, and paper came into widespread use with the introduction of printing in the mid-15th century.

The oldest vellum codex known to exist is the *Codex Sinaiticus*, a Greek Old and New Testament of the mid-4th century written in *scriptio continuo* in four columns per page, currently in The British Library, although some scholars consider the *Codex Vaticanus* in the Vatican Library to be older. The term also refers to the form of the modern book, consisting of individual leaves of writing material bound together along one edge and enclosed in a protective cover. *See also*: *pugillaria*.

codicology   Analysis of the physical structure and characteristics of a book as a means of understanding its production and to establish date and place of origin and determine subsequent history (provenance). By examining the materials used in making a book, and its page design, artistic style(s), and methods of construction, *codicologists* are able to identify the scribes and workshops that produced them, establish relationships between manuscripts, and assist scholars in detecting alterations (accidental or intentional) in classical and medieval texts. In the case of books that survive in altered condition, such study may also help determine the original appearance for purposes of documentation or restoration. Compare with *bibliology*. *See also*: *paleography*.

codification   The process of creating systematic rules to govern a specific activity, such as the cataloging of bibliographic materials. In the United States, Britain, and Canada, the joint efforts of the American Library Association, the Library Association (UK), and the Canadian Library Association have produced *Anglo-American Cataloguing Rules*, which apply to library materials in various formats (books, manuscripts, cartographic materials, music, sound recordings, motion pictures and videorecordings, graphic materials, computer files, three-dimensional artifacts and realia, microforms, and serials).

co-edition   An edition for which two or more publishers share responsibility, for example, *The Great Libraries: From Antiquity to the Renaissance*, published in 2000 by Oak Knoll Press and The British Library. In most cases, the original publisher grants the exclusive right to market and distribute the publication within a specific sales territory to one or more other publishers (see *co-publishing*). The title page of a co-edition may bear the imprint of the originator, of one of the companies granted distribution rights, or of all the co-publishers. Compare with *export edition* and *joint publication*. *See also*: *joint imprint*.

coextensive entry   The principle in indexing that the subject heading or descriptor assigned to a work should encompass *all* the significant concepts covered in the item (and no more). Thus a book about painters and poets would require the heading "Painters and poets," rather than separate headings for "Painters" and "Poets." Coextensive indexing is attempted in the PRECIS system. Also spelled *co-extensive entry*. Compare with *specific entry*.

coextensive heading   A subject heading that indicates all or most of the subjects of a bibliographic item, for example, the Library of Congress subject heading **United States—History—Civil War, 1861–1865—Participation, African American—Juvenile literature** assigned to the juvenile book *Black, Blue & Gray: African Americans in the Civil War* (Simon & Schuster, 1998). Also spelled *co-extensive heading.* Compare with *post-coordinate indexing. See also: exhaustivity.*

coffee table book   An expensive book on a popular subject, usually oversize and lavishly illustrated, with the text clearly subordinate to the illustrations. Designed primarily for display and casual browsing rather than cover-to-cover reading, coffee table books are often marketed on the decorative appeal of their colorful dust jackets. In trade bookstores, they may be sold at a deep discount, especially at Christmas to attract gift buyers. Public libraries may add them to the collection when received as gifts, provided demand exists for the subject and their condition is good. Academic library approval plans generally exclude them. Compare with *table book.*

cognitive style   The way a person habitually organizes a problem-solving or learning experience, or consistently receives and responds to information, especially whether the individual prefers content already structured (lecture-style) or is more likely to impose his/her own structure on the material (hands-on approach). Differences in learning style have important implications for the delivery of reference services and bibliographic instruction and for the design of online tutorials and library Web pages.

coil binding   *See*: spiral binding.

cold boot   To restart a computer by turning the power off and turning it back on again, causing the files in its operating system to be re-executed. This procedure is sometimes helpful in getting a computer "unstuck" when it locks up unexpectedly during processing and rebooting fails to get it going again, but the user should be aware that powering down will result in loss of unsaved data.

cold-crack   The tendency of the adhesive on the spine of a perfect-bound book to split at very low temperatures, reducing the text block to a pile of loose leaves. The inability of hot-melt adhesives to withstand cold temperatures makes them unsuitable for use in bindings marketed in countries like Finland and Russia where winter temperatures can be severe. The problem is eliminated in Otabind adhesive binding, which uses slower-drying, cold-resistant polyvinyl acetate (PVA) adhesive.

collaborative reference   A mode of digital reference in which reference questions are routed to reference librarians at different institutions, based on such criteria as expertise, availability, etc. The *QuestionPoint* service developed by OCLC and the Library of Congress, with input from participating members of the Global Reference Network, is an example of such a service. Compare with *cooperative reference.*

collaborator   A person who works closely with one or more associates in producing a work to which all who participate make the same kind of contribution (shared responsibility) or different contributions (mixed responsibility), for example, essays written by different authors for publication in a collection or illustrations for a children's book in which the text is written by a person other than the illustrator. *See also*: *joint author*.

collate   To determine, usually by close examination of signatures, leaves, illustrations, and other characteristics, if a copy of a book is complete and perfect, or to compare it with descriptions of ideal copies found in bibliographies for the same purpose. Also, to compare two printed works page by page and line by line, to establish whether they are identical copies or variants of the same text.

Also, to check a book for completeness before binding, and to make sure the signatures are gathered in correct sequence, a task is made easier by *collating marks* printed along the back fold or in the tail margin, making misplaced sections easier to spot. The marks are concealed when the lining is applied to the binding edge, or removed in trimming.

Also, to merge two or more ordered sets of documents, records, pages, or data into a single desired sequence. High-end photocopiers usually have collating capability.

collating mark   *See*: collate.

collation   In codicology, a complete description of both the current and the original structure of a manuscript or book, especially the arrangement of its leaves and sections. Separate descriptions may be given of current and original structures or information about both states conveyed in a single collation.

In binding, a list of the signatures of a book, indicating the number of leaves in each. Also, the process of checking the physical make-up of a book for correct sequence and completeness before binding, particularly the presence of all illustrations, plates, and maps not printed with the text.

In analytical bibliography, the comparison of two texts of the same work to determine which is the first edition or the definitive text.

In library cataloging, a synonym for the *physical description area* of a bibliographic record, now fallen into disuse.

Also refers to the merger of two ordered sets of documents, records, pages, or data into a single desired sequence.

collected edition   An edition of the previously published works of an author, issued in a single volume or uniform set of volumes, usually under a collective title. Compare with *author's edition*.

collected work   *See*: collection.

collected works   *See*: author's edition.

collectible   Any class of things, usually old or rare but lacking intrinsic value, that people accumulate as a hobby or in the expectation that the value will rise (autographs, comic books, phonograph records, etc.). Also used as an adjective to describe something sought by collectors, for example, first editions and incunabula. Also spelled *collectable*.

collecting archives   An independent organization, or unit within a larger organization or institution, responsible for building a collection of records and documents from a variety of sources, in keeping with the mission of the parent institution, for example, a manuscript repository in the library of a major university. Archives of this type may provide online access to a portion of their resources (see *Declaring Independence: Drafting the Documents*, sponsored the Library of Congress at: www.loc.gov/exhibits/declara/declara1.html) or be completely electronic (*USGenWeb Archives* hosted by RootsWeb at: www.rootsweb.com/~usgenweb). *See also*: *personal archives*.

collecting level   The thoroughness with which materials published in a given field or subject area are selected by a library for inclusion in the collection. The following levels are generally recognized in the library literature:

0 Out of scope
1 Minimal information
2 Basic information
3 Study or instructional support
4 Research support
5 Comprehensive

Synonymous with *collecting intensity*.

collection   In library cataloging, three or more independent works or long excerpts from works by the same author, or two or more independent works or excerpts from works by different authors, not written for the same occasion or for the publication in hand, published together in a single volume or uniform set of volumes, for example, a book of essays written by one or more essayists. Selected by an editor, the works are listed in the table of contents in order of appearance in the text. Synonymous with *collected work*. Compare with *anthology* and *compilation*. *See also*: *analytical entry*.

Also refers to a number of documents (books, reports, records, etc.) assembled in a single physical or virtual location by one or more persons, or by a corporate entity, and arranged in some kind of systematic order to facilitate retrieval. *See also*: *library collection*.

collection agency   A commercial enterprise that specializes in collecting past-due bills from people who owe them, usually by informing them that their credit record will suffer unless prompt payment is received. Most public libraries enter into a contractual agreement with such an agency to handle the collection of unpaid bills for items lost, damaged, or long overdue. Academic institutions have the option of withholding grades or diploma from a student until library fines are paid.

collection assessment   The systematic evaluation of the quality of a library collection to determine the extent to which it meets the library's service goals and objectives and the information needs of its clientele. Deficiencies are addressed through collection development. Synonymous with *collection evaluation*.

collection development   The process of planning and building a useful and balanced collection of library materials over a period of years, based on an ongoing assessment of the information needs of the library's clientele, analysis of usage statistics, and demographic projections, normally constrained by budgetary limitations. Collection development includes the formulation of selection criteria, planning for resource sharing, and replacement of lost and damaged items, as well as routine selection and deselection decisions.

Large libraries and library systems may use an approval plan or blanket order plan to develop their collections. In small- and medium-sized libraries, collection development responsibilities are normally shared by all the librarians, based on their interests and subject specializations, usually under the overall guidance of a written collection development policy. Compare with *collection management*.

collection development bias   Partiality in the selection of materials for a library collection, whether against or in favor of materials presenting a particular point of view or with respect to a specific type of resource, category of publisher, etc. Although the *Library Bill of Rights* of the American Library Association charges librarians in the United States to "provide materials and information presenting all points of view on current and historical issues," some studies suggest that librarians tend to avoid selecting potentially controversial books and media, for reasons conscious or unconscious, undermining the goal of developing a balanced collection. *See also*: *precensorship*.

collection development policy (CDP)   A formal written statement of the principles guiding a library's selection of materials, including the criteria used in making selection and deselection decisions (fields covered, degrees of specialization, levels of difficulty, languages, formats, balance, etc.) and policies concerning gifts and exchanges. An unambiguously worded collection development policy can be very helpful in responding to challenges from pressure groups.

collection evaluation   *See*: collection assessment.

collection level cataloging   The encoding level used to control separately published documents (maps, pamphlets, ephemera, etc.) that are unrelated bibliographically and do not warrant the expense of full level or even minimal level cataloging but have research value and can be cataloged as a single item under a collective title because they share at least one unifying characteristic (author, issuing body, language, subject, genre, etc.). Synonymous with *collective cataloging*.

collection maintenance   Measures taken on a routine basis or as needed to preserve the materials in a library collection in usable condition, including mending, repairing, binding, rebinding, and reformatting, usually the responsibility of the technical processing and serials departments.

collection management   The application of quantitative techniques, such as statistical and cost-benefit analysis, to the process of collection development, usually limited to large libraries and library systems. In a more general sense, the activity of planning and supervising the growth and preservation of a library's collections based on an assessment of existing strengths and weaknesses and an estimate of future needs.

collective bargaining agreement   A legally binding contract signed on behalf of library staff organized in a *collective bargaining unit* by elected representatives authorized to negotiate terms of employment with management, including salaries and wages, benefits, job responsibilities, evaluation for promotion and tenure, grievance procedures, etc. Librarians employed at colleges and universities that grant librarians faculty status may be members of the same bargaining unit as the teaching faculty. *See also*: *American Association of University Professors* and *compulsory arbitration*.

collective bargaining unit   *See*: collective bargaining agreement.

collective biography   A work in one or more volumes containing separate accounts of the lives of two or more individuals who lived within a specific time period, distinguished themselves in the same field or activity, or have some other characteristic in common (*example*: *Ordinary Women, Extraordinary Lives: Women in American History* edited by Kriste Lindenmeyer). Written by one or more biographers, the essays in a collective biography are usually longer than the entries in a *biographical dictionary* and may include a biobibliography or list of references for further reading.

collective cataloging   *See*: collection level cataloging.

collective name   *See*: corporate name.

collective title   In library cataloging, the title proper of a bibliographic item containing several works by one or more authors issued in a single volume or uniform set of volumes, each with its own title distinct from that of the whole. Also refers to the title assigned by a cataloger to a group of separately published materials cataloged collectively.

college bookstore   A retail outlet operated in association with a college or university, selling new and secondhand textbooks and trade editions assigned by professors as reading in their courses. College bookstores also sell popular reference books, school supplies, greeting cards, college memorabilia, general interest magazines, bestsellers, and nonfiction trade titles of interest to the student market. They can be owned and managed by the institution served, operated by an independent contractor, or run as a cooperative. Compare with *trade bookstore*.

college catalog   *See*: course catalog.

college dictionary   *See*: desk dictionary.

college library   A type of academic library maintained by an independent four-year college, or by one of several colleges within a larger university, for the use of students and faculty. Compare with *undergraduate library*.

collegiality   From the Latin *collegium*, meaning "community," "association," or "fraternity." Engagement by the members of a group in relations based on civility and an awareness of common interests, as between *colleagues*.

collocation   In library cataloging, the process of bringing together all the bibliographic records representing works by the same author, of variant titles, of different editions, of the same series, or on closely related subjects, by assigning the same access point to facilitate retrieval. For example, the preparation of entries under a heading for the predominant name of an author who wrote under one or more pseudonyms. Collocation often requires the use of cross-references to direct the user to the authorized form of the name, title, subject heading, etc. *See also*: *authority control*.

In classification, the arrangement of the subdivisions of a hierarchical classification system in a manner that places classes and subclasses of equal rank together and shows the degree to which they are logically removed from the main class.

colloquy A literary work written in the form of a conversation or dialogue (*example*: *Aelfric's Colloquy*). Plural: *colloquies*.

Also refers to a conference in the form of a seminar, with several speakers participating in a discussion that is conversational in style and tone. Synonymous in this sense with *colloquium*.

Colon Classification A classification system in which subjects are analyzed into facets based on their uses and relations, then represented by synthetically constructed classes with the parts separated by the colon (:). Developed by S.R. Ranganathan in the 1930s, Colon Classification is used in libraries in India and in research libraries throughout the world.

colophon A Greek word meaning "finishing touch." A statement given at the end of the text of an early manuscript, usually giving details of production (name of scribe, illuminator, and binder; date and place of production; etc.). The colophon may also include an expression of gratitude to the patron or client commissioning the work, a warning against unauthorized copying, or a brief comment by the scribe (usually an expression of relief at having completed the task). Colophons occur sporadically in medieval manuscripts and were sometimes decorated or embellished with flourishes. Early printed colophons followed the manuscript tradition, giving the name and emblem (imprint) of the printer, date of printing, number of copies printed, and sometimes an apology to the reader for any errors in the text. Synonymous with *explicit*. *See also*: impensis.

In modern printing, a statement printed at the end of the text, or on the verso of the title page of a book, giving the name of the printer, typeface, grade of paper, materials used in binding, and sometimes the names of those responsible for producing the edition. Also refers to a printing device, usually an emblem, used to represent a publisher's imprint.

color plate An illustration in color, usually printed separately from the text on a different grade of paper and bound with others in one or more sections of a book. Color plates are often numbered and listed by number in the front matter of a book. In publishing, color printing almost always increases cost of production. In the 19th century, when color lithography reached its peak, editions consisting of color plates with little or no text were common. Also spelled *colorplate*. Compare with *duotone* and *monochrome plate*.

color supplement A magazine printed in color to be issued with a Sunday newspaper (*example*: *The New York Times Magazine*). Also refers to a section of illustrations printed in color for insertion in the center of a magazine or book, whether removable or not.

colporteur From the French words *col* ("neck") and *porter* ("to carry"). A peddler of newspapers and books printed in inexpensive edition (almanacs, primers, Bibles, etc.) who traveled about the countryside in Europe, carrying his wares in a box or basket attached to a neck strap as he hawked them in the streets and door to door. In Britain, itinerant salesmen were sometimes employed by religious societies to sell or distribute religious tracts on foot. *Colportage* flourished from the late 15th century, when printed works first became available, until the end of the 18th century despite unsuccessful efforts by the French government to suppress the trade because it helped spread the revolutionary new ideas that eventually led to reformation and revolution.

column   One of two or more vertical sections of written or printed text separated from each other by a ruled line or blank space, as in ancient scrolls, newspapers, and language dictionaries. The length of a newspaper article is expressed in column inches. *See also*: *double column*.

Also refers to an essay providing commentary on a current issue, sometimes from a political point of view (Left, Right, or Center), usually printed on or near the editorial page of a newspaper or in a magazine or trade journal (*example*: Carol Tenopir's *Online Databases* column in **Library Journal**). National political columnists are often syndicated. Compare with *editorial*.

column inch   In newspaper and magazine publishing, the unit of measurement in which the length of an article or size of a paid advertisement is expressed, equivalent to the width of a column of type multiplied by one inch of depth.

columnist   A journalist who writes regular commentary on current issues for publication in a magazine or newspaper, or in more than one newspaper, usually from a political position left or right of center, or expressing an original point of view on a matter of interest to readers. National political columnists are often syndicated. Also refers to a specialist in a particular field or on a given subject who writes regular commentary for a magazine or trade journal (*example*: Roy Tennant who writes the *Digital Libraries* column in **Library Journal**).

COM   *See*: computer output microform.

comb binding   A form of mechanical binding in which a row of interconnected curved plastic teeth is inserted into slots punched along the binding edge of the leaves of a publication to hold them together, used for binding calendars, lab manuals, instruction manuals, and workbooks that must open flat to be used conveniently. If the plastic spine is wide enough, the title may be printed on it. Plastic comb bindings are easily broken. Compare with *loose-leaf* and *spiral binding*.

combination rate   The special discounted price offered by a publisher when subscriptions to two or more serial publications are purchased by the same subscriber. The publisher normally determines the eligibility of a specific title for such a discount.

comcatalog   *See*: computer output microform catalog.

comedy   A dramatic work in which an amusing event or series of events with a happy ending is presented for the enjoyment of the audience or reader. Comic effect is usually achieved by emphasizing incongruity of character in dialogue and/or action. When such an effect is achieved with subtle insight, the result is "high" comedy, as distinct from "low" comedy, which appeals to cruder perceptions. The earliest surviving examples of classical comedy are the 11 plays of Aristophanes, thought to have been written and performed in Athens in the 5th century B.C. Compare with *farce*. *See also*: *tragedy* and *tragicomedy*.

comic book   A booklet, usually printed in color on paper made from wood pulp, containing one or more stories told pictorially in a continuous strip of panels drawn in cartoon style, with dialogue or monologue enclosed in balloons or given in captions. An extended form of the *comic strip* published in daily newspapers, comic books are often issued in series and classified by genre (adventure, fantasy, romance, science fiction, etc.). They are acquired by libraries for special collections on popular culture and are of considerable interest to private collectors. *See also*: *comic strip* and *graphic novel*.

comic strip   A succession of cartoon panels that tells a story graphically, with monologue or dialogue provided in balloons or captions. A comic strip may be complete in itself or part of a longer narrative published serially. The comics section of the Sunday issue of most major newspapers provides a selection of syndicated comic strips printed in color. The most famous American comic strip was "Peanuts," created by Charles Schulz. Other classics include "Li'l Abner" by Al Capp and "Pogo" by Walt Kelly. *See also*: *comic book*.

command-driven   A computer interface in which the user must type a command statement or query to achieve the desired result, usually faster than a menu-driven interface but not as user-friendly for novices who must invest time and effort in learning the system's command language.

commentary   A critical or explanatory note or collection of notes on a sacred or literary work, accompanying the text or issued separately, usually written by a person or persons other than the author. Commentaries are generally devoted to major works that have been the subject of considerable interpretation (*Bhagavad-Gita*, *Bible*, *Koran*, etc.). In medieval manuscripts, commentaries are often written as glosses alongside the text to which they refer (see *glossed bible*). Also refers to a historical narrative written largely from personal experience, for example, *Seven Commentaries on the Gallic War* by Julius Caesar. Synonymous in this sense with *memoirs*.

In a more general sense, a series of remarks or observations made by someone with authority to speak and be heard on the subject, for example, a journalist writing a column on a political or social issue.

commercial journal   A scholarly journal or trade journal published by a for-profit company, as opposed to a journal published by a university press or nonprofit organization, such as a scholarly society or professional association. Relentless price increases have become an important issue for libraries that subscribe to commercially published journals.

commercial publisher   A publisher in the business of producing and selling books and/or other publications for profit, as opposed to a university press or the publishing arm of a scholarly society, professional association, or other nonprofit organization that operates on a cost-recovery basis. The term includes trade publishers and popular presses. In commercial publishing, the decision to publish is influenced by sales potential, sometimes at the expense of originality and quality.

commercial television   Television broadcast stations for which profit is the prime concern. In the selection of programming, commercial stations rely heavily on ratings because their advertisers are motivated by the desire to reach the widest possible viewing audience. Compare with *public television*.

Committee on Accreditation (COA)   The official body within the American Library Association responsible for accrediting graduate programs leading to the first professional degree in library and information science offered at universities in the United States, under the ALA's *Standards for Accreditation of Master's Programs in Library and Information Studies* (1992). The COA statement on *Accreditation Process, Policies & Procedures* (2002) is available online at: www.ala.org.

common carrier (CC)   A telecommunication service, such as a telephone or cable company, that provides wire and/or microwave services to businesses and the general public, usually at rates regulated by federal, state, or local government.

Common Gateway Interface (CGI)   A program interface installed on a Web server that allows Web pages to be linked to databases and other programs in such a way that input can be entered via the Web page and sent to a database management system for searching. Results are sent back by the DBMS and presented to the user in HTML format.

commonplace book   A book with blank pages in which passages in prose or verse are recorded irregularly by its owner as ideas for future exploration or contemplation, sometimes arranged by subject. The writer may note only his own thoughts and ideas or excerpt those of other writers or speakers. Commonplace books kept by persons of literary or historical importance, such as Ralph Waldo Emerson and Thomas Jefferson, have been deemed worthy of publication. Although interest in this form of literary expression has waned, it is still used by poets (*example*: *A Certain World* by W.H. Auden). *See also*: *diary* and *journal*.

communications   The transfer of information from one physical location to another by electronic means. The term *telecommunication* refers to both analog and digital communications, including the transmission of voice and video. *Data communications* refers to digital communications only, occurring via modem over a telephone line, by direct cable to another PC equipped with file transfer software, from a remote terminal connected to a minicomputer or mainframe, from one node to another on a local area network (LAN), or between client and server in a network environment. A *communications device* is a piece of hardware, such as a modem, cable, or port, designed to facilitate data transmission.

Communications Decency Act (CDA)   Part of the *Telecommunications Act of 1996*, the *Communications Decency Act* made it a federal offense to transmit content over the Internet deemed "indecent" on the basis of "community standards" and made it a criminal offense to have transmitted such material if it was received by a minor. In a suit filed by the Citizens Internet Empowerment Coalition (CIEC), the American Library Association took the lead, joined by 22 co-plaintiffs, in challenging the *CDA* in federal district court, consolidating its action with a similar suit by the American Civil Liberties Union (ACLU). In June 1996, a three-judge panel ruled that the term "indecent" was unconstitutionally vague and unenforceable but upheld the portion of the *CDA* making it a felony to display or transmit "offensive" materials to minors. On appeal, the *CDA* was declared unconstitutional in June 1997 by unanimous decision of the U.S. Supreme Court, whose members agreed with the plaintiffs' argument that the law was so broad and poorly defined that it violated the First Amendment rights of adults and would subject librarians to criminal prosecution for posting materials online that are not illegal in other media. *See also*: Child Online Protection Act and Children's Internet Protection Act.

community service volunteer (CSV)   A person convicted of a misdemeanor assigned volunteer work in his or her community as a form of restitution. Community service volunteers are typically recommended by a probation officer based on criteria established by the library, with most libraries reserving the right of refusal. Because one of the goals of such work is to teach responsibility, attendance is closely monitored, but duties that involve handling money or accessing nonpublic computer systems are generally not assigned. Some libraries accept adult offenders but not teenagers. In most cases, the program coordinator and supervising librarian are the only employees in the library who know the volunteer is completing community service. The library benefits from unpaid labor, but CSVs often require closer supervision than paid employees. Synonymous with *probation volunteer*.

compact disc (CD)   A digital audiorecording medium introduced in 1982 capable of storing up to 74 minutes of high-fidelity stereophonic sound in a single spiral track on one side of a 4.75-inch disc, similar to the track on a phonograph record. Designed to be read by a laser beam and decoded inside a device called a *CD player*, compact discs not only provide clearer sound than phonograph records and audiotape but are capable of recording a much wider range of volume. In libraries, CDs are usually shelved separately, often in specially designed display cases. Some libraries provide listening equipment on the premises. In *AACR2*, the term "sound disc" is used in the physical description area of the bibliographic record representing a compact disc, with "digital" given as type of recording. *See also*: *optical disk*.

compact edition   An edition in which the physical size of a long work is reduced, usually by altering the format without changing the content, for example, *The Compact Oxford English Dictionary* (second edition), reproduced micrographically and issued in a slipcase with a microprint reader. Compare with *concise edition*.

compact shelving   Library shelving designed to maximize the storage capacity of a given space by incorporating movable elements such as shelf ranges on tracks. Because it is considerably heavier than normal shelving when filled, compact shelving requires more structural support, an important design consideration in the construction of a new library facility. *See also*: *compact storage*.

compact storage   A library shelving area, often reserved for low-use materials, in which narrow aisles, higher-than-normal shelves, and/or compact shelving is employed to maximize storage capacity. The building must be structurally capable of supporting the additional weight. Compact storage with movable parts may be subject to electrical or mechanical failure.

companion book   A book published in conjunction with a motion picture or television program or series, usually a work of nonfiction intended to complement documentary or instructional content, for example, *Lewis and Clark: An Illustrated History* by Dayton Duncan, based on the PBS television series *Lewis and Clark: The Journey of the Corps of Discovery* by Ken Burns. In library cataloging, the note *Companion volume to:* is included in the bibliographic description, followed by the title of the work on which the book is based. Compare with *tie-in*.

company file   A collection of information about one or more commercial enterprises, usually maintained by a corporation or business library, for the use of employees, business students, investors, career counselors, job seekers, etc. Annual reports, SEC filings, trade catalogs, issues of house organs, news clippings, photographs, etc., are usually organized alphabetically by name of firm. Synonymous with *corporation file*.

company library   *See*: corporation library.

comparative librarianship   The study and analysis of similarities and differences in librarianship as practiced in different countries to identify or clarify underlying principles, expand awareness of successful practices, facilitate cooperation, etc.

comparative table   An alphabetical list of selected topics in a complete or extensive revision of Dewey Decimal Classification, giving the class number in the current edition and the corresponding number used in the preceding edition. In most cases, only numbers for comprehensive works are given. *See also*: *equivalence table*.

compatibility   The ability of computer software to run on hardware other than that for which it was originally designed. Compatibility can be *upward* (or *forward*) in programs capable of running on newer, more powerful machines, or *downward* (*backward*) in programs that will run on older, less powerful machines.

compendium   A work that presents in condensed form the main points of a longer work, prepared by a person other than the original author. Also, a work that treats a broad subject or entire field of knowledge briefly and concisely, sometimes in the form of an outline. Used synonymously with *digest* and *epitome*.

competencies   The capabilities expected of a person hired to perform a specific job or upon successful completion of a course of study or training. In librarianship, the knowledge, skills, and experience necessary to effectively handle professional responsibilities, usually within a specialization, expressed inclusively rather than as a set of minimum standards, as in *Competencies for Librarians Serving Children in Public Libraries* (1999), approved by the board of the Association for Library Service to Children (ALSC) in a revised version.

compilation   A work assembled from the works of various authors, or the various works of a *single* author, into an ordered whole by a person other than the original author, without editorial alteration of the original text. Laws, rules, procedures, regulations, and technical data are particularly subject to compilation. The person who puts such a work together is a *compiler*. In a broader sense, any book or other written work assembled, sometimes over an extended period of time, from materials gathered from a variety of sources, for example, a bibliography or index. Compare with *anthology* and *collection*.

compile   To gather and put together pieces of information or materials from various sources in an orderly structured whole, as in the creation of a bibliography or index. The person who assembles such a work is the *compiler*, and the resulting work is called a *compilation*.

compiler   A person who selects and assembles written or printed material from the works of various persons or bodies, or the various works of a *single* person or body, into a ordered whole, without editorial alteration of the original text. The resulting document is called a *compilation*. When the compiler's name is indicated in or on the chief source of information, it is entered in the statement of responsibility area of the bibliographic record that represents the item in the library catalog. Compare with *editor*.

completeness   An indication of how much of the published run of a serial title is held by a library, usually given in the holdings statement as: *complete* (95–100 percent held), *incomplete* (50–94 percent held), or *scattered* (less than 50 percent held).

complete works   *See*: author's edition.

complex subject   In library classification, a subject that has more than one defining characteristic, for example, the subject "unemployed librarians," which has the facets "employment status" and "occupation." *See also*: preference order.

complimentary copy   Any copy of a book or periodical given free of charge by the publisher, usually to promote sales. The category includes *author's copies*, *desk copies*, *examination copies*, and *review copies*. Faculty members sometimes donate complimentary copies to the library at the institution with which they are affiliated. Abbreviated *comp*.

composer   The original creator of a musical work in any form, entered as author in the bibliographic record created to represent the work in the library catalog. Compare with *arranger* and *performer*.

composite book   A book assembled from portions of other books. Because page size may vary slightly, the edges are apt to be irregular.

composite volume   A bound volume containing two or more separately published works, for example, a collection of brochures or music scores.

composite work   An original work produced as the result of a collaboration between two or more authors or composers in which the contribution of each is a separate and distinct part of a planned whole (*example*: **Festschrift**). Compare with *joint author*. *See also*: *shared responsibility*.

composition   The putting together of words to express an idea, sentiment, thesis, analysis, or conclusion, as in a work of poetry or prose, or in the form of a writing exercise assigned as school work. In a musical composition, the message is expressed in musical notation. Also refers to the piece of writing or music that is the result of such activity.

In printing, the process of preparing copy, assembling type, and making up type and display matter into pages. In letterpress, these tasks are accomplished by the *compositor*.

In medieval manuscript illumination, the overall design of a page or miniature, especially the *ensemble* formed by its parts.

compositor   The worker responsible for setting (*composing*) the type used to print a book or other publication. In letterpress, the compositor holds the *composing stick* in his left hand and removes the individual elements of type, called *sorts*, each bearing an individual letter or other character, from the *case* with his right hand, assembling each line in sequence until the stick is full and ready to be transferred to a tray called a *galley*. The compositor is also responsible for making up the galleys into pages, a process that includes inserting display matter, dividing the matter into page lengths, adding running heads, page numbers, footnotes, etc., and imposing the pages in a frame called a *chase*, which, when *locked up*, constitutes a *forme* ready to be placed on the bed of the press for printing.

compound name   A name formed by joining two or more proper names with a hyphen (*example*: **Marie-Louise**), conjunction (**Simon & Schuster**), or preposition (**Alcuin of York**). *See also*: *compound surname*.

compound subject heading   A subject heading consisting of two or more words that together represent a single concept (*example*: "Book reviewing") or two related concepts ("Libraries and adult education"). In some cases, semantic factoring yields false drops (School + Library → "Library school" and "School library").

compound surname   A surname composed of two or more proper names, usually joined by a hyphen (*example*: **Smith-Bannister**), preposition (**Ruiz de Alarcón**), or conjunction (**Ortega y Gasset**). In *AACR2*, compound surnames are entered under the element preferred by the person, with cross-references from the other elements, for example, **Lloyd George, David, 1863–1945** with a reference from George, David Lloyd, his correct paternal surname. Hyphenated surnames are entered under the first element (**Bourke-White, Margaret, 1904–1971**).

comprehensive   All-inclusive or all-encompassing. An index, bibliographic database, or other work of reference compiled with the stated goal of covering all possible aspects of a subject or all the published literature on a subject or in a field or discipline. In bibliography, an attempt to list of *all* the works that meet the criteria for inclusion established by the bibliographer as to author, subject, publication type, currency, etc. The opposite of *selective*.

comprehensive number   In Dewey Decimal Classification, a class number (often identified by a "Class here comprehensive works" note) covering all the components of the subject treated within the discipline, whether those components are represented by a span of consecutive class numbers or distributed throughout the schedule or table, for example, **305.2** representing the heading "Age groups," also used for comprehensive works on the generation gap (DDC).

compression   *See*: data compression.

comp time   *See*: flextime.

compulsory arbitration   The process in which representatives of organized labor and management, having reached an impasse in contract negotiations, submit their differences to a legally designated *arbitrator* or *arbitration board* authorized to hear arguments from both sides on unresolved issues and reach a final binding decision. Both sides are required to accept the outcome. *See also*: *collective bargaining agreement*.

compulsory retirement   Mandatory retirement at a fixed age, usually established by the employer and stipulated in its personnel policy. Compulsory retirement is a controversial legal issue in the United States. Organizations with no mandatory retirement age may offer periodic retirement incentives to longtime employees, usually to reduce payroll costs.

computer crime   *See*: cybercrime.

computer file   Data or programs encoded in machine-readable format for processing by a computer. Data files stored on a computer are usually organized by topic or other characteristic in directories and subdirectories. Synonymous with *machine-readable data file*.

computer literacy   The skills required to retrieve information efficiently and communicate effectively using computer hardware and software, based on a conceptual understanding of computer technology and how it can be used to accomplish specific tasks, including an awareness of its inherent limitations, as well as its advantages. Because most hardware and software are progressively upgraded, an ongoing effort is required of the user to remain computer literate. Compare with *information literacy*.

computer output microform (COM)   Computer output produced directly on microfiche or microfilm without ever having been printed on paper. A device called a *COM recorder* converts digital data into a form that can be read by the human eye before recording it on film. *See also*: *computer output microform catalog*.

computer output microform catalog   A library catalog produced directly on microfiche or microfilm from a file of machine-readable bibliographic records, using a special recording device called a *COM recorder. Comcatalog*s are more compact than card catalogs, but a microform reader-printer machine is required to display and print individual catalog records. Prior to the development of online catalogs, this format was preferred for state, regional, and consortial union catalogs.

computer program   A set of instructions written in a programming language to enable a computer to process data, perform operations, and solve logical problems. Synonymous with *software*. *See also*: *application* and *operating system*.

computus text   A medieval manuscript or early printed book devoted to the calculation of time and/or date. The category includes calendars, Easter tables, almanacs, and various astronomical/astrological texts used in medicine and for other purposes, often illustrated with diagrams. Some were designed to be portable (see *vade mecum*). *See also*: *volvelle*.

Comstock, Anthony (1844–1915)   An American reformer with a high school education who in 1873, after serving in the Union army during the Civil War, founded the New York Society for the Suppression of Vice and devoted the rest of his life to waging an aggressive crusade against pornography, abortion, gambling, swindling, medical quackery, and other activities he considered morally offensive. Comstock used his influence to persuade Congress to pass what became known as the "Comstock laws" empowering the U.S. Postal Service to exclude from the mail books and other publications what he considered indecent or obscene, including information about contraception. After Comstock publicly attacked the first American production of George Bernard Shaw's play *Mrs. Warren's Profession*, the British playwright dubbed his rigid views and repressive methods "comstockery," turning his name into a public symbol of censorship based on prudery.

comstockery   *See*: Comstock, Anthony.

concatenate   From the Latin *con* ("together") and *catenare* ("to chain"). To join two or more data fields within a record to create a single field. In a more general sense, to link items together in a series, for example, several related essays or long excerpts for publication in a collection.

concertina   A form of bookbinding in which the spine is continuous with the front and back covers but folded in narrow accordion-style pleats to which the leaves or folios are attached along the peaks or valleys of the folds. Also used synonymously with *accordion fold*. Compare with *zig-zag book*.

concise edition   An edition in which the content of a longer work is stated in the fewest possible words, sometimes aimed at beginners in the field (*example*: *The Concise AACR2* published by ALA Editions). In the concise edition of a dictionary, infrequently used words and phrases in the full edition are omitted, and long definitions may be shortened. In a concise encyclopedia, the text is shortened and less important entries may be dropped entirely. The adjective *concise* is sometimes used in the titles of works *not* based on a longer work to indicate that the content is expressed succinctly. Compare with *compact edition*. *See also*: *abridgment*.

concordance   An alphabetically arranged index of the principal words or selected words in a text, or in the works of an author, giving the precise location of each word in the text, with a brief indication of its context. A *glossarial concordance* includes a brief definition of each term. Concordances are usually devoted to very well known works, such as the Bible, or to the works of a major writer (Chaucer, Shakespeare, etc.). The first Bible concordance was completed in A.D. 1230 under the guidance of Hugo de Saint-Cher while he was Prior of the Dominican Order in France. It was an index to passages in which a word could be found, indicated by book and chapter. Compare with *dictionary*.

condensation   *See*: abridgment.

condensed   A typeface narrower in proportion to its height than the normal version of the same style, used in printing to fit more text than normal in a column or on a page. The opposite of *expanded*. Compare with *full face*.

condensed book   A single volume, usually published in inexpensive hardcover edition, containing abridgments or long extracts from several separately published works, usually of fiction. In the United States, the *Reader's Digest Condensed Book Club* is a prolific distributor of condensed books. Most libraries specify in their collection development policy that works are to be purchased in *unabridged* form.

condensed score   The score of a musical work composed for orchestra or band in which the principal parts, usually organized by type of instrument (woodwind, brass, strings, percussion), are reduced to a minimum number of staves.

condition   The physical state of existence of a book or other document at a particular point in time, indicated in the antiquarian and used book trade by a two-part code (*example*: **VG/G**) in which the first part (**VG**) indicates the condition of the book itself and the second part (**G**) the condition of its dust jacket. A hyphen or dash following the slash indicates that the dust jacket is missing. Antiquarian book dealers grade the condition of hardcover books as follows:

As New/Mint—in the same flawless condition as when published (no defects, missing pages, or ownership marks); dust jacket in perfect condition (no chips, marks, or tears).

Fine (F or FN)—nearly new but not as crisp and clean as mint; small defects in dust jacket are noted.

Very Good (VG)—shows some signs of wear but has no tears in paper or binding; defects are noted.

Good (G)—an obviously worn book in which all the pages or leaves are present; defects must be noted.

Fair—worn but all pages present; may lack endpapers, half title, etc.; binding and jacket also show signs of wear; defects must be noted.

Poor—text complete but so worn that it can be sold only as a reading copy; missing parts must be noted.

Booksellers may use a simpler letter system for grading used paperbacks. *See also*: *as issued, brittle, chipped, cracked, damaged, doctored, dog-eared, fallen in, foxing, mildew, rubbed, shaken, sunned, thumbed, warping, water-damaged, with all faults*, and *worming*.

conference   A formal meeting of a group of individuals, or representatives of various bodies, for the purpose of discussing topics and/or making decisions on issues of mutual interest, for example, the Charleston Conference, an annual meeting of librarians, publishers, and vendors. When published collectively, any papers presented at such a meeting are known as *proceedings*. Abbreviated *conf.* Compare with *workshop*. *See also*: *conference name*, *library conference*, and *preconference*.

Also refers to a formal meeting of the representatives constituting the legislative or governing authority of a corporate body, usually for the purpose of discussing and acting on matters of importance to the organization.

conference name   The official name of a meeting, conference, workshop, symposium, exhibition, exposition, festival, athletic contest, scientific expedition, etc., used as the name heading in cataloging any publication issued in its name. Form of heading is subject to authority control.

conference proceedings   *See*: proceedings.

confidentiality   In the delivery of library services, the right of patrons to have the nature of their research and library transactions remain private. Under the guidance of the *ALA Code of Ethics*, librarians and library staff members are encouraged to "protect each library user's right to privacy and confidentiality with respect to information sought or received and resources consulted, borrowed, acquired or transmitted." For this reason, automated circulation systems are designed to delete from the patron record all indication that a specific item has been borrowed once it has been returned to the library and to limit access to borrower accounts to authorized personnel. *See also*: *Library Awareness Program* and USA Patriot Act.

configuration   The physical arrangement and functional relationships of the various components of a computer system, usually established to meet the needs and preferences of its users. The term *configurability* has been coined to refer to the ease with which a computer system can be modified or customized to meet changing needs and requirements.

conjoint leaves   Two leaves formed by one piece of parchment, vellum, or paper, usually folded lengthwise down the center. In a book, they may be bound into a section in such a way that they are not adjacent in the resulting sequence of leaves but when traced through the back of the volume are found to be of a single piece, for example, in a 16-page signature, pages 3–4 (leaf 2) would be the *conjugate* of pages 13–14 (leaf 7), and vice versa. Compare with *singleton*.

conjugate   *See*: conjoint leaves.

connect time   The length of time a user is logged on to a remote computer network or system. Some Internet service providers began by charging subscribers on the basis of connect time, but most ISPs now provide unlimited access for a fixed monthly fee. Connect time is still used by some database vendors as the basis for billing (*example*: **DIALOG**).

Connexion   An OCLC interface that provides one-stop access to integrated cataloging tools and to *WorldCat*, the world's largest online union catalog and bibliographic database. Functions of the OCLC CORC service, CatExpress, and other options, such as Dewey services, are included in *Connexion*. The interface is available in browser and client versions. URL: www.oclc.org/connexion.

CONSER An acronym for Cooperative Online Serials, a cooperative online serials cataloging program that began in the early 1970s as a project to convert manual serials cataloging to machine-readable format. Since then it has evolved into a program for creating and maintaining high-quality bibliographic records for serial publications. CONSER also establishes standards for serials.

Residing within the OCLC Online Union Catalog, the CONSER database is maintained by program members, which include the national libraries of the United States and Canada and their respective ISSN centers; selected academic, U.S. federal, and special libraries; participants in the U.S. Newspaper Program (USNP); and selected library associations, subscription services, and abstracting and indexing services. CONSER is a component of the Program for Cooperative Cataloging (PCC). URL: lcweb.loc.gov/acq/conser/homepage.html.

conservation The use of physical or chemical methods to ensure the survival of manuscripts, books, and other documents, for example, the storage of materials under controlled environmental conditions or the treatment of mildew-infected paper with a chemical inhibitor. Non-invasive techniques are preferred as a means of preserving items in their original condition. In a more general sense, any measures taken to protect archival or library collections from damage or deterioration, including initial examination, documentation, treatment, and preventive care supported by research. A person educated, trained, and experienced in such procedures is a *conservator*. See *Conservation OnLine (CoOL)* at: palimpsest.stanford.edu. *See also*: *conservation binding* and *conservation center*.

conservation binding Binding or rebinding intended to ensure the long-term survival of a manuscript or book while maintaining the integrity of its original form, as opposed to binding or rebinding for appearance or durability regardless of the consequences for conservation. Ideally, no adhesives are used in contact with the book block, and the materials selected are as stable as possible.

conservation center An organization that specializes in the protection and rehabilitation of printed and photographic materials, especially damaged or deteriorating items. Conservation centers support the enhancement of preservation programs in libraries, archives, museums, and other historical and cultural organizations. Some conservation centers also provide disaster assistance, for example, the Northeast Document Conservation Center in Andover, Massachusetts (www.nedcc.org).

conservator *See*: conservation.

consignment list *See*: box list.

consistency The quality of being in agreement or conformity with previous or existing practice. Catalog code is adopted to ensure that bibliographic description and classification remain *consistent* over time and across participating libraries. Standards are created to govern the form in which bibliographic information is recorded and displayed. Style manuals are written to encourage consistency of citation in scholarly communication.

In indexing, the degree of similarity between the index terms (subject headings or descriptors) assigned to the same item or document by different indexers or at different times by the same indexer.

consolidated shipment   In the book trade, a batch of materials sent by a publisher, jobber, or other vendor to a library or bookseller that includes both recently ordered titles and items on back order, combined to reduce shipping costs.

consolidation   The merger of two or more separately administered libraries, or organizational units within a library, into one unit under a single administration, usually for reasons of efficiency and/or economy or to improve quality of service.

consortium   An association of independent libraries and/or library systems established by formal agreement, usually for the purpose of resource sharing. Membership may be restricted to a specific geographic region, type of library (public, academic, special), or subject specialization. One of the leading examples in the United States is OhioLINK, which includes Ohio's college and university libraries and the Ohio State Library. Plural: *consortia*. Compare with *network*.

conspectus   A survey of a topic or body of literature that takes a general or comprehensive view of the subject. Also, a summary or digest that retains the basic pattern or structure of a larger work but condenses the content considerably.

In libraries, a method of uniform collection assessment developed in North America in 1979 to facilitate resource sharing. The system uses codes to survey strengths, levels of difficulty, linguistic and geographical coverage, etc., recorded on worksheets in subject areas based on Library of Congress Classification. In 1982, the Research Libraries Group initiated the RLG Conspectus Online to provide electronic access to data on the collections of research libraries in the United States. The system was subsequently adopted by the Association of Research Libraries for its North American Collection Inventory Project (NCIP). It has also been adapted by the National Library of Canada and is used in the UK, Australia, and some European countries. In the 1990s, after the Western Library Network (WLN) developed PC software that enables libraries to develop and maintain local collection assessment databases, use of RLG Conspectus Online dwindled, and the files were removed from the *Research Libraries Information Network* (RLIN) database in 1997.

constituency   The persons represented by a library or library system when it seeks funding for daily operations, new programs, and capital improvements and when it lobbies for legislation favorable to its interests. Successful library administration depends on winning the approval of the library's *external* constituency (voters, users, supporters, etc.) through quality of service, public relations, and community outreach programs. A library also has an *internal* constituency consisting of its employees and management. *See also*: *library advocate*.

consultant   A person with knowledge and experience in a specialized field, hired by a library or other institution to analyze a problem and provide professional or technical advice concerning possible solutions, especially when the required level of expertise is not available within the organization or the opinion of an outsider is desirable. A consultant may also participate in the planning and implementation phase of a recommended change.

consumer guide A publication containing practical information and advice for prospective purchasers concerning the quality of products and services available in the market place. Some consumer guides are published serially (*example*: ***Consumer Reports Buying Guide***). High-demand consumer guides may be shelved in the reference section of a library, sometimes in ready reference. Used synonymously with *buying guide*.

container A box or holder designed for storing a bibliographic item, group of items, or part of an item, for example, a *pull-case*, *slipcase*, or *solander*. Physically separable from its contents, a container can be open or lidded. Compare with *physical carrier*. *See also*: *archival box* and *pull*.

conte The French term for a narrative tale or short story of the medieval period, originally dealing with events of an imaginative nature (*example*: ***Guigemar*** by Marie de France, as distinct from her *lais*). In modern usage, the term is associated with any brief story of a few printed pages, regardless of genre. *See also*: *short short story*.

contemporary In the antiquarian and used book trade, a work published within the most recent decade. Also refers to a book in which all the parts, particularly the illustrations and binding, were created at the time the edition was published and to an author inscription dated the year of publication.

content The essential matter or substance of a written work or discourse, as opposed to its form or style. In a more general sense, *all* the ideas, topics, facts, or statements contained in a book or written work. Synonymous in this sense with *subject matter*. Also refers to the matter that is the subject of a course of study. Compare with *contents*. *See also*: *content analysis* and *editorial content*.

content analysis Close analysis of the explicit and implicit message of a work or body of communicated information through classification and evaluation of the important concepts, symbols, and themes it addresses to determine its meaning and account for the effect it has on its audience.

content designator Characters used as tags, indicators, and subfield codes in a machine-readable bibliographic record to identify or provide additional information about the data elements of which it is composed. *See also*: *parallel content*.

content enrichment Information added to the bibliographic description of an item not included in the original machine-readable record format, for example, image of cover or dust jacket, table of contents, first page or chapter, excerpts from or links to reviews, biographical information about the author(s) and/or illustrator, etc. Synonymous with *record enrichment*.

content rating A labeling system that uses ranks, grades, or classes to index media content, primarily as a means of controlling access by minors to material considered suitable only for adults. In the United States, most motion pictures produced for theatrical distribution are rated by the Motion Picture Association of America (MPAA) according to a voluntary system introduced in 1968, using five categories to indicate the age-appropriateness of movie content: **G**: General Audiences; **PG**: Parental Guidance; **PG-13**: Parents Strongly Cautioned; **R**: Restricted (anyone under 17 must be accompanied by a parent or adult guardian); and **NC-17**: No One 17 and Under Admitted.

In response to growing evidence that viewing violence on television has a negative effect on the psychological development of children and adolescents, Congress included a provision for "Parental Choice in Television Programming" in the *Telecommunications Act of 1996 (TCA)* to give parents greater control over content available on their home television receivers. The legislation required manufacturers to include a V-chip in new TV sets and recommended that the television industry develop a voluntary rating system readable by the V-chip. In January 1997, entertainment industry executives began implementing "TV Parental Guidelines," a controversial four-level rating system based on the MPAA movie ratings. Many child advocacy organizations preferred ratings modeled on the premium channel system, designed to indicate the amount of sex, violence, and vulgar language by such labels as: **SC**: Strong Sexual Content; **MV**: Mild Violence; **AL**: Adult Language; etc. In July 1997, the industry and public advocacy groups agreed on a compromise that adds content indicators to age-based guidelines.

Video games, software, and the Internet have created additional pressure for ratings and generated debate over descriptive versus evaluative labeling. The Internet Content Rating Association (www.icra.org), a global consortium of representatives from the Internet industry and the public sector, has focused on describing Web site content, leaving judgment concerning appropriateness for the child to the parent. Also at issue is whether ratings should be administered by a neutral third party or by individuals involved in producing and/or distributing Internet content. ICRA is developing a system of voluntary, descriptive self-ratings to operate within the PICS open labeling platform. Compare with *filtering*.

contents   All the divisions, chapters, articles, or individual works contained in a book, periodical, or other publication, usually listed in order of appearance with locators (page numbers) in the *table of contents* in the front matter of a book or on a page near the front of an issue of a periodical. Compare with *content*.

Also refers to all the items physically contained in a box, binder, case, or holder designed for loose materials, for example, a pamphlet file or portfolio.

contents note   A note in the bibliographic record for a book listing its major divisions (books, chapters, etc.) or the works contained in it (essays, interviews, short stories, poems, plays, etc.), usually by title in order of appearance in the text.

context   In the most general sense, the entire situation, background, or environment relevant to an event, action, statement, work, etc. In a literary sense, the parts of a sentence, paragraph, or text that occur just before and after a specific word, phrase, or passage and determine its precise meaning. Quoting *out of context* may give a misleading impression of the intentions of the original speaker or author. Context is included in certain types of keyword indexing (see *KWAC*, *KWIC*, and *KWOC*).

context-sensitive   In computing, an interface designed to provide assistance to the user at the point when help is needed, as opposed to a program that provides a general help screen that the user must locate and navigate to find instructions or advice about how to solve a problem. *See also*: *wizard*.

contingency fund   A special fund set aside in a library budget to cover unanticipated expenditures and emergencies. Contingency funds are commonly included in budgets for major capital improvements to allow for possible cost overruns.

contingency plan   An alternative plan of action prepared in advance to be put into effect should it become impossible to implement normal arrangements or when certain predetermined conditions arise. An example might be the decision of a library to cut spending on monographs rather than cancel serials subscriptions in the event of an unexpected budget cut. Compare with *disaster plan* and *emergency plan*.

continuation   A book or other uncompleted work continued by another writer, usually after the death of the original author. Compare with *sequel*. *See also*: *posthumous*.

Also, a work issued as a supplement to one previously published or a part issued in continuance of a monographic set or series. Libraries normally place such materials on *continuation order*. In the catalog record for such a publication, a library's holdings are indicated in an open entry for a publication that is ongoing or in a closed entry for one that has ceased.

continuation order   An order placed by a library with a publisher or vendor to automatically supply until further notice each succeeding issue, volume, or part of a serial or series as published. If a continuation order does not specify a maximum price, it is assumed that the item may be shipped regardless of price. Some publishers offer a discount on continuation orders (usually 5 to 10 percent). Annuals (*example*: **Literary Market Place**) and reference serials are often purchased in this way. A special order record is created and maintained to track receipt of individual items. Sometimes used synonymously with *standing order*. *See also*: *open entry*.

continuation order discount   *See*: discount.

continuing education   Formal instruction for persons who have completed an academic degree, moved into the workplace, and wish to keep up with changes and innovations in their field. For librarians, continuing education opportunities include courses offered online or traditionally through a library school, training provided by commercial vendors, and workshops sponsored by bibliographic service centers and library associations, as well as independent study.

continuing resource   A publication in any medium, defined in *AACR2 2002* as issued over time with no predetermined conclusion, including bibliographic resources issued successively in discrete parts and integrating resources into which updates are incorporated without remaining discrete. Examples include serials (periodicals, newspapers, etc.), monographic series, and updating loose-leaf services, databases, and Web sites.

continuous pagination   Numbering the pages of two or more volumes or parts of a set, or the issues of a periodical comprising a volume, in a single unbroken sequence, beginning with number one. Compare with *separately paginated*. *See also*: *journal pagination*.

continuous revision   The process of updating a textbook or reference work by revising a portion of the text and/or illustrations with each printing, as opposed to updating the entire content of the work all at once and publishing the result as a revised edition.

contour map   A topographic map that indicates relief by continuous lines, traditionally shown in brown ink, connecting points of equal elevation, with or without shading. The number of feet represented by the intervals between contour lines varies with the scale of the map. A topographic map of the sea floor is called a *bathymetric map*. Compare with *relief map*.

contract   A legally binding written agreement between an employer and (1) an individual librarian or other member of the library staff or (2) librarians and/or staff organized in a collective bargaining unit for the purpose of negotiating terms of employment (salaries and wages, duties and responsibilities, promotion and tenure, vacation and sick leave, benefits, etc.), usually for a specified period of time. *See also*: *book contract* and *breach of contract*.

contraction   A shortened form of a word or phrase used for brevity in place of the whole, formed by the omission of one or more letters or sounds, usually replaced by a hyphen (**e-mail** for *electronic mail*) or an apostrophe (**isn't** for *is not*). Compare with *abbreviation* and *elision*.

contraries   Impurities in the rag, waste paper, or other fibrous material from which paper is made, usually bits of wool, feathers, or twine, or hard materials such as metal staples, bone, or plastic that must be removed in the papermaking process to maintain quality of product. Contraries occasionally show as blemishes in a sheet of finished paper.

contrast   The degree of difference between the high and low tonal values in a print, photograph, or image on motion picture film, video, or television, maximum contrast being black and white with no intermediate gray tones.

contribution   An article, column, editorial, entry, or other composition written for publication with works by other authors in a serial, reference work, or collection. Usually written by a freelance writer or academic professional, a contribution may be signed or unsigned. *Contributors* are usually listed by name with credentials in the front or back of the issue, volume, or set of volumes that includes their work(s).

contributor   One of several persons, each of whom writes one or more signed or unsigned portions of a book, periodical, or other edited work. A *contribution* may consist of an article or column in a magazine or journal, an essay in a collection, a poem or story in an anthology, an entry in an encyclopedia, or one or more terms and definitions in a dictionary or glossary. Contributors are usually listed by name in the front matter or back matter of a book, on one page of a periodical, or in the last volume of a reference set, alphabetically by name or in the order in which their works appear. Compare with *joint author*.

control field   A field of the MARC record (tagged **00X** with **X** in the range of **1–9**) containing neither indicators nor subfield codes, reserved for a single data element or series of fixed-length data elements identified by the relative position of characters. For example, **field 008** containing 40 characters of encoded information about the record as a whole, such as the date it was entered into the database, frequency of publication, etc. A control field containing a fixed number of characters, as in 008, is called a *fixed field*. Compare with *variable data field*.

control key   A key located in the lower left-hand corner of a standard computer keyboard, usually labeled **Ctrl** or **Ctl**, that can be used simultaneously with one or more other keys to give a specific command, for example, **Ctrl+Alt+Del** to reboot the operating system.

controlled access   Entry into a library, or use of a library collection, that is limited to registered members of the library's user group or some other category of user specifically granted access. The libraries of large private universities may extend access to all or part of their collections only to registered students, faculty, and staff. Use of special collections may be limited to authorized library staff, except by appointment. Compare with *restricted access*. *See also*: *closed stacks*.

controlled vocabulary   An established list of preferred terms from which a cataloger or indexer must select when assigning subject headings or descriptors in the bibliographic record to indicate the content of a work in the library catalog or in an index or bibliographic database. Synonyms are included as *lead-in vocabulary*, with instructions to *see* or *USE* the authorized heading.

     For example, if the authorized subject heading for works about dogs is "Dogs," then all items about dogs will be assigned the heading "Dogs," including a work titled *All about Canines*. A cross-reference to the heading "Dogs" will be made from the term "Canines" to ensure that anyone looking for information about dogs under "Canines" will be directed to the correct heading. Controlled vocabulary is usually listed alphabetically in a subject headings list or thesaurus of indexing terms. The process of creating and maintaining a list of preferred indexing terms is called *vocabulary control*. Synonymous with *controlled terms*. Compare with *free-text search*.

conventional name   A name, distinct from the real or official name by which a thing, place, or corporate body has become known, for example, "Wall Street" for the New York Stock Exchange. Compare with *nickname*.

conventional title   *See*: uniform title.

convention discount   A discount given on orders placed at a publisher's exhibit booth during a conference or convention, usually 10 to 20 percent, with 15 percent the norm. Librarians sometimes compile lists of selected new books prior to attending a major library conference to be prepared to take advantage of the anticipated discount. At the end of the conference, display copies may be sold at an even deeper discount, especially if the dust jackets are no longer in perfect condition. Synonymous with *show discount*.

convention issue　An issue of a trade journal devoted to a forthcoming conference or convention, providing a brief description of the program, information about exhibits, registration procedures, advice about travel and accommodations, and whom to contact for more details. Follow-up articles usually appear in the issue immediately following the event.

conversion table　A cataloging tool that lists the class numbers of one classification system in order of notation, giving the corresponding class number in a second classification system, usually in a separate column on the same line, and sometimes vice versa, for example, Mona L. Scott's *Conversion Tables* published in three separate volumes by Libraries Unlimited, converting (1) Library of Congress Classification to Dewey Decimal Classification and Library of Congress Subject Headings, (2) DDC to LCC and LCSH, and (3) LCSH to LCC and DDC. Conversion tables facilitate reclassification, especially in projects involving very large collections or entire libraries.

cookbook　A type of how-to book that gives instructions for preparing food, including recipes for specific dishes, notes about tools and ingredients, weights and measures, and sometimes directory information for culinary suppliers. Most cookbooks are specialized, focusing on a particular cuisine, type of dish, or category of food. Cookbooks for beginners often include color illustrations, but those intended by the author to be comprehensive are usually sparsely illustrated. Most public libraries include a diverse selection of cookbooks in the nonfiction section. Synonymous with *recipe book*.

In computing, a how-to manual that often includes boilerplate code, templates, style sheets, and other software tools, assembled to help implement a particular standard or technology.

cookie　A small string of data created by a Web server, transmitted to a computer connected to the Internet, and stored in the cookie file of its Web browser. Originally intended to reduce the amount of time required for Web site registration by retrieving from the user's hard drive input provided in a previous visit, cookies can also be used to determine what a user viewed on previous visits and on visits to other Web sites. Potential invasiveness has made cookies the subject of debate over privacy. Web browser software can be set to allow the user to accept or reject a cookie at the time it is offered or to reject *all* cookies automatically. "Cookie manager" software provides a wider range of options.

cooperative cataloging　An arrangement in which a library or library system agrees to follow established cataloging practices and work in automated systems or utilities that facilitate the creation of bibliographic and authority records in a form that can be shared with other libraries. In North America, cooperative cataloging is facilitated by the uniform cataloging practices established under *AACR2R*. OCLC is the bibliographic utility used for cooperative cataloging in the United States. *See also*: *National Union Catalog of Manuscript Collections*.

Cooperative Online Resource Catalog (CORC)　A Web-based metadata project undertaken by OCLC in 1998 to facilitate access to electronic resources, CORC provided a catalog of bibliographic records for electronic resources, an authority file, a path-finder database, and an enhanced version of Dewey Decimal Classification called *WebDewey*. The *CORC* toolkit was designed to support flexible automated bibliographic record creation, authority control, URL maintenance, subject heading assignment, and pathfinder creation. CORC functions are now available in the integrated OCLC cataloging interface called *Connexion*.

cooperative reference   Reference services provided by referring the user or the user's question(s) to library or information personnel at another institution, according to a formally established system of protocols, rather than on an informal case-by-case basis. When such services are provided digitally, the service is known as *collaborative reference*. To assist libraries in establishing and evaluating cooperative reference service, the Reference and User Services Association (RUSA) of the American Library Association has developed *Guidelines for Cooperative Reference Service Policy Manuals* available online at: www.ala.org.

coordinate   One of a number of quantities used to indicate the position of a point, line, or plane with reference to a fixed system, such as a grid. On maps and charts of the surface of the earth and other heavenly bodies, the quantities are usually degrees, minutes, and seconds of *latitude* and *longitude* or angles of declination and ascension.

coordinate indexing   *See*: post-coordinate indexing.

COPA   See: Child Online Protection Act.

Coptic binding   The earliest form of codex binding, in use from the 4th to the 11th century, developed in the Coptic monasteries of Egypt and North Africa. Gatherings of papyrus or vellum bifolia, sewn through the fold, were linked together by a chain stitch running at intervals perpendicular to the binding edge. The boards were made of wood or layers of discarded papyrus glued together (*cartonnage*) and attached to the book block by knotting the ends of the chain stitches through holes pre-bored along the inner edge. The spine was lined with a strip of linen, vellum, or leather, with the endbands extending onto the boards. Spine and boards were covered in goat-skin decorated with blind tooling or pierced leatherwork.

Coptic binding spread to northwestern Europe in the early Christian period, the 7th-century *Stonyhurst Gospel* being the earliest-known English example. The method has been revived in the United States for sewing single sheets (see *Non-Adhesive Binding Volume IV: Smith's Sewing Single Sheets*, Keith Smith Books, 2001).

co-publishing   The simultaneous publication of an edition by two or more publishers, usually in different countries, to achieve economies of scale when the home market is not sufficient to guarantee a reasonable profit. Typically, a work is printed in the country of the originating publisher and then supplied to a publisher in another country with a title page bearing the imprint of the second publisher (or both). Subsequent printings may occur independently or cooperatively. In journal publishing, the result may be separate editions for each country or a bilingual edition marketed in both countries. Compare with *export edition*.

copy   To make a duplicate of a document or other work by hand or any other process. Many early books were produced in only one copy. In medieval Europe, devotional works and the classics were laboriously hand-copied by monks and *copyists* known as scribes. Modern methods rely on printing and reprography. In data processing, to reproduce data from one file, location, or storage medium to another without alteration. Compare with *original*.

Also refers to a single specimen of a manuscript or printed document. Libraries sometimes purchase heavily used items in multiple copies. Copy number is indicated in the catalog record and at the end of the call number, beginning with the second copy. In limited editions, the total number of copies printed and the number of each copy are recorded in the certificate of issue, usually on the verso of the leaf preceding the title page. *See also*: *aberrant copy*, *advance copy*, *association copy*, *author's copy*, *complimentary copy*, *desk copy*, *distribution copy*, *examination copy*, and *review copy*.

In publishing, matter that is to be typeset in preparation for printing or incorporated as text into a hypertext document. *See also*: *fair copy* and *printer's copy*.

In computer applications, an operation in which data stored in memory is transferred elsewhere (usually to another location within the same document, to another document, or to another application) without being erased from memory. Compare with *cut-and-paste*.

copy card   A small plastic debit card available for purchase from a vending machine or at the circulation desk of a library that can be used in photocopiers and microform reader-printer machines instead of cash to pay for paper copies of documents.

copy cataloging   Adaptation of a pre-existing bibliographic record (usually found in OCLC, *RLIN*, NUC, or some other bibliographic database) to fit the characteristics of the item in hand, with modifications to correct obvious errors and minor adjustments to reflect locally accepted cataloging practice, as distinct from *original cataloging* (creating a completely new record from scratch). Synonymous with *derived cataloging*.

copy editor   A person employed by a publisher to meticulously edit and mark up an author's typescript in preparation for printing, usually in accordance with house style as to spelling, abbreviation, punctuation, grammar, syntax, usage, citation style, etc. A good copy editor also checks the accuracy of facts, quotations, and citations and is alert to possibilities of libel, plagiarism, etc.

copyist   *See*: scribe.

copy number   When multiple copies of the same edition are added to a library collection, the cataloger numbers each copy sequentially, beginning with the second. In the catalog record for the edition, each copy is listed separately in the holdings, with the copy number given at the end of the call number, following the abbreviation *cop*. It is also printed at the end of the call number on the spine label attached to the outside of the physical item.

copyright   The exclusive legal rights granted by a government to an author, editor, compiler, composer, playwright, publisher, or distributor to publish, produce, sell, or distribute copies of a literary, musical, dramatic, artistic, or other work, within certain limitations (*fair use* and *first sale*). Copyright law also governs the right to prepare derivative works, reproduce a work or portions of it, and display or perform a work in public.

Such rights may be transferred or sold to others and do not necessarily pass with ownership of the work itself. Copyright protects a work in the specific form in which it is created, not the idea, theme, or concept expressed in the work, which other writers are free to interpret in a different way. A work never copyrighted or no longer protected by copyright is said to be in the *public domain. See also*: *copyright compliance, copyright depository, copyright notice, copyright piracy, digital rights, infringement, intellectual property, international copyright*, and *Public Lending Right.*

In 1710, the first copyright law in England gave protection to the author for 14 years, renewable for a second period of equal length. In the United States, the first federal copyright law, passed in 1790, also provided protection for 14 years, renewable for an additional 14 years if the author survived the first term. Congress extended the term in 1831 and 1909, then changed the duration of copyright to life of the author plus 50 years, effective January 1, 1978. In 1998, the controversial *Copyright Term Extension Act (CTEA)* lengthened the period to life of the author plus 70 years for works published on or after January 1, 1978, the same as in Europe. For anonymous works, pseudonymous works, and works for hire the period is 95 years from year of first publication or 120 years from year of creation, whichever expires first. Library and consumer groups including the American Library Association filed amicus briefs in support of a challenge (*Eldred v. Ashcroft*), but on January 15, 2003 the U.S. Supreme Court upheld the *CTEA* by a 7–2 vote. Copyright is controlled by Congress and administered by the U.S. Copyright Office of the Library of Congress. International copyright is governed by the *Berne Convention* and the *Universal Copyright Convention.*

Notice of copyright usually appears on the verso of the title page of a book in the form of a small "c" inside a circle ©, the abbreviation "Copr.," or the word "Copyright" followed by the year of publication, the name of the owner of copyright, and the phrase "all rights reserved." Because copyright law is highly complex, accurate interpretation often requires the advice of a legal specialist. The Stanford University Libraries maintain a Web site on *Copyright & Fair Use* at: fairuse.stanford.edu. *See also*: *Copyright Clearance Center*, Digital Millennium Copyright Act, and *International Copyright Information Centre.*

Copyright Clearance Center, Inc. (CCC)   The largest licenser of photocopy reproduction rights in the world, CCC was established in 1978 by a group of authors, publishers, and users of copyrighted material in an effort to facilitate compliance with U.S. copyright law. CCC manages the rights to over 1.75 million works and represents approximately 9,600 publishers and hundreds of thousands of individual authors and creators. URL: www.copyright.com. *See also*: *fair use* and *International Copyright Information Centre.*

copyright compliance   The responsibility of a library to ensure that its interlibrary loan requests, reserve materials, instruction guides, Web pages, etc., conform to existing copyright law. In the OCLC interlibrary loan system, the codes *ccg* ("conforms to copyright guidelines") and *ccl* ("conforms to copyright law") are used by the borrowing library to inform the lending library that a request is compliant. *See also*: *Copyright Clearance Center, Inc.*

copyright date   The year in which a specific work was granted copyright protection, usually printed on the verso of the title page, sometimes following the letter "c" with a circle around it. If more than one copyright date is given, the earliest is the date of the first edition, which is the same as the date of first publication. Subsequent dates indicate revisions in the text of an extent requiring renewal of copyright.

copyright depository   A library designated by law or custom to receive and preserve a specified number of free deposit copies of works published under national copyright law. In the United States, the copyright depository is the U.S. Copyright Office at the Library of Congress. In Great Britain it is the Bodleian Library. In Canada, copyright law is administered by the Canadian Intellectual Property Office (CIPO). Synonymous with *copyright library*.

copyright fee   The payment required by a national copyright depository to register copyright of a creative work, which must be submitted with the completed application form and a deposit copy of the work. Also refers to the fee that must be paid to the holder of copyright in exchange for the right to use all or part of a work in a manner *not* defined under U.S. copyright law as fair use, for example, the right to include a poem or short story in an anthology, or an excerpt or quotation in a published work. *See also*: *permission*.

copyright holder   The person(s) or corporate body possessing the exclusive legal rights granted by a government to publish, produce, sell, or distribute copies of a literary, musical, dramatic, artistic, or other work, within certain limitations (fair use), usually the author, editor, compiler, composer, playwright, publisher, or distributor. In the United States, such rights are granted by the U.S. Copyright Office when a work is registered for copyright. The name of the copyright holder is given in the *copyright notice*, usually printed on the verso of the title page of a book. Synonymous with *copyright owner*.

copyright notice   A formal announcement of legal status appearing conspicuously on all copies of a work protected by copyright, published by authority of the copyright owner. In the United States, it consists of three parts: (1) the symbol "c" inside a small circle © and the abbreviation *Copr.* or the word *Copyright*, followed by (2) year of first publication and (3) name of copyright holder. In printed books, the copyright notice appears on the verso of the title page.

Copyright Office   *See*: U.S. Copyright Office.

copyright page   The page of a book, in most editions the verso of the title page, bearing official notice of copyright, usually the copyright symbol ("c" inside a small circle) or the word *Copyright* or its abbreviation (*Copr.*), followed by year of first publication and name of copyright holder.

copyright piracy   The systematic unauthorized reproduction or use, without permission and recompense, of a work protected by copyright law, usually for the purpose of profiting from such activity. This type of egregious infringement is subject to legal action by the copyright owner(s) in countries that have accepted international copyright agreements, but in countries that have not, the holder of intellectual property rights may have little recourse. *See also*: *pirated edition*.

Copyright Term Extension Act (CTEA)   *See*: copyright.

CORC   *See*: Cooperative Online Resource Catalog.

cords   *See*: sewing supports.

core collection   A collection representative of the basic information needs of a library's primary user group. In public libraries, core collections are selected in anticipation of popular demand and maintained on the basis of usage. In academic libraries, selection is based on curriculum need, and collections are maintained to meet the research interests of students and faculty. Also refers to an initial collection developed for a new library, usually with the aid of standard lists and other selection aids (*example*: ***Books for College Libraries: A Core Collection*** . . . published by the American Library Association).

core curriculum   *See*: curriculum.

core document   An important record, usually one of several, widely regarded as defining a subject because it contains information vital to understanding the topic, for example, the list of *Core Documents of U.S. Democracy* available online from *GPO Access* at: www.gpoaccess.gov/coredocs.html. Print collections of core documents are often shelved in the reference section of a library.

core journal   A scholarly journal that reports original research of such significance to the academic community that the publication is considered indispensable to students, teachers, and researchers in the discipline or subdiscipline. For this reason, it is included in the serials collections of academic libraries supporting curriculum and research in the field (*example*: ***American Historical Review*** in American history). Compare with *primary journal*.

In public libraries, a periodical so essential to meeting the information needs of a wide range of users that it is included in most general serials collections (*example*: ***Scientific American***).

core level cataloging   An encoding level developed for use in the Program for Cooperative Cataloging (PCC) that allows the cataloger to create bibliographic records containing fewer data elements than in *full level cataloging* but more than in *minimal level cataloging*. Fields of fixed length are fully coded, but a list of exceptions applies to certain fields of variable length.

core list   A list of the best books, periodicals, etc., on a subject or in a discipline, usually compiled as a selection aid for librarians whose responsibilities include collection development (*example*: **Core List of Best Books and Journals in Education** by Nancy O'Brien and Emily Fabiano). Although useful when first published, such lists become outdated within a few years. *See also*: *core collection*.

corner   The juncture of two edges of the cover of a book. Corners can be rounded, square, or mitered and are sometimes covered in contrasting material, such as leather or heavier cloth, for protection and decorative effect. To make *library corners*, the turn-in is folded; on *Dutch corners*, it is cut. *See also*: *boss*, *cornerpiece*, and *Oxford corners*.

cornering   A binding technique in which the outer corners of the boards of a book are rounded before the covering material is applied.

cornerpiece   In bookbinding of the late 16th and early 17th centuries, an ornamental design tooled or stamped on each of the four corners of a book cover, sometimes as part of a design that includes a matching centerpiece. Also refers to metal corners attached to the binding of a book to protect it from wear, sometimes with a decorative centerpiece and matching clasps. In modern usage, a temporary guard made of metal, plastic, or some other hard material, attached to the corners of a book to protect against damage in shipping. Compare with *boss* and *shoe*.

Also refers to an ornament or flourish printed or drawn by hand at the corner of a border around a portion of printed or handwritten text.

corpora   Initial capital letters inserted by a rubricator in blank spaces left for that purpose by the copyist in a manuscript or by the printer in an early printed book.

corporate author   A corporate body such as an association, company, government agency, institution, or nonprofit organization in whose name a publication is issued. In libraries, the official name or title of such a body is used as the corporate name in cataloging publications issued in its name. Compare with *personal author*.

corporate body   A commercial enterprise, government agency, association, nonprofit organization, institution, or group of individuals identified by a collective name that has the capacity to act as a single entity, including territorial authorities and groups constituted as meetings, conferences, congresses, expeditions, exhibitions, etc., whether operating or defunct. In libraries, the official name or title of such a body is used as the corporate name in cataloging publications issued in its name. *See also*: *related body* and *subordinate body*.

corporate name   The official name by which a corporate body such as an association, commercial enterprise, government agency, institution, or organization is identified, used by libraries in cataloging publications issued in its name (*example*: **American Library Association**). Form of entry is subject to authority control. Synonymous with *collective name*. *See also*: *geographic name* and *personal name*.

corporation library   A type of special library established and maintained as a unit within an incorporated company or organization to meet the information needs of its employees and facilitate the achievement of its mission and goals. Some corporation libraries also serve as the repository for the official records of the organization. For internal security reasons, most corporation libraries are closed to the public except by special appointment. Synonymous with *company library*. Compare with *business library*.

correction   A change made in a manuscript or proof, usually to correct an error of spelling, punctuation, or grammar or to insert or delete a word, phrase, sentence, etc. Word processing software makes correction easy. In letterpress printing, type has to be reset. In medieval manuscripts, the scribe, stationer, or reader made corrections by erasing and rewriting, by inserting omissions in margins, by crossing out repetitions, or by adding an unobtrusive row of dots under the word or phrase to be deleted (expunction). Errors were detected by comparing the text against the exemplar or another copy, but in some cases corrections were based on independent judgment.

correctional library   A type of special library maintained inside the walls of a prison or other correctional institution for the use of inmates and staff, usually managed by a *prison librarian* (*example*: **Federal Bureau of Prisons Library**). The collection usually includes general interest titles for recreational reading, educational and vocational materials, and legal resources. Synonymous with *prison library*.

correspondence   Letters, memoranda, and other recorded messages exchanged between two or more people, usually archived with the personal papers of the *correspondents*. Often used in preparing in biographical and historical works, correspondence may be published separately or with other papers. In *AACR2*, collected correspondence is cataloged under the name that appears first on the title page, with an added entry for each of the other correspondents and for the editor or compiler. *See also*: *letterbook*.

corrigenda   *See*: errata.

corrupted text   A text in which words or passages have been added, deleted, or altered to suggest a meaning other than the one intended by the original author. In medieval manuscripts, this was sometimes the result of accidental copying errors, but in modern texts tampering may be done by an individual or organization for other purposes, such as propaganda or public relations. *See also*: *censorship* and *expurgated*.

COSLA   *See*: Chief Officers of State Library Agencies.

cost-effective   A decision or practice that reduces expenditure in relation to the amount of resources invested (time, money, materials, etc.). Monetary savings can be difficult to determine when costs are intangible, intermittent, or incurred over an extended period of time.

cost-recovery   A product or service offered at a price that allows the vendor or provider to cover costs incurred without generating a profit, for example, document delivery service in most academic libraries.

cottage binding   A style of leather binding, popular in England during the 17th and 18th centuries, in which the center panel is surrounded by decoration tooled to resemble the gables of a building, there being no relationship between design of binding and content of work. According to *The Bookman's Glossary* (R.R. Bowker, 1983), this ornamental style, developed by Samuel Mearne, binder to King Charles II, was particularly popular on Bibles and prayer books. Synonymous with *cottage style*.

cottage style   *See*: cottage binding.

Council on Library and Information Resources (CLIR)   Originally named the Council on Library Resources, CLIR is an independent foundation that supports initiatives in preservation awareness, digital libraries, information economics, resources for scholarship, and international developments in library and information science. CLIR publishes the bimonthly newsletter *CLIR Issues*. URL: www.clir.org.

Council on Library Resources (CLR)   *See*: Council on Library and Information Resources.

counter   A long cabinet top, shelf top, or other horizontal work surface of sufficient height to accommodate a person standing in front of it who wishes to transact business with the person standing or sitting behind it. In most libraries, the circulation desk is a long counter near the entrance to the building. In the children's room of a library, countertops (and furniture) are usually lower than normal to accommodate persons of small stature.

    Also, an automatic feature built into the HTML code of a Web page, or into the software running some other type of online resource, that allows the number of visits or uses to be counted for statistical purposes.

    In typography, the space enclosed by the strokes of a unit of type, for example, the center of the "p" or the space between the vertical strokes of the "h."

COUNTER   *See*: Counting Online Usage of Networked Electronic Resources.

countermark   A smaller, secondary watermark on antique papers, usually located in the center or lower center of the half-sheet opposite the watermark, indicating the name of the papermaker and sometimes the date and place of hand manufacture.

countersunk   Said of a depression stamped or impressed on the surface of a book cover to display a label, inlay, or decoration.

counting book   A picture book designed to teach preschool children to count (usually from 1 to 10 or 12) by providing illustrations in which the number of objects displayed on each page or double spread corresponds to the numeral printed with them. Compare with *alphabet book*. *See also*: *horn book*.

Counting Online Usage of Networked Electronic Resources (COUNTER)   An international initiative launched in March 2002 to serve librarians, publishers, and intermediaries by developing more consistent, reliable, and meaningful measures of online resource usage to facilitate the recording and exchange of e-usage statistics. The project initially focused on journals and bibliographic databases but will include other types of networked resources, such as e-books. Librarians can encourage the adoption of this new code of practice by requiring vendors to be COUNTER-compliant in licensing agreements. URL: www.projectcounter.org/about.html.

country code   The top level domain for an Internet site outside the United States, indicated by two alphabetic characters at the end of the address, representing the country or external territory in which the network host is located (*examples*: **.au** for Australia, **.ca** for Canada, **.uk** for Great Britain, **.vg** for British Virgin Islands). Some

Web search engines allow the user to specify country code in a query. Country codes are maintained by the Internet Corporation for Assigned Names and Numbers (www. icann.org). A worldwide list of ISO two-letter country codes is available online at: www.bcpl.net/~jspath/isocodes-table.html.

country of origin   The country in which a book, pamphlet, serial, etc., is published, determined by the geographic location of the editorial office responsible for producing its intellectual content (ALCTS *Serials Acquisitions Glossary*, Chicago, 1993).

country study   A publication that provides factual information about a specific nation, including its history, geography, demography, society and culture(s), economy, government and politics, etc., with statistical information sometimes given in an appendix. Country studies often include at least one map and may be published in series, for example, the Country Studies/Area Handbook Program sponsored by the U.S. Department of the Army and issued by the Federal Research Division of the Library of Congress. Compare with *area study*.

courier   A person or service hired by a library to retrieve materials on request from an off-site storage facility or to transport materials from one library to another within a library system or consortium, as opposed to relying on the postal service or a commercial delivery service.

course catalog   A comprehensive list, usually published annually, of all the courses taught at a school, college, or university during a given academic year, usually arranged by department and course number, with brief descriptions of course content and a list of instructors and their credentials at the end. Institutions offering both undergraduate and graduate programs may publish separate catalogs. Course catalogs for educational institutions in the United States and around the world are available online in *CollegeSource*, a searchable database provided by the Career Guidance Foundation.

course-integrated   Bibliographic instruction designed to complement the content of a specific course of study, integral to completing the library research component embedded in the course. Compare with *course-related*.

coursepack   A collection of readings from a variety of sources, selected by the instructor(s) of an academic course of study to supplement or serve in place of a textbook. The readings are reproduced, usually by a college/university duplicating service or commercial photocopy shop, for sale under a single cover to students enrolled in the course. Kinko's, a leading producer of coursepacks, was sued by eight publishers for violating U.S. copyright law and in the 1991 settlement, the company agreed to pay the plaintiffs $1.875 million and cease producing coursepacks for ten years. In 2003, Kinko's re-entered the coursepack market, promising full compliance with copyright law.

course-related   Bibliographic instruction designed to support the needs and objectives of a specific course of study but not essential to the completeness of the course. Compare with *course-integrated*.

courseware   A computer application designed to assist teachers and librarians in creating Web-based courses and online tutorials, either in conjunction with a traditional textbook or independently of other instructional materials. Courseware requires little knowledge of HTML and may include presentation management software, the ability to include graphics and audio/video files, online chat and threaded discussions, automarked quizzes, course calendaring, and grading (*examples*: **Blackboard** and **WebCT**). Synonymous with *authorware*.

courtesy book   A literary genre popular during the Renaissance devoted to the detailed description of the code of personal conduct, training, and view of life expected of a gentleman, soldier, and courtier by the society in which he lived (*example*: Castiglioni's **The Courtier**).

court hand   The cursive style of writing used by scribes from about A.D. 1100 until the end of the 16th century for making charters, keeping legal records, and writing other official documents, in contrast to the book hand used for copying liturgical, devotional, and literary works in manuscript form. Marc Drogin notes in *Medieval Calligraphy: Its History and Technique* (Allanheld & Schram,1980) that during the early Middle Ages court hands were highly ornate, making them indecipherable to most outsiders, but by the late Middle Ages, they had become models of elegance and clarity.

court library   A large private library housed in a monumental building, similar to the libraries known to have existed in ancient Rome, financed by a wealthy nobleman, aristocratic family, or high-ranking Church dignitary of the Italian Renaissance whose love of books manifested itself in collecting. An expression of the humanist revival of interest in classical culture, court libraries were open for use by outsiders at the discretion of the owner and, according to Konstantinos Staikos (*The Great Libraries: From Antiquity to the Renaissance*, Oak Knoll/British Library, 2000), some even functioned as lending libraries for educated readers.

cover   The outer protective material attached to the sewn, stitched, or adhered leaves of a manuscript or printed publication, consisting in books of two panels (front and back), each attached to an inlay over the spine along a flexible joint. Books covered in cloth, paper, leather, or vellum over stiff boards are bound in *hardcover*. Covers can also be *limp* or *semi-limp*. In *full binding*, the material used to cover the boards is all of a kind (see also *half-binding*, *quarter binding*, and *three-quarter binding*). The cover of a machine-bound book is called a *case*. Books bound in flexible paper covers are called *paperbacks*. Periodicals are almost always issued in *softcover*. **See also**: *all over* and *covers bound in*.

coverage   The extent of a library collection (or section of a collection), or of a catalog, index, abstracting service, database, bibliography, or other finding tool, usually indicated by the number and types of publications indexed and a publication date range. The range of subjects or fields indexed determines the *scope* of such a resource.

Also refers to the amount of attention (time, space, number of commentators, etc.) given a specific topic in the media.

cover letter   A letter of introduction, usually no longer than one page, sent with a resume or *curriculum vitae* when applying for employment. A good cover letter usually indicates that the applicant meets all the qualifications listed in the job posting, and expresses an interest in being considered for the position. In a more general sense, a brief letter of explanation sent with a document.

cover paper   Heavier grades of paper used for the outer cover of pamphlets, trade catalogs, and paperback books. Also, any paper used to cover the outer surface of the boards of a book bound in hardcover. Available in a wide range of colors, cover papers often have a finish designed for durability or to enhance marketability.

cover price   The retail price of a book as suggested by the publisher, usually printed on the dust jacket in hardcover editions or on the back cover in paperback editions. In most cases, cover price is the same as *list price*.

covers bound in   A term used in the book trade to describe a volume in which the original covers are enclosed in a later binding. This usually occurs in rebinding when the bindery decides to retain the original covers as endpapers or flyleaves.

cover story   The article in a magazine or trade journal that corresponds to the headline and illustration on the cover, usually longer and more extensively illustrated than other feature articles in the same issue. Some periodical indexes and bibliographic databases are designed to indicate whether an article is a cover story.

cover title   The title printed or impressed on the cover of a publication as issued by the publisher, which may be a shortened form of the title proper. Compare with *binder's title*. **See also**: *side title*.

CPC   *See*: Canadian Publishers' Council.

CPU   *See*: central processing unit.

cracked   The condition of a book that has developed one or more long, narrow breaks in the cover or down the length of the spine. The usual method of rehabilitation is rebinding. **See also**: *cold-crack*.

cracker   A slang term for a person who tries to gain access to a supposedly secure computer system without proper authorization, usually with malicious or criminal intent. Compare with *hacker*. **See also**: *security*.

crash   In bookbinding, a narrow strip of thin, loosely woven, starched muslin attached with adhesive to the back of a book after the sections have been sewn to help hold them together. In some editions, a strip of kraft paper is applied to the layer of fabric as a liner for added strength. Synonymous with *gauze*, *mull*, and *super* (in the United States).

  In computing, a slang term for the unanticipated breakdown of a system, usually caused by hardware failure, a serious software defect, or a network error. **See also**: *dump*.

crawler   A robot software program that searches "intelligently" for information on the World Wide Web, for example, one that looks for new documents and Web sites by following hypertext links from one server to another, indexing the files it finds according to pre-established criteria. The crawlers used to fetch URLs listed as entries by Web search engines are designed to adhere to standard rules of politeness by asking each server which files may not be indexed, observing firewalls, and allowing an interval of time to pass between requests to avoid tying up the server. Synonymous with *harvester*, *spider*, and *webcrawler*. *See also*: *harvesting*.

CRC   *See*: camera-ready copy.

creasing   In binding, the process of impressing a dull rule or disk on a sheet or leaf of paper to create an indentation along the line where a fold is to be made. By compressing the fibers, creasing produces a cleaner fold and increases the number of times the sheet can flex before it detaches at the fold. Compare with *scoring*.

creator   In archives, the individual or agency responsible for creating, receiving, accumulating, or otherwise producing records or documents for which some form of disposition must be made once their archival value has been appraised. Also refers to the person responsible for producing an original work of visual art.

credential   A letter, certificate, degree, or other document certifying that a person, organization, or institution is qualified to fill a specific position, offer a service, or exercise authority in a given field. For librarians in the United States, the most desirable credential is the M.L.S. or M.L.I.S. degree from an ALA-accredited library school. The term is usually used in the plural: *credentials*.

credenza   Originally, a sideboard from which a lord's food was tested for poison ("credence"). In libraries, a furnishing that doubles as a bookshelf and study table, having two or three tiers of shelves under a flat surface low enough to accommodate a person standing or seated on a high stool or chair.

credibility   The state or quality of being worthy of trust or belief. The reliability of information content usually depends on the motives and credentials of the author or provider. In 2001, Consumers Union launched a three-year Web Credibility Program with $4.8 million in grant support from the Pew Charitable Trusts, the Knight Foundation, and the Open Society Institute. Its goals are to investigate the business practices of Web sites and report findings to the public, develop disclosure standards for the Internet, and make the public more aware of disclosure issues. Academic librarians have responded to lack of disclosure in the online environment by emphasizing critical thinking skills and verification techniques in information literacy instruction. The Persuasive Technology Lab at Stanford University maintains *Web Credibility Research* (www.webcredibility.org), a site devoted to understanding what leads people to accept information they find on the Web.

credit   Any textual statement at the beginning or end of a motion picture, videorecording, or television program identifying by name the director, producer, screenwriter, performers, narrator, and other persons responsible for creating the work, usually with musical accompaniment. In filmmaking, considerable artistic attention is devoted to the style in which credits are presented, to set the tone for what is to follow (or add a final touch).

Also refers to an amount printed on a vendor's monthly statement, or on a separate *credit memo*, usually following a minus sign, indicating that it has been deducted from the total amount owed, for items returned or prepaid but not shipped.

credit line   A brief statement giving the name of the author, artist, agency, or publication that is the source of a picture, photograph, or quotation reproduced in an article or book, or on a Web page, usually displayed immediately below the illustration or portion of text or given at the end of the caption. Credit lines are sometimes printed together in a separate section in the front matter or back matter of a book or in a paragraph on another page in a periodical.

credit memo   A written or printed statement sent by a publisher or vendor to confirm an amount credited to the library's account. A credit is often taken by submitting a copy of the credit memo with an invoice and deducting the amount of the credit from the total amount due.

crime   Because many libraries in the United States and other countries are open to the public, they are not immune to the disruption caused by unlawful behavior, including theft of materials and equipment, verbal abuse and assault on patrons and staff, indecent exposure, drug use and sale by patrons and staff, mutilation of materials, vandalism of equipment and facilities, arson, and more recently, computer crimes. Statistics indicate that crime is increasing in libraries, placing an additional burden on library budgets to provide adequate security. *See also*: *cybercrime* and *problem patron*.

crime fiction   A popular novel, short story, or drama about a criminal act that has been committed or is about to be committed, usually homicide but abduction, theft, assault, and confidence games are also common themes. The category includes murder mysteries, detective fiction, courtroom dramas, legal thrillers, and crime capers. Although "crime" is widely used in publishing and reviewing for thrillers in general, Diana Tixier Herald recommends limiting the scope of the term to fictional works in which the perpetrator of a crime is the primary focus (*Genreflecting: A Guide to Reading Interests in Genre Fiction*, Libraries Unlimited, 2000). The criminal can be a professional or amateur (psychopathic or an ordinary person compelled by circumstance). Compare with *true crime story*.

critical abstract   An abstract that includes a brief evaluation of the content and/or style of presentation of the work abstracted, usually written by a subject specialist. Compare with *indicative abstract* and *informative abstract*.

critical annotation   In a bibliography or list of references, an annotation that includes a brief evaluation of the source cited, as opposed to one in which the content of the work is described, explained, or summarized.

critical bibliography   *See*: analytical bibliography.

critical edition   An edition of a work based on scholarly research and close examination of earlier manuscripts, texts, documents, letters, etc., that sometimes includes analysis and commentary by one or more qualified scholars who have studied and interpreted its meaning and significance.

critical thinking   In research and scholarship, the skill required to develop effective and efficient search strategies, assess the relevance and accuracy of information retrieved, evaluate the authority of the person(s) or organization responsible for producing information content, and analyze the assumptions, evidence, and logical arguments presented in relevant sources. Critical thinking is essential in evaluating information available online because the process of peer review that exists in print publishing is yet to be established in electronic publishing. For this reason, instruction librarians have focused an increasing amount of attention on teaching critical thinking skills in recent years.

CRÍTICAS: An English Speaker's Guide to the Latest Spanish Language Titles   Published bimonthly by Reed Business Information, *CRÍTICAS* was created in 2001 by the editors of *Publishers Weekly*, *Library Journal*, and *School Library Journal* as an English-language magazine providing news, reviews, feature articles, author interviews, and other information about Spanish-language books, audiobooks, and videorecordings for adults and children. ISSN: 1535–6132.

criticism   From the Greek word *kritikos*, meaning "judge." The thoughtful analysis, interpretation, and evaluation of an artistic or literary work in which the primary considerations are its essential nature ("message"), the intentions of the artist or author, the effect of the work on its audience, its relationship to works of similar style or content, its influence on subsequent works, and its implications for critical theory. Literary criticism is considered to have originated with the ancient Greeks (Aristotle's ***Poetics***). Modern criticism is classified by school or type, depending on the approach taken by the *critic*.

In the performing arts, initial critical response may determine the success or demise of a production, though a work that fails on first exposure may receive wider acclaim if revived. In publishing, works rejected by critics and readers when first published sometimes become classics with the passage of time. Unlike reviews, which appear during the months immediately following first publication, serious criticism of an enduring literary work may continue indefinitely. Compare with *explication*.

critique   A critical examination of a topic, idea, thing, or situation by a person intent on determining its essential nature, its strengths and/or limitations, and the degree to which it conforms to accepted standards or prevailing beliefs or assumptions. Sometimes used synonymously with *review*.

CRL   *See*: **C**enter for **R**esearch **L**ibraries.

crocodile   *See*: alligator.

cropped   A photograph or illustration from which a portion of the top, bottom, or sides has been eliminated in the process of reproduction to omit unnecessary detail or make its proportions fit the space available in the layout of a printed page. Also refers to a book trimmed to such an extent that the text is cut into, causing it to *bleed*. Compare with *shaved*.

cross aisle   A corridor or passageway that intersects at a 90-degree angle the ranges and range aisles in the stack area of a library, allowing staff and patrons to move from one range to another without walking to the end of the range.

cross-check   To verify the results of an investigation by using an alternative source or method. In library research, facts are usually confirmed or disconfirmed by consulting a second (independent) source. When conflicting evidence or opinion is found, a third or fourth source may be required to resolve the discrepancy.

cross classification   In Dewey Decimal Classification, the assignment of two different class numbers to works on the same subject, an accident most likely to happen when the works deal with two or more characteristics (facets) of the subject in the same class. Notes on preference order are intended to prevent this type of classification error.

cross-classification   The inclusion of a subclass under more than one class in a hierarchical classification system, for example, the subject heading "Library bonds" under the broader terms "Library finance" and "Municipal bonds" in the list of *Library of Congress Subject Headings*.

cross-grain   A book or other bound publication in which the grain of the paper runs perpendicular to the spine, instead of parallel to it, reducing its openability and making the leaves more difficult to turn.

cross-index   A book index that covers the contents of more than one bibliographic item, such as a group of related reference works. The author and title indexes to the various parts of the Gale *Literary Criticism Series* are a good example.

cross-reference   A reference from one heading to another in the same catalog, index, or reference work. The most common are *see* references, instructing the user to look elsewhere for the preferred form of the heading, and *see also* references, directing the user to related headings under which additional information may be found. A work containing cross-references is said to have *syndetic structure*. Abbreviated *x-ref. See also*: *blind reference*, *explanatory reference*, and *omnibus reference*.

Examples:
Librarianship
See Library science
Library catalogs
See also Cataloging

cross-reference directory   *See*: city directory.

crosswalk   In the management of metadata, a human-generated table indicating equivalencies and relationships between the data elements of two (or more) different metadata standards, for example, between FGDC content standards for digital geospatial metadata and USMARC. Crosswalks enable search engines to operate across databases that use dissimilar record formats. *See also*: *interoperability*.

cryptography   Writing in cipher, usually for the purpose of concealment. Also refers to the study and decoding of such writing. In computing, the conversion of data into a code that can be deciphered only by those who have the key, usually to ensure confidentiality when it is transmitted over a publicly accessible network. *See also*: *encryption*.

cryptonym   A secret name, for example, a name written in code or cipher or in the form of an anagram. *See also*: *cryptography*.

CSLA   *See*: Church and Synagogue Library Association.

CSNA   *See*: Classification Society of North America.

CSS   *See*: cascading style sheets.

CSV   *See*: community service volunteer.

CTEA   Copyright Term Extension Act. See: copyright.

cubook   A unit of volume used to measure library stack capacity, equal to one-hundredth of a standard section of shelving (3 feet wide by 7.5 feet high), the amount of space needed to shelve a book of average height and depth (thickness), assuming 10 percent of the length of each shelf remains unoccupied.

cuir bouilli   A French term meaning "boiled skin." An early form of bookbinding in which the leather used for the cover was soaked in scalding water, then hammered or molded on a die to create a design in relief, usually incorporating motifs popular in the medieval book arts (vines, leaves, flowers, birds, mythical beasts, etc.). When the skin dried, it became so hard that boards were unnecessary.

cuir ciselé   A style of leather binding in which the cover is decorated by using a punch to depress the area around the outline of a design scored in the dampened surface, throwing it into relief against a textured background. When hammered from the reverse side, the design appears embossed. Geoffrey Glaister notes in *Encyclopedia of the Book* (Oak Knoll/British Library, 1996) that the technique was used during the 15th century in Germany, Austria, and Spain. Synonymous with *cut leather* and *Lederschnitt*.

cumdach   An Irish word for a rectangular box made of bronze, brass, or wood, elaborately ornamented in gold, silver, and jewels, used in 9th-century Ireland and Northumbria to store and protect precious manuscript books, especially elaborately decorated liturgical works like the *Book of Kells* and *Lindisfarne Gospels*. Synonymous with *book shrine*.

cum licentia   See: *cum privilegio*.

cum privilegio   A Latin phrase meaning "with permission," printed in old books to inform readers that the work was published with the approval of existing secular or ecclesiastical authorities. The Roman Catholic Church still requires "imprimatur" and *"nihil obstat"* in books representing its official teachings. Synonymous with *cum licentia*.

cumulative index   An index designed to save the user's time by combining in a single sequence the entries listed in two or more previously published indexes, for example, the 10-year indexes to *Current Biography Yearbook*. Most printed periodical indexes are issued in monthly or quarterly paperback supplements, *cumulated* at the end of the publication year in one or more annual volumes. In a more general sense, any index that combines in a single sequence entries for previously published volumes of a book or periodical.

cuneiform From the Latin *cuneus* ("wedge") and *forma* ("shape" or "form"), referring to the pictographic characters used in ancient Akkadian, Assyrian, Babylonian, Persian, and Sumerian inscriptions from about 4,000 to 100 B.C., each of which consisted of an arrangement of wedge-shaped marks incised in a wet clay tablet using a sharp, pointed implement called a stylus. If a text was long enough to be continued on more than one tablet, each tablet was numbered and incised with a catchword at its foot to link it to the next. The last tablet usually ended with a colophon. The University of Minnesota provides an online exhibit of cuneiform inscriptions at: special.lib.umn. edu/rare/cuneiform.

curator A person responsible for the development, care, organization, and supervision of a museum, gallery, or other exhibit space and all the objects stored or displayed in it. Also, a person in charge of a special collection, trained to assist users in locating and interpreting its holdings.

curiosa Books or pamphlets that are highly unusual in subject or treatment, usually somewhat indecent by conventional standards. *See also*: *erotica* and *pornography*.

currency The quality of being in progress, recent, or up-to-date. In information retrieval, the extent to which the content of a document or source reflects the existing state of knowledge about the subject. In research, the importance of currency varies, depending on the discipline. Medical and scientific information can become outdated in less than five years, but in the arts and humanities, materials decades old may be just as useful as recent information.

Because newspapers and periodicals are issued at regular intervals, they provide more current information than books, which must be updated in supplements and revised editions. Some online catalogs and bibliographic databases allow the user to limit search results by publication date to retrieve only recently published materials. The opposite of *noncurrent* and *outdated*. *See also*: *current awareness service*, *current bibliography*, *current contents*, and *current issue*.

In archives, newly acquired records usually remain current for a designated period of time, after which their status is changed to "semicurrent," and they are moved to a temporary holding area to await final disposition.

current awareness service A service or publication designed to alert scholars, researchers, readers, customers, or employees to recently published literature in their field(s) of specialization, usually available in special libraries serving companies, organizations, and institutions in which access to current information is essential. Such services can be tailored to fit the interest profile of a specific individual or group. Some online catalogs and bibliographic databases include a "preferred searches" option that allows the library user to archive search statements and re-execute them as needed. Synonymous with *selective dissemination of information*. *See also*: *current contents*.

current bibliography   A bibliography that includes only references to recently published sources on a subject or in a specific field or discipline (*example*: ***Annual Bulletin of Historical Literature*** published by the Historical Association, London). The opposite of *retrospective bibliography*.

current contents   A periodical that reproduces the tables of contents of the leading scholarly journals in an academic field or discipline to assist researchers in keeping abreast of the most recently published literature in their areas of interest or specialization, usually published weekly or monthly. Because currency is the raison d'être of this type of publication, libraries may limit back files to the most recent three to five years. *See also*: *current awareness service*.

current issue   The latest number of a serial publication, bearing the most recent issue date. In some libraries, current issues are displayed with the front cover facing forward on sloping shelves or on a periodical stand to facilitate browsing. Back files are typically stored in a different location, sometimes on microfilm or microfiche to conserve space. Synonymous with *current number*. Compare with *back issue*. *See also*: *first issue*.

current number   *See*: current issue.

curriculum   All the required and elective subjects/courses taught at a school or institution of higher learning, usually listed by department and course number in an annual course catalog. Courses required of all students for graduation constitute the *core curriculum*.

curriculum guide   A written plan covering one or more facets of curriculum and instruction (goals and objectives, teaching strategies, learning activities, specific resources, evaluation and assessment techniques) for use within an instructional unit as small as a classroom or as large as a school district or state. Curriculum guides are indexed and abstracted as documents in *ERIC*.

curriculum lab   *See*: curriculum room.

curriculum room   A room or designated area within an academic library containing curriculum-related materials such as kits, textbooks, workbooks, educational software, and juvenile fiction and nonfiction for the use of students enrolled in teacher education courses. Synonymous with *curriculum lab*.

curriculum vitae (c.v.)   A brief summary of a person's professional career, including basic biographical information, degrees and postgraduate education, honors and awards, employment history, publications and presentations, memberships, service, etc., for use in employment (hiring, tenure, promotion, etc.). Compare with *resume*.

cursive   A right-sloping style of handwriting, also known as *running script*, in which the letters within words are connected, having been written continuously without lifting pen or pencil from paper (or other writing surface), used in humanist manuscripts and papal documents of the Renaissance and for writing letters and other informal documents. Cursive hands are functional rather than calligraphic, the form of each letter of less importance than the speed with which it can be written. In printing and word processing, a cursive typeface or font is designed to imitate handwriting done with a pen or brush. *See also*: *court hand*.

cursor   A small illuminated point, vertical bar, underline, or other symbol on a computer screen that can be positioned by the user via a keyboard, mouse, or other control device to indicate where a new character will appear when typed as input or a new operation is to occur when initiated by the user. In Windows and other graphical user interfaces, the cursor may change shape when moved from one window or dialog box to another, turning into an I-beam for text editing, an arrow or finger for selecting an option from a menu or toolbar, an hourglass while an operation is in progress, or a small pen in graphics programs. In many applications, the symbol blinks steadily to make it easier to locate on the screen. Synonymous with *pointer*. *See also*: *prompt*.

CUSTARD   *See*: Canadian-U.S. Task Force on Archival Description.

custodian   The person responsible for the care and protection of something of value. Over the past 100 years, the model of librarianship has evolved from *custodianship* of materials in physical form to one in which the librarian is seen as a mediator of access to information in a wide range of formats, including electronic resources. However, custodianship remains a high priority in archival and special collections.

custody   In archives, the official guardianship of books, manuscripts, papers, records, and other documents, based on physical possession, with or without legal title or the right to control access or disposition. The person responsible for such care is their *custodian*.

custom binding   A book bound to the specifications of its owner or a dealer or in accordance with special instructions from the publisher, rather than the general instructions for the edition.

cut   An illustration printed (captioned or uncaptioned) with the text page, as opposed to a plate printed on a separate leaf, usually of different quality paper, to be added to the publication in binding. The term is also used in reference to the woodcut illustrations in chapbooks and 19th-century publications for children.

cut-and-paste   A feature built into most graphical user interfaces allowing the user to move an element displayed on the computer screen, such as a portion of text or graphic, from one location to another within the same document, from one document to another, or even from one application to another, usually by highlighting the element to be moved, selecting the option "Cut" under "Edit" in the toolbar, and then "Paste" after positioning the cursor at the point to which the element is to be moved. The element cut is transferred to a temporary storage area called a *clipboard* until the next cut-and-paste operation is initiated. Most software includes an "Undo" option that allows the user to reverse the operation if a mistake is made. Compare with *copy*.

cutaway   An illustration of a mechanical device, physical structure, or other enclosed system in which the outer covering or wall is shown removed (like the back of a doll's house) to reveal inner details. Also spelled *cut-away*.

cut edges   Outer edges of the sections of a book, trimmed smooth in binding using a tool called a *guillotine* or its predecessor, the *plough*. Compare with *deckle edges* and *uncut*.

cut flush   Said of a book cover that has edges perfectly even with the edges of the leaves, the result of having been cut after it was attached to the sections in binding. Most paperback books are cut flush. Synonymous with *flush boards* and *trimmed flush*. Compare with *squares*.

cut-in note   A side note printed wholly or partially inside the edge of a paragraph of text, instead of in the margin, usually in a typeface heavier and smaller in size than the text type. Synonymous with *cut-in side note*, *in-cut note*, and *let-in note*.

cut leather   *See*: *cuir ciselé*.

cut line   *See*: caption.

Cutter number   A system of alphanumeric author marks developed by Charles A. Cutter to permit the subarrangement of items of the same classification, alphabetically by author's last name. A Cutter number consists of one to three letters from the name, followed by one or more arabic numerals from the Cutter Table added to the end of the call number by a cataloger. Synonymous with *Cutter author mark*. ***See also***: *work mark*.

Cutter-Sanborn Table   *See*: Cutter Table.

Cutter Table   In 1880, Charles A. Cutter first circulated a two-figure table designed to assist catalogers in adding author marks to call numbers to differentiate items of the same classification by author. The Cutter Table was extended to allow the assignment of three arabic numerals following the initial letters of the author's last name and later revised by Kate A. Sanborn. The OCLC Four-Figure Cutter Tables are revised and expanded versions of the Cutter Three-Figure Author Table and the Cutter-Sanborn Three-Figure Author Table. DDC provides a software program that automatically provides Cutter numbers from the OCLC Four-Figure Cutter Tables.

cutting   A piece sliced from a leaf of a medieval manuscript, usually a miniature or illuminated initial letter removed by a collector or person intent on selling the illustrations individually, a destructive practice condemned by antiquarians and preservationists. Cuttings were collected for their independent aesthetic value, particularly during the 18th and 19th centuries. Compare with *clipping*.

c.v.   *See*: curriculum vitae.

cybercafe   A "high-tech" coffee house equipped with microcomputers for the use of its customers. Cybercafes originated in New York City in the 1990s and have since spread throughout the world. Some large academic libraries have installed them on their premises to give students a place to relax and read their e-mail. Synonymous with *Internet cafe* and *netcafe*.

cybercrime   Illegal activities carried out over the Internet, such as malicious hacking, virus distribution, data theft, extortion, fraud, forgery, child pornography, trafficking in illegal substances, digital copyright infringement, etc. Libraries providing computers for public use must be particularly vigilant. In 2001, the United States, Canada, Australia, Japan, and the 43 member nations of the Council of Europe approved the *European Cybercrime Treaty*, the first international agreement on Internet-related criminal offenses, providing comprehensive global laws governing Internet use, including enforcement provisions that allow violators to be extradited. Synonymous with *computer crime*.

cybernetics   From the Greek word *kybernetes*, meaning "helmsman." A branch of science developed by Norbert Wiener in the 1940s that utilizes the concept of feedback in comparing human and machine processes, particularly mental processes, to understand their similarities and differences, with the ultimate goal of creating machines capable of imitating human behavior and intelligence. *See also*: *artificial intelligence*.

cyberplagiarism   *See*: plagiarism.

cyberporn   A neologism coined from the terms "cyberspace" and "pornography" to refer to sexually explicit materials available electronically over the Internet. Cyberporn is of particular concern to parents who would like to see their children become computer literate but hesitate to expose them to adult influences prematurely. Filtering software designed to block access to adult material remains controversial. *See also*: *censorship*, Children's Internet Protection Act, and *intellectual freedom*.

cyberspace   A neologism coined by the writer William Gibson in his science fiction novel *Neuromancer* (1984) to refer to the virtual world of digital communication, in which human beings interact with one another electronically via computer networks instead of face-to-face.

cybrarian   A shortened form of *cyberlibrarian*, coined from the terms "cyberspace" and "librarian" to refer to a librarian whose work routinely involves information retrieval and dissemination via the Internet and the use of other online resources. Despite its catchy sound, the appellation has *not* been widely adopted within the library profession.

cycle   A group of literary works (poems, plays, stories, novels) that share a unifying theme, for example, the Yoknapatawpha stories of William Faulkner. An *epic cycle* is a group of individual epics or ballads joined, usually by a process of accretion, to form a whole, as in the *Iliad* of Homer or the narratives comprising the Arthurian legend.

cyclopedia   *See*: encyclopedia.

Cyrillic   An alphabet used in Russia and countries formerly part of the Soviet Union, Cyrillic evolved from the Greek uncial alphabet. Formalized during the 9th or 10th century, it contains characters not included in the Latin alphabet that represent sounds peculiar to the Slavic languages. Cyrillic typefaces of 43 letters were introduced in the 18th century, based on the civil script established by Peter the Great in 1710. In 1918, the alphabet was reduced to its present 32 letters as a result of reforms introduced after the Russian Revolution. *See also*: *romanization* and *transliteration*.

D

---

daemon The Greek word for "guardian spirit." In computing, an auxiliary systems program initiated at startup and executed in the background that performs a specific task when needed, for example, running a scheduler to start another process automatically at a pre-established time, checking incoming e-mail messages for addresses that cannot be found, or notifying the sender that a message could not be delivered. Pronounced "demon."

dagger (†) In printing, a character in the shape of a vertical stroke crossed above its midpoint, used in text as a second-order reference mark following use of the asterisk. When it appears before a personal name in the English language, the dagger indicates that the individual is deceased. Also called an *obelisk* or *long cross*. ***See also***: *double dagger*.

daguerreotype Historically, the first photographic process that actually worked, producing a positive image directly on a highly polished, silvered copper plate sensitized with iodide vapor. By exposing the plate to light in a *camera obscura*, an image was captured in the photosensitive layer of silver iodide that could be developed through the application of mercury vapor. Made public in 1839, the process was named after its French inventor, the painter of dioramas Louis Jacques Mande Daguerre, who relied heavily on earlier experiments by Joseph Nicephore Niepce. Easily scratched and tarnished, daguerreotypes were normally protected by a metal mat and a sheet of glass. Early examples are valued by collectors because each one is unique, not having been made from a negative. Also spelled *daguerrotype*. ***See also***: *tintype*.

daguerrotype *See*: daguerreotype.

DAI *See*: ***Dissertation Abstracts International***.

daily Issued on a daily basis, with the possible exception of Sundays. Also refers to a serial issued daily, especially a newspaper.

damaged An item returned to the library in such poor condition that it cannot be placed back on the shelf for circulation, for example, a water-soaked or pet-chewed book. The borrower is normally charged the cost of repair or replacement. New items received from the shipper in damaged condition are returned by the library to the seller for credit or replacement.

Dana, John Cotton (1856–1929)   A public librarian for over 40 years, John Cotton Dana began his career in 1889 as head of the Denver Public Library, moved to the City Library of Springfield in 1898, and ended his career at the Free Public Library in Newark, New Jersey. A leader in the library profession, he served as president of the American Library Association from 1895 to 1896, as a member of its council from 1896 to 1902, and as president of the Special Libraries Association from 1909 to 1910, an organization he helped establish. His philosophical approach to librarianship is best expressed in his book *Suggestions*, published in 1921 by F.W. Faxon.

dandy roll   The cylinder that exerts pressure in mechanized papermaking, smoothing the surface and creating designs such as the watermark, countermark, and the lines characteristic of laid and wove paper.

Dartmouth Medal   A literary award presented annually since 1974 by the Reference and User Services Association (RUSA), a division of the American Library Association, to the most outstanding reference work published during the preceding calendar year.

dash   A short length of horizontal rule used for punctuation, to separate text, and for decorative effect. In printing, dashes vary in length from the three-em (longest) to the hyphen (shortest). In typing, a dash is made by striking the hyphen key twice (--) in succession. In descriptive cataloging, the dash is given a space on either side, but when used in subject headings to indicate subdivision, no spaces are included.

dashed-on entry   A pre-*AACR2* convention of indicating accompanying material and additional versions on the catalog entry for the main item, a practice that economized on the number of catalog cards needed for items sharing basic bibliographic description. This type of entry was eliminated in *AACR2*, reflecting a shift from card catalogs to MARC-based electronic catalogs. Synonymous with *dash entry* and *dash on entry*.

dash entry   *See*: dashed-on entry.

dash on entry   *See*: dashed-on entry.

data   The plural of the Latin word *datum*, meaning "what is given," often used as a singular collective noun. Facts, figures, or instructions presented in a form that can be comprehended, interpreted, and communicated by a human being or processed by a computer. Compare with *information* and *knowledge*. *See also*: *data bank*, *database*, *data set*, and *metadata*.

data bank   Sometimes used synonymously with *database*, the term applies more specifically to a collection of nonbibliographic data, usually numeric (*example*: the *Global Soil Moisture Data Bank* available online from the Department of Environmental Studies at Rutgers University). Large data banks containing information about individuals (social security numbers, credit history, health records, etc.) have become the subject of controversy as the rapid development of high-speed information technology poses new threats to personal privacy.

database   A large, regularly updated file of digitized information (bibliographic records, abstracts, full-text documents, directory entries, images, statistics, etc.) related to a specific subject or field, consisting of records of uniform format organized for ease and speed of search and retrieval and managed with the aid of database management system (DBMS) software. Content is created by the database producer (for example, the American Psychological Association), which usually publishes a print version (*Psychological Abstracts*) and leases the content to one or more database vendors (EBSCO, OCLC, etc.) that provide electronic access to the data after it has been converted to machine-readable form (*PsycINFO*), usually on CD-ROM or online via the Internet, using proprietary search software.

Most databases used by libraries are catalogs, periodical indexes, abstracting services, and full-text reference resources leased annually under licensing agreements that limit access to registered borrowers and library staff. Abbreviated *db*. Compare with *data bank*. **See also**: *bibliographic database* and *metadatabase*.

database management system (DBMS)   A computer application designed to control the storage, retrieval, security, integrity, and reporting of data in the form of uniform records organized in a large searchable file called a database. The range of available DBMS software extends from simple systems intended for personal computers to highly complex systems designed to run on mainframes.

data compression   The algorithmic re-creation of a data file to reduce the amount of memory required for storage. Exchange of compressed data requires less transmission time but more computation time to restore it to its original form for processing. In digital imaging, a number of compression methods are used, including JPEG, GIF, and LZW. Compression algorithms are classified as *lossless* or *lossy*, depending on whether data is lost in compression.

data conversion   The process of translating data from one form to another, usually from human-readable to machine-readable format (or vice versa), from one file type to another, or from one recording medium to another, for example, from film to videotape or videodisc.

data dictionary   A set of data descriptions documenting the fields (columns) in the tables of a database system. A data dictionary may describe the *data type* and other physical characteristics of fields, enumerate allowed values, and specify appropriate usage.

Data Documentation Initiative (DDI)   A project of the social science community to develop a standardized XML markup and representation for codebooks, the primary metadata describing social science data sets. URL: www.icpsr.umich.edu/DDI.

data processing   The systematic performance of a single operation or sequence of operations by one or more central processing units on data converted to machine-readable format to achieve the result for which the computer program that controls the processing was written, for example, the compilation of circulation statistics from records of circulation transactions occurring in a library over a given period of time.

data set   A logically meaningful collection or grouping of similar or related data, usually assembled as a matter of record or for research, for example, the *American FactFinder Data Sets* provided online by the U.S. Census Bureau at: factfinder. census.gov. Also spelled *dataset*. *See also*: *social science data set*.

date due slip   A card or slip of paper inserted in an item charged from a library collection or a small printed form attached to the inside of the front or back cover (or to one of the endpapers), on which is stamped the date the item is due back in the library. The paper on which they are printed should be acid-free. Date due slips are sometimes removed by borrowers in an attempt to avoid overdue fines, but the advent of automated circulation systems has nixed this strategy. Synonymous with *charge slip*.

date line   The line printed at the beginning of a story in a newspaper or article published in a magazine, indicating the date and place of origin of news that is not local. *See also*: *byline*.

date range   An interval of time marked by a beginning and ending date. Some online catalogs and bibliographic databases allow the user to limit a search to a specific range of publication dates. A year followed by a hyphen (1946–) limits retrieval to information published in the year specified or any succeeding year, a year preceded by a hyphen (–1945) limits retrieval to sources published up to and including the year specified, and a year followed by a hyphen and a subsequent year (1939–1945) limits retrieval to sources published in those or any intervening years.

DBMS   *See*: **d**ata**b**ase **m**anagement **s**ystem.

DBV   *See*: **D**eutscher **B**ibliotheks**v**erband e.V.

DCMI   *See*: Dublin Core.

DDC   *See*: **D**ewey **D**ecimal **C**lassification.

DDI   *See*: **D**ata **D**ocumentation **I**nitiative.

DDS   *See*: **d**ocument **d**elivery **s**ervice.

deaccession   The process of deleting from an accession record documents and other materials that are to be removed from a library collection. Also refers to any item so removed. The opposite of *accession*.

   In archives, the process of removing records or documents from official custody, undertaken after careful consideration, usually as the result of a decision to transfer the material to another custodian or because the legal owner desires its return or the material is found upon reappraisal to be of doubtful authenticity or inappropriate for the collection.

deacidification   A general term for a variety of costly preservation processes that chemically reduce the acid content of paper documents to a pH of 7.0 (neutral) or higher, usually undertaken at a professional conservation center to prevent further deterioration. An alkaline buffer may be deposited in deacidification to neutralize any acids that develop in the future. Brittleness is not reversed by deacidification. *Mass deacidification* is the shipment of a quantity of documents to a center for processing in small batches, rather than individually.

Dead Sea Scrolls   Ancient papyrus and parchment manuscripts discovered in caves in the Judean Desert in 1947 by Bedouin shepherds, stored inside large pottery jars. Radiocarbon dating has established that the scrolls, and the Essene community at wadi Quram with which they are believed to be associated, date from 250 B.C. to A.D. 65. Written in Aramaic, the scrolls comprise about 800 documents of which most are in fragmentary condition. They include the oldest extant text of the Old Testament. The scrolls are in the possession of the Israel Antiquities Authority in Jerusalem, where they are being prepared for publication. The tedious work of piecing them together has taken decades.

dealer   An individual or commercial company in the business of buying and selling new and used books to libraries, collectors, and other booksellers. Although the term is sometimes used synonymously with *vendor* or *jobber*, it is usually reserved for specialists who deal in out of print titles, rare books, periodical back issues, etc. *See also*: *antiquarian bookseller*.

decennial   Issued every 10 years (*example*: **U.S. Census**). Also refers to a serial publication issued every 10 years. *See also*: *annual, biennial, triennial, quadrennial, quinquennial, sexennial*, and *septennial*.

decimal point   The period used in the numeric portion of Library of Congress Classification notation (*example*: **DK 265.9**) and following the third digit of a class number in Dewey Decimal Classification (**947.084**) to indicate that succeeding digits are to be treated as a decimal fraction.

deckle edges   The uneven or feathered edge of a sheet of handmade paper, created by the flow of liquefied fibrous stock between the frame (deckle) and sieve of the mould used in manufacture. The same effect is achieved in machine-made paper by exposing the edge to a jet of air or water. In quality bookbinding, deckle edges are considered tasteful, but since books tend to collect dust when stored on an open shelf, and rough edges are difficult to clean, this feature is not practical. Compare with *cut edges*.

declassified   A document no longer protected against unauthorized disclosure because the security classification assigned to maintain confidentiality has been officially changed or canceled. The opposite of *classified*.

decorated initial   An initial letter in an illuminated manuscript or early printed book embellished in an abstract, nonrepresentational style, rather than with foliate, zoomorphic, and/or anthropomorphic motifs or pictorial elements.

decorated paper   Fine paper hand-printed in Germany, France, and Italy from patterns carved in woodblocks, used in luxury bookbinding from the 18th century on for doublures and flyleaves. Dutch gilt was a multicolored floral pattern blocked in gold, shipped from Germany to the Netherlands for re-export. *See also*: *marbling*.

decretals   A book containing a collection of letters written to transmit papal decrees, usually concerning canon law, often made in response to a specific appeal. Michelle Brown notes in *Understanding Illuminated Manuscripts* (Getty Museum/British Library, 1994) that copies of decretals used by ecclesiastical and civil officials, and for purposes of study in universities, often included commentaries written as glosses alongside the text and also decoration (miniatures, bas-de-page scenes, grotesques, etc.).

dedicated   In computing and communications, a device or channel reserved for a specific use. In libraries, dedicated servers are used to run the online catalog and provide access to the library's Web site. *See also*: *dedicated line*.

dedicated line   A direct pathway to the Internet or some other computer network via a separate telecommunications channel not shared with multiple users as in dial-up access but available around the clock to a specific user or group of users for a designated purpose. When accessed through a common carrier, the channel is called a *leased line*.

dedication   A brief note in which the creator of a work addresses it to one or more persons, usually a colleague, mentor, or family member, as a sign of honor, appreciation, or affection. In books, the author's dedication appears in the front matter, usually printed on the recto of the leaf following the title page. Compare with *acknowledgments*.

dedication copy   A copy of a book or other work inscribed by the author, editor, or illustrator to the person or persons to whom the work is dedicated. In the antiquarian book trade, a dedication copy may be of substantially greater value than a copy with no inscription and is considered one of the most collectible presentation copies of an edition.

deduping   Removal of all but one occurrence of a bibliographic record from a file of machine-readable records, one of the initial steps in processing a MARC database. Deduping is a batch process that prevents confusion in the minds of users, conserves computer storage, and allows reliable usage statistics to be collected. Duplicate records are not uncommon because the "cancel holdings" command in OCLC software does not delete a record from the library's OCLC tapes. Synonymous with *duplicate removal* and *duplicate resolution*.

deed of gift   A signed document stating the terms of agreement under which legal title to real or personal property, such as a gift to a library or archives, is transferred, voluntarily and without recompense, by the donor to the recipient institution, with or without conditions specifying access, use, preservation, etc.

deep linking   A link made from a Web document to the interior of another Web site, bypassing the second site's homepage, usually without any indication that a shortcut has been taken. Deep linking raises digital rights issues, particularly for commercial entities that derive income from advertising on their main page. Likelihood of litigation depends on the type of site involved and the nature of the content accessed. Libraries should seek permission before deep linking from their Web pages.

deep Web   Publicly accessible information available via the World Wide Web but not retrievable using search engines that rely on crawlers or spiders, for example, data in file formats such as PDF, database content accessible only by query, information contained in frames, etc. The number of documents available in the deep Web is estimated to be 400–500 times greater than the amount of content retrievable via conventional search engines (the "surface Web"), with over half of the "hidden" content residing in topic-specific searchable databases. *CompletePlanet* and *InvisibleWeb. com* are examples of Internet services specifically designed to provide access to information in the deep Web. Synonymous with *invisible Web*.

The term is also used for password-protected Web content available only to authorized users (members, subscribers, etc.).

default   A value, option, or setting automatically selected in a hardware or software system in the absence of specific instructions from the user. The default setting may be displayed on the data entry screen to allow the user to see what action will be taken if no input is provided.

definition   One meaning of a word expressed clearly and concisely. Because some words have more than one meaning, a word may have more than one definition. In lexicography, a word or phrase is defined by first specifying the class (genus) to which its referent belongs, then indicating the characteristics that distinguish the referent from others of the same class. Definitions are listed in dictionaries and glossaries and are also provided in some concordances and thesauri. In most dictionaries, the modern definition of a word is given first and the oldest last, but there are notable exceptions to this rule. Abbreviated *def*. *See also*: *headword*.

Also refers to the distinctness of a printed or photographic image.

definitive edition   An edition of the complete text of an author's work or works usually edited and published after the person's death in a form considered final and authoritative. Also refers to the text of an anonymous work considered by scholars or other experts to be closest to the original version. Compare with *authorized edition*. *See also*: *critical edition* and *variant edition*.

dehumidify   *See*: humidity.

delayed publication   A book or periodical not issued on schedule, usually due to delays in production. Also refers to new information not published in a timely manner, for whatever reason.

delete   To remove, erase, or omit a character, word, or passage from a text or document. In computing, to erase a character, word, passage, or entire file from memory, usually by pressing the "Backspace" key on a keyboard or by highlighting text and pressing the "Delete" key or selecting the "Delete" option from a menu or toolbar. Some software systems allow the user to "Undo" a deletion while the application remains open.

delimiter   In a general sense, any character or sequence of characters used in an electronic database to separate discrete elements of data within a field (or fields) of a record. In the MARC record, a character used as the first character of a two-character *subfield code* to indicate the beginning of a *subfield*, separating one data element from another within the field. Because the *subfield delimiter* value has no standard display representation, it is represented as a double dagger (‡) by OCLC and as a dollar sign ($) in Library of Congress cataloging.

deluxe binding   French for "of elegance." A binding of very fine quality, usually covered in leather or fine cloth stamped or tooled in gold, sometimes with gilt edges and doublures or endpapers of marbled or decorated paper. Also spelled *de luxe binding*. *See also*: *deluxe edition*.

deluxe edition   An edition printed on better quality paper than the standard trade edition, sometimes from specially cast type, usually bound in leather or some other material of fine quality. Deluxe editions may also be larger in size, more lavishly illustrated, and published in limited edition. Also spelled *de luxe edition*. Synonymous with *fine edition*. *See also*: *deluxe binding*.

demand   The number of people who need or request a product or service. In libraries, *high-demand* items may be ordered in multiple copies or placed on reserve to ensure access. In public libraries, low-demand items in the circulating collection may be candidates for weeding. Demand for library services usually peaks at different times during the day, week, month, and year. Transaction logs can be helpful in tracking and anticipating patterns of usage.

demand publishing   A commercial service that supplies single copies of rare or out of print books in response to individual demand, usually by photocopying prints made from a microform master, for example, *Dissertation Express* from ProQuest.

DEMCO   A commercial company that provides furniture, equipment, and supplies for the library, school, office, and home. DEMCO also provides periodical subscription services. URL: www.demco.com.

density   In typography, the number of characters filling a given space, a variable affecting legibility of type. In photography, the degree of opacity of a developed photosensitive medium, such as film. In printing and photography, the density of an image is measured by an instrument called a *densitometer*.

In computing, the amount of data, usually measured in bits or bytes, that can be stored in or on a given storage medium, such as a memory chip or portable disk. A floppy disk can be *single-density*, *double-density*, *high-density*, or *extra-high-density*. A disk drive designed to support the specific density level is required.

dentelle binding   A style of 18th-century leather binding in which the covers are decorated on the outer and/or inner surface with broad, full borders gold-tooled in a finely detailed pattern resembling lacework.

departmental library   A type of academic library that serves the information and research needs of the faculty members of a specific department within an institution of higher learning, usually a large university. Departmental libraries are also used by students enrolled in courses in the discipline(s) taught by the department, especially graduate students. If acquisitions are funded through the department, selection is usually the responsibility of the teaching faculty in collaboration with the departmental librarian.

dependent work   In library cataloging, a work that is contingent in some way on a previously published work by another author. Included in this category are: abridgments, arrangements, commentaries, continuations, dramatizations, sequels, revised editions, and supplements. Synonymous with *related work*. Compare with *derivative work*.

deposit   Any addition to archival holdings, usually a transfer of materials from some other location or agency, but the term also applies to materials on loan for a period of fixed or indefinite duration. The *depositor* usually retains legal ownership and responsibility, except in the case of gifts. *See also*: *deposit copy*.

deposit account   In acquisitions, a vendor prepayment account into which the customer deposits a substantial sum, against which orders are subsequently charged. When the balance in the account reaches zero, an additional amount must be deposited for fulfillment to continue. In return, the library receives a financial incentive in the form of an annual credit based on an agreed rate, a larger than normal discount on purchases, or interest paid on the balance in the account. A library's funding authority usually dictates the feasibility of this type of account (some institutions prefer to earn interest on the money rather than allow the library to expand its purchasing power). There is risk to the customer, should the vendor go out of business before the end of the deposit period.

deposit copy   A copy of a new publication sent without charge to a copyright depository or other designated library by the author or publisher in compliance with national copyright law. In the United States, the deposit copy is sent with the completed copyright application form and copyright fee to the U.S. Copyright Office of the Library of Congress in Washington, D.C. Synonymous with *statutory copy*.

depository library   A library legally designated to receive without charge all or a portion of the government documents provided by the U.S. Government Printing Office (GPO) and other federal agencies to the Superintendent of Documents for distribution under the Federal Depository Library Program (FDLP). Some federal depositories also collect publications issued by state government agencies. *GPO Access* provides an online Federal Depository Library locator service at: www.gpoaccess.gov/libraries.html. Compare with *repository*.

depth   The thickness of a bound volume at its thickest point (usually at the spine) with the covers included. Average depth determines how many volumes will fit on a shelf of given length. Also refers to the width of a bookshelf from front to back. Most library shelving is 8, 9, 10, or 12 inches deep. *See also*: *height*.

In indexing, a combination of the average number of index terms (subject headings or descriptors) assigned to documents indexed and the specificity of the terms used (*ASIS Thesaurus of Information Science and Librarianship*, Information Today, 1998).

depth indexing   An indexing system that attempts to extract *all* the concepts covered in a work, including any subtopics, as opposed to *summarization*, in which a work is indexed only under its dominant subject. Library catalogers have traditionally looked for the single concept that best describes the entire content of an item, leaving depth indexing to commercial services that index parts of items (articles in periodicals, book chapters, essays in collections, etc.).

derivative indexing   A method of indexing in which a human indexer or computer extracts from the title and/or text of a document one or more words or phrases to represent subject(s) of the work, for use as headings under which entries are made. Synonymous with *derived indexing* and *extractive indexing*. Compare with *assignment indexing*. *See also*: *automatic indexing* and *machine-aided indexing*.

derivative work   A work based on another work that transforms the content of the original in a significant way (abridgment, adaptation, arrangement, revision, translation, etc.). Under U.S. copyright law, the rights to produce derivative works are retained by the copyright holder. Compare with *dependent work*.

derived cataloging   *See*: copy cataloging.

derived indexing   *See*: derivative indexing.

descender   In typography and calligraphy, the stroke of a lowercase letter that extends below the lowest point of an x-height letter (**a**, **c**, **e**, **m**, etc.). The letters of the roman alphabet that have descenders are: **g**, **j**, **p**, **q**, and **y**. The *descender line* is an imaginary horizontal line connecting the bottoms of descender letters, not to be confused with the base line. Compare with *ascender*. *See also*: *primary letter*.

descriptive bibliography   The close study and description of the physical and bibliographic characteristics of books and other materials, including detailed information about author, title, publication history, format, pagination, illustration, printing, binding, appearance, etc., as opposed to an examination of content. Also refers to a work that is the result of such study. Descriptive bibliography is considered a branch of *analytical bibliography*.

descriptive cataloging   The part of the library cataloging process concerned with identifying and describing the physical and bibliographic characteristics of the item, and with determining the name(s) and title(s) to be used as access points in the catalog, but not with the assignment of subject and form headings. In the United States, Great Britain, and Canada, descriptive cataloging is governed by *Anglo-American Cataloguing Rules* (*AACR2*). *See also*: *authority control* and *subject analysis*.

descriptor   In indexing, a preferred term, notation, or sequence of symbols assigned as an access point in the bibliographic record representing a document to indicate one of the subjects of its text (synonymous in library cataloging with the term *subject heading*). In bibliographic databases, descriptors appear in the DE or SUBJECT field of the record. Major descriptors are distinguished from minor descriptors by a special character, usually the asterisk. Some abstracting and indexing services, such as *ERIC* and *Psychological Abstracts*, provide a list of authorized indexing terms in the form of a printed or online thesaurus. Compare with *identifier*. *See also*: *aboutness*, *controlled vocabulary*, and *descriptor group*.

descriptor group   In some indexing systems, the preferred terms are grouped in broad subject categories that together serve as a "table of contents" to the controlled vocabulary. The group to which a specific descriptor is assigned is usually indicated by a code in the entry for the term in the thesaurus of indexing terms; for example, the group code **GC: 730** in the entry for the term "Literature Reviews" in the *Thesaurus of ERIC Descriptors* indicates that it is assigned to the descriptor group "Publication/ Document Types."

deselection   In serials, the process of identifying subscriptions for cancellation, usually in response to subscription price increases and budgetary constraints. In book and nonprint collections, the process of identifying titles for weeding, usually on the basis of currency, usage, and condition. The opposite of *selection*.

desensitization   The process of deactivating the magnetic strip affixed to a book or other printed item to prevent the security alarm from sounding when the borrower exits the library, a step performed by circulation staff when the item is checked out, using a device called a *desensitizer*. A different machine is required to desensitize magnetic media (audiocassettes, videocassettes, etc.).

desiccant   A drying agent such as silica gel used in museums and libraries to remove water vapor from a small enclosed space when control of relative humidity is an important factor in the preservation of specimens, documents, and other materials in storage or on exhibit. Because desiccants release moisture when heated, they can usually be reused.

desiderata   A list of books and other materials needed and wanted by a library, to be purchased when budget permits or a cash donation is received. Synonymous in this sense with *waiting list* and *want list*. Also refers to a list of subjects or topics on which a writer or researcher requires information.

designer binding   A bookbinding bearing decoration done by an artist skilled in graphic design, usually in a style contemporary with the period in which it was made. This type of binding began to appear in trade editions in the second half of the 19th century and remained popular into the early 20th century.

desk copy   A complimentary copy of a new book or recently revised edition provided without charge by the publisher as an instructor's copy when additional copies are ordered by a college or university bookstore for students enrolled in a course of study. An *examination copy* may become a desk copy once an instructor decides to assign the work as required reading.

desk dictionary   A single-volume dictionary of approximately 150,000 words intended for use by an individual sitting at a desk or in a workspace (*example*: ***Webster's New World Dictionary of the American Language***). Entries usually indicate orthography, syllabication, pronunciation, etymology, and definition. Synonyms, antonyms, and brief biographical and gazetteer information are included in some editions. Synonymous with *college dictionary*. The online version of ***Merriam-Webster's Collegiate Dictionary and Thesaurus*** is available at: www.m-w.com/dictionary.htm. Compare with *pocket dictionary* and *unabridged dictionary*.

desk schedule   A list of the hours during which librarians and other public services staff are regularly assigned to assist users at the circulation desk, reference desk, information desk, or other public service point in a library, usually prepared by the staff member responsible for supervising the operations performed at the location. *See also*: rotation.

desktop binding   Office technologies designed to allow the producer of a multipage document to securely fasten its leaves together, without sending it to a professional binder. One example is VeloBind, an electric punch and strip, hot-knife process often used to custom bind legal documents up to three inches (750 sheets) thick.

desktop computer   *See*: personal computer.

desktop publishing (DTP)   The use of microcomputer hardware and software for page layout, graphic design, and printing to produce professional-quality camera-ready copy for commercial printing at a fraction of the cost of using the services of a commercial publisher. Used extensively to produce in-house brochures, fliers, newsletters, posters, etc., DTP requires desktop publishing software and a high-speed PC equipped with a large monitor and high-resolution laser printer to produce text and graphics in WYSIWYG format. *See also*: *self-publishing*.

destruction   In archives, the process of physically doing away with records that are no longer of value but remain too sensitive to be simply discarded as trash. For paper records, the most common methods are shredding and pulping. Incineration is used for records in other formats.

detective fiction   A popular novel, short story, or drama in which the details of a crime (or suspected crime) are uncovered by an amateur or professional sleuth who searches for clues and interprets them, often using ingenious methods to solve the mystery of "Who done it?" The modern detective story began with Edgar Allan Poe's *Murders in the Rue Morgue* (1841) and is now a popular subgenre of crime fiction. Sherlock Holmes, the eccentric sleuth created by Sir Arthur Conan Doyle, has become a household word in many English-speaking countries. The hard-boiled detective, at home in the criminal underworld, first appeared in pulp magazines in the 1920s and was brought to life in *film noir* classics such as Alfred Hitchcock's *The Maltese Falcon*, based on the novel by Dashiell Hammett. Period detective novels may qualify as historical fiction (*example*: ***The Chronicles of Brother Cadfael*** by Ellis Peters). Detective fiction is reviewed in *The Mystery Review* and *The Drood Review of Mystery*. *See also*: *suspense*.

deterioration   Damage that occurs to an item by physical, chemical, or biological means after it has been produced, usually over a period of time. Examples include bindings weakened by adhesives that dry out and crack, printing papers embrittled by acid, and paper documents discolored by the growth of mildew under damp conditions. Data recorded on some digital storage media also deteriorates over time, a phenomenon known as "bit rot." *See also*: *inherent vice* and *stabilization*.

Deutscher Bibliogtheksverband e.V. (DBV)   Founded in 1949 with headquarters in Berlin, the DBV (German Library Association) promotes library services and professional librarianship in Germany and publishes the journal *Bibliotheksdienst*. URL: www.bibliotheksverband.de/index.html.

device   An ornament or symbol used in printing, such as the north pointer used on maps to indicate compass orientation. Also refers to an insignia used as a publisher's identifying mark, for example, the small design of a house stamped on the spine and printed on the title page of books published by Random House. *See also*: *colophon*.

Also refers to any electronic or electromagnetic machine or hardware component. Computer peripherals (printer, scanner, disk drives, etc.) require a program routine called a *device driver* to connect to the operating system.

Dewey, Melvil (1851–1931)   One of the founders of the American Library Association, Melvil Dewey served as editor of *Library Journal* from 1876 to 1881, published the Dewey Decimal Classification system in 1876, and served as librarian at Columbia University from 1883 to 1888, where he founded the first professional library school in 1887. He became the director of the New York State Library in Albany in 1888, taking the library school with him. Dewey was also a spokesman for professionalism in librarianship, for library education, and for equality of opportunity for women in the profession. A dynamic man, he also advocated standardization of library education, methods, tools, equipment, and supplies and was an advocate of spelling reform.

Dewey Decimal Classification (DDC)   A hierarchical system for classifying books and other library materials by subject, first published in 1876 by the librarian and educator Melvil Dewey, who divided human knowledge into 10 main classes, each of which is divided into 10 divisions, and so on. In Dewey Decimal call numbers, arabic numerals and decimal fractions are used in the class notation (*example*: **996.9**). An alphanumeric book number is added to subarrange works of the same classification by author and by title and edition (**996.9 B3262h**).

Developed and updated continuously for the past 125 years, most recently by a 10-member international Editorial Policy Committee (EPC), DDC is the most widely used classification system in the world. According to OCLC, it has been translated into 30 languages and is used by 200,000 libraries in 135 countries. The national bibliographies of 60 countries are organized according to DDC.

In the United States, public and school libraries use DDC, but most academic and research libraries use Library of Congress Classification because it is more hospitable. The abridged edition (ADC), intended for general collections of 20,000 titles or less, is a logical truncation of the notational and structural hierarchy of the *full edition*. OCLC has also developed *WebDewey* for classifying Web pages and other electronic resources. URL: www.oclc.org/dewey. *See also*: *Universal Decimal Classification*.

diacritical mark   A mark written or printed above or below an alphabetic character to indicate its semantic or phonetic value, for example, the *cedilla* used in French under the letter *ç* (as in *français*) to indicate that it is pronounced like *ts* or *s*, instead of *k*.

diagnostics   Software designed to automatically test hardware components (disks, keyboard, memory, etc.) whenever a computer session begins, to determine if they are functioning properly. If a component fails on startup, a warning message appears on the screen.

diagram A figure, chart, or graphic design intended to explain or illustrate a principle, concept, or set of statistical data. Also, a drawing, sketch, or plan that shows the steps in a process or the relationship of the parts of an object or structure to the whole, usually simplified for the sake of clarity and utility. A diagram is usually accompanied by a line or two of explanation or by explanatory text, and the various parts of the illustration may be keyed to the text or caption by means of numbers or letters with lines or arrows pointing to the appropriate features.

DIALOG A vendor that provides per-search access to a wide selection of online databases via a proprietary interface. Established in 1972, DIALOG led the market for many years in online information retrieval and remains strong in business, science, and technology. The company also provides technical support for Internet users and e-commerce. In most libraries, DIALOG searches are mediated by a specially trained librarian to keep costs down. URL: www.dialog.com.

dialog box A small square or rectangular area that opens in a graphical user interface in response to a selection made by the user, usually providing additional information or listing other options and/or settings available at that point in the program. A dialog box differs from a window in being neither movable nor resizable. Some applications are designed to open a dialog box automatically when certain operations are selected, but this feature can usually be set "off" when not desired.

dialogue Conversation, real or imagined, between two or more persons, especially the exchange of ideas and opinions between individuals who do not share the same point of view. Also refers to a written work in the form of a conversation between two or more people or to the portions of a work of fiction (novel, short story, play, etc.) consisting of words spoken by the characters, as opposed to passages of narrative or description. In the text of a narrative work, dialogue is set apart by the use of quotation marks. Compare with *monologue*.

dial-up access Connection to a network, online service, or computer system from a terminal or workstation via a telephone line, usually in exchange for payment of a monthly fee to a service provider, as opposed to access via a dedicated line. Dial-up access requires a modem to convert the digital signals produced by the computer into the analog signals used in voice transmission, and vice versa.

diamond In bookbinding, an ornament in the shape of a rhombus, usually built up of small massed tools done in blind, ink, or gold. A *lozenge* is a rhombus-shaped decorative design with one axis longer than the other.

Diamond Sutra The earliest-dated printed book known to exist, the *Diamond Sutra* was discovered in 1907 by British archaeologist Sir Marc Aurel Stein in the walled city of Dunhuang, an important military base on the Silk Road. Printed on seven strips of paper joined to form a scroll approximately 16 feet long and about 10½ inches wide, its extraordinary state of preservation is attributed to the dryness of the climate in northwest China and the fact that it remained sealed inside a cave with thousands of Buddhist manuscripts and silk paintings for approximately 900 years. Earlier examples of block printing survive, but this Chinese translation of a work originally written in Sanskrit is the first bearing a date. Decorated with an elaborate frontispiece, the scroll has a colophon at the inner end, establishing the date of its creation as A.D. May 11, 868.

diapering   From the French *diapré*, meaning "variegated." In manuscript illumination, a repetitive geometric pattern used as background in a miniature, initial letter, or border or as a filler for empty spaces. Michelle Brown notes in *Understanding Illuminated Manuscripts* (Getty Museum/British Library, 1994) that this style of decoration, used as early as the 11th century, was especially popular in gothic illumination.

diary   A private written record of day-to-day thoughts, feelings, and experiences kept by a person who does not expect them to be published. Also refers to the blankbook or notebook in which such experiences are recorded. Diaries are sometimes published posthumously, and some have become famous literary and historical works, for example, the *Diary of Samuel Pepys* and more recently that of Anne Frank. Compare with *journal* and *memoirs*.

Also refers to a small notebook in which the consecutive dates of the year are listed, with blank space for scheduling appointments, meetings, important deadlines, etc.

diced   A leather bookbinding decorated in a crisscross pattern of parallel diagonal lines forming rows of small diamonds across the surface.

dictionary   A single-volume or multivolume reference work containing brief explanatory entries for terms and topics related to a specific subject or field of inquiry, usually arranged alphabetically (*example*: *Dictionary of Neuropsychology*). The entries in a dictionary are usually shorter than those contained in an encyclopedia on the same subject, but the word "dictionary" is often used in the titles of works that should more appropriately be called encyclopedias (*Dictionary of the Middle Ages* in 13 volumes). *See also*: *biographical dictionary*.

A *language dictionary* lists the words of a language in alphabetical order, giving orthography, syllabication, pronunciation, etymology, definition, and standard usage. Some dictionaries also include synonyms, antonyms, and brief biographical and gazetteer information. In an unabridged dictionary, an attempt is made to be comprehensive in the number of terms included (*example*: *Webster's Third New International Dictionary*). An abridged dictionary provides a more limited selection of words and usually less information in each entry (*Webster's New College Dictionary*). In a visual dictionary, each term is illustrated. *See also*: *desk dictionary* and *pocket dictionary*.

Dictionaries are known to have developed from Latin glossaries as early as the 13th century. Dictionaries of the English language, limited to difficult words, were first compiled in the 17th century. The most famous is the *Oxford English Dictionary* (1989), conceived in Britain in 1857 by the Philological Society. Some English dictionaries are limited to a specialized vocabulary (*example*: *Dictionary of American Slang*). In libraries, at least one large printed dictionary is usually displayed open on a dictionary stand. Smaller portable editions are shelved in the reference section. The online version of *Merriam-Webster's Collegiate Dictionary and Thesaurus* is available at: www.m-w.com/dictionary.htm. Abbreviated *dict*. Compare with *concordance* and *thesaurus*. *See also*: *lexicography*, *metadictionary*, *polyglot dictionary*, and *rhyming dictionary*.

dictionary catalog   A type of catalog, widely used in the United States before the conversion of the card catalog to machine-readable form, in which all the entries (main, added, subject) and cross-references are interfiled in a single alphabetic sequence, as opposed to one divided into separate sections by type of entry (author, title, subject). Compare with *classified catalog*.

dictionary stand   A free-standing piece of display furniture usually made of wood, at least waist-high with a sloping top and a book stop, used in libraries to display an open dictionary or other large reference work. A dictionary stand is narrower than an atlas case and may contain shelves for storing other volumes. Small revolving table-top models are also available from library suppliers.

differential pricing   The controversial practice of charging libraries a substantially higher price for periodical subscriptions than the amount an individual subscriber is required to pay, which some journal publishers claim is justified because a library subscription makes the publication available to more readers, an effect known in the publishing trade as *pass-along*. Also refers to the practice in Europe of charging North American subscribers a rate substantially higher than normal, presumably because they can afford to pay more.

diffuse authorship   A work created by four or more persons or corporate bodies in which no single individual or body can be identified as the primary author. In libraries, such works are cataloged under the title, with an added entry for the first-named person or body. Under *AACR2*, if three or fewer persons or bodies are primarily responsible for a work, the main entry is under the heading for first-named author, with added entries for the other principal authors. Compare with *unknown authorship*. *See also*: *mixed responsibility* and *shared responsibility*.

digest   An orderly, comprehensive abridgment or condensation of a written work (legal, scientific, historical, or literary), broader in scope than a synopsis, usually prepared by a person other than the author of the original. Headings and subheadings may be added to facilitate reference. In law, a summary of existing laws, reported cases, and court decisions arranged systematically for quick reference. The earliest digests, treatises on Roman law compiled by classical Roman jurists, were copied by medieval scribes in manuscripts, sometimes with glosses and illumination.

Also refers to a periodical or index containing excerpts or condensations of works from various sources, usually arranged in some kind of order (*example*: ***Book Review Digest***).

digital   Data recorded or transmitted as discrete, discontinuous voltage pulses represented by the binary digits 0 and 1, called *bits*. In digitized text, each alphanumeric character is represented by a specific 8-bit sequence called a *byte*. The computers used in libraries transmit data in digital format. Compare with *analog*. *See also*: *born digital*.

The term is also used in a general sense to refer to the wave of information technology generated by the invention of the microcomputer in the second half of the 20th century, as in the expressions "digital divide" and "digital library."

digital archive   A system designed for locating, storing, and providing access to digital materials over the long term. A digital archive may use a variety of preservation methods to ensure that materials remain usable as technology changes, including emulation and migration. The National Digital Information Infrastructure and Preservation Program (NDIIPP) led by the Library of Congress is an example of a program aimed at preserving digital content. Synonymous with *digital repository*. Compare with *digital archives*.

digital archives   Archival materials that have been converted to machine-readable format, usually for the sake of preservation or to make them more accessible to users. A prime example is *American Memory*, a project undertaken by the Library of Congress to make digital collections of primary sources on the history and culture of the United States available via the Internet. Also refers to information originally created in electronic format, preserved for its archival value (see *digital archive*).

digital collection   A collection of library or archival materials converted to machine-readable format for preservation or to provide electronic access, for example, the *Thomas Jefferson Digital Archive*, a project of the Electronic Text Center at the University of Virginia Library (etext.virginia.edu/jefferson). Also, library materials produced in electronic formats, including e-zines, e-journals, e-books, reference works published online and on CD-ROM, bibliographic databases, and other Web-based resources. In the United States, the Digital Library Federation (DLF) is developing standards and best practices for digital collections and network access.

digital divide   A term coined by former Assistant Secretary of Commerce for Telecommunication and Communication Larry Irving, Jr., to focus public awareness on the gap in access to information resources and services between those with the means to purchase the computer hardware and software necessary to connect to the Internet and low-income families and communities that cannot afford network access. Public libraries are helping to bridge the gap between information "haves" and "have-nots" with the assistance of substantial grants from industry leaders such as Microsoft's Bill Gates. The E-rate established by the *Telecommunications Act of 1996* has helped schools, public libraries, and rural health care institutions bridge the gap. For a Web site devoted to the issue, see the *Digital Divide Network* at: www.digitaldivide network.org. Synonymous with *information gap*.

digital imaging   The field within computer science covering all aspects of the capture, storage, manipulation, transmission, and display of images in digital format, including digital photography, scanning, and bitmapped graphics. In libraries, images of text documents are created for electronic reserve collections and digital archives. They are also available in full-text bibliographic databases and reference resources. The University of Illinois Library maintains the *Digital Imaging & Media Technology Initiative* Web site at: images.library.uiuc.edu.

Digital Libraries Initiative (DLI) A multi-agency interdisciplinary research program of the National Science Foundation (NSF) that provides grants to facilitate the creation of large knowledge bases, develop the information technology to access them effectively, and improve their usability in a wide range of contexts. URL: www.dli2.nsf. gov.

digital library A library in which a significant proportion of the resources are available in machine-readable format, as opposed to print or microform, accessible by means of computers. The digital content may be locally held or accessed remotely via computer networks. In libraries, the process of digitization began with the catalog, moved to periodical indexes and abstracting services, then to periodicals and large reference works, and finally to book publishing. Abbreviated *d-lib*. Compare with *virtual library*. *See also*: *Digital Library Federation* and *National Science Digital Library*.

Digital Library Federation (DLF) A consortium of major libraries and library-related agencies dedicated to promoting the use of electronic technologies to extend collections and services, DLF is committed to identifying standards and best practices for digital collections and network access, coordinating research and development in the use of information technology by libraries, and assisting in the initiation of projects/ services that individual libraries lack the means to develop on their own. URL: www. diglib.org/dlfhomepage.htm.

digital media *See*: multimedia.

Digital Millennium Copyright Act (DMCA) Legislation passed by Congress and signed into law in October 1998 to prepare the United States for the ratification of international treaties protecting copyrights to intellectual property in digital form, drafted in 1996 at a conference of the World Intellectual Property Organization (WIPO). The bill was supported by the software and entertainment industries and opposed by the library, research, and education communities. *See also*: Technology, Education and Copyright Harmonization Act.

digital object In the technical sense, a type of data structure consisting of digital content, a unique identifier for the content (called a "handle"), and other data about the content, for example, rights metadata. *See also*: *Digital Object Identifier*.

Digital Object Identifier (DOI) A unique code preferred by publishers in the identification and exchange of the content of a digital object, such as a journal article, Web document, or other item of intellectual property. The DOI consists of two parts: a prefix assigned to each publisher by the administrative DOI agency and a suffix assigned by the publisher that may be any code the publisher chooses. DOIs and their corresponding URLs are registered in a central *DOI directory* that functions as a routing system.

The DOI is *persistent*, meaning that the identification of a digital object does not change even if ownership of or rights in the entity are transferred. It is also *actionable*, meaning that clicking on it in a Web browser display will redirect the user to the content. The DOI is also *interoperable*, designed to function in past, present, and future digital technologies. The registration and resolver system for the DOI is run by the International DOI Foundation (IDF). URL: www.doi.org.

digital preservation   The process of maintaining, in a condition suitable for use, materials produced in digital formats, including preservation of the bit stream and the continued ability to render or display the content represented by the bit stream. The task is compounded by the fact that some digital storage media deteriorate quickly ("bit rot"), and the digital object is inextricably entwined with its access environment (software and hardware), which is evolving in a continuous cycle of innovation and obsolescence. Also refers to the practice of digitizing materials originally produced in nondigital formats (print, film, etc.) to prevent permanent loss due to deterioration of the physical medium. Synonymous with *e-preservation* and *electronic preservation*. *See also*: *digital archive*, *LOCKSS*, *National Digital Information Infrastructure and Preservation Program*, and *preservation metadata*.

digital reference   Reference services requested and provided over the Internet, usually via e-mail, instant messaging ("chat"), or Web-based submission forms, usually answered by librarians in the reference department of a library, sometimes by the participants in a collaborative reference system serving more than one institution. Synonymous with *chat reference*, *e-reference*, *online reference*, and *virtual reference*.

digital rights   Ownership of information content published and distributed in electronic format, protected in the United States by copyright law. *Digital rights management (DRM)* uses technologies specifically designed to identify, secure, manage, track, and audit digital content, ideally in ways that ensure public access, preserve fair use, and right of first sale, and protect information producers from uncompensated downloading (copyright piracy).

The Copyright Clearance Center (CCC) provided one of the earliest solutions used by libraries to obtain permissions. Since the late 1990s, a variety of models have emerged to facilitate the complex relationships and transactions among rights, works, and the parties that produce and use information, including encryption schemes and plug-ins. ContentGuard has based its software approach on XrML (e**X**tensible **r**ights **M**arkup **L**anguage), originally developed at Xerox PARC, which the company hopes will become the open standard for interoperability, giving customers a common platform for receiving content under conditions that protect copyright.

digital rights management (DRM)   A system of information technology components (hardware and software) and services designed to distribute and control the rights to intellectual property created or reproduced in digital form for distribution online or via other digital media, in conjunction with corresponding law, policy, and business models. DRM systems typically use data encryption, digital watermarks, user plug-ins, and other methods to prevent content from being distributed in violation of copyright.

Unfortunately for consumers and libraries, "quick fix" DRM solutions often fail to distinguish between copyright piracy and fair use, may undermine the first sale provision of U.S. copyright law, and can be draconian. For example, many e-book editions completely forbid copying, even for works in the public domain. Carrie Russell, copyright specialist for the American Library Association, also contends that some DRM solutions threaten "to reduce the functionality of consumer and library electronic equipment, including desktop computers" (*Library Journal*, August 2003).

digital thesis   A master's thesis or Ph.D. dissertation created in electronic form ("born digital"). Most universities require a paper or microform copy for archival purposes, but for some hypermedia theses, a print version may not be an accurate representation of the original (or even possible). Preservation dilemmas posed by the rapid obsolescence of digital equipment and formats underscore the need for standards.

digital videodisc   *See*: DVD.

digital watermark   *See*: watermark.

digitization   The process of converting data to digital format for processing by computer. In information systems, digitization usually refers to the conversion of printed text or images (photographs, illustrations, maps, etc.) into binary signals using some kind of scanning device that enables the result to be displayed on a computer screen. In telecommunication, digitization refers to the conversion of continuous analog signals into pulsating digital signals.

dime novel   A melodramatic fictional narrative of adventure, romance, and action published in inexpensive paperback edition in the United States during the second half of the 19th century, sold mainly at newsstands for 10 to 25 cents a copy. The term originated with the *Dime Novel Library* introduced in 1860 by Beadle and Adams of New York. Hundreds of thousands of titles, written according to formula, were issued before this pulp fiction genre waned in the early 20th century. Among the most popular was *Buffalo Bill, King of the Border Men* (1869) by E.Z.C. Judson, writing under the pseudonym Ned Buntline. His other works included *Bigfoot Wallace: Giant Hero of the Border* (1891) and *The Red Warrior, or, Stella DeLorme's Comanche Lover: A Romance of Savage Chivalry* (1869). The influence of the dime novel on popular culture is studied by literary historians. Compare with *penny dreadful* and *yellowback*.

dimensions   The actual physical size of a bibliographic item, given in centimeters in the physical description area of the bibliographic description unless some other unit of measurement is more appropriate. *See also*: *height* and *width*.

diminuendo   The practice of gradually reducing the height of the letters following a large initial letter in a medieval manuscript or early printed book until they are the same size as the script or type used for the text. Michelle Brown notes in *Understanding Illuminated Manuscripts* (Getty Museum/British Library, 1994) that this practice was particularly popular among the scribes of Ireland and Britain from about A.D. 550 to 900. Prime examples are the incipit pages in the *Lindisfarne Gospels*, an illuminated masterpiece produced in Northumbria at the end of the 7th century, currently in the custody of The British Library.

diorama   A three-dimensional museum exhibit or display on any scale in which inanimate objects and lifelike figures are carefully arranged in front of a two-dimensional background scene drawn or painted in perspective on a flat or curved surface to create the illusion of greater depth of field than actually exists. Special lighting and recorded sound effects are often added to make the impression more realistic. Small portable examples are made for traveling exhibits.

diptych   A portable tablet consisting of two shallow hinged boxes made of wood, ivory, or metal filled with a layer of beeswax on the inside, on which the ancient Greeks and Romans wrote with a stylus. When warm, the wax surface could be easily erased by rubbing, and written over. Also refers to a picture or design painted or carved on the inside surfaces of two hinged tablets. In medieval Europe, three tablets called a *triptych* were also used for the same purpose, hinged in such a way that the outer tablets folded over the center panel. Compare with *pugillaria*.

direct access   The use of an electronic resource by means of a physical carrier (disk, cassette, cartridge, etc.) designed to be inserted into a computer or its auxiliary equipment, as opposed to accessing the resource remotely via a network (*AACR2*). Although floppy disks and CD-ROMs are still used for some applications, most libraries in the United States have shifted to networked digital resources available from vendors on subscription. Compare with *remote access*.

direct delivery   Putting library materials directly into the hands of the patron who requests them, without requiring a trip to the library to pick them up, for example, through a books-by-mail program. Direct delivery is practical for special libraries located on the premises of the host organization. It is also used by public libraries on a limited scale to serve homebound users.

direct edition   An edition of a work for which the author provides the publisher with camera-ready copy produced on a computer with the aid of word processing software. Used mainly for works that cannot be produced economically from type.

direct entry   The principle in indexing that a concept describing the content of a bibliographic item should be entered under the subject heading or descriptor that names it, rather than as a subdivision of a broader term; thus a book about "academic libraries" would be assigned the heading **Academic libraries**, not **Libraries—Academic**.

directional   Said of a question that can be answered at the information desk or reference desk by directing the patron to the location of specific resources, services, or facilities within the library, as opposed to a question requiring substantive information, instruction in the use of library resources, or referral to an outside agency or authority. *See also*: *signage*.

director   The person who has overall responsibility for directing the performance of a work written for stage or screen. The director's name appears in the credits at the beginning or end of a motion picture, videorecording, or television program and is indicated in the note area of the bibliographic record created to represent the work in the library catalog. Compare with *producer* and *screenwriter*. *See also*: *library director*.

direct order   An order for materials placed by an acquisitions librarian directly with the publisher, rather than through a jobber or subscription agent. The percentage of orders placed in this manner has declined as wholesalers and subscription services have positioned themselves to offer economies of scale to their customers and provide services that add value. Some publishers no longer accept direct orders and sell only to wholesalers (*example*: **Random House**).

directory A list of people, companies, institutions, organizations, etc., in alphabetical or classified order, providing contact information (names, addresses, phone/fax numbers, etc.) and other pertinent details (affiliations, conferences, publications, membership, etc.) in brief format, often published serially (*example*: *American Library Directory*). In most libraries, current directories are shelved in ready reference or in the reference stacks. *See also*: *city directory*, *telephone directory*, and *trade directory*.

In data storage and retrieval, a catalog of the files stored on the hard disk of a computer, or on some other storage medium, usually organized for ease of access in a hierarchical tree of *subdirectories*. The topmost directory is called the *root directory*. *See also*: *FTP*.

In library cataloging, the portion of the MARC record following the leader, which serves as an index to the tags included in the record, normally hidden from view of cataloger and catalog user. Constructed by the cataloging software from the bibliographic record at the time the record is created, the directory indicates the tag, length, and starting location of each variable field. Whenever a change is made in the record, the directory is automatically reconstructed.

dirty proof In printing, a proof of typeset copy containing many errors or one returned to the printer heavily corrected. A *clean proof* contains no errors or corrections.

disaster plan A set of written procedures prepared in advance by the staff of a library to deal with an unexpected occurrence that has the potential to cause injury to personnel or damage to equipment, collections, and/or facilities sufficient to warrant temporary suspension of services (flood, fire, earthquake, etc.). In archival records management, securing vital records in the event of disaster is one of the highest priorities. An effective disaster plan begins with a thorough risk assessment to identify the areas most susceptible to various kinds of damage and evaluate measures that can be taken in advance to ensure preparedness. Both an initial action plan and a recovery plan should be included. Compare with *contingency plan* and *emergency plan*.

disaster preparedness Steps taken by a library or archives to prepare for serious damage to facilities, collections, and/or personnel in the event of a major occurrence such as a fire, flood, or earthquake, including preventive measures, formulation of an effective disaster plan, maintenance of adequate insurance, etc. *Conservation OnLine (CoOL)* maintains a Web page on disaster preparedness at: palimpsest.stanford.edu/bytopic/disasters.

disbound A book or other printed publication from which a previous binding has been removed, usually in preparation for rebinding, part of the process called *pulling*. Compare with *unbound*.

disc A generic term used in computing to distinguish read-only digital storage media (audio compact discs, CD-ROMs, videodiscs, etc.) from those that are rewritable. Also, an alternate spelling of *disk* ("optical disc" or "optical disk").

discard   To officially withdraw an item from a library collection for disposal, a process that includes removing from the catalog all references to it. Also refers to any item withdrawn for disposal, usually stamped "discard" to avoid confusion. Materials are usually withdrawn when they become outdated, cease to circulate, wear out, or are damaged beyond repair. When shelf space is limited, duplicates may be discarded to make room for new acquisitions. Withdrawn items may be exchanged or given as gifts to other libraries, but the most common method of disposal is in a book sale. Unsold items may be given to a thrift store or thrown away as trash, depending on the policy of the library. *See also*: *weeding*.

discharge   In circulation, to cancel the record of a loan upon return of the borrowed item and payment of any overdue fine. Compare with *charge*. *See also*: *patron record*.

discipline   An organized branch of human knowledge, developed through study and research or creative endeavor, constituting a division of the curriculum at institutions of higher learning. A discipline may be divided into subdisciplines, for example, *botany* and *zoology* within the *biological sciences*. In Western scholarship, the disciplines are traditionally organized as follows:

Arts and humanities: archaeology, classical studies, communication, folklore, history, language and literature, performing arts (dance, film, music, theater), philosophy, religion and theology, visual arts

Social sciences: anthropology, criminology and criminal justice, economics, international relations, law, political science, psychiatry, psychology, public administration, social work, sociology, urban studies, women's studies

Sciences: astronomy, biology, chemistry, computer science, earth sciences, mathematics, medicine and health, physics

In Dewey Decimal Classification, the classes representing subjects are arranged according to discipline.

disclaimer   A legal notice posted on a Web page, appended to an e-mail message, given on a product, or provided with a service informing the reader or consumer that the host or producer does not guarantee and cannot be held responsible for all aspects of its content or performance.

disclosure   The act of making something known by revealing it to public scrutiny. In the information sector, disclosure is usually made by the provider in a voluntary statement informing the user of any financial or personal interest in the content provided or in its provision, for example, payment made by the owners of a Web site to a Web search engine to get the site listed or payment received by the owners of a Web site from the manufacturer or distributor of a product or service recommended by the site. Lack of disclosure, a common problem on the Internet, may affect the credibility of information available online.

discography   A list or catalog of audiorecordings, usually of works by a specific composer or performer, of a certain style or genre, or of a specific time period. Each entry in a discography provides some or all of the following descriptive elements: title of work, name of composer and performer(s), date of recording, name of manufacturer,

manufacturer's catalog number, and release date. Also refers to the systematic cataloging of audiorecordings and to the study of sound recording as a medium of expression. The person who compiles such a catalog is called a *discographer*. Compare with *filmography*.

discontinuation   In Dewey Decimal Classification, the shifting of a topic or the entire contents of a class number to a more general number in the same hierarchy, or the complete removal of the topic or number from the schedule, usually because the current literature on the topic or concept has dwindled significantly or because the distinction represented by the number is no longer valid or recognized in the field. A note is added to explain the shift or removal, and the discontinued number is enclosed in square brackets. *See also*: *relocation* and *schedule reduction*.

discontinued   A serial publication for which a library subscription or continuation order has ended. In the catalog record for the title, the library's holdings are indicated in a closed entry. *See also*: *canceled* and *ceased publication*.

discontinued number   In Dewey Decimal Classification, a class number from an earlier edition no longer used, indicated at the appropriate location in the schedules by a note to "class in" a more general number. A discontinued number is enclosed in square brackets. *See also*: *schedule reduction*.

discount   A percentage deducted from the price of any product or service, for example, the reduction in the rate paid for telecommunication services by schools and public libraries under the federal E-rate program. In publishing, a percentage deducted from the publisher's list price for an item as an inducement to purchase. In book sales, the discount system includes:

Cash discount—usually 1–2 percent, offered by publishers to booksellers in exchange for payment within 30 days or less

Continuation order discount—for automatic shipment of works published as serials (usually 5 percent)

Convention discount—on orders placed at a publisher's exhibit during a conference or convention (usually 15 percent)

Library discount—on purchases by libraries and related institutions (usually 5–10 percent)

Prepayment discount—for payment with order (usually 5 percent or free shipping)

Prepublication discount—on orders placed prior to the publication date to encourage advance sales

Professional or *courtesy discount*—offered to individuals at publisher's discretion

Quantity discount—on purchases of a required number of copies or titles

Short discount—on professional books and textbooks sold directly to individuals and sometimes on special orders

Trade discount or *long discount*—to jobbers and retail outlets, usually 30–45 percent or better, depending on publisher and quantities ordered

discourse analysis   Linguistic analysis of segments of spoken or written language that are longer than one sentence and form a unit having recognizable structure for the purpose of identifying regularities in the occurrence of phonological, grammatical, and semantic elements. In computer science, the results of discourse analysis have been applied to the study of human/computer interaction, for example, in the development of voice recognition systems.

discussion list   *See*: mailing list.

discussion paper   *See*: working paper.

disinformation   The deliberate, often covert, dissemination of erroneous information, usually with the intention of influencing by deception the actions or opinions of another, a technique used in foreign relations and armed conflict to mislead an adversary. Compare with *misinformation*. *See also*: *propaganda*.

disintermediation   Elimination of the mediator or "middleman." In the delivery of information services, the need for professional assistance is minimized in user-friendly systems designed to facilitate end-user searching. *See also*: *mediated search*.

disk   A generic term used in computing for a digital storage medium that is *rewritable*, as opposed to *read-only*. Compare with *disc*. *See also*: *magnetic disk* and *optical disk*.

disk drive   In computing, a generic term for the hardware component that physically manipulates a specific type of magnetic disk (hard, floppy, WORM, Zip), allowing the user to read data from and write data to it. Disk drives can be internal or external. Also spelled *disc drive*.

diskette   *See*: floppy disk.

display case   A box or set of shelves enclosed in glass or plexiglass to allow books and other items to remain protected while on exhibit. A display case can be free-standing, wall-mounted, or built-in. Modern designs are usually lockable. Cases used for perishable museum specimens may be climate-controlled to prevent deterioration. Synonymous with *exhibit case*. Compare with *display rack*.

display copy   A copy of a new book or other publication put on view, usually in a bookstore or as part of publisher's exhibit at a conference or convention. At the end of the event, display copies are sometimes sold to conference participants at a discount, especially if their dust jackets are no longer in new condition.

display matter   Any printed matter that is not part of the text of a work, including illustrations, headings, captions, printer's ornaments, etc. To distinguish it from body matter, textual display matter is set in type of a different size and/or font.

display rack   A library furnishing in metal, wood, or plastic designed to display printed material, such as brochures, announcements, instructional handouts, reading lists, etc., face-forward to encourage users to browse and select what they need. Sold by library suppliers, display racks are available in wall-mounted and free-standing designs, from small countertop models to large floor units. Compare with *display case*.

display script   A decorative calligraphic script in which the letterforms are more elaborate and generally larger than the script used for the text. In medieval manuscripts, display script often followed a large initial letter, emphasizing a major division of the work. Each letter was sometimes written in ink of a different color, and the script might be enclosed in a decorative *display panel*. The corresponding term in printing is *display type*.

display type   Type sizes larger than 14-point, used mainly for headings, titles, banners, and other display purposes, in contrast to the smaller text type used to print the body of the text and even smaller extract type used for quotations, notes, etc. The corresponding term in calligraphy is *display script*. *See also*: *fancy type*.

disposal   In U.S. government archives, the destruction of noncurrent records that are no longer needed. Also used synonymously with *disposition*.

disposition   The manner in which the noncurrent records of an agency or individual are handled once their utility has been appraised, whether stored (temporarily or permanently) in a repository in their original format, reproduced and stored on microform, sold, donated, or destroyed. Compare with *disposal*. *See also*: *disposition schedule*.

disposition schedule   A systematic list of documents used by an archivist to determine: (1) which of the recurring records of an agency or individual will be retained, (2) the period of time for which they will be held, (3) where they will be housed during the retention period (archives or intermediate storage), and (4) any other decisions concerning their disposition, based on their utility and value to the organization. Synonymous with *retention schedule*. *See also*: *sentencing*.

dissertation   A lengthy, formal written treatise or thesis, especially an account of scholarly investigation or original research on a specialized topic, submitted to a university in partial fulfillment of the requirements for a Ph.D. degree. Dissertations submitted at universities in the United States, Canada, Great Britain, and other European countries are indexed and abstracted in *Dissertation Abstracts International* (*DAI*), available in print, on CD-ROM, and online from ProQuest. In most academic libraries, copies of dissertations may be requested on interlibrary loan or ordered via document delivery. Abbreviated *diss*. Compare with *thesis*.

***Dissertation Abstracts International* (*DAI*)**   A service that provides indexing and abstracting of Ph.D. dissertations and master's theses in all academic disciplines submitted at universities in the United States, Canada, Great Britain, and other European countries since 1861 (dissertations abstracted since 1980, theses since 1988). *DAI* is available from ProQuest in print, on CD-ROM, or as an online bibliographic database, or via OCLC *FirstSearch* (updated monthly). Paper copies of dissertations can be ordered from *Dissertation Express* (www.proquest.com/hp/Products/DisExpress.html) on a fee-per-item basis.

distance education   *See*: distance learning.

distance learning   A method of instruction and learning designed to overcome barriers of time and space by allowing students to study in their own homes or at local facilities, often at their own convenience, using materials available electronically or by mail. Communication with the instructor is normally by telephone or e-mail. Telecommunication networks and teleconferencing have facilitated distance learning. Libraries are working to support distance learning by providing online catalogs and databases, electronic reserves, electronic reference service, online tutorials, and electronic document delivery service. *See also*: *continuing education*.

distinctive title   A title that is unique to a specific work. Distinctiveness of title is important in registering copyright and makes the entry for a document easier to retrieve from a library catalog or other finding tool in a search by title.

distribution copy   In reprography, a microform copy from which additional copies of equal legibility can be reproduced.

distribution imprint   The statement printed on the verso of the title page of a book giving the official name(s) of the distributor(s) from which copies can be obtained, as distinct from the imprint of the publisher that issued the edition or the printer responsible for printing the edition.

distribution list   In e-mail software, a feature that allows the user to establish a list of e-mail addresses under a common name, enabling messages to be sent simultaneously to everyone on the list when addressed to the list name. Although the term is sometimes used synonymously with *mailing list*, the latter generally supports a much larger group, requiring special software for automatic maintenance.

distribution rights   Legal arrangements made by a publisher to transfer to another company or person the exclusive right to market a publication, usually within a designated geographic area. In books, distribution rights are usually indicated in the distribution imprint on the verso of the title page.

distributor   An agent or agency that owns the exclusive or shared rights to market a publication or other item, usually within a designated geographic area. In domestic publishing, the distributor is usually but not always the publisher. Foreign publications are often distributed by a domestic publishing company under an agreement with the original publisher. Abbreviated *distr*. *See also*: *distribution imprint*.

diversity   Inclusiveness with regard to variation in age, gender, sexual orientation, religious belief, and ethnic, racial, or cultural background within a given population. In the United States, libraries strive to achieve diversity in library school admissions, hiring, collection development, services, and programs. *See also*: *affirmative action*.

divided catalog   In the 1930s, when it became apparent that dictionary catalogs were becoming cumbersome, large libraries in the United States began dividing their catalogs into two sections, one for subject entries and the other for main and added entries other than subject (authors, titles, series, etc.). Eventually, some libraries divided their catalogs into *three* sections (author, title, and subject). Divided catalogs have the disadvantage of requiring that the user know in advance which type of entry is required (entries for works written *by* a specific author are filed separately from works written *about* the same person), but once the initial determination is made, the user is spared the time and effort of looking through entries that are not of the type desired. Synonymous with *split catalog*. *See also*: *classified catalog*.

divide-like note   A note added to a heading in a classification schedule to inform the cataloger that the heading is subdivided in the same way as another heading in the same schedule. *See also*: *pattern heading*.

Divine Office   Literally, a duty performed for God. Prayers performed daily at certain hours of the day and night by priests, clerics, and members of monastic orders. The Divine Office and the Mass form the basis of Roman Catholic liturgy. The practice originated in services performed in the Jewish synagogue and the Apostolic Church, each office consisting of a recitation of Psalms and lessons read from Scripture. Over the centuries, hymns, antiphons, canticles, and other elaborations were added. By the close of the 6th century, the eight canonical hours were fixed at: matins (2:30 A.M.), lauds (5:00 A.M.), prime (6:00 A.M.), terce (9:00 A.M.), sext (12:00 noon), none (3:00 P.M.), vespers (4:30 P.M.), and compline (6:00 P.M.). The prayers of the Divine office are contained in the *breviary*. Its lay counterpart is the *Book of Hours*.

divinity calf   A style of binding used in the mid-19th century for theological and devotional works characterized by plain covers in smooth khaki or dark brown calfskin, usually with beveled boards, blind-tooled single-line borders ending in Oxford corners, and the edges of the sections often stained red.

divinity circuit   *See*: circuit edges.

division   In Dewey Decimal Classification, the first level of subdivision of the 10 main classes, usually representing a discipline or subdiscipline, indicated by the first two digits in the notation (*example*: **94** in **940** European history). There are 100 divisions in DDC (10 × 10). The next level of subdivision, indicated by a third digit other than zero, is a *section* (**944** for works on the history of France).

divisional title   The title printed on the recto of the leaf preceding the first page of the text of a major division of a book, sometimes with the number of the division, if numbered. The verso is normally left blank. Synonymous with *part title* and *section title*.

DLF   *See*: **Digital Library Federation**.

DLI   *See*: **Digital Libraries Initiative**.

DMCA   *See*: *Digital Millennium Copyright Act*.

DNS   *See*: **Domain Name System**.

docking station   A piece of computer hardware that enables a laptop to function as a desktop computer by providing a single large plug and socket that duplicates the individual cable connections to monitor, keyboard, mouse, and printer. Some docking stations include built-in peripherals such as audio speakers and CD-ROM drive and a network interface card to allow the user to connect to a local area network. Because no standard exists for docking stations, compatibility with the specific type of laptop is an important consideration in making a purchase decision.

doctored   A book that has been altered from its original condition, usually as a consequence of mending, repairs, restoration, or the addition or removal of parts. Compare with *as issued*. *See also*: *made-up copy*.

docudrama   A shortened form of the term *documentary drama*, a dramatization of events that actually happened, usually produced for film or television. Although some elements may be fictionalized, a serious attempt is made to be historically accurate (*example*: ***Edward Hopper, the Silent Witness***, a film by Wolfgang Hastert). Compare with *documentary* and *feature film*.

document A generic term for a physical entity consisting of any substance on which is recorded all or a portion of one or more works for the purpose of conveying or preserving knowledge. In the words of the communication theorist Marshall McLuhan, a document is the "medium" in which a "message" (information) is communicated. Document formats include manuscripts, print publications (books, pamphlets, periodicals, reports, maps, prints, etc.), microforms, nonprint media, electronic resources, etc. Abbreviated *doc*. *See also*: *core document, document delivery service, government documents*, and *internal document*.

Also, any form printed on paper, once it has been filled in, especially one that has legal significance or is supplied by a government agency, for example, an application for copyright protection.

Also refers to a word processing text file (file type **.doc**) or any file created on a Macintosh computer.

documentary A motion picture that records actual events or depicts social conditions without fictionalization, often through the use of historical footage and still photographs, usually accompanied by a narration dramatically structured to highlight important individuals who participated in the action. The term was coined by the Scottish filmmaker John Grierson in the late 1920s to describe the cinematic works of Robert Flaherty, the first person to produce films of social commentary depicting actual people in real-life situations (*example*: ***Louisiana Story***). Compare with *docudrama* and *feature film*.

documentary fiction *See*: faction.

documentation The process of systematically collecting, organizing, storing, retrieving, and disseminating specialized documents, especially of a scientific, technical, or legal nature, usually to facilitate research or preserve institutional memory. Also refers to a collection of documents pertaining to a specific subject, especially when used to substantiate a point of fact. *See also*: *documentation center*.

In scholarly publication, the practice of citing the source of a direct quotation or excerpt, an idea that is not original, or factual information, to support a thesis or argument and/or avoid plagiarism or infringement of copyright, particularly important in the writing of history and biography.

In archives, the process of writing and organizing descriptions of records for reference purposes and to facilitate the development of finding aids for users.

In data processing, detailed descriptive information required to develop, operate, and maintain machine-readable data files and systems. In a more general sense, a systematic written description of any procedure (or set of procedures and/or policies), including the history of its application within a specific context.

In France, a term used in nearly the same sense as *information science*.

documentation center An organization or agency that specializes in receiving, processing, preserving, abstracting, and indexing publications, usually within a scholarly discipline or field of research and study (*example*: **ERIC**). Documentation centers also issue bulletins on the progress of such work for distribution to interested parties and may also prepare bibliographies on special topics, make copies or translations, and engage in bibliographic research.

document camera   A tabletop device used in bibliographic instruction and other visual presentations to project text and/or images from an opaque surface or transparency onto a large screen using an LCD projector. Document cameras have superseded overhead projectors in well-equipped libraries.

document delivery service (DDS)   The provision of published or unpublished documents in hard copy, microform, or digital format, usually for a fixed fee upon request. In most libraries, document delivery service is provided by the interlibrary loan office on a cost-recovery basis. The patron is usually required to pick up printed material at the library, but electronic full-text may be forwarded via e-mail. Also refers to the physical or electronic delivery of documents from a library collection to the residence or place of business of a library user, upon request. For a directory of document suppliers, see *DocDel.net* at: www.docdel.net. *See also*: *Ariel* and *electronic document delivery*.

document supplier   A commercial company, agency, or library that provides copies of documents on request, usually for a fixed fee, for example, the ERIC Document Reproduction Service (EDRS), which provides copies of ERIC documents on microfiche and online. A list of document suppliers is provided in the front matter of the reference serial *Magazines for Libraries* and in the *DocDel.net* directory available online at: www.docdel.net.

document trail   All the authenticated sources of information about a topic, recorded in any medium, traced backward in time to determine conclusively the origins of an existing state of affairs, a technique used in archives to establish provenance and in news reporting to uncover the details of a story.

Document Type Definition (DTD)   A formal description of a particular type of document content, for example, a metadata record in SGML or XML declaration syntax, giving the names of data elements and rules for their use (where they may occur, whether they may repeat, etc.). DTDs are expected to be replaced by a new standard called *XML Schema*, a superset of DTD.

dog-eared   The condition of a book that shows definite signs of wear, especially pages that have been folded down at a corner to mark a place.

doggerel   Versification that is loose, irregular, crude, and/or superficial due to the writer's ineptitude or by intention, usually for comic effect, as in John Skelton's *Colin Clout*:

> For though my rhyme be ragged,
> Tattered and jagged,
> Rudely rain-beaten,
> Rusty and moth-eaten,

> If ye take well therewith,
> It hath in it some pith.

Also spelled *doggrel*.

DOI   *See*: **D**igital **O**bject **I**dentifier.

domain   All the hardware and software resources controlled by a single computer system. In a local area network (LAN), all the clients, servers, and devices under the control of a single security database, administered under a common set of rules and procedures. On the Internet, all the clients, servers, and devices sharing a common portion of the IP address, the highest level domain being the type of entity serving as network host, indicated by the top level domain code at the end of the domain name. In database management, all the possible values of the data contained in a specific field present in every record in a file.

In indexing, the range or extent within which documents or items are selected for inclusion in a bibliography, index, or catalog. When the domain is one or more tangible collections, the result is a catalog. In an abstracting and indexing service, the domain is usually the published literature of an academic discipline (*example*: *Sociological Abstracts*) or group of related disciplines (*Child Development Abstracts and Bibliography*). In a national bibliography, the domain is the published output of an entire country. *See also*: *scope*.

domain name   The address identifying a specific site on the Internet. In the United States, domain names usually consist of three parts separated by the period (full stop). In the address **www.thisuniversity.edu**, the first part (**www**) indicates the protocol or language used in accessing the address, the second part (**.thisuniversity**) represents the name of the institution or organization hosting the site, and the last part (**.edu**) is a top level domain code indicating type of entity serving as network host. For the United States, the six basic top level domain codes are:

.com—commercial enterprise
.edu—educational institution
.gov—government agency
.mil—military installation
.net—network
.org—nonprofit organization

The top level domain for a country other than the United States is represented by a two-character country code. For example, in the URL **www.bbc.co.uk**, the code **.uk** indicates that the commercial Web site is hosted in the United Kingdom. Other top level domain codes have been approved by ICANN, the technical body authorized to assign globally unique Internet identifiers, but the new codes are not widely used. For more information on the assignment of domain names, see *ICANN Watch* at: www.icannwatch.org.

Domain Name System (DNS)   A distributed Internet directory service used primarily to translate numerical IP (Internet Protocol) addresses (*example*: **123.456.78.9**) into the alphanumeric domain name addresses (**www.thisuniversity.edu**) familiar to Internet users, and vice versa. The **DNS** is administered by the Internet Corporation for Assigned Names and Numbers (ICANN). URL: www.icann.org.

donation   In archives, a voluntary deposit of records by a person or organization in which both legal title and physical custody are formally transferred by the *donor*. Compare with *gift*. *See also*: *donor file*.

donor file   A systematic record of the names of persons and/or organizations that have donated materials to a library or archives. A well-maintained donor file should document any restrictions on the preservation, use, or disposition of donated items or files and provide current contact information. In a weeding project, it is wise to check discards against such a file to ascertain if a prior agreement was made with the donor concerning their final disposition.

door count   *See*: gate count.

door stop   Library slang for a piece of equipment so obsolete that it cannot be given away. Such items are usually consigned to a storage room in the basement until renovation or a move into a new facility makes disposal unavoidable.

DOS   An acronym for **D**isk **O**perating **S**ystem (pronounced "dahss"), the first operating system for IBM-compatible personal computers, developed for IBM in a version called PC-DOS by Bill Gates' fledgling company Microsoft. Gates subsequently marketed the Microsoft version (MS-DOS) that became the underlying control program for early versions of Windows. Windows NT and later versions of Windows are not dependent on DOS, although they are capable of supporting DOS applications. Because it is nongraphical, line-oriented, and command-driven, the DOS interface is not as user-friendly as Windows.

dos-à-dos   An English term for a type of binding in which two books are bound back-to-back, sharing the back cover, with the fore-edges of one aligned with the spine of the other, so that they open in opposite directions. Popular during the 17th century, this style was used to bind in a single volume the *New Testament* with the *Prayer Book and Psalms*. Compare with *tête-bêche*.

dot   A full stop used to divide the elements of an Internet address.

dot.com   A commercial enterprise that does all or a substantial portion of its business over the Internet, mostly sales by credit card (*example*: **Amazon.com**).

dots per inch (dpi)   In computing, a measure of image quality (resolution) in display and printing. On a typical computer screen, 72 dpi is acceptable, with 96 dpi the norm. In flat panels displays, 110 to 200 dpi is common. By comparison, 300 to 600 dpi is standard in printing.

dotting   *See*: rubrication.

double column   A book or other publication in which the text is set to half the width of a page, usually with a blank space or rule dividing the two columns, a format commonly used in dictionaries, encyclopedias, and other large-format reference works.

double dagger (‡)   In printing, a character in the shape of a vertical stroke crossed twice, above and below the midpoint, used as the third-order reference mark, following the use of the asterisk (*) and the dagger (†). The double dagger is also known as a *double obelisk* or *diesis*.

double-fan adhesive binding   A type of adhesive binding in which the binding edge of the text block is milled and splayed, first in one direction while a slow-drying adhesive is applied, and then in the opposite direction as a second application is made, allowing the adhesive to penetrate no more than one thirty-second of an inch between the leaves, so that each leaf is tipped to the next. The method is not practical for books with a text block more than two inches thick. The strength of fan adhesive binding can be enhanced by notching the binding edge, but this technique has the disadvantage of restricting openability. Compare with *perfect binding*.

double fold   *See*: double leaf.

double leaf   A leaf twice the page size in a book, folded in half at the fore-edge or top edge, with the fold uncut and no printing inside the fold. When such a leaf is unnumbered, it is counted as two pages. In the bibliographic description of the item, the total number of pages is recorded as in the following example: **[32] pp. (on double leaves)**. Synonymous with *double fold*. *See also*: *Chinese style*.

double numeration   A system of enumeration, used mainly in textbooks, law books, and technical publications, in which *two* numbers are assigned, usually separated by a period, hyphen, or other symbol, the first being the number of the chapter or other major division of the work, and the second indicating a section of the text or one of several illustrations, maps, graphs, charts, etc., numbered in the sequence in which they appear within the division, for example, *Fig. 12.10* to indicate the tenth figure in chapter 12.

double plate   A single illustration that extends across facing pages in an open book or other publication, usually printed on a double-size leaf folded down the center and bound at the fold. A caption may be printed on the preceding or following page. Compare with *double spread* and *face up*. *See also*: *plate*.

double shelving   Storing books two rows to a shelf, one behind the other, a shelving method used in libraries only when space is severely limited. Shelves must be at least 10 inches deep for this alternative to work. The method can potentially double shelf capacity, but it reduces browsability and makes materials more difficult to locate and reshelve. These drawbacks can be minimized by installing graphic signage or limiting its use to series, such as legal case law, or to the back files of bound periodicals and reports. *See also*: *flat shelving*, *fore-edge shelving*, and *shelving by size*.

double spread   Text and/or illustration printed across facing pages in a book or other publication, as if on a single page, usually for visual effect. Compare with *double plate*.

doublure   From the French *doubler*, meaning "to line." An ornamental lining of watered silk, satin, vellum, leather, decorated paper, or some other material of fine quality, used in place of the paste-down endleaf to cover the inside of the boards in deluxe bindings. Morocco doublures were introduced in Europe during the late 15th century by Moorish binders working in Spain. Jane Greenfield notes in *ABC of Bookbinding*

(Oak Knoll/Lyons Press, 1998) that doublures were popular from 1750 on, particularly in France, and that the turn-ins surrounding them were often gold-tooled. Synonymous with *ornamental endpaper*. *See also*: *marbling*.

doubtful authorship A work for which authorship has *not* been conclusively established, which is ascribed to one or more persons on the basis of incomplete or unconvincing evidence. Some scholars believe the works of William Shakespeare to have been written by another author, but the evidence in support of this contention is inconclusive.

download To transfer one or more files from a mainframe computer to a terminal, from a network server to a client computer, or from the hard disk of any computer to another storage medium. In libraries, downloading bibliographic data to floppy disk is a low-cost alternative to printing the output of an online search, and users are generally encouraged to do so. The opposite of *upload*.

down time Any period during which a computer or system is out of operation, usually due to hardware or software failure or regular maintenance. In libraries, the amount of time a public access workstation or system is "down" is a measure of its reliability and can directly affect quality of service, particularly during periods of peak use. Also spelled *downtime*.

dpi *See*: **d**ots **p**er **i**nch.

draft A version of a document, in handwritten, typed, printed, or digital form, not intended to be final but instead subject to future modification (correction, revision, etc.), sometimes by a person or persons other than the original author. A *rough draft* usually provides only a preliminary or sketchy version of the work or plan. The last version of a work that has seen multiple revisions is the *final draft*. To avoid misunderstanding, a document not yet completed should be clearly marked "Draft." *See also*: *bill*.

drama *See*: play.

dramatization An adaptation of a nondramatic work of fiction or nonfiction for performance on stage or screen, usually by a person other than the original author. In library cataloging, a dramatization is entered under the name of the playwright, with added entries under the author and title of the work on which it is based. *See also*: *novelization*.

dress code A set of written standards governing the proper attire and personal grooming of library employees when on duty, usually established by the library board and enforced by the library administration, to help maintain professionalism. Most codes require employees to be neat and clean and wear clothing in good condition and appropriate to their duties. Some codes also address recent fads such as body piercing and tattooing. Not all libraries have such a code.

driver A program routine specifically designed to link a peripheral device to the operating system of a computer, allowing it to perform the functions requested by application software. Some drivers, such as the keyboard driver, are included in the operating system, but when a new piece of hardware is added to a computer (printer, scanner, disk drive, etc.), the appropriate driver must usually be installed on the CPU so that the operating system can call upon it to run the device. Also called a *device driver*.

DRM   *See*: digital rights management.

drollery   A small comic figure (or part of a figure) drawn or painted in the margin of an illuminated manuscript or hidden in a border or in the decoration of an initial letter. Christopher de Hamel suggests that drolleries and grotesques may have served as mnemonic devices, since medieval manuscripts were neither foliated nor paginated (*The British Library Guide to Manuscript Illumination*, University of Toronto, 2001).

Drood Review of Mystery, The   Published since 1982, the bimonthly *Drood Review of Mystery* provides reviews of new mystery, suspense, and detective fiction, as well as author interviews, commentary on the genre, and guides to new titles for use in collection development, readers' advisory, and book discussions. ISSN: 0893–0252. URL: www.droodreview.com. *See also*: Mystery Review, The.

drop   A telecommunication outlet in a library or other facility usually consisting of a voice jack and at least one data jack to allow users to connect to a computer network.

drop cap   *See*: drop initial.

drop-down title   The shortened version of the title of a book, printed on the first page of the text, usually the same as the running title. Compare with *caption title*.

drop initial   A large decorated or undecorated initial letter in a manuscript or printed work aligned horizontally with the tops of succeeding letters in the same line but extending below the line into a space left by indenting the next line (or lines). Drop initials are used mainly at the beginning of a chapter or other major division of a work. Synonymous with *drop cap*. Compare with *raised capital*.

drop shipment   Publications ordered from a jobber by the acquisitions department of a library, sent by the publisher directly to the library at the request of the jobber, usually to reduce shipping costs when the jobber does not have the items in stock. Compare with *reshipment*.

DTD   *See*: Document Type Definition.

DTP   *See*: desktop publishing.

dual editions   *See*: multiple editions.

Dublin Core (DC)   A standard set of 15 interoperable metadata elements designed to facilitate the description and recovery of document-like resources in a networked environment. The descriptive elements are:
- **Title** (name given to the resource)
- **Creator** (entity primarily responsible for making the content of the resource)
- **Subject** (topic of the content of the resource, typically expressed as keywords, key phrases, or classification codes)
- **Description** (abstract, table of contents, free-text account of the content, etc.)

- **Publisher** (entity responsible for making the resource available)
- **Contributor** (entity responsible for making contributions to the content of the resource)
- **Date** (typically associated with the creation or availability of the resource)
- **Type** (nature or genre of the content of the resource)
- **Format** (physical or digital manifestation of the resource)
- **Identifier** (an unambiguous reference to the resource within a given context, such as the URL, ISBN, ISSN, etc.)
- **Source** (reference to a resource from which the present resource is derived)
- **Language** (the language of the intellectual content of the resource)
- **Relation** (reference to a related resource)
- **Coverage** (extent or scope of the content of the resource)
- **Rights** (information about rights held in and over the resource)

Dublin Core is the result of an international cross-disciplinary consensus achieved through the ongoing efforts of the Dublin Core Metadata Initiative (DCMI), aimed at providing a foundation for standardized bibliographic description of information resources available via the Internet. URL: dublincore.org.

ductus   In calligraphy, the number of pen strokes required to write a character and the direction and sequence in which they are executed by the scribe. In medieval manuscripts, the ductus of each script was in its time considered by experienced scribes to be the most effortless way of writing it. However, as Marc Drogin notes in *Medieval Calligraphy: Its History and Technique* (Allanheld & Schram, 1980), two scribes might write a letter differently, or ductus might depend on the letter preceding or following it. On an exemplar, ductus is shown by surrounding the completed letter with numbered arrows indicating the sequence and direction of strokes or by displaying the letter in the process of creation (first stroke, then first and second, and so on, until the final stroke is added). Plural: *ducti*. Compare with *aspect*.

due date   The date of the last day of the loan period, stamped or written by a library staff member on the date due slip affixed to an item when it is checked out at the circulation desk. Fines may be charged for materials returned after the due date if they are not renewed. In the online catalog, the due date is displayed to indicate the circulation status of an item currently checked out. Synonymous with *date due*. *See also*: *overdue*.

dues   Titles ordered from a publisher that cannot be supplied until additional stock arrives from the printer, usually new books for which stock has not been received or backlisted titles in the process of being reprinted. Such items are usually *back ordered*.

Also refers to the annual fee that a member of a professional organization, such as the American Library Association, must pay to keep his or her membership current. Some organizations offer a sliding scale allowing each member to pay an amount corresponding to length of service or level of participation, with students and recent graduates paying the least.

dumb terminal   *See*: terminal.

dummy   A single prototype of a book made up of the same number of leaves (usually blank) of the same grade of paper as the final product, trimmed and sewn but usually unbound, to give the binder an idea of bulk and page size and to assist the graphic designer in planning the layout of the dust jacket.

Also refers to the complete layout of every page of a print job, including typeface, type size, and the position of text block, headings, illustrations, captions, etc. *See also*: *shelf dummy*.

dump   A computer operation that copies raw data from one location to another in a system, usually with little or no formatting, for example, the transfer of the contents of memory to a printer or computer screen to display the status of a program at the moment it crashed, useful in diagnosing the nature of a problem.

duodecimo (12mo)   A book, approximately eight inches high, made by folding a full sheet of book paper to form signatures of 12 leaves (24 pages). *See also*: *folio*, *quarto*, *octavo*, and *sextodecimo*.

duotone   An illustration in which the image is printed in two colors, usually black and either dark blue or dark green, a method that allows tint to be applied to a black and white image at considerably less expense than full-color printing. Also refers to the process used to produce such an image. *See also*: *halftone*.

duplex   In communications, a channel capable of transmitting signals in both directions (sending and receiving) at the same time. In computer networks, this is usually achieved by using paired wires or by dividing bandwidth into two frequencies. A *half-duplex* connection is capable of transmitting signals alternately but not simultaneously in either direction, for example, two-way radio. Synonymous with *full-duplex*. Compare with *simplex*.

Also refers to a printer attached to a computer or computer network that has the capability to print both sides of a sheet of paper, a means of conserving paper in libraries that allow printing from public access workstations.

duplicate   An additional copy of an item already in a library collection that is not needed. Public libraries often order high-demand items in multiple copies, then weed duplicates as they cease to circulate. Compare with *added copy*.

In reprography, an exact copy of an original document (either positive or negative) that can be used in place of the original. Also refers to the process of making single or multiple copies of an original document.

duplicate paging   The numbering of pages in duplicate, usually on facing pages, used mainly in books containing parallel texts, for example, a text in translation and the same text in the original language.

duplicate record   A bibliographic record that occurs more than once in a library's catalog. In MARC files, this usually occurs when a record is used more than once in OCLC cataloging procedures. When a bibliographic database is created or updated, duplicate records are removed in a batch process known as *deduping*.

durability   The degree to which a material retains its physical integrity when subjected to stress, for example, heavy use in the case of some library materials. A *durable* material, such as the buckram used as a covering in some library bindings, will generally last a relatively long time under conditions of normal use. The opposite of *fragile*.

durable paper   *See*: permanent paper.

dust cover   *See*: dust jacket.

dust jacket   The removable paper wrapper on the outside of a hardcover book, usually printed in color and given a glossy finish to market the work to retail customers and protect it from wear and tear. The front of the dust jacket bears the title, the author's full name, and a graphic design. The title also appears on the spine of the jacket, with the author's last name and the publisher's name or symbol. For most trade titles, a promotional blurb written by the publisher appears on the inside flap. The back flap usually provides brief biographical information about the author, which may include a small portrait photograph. The ISBN is printed on the back of the dust jacket, usually in the lower-right-hand corner, following brief quotes from positive reviews of the work. Textbooks, reference books, and sci-tech books are usually published without a dust jacket.

The first protective paper jacket was provided by a publisher in England in 1833. Since then, dust jacket design has become a highly skilled form of graphic art and a significant factor in the cost of book production. In illustrated children's books, the design used on the dust jacket is usually done by the illustrator. Public libraries usually cover the dust jacket with polyester film for protection against abrasion and fading and to enhance visual appeal. In academic libraries, dust jackets are usually removed in processing and used for display or discarded. Synonymous with *book jacket* and *dust cover*. Abbreviated *dj*. Compare with *wrapper*. *See also*: sleeve.

DVD   An abbreviation of *digital videodisc*, a type of optical disk of the same size as a compact disc but with significantly greater recording capacity, partly because it is double-sided. Although DVD requires special equipment for playback, most DVD players can also read CD media. According to the Video Software Dealers Association's weekly VidTrac report, the number of commercial DVD rentals exceeded those of VHS for the first time in June 2003. DVD is expected to become the preferred medium for motion pictures distributed for home use. The new format is also gaining rapidly on VHS in public library collections in the United States.

dwarf book   *See*: bibelot.

dwell   In tooling, the length of time the heated finishing tool is in contact with the leather or cloth surface being decorated.

dynamic map   A map on which flow lines and/or arrows of varying width are used to indicate the direction and amount of movement (migration), action (military maneuvers), or change in conditions (weather). Synonymous with *flow map*.

E

EAD *See*: Encoded Archival Description.

ear A small decorative design printed on either side of the title in the flag at the head of the front page of a newspaper. Also refers to a small projection found on the upper-right-hand edge of the lowercase "g" in some typefaces.

earliest entry A method of cataloging serials that have undergone title changes, in which the bibliographic description is based on the earliest issue and all subsequent titles are recorded as notes in the single bibliographic record. This convention was followed in the United States in the early part of the 20th century but eventually replaced, first by *latest entry* cataloging in the *ALA Rules* and then by *successive entry* cataloging in *AACR*.

early adopter A person, organization, or institution that begins using a new technology at or near the time of its introduction in the market place, rather than waiting to see if it will be successful.

early book Books produced during the earliest periods in which human activities were recorded—on clay tablets in Mesopotamia, on papyrus scrolls in ancient Egypt, on tree bark or palm leaves in Asia, etc.—usually to record sacred prayers and rituals, traditional sagas and epics, lists of dynastic succession, laws and legal decisions, property ownership and taxation, magical incantations, astronomical observations and astrological predictions, important medical knowledge, etc. Because of the amount of labor required, early books were usually produced in single copies.

early copy *See*: advance copy.

early journal A journal that began publication during the 17th, 18th, or 19th century (*example*: ***Philosophical Transactions of the Royal Society of London*** issued for the first time in 1665). In a library, copies of early periodicals may be stored in special collections, or accessible in digital format or on microform, to protect the originals from damage. The Bodleian Library at Oxford University provides online access to the *Internet Library of Early Journals (ILEJ)* at: www.bodley.ox.ac.uk/ilej.

easel   A metal, wood, or plastic rack or stand on a tripod base designed to allow an open book or periodical to be displayed face-out as part of an exhibit or presentation. Large models are used to display flip charts in presentations.

easel binding   A type of comb or spiral binding designed with rigid extended covers that can be folded back to form the base of a triangle, allowing the book or notebook to stand upright when opened, with the spine across the top. The text is printed parallel with the spine, and the pages are turned up and over, instead of from side to side.

easy book   A heavily illustrated book with limited text written to appeal to the interests and reading ability of children from preschool to third grade, usually shelved in a separate section of a school library or children's room in a public library.

e-book   *See*: electronic book.

EBSCO   A commercial company that provides subscription management services, electronic journal access, online bibliographic and full-text databases, and an online book ordering service to libraries and related institutions. EBSCO is currently one of the three leading aggregators of journals available in electronic full-text. URL: www-us. ebsco.com/home. *See also*: *Gale Group* and *ProQuest*.

eclogue   A short pastoral poem, or part of a longer one, traditionally in the form of a dialogue between a pair of shepherds, for example, Spenser's *The Shepheard's Calendar* (1579). The term lost its pastoral connotation in the 18th century and now refers to a poem in which a serious theme is developed through a monologue or dialogue, as in *Rosalind and Helen* (1819) by Percy Bysshe Shelley.

e-collection   *See*: digital collection.

e-conference   *See*: mailing list.

economies of scale   The decrease in cost of production that occurs as the extent of an operation is enlarged, for example, reduction in the cost of preparing new items for circulation, achieved by processing them in large batches rather than a few at a time, an argument used to justify centralized ordering and processing in library systems. If marginal cost (cost of producing an additional unit) is less than average cost, an economic incentive exists to produce additional output. *Diseconomies of scale* occur when average cost increases as output increases. In large libraries, efficiency can be enhanced by taking advantage of economies of scale. Synonymous with *scale economies*.

edge   The outermost limit of the cover or sections of a book, or of one of its leaves, or of an unbound sheet. The *fore-edge* is opposite the binding edge of the text block (the spine of a bound volume). The other two edges are the *head* and *tail*. *See also*: *deckle edges*, *edge decoration*, *gauffered edges*, and *gilt edges*.

edge decoration   Ornamentation applied to one or more of the trimmed edges of the sections of a book, a general term that includes gilding, gauffering, edge painting, sprinkling, staining, daubing, etc.

edge painting   A picture drawn or painted on the edges of the sections of a book with its leaves closed, a common form of decoration in the Middle Ages. On some books, painting was done on all three edges but on most only on the fore-edge. In England during the late 18th and early 19th centuries, the technique was refined to make the picture visible only when the leaves were slightly fanned. In *double fore-edge painting*, two different images are displayed by fanning the leaves first in one direction, then the other.

edge title   A title written in ink on one or more edges of the sections of a book, not by the binder but by the owner. This method of marking the outside of a volume was used until the 16th century when books began to be shelved upright with the spine out, instead of flat with one of the edges facing out.

edited   A single work, or two or more shorter works by the same or different authors, prepared for publication by a person other than the author, whose name usually appears as editor on the title page. In the bibliographic description, the editor's name is given in the title and statement of responsibility area (field 245 of the MARC record) following the phrase "edited by." For works with more than one editor, the names are listed in order of appearance on the chief source of information, followed by the word "editors."

editing   In publishing, the process of revising and preparing for publication material submitted by an author in manuscript or typescript form, usually performed by one or more *editors*. Also refers to the work of gathering together and preparing for publication in a single volume or uniform set of volumes the previously published works of one or more authors, usually done by someone else.

In data processing, the revision of a document, such as a machine-readable bibliographic record, usually by selecting from an *edit* menu an option to *cut, copy, paste,* or *delete* portions of text or by reformatting the text in some manner.

Film editing is the process of selecting from the total footage shot those portions that are to be included in a motion picture, then splicing them together in a sequence of scenes that tells a story (feature film) or conveys factual information about the subject (documentary). A similar process occurs in the production of audio- and videorecordings.

edition   All copies of a book, pamphlet, fascicle, single sheet, etc., printed from the same typographic image and issued by the same entity in the same format at one time or at intervals without alteration. An edition may consist of several impressions in which the text and other matter are not substantially changed. In older publications, the terms *impression* and *edition* are virtually synonymous since type was broken up for reuse after the first printing. For some books, especially reference books and textbooks, the content of the *original edition* may be revised and the text republished under the same or an altered title. Unless the publisher states that a work is a revised edition or expanded edition, the first revision is known as the *second edition*. Subsequent revisions are numbered in the order in which they are published. The latest edition is the most current, but older editions may contain useful information deleted from later ones. *See also*: *facsimile* and *reprint*.

In the case of electronic resources, all copies of a work embodying essentially the same content, issued by the same entity, for example, a version of a Web page updated

on a specific date. For unpublished items, all copies made from essentially the same master production, for example, the original and one or more carbon copies of a typescript (*AACR2*). For other materials, including nonprint items, all copies produced from essentially the same master copy and issued by the same entity, whether distributed by the same entity or not. In a more general sense, the format (particularly the size and shape) in which a work is published.

Also applies to one of the formats in which a literary work or collection of works is published, usually for a specific purpose or market, for example, a *book club edition*, *deluxe edition, export edition, library edition, limited edition, paperback edition, trade edition*, or *special edition*. In library cataloging, the edition is indicated by ordinal number and/or description in the edition area of the bibliographic record. Abbreviated *ed*. *See also*: *co-edition*.

In newspaper publishing, one of two or more printings issued on the same day, for example, the "Early Edition" or the "Late Edition." In radio and television, a program broadcast at a particular time of day ("Morning Edition").

edition area   In library cataloging, the area of bibliographic description in which information pertaining to the edition is entered, usually by ordinal number (*15th ed.*) and/or description (*Rev. ed.*), including the edition statement and statements of responsibility relating to the edition. In the MARC record these data elements are given in field 250.

edition binding   *See*: publisher's binding.

edition statement   In library cataloging, the portion of the bibliographic record in which the edition of the work is indicated by ordinal number (*7th ed.*) and/or description (*Rev. ed.*) as found on the item, using standard abbreviations found in *Appendix B* of *AACR2*. If an item lacks an edition statement but is known to include important changes from previous editions, a brief statement in the language and script of the title proper is provided by the cataloger in square brackets. In the MARC record, the edition statement is given in subfield *a* of field 250.

editio princeps   Latin for "original edition." Usually reserved for the first printed edition of a work that existed in manuscript before the invention of printing. For other works, the term *first edition* is preferred in analytical bibliography and the antiquarian book trade.

editor   A person who prepares for publication the work(s) of one or more other authors. An editor may be responsible for selecting material included in a collection or for preparing manuscript copy for the printer, including annotation of the text, verification of the accuracy of facts and bibliographic citations, polishing grammar and style, organizing front and back matter, etc. Periodicals and large reference works often have a *general editor* or *editor-in-chief* who supervises the work of an editorial staff. Compare with *compiler*. *See also*: *author's editor*.

In large publishing houses, the editing process may be divided into separate functions, each performed by a different person:

Acquisition editor—scouts and evaluates new works for recommendation to the publisher

Manuscript editor—assists the author in developing and organizing the work

Copy editor—perfects details of grammar and style, checks the accuracy of facts, quotations, citations, etc.

Managing editor—coordinates resources required for publication and develops the publication schedule

Production editor—oversees the transition from editorial process to production (printing, binding, distribution)

Also refers to the individual in charge of the content of a newspaper, magazine, or journal, and in some cases its publication, whose name is given in the masthead. *See also*: *editorial, editorial board*, and *letter to the editor*.

editorial   A brief essay expressing clearly and unequivocally, and sometimes with artful persuasiveness, the opinion or position of the chief editor(s) of a newspaper or magazine with respect to a current political, social, cultural, or professional issue. Editorials appear on the *editorial page* of a newspaper, usually printed at the end of the news section. The editorial page may also include letters to the editor. Syndicated columns and political cartoons usually appear on the *op-ed page*. In newsmagazines, editorials and columns usually precede the feature articles or appear on the last page(s). Compare with *advertorial. See also*: *journal of commentary*.

editorial board   A group of people responsible for controlling the editorial content and overseeing the publication of a newspaper or periodical whose names are usually given in the masthead. In magazine publishing, the editorial board establishes the overall editorial policy and tone to be followed by staff writers, selects columnists, and decides which letters to the editor will be published. In journal publishing, the board usually controls the evaluation and selection of articles submitted by independent scholars for publication.

editorial content   The portions of a newspaper or periodical containing content controlled by the editor(s) or editorial board (articles, columns, editorials, letters to the editor, illustrations, political cartoons, etc.), as opposed to the space devoted to advertisements, notices and announcements, etc.

editorialize   To put forth an opinion or position on a subject, usually with intent to persuade the listener or reader to adopt or at least consider the point of view of the speaker or writer. Also, to inject personal opinions or comments into an otherwise objective discussion or account, a technique used in essays, editorials, columns, letters to the editor, and other forms of persuasive writing but considered inappropriate in scholarly publication and works of fiction.

editorial page   *See*: editorial.

educational videotape   A videotape designed and marketed to schools and libraries as a teaching tool, sometimes for use in conjunction with a specific curriculum unit. Educational videos tend to be priced higher than feature films and mass-market nonfiction videos.

e.g.   An abbreviation of the Latin phrase *exempli gratia*, meaning "for the sake of example."

eggshell   A smooth, slightly pitted finish given to uncoated paper or board that produces a soft, nonglossy surface resembling the shell of a bird's egg. Most antique papers have this type of finish.

Eighteenth Century Short-Title Catalogue   See: *English Short Title Catalogue.*

e-journal   *See*: electronic journal.

electronic book   A digital version of a traditional print book designed to be read on a personal computer or an e-book reader (a software application for use on a standard-sized computer or a book-sized computer used solely as a reading device). Although the first hypertext novel was published in 1987 (*Afternoon, A Story* by Michael Joyce), electronic books did not capture public attention until the online publication of Stephen King's novella *Riding the Bullet* in March 2000. Within 24 hours, the text had been downloaded by 400,000 computer users. Some libraries offer access to electronic books through the online catalog. A universally accepted format and simple delivery system are needed. Synonymous with *e-book*, *ebook*, and *eBook*.

electronic collection   *See*: digital collection.

electronic conference   *See*: mailing list.

electronic discussion list   *See*: mailing list.

electronic document delivery   The transfer of information traditionally recorded in a physical medium (print, videotape, sound recording, etc.) to the user electronically, usually via e-mail or the World Wide Web. Libraries employ digital technology to deliver the information contained in documents and files placed on reserve and requested via interlibrary loan.

electronic journal   A digital version of a print journal, or a journal-like electronic publication with no print counterpart, made available via the Web, e-mail, or other means of Internet access. Some Web-based electronic journals are graphically modeled on the print version. The rising cost of print journal subscriptions has led many academic libraries to explore electronic alternatives. Directories of electronic journals are available online. Synonymous with *e-journal*. Compare with *electronic magazine*.

electronic magazine   A digital version of a print magazine, or a magazine-like electronic publication with no print counterpart, made available via the Web, e-mail, or other means of Internet access. Some Web-based electronic magazines are graphically modeled on the print version. Directories of electronic magazines are available online. Synonymous with *e-zine* and *Webzine*. Compare with *electronic journal.*

electronic mail   *See*: e-mail.

electronic newsletter   A newsletter published online, usually via the Internet, with or without a print counterpart (*example*: *LITA Newsletter*).

electronic preservation   *See*: digital preservation.

electronic publication A work in digital form capable of being read or otherwise perceived, distributed to the general public electronically. The category includes electronic journals and e-prints, electronic magazines and newspapers, electronic books, Web sites, Weblogs, etc. Some electronic publications are online versions of print publications; others are "born digital." Synonymous with *e-publication*.

electronic publishing The publication of books, periodicals (e-journals, e-zines, etc.), bibliographic databases, and other information resources in digital format, usually on CD-ROM or online via the Internet, for in-house users, subscribers, and/or retail customers, with or without a print counterpart (*example*: **Journal of Electronic Publishing**). Synonymous in this sense with *e-publishing*. Also used synonymously with *desktop publishing*.

electronic records Bibliographic or archival records stored on a medium, such as magnetic tape/disk or optical disk, that requires computer equipment for retrieval and processing. Compare with *machine-readable records*.

electronic reference *See*: digital reference.

electronic reserves Items placed on reserve that an academic library makes available online to be read on a computer screen, downloaded to diskette, or printed as needed. Permission may be required to use works not in the public domain. Software for electronic reserves systems is available from commercial vendors (*example*: **ERes** from Docutek Information Systems). Synonymous with *e-reserves*.

electronic resource Material consisting of data and/or computer program(s) encoded for reading and manipulation by a computer by the use of a peripheral device directly connected to the computer or remotely via a network such as the Internet (*AACR2*). The category includes software applications, electronic texts, bibliographic databases, etc. Abbreviated *e-resource*. *See also*: *file*.

electronic style Accepted format for citing (in footnotes, endnotes, and bibliographies) information available in digital formats, such as computer software, abstracts and full-text articles retrieved from bibliographic databases, messages posted to newsgroups and mailing lists, and documents available on the World Wide Web. To find an online list of electronic style guides, try the phrase "Internet style" as a search in *Yahoo!* (www.yahoo.com).

The most recent print editions of the *Publication Manual of the American Psychological Association* and the *MLA Handbook for Writers of Research Papers* also include sections on citing electronic resources.

electronic text The words used by an author to express thoughts and feelings in digital form, as opposed to printed or handwritten form. In order to be displayed with formatting on a computer, text must first be encoded in a markup language. Electronic text can be "born digital" or converted from another format. Abbreviated *e-text*.

electronic theses and dissertations (ETD) Master's theses and Ph.D. dissertations submitted in digital form rather than on paper, as opposed to those submitted in hard copy and subsequently converted to machine-readable format, usually by scanning. Forty universities in the United States and over 100 institutions worldwide currently participate in the Networked Digital Library of Theses and Dissertations (NDLTD), an initiative to require that *all* theses and dissertations be submitted in electronic format.

elegy In classical literature, a lyric poem composed in couplets of alternating hexameter and pentameter lines, a form known as *elegiac meter*. In English literature through the 17th century, a song or poem of melancholy or solemn contemplation. In contemporary usage, a formal poem lamenting the death of a particular person (*example*: *In Memory of W.B. Yeats* by W.H. Auden) or the phenomenon of mortality in general (*Elegy Written in a Country Churchyard* by Thomas Gray). Compare with *eulogy*.

element In library cataloging, a discrete unit of data (word, phrase, or group of characters) constituting part of an area of description within the bibliographic record created to represent an item, for example, the publication date in the edition statement or the number of pages or plates in the physical description. Similarly, a unit of information within a field of a record in a bibliographic database, for example, the journal title or volume number in the source field of an entry representing a periodical article.

elephant folio In nonspecialty publishing, a large folio usually about 23 × 14 inches (58 × 35 centimeters) in size. The term *double-elephant* refers to the very large paper size used in printing works such as *Birds of America* by John James Audubon. Compare with *atlas folio*.

el-hi book *See*: elhi book.

elhi book A term used in the educational book trade in the United States to refer to a textbook published specifically for **el**ementary and **hi**gh school students, usually revised and updated regularly by publishers anxious to retain market share. In a more general sense, *any* book published for elementary and/or high school age readers. Also spelled *el-hi*. *See also*: El-Hi Textbooks & Serials in Print.

El-Hi Textbooks & Serials in Print A reference serial published by R.R. Bowker since 1985, indexing elementary and high school textbooks currently in print, by author, title, and a classified list of subjects. Textbooks published in series are indexed separately. Elhi serials are indexed by subject and title. ISSN: 0000–0825. Former titles: *Textbooks in Print* (1956–1968) and *El-Hi Textbooks in Print* (1969–1984). *See also*: Children's Books in Print.

elision From the Latin *elisio*, meaning "a striking out." The omission of a vowel or silent consonant at the beginning or in the middle of a word (*example*: **you've** for *you have* or **ne'er** for *never*), or the omission of a vowel, consonant, or syllable in the pronunciation of a word or phrase. In orthography, the omission is indicated by an apostrophe. Compare with *contraction*. *See also*: *ellipsis*.

ellipsis The use of square brackets ([ ]) or three full points (. . .) or a series of asterisks (****) in handwritten or printed text to indicate the omission or suppression of a word or words (four points if the omission ends a sentence). Often used to reduce the length of a quotation without altering its meaning or significance. Compare with *elision*.

e-magazine   *See*: electronic magazine.

e-mail   An abbreviation of *electronic mail*, an Internet protocol that allows computer users to exchange messages and data files in real time with other users, locally and across networks. E-mail requires a *messaging system* to allow users to store and forward messages and a *mail program* with an interface for sending and receiving. Users can send messages to a single recipient at a specific e-mail address or multicast to a distribution list or mailing list without creating a paper copy until hard copy is desired. Faster and more reliable than the postal service, e-mail can also be more convenient than telephone communication, but it has raised issues of security and privacy. Commonly used e-mail programs: **Lotus Notes**, **Eudora**, **Sendmail**, **Critical Path**. Most Internet service providers offer an e-mail option to their subscribers. Also spelled *email*. *See also*: *attachment*, *body*, *encryption*, *footer*, *header*, and *SMTP*.

e-mail address   A string of characters used to route messages from one computer to another over a network governed by the Internet protocol for electronic mail (SMTP).
E-mail addresses follow a standard format containing *no* spaces:

United States: **username@domainname.domaincode**
Other countries: **username@domainname.countrycode**

Examples:
smithj@myuniversity.edu
duboisf@universite.fr

To find an online list of e-mail directories, try a search on the phrase "email addresses" in *Yahoo!* (www.yahoo.com).

embargo   The period during which the articles published in a periodical are not available in online full-text from a journal aggregator, usually the most recent one to three years. Journal publishers have established such periods to prevent libraries from canceling print subscriptions. In most periodical databases, this restriction applies only to a small proportion of the titles indexed, but in *JSTOR* nearly all of the journals are embargoed. Not to be confused with an exclusive agreement between a journal publisher and an aggregator.

emblem   A moral fable, allegory, or abstract quality expressed pictorially, sometimes with an accompanying motto or verse. Also, a figure of an object (or objects) representing symbolically a person, family, people, or nation, as on a heraldic device (coat of arms) or image of a saint or hero.

emblem book   A type of illustrated book, popular from the early 16th century to about 1700, containing a collection of symbolic engravings or woodcuts called *emblems*, each expressing a moral adage or principle, accompanied by an epigram, motto, proverb, or brief explanatory text in prose or verse. Included in this category are books with the text arranged in symbolic designs, for example, crosses. The form was revived by the poet William Blake in *Gates of Paradise*. Emblem books are studied as cultural artifacts providing information about popular culture, the use of allegory, the relationship of word to image, reading practices, and printing history.

embossed A decorative design or lettering raised in bas-relief above the surface of a sheet or page, or the cover of a book, an effect produced by the use of printing or stamping dies. Employed throughout the history of binding and printing, embossing is a mechanical technique now used mainly in the production of art books, elegant greeting cards, and other decorative items. *See also*: cuir ciselé.

embrittlement *See*: brittle.

embroidered binding A book with boards covered in cloth decorated with raised stitching in designs executed by a professional embroiderer, usually from a pattern book, in thread of colored silk and/or metal (gold or silver), sometimes with pearls and sequins sewn on, a style commonly used during the late Middle Ages and Renaissance for devotional books. Canvas was used as the fabric base from the 14th to the mid-17th centuries, but velvet was preferred during the Tudor period in England and satin in the Stuart.

emendation Correction or improvement, especially of a literary or artistic work or written document, by alteration of the text, whether done by the author or another person, such as an editor. Also, a specific instance of such an alteration. In textual criticism, the correction, usually by judicious inference or informed conjecture, of a text found to have been corrupted in transmission, restoring it to a state presumed to be closer to the original.

emergency plan A set of guidelines or steps prepared in advance to help the staff of a library deal with unusual occurrences that may temporarily disrupt normal operations (assaults, bomb threats, security violations, etc.) but are not usually disastrous. Compare with *contingency plan* and *disaster plan*.

Emmy Award One of several awards given annually in the United States by the Academy of Television Arts and Sciences for outstanding programming in news and documentaries, sports, and daytime television. A list of the most recent Emmy Award winners is available online at: www.emmyonline.org.

emoticon An abbreviation of the term *emotional icon. See*: smiley.

employee handbook A manual, often printed in loose-leaf form, describing the rights, responsibilities, privileges, rules, expectations, etc., associated with employment in a company, organization, agency, or institution, usually distributed to employees at the time they are hired. At academic institutions that grant faculty status to librarians, the *faculty handbook* usually serves this function and may also cover governance. Compare with *procedure manual*.

emulation The process by which a computer program or device designed to allow one system to imitate another accomplishes that task. *Terminal emulation* software allows a PC user to log on to a mainframe as if it were the type of terminal normally used for that purpose.

In digital archiving, a preservation technique that employs special software, called an *emulator*, to translate instructions from an original archived software program to enable it to run on a newer platform, obviating the need to preserve obsolete hardware and system software.

emulsion   A stable colloidal suspension of one immiscible liquid in another. In photography, the light-sensitive coating on a plate or base of plastic film consisting of very fine silver halide crystals dispersed in a gelatin medium. Considered a scientific art, the making of photographic emulsions often involves trade secrets jealously guarded by commercial film manufacturers.

encapsulation   The process of enclosing a flat document in a thin polyester envelope, the edges of which are sealed to protect it from damage, used in conservation and preservation to provide support for large, fragile sheets such as maps, charts, posters, etc., while allowing them to remain visible on both sides. The procedure does not alter the condition of the document by adhering it to the film, as does *lamination* (the sheet can easily be removed by slitting one or more sides of the envelope). When this method is used to preserve a bound item, the leaves must be cut apart and each one encapsulated separately. The envelopes can then be bound together again. Although encapsulation provides protection from impurities in the atmosphere, it does not retard processes of deterioration inherent in the object.

encaustum   From the Latin *encausticus*, meaning "burnt in." A purplish-black, highly durable ink made from a mixture of iron salts and gallic (tannic) acid, preferred by Irish and Anglo-Saxon scribes during the early Middle Ages because it bonded well with the surface of parchment or vellum and was not grainy, in comparison with ink made from lampblack. Also spelled *incaustum*.

enchiridion   From the Greek word for "handbook," a volume of a size that can be easily carried in a person's hand. In the Christian religious tradition, a manual of devotions (*example*: Saint Augustine's **Enchiridion on Faith, Hope, and Love**).

Encoded Archival Description (EAD)   The EAD Document Type Definition (DTD) is a nonproprietary standard for encoding in Standard Generalized Markup Language (SGML) or Extensible Markup Language (XML) the finding aids (registers, inventories, indexes, etc.) used in archives, libraries, museums, and other repositories of manuscripts and primary sources to facilitate use of their materials. EAD was developed in 1993 on the initiative of the UC Berkeley Library and is maintained by the Library of Congress, in partnership with the Society of American Archivists. URL: lcweb.loc.gov/ead.

encoding   In information retrieval, the process of converting a message or data into electronic signals that can be processed by a computer or transmitted over a communications channel. The opposite of *decoding*. Compare with *encryption*.

encoding level   One of several modes of library cataloging recognized by the Library of Congress as appropriate, depending on a library's resources and needs and the amount of descriptive detail available to the cataloger. The levels are: *full level*, *core level*, *minimal level*, *collection level*, and *copy cataloging*.

encryption   The process of converting data contained in a message into a secret code prior to transmission via public telecommunication channels to make the content incomprehensible to all but authorized recipient(s). In computing, the modification is often done by means of a transformation algorithm. Encryption is a security measure taken to protect confidential information, such as credit card numbers used in online business transactions and to ensure that only those who have paid for a fee-based service can obtain it. The opposite of *decryption*.

encumbrance   In library acquisitions, an amount charged against a budgetary fund to cover a prior commitment to purchase materials, equipment, services, or supplies, removed once full payment is made or the order is canceled. Encumbrances are tracked to prevent over-expenditure.

encyclopedia   A book or numbered set of books containing authoritative summary information about a variety of topics in the form of short essays, usually arranged alphabetically by headword or classified in some manner. An entry may be signed or unsigned, with or without illustration or a list of references for further reading. Headwords and text are usually revised periodically for publication in a new edition. In a multivolume encyclopedia, any indexes are usually located at the end of the last volume. Encyclopedias may be general (*example*: **Encyclopedia Americana**) or specialized, usually by subject (**Encyclopedia of Bad Taste**) or discipline (**Encyclopedia of Social Work**). In electronic publishing, encyclopedias were one of the first formats to include multimedia and interactive elements (*example*: **Grolier Multimedia Encyclopedia Online**). Also spelled *encyclopaedia*. Synonymous with *cyclopedia*. Compare with *dictionary*.

Encyclopedia of Associations   An annual reference serial published by the Gale Group providing detailed directory information on over 22,000 nonprofit American membership organizations of national scope. Each entry typically includes the organization's official name, address, and phone/fax numbers; the primary official's name and title; founding date, purpose, and activities; size of membership and dues; national and international conferences; and publications. Each edition includes an alphabetically arranged name index and keyword index and a separate volume containing geographic and executive indexes. Companion volumes are available from the same publisher for international organizations and regional, state, and local organizations.

endangered   In libraries and archives, a category of item, or group of items, whose continued existence is threatened, usually by deterioration or the obsolescence of equipment required to read the format. Preservation may require conversion to a format of greater permanence. Synonymous with *at risk*.

endbands   A collective term for the protective *headband* and *tailband* attached to the top and bottom of the spine of a book that has a sewn binding. They were originally made of a core of leather, parchment, cord, rolled paper, or cane covered in decorative linen or silk embroidery and sewn to the quires with the ends laced into the boards, but in modern binding they are machine-made and simply glued on.

end matter   *See*: back matter.

endnote   A statement printed at the end of a chapter or book to explain a point in the text, indicate the basis of an assertion, or cite the source of a concept, idea, quotation, or piece of factual information. Like footnotes, endnotes are numbered, usually in superscript, and listed in the sequence in which they appear in the text. Compare with *in-text citation*.

endowment   A permanent fund accumulated by an institution over an extended period of time consisting of gifts and bequests invested to provide an ongoing return, all or a portion of which is expended, sometimes for purposes specified by the donor(s), leaving the principal intact to generate further income. A library may be separately endowed or share in the endowment of its parent institution. *See also*: *fund-raising*.

end panel   A single- or double-faced flat piece of wood, steel, or other rigid material securely attached to the end of a range of library shelving, usually extending from floor to top of unit to cover the shelf ends facing an aisle or open area. End panels also help provide structural rigidity to shelving, important in regions prone to earthquake. The panels may be painted or covered with material that aesthetically enhances the library's decor. End panels in wood may be custom-made to match library furnishings.

endpaper   In binding, a sheet of thick, strong paper folded down the center, one-half of which is pasted to the inside of the front or back board of a book, the other half forming the first or last leaf (the *flyleaf*), protecting the text from the boards. The folds function as hinges, joining the text block to the covers and allowing the boards to swing open and closed. For extra strength, some books have *double endpapers*.

From the 17th century on, decorated endpapers were used in hand-binding (see *marbling*). In modern book production, the color of the endpapers often complements the material covering the boards. Maps, genealogies, tables, or illustrations are sometimes printed on the endpapers, especially in biographies and historical works. Also spelled *end-paper*. Synonymous with *endleaf* and *endsheet*. Compare with *doublure*.

end-user   In information retrieval, the person or persons for whom a mediated literature search is conducted and to whom the results are delivered. In a more general sense, the person for whom *any* search requiring the use of library resources or other information services is performed.

end-user search   In information retrieval, a literature search conducted by the person who actually intends to use the results, as opposed to a mediated search conducted by a trained specialist on behalf of the user.

e-newsletter   *See*: electronic newsletter.

English Short Title Catalogue (ESTC)   A project begun in 1977 by The British Library under the title *Eighteenth Century Short-Title Catalogue* for the purpose of compiling a comprehensive record of books, pamphlets, and other printed material published in Great Britain and its colonies and printed in the English language anywhere else in the world, from 1701 to 1800. When the decision was made to include monographs and serials printed prior to 1701, the title changed to *English Short Title Catalogue*. Produced by the *ESTC* editorial offices at the University of California, Riverside, and The British Library, in partnership with the American Antiquarian Society and over 1,600 libraries worldwide, the *ESTC* represents all recorded English monographs printed between 1475 and 1700. Updated and expanded daily, the extensively indexed file is available from the Research Libraries Group (RLG) in *RLIN*. Plans are under way to digitize images of sample publications from the collections of various research libraries. *See also*: Short-Title Catalogue.

engraving   An illustration or print made from a design incised with a sharp, pointed tool called a *burin* or *graver* on the surface of a metal plate or hardwood block. The lines are inked and an impression made by pressing a sheet of paper or some other printing surface against the plate, in a process known as *intaglio*. Compare with *etching*. *See also*: *stipple engraving*.

enlarged edition   *See*: expanded edition.

enlargement   A reproduction or copy produced on a larger scale than the original. Some photocopiers have the capacity to enlarge an original. The opposite of *reduction*. Synonymous, in photography, with *blowup*.

ensemble work   A musical work composed for more than one voice and/or instrument singing or playing together, for example, soprano and piano, or a string quartet.

entity   As defined in *FRBR* (*Functional Requirements for Bibliographic Records*), one of the key objects of interest to users of information within a given domain of "things" described by bibliographic data. In *FRBR*, entities are divided into three groups: (1) the products of intellectual or artistic endeavor (work, expression, manifestation, item); (2) the individual(s) or corporate bodies responsible for creating intellectual/artistic content, for producing or disseminating the content in physical form, or for maintaining custody of the products; and (3) the subjects of intellectual or artistic expression (concept, object, event, place). Each type of entity has a defining set of *attributes*, for example, the attributes of a "work" include the title, form, date of work, intended audience, etc. The nature of the link between entities is their *relationship*; for example, an expression may be an "adaptation of" a pre-existing work.

entrance level   *See*: entry level.

entry   A single record in the library catalog representing an item in one of its collections. *See also*: *added entry* and *main entry*. Also, a record in a bibliographic database representing a work indexed and/or abstracted.

Also refers to a reference in a bibliography or printed index or to the information given under a headword in a dictionary or under a heading in a reference work such as an encyclopedia or handbook.

In a more general sense, any point of access to a file of bibliographic records or other data (name of author, title of work, series title, assigned subject heading or descriptor) under which a record representing a specific item may be searched and identified, manually or electronically.

entry level   Employment at the lowest grade in a system of classified positions, suitable for candidates who are beginning their careers and lack experience. Promotion usually depends on a vacancy occurring at a higher grade or classification, rather than on the development of the initial position into one requiring greater skill or responsibility. Synonymous with *entrance level*.

entry word   The word under which a record in a catalog, index, or bibliography is filed and searched, usually the first word of the heading (initial articles excluded). In retrieving information from an online catalog or bibliographic database, the order of terms typed as input may determine the success or failure of a search by author, title, subject heading, or descriptor, but in a keywords search, word order should not affect results if Boolean logic is used correctly. Synonymous with *filing word*.

enumeration   A naming or counting of items, one by one, as in a list, in any amount of detail but without systematic arrangement. Also, the volume numbering of a serial issue. *See also*: *enumerative classification*.

enumerative classification   A classification system in which each subject is developed to the point of indivisibility and a notation assigned for every subdivision (*example*: **Library of Congress Classification**). In such a system, class numbers representing complex subjects are precombined. Compare with *synthetic classification*. *See also*: *hierarchical classification*.

environmental control   In the preservation of library and archival collections, creating and maintaining hospitable storage conditions is the most effective strategy for promoting the longevity of materials. Deterioration of paper, leather, cloth, plastic, etc., can be dramatically reduced by controlling temperature, relative humidity, light, and air quality in storage. Monitoring devices should be installed to ensure that materials remain cool and dry. Low illumination, ventilation that removes atmospheric pollutants, and effective pest management are also essential.

ephemera   From the Greek *ephemeron*, meaning "something short-lived." The printed materials of everyday life, generally regarded as having little or no permanent value because they are produced in large quantities or in disposable formats. The category includes pamphlets, leaflets, broadsides, fliers, playbills, performance programs, posters, postcards, greeting cards, menus, tickets, comic books, paper toys, etc. Ephemeral items are sometimes retained and exhibited for their graphic qualities or for their association with a specific person, event, or activity. When collected by libraries, they are usually stored in special collections. Also refers to material of brief currency that has reference value or sufficient literary or historical importance to merit permanent archival storage, for example, academic course catalogs and schedules, newsletters, staff directories, etc. The Ephemera Society of America maintains a Web site at: www.ephemerasociety.org. Compare with *gray literature*.

epic   A lengthy narrative poem in which the language, characters, and action are heroic and exalted in style. Most epics have a comparatively simple plot, a theme (or themes) reflecting the universal human condition, a hero of superhuman mental and physical capacity who is nonetheless fatally flawed, a setting imaginary or remote in time and place, with supernatural forces playing a decisive role in the action, upon which may depend the fate of an entire society or people. Epics are usually closely tied to the legends, oral traditions, and history of a specific culture (***Iliad*** and ***Odyssey*** of Homer, ***Beowulf***, etc.). Literary epics, such as the ***Aeneid*** of Virgil and ***Paradise Lost*** by John Milton, are consciously modeled on traditional examples.

epigram In the classical period, an inscription or epitaph, but in modern usage a tersely witty, often antithetical saying, ingeniously composed in prose or verse, delivered with aplomb to make a point in a manner calculated to enhance one's reputation in the company of people who value feats of intellectual and literary virtuosity. The satirical form, established in ancient Rome by Martial, was cultivated in England from the late 16th to the early 20th century. An example by Hilaire Belloc:

ON OLD LADY POLTAGRUE, A PUBLIC PERIL

The Devil, having nothing else to do,
Went off to tempt my Lady Poltagrue.
My Lady, tempted by a private whim,
To his extreme annoyance, tempted him.

epigraph A brief quotation or motto included in the front matter of a book, usually following the dedication, or at the beginning of each chapter, suggesting an idea or theme that the author intends to develop more fully in the following text.

epilogue A part added as a conclusion at the close of a literary work, for example, the statement of the moral at the end of a fable. Compare with *afterword*.
  The term also refers to the final section of a speech, also called the *peroration*, and to a brief speech delivered at the end of a dramatic performance, requesting the approval of audience and critics. Compare in this sense with *prologue*.

episodic A literary work consisting of a number of more or less self-contained but loosely connected incidents (*episodes*) strung together by the author to form a narrative (*example*: *Idylls of the King* by Alfred, Lord Tennyson).

epistemology From the Greek *episteme* ("knowledge") and *logos* ("theory"), the branch of philosophy devoted to the theoretical study of the nature, methods, and validity of human knowledge, including the relationship between the knower (subject), the known (object), and the process of knowing.

epistle A composition in poetry or prose written in the form of a letter so elegant in style that it is considered a literary work worthy of publication, for example, the epistles of Cicero, Horace, Ovid, and Pliny. Also refers to one of the letters from the apostles included in the *New Testament* of the Christian Bible. In a more general sense, a written letter addressed to an absent person or, when published, an open letter meant to be read by persons in addition to the addressee.

epistolary A liturgical book containing readings for the Mass from the *Epistles* of the New Testament and sometimes from other books of the Bible, arranged according to the liturgical year and read by the subdeacon. The Gospel reading was normally done by the deacon from a separate book called the *lectionary*. From the 10th century on, the *Epistles* were combined with other liturgical readings in the *missal*. Synonymous with *Apostle*.

epistolary novel A form of novel that reached its greatest popularity during the 18th century in which the narrative is developed by the author in a series of letters (*example*: *Clarissa* by Samuel Richardson). Sometimes a novelist begins a work in epistolary style, then switches to conventional narrative (***Busman's Honeymoon*** by Dorothy L. Sayers).

epitaph   From the Greek *epi* ("upon") and *taphos* ("tomb"), a brief valedictory verse on the life and death of a person (or persons), composed as an inscription on a grave marker, sometimes by the deceased before death. Epitaphs are usually complimentary but may be humorous or ironic. One of the most famous was written by Simonides of Ceos (556–468 B.C.) commemorating the 300 warriors who died at Thermopylae:

> Go, tell the Lacedaimonians, passer-by,
> That here obedient to their laws we lie.

epithet   From the Greek word *epitheton*, meaning "something added." A descriptive name or title expressing an important quality or attribute, usually added to distinguish a person (William *the Conqueror*), epoch (Age of *Enlightenment*), or thing (*John Knox* cap) from others of the same name or class. In library cataloging, the epithet follows the personal name in the heading under which the item is cataloged.

epitome   A statement of the essence of a subject in the briefest possible form. Also refers to a very brief but accurate written statement of the main points of a work, usually prepared by a person other than the author.

eponym   A single name under which several authors are published. Also, the name of a person or character so closely associated with a quality, process, or activity that the name is used in signifying it (*Herculean, pasteurization, Platonic, Romeo*).

Also refers to a person who gives, or is reputed to have given, his or her name to an institution, structure, place, etc. (*Guggenheim Museums*), or to a distinguishing title derived from the name of a person, designating a people, place, thing, or period (*Periclean* Athens, *Carolingian* minuscule, *Elizabethan* drama). ***See also***: *eponymous imprint*.

eponymous imprint   A publisher's imprint that carries a personal name or names, often of the founder(s) (*examples*: **J.B. Lippincott** and **R.R. Bowker**). More recently, eponymous imprints under the editor's name have been set up as one-person shops within larger publishing houses to give exceptionally talented editors the freedom to publish without the approval of an editorial committee and to develop an individual voice within the industry. Editor's imprints are often given distinctive names like Apple Soup, Greenwillow, and Silver Whistle, but publishers increasingly encourage star editors to use their own names. Books published under such imprints have received many top awards in children's book publishing where the practice began in 1972 with the creation of Margaret McElderry Books at Atheneum, followed in 1973 by Ursula Nordstrom Books at Harper & Row. The recent success of the Harry Potter series, published by Arthur A. Levine Books at Scholastic, demonstrates the important role of imprinted editors in the promotion of quality works by new authors.

e-preservation   A shortened form of *electronic preservation*. *See*: digital preservation.

e-print   A preprint in digital format, distributed electronically. The use of e-print servers to provide access to collections of preprints is a comparatively new mode of scholarly communication, developed in the physical sciences to circumvent the delays and high cost of commercial publishing. One of the earliest and best-known e-print repositories was created at the Los Alamos National Laboratory in New Mexico. The Open Archives Initiative (OAI) aims to facilitate the retrieval of scholarly papers from disparate digital archives. Also spelled *eprint*.

e-publication   *See*: electronic publication.

e-publishing   *See*: electronic publishing.

equivalence table   A list in numerical order of the classes altered in a complete or extensive revision of Dewey Decimal Classification, giving the class number in the current edition and its equivalent in the preceding edition (and vice versa). *See also*: *comparative table*.

erasure   Names or words written, stamped, or printed in a book and subsequently removed, usually with a gum eraser if in pencil or by some other abrasive means if in ink. Erasures almost always decrease the value of an item in the used book market. John Carter warns in *ABC for Book Collectors* (Oak Knoll, 1995) that erasures near the center of the title page, or in the upper half of the verso of the title page, should be regarded with suspicion because the intent may have been to remove the words *Second* (or *nth*) *Edition* from the imprint. *See also*: *correction* and *palimpsest*.

E-rate   An abbreviation of *education rate*. A federal program established under the *Telecommunications Act of 1996 (TCA)* and implemented in 1998, with oversight by the Federal Communications Commission (FCC), E-rate allows schools, public libraries, and rural health care institutions to apply for substantial discounts on rates paid for telecommunication services, including Internet access, communications equipment, and internal wiring. The program is funded by the Universal Service surcharge on telephone bills and administered by the Universal Service Administrative Company (USAC) in Washington, D.C. Although it has been hampered by a byzantine application process and subjected to filtering requirements under the *Children's Internet Protection Act of 1999 (CIPA)*, the program has helped many schools and libraries build technological infrastructure, particularly in low-income areas.

e-reference   *See*: digital reference.

ERes   *See*: electronic reserves.

e-reserves   *See*: electronic reserves.

e-resource   *See*: electronic resource.

ergonomics   The systematic study of the relationship between people and the environment in which they work, serving as the basis for the design and arrangement of equipment, furnishings, and workspaces with the aim of enhancing productivity and avoiding negative effects on safety, health, comfort, and efficiency. Synonymous with *human engineering*.

ERIC   The **E**ducational **R**esources **I**nformation **C**enter is a national information service consisting of a group of federally funded clearinghouses administered by the National Library of Education (NLE) that indexes and abstracts journal articles and research reports in education and related fields and publishes the results in the print publications

CIJE (*Current Index to Journals in Education*) and *RIE* (*Resources in Education*), and in the *ERIC* database, available online or on CD-ROM in most academic libraries supporting education curriculum in the United States.

Items indexed in *ERIC* are assigned at least one subject descriptor from the *Thesaurus of ERIC Descriptors* and a six-digit *EJ number* for journal articles, or a six-digit *ED number* for research reports (documents). Available on microfiche, ERIC documents are filed by ED number in microfiche cabinets usually located in the microforms section of the library. A reader-printer machine is required to enlarge and make copies of documents on microfiche. ERIC documents are also available online from the ERIC Document Reproduction Service (EDRS). URL: www.eric.ed.gov.

ERIC document (ED)   A separately published or unpublished research report on a topic in education or a related field, available on microfiche and online by subscription from the ERIC Document Reproduction Service (EDRS). Access to ERIC documents is provided by most academic libraries in the United States that support curriculum in education. ERIC microfiche is filed by six-digit *ED number* in microfiche cabinets usually located in the microforms section of the library.

erotica   Works containing sexual content calculated to stimulate the passions of the reader but that also have some artistic value and integrity (*example*: **Fanny Hill, or, Memoirs of a Woman of Pleasure** by John Cleland). Examples are usually found in private collections and in the special collections of libraries that specialize in the history of books and publishing. Compare with *curiosa* and *pornography*.

errata   The plural of *erratum*. Errors discovered after a book or periodical has gone to press but before it is distributed, brought to the reader's attention by the insertion of a list of corrections, separately printed on a small piece of paper known as an *errata slip*, usually tipped in at the beginning of the text or in the front matter. Synonymous with *corrigenda*. Compare with *paste-in*.

error message   A text message displayed automatically by a computer system to indicate that the operation initiated by the user could not be completed for some reason. Common error messages in Web browser software include:

400—Bad File Request
Usually means the URL contains an error in syntax. Check punctuation marks and case (URLs are often case-sensitive).

403—Forbidden/Access Denied
User not authorized to view requested file. The site may require a password, the user's domain may be blocked, or the file may be available only to internal users.

404—File Not Found
Host server cannot locate the requested file, usually because it has been renamed, no longer exists, or has been moved to another server or because the user made an error in entering the URL.

500—Internal Error
HTML document could not be retrieved due to server-configuration problems. User should consult site administrator.

Bad File Request
  Web form uses nonstandard form entry elements or has errors in HTML code. Notify Webmaster of programming error.
Connection Refused by Host
  User does not have permission to access file or password is incorrect.
Failed DNS Lookup
  Servers that translate domain names into IP addresses may be overloaded. Wait a few seconds, then select "Reload" or "Refresh" in browser toolbar.
File Contains No Data
  The browser located the site but found no data in requested file. Try adding ":80" (without the quotation marks) to the URL immediately preceding the first slash.
Network Connection Refused or **Too Many Users**
  Host server is overloaded and unable to handle user's request. Try "Reload" or "Refresh" or wait and try again later.
Unknown Host or **Unable to Locate Server**
  Host server is not accessible for some reason. Try "Reload" or "Refresh" or wait awhile before trying again. If site remains inaccessible for several days, it has probably been shut down permanently.

ERT   *See*: Exhibits Round Table.

ES   *See*: expert system.

escape key   A key located in the upper-left-hand corner of a standard computer keyboard, usually labeled **Esc**, that allows the user to go backward one step in a sequence of operations, terminating the current operation.

escapist literature   Fiction written as light entertainment, intended mainly to divert the mind of the reader into a world of imagination and fantasy. Popular genres include romance, science fiction, thrillers, etc.

ESL   An abbreviation of *English as a Second Language*, a branch of English-language study and teaching.

esparto   A type of paper named after a coarse, short-fibered grass grown in the Mediterranean region that, when mixed with chemical wood pulp, produces the bulk and smooth finish suitable for printing fine-quality books and plates.

espionage   The practice of spying or using spies (or listening devices) to systematically collect strategic information that the government of a country or the management of a commercial entity would prefer to keep secret. When such information is used in military planning and decision-making, it is called "intelligence." Because some research libraries in the United States provide public access to scientific and technical information that could be used by an aggressor, their policies have been scrutinized (see *Library Awareness Program* and USA Patriot Act).
  Also refers to a subgenre of mystery fiction and motion picture devoted to tales of spies and spying (*example*: **Reilly: The Ace of Spies**). *See also*: *thriller*.

essay   A short literary composition written in expository prose addressed to the general reader, usually dealing thoughtfully and in some depth with a single theme, seen from the personal point of view of the *essayist* who does not necessarily attempt the systematic or comprehensive analysis one would expect in a dissertation or treatise. There are no limitations on style or content—essays can be formal or informal, descriptive, narrative, persuasive, humorous, satirical, historical, biographical, autobiographical, or critical. In some cases, essays that appear on the surface to be straightforward have a deeper, more philosophical meaning. Essays published in collections and Festschriften are indexed in *Essay and General Literature Index*, published by H.W. Wilson.

ESTC   *See*: *English Short Title Catalogue.*

estimated price   The price that the acquisitions department of a library anticipates will be charged when an item or subscription is ordered from a publisher, jobber, dealer, or subscription agent. The price actually paid may be higher or lower due to a discount, shipping charges, etc. *See also*: *list price*.

estray   In archives, the legal term for a record or document no longer in the possession of its original creator or legitimate custodian.

et al.   An abbreviation of the Latin phrase *et alii*, meaning "and other people," used in bibliographic citations after the first of more than three collaborators, instead of listing all the names. Also, an abbreviation of *et alibi* ("and elsewhere") and *et alia* ("and other things").

etc.   An abbreviation of the Latin phrase *et cetera*, meaning "and the rest" or "and so forth," used to shorten a list. Also abbreviated *&c.*

etching   An illustration or print made from a metal or glass plate on which a design is made with a needle or other pointed tool through a layer of wax, varnish, or other resistant material (the *etching-ground*). When subjected to an acid bath, areas of the surface exposed by the action of the needle are eaten away, becoming design elements that can be inked to produce an impression on paper in intaglio printing. Compare with *engraving*.

ETD   *See*: electronic theses and dissertations.

e-text   *See*: electronic text.

Ethernet   Conceived at Xerox PARC in 1976 and developed in cooperation with Intel and DEC, Ethernet has become the industry standard for network architecture. It is the most widely installed local area network (LAN) technology in the world, connecting nodes over twisted pair, coaxial, or fiber optic cable. *See also*: *packet switching*.

ethics   *See*: code of ethics.

Etruscan binding   A style of leather binding developed during the late 18th century by William Edwards of Halifax in which the panel on each cover, decorated by means of acid staining, is surrounded by borders of classical design (fretwork, etc.). A vase of classical shape sometimes adorns the center of each panel.

et seq.   An abbreviation of the Latin phrase *et sequens*, meaning "and the following one." Plural: *et seqq.* ("and those that follow").

etymology   The origin of a word traced back as far as possible in time, usually by the methods of comparative linguistics. Most language dictionaries provide some information about word derivation but often differ in how far back origin is traced and the amount of historical detail. Most English-language dictionaries trace the origin of a word back to Latin or ancient Greek, but not as far back as Proto-Indo-European (PIE). The *Oxford English Dictionary (OED)* is the leading example of an English-language dictionary constructed on historical principles. Specialized etymological dictionaries provide the most complete description of the evolution of words (*example*: **The Oxford Dictionary of English Etymology** edited by C.T. Onions).

eulogy   A written or spoken composition in praise of someone or something, especially a person who is deceased, for example, Ben Jonson's eulogy on Shakespeare. Compare with *elegy*.

e-usage   The extent to which an online resource, such as an aggregated database, is used by a library's clientele. Because e-content is expensive to provide, librarians are under pressure to document usage in order to justify funding. Counting Online Usage of Networked Electronic Resources (COUNTER) is a cooperative endeavor on the part of publishers, librarians, and vendors to develop international cross-platform standards for generating usage statistics for online resources.

evangelary   A liturgical book containing the passages from the Gospels read during the Mass, arranged in order of the liturgical year, easier to use than the earlier Gospel Book that had capitularies added at the end to indicate the time of year or celebration for which specific passages were to be read. Medieval evangelaries were often beautifully illuminated. Also spelled *evangeliary*. Synonymous with *Gospel lectionary* and *pericope book*.

evangeliary   *See*: evangelary.

evidential value   *See*: archival value.

exact size   The actual size of the binding of a book as measured in inches or centimeters, independent of the dimensions of the leaves or any other size designation. In library cataloging, exact size is given in centimeters in the physical description area of the bibliographic record. Synonymous with *absolute size*. Compare with *book size*.

examination copy   A copy of a book sent by a publisher on approval or at no charge to a prospective customer for consideration. Educators are the primary recipients of this type of promotion because they are often in a position to adopt an edition as a textbook for courses on the subject. Synonymous with *inspection copy*. *See also*: desk copy.

example   In printing and the book trade, a specific copy of a given edition, no different in any respect from other copies of the same edition.

excerpt   A lengthy verbatim selection taken from a speech or written work, usually longer than a quotation. Reprinting an excerpt without permission may be an infringement of copyright. Excerpts are sometimes published in the form of a digest (*example*: **Book Review Digest**). Compare with *extract*.

exchange   An arrangement in which a library sends items it owns to another library and receives in return items owned by the other library, or sends duplicate copies to another library and receives duplicate materials in return. Also refers to any publication given or received in this manner. Compare with *gift*.

In acquisitions, an agreement with a publisher or jobber allowing the return of an item to receive another item of comparable value, for example, when a library orders the wrong title or a duplicate copy by mistake.

exclusive   An agreement in which a journal publisher agrees to make the content of one or more of its periodical titles available in online full-text from a *single* journal aggregator, as opposed to multiple aggregators, a practice that has become the subject of debate among serials librarians. Not to be confused with the term *embargo*.

exegesis   Scholarly explanation or interpretation of a word, phrase, sentence, or passage in a written work, based on close study and critical analysis of the text, especially to clarify an obscure point in the Bible or some other sacred work. *See also*: *scholium*.

exemplar   In the context of medieval manuscript production, a masterwork from which another was copied. The scribe kept the exemplar propped open on a lectern or close at hand on a sloping writing desk, consulting it frequently. In the early Middle Ages, monks working in scriptoria obtained exemplars by borrowing them from other monastic establishments. When book production became a commercial activity in the 12th century, copies of scholastic texts made by stationers on the authority of the university were rented as exemplars to students in need of textbooks, to be copied under the *pecia system*. *See also*: *apograph*.

In calligraphy, an alphabet or lettering style used for the purpose of study or decoration. In a more general sense, someone or something that serves as a model, type, specimen, instance, or example of a quality, category, or group.

exemplum   A story or anecdote told to illustrate a moral point, especially in the context of a sermon given by a medieval preacher. An exemplum differs from a parable in having the moral stated at the beginning, rather than at the end. It is also presumed to be based on actual events. Plural: *exempla*.

exhaustive   A search of an index, catalog, bibliographic database, or library collection with the aim of identifying *all* the records or items relevant to the topic. An exhaustive literature search, using all the finding tools at the scholar's disposal, is one of the first steps in a major research project.

exhaustivity   In subject analysis, a measure of the level of detail with which a cataloger or indexer describes the content of a document to facilitate retrieval by subject, expressed as the average number of terms extracted from the title and text or the average number of preferred terms (subject headings or descriptors) selected from a controlled list, for assignment in the bibliographic record representing the item.

exhibit   A physical object placed on display in a museum, gallery, or other public place, usually because of its historical, cultural, or scientific importance or its aesthetic qualities, extraordinary characteristics, or monetary value. Libraries typically exhibit rare or valuable books, manuscripts, personal papers, and memorabilia associated with authorship, publishing, book history, and reading. Exhibits may be permanent or rotated periodically, depending on the availability of materials suitable for display and the policy of the library. Also refers to the event during which such objects are displayed. A list of online exhibits sponsored by the Library of Congress is available at: www.loc.gov/exhibits. Synonymous with *exhibition*. *See also*: *display case* and *exhibit catalog*.

Also, a booth or table at which a book publisher, jobber, or dealer, or a library vendor or supplier, displays its products and services at a conference to attract prospective customers. Companies and organizations that lease exhibit space are called *exhibitors*. *See also*: *display copy* and *Exhibits Round Table*.

exhibit case *See*: display case.

exhibit catalog An art book in hard or softcover containing reproductions of the works of art displayed in an exhibition or series of exhibitions held at a museum or gallery. The illustrations are usually numbered and may be arranged in the order in which the items are exhibited, with or without prices. Accompanying text may be minimal. Exhibit catalogs are often issued by museum publishers. Synonymous with *exhibition catalog*.

Exhibits Round Table (ERT) A permanent round table of the American Library Association, ERT provides a venue for cooperation between the Association and exhibitors, with the aim of making exhibits an effective part of state, regional, and national library conferences. URL: www.ala.org.

exit A door or set of doors through which patrons are permitted to leave a library facility under normal conditions, usually located near the circulation desk and equipped with a security alarm to detect unauthorized removal of library materials. In the United States, special *emergency exits* are required by law in libraries open to the public.

Also, to end a session using a computer application by closing the program. The procedure for ending a session on the computer itself is called *logging off*.

exit interview An interview conducted by a personnel director, or some other person designated by management, at the time an employee leaves employment (voluntarily or involuntarily), usually to determine the reason(s) for leaving, in particular whether separation is the result of grievances that might have been resolved or prevented. For retirees, the interview also provides a final opportunity to discuss with the employer matters concerning pension, health insurance, etc.

ex-library copy A copy of a book or other item once owned by a library and subsequently acquired by a dealer in used books, usually identified by an ownership mark, library binding, or spine label. An ex-library copy may also show signs of heavy use. Condition may reduce its value to collectors. If not stamped "discard," the volume may still belong to the library. Abbreviated *ex-lib* or *x-lib*.

ex libris A Latin phrase meaning "from the books of," usually printed on a bookplate followed by a blank space for the owner's name. An *ex libris inscription* is a note written in or on a book to record its inclusion in a private or institutional library, sometimes providing evidence of the provenance of medieval manuscripts and early printed books. Abbreviated *ex lib.*

exotics   In the printing trade, a general term for non-Latin alphabets (Arabic, Chinese, Cyrillic, Hebrew, Japanese, etc.).

expanded   A typeface wider in proportion to its height than the normal version of the same style. The opposite of *condensed.* Synonymous with *extended.* Compare with *full face.*

expanded edition   A previously published work enlarged by the addition of a significant amount of new material, sometimes in the form of at least one supplement or appendix, with little or no revision of the existing text. Compare with *revised edition.*

expansion   Enlargement of the space available in an existing library facility. The amount of floor space in a library is usually increased by moving nonlibrary functions such as a computer lab or offices to other facilities or by adding a new wing or floor to the existing structure. Some libraries are designed with a knock-out wall and sited on property large enough to accommodate future expansion. In libraries critically short of space, a new addition may dwarf the original structure. Major library expansions are reported annually in *Library Journal* and in *The Bowker Annual Library and Book Trade Almanac.* Compare with *new construction* and *renovation.*

Also refers to the development of an existing class or subdivision in the schedules or tables of Dewey Decimal Classification, usually to accommodate advances in the literature on the subject that require more specific notation.

expert system (ES)   A computer system or application based on artificial intelligence designed to replicate the ability of a human expert to solve a problem or perform a specific task (or sequence of tasks), for example, financial analysis and forecasting. An expert system requires a knowledge base (KB) composed of facts and rules bases, plus an inference engine to run the KB. In the plural, the term refers to the science of creating such systems.

expert user   A person with sufficient knowledge and experience to be able to use a library or computer system effectively and efficiently, with only occasional assistance. The opposite of *novice.*

expiration date   The date on which delivery of a periodical subscription ceases if payment is not received from the subscriber in response to a final renewal notice. Also, the date after which a library is no longer eligible to receive a prepublication price, special discount, or other promotional incentive for ordering an item. Also, the date after which a library card, password, membership, software license, document, etc., is no longer valid. Synonymous with *expiry date.*

explanatory reference   A cross-reference provided in a library catalog or index when more information is required than is normally given in a *see* or *see also* reference, usually an explanation of the circumstances under which the heading(s) should be consulted.

Example:
Klama, John
   The joint pseudonym of John Durant, Peter Klopfer, and Susan Oyama.
For separate works entered under each name see
   Durant, John
   Klopfer, Peter
   Oyama, Susan

explication   A form of critical analysis requiring close examination of the language, style, symbolism, and structure of a literary text, intended to provide a clear and detailed exposition of its meaning and significance. Examples can be found in the literary quarterly titled *The Explicator*.

explicit   An abbreviation of the Latin phrase *Explicitus est liber*, meaning "the book is unrolled to the end." Originally used to signify the end of a text written on a continuous papyrus or parchment scroll or volumen, the expression continued to be used in codex manuscripts and early printed books to indicate the end of the work or the conclusion of one of its major divisions. The explicit sometimes included the author's name and title of work but more often the place and date of production/publication and name of printer. Compare with *incipit*. *See also*: *colophon* and *finis*.

explode   A command available in some bibliographic databases, such as *MEDLINE*, that automatically creates and executes a search statement in which the Boolean OR is used between a given subject heading and each and every one of the headings indented under it in the hierarchical tree structure, expanding retrieval to include narrower subdivisions of the topic.

export   To send data in digital format from one application or computer system to another, usually by means of a specific command, for example, bibliographic records retrieved from an online catalog or database to an e-mail address or storage medium (usually floppy disk). The export process may require the conversion of data into a format compatible with the receiving application or system. Most applications have the capacity to convert a variety of popular formats. The opposite of *import*.

export edition   An edition of a publication prepared by the publisher specifically for distribution and sale in another country (or countries). Compare with *co-edition*.

expression   As defined in *FRBR* (*Functional Requirements for Bibliographic Records*), the form in which a creative work is realized, for example, a single variant of the text of a literary work (Shakespeare's **Hamlet**) or a composer's score or a specific performance of a musical work (original Broadway production of **West Side Story**). Any alteration of the intellectual or artistic content of a work (abridgment, adaptation, revision, translation, etc.) produces a new expression. The term is abstract in the sense of excluding aspects of physical form not essential to the intellectual/artistic content, such as the typeface, type size, and page layout used in printing the words and sentences of a written work. Compare with *manifestation*.

expressive notation   In some classification systems, the structure of the letters, numerals, and/or symbols used to indicate the classes is designed to show the hierarchical position or facets of each class and subclass. For example, in Dewey Decimal Classification, the successive subdivisions of a class are indicated by arabic numerals and decimal fractions. In the DDC notation **782.42**, assigned to the book titled ***Broadway Love Songs***, **700** indicates that the work is about a topic in *the arts*, **780** that it concerns *music*, **782** *vocal music*, and the decimal fraction *.42 songs*.

expunction   An unobtrusive method of correction used in medieval manuscripts in which a dot was written beneath one or more letters or words to indicate deletion.

expurgated   A text or edition from which portions have been deleted ("purged") usually to satisfy moral or political objections, an alternative to banning the work completely from publication or distribution. The opposite of *unexpurgated*. ***See also***: *bowdlerize* and *censorship*.

extended   *See*: expanded.

extended binding   A binding in which the front and back covers extend beyond the trimmed edges of the leaves it encloses. Compare with *flush binding*. ***See also***: *squares*.

extended cover   *See*: extended binding.

extended offer   In publishing, an introductory offer or prepublication price continued beyond the originally announced expiration date, usually in response to strong demand. Sometimes a publisher reissues an entire sale catalog with an extended expiration date.

extended subscription   Instead of resupplying claimed issues or parts, or issuing a credit, the publisher of a periodical may compensate the subscriber by lengthening the period of the current subscription.

extender   A decorative addition to an initial letter in a medieval manuscript continuing the letterform into the margin of the page. In some manuscripts, extenders have been carried even further, forming a decorative border along the margin and corners of the text. ***See also***: *bar border*.

Extensible Markup Language (XML)   A subset of the SGML markup language in which the tags define the kind of information contained in a data element (i.e., product number, price, etc.), rather than how it is displayed. "Extensible" means that XML tags are not limited and predefined as they are in HTML—they must be created and defined through *document analysis* by the person producing the electronic document. Designed to meet the needs of large-scale electronic publishing, XML is a flexible text format that can be used with HTML in the same Web page. Document structure can be defined in a Document Type Definition (DTD) or XML Schema capable of handling document hierarchies. The most elaborate XML vocabularies have been developed to support business-to-business transactions. The World Wide Web Consortium (W3C) provides information on the development of XML at: www.w3.org/XML. ***See also***: *Encoded Archival Description* and *MARCXML*.

Extensible Stylesheet Language (XSL)   A language for expressing style sheets to determine the presentation of XML documents or data files, for example, how the content is formatted, laid out, and paginated in a presentation medium, such as a window in a Web browser or hand-held device or a set of printed pages. URL: www.w3.org/TR/xsl.

extension   A three- or four-character code added to a filename following a period (full stop) to indicate file type, for example, **.txt** to indicate a file in plain ASCII text, **.doc** for a document file created in MS-Word, or **.html** for a file in HTML script. For a more complete list of extensions, see *Every File Format in the World* from ***whatis?com*** (whatis.techtarget.com/fileFormatA).

extent   A publishing term for the length of a book or other printed publication expressed as the total number of pages. Type size and width of margins can be manipulated by the typographer to make a work appear longer or shorter than it actually is. In library cataloging, number of pages is given in the physical description area of the bibliographic record. In a more general sense, the length of any bibliographic item, print or nonprint. *See also*: *extent of item*.

extent of item   The first element in the physical description area (MARC field 300) of the bibliographic record, giving in arabic numerals the number of physical units comprising the item, the specific material designation, and any other details of extent, such as playing time in the case of sound recordings, motion pictures, videorecordings, and DVDs.

external decoder   An electronic device that connects one or more barcode scanners by cable to a computer or computer system and translates input from the scanner into digital signals that can be processed by the computer. Some barcode scanners come with a built-in decoder.

extract   One or more lengthy quotations from a book or other work set within the main text of another work, usually indented and sometimes printed in distinguishing type. When printed in the same type size as the text and without indention, an extract is enclosed in quotation marks and preceded and followed by a blank line. In a more general sense, any piece taken from one work and used in another, sometimes to represent the whole, as in a scene from a motion picture used in a trailer. Compare with *excerpt*.

extract type   In printing, notes and lengthy quotations or extracts are distinguished from the body of the text by setting them in a smaller size of the same typeface. Compare with *text type*. *See also*: *display type*.

extra-illustrated   A volume into which additional illustration and sometimes printed matter have been inserted, not part of the publication as issued. Synonymous with *privately illustrated*. *See also*: *grangerized*.

extranet   A private computer network designed to serve the employees of a company or members of an organization (as in an intranet) and also to provide various levels of accessibility to selected persons *outside* the organization (business partners, customers, clients, etc.) but not the general public. When transmission occurs over public telecommunication channels (the Internet), the system is passworded to exclude unauthorized users. Services may be fee-based or offered at no charge.

extrapolation   The addition of one or more new subjects at the end of an array in a classification system, based on a shared characteristic or characteristics. Compare with *interpolation*.

e-zine   *See*: electronic magazine.

F

fable   A fictitious story that uses animal characters to express or teach a moral lesson (*example*: **Animal Farm** by George Orwell). Compare with *bestiary*. **See also**: *allegory* and *parable*.

fabliau   In medieval literature written in old French, a humorous metrical story told in eight-syllable lines that relates incidents of ordinary life in a realistic style and at the same time conveys a moral message. *Fabliaux* often satirize the faults of clergymen or other prominent persons or the foibles of ordinary people. They can be broadly humorous, as in some of *The Canterbury Tales* by Geoffrey Chaucer.

face   In publishing, the outside of the front cover of a book. In printing, the raised surface of a unit of metal type from which the impression of a single character is taken in printing. Also used as an abbreviation of *typeface*. In binding, the outer side of one of the boards of a book, as opposed to the inside surface or the edge.

Also refers to the unbroken front of a single-sided bookcase or shelving unit, or one side of a double-sided bookcase or shelving unit, or range of double-sided units.

face out   Placement of a book or periodical on edge with the front cover forward, usually to attract browsers to a library display or exhibit or to encourage sales in a retail outlet. In some libraries, current issues of periodicals are displayed on sloping shelves designed to allow the front covers to face forward. Compare with *spine-out*.

facet   In indexing, the entire set of subclasses generated when a class representing a subject in a classification system is divided according to a single characteristic, for example, the subclasses "children," "adolescents," and "adults" generated by the division of the class "people" according to the characteristic "age." The number of subclasses depends on the specific characteristic applied. In his *Colon Classification*, S.R. Ranganathan identified five basic characteristics recognizable in any class: personality, matter, energy, space, and time (abbreviated PMEST). In a more general sense, any one of several distinct aspects of a subject.

facet analysis   Examination of the various aspects of a subject to identify the basic characteristics by which it can be divided into subclasses, the first step in developing a faceted classification system.

faceted classification A classification system developed through analysis of the fundamental characteristics of subjects by which they can be divided into subclasses. For example, in his *Colon Classification*, S.R. Ranganathan identifies five basic characteristics: personality, matter, energy, space, and time (abbreviated PMEST). In such a system, the notation representing a subject is created by combining the notations of its facets.

faceted initial An initial letter in an illuminated manuscript or early printed book drawn to appear three-dimensional, like a gemstone cut into a number of small, intersecting plane surfaces.

faceted notation A notation in which the facets of a classification system are indicated by symbols, for example, the colon in S.R. Ranganathan's *Colon Classification*.

facetiae Witty sayings or writings, sometimes of a coarse, indecent, or blasphemous nature. In bookselling, the term is sometimes used as a euphemism for *erotica* and *pornography*. *See also*: *jestbook*.

facet indicator In Dewey Decimal Classification, a digit used to introduce notation representing a characteristic of the subject, for example, the "0" often used to introduce concepts represented by standard subdivisions (DDC).

face up In printing, the position of a full-page illustration printed on the recto of a leaf so that it appears on the right-hand side of the opening in a book or other publication. Compare with *double spread*.

facilitator A person who makes it easier for others to do their work and accomplish their goals. Ideally, a library director should facilitate the work of staff under his or her supervision. Also refers to a person with exceptional communication skills selected to lead the discussion at a conference or workshop.

facsimile A reproduction or copy intended to simulate as closely as possible the physical appearance of a previous work. A facsimile of a handwritten or printed document is an exact replica of the original text, without reduction or enlargement. A *facsimile edition* duplicates as closely as possible the appearance and content of the original edition. Abbreviated *facsim*. Compare with *forgery*. *See also*: *facsimile binding* and *facsimile catalog*.

facsimile binding A binding intended to duplicate as closely as possible the binding on a previously published edition of the same work or an earlier style of binding typical of the period in which the work was first published. Compare with *retrospective binding*.

facsimile catalog A catalog that includes in each entry a small reproduction of the picture, slide, map, or other item it represents, usually affixed to or printed on cards larger than standard size or on sheets of heavy paper filed in a loose-leaf or other type of binder.

facsimile edition *See*: facsimile.

facsimile reprint *See*: type facsimile.

facsimile transmission (fax) The transfer, over telephone lines, of text and/or images printed or handwritten on a sheet of paper, producing output that is an exact reproduction of the original. The method requires a *fax machine* at each location (sending and receiving), consisting of a scanner, printer, and modem with a dedicated line and *fax number*. Transmission speed depends on the standard of the sending machine, with Group 3 (9600 bits per second) the most common.

faction A term coined in the 1960s with the publication of Truman Capote's novel *In Cold Blood* to describe a new literary genre consisting of fictional narrative based on real events and/or characters, depicted without disguise. Unlike historical fiction in which the author attempts to interpret a more distant past with a reasonable degree of accuracy, faction is based on contemporary events or the recent past, often leaving the distinction between what is real and imaginary to the reader. Some critics and serious writers consider it a "mongrel genre." Synonymous with *documentary fiction*. *See also*: *nonfiction novel* and *roman à clef*.

factotum A printer's ornament in wood or metal, designed with a space in the center, into which a unit of type bearing any letter of the alphabet can be inserted to print a large capital letter at the beginning of a chapter. In early printing, *factotum initials* were usually decorated.

faculty status Official recognition by a college or university that the librarians in its employ are considered members of the faculty, with ranks, titles, rights, and benefits equivalent to those of teaching faculty, including tenure, promotion, and the right to participate in governance. Compare with *academic status*.

FAFLRT *See*: Federal and Armed Forces Libraries Round Table.

fair copy In publishing, the final version of the manuscript or typescript of an original work, containing few mistakes and no corrections, having been carefully prepared from the final draft by the author, or by a copy editor, for the use of the printer. Synonymous with *clean copy*.

fair use Conditions under which copying a work, or a portion of it, does *not* constitute infringement of copyright, including copying for purposes of criticism, comment, news reporting, teaching, scholarship, and research. The Stanford University Libraries maintain a useful Web site on *Copyright & Fair Use* at: fairuse.stanford.edu.

U.S. Copyright Act: Fair Use
Title 17. Chapter 1. Section 107. Limitations on exclusive rights: Fair use

Notwithstanding the provisions of sections 106 and 106A, the fair use of a copyrighted work, including such use by reproduction in copies or phonorecords or by any other means specified by that section, for purposes such as criticism, comment, news reporting, teaching (including multiple copies for classroom use), scholarship, or research, is not an infringement of copyright. In determining whether the use made of a work in any particular case is fair use the factors to be considered shall include:

(1) the purpose and character of the use, including whether such use is of a commercial nature or is for nonprofit educational purposes;

(2) the nature of the copyrighted work;

(3) the amount and substantiality of the portion used in relation to the copyrighted work as a whole; and

(4) the effect of the use upon the potential market for or value of the copyrighted work.

The fact that a work is unpublished shall not itself bar a finding of fair use if such finding is made upon consideration of all the above factors.

fairy tale   A fanciful story written for or told to children, usually containing at least one supernatural element (magic, dragons, elves, ghosts, hobgoblins, witches, etc.) affecting adults and children, animals, and/or inanimate objects. Most fairy tales are based on the traditional folklore of a specific culture. Some are didactic (*example*: "The Three Little Pigs"). Often published in illustrated collections, fairy tales are usually shelved in the children's room of a public library or in the curriculum room of an academic library. Compare with *folktale*.

fallen in   The condition of the spine of a book that has become concave with use, usually the result of faulty binding or improper handling by the owner. Thick volumes are especially prone to this problem, which may be due in part to the force of gravity on the sections as the book sits upright on the shelf. *See also*: *rounding*.

fallout   A measure of the effectiveness of information retrieval, computed as the ratio of nonrelevant entries or items retrieved in response to a query to the total number of nonrelevant items indexed in the database (adapted from the *ASIS Thesaurus of Information Science and Librarianship*, Information Today, 1998). As a practical matter, the number of nonrelevant items in a given database is often difficult (if not impossible) to ascertain, except in very small databases, so this measure remains largely conceptual. *See also*: *precision* and *recall*.

false bands   Fake ridges added to the spine of a decorative binding in imitation of the *raised bands* produced by an older method in which the cords (sewing supports) were not recessed in grooves cut into the sections perpendicular to the binding edge. Compare with *half bands*.

false date   A date such as a birth or death date or publication date given incorrectly, whether intentionally or inadvertently. In library cataloging, the correct date is interpolated in square brackets following the incorrect date in the bibliographic record (*example*: **1950 [1952]**).

false drop   In information retrieval, a bibliographic record retrieved in a keywords search that is unrelated to the subject of the search, usually because it meets the syntactic requirements of the query but not its semantic requirements. False drops generally occur when meaning is contingent on the order of search terms (library + school retrieves "library school" and "school library") or when a term used in a search statement has more than one meaning. For example, a search on the keyword "aids" will retrieve records for items about HIV infection and also items about *hearing aids*, *teaching aids*, *band-aids*, etc. To avoid this problem, a qualifier such as "disease" must be added to the search statement to make retrieval more precise. Synonymous with *false combination*. *See also*: *semantic factoring*.

false imprint   *See*: fictitious imprint.

family   *See*: type family.

family name   *See*: surname.

fan   A book bound at only one point, usually one of the four corners.

fan binding   A style of leather binding developed in France and Italy during the second half of the 17th century in which the center of the boards is embellished with a design in the shape of a fan open 360 degrees composed of small hand-tooled motifs repeated to resemble lacework. The four corners were often tooled in matching quarter-fans. Geoffrey Glaister notes in *Encyclopedia of the Book* (Oak Knoll/British Library, 1996) that the style was adopted by Scottish binders of the 18th century. *See also*: *wheel binding.*

fancy type   In printing, a general term for decorative type, in any size, used mainly for display purposes (ornamental book titles, chapter headings, etc.).

fan drying   When a book has become wet but not saturated, it can usually be dried by standing it on its head on several layers of clean paper toweling or unprinted newsprint, with the covers open wide and the leaves fanned out to expose them to the air. Electric fans hasten drying by increasing air circulation. Former Yale University conservator Jane Greenfield recommends supporting the book block to the height of the squares, if possible, by resting it on one or more thin, pie-shaped pieces of styrofoam (*The Care of Fine Books*, Nick Lyons Books, 1988). Fan drying will reduce some of the swelling caused by exposure to water but does not return the book to its former condition. Vacuum drying must be used for books printed on coated papers that fuse when wet.

fanfare binding   A style of leather binding developed in France during the late 16th and early 17th centuries, featuring interlaced ribbons dividing nearly the entire surface of the cover into compartments of various shapes, each filled with small tooled foliate designs, except for the compartment in the center. Geoffrey Glaister notes in *Encyclopedia of the Book* (Oak Knoll/British Library, 1996) that the interlace was typically bounded by a single line on one side and a double line on the other.

fan fold   *See*: accordion fold.

fantasy   A highly imaginative novel, short story, poem, etc., in which the action occurs in an unreal and nonexistent time and/or place outside the realm of possibility (*example*: **The Hobbit** by J.R.R. Tolkien). Also refers to genre fiction in which the writer's imagination is not constrained by the limitations of conventional reality. *See also*: *science fiction* and *utopia.*

fanzine   A contraction of "fan magazine." A serial publication in electronic or print format containing news and information of interest to enthusiasts of a particular pastime, phenomenon, or notable person or group (living or dead), which may also serve as a forum enabling readers to share their common interest. When published on the Web, such a publication may be called a *fansite*. *See also*: *zine.*

FAQ   Frequently Asked Questions, a text file available online or in print, containing answers to commonly asked questions about a specific topic, that serves as a mini–help file for inexperienced users of a computer system or software program. Usually maintained by one or more persons who have an active interest in the subject.

farce   A light, boisterous form of comedy in which the characters are exaggerated stereotypes, the action improbable to the point of being ludicrous, and the verbal and visual humor lacking in subtlety (*example*: ***Charley's Aunt*** by Brandon Thomas). Farce bears the same relationship to "high" comedy as melodrama to tragedy.

farrago   In literature, an unorganized mixture ("hodgepodge") of humorous prose and light verse. Also used in the context of vaudeville and musical theater to indicate a disjointed medley of tunes, dramatic skits, and comedy routines.

fascicle   For convenience in publishing or printing, a book or other item is sometimes issued in numbered or unnumbered installments, each of which is incomplete and does not necessarily coincide with any formal division of the work. Usually issued in paper wrappers, fascicles may eventually be bound together in correct sequence to form a complete volume or uniform set of volumes (*example*: ***Middle English Dictionary***, published by the University of Michigan Press). They differ from parts in being temporary rather than permanent. Abbreviated *fasc.* Synonymous with *fascicule* and *fasciculus.*

fascicule   *See*: fascicle.

fastening   A device used to keep a book closed. The earliest fasteners were wrapping bands, thongs, and ties made of fabric or leather. Metal clasps eventually replaced leather strap-and-pin fittings on medieval manuscript books. Their use helped prevent the parchment or vellum leaves from cockling due to changes in temperature and humidity. As paper replaced parchment in the 16th century, the use of fastenings declined. Today, they are seen mainly on portfolios and on personal diaries and albums.

fat face   A novelty typeface in which the degree of contrast between the thick and thin strokes of each character is highly exaggerated.

fat matter   A printer's term for copy that does not take long to set because it contains a high proportion of white space, for example, extended passages of dialogue in a work of fiction. The opposite of *lean matter*.

fax   *See*: facsimile transmission.

FDLP   *See*: Federal Depository Library Program.

feasibility study   A preliminary investigation and report on a proposed policy, project, or plan to ascertain if it can be successfully carried out, for example, to determine if a library building can be constructed on a particular site.

feature   A comparatively long article in a magazine or newspaper given special emphasis by the editor(s) or publisher, as opposed to a short article, regular column, or editorial. In magazines, the article illustrated on the front cover is called the *cover* *story*. Other feature stories in the same issue may also be noted on the front cover, usually by subject.

feature film   A motion picture in which the dialogue and characters are largely fictional, although the plot may be derived from a true story adapted as a screenplay. Feature films vary in length, but most are at least 90 minutes long. Libraries that circulate feature films usually make them available on videocassette or DVD. Compare with *documentary* and *short film*. *See also*: *credit*, *director*, and *performer*.

Federal and Armed Forces Libraries Round Table (FAFLRT)   A round table of the American Library Association, FAFLRT is dedicated to promoting library and information services and the LIS profession within the U.S. federal government/military community, to encouraging appropriate utilization of federal and military library and information facilities and resources, and to stimulating research and development related to the planning, development, and operation of federal and military libraries. FAFLRT publishes the quarterly newsletter *Federal Librarian*. URL: www.ala.org.

Federal Depository Library Program (FDLP)   Established by Congress as part of the Printing Act of 1895 to assure that the American public has access to federal government information, the FDLP provides copies of federal government documents without charge to designated depository libraries in the United States (and its territories) that provide unrestricted access and professional assistance at no charge to the user. There are currently about 1,350 depository libraries, some receiving less than the full complement of available publications. The FDLP also provides free online public access to government information via *GPO Access*. The Public Printer and Superintendent of Documents are advised on policy matters concerning the FDLP by the Depository Library Council (DLC) established in 1972. URL: www.access.gpo. gov/su_docs/fdlp.

federal library   A library owned and operated by the federal government of the United States, usually containing a collection of government documents pertaining to the field(s) it is mandated to cover. The largest are the Library of Congress, the National Library of Medicine, the National Library of Education, and the National Agricultural Library. The Federal Library and Information Center Committee (FLICC) of the Library of Congress has provided the FEDLINK guide to federal libraries since 1965. Federal librarians are organized in the Federal and Armed Forces Libraries Round Table (FAFLRT) of the American Library Association.

Federal Library and Information Center Committee (FLICC)   Created in 1965 as the Federal Library Committee, FLICC is composed of the directors of the four national libraries (Library of Congress, National Library of Medicine, National Library of Education, and National Agriculture Library) and representatives of cabinet-level executive departments and federal agencies with major library programs, chaired by the Librarian of Congress.

   The mission of FLICC is to enhance utilization of federal library and information center resources and facilities through professional development, publicity, and coordination. FLICC is also responsible for recommending policies, programs, and procedures to federal agencies concerning libraries and information resources and for providing guidance and direction for the Federal Library and Information Network (FEDLINK), the purchasing, training, and resource sharing consortium of federal libraries and information centers. URL: lcweb.loc.gov/flicc/mmabout.html.

FEDLINK   *See*: Federal Library and Information Center Committee.

fee   A sum of money paid for a service. The amount may be fixed, depending on type of service, or variable, depending on the amount of time required to perform the service. In some libraries, document delivery service is fee-based. Fees may also be charged for the use of items in rental collections, but for the most part, libraries in the United States are committed to offering basic services at no charge to their clientele. Persons who live outside a public library's service area, or who are not faculty or students entitled to use the resources and services of an academic library, may be charged a fee for limited borrowing privileges. *See also*: *copyright fee*.

fee-based service   An information service provided by a library or information broker in exchange for monetary payment. In most academic and public libraries in the United States, fee-based services, provided on a cost-recovery basis, are limited to document delivery and rental collections. *See also*: *fee-or-free*.

feedback   In computing, output put back into the same system as input to achieve a degree of self-regulation. In library operations, the views (solicited or unsolicited) of the users of a resource or service concerning its quality and/or usefulness, whether positive or negative. Libraries rely on user surveys and the suggestion box to obtain feedback from patrons.

fee-or-free   The ongoing debate in libraries over the ideal of providing unlimited free access to information versus charging, usually on a cost-recovery basis, for certain services. In the United States, most libraries limit fee-for-service to document delivery, interlibrary loan when the lender charges, and rental collections. Libraries may also charge users to print from computer workstations, and in most libraries, photocopiers and reader-printer machines are coin-operated.

feint   Parallel horizontal lines drawn lightly with a ruler or printed in light-colored ink across a sheet or page, as in an account book to keep entries separate or in a medieval manuscript to guide the hand of the scribe.

feltboard   *See*: flannel board.

Feminist Task Force (FTF)   Founded in 1970 as a task force of the Social Responsibilities Round Table of the American Libraries Association, FTF focuses on women's issues, including sexism in libraries and librarianship. FTF hosts an electronic mailing list and publishes the quarterly newsletter *Women in Libraries*. URL: libr.org/FTF.

ferrotype   *See*: tintype.

Festschrift   From the German words *Fest* ("festival") and *Schrift* ("writing"). A memorial publication, usually in the form of a collection of essays or speeches by distinguished persons, issued in honor of a scholarly person or society, sometimes on the occasion of an anniversary, birthday, or retirement celebration. The subject or theme encompassing the collected works is usually related to the field in which the person (or organization) achieved distinction. The contributors are often friends, colleagues, and former students of the person (or entity) honored. Plural: *Festschriften*.

FIAF   *See*: International Federation of Film Archives.

fiberboard   A very rigid form of paperboard made from heavily pressed sheets of pulped vegetable fiber, laminated together.

fiber content   A statement of the various kinds of fiber present in a material manufactured from fiber (paper, board, cloth, thread), usually expressed in percentages to indicate relative proportions, important information because type of fiber affects the properties of a product, for example, its color, chemical stability, strength, and durability. Synonymous with *fiber composition*. *See also*: *pulp*.

fiber optics   The high-speed transmission of data encoded in pulses of laser light via cable constructed of optical fiber made of pure silicon dioxide, a technology that revolutionized the telecommunication industry in the late 20th century, making it possible to interconnect computers large and small in a worldwide network.

fiche   *See*: microfiche.

fiction   From the Latin *fictio*, meaning to "make" or "counterfeit." Literary works in prose, portraying characters and events created in the imagination of the writer, intended to entertain and vicariously expand the reader's experience of life. In historical fiction, characters and events usually bear some relationship to what actually happened, but any dialogue is reconstructed or imagined by the author. All fiction is fictitious in the sense of being invented, but good fiction remains "true to life." In the Western tradition, the traditional forms of literary fiction include the novel, novelette, and short story. Compare with *nonfiction*. *See also*: *faction*, *genre*, *popular fiction*, and *pulp fiction*.

In libraries that use Library of Congress Classification, fiction is shelved in the Ps, the section for language and literature, subdivided by language. To locate a specific work of fiction in the stacks, the patron must first look up the LC call number in the catalog. In libraries that use Dewey Decimal Classification, long fiction is shelved separately from nonfiction, alphabetically by last name of author, to facilitate browsing. In some public libraries, genre fiction is shelved separately from general fiction, usually by category (mystery, science fiction, etc.), sometimes indicated by a graphic label on the spine.

fictitious imprint   An imprint that has no real existence because the publisher has given incorrect information about when, where, or by whom the edition was printed or issued, usually to evade legal or other restrictions, avoid charges of copyright piracy, or conceal the identity of the author. In library cataloging, the real imprint, when known, is given following the fictitious one in the bibliographic description as an interpolation inside square brackets ([]). Synonymous with *false imprint*.

field   In library cataloging, a relative location of fixed or variable length in a machine-readable record, reserved for a specific data element or group of elements that constitute a single logical category of bibliographic description, for example, the area of physical description reserved for information about the physical characteristics of an item. In the MARC record, each field is indicated by a three-digit tag, but in the catalog display, textual field labels are provided to assist users in identifying the various categories of description.

Repeatable fields (R) may appear more than once in the same record; for example, there is no restriction on the number of topical subject headings (MARC field 650) that may be assigned to a work. Nonrepeatable (NR) fields can be used only once and may be mutually exclusive, for example, the personal name main entry (field 100) and uniform title main entry (field 130). Fields for areas of description containing more than one data element are divided into *subfields*. Only about 10 percent of available MARC fields are used in most bibliographic records; the other 90 percent are used infrequently. ***See also***: *control field*, *directory*, *leader*, *local field*, and *variable data field*.

In a more general sense, a logical unit of data that, together with other units, comprises a record in a database or other system of recordkeeping, for example, the name, address, or phone number field of each patron record in a library's patron database.

In academic research, a subject or group of related subjects studied in depth, for example, "anthropometry" in the subdiscipline "physical anthropology" within the discipline of anthropology.

field guide   A handbook designed to help readers identify and learn about the flora and/or fauna of a specific geographic area, often published as part of a series. The content of a field guide is usually arranged according to biological classification, with each entry describing a single species or group of related species (genus). Entries typically include the Latin species name, descriptive text, at least one illustration intended to facilitate identification, and one or more maps showing geographic distribution. Field guides are shelved in the reference section or the circulating collection, depending on local library policy.

field label   An abbreviation or descriptive word or phrase appearing in the record display in an online catalog or bibliographic database, usually in italics or distinguished typographically in some other way, aligned with the left-hand margin to indicate the category of data that follows, for example, *Source* used in periodical databases to indicate the journal title, volume number, publication date, and page numbers of the article indexed. In the MARC record, a numeric tag is used instead of a textual label to indicate a specific field of the record.

fieldwork   The gathering of information or scientific data about a subject through observation, interviewing, and other methods of direct investigation, usually conducted in a location closely associated with the topic, as opposed to researching the subject in books and other publications, conducting experiments in a laboratory setting, administering mail surveys, etc.

In archives, the process of locating, identifying, and securing materials for an archival collection, including any negotiations required to acquire custody if the materials have monetary value. Also spelled *field work*.

figure   Illustrative matter printed *with* the text, rather than separately in the form of plates. Figures are usually fairly simple line drawings, numbered consecutively in arabic numerals in order of appearance to facilitate reference. Figures not individually captioned may be listed with captions on a separate page, usually in the front matter of a book. Abbreviated *fig*. Also, synonymous in printing with *numeral*.

figure initial   An initial letter in an illuminated manuscript or early printed book composed wholly or in part of designs representing animals, humans, and/or imaginary beings unrelated to the text. Figure initials can be anthropomorphic, zoomorphic, or zoo-anthropomorphic. Compare with *historiated initial* and *inhabited initial*. **See also**: *gymnastic initial*.

figure of speech   A form of expression employed mainly in rhetoric and literary writing in which words or entire sentences are used in a way that deviates from conventional order or literal meaning to achieve an unusual or unexpected poetic or aesthetic effect, for example, the phrase "a flood of tears." *Wikipedia: The Free Encyclopedia* provides a Web site devoted to figures of speech at: en.wikipedia.org/wiki/Figure_of_speech. *See also*: *metaphor*.

file   A collection of documents usually related in some way, stored together, and arranged in a systematic order. In computing, a collection of structured data elements stored as a single entity or a collection of records related by source and/or purpose, stored on a magnetic medium (floppy disk, hard disk, Zip disk, etc.). File type, indicated by an extension on the end of the filename, depends on the code in which the data is written (*example*: **.html** for HTML script). In *AACR2*, the term is defined as a basic unit in which electronic resources are organized and stored, some e-resources containing more than one file.

In manual data systems, the contents of a manila file folder or other physical container used to organize documents, usually of a size and shape designed to fit inside the drawer of a standard-sized filing cabinet or other storage space. Also refers to a collection of information about a specific subject or person, for example, a *personnel file* kept by an employer.

file copy   A copy of a document, report, periodical article, etc., kept on file, usually with related items, for reference or future use.

file name   *See*: filename.

filename   A brief name assigned by a programmer or computer user to a data file to identify it for future retrieval. Filenames usually provide a clue to the content of the file (*example*: **resume.txt** or **home.html**). The three- or four-letter extension added to the end of a filename indicates file type (*example*: **.txt** for a file in ASCII or **.html** for a file in Hypertext Markup Language). Also spelled *file name*.

file server   *See*: server.

File Transfer Protocol   *See*: FTP.

file type   In electronic data processing, the type of code in which a data file is written, indicated by a three- or four-letter extension at the end of the filename (*example*: **dictionary.html** for a file in HTML script). Synonymous with *file format*. Compare with *Internet media type* and *MIME media type*.

Common file types and their extensions:

File Type	Extension
Plain ASCII text	**.txt**
Document in Hypertext Markup Language	**.htm** or **.html**
Document in Standard Generalized Markup Language	**.sgml**
Document in Extensible Markup Language	**.xml**
GIF image	**.gif**
JPEG image	**.jpg** or **.jpeg**
TIFF image	**.tif** or **.tiff**
Bitmap	**.bmp**
PostScript file	**.ps**
AIFF sound file	**.aif** or **.aiff**
AU sound file	**.au**
WAV file	**.wav**
QuickTime movie	**.mov**
MPEG movie	**.mpg** or **.mpeg**

filigree   An elegant style of decoration used in manuscripts and fine printing in which an initial letter or border is edged with a delicate tracery of curved lines resembling lacework. In medieval manuscripts and early printed books, this type of decoration was usually done in pen using colored ink.

filigree letter   An initial letter in a manuscript or printed book given a decorative outline or background of delicately interlaced lines resembling lacework.

filing rule   A guide established to determine how a specific type of decision is to be made concerning the order in which entries are filed in a library catalog. Published in 1942, the first edition of the *A.L.A. Rules for Filing Catalog Cards* was revised in 1967 to correlate with *Anglo-American Cataloguing Rules*. New *ALA Filing Rules* published in 1980 apply to all bibliographic display formats (print, microform, digital, etc.). Under the current guidelines, filing is character-by-character to the end of each word, and word-by-word to the end of each filing element. Numerals precede letters, and letters of the English alphabet precede those of nonroman alphabets.

filing title   *See*: uniform title.

filing word   *See*: entry word.

filler   Blank unnumbered leaves added at the end of a publication to increase its bulk when bound, known in the book trade as *padding*.

fillet   In bookbinding, one or more thin bands or lines impressed on the covers and/or spine of a book for decorative effect. Also refers to the rolling tool used, when heated, to apply such lines. A *French fillet* consists of three unevenly spaced gilt lines. *See also*: *Oxford corners*.

fill rate   In acquisitions, the percentage of materials ordered by a library from a publisher, jobber, or other vendor actually supplied within a specified period of time. *See also*: *back order* and *canceled*.

film   A thin strip or sheet of flexible, transparent or translucent material (usually plastic) coated with a light-sensitive emulsion that, when exposed to light, can be used to develop photographic images. The instability and flammability of the cellulose nitrate used as a film base prior to 1950 has created a preservation imperative of massive proportions. To prevent deterioration, older films must be copied onto a more permanent base such as acetate or polyester, a time-consuming and expensive process.

Also refers to commercial and educational motion pictures in widths of 8, 16, 35, or 70 mm, including documentaries, feature films, and short films. *See also*: *film archives*, *film library*, *filmography*, *filmstrip*, *International Federation of Film Archives*, *microfilm*, *National Film Preservation Board*, *National Film Registry*, and *orphan film*.

film archives   An organization or unit within a larger organization or institution responsible for maintaining a permanent film collection, usually of motion pictures, documentaries, cartoons, and associated materials. Environmental control is essential in film archives to prevent deterioration of the medium. The UCLA Film & Television Archive (www.cinema.ucla.edu) maintains the largest university-held moving image collection in the world. For an international list of film archives, see the directory of the International Federation of Film Archives (FIAF) at: www.fiafnet.org/uk/members/directory.cfm. *See also*: *National Film Preservation Foundation*.

film clip   A short piece of motion picture footage taken from a longer work, usually for promotional use or for review purposes, to give viewers a brief impression of the whole. Compare with *trailer*. *See also*: *video clip*.

film library   A type of special library containing a collection of 8, 16, 35, or 70 mm motion pictures, videorecordings, DVDs, and materials related to filmmaking and film studies, classified for ease of access and retrieval. Borrowing privileges may be restricted to registered members or subscribers required to pay a rental fee per item. *See also*: *film archives*.

filmography   A list of motion pictures, usually limited to works by a specific director or performer, in a particular genre, of a specific time period or country, or on a given subject, usually listed alphabetically by title or chronologically by release date. The entries in a filmography include some or all of the following elements of description: producer, distributor, director, cast, release date, running time, language, color or black and white, etc. Compare with *discography*.

filmslip   A very short filmstrip mounted like a slide in a rigid holder instead of stored in a short flexible roll.

filmstrip   A length of 35 mm or 16 mm black and white or color film consisting of a sequence of related still images, with or without text or captions, intended to be projected one at a time at slow speed using a *filmstrip projector*. Filmstrips are of variable length, usually no longer than 50 frames. Some include a signal that automatically advances the projector in synchrony with recorded sound. Compare with *filmslip*.

filmstrip projector *See*: filmstrip.

filter A computer program designed to allow only selected data to pass through to the user, for example, an e-mail system that alerts the recipient to selected incoming messages or software that blocks access to Web sites containing certain types of content, usually violent or sexually explicit material considered unsuitable for young children. In the United States, filtering has become the focus of a national debate over intellectual freedom and censorship. *See also*: *adult content filter*, Children's Internet Protection Act, and *V-chip*.

filtering In computing, the use of specially designed software to prevent the user of a specific computer, network, or system from viewing certain types of content by blocking access. Filters are used primarily to prevent children from viewing violent and/or sexually explicit material and by employers to prevent employees from engaging in non-work-related activities on the job. In libraries, the passage by Congress of the *Children's Internet Protection Act* has made filtering a controversial issue. Compare with *content rating*. *See also*: *censorship* and *intellectual freedom*.

finding aid A published or unpublished guide, inventory, index, register, calendar, list, or other system for retrieving archival primary source materials providing more detailed description of each item than is customary in a library catalog record. Finding aids also exist in nonprint formats (ASCII, HTML, etc.). In partnership with the Society of American Archivists, the Library of Congress maintains a standard known as Encoded Archival Description (EAD) for encoding archival finding aids in Standard Generalized Markup Language (SGML) and/or Extensible Markup Language (XML). *EAD Finding Aids* for Library of Congress collections are available online at: lcweb. loc.gov/rr/ead/eadhome.html.

finding list A list of a library's holdings in which each item is represented by a very brief entry containing incomplete bibliographic information (usually just the author's name, the title, and its location within the library). Compare with *catalog*.

findings Information or evidence uncovered as a result of systematic research or investigation. Also, the conclusions of an official inquiry or hearing on a particular topic or issue, usually presented in the form of a report that may be preserved as a legal document.

finding tool A general term for a resource designed to be used in a library to locate sources of information, usually in a search by author, title, subject, or keywords. The category includes catalogs, bibliographies, indexes, abstracting services, bibliographic databases, etc. The corresponding term in archives is *finding aid*.

fine book A book of exceptional quality with respect to its design, printing, illustration, and binding, often a copy of a deluxe edition. Very fine books are usually sold by antiquarian booksellers and at book auctions. Libraries preserve them in special collections. Compare with *rare book*.

fine copy   In the used book trade, a copy in clean, crisp condition that surpasses "good" but falls short of *mint*.

fine edition   *See*: deluxe edition.

fine-free period   *See*: grace period.

fine press   A publisher/printer that specializes in the production of books of exceptional quality, designed to meet the highest aesthetic standards and serve as an inspiration to the book arts (*example*: **Kelmscott Press** established in 1891 by William Morris). Fine presses are often private. *See also*: *Limited Editions Club*.

fine print   Information printed in very small type, usually at the end of a document or in an inconspicuous place within it, containing details of which the reader must be informed but to which the source or publisher may not wish to call attention. The term is also used to refer to the details of a document, printed in any type size, as opposed to its main points. Failure to read fine print can have serious consequences for a person signing a legal document. *See also*: *mouse type*.

fines   To encourage borrowers to return materials promptly, most libraries charge a small amount for each day that a circulating item is kept past its due date. The amount may vary depending on the format of the material checked out. Overdue fines for items on reserve may be charged by the hour. Fines can be avoided by renewing items on or before the due date. Most automated circulation systems are programmed to block a borrower account if unpaid fines accumulate beyond a certain amount. *See also*: *grace period*.

fingerprint   A unique identifier constructed according to formula, used in historical bibliography to identify copies of early printed books as belonging to a specific edition or issue. Fingerprint formulas are usually in two parts: the year in which the edition appeared plus size of book (*example*: **157504** for a quarto edition of the year 1575), followed by three groups of characters transcribed from the line of text immediately above the signature marks printed at the foot of certain pages in the front matter, main text, and back matter to assist the binder in assembling the gatherings in correct sequence. Even when a text is reprinted exactly as it appeared in a preceding edition, the signature marks added after the text is composed rarely fall in the same place, creating a variance that can be used for identification. Synonymous with *signature position*.

For more information, please see *Fingerprints = Empreintes = Impronte* (Paris: Institut de Recherche et d'Histoire des Textes, 1984) and the critique by Ben J.P. Salemans of the technique in the June 1994 issue of the journal *Computers and the Humanities*.

finger tab   A small marker attached to the fore-edge of a book to aid the reader in locating a particular passage or division of the text. In medieval manuscripts, they were usually made of vellum, tawed skin, or cloth, sometimes in the form of a small knot. In modern binding, finger tabs are usually made of paper, card, fabric, or plastic stamped or printed with letters, words, numbers, or other characters indicating the alphabetic, numeric, subject, or other arrangement of the text, to facilitate reference. Synonymous with *extension tab*. *See also*: *tab index*.

Also refers to a projecting part of a card, folder, divider, etc., large enough to bear a label indicating the contents, used in filing and retrieval.

finis   A French word printed at the end of an old book, or appearing at the end of an early motion picture, meaning "the end" or "conclusion." Compare with *explicit*.

finish   A general term for the texture of the surface of a grade of paper, determined by the materials and techniques used in manufacture (fiber content, sizing, calendering, coating, drying, etc.). The terms used to describe finish are descriptive: antique, cockle, eggshell, glossy, matte, stipple, etc.

In binding, to apply lettering and/or ornamentation to the cover of a book in a process known as *finishing*.

finishing   In hand-binding, the process of applying lettering and/or decorative elements to a book cover by blocking, tooling, inlaying, or onlaying, done by a person known as a *finisher*. Compare with *forwarding*.

Also, a general term for the final steps in the processing of type matter once it has been printed, including cutting, folding, machine binding, stamping, laminating, application of the dust jacket, etc.

finite resource   *See*: seriality.

fire   One of the worst disasters a library or archives can experience, usually caused by incendiarism, defective electrical equipment, careless smoking, or the exposure of paper-based materials to overheating. The best defense is an effective fire prevention program that includes systematic inspection and removal of hazards and a detection system designed to give early warning. Because the chemicals used in some hand fire extinguishers damage books, their use is recommended only as a last resort. An on–off sprinkler system detects fire at its point of origin and minimizes the amount of water damage by automatically shutting off as soon as temperature returns to normal. To prevent arson, book drops that empty into the building through an exterior wall should be kept locked when the library is unstaffed.

firewall   A dedicated computer that functions as a security boundary, blocking traffic from one part of a network to another, usually the transmission of data from a larger network to a local area network. Firewalls are installed to restrict access to private computer network(s) and proprietary files by screening incoming traffic and denying access to unauthorized users. They also help prevent confidential information from passing out.

firm order   In acquisitions, an order placed with a publisher, jobber, or dealer for a specific title and number of copies, specifying a maximum price and time limit for delivery, not to be exceeded without prior approval of the ordering library. Firm orders are placed for materials requested by individual selectors responsible for collection development. Compare with *continuation order* and *subscription*.

First Amendment   Amendment I to the *United States Constitution*, ratified in 1791, which guarantees freedom of speech: "Congress shall make no law respecting an establishment of religion, or prohibiting the free exercise thereof; or abridging the freedom of speech, or of the press; or the right of the people peaceably to assemble, and to petition the government for a redress of grievances." The *Freedom to Read Statement* and the *Library Bill of Rights* of the American Library Association are based on this constitutional protection.

first American edition   The first edition published in the United States of a work previously published in another country.

first appearance   A term used in the book trade to mean: (1) an author's initial appearance in print; (2) the first time a given work by an author appears in print, especially a short work (essay, poem, or short story); or (3) the first treatment of a subject to be published in book form.

first book   In publishing, the first appearance in print of a book-length work written entirely by the author. The initial books of many well-known writers remain comparatively obscure (*example*: **Fanshawe: A Tale** by Nathaniel Hawthorne).

first edition   All the copies of the edition of a book or other publication printed and issued at the same time, before any other printings. Subsequent printings from the same set of type are considered new impressions but are still part of the first edition. The *second edition* is printed from a new setting of type or includes significant changes in text or format. Also refers to an individual copy of a work printed from the initial setting of type. In the antiquarian book trade, first editions are usually more valuable than later editions. Synonymous with *princeps edition* and editio princeps. Compare with *reprint* and *revised edition*. *See also*: *all firsts*.

Also refers to the first printing of a newspaper on a specific date when two or more editions are issued each day.

First Folio   The common name for the first collected edition of Shakespeare's dramatic works, containing 36 plays assembled by actor-editors John Heminge and Henry Condell, 18 of which had never been published. Issued in London in 1623, it is one of the most famous and valuable printed books in the world. *See also*: *Folger Shakespeare Library*.

first impression   All the copies of a book made at the first printing, before any alterations in the text. Subsequent impressions made from the same setting of type soon after the first are numbered sequentially and may contain slight changes to correct errors detected after the first printing. Compare with *first edition*.

first issue   The first installment of a newly published periodical (issue number one of volume one). Also refers to the first installment received by a library in response to a new periodical subscription, not necessarily the first issue published. *See also*: *back issue* and *current issue*.

first-line index   An index in which the opening lines of poems (songs, hymns, etc.) are listed in alphabetical order, each entry giving the title of the work and the name of the poet, usually shelved in the reference section of a library. In *The Columbia*

Granger's Index to Poetry in Anthologies, poems are indexed by first line, last line, and title, in a single alphabetical sequence.

first name   The first of one or more given names or Christian names, as distinct from the surname identifying members of the same family. In *AACR2*, personal name headings for persons known by their initials begin with the surname, followed by a comma, then the initials, followed by the full given names (*example*: **Eliot, T.S. Thomas Stearns**).

first-of-two rule   The instruction in Dewey Decimal Classification that works dealing in equal measure with two subjects, neither used to introduce or explain the other, are given the class number appearing first in the schedules, whether the subjects are close in the list of classes or widely separated. *See also*: *rule of three*.

first published edition   An edition issued for sale to the general public after the work has been distributed to a restricted audience, for example, a motion picture released for public viewing after it has been previewed by a limited audience, usually selected by the producer.

firsts   *See*: first edition.

first sale   Under *Section 109* of the *U.S. Copyright Act*, users who have lawfully acquired a copy of a work are allowed to sell, trade, rent, loan, or dispose of the item without the prior consent of the copyright holder. Without right of first sale, libraries could not legally lend materials protected by copyright, sell their used books, or exchange materials with other libraries. It would also be unlawful for owners to donate copyrighted materials to libraries.

FirstSearch (FS)   A service of OCLC that provides access to over 40 online bibliographic databases in a wide range of disciplines via a proprietary interface, on a per search or subscription basis, by licensing agreement. Some of the databases in *FirstSearch* include full-text. *WorldCat*, the largest union catalog in the world, is available in *FS*. URL: www.oclc.org/firstsearch.

first trade edition   The first edition of a book to be published for sale to the general public, as distinct from a previously issued limited edition.

fiscal value   *See*: archival value.

fiscal year   A period of 12 months, not necessarily coincident with the calendar year, used by a library or library system for financial accounting purposes. In the United States, most public and academic libraries that depend on public funding use a fiscal year beginning on July 1 and ending on June 30. Academic libraries at privately funded colleges and universities may use a fiscal year that coincides with the academic calendar. In federal libraries, the fiscal year may begin on October 1 and end on September 30. In special libraries, the fiscal year usually corresponds with that of the parent organization. Synonymous with *accounting year*.

fist   Printer's slang for a symbol in the form of a closed hand with the index finger extended, used to draw attention to something on a printed page, and in signage to indicate direction. In medieval manuscripts, this symbol (called a *manicula*) was inserted in the margin to draw attention to an important passage in the text. Also known as a *digit* or *hand*.

fittings   *See*: furniture.

Five Laws of Library Science   *See*: Ranganathan, S.R.

fixed field   A field of the MARC record containing a fixed number of characters, as opposed to a field of variable length, for example, the 24-character leader (field 001) or the 005, 006, 007, and 008 fields. Because the function of each character in a fixed field is defined by its relative position, subfield codes are not required to distinguish data elements. Cataloging software usually provides prompts or windows to assist catalogers entering data in fixed fields.

fixed-length data elements   Field 008 of the MARC record, containing 40 characters used to encode information that allows records meeting certain criteria to be identified and retrieved, for example, materials in a specific format, published in a specific language or country, or intended for a particular audience.

fixed location   A specific physical location to which an item in a library collection is permanently assigned, for example, a dictionary stand on which a large dictionary is displayed or an atlas case in which several large atlases are stored for ease of access. In medieval libraries, manuscript books were sometimes chained to a shelf, table, or carrel to prevent removal. In most modern libraries, items have a *relative location* determined by the classification notation assigned in cataloging, their actual physical position on the shelf changing as other items are acquired or withdrawn or when the collection is shifted. Synonymous with *absolute location*.

fixed shelving   Shelving in which each shelf is permanently attached to the uprights in a range, or to the vertical side of a bookcase, as opposed to *adjustable shelving* in which the shelves are detachable and can easily be moved up or down to accommodate materials of varying height.

flag   The title of a newspaper exactly as printed across the top of the front page, including any design elements on either side, called ears. Synonymous with *nameplate*. *See also*: *masthead*.

Also refers to a long, narrow strip cut with the grain from a sheet of stiff paper or thin pasteboard, inserted in a book or other item to alert library staff to the existence of special characteristics, status, or instructions, usually in technical processing or shelving. The strips may be color-coded to communicate specific information to the person doing the processing or shelving. Acid-free paper or board should be used for this purpose.

In data processing, a special character used to mark the occurrence of a condition specified in advance.

flame   To communicate via e-mail in an angry, sarcastic, or critical tone. A protracted dispute in a newsgroup or mailing list discussion is known as a *flame war*. Such disputes are usually mediated or terminated by the other participants or by the moderator. *See also*: *netiquette* and *shouting*.

flannel board   A large square or rectangular board covered in felt, used in storytelling and instruction to display letters, symbols, and shapes cut from fabric or some other textured material that sticks to the felt surface when the board is held in an upright position. Synonymous with *feltboard* and *cloth board*.

flap   One of the two ends of the paper dust jacket wrapped around the cover of a book bound in hardcover. The list price and the publisher's promotional blurb are usually printed on the front flap. The back flap provides brief biographical information about the author and/or illustrator, usually with a small portrait photograph of each person.

flap binding   A style of binding in which the back cover of a book extends beyond the sections in a wide flap that folds over the fore-edge and is usually fastened to the front cover in some fashion. In Islamic binding, an envelope flap often fits inside the upper board. The category includes *wallet* bindings.

flash card   A small card or piece of stiff, opaque material bearing a letter, word, phrase, numeral, symbol, picture, or combination of characters and images, usually part of a set designed for rapid display in mnemonic drill and recognition training. Flash cards are also used in presentations to provide visual cues to the audience. Libraries that include flash cards in their collections usually make them available in the curriculum room or children's room. Compare with *activity card*.

flat back   A type of binding in which the back of a book is not rounded or backed after gluing, leaving the front and back covers to meet the spine at a right angle. Synonymous with *square back*. *See also*: *hollow back* and *tight back*.

flat panel   A computer peripheral device in the form of a thin, flat screen that uses LCD or plasma technology, rather than a cathode ray tube, to display output. In laptops, the flat panel folds down to cover the keyboard.

flat shelving   Storing books stacked flat on the shelf, one on top of another with the lower edges (tails) facing outward, used mainly for large sets and series such as law books. The volume number may be written large on the lower edge to facilitate retrieval. This method of shelving can increase shelf capacity by as much as 28 percent, but it makes browsing difficult because the spines are not visible. *See also*: *double shelving*, *fore-edge shelving*, and *shelving by size*.

fleuron   A small stylized ornament in the form of a symmetrical spray of leaves and/ or flowers, usually used in bookbinding as a repeating pattern in blind- or gold-tooling. The French *fleur-de-lis*, representing the iris plant, is an example of a fleuron. Also used synonymously with *printer's flower*.

flex-cover   *See*: flexible binding.

flexible binding   A cloth or leather covered book bound in a material that bends easily, rather than the rigid boards used in most hardcover editions. Synonymous with *flexcover*. Compare with *limp binding* and *softcover*. *See also*: *bible style*.

flextime   Time worked in excess of the maximum number of hours per day, week, or month specified under the terms governing employment, for which the employee is granted time off at a later date. Synonymous with *comp time*. Compare with *overtime*.

FLICC   *See*: Federal Library and Information Center Committee.

flicker book   A type of toy book published during the 19th century containing a sequence of closely related cartoon-style illustrations designed to give the impression of animation when the pages are fanned from cover to cover, similar to the visual effect created by the rapid projection of frames in a motion picture. Synonymous with *flip book*.

flier   An inexpensive, widely distributed handbill or circular of small size (usually 8½ × 11 inches), used flat or folded for advertising and announcements. Also spelled *flyer*. Synonymous in the UK with *leaflet*. *See also*: *ephemera*.

flip chart   A large-sized pad of paper designed to be mounted on an easel to display information in graphic or tabular format during a presentation. As the session proceeds, pages are either torn off or turned over the top. Unlike slide projection or presentation software, a flip chart allows the presenter to manipulate information content manually as it is presented, sometimes in response to feedback from the audience. Transparencies are visible to a larger audience but require overhead projection equipment. Also spelled *flipchart*.

floor plan   A drawing of the layout of a library building showing the location of collections, services, and facilities on each floor, helpful to first-time users, sometimes displayed on the library's Web site with links to descriptive text.

floppy   *See*: floppy disk.

floppy disk   A 3½-inch external metallic disk encased in a rigid plastic envelope designed for use in a personal computer as a portable storage medium for data in digital format. The most commonly used sizes are 720K (double-density) and 1.44MB (high-density). Before 1987, most PCs used flexible 5¼-inch *floppies*. To conserve paper, library users are encouraged to save the results of a search of an online catalog or bibliographic database to floppy disk (or export output to an e-mail account), instead of printing it. In microcomputers, the floppy disk drive is the **a:** drive. Synonymous with *diskette*. Compare with *hard disk*.

floret   *See*: printer's flower.

flourish   A decorative tail or ornamental extension on a swash letter, usually in the form of one or more swirling curves. A flourish is often an extension of an ascender or descender. Pen-flourished initial letters are common in medieval manuscripts. In older signatures, flourishes were used as a mark of distinction and to prevent forgery. *See also*: *paraph*.

flowchart   A diagram showing the complete series of steps in a process, such as a computer program, or the sequence in which the components of a system function, usually in the form of symbols of various shapes, each representing a specific type of operation or component, connected by directional lines indicating movement.

flow map   *See*: dynamic map.

flush   Said of a line of type aligned along a right or left margin without indention.

flush binding   A binding in which the covers are trimmed even with the leaves after having been attached to the sections. Most paperback books have *flush covers*. Compare with *extended binding*. *See also*: *cut flush*.

flush boards   A bookbinding with boards cut even with the edges of the sections, used in Europe until about the 15th century, after which time the boards extended beyond the edges of the book block, forming squares.

flush cover   *See*: flush binding.

flyer   *See*: flier.

flyleaf   Often used in reference to the free half of an endpaper, not pasted to the inside of one of the boards of a book, but according to *The Bookman's Glossary* (R.R. Bowker, 1983), the term applies only to the binder's blank leaf at the beginning of a book, following the front free endpaper, and by analogy at the end of the text, preceding the back free endpaper, when the text does not fill the last page or pages. Their purpose is to protect the first and last leaves of the text block from damage. In medieval manuscripts, the flyleaves sometimes bear pen trials and inscriptions that can be helpful in establishing provenance. Also spelled *fly leaf*. Synonymous with *free endleaf*.

fly-title   An additional half title sometimes printed on the recto of an otherwise blank leaf following the last page of the front matter and preceding the first page of the text in a book. Also refers to a similarly printed leaf at the beginning of a chapter or other major division of a book, bearing the title of the division. In England, synonymous with *bastard title* and *half title*.

focus group   A small group of people assembled by a researcher to identify through informal discussion the key issues and/or themes related to a research topic, often to facilitate development of a more quantitative methodology, such as a survey. An effort may be made to select a representative sample of the larger cohort used in subsequent research. Focus groups are sometimes used in library research and strategic planning, for example, to determine user needs and preferences in the development of a technology plan. The technique is also used extensively in business for qualitative research on consumer behavior. Online focus groups are used in the evaluation of Web-based services.

fog index   A numeric formula used in publishing to gauge the degree of readability (clarity) of a piece of writing, based on average sentence length and number of words of three or more syllables per sentence. The higher the index number, the less intelligible the writing, an important consideration in judging the sales potential of a work. The measure is imprecise because it does not take into consideration the writer's style, which may break long sentences into phrases and make difficult words easier to comprehend from the context.

FOIA   *See*: *Freedom of Information Act*.

FOL   *See*: Friends of the Library.

fold   The crease formed when two edges of a sheet of paper, parchment, or vellum are brought together along a line and pressed together. A *bifolium* is created by a single fold down the center of a sheet. Early manuscript books consisted of gatherings of *bifolia* placed one within another. When paper replaced parchment and vellum in book production, a full sheet could be printed and folded more than once to make a quire of a given number of pages, depending on how the printed matter was arranged:

Folio. One fold: 2 leaves, 4 pages
Quarto (4to). Two folds: 4 leaves, 8 pages
Octavo (8vo). Three folds: 8 leaves, 16 pages
Sextodecimo (16mo). Four folds: 16 leaves, 32 pages

In modern binding, folding is done by machine. *See also*: *back fold*, *bolt*, and *fold sewn*.

folded book   A novelty book format consisting of one long strip of paper folded accordion-style, with one or both ends attached to separate rigid covers, and no back. Used for pictorial display of wide-angle panoramas, particularly in China. More complex folded books have been created by contemporary artists for whom the book is a form of visual art (see *artist's book*). Synonymous with *folding book*.

fold endurance   A measure of the strength of a grade of paper, based on the number of times a sheet can be folded in both directions along the same fold line before the fibers detach at the crease, usually tested mechanically. Fold endurance was dropped as a criterion in the 1992 revision of the ANSI/NISO Z39.48 standard for permanence of paper. *See also*: *two-double fold test*.

folder   A publication consisting of a single sheet of paper folded, usually down the center, into two or more leaves, not cut or stitched. Examples include performance programs, restaurant menus, etc. Also refers to a sheet of heavy paper such as manila, folded once, sometimes with a flap across the bottom and a projecting tab for labeling, used to file loose papers. Standard sizes in the United States are 9 × 11¾ and 9 × 17¾ inches.

In software applications, a heading created by the user under which data files, e-mail messages, Web bookmarks, and other information in digital format can be filed and stored for future retrieval.

fold-out   Also spelled *foldout*. *See*: throw-out.

fold sewn   A binding in which the gathered sections are attached to each other by sewing through the back fold, with a kettle stitch linking adjacent sections at the end of each pass of the thread. Fold sewing allows greater ease of opening than *side sewing*. Hand fold sewing can be *all along*, *two on*, or *three on*.

Folger Shakespeare Library   Founded in 1932, the Folger Library in Washington, D.C., is an independent research center for Shakespeare scholars containing the largest collection of printed materials in the world on "The Bard" and his works. The Folger also collects research materials on British civilization and the culture of the Renaissance, including rare books and manuscripts. A substantial gift from the private library of Henry and Emily Folger forms the nucleus of the collection. The Folgers also established an endowment in support of the library, administered by the Trustees of Amherst College. The library includes a small theater in which Shakespeare's plays are publicly performed. Poetry readings and concerts of early music are also scheduled. The Folger Library is housed in a building listed on the National Register of Historic Places. URL: www.folger.edu.

foliate border   An ornamental band around a miniature and/or portion of text on a page of an illuminated manuscript or early printed book, decorated with painted vines, leaves, fruit, and/or flowers, often intertwined with insects, animals, humans, and grotesques. Acanthus and *rinceaux* are the most common styles. Trompe l'oeil floral borders are common in Flemish manuscripts. Synonymous with *foliated border*. *See also*: *foliate initial*.

foliated initial   *See*: foliate initial.

foliate initial   An initial letter in an illuminated manuscript or early printed book embellished with vine, leaf, fruit, and/or flower scrollwork. Foliate designs are also used in ornamental borders and as line fillers. Synonymous with *foliated initial*. Compare with *figure initial*. *See also*: *historiated initial* and *rustic capital*.

foliation   The precursor of pagination in which the leaves, rather than the individual pages, of a manuscript or early printed book were numbered consecutively on the recto only, usually in roman numerals following the word "Folio" or the abbreviation *F.*, *f.*, *fo.*, or *fol.* Foliation in arabic numerals was introduced in Italy during the late 15th century. Pagination in arabic numerals began about 100 years later but did not become widespread until the 18th century. Also refers to the total number of leaves in a manuscript or book, numbered or unnumbered. *See also*: *blind folio*.

folio   Latin for "leaf." A single leaf of a book or manuscript (of paper, parchment, vellum, etc.), usually one-half of a sheet folded down the center to form a *bifolium*. In manuscript books, several *bifolia* nested together, to be sewn through the fold in binding, constitute a *quire* or *gathering*. When numbered at the top or bottom on the recto only, a leaf is said to be *foliated*. Numbering on the recto and verso is called *pagination*. The term also refers to a blank sheet of printing paper in its full, unfolded size and to a single sheet of a writer's manuscript or typescript with writing or printed matter on one side only. Abbreviated *F.*, *f.*, *fo.*, or *fol.* Plural: *folios* or *folia*, abbreviated *ff*.

Also refers to the size of book, approximately 15 inches in height, made by folding a full sheet of book paper in half once to form signatures of two leaves (four pages). The precise size of each leaf in a folio edition depends on the size of the original sheet. Some early editions are known by the number of leaves in their sections, as in the First Folio edition of Shakespeare's plays. Compare with *quarto, octavo, duodecimo*, and *sextodecimo*.

folio number   *See*: foliation.

folklore   A collective term applied since the mid-19th century to the traditions, beliefs, narratives, etc., passed from one generation to the next within a community by word of mouth, without being written down. Folklore includes legends, folktales, songs, nursery rhymes, riddles, superstitions, proverbs, customs, and forms of dance and drama performed at traditional celebrations. Because folklore flourishes in communities with a low literacy rate, it is disappearing in many parts of the world. Dictionaries of folklore are available in the reference section of most large libraries. Compare with *myth*.

folktale A short narrative rooted in the oral tradition of a particular culture that may include improbable or supernatural elements. The category includes a range of forms, from fairy tale to myth. Some have historical roots (*example*: **John Henry**), others are purely imaginative (**Pecos Bill**). Folktales are usually published in collections. In libraries, they are shelved in either the adult or juvenile collection, depending on reading level and format. Also spelled *folk tale*.

follow through *See*: letter-by-letter.

FOLUSA *See*: Friends of Libraries **USA**.

font From the French word *fondre*, meaning "to cast." In printing, all the characters of a specific typeface in a given size, including uppercase and lowercase, small capitals, numerals, punctuation marks, reference marks, and any special characters, as opposed to a type family that includes different variations and sizes of the same type style (roman, italic, boldface, etc.). In books, the text is set in a single font, with any long quotations and notes in a smaller size of the same font. Older spelling: *fount*.

In computers, fonts come built into the printer, usually in the form of exchangeable plug-in cartridges or as "soft" fonts residing on the computer's hard disk or on a hard disk built into the printer. By embedding fonts in a document before it is transmitted, document exchange software such as *Adobe Acrobat* allows text to be displayed and printed in its original form without having to install fonts on the receiving machine.

foolscap Formerly, a sheet of printing paper of standard size, which varied from 13 × 15 to 13½ × 17 inches, producing two leaves of roughly 13 x 8 inches when folded once down the center. The word is derived from the watermark traditionally used by papermakers, showing the distinctive multi-pointed cap with bells worn by medieval jesters. Abbreviated *fcap* or *fcp*.

foot The bottom edge of a book or page in a bound publication. The opposite of *head*. Synonymous with *tail*.

footage A length or quantity expressed in feet, for example, the number of running feet in a segment of film joined to other segments in editing to create a motion picture.

footer A line or lines at the bottom of a Web page giving the name of the person (or persons) responsible for creating and maintaining the site, and its host. The footer may also include the date of last update, a copyright notice, and a contact link or Internet address. Also refers to the lines at the bottom of an e-mail message indicating the name, title, and affiliation of the sender and any contact information, as distinct from the *header* at the beginning of the message and the *body* containing the text. Also used synonymously in printed documents with *running foot*.

footline *See*: running foot.

footnote   A brief note at the bottom of a page explaining or expanding upon a point in the text or indicating the source of a quotation or idea attributed by the author to another person. Footnotes are indicated in the text by an arabic numeral in superscript, or a reference mark, and are usually printed in a smaller size of the font used for the text. When numbered, the sequence usually starts with 1 at the beginning of each chapter but may occasionally start with 1 at the beginning of each page. Compare with *endnote* and *in-text citation*.

In Dewey Decimal Classification, an instruction that applies to many subdivisions of a class, or to a topic within a class, marked in the schedules with a symbol such as the asterisk. In the print version of DDC, a footnote appears at the bottom of the page; in the electronic version, it is given in the notes section of the class to which it applies.

In a more general sense, any afterthought or minor but related comment on, or confirmation of, a primary statement, in writing or in speech.

footprint   The amount of surface area on a desktop or table required to accommodate a computer or peripheral device, less for a laptop than for a conventional PC, an important consideration in designing and equipping library instruction labs.

Also refers to the geographic area in which the signal transmitted by a telecommunication satellite can be received.

fore-edge   The outer edge of a leaf in a bound publication, or of the sections or cover of a book, opposite the spine or binding edge, the other two edges being the *head* and *tail*. The fore-edges of medieval manuscripts were sometimes decorated or labeled in ink, often with the title, because prior to the 16th century books were shelved flat with the fore-edge facing out. Synonymous with *front edge*.

fore-edge binding   A style of half binding in which the fore-edges of the boards, instead of the corners, are covered in a strip of the same material as the spine of the book, with the remainder of the boards covered in a different material.

fore-edge painting   *See*: edge painting.

fore-edge shelving   Storing books with their spines parallel with the surface of the shelf, rather than perpendicular to it. To prevent the force of gravity from causing the book block to pull away from the case or cover, the spine should rest on the shelf with the fore-edge up. This method preserves call number sequence and adds at least two shelves to a standard 90-inch-high section when space is limited but makes browsing and locating a specific item difficult because the spines are not visible. For this reason, it is usually restricted to portions of the collection that are not heavily used. *See also*: *double shelving*, *flat shelving*, and *shelving by size*.

fore-edge title   The title hand-lettered on the fore-edge of a volume to facilitate identification when it was standard practice to shelve books fore-edge out.

foreign book   A term used in acquisitions to refer to a book published outside the United States. Certain vendors specialize in supplying libraries and bookstores with titles published in specific countries (*example*: **China Books & Periodicals, Inc.** of San Francisco).

foreign language dictionary   *See*: language dictionary.

foreign subsidiary   A publisher wholly or partially owned by a company that has its headquarters in another country (*example*: **Random House** owned by Bertelsmann AG of Germany). The trend toward globalization of corporate ownership has profoundly affected the media, including publishing.

forename   A name preceding a person's surname (family name), given at birth to distinguish him or her from others of the same family or clan. Synonymous with *given name*. *See also*: *first name*.

forename entry   A personal name entry in a library catalog, index, or bibliographic database under a person's given name (forename). In *AACR2*, this practice is reserved for names that do not include a surname (*example*: **Plato**), names that include a patronymic (**Isaac ben Aaron**), and royal persons (**Liliuokalani, Queen of Hawaii**). Any word or phrase commonly associated with the name in works by the person, or in reference sources, such as place of origin, domicile, occupation, etc., is added in parentheses, as in **Ezekiel (Biblical prophet)**, or following a comma (**Eleanor, of Aquitaine**).

foreword   Introductory remarks preceding the text of a work, usually written by a person other than the author. When written by the author, introductory remarks constitute the preface. The foreword differs from the preface in remaining unchanged from one edition to the next. In the front matter of a book, the foreword or preface usually follows the dedication and precedes the introduction. Abbreviated *fwd*.

forgery   The deliberate counterfeit or imitation of a signature, or fabrication or alteration of a document or other work, with intent to deceive or harm the interests of another person or persons. The creation of fake first editions of rare and valuable books is considered forgery. In most countries, the act of forgery, or the sale of a forged work with intent to deceive, is a crime. Also refers to that which is forged. *See also*: *authenticity*.

form   A term used in library cataloging to refer to the manner in which the text in a book is arranged (dictionary, encyclopedia, directory, anthology), the genre in which a literary work is written (novel, poetry, drama, etc.), or the structure of a musical composition (concerto, symphony, opera, etc.). *See also*: *form heading* and *form subdivision*.

format   A general indication of the size of a book, based on the number of times the printed sheets are folded in binding to make the leaves (folio, quarto, octavo, duodecimo, sextodecimo, etc.).

   Also refers to the particular physical presentation of a bibliographic item (*AACR2*). For printed publications, format includes size, proportions, quality of paper, typeface, illustration, layout, and style of binding. Synonymous in American usage with *get up* (books). In a more general sense, the physical medium in which information is recorded, including print and nonprint documents. *See also*: *original format* and *reformat*.

   In data processing, the manner in which data is arranged in a medium of input, output, or storage, including the code and instructions determining the arrangement (see *file type*). Also, to prepare a floppy disk for the recording of data (most floppies are sold preformatted) and to arrange text on a computer screen in the form in which it will be printed on paper (font, margins, alignment, type size, italic, boldface, etc.).

format integration   The concept that separate cataloging rules and documentation should not be maintained for each bibliographic format (books, scores, maps, etc.) but that any MARC field can be used for any format for which it is appropriate. In the United States, MARC format integration was defined in the 1980s and implemented in the 1990s.

formatting   The appearance of printed text, including font, type size, alignment, boldface, italic, underlining, etc. In word processing software, options allow the user to specify formatting. In HTML documents, the same effects are achieved through the use of fixed tags embedded in the text.

forme   In letterpress, assembled type and display matter that has been made up into pages, imposed in a chase, and firmly locked up for transfer to the bed of the press for printing.

form heading   In library cataloging, an access point added to a bibliographic record, consisting of a word or phrase that indicates type of composition (*example*: **Children's poetry**) or format of item (*example*: **Astronomy charts, diagrams, etc.**). Compare with *subject heading*. *See also*: *form subdivision*.

form of composition   The structural form or shape in which a musical work is composed, given in the note area of the bibliographic record if it is not apparent from the title or other parts of the bibliographic description (concerto, fantasia, fugue, nocturne, prelude, rondo, sonata, variations, etc.).

form of entry   The specific words and spelling used to create headings that serve as access points in a catalog or index, governed by rules concerning singular and plural forms, verb tense, syntax, punctuation, etc. In most cataloging and indexing systems, form of entry for names (personal and corporate), titles, and subjects is also subject to authority control.

form subdivision   In library cataloging, a word or phrase added to a subject heading to divide works on the same subject by type of composition (*example*: **Hughes, Langston, 1902–1967—Biography**) or format (**Psychology—Encyclopedias**). In Library of Congress subject headings, a form subdivision is usually the final element in a heading (**Libraries—Automation—Directories**). Sometimes, two subdivisions are required to designate form (**Libraries—Periodicals—Bibliography**). In a classification system, a similar subdivision of a class. *See also*: *form heading*.

forthcoming   Soon to be published. Usually refers to new titles included in a publisher's frontlist for the next season. R.R. Bowker publishes a bimonthly author and title index of *Forthcoming Books*.

Forthcoming Books   A bimonthly author and title list of books to be published in the United States within the next five months and books published since the most recent edition of *Books in Print*. Published in softcover by R.R. Bowker, *Forthcoming Books* lists approximately 200,000 titles annually. Entries include name of publisher, month and year of publication, price, and ISBN.

fortnightly   Occurring once in a fortnight (every fourteenth night). The frequency of a serial publication issued at two-week intervals (26 times per year). Abbreviated *fortn*.

forwarding   In bookbinding, the intermediate steps in the physical production of a book following the sewing of the leaves or sections and preceding finishing. Forwarding includes attaching the endleaves, rounding and backing, gluing the lining and endbands to the binding edge, and attaching the boards and covering material. The sequence of operations is slightly different in case binding than in hand-binding.

foxing   Reddish-brown or yellowish spots resembling freckles on the paper of old documents (books, prints, etc.), a condition probably caused by fungus and/or a chemical reaction under humid conditions, particularly common in paper made by machine during the late 18th and 19th centuries. Although the cause (or causes) are not fully understood, the fact that foxing often begins near the edge of a leaf or sheet and spreads inward suggests that exposure to the atmosphere may play an important role. In some types of documents, foxing can be reduced or eliminated by a technique called *washing*, but preservationists proceed with caution because some methods can cause further damage. Synonymous with *foxmarks*.

fps   An abbreviation of *frames per second*. *See*: projection speed.

fragile book   A book in such delicate or poor condition that even normal handling is likely to cause further deterioration. Libraries sometimes affix a bookplate to warn the user that gentle treatment is required. If the book is valuable, it may be kept in the rare books and special collections section to allow supervision of its use.

fragment   A detached, incomplete portion of a manuscript or inscription that can sometimes be reassembled with other pieces of the same object to get a sense of the whole. Many ancient manuscripts written on papyrus survive only in fragments (see the *Duke Papyrus Archive* at: odyssey.lib.duke.edu/papyrus). Fragments of codices also exist in great numbers. *See also*: cutting.

Also refers to a literary work left unfinished by the author, especially a poem. During the Romantic period, the fragment poem was developed as a literary form (see *The Romantic Fragment Poem: A Critique of a Form* by Marjorie Levinson, University of North Carolina Press, 1986).

frame   A separately scrollable area in the window of a computer application or in a Web page that has been divided into more than one scrollable area.

In filmstrips, motion pictures, and videorecordings, one of the individual still images arranged in sequence to tell a story or create the illusion of movement when projected in rapid succession. Projection speed is measured in *fps* (frames per second). Librarians use the frame (or frames) bearing the title of the work as the chief source of information in cataloging such an item. Also refers to a single subdivision of the grid on a sheet of microfiche, or one of the units comprising a length of microfilm. Abbreviated *fr*.

In binding, an ornamental rectangle impressed in the surface of the cover of a book some distance from the edges. Compare in this sense with *border*. Also refers to a rigid border of wood, metal, plastic, cardboard, etc., used to mount a picture, print, photograph, slide, etc.

In medieval manuscripts, a decorative border painted around a miniature, sometimes in imitation of an actual picture frame. Architectural motifs, such as gothic cathedral arches, were sometimes used to frame miniatures in manuscripts produced during the late Middle Ages.

Frankfurt Book Fair   The largest and one of the oldest book trade fairs in the world, held annually in Frankfurt, Germany, in October, providing an opportunity for publishers to exhibit their publications, negotiate international sales rights, make arrangements for co-published editions, etc. URL: www.frankfurt-book-fair.com.

Franklin, Benjamin (1706–1790)   A man of many talents who combined intellectual genius with practicality, Benjamin Franklin was a champion of American independence and is considered one of the founding fathers of the United States. At various periods in his life he was printer and publisher, diplomat and statesman, scientist and philosopher. Born in Boston, the son of a Puritan candlemaker and mechanic, Franklin was apprenticed at age 12 to his brother James, printer of an early Boston newspaper *The New England Courant*.

Franklin eventually settled in Philadelphia, where he owned a printing business and published the *Philadelphia Gazette* from 1730 until 1748. His best-known publication was the highly successful series *Poor Richard's Almanack* issued from 1733 to 1758 under the pseudonym Richard Saunders. During this period of his life, Franklin also established one of the earliest circulating libraries in the colonies, which became the Library Company of Philadelphia, and in 1743 he helped found the American Philosophical Society.

After selling his press in 1748, Franklin devoted himself to public life and to scientific experimentation. In 1757, he was sent to England to enlighten the government concerning conditions in the colonies. Franklin was chosen a member of the Continental Congress and dispatched to France in 1776 to negotiate a treaty. Remaining as plenipotentiary until 1785, he secured considerable foreign support for the American cause in the War of Independence. The text of his *Autobiography* is available online at: eserver.org/books/franklin.

frayed   The condition of a cloth book cover on which the threads along at least one edge have broken and pulled loose due to abrasion, exposing the board underneath.

FRBR   Pronounced "furbur." *See*: *Functional Requirements for Bibliographic Records*.

FRBRization   The attempt to model in bibliographic systems the entity structure described in *Functional Requirements for Bibliographic Records (FRBR)*, based on the concepts of work, expression, manifestation, and item. Pronounced "furburization."

Frederick G. Kilgour Award for Research in Library and Information Technology   An annual award sponsored by the Online Computer Library Center (OCLC) and the Library and Information Technology Association (LITA), established in 1998 in honor of Frederick G. Kilgour, founder of OCLC and a seminal figure in library automation. The award is bestowed on a person who has contributed a body of research in the field of library and information technology that has significantly influenced the way information is published, stored, retrieved, disseminated, or managed. The award consists of $2,000 in cash, an expense-paid trip to the ALA Annual Conference, and a citation of merit.

freedom of information   The statutory right of public access to official information compiled and maintained by federal government agencies, embodied in the *Freedom of Information Act (FOIA)* passed by the U.S. Congress in 1966 and subsequently enacted in most European and UK countries. Under *FOIA*, applicants who request in writing specific information must be supplied with copies of the requested documents or records within a designated period of time. Disclosure of information that might prove harmful to national defense, foreign relations, law enforcement, commercial activities of third parties, or personal privacy is exempted. Compare with *intellectual freedom*. *See also*: *information law*.

Freedom of Information Act (FOIA)   Passed by Congress in 1966, *FOIA* guarantees right of access to unclassified government information to any American who submits a written request to see copies of specific records or documents. The *Act* exempts from disclosure information that might prove harmful to national defense, foreign relations, law enforcement, commercial interests of third parties, or personal privacy. The intent behind *FOIA* is to make government more transparent and accountable to citizens and to prevent secrecy from being used for illegitimate purposes. Similar legislation has been enacted in most European and UK countries. *FOIA* applies only to federal agencies and does not create right of access to records held by Congress, the courts, or state or local government agencies (each state has enacted its own access laws). URL: www.usdoj.gov/04foia/index.html.

Freedom to Read Foundation (FTRF)   A nonprofit organization founded in 1969 by the American Library Association in support of the First Amendment right of all Americans to read and hear the ideas of others without government interference. The FTRF also fosters libraries in which the individual's First Amendment rights can be fulfilled and supports the right of libraries and librarians to include in their collections any work that can be legally purchased in the United States, despite objections from individuals and groups with an axe to grind. URL: www.ala.org. *See also*: *intellectual freedom, Intellectual Freedom Round Table*, and Library Bill of Rights.

Freedom to Read Statement   A formal declaration originally issued in May 1953 by the Westchester Conference of the American Library Association and the American Book Publishers Council (now the Association of American Publishers) that affirms the First Amendment right of every American to choose without interference whatever he or she wishes to read. The *Statement* was adopted by the ALA and the ABPC in June 1953 and revised in 1972 and 1991 by the ALA Council and the AAP Freedom to Read Committee. The text of the *Statement* is available at: www.ala.org. *See also*: *Freedom to Read Foundation* and Library Bill of Rights.

free-floating subdivision   A form or topical subdivision that may be assigned under designated subjects in accordance with established subject cataloging rules, policies, and practices, without the specific usage having been editorially established and without creating an authority record for each main heading/subdivision combination. Five types of free-floating subdivisions are used in Library of Congress subject headings:

- Form and topical subdivisions of general application (*example*: **Globalization—Economic aspects**)
- Subdivisions used under classes of persons and ethnic groups (*example*: **Asian Americans—Civil rights**)
- Subdivisions used under names of individual corporate bodies, persons, and families (*example*: **United States—Constitution**)
- Subdivisions used under place names (*example*: **New York (N.Y.)—Anecdotes**)
- Subdivisions controlled by pattern headings (*example*: **Liver—Biopsy** controlled by the pattern heading **Heart**)

freehand   Handwriting of any period that does not follow established rules with respect to abbreviation, contraction, punctuation, uppercase and lowercase, etc.

freelance   A form of self-employment in which a person, acting as an independent contractor, markets and sells a specific product, skill, or service to more than one employer (usually by the project) for a fixed fee that may be payable in advance. In the information sector, this mode of operation is commonly used by literary agents, information brokers, journalists, photographers, illustrators, and even editors. Freelancers often work from home, rather than from a commercial address.

free resource   A source of reliable information that can be obtained without charge (*example*: **telephone directories**). Prior to the emergence of the Internet, government, business, and nonprofit organizations provided most of the free information available to librarians and library users. Today, information is available at no charge from a considerably wider range of sources via the World Wide Web, but the user must exercise discrimination in assessing accuracy and authority.

free speech   Freedom under the First Amendment to the U.S. Constitution to write or say whatever one wishes without fear of censorship or prosecution, within certain limitations (libel, slander, etc.). *See also*: *intellectual freedom*.

free-standing shelving   Shelving designed to stand on its own, away from a wall or other support. Most free-standing shelving is double-sided and available in sections to allow the assembly of ranges of variable length. In libraries in the United States, minimum aisle width between ranges is 36 inches. Building safety codes in earthquake-prone areas may require special bracing to stabilize free-standing shelving. Compare with *wall shelving*. *See also*: *compact shelving*.

free-text search   A search of a bibliographic database in which natural language words and phrases appearing in the text of the documents indexed, or in their bibliographic descriptions, are used as search terms, rather than terms selected from a list of controlled vocabulary (authorized subject headings or descriptors). Compare with *full-text search*. *See also*: *keyword(s)*.

freeware   A term coined in the 1980s to refer to software available at no cost, usually distributed over the Internet by the developer who retains copyright. Compare with *shareware*.

freeze   A cessation in the hiring of new personnel or the payment of funds, usually necessitated by budgetary constraints. In most cases, normal operations resume after the cause of the problem is resolved.

Also, to stop the action and display a single frame in film, television, or video production, a technique used for dramatic effect.

freezing   A technique used in conservation to eliminate book-eating insects. According to former Yale University conservator Jane Greenfield (*The Care of Fine Books*, Nick Lyons Books, 1988), freezing at minus 6 degrees Fahrenheit in a domestic freezer unit will kill insects at all stages of development (eggs, larvae, pupae, and adult). To prevent the formation of ice crystals, damp books should be allowed to dry for at least a week before freezing. She recommends sealing items for freezing in polyethylene bags and leaving them in the bags after removal from the freezer until condensation on the outside has evaporated. Freezing is also used to prepare water-damaged books for vacuum drying.

french fold   A single sheet of paper printed on one side and folded into quarters, first down the length and then at a right angle to the initial fold, producing a single section with the unprinted side folded in and the bolts left uncut to form four pages, as in wedding invitations and greeting cards.

frequency   The interval at which a newspaper, periodical, or other serial publication is issued (daily, semiweekly, weekly, semimonthly, monthly, bimonthly, triquarterly, quarterly, semiannually, annually, irregularly, etc.). Scholarly journals are usually published quarterly, magazines weekly or monthly, and newspapers daily or weekly. Frequency and changes of frequency are indicated in the note area of the bibliographic description of a serial.

In statistics, the number of times a unit of measurement occurs within a class or during a specified period of time. In electronics, the number of repetitions of the period of an alternating current (signal), expressed in *Hertz* (cycles per second). *See also*: *MegaHertz*.

Friends of Libraries USA (FOLUSA)   Established in 1979, with headquarters in Philadelphia, FOLUSA is an affiliate of the American Library Association with a membership consisting of Friends of the Library groups, libraries, clubs, associations, corporations, and individuals interested in promoting quality library service to all residents of the United States. URL: www.folusa.com.

Friends of the Library (FOL)   An organization whose members share an interest in supporting a particular library or library system through fund-raising and promotional activities. In some libraries, the Friends group operates a small gift shop or conducts an annual book sale, using the proceeds to support library programs and services. Friends members often serve as volunteers in the library, performing a variety of tasks from mending to storytelling. *See also*: *Friends of Libraries USA*.

fringes   *See*: benefits.

frontis   *See*: frontispiece.

frontispiece   In printed books, an unnumbered illustration appearing on the unpaginated verso of the leaf immediately preceding the title page or first page. This type of frontispiece is also found in some Renaissance manuscripts. In earlier manuscripts, the frontispiece sometimes appears on the first page above the text. Abbreviated *front*. Compare with *headpiece*.

frontlist   A publisher's list of all the new books published (or about to be published) during the most recent publishing season or cycle, usually heavily promoted by sales staff. The most important titles in the frontlist are called *leaders*. Also spelled *front-list*. Compare with *backlist*. *See also*: *midlist*.

front matter   The parts of a book preceding the first page of the text. They include, in customary but not immutable order, the half title, series title or frontispiece, title page, imprint and copyright notice, dedication, epigraph, table of contents, list of illustrations and/or tables, foreword, preface, acknowledgments, introduction, list of abbreviations, translator's note, errata or corrigenda, and half title repeated (optional). Front matter is usually paginated in lowercase roman numerals. Synonymous with *preliminary matter*, *preliminaries*, and *prelims*. Compare with *back matter*. *See also*: *parts of a book*.

front page   The first page of the first section of a newspaper, bearing the flag and headlines of the major news stories of the day. Also, the first page of a newsletter, magazine, or journal. Compare with *title page*. *See also*: *back page*.

frozen catalog   A library catalog to which no new bibliographic records are added and from which no existing records are removed, even when revisions or corrections are made or existing records are converted to machine-readable format. Compare with *closed catalog* and *open catalog*.

FTE   *See*: full-time equivalent.

FTF   *See*: Feminist Task Force.

FTP   File Transfer Protocol, the TCP/IP protocol that allows data files to be copied directly from one computer to another over the Internet regardless of platform, without having to attach them as in e-mail. A computer that functions as a file server, storing files available to other computers, is called an *FTP site* or *FTP server*. If no username or password is required for access, such a computer is an *anonymous FTP site*—its files may be downloaded by anyone with access to the Internet. Although still widely available, anonymous FTP has been supplanted by the World Wide Web as the most popular mode of disseminating information in digital format.

fugitive material   Publications such as pamphlets, posters, performance and exhibit programs, and duplicated material produced in small quantities, that are of immediate, local, or transitory interest and therefore difficult for libraries to collect and catalog. *See also*: *ephemera*.

fulfillment   All the activities undertaken by a publisher or vendor in supplying materials to a library or library system, including order processing, shipping and warehousing, maintaining sales and inventory records, invoicing, accounts receivable and collections, credit control, processing claims, renewing and cancelling subscriptions, etc. *See also*: *fulfillment year*.

fulfillment year   The period of time for which a subscriber who has paid for an annual periodical subscription is entitled to receive issues. Compare with *subscription period*. *See also*: *renewal*.

full binding   A style of bookbinding in which the spine and boards are covered in material entirely of one kind, originally leather but in modern binding usually some kind of cloth. Compare with *half-binding*, *quarter binding*, and *three-quarter binding*. Synonymous with *whole bound*.

full border   Continuous ornamentation, plain or simple, extending around the perimeter of a page on all four sides. In medieval illuminated manuscripts, a decorative band surrounding text and/or graphic elements (miniatures, initial letters, line fillers, etc.) on all four sides of a page, usually consisting of a dense carpet of multicolored vines, leaves, flowers, birds, animals, human forms, and/or other designs, leaving very narrow margins. A *three-quarter border* extends around three of the four sides. Synonymous with *full-page border*.

full-color printing   A method of reproducing in print an infinite range of colors by controlling the overprinting of three colors of ink (yellow, magenta, and cyan), with black added to create gradations of light and dark. The term *color separation* refers to the process by which a full-color original is photographed through colored filters or scanned by a color sensing machine to separate the colors and allow negatives to be produced that define the area to be printed with each color of ink. Compare with *black and white* and *duotone*.

full-duplex   *See*: duplex.

full face   A typeface that has not been condensed and is therefore more readable than a version of the same style in which the characters are narrower than normal. *See also*: *expanded*.

full level cataloging   The most complete form of general cataloging, applied to library materials not designated for one of the other encoding levels, producing a bibliographic record that contains the fullest set of data elements, including a complete bibliographic description of the item in a record structured to facilitate descriptive and subject access. Compare with *core level cataloging* and *minimal level cataloging*.

full measure   *See*: measure.

full-motion video   Video transmission in which the image changes at the rate of 30 frames per second (fps). Motion pictures run at 24 fps. Video that has been digitized and stored on computer can be displayed at varying frame rates, depending on the speed of the computer.

full-page   A term used in printing to refer to an illustration, plate, or map that fills an entire page in a book or other publication, with or without margins and caption. Also refers to an article that fills all the available space on one page of a newspaper.

full-page border   *See*: full border.

full point   A printer's term for the punctuation mark used to indicate the end of an ordinary sentence and as a mark of abbreviation. Synonymous with *period* and *full stop*.

full record   The most complete display of data elements contained in the bibliographic record created to represent an item, including all the fields and subfields needed to identify and describe the item, as opposed to a *brief record* in which only a portion of the available bibliographic description is shown. Most online catalogs and bibliographic databases provide both formats.

full score   A music score in which each of the parts is written on a separate stave, usually for the use of the conductor. For orchestral and choral works, this usually requires a large page size. From top to bottom, the standard arrangement of instrumental parts in a full score is: woodwinds, brass, percussion, and strings, with any solo part in a concerto appearing above the violins. Voice parts, arranged in descending order of vocal register, are placed above the string section, with any solo parts given above the chorus. Only the largest music libraries collect this type of score.

full stop   The period, a punctuation mark used in text to indicate the end of a sentence and in bibliographic records to separate elements of description. When used to divide the parts of an Internet address, it is called a *dot*. Synonymous with *full point*.

full-text   An electronic resource that provides the entire text of a single work (*example*: **Britannica Online**) or of articles in one or more journals, magazines, and/or newspapers, for example, a bibliographic database that provides the complete text for a significant proportion of the works indexed, besides the bibliographic citation and (in many cases) an abstract of the content (*example*: **JSTOR**). Also spelled *fulltext*.

full-text search   A search of a bibliographic database in which the entire text of each record or document is searched and the entry retrieved if the terms included in the search statement are present. Most Web search engines are designed to perform full-text searches. This can pose a problem for the user if a search term has more than one meaning, resulting in the retrieval of irrelevant information (false drops). For example, in a medical database, the query "treatment of AIDS" might retrieve entries for sources containing the phrase "treatment aids in geriatrics" (with "of" a stopword). Compare with *free-text search*.

full-time   Employment for the number of working hours considered normal for a given position, in the United States no more than 40 hours per week without overtime or flextime. Full-time employees are usually entitled to full benefits. At some academic institutions, the ratio of full-time to part-time (adjunct) faculty, including librarians, is governed by a collective bargaining agreement.

full-time equivalent (FTE)   A measure of the total number of students, undergraduate and graduate, enrolled for the number of credit hours considered by an institution of higher learning to be a full schedule, sometimes used by vendors to determine subscription rates charged on a sliding scale for access to electronic resources such as bibliographic databases. In the United States, there is no national standard for computing FTE—each institution has devised its own formula. A typical example: FTE = total number of undergraduate credit hours divided by 15, plus total number of graduate credit hours divided by 12.

fumigation   In conservation, the process of exposing items made of paper and other materials to a toxic vapor within an airtight container to eliminate insects, mildew, mold, and other organisms that damage collections. When an infestation is extensive, fumigation of the area(s) in which the affected items are stored may also be necessary. Fumigants used in book preservation include thymol, methyl bromide, chloropicrin, carbon tetrachloride, ethylene dichloride, and hydrogen cyanide.

functionality   Features built into a search interface that determine the ease with which users may formulate queries and obtain results. Well-designed search software enables the user to:

- Identify the database(s) most appropriate to the subject of the search
- Search more than one database simultaneously
- Remove duplicate records from results when searching multiple databases
- View a current list of the publications indexed in each database
- Choose search mode based on proficiency (basic or advanced)
- Access well-organized contextual help at each stage of the search process
- View an online thesaurus or use vocabulary mapping to identify appropriate search terms
- Limit search results by relevance, material type, publication date, language, institutional holdings, latest update, full-text, etc.
- Sort results by author, title, publication date, etc.
- View search terms highlighted in results
- Select/deselect records as output
- View and save search history
- Save results independent of Web browser
- Print, e-mail, and download results in various formats

Functional Requirements for Bibliographic Records (FRBR)   The principles espoused in the 1998 report of the IFLA Study Group on Functional Requirements for Bibliographic Records titled *Functional Requirements for Bibliographic Records*. Although the report covers the user-oriented functions that bibliographic records should fulfill, and the data elements necessary to fulfill these functions, the term *FRBR* is usually used to refer to the *entity-relationship model* described in the report, which defines the characteristics of *works*, *expressions*, *manifestations*, and *items*.

In the years following the publication of *International Bibliographic Description for Monographic Publications* in 1971, major changes occurred in the environment in which cataloging principles and standards operate, such as the expansion of automated systems, the development of large-scale bibliographic databases by national cataloging agencies, and the emergence of networked access to electronic information and new forms of electronic publishing. These changes necessitated a comprehensive re-examination of cataloging theory. In 1990, a resolution was passed at the Stockholm Seminar on Bibliographic Records calling for a clear delineation of the functions performed by the bibliographic record with respect to media, applications, and user needs.

In the user-focused study that produced *FRBR*, no a priori assumptions were made about the nature of the bibliographic record. The study group used *entity analysis*, a technique for constructing conceptual models of relational databases, to generate a model based on three basic elements: the *entities* of interest to users of bibliographic records, the *attributes* of each entity, and the *relationships* between entities. Published by K.G. Saur München (1998), the final report of the IFLA Study Group is available online at: www.ifla.org/VII/s13/frbr/frbr.htm. *FRBR* is pronounced "furbur." *See also*: *FRBRization*.

function key   One of 12 keys numbered F1 to F12 from left to right across the top row of a standard PC keyboard that allows the user to execute a specific task or routine in a computer program as a shortcut by pressing the appropriate key. The program-specific function associated with each key in a specific program is explained in the documentation provided with the software.

funding   The money that supports the daily operations of a library or library system and its capital projects. Most institutional libraries are supported by revenue generated by taxation or collected by the organization of which they are a part. Library funding is subject to the economic vicissitudes of its source. *See also*: *endowment*, *fundraising*, *grant*, *grant-in-aid*, and *underfunded*.

fund-raising   Programs and activities intended to encourage benefactors to contribute a portion of their wealth to a library or library system in support of capital projects and operating expenditures. Some academic libraries and large public libraries have an endowment fund to which potential benefactors are encouraged to contribute. LSTA grants-in-aid often require the local community to provide matching funds. Also spelled *fundraising*.

furlough   A temporary leave of absence granted without pay to an employee. Some libraries and library systems use mandatory furloughs to cut costs in a budget crisis, electing to close for one or more weeks, usually during periods of low usage (end of summer, week before Christmas, etc.), instead of laying off workers. This option spreads the impact of cuts over all employees and administrative units within the organization.

furniture   A collective term for anything attached to the outside of a book in binding (clasps, bosses, cornerpieces, plaques, chains, etc.). Fittings in plain or precious metal were used from the 8th to the 16th century to protect book covers from abrasion and as decoration.

further reading   A bibliography of sources provided by the author for the benefit of readers who wish to expand their knowledge of the subject(s) treated in the work to which it is appended, distinct from a list of works cited, a common feature of introductory works used as textbooks at the undergraduate level.

fuzzy logic   The branch of logic that recognizes a possible range of intermediate values between the logical extremes of true and false, similar to the way the human mind evaluates complex situations. Because fuzzy logic allows degrees of uncertainty and imprecision to be expressed in the representation of knowledge, it has proved useful in artificial intelligence and the design of expert systems. In application software, it has been incorporated into some spell checkers to suggest to the user the most likely substitutions for a misspelled word.

G

Gale Group　A publisher of major reference serials (*Contemporary Authors, Encyclopedia of Associations, Market Share Reporter*, etc.), in print and online, for libraries, educational institutions, and businesses worldwide. Gale is also one of the three leading aggregators of journals in electronic format, providing online access to a range of bibliographic and full-text databases. URL: www.galegroup.com. *See also*: *EBSCO* and *ProQuest*.

galley　In printing, a long, narrow tray open at one end into which assembled lines of type are transferred by the compositor from a manual composing stick, or from a typesetting machine, to await make-up into pages. Galleys were originally about 10 × 6 inches in size and made of wood, but in the early 19th century, metal trays came into use and their length was extended to about 22 inches to accommodate several pages of type. Also used as a shortened form of *galley proof*.

galley proof　An impression taken from type composed in long columns, arranged in trays called *galleys*, before it has been made up into pages, to allow the author and proofreader to inspect the text and make any corrections before the work goes to press. Although galley proofs usually do *not* include illustrations and indexes, reviews may be written from them. Synonymous with *galleys* and *slip proof*.

galleys　*See*: galley proof.

game　A single physical item or set of materials designed for recreational or instructional play according to a prescribed or implicit set of rules (*AACR2*), usually stored in a container to keep the pieces together. The category includes puzzles and simulations. Games are usually stored in the curriculum room or children's room of a library. Compare with *kit*. *See also*: *activity card* and *toy*.

gap　A set of issues or entire volumes missing from a library's holdings of a serial title. This can occur when a subscription is canceled and later resumed or when items are lost or stolen. Most libraries try to fill gaps in periodical subscriptions with microfilm or microfiche, or by relying on the services of a back issues dealer, when online full-text is not available. Compare with *nongap break*.

Garfield, Eugene (1925–)   Born in New York City, Eugene Garfield earned a B.S.
in Chemistry from Columbia University in 1949. His career in scientific communication and information science began in 1951 when he joined the Welch Medical
Indexing Project at Johns Hopkins University. After receiving an M.S. in Library
Science from Columbia in 1954, he founded his own company, Eugene Garfield Associates, and began work on what was to become *Current Contents* while studying
for a Ph.D. in Structural Linguistics from the University of Pennsylvania (1961).
Having produced *Genetics Citation Index* with funding from the National Institutes
of Health, Garfield expanded his scope to produce the multidisciplinary *Science Citation Index*, published in 1964 by the Institute for Scientific Information, the name
his firm assumed in 1960. The success of *Current Contents* and *Science Citation Index*
made ISI a major information company, but Garfield's greatest achievement is his
development of the concept of citation indexing, which has given generations of researchers access to current bibliographical information and facilitated quantitative
analysis in the study of scholarly communication. Garfield is currently Editor-in-Chief
of *The Scientist*, a biweekly professional newsmagazine he founded. More information
about Garfield's career can be found at: www.garfield.library.upenn.edu.

garland   A type of anthology containing a collection of prose extracts or short literary
compositions, usually ballads or poems (*example*: *A Little Garland of Celtic Verse*
published in 1905 by T.B. Mosher).

gate count   The number of times a mechanical counting device, located at the entrance
to or exit from a library, is automatically activated whenever a person enters or leaves
during a designated period of time (day, week, month, year), an important measure
of library use. In most facilities, the counter is located near, attached to, or part of
the security gate. Totals are recorded at regular intervals, usually by the staff at the
circulation desk. Gate counts provide statistical information on traffic patterns, helpful
in establishing library hours and anticipating staffing needs. Synonymous with *door
count*.

gatefold   An illustration, map, or other insert, larger than the volume in which it is
bound, that must be unfolded horizontally to the left or right to be fully viewed. Also,
a method of folding a sheet of paper into three sections in which the two ends are
folded toward each other over the center, like a triptych, used in advertising, performance programs, restaurant menus, etc.

gateway   Computer software that allows a user to access data stored on a host computer
via a network. Also refers to the hardware device that interconnects two separate
networks, providing a pathway for the transfer of data and any protocol conversion
required, for example, between the messaging protocols of two different e-mail systems.

gathering   In binding, the process of assembling and arranging in correct sequence the
folded sections of a book prior to sewing them through the back fold or milling the
clamped back folds preparatory to gluing sections to cover in adhesive binding. Used
synonymously with *signature* in bibliography.

In medieval manuscripts, a gathering (called a *quire*) consisted of one or more parchment or vellum *bifolia* (usually four) nested inside each other, hair side facing hair side and flesh side facing flesh side, sewn through the back fold to leather or hemp cords that attached the book block to the boards. The unit of work in medieval scriptoria was usually the gathering—a change of scribe can sometimes be detected from one quire to the next.

gauffered edges   A small wavy or crimped repeating pattern impressed as decoration on the gilt edges of a book by the use of heated finishing tools called *gauffering irons*, popular on ornamental bindings of the late 15th through the 17th century. The designs were sometimes built up through repeated impressions. Also spelled *goffered edges*. Synonymous with *chased edges*.

gauffering   *See*: gauffered edges.

gauze   *See*: crash.

Gay, Lesbian, Bisexual, and Transgendered Round Table (GLBTRT)   Founded in 1970 as the Task Force on Gay Liberation of the American Library Association, GLBTRT is a permanent round table that serves as an advocate for gays, lesbians, and bisexuals employed in libraries and for the inclusion of materials on gay, lesbian, and bisexual issues in library collections. GLBTRT hosts the electronic mailing list GLBTRT-L, sponsors annual literary awards in fiction and nonfiction, and publishes the quarterly *GLBTRT Newsletter*. URL: www.niulib.niu.edu/lgbt. *See also*: Lambda Book Report.

Gaylord   A library supplier that provides office and library supplies, furniture, security systems, and automation software to libraries, schools, and other educational institutions largely through its trade catalog. URL: www.gaylord.com.

gazette   A news sheet in which current events, legal notices, public appointments, etc., are recorded on a regular basis. Formerly, a journal devoted to current news. Also, a journal officially issued by a government, particularly in Great Britain. The word is derived from the name of an Italian coin that was equivalent at one point in time to the price of a news sheet.

gazetteer   A separately published dictionary of geographic names that gives the location of each entry (*example*: ***The Columbia Gazetteer of the World***). Also, an index of the names of the places and geographic features shown in an atlas, usually printed in a separate section following the maps, with locations indicated by page number or map number and grid coordinates. Some book-length gazetteers include basic information about major geographic features such as rivers, lakes, mountains, cities, etc. Abbreviated *gaz*. The *U.S. Gazetteer*, provided by the U.S. Census Bureau, is searchable online at: www.census.gov/cgi-bin/gazetteer.

Also refers to person who writes or publishes a news sheet called a *gazette*.

genealogical table   A diagram, usually in the form of an inverted tree, with branches showing the lineage of a person or group of persons who share a common ancestor, sometimes printed on the endpapers of biographical or historical works, particularly those concerning the reigns of sovereigns or the lives of titled nobility.

genealogy   The study of the descent from a common ancestor (or ancestors) of a specific individual, family, or group of persons. Genealogical research often requires the use of archival materials. Genealogical resources are increasingly available in digital form (see *US GenWeb Archives* at www.rootsweb.com/~usgenweb and *Ancestry. com* at www.ancestry.com). *See also*: *National Genealogical Society*.

Also refers to an enumeration of ancestors and their descendants in natural order of succession, usually in the form of a "family tree." In works of history and biography, genealogical tables are sometimes printed on the endpapers or at the beginning of the text.

general encyclopedia   An encyclopedia that provides basic information on a broad range of subjects but treats no single subject in depth (*example*: ***Encyclopedia Americana***), as distinct from a subject encyclopedia that provides greater depth of coverage within a limited scope (*example*: ***Encyclopedia of 20th Century American Humor***).

generalia   Works that cannot be assigned to a particular class on the basis of subject, theme, or treatment because their nonspecialized or diverse nature defies specific classification, for example, general encyclopedias and world almanacs. In library classification and bibliography, a separate category is reserved for general works, usually appearing at the beginning of the schedule or list. Synonymous with *generalities*.

general interest magazine   A magazine of interest to a wide audience (*example*: ***Reader's Digest***). Most public libraries make an effort to subscribe to the most popular general interest magazines but are more selective in subscribing to special interest magazines. Compare with *newsmagazine*.

general material designation (GMD)   An optional term added in square brackets to the bibliographic description of a nonbook item following the title proper to indicate type of material (*example*: **[videorecording]**). Separate lists of general material designations are provided in *AACR2* for British and North American libraries. In some categories, the British list is more general (*object* includes diorama, game, microscope slide, model, and realia). The Library of Congress does *not* include the GMD in catalog records for manuscripts, maps, music, and text. Compare with *material type*. *See also*: *specific material designation*.

generation   In reprography, the degree to which a copy is removed from the original document. In microfilm, the master negative developed from film taken of the original image is *first-generation*, print masters made from the master negative are *second-generation*, and service copies made from a print master for use in libraries are *third-generation*. Sharpness of image usually declines with each succeeding generation.

generic relation   *See*: semantic relation.

genre   A type, class, or style of literature, music, film, or art. Genre criticism originated with Aristotle, who divided literature into three basic categories: dramatic, epic, and lyric. Today, literary works are classified by form (novel, short story, etc.), by theme (adventure, fantasy, horror, mystery, romance, science fiction, western, etc.), and less often by subject (carpe diem poem). In modern *genre fiction*, plot is the driving force, leading literary critics to dismiss such works as formulaic. For more on genre fiction, see *Genreflecting: A Guide to Reading Interests in Genre Fiction* by Diana Tixier Herald (Libraries Unlimited, 2000). *See also*: *subgenre*.

Also, a painting in which the subject is a person (as in a portrait), an object (as in a still-life), or a scene from daily life, rather than a theme derived from history, mythology, imagination, etc. By extension, a *genre piece* is a work that has as its subject people and incidents from everyday life.

geographic index   An index in which the entries are listed by their geographic location (city, state, country, etc.). Also refers to an index that lists the geographic locations mentioned in the text of a document. Synonymous with *place index*. *See also*: *gazetteer*.

geographic information system (GIS)   A computer-based system (hardware *and* software) designed to facilitate the mathematical manipulation and analysis of spatially distributed data, providing an automated link between the data and its location in space, usually in relation to a system of coordinates (latitude, longitude, elevation or depth, etc.). The data can be on any scale, from microscopic to global.

A GIS differs from a map in being a digital, rather than an analog, representation. Each spatial feature is stored as a separate layer of data that can be easily altered using techniques of quantitative analysis. A map can be input or output in a GIS, but the output may also be one or more *data sets*. In the plural, the term refers to the field within the earth sciences devoted to the study of computer-based systems for analyzing spatial data. GIS technology is used in scientific investigation, resource management, and development planning. Compare with *spatial information system*.

geographic name   The name most commonly used to identify a specific geographic location, feature, or area, preferred by catalogers in establishing the correct form of entry, not necessarily the same as the political name (*example*: **France** instead of République française). The Library of Congress provides information about *Geographic Names and the World Wide Web* at: lcweb.loc.gov/catdir/cpso/geogname. html. Synonymous with *place name*. *See also*: *corporate name*, Getty Thesaurus of Geographic Names, and *personal name*.

geographic subdivision   In library classification, the division of a class by geographic area (region, country, state, city, etc.). For example, in Library of Congress Classification, the division of the class **P** (Literature) into **PR** (English literature), **PS** (American literature), etc. Also, the extension of an existing subject heading by the addition of a subheading indicating the geographic area to which treatment of the topic is limited (*example*: **Libraries—United States**). A geographic subdivision may designate where something is located or where it is from, depending on the subject. In the *Library of Congress Subject Headings* list, the option to subdivide geographically is indicated by the note *"(May Subd Geog)"* or *"(Not Subd Geog)."* Synonymous with *local subdivision* and *place subdivision*.

geological survey   An organization that prepares and publishes maps, charts, and other cartographic materials concerning the geography of a specific nation and its territories, usually with government approval or sponsorship (*example*: **U.S. Geological Survey**).

In libraries without a separate map section, publications of the USGS may be shelved in the government documents collection. Also refers to the activity of gathering data for the production of cartographic materials and for geological research.

geologic map   A map that shows the distribution of the different types of rock and sediment lying beneath the surface of a specific region, usually by means of color, shading, and/or printed symbols. Major fault lines, mineral deposits, fossils, and the age of rock formations may also be indicated.

German Library Association   *See*: Deutscher Bibliotheksverband e.V.

gesso   A water-based preparation made from slaked plaster of Paris, white lead, and bole (soft greasy red or yellow clay), used in medieval manuscript illumination as a flexible ground for raised gilding. Gesso was laid down in layers to build up the portions of an underdrawing to which metallic leaf was later applied. Because of its color, it could easily be seen by the gilder and imparts a warm pinky glow to pages from which the gilding has begun to wear away.

Getty Thesaurus of Geographic Names (TGN)   A searchable database of controlled vocabulary, containing over 1 million names and other details concerning places, maintained on the Internet by the Getty Research Institute in Los Angeles, California. Although the terms are not linked to maps, latitude and longitude are given in each entry, with the place name's position in a hierarchy of geographic names. URL: www. getty.edu/research/conducting_research/vocabularies/tgn.

ghost   A work or edition of a work recorded in bibliographies, catalogs, or other sources of whose actual existence there is no conclusive evidence. A 20th-century example is a book titled *Poetics* supposedly written by the poet and literary critic John Crowe Ransom. Announced in 1942 by the publisher New Directions, it was never published but found its way into *Cumulative Book Index* and was cited in a biographical essay in *Contemporary Authors* in 1962 and in the *Dictionary of Literary Biography* in 1986. Synonymous with *bibliographical ghost*.

ghost writer   A person who writes or prepares a work for, and in the name of, another person who may be famous but is usually not a writer by profession. Autobiographies and memoirs are often written in this way. Although a ghost writer normally receives compensation for services rendered, sometimes even a share of royalties, the writer's name may or may not be listed as joint author on the title page.

GIF   An acronym for Graphics Interchange Format, one of the two most commonly used file formats for storing graphic images displayed on the World Wide Web (others being JPEG and TIFF). An algorithm developed by Unisys, GIF is protected by patent, but in practice the company has not required users to obtain a license. The most recent version of GIF supports color, animation, and data compression. Pronounced *jiff* or *giff* (with a hard *g*).

gift   One or more books or other items donated to a library, usually by an individual but sometimes by a group, organization, estate, or other library. In academic libraries, desk copies and review copies are sometimes received as gifts from members of the teaching faculty. Donated items are usually evaluated in accordance with the library's collection development policy and either added to the collection or disposed of, usually in a book sale or exchange with another library. Compare with *donation*.

gift book   An elaborately printed, expensively illustrated, ornately bound book of poetry or prose, usually published annually, popular as a gift item during the early part of the 19th century. Also known as a *keepsake*. In modern usage, a book purchased as a gift for another person (or persons). Coffee table books are often purchased for this purpose. Also spelled *giftbook*.

gigabyte (GB)   *See*: byte.

GIGO   In computing, an initialism that stands for "garbage in, garbage out," a slang expression for the axiom that the quality of output a user receives from a computer is directly proportional to the quality of the input submitted.

gilding   The application of gold or silver to a surface as decoration. Three methods were used in medieval manuscripts to gild initial letters, decorative borders, and miniatures. In flat gilding, a thin adhesive such as glair was applied to the underdrawing and the leaf laid on. Flat gilding could be left antique or burnished to a shimmering brightness. In raised gilding, gesso was built up in layers to make the burnished surface appear three-dimensional. Gold was always the first color applied to an underdrawing. Ink made from powdered gold mixed with a binding medium was used for detail work and in chrysography. Gilding was used in illuminated manuscripts to depict crowns and other metallic objects; to show light not visible to normal sight (halos and other forms of radiance); on drapery to give the impression of opulence; as highlighting on decorative elements; and as a background. Metallic leaf was also used in tooling and blocking to decorate leather and vellum book covers. Unlike silver, gold never tarnishes. *See also*: *gilt edges*.

GILS   *See*: Government Information Locator Service.

gilt edges   In deluxe editions, gold leaf is sometimes applied to the head, tail, and/or fore-edge of the sections and burnished to create an especially luxurious appearance. In the book trade, the following abbreviations are used to describe gilt edges:

aeg or *ae*—all edges gilt
ge—gilt edges
gt—gilt top
teg—top edge gilt

Left unburnished, a gilt edge is *antique*. *See also*: *gauffered edges*.

girdle book   A book with an outer wrapper of cloth or soft, flexible leather extending beyond the edges of the inner cover far enough to be knotted, allowing the volume to hang upside down when the knot was slipped under a belt or girdle tied round the waist. Geoffrey Glaister writes in *Encyclopedia of the Book* (Oak Knoll/British Library, 1996) that this type of binding was used by medieval clerics to protect breviaries, especially in Germany. Michelle Brown notes in *Understanding Illuminated Manuscripts* (Getty Museum/British Library, 1994) that it was also employed by wealthy women for carrying prayer books used in private devotion, sometimes very small volumes in bindings made of precious metals. Synonymous with *pouch binding*. *See also*: *polaire* and *vade mecum*.

GIS *See*: geographic information system.

given name One or more names chosen for a person, usually by the parents at birth or christening (*example*: **Emily**), sometimes the same as that of a living relative or ancestor but distinct from the surname identifying members of the same family (*example*: **Dickinson**). Given names can be compound (*example*: **Marie-Louise**). Compare with *first name*.

glair An adhesive preparation made from egg white (albumen in colloidal solution) used in tooling and edge gilding to permanently affix metallic leaf. Glair is usually purchased dry as albumen and mixed with water or vinegar prior to use. It melts with the application of heat and sets up quickly as soon as the hot finishing tool is removed, securing the leaf firmly to the surface. Glair was also used to bind pigments used in medieval manuscript illumination. Also spelled *glaire*. Synonymous with *clarea*.

glaire *See*: glair.

glassine A type of thin, dense, translucent glazed paper sometimes used to protect the covers of new books. Also used for panels in window-envelopes and as wrapping material because it is resistant to the passage of air, water, grease, etc.

GLBTRT *See*: Gay, Lesbian, Bisexual, and Transgendered Round Table.

glitch A malfunction in the hardware of a computer system, usually temporary or random, sometimes difficult to distinguish from a bug in the software. In a more general sense, any unanticipated problem that brings a process to a halt. Also spelled *glytch*.

globe A representation of the surface of the earth, or of another celestial body, on a relatively permanent spherical object, usually a more accurate depiction than a map because it lacks the distortion inherent in any two-dimensional representation of a three-dimensional object. Globes are made of heavy paper, papier-mâché, cardboard, plastic, metal, or glass, mounted on a full- or half-meridian axel, in a free cradle, or with gyroscopic support. Expensive models may be illuminated and/or animated for special effect. In the United States, the most common sizes are 12 inches and 16 inches in diameter.

gloss In old manuscripts, an explanation, definition, or interpretation of a word or phrase, sometimes in a more familiar language, written in a margin, above the line of text to which it refers (interlinear), or in a special appendix called a *glossary* compiled by a *glossator*, *glossographer*, or *glossarist*. Glosses were common in medieval Bibles and legal texts. In a heavily glossed book, text and commentary might be written in parallel columns, with the glosses in a different script or in a smaller version of the script used for the text. In modern printing, a note in the left- or right-hand margin is called a *side note* and is usually set in a type size smaller than that of the text to which it refers.

The term can also mean a deliberately misleading interpretation. Also refers to the degree to which paper reflects light, a function of the smoothness of its surface.

glossarial concordance   *See*: concordance.

glossarial index   An index at the end of a book (or set of books) that includes in each entry a definition or description of the term indexed, as well as the page number(s) referenced.

glossary   An alphabetical list of the specialized terms related to a specific subject or field of study, with brief definitions, often appearing at the end of a book or at the beginning of a long entry in a technical reference work. Long glossaries may be separately published (*example*: ***The ALA Glossary of Library and Information Science***, 1983). Compare with *dictionary*, *lexicon*, and *vocabulary*. *See also*: *gloss*.
   Also refers to a list of equivalent synonyms in more than one language.

glossed bible   A bible that includes commentary and/or translation, usually written in smaller script or printed in smaller type on the same page as the text. Prior to the 12th century, two types of glossed bibles were used: the *Glossa Ordinaria*, containing marginal notation throughout, and the *Glossa Interlinearis*, with notation written over the lines, the work of Anselm of Laon (d. 1117). After the 12th century, copies of the Vulgate usually contained both glosses. From the 14th century on, additional glosses were added at the foot of the page. Early printed bibles sometimes included all the exegetical glosses.

gloss ink   Printing ink that appears shiny even when dry because it contains a higher-than-normal proportion of varnish, used mainly in display work.

glossy   A finish in which the surface of paper or board is given a smooth, shiny coat of varnish to enhance the appearance of visual material (illustrations, posters, etc.). Most magazines are printed on glossy paper to attract readership, as are dust jackets to heighten the sales appeal of new books. In publishing, the term also refers to a photograph printed on smooth, shiny paper, the format preferred by printers in reproduction work.

glue   A type of adhesive made from protein derived from the collagen in animal by-products (bone, hooves, hides, etc.) boiled to form a brownish gelatin that can be thinned with water. Most glues are not suitable for use in binding because they become brittle with age. Compare with *paste*.

gluing off   In bookbinding, the application of adhesive to the binding edge of a book after the sections are sewn and before rounding and backing. The adhesive is forced between the sections to help hold them together. In adhesive binding, gluing replaces sewing. Compare with *pasting down*.

glyph   A visual representation of a textual element (letter, character, ideograph) made by any means: handwritten, inscribed, printed, electronically displayed, etc. In computing, the standard code for a character set does not define the appearance (size, shape, or style) of the individual characters. Image is rendered by the software or hardware using the code. Also used as a shortened form of *hieroglyph*.

glyphic In printing, a typeface derived from a carved or chiseled form, rather than from a calligraphic hand.

GMD *See*: general material designation.

gnawed A book that shows signs of having been chewed by an animal on at least one edge or corner, a condition that reduces its value considerably in the used book market and makes it a candidate for weeding in libraries.

goal In strategic planning, a general direction or aim that an organization commits itself to attaining in order to further its *mission*. Goals are usually expressed in abstract terms, with no time limit for realization. The specific means by which they are to be attained is also left open. Compare with *objective*.

goatskin Leather made from the skin of a goat, used extensively in hand bookbinding from the mid-16th century on. Imported into Europe from Turkey and North Africa via Venice and Spain, the names of the various types often reflect place of origin (levant, niger, etc.). Goatskin has a distinctive furrowed grain and, though spongy to the touch, can dry out and harden with age if not kept polished. Because it takes dye well, goatskin used in binding is often richly colored in red, blue, or green. The most common form of decoration is gold tooling. Older books elegantly bound in fine-quality goatskin, known in the antiquarian book trade as *morocco*, can be very valuable.

GODORT *See*: Government Documents Round Table.

goffered edges *See*: gauffered edges.

gold foil An inexpensive substitute for gold leaf, made by spraying a thin deposit of gold or a look-alike substitute onto an adhesive backing, used extensively to decorate edition bindings and library bindings and also in hand-binding when economy is desired. Synonymous with *blocking foil*.

gold leaf Gold beaten by hand or mechanical means into very thin sheets, used in bookbinding to embellish lettering, tooling, and the edges of the sections (silver is used less often for the same purpose). Gold leaf is sold in sheets 3½ inches square, made from an alloy of 23 carat gold and 1 carat silver and copper, beaten to a thinness of 1/200,000 to 1/250,000 of an inch. When rubbed between the fingers, gold leaf disintegrates. When dropped, it floats gently to a surface and can be unruffled like a blanket. Unlike silver, gold never tarnishes.

In medieval manuscripts, gold leaf was used to decorate miniatures, initial letters, and ornamental borders in a process called *gilding*. Medieval illuminators applied it to layers of gesso to give it a three-dimensional appearance on the page. Gold leaf could be left *antique* but was usually burnished to a brilliant shine. Goldbeaters used gold coins (florins and ducats) as a convenient source of supply, producing as many as 145 leaves from a single coin. Compare with *gold foil*.

gone to press A term used in printing to indicate that the process of preparing the final plates for a work has commenced. Subsequent changes or corrections must be added as *errata* after printing is completed. In newspaper publishing, the corresponding term is *gone to bed*.

Gopher   Before the World Wide Web was developed, files and resources available on the Internet were accessed by means of a hierarchical menu system installed on a *Gopher server* (named after the mascot of the University of Minnesota where the software was developed). Although they have fallen into disuse since the introduction of graphical Web browsers, Gopher servers have two advantages over Web search engines: they list Internet resources of *all* types (FTP files, Usenet newsgroups, etc.), not just Web sites, and they present resources in a logical hierarchy of directories created by a human being, rather than relying on an automated Web crawler ("spider") to locate information. The tools developed for searching Gopher file directories are named *Veronica* and *Jughead*. Gopher addresses begin with **gopher://**.

Gospel book   The text of the canonical Gospels, accounts of the life of Christ attributed to Matthew, Mark, Luke, and John, reproduced separately from the rest of the Bible, often preceded by introductory texts such as the *Prefaces* of St. Jerome, Eusebius' canon tables, and chapter lists, called *capitula*. From the 7th to the 12th century, the most important and beautifully illuminated manuscripts produced in western Europe were the large Gospel books used in Church services, in which each of the four Gospels often began with an author portrait and a lavishly decorated incipit page. The most famous examples are the *Book of Kells* and the *Lindisfarne Gospels*. *See also*: *evangelary*.

gothic   A bold, dark, angular script executed with a broad-nib pen. Developed in northern Europe during the 12th and 13th centuries, gothic was widely used as a book hand during the late Middle Ages and adapted as a typeface in early printed books, particularly Bibles and other liturgical and devotional works. It is characterized by compression, lack of curves, contrast between broad main strokes and fine hair strokes, regular verticals, uniform counters, diagonal couplings, and extensive use of abbreviation. Emphasis is on the uniformity of the word, rather than the distinctiveness of individual letterforms. In its fully developed form, gothic is called *textura*. Also refers to any modern typeface resembling gothic script. The first book printed in Europe from movable type, the *Gutenberg Bible*, was set in gothic type. Synonymous with *black letter* and *lettre de forme*. Compare with *roman* and *white letter*. *See also*: *bastarda* and *rotunda*.

gothic novel   Originally, a type of novel in which a medieval castle formed the setting for a plot with chillingly sinister overtones, intended to evoke irrational fear in the heart of the reader. Horace Walpole's *Castle of Otranto, A Gothic Story* (1764) established this genre. In modern usage, a subgenre of romance fiction, popular during the 18th and early 19th centuries, in which the setting is dark and gloomy, the action grotesque or violent, the characters strange or malevolent, the plot mysterious, and the mood often one of decadence or degeneration, for example, *Wuthering Heights* by Emily Brontë. Synonymous with *roman noir*. *See also*: *mystery*.

gouge   A nick or hole made accidentally in the cover or spine of a book. Also refers to a finishing tool used in bookbinding to make curved lines on a book cover.

govdocs   *See*: **gov**ernment **doc**uments.

governance   The arrangements by which the faculty and administration of an academic institution control and direct institutional affairs (bylaws, elective offices, committees, etc.). In some academic libraries, participation in governance may be a factor in tenure and promotion decisions affecting librarians who have faculty status.

government agency   A unit of government authorized by law or regulation to perform a specific function, for example, the U.S. Government Printing Office (GPO) authorized to collect, publish, and distribute government documents to the American public. Each agency of the U.S. federal government normally maintains its own records, which may or may not be publicly accessible, depending on whether its activities are exempted from public disclosure under the *Freedom of Information Act (FOIA)*.

government archives   A government agency authorized by legislation to provide centralized archival services for all, or a portion of, the agencies or units that administer a country's government (legislative, executive, and judicial). For the federal government of the United States, that agency is the National Archives and Records Administration (NARA). Each of the 50 U.S. state governments maintains its own state archives, sometimes as a unit of the state library.

government documents   Publications of the U.S. federal government, including transcripts of hearings and the text of bills, resolutions, statutes, reports, charters, treaties, periodicals (*example*: ***Monthly Labor Review***), statistics (**U.S. Census**), etc. In libraries, federal documents are usually shelved in a separate section by SuDocs number. The category also includes publications of state, local, territorial, and foreign governments. Abbreviated *govdocs*. ***See also***: *depository library*, *Government Documents Round Table*, and *GPO*.

Government Documents Round Table (GODORT)   A permanent round table within the American Library Association, GODORT has a membership of government documents librarians and others who have an interest in government documents collections and librarianship. GODORT publishes the quarterly journal *DttP: Documents to the People*. URL: sunsite.berkeley.edu/GODORT.

Government Information Locator Service (GILS)   A decentralized collection of agency-based information locators that uses network technology and international metadata standards based on *ANSI Z39.50* to direct users to publicly accessible information resources available from the U.S. federal government. The core data elements of the GILS system are: title, control identifier, abstract, purpose, originator, use constraints, availability, point of contact for further information, record source, and date last modified. The system also includes optional core elements.

The records of over 30 federal agencies have been mounted on the *Government Information Locator Service* (www.access.gpo.gov/su_docs/gils), a Web site maintained by *GPO Access*, which also provides pointers to GILS sites maintained by other federal departments and agencies. The National Biological Information Infrastructure (www.nbii.gov) is an example of an online government information service based on the GILS standard. Some state governments have established Internet sites based on the GILS model, enabling users to discover, identify, locate, and access publicly available state government information.

In 1995, the G7 (Canada, France, Germany, Italy, Japan, United Kingdom, and United States.) commissioned several pilot projects to demonstrate the potential of a global information infrastructure. One of these, the Environment and Natural Resources Management Project, was an attempt to use the GILS format to establish an international distributed database of information about the earth, a first step toward a Global Information Locator Service.

government library   In the United States, a library maintained by a unit of government at the local, state, or federal level, containing collections primarily for the use of its staff. Some government libraries have a wider mandate that includes accessibility to the general public (*example*: **Smithsonian Institution Libraries**). Government librarians are organized in the Government Documents Round Table (GODORT) of the American Library Association. *See also*: *federal library*, *military library*, *national library*, and *state library*.

government publication   Under *Title 44, Section 1901* of the *United States Code*, a government publication is defined as "information matter" published as a separate document at government expense or as required by law. *Section 1902* states that government publications, except those "required for official use only or for strictly administrative or operational purposes which have no public interest or educational value and publications classified for reasons of national security," are to be made publicly available to depository libraries by the Superintendent of Documents. The term is also used in a broader sense to include documents published by local, state, territorial, and foreign governments.

GPO   The U.S. **G**overnment **P**rinting **O**ffice, the government agency responsible for collecting, publishing, and distributing federal government information. The GPO publishes a printed index to government documents under the title *Monthly Catalog of U.S. Government Publications*. Its online equivalent is *GPO Access*, funded by the Federal Depository Library Program. The British counterpart is Her Majesty's Stationery Office. URL: www.gpoaccess.gov/index.html.

GPO Access   A service of the U.S. Government Printing Office that provides free electronic access to over 1,500 databases containing information from the three branches of the federal government, including the *Federal Register*, *Code of Federal Regulations*, and *Congressional Record*. *GPO Access* is funded by the Federal Depository Library Program under the *Government Printing Electronic Information Enhancement Act of 1993*. URL: www.gpoaccess.gov/index.html.

grace period   A designated period of time following the due date during which a borrower may renew an overdue item or return it to the library without incurring a fine. To encourage the return of long-overdue materials, some libraries also set aside one day (or several days) each year during which overdue items may be returned without penalty. Not all libraries provide a grace period. Synonymous with *amnesty period* and *fine-free period*.

gracing policy   The number of issues the publisher of a magazine or journal will allow a subscriber to receive following the expiration date of a subscription that has not been renewed.

gradient tint   The use of different colors and shades on a relief map, usually between contour lines, to indicate elevation. Care must be taken in the choice of color to avoid misleading the user. For example, the choice of green to indicate low elevation might lead an inexperienced user to assume that a desert area is verdant, with potentially fatal results. Synonymous with *hypsometric tint*.

gradual   A liturgical book containing a complete collection of the chants used for the Catholic Mass, arranged according to the liturgical year. Graduals were among the largest books produced during the Middle Ages because the musical notation and script had to be of a size that could be read from a single copy by members of the choir. Often beautifully illuminated, many graduals survive only in fragments.

graduate library   The academic library at a university that maintains separate collections (and usually facilities) for undergraduates and graduate students, containing the major research collections, staffed and equipped to meet the information needs of graduate students and faculty but also open to undergraduates.

grain   In a sheet of machine-made paper or board, the direction in which most of the fibers lie, determined by forward movement of the papermaking machine in manufacture. Books are printed with the grain parallel to the spine because paper bends more readily with the grain than against it. One way to determine the grain in a sheet of paper is to do a *tear test*—paper tears more cleanly with the grain than across it. There is little or no grain in a sheet of handmade paper. Woven material used as covering material in bookbinding also has grain—as a general rule, the warp threads run parallel to the spine. Grain in leather depends on the direction in which the hairs lay before removal, indicated by tiny puncture marks in the surface. *See also*: *against the grain*, *cross-grain*, and *grained*.

grained   Leather used in bookbinding that has been processed to accentuate the natural grain or give the surface an artificial texture, either as decoration or to enhance its durability. Pebble-grained goatskin is an example. *Graining* is accomplished by working a cork-covered board across the tanned skin or by using engraved metal plates or rollers to impress the desired pattern.

grammar   A book written to instruct students in the formal rules of speaking and writing a language, based on scholarly study of its morphology and syntax. During the Middle Ages, the term referred to the study of classical Latin, the language in which most books were written. Also refers to the rules themselves and to a person's use of them.

gramophone record   *See*: phonograph record.

grangerized   An edition into which illustrations, letters, and/or other matter is inserted after publication. The practice began in 1769 when James Granger (1723–76) published *A Biographical History of England* containing blank leaves for the insertion of portrait engravings after printing. Synonymous with *privately illustrated*. *See also*: *extra-illustrated*.

grant   Funds received from a private foundation (*example*: **Council on Library and Information Resources**) or government-sponsored organization (**National Endowment for the Humanities**) by an individual, group, or institution in support of a worthy project or cause. In most cases, the recipient must compete for such funds by submitting a proposal. The art of obtaining grants is called *grantsmanship*. Guides for proposal writing are available in academic libraries and large public libraries. Information on funding sources can be found in the *Annual Register of Grant Support* published by R.R. Bowker and *The Foundation Directory* published annually by The Foundation Center. *See also*: *matching grant*.

grant-in-aid   Funds received by a library or library system from a state or federal government agency in support of regular operations, or a special project or program, as opposed to funds derived from the community or district served. In most cases, the library must apply in a competitive process by submitting a proposal (*example*: certain **LSTA funds**).

grantsmanship   The art of successfully obtaining and administering grants and grants-in-aid, including the ability to recognize when an idea is fundable, locate funding sources, research the information necessary to fill out the application, establish a realistic timetable, write the proposal, and manage the grant process once funding is approved. When grant funding is a high priority, a college or university usually employs a trained and experienced *grants administrator* to help teaching faculty and librarians negotiate the process.

granularity   The level of descriptive detail in a record created to represent a document or information resource for the purpose of retrieval, for example, whether the record structure in a bibliographic database allows the author's name to be parsed into given name and surname.

graph   A diagram that shows (1) quantity in relation to a whole (pie graph), (2) the distribution of separate values of a variable in relation to another (scatter graph), or (3) change in the value of a variable in relation to another, for example, the change in the average price of a journal subscription over time (coordinate graph, histogram, etc.).

    The suffix **-graph**, derived from the Greek word *graphos* ("writing"), refers to something written, as in *autograph* or *monograph*, or something that writes or records, as in *photograph*.

graphic   Any two-dimensional nontextual, still representation. Graphics can be opaque (illustrations, photographs, diagrams, maps, charts, graphs, etc.) or designed to be viewed or projected without motion using optical equipment (slides, filmstrips, etc.). Magazines and art books usually contain a high proportion of graphic material. In marketing new books, the graphic appeal of the dust jacket is an important factor. Computer graphics are created with the aid of graphic design software. *See also*: *American Institute of Graphic Arts*, *animated graphics*, *graphical user interface*, and *thumbnail*.

In printing, a typeface that appears to have been drawn, rather than derived from a calligraphic hand or lapidary precursor.

graphical user interface (GUI)   A computer interface that allows the user to provide input and receive output interactively by manipulating menu bars, icons, and movable, resizable windows by means of a keyboard or pointing device such as a mouse. GUIs are used in Web browsers and in most word processing, spreadsheet, and graphics applications. The quality of a GUI depends on its functionality and usability. Pronounced "gooey." Synonymous with *graphic user interface* and *WIMPS*. *See also*: *Macintosh* and *Windows*.

graphic novel   A term coined by Will Eisner to describe his semi-autobiographical novel *A Contract with God* (1978), written and illustrated in comic book style, the first work in a new genre that presents an extended narrative as a continuous sequence of pictorial images printed in color and arranged in panel-to-panel format, with dialogue enclosed in balloons. A precursor can be found in the *picture story* albums of the 19th-century Swiss writer Rodolphe Topffer, who also wrote novels in conventional form. This new literary form is viewed with suspicion by traditionalists who regard it as a marketing ploy aimed at attracting adult readers to comic books by removing the stigma attached to them.

graticule   A grid composed of horizontal and vertical lines printed over an image, such as a map, to assist the viewer in locating the position of a specific feature. In an atlas, the grids are usually keyed to a gazetteer of place names giving the page number and grid coordinates for each entry. On maps intended for navigation, the lines represent degrees of latitude (parallels) and longitude (meridians).

gray literature   Printed works such as reports, preprints, internal documents, Ph.D. dissertations, master's theses, and conference proceedings, not readily available through regular market channels because they were never commercially published or listed or were poorly distributed. Alternative methods of supply and bibliographic control have evolved in response to the need of libraries to preserve and provide access to such material. In the United States, the gray literature of science and technology is indexed in the NTIS database. Theses and dissertations are indexed and abstracted in *Dissertation Abstracts International* and are available on demand via *Dissertation Express*. Also spelled *grey literature*. Compare with *ephemera*. *See also*: *semipublished*.

gray scale   Variations in the density of black, arranged in sequence (usually from 10 to 90 percent) for use in printing and film developing.

Great Books   A nonprofit foundation established in 1947 by Robert Maynard Hutchins, then president of the University of Chicago, and professor and author Mortimer J. Adler to encourage lifelong learning at the grass-roots level through the reading and discussion of enduring works of literature and philosophy. The Foundation provides reading materials for over 850 Great Books discussion groups that meet regularly in libraries, homes, schools, and community centers. Not all the selected readings are classics—the Foundation strives to select works of high literary merit, rich in discussable ideas.

In 1962, the Foundation introduced Junior Great Books to extend the benefits of its programs to elementary, middle, and high school students. The junior program is used in thousands of public and private schools in the United States. The Great Books Foundation publishes the quarterly magazine *The Common Review*. It is not the publisher of *Great Books of the Western World*, a set of hardbound books published by Encyclopaedia Britannica, Inc. URL: www.greatbooks.org.

Greek style   Derived from Coptic binding, Greek style was an early form of bookbinding with many distinctive characteristics. The sections were sewn together using a recessed chain stitch, producing a smooth, rounded spine that was lined with a wide band of coarse cloth. Prominent endbands sewn to the body through each gathering were fastened into grooves in the thick boards. Flush with the edges of the sections, the wooden boards often had grooved edges. The cover, usually in red or brown calf or goatskin, had projecting head- and tailcaps to protect the endbands. Strap-and-pin fastenings made of braided leather were often attached to the head and tail, as well as to the fore-edge of the binding. Geoffrey Glaister notes in *Encyclopedia of the Book* (Oak Knoll/British Library, 1996) that this style was used on the earliest Greek bindings and in Russia from the 11th to 15th century for theological works. It was also revived in 16th-century Europe for binding classical Greek texts.

Greenaway Medal   A literary award presented annually since 1956 by the Library Association (UK) to the artist judged to have produced the most distinguished work in the illustration of children's books published in the United Kingdom during the preceding calendar year. Compare with *Carnegie Medal*. **See also**: *Amelia Frances Howard-Gibbon Illustrator's Award* and *Caldecott Medal*.

Greenaway Plan   A form of blanket order plan in which a large library or library system agrees to receive from a publisher for a nominal price one advance copy of all the trade books it publishes, to encourage acquisitions librarians to order selected titles in advance of publication. The publisher relies on the probability that enough titles will be ordered in multiple copies to cover its costs. The plan is named after Emerson Greenaway, the librarian at the Philadelphia Free Library who conceived the idea in 1958.

green paper   A printed document issued in green paper covers by a ministry or department of the British government to elicit public comment and debate on a proposed new policy (or change in an existing one). The practice began in 1967. Compare with *white paper*.

grey literature   *See*: gray literature.

grid   Two sets of parallel lines intersecting at right angles, usually at regular intervals, that when superimposed on a map or other two-dimensional surface can be used to locate specific points by means of coordinates, usually a sequence of numbers or letters printed across the top and/or bottom margin, with a second sequence along one or both sides.

grievance   In the workplace, a formal complaint concerning a specific action or policy, set of circumstances, or persistent condition addressed by an employee or group of employees to management, to a special committee established to hear grievances, or to some other appropriate authority, to protest its unfairness and request a remedy. Most organizations have an established procedure for filing grievances and negotiating settlement. In library employment governed by collective bargaining agreement, the grievance procedure and conditions under which it applies may be explicitly stated in the contract.

grisaille   From the French *gris*, meaning "gray." Monochrome painting done entirely in tones of gray (or another neutral color) as a means of depicting objects in relief. The effect was achieved by combining dark pigment and an inert white, with touches of color sometimes added to create highlights. In *semi-grisaille*, portions of the image (usually flesh and/or background) are done in color and the rest in shades of gray. The technique was used in medieval illuminated manuscripts and stained glass church windows from the late 13th century on.

Grolier binding   A style of ornamental bookbinding named after bindings commissioned by the 16th-century French bibliophile Jean Grolier, Vicomte d'Aguisy (1479–1565) for books in his personal collection, the decoration typically consisting of open interlace strapwork, plain or polychromatic, in a geometrical pattern (circles, squares, lozenges), often with a tooled central motif, plain gilt edges, and vellum paste-down endleaves.

Grolier Club   Founded in 1884, the Grolier Club of New York City is named for the French Renaissance bibliophile and book collector Jean Grolier, Vicomte d'Aguisy (1479–1565), known for his willingness to share his library with friends. With over 700 members, the Club is the oldest and largest society for bibliophiles and graphic arts enthusiasts in the United States. Its primary goal is to advance study and appreciation of the book arts. Membership is by nomination, with recommendation based on the candidate's demonstrated passion for books and collecting. The Club maintains a library of over 100,000 volumes in a townhouse at East 60th Street in midtown Manhattan, where it sponsors book-related lectures and public exhibitions. URL: www.grolierclub.org.

grotesque   A distorted, fantastic, or incongruous figure drawn or painted in the margin of an illuminated manuscript, incorporated into the decoration of an initial letter, or hidden in an ornamental border. According to Geoffrey Glaister (*Encyclopedia of the Book*, Oak Knoll/British Library, 1996), the word *grottesca* was first used in Italy to describe the images in murals found in buildings constructed during the reign of Nero (A.D. 37–68). Michelle Brown notes in *Understanding Illuminated Manuscripts* (Getty Museum/British Library, 1994) that the grotesques found in medieval manuscripts are usually unrelated to the text, but some may have meaning associated with their appearance in bestiaries. Christopher de Hamel suggests that some may have been mnemonic devices, since medieval manuscripts were neither foliated nor paginated (*The British Library Guide to Manuscript Illumination*, University of Toronto Press, 2001). Compare with *drollery*.

groupware   Computer software designed to support more than one user connected to a LAN, usually colleagues working together on related tasks whose offices are not in the same location. Although groupware is an evolving concept, most products include a messaging system, document sharing and management software, a calendaring and scheduling system for coordinating meetings and tracking the progress of group projects, electronic conferencing, and an electronic newsletter (*example*: **Lotus Notes**).

Grub Street   According to Samuel Johnson, the name of a street near Moorfields in London "much inhabited by writers of small histories, dictionaries, and temporary poems" (*Encyclopaedia Britannica*). The term has been used since the 18th century as a pejorative for pamphleteers, literary hacks, and writers who work for hire, as in the title of the book *Women of Grub Street: Press, Politics, and Gender in the London Marketplace, 1678–1730*, published in 2002. Also spelled *Grub-street* and *Grubstreet*.

guard   A flexible paper or muslin strip inserted along the inner margin between two leaves prior to sewing the sections of a book, used to mount a text leaf plate, or an insert too stiff to turn like a normal page. Synonymous in this sense with *hinge*. Also refers to a strip of paper or other material added to reinforce a signature in a book or to compensate for the thickness of material added after binding. In medieval manuscripts, parchment guards were sometimes folded around the binding edge of a quire or bifolium for strength, especially when the leaves were of paper. In preservation rebinding, the leaves of a manuscript may be mounted on guards to retain information of interest to codicologists. *See also*: *security guard*.

guard book   A volume that includes *compensation guards* sewn with the sections, equal in thickness to material to be added between the leaves following binding, to prevent the book from bulging open.

GUI   *See*: graphical user interface.

guide   Information provided by a library, usually in the form of a printed handout or leaflet, that (1) explains how to use a library service (online catalog, interlibrary loan, etc.); (2) describes important resources on a subject (**World War II**), in a discipline (**history**), or of a specific form (**periodical articles**, **government documents**, **biography**, etc.); or (3) explains how to accomplish something (compile an annotated bibliography, cite sources in a particular bibliographical style, etc.).

In archives, a type of finding aid that provides a summary or general description of the contents of an archival collection or that describes archival holdings related to a specific subject, geographic area, period in history, etc., or of a certain type of material (diaries, letters, photographs, etc.).

guidebook   A handbook that provides useful current information for travelers to a city, state, region, country, or other geographic area or for visitors to a museum, park, historical site, etc.

guide letter   In medieval manuscripts and early printed books, a small letter written in cursive or printed in small type in the center of a space left blank at the beginning of a paragraph or other division, indicating the initial letter to be added by a rubrisher or illuminator after the text has been copied or printed. Painted over on the finished page, guide letters are seen only in copies with incomplete rubrication and/or illumination. Guide letters were necessary in manuscript production when the exemplar was no longer available. Additional instructions for decorating initials (subject, style, color, etc.) might also be provided, usually unobtrusively in hard point or metal point.

guidelines   Recommended procedures for accomplishing a given task or achieving a set of goals and objectives, formulated by a body with authority to speak on the subject but less binding than the formal *standards* used in evaluation and assessment, for example, *Guidelines Regarding Thefts in Libraries* approved in 2003 by the Association of College and Research Libraries (ACRL) and the American Library Association (ALA). Compare with *best practices* and *standards*.

Guide to Reference Books   First published in 1907 by the American Library Association, *Guide to Reference Books* is the definitive selection aid for developing reference collections in North America. For decades, it was compiled in the Reference Department of the Columbia University Library, but the eleventh edition published in 1996 is the work of 50 reference librarians from major academic libraries across the United States, many of them subject specialists who based their selections primarily on the collections of their own research libraries. Emphasis is on English-language printed works published in North America. Entries are based on MARC records cataloged by the Library of Congress. Each entry includes an annotation intended to acquaint the reader with the purpose, scope, coverage, arrangement, special features, audience, and usefulness of the work. The list is classified in five parts (General Reference; Humanities; Social and Behavioral Sciences; History and Area Studies; and Science, Technology, and Medicine), with a combined author, title, and subject index at the end.

guideword   *See*: catchword.

guillemets   French quotation marks printed «like this», also seen in some German texts. Synonymous with *duck-foot quotes*.

guillotine   A power-driven or hand-operated machine with a long, sharp-edged blade, used in binding since 1840 to cut and trim large numbers of flat or folded sheets to the desired dimensions. A guillotine makes a straight cut, as distinct from other methods of cutting used in binding, such as die-cutting, slitting, perforating, etc. Before the guillotine was invented, binders used a tool called a "plough" consisting of a cutting blade held between two blocks of wood, drawn manually along the edges of the sections, with the text block firmly clamped in a press.

gum arabic   *See*: binding medium.

Gutenberg, Johann (c. 1399–1468)   A goldsmith by trade, Johann Gensfleisch zum Gutenberg is credited with the invention of printing from movable type, probably at Mainz in Germany. His first printed work was a 42-line Bible set in gothic type probably printed no later than 1456. Uncertainty regarding Gutenberg's accomplishment arises from the lack of recorded information about his life and the fact that no extant work bears his name, nor have any of his presses survived. The printing press spread rapidly to the Netherlands, Italy, France, and England, becoming well established in Europe by the 1480s. The Gutenberg Museum was established in Mainz in 1900 as a center for the study of Gutenberg's life and work and the early history of typography.

Gutenberg Bible   The earliest known book produced in Europe from movable type, probably printed between 1450 and 1455 at Mainz, Germany, by Johann Gutenberg and his associate Peter Schöffer, with the financial assistance of a merchant named Johann Fust, also known as the *Mazarin Bible* because a copy was found by a French bookseller in the private library of the bibliophile Cardinal Mazarin (1602–61) 100 years after his death. Because no date, place of printing, or name of printer appears on the work, the circumstances under which it was produced cannot be determined with precision.

The *Gutenberg Bible* is a Latin bible printed in black ink in gothic type set in two 42-line columns per page. Of approximately 180 copies printed, only 48 are known to have survived, which makes them very rare and valuable. Twelve are printed on vellum and 36 on paper. The British Library owns 2 copies, and the Bibliothèque Nationale de France 1. In the United States, there are 13 copies, 1 each at the Library of Congress, the New York Public Library, the Huntington Library in California, and at the libraries of Harvard, Princeton, and Yale. The Morgan Library in New York City owns 3 copies. Digital images of the illuminated copies held by The British Library are on display at: prodigi.bl.uk/gutenbg. *See also*: *incunabula*.

gutter   The blank space formed by the inner margins of facing pages in an open book, from the binding edge to the area that bears printed matter. The width of the gutter is an important factor in determining whether a book can be rebound.

gutter press   Tabloid newspapers and magazines that publish salacious gossip, usually of a personal nature concerning the lives of prominent people. Synonymous with *yellow press*.

gutting   The practice, abhorred by publishers, of reviewing a book, not by critically evaluating its strengths and/or weaknesses but by revealing the main lines of its plot, ruining the experience of first-time readers. Also refers to the practice in publishing of carefully quoting out of context, in the blurb on the dust jacket and in advertising, only the most complimentary passages from reviews that, in their entirety, expressed mixed or even negative opinions of the work.

gymnastic initial   A figure initial in a medieval manuscript or early printed book composed of anthropomorphic, zoomorphic, or zoo-anthropomorphic forms, stretched or contorted by the illuminator into impossible or unlikely positions to create the letterform. Gymnastic motifs also occur in decorative borders.

H

hachure   A series of short lines drawn or printed on a land map to indicate gradient: long thin, widely spaced lines indicating a moderate grade and short, thick, closely spaced lines a steep grade, with direction of slope indicated by direction of line. *Hachuring* is common on maps produced by the National Geographic Society and the U.S. Forest Service.

hack   From the English word *hackney*, meaning "a horse let out for hire." A writer engaged in churning out fiction or nonfiction for the market place, originally at a bookseller's request, with little regard for literary quality. The term is still used in journalism. Synonymous with *hired pen*. In a more general sense, a drudge in any occupation. *See also*: *Grub Street*.

hacker   A slang term for a person with extensive knowledge of computers and computing who uses his skills to access supposedly secure computer systems for the intellectual challenge such activities provide. The best hackers take pride in leaving no "tracks" to reveal their presence. Compare with *cracker*. *See also*: *security*.

hagiography   A form of biography, popular during the Middle Ages and Renaissance, in which the life described is that of a saint. Also refers to a book containing such accounts, often a collective biography covering the lives of two or more saints. The lives of early saints were included in the Martyrology, which became one of the liturgical readings in the Divine Office. As new saints were canonized, accounts of their lives (*vitae*) were written in Latin by *hagiographers* and translated into the vernacular for the laity.

half bands   Narrow ridges across the spine of a book added between the sewing supports as a form of decoration, popular in Italian bookbinding of the 17th century. Unlike *false bands*, half bands are not an imitation of the *raised bands* produced by unrecessed sewing supports.

half-binding   A style of bookbinding in which the spine and corners are covered in a different material than the sides, usually selected for greater durability. Compare with *full binding*, *quarter binding*, and *three-quarter binding*. **See also**: *fore-edge binding*, *half cloth*, and *half leather*.

half cloth   A book bound in a cloth spine and paper-covered boards. Synonymous with *half linen*.

half-duplex   *See*: duplex.

half leather   A book with spine and corners covered in leather and the rest of the binding in paper or cloth. Compare with *quarter leather*.

half title   The title of a book as printed, in full or in brief, on the recto of a leaf preceding the title page, usually in a smaller size of the font in which the title proper is printed on the title page. In books published in series, the series title page often appears on the verso of the leaf bearing the half title.

The use of half titles dates from the 17th century and may have evolved from the practice of including a blank leaf to protect the title page from wear. In modern printing, the half title helps the printer identify the work to which the first sheet belongs. In some editions, the half title also appears on the recto of a leaf separating the front matter from the first page of the text. Also spelled *half-title*. Synonymous with *bastard title* and *fly-title*.

halftone   Art made ready for printing by photographing the image through the fine, diagonally crossed lines of a screen made of glass or film, converting it into a field of tiny graded dots that reproduce by optical illusion the tonal values of the original. Halftone screens range from 50 to 200 rulings per inch. The finer the screen, the greater the range of tonal values. Printing papers with a smooth finish require a finer screen than coarse papers. Also refers to a print made by this process. Also spelled *half-tone*. Compare with *line art*.

half uncial   The stage in the development of Latin calligraphic letterforms at which cursive characteristics and ligatures were added to the uncial script and the beginnings of ascenders and descenders appeared. A transitional phase on the path to roman minuscules, half uncial began in the early 6th century as a script for writing less formal manuscripts. It may have been brought to Britain by St. Augustine and was subsequently introduced in Europe as a book hand by St. Boniface in the 8th century. Marc Drogin notes in *Medieval Calligraphy: Its History and Technique* (Allanheld & Schram, 1980) that aspects of half uncial are evident in many subsequent scripts. It was abandoned in the 9th century with the adoption of Carolingian minuscule throughout much of Europe. The *Book of Kells* is written in Irish half uncial. Synonymous with *semi-uncial*.

half yearly   *See*: semiannual.

hand   The way a script is actually written on the page, as opposed to the model a particular scribe has in mind when engaged in writing. **See also**: *book hand* and *court hand*.

handbill   A small notice or advertisement printed on a single unfolded sheet intended for distribution by hand but also used as a poster. **See also**: *broadside*.

hand-binding   The art and craft of binding books by hand without the aid of mechanization. Medieval manuscripts and early printed books were hand-bound in wooden boards covered in leather. Today, trade editions are case bound, and hand-binding is limited to fine books. Synonymous with *craft binding*.

handbook   A single-volume reference book of compact size that provides concise factual information on a specific subject, organized systematically for quick and easy access. Statistical information is often published in handbook form (*example*: ***Statistical Handbook on the American Family***). Some handbooks are published serially (***CRC Handbook of Chemistry and Physics***). Synonymous with *vade mecum*. *See also*: *manual*.

handheld computer   *See*: personal digital assistant.

handout   A printed sheet, or group of sheets, usually stapled together at one corner, intended for distribution during an oral presentation or instruction session to give the attendees a record of content covered (summary, outline, hard copy of *PowerPoint* slides, etc.) or provide supplementary or complementary information (supporting data, examples, suggestions for further reading, contact information, etc.).

hands-on   A library instruction session or one-on-one reference transaction in which the student or patron has the opportunity to practice, usually at a computer workstation, research techniques demonstrated by the instructor or reference librarian.

hang   Having a computer freeze during a session so that it does not respond to user input, usually with no indication of the probable cause. Downloading a very large data file can create the appearance of a *hang-up*. Closing the application or rebooting will usually get the system unstuck, but unsaved data will be lost in the process.

hanging-in   *See*: case binding.

hanging indention   A form of indention in which the opening line is flush with the left-hand margin and subsequent lines are indented one or more spaces. Used in typed and printed catalog cards and in some styles of bibliographic entry.

HAPLR   *See*: library rating.

hard copy   A human-readable copy on card or paper of a document or record in machine-readable format (digital, microform, etc.) or in a form not easily readable. Also used in a more general sense to refer to printed matter, as opposed to its nonprint equivalent. Compare with *printout*.

hardcover   A book bound in an inflexible board case or cover, usually covered in cloth, paper, plastic, leather, or some other durable material, as distinct from a book bound in a cover made of flexible material. In modern publishing, a new trade title is usually issued first in hardcover, then in a paperback edition after sales in hardcover decline. Synonymous with *cloth bound*, *hardback*, and *hard bound*. Compare with *softcover*.

hard disk   A magnetic medium capable of storing a large quantity of data, which resides permanently within a computer, as opposed to a portable disk (floppy, Zip, etc.) that can be inserted in a disk drive by the user whenever a data file needs to be opened or saved and removed once the operation is completed. In microcomputers, the hard disk is usually the **c:** drive. In networked systems, users may also have access to a portion of the *hard drive* on a shared server.

hard point   A pointed implement made of metal or bone used during the Middle Ages for underdrawing and ruling blank pages in preparation for work on a manuscript. Hard point does not leave a graphic mark on the writing or drawing surface; instead, the application of pressure creates a visible furrow on one side of the sheet and a corresponding ridge on the other, a technique called *scoring*. The scribe may cut through the parchment if the implement is too sharp or if excessive pressure is applied. Synonymous with *dry point*. Compare with *metal point*.

hardware   Mechanical, electrical, electronic, or other physical equipment and machinery associated with a computer system or necessary for the playback or projection of nonprint media. Basic microcomputer hardware includes a central processing unit (CPU), keyboard, and monitor. In TechWeb's *TechEncyclopedia* (www.techweb. com/encyclopedia) the distinction between hardware and software is described as the difference between "storage and transmission" and "logic and language." *See also*: *peripheral*.

hardwired   A term that originally referred to a computer device containing unalterable circuitry designed to perform a specific task, as opposed to circuits that are programmable or controlled by a switch. However, the meaning has broadened to include constants built into computer software. Synonymous in this sense with *hard-coded*. In a more general sense, hardware or software that cannot be modified.

harmony   An arrangement of biblical passages on the same topic in parallel columns to facilitate comparison. Also, an interweaving of such passages into a continuous text (*AACR2*).

harvesting   The process of gathering data from Web pages and other Internet sources and sending it back to a central site for indexing. An Internet crawler harvests Web pages for indexing in Internet search engines. Spammers use harvesting to pull e-mail addresses off Web pages for use in mass mailings. In the Open Archives Initiative (OAI), metadata is harvested from distributed repositories such as e-print servers and from library catalogs.

hash   *See*: hashmark.

hashmark   The symbol # used to represent the word "number" in lists and street addresses, in touch-tone telephone systems that allow the caller to key input, in Web addresses (URLs) to create a link to another location in the same document, etc. Abbreviated *hash*.

head   The top edge of a book. Also refers to the margin at the top of a page, as opposed to the margin at the tail or foot of the page. Also, a word or phrase used as a brief headline in a book or periodical.

headband   In bookbinding, a band of woven cotton or silk, sometimes colored or multicolored, glued or sewn to the back of a book at the head, to protect the end of the bound sections and take the strain off the covering material at the top of the spine when the volume is pulled from the shelf. The corresponding band at the lower end of the spine is called the *tailband*. Collectively, the headband and tailband are known as *endbands*.

Originally, the headband and tailband were a part of the sewing of a book, holding the sections together securely, but because they prevented the edges of the sections from being trimmed after sewing, their primary function was transferred to the kettle stitch, and endbands began to be glued on with the lining. In early binding, headbands were laced into the boards, and in fine binding they may still be embroidered for decorative effect. Compare with *headcap*.

Also refers to a decorative band printed at the top of a page or at the beginning of a chapter in older books. Synonymous in this sense with *headpiece* and *head ornament*.

headcap   The thickened edge at the upper end of the spine of a leather-bound book, created by inserting a piece of cord inside the turned-in end of the covering material after the text block has been attached to the cover. The same edge at the lower end of the spine is called the *tailcap*. Compare with *headband*. **See also**: *Greek style*.

header   The lines at the beginning of an e-mail message that display the e-mail address and (in some mail systems) the name of the sender (To:) and recipient (From:), any delivery options (CC:), and the subject of communication (Subj:), as opposed to the *footer* at the end of the message and the *body* containing the text.

heading   The name of a person, corporate body, or geographic location; the title proper of a work; or an authorized content descriptor (subject heading), placed at the head of a catalog entry or listed in an index, to provide an access point. In library cataloging, form headings are also used. In *AACR2*, form of entry is subject to authority control. **See also**: *main heading* and *subheading*.

In Dewey Decimal Classification, a word or phrase used as a description of a class, given in the schedules in conjunction with the class number, for example, "Library and information sciences" for which the class notation is **020**.

Also, a line of type printed on a separate line at the beginning of a section of text in a chapter or other division of a work, indicating the following content in a few descriptive words, usually distinguished from the text typographically (larger type size, boldface, italic, etc.).

headline   A few words printed in large display type across the top of the front page of a newspaper to give prominence to the most important news story of the day, or above the text of one of the other articles in the newspaper to give the reader a sense of its content. Headlines are carefully worded to capture the reader's interest. *See also*: *banner*.

Also refers to a uniform line of type printed at the top of the page in a book, giving the page number and running title, usually on the verso, or the chapter title or subject of the chapter or page, usually on the recto. Synonymous in this sense with *page head* and *running head*.

headnote   A brief explanatory note printed at the beginning of a chapter, short story, poem, or other work to serve as a preface.

headpiece   A decoration printed in the blank space at the beginning of a chapter or other division of a book, usually a printer's ornament or a small illustration done by a professional illustrator. Michelle Brown notes in *Understanding Illuminated Manuscripts* (Getty Museum/British Library, 1994) that decorative panels began appearing at the beginning of texts in late Antiquity, a practice that continued in medieval manuscript and Renaissance book production. Also spelled *head-piece*. Synonymous with *headband* and *head ornament*. Compare with *tailpiece*. *See also*: *sinkage*.

headword   A word or phrase used as a main entry in a dictionary or encyclopedia, usually printed in boldface or some other distinctive type at the beginning of a definition or other entry. In most dictionaries, headwords are arranged in a single alphabetical sequence. In classified reference works, headwords may be listed alphabetically within each section, usually with a subject or keyword index to the entire work at the end of the last volume.

health science library   *See*: medical library.

hearings   Publications of the U.S. federal government containing the transcripts of testimony given before congressional committees and subcommittees, usually available in the government documents section of a library. Congressional hearings are also available online via *GPO Access* at: www.access.gpo.gov/congress/cong017.html. Not all hearings are published by the U.S. Government Printing Office. In a more general sense, the printed transcript of testimony given before any government committee or executive body authorized to hold investigative or fact-finding proceedings. *See also*: *freedom of information*.

HEGIS   *See*: Higher Education General Information Survey.

height   The dimension of a book or other bound item from head to tail, usually greater than its width, the exception being volumes square or oblong in shape. In the library cataloging, the height of a book is given in centimeters in the physical description area of the bibliographic description. In many libraries, books over a certain height are labeled oversize and shelved in a separate section. Also refers to the vertical dimension of a unit of single- or double-faced shelving. Most commercially made library shelving is sold in units 42, 60, 72, or 84 inches high. *See also*: *depth* and *shelf height*.

help line   A telephone number that a person may call to receive assistance of a certain kind, for example, instructions or advice on how to use a specific type of computer hardware or software. Some help lines are more helpful than others. *See also*: *help screen*.

help screen   The screen or sequence of screens in an online catalog, bibliographic database, or other application program providing instructions to users who need assistance in learning how to use the system. In well-designed software, the help screens are context-sensitive. In Windows, the help menu can be accessed by pressing the **F1** key or **Alt+H**. Compare with *wizard*. *See also*: *tutorial*.

herbal   A text containing practical information about herbs and other plants, especially their properties and medicinal uses, providing both common and scientific names and a physical description, with illustrations drawn or painted from actual specimens to aid identification. Botanical texts survive from Antiquity and were produced throughout the Middle Ages, often containing picture cycles based on classical models. Modern herbals are illustrated with drawings, watercolors, or photographs.

Her Majesty's Stationery Office (HMSO)   The government agency in the United Kingdom responsible for printing official government publications and for regulating and licensing the reuse of all information produced by the government, the British equivalent of the U.S. Government Printing Office. URL: www.hmso.gov.uk.

hermeneutics   The study of the art and science of interpretation and understanding, as opposed to the practice of exposition. The term originally applied to biblical exegesis but was subsequently extended to secular texts. In the 19th century, literary theorists recognized the paradox that understanding a work as a whole requires knowledge of its parts, but understanding the parts presupposes at least some knowledge of the whole. In the 20th century, as objectivity gave way to subjectivity in literary theory, interpretation was found to be rooted in culture and history, turning the meaning of a text into the history of its interpretations.

herringbone   In bookbinding, a design resembling the skeleton of a fish, consisting of a vertical line up the center with horizontal ornaments arranged like ribs. Built up of small tools, herringbone was used on the spine in Byzantine binding and on the covers of late-17th- and 18th-century Scottish bindings.

heuristic   From the Greek word *heuriskein*, meaning "to discover." A course of action or method of problem solving in which progress toward the best possible outcome or solution is continuously evaluated through trial and error. Both positive and negative results are incorporated as feedback into the discovery process, allowing procedure to be adjusted as the best next step is determined. Library research is ideally a heuristic process.

Hexateuch   The first six books of the Old Testament of the Bible (the Pentateuch plus the book of Joshua), sometimes produced as a separate manuscript by medieval scribes. *See also*: *Octateuch*.

hickie   Printer's slang for an unintended spot or defect on a printed page, usually caused by a speck of dust, lint, or dried ink on the printing plate or negative. Also spelled *hickey*.

hidden agenda   *See*: agenda.

hierarchical classification   A classification system in which the classes are subdivided on the principle of logical subordination, from the most general subjects to the most specific (*example*: **Dewey Decimal Classification**). Hierarchical classification can be broad or close. Synonymous with *analytic classification*. *See also*: *enumerative classification*, *synthetic classification*, and *tree structure*.

hierarchical force   In classification systems based on logical subordination (including Dewey Decimal Classification), the principle that the attributes of a class identified in the heading assigned to represent it (*example*: **Political ideologies**), and in certain explanatory notes, apply to all its subdivisions (**Liberalism, Conservatism, Nationalism**, etc.) and to all other classes to which reference is made in the notes.

hierarchic relation   A semantic relation between two terms in which the concept represented by one is a subclass of the concept represented by the other (*example*: **Library books / Books**).

hierarchy   The arrangement of classes in a classification system, from the most general to the most specific. In a classification schedule, hierarchy is usually indicated by length of notation and depth of indention, as in the following example from Dewey Decimal Classification:

700 The Arts
  720 Architecture
    725 Public structures
      725.8 Recreation buildings
        725.82 Buildings for shows and spectacles
        725.822 Theaters and opera houses

In an indexing language, logical hierarchy is indicated in the list of subject headings or descriptors by the codes BT (broader term) or NT (narrower term). In a more general sense, the arrangement of a set of terms or items by degree of specificity according to a given characteristic, for example, the sequence United States—New England—Massachusetts—Boston—Beacon Street, according to geographic location. *See also*: *tree structure*.

hieroglyph   *See*: hieroglyphics.

hieroglyphics   From the Greek *hieros* ("sacred" or "powerful") and *glyphikos* ("carving"). A writing system in which pictures or symbols, rather than letters of a phonetic alphabet, are used to represent words, syllables, and sounds. The ancient Egyptians wrote in *hieroglyphs* that were not deciphered until after the discovery of the Rosetta Stone in 1799, bearing the same inscription in three different scripts: *hieratic* Egyptian (formal), *demotic* Egyptian (cursive), and ancient Greek.

In a more general sense, any form of written expression that is difficult to read or understand.

hieronym   A surname based on a sacred name (*example*: **Perse Saint John**).

high-demand   *See*: demand.

Higher Education General Information Survey (HEGIS)   Part of the comprehensive nationwide system of collecting data on higher education in the United States, HEGIS was widely used by administrators, planners, researchers, and guidance counselors from its inception in 1966 until its replacement by IPEDS in 1986. Composed of a number of surveys conducted by the U.S. Office of Education and other federal agencies, HEGIS covered fall enrollment, completions, revenues and expenditures, institutional characteristics, staffing, and faculty compensation. It also included a component on library resources, facilities, and personnel. The fund accounting systems used today in some academic libraries evolved from the six-digit codes for classifying academic fields developed for HEGIS.

high fidelity   Any method of sound recording that minimizes distortion by reproducing such a wide range of audible frequencies that the result is very faithful to the original.

high-level domain   *See*: top level domain.

highlight   To use a broad-tipped pen to mark in light-colored ink a section of text in a book or document, usually for future reference. College textbooks donated to libraries are often heavily highlighted. In a similar fashion, the "edit" option in some computer applications allows the user to mark in a shaded or contrasting background portions of electronic text to be cut or copied. In a more general sense, to give prominence to the part of a whole that is the most outstanding, interesting, pertinent, useful, etc.

highlighting   Words, phrases, or passages of text marked in a book with a broad-tipped, brightly colored pen for future study. The presence of highlighting diminishes the value of a book for resale, particularly for collectors. As a general rule, donated materials containing highlighting are added to a library collection only in exceptional cases. Compare with *underlining*

Highlighting is also used in some computer applications to edit text by positioning the cursor at the beginning of a word, phrase, or entire passage, holding down on the mouse button, and dragging the cursor to the end of the desired portion of text.

high-risk collection   An archival or library collection for which the likelihood of vandalism or theft is higher than normal due to its exceptional value (rare books) or unusual content (special collections). Tighter security precautions are taken, especially when such items are placed on exhibit.

Highsmith   A commercial company in the business of providing equipment, supplies, and furnishings to libraries and schools, marketed through its trade catalog. URL: www.highsmith.com. *See also*: *Brodart* and *DEMCO*.

high-speed   In computing, equipment that functions at a higher-than-normal speed, usually purchased at a premium. Also refers to a fast Internet connection (compare *T3* with *T1*).

hinge   A narrow strip of muslin or paper attached with adhesive along the line dividing the two halves of an endpaper to reinforce the flexible joint along which the body of a book is attached to the cover. In volumes lacking this reinforcement, the hinge is formed by adhering the covering material (leather, cloth, paper, etc.) directly to the fold in the endpaper.

Also refers to a narrow cloth or paper stub inserted along the binding edge between the pages of a book to allow a map or added leaf to flex easily when the volume is opened. Synonymous in this sense with *guard*.

hiring freeze   The temporary cessation of activities aimed at employing personnel to fill vacancies and new positions on the staff and/or faculty of a library or library system, usually in response to a major budget cut. An "across-the-board" freeze has the potential disadvantage of distributing the impact of cuts unequally across the administrative units within the library, sometimes necessitating the temporary reorganization of duties. When funds are restored, hiring resumes, usually according to priorities based on need.

histogram   A graph representing quantitative data in a series of vertical or horizontal bars or lines drawn from a base line. The position of each bar (or line) along the base indicates the class or value of one variable, with the length of the bar (or line) indicating the corresponding value of a second variable. A third variable can be added if the bars are displayed in groups and distinguished graphically, by color, shading, etc. Synonymous with *bar graph*.

historiated border   An ornamental band around a miniature and/or portion of text on the page of an illuminated manuscript or early printed book, decorated with figures of animals and/or human beings in a scene that illustrates the accompanying text or tells a story. *See also*: *historiated initial*.

historiated initial   An initial letter in an illuminated manuscript or early printed book containing an identifiable figure or group of figures (human, animal, and/or imaginary) in a narrative scene that may be related to the text. Compare with *figure initial* and *inhabited initial*. *See also*: *historiated border*.

historical atlas   A book of maps showing the progressive changes that have occurred over a given period of time in a geographic area or in the development of a spatial phenomenon (*example*: ***Historical Atlas of United States Congressional Districts, 1789–1983***).

historical bible   *See*: *Bible historiale*.

historical bibliography   The branch of bibliography devoted to the study of the history and methods of book production, including hand-copying, illustration, publishing, printing, papermaking, binding, and preservation. Historical bibliography has merged with the field of book history.

historical fiction   A narrative in the form of a novel set in a specific place and period in history, or based on an event or sequence of events that actually happened. The characters may be completely fictional, but if they are known to have existed, their feelings, words, and actions are reconstructed and to some degree imagined by the author. The presence of dialogue in a historical work is usually a clue that the account is fictionalized. Sir Walter Scott established the genre in 1814 with the publication of *Waverly*, a novel of life in the Scottish borderlands, followed by several more historical romances, including *Ivanhoe* (1819). Compare with *nonfiction*.

historical society   A nonprofit organization devoted to preserving the historical record of a state or municipality, place, institution, people, activity, or thing. Well-established historical societies often support a public museum, maintain an archive or library for the use of members, and may publish books and other materials related to their sphere of interest. For a directory of the affiliates of the American Historical Association (AHA), please see: www.theaha.org/affiliates.

historical value *See*: archival value.

history *See*: search history.

history note A brief note in an entry in a thesaurus of indexing terms giving the date the descriptor was added to the list of preferred terms and indicating any changes that have occurred in its meaning, scope, relationships to other terms, etc.

history of the book *See*: book history.

history play *See*: chronicle play.

hit In information retrieval, a record retrieved from a database that matches the information need expressed in the query. The term is sometimes used loosely to refer to a record that satisfies the syntactic requirements of the query without necessarily meeting its semantic requirements (a *false drop*), but this is an imprecise use of the term. *Hit rate* is the percentage of all the records retrieved in a search that are relevant to the query. *See also*: *precision* and *recall*.

hits In information retrieval, the number of records retrieved from a database that are relevant to the query. In some databases, the number of hits is indicated *before* records are displayed, to enable the user to modify the search statement before viewing search results. When *zero hits* are retrieved, the reason may be the misspelling of one or more search terms, a query that contains syntactical or semantic errors, or indexing of sources under a synonym or related term. Compare with *false drop*. *See also*: *precision* and *recall*.

On the Internet, the number of times a particular site is visited during a designated period of time, which can be recorded by an automatic counter supported by the software running the site.

HMSO *See*: Her Majesty's Stationery Office.

hold When a book or other item is currently on loan, most libraries permit another borrower to place a "hold" on it by contacting the circulation desk. The patron who has the item checked out will not be permitted to renew it, and the person placing the "hold" will be entitled to check it out after it has been returned. Some online catalogs include a feature that allows the user to place an item on hold without staff assistance.

holding area In archives, a location specifically designated for the temporary storage of semicurrent records and materials, usually less accessible than the space allocated for current records.

holdings The total stock of materials, print and nonprint, owned by a library or library system, usually listed in a catalog. Synonymous in this sense with *library collection*.

In a narrower sense, all the copies, volumes, issues, or parts of an item owned by a library, especially a serial publication, indicated in a *holdings statement* in the record representing the item in the catalog. Holdings can be recorded in the MARC21 Format for Holdings Information. *See also*: *closed entry* and *open entry*.

holdings display   In a union catalog, a list of all the libraries and other participating institutions that own a specific item, for example, in the OCLC *WorldCat* database, the OCLC symbols attached to the bibliographic record for an item, representing institutions that own at least one copy, used in interlibrary loan to generate lender strings.

holdings rate   The percentage of items requested by the users of a library that are in its collections. In most libraries, items not held locally may be borrowed on interlibrary loan (ILL) or obtained via document delivery service (DDS).

holdings record   In cataloging, a separate record attached to the bibliographic record for a serial title or multivolume item to track the issues, parts, volumes, etc., acquired by the library. A format for holdings is defined in MARC21. In most libraries, the holdings record is separate from the *check-in record* used for current receipts of serials. As successive issues or parts are received and volumes are completed, the record of receipt is moved from the check-in record to the holdings record. Compare with *item record*.

holdings statement   A note added to the catalog record for an item in a library collection indicating the copies, volumes, issues, or parts held by the library or library system in an open or closed entry, usually with information concerning the location of the item. For serials, separate notes may be provided for print and microform holdings. The ANSI/NISO standard Z39.71-1999 *Holdings Statements for Bibliographic Items* specifies rules for the construction and display of holdings statements for all non-unitary publications. Compare with *numeric and/or alphabetic, chronological, or other designation*.

hollow   The open space between the cover and the back of a book in which the sections are not glued directly to the cover. A hollow back allows a book to open flat and stay open without damaging the spine.

hollow back   A type of binding in which the cover is *not* glued to the back of a book, leaving an open space that allows the binding to flex easily when the volume is opened, without cracking the spine. Most hardcover trade editions are bound with a hollow back. Synonymous with *loose-back* and *open back*. Compare with *tight back*.

holograph   A document written entirely in the handwriting of the person (or persons) to whom it is attributed. A holographic reprint is a reproduction of such a document, made by mechanical means. Also refers to a three-dimensional image of an object recorded on photosensitive film by the pattern of interference made by a split laser beam in a process called *holography*.

holograph manuscript   The text of an original work written entirely in the hand of the author. For photographic illustration of sample pages, see entries in the *Dictionary of Literary Biography*, a reference serial published by the Gale Group.

homebound   A person unable to leave home to come to the library, usually for reasons of disability or ill health. To reach homebound patrons, public libraries have developed extension services such as books-by-mail, bookmobiles, and direct delivery.

homepage   The first or main page of a site on the World Wide Web, displayed whenever a user logs on to a Web browser and opens the site address (URL). The filename at the end of a homepage address is often *home.html*, *index.html*, *main.html*, or something similar. A well-designed homepage gives the title of the site, name of author, host, date of last update, notice of copyright, table of contents, and links to subpages providing more detailed information about the site, usually the best starting point when navigating the site for the first time. Also spelled *home page.*

homework center   A space set aside for study in a public library, usually with established hours and assigned staff trained to provide clearly defined services to students in need of assistance with their homework assignments.

homilary   A book containing a collection of homilies (sermons or discourses on religious themes or biblical passages) to be read on Sundays and feast days, arranged according to the ecclesiastical year. Synonymous with *sermologus.*

homily   A sermon explaining or discussing a point in the Christian Bible, usually accompanied by instructions for the congregation hearing it. In a more general sense, any tendentious, moralizing speech or lecture. *See also*: *homilary.*

homograph   A word spelled the same as one or more other words but different in meaning and sometimes in origin, for example, *current* (ocean) and *current* (up-to-date) but not *currant* (the fruit). Every effort is made to avoid homographs in indexing, but when necessary, a parenthetical qualifier is added to the heading, as in the Library of Congress subject heading **Mice (Computers)**. Compare with *homonym* and *homophone.*

homonym   A word pronounced the same as one or more other words but different in meaning and origin (and usually in spelling), for example, *plate* (illustration) and *plait* (braid or pleat). The word "plate" is also a homograph: *plate* (dish for eating). Synonymous with *homophone.* Compare with *synonym.*

homophone   A word pronounced the same as one or more others but which has a different spelling, meaning, and derivation (**toad**, **toed**, and **towed**). Synonymous with *homonym.*

honorific title   A formal title conferred on a person by a recognized authority as a mark of honor, rank, nobility, or royalty (*example*: **Cardinal** Richelieu). In *AACR2*, an honorific title is included in a personal name heading only when commonly used in referring to the person. In such cases, the title follows the personal name and precedes the birth and death dates (**Newton, Isaac, Sir, 1642–1727**).

horae   *See*: Book of Hours.

horn book   A type of child's primer used in England and America from the 15th to the 18th century, consisting of a sheet of parchment or paper bearing the letters of the alphabet, usually the first 10 numerals, basic spelling rules, the Lord's Prayer, and sometimes a hand-colored illustration, protected by a thin, transparent sheet of cattle horn, mounted on an oblong bat of wood or leather with a projecting handle by which it could be fastened to a child's girdle. Its paddle shape suggests that it may have been used in playing the game *shuttlecock*. The term is used in the title of *Horn Book Magazine*, a review publication devoted to children's literature. Also spelled *hornbook*. *See also*: *abecedary* and *battledore*.

hornbook   *See*: horn book.

Horn Book Magazine, The   Published since 1924, *The Horn Book Magazine* provides articles, author interviews, editorials, columns, and lengthy reviews of children's books in each bimonthly issue. The title is derived from the name of an educational toy, called a *horn book*, used by young children from about the 15th to the 18th century. ISSN: 0018–5078. URL: www.hbook.com.

horror   A subgenre of gothic fiction in which supernatural events, macabre effects, and obsessive introspection are combined with chilling suspense to produce visceral sensations of fear and revulsion in the reader. Ghosts, hallucinations, monsters, mummies, nightmares, witches, werewolves, vampires, demons, and black magic are common themes. Early literary examples include Mary Shelley's novel *Frankenstein* (1818), Edgar Allan Poe's short story "The Fall of the House of Usher" (1839), and *Dracula* (1897) by Bram Stoker. In motion pictures, the earliest examples are *The Cabinet of Dr. Caligari* (1919) directed by Robert Wiene and *Nosferatu* (1922) by F.W. Murnau, both classics of German expressionism. More recent examples include Alfred Hitchcock's *Psycho* (1960) and Rod Serling's television series *The Twilight Zone*. The contemporary master of horror fiction is Stephen King. Synonymous with *weird fantasy*. Extreme graphic horror has been dubbed *splatterpunk*. Compare with *thriller*.

hors texte   A French phrase meaning "outside the text," referring to illustrations not printed with the text, such as plates. They are usually numbered in roman numerals to distinguish them from illustrations printed with the text, which are numbered in arabic numerals or referenced by page number. The phrase *hors texte, versos blank* is used in the book trade to refer to plates without printing on the reverse side, sometimes tipped in to paper of different stock than that used for the text.

hospitality   In classification, the property that allows new classes to be added to a system of notation as needed, without requiring the alteration of previously established schedules.

hospital library   A medical library maintained within the walls of a hospital containing a collection of print and online resources on medicine and allied health to serve the information and research needs of doctors, nurses, patients, and staff, usually managed by a medical librarian.

host   A computer that serves as a source of data for other terminals or computers, for example, a central computer providing files to terminals connected directly to it, or a network server accessed by client machines. Also refers to the organization or institution that provides the server on which a Web site is installed, usually indicated in its Internet address.

hostile work environment   Conditions in the workplace found to be detrimental to the safety and well-being of employees, due to discrimination on the basis of age, gender, race, or national origin. In 2003, a group of 12 library staff members (including 6 librarians) won $435,000 in damages from the Minneapolis Public Library over failure to control persistent public use of the library's computers by patrons to access sexually explicit images (pornography). Unable to convince their library administration of the seriousness of the problem, the employees complained of sexual harassment and intimidation to the local office of the Equal Employment Opportunity Commission in 1997, and the EEOC found probable cause that the women faced a hostile work environment. When the U.S. Department of Justice failed to take action, the staffers filed suit in federal court and won their case.

host organization   The organization in which a special library functions as an administrative unit, for example, a museum that maintains a library on its premises for the use of curators, researchers, and members or a corporation that maintains a library for the use of employees in their work.

hot-melt   A tough, flexible chemical adhesive used in commercial bookbinding. Solid at room temperatures, hot-melt adhesive liquifies under high heat. In perfect binding, it is applied to the binding edge of a book in a single shot at temperatures of 135 to 175 degrees Centigrade. Unlike the adhesives used in sewn bindings, which take time to dry, hot-melt adhesive sets up in seconds as it cools, significantly reducing production costs. Unfortunately, it has a clamping effect that reduces openability, and it is not resistant to cold-crack, which makes it unsuitable for bindings marketed in countries where winter temperatures are severe. Also spelled *hotmelt*. *See also*: *Otabind*.

hot spot   An icon of any size, or portion of a larger image displayed on a computer screen, that functions as a live link to another file or document available on the same or a different server. When it is clicked with a pointing device such as a mouse, a coded instruction is executed to retrieve and display the linked material. Also refers to the precise pixels within a clickable icon or image that are sensitive to selection by the user.

hours   The times during a day, week, and year that a library is open to its users, usually posted near the front entrance and available by phone or via the library's Web site, including any days the library is not open (usually holidays). A library's hours are determined by the needs of its users and by budgetary constraints. Also refers to the times during which a specific service is available from a library, which may be shorter (or longer) than the hours the facility is open.

housekeeping   Routine chores that must be performed methodically in a library to maintain manual or automated systems in good order, usually delegated to a trained assistant, for example, the task of checking in serial parts in a timely manner to make them available to users and to identify missing issues that need to be claimed.

house organ   A periodical issued by a commercial or industrial organization for distribution internally to its employees and/or externally to its customers, not intended for wider publication. Synonymous with *house journal*. Compare with *trade journal*.

house style   The uniform standards of a publisher, printer, company, or organization with reference to writing style (grammar, syntax, usage, punctuation, etc.) and presentation (spelling, abbreviation, uppercase/lowercase, citation format, etc.) to be followed, in the absence of contrary instructions, in publications issued in its name, usually explained in a *style sheet*.

how-to publication   A book, pamphlet, or videocassette that provides practical information and advice about how to accomplish a task, acquire a skill, or achieve a desired result, usually in the form of step-by-step instructions accompanied by diagrams, for example, home improvement and auto repair manuals. How-to titles are available in public libraries, shelved by call number in the nonfiction section. Compare with *self-help publication*.

HTML   *See*: Hypertext Markup Language.

HTML editor   Computer software designed to facilitate the creation of Web pages by relieving the designer of the necessity of typing the required HTML code from scratch (*examples*: **Dreamweaver**, **FrontPage**, **Netscape Composer**).

HTTP   *See*: Hypertext Transfer Protocol.

Hufnagel   A form of musical notation used mainly in German choir books of the late Middle Ages, named for its resemblance to the horseshoe-nail. David Hiley notes in *The New Grove Dictionary of Music and Musicians* (Macmillan, 2001) that it was written in right-angle strokes without curves and used as late as the 18th century. Compare with *neume*.

humanistic script   In the late 14th and 15th centuries, the renaissance of interest in classical art and literature in Italy had a profound effect on calligraphy, producing a script that abandoned many characteristics of gothic letterforms, returning instead to the simplicity and clarity of the Carolingian minuscule of the 8th and 9th centuries, though in a more compressed form. Appearing concurrently with the invention of movable type, *scrittura umanistica* was quickly adapted by type founders, particularly the lowercase letters, which are very close to the forms used in modern printing. Warren Chappell notes in *A Short History of the Printed Word* (Knopf, 1970) that chancery script, from which italic developed, was a direct descendant of *scrittura umanistica*.

human resources   A collective term for all the people employed by a company, agency, organization, or institution. Also, the administrative department responsible for matters pertaining to employment (hiring, evaluation, promotion, termination, etc.). Large independent libraries and library systems usually have their own human resources office. Libraries that function as a unit within a larger organization may rely on the parent organization for such services. Synonymous with *personnel*.

humidify   *See*: humidity.

humidity   The amount of water vapor held in air. *Absolute humidity* is the weight (mass) of water vapor in a given volume of air, usually expressed as grams of water per cubic meter of air. *Relative humidity* (RH) is the ratio of the amount of water vapor present in a given volume of air to the amount required to reach saturation (condensation into droplets) at the same temperature, expressed as a percentage. Relative humidity varies with temperature and air pressure—warm air can hold more water vapor than cooler air. It is the most important factor in providing a suitable environment for books and other items made of paper, with 40 to 45 percent RH considered ideal for permanent storage of library and archival materials. Mold can become a serious problem when RH exceeds 70 percent.

To *humidify* is to put moisture into the atmosphere, usually done with a device called a *humidifier* to prevent paper documents from becoming brittle. *Dehumidification* takes moisture out of the atmosphere. It is done with desiccants or a *dehumidifier* to prevent mildew, warping, etc. Measured by an instrument called a *hygrometer*, humidity is carefully controlled in areas where archival and special collections are stored and used.

Huntington Library   Located in San Marino, California, the Huntington Library is one of the world's leading libraries of Americana and English literature, surpassed only by The British Library and the Bodleian. Its collections include over 5 million manuscripts, rare books, reference works, and other materials on Anglo-American history, literature and the arts, the history of science, and maritime history. The library includes a conservation center, exhibition hall, art collection, and botanical gardens. URL: www.huntington.org/LibraryDiv/LibraryHome.html.

H.W. Wilson   A commercial publishing company that began issuing reference serials for libraries and researchers (especially periodical indexes) long before library finding tools were automated. Most of its publications are now available online and on CD-ROM. Some of its bibliographic databases include full-text. URL: www.hwwilson. com.

hybrid journal   A periodical that functions as both a magazine and a journal by including features typical of both. A prime example is *Analytical Chemistry* published by the American Chemical Society, which includes a magazine section in the front of each issue, followed by a longer section of research articles with its own table of contents and separate pagination.

hydrologic map   A map showing the drainage of surface waters (streams, rivers, etc.) and other features related to hydrology in a geographic area (lakes, reservoirs, glaciers, ground water, springs, wetlands, water quality, etc.).

hygrometer   Any one of several meteorological instruments designed to measure atmospheric humidity. Hygrometers are used to monitor conditions in facilities such as libraries and museums that house materials easily damaged by water vapor (rare books, manuscripts, specimens, film, etc.). *See also*: *preservation*.

hygroscopic   A material that readily absorbs and retains moisture from the air, often changing in form or consistency. For example, vellum used as a writing surface in manuscript books and in early bookbinding, which cockles with changes in relative humidity.

hymnal   A separate collection of the metrical hymns sung in the Divine Office (canonical hours) of the Catholic Church, arranged according to the liturgical calendar. Incorporated into Church liturgy in the 5th century, hymns were also contained in antiphonals and psalters. The contents of the hymnal were eventually incorporated into the breviary. In Protestant churches, a book of hymns sung during worship services. Latin: *hymnarium*. Synonymous with *hymnary* and *hymnbook*.

hymnary   *See*: hymnal.

hype   An abbreviation of *hyperbole*. Publisher's slang for advertising copy written in an exaggerated style for effect, usually to attract attention to a new publication, not intended to be taken literally by prospective customers. Objective reviews are the best antidote. Compare with *puff*.

hyperlink   *See*: link.

hypermedia   A hypertext document in which text is combined with graphics, audio, animation, and/or full-motion video (*example*: **National Geographic Channel** at: www.nationalgeographic.com/channel).

hypermodern   A term used in the book trade for collected first editions published within the last decade, or so recently that the author or title does not have a well-established reputation.

hyperonym   *See*: broader term.

hypertext   A method of presenting digital information that allows related files and elements of data to be interlinked, rather than viewed in linear sequence. Text links and icons embedded in a document written in HTML script allow information to be browsed in nonlinear, associative fashion similar to the way the human mind functions, by selecting with a pointing device or using a computer keyboard. Hypertext is the basic organizing principle of the World Wide Web. *See also*: *hypermedia* and *Web browser*.

Hypertext Markup Language (HTML)   Used to create the hypertext documents accessible on the World Wide Web and via intranets, HTML script is a cross-platform presentation markup language that allows the author to incorporate into a Web page text, frames, graphics, audio, video, and links to other documents and applications. Formatting is controlled by "tags" embedded in the text. To see the HTML code in which a Web page is written, click on "View" or its equivalent in the toolbar of a Web browser, then select "Document source" or "Page source." *See also*: *HTML editor* and *Standard Generalized Markup Language*.

Hypertext Transfer Protocol (HTTP)   The communications protocol used in Web browser software to establish the connection between a client computer and a remote Web server, making it possible for data files in HTML format to be transmitted over the Internet from the server to the client machine on which the browser is installed. Most Web browsers are designed to default to **http://** whenever a user enters a Web address (URL) without the protocol.

hyphen   In printing, the shortest rule used as punctuation. Also used to join the parts of a compound name (Jean-Pierre) or compound word (dog-eared) and to divide a long word at the end of a line of written or printed text. Compare with *dash*.

hyphenation   Use of the hyphen to divide a word (*co-opt*), to compound two or more words (*son-in-law*), to give the impression of stuttering or faltering speech (*n-n-no*), or to indicate that a word is to be spelled out (*h-y-p-h-e-n-a-t-e*). In computerized typesetting, word division is done automatically by a system that applies a set of rules, with an exception dictionary of words that do not follow the rules.

hyponym   A word or phrase that can be replaced without exception by another, without changing the meaning of a sentence, but not vice versa, for example, *azure* by *blue* or *sparrow* by *bird*. ***See also***: *narrower term*.

I

I2 *See*: Internet2.

IATUL   *See*: International Association of Technological University Libraries.

ibid.   An abbreviation of the Latin *ibidem*, meaning "in the same place," used with a page number (or numbers) in footnotes, endnotes, and bibliographies to indicate a source that has been cited fully in a preceding note or entry.

ICIC   *See*: International Copyright Information Centre.

icon   A small graphic element or symbol displayed on a computer screen that the user can select with a pointing device such as a mouse to summon a menu of options, access a data file, or initiate a process or operation in an application program that uses a graphical user interface, for example, a small image of a trash can or recycle bin to which unwanted documents can be moved for disposal.

   Also refers to a picture, image, figure, or representation. In Eastern Orthodox religious imagery, a picture of Jesus, Mary, or an apostle or saint. Also spelled *ikon* or *eikon*.

iconic document   A publication or other document in which the content is presented in predominantly graphic or pictorial form. Examples include atlases, children's picture books, exhibit catalogs, visual dictionaries, posters, postcards, etc.

iconography   The art of illustration or representation by means of pictures, figures, or images, developed to a high degree in the artistic tradition of the Eastern Orthodox faith. Also refers to the study of the pictorial representation of objects or people, in portraits, paintings, photographs, sculpture, coins, etc., and to the result of such study, especially when it takes the form of detailed lists of representations.

ideal copy   In analytical bibliography, a detailed description of the most perfect copy of the first impression of an edition, based on close inspection of as many copies as possible, to which all other copies of the same impression, and any subsequent impressions, are compared in determining issue and state (adapted from *The ALA Glossary of Library and Information Science*). In *ABC for Book Collectors* (Oak Knoll, 1995), John Carter writes that the term applies only to books printed before about

1800, when it was not unusual for corrections to be made in the type while printing was in progress.

identifier   A keyword or indexable concept assigned to a document to add depth to subject indexing, not listed in the thesaurus of indexing terms because it either represents a proper name (geographic name, personal name, test or program name, piece of legislation, etc.) or a concept not yet approved as an authorized descriptor. Identifiers are usually listed in a separate field of the index entry or bibliographic record, immediately following the descriptors. Major identifiers may be marked with an asterisk or distinguished in some other manner. Form of entry may be subject to authority control. In some indexing systems, identifiers are periodically reviewed for suitability as new descriptors. Not all indexing systems use identifiers. Compare with *provisional term*.

Also, a string of characters intended to uniquely identify a bibliographic resource. There are many identifier systems in use for different types of library materials, including the International Standard Book Number (ISBN) for books, the International Standard Serial Number (ISSN) for serial titles, the Serial Item and Contribution Identifier (SICI) for serial issues and articles, and the Digital Object Identifier (DOI) for journal articles and other digital content.

ideogram   A picture or symbol that represents an object or idea without expressing phonetically the sounds of its name, for example, the characters used in Chinese and Japanese writing systems. Also refers to a symbol that represents an idea, for example, the equal sign = or the plus sign +. Synonymous with *ideograph*. Compare with *phonogram*.

ideograph   *See*: ideogram.

idiom   A well-known expression that has a different meaning than the literal interpretation of its words (*example*: **holy terror**). Idioms are sometimes coined from the lexicon of a particular occupation or pastime (*example*: **Monday morning quarterback**). Because idioms are specific to a given language, they can be difficult to translate. Dictionaries of idioms are usually shelved in the reference section of a library.

Also refers to a characteristic style, particularly in the arts, or to the language or dialect peculiar to a specific people, geographic region, or social class.

idyl   From the Greek word meaning "little picture"—a short poem describing the simplicity and innocence of rural, pastoral, or domestic life. The origin of this literary form can be traced to Theocritus, who described pastoral life in Sicily for readers in Alexandria during the 3rd century B.C. An *eclogue* is a type of idyl. Compare with *idyll*.

idyll   A narrative poem based on a romantic, epic, or tragic theme, for example, *Idylls of the King* (1859) by Alfred, Lord Tennyson, an episodic retelling of the fables of the Holy Grail, Camelot, Round Table, and Morte d'Arthur. Compare with *idyl*.

i.e.   An abbreviation of the Latin phrase *id est*, meaning "that is."

IETF   *See*: Internet Engineering Task Force.

IFCS   *See*: International Federation of Classification Societies.

IFLA   *See*: International Federation of Library Associations and Institutions.

IFRT   *See*: Intellectual Freedom Round Table.

IL   *See*: information literacy.

ILAB   *See*: International League of Antiquarian Booksellers.

ILL   *See*: interlibrary loan.

illiteracy   *See*: literacy.

illuminate   To decorate an initial letter or word in a manuscript with designs or tracings in bright colors and gold or silver or to decorate a border or an entire page with initial letters, hand-painted miniatures, and/or colorful designs highlighted in gold or silver, techniques commonly used in medieval manuscripts and incunabula. An artist who decorates books by hand is an *illuminator*. *See also*: *illuminated* and *rubric*.

illuminated   From the Latin *illuminaire*, meaning "to give light." A manuscript or incunabulum richly decorated by hand with ornamental polychrome letters, designs, and/or illustrations highlighted in gold or silver. Illumination flourished during the medieval period when books were hand-copied on parchment and vellum, originally by Christian monks who produced books for liturgical and devotional use and for exchange with other monasteries (*example*: **Book of Kells**). Illumination was of three main types: small paintings called *miniatures* (usually illustrative) occupying all or part of a page; decorated initial letters, often containing figures or scenes related or unrelated to the text; and ornamental borders around text and/or images on one or more sides, usually incorporating a variety of motifs.

During the early Middle Ages, illumination was done in monastic scriptoria, where most books were produced, but early in the 12th century independent artists began trading on their skill as *illuminators*, working mainly for wealthy patrons who filled their private libraries with fine books (*example*: **Les très riches heures du Duc de Berry**). The Morgan Library in New York City holds one of the largest collections of illuminated manuscripts in the United States. The Getty museum provides an online exhibition of illuminated manuscripts at: www.getty.edu/collections. Abbreviated *illum*. *See also*: *chrysography* and *gilding*.

illuminated initial   An initial letter in a medieval illuminated manuscript painted in bright colors and embellished in gold or silver. Compare with *rubric*. *See also*: *figure initial*, *foliate initial*, and *historiated initial*.

illumination   *See*: illuminated.

illustration   A picture, plate, diagram, plan, chart, map, design, or other graphic image printed with or inserted in the text of a book or other publication as an embellishment or to complement or elucidate the text. Also refers to the fine art of creating such visual works.

The earliest examples of illustrated texts date from the second millennium B.C. Medieval manuscripts were illustrated with illuminated miniatures. Early printed books were illustrated with woodcuts or wood engravings. In modern books, illustrations are often numbered and listed by number in the front matter. Photographs or plates may be printed on a different grade of paper than the text and added to the sections of a book in one or more groups. Maps, tables, and genealogies are sometimes printed on the endpapers. Magazines, art books, and books for young children are usually heavily illustrated. The use of illustration in works of general fiction has declined since the early 20th century but continues unabated in children's books. Abbreviated *ill.* or *illus. See also*: *artwork.*

illustrator   An artist who creates drawings, paintings, or designs to elucidate or embellish the text of a book or other printed publication. The illustrator of a children's picture book may receive higher honors than the author of the text. In *AACR2*, when illustration is added to the text of a work, main entry is made under the heading appropriate to the text, with an added entry for the illustrator if appropriate. However, if the work is the result of a collaboration between author and illustrator, main entry is under the person named first on the chief source of information unless greater prominence is given to the other by typography or some other means. *See also*: *Caldecott Medal* and *Greenaway Medal.*

ILMP   See: *International Literary Market Place.*

IM   *See*: instant messaging.

image   For many years, librarians have been consciously depicted in the mass media as female in gender, mousy in appearance, dowdy in dress (orthopedic shoes), know-it-all in attitude, overly serious, and too strict in the enforcement of rules. Although this negative stereotype may in part be a manifestation of anti-intellectualism in American society, many members of the profession consider it unfair and would like to see it change. Although the topic is often treated humorously in the library literature (see the chapter on "Image" in Will Manley's *The Manley Art of Librarianship*, McFarland, 1993), the effect of professional image on recruitment and morale has yet to be measured systematically.

Interestingly, research conducted by Mary Jane Scherdin in 1992 under the aegis of the Association of College and Research Libraries (ACRL) reveals that the personality profiles of librarians as a group differ significantly from data on the general population. Using the Myers Briggs Type Indicator (MBTI) to measure personal preferences, Scherdin found that librarians scored substantially higher on introversion, intuitiveness, and thinking than the population at large and that individuals with extroverted, sensing, feeling, and perceiving preferences are rare in the library profession. Assuming that introverts are likely to be perceived by extroverts as timid or reserved, that those who prefer emotion over reason may find thinkers too serious, and that individuals who are flexible and spontaneous tend to regard those who are systematic and well organized as rigid or controlling, Scherdin's findings suggest that the popular stereotype may have some basis in reality (see "Shattering Our Stereotype: Librarians' New Image" in the July 1995 issue of *Library Journal*).

Also refers to a visual impression of something real or imagined. *See also*: *picture.*

image search engine   *See*: image searching.

image searching   In library cataloging, the bibliographic record is designed to indicate whether an item contains illustrations, and if so, the number of plates and whether they are in color, but pictorial content is not described in detail. Some Web search engines, however, include an optional feature that allows the user to retrieve images from Web pages by entering descriptive keywords.

The "Image" feature in *AltaVista* (www.altavista.com) provides both basic and advanced search modes, allowing the user to specify color or black and white and choose between photographs, graphics, and/or buttons and banners. Some image search engines even allow the user to specify file type (JPEG, GIF, etc.) and other characteristics (see "Advanced Image Search" in *Google Image Search* at: images.google.com). Most have a default adult content filter that can be turned off by the user. Results usually include a thumbnail of the image, its filename and size, and the URL of the Web page in which it appears. Because most image search engines locate pictorial content by analyzing text adjacent on the same page (including any captions), false drops are common. Like text, online images are usually protected by copyright.

imbrication   In the book arts, a decorative pattern designed to give the impression of overlapping scales, tiles, shingles, leaves, etc.

imitation binding   A contemporary binding executed in a style intended to closely resemble that of an earlier period.

imitation leather   A synthetic or partly synthetic binding material manufactured to resemble leather, for example, a fabric base given a textured coating, usually more washable than real leather. Synonymous with *artificial leather*.

IMLS   *See*: Institute of Museum and Library Services.

impact factor   In citation analysis, a quantitative measure of the frequency with which the "average article" published in a given scholarly journal has been cited in a particular year or period, developed by the Institute for Scientific Information (ISI) for use in *Journal Citation Reports*, a multidisciplinary tool for ranking, evaluating, and comparing journals within subject categories. The indicator is used by serials librarians in collection management, journal publishers in marketing, information analysts in bibliometric research, and authors in identifying journals in which to publish. Eugene Garfield advises caution in using the indicator as a measure of the prestige of a journal for purposes of academic evaluation for promotion and tenure (*Current Contents*, June and July 1994).

impensis   Latin for "at the expense of," a word appearing in an imprint or colophon at the end of a work printed prior to the end of the 17th century, followed by the name of the person or entity responsible for financing the publication, usually the publisher or a bookseller or patron.

imperfect   Said of a book discovered upon examination to have pages or sections missing, duplicated, or bound out of order or upside-down. The publisher will usually exchange or perfect copies containing binding errors and reimburse the purchaser for shipping costs. Compare with *imperfections*.

imperfections   Printed sheets rejected in the binding process because they contain defects or errors that require replacement sheets.

Also refers to copies of a book that contains printing or binding defects, for example, the accidental omission or duplication of a signature or insert. The publisher will usually exchange or perfect such copies and reimburse shipping costs when booksellers or retail purchasers return them, but only for defective make-up, not the insertion of errata slips (corrigenda). *See also*: *out*.

import   A publication produced and issued in one country and brought into another for sale in the same unaltered form. The name of the importer may be printed on the title page in addition to, or in place of, the original publisher or indicated on a label added to the title page after printing. Compare with *co-publishing*.

In computing, to read or receive data from a different application or computer system, which may require that it be converted into a compatible format. Popular applications are usually equipped to convert a variety of formats. Compare with *export*.

impression   All the copies of a book or other publication printed in the same press run from the same setting of type or plates. An edition may comprise several impressions in which the typesetting remains unchanged. Compare with *reprint*. *See also*: *issue*.

Also refers to the result of the transfer of wet ink under pressure from type or plates to the surface of a sheet or roll of paper, as in printing, engraving, etching, etc.

imprimatur   A Latin phrase meaning "let it be printed." The license for publication granted by an ecclesiastical or secular authority, usually printed on the verso of the title page of a book, indicating the name of the licenser and the date on which it was granted. Found most often in books printed during the 16th and 17th centuries, *imprimatur* is still used in the doctrinal publications of the Roman Catholic Church to indicate official approval (*example*: **New Catholic Encyclopedia**). *See also*: cum privilegio *and* nihil obstat.

imprint   The statement in a book that identifies the publisher and/or printer. The *publisher's imprint* consists of the official name of the publishing company and the date and place of publication. It usually appears at the foot of the title page and more completely on the verso of the title page. The *printer's imprint*, indicating the name of the printing company and the place of printing, usually appears on the verso of the title page, at the foot of the last page of text, or on the page following the text. By extension, the actual item printed or published, as in "early 19th-century imprint." Synonymous with *biblio*. *See also*: *colophon, distribution imprint, eponymous imprint, fictitious imprint*, and *joint imprint*.

In binding, the name of the publisher and/or the publisher's device stamped at the base of the spine, or the name of the binder stamped on the inside of the back board of the cover, usually near the bottom.

imprint date   *See*: publication date.

inactive records   Records no longer required by an agency or individual in the daily conduct of business or affairs, which may be placed in intermediate storage, transferred to archival custody, destroyed, or disposed of in some other way without affecting normal operations. The opposite of *active records*. Synonymous with *nonactive records*. *See also*: *intermediate records*.

incipit   Latin for "here begins." The opening words or phrase of a text, or of one of its divisions, providing a clue to its content. In the absence of a title page, medieval manuscripts and incunabula often began with the word "incipit" written or printed in majuscules and/or in a distinguishing color. The incipit often included the name of the author and the title of the work. Compare with *colophon* and *explicit*. *See also*: *incipit page*.

incipit page   The beginning of a major section of text in a medieval manuscript or early printed book, embellished with a particularly large initial letter, often followed by display script in diminuendo to emphasize the importance of the division. In Gospel books, the incipit page sometimes begins with a monogram or initial capital representing the evangelist's name. Elaborate examples are found in the *Book of Kells* and the *Lindisfarne Gospels*.

incomplete   *See*: completeness.

incunabula   From the Latin word *cunae*, meaning "cradle." Books, pamphlets, calendars, and indulgences printed from movable type in Europe prior to 1501, during the earliest years (infancy) of printing. The earliest example is the *Gutenberg Bible* believed to have been printed before 1456 in Mainz, Germany, by Johann Gutenberg, who is credited with the invention of modern printing. Singular: *incunabulum*. Synonymous with *cradle books* and *incunables*. *See also*: *xylograph*.

incunabulum   *See*: incunabula.

in-cut note   *See*: cut-in note.

indent   To set back a line of type or column of figures by one or more spaces from a margin to mark or distinguish it from preceding and succeeding lines or columns, as at the beginning of a new paragraph. Indention is used in outlines and classification schedules to indicate logical hierarchy, and in subject thesauri to show semantic relations. It is also used on typed and printed catalog cards to designate specific areas of bibliographic description.

indention   A space between the margin on a page and the beginning of a line of type, as at the beginning of a paragraph of text. The points listed in an outline are usually indented to indicate the logical structure of the content covered. Indention is also used in subject thesauri to indicate semantic relations, in classification schedules to show the logical subordination of classes, and on typed and printed catalog cards to designate specific areas of bibliographic description. *See also*: *hanging indention*.

independent librarian   A provider of library services who works outside traditional library settings, for example, an information broker who works from a home office. Independent librarians are organized in the Independent Librarian's Exchange (ILEX), a section of the Association of Specialized and Cooperative Library Agencies (AS-

CLA) of the American Library Association. Also used synonymously with *solo librarian*.

Recently, the term has been used in reference to Cubans who, in response to Fidel Castro's 1998 announcement that there are no prohibited books in Cuba (only books that no one had the money to buy), began lending banned materials from their homes. The following year, human rights activists in the United States formed the group Friends of Cuban Libraries to oppose the intimidation and arrest of "independent librarians" in Cuba, including confiscation of their book collections, and began lobbying the ALA in support of the position that intellectual freedom was at issue. After hearing arguments on both sides of the controversy at its January 2001 meeting, the International Relations Committee (IRC) of the ALA issued a report recommending no action be taken, based on information that the Cubans suffering persecution were not librarians but political dissidents supported by anti-Castro groups.

Independent Publisher A trade publication, formerly titled *Small Press*, that provides articles, announcements of new books, excerpts, and over 100 reviews of small press publications in each bimonthly issue. *Independent Publisher* is known for reviewing works not reviewed elsewhere. ISSN: 1098–5735. URL: www.independentpublisher. com.

index An alphabetically arranged list of headings consisting of the personal names, places, and subjects treated in a written work, with page numbers to refer the reader to the point in the text at which information pertaining to the heading is found. In single-volume works of reference and nonfiction, any indexes appear at the end of the back matter. In a multivolume work, they are found at the end of the last volume. In very large multivolume reference works, the last volume may be devoted entirely to indexes. Works of fiction are rarely indexed. The publisher of a periodical may provide an index to each volume at the end of the last issue of the publication year. For best results, indexing should be done by a professional *indexer*. Alternate plural: *indices*. *See also*: *American Society of Indexers*.

Also refers to an open-end finding guide to the literature of an academic field or discipline (*example*: ***Philosopher's Index***), to works of a specific literary form (***Biography Index***) or published in a specific format (***Newspaper Abstracts***), or to the analyzed contents of a serial publication (***New York Times Index***). Indexes of this kind are usually issued in monthly or quarterly paperback supplements, cumulated annually. Citations are usually listed by author and subject in separate sections, or in a single alphabetical sequence under a system of authorized headings collectively known as *controlled vocabulary*, developed over time by the indexing service. Indexing can be either *pre-coordinate* or *post-coordinate*. Compare with *abstracting service* and *catalog*. *See also*: *author index*, *classified index*, *cross-index*, *geographic index*, *meta-index*, *name index*, *periodical index*, *subject index*, and *title index*.

indexable matter The parts of a book or other publication included when the document is analyzed for indexing, not necessarily limited to the text. Notes, appendices, and other complementary or supplementary material may or may not be indexed, depending on its potential usefulness to readers and the policy of the publisher. Bibliographies and glossaries are rarely indexed.

Index Expurgatorius *See*: *Index Librorum Prohibitorum*.

indexing   The process of compiling one or more indexes for a single publication, such as a monograph or multivolume reference work, or adding entries for new documents to an open-end index covering a particular publication format (*example*: **newspapers**), works of a specific literary form (**biography**, **book reviews**, etc.), or the literature of an academic field, discipline, or group of disciplines.

The professionally trained *indexer* reads or scans the text of each document to determine its content, then selects appropriate headings (names, places, subjects) to facilitate retrieval. Cross-references are made from synonyms, and the entries are arranged in the desired sequence (alphabetical, numerical, classified, etc.). In an open-end index, content descriptors are usually selected from a list of preferred terms (controlled vocabulary), developed over time by the indexing service.

Indexing can be *pre-coordinate* or *post-coordinate*. ***See also***: *assignment indexing*, *automatic indexing*, *derivative indexing*, *indexable matter*, *machine-aided indexing*, and *string indexing*.

indexing language   An artificial language consisting of subject headings or content descriptors selected to facilitate information retrieval by serving as access points in a catalog or index, including any lead-in vocabulary and rules governing form of entry, syntax, etc. ***See also***: *controlled vocabulary*.

Index Librorum Prohibitorum   A "list of forbidden books" prepared in 1558 at the request of Pope Paul IV by a special Congregation of the Inquisition. First published in 1559, the "Pauline index" included works that Catholic laypersons were prohibited from owning or reading because ecclesiastical authorities considered them detrimental to faith and morals, usually because they contained teachings condemned as heretical. In 1562, the Council of Trent took up the issue of censorship and appointed a commission to draft a new index. Approved by Pope Pius IV, the "Tridentine index" was published in Rome by Paulus Manutius in 1564. Also known as the *Index Expurgatorius*, the list was not abolished by the Vatican until 1966. ***See also***: *imprimatur* and nihil obstat.

index map   A map showing the complete extent of the geographic coverage of a set or series of more detailed maps, with or without segmentation. Compare with *map index*.

Index of Prohibited Books *See*: *Index Librorum Prohibitorum*.

India paper   *See*: bible paper.

indicative abstract   An abstract that describes the type and form of the work abstracted, indicating the main topics covered and providing a brief description of the treatment, but that does not summarize the content or evaluate quality. Compare with *critical abstract* and *informative abstract*.

indicator   One of two single-character positions at the beginning of a field in a MARC record (except fields 001 to 009), which can be used to specify certain conditions for the field. The positions nearly always contain a digit from 0 to 9, although alphabetic characters are permitted. The meaning of the indicators is always field-dependent; for example, in the personal name main entry field (100), the first indicator specifies the type of name, while in the uniform title main entry field (130), the first indicator specifies the number of nonfiling characters to skip in sorting. In some fields, the first or second position is used, in others, both or neither. When one of the positions is not used, the indicator is *undefined* and the position is left blank. In some fields, the absence of a character in one of the indicator positions has a specific meaning.

inedita   The plural of the Latin word *ineditum*, meaning "not made known," literary works not published, for example, the personal papers of a writer or well-known person. Works of this kind are usually available in the special collections of the library that purchased them or received them as a gift.

inedited   A work published as submitted by the author, without editorial changes. Such works may include passages objectionable to some readers or containing errors of fact, which an editor might have altered or omitted. *See also*: editing.

Also refers to unpublished works, especially the memoirs or correspondence of a writer who is deceased.

infomercial   An advertisement on film usually aimed at television audiences, promoting a product or service informatively, usually in a spontaneous soft-sell style intended to create the impression of objectivity. When infomercials masquerade as television programs, they often include panel discussions, demonstrations, etc., to bolster credibility.

infometrics   *See*: informetrics.

informatics   The *ASIS Thesaurus of Information Science and Librarianship* (Information Today, 1998) defines informatics as the area of activity that "represents the conjunction of information science and information technology." It is the formal study of information, including its structure, properties, uses, and functions in society, in particular the technology used to record, organize, store, retrieve, and disseminate it. Some academic institutions offer a separate degree in the subject as one of the tracks in an information studies program or school. For a discussion of the history and current state of informatics, please see the entry in the *International Encyclopedia of Information and Library Science* (Routledge, 2003).

information   Data presented in readily comprehensible form to which meaning has been attributed within a context for its use. In a more dynamic sense, the message conveyed by the use of a medium of communication or expression. Whether a specific message is *informative* or not depends in part on the subjective perception of the person receiving it.

More concretely, all the facts, conclusions, ideas, and creative works of the human intellect and imagination that have been communicated, formally or informally, in any form. In his inaugural address of 1801, Thomas Jefferson listed the "diffusion of information" as one of the fundamental principles of the republican form of government established under the Constitution of the United States. Compare with *knowledge*. *See also*: *disinformation* and *misinformation*.

informational value   *See*: archival value.

information and referral (I&R)   A service available at no charge, usually from a public library or other public service agency, providing contact information about *other* organizations, agencies, and individuals qualified to offer specific information and services, both free and fee-based, usually within a local community.

information broker   A self-employed professional skilled in information retrieval and delivery who markets his or her research services commercially, usually on a freelance basis. Information brokers are organized in the Association of Independent Information Professionals (AIIP).

information desk   A desk in a large public or academic library, usually located near the main entrance, staffed by a nonprofessional trained to screen questions, provide basic information about library services and collections, and direct users to the reference desk or some other public service point when further assistance is needed. The presence of an information desk reduces the number of directional questions received by reference librarians, freeing them to focus on the needs of patrons who require professional services.

information ethics   The branch of ethics that focuses on the relationship between the creation, organization, dissemination, and use of information, and the ethical standards and moral codes governing human conduct in society. In the United States, the *ALA Code of Ethics* is the leading statement of ethical standards for the library profession. Compare with *information law*. *See also*: *censorship*, *intellectual freedom*, *intellectual property*, *plagiarism*, and *privacy*.

information gap   *See*: digital divide.

information industry   A broad term covering all the companies and individuals in the business of providing information and access to information for a profit, including the mass media, commercial publishers, software and database producers and vendors, indexing and abstracting services, and freelance information brokers. Public libraries, academic libraries, and many types of special libraries function outside the information industry because they operate on a nonprofit basis. Because the industry encompasses such a wide range of commercial enterprises, it has no single trade journal.

information law   The regulation and control of information by the state, including laws concerning censorship, copyright and intellectual property, forgery, freedom of information, intellectual freedom, privacy, computer crime, and public funding of information providers, such as libraries and museums. Also refers to a specialized branch of legal studies dealing with the regulation of information. *See also*: *information ethics*.

information literacy (IL)   Skill in finding the information one needs, including an understanding of how libraries are organized, familiarity with the resources they provide (including information formats and automated search tools), and knowledge of commonly used research techniques. The concept also includes the skills required to critically evaluate information content and employ it effectively, as well as an understanding of the technological infrastructure on which information transmission is based, including its social, political, and cultural context and impact. Synonymous with *information skills*. Compare with *computer literacy*.

information management   The skillful exercise of control over the acquisition, organization, storage, security, retrieval, and dissemination of the information resources essential to the successful operation of a business, agency, organization, or institution, including documentation, records management, and technical infrastructure. For a detailed discussion of information management as a field, please see the entry by T.D. Wilson in the *International Encyclopedia of Information and Library Science* (Routledge, 2003). *See also*: *Association for Information Management*.

information need   A gap in a person's knowledge that, when experienced at the conscious level as a question, gives rise to a search for an answer. If the need is urgent, the search may be pursued with diligence until the desire is fulfilled. Persons with information needs often end up at the reference desk of a library where it is the responsibility of the reference librarian to determine the precise nature of the need, usually by conducting an informal reference interview, as a basis for recommending relevant sources. In order to search the online catalog or bibliographic databases, the need must be expressed in the form of a query.

It is the job of collection development librarians to anticipate the information needs of a library's clientele, sometimes with the aid of survey research, in order to select materials to meet those needs. Patrons with questions that cannot be answered using the resources of the library may be referred to other information providers in the local community or elsewhere.

information overload   A condition in which too much information is available on a topic, a common occurrence in online searching, particularly when the query is expressed in terms that are too broad. Systems that facilitate the retrieval of high-quality resources, sifting out the chaff, are badly needed. In the meantime, consumers of information must develop their own analytical and critical skills.

information policy   A governing principle, plan, or course of action concerning information resources and technology adopted by a company, organization, institution, or government, for example, the political decision to use public funds to subsidize Internet access for schools and public libraries. In the United States, Congress and the president are advised by the National Commission on Library and Information Science (NCLIS) on decisions concerning national library and information policy. For a detailed discussion of information policy, please see the entry by Ian Rowlands in the *International Encyclopedia of Information and Library Science* (Routledge, 2003).

information retrieval (IR)   The process, methods, and procedures used to selectively recall recorded information from a file of data. In libraries and archives, searches are typically for a known item or for information on a specific subject, and the file is usually a human-readable catalog or index, or a computer-based information storage and retrieval system, such as an online catalog or bibliographic database. In the design of such systems, a balance must be attained between speed, accuracy, cost, and effectiveness.

information science The systematic study and analysis of the sources, development, collection, organization, dissemination, evaluation, use, and management of information in all its forms, including the channels (formal and informal) and technology used in its communication. Compare with *informatics* and *library science*. *See also*: *information theory*.

Information Science & Technology Abstracts (ISTA) An abstracting and indexing service established in 1966 that provides abstracts of books, conference proceedings, and articles from over 450 journals and trade publications in information science, *ISTA* covers abstracting and indexing, bibliometrics, cataloging, classification, electronic publishing, information management, the information industry, Internet search engines, and online information retrieval. Published nine times per year in print by Information Today, Inc., *ISTA* provides author and subject indexes in the last issue of each annual volume. The service is also available online from DIALOG. Formerly *Information Science Abstracts (ISA)*. URL: www.infotoday.com/ISTA.

information storage and retrieval (ISAR) Operations performed by the hardware and software used in indexing and storing a file of records whenever a user queries the system for information relevant to a specific topic. For records to be retrieved, the search statement must be expressed in syntax that is executable by the computer.

information studies An umbrella term used at some universities for a curricular division that includes library and information science (LIS) and allied fields (informatics, information management, etc.), for example, the School of Information Studies at Syracuse University and the iSchool, a new incarnation of the former Graduate School of Library and Information Science at the University of Washington. Accredited library and information studies programs in the United States and Canada are listed in *American Library Directory* and *The Bowker Annual Library and Book Trade Almanac*, both published by R.R. Bowker. For an online *World List of Departments and Schools of Information Studies, Information Management, Information Systems, etc.*, see: informationr.net/wl.

information superhighway *See*: Internet.

information system (IS) A computer hardware and software system designed to accept, store, manipulate, and analyze data and to report results, usually on a regular, ongoing basis. An IS usually consists of a data input subsystem, a data storage and retrieval subsystem, a data analysis and manipulation subsystem, and a reporting subsystem. Widely used in scientific research, business management, medicine and health, resource management, and other fields that require statistical reporting, information systems can be broadly classified as *spatial* or *nonspatial*, depending on whether the data refers to a system of spatial coordinates. *See also*: *geographic information system*, *management information system*, and *spatial information system*.

information technology (IT)   A very broad term encompassing all aspects of the management and processing of information by computer, including the hardware and software required to access it.

information theory   The systematic statement of principles concerning the phenomenon of information and its transmission, based on the collection and analysis of quantitative and qualitative data as a means of testing hypotheses about its nature and properties. Compare with *informatics*.

informative abstract   An abstract that summarizes as much of the essential content of a work as possible, within the limitations of a single paragraph. Compare with *critical abstract* and *indicative abstract*.

informetrics   The use of mathematical and statistical methods in research related to libraries, documentation, and information. Synonymous with *infometrics*. ***See also***: *bibliometrics*.

infrastructure   A collective term borrowed from military parlance, encompassing all the components that support a particular activity, especially the permanent systems and structures that constitute its foundation. In modern information technology, all the hardware and software developed and maintained to keep a communication system (large or small) operating smoothly. The state of a society's infrastructure represents its commitment to investing in the future.

infringement   The use without permission of material protected by copyright or patent in a manner reserved under law to the holder of rights in the work. Such use may be subject to legal action at the discretion of the copyright owner. ***See also***: *all rights reserved* and *fair use*.

Ingram   A wholesaler of trade books, audiobooks, and periodicals to libraries, booksellers, and specialty retailers, Ingram passes on economies of scale to its customers in the form of a substantial discount off the list price. URL: www.ingrambookgroup.com.

inhabited initial   An initial letter in an illuminated manuscript or early printed book containing within its contours one or more decorative animal, human, or imaginary figures, not necessarily related to the text, often depicted fancifully. Ornamental borders can also be inhabited. Compare with *figure initial* and *historiated initial*.

inherent vice   A weakness in the chemical or physical composition of a document or other item that causes it to deteriorate from within over time, for example, the chemical instability of cellulose nitrate film used in early cinematography. Impurities introduced in book manufacture include acid in papers made from untreated wood pulp, alum rosin sizing, acid adhesives, chemicals used in tanning, etc. Incorporation of damaging elements reached a peak from about 1850 to 1900 and again during World War II. When conservation measures fail, reformatting may be required to preserve the item.

in-house   Refers to something accomplished on the premises, usually by library staff, rather than outside the library by an independent contractor, for example, binding done in the library, rather than sent to an offsite commercial bindery. *See also*: *in-house use*.

in-house archives   The unit within a company, agency, or institution responsible for retaining the noncurrent records of the parent organization and sometimes those of other corporate bodies and individuals with which it is closely associated, as opposed to an outside repository.

in-house use   The number of times an item is used within the walls of a library during a given period of time (usually a month or year), as opposed to the number of times it is checked out. In-house use is tracked by counting the number of times an item is left lying on a table, carrel, or reshelving cart in a public area of the library, to be reshelved by a member of the library staff. Although this method is never completely accurate (some patrons return materials to the shelf after using them), statistics on in-house use can be helpful in developing periodical and reference collections. Compare with *circulation statistics*. *See also*: *usage*.

initial article   An article appearing in first-word position in a title or corporate name, usually *a*, *an*, or *the* (or the equivalent in another language), ignored in indexing and filing under most filing rules. *See also*: *nonfiling character*.

initialism   A shortened form of a phrase or compound term composed of the initial letters of its words or parts spoken *letter-by-letter*, rather than pronounced as a word (*example*: **IPO** for **i**nitial **p**ublic **o**ffering or **ADA** for *Americans with Disabilities Act*). Compare with *abbreviation* and *acronym*.

initialize   To start a computer system, program, or disk anew, an operation that usually requires erasing all or part of the data stored in memory. In Apple Macintosh computers, initializing a disk formats it. In computer programming, a variable is *initialized* when it is given its first value.

initial letter   A large capital letter at the beginning of the first word of a paragraph, chapter, or other division of a text. In medieval manuscripts and early printed books, initial letters were often decorated or illuminated, for example, the "B" at the beginning of the text of a psalter (the first letter of *Beatus*, the first word of the first Psalm). Size of letter and amount of decoration indicate the relative significance of the division within the text, with gradations measured in number of lines (height). In manuscripts and incunabula, large initial letters were inserted by a rubricator or illuminator in spaces left blank when the sheets were hand-copied or printed. *See also*: *anthropomorphic initial, architectural initial, armorial initial, drop initial, faceted initial, figure initial, foliate initial, gymnastic initial, inhabited initial, pen-flourished initial, penwork initial, raised capital, zoo-anthropomorphic initial*, and *zoomorphic initial*.

initial title element   The word or words selected by the cataloger from the title of a musical work to be placed first in the uniform title for the work, for example, the word *Nocturne* from the title *Troisième nocturne*. If no additions are required by the rules, the element becomes the uniform title for the work (*AACR2*).

ink   From the Latin *encaustum*, meaning "burnt in." A colored liquid used for writing and drawing and in printing to create an impression on a flat surface (usually a sheet or roll of paper). The ink used in medieval manuscripts was made by mixing tannic acids from pulverized oak gall with iron sulfate or *copperas* (ferrous sulfate) and gum arabic (dried sap of the acacia tree). Iron gall ink darkens and bonds with the writing surface when exposed to air, but because ferrous ink has a tendency to fade to brown over time, some pure carbon in the form of lampblack was often added.

Prior to the late 19th century, printing ink was traditionally made from lampblack mixed with a linseed oil base. To create colors, lampblack was replaced with other substances, such as vermilion (mercuric sulfide) to produce red. The quality of printing ink depended on the quality of the oil base, which varied because most printers made their own ink according to recipes handed down from master to apprentice. Although lampblack remains the basic ingredient of black printing ink, the complex formulas used today are the product of chemical technology. The typographer must carefully match choice of ink to grade of paper in planning a print job. *See also*: *inkhorn*, *permanent ink*, and *show through*.

ink ball   A large, round pad made of buckskin or sheepskin firmly stuffed with a wad of cotton or wool and fastened to a short wooden handle, used by the pressman in hand printing to apply ink to type set in wooden formes. Most pressmen worked two-handed with an ink ball in each hand.

inkhorn   A small receptacle made from the inverted horn of an animal, used to hold ink in the medieval scriptorium. Because manuscripts were written in both black and red ink, and sometimes in other colors, a scribe needed more than one ink pot. Ink-horns were usually inserted into metal hoops attached to the edge of a writing desk, into holes cut through its surface, or into free-standing holders to prevent them from overturning.

inlay   A picture or decorative element of contrasting color set into the cover of a book, usually in leather with or without tooling. Synonymous in this sense with *mosaic binding*. Also, an illustration set into a border or frame of paper, the overlapping edges shaved thin to make the resulting sheet uniform in thickness. Compare with *onlay*.

In case binding, the strip of heavy paper or card added as a lining between the inner edges of the boards to stiffen the spine when the case is covered in cloth, paper, or some other protective material. *See also*: *backstrip*.

inline   An elegant display typeface in which each broad stroke has a white line down its center. Compare with *outline letter*.

in loco parentis   Latin for "in place of a parent," usually a person who temporarily assumes parental authority. *See*: *parental mediation*.

INPL   *See*: International Network of Public Libraries.

in press   A book or other publication in the process of being printed, usually listed in *Forthcoming Books* published by R.R. Bowker.

in print   A book currently available from the publisher, either as a frontlist or backlist title, as opposed to a title no longer available. Books currently in print in the United

States are listed annually in *Books in Print, Children's Books in Print*, and *El-Hi Textbooks & Serials in Print*. The opposite of *out of print*.

in process   Newly ordered library materials shipped by the vendor and received by the library but not yet ready for circulation because technical processing has not been completed. In some online catalogs, the phrase "in process" is added in the temporary catalog record to indicate the circulation status of a new item that has arrived but is not ready to be checked out. Most libraries will expedite processing at the request of a registered borrower. *See also*: *arrears*.

in progress   A term used by library catalogers to indicate that a serial publication or set is as yet incomplete, usually because parts or volumes remain to be issued by the publisher. Compare with *work in progress*. *See also*: *checklist*.

input   Data transferred to or entered into a computer system for processing, as opposed to the *results* of processing, known as *output*. The most commonly used *input devices* in personal computing are the keyboard and mouse. Scanners are also becoming more widespread, and significant advancements have recently been made in voice recognition technology.

input standards   OCLC has established the following set of standards for entering bibliographic data into its online union catalog:

SS—*System-supplied*—data generated by the cataloging system that cannot be altered by the cataloger.

M—*Mandatory*—data the cataloger must enter to meet the designated standard for a specific encoding level.

R—*Required if applicable or readily available*—must be entered if appropriate under *AACR2* and available on the item or from other records.

O—*Optional*—cataloger may decide whether to enter.

C—*From copy only*—data entered from cataloging copy, usually provided by the Library of Congress, National Library of Medicine, etc.

X—*Obsolete*—not used (older records may contain data elements no longer used).

in quaternis   A Latin phrase used in catalogs compiled in medieval monastic libraries to refer to unbound books that may have been stitched into some kind of flexible wrappers made of parchment or vellum, rather than left loose in quires (Christopher de Hamel, *Scribes and Illuminators*, University of Toronto Press, 1992).

in quires   *See*: in sheets.

inscribed copy   A copy of a book that bears, as a presentation inscription, the name of the recipient and sometimes an appropriate comment or remark, followed by the signature of the donor, who may or may not be the author. The inscription is usually written on the flyleaf. Abbreviated *insc*. Compare with *presentation copy*.

inscription   A brief, informal dedication written inside a book, usually on the flyleaf. Also, words engraved in stone or on some other hard surface, usually as a greeting or to commemorate an important event or person (*example*: the **Rosetta Stone**). *See also*: *inscribed copy*.

insert   Any printed material, such as a map, illustration, subscription blank, advertising supplement, etc., slipped loose (unbound) into a book or periodical, which is not an integral part of the publication. Synonymous with *loose insert* and *throw-in*.

Also refers to a phrase, sentence, or paragraph added to the text of a publisher's proof and included in the revised or final proof before the work goes to press.

in-service training   Formal instruction provided by a company, agency, organization, or institution at its own expense to enable its employees to become more proficient or qualified, especially in a new skill or set of skills. The sessions may be designed in-house and conducted on the premises by employees with the necessary expertise, presented by a vendor's traveling representative, or conducted by an outside training firm hired specifically for the purpose. *See also*: *professional development*.

inset   In bookbinding, a section of two or more leaves placed within another section in such a way that the back folds of both are sewn in the same pass of the thread. The inset section can wrap around the outside of the main section ("outsert") or be placed in its center or at some intermediate location within it. Insetting is used to include plates without having to go through the time-consuming process of tipping them in. Also refers to a small diagram, map, or illustration printed within the area of a larger illustration, usually enclosed in a border of ruled lines. *See also*: *inset map*.

inset map   A small map drawn or printed within the border of a larger map, usually showing in greater detail a specific feature or portion of the larger one, for example, a major metropolitan area within the borders of a map of a state or province. The same purpose may be served by an *ancillary map* printed on the same sheet or page outside the borders of the main map.

in sheets   A book in flat or folded unbound sheets, before the sections have been gathered. Synonymous with *in quires*.

inspection copy   *See*: examination copy.

installment   One portion of a literary work divided into parts for publication in consecutive issues of a periodical or one part or fascicle of such a work published separately, usually at regular intervals. During the 19th century, novels were often published in this fashion. *See also*: *original parts*.

installment sale   A sale in which the purchaser pays for an item in two or more payments, usually at regular intervals of a month or more. Under this arrangement, the item is shipped when the order is received, without waiting for final payment. In the book trade, this practice is usually limited to very expensive multivolume reference works.

instant book   A book written, produced, and marketed within weeks of an important event to capitalize on current interest in the subject. Because careful research generally requires an investment of time and effort, works prepared in haste may contain errors of fact or lack depth of treatment. A perceptive reviewer will note such deficiencies.

instant messaging (IM)   A real time computer conferencing system that enables two or more persons to "chat" online via the Internet, IM allows the user to add the name of another person to a messaging list and be instantly notified whenever the person logs on. A chat session is initiated by typing a message in a designated window or "chat room" generated by the IM software. The message is displayed almost instantaneously on the screen of each person on the list, and the recipient(s) may respond quickly by typing a message. Most IM systems are designed to emit an auditory signal whenever a message is transmitted or received. Some systems allow the user to exchange data files, synchronize Web browsing, send images and video, and play computer games. Instant messaging is used in libraries to deliver digital reference services to remote users and to persons who prefer to communicate online.

Institute for Scientific Information (ISI)   Established by Eugene Garfield in 1958, ISI is a commercial company providing citation indexing, current contents services, and information management tools in the sciences, social sciences, and arts and humanities. URL: www.isinet.com.

Institute of Museum and Library Services (IMLS)   An independent federal grant-making agency created under the Museum and Library Services Act of 1996 to foster leadership, innovation, and lifelong learning by supporting museums, archives, and libraries of all types and encouraging partnerships among them. IMLS administers four grant-in-aid programs for libraries, including LSTA grants to state library agencies. IMLS publishes the monthly e-mail newsletter *Primary Source*. URL: www. imls.gov.

institutional memory   A collection of official materials assembled to document the current and historical activities and intellectual production of an organization, including legal and policy documents, reports, proceedings, books, periodicals, articles, non-print media, technical documents, membership and employment records, etc., usually organized to facilitate access and sometimes available in digital form. E-mail communication and electronic recordkeeping pose challenges to traditional paper-based methods of preserving institutional memory. *See also*: *archives*.

in stock   An item for which a publisher, dealer, jobber, distributor, or bookseller has a sufficient number of copies in inventory to fill an order at the time it is placed. Compare with *out of stock* and *temporarily out of stock*.

instruction lab   A library instruction classroom equipped with computer workstations (PCs or laptops) for the hands-on use of students, usually with an instructor station connected to an LCD projector for the demonstration of online search techniques.

Insular majuscule   A variety of half uncial script developed and used by the scribes of Ireland and Britain for writing biblical, liturgical, and patristic texts from about A.D. 550 to 900. The most formal examples are found in the *Book of Kells* and the *Lindisfarne Gospels*. Marc Drogin notes in *Medieval Calligraphy: Its History and Technique* (Allanheld & Schram, 1980) that the script is characterized by ligatures, triangular or wedge-shaped serifs, and creative stretching and shaping of letterforms. Insular scripts replaced uncial in England shortly after the synod of Whitby in 664. Synonymous with *Irish half-uncial* and *Irish majuscule*.

intaglio From the Italian *intagliare*, meaning "to cut in." A printing technique used mainly for graphic purposes in which the areas to be printed are engraved or etched below the surface level of a plate. The plate is inked and then the surface is wiped clean, leaving a residue only in the engraved portions, which is then transferred to a sheet of paper or other printing surface under pressure, usually on a rolling press. The only intaglio printing process still in commercial use is *photogravure*.

integral Said of a leaf or page sewn or bound into a book or pamphlet when the publication was first printed. Compare with *insert*.

integrated access An information retrieval system that allows users to search for books, periodical articles, and electronic resources such as computer files and Web sites, in one operation using a single interface, instead of searching online catalogs, bibliographic databases, and Web search engines separately. Seamless access is a goal yet to be realized in most libraries.

integrated library system (ILS) *See*: library management system.

Integrated Postsecondary Education Data System (IPEDS) A system for collecting data on approximately 10,000 primary providers of postsecondary education in the United States (colleges, universities, and institutions offering technical and vocational education), administered by the National Center for Education Statistics (NCES). The IPEDS annual surveys cover fall enrollment, completions by type of program, revenues and expenditures, institutional characteristics, staffing, salaries, tenure, benefits, and library resources. Prior to the adoption of IPEDS in 1986, much of the same information was collected in the Higher Education General Information Survey (HEGIS). URL: nces.ed.gov/ipeds.

integrating resource As defined in *AACR2 2002*, a category of *continuing resource* added to or changed over time by means of updates incorporated into the whole without remaining discrete. Examples include updating loose-leaf services, databases, Web sites, etc. *See also*: *iteration*.

intellectual freedom The right under the First Amendment to the U.S. Constitution of any person to read or express views that may be unpopular or offensive to some people, within certain limitations (libel, slander, etc.). Legal cases concerning free speech issues are heard by the U.S. Supreme Court. The Office for Intellectual Freedom of the American Library Association maintains a Web page on intellectual freedom at: www.ala.org. Compare with *freedom of information*. *See also*: *banned book*, *censorship*, *challenge*, *filtering*, Freedom to Read Statement, and Library Bill of Rights.

Intellectual Freedom Round Table (IFRT) Founded in 1973 as a permanent round table of the American Library Association, IFRT advocates freedom of access and expression in libraries and provides support to librarians and other library employees who become embroiled in controversies involving censorship. IFRT also serves as a forum for the discussion of intellectual freedom issues at the state and local levels and monitors developments in intellectual freedom that affect libraries, including legislation and court decisions. IFRT is affiliated with the Office for Intellectual Freedom of the ALA, which publishes the *Library Bill of Rights*, the *Freedom to Read Statement*, and other ALA policies concerning the freedom to read. URL: www.ala.org. *See also*: *Freedom to Read Foundation*.

intellectual property   Tangible products of the human mind and intelligence entitled to the legal status of personal property, especially works protected by copyright, inventions that have been patented, and registered trademarks. An idea is considered the intellectual property of its creator only after it has been recorded or made manifest in specific form. Abbreviated *IP*. *See also*: *information law*.

intelligence   Information about events or about the activities of a government or political group gathered systematically and often covertly, especially for its value in military planning. When recorded, military intelligence usually remains classified until it becomes publicly known. *See also*: *leak*.

interactive   A computer interface designed to respond to input from a human being, usually in the form of commands and/or data. A back-and-forth dialogue between a computer program and its human user is an *interactive session*. Highly interactive systems, such as computer games, are designed to anticipate the user's needs, instead of responding in a prescribed way. Once started, a program that is *not* interactive proceeds without further human input. *See also*: *expert system*.

interactive map   A map in digital format designed to allow the user to view a portion of its surface on another scale or gain access to additional information, usually by selecting a hot spot on its surface with a pointing device such as a mouse (*example*: *Mapquest* at: www.mapquest.com).

interdisciplinary   Research or course work requiring the resources of more than one academic discipline, for example, a topic in *American studies*, a field that overlaps American history, politics, literature, art, music, popular culture, etc. Although most abstracting and indexing services limit their scope to a specific discipline (*example*: **Psychological Abstracts**) or field (**Child Development Abstracts & Bibliography**), pertinent literature from allied disciplines may also be included. Also refers to a reference work on a subject that overlaps two or more disciplines (*example*: **Encyclopedia of Violence, Peace, and Conflict**).

interdisciplinary journal   A scholarly periodical that publishes articles of primary interest to researchers in two or more specific academic disciplines or fields (*examples*: **Language & Cognitive Processes** and **Medical Engineering & Physics**). Compare with *multidisciplinary journal*.

interdisciplinary number   A class number in Dewey Decimal Classification used for works that cover a subject from the point of view of two or more disciplines, for example, **305.231** in *sociology*, reserved for interdisciplinary works on *child development*. In the schedules, such numbers are identified by a "Class here interdisciplinary works" note. They are to be used only when the author devotes a significant amount of content to the discipline in which the number is found.

interest profile   A list of keywords or descriptors selected from a subject thesaurus to represent topics of interest to the user of a current awareness service. As part of the service, regular searches are performed on the terms. Based on the results, the user is notified of the existence of new publications as soon as they are indexed, and current information is forwarded on the desired topic(s). Synonymous with *user profile*.

interface   The point or process that joins two components of a data processing system, for example, the screen display that functions as an intermediary between a software program and its human users. Some interfaces are more user-friendly than others. *See also*: *graphical user interface* and *usability*.

interlace   A decorative design in a medieval manuscript or early printed book composed of an intricate pattern of intertwined vines, snakes, animal or human limbs, or purely abstract lines, sometimes in the form of a complex knot. Interlaced designs were also used on hand-tooled leather bindings (see *Grolier binding*). Interlace was a favorite decorative motif of the scribes of Ireland and England from the 6th to 10th centuries and is also a hallmark of Islamic decorative arts, including calligraphy. *See also*: *white vine*.

interleaving   In fine editions, a protective sheet of tissue or blank paper pasted or inserted loose between a plate and a page of text to prevent rubbing. Interleaving is sometimes done with buffered paper between acidic and acid-free materials to prevent acid migration. Also refers to blank leaves that are sometimes bound between the printed pages of a book for use in note taking.

interlibrary loan (ILL)   When a book or other item needed by a registered borrower is checked out, unavailable for some other reason, or not owned by the library, a patron may request that it be borrowed from another library by filling out a printed interlibrary loan request form at a service desk, or electronically via the library's Web site. Some libraries also accept ILL requests via e-mail or by telephone, usually under exceptional circumstances. Materials borrowed on interlibrary loan may usually be renewed on or before the due date. Interlibrary loan is a form of resource sharing that depends on the maintenance of union catalogs. The largest interlibrary loan network in the world is maintained by OCLC, which uses the *WorldCat* database as its union catalog. Compare with *document delivery service* and *intralibrary loan*. *See also*: Ariel, *borrowing library*, *lending library*, and *reciprocal agreement*.

interlinear   A form of gloss in which translation, commentary, or explanatory notes are handwritten or printed above the lines of text to which they refer, usually in a different script or typeface or in letters of smaller size.

intermediary   A person or software program that functions *between* the end-user and an online bibliographic retrieval system to assist in database selection, establish telecommunication connections, formulate useful queries in correct syntax, and evaluate the relevance of information retrieved. Mediated searching is provided on request in most academic libraries by a public services librarian specially trained in online searching.

intermediate records   Records used so infrequently by an agency or individual in the conduct of business or affairs that normal operations are not hampered by their transfer to a storage area less accessible than the location where *active records* are housed. Synonymous with *semicurrent records*. *See also*: *inactive records*.

intermediate storage   In archives, a separate area where inactive or intermediate records are stored temporarily prior to final disposition, often less accessible than the location where active records are housed. Synonymous with *secondary storage*.

intern   *See*: internship.

internal document   A document, such as a memorandum or report, intended for distribution *within* an organization, rather than for wider publication. Sensitive internal documents may be classified to restrict access to authorized personnel.

International Association of Technological University Libraries (IATUL)   Founded in Germany in 1955, IATUL provides an international forum for the exchange of ideas pertinent to librarianship in technological universities and the discussion of opportunities for collaboration in the solution of common problems. Its member libraries are represented by their directors and senior managers. IATUL publishes the quarterly newsletter *IATUL News*. URL: www.iatul.org.

international copyright   Copyright protection extended to works published outside a country's borders, currently governed by national copyright law and international agreements, such as the *Berne Convention* and the *Universal Copyright Convention*.

International Copyright Information Centre (ICIC)   A clearinghouse with headquarters in Paris, established by UNESCO in 1971 to offer assistance to publishers from developing countries in securing rights to books and other publications protected by copyright in other countries. *See also*: *Copyright Clearance Center*.

International Federation of Classification Societies (IFCS)   Founded in 1985, IFCS is a federation of national, regional, and linguistically based classification societies devoted to promoting research in classification. The IFCS publishes the *IFCS Newsletter* and supports the *Journal of Classification* published by the Classification Society of North America. URL: www.classification-society.org.

International Federation of Film Archives (FIAF)   Founded in Paris in 1938, FIAF has an international membership of the world's leading museums and film archives. Its goals are to preserve the moving image in all its forms, facilitate research on the history of motion pictures, encourage the collection of documents on cinema history and film preservation, foster the accessibility and exchange of films and cinema-related material, and help create new film archives around the world. FIAF publishes the biannual *Journal of Film Preservation*. URL: www.fiafnet.org/uk. *See also*: *National Film Preservation Board*.

International Federation of Library Associations and Institutions (IFLA)   An independent international nongovernmental association of library associations, libraries and related institutions, sponsors, and individuals, IFLA was founded in 1927 by 15 countries as the International Library and Bibliographical Committee to promote global cooperation, communication, and research in library science and librarianship. With association and institutional members in over 130 countries, IFLA has a democratic structure in which a general assembly of members (the Council) is the highest governing organ. The organization maintains a Secretariat headed by a Secretary-General in The Hague and sponsors an annual conference, the World Library and Information Congress, in a different member country each year. URL: www.ifla.org.

International League of Antiquarian Booksellers (ILAB)   An organization encompassing 20 national associations representing antiquarian booksellers in 30 countries, ILAB was founded in Amsterdam in 1947 to uphold and improve professional standards in the antiquarian book trade, promote honorable conduct in business, and contribute to a broader appreciation of the art and history of the book. URL: www.ilab-lila.com.

International Literary Market Place (ILMP)   A directory of the international book publishing industry issued annually by R.R. Bowker, *ILMP* provides information on publishers, literary agents, book manufacturing, book clubs and dealers, major libraries and library associations, and literary associations, periodicals, and awards for over 180 countries. The directory also includes an industry yellow pages. The most recent edition of *ILMP* is usually shelved in the reference section of most large academic and public libraries. *See also*: Literary Market Place.

International Network of Public Libraries (INPL)   Created in 1996 by the Bertelsmann Foundation, INPL is a network of 15 public library participants with a mission of developing and nurturing innovative practices (a "think tank" for librarians). The Bertelsmann Foundation is a 26-year-old nonprofit foundation established by the multinational media publishing giant Bertelsmann AG. The network was established to facilitate cooperation and exchange of experience among public library experts across national boundaries. Membership changes on an 18-month cycle. The Foundation accepts applications from interested librarians. URL: www.public-libraries.net/en.

International Organization for Standardization (ISO)   A name derived from the Greek word *isos*, meaning "equal." Founded in London in 1947 with headquarters in Geneva, ISO is a nongovernmental federation of national standardization organizations in 130 countries, dedicated to establishing international standards to facilitate commerce and cooperation in scientific, technical, and economic endeavors. The United States is represented in ISO by the American National Standards Institute (ANSI). ISO operates through approximately 160 technical committees and 2,300 subcommittees that recommend standards and standardization policy to its national members. URL: www.iso.ch/iso/en/ISOOnline.frontpage.

International Relations Round Table (IRRT)   A round table of the American Library Association created in 1949, IRRT develops the interests of librarians in activities and problems related to international library relations by providing hospitality to visitors to the United States from the library community abroad and by facilitating communication between the International Relations Committee of the ALA and individual ALA members. URL: www.ala.org.

International Serials Data System (ISDS)   An intergovernmental network established under the auspices of UNESCO to develop and maintain an international registry of serial publications containing the information necessary for identification and bibliographic control, including the International Standard Serial Number (ISSN) and key title. The ISSN center for the United States is the National Serials Data Program (NSDP) administered by the Library of Congress (lcweb.loc.gov/issn). The ISSN International Centre located in Paris, France, maintains a Web site at: www.issn.org.

International Standard Bibliographic Description (ISBD)   A set of standards adopted in 1971 by the International Federation of Library Associations (IFLA), governing the bibliographic description of items collected by libraries. The general standard ISBD(G) serves as a guide for describing *all* types of library materials. Standards have also been developed for specific formats: ISBD(CM) for cartographic materials, ISBD(PM) for printed music, ISBD(S) for serials, etc. ISBDs have been integrated into several catalog codes around the world, including *AACR2*.

International Standard Book Number (ISBN)   A unique 10-digit standard number assigned to identify a specific edition of a book or other monographic publication issued by a given publisher, under a system recommended for international use by the International Organization for Standardization (ISO) in 1969. In the ISBN system, media such as audiorecordings, videorecordings, microfiche, and computer software are considered monographic publications, but serials, music sound recordings, and printed music are excluded because other identification systems have been developed to cover them. The ISBN is usually printed on the verso of the title page and on the back of the dust jacket of a book published in hardcover, or at the foot of the back cover in a paperback edition. In *AACR2*, the ISBN is entered in the standard number and terms of availability area of the bibliographic record.

The ISBN is divided into four parts separated by a space or hyphen: a *group identifier* one to five digits in length identifying the national, language, geographic, or other area in which the edition is published; a *publisher prefix* one to seven digits in length uniquely identifying the publisher; a *title number* one to six digits in length identifying the title, volume, or edition of the work; and a *check digit* that allows any errors in the preceding sequence to be detected by a computer. For example, in the ISBN **0-8389-0847-0**, the **0** at the beginning identifies the United States as the country of publication, the second element (**8389**) identifies the American Library Association as the publisher, the third element (**0847**) identifies the 2003 edition of the book *Metadata Fundamentals for All Librarians* by Priscilla Caplan, and the **0** at the end is the check digit. When a calculated check digit is the number 10, the letter X is used, but in the other parts of the ISBN only the arabic numerals 0–9 may be used.

The 10-digit ISBN system has a theoretical numbering capacity of 1 billion. Over the past 35 years, numbers have been assigned in over 150 countries and the rate of depletion has accelerated with the proliferation of new publishing formats. To increase numbering capacity, ISO has announced a transition to a 13-digit ISBN, to be implemented worldwide on January 1, 2007. The 13-digit number will be identical to the Bookland EAN barcoded version of the current 10-digit ISBN, which has an added 3-digit prefix and a recalculated check digit. In the United States, the allocation of publisher prefixes and the assignment of ISBNs are managed by R.R. Bowker. ISBN codes for publishers are listed in the *Publishers' International ISBN Directory* available from Bowker. To learn more about the ISBN, log on to: www.isbn.org/ standards/home/index.asp. *See also*: *International Standard Music Number* and *International Standard Serial Number*.

International Standard Music Number (ISMN)   An alphanumeric code assigned to identify printed music available for sale, hire, or free of charge. Used in music publishing, the music trade, and libraries, the ISMN uniquely identifies a title issued by a given publisher in a particular edition. The ISMN is not used for sound recordings (audiotapes, CDs, etc.), videorecordings, or books about music. Music publications issued in series can have both an International Standard Serial Number and an ISMN, the ISSN identifying the ongoing serial and the ISMN an individual title in the series. When both are assigned, the two numbers are printed clearly on the copyright page.

Composed of the letter *M* followed by nine digits, the ISMN is divided into four parts (two of which are variable length) separated by the hyphen. In the example **M-2306-7118-7**, the letter **M** distinguishes the code from standard numbers used to identify other types of material, the second part (**2306**) is a unique *publisher identifier* assigned by an *ISMN agency* coordinated by the international ISMN Agency in Berlin, the third part (**7118**) is an *item identifier* assigned by the publisher, and the fourth part (**7**) is a computer-generated check digit that allows any errors in the preceding sequence to be detected. R.R. Bowker is the independent agent for the ISMN system in the United States. URL: www.ismn-international.org. *See also*: *International Standard Book Number*.

International Standard Serial Number (ISSN)   A unique eight-digit standard number assigned by the International Serials Data System (ISDS) to identify a specific serial title, for example, **0363–0277** to identify the publication *Library Journal*. In 2001, the scope of the ISSN was extended to cover continuing resources in general. The ISSN is usually given in the masthead of each issue or on the copyright page of each volume or part of a series. When a continuing resource undergoes a title change, a new ISSN is assigned. In library cataloging under *AACR2*, the ISSN is entered in the standard number and terms of availability area of the bibliographic record. *See also*: *International Standard Book Number* and *International Standard Music Number*.

International Standard Text Code (ISTC)   A numeric code system under development by the International Organization for Standardization (ISO) for the unique identification of individual textual works (novels, short stories, plays, poems, essays, articles, etc.), to distinguish them within computer applications and to facilitate the administration of rights. The ISTC differs from most identifiers in identifying a work, rather than a specific manifestation of the work, and can therefore be used to bring together various versions of the same creative output.

Internet   The high-speed fiber-optic network of networks that uses TCP/IP protocols to interconnect computer networks around the world, enabling users to communicate via e-mail, transfer data and program files via FTP, find information on the World Wide Web, and access remote computer systems such as online catalogs and electronic databases easily and effortlessly, using an innovative technique called packet switching. The Internet began in 1969 as ARPAnet, a project of the U.S. Department of Defense. It now has hundreds of millions of regular users worldwide. The Internet Society provides *A Brief History of the Internet* at: www.isoc.org/internet/history/brief.shtml. Abbreviated *Net*. Synonymous with *information superhighway*. *See also*: *backbone* and *domain name*.

Broadly speaking, an "internet" is any group of interconnected but logically independent networks. Compare with *extranet* and *intranet*.

Internet2 (I2)   A consortium of over 200 research universities in the United States working with government and industry to develop and deploy a next-generation backbone network capable of carrying very high speed traffic and guaranteeing quality of service. The national academic and research network being built by the consortium is often called I2, although its formal name is *Abilene*. URL: www.internet2.edu.

Internet address   The unique code assigned to a specific computer connected to the Internet to identify it as a sender and/or receiver in the transmission of data or program files. Two categories of addresses are used: e-mail addresses of specific individuals (*example*: **presleyelvis@aol.com**) and the URLs of FTP sites, Telnet sites, and Web sites (*example*: **www.aol.com**). The form of Internet addresses is governed by the Domain Name System (DNS). *See also*: *IP address*.

Internet cafe   A retail business that sells coffee, snacks, and light meals and provides computer equipment and Internet access to customers while they dine, at no charge or for a reasonable fee. Some large academic and public libraries have installed such facilities on their premises to allow patrons to read their e-mail without monopolizing equipment needed in other locations for library research. To find links to Internet cafes worldwide, try a keywords search on "Internet cafes" at *Yahoo!* (www.yahoo.com). Synonymous with *cybercafe* and *netcafe*.

Internet Engineering Task Force (IETF)   A large international community of network designers, operators, vendors, and researchers concerned with the evolution of Internet architecture and the smooth operation of the Internet. The IETF is open to any interested individual. The actual technical work of protocol engineering and development is done in working groups organized by topic within several areas (routing, transport, security, etc.). Although the IETF holds meetings three times a year, much of its work is accomplished via e-mail (mailing lists). URL: www.ietf.org.

Internet Explorer   *See*: Web browser.

Internet media type   A general category of Internet content (application, image, text, audio, etc.). For each media type, a number of subtypes are defined to further refine the categorization, for example, "application/pdf," "image/tiff," and "text/sgml." The Internet media type and subtype are often used synonymously with *MIME media type*.

Internet Protocol   *See*: IP address.

Internet resource   A digital document (Web page, FTP file, e-mail message, etc.) that can be downloaded from a remote server over the Internet. Rules for cataloging Internet resources are available online from OCLC in *Cataloging Internet Resources: A*

Manual and Practical Guide, edited by Nancy Olson. Most writing style manuals have been updated to include a section on citing electronic sources ("electronic style").

Internet service provider (ISP)   A company in the business of providing Internet access to computer users who do not have a direct connection, usually via a telecommunication channel in exchange for payment of a modest monthly fee. The ISP with the largest number of subscribers is America Online (AOL). Most ISPs also provide proprietary software to facilitate use of the Internet. *See also*: *dial-up access*.

Internet TV   *See*: WebTV.

Internet use policy   *See*: acceptable use policy.

internship   A limited period of supervised training in a library or other information agency intended to facilitate the application of theory to practice following completion of formal course work toward a master's degree in library and information science. An *intern* may be paid and/or receive graduate credits based on the number of hours worked. *See also*: *M.L.I.S.* and *M.L.S.*

interoperability   The capability of a computer hardware or software system to communicate and work effectively with another system in the exchange of data, usually a system of a different type, designed and produced by a different vendor.

interpolation   Information not explicitly stated in or on an item, added to the bibliographic description of the item by the cataloger, for example, the number of pages in a book without page numbers or a publication date not given in the item but believed on the basis of investigation to be correct. In the bibliographic record, interpolations are made inside square brackets (*examples*: **[32] p**. and **[1974?]**). Compare with *extrapolation*.

Also refers to the insertion of a new subject at any point in an existing library classification system. *See also*: *hospitality*.

in-text citation   A reference to an outside source made by the writer within the text of a paper or publication, usually by enclosing name of author with page number(s) in parentheses immediately following the portion of text to which the citation refers, as opposed to indicating the source in a footnote or endnote. Proper form can be found in a suitable style manual.

intralibrary loan   The loan of an item by a library to another library within the same library system, or directly to a patron of another library within the same system, on request, usually faster than interlibrary loan if the system has its own delivery service. In some online catalogs, the user may initiate this type of transaction without staff assistance.

intranet   An in-house Web site designed to be used only by the staff or employees of an organization, institution, or commercial enterprise. Intranets use the same TCP/IP and hypertext protocols as the Internet, but access by unauthorized users is usually blocked by a firewall. Also used in a more general sense to refer to any in-house LAN or client-server system. Compare with *extranet*.

intrinsic value   *See*: archival value.

introduction   The part of a book in which the subject, purpose, and limits of the work are briefly stated, and the reader prepared for the treatment of the subject that follows in the text, usually written by the author or by a recognized authority in the field. The introduction normally appears in the front matter, following the preface or foreword, but may sometimes take the form of the first chapter. In either case, it is considered an integral part of the work and is not necessarily changed in subsequent editions, as is the preface. Abbreviated *introd*. Compare with *prologue*.

Also refers to a book written for persons unfamiliar with its subject to provide information at an elementary level, the title often beginning with the words *Introduction to . . .* or ending in the subtitle *An Introduction*.

introductory offer   A promotional tool used by book clubs to attract new subscribers by allowing the customer to select a certain number of books at a very low price (sometimes at no charge), usually from a list of popular titles, in exchange for a commitment to purchase a minimum number of additional titles within a designated period of time, usually one year.

In magazine publishing, a similar promotional device in which a heavily discounted price is offered to new subscribers, usually for a one- or two-year subscription, after which the subscriber is billed at the normal rate.

introductory price   A lower price offered by the publisher of a new book or other publication prior to the announced publication date, or for a limited period before *and* after publication, to encourage advance sales, after which the item is sold at list price. The period during which an introductory price is offered may be extended when advance orders warrant, in contrast to a prepublication price that expires on a specific date designated by the publisher.

introductory title   *See*: lead-in title.

inventory   The process of checking all the items on a library's shelves against a list of holdings to identify for replacement or deselection those missing and not checked out. A similar procedure is used to check other library property such as furniture and equipment against an authority list to identify missing items. Also refers to the list itself, which may include descriptions, quantities, prices paid, etc.

In the book trade, the total stock of materials available from a publisher, jobber, or dealer at a particular point in time. In the United States, publishers strive to keep the size of a printing as close as possible to estimated demand to avoid paying *inventory tax*, a practice that has caused books to go out of print more rapidly than they did before inventories were taxed. ***See also***: *out of stock*.

inverted heading   In indexing, a multiword heading in which conventional word order is transposed to bring the most significant word into first-word position (*example*: the Library of Congress subject heading **Combustion, Spontaneous human**).

inverted title   A title divided by a bibliographer or indexer into two parts and transposed to bring a significant word into first-word position, for use as an entry in a bibliography or as a heading in an index (*example*: ***Language and Linguistics, Dictionary of***).

invisible Web *See*: deep Web.

invoice A document or form sent to a purchaser by a vendor indicating the order number, description, quantity, price, terms of sale, method of delivery, cost of shipping, and total amount owed for items shipped and/or services rendered. Most libraries require an itemized invoice before payment can be authorized. Compare with *purchase order*. *See also*: *annual invoice* and *supplemental invoice*.

Symbols and abbreviations commonly used on publisher's invoices:

BO—back order
C or **OC**—order canceled
CWO—cash required with order
EX—see explanation or full exchange on returns
NEP or **NE**—new edition pending
NOP—not our publication
NR—nonreturnable (no returns allowed)
NYP—not yet published
OP—out of print
OPP—out of print at present
OPS—out of print, searching
OS—out of stock
OSC—out of stock, canceled
OSI—out of stock indefinitely
TOP—temporarily out of print
TOS—temporarily out of stock
W—will advise shortly
XR—nonreturnable

invoice symbol *See*: invoice.

IP *See*: intellectual property *and* IP address.

IP address IP stands for Internet Protocol, the physical address of a client or server computer attached to a network governed by the TCP/IP protocol, written as four sets of arabic numerals separated by dots (*example*: **123.456.78.9**). Each IP address has an associated alphanumeric Internet address in the Domain Name System (DNS), which is easier to remember.

IPEDS *See*: Integrated Postsecondary Education Data System.

IPM An abbreviation of *integrated pest management*. *See*: pest management.

ips An abbreviation of *inches per second*. *See*: playing speed.

IR *See*: information retrieval.

irregular The frequency of a serial publication issued at intervals of uneven length that follow no established rule. The opposite of *regular*.

irreversible A change in the chemical or physical state of an item that cannot be undone, for example, an embossed or perforated ownership mark or worming in a book. In conservation, reversibility is a priority in the treatment of materials for which the original condition is of evidential or historical value.

IRRT   *See*: International Relations Round Table.

IS   *See*: information system.

ISA   *See*: *Information Science & Technology Abstracts.*

ISAR   *See*: information storage and retrieval.

ISBD   *See*: International Standard Bibliographic Description.

ISBN   *See*: International Standard Book Number.

ISDS   *See*: International Serials Data System.

ISI   *See*: Institute for Scientific Information.

ISMN   *See*: International Standard Music Number.

ISO   *See*: International Organization for Standardization.

isogram   A line on a graph or map connecting points of equal or corresponding average value for a specific variable. *Isorithms* show amount, for example, temperature (*isotherms*), barometric pressure (*isobars*), sunshine (*isohels*), etc. *Isopleths* show frequency (hurricanes, marriages, power plants, etc.). Synonymous with *isoline*. *See also*: *choropleth map.*

isopleth   *See*: isogram.

isorithm   *See*: isogram.

ISP   *See*: Internet service provider.

ISSN   *See*: International Standard Serial Number.

issue   To produce books or other printed materials for public sale or distribution.

Also, all the copies of an edition of a book printed as a unit from the same setting of type as the first impression, with minor variations or revisions such as a redesigned title page, supplemental material added as an appendix, an updated bibliography, or a slightly different format. Also used synonymously with *state* to refer to the priority of copies within a first edition. Compare with *variant*. *See also*: *as issued* and *reissue.*

Also refers to all the copies of a newspaper or periodical published on the same date and bearing the same *issue number*. Purchase of a subscription entitles the subscriber to receive one copy of each successive issue for a prescribed period of time. In libraries, all the issues for the same publication year may be bound in one or more physical volumes, with the bibliographic volume number stamped on the spine(s), to create a back file. *See also*: *back issue, convention issue, current issue, first issue, sample issue,* and *special issue.*

issue date   The specific date or period (spring, summer, fall, winter) by which a particular issue of a serial publication is identified, usually printed on the front cover, on the same page as the table of contents, and on each page as a running foot. *See also issue number.*

issue number   The number assigned by the publisher to a separately issued part of a serial publication to distinguish it from other parts published at different times. Issue numbers are assigned consecutively, starting with the first issue of each publication period. When a serial is published in volumes, issue numbers recommence with each volume.

When an article published in a numbered issue of a periodical is cited, the issue number is usually given in the citation following the volume number and a colon or period. In the following example, the article appeared on pages 116–123 in the *third issue* of volume 9 of the journal *Research Strategies*, published in the summer of 1991:

Example:
> **O'Hanlon, Nancy. "Begin at the End: A Model for Research Skills Instruction."** *Research Strategies* **9:3 (Summer 1991), 116–123.**

ISTA   *See*: *Information Science & Technology Abstracts.*

ISTC   *See*: International Standard Text Code.

IT   *See*: information technology.

italic   A cursive form of type, first used by Aldus Manutius in an edition of Virgil printed in 1501, in which the characters slant heavily to the right. In modern printing, italic is used in combination with roman type for *emphasis* and to indicate foreign words or phrases in a text. In the preceding sentence, the word "emphasis" is in italic, and in the following sentence, the book title appears in boldface italic. Warren Chappell states in ***A Short History of the Printed Word*** (Knopf, 1970) that italic is rooted in a humanistic script known as *cancellaresca* or "chancery" that reached its highest state of development in 16th-century Italy when rounded letterforms were elongated to become elliptical. Abbreviated *ital.* or *it.*

item   *See*: bibliographic item *and* record item.

item record   In cataloging, a record attached to the bibliographic record to track a single copy of a one-volume work, or a single copy of one volume of a work published in more than one separately bound volume, after the item has been acquired and processed by the library. The item record usually indicates item type, volume number, copy number, barcode, location, price, status, applicable loan rule, and information about borrowing transactions, such as patron ID, due date, year-to-date circulation, etc. When item records are used in serials cataloging, each record usually represents a single serial title, and a separate check-in record is created to track individual issues. Compare with *holdings record. See also*: *order record.*

item type   A code in the item record for a bibliographic item in a library collection that, in conjunction with patron type, determines the loan rule applied when the item is checked out by a specific borrower. Each library or library system develops and maintains its own set of item types based on the nature of its collection(s).

iteration   A single instance of an integrating resource, either as first published or as subsequently updated (*AACR2*).

iterative search   A search for information in which the researcher or investigator repeatedly poses questions until an answer or solution is found.

J

jacket   *See*: dust jacket *and* sleeve.

jacket cover   A removable covering made of thin, transparent, flexible plastic designed to fit over the dust jacket of a book published in hardcover, to extend the life of the binding and enhance the visual appeal of the jacket design, available from library suppliers in a range of sizes. Used more extensively in public and school libraries than in academic and special libraries, it allows the outside surface of a book to be easily cleaned with a damp rag or paper towel and disinfectant cleaning solution. The ends should be securely fastened to the cover with adhesive tape of a type that can be removed without damage.

jade book   A book consisting of text inscribed on thin jade tablets strung together on one or more cords, a luxury format reserved in traditional Chinese society for the most highly esteemed texts.

Japanese style   *See*: Chinese style.

jargon   The specialized vocabulary and idioms of a group of people engaged in the same activity or line of work, for example, the "MARCese" used by library catalogers in reference to the bibliographic record and its component fields. In a more general sense, speech that is unintelligible or incoherent. Compare with *slang*.

Java   A high-level programming language widely used for writing application software for the World Wide Web. Introduced in 1995 by Sun Microsystems, Java enables programs to run on a Java-enabled Web browser regardless of platform (Windows, Macintosh, or UNIX), eliminating the need to write platform-specific versions of the same program. Netscape developed the JavaScript language to make programming in Java easier, especially in the design of interactive Web pages, but it is less powerful and limits the designer to the HTML interface. Sun Microsystems maintains a Web page on Java at: java.sun.com. *See also*: *applet*.

JavaScript   *See*: *Java*.

jeremiad   A fierce denunciation of a particular evil, or the evils of society in general, in which current misfortunes are considered a just penalty for past misdeeds and repentance extolled as the only road to a happier, more secure future. The term is derived from the *Lamentations of Jeremiah* in the Old Testament. The sermons of Puritan preachers in colonial New England provide abundant examples of this literary form.

jestbook   A collection of jokes, witty anecdotes, epigrams, exempla, and ribald tales, usually with didactic endings. Introduced into Europe from the Muslim world during the 8th century, jestbooks enjoyed greatest popularity during the 16th and 17th centuries. Because of their ephemeral nature, few early examples survive. Also spelled *jest book*. Synonymous with *facetiae*.

jeweled binding   A binding in which the boards are covered in designs done in gold or silver inset with ivory and/or precious or semiprecious stones, usually with a similarly decorated clasp to keep the leaves pressed firmly together. During the Middle Ages, this style was used for liturgical and devotional books commissioned by the Catholic Church and by members of the nobility from the 6th century on. The lavish use of costly materials was considered an act of religious piety rather than ostentation, and the colors of the gems often had symbolic significance. Extremely valuable, the rare survivals are sold by the world's most prestigious auction houses. Jeweled binding underwent a revival in the late 19th and early 20th centuries. Compare with *treasure binding*.

jobber   In the United States, a wholesaler that stocks large quantities of new books and nonprint materials (audiobooks, videotapes, music CDs, etc.) issued by various publishers and supplies them to retail bookstores and libraries on order, usually at a substantial discount (10–40 percent). Titles out of print from the publisher may still be available in limited quantity from a book jobber. Large jobbers also offer customized services such as continuation orders, approval plans, cataloging, technical processing, etc. Using a book jobber allows a library to operate more efficiently by consolidating orders. Directory information on book wholesalers is available in the reference serial *Literary Market Place*. Synonymous in the UK with *library supplier*. Compare with *dealer*. **See also**: *Baker & Taylor* and *Ingram*.

job description   A detailed description of the duties and responsibilities associated with a specific position in an organization, used in training, performance evaluation, and the allocation of workload. Compare with *position description*.

job lot   Copies of a book or other publication offered by the publisher at lower than list price to a wholesale bookseller known as a *jobber*, usually to reduce or close out stock of the title. Compare with *remainders*.

job rotation   The systematic movement of employees from one job to another within an organization or between organizations usually to a new position for a fixed period of time and then back to the former position. Uncommon in libraries, the practice has been tried with veteran librarians in both public and academic libraries. Participants report that the voluntary experience can provide a broader perspective on the profession, clarify job content and process, lead to improvements in procedures and collections, enhance capacity to cope with change, provide networking opportunities, and renew commitment. Rotation can be particularly rewarding for employees at risk of stagnation, whose careers have reached a plateau. Disadvantages include temporary loss of productivity and increased stress for co-workers. Planning can mitigate negative effects. Compare with *job sharing*.

job sharing   An alternative work arrangement in which two qualified people are hired to fill a single full-time, often permanent, position, sharing duties and responsibilities usually according to a prearranged schedule. The voluntary practice began in the 1970s as a means of accommodating talented women who wished to pursue careers while rearing a family. Unlike most part-time employment, job sharing includes benefits (salary and benefits are usually prorated). The arrangement often increases job satisfaction and enhances productivity, reducing absenteeism and turnover and providing coverage for vacations, illnesses, conference attendance, etc. Communication needs are often met by scheduling a few hours of overlap between participants. Compare with *job rotation*.

joint   In bookbinding, the narrow portion of covering material affixed directly to the endpaper along the groove separating the board from the inlay over the spine, forming the hinge that allows the cover to open and close like a door. A book has a *front joint* connecting the front board to the spine and a *back joint* connecting the back board to the spine. On the inside, the hinge is formed by the fold in the endpaper, reinforced in some editions with a cloth strip.

joint author   In *AACR2*, a person who collaborates with one or more others to produce a work in which all who contribute perform the same function. The contributions of the individual collaborators may not be indicated and are usually not separable. In cataloging, the main entry is made under the name of the author listed first on the chief source of information (the *primary author*), with added entries for the other authors, unless the primary responsibility clearly rests with one author. Bibliographic style manuals differ in the maximum number of joint authors included in a citation. Synonymous with *coauthor*. Compare with *composite work*. **See also**: *et al.* and *shared responsibility*.

joint imprint   The imprint of two or more publishers appearing on the title page of the same edition of a work. In most instances, the co-publishers market and distribute the work in different countries or regions of the world. For a recent example, see *The Great Libraries: From Antiquity to the Renaissance*, published in 2000 by Oak Knoll Press and The British Library and assigned separate ISBNs for the United States and the United Kingdom.

joint pseudonym   *See*: pseudonym.

joint publication   Publication (by prior agreement) of the same work by two different publishers in separate editions, often in hardcover by a university press and in paperback by a trade publisher. Compare with *co-edition*. **See also**: *simultaneous publication*.

joint use   A cooperative arrangement between a library and another institution, such as a school, community college, or university, in which both institutions share the same facility and/or collections, for example, the Dr. Martin Luther King, Jr. Library in San Jose, California, a partnership between the City of San Jose and San Jose State University in which the San Jose Public Library and the University library share the same building and collections.

journal   A periodical devoted to disseminating original research and commentary on current developments within a specific discipline, subdiscipline, or field of study (*example*: ***Journal of Clinical Epidemiology***), usually published in quarterly, bimonthly, or monthly issues sold by subscription. Journal articles are usually written by the person (or persons) who conducted the research. Longer than most magazine articles, they almost always include a bibliography or list of works cited at the end. In journals in the sciences and social sciences, an abstract usually precedes the text of the article, summarizing its content. Most scholarly journals are peer-reviewed. Scholars often use a current contents service to keep abreast of the journal literature in their fields of interest and specialization. *See also*: *impact factor*.

A library usually binds all the issues for a given publication year in one or more annual volumes or converts its print issues to microform. Articles from some journals are available in digital format in full-text bibliographic databases, usually by licensing agreement. Some journal publishers also provide an electronic version accessible via the World Wide Web. Abbreviated *jour*. Compare with *journal of commentary* and *magazine*. *See also*: *archival journal, commercial journal, core journal, early journal, electronic journal, hybrid journal, interdisciplinary journal, letters journal, library journal, methods journal, multidisciplinary journal, synoptic journal, technical journal*, and *trade journal*.

Also refers to a record of events, experiences, thoughts, and observations kept on a regular basis by an individual for personal use. Writers often keep a daily journal to record ideas and material that may subsequently be incorporated into their works. Synonymous in this sense with *diary*.

journalese   The rather trite style of writing used by some newspaper and broadcast journalists who rely on clichés and hackneyed expressions to pitch a story to the widest possible audience ("rattlesnake roundup rattles rights groups"), avoided in serious journalism.

journalism   The art of gathering news, writing and editing copy, or directing the publication of a newspaper, magazine, or journal. A person who turns news into copy is a *journalist* (also refers to the person who keeps a journal or diary). A photographer who specializes in capturing news on camera is a *photojournalist*. In the United States, Pulitzer Prizes are awarded annually for distinguished public service in journalism and for reporting in a variety of categories (feature writing, commentary, criticism, editorial writing, cartooning, and photography).

journalist   *See*: journalism.

journal of commentary   A periodical that specializes in the publication of news analysis and discussion of political, social, and cultural issues, usually from an editorial position somewhere on the political spectrum, for example, the *National Review* on the Right or *The Progressive* on the Left. Journals of commentary are usually issued monthly and sold at newsstands, in bookstores, and by subscription. Compare with *journal* and *magazine*.

journal pagination In journal publishing, page numbers often begin with the first page of the first issue in a volume and continue in a single numeric sequence through the last page of the last issue in the volume. This means that the pagination in each issue (except the first) begins where the previous issue ended. Since most journals are published quarterly and bound into annual volumes, continuous pagination makes it easier for the user to find a specific article by page number in the appropriate volume. Compare with *magazine pagination*.

journals consortium An organization that handles the production and distribution of a number of journals but does not necessarily exercise editorial control over them if they are owned by other organizations. In the United States, perhaps the best-known example is the journals publishing division of the Johns Hopkins University Press, which provides online access through *Project MUSE* to the full-text of its own journals, plus 60 titles from other scholarly publishers.

JPEG An acronym that stands for **J**oint **P**hotographic **E**xperts **G**roup, a standard for compressing still images in digital format at ratios of 100:1 and higher. Data compression is accomplished by dividing the image into small blocks of pixels, halved again and again until the desired ratio is reached. Data is lost each time the compression ratio increases. Pronounced "jay-peg." Compare with *MPEG*. *See also*: *GIF* and *TIFF*.

JSTOR A nonprofit organization that began as a digital text initiative of the Andrew W. Mellon Foundation aimed at easing the space problems faced by libraries that own long runs of journal backfiles, ***JSTOR*** provides searchable bibliographic databases containing the complete full-text of core scholarly journals in a wide range of disciplines, current to within 2–5 years. URL: www.jstor.org. *See also*: *Project MUSE*.

jukebox *See*: CD-ROM changer.

jumbo file A collection of prints, pictures, and/or documents of unusually large size, organized for ease of access in a folder, portfolio, or other container of a size sufficient to accommodate them.

jump page The page of a newspaper, magazine, or journal on which a story or article that begins on the first page (or near the front of the issue) is continued, usually indicated by the references "Continued on page . . ." and "Continued from page . . ." at the break in the text.

junk mail Unwanted e-mail messages, usually advertising not solicited by the recipient. *See also*: *spam*.

juried *See*: peer-reviewed.

justification In typesetting, the equal and exact spacing of words and letters in a line of type to make the text block appear vertically even at the right- and/or left-hand margins. Type aligned with the left margin is said to be *left-justified*. Aligned with the right-hand margin, it is said to be *right-justified*. Type can also be *centered* on a page, as in headings. Compare with *alignment*. *See also*: *ragged*.

justified   *See*: justification.

juvenile collection   A library collection of books and other materials intended specifically for children under 12–13 years of age, shelved separately from the adult and young adult collections, sometimes in a children's room with separate sections for juvenile fiction and nonfiction, beginning readers and easy books, picture books, and books for very young children (alphabet books, counting books, board books, cloth books, etc.). Juvenile collections are usually managed by a librarian with specialized training in children's services. *See also*: *Association for Library Service to Children*.

juvenile literature   *See*: children's literature.

juveniles   A term used by publishers and serious collectors to refer to children's books as a type of publication. Compare with *juvenilia*.

juvenilia   Works produced during the childhood or youth of an artist or writer, which may reveal literary or artistic immaturity but often compensate with an abundance of youthful enthusiasm and a style or approach that is highly innovative (*example*: ***Evelyn*** by Jane Austen).

K

kanji   A subset of approximately 5,000 Chinese ideograms borrowed or adapted by the Japanese for use in their own written language. In 1946, the Japanese government selected a smaller subset of 1,850 for use in official publications and in newspaper/ magazine publishing. Also refers to any one of these loan characters.

keep down   In typesetting, an instruction to the typesetter to use capital letters sparingly in the titles of works mentioned in the text. The opposite of *keep up*.

keepsake   An item given or kept as a memento, especially something printed for distribution by a club or organization on a special occasion (commemorative dinner, dance, concert, etc.). Also used synonymously with *giftbook*.

keep up   In typesetting, an instruction to the typesetter to use capital letters at the beginning of each word of the title of any work mentioned in the text. Prepositions, conjunctions, and initial articles are usually *kept down*, making "The Adventures of Huckleberry Finn" an *all up* setting. In modern British practice, only the first word and proper names are capitalized ("The adventures of Huckleberry Finn"). In French, only the first word following the initial article and proper names are capitalized. In Italian, only the initial article is capitalized. In German, all nouns are capitalized. The opposite of *keep down*.

Kelmscott Press   A private press founded in 1891 by the architect, designer, writer, calligrapher, and typographer William Morris (1834–96), who sought to revive, in modern book production, the aesthetic of the medieval period and early printing. Although the press survived only until 1894, the 53 books it issued set a very high standard of beauty and craftsmanship. For more information about the Kelmscott Press, please see the entry in *A Dictionary of Book History* (Oxford University Press, 1986) by John Feather. For images of works produced by the Press, see the exhibit catalog *William Morris and the Art of the Book* published in 1976 by The Morgan Library.

kerf   A shallow groove cut into the binding edge of the sections of a book, perpendicular to the spine near the head and tail of the text block, to allow the kettle stitching to be recessed. Also spelled *cerf*.

Kermit   An asynchronous communication protocol developed and maintained by the Kermit Project at Columbia University that enables files to be transferred from one computer system to another. Accurate, flexible, and customizable, Kermit includes terminal emulation and can be installed on almost any operating system. Although it is not in the public domain, Columbia University allows Kermit to be used as shareware but encourages users to purchase the product in support of the Project. URL: www.columbia.edu/kermit.

kern   The portion of the face of a unit of type that extends beyond the edge of its body to overlap an adjacent character, for example, the lowercase italic *f* in many typefaces. *Kerning* also refers to the practice in typesetting of backspacing to tuck one character into another to avoid the appearance of irregular spacing in a line. Pairs of letters close-fitted in this way include *AT*, *AV*, *Ta*, *Wa*, etc. The term is also used in type-setting for the practice of reducing the space between characters to make copy fit a given line length.

kettle stitch   In hand-binding, a special end stitch taken near the head and foot of each section to lock the sewing thread after it passes down the fold, linking adjacent sections through their folds and producing two rows of kettle stitches perpendicular to the binding edge, one near the top and the other at the bottom of the spine. In some editions, a shallow groove called a *kerf* is cut into the binding edge at each end of the spine to recess the kettle stitching. Synonymous with *catch stitch*.

keyboard   A thin, flat peripheral device that allows a computer user to enter input by manually depressing keys marked with letters, numerals, and special characters. The keys can be arranged in a single set of parallel rows or split into two sets of rows (fixed or adjustable) to make them more ergonomic. A computer keyboard can be built in, as in a laptop, or a separate piece of equipment, as in most desktop personal computers.

key control   The process of establishing and maintaining the list of persons authorized to access keys to the door locks and lockable equipment in a library, as a means of securing the facility's locking system. A full survey of all locks and lock locations must first be conducted and an inventory made of all existing keys. Then key distribution is carefully recorded, including keys retrieved from employees who leave library employment. Access to master keys is limited to essential personnel, using a two-key system in areas where security is especially important (rare books, special collections, computer equipment rooms, etc.). When not in use, keys are stored in a secure cabinet, with a log for recording name of borrower, date of issue, and date of return.

keypad   A small handheld infrared device used in large-screen demonstrations of online systems to enable the instructor to control electronic equipment installed on the demonstration console. Also, the part of a full-size computer keyboard consisting of a set of programmable numeric keys, usually arranged in four rows on the far right-hand side.

Also refers to a security device consisting of a small set of numeric keys, usually mounted on a wall near a door, to allow the automatic alarm system to be deactivated and reactivated by a person typing a valid authorization code.

key title   The unique name assigned to a serial publication by the centers of the ISSN Network under the International Serials Data System (ISDS), usually (but not always) the same as the title proper. In library cataloging, the key title is entered immediately following the ISSN in the bibliographic record. If there is no ISSN, the key title is not added. Also spelled *key-title*.

keyword(s)   A significant word or phrase in the title, subject headings (descriptors), contents note, abstract, or text of a record in an online catalog or bibliographic database that can be used as a search term in a free-text search to retrieve all the records containing it. *See also*: *stopword*.

Most online catalogs and bibliographic databases include an option that allows the user to type words that describe the research topic (in any order) and retrieve records containing the search terms in the data fields the system is designed to search whenever the keywords option is selected. One disadvantage of a keywords search is that it does not take into account the *meaning* of the words used as input, so if a term has more than one meaning, irrelevant records (false drops) may be retrieved. Keywords are also used as access points in *KWAC*, *KWIC*, and *KWOC* indexing. *See also*: *Boolean* and *truncation*.

keyword index   A type of subject index in which significant words, usually from the titles of the works indexed, are used as headings. When a string of keywords is rotated, such an index is said to be *permuted*. *See also*: *KWAC*, *KWIC*, and *KWOC*.

kickstool   A step stool designed to move on casters when gently pushed, often available in the stacks of libraries that have shelving too high to be reached by persons of average height. Many libraries in the United States favor a circular metal design with casters that retract under the downward pressure of a person's weight, a rubber bumper around the bottom that grabs the floor for steadier footing, and a nonskid plastic top tread for safety. Some models also have a rubber belly band to protect adjacent furniture from scratches and dents. Metal kickstools are available from library suppliers in a variety of colors to match interior decor.

Kilgour, Frederick G. (1914–   )   A chemistry major at Harvard University, Frederick Kilgour worked at the Harvard University Library from 1935 to 1942, then as chief of the Interdepartmental Committee of the Office of Strategic Services (OSS), where he applied his knowledge and experience to the problem of importing strategic enemy publications for military use during World War II. He served in the intelligence branch of the U.S. State Department after the war, then worked as librarian at the Yale Medical Library from 1948 to 1965 and was Associate Librarian for Research and Development at the Yale University Library in 1967 when offered the position of executive officer of the fledgling Ohio College Library Center (OCLC), an initiative of the Ohio College Association to make the books and journals of academic libraries in Ohio available to students and faculty at all the state's colleges and universities.

To achieve that goal, an online union catalog of the holdings of 37 Ohio academic libraries was created in 1971, dramatically decreasing the cost of cataloging in Ohio and later throughout the United States when the system was expanded. In 1978, an Interlibrary Loan Subsystem was added to the union catalog. OCLC evolved into the Online Computer Library Center and has grown into the largest bibliographic utility in the world. Kilgour ended his career as distinguished research professor at the University of North Carolina at Chapel Hill. *See also*: *Frederick G. Kilgour Award for Research in Library and Information Technology.*

kilobyte   *See*: byte.

kinescope   A motion picture made by filming the images displayed on a television monitor.

kiosk   A small circular pavilion, usually located near the entrance to a library, used for displaying announcements, dust jackets removed from new books, reading lists, comments and suggestions from library users (sometimes with responses from library administration), and other information concerning library operations and programs. *See also*: *bulletin board.*

Also refers to a free-standing furnishing equipped with a multimedia computer to allow users to retrieve information "on the run" via a touch screen, used in airports and other public locations to provide directions, scheduling information, etc.

Kirkus Reviews   Published since 1933 under various titles, *Kirkus Reviews* is a semi-monthly review publication covering books for adults, young adults, and children. ISSN: 0042–6598.

kit   A set of related materials in more than one medium designed to be used as a unit with no single medium predominating, often stored in a container to keep the parts together. The category includes laboratory kits and packages of curriculum materials. In *AACR2*, the term also applies to a single-medium package of textual material, for example, a press kit or set of printed test materials. In academic libraries, instructional kits are usually housed in the curriculum room. Synonymous with *multimedia item.* Compare with *game.*

KLIATT   Published since 1967, *KLIATT* reviews paperback books, hardcover fiction, audiobooks, and educational CD-ROMs and software recommended for libraries and classrooms serving young adults. Each bimonthly issue also includes a feature article. ISSN: 1065–8602. URL: www.hometown.aol.com/Kliatt.

knowledge   Information that has been comprehended and evaluated in the light of experience and incorporated into the knower's intellectual understanding of the subject. *See also*: *epistemology.*

known-item search   A search in a library for a specific work, as opposed to a search for *any* work by a known author or for works on a particular subject. If the title of the work is known, the easiest way to locate a copy is to search a library catalog or bibliographic database by title. When the user is uncertain of the precise wording of the title, the best strategy may be to search by author's name. If at least two or three significant words in the title are known with certainty, a keywords search may retrieve an entry for the work.

kraft paper   A heavy, unbleached grade of coarse paper, usually mocha brown in color, used for paper bags and wrapping paper because of its strength and fold endurance and also for the outer wrapper on magazines to protect the glossy cover from damage in mailing. In binding, a narrow strip of kraft paper may be used as a *liner* to reinforce the layer of thin fabric (known as *crash* or *super*) applied with adhesive to the binding edge of the sewn sections to hold them firmly together.

Kunstlerroman   From the German word *Kunstler* ("artist") and the French word *roman* ("novel"), a novel that traces the growth of a writer's creative genius from childhood to maturity, with particular attention to major trials and obstacles and their influence on the development of the artist's character and work (*example*: *A Portrait of the Artist as a Young Man* by James Joyce). Compare with *Bildungsroman*.

KWAC   An acronym for *Keyword and Context* (also known as *Keyword alongside Context*), an algorithmically generated index in which keywords from the title (and sometimes the text) of a document are printed as headings along the left-hand margin of the page, with the portion of the title or text following each keyword indented under the heading, followed by the portion of the title or text preceding the word. Unlike KWOC indexing, this method preserves multiword terms and phrases in the alphanumeric sequence of headings. Compare with *KWIC*.

Example:
   academic
      support systems for distance learning. Libraries and
   distance
      learning. Libraries and academic support systems for
   learning
      Libraries and academic support systems for distance
   libraries
      and academic support systems for distance learning

KWIC   An acronym for *Keyword in Context*, a type of permuted index in which the title of a document (and sometimes the text) is used to illustrate the meaning of a keyword used as an entry. Tagged by hand or extracted from the document algorithmically, keywords are printed in alphabetical order at a fixed position in a line of fixed length (usually at the center), so that they appear in a column with as much of the context as can be accommodated preceding and following each word. The keywords in the column may be distinguished typographically to make them easier to read. Keyword and context are usually coded to identify the document indexed. Compare with *KWAC* and *KWOC*.

Example:
   Libraries and   **ACADEMIC** support systems for distance learning.
   ort systems for   **DISTANCE** learning. Libraries and academic supp
   ems for distance   **LEARNING**. Libraries and academic support syst
   stance learning.   **LIBRARIES** and academic support systems for di

KWOC   An acronym for *Keyword out of Context*, a variation on the KWIC (Keyword in Context) index, in which keywords extracted algorithmically from the title of a document (and sometimes the text) are printed as headings along the left-hand margin of the page, with the titles or portions of text containing each keyword indented under the corresponding heading. A symbol may be substituted for the keyword in the string of text. Unlike KWAC indexing, this method does *not* preserve multiword terms and phrases in the alphanumeric sequence of headings.

Example:

libraries

academic support systems for distance learning. **Libraries** and distance learning. **Libraries** and academic support systems for learning. **Libraries** and academic support systems for distance support systems for distance learning. **Libraries** and academic systems for distance learning. **Libraries** and academic support

L

LA *See*: Library Association.

lab *See*: instruction lab.

label A small paper form on which information can be written, typed, or printed, designed to be affixed to the surface of an item such as a book, usually for purposes of identification or classification. Libraries use labels extensively in technical processing. They are available precut from library suppliers in various colors, shapes, and sizes, either blank or preprinted, with or without adhesive backing. Labeling tape is also available for making customized labels mechanically. When labels are used in preservation, they should be acid-free. In a broader sense, any identifying mark attached to a thing, usually to set it apart or provide information to those using or viewing it (see *labeling*). *See also*: *spine label*.

    Also refers to a piece of material (leather, parchment, or paper) not integral to the cover of a book that is printed, stamped, or engraved, usually with the title and name of author, and affixed to the spine or front cover.

labeling The controversial practice of affixing a warning mark or label to library materials considered unsuitable for young children or that contain language or images that some readers or viewers might find offensive or distressing. The practice is followed by some public television stations in the United States when programs containing adult language or graphic images of sex and/or violence are broadcast at times when children are likely to be watching. *See also*: *content rating*.

lab manual A book of exercises that includes instructions for laboratory experiments to be carried out, usually under the supervision of an instructor, by a student enrolled in a course in the sciences, often published in softcover in conjunction with a textbook.

lacing in In hand-binding, the attachment of the sewing supports to the boards. In early Coptic bindings, this was done by lacing the sewing threads through pre-bored holes in the edges of the boards and tying them down. In medieval bindings, thongs or cords were threaded through grooves called "channels" cut into the boards and secured with pegs or nails. When pasteboard replaced wooden boards, the cords were threaded through holes pierced in the pasteboard and the ends attached by various means.

lacquered   A 19th-century style of bookbinding in which the covers, decorated in metalwork or papier mâché, were protected by layers of resinous varnish given a high polish. Lacquer ware was introduced into Europe and the United States from China and Japan.

lacuna   A gap in a library collection, usually in the holdings on a specific subject or by a particular author, which the library seeks to fill in order to meet the needs of its users. Also refers to a missing portion of a page, or missing pages, in a manuscript or text, especially when caused by damage or normal wear and tear. Plural: *lacunae*.

lai   In medieval French literature of the late 12th to 13th century, a short poem composed in octasyllabic couplets. Provençal lais were love poems composed to be sung to music. Marie de France, who wrote in old French at the court of Henry II (Plantagenet), is famous for her short romantic narratives on themes drawn from Arthurian and other Celtic legends. The International Marie de France Society provides the text of some of her lais at: www.people.vcu.edu/~cmarecha.

The term *lay* was also used by English poets of the 18th and 19th centuries in reference to a song or relatively short narrative poem with romance or adventure as its central theme (*example*: **Lay of the Last Minstrel** by Sir Walter Scott).

laid in   A single sheet inserted but not glued into a book or other printed publication. Compare with *integral*.

Also used in a note in a catalog entry to indicate a leaflet or pamphlet included in a record album or musical publication, usually containing information about the contents.

laid paper   Handmade paper that, when held up to a light source, reveals a grid of fine, faintly translucent parallel lines intersecting at right angles, made by the wires of the papermaking mold. The same effect is achieved in machine-made paper by the dandy roll, a cylinder that smoothes the surface and impresses designs such as the watermark and countermark. Although it is more elegant in appearance, laid paper is not superior to other papers in a practical sense. Compare with *wove paper*.

LAMA   *See*: Library Administration and Management Association.

Lambda Book Report   A monthly review publication published by the Lambda Literary Foundation, a nonprofit organization supporting gay and lesbian literature. The Foundation also sponsors the annual Lamda Literary Awards and Behind Our Masks, an annual writers conference. ISSN: 1048–9487. URL: www.lambdalit.org.

lamination   A method of preserving old and fragile documents by adhering a layer of thin transparent plastic film to one or both sides of each sheet by the application of pressure and/or heat, sealing the surface against dust and atmospheric conditions. Processes of deterioration inherent in the object are not arrested by lamination. Encapsulation is preferred in preservation work because it is reversible. Lamination is also used in libraries to protect and enhance the appearance of dust jackets on hardcover books and the covers of paperbacks. Available in rolls from library suppliers, *laminate* is applied by hand or on a machine called a *laminator*.

lampoon   A biting satire written in prose or verse, usually directed against an individual in public life or an institution that has become the object of public scrutiny. Lampoons written in verse were popular in England during the 18th century. The form was given new life in 20th century by publications such as the *Harvard Lampoon* and its close relative, the *National Lampoon*. Because this form of humor exposes its subject(s) to public ridicule, libel laws impose restraint. *See also*: *caricature*.

LAN   *See*: local area network.

landmark building   A library facility preserved because it has architectural and historical significance, for example, the New York Public Library building at 5th Avenue and 42nd Street in Manhattan, which houses the humanities and social sciences research collections. Designed in the beaux-arts style by John Merven Carrère and Thomas Hastings and constructed on the site of the old Croton Reservoir, the building opened in the spring of 1911.

landscape binding   A book with a decorative panel on the front cover bearing a picture of scenery. The horizon of the landscape is sometimes aligned with the spine to give the artist greater breadth of field.

language   The system of conventional sounds and symbols developed over time by a specific human population as a means of expressing and exchanging thoughts, feelings, information, and knowledge. A language consists of a vocabulary and rules of grammar, syntax, and orthography. A *national language* is the official language of a specific country, used in its government publications and educational institutions. Some countries have more than one national language, for example, Canada where both English and French are officially recognized.

In library cataloging, the language in which a work is written or spoken is indicated by a three-letter code in the 041 (Language code) field of the MARC record. A note is made in the bibliographic record only when the language of the text is not apparent from the rest of the bibliographic description, as in the case of a film subtitled in a language different from that of the dialogue or narration. In some online catalogs and bibliographic databases, it is possible to limit search results by language. The *MARC Code List for Languages* is available online at: lcweb.loc.gov/marc/languages. Abbreviated *lang*. *See also*: *artificial language*, *indexing language*, *natural language*, *original language*, and *programming language*.

language code   One of a set of over 450 three-letter lowercase codes developed for use in the 041 (Language code) field and in other fields of the MARC record to indicate the modern or ancient language in which a work is written or spoken. In most cases, the code is the first three letters of the English name of the language as it appears in the *Library of Congress Subject Headings* (*example*: **ger** for German) or the initial letters of the parts of the language name (**goh** for German, Old High). Usually only one code is provided for a given language, even if that language can be written in more than one set of characters; however, in a few cases, separate codes are provided for the same spoken language written in different characters. Some individual languages are assigned a *group code* because it is not practical to establish a separate code for each (**myn** for Mayan languages). A list of the MARC language codes is available online at: lcweb.loc.gov/marc/languages. The Library of Congress has been designated the registration authority for processing requests for alpha-3 language codes comprising the ISO 639-2 international standard *Codes for the Representation of Names of Languages—Part 2: Alpha-3 Code* (www.loc.gov/standards/iso639-2).

language dictionary   A reference work that lists the words of a language in alphabetical order, providing information about orthography, syllabication, pronunciation, etymology and history, definition, standard usage, abbreviation, and sometimes synonyms and antonyms. Language dictionaries differ in period of the language covered, extent and characteristics of the vocabulary included (slang, idioms, etc.), amount of illustration (see *visual dictionary*), and special features. The division of dictionaries of the English language into American and English reflects slight differences in spelling, pronunciation, and usage.

A *foreign language dictionary* lists the words of a language in alphabetical order, with each entry containing a translation of the word into a second language. Some are divided into two parts, giving translation into a second language, and vice versa. Foreign language dictionaries are often published in pocket-size for the convenience of travelers. Visual foreign language dictionaries are available for some languages. Compare with *thesaurus*. ***See also***: *polyglot dictionary*.

lapsit services   Library services and programs designed for very young children (12–24 months old) in conjunction with their adult caregivers, including nursery rhymes, songs, finger plays, and storytelling, often with the aid of a flannel board or puppets.

laptop   A small, portable battery-operated personal computer, usually equipped with a built-in keyboard and mouse and a flat panel monitor that folds over the keyboard to form a cover. Modern research libraries are retrofitting study areas to provide network connectivity for patrons who use laptops, and some academic libraries are installing them in classrooms used for bibliographic instruction. Synonymous with *notebook*. Compare with *personal digital assistant*. ***See also***: *docking station*.

large paper copy   A copy of a book printed on paper of larger size (and usually finer quality) than the rest of the edition, for use as a presentation copy or to be sold by subscription or at a higher price. Large paper copies are printed in small numbers from the same setting of type (usually following copies of regular size) for simultaneous publication. According to John Carver (*ABC for Book Collectors*, Oak Knoll, 1995), the term was used synonymously during the 18th century with *fine*, *royal*, and *imperial paper copy*. Compare with *large paper edition*.

large paper edition   An edition printed from the same setting of type as the trade edition but on leaves of larger size (and usually paper of superior quality), making the margins wider than normal. Limited and deluxe editions are often printed in this way. Compare with *large paper copy*.

large print (LP)   Any type size larger than 16-point. Also refers to books printed in type larger than the 9-, 10-, or 11-point size normally used for text, mostly publications for visually impaired, elderly, and young readers (picture books, beginning readers, etc.). The National Association for Visually Handicapped has established standards for LP materials. English-language LP materials currently in print (and forthcoming) are listed in *The Complete Directory of Large Print Books and Serials*, a biennial reference serial published by R.R. Bowker, arranged by subject (with author and title indexes) and printed in 14-point type to accommodate use by sight-impaired readers.

laser disk   *See*: optical disk.

laser pointer   A small battery-operated metal wand about the size of a fountain pen, designed to project a narrow laser beam of intense red light onto a wall screen or other display surface, in daylight or a darkened room, from a distance of over 100 yards, used for emphasis by speakers during presentations including visual aids. Most models include a pocket clip or come with a carrying case.

laser printer   An output device introduced by IBM in 1975 that uses a laser beam and electrostatic imaging to print text and/or image(s) by transferring and fusing toner to the surface of paper, one sheet at a time. Resolution is determined by the spot size of the laser. Print quality is superior to that of dot-matrix and ink-jet printers. Hewlett-Packard is currently the major manufacturer of personal laser printers, from low-end desktop models, capable of printing 4 to 8 pages per minute, to large office units, capable of printing up to 32 pages per minute.

latchkey child   A young person left unattended by a parent or other adult caregiver, at home or in a public place. In libraries, the presence and behavior of latchkey children may create disciplinary problems and pose issues of legal liability. In the United States, many libraries require children under a certain age (usually 9 or 10) to be accompanied by an adult. However, public libraries that perceive such children as an opportunity rather than a problem, and invest in programs that reach out to them, often experience a decline in problem behavior and improved community relations. The child benefits from homework help and learns to value the library as a welcoming and nurturing place.

latest entry   A method of cataloging serials that have undergone title changes, in which the bibliographic description is based on the most recent issue, with the publication's relationship to earlier titles established in explanatory notes or by added entries. This convention was followed under the *ALA Rules* but replaced in *AACR* by successive entry cataloging of serials. *AACR2 2002* prescribes latest entry cataloging for integrating resources. Compare with *earliest entry*.

latin   A general term used in typography to refer to all typefaces that have their origin in the Latin alphabet, as opposed to those that do not (Arabic, Chinese, Greek, Hebrew, etc.). Also refers to typefaces that have wedge-serifs.

Laubach Literacy (LL)   A nonprofit educational corporation dedicated to helping adults of all ages improve their lives and communities by learning essential literacy skills (reading, writing, math, and problem solving). Its publishing division, New

Readers Press, distributes over 500 titles to literacy programs, libraries, schools, prisons, and religious organizations in the United States. LL is an affiliate of the American Library Association. URL: www.laubach.org/home.html.

lavage   Erasure by washing a sheet, roll, or leaves to remove the ink. In Antiquity and the early Christian period, the method was applied to papyrus manuscripts. To erase text written on parchment or vellum, rubbing with an abrasive such as pumice was required.

law binding   A style of binding used for law books in which the boards are covered in leather or imitation leather of a medium to light color, with two contrasting bands of a darker color on the spine (usually dark red, green, or blue).

law library   A type of special library with a collection consisting primarily of materials for legal research and study, including case law, federal and state statutes, international legal agreements, treatises, reference works, legal periodicals, and electronic search tools. A law library maintained by a court, law school, or legal firm is normally managed by a *law librarian* who may hold a J.D. degree in addition to the M.L.S. or M.L.I.S. *See also*: *American Association of Law Libraries*.

lay   *See*: lai.

layoff   Separation from employment at the discretion of the employer, usually for budgetary reasons. Libraries may be forced to reduce staff when tax revenue declines or funding is cut by the primary source(s) of support. In employment governed by collective bargaining agreement, layoffs are usually decided on the basis of seniority.

layout   In typography, the overall plan of a printed publication showing the placement of text blocks, illustrations, captions, running heads, etc., and indicating fonts and font sizes, intended to be followed by the printer. Also refers to the process of preparing copy for typesetting and to the preliminary rough sketch and eventually to the more precise drawing called a "comprehensive" showing the general appearance of a printed page, usually done on special paper ruled in 12-point squares. Compare with *make-up*.

Also, the manner in which components of an interface or online document, such as a Web page, are arranged by the designer for viewing on the user's computer screen.

LBI   *See*: Library Binding Institute.

LC   *See*: Library of Congress.

LCC   *See*: Library of Congress Classification.

LCCN   *See*: Library of Congress Control Number.

LCD   *Liquid crystal display*, a technology used in display panels and projectors that enables the output from a computer or other digital device to be projected onto a large screen. LCD technology is used in laptops because it requires less power than a conventional light-emitting monitor and occupies less space, allowing a flat panel to be used as the display unit; however, an external light source is required (ambient light is usually sufficient).

LCRI   *See*: *Library of Congress Rule Interpretations*.

leader   The first field (001) of a MARC record, consisting of 24 character positions, each of which encodes data of a specific type, mostly information of use to catalogers, such as record status (new, corrected or revised, deleted, etc.) and descriptive cataloging form (*AACR2*, *ISBD*, etc.), or codes to facilitate record interpretation (character coding scheme, base address of data, etc.). Cataloging software usually provides prompts or windows to assist catalogers as they enter information in the leader. *See also*: *fixed field*.

Also refers to the strip of film without images at the beginning of a filmstrip, motion picture, or roll of unexposed film, used to thread the projector, processing machine, or camera. Compare with *trailer*.

leaders   In typesetting, a line of dots or dashes intended to direct the reader's eye across the page, as from a chapter title in a table of contents to the appropriate locator (usually a page number) in the right-hand column. In publishing, the books on a publisher's frontlist, considered to have the most sales potential, as distinct from midlist titles.

leading   In printing, the amount of vertical space allowed by the typesetter between lines of type in a column or on a page. Pronounced "ledding."

lead-in title   Backlisted titles offered in a book club mail advertising campaign at very low prices or no charge, as an inducement to potential subscribers or as bonuses or dividends to existing members. Synonymous with *introductory title*.

lead-in vocabulary   In a thesaurus of the controlled vocabulary used in indexing the literature of an academic discipline (or group of disciplines), cross-references are included to direct or "lead" the user from synonyms and quasi-synonyms to the authorized subject heading or descriptor, usually by means of an instruction to *see* or USE the preferred term. A thesaurus containing such cross-references is said to have *syndetic structure*.

lead point   *See*: plummet.

lead story   The most important item of news reported in an issue of a newspaper or newsmagazine, or in a television news broadcast, usually printed on the front page, featured on the front cover, or introduced in the opening minutes of the program. The lead story is usually longer and more detailed than the other stories published in the same issue or broadcast on the same program.

lead term   In indexing, the first word in a heading or content descriptor, which determines the position of the heading when it is listed or filed in alphanumeric sequence. In headings of two or more words, conventional word order is sometimes inverted to bring the most significant word into first-word position (*example*: **Law, Spartan** as opposed to **Spartan Law**).

leaf   One of the units formed when a sheet or half-sheet of paper, parchment, etc., is folded in half to become part of a book, pamphlet, or periodical. Of single thickness, each leaf consists of two pages, one on each side, either blank or printed. In early books, the leaves were consecutively numbered only on the recto or right-hand page of an opening (foliation), but in modern book production, the recto usually bears an *odd* page number and the verso or left-hand page an *even* number (pagination), a convention sometimes reversed in reprints. As a general rule, blank leaves are not numbered. *See also*: *double leaf* and *folio*.

Also refers to very thin sheets of silver or gold used to highlight lettering or ornamentation stamped on a book cover or applied to one or more of the edges of a bound volume to give the appearance of luxury. *See also*: *burnish*.

leaf book   A book written about another book, with a leaf from the subject volume included (adapted from Jane Greenfield's *ABC of Bookbinding*, Oak Knoll/Lyons Press, 1998).

leaflet   A publication of two to four pages, unstitched and unbound, usually folded or stapled together, as in the program notes distributed to attendees at a performance. Also refers to a thin pamphlet of comparatively small size.

leak   In information systems, the loss of confidentiality that results when security precautions are breached. When sensitive information falls into unauthorized hands, the consequences can be devastating for those who have a stake in maintaining secrecy, but leaks can also be intentional (to divert attention, preempt criticism, etc.).

lean matter   A printer's term for copy that takes longer than usual to set because it does not contain much white space, for example, a scholarly essay or treatise, as opposed to dialogue or poetry. The opposite of *fat matter*.

learning curve   A graphical representation of the rate at which learning occurs, particularly in a new environment or subject area. A learning curve may be *steep*, *moderate*, or *gentle*, depending on the amount of new knowledge to be acquired, its complexity, and the time available to complete the task.

learning management system (LMS)   An integrated set of online applications providing access to course assignments and materials, tests and test results, e-discussion and chat space, and other features in support of education, particularly in colleges and universities. Learning management systems offer some functions that overlap with library systems, such as the provision of electronic reserves, and their content may overlap with that delivered through library portals.

learning resources center (LRC)   Synonymous in the United States with *school library*.

learning style   *See*: cognitive style.

leased line   *See*: dedicated line.

leasing plan   *See*: book lease plan.

leather   The skin of an animal (calf, sheep, goat, pig, seal, reptile, etc.), processed for use in bookbinding. Often dyed an attractive color, the leather used on book covers may also be embellished with inlay and/or tooling, blind or highlighted in gold or silver. Leather-bound books were common up to the mid-19th century. Today, cloth, paper, or synthetic material is used to cover the boards of trade books published in hardcover. Real leather is used only in hand-binding. Compare with *imitation leather* and *leatherette*. *See also*: *ooze leather*, *skiver*, and *tanning*.

leather-bound   A book bound, fully or partially, in the processed skin of an animal, with the back of the spine always in leather. Medieval manuscripts and early printed books were bound in wooden boards covered in leather or parchment. In modern book production, leather is used mainly in hand-bound books of fine quality. Leather bindings can be plain or tooled, with any tooling left blind or gilt. Compare with *imitation leather* and *leatherette*. *See also*: *calf*, *goatskin*, *morocco*, *ooze leather*, and *pigskin*.

leatherette   A durable bookbinding material available in various colors, made from strong machine-glazed paper, embossed to give the appearance of a leather surface.

LEC   *See*: Limited Editions Club.

lectern   A reading stand in a Christian church, especially one from which portions of the Scriptures are read aloud during services. In a more general sense, any sloping stand or desk, usually with a narrow ledge called a *book stop* along the bottom edge to support an open book or sheaf of papers, allowing the reader free use of the hands. In medieval manuscript illustrations, lecterns are shown in a variety of designs and styles.

lectionary   A liturgical book containing lessons and selections from the Bible, also indicating the sequence in which they are to be read by the congregation in services throughout the year. In the Catholic Church, the lectionary is used in the Mass and for Matins of the Divine Office. Medieval lectionaries were often beautifully illuminated.

legal value   *See*: archival value.

legend   A visual aid that explains to the reader the symbols used on a map or in a diagram. Also refers to the identifying title or explanatory caption printed beneath an illustration or on a coin or medal.

Also, a traditional story of a well-known event, sometimes concerning the life of a national folk hero, which may contain fictional or supernatural elements but is considered to have some basis in historical fact (*example*: **Paul Bunyan**). Compare with *folktale* and *myth*.

legibility   The cumulative visual effect of the physical appearance of written or printed text, which allows the human eye to comprehend a few words or phrases on a page quickly and accurately. Legibility depends on the size, shape, and darkness of the characters, their distance from each other, length of line, and the amount of spacing between words and between lines. Other factors determining legibility are the color and finish of paper, available illumination, and the experience and skill of the reader. In printing, legibility of text is enhanced by no more than 13 words per line, adequate type size (9- to 12-point), margins of sufficient width and balance, clarity of type, density of ink, and paper finish that reduces glare (matte rather than smooth). Compare with *readability*.

legible   Writing or printing that can be easily read or deciphered by the human eye, the opposite of *illegible*. Legibility is an important consideration in the design of printed material. Compare with *readable*.

legislative history   A chronological account of the steps involved in the passage of a bill into law, including events leading up to the first draft, committee hearings, lobbying efforts, floor debates, compromises, final vote, enactment, and any subsequent history, such as a presidential veto or court test. *See also*: *legislative reference service*.

legislative reference service   An agency or unit of government that provides research assistance to legislatures and other government agencies on issues related to proposed legislation. This function may include assistance in drafting and indexing bills. At the federal level, legislative reference service is provided by the Congressional Research Service (CRS), a division of the Library of Congress. *See also*: *legislative history* and THOMAS.

lemma   A passage (or passages) excerpted from a text, appearing as the heading or theme of a marginal gloss or annotation, usually underlined to set them apart from the gloss or commentary. Also, the argument or subject of a literary composition, given as a heading or title. In logic, a secondary premise, used to demonstrate the truth of the primary proposition. Plural: *lemmata*.

lender string   In interlibrary loan, a list of the OCLC symbols of up to five libraries, selected by the borrowing library from the holdings display in the OCLC *WorldCat* database as potential lenders for an item requested by a library patron. OCLC queries the first prospective lender on the list, and if the request is not filled, the second is automatically queried, and so on. Should the request remain *unfilled* after the first five libraries have been contacted, the borrowing library has the option of selecting a second string of five new OCLC symbols from the holdings list and repeating the process.

lending library   A library or other institution that sends materials on request to another library, usually via interlibrary loan. Compare with *borrowing library*. *See also*: *net lender*.

letter   In writing and printing, a character or symbol used to represent a speech sound. All the letters of a written language constitute its alphabet. The Latin alphabet used to write the English language contains 26 letters, each with an uppercase and lowercase form. *See also*: *lettering*.

Also refers to a handwritten, typewritten, or printed personal or business message of one or more persons, usually enclosed in an envelope and delivered to the addressee by post or courier. Compare with *correspondence*. *See also*: *cover letter*, *epistle*, *letter to the editor*, and *missive*.

letterbook   A type of manuscript common in the 16th and 17th centuries containing handwritten copies of letters from the author to the recipient and originals of the replies. Copies of pertinent letters from third parties, diary entries, financial records, and memoranda might also be included.

letter-by-letter   A method of alphabetization in which any punctuation marks and divisions are ignored in a heading consisting of two or more words, and the heading treated as a single word ("newt" appearing before "New Testament"). *The Chicago Manual of Style* recommends a modification in which the method is followed only to the first comma or parenthesis, to keep identically spelled surnames together. Most dictionaries are alphabetized in this fashion. Synonymous with *all through* and *follow through*. Compare with *word-by-word*.

lettered   Inscribed with letters of the alphabet, especially the title on the spine of a book, usually done in letters of contrasting color or gilt. Also refers to a person who is educated or literate. Compare with *unlettered*.

letterform   The shape of the uppercase and lowercase letters of the Latin alphabet, especially with reference to their evolution in calligraphy and their design in typography. Also spelled *letter form*. For a brief but informative treatment of the history of letterforms, please see the entry on "Letters" in Geoffrey Glaister's *Encyclopedia of the Book* (Oak Knoll/British Library, 1996).

lettering   The act of making letters or of inscribing with letters, numerals, and special characters, especially by hand-printing, painting, or calligraphy. In binding, the process of marking the cover of a volume with the title, name of author, volume number, etc. To remain sharp and legible, lettering on the outside of a book should be applied with sufficient pressure, temperature, and dwell to ensure permanent adhesion of the stamping foil to the covering material.

letterpress   The process of printing from a raised surface, first used in China to print entire texts or portions of text from a carved block, then in Europe to print illustrations from wood blocks. The process of printing from raised metal movable type was invented by Johann Gutenberg, probably at Mainz, Germany, in the mid-15th century. In relief printing, the printing surface (block, plate, or type) is coated with ink that is transferred directly to paper or some other flat surface by the application of pressure. After a press run, type may be left standing for subsequent reuse or broken up for use on another job. Letterpress was used for books until the mid-20th century when it was superseded by offset lithography. Also spelled *letter-press*. **See also**: *intaglio*.

letters   The handwritten, typewritten, or printed personal or business messages of one or more persons. A letter is usually enclosed in an envelope and sent to the addressee by post or courier. In *AACR2*, the collected letters of a single person are cataloged under the name of the writer, with an added entry for the editor or compiler. If the letters are addressed to the same person, an added entry is also made under the name of the addressee. The collected letters of several writers are cataloged under the name of the editor or compiler. Compare with *correspondence*.

   Also refers to learning or knowledge in a general sense (as in the phrase "arts and letters") and to the profession of the writer, with reference to literary works.

letters journal   A scholarly periodical devoted to publishing short articles containing interim reports of research results, usually in a specific academic field, including negative and inconclusive results likely to be of interest to other researchers (*example*: the weekly ***Applied Physics Letters***). Speedy review and publication processes are essential for this type of journal.

letters patent   A written document of record issued by a government or monarch to confer a right, privilege, title, office, or property on a person or corporate entity, in a manner that is open for inspection.

letter to the editor   A letter, usually printed at the discretion of the publisher on the editorial page of a newspaper or magazine, in which a reader expresses his or her views on the subject of a previously published article or editorial, or on the editorial policy of the publication in general, sometimes followed by a brief response from the editor(s).

levant   A high-quality open-grained morocco leather made from the skin of the Angora goat, used in bookbinding to achieve an elegant, highly polished look.

level of description   In library cataloging, the amount of detail given in a bibliographic record, indicated by the number of data elements included in the bibliographic description of the item. *Anglo-American Cataloguing Rules* specify three distinct levels of description: full level, core level, and minimal level.

lexicography   The process of writing and compiling a dictionary or glossary, including the selection of terms and the preparation of an entry for each word, giving the correct spelling, pronunciation, derivation, one or more definitions, and sometimes antonyms and examples of usage. The person who writes or compiles such a work is a *lexicographer*. Compare with *lexicology*.

lexicology   The field of study devoted to the origins, form, and meaning of words in any language. Compare with *lexicography*. *See also*: *etymology*.

lexicon   Originally, a dictionary of Greek, Hebrew, Arabic, or some other literary language. In modern usage, a specialized dictionary or glossary of the words of a specific subject or field of study. In linguistics, a list of all the lexical items (*lexemes*) in a given language. *See also*: *vocabulary*.

LHRT   *See*: Library History Round Table.

liaison   In academic libraries, librarians are often assigned one or more academic departments for which they serve as intermediary between the teaching faculty and the library. Liaison responsibilities may include bibliographic instruction, collection development (including reference and electronic resources), current awareness, and faculty training in the use of library resources. Most liaison librarians have academic preparation or at least some level of expertise in the disciplines they serve.

LibDex: The Library Index   A searchable worldwide online directory of library homepages, Web-based OPACs, Friends of the Library homepages, and library e-commerce affiliates, *LibDex* is maintained by Peter Scott of the University of Saskatchewan Library. URL: www.libdex.com. *See also*: Libweb.

libel   A written or printed statement or representation intended to expose a person, group of persons, or corporate entity to public ridicule or contempt, or to damage in some other way the reputation of its subject, or cause pecuniary loss. Also refers to the act of publishing such a statement. Burden of proof is on the plaintiff to show that actual damage occurred. In the United States, the constitutional guarantee of freedom of speech and press provides no protection for libelous statements. *Slander* is defamatory words spoken but not published in writing or in print.

libelli   Booklets originally created as discrete units, subsequently bound together within a larger composite manuscript. Medieval tropes (musical and textual additions to liturgical chants) were often produced in this form. French: *livret*.

LIBER   *See*: **L**igue des **B**ibliothèques **E**uropéennes de **R**echerche.

libraire   *See*: stationer.

librarian   A professionally trained person responsible for the care of a library and its contents, including the selection, processing, and organization of materials and the delivery of information, instruction, and loan services to meet the needs of its users. In an online environment, the role of the librarian is to manage and mediate access to information that may exist only in electronic form.

In the United States the title is reserved for persons who have been awarded the M.L.S. or M.L.I.S. degree or certified as professionals by a state agency. Also refers to the person responsible for the overall administration of a library or library system, synonymous in this sense with *library director*. Classified by functional specialization (acquisitions librarian, cataloger, instruction librarian, reference librarian, serials librarian, systems librarian, etc.), librarians in the United States are organized in the American Library Association (ALA) and its affiliates. Compare with *support staff*. *See also*: *Librarian of Congress* and *solo librarian*.

librariana   A catch-all term for the body of information, works, and memorabilia that has accumulated on the subject of libraries, librarians, and related topics, particularly items of historical interest.

Librarian of Congress   An office created in 1802, two years after the Library of Congress was established, for which no qualifications were specified. The position is filled by presidential appointment for no fixed term. In 1897, the Senate acquired the power to approve the president's nomination, and the Librarian of Congress was given the authority to appoint the staff of the Library of Congress and to establish its rules and regulations. In the 20th century, a precedent was established for appointing the Librarian of Congress for life. Biographical information about past Librarians of Congress is available online at: lcweb.loc.gov/loc/legacy/librs.html.

librarianship   The profession devoted to applying theory and technology to the creation, selection, organization, management, preservation, dissemination, and utilization of collections of information in all formats. In the United States, often used synonymously with *library science*. A person formally trained or certified to perform such services is a *librarian*. Librarianship is a very old profession. The founder and organizer of the great classical library at Alexandria (c. 300 B.C.) was Demetrius of Phaleron. The ancient Egyptians and Babylonians probably had librarians to organize and preserve their extensive collections of papyrus scrolls and clay tablets. *See also*: *comparative librarianship*.

Librarians' Index to the Internet (lii.org)   A searchable, annotated subject directory of over 11,000 Internet resources, carefully selected and evaluated by librarians for users of public libraries. A resource used by both librarians and the general public, *lii.org* prides itself on its commitment to quality. Each site is reviewed at least twice (sometimes three or four times) before it is added. The index includes a "Quick Facts & Ready Reference" section and a sidebar featuring new sites and special themes.

The resource began in 1990 as the bookmark file of reference librarian Carole Leita, then migrated to the Berkeley Public Library's Web server in 1993 under the title *Berkeley Public Library Index to the Internet*. In 1996, work began with Roy Tennant at Digital Library SunSITE to include a search engine. Library of Congress subject headings were also added and a virtual workspace created to facilitate team-based record creation and maintenance. In 1997, the index was moved to Berkeley SunSITE and given its current name. Since October 2000 much of the operational funding for *lii.org* has been provided by the Library of California. The project has also received LSTA grants. URL: lii.org.

library   From the Latin *liber*, meaning "book" (in Greek and the Romance languages the corresponding term is *bibliotheca*). A collection or group of collections of books and/or other materials organized and maintained for use (reading, consultation, study, research, etc.). Institutional libraries, organized to facilitate access by a specific clientele, are staffed by librarians and other personnel trained to provide services to meet user needs. By extension, the room, building, or facility that houses such a collection, usually but not necessarily built for that purpose. Directory information on libraries is available alphabetically by country in *World Guide to Libraries*, a serial published by K.G. Saur. Two comprehensive online directories of library homepages are *LibDex* (www.libdex.com) and *Libweb* (sunsite.berkeley.edu/Libweb). Abbreviated *lib*. *See also*: *academic library*, *government library*, *public library*, and *special library*.

Also, a collective noun used by publishers, particularly during the Victorian period, for certain books published in series (*example*: *Everyman's Library*).

Also refers to a collection of computer programs or data files, or a set of ready-made reusable routines, sometimes called *modules*, that can be linked to a program at the time it is compiled, relieving the programmer of the necessity to repeat the same code each time the routine is used in the program.

library administration   The control and supervision of a library or library system, including planning, budgeting, policymaking, personnel management, public relations, and program assessment, with responsibility for results. Also refers collectively to the persons responsible for managing a library, usually a board of trustees or dean, library director, and his or her immediate staff. *See also*: *Library Administration and Management Association*.

Library Administration and Management Association (LAMA)   A division of the American Library Association founded in 1957, LAMA has a membership consisting of library directors and persons with an interest in improving the quality of administration and management in libraries of all types. LAMA publishes the quarterly journal *Library Administration & Management (LA&M)*. URL: www.ala.org.

library advocate   A person who appreciates libraries and their role in society to the extent of speaking and acting publicly in their support, especially when funding and the freedom to read are at stake. *See also*: *Friends of the Library* and *library trustee*.

Library and Information Science Abstracts (LISA)   An abstracting and indexing service devoted to the literature of library science and information science, published quarterly from 1950 to 1968 under the title *Library Science Abstracts*, and bimonthly from 1969 to 1982 and monthly since 1982 under the current title, by the Library Association of Great Britain. Available online from R.R. Bowker, *LISA* provides abstracts of articles from over 500 periodicals published in 68 countries, as well as papers from major English-language conference proceedings, updated biweekly. ISSN: 0024–2179. *See also*: Library Literature & Information Science.

Library and Information Technology Association (LITA)   A division of the American Library Association since in 1966, LITA has a membership consisting of librarians and other information professionals concerned with all aspects of the acquisition, organization, storage, retrieval, and dissemination of information in electronic formats, including digital libraries, metadata, authorization and authentication, electronic journals and electronic publishing, telecommunications, networks, computer security and intellectual property rights, technical standards, online catalogs and bibliographic databases, optical information systems, desktop applications, software engineering, etc. LITA publishes the quarterly journal *Information Technology and Libraries (ITAL)* and also the *LITA Newsletter*. URL: www.ala.org.

library anxiety   Confusion, fear, and frustration felt by a library user, especially one lacking experience, when faced with the need to find information in a library. Among college and university students, library anxiety may be a cause of academic procrastination. The first formal study of this phenomenon was conducted by Constance Mellon in the mid-1980s using qualitative methods. In 1992, Sharon Bostick developed the Library Anxiety Scale (LAS) to quantitatively measure: (1) barriers with library staff, (2) affective barriers, (3) comfort with the library, (4) knowledge of the library, and (5) mechanical barriers. In 2001, Doris Van Kampen developed the Multidimensional Library Anxiety Scale (MLAS) to reflect changes in information theory and search methods. The new questionnaire instrument was successfully pilot-tested on doctoral students in 2002. For more information, see Van Kampen's article in the January 2004 issue of *College & Research Libraries*.

library association   A membership organization consisting of a group of librarians, library directors, and other persons involved with libraries who meet periodically to discuss matters of professional interest. Library associations elect officers, sponsor conferences, select committees to address specific issues, publish newsletters and professional journals, and charge dues to support the organization's activities. The largest library association in the United States is the American Library Association (ALA). Its counterparts in Canada and Great Britain are the Canadian Library Association (CLA) and the Chartered Institute of Library and Information Professionals (CILIP). The major library and information industry associations in the United States and Canada are listed in *The Bowker Annual Library and Book Trade Almanac*. *See also*: *American Society for Information Science and Technology* and *Special Libraries Association*.

Library Association (LA)   Founded in 1877, LA is the leading library association in the United Kingdom, with a membership of 25,000 librarians and other information professionals, approximately 5.5 percent of whom are employed overseas. Divided into 12 geographic branches and over 20 special interest groups with headquarters in London, LA publishes the monthly journal *Library Association Record*. Its publishing arm, Library Association Publishing Limited (LAPL), issues approximately 30 new titles each year and maintains a backlist of over 200 titles. In April 2002, LA merged with the Institute of Information Scientists (IIS) to form the Chartered Institute of Library and Information Professionals (CILIP). URL: www.cilip.org.uk.

library automation   The design and implementation of ever more sophisticated computer systems to accomplish tasks originally done by hand in libraries. Beginning in the 1960s with the development of the machine-readable catalog record (MARC), the process of automation has expanded to include the core functions of acquisitions, cataloging and authority control, serials control, circulation and inventory, and interlibrary loan and document delivery. The library automation field is currently dominated by a handful of systems vendors (Brodart, Dynix, Endeavor, Ex Libris, Follett Software, Innovative Interfaces, The Library Corporation, SIRSI, VTLS).

Recent trends in library automation include the growing importance of "add-ons" mostly related to the delivery of digital content (link resolvers, portal and metasearch interfaces, and e-resource management modules often provided by third-party vendors), better integration with the Web environment (rewriting fat PC clients as browser applications, using XML and style sheets for display, and developing XML import and export capabilities) and for academic libraries, closer integration of library systems with learning management systems.

library award   Special recognition given to an individual, group, or library in honor of outstanding achievement and/or distinguished service to the profession. Major awards given annually often include a monetary prize funded by an individual or corporate donor or by a library association. Recipients of library awards and scholarships are listed in *The Bowker Annual Library and Book Trade Almanac*. A less extensive list is provided in the *American Library Directory*. Awards and scholarships in the Awards Program of the American Library Association are listed on the ALA Web site (www.ala.org).

Library Awareness Program   An attempt by the FBI to recruit librarians in the United States as "cold warriors" during the 1970s and 1980s by suggesting that they restrict public access to unclassified scientific research, particularly information available from the National Technical Information Service (NTIS). Librarians were asked to report on individuals requesting certain categories of scientific information, especially foreign nationals from countries in the Soviet Union. The FBI had the support of the National Commission on Libraries and Information Science (NCLIS) in this effort, which undermined the confidentiality of library lending records and open access to library resources.

In *Free Expression and Censorship in America: An Encyclopedia* (Greenwood, 1997), Herbert Foerstel writes that the FBI conducted a 16-month investigation of librarians who openly opposed the Library Awareness Program, even accusing them of being dupes of the Soviet Union. The program was also opposed by the American Association of University Professors, the American Federation of Teachers (AFT), and other organizations. In response to public indignation, many state legislatures passed statutes making it illegal for any librarian to reveal library records or patron requests without a court order. For more information, see *Surveillance in the Stacks: The FBI's Library Awareness Program* by Herbert Foerstel (Greenwood Press, 1991). *See also*: USA Patriot Act.

Library Bill of Rights   A formal statement adopted by the American Library Association in 1948 and amended in 1961, 1990, and 1996, affirming the right of libraries in the United States to provide, to all members of the communities they serve, materials expressing diverse points of view and to remain free of censorship. Implementation of the *Library Bill of Rights* is the work of the Office for Intellectual Freedom of the ALA. The full text of the statement is available online at: www.ala.org. *See also*: Freedom to Read Statement and *Intellectual Freedom Round Table*.

library binder   A commercial binder that specializes in serving the needs of libraries. Many libraries regularly send their periodical back files to a library binder to be bound into annual volumes. Special binding may also be needed for heavily used items and trade paperbacks. Library binders are organized in the Library Binding Institute. *See also*: *library binding*.

library binding   An especially strong, durable binding used for periodical back files and for rebinding worn volumes and new paperbound publications for which circulation is expected to remain high over a comparatively long period of time. Includes *prelibrary binding*.

The ANSI standard for library binding, established by the American Library Association and the Library Binding Institute, requires that a book have a spine glued with polyvinyl acetate adhesive, strong endpapers, reinforced hinges, and boards covered in buckram, coated or impregnated with nonmigratory resin. Library binding is usually more expensive than the standard publisher's binding. Compare with *library edition*. *See also*: *oversewing*.

Library Binding Institute (LBI)   A trade association of commercial library binders doing business in the United States, Canada, and the United Kingdom, LBI was established in 1935 to create and maintain standards for library rebinding and prebinding, improve binding methods, and facilitate cooperation between library binders and between binders and their customers. Membership is also open to suppliers of library binders and organizations with an interest in the preservation of books and periodicals. LBI developed the ANSI standard for library binding in cooperation with the American Library Association. The Institute publishes the magazine *The New Library Scene* and technical papers on binding and related topics. URL: www.lbibinders.org.

library bond   An interest-bearing or discounted security issued by a library district, or by the government entity of which a library or library system is a part, usually to finance the construction and/or renovation of facilities or some other major capital project. A bond places the library district under a general obligation to pay the bond-holder (investor) a specified amount of interest, usually at regular intervals, and to repay the principal amount of the loan within a designated period of time. The bond is backed by a majority of voters in the district, who consent to be taxed at a slightly higher rate to raise sufficient revenue to pay the interest and principal on the loan. Bond measures pass more easily in times of prosperity than in economic recession.

library book   A book that is the property of a library, usually bearing an ownership mark and labeling. Library books allowed to circulate are usually barcoded, with a date due slip attached inside the cover. Some are given a more sturdy binding than the trade edition, or a plastic sleeve to protect the dust jacket and cover. A book no longer owned by a library is usually stamped "discarded" or "withdrawn." *See also*: *ex-library copy*.

library card   A small paper or plastic card issued by a library to a registered borrower that must be presented at the circulation desk in order to check out materials from its collections. Identification is usually required of new applicants. In most libraries in the United States, library cards are barcoded for electronic circulation. Periodic renewal may be required to verify current street address and telephone number. Synonymous with *borrower card*. *See also*: *library card campaign* and *patron ID*.

library card campaign   An organized publicity effort conducted by a public library or library system over a finite period of time aimed at encouraging the adult and juvenile residents of the district or area served to become registered borrowers and active library users. Successful library card campaigns have been conducted in many communities in the United States, sometimes in conjunction with National Library Week. Collateral benefits often include increased visibility and enhancement of the library's image in the community. For more information, see *Running a Successful Library Card Campaign: A How-to-Do-It Manual* by Patrick Jones (Neal-Schuman, 2002).

library closure   The closing of a library or branch in a library system, temporarily or permanently, usually due to budgetary constraints or demographic changes in the area served. Library closings are announced in the news section of *American Libraries*, the monthly magazine of the American Library Association.

library collection   The total accumulation of books and other materials owned by a library, cataloged and arranged for ease of access, which often consists of several smaller collections (reference, circulating books, serials, government documents, rare books, special collections, etc.). The process of building a library collection over time is called *collection development*. Synonymous with *holdings*. Compare with *collection*. *See also*: *digital collection*, *high-risk collection*, *rental collection*, *subject collection*, and *test collection*.

library conference   A formal gathering of librarians, library directors, and others associated with libraries for the purpose of meeting colleagues, discussing issues and events, and learning about new products, services, technologies, and recent developments in the library science and information science profession. Most library associations sponsor regular conferences at which officers are elected, committees and task forces formed, policies formulated, awards announced, etc. *Conferees* are generally charged a registration fee based on the sections of the conference that they plan to attend. *See also*: *preconference* and *proceedings*.

The American Library Association sponsors two national conferences each year, one during the summer in a different city each year, the other at midwinter, often in Chicago. The state chapters of the ALA, and some of its major divisions, sponsor their own conferences, as does the Special Libraries Association and ASIST. The permanent round tables of the ALA convene concurrently with the national conferences.

library cooperation   Methods by which libraries and library systems work together for the mutual benefit of their users, including centralized processing, cooperative cataloging, international exchange of bibliographic information, union catalogs, resource sharing, etc.

library director   The person who has overall responsibility for supervising the operations of a library or library system, including planning, budgeting, policymaking, personnel management, and program assessment. In public libraries, the library director is usually subject to the oversight of a board of trustees; in academic libraries, by a dean of academic affairs or provost. *See also*: *library administration* and *Library Administration and Management Association*.

library discount   A discount off the list price of a book or other publication, given by most publishers and jobbers on purchases made by an institutional library. Most publishers offer a flat rate, usually 5–10 percent. Jobbers may link the discount rate to size of order or volume of purchasing. As a general rule, specialized titles are given a shorter discount than trade books or not discounted at all because of their limited sales potential.

library district   An officially delineated geographic area in which the residents decide by popular vote whether to provide tax support for a public library or library system, or one of the geographical areas into which a state is divided for the purpose of administering libraries in accordance with a comprehensive statewide tax plan. *See also*: *service area*.

library edition   An edition, often of a children's book, published in a binding stronger and more durable than the usual publisher's binding, for marketing specifically to libraries, usually more expensive than the trade edition of the same title. *See also*: *library binding* and *prelibrary binding*.

library education   Educational programs designed to prepare students for the postbaccalaureate degree of M.L.S. or M.L.I.S., taught by the faculty of a university department known as a *library school* (or school of librarianship). Modern library education began in 1887 when Melvil Dewey founded the first school for training professional librarians at Columbia University. *See also*: *Association for Library and Information Science Education* and *information studies*.

library equipment   Mechanical and electronic devices purchased by a library for staff use or to facilitate patron use of its services and collections, including photocopy machines, microform reader-printers, video and CD players, projection equipment, computers and computer peripherals, security devices, etc.

library extension   Programs and activities that enable a library or library system to deliver traditional services outside the physical walls of its facilities, including bookmobiles, books-by-mail, and direct delivery of library materials to patrons. Compare with *outreach*.

library faculty   The professionally trained librarians employed at an academic institution that grants faculty status to librarians. One of the advantages of faculty status is the right to participate in governance. At some institutions, library faculty are members of the same collective bargaining unit as the teaching faculty. Whether they are eligible for tenure and promotion to the same ranks as the teaching faculty depends on the contract governing employment. *See also*: *academic status*.

library hand   A highly legible, uniform style of handwriting traditionally used by librarians for making entries in manuscript catalogs before the typewriter came into widespread use. With the conversion of card catalogs into files of machine-readable records, catalog cards have fallen into disuse, and handwritten catalog entries are rarely seen.

library historian   A researcher who writes about the history of libraries and librarianship, from ancient to modern times. Librarians with an interest in library history are organized in the Library History Round Table (LHRT) of the American Library Association.

Library History Round Table (LHRT)   A round table of the American Library Association dedicated to facilitating communication among scholars and students of library history, supporting research in library history, and addressing current issues of concern to library historians, such as conservation and preservation. LHRT publishes the semiannual *LHRT Newsletter*. URL: www.ala.org.

library hours   The hours during which a library is open to its users, and any days when it is *not* open, usually posted near the entrance or at the circulation desk. Libraries also make their hours available by telephone and via their Web pages. Because staffing is required to keep a library facility open, hours often reflect budgetary constraints. Most libraries are equipped with a book drop for returning items when the facility is closed.

library humor   Jokes, cartoons, anecdotes, unusual reference questions, witticisms, satire, occupational folklore, etc., having to do with libraries and librarianship. The Michigan Electronic Library maintains a list of Web sites on "Humor and Culture in Libraries" at: mel.lib.mi.us/libraries/LIBS-humor.html.

library instruction *See*: bibliographic instruction.

Library Instruction Round Table (LIRT) A round table of the American Library Association dedicated to promoting formal and informal library instruction in all types of libraries as a means of helping library users acquire the information literacy skills essential for lifelong learning. URL: www3.baylor.edu/LIRT.

library journal A professional journal devoted to the publication of articles about library and information science, librarianship, and related topics. Most library journals also publish reviews of new publications, including books of professional interest to librarians. *Yahoo!* provides a list of links to online library journals under Reference>Libraries>Library and Information Science (www.yahoo.com).

Library Journal (LJ) Founded in 1876, *Library Journal* is a combination trade journal/review publication published in 20 issues per year by Reed Business Information. *LJ* publishes news and announcements of interest to library professionals, feature articles, commentary, analysis of trends, regular columns, and approximately 7,500 reviews per year of new books, magazines, databases and CD-ROMs, videocassettes, and audiobooks suitable for general library collections aimed at adult readers. The reviews are short but evaluative, written by and for librarians. ISSN: 0363–0277. Materials published for children and young adults are reviewed in *School Library Journal*. The online version of *LJ* is available at: www.libraryjournal.com/index.asp.

library law *See*: library legislation.

library legislation Laws passed by a federal or state legislative body pertaining to or affecting the interests of libraries and related institutions (*example*: *Digital Millennium Copyright Act* of 1998). Through their professional associations, librarians and library advocates seek to influence legislative decision-making in ways that will benefit libraries and their users. Federal legislation affecting libraries is summarized in *The Bowker Annual Library and Book Trade Almanac*. The legislative priorities and activities of the American Library Association can be explored online under "Issues & Advocacy" at: www.ala.org. Synonymous with *library law*.

library literature The body of published information pertaining to libraries, library and information science, and librarianship, including books, journal articles, conference proceedings, reports, guidelines and standards, etc. The literature of the profession is indexed in *Library Literature & Information Science (LLIS)*, published by H.W. Wilson, and in *Library and Information Science Abstracts (LISA)*.

Library Literature & Information Science (LLIS) Published by H.W. Wilson, *Library Literature & Information Science* is an author and subject index to the English-language literature of library science and information science, covering books, periodical articles, pamphlets, and library school theses, with book reviews listed in a separate section at the end of each volume. Published from 1932 to 1998 under the title *Library Literature*, *LLIS* is available in print in bimonthly paperback supplements cumulated annually. It is also available as an online database directly from the Wilson Company or via OCLC *FirstSearch* (1980 to the present). ISSN: 1528–0659. *See also*: Library and Information Science Abstracts.

library management   *See*: library administration.

library management system (LMS)   In automated systems, an integrated set of applications designed to perform the business and technical functions of a library, such as acquisitions, cataloging, circulation, and the provision of public access. Synonymous with *integrated library system (ILS)*.

library market   The portion of the market for books and other publications generated by sales to libraries, library systems, and related organizations such as museums, archives, and research institutions. The library market is segmented by type of library (public, academic, school, special, etc.). Publishers and jobbers market their products to libraries by exhibiting at library conferences, advertising in library trade journals and review publications, offering special library discounts and prepublication prices, and direct mail advertising (trade catalogs and brochures).

library materials   All the items purchased by a library or library system to satisfy the information needs of its users, including books, newspapers and periodicals, reference materials, music scores, maps, microforms, and nonprint media, as distinct from equipment and supplies. Some libraries include subscriptions to electronic resources in the materials budget; others fund them separately. Except for gifts and special endowments, the acquisition of library materials is normally funded through the operating budget. The rapid escalation of journal subscription prices over the past decade has forced many academic libraries to cancel periodical subscriptions to maintain balance between expenditures for books and serials.

Library of Congress (LC)   Established by Congress in 1800 to function as a research library for the legislative branch of the federal government, the Library of Congress eventually became the unofficial national library of the United States. Located in Washington, D.C., LC houses a collection of over 120 million items and administers the U.S. copyright system, serving as the nation's copyright depository. LC is also the primary source of original cataloging in the United States. The machine-readable cataloging (MARC) and cataloging-in-publication (CIP) programs originated at LC. URL: www.loc.gov. Compare with *National Archives and Records Administration*. *See also*: *Librarian of Congress*.

Library of Congress Catalog Number   *See*: Library of Congress Control Number.

Library of Congress Classification (LCC)   A system of classifying books and other library materials developed and maintained over the last 200 years by the Library of Congress in Washington, D.C. In LCC, human knowledge is divided into 20 broad categories indicated by single letters of the roman alphabet, with major subdivisions indicated by a second letter, and narrower subdivisions by decimal numbers and further alphabetic notation.

Example: *LC call number*: **PE 3727.N4 M34 1994**

In the example given above, assigned to the book *Juba to Jive: A Dictionary of African-American Slang* edited by Clarence Major, **P** represents the main class "Language and literature," **PE** the class "English language," **3727** the subclass "English slang," and **N4** African Americans as a special group. **M34** is the Cutter number for the editor's surname and **1994** the year of publication. In the United States, most research libraries and academic libraries use LCC, while most school libraries and public libraries use Dewey Decimal Classification. An outline of LC Classification is available online at: lcweb.loc.gov/catdir/cpso/lcco/lcco.html. The *LC Classification Weekly Lists* are available at: lcweb.loc.gov/catdir/cpso/cpso.html#subjects.

Library of Congress Control Number (LCCN)   When the Library of Congress began printing catalog cards in 1898 and distributing them in 1901, a unique Library of Congress Card Number was assigned to each item for identification and control. With the development of machine-readable cataloging in the late 1960s, LCCN became the Library of Congress Control Number. It is used in bibliographic records and also in authority and classification records. The LCCN is assigned to a publication after the deposit copy is received by the U.S. Copyright Office or in advance of the publication date if a publisher requests cataloging-in-publication. *See also*: *accession number*.

Library of Congress Rule Interpretations (LCRI)   A loose-leaf service that provides current information on recent decisions of the Library of Congress concerning the interpretation of the most recent revision of *Anglo-American Cataloguing Rules (AACR2)*. *LCRI* is published in print and as part of *Cataloger's Desktop* available on CD-ROM.

Library of Congress subject heading (LCSH)   A descriptive word or phrase selected by a subject specialist at the Library of Congress from the list of *Library of Congress Subject Headings* and assigned to a book or other item when first published to indicate its subject. Multiple subject headings are assigned when necessary or desirable. The complete list of LC subject headings is published annually in a multivolume set colloquially known as "the big red books," usually available in the reference section of most large public and academic libraries and in the cataloging department of smaller libraries. Compare with *Sears subject heading*. *See also*: *controlled vocabulary*.

library orientation   *See*: bibliographic instruction.

library portal   Software that allows a computer user to customize online access to collections of information resources by creating a list of Internet connections, much like a personalized directory of street addresses and telephone/fax numbers (*example*: *MyLibrary*). Library portals are designed to reduce information overload by allowing patrons to select only the resources they wish to display on their personal interface.

library publication   A work produced and distributed by a library, for example, a brochure intended for users, describing the library facility, its resources, and the services provided by its staff. Most library publications are ephemeral, but large academic and research libraries publish more permanent works. A recent example: Alixe Bovey's *Monsters and Grotesques in Medieval Manuscripts* published by The British Library in 2002.

library rate   A significantly lower postal rate charged to libraries and related nonprofit institutions by the U.S. Postal Service for books and other educational materials sent by mail. The law was amended in 1976 to allow publishers and distributors to use the rate when shipping books and other materials to libraries. The lower rate has allowed public libraries to offer books-by-mail programs to homebound patrons and has helped keep down the cost of interlibrary loan service. Compare with *media mail.*

library rating   The practice of evaluating libraries on the basis of formal criteria and ranking them according to the results. A prime example is *Hennen's American Public Library Ratings (HAPLR).* Created and maintained by library administrator Thomas J. Hennen, Jr., *HAPLR* ranks U.S. public libraries on 15 weighted input and output measures based on statistical data from the U.S. Federal-State Cooperative Service. Published annually, *HAPLR* also lists the top 10 public libraries in the United States by size of community. For more information, see the *HAPLR Homepage* at: www. haplr-index.com.

library rep   *See*: library representative.

library representative   A publisher's sales representative responsible for calling on libraries, usually within an established territory, to solicit orders for titles on the publisher's list. Contacts are made, usually by telephone or in person, with librarians responsible for collection development and acquisitions. Also refers to a vendor's representative, responsible for soliciting subscriptions to online bibliographic databases and full-text resources, usually trained to give demonstrations to library selection committees. Abbreviated *library rep.*

library research   Systematic study and investigation of some aspect of library and information science in which conclusions are based on the statistical analysis of data collected in accordance with a pre-established research design and methodology. Results are usually published in a professional library journal or presented at a library conference and subsequently published in its proceedings. Library research helps expand the theoretical base of library and information science and also provides data necessary for effective administrative decision-making and problem solving. Research on libraries and librarianship published in the previous year is reported in an essay in *The Bowker Annual Library and Book Trade Almanac.* *See also*: *Library Research Round Table* and *library survey.*

Library Research Round Table (LRRT)   Founded in 1968 as a permanent round table of the American Library Association, LRRT is dedicated to fostering library research by providing program opportunities for researchers to describe and disseminate their work and by informing and educating ALA members about research techniques and the importance of research as a foundation for effective administrative decision-making and problem solving. LRRT also gives annual awards for distinguished published research and excellence in doctoral research. URL: www.ala.org.

library school   A professional school or department qualified to grant the postbaccalaureate degree of M.L.S. or M.L.I.S., supported and administered by an institution of higher learning to prepare graduate students for employment in professional positions in libraries and as information service providers. The first modern library school was established by Melvil Dewey at Columbia University in 1887. Library schools may be *accredited* or *approved* (or both). Length of program varies. Synonymous with *school of librarianship.*

The term is becoming archaic as more and more institutions use "library and information studies" or simply "information studies" to describe the expansion of their LIS schools to include allied fields (informatics, information management, etc.). Accredited library and information studies programs in the United States and Canada are listed in *American Library Directory* and *The Bowker Annual Library and Book Trade Almanac*, both published by R.R. Bowker. For an online *World List of Departments and Schools of Information Studies, Information Management, Information Systems, etc.* see: informationr.net/wl.

library science   The professional knowledge and skill with which recorded information is selected, acquired, organized, stored, maintained, retrieved, and disseminated to meet the needs of a specific clientele, usually taught at a professional library school qualified to grant the postbaccalaureate degree of M.L.S. or M.L.I.S. The term is used synonymously in the United States with *librarianship*. Compare with *information science*.

library security officer (LSO)   The person appointed by the director of a library or library system who is authorized by the library and its parent institution to act on their behalf in working with the institution's administration and staff, legal counsel, security force, and outside agencies to develop and implement an effective *security plan*, based on a thorough knowledge of security needs, particularly those of special collections. Such a plan should include a survey of the library's collections, a review of the layout of the physical facility, staff training, and standard operating procedures for dealing with theft and other common security problems.

Library Services and Construction Act (LSCA)   Passed by Congress in 1956, the *Library Services Act (LSA)* provided federal funding for the extension of public library services to the unserved, mainly in rural areas. In 1964, Congress expanded its scope to permit federal grants-in-aid for construction *and* expansion of library services in all areas with inadequate services, including urban communities. Over a period of 30 years, the effect of *LSCA* on public library construction was comparable to the era of Carnegie philanthropy in the early 20th century. In its final phase, *LSCA* funding was extended to adult literacy programs and outreach services to the children and youth of poor families, homeless persons, and the physically disabled.

In 1996, following a proposal by a task force consisting of the Chief Officers of the State Libraries (COSLA), the American Library Association (ALA), and the Urban Libraries Council (ULC), Congress passed the *Library Services and Technology Act (LSTA)* as part of the *Museum and Library Services Act*, replacing the eight titles of the *LSCA* with two new titles and consolidating the administration of federal library programs under the Institute for Museum and Library Services (IMLS).

Library Services and Technology Act (LSTA)   A section of the *Museum and Library Services Act* of 1996, *LSTA* promotes access to learning and to the information resources provided by all types of libraries by distributing federal funds to state library agencies under a formula based on population. State libraries may use the appropriations to support statewide initiatives and services or distribute funds to public, academic, research, school, and special libraries within their state, through subgrant competitions and cooperative agreements. In the year 2000, more than $138 million in *LSTA* funds was distributed to state library agencies. The Institute of Museum and Library Services maintains a Web page on *LSTA* grants-in-aid at: www.imls.gov/grants/library/lib_gsla.asp. For a brief history of the origins of *LSTA*, see the entry for *Library Services and Construction Act*.

library staff   The entire group of paid employees responsible for the operation and management of a library or library system, including its director, librarians, paraprofessionals, technical assistants, clerical personnel, and pages or student assistants. In academic libraries at institutions that grant librarians faculty status, a distinction is usually made between faculty members and nonfaculty staff. In other types of libraries, a distinction may be made between professionally trained librarians and support staff. Volunteers are not considered part of the staff because they are unpaid.

library statistics   Numerical data assembled, classified, and tabulated to present useful facts and information about the operation of a library or library system or about the activities of libraries at the local, state, provincial, or national level, usually presented in the form of a periodic report. The ANSI/NISO Z39.7 standard identifies data categories for basic library statistics applicable to four types of libraries (academic, public, school, and special) and additional data categories that may be collected by one or more types of libraries but not by all. The National Center for Educational Statistics (NCES) maintains a Web site on library statistics as part of the Library Statistics Program (URL: nces.ed.gov). *See also*: *circulation statistics*.

library supplies   Expendable materials such as labels, book cards and pockets, date due slips, rubber stamps, mending tape, magnetic strips, plastic sleeves, laminate, paper for printing and photocopying, etc., that a library must order from a library supplier in order to prepare new items for circulation, maintain collections, and provide services. *See also*: *Brodart*, *Gaylord*, and *Highsmith*.

Library Support Staff Interests Round Table (LSSIRT)   A permanent round table of the American Library Association, LSSIRT provides a forum for addressing issues of concern to library support staff such as training and continuing education, career development, job responsibilities, and compensation. URL: www.ala.org. *See also*: *paraprofessional*.

library survey   A written or oral question-and-answer instrument designed to elicit feedback from library users. Library surveys are administered by staff, or by an outside agency, to determine how well the library's services, programs, and collections meet user needs and any objectives established by the library administration and/or governing institution. They are also used to generate data in library research. Also refers to the report produced as the result of such a study.

library system   A group of libraries administered in common, for example, a central library and its branches or auxiliary outlets. Also, a group of independently administered libraries joined by formal or informal agreement to achieve a common purpose. Under such an arrangement, each library is considered an *affiliate*. Compare with *consortium*.

library tour A guided walk through a library facility, usually conducted by a librarian or library assistant, to orient new users to the location of services and resources. Some libraries have installed online library tours on their Web sites, which include clickable floor plans linked to photographs and descriptive text. Not to be confused with *bibliographic instruction*.

library trustee A member of an appointed or elected board responsible for overseeing the growth and development of a library or library system, including long-range planning and policymaking, public relations, and fund-raising. Trustees are usually library advocates but may sometimes be political appointees. *See also*: *Association for Library Trustees and Advocates*.

library use The extent to which the facilities and resources of a library are actually used by its clientele. Common measures include overall or per capita circulation, turnover of collection(s), gate count, program attendance, Internet use within the building, interlibrary loan and reference transactions, etc. Statistics on library use are important in documenting effectiveness and justifying funding.

library use only A circulation status code written on or affixed to a physical item in a library collection and entered in the item record in the catalog, indicating that it is available for use within the walls of the library but may not be checked out and removed from the premises except by special arrangement. The use of reference books, periodical indexes, and in some cases bound and/or unbound periodicals is generally restricted to the library. Use of items in special collections, such as rare books and manuscripts, may even be restricted to a designated room or area of the library. Compare with *noncirculating*. *See also*: *in-house use*.

library without walls *See*: virtual library.

libretto The words or text to which a cantata, oratorio, opera, operetta, or other work for the musical stage is set, often published in the form of a small booklet for enthusiasts who wish to follow along while attending a performance or listening to a sound recording. The person who writes a libretto is the *librettist*, for example, Edna St. Vincent Millay in the case of *The King's Henchman*, an opera composed by Deems Taylor. To find *libretti* online, try a keywords search on "libretti or librettos" at *Yahoo!* (www.yahoo.com).

libricide The systematic state-sponsored destruction of books and libraries. Twentieth-century examples include book burnings and attacks on libraries in Europe by the Nazis and the destruction of the National Library of Bosnia and Herzegovina in 1992 by the Serbs during the siege of Sarajevo. The term is used by author Rebecca Knuth in her study *Libricide: The Regime-Sponsored Destruction of Books and Libraries in the Twentieth Century* (Praeger, 2003). *See also*: *biblioclast*.

Libweb A very comprehensive worldwide directory of library homepages, updated daily on the Berkeley Digital Library Web site. URL: sunsite.berkeley.edu/Libweb. *See also*: *LibDex*.

license *See*: licensing agreement.

licensed book   A book in which the author makes use of a character or product subject to copyright restrictions, for example, a children's book based on a motion picture character (Mickey Mouse) or a commercially successful toy (Barbie). Use is by permission of the copyright holder under the terms of a *licensing agreement* handled by the copyright owner's *licensing agent*. Although the sales potential of licensed books makes them popular with retail booksellers, they are as a general rule not purchased for library collections.

licensing agreement   A formal written contract between a library and a vendor for the lease of one or more proprietary (copyrighted) bibliographic databases or online resources, usually for a fixed period of time in exchange for payment of an annual subscription fee or per-search charge. Vendors typically charge libraries on a sliding scale based on number of registered borrowers or FTE enrollment, number of institutions or facilities served, and number of simultaneous users. Most licensing agreements limit remote access to authorized users. For more information about licensing, see the final draft of *Principles for Licensing Electronic Resources* developed by the AALL, ALA, AAHSL, ARL, MLA, and SLA available online at: www.arl.org/scomm/licensing/principles.html. Compare with *site license*. **See also**: *authorized use*.

lifelong learning   One of the goals of bibliographic instruction and information literacy programs is to help library users obtain the skills they need to pursue knowledge at any age, independent of a formal educational institution. Public libraries play an important role in meeting this need because they provide access to materials in a wide range of subjects at various reading levels, not only for students enrolled in a formal curriculum but for anyone interested in reading and learning.

ligature   Two or more letters joined together in printing, such as *ff* joined at the cross-stroke in some fonts. Also refers to the stroke that joins the two letters. In letterpress, a ligature is cast as a single unit of type. Compare with *logotype*.

light   *See*: ambient light.

lightface   A typeface in which the characters are the same size as medium-weight and boldface type of the same font but composed of thinner strokes that do not appear as dark on the printed page.

light pen   A metal stylus equipped with a light sensor on one end for scanning barcodes at the circulation desk. Some models require an external decoder. Synonymous with *bar code wand*.

lignin   An organic substance contained in wood pulp, considered undesirable in all but the lowest grades of paper because it contains acid, which weakens the cellulose in vegetable fiber, causing paper, board, and cloth to yellow and become brittle over time. Lignin is removed in the manufacture of chemical pulp but not in the production of groundwood pulp from which inexpensive papers such as newsprint are made.

Ligue des Bibliothèques Européennes de Recherche (LIBER)   The European version of the Association of Research Libraries, LIBER is a nongovernmental association of the national, university, and research libraries of Europe, founded in 1971 by an IFLA steering group under the auspices of the Council of Europe. Its goal is to assist in establishing a functional network of research libraries throughout Europe, improve access to research collections and services, facilitate research librarianship, and help preserve the European cultural heritage. LIBER publishes *LIBER Quarterly* and sponsors a conference in a different country each year. URL: www.kb.dk/liber.

lilliput edition   *See*: miniature edition.

limerick   A five-line poem written in light verse in which the rhymes (in a/a/b/b/a scheme) are highly original and often irreverent to the point of being unprintable. The earliest examples are from the 18th-century nursery rhyme collection *Mother Goose Melodies for Children* ("Hickory dickory dock . . ."").

limitation   The statement that certifies the total number of copies printed in a limited edition, usually appearing on the verso of the leaf preceding the title page. The statement usually notes any special qualities of the edition (large paper, special binding, etc.) and provides a blank space for the number of each copy to be entered by hand. In some limited editions, the statement is signed by the author and/or illustrator. Synonymous with *certificate of issue*.

limited edition   An edition consisting of a predetermined number of copies (usually 200 to 500, seldom more than 1,500) that the publisher intends not to reprint in exactly the same form. If the individual copies are consecutively numbered, each copy usually bears a certificate of issue on the verso of the leaf preceding the title page, indicating the size of the edition and copy number. Individual copies may also be autographed by the author. If a trade edition of the same work is also issued, the limited edition is usually printed on finer paper, given a better quality binding, and sold at a higher price. In the antiquarian book trade, a copy of a limited edition usually commands a higher price because of its rarity. Compare with *deluxe edition*. **See also**: *Limited Editions Club*.

Limited Editions Club (LEC)   A New York–based subscription book club established in 1929 by the bibliophile George Macy, specializing in the publication of finely printed, illustrated, and crafted collectible editions of literary classics, originally issued one title per month and limited to no more than 1,500 numbered and signed copies (later increased to 2,000). Among the most famous of the Club's early editions are Aristophanes' *Lysistrata* (1934), with pencil drawings and etchings by Picasso, and James Joyce's *Ulysses* (1935), with etchings and lithographic drawings by Matisse.

In 1978, the Club was purchased by Wall Street investment banker Sidney Shiff, who focused on works by contemporary writers. Commissioning leading graphic artists to oversee the design of each book, Shiff began to produce beautiful *livres d'artiste*, advancing the book arts in the United States. He also raised the annual subscription fee to $5,000, reduced the number of books produced to 1 to 4 per year, and limited press runs to 300 copies. Distinguished in appearance but sharing a recognizable style, LEC editions are published in large octavo or quarto formats in dust jackets and slipcases. More affordable reprints were produced by The Heritage Press. Many libraries in the United States have LEC editions in their special collections.

limiter   *See*: limiting.

limiting   A feature of a well-designed online catalog or bibliographic database that allows the user to employ various parameters to restrict the retrieval of entries containing terms included in the search statement. Limits may be set *before* a search is executed, *after* results are displayed, or both, depending on the design of the system. *Limiters* are not standardized but typically include: publication date, material type, language, full-text, peer-reviewed (journal articles), and locally held.

limp binding   A book bound without boards in flexible leather, vellum, or cloth covers, lined or unlined, a style used mainly for diaries, devotional works, and light verse. The squares in limp binding often extend further beyond the edges of the sections than in a normal binding. Inexpensive and surprisingly durable, limp bindings were used as early as the late Middle Ages for books not considered worth the expense of full binding (music scores, academic textbooks, etc.). Vellum covers had a tendency to curl under warm conditions. Compare with *flexible binding*. *See also*: *Yapp binding*.

Lindisfarne Gospels   A 259-page Gospel book written in honor of St. Cuthbert on vellum at the Monastery of Lindisfarne on Holy Island off the coast of Northumbria by a monk named Eadfrith who became Bishop of Lindisfarne in A.D. 698. A stunning example of the skill of Celtic scribes, illuminators, and book binders, the *Lindisfarne Gospels* includes 15 lavishly decorated pages marking major divisions of the text. During the 10th century, a translation of the original Latin into a form of old English was added as a gloss above the lines. Now lost, the original leather binding was decorated with jewels and precious metals. The present jeweled silver binding was added in 1852 at the expense of Edward of Maltby, Bishop of Durham. The *Lindisfarne Gospels* is one of the treasures of The British Library.

line art   In printing, an illustration of reproduction quality done in black and white, as opposed to a halftone in which the range of tonal values in the original is rendered by converting the image into a field of minutely graded dots.

line drawing   A drawing executed entirely in lines without the use of shading, hatching, or some other graphic technique to add depth or volume to the image. Cartoons, caricatures, and diagrams are often done in this style. In printing, any drawing that can be reproduced without using halftone.

line filler   A decorative device, usually of oblong shape, employed in a medieval manuscript or early printed book to fill the blank space at the end of a line of script or type of less than full line length. Fillers can be foliate, zoomorphic, or anthropomorphic in design but most are nonrepresentational. Michelle Brown notes in *Understanding Illuminated Manuscripts* (Getty Museum/British Library, 1994) that scribes working in Ireland and Britain from about A.D. 550–900 were the first to popularize the use of line fillers.

line-item budget   A method of budgeting used in some libraries and library systems in which anticipated expenditures are divided into discrete functional categories called "lines" (salaries and wages, materials, equipment, etc.) for the purpose of systematically allocating resources and tracking operating expenditures.

liner   A strip of kraft paper glued to the back of a book, to reinforce the layer of thin gauzy fabric, called *crash* or *super*, applied to the binding edge of the sections as lining.

lining   Material applied with adhesive to the binding edge of a book, following rounding and backing, to hold the sewn sections together securely, usually a piece of thin, loosely woven fabric called *crash* (also *gauze*, *mull*, or *super*). In better quality bindings, a strip of kraft paper called a *liner* is added as a second layer for extra strength. Synonymous in this sense with *back-lining*. The term is also used synonymously with *endpapers*.

link   A direct connection in a hypertext document or hypermedia file to the Internet address (URL) of another document or file, embedded as a word or phrase in the text, or appearing as a symbol, icon, or other graphic element that can be activated by the click of a mouse or some other pointing device. Text links usually appear underlined and in a distinctive color on the computer screen. A link is *broken* if it does not take the user to the desired destination when clicked. *Link rot* is a colloquial expression for the tendency of links to become broken due to address changes and the removal of HTML files from access. The remedy is regular *link checking*. Synonymous with *hyperlink*. **See also**: *deep linking* and *hot spot*.

link checking   The process of testing the links in an HTML document to determine if they are functioning properly. Software has been developed to check links automatically. Without regular checking and updating, URL changes and dead links may accumulate in a Web page.

link resolution system   A software application designed to match source citations with target resources, taking into account which materials the user is authorized by subscription or licensing agreement to access. Most link resolution systems accept citation information in the form of an OpenURL and store extensive databases describing a library's electronic journal holdings. Examples include *SFX* from Ex Libris, *Link-Finder Plus* from Endeavor, and *1Cate* from Openly Informatics. Synonymous with *link resolver*.

link resolver   *See*: link resolution system.

link source   An information resource, such as an abstracting and indexing database, capable of detecting that the user has an available *link resolution system* and of sending citation information in the form of an OpenURL to the system.

link target   An information resource that can be linked via a *link resolution system*. Link targets are often collections of full-text electronic journal articles but may also be abstracting services, citation indexes, document delivery services, library catalogs, and other useful sources of information.

Lion and the Unicorn, The   Published since 1977, *The Lion and the Unicorn* is a theme- and genre-centered journal of international scope, devoted to scholarly discussion of children's literature. Published three times a year by Johns Hopkins University Press, each issue includes a book review section. Some issues include interviews with authors, editors, and other major contributors to the field. The publication is available online in full-text as part of *Project MUSE*. ISSN: 0147–2593. URL: www.press.jhu.edu/journals/lion_and_the_unicorn.

LIRT   *See*: Library Instruction Round Table.

LIS   An abbreviation of *library and information science and library and information studies*. *See*: information science, information studies, *and* library science.

LISA   *See*: *Library and Information Science Abstracts*.

list   All the publications currently available for purchase from a given publisher, including the frontlist, backlist, and forthcoming titles. Publishers of trade books in hardcover and paperback generally issue seasonal lists twice a year in the spring and fall, or three times a year (spring, fall, and winter). *See also*: *midlist*. Also used as a shortened form of *list price* and *mailing list*.

listening room   A special soundproof room or area in a library, equipped with playback equipment (players, speakers, headphones, etc.) for listening to audiorecordings (compact discs, audiocassettes, LPs, etc.). Registered borrowers and sometimes members of the general public are permitted to use the equipment, individually or in groups, usually for a limited period of time. *See also*: *viewing room*.

list price   The undiscounted price at which a new publication is offered for sale to the public, established by the publisher at the time the edition is issued. The list price is quoted in the publisher's catalog and printed on the front flap of the dust jacket in hardcover editions and usually on the back cover in softcover editions. Discounts offered to libraries, booksellers, and jobbers are computed as a percentage off the list price. In library cataloging, the list price of an item is indicated (when available) in the standard number and terms of availability area of the bibliographic description (field 020 or 022 of the MARC record). Synonymous with *published price* and *retail price*. *See also*: *introductory price* and *prepublication price*.

LISTSERV   Mailing list management software that runs on a variety of platforms, designed to scan incoming e-mail messages for the words "subscribe," "unsubscribe," and other housekeeping commands and update the subscriber list automatically. Also used as a general term for any mailing list that runs on LISTSERV software. Two excellent online directories of e-mail discussion lists are LISZT (www.liszt.com) and Tile.Net/Lists (tile.net/lists). *See also*: *Majordomo*.

LITA   *See*: Library and Information Technology Association.

literacy   The ability to read and write with a minimal level of proficiency. *Illiteracy* is the *in*ability to read and write. The *literacy rate* of a nation or other geographic area is usually expressed as the percentage of its adult citizens who know how to read and write. In the United States, adult literacy programs have been available for many years, and public libraries have been heavily involved in promoting literacy. In recent years, such efforts have focused on adults for whom English is not the first language. Compare with *computer literacy* and *information literacy*. *See also*: *Laubach Literacy*, *Literacy Volunteers of America*, and *new adult reader*.

Literacy Volunteers of America (LVA)   A national network of over 350 locally based programs that provide professionally trained volunteer tutors to teach basic literacy and English to speakers of other languages. LVA is an affiliate of the American Library Association. URL: www.literacyvolunteers.org/home/index.htm.

literal   Following the exact words and ordinary meaning of a text or speech, without taking into account possible figurative or symbolic use of language, as in a literal interpretation of a passage from the Bible. The interpretation of words or statements according to their denotation rather than their connotation. Also refers to an approach that is prosaic or matter-of-fact, rather than intuitive.

literary agent   An organization or person in the business of offering professional advice to writers on the suitability of manuscripts for publication. An agent may also provide guidance and/or assistance in locating and selecting a publisher, negotiating a book contract, arranging the sale of subsidiary rights, and handling the business of authorship in general, usually in exchange for a commission paid by the author or a portion of the proceeds derived from the work. A literary agent may also act on behalf of a publisher to find works to fill a specific need. Not all authors use an agent; some prefer to deal directly with the publisher. Directory information for literary agents is available in the reference serials *Literary Market Place* and *Writer's Market*.

literary award   A special honor and/or reward given to an author or illustrator for creating a specific work or in recognition of a distinguished career, usually based on the decision of a qualified panel of judges. Most literary awards and prizes given annually are funded by private individuals or foundations. Rewards may include a medal, grant, and/or cash prize. Recognition usually boosts the sale of the recipient's works and can mean larger advances on royalties from publishers. *See also*: *children's book award*.

    The most prestigious literary awards are the Nobel Prize for Literature and in the United States the Pulitzer Prize. The Christchurch City Libraries in New Zealand maintain an online list of literary prizes and awards at: library.christchurch.org.nz/LiteraryPrizes. The annual reference serials *Literary Market Place* and *Writer's Market* also list literary awards and contests. In library cataloging, awards received by a work are entered in the 586 field of the MARC record. In the bibliographic display, they appear in an *Awards*: note.

literary epic   *See*: epic.

literary form   A mode of literary expression characterized by elements of internal structure, rather than by content, for example, drama, poetry, fiction, essay, etc. The major literary forms are further subdivided (one-act play, sonnet, novel, etc.). *See also*: *genre*.

literary magazine   *See*: little magazine.

Literary Market Place (LMP)   Published annually by R.R. Bowker, *LMP* is a directory of the book publishing industry in the United States and Canada, containing an alphabetic list of U.S. publishers, indexed by subject, type of publication, and geographically by state. It also lists Canadian publishers, small presses, editorial services, literary agents, book trade associations, writer's conferences and workshops, literary awards and prizes, fellowships and grants, and provides a calendar of book trade and promotional events. The section on advertising, marketing, and publicity lists book review publications, news services, book clubs, book exhibits, etc. *LMP* also includes an industry yellow pages, with separate sections for companies and key personnel. Bowker also publishes the companion *International Literary Market Place*. The most recent edition of *LMP* is shelved in the reference section of most large- and medium-sized academic and public libraries. ISSN: 0000–1155. *See also*: Writer's Market.

literary prize   *See*: literary award.

literary review   A periodical devoted to publishing contemporary poetry, short fiction, drama, essays, reviews, interviews, and sometimes art (*example*: *The Hudson Review*). Most are published quarterly and many are affiliated with institutions of higher education, for example, *The Sewanee Review* affiliated with the University of the South in Tennessee. A selection of literary reviews is provided in the reference serial *Magazines for Libraries*. Compare with *little magazine*.

literary warrant   The quantity of works that have been written on a specific subject or topic. In library cataloging, the development of portions of a classification system in response to the content of the materials requiring classification. A body of literature must exist on a topic for a new class to be added. In indexing, the addition of a subject heading or content descriptor to an indexing language, based on the frequency of its occurrence in the title or text of the documents indexed. Compare with *user warrant*.

literary work   A nonsacred work written in literary form (poem, play, essay, novel, story) recognized and appreciated by educated readers and lovers of literature for the superior quality of its style and treatment of an enduring theme. Compare with *popular fiction* and *pulp fiction*.

literati   Men of letters. Scholarly, learned, and/or well-educated people.

literature   Enduring works of poetry or prose that express ideas and emotions of universal human interest in a form and style embodying excellence. Also refers to the body of works written and/or produced on a subject, in a given field of inquiry, or in a specific language, country, period, etc. Abbreviated *lit*.

literature review   A comprehensive survey of the works published in a particular field of study or line of research, usually over a specific period of time, in the form of an in-depth, critical bibliographic essay or annotated list in which attention is drawn to the most significant works. An *annual review* is a type of serial devoted to the publication of literature reviews. Synonymous with *review of the literature*.

In scholarly journals, particularly those publishing original research in the physical and social sciences, the first section of each article, devoted to a review of the previously published literature on the subject, with references in the text to footnotes or to a list of works cited at the end.

literature search   An exhaustive search for published information on a subject conducted systematically using all available bibliographic finding tools, aimed at locating as much existing material on the topic as possible, an important initial step in any serious research project. Compare with *ready reference*.

lithography   A planographic (as opposed to *intaglio*) method of creating illustrations or prints by drawing on the surface of fine-grained limestone or on a zinc plate with a water-repellent substance to which ink adheres. When the stone is wetted, ink is repelled by the moist areas and attracted only by the design. An impression is made by applying dampened paper to the stone under pressure. In *chromolithography*, separate stones are used to produce multiple colors. Developed in Germany in the 1840s, the process is used today mainly by artists.

littera bastarda   *See*: bastarda.

littera florissa   A pen-flourished initial or letter in a medieval manuscript, embellished with tracery in geometric and/or foliate patterns. Plural: *litterae florissae*.

litterateur   A man of letters, especially one who devotes himself to the study and writing of literature in the capacity of an amateur or dilettante.

little magazine   A periodical of limited circulation devoted to experimental or avant-garde poetry, fiction, essays, humor, photography, and art. Little magazines flourished in the United States, Britain, and France during the 1920s, but most disappeared before the beginning of World War II. Desktop publishing has given new life to this form of publication. According to *Magazines for Libraries*, over 5,000 little magazines are currently published in the United States, with some available online (*example*: **Ploughshares**). For libraries, indexing is a problem because they fall outside the mainstream press. Synonymous with *literary magazine*. Compare with *zine*.

little press   *See*: small press.

liturgical work   A book used in the worship services of an organized religion. In *AACR2*, liturgical works are entered under the name of the body with which they are associated (*example*: **Catholic Church**). If a well-established title exists in English, it is used as the uniform title (*example*: **Breviary**). If there is no well-known title in English, or the name of the body is given in another language, a brief title is entered in the language of the liturgy, followed by a word or phrase in parentheses indicating the variant or special text (if applicable), for example, **Book of hours (Ms. Rohan)**. Synonymous with *service book*. Compare with *sacred text*.

An understanding of the liturgical books of the Catholic Church is essential to the study of medieval manuscripts because book production in Europe occurred mainly in monastic scriptoria from the early Christian period until about 1200. *See also*: *antiphonal, benedictional, Book of Hours, breviary, epistolary, evangelary, gradual, lectionary, martyrology, missal, ordinal, pontifical, processional, psalter,* and *sacramentary*.

live action   A motion picture or videorecording made by photographing sequences of action that occur in the living world, as opposed to one in which the optical illusion of motion is created through the use of animation techniques. A bibliographic item may consist of a combination of live action *and* animated sequences.

LJ   *See*: *Library Journal*.

LMP   *See*: *Literary Market Place*.

LMS   *See*: learning **m**anagement system *and* library **m**anagement system.

loan character   A character from one writing system used in writing another language, for example, the Chinese characters used by the Japanese to write their own language (kanji).

loan desk   *See*: circulation desk.

loan period   The length of time for which an item in the circulating collection of a library may be checked out by a borrower. Under normal circumstances, loan period is determined by the loan rule applied to a specific item, based on item type and the borrower's patron type. In most libraries, circulating items (except reserves) may be renewed for an additional loan period, provided no holds have been placed by other borrowers. Most libraries charge fines for items returned after the due date. Synonymous with *borrowing period* and *checkout period*.

loan rule   In library circulation systems, the decision governing the prescribed period of time for which an item of a specific item type may be checked out by a borrower, depending on the patron type. The loan rule also determines the form of the notice sent when an item is kept past its due date and the amount of any overdue fine charged to the patron. The cost of replacing a lost or damaged item may also be determined in part by the loan rule. Each library or library system establishes and maintains its own set of loan rules for the various categories of materials in its collections.

loan status   The type of loan in effect at a particular time for a specific item in a library collection. In public and academic libraries, most items are available for general circulation, but some may be on reserve or on loan to other libraries via interlibrary loan. Noncirculating items such as reference books are for *library use only*.

local area network (LAN)   A communications network restricted to a relatively small geographic area, often within a single building or group of adjacent buildings such as a college, university, or corporate campus, consisting of at least one high-speed server, client workstations, a network operating system, and a communications link. LANs handling communication over the Internet use optical fiber as a transmission medium. Compare with *wide area network*.

local bibliography   A bibliography of books and other materials about a specific geographic area smaller than a country, usually including material about the history, geography, architecture, and environment of the area, as well as works about the people born or residing in it. Useful in genealogical research. *See also*: *regional book*.

local collection   A library collection of books, prints, maps, photographs, and other materials related to a specific geographic area and its inhabitants, usually the community in which the library is located, useful in historical and genealogical research. *See also*: *regional book*.

local field   In library cataloging, a field of the machine-readable bibliographic record tagged **9XX** (with XX in the range of 01–99), not technically part of the MARC record format, defined by OCLC for (1) the Library of Congress, (2) local processing, and (3) OCLC-MARC record delivery services. For example, the **910** field used for data of local interest, such as funding source (grant, endowment, etc.) or the **938** field reserved for vendor-specific ordering data. OCLC does not retain 9XX fields in the master record, but they may be retained in archival records.

local serial control number   A unique identification number assigned by a library to a specific serial title, used as a code for serials control within the library but not in data exchange or communication outside the library or local system. Compare with *International Standard Serial Number*.

location code   *See*: location symbol.

location symbol   A code consisting of a few letters or a word displayed in a catalog record or added to an entry in a bibliography, indicating the specific location or collection in which the item is shelved (*example*: **Ref** for items in the reference stacks). In a union catalog, location symbols are used to indicate the libraries in the system or consortium owning at least one copy of the item. Synonymous with *location code*.

locative relation   *See*: semantic relation.

locator   The portion of an entry in a catalog or index that gives the location of the unit indexed. In the library catalog, it is the call number. In a *single index*, the locator is usually a page or paragraph number, or a figure or table number. In an *abstracting service*, the locator is the abstract number under which the full bibliographic description of a document can be found. In an *open-end index*, the locators may be the bibliographic descriptions themselves.

A *sequential locator* is a pair of locators separated by a hyphen, indicating the first and last pages, paragraphs, or sections of the book or other document in which the indexed topic is mentioned. To avoid ambiguity, it is standard practice to give the second part of a sequential locator in full (*example*: **396–409** instead of **396–09**).

loc cit.   An abbreviation of the Latin phrase *loco citato*, meaning "in the place cited."

locked up   Said of assembled type and display matter made up into pages and imposed in a *chase* once it has been tightly secured by adjusting small expandable wooden or metal boxes called *quoins* positioned between the imposed type and the sides of the chase. The resulting *forme* is ready to be placed on the *bed* of the press for printing.

LOCKSS   An acronym for **L**ots **o**f **C**opies **K**eeps **S**tuff **S**afe, an application designed to create low-cost, persistent digital "caches" of electronic journal articles, housed locally at institutions that have authorized access to the content and elect to preserve it. The idea behind LOCKSS is that e-journal content is more likely to be preserved if there are many distributed copies of the material. If a particular document ceases to be available from the publisher's site, it can be accessed from the LOCKSS cache. URL: lockss.stanford.edu.

LOEX   An acronym for **L**ibrary **O**rientation **Ex**change (pronounced "low-ex"), a "library outreach" office established in 1971 at Eastern Michigan State University with the aid of a grant from the Council on Library Resources (CLR) and the National

Endowment for the Humanities (NEH). Since its inception, LOEX has sponsored the annual *LOEX Conference*, attended by bibliographic instruction librarians and other individuals with an interest in library instruction, and has served as a clearinghouse for bibliographic instruction materials and resources. URL: www.emich.edu/public/ loex/loex.html.

logical difference   In Boolean logic, the result obtained when the **NOT** command is used to separate members of a set of entities from those of another. It is the search strategy used to determine which records in a library catalog or bibliographic database contain term **A** but not term **B**. Synonymous with *logical subtraction* and *negation*. Compare with *logical product* and *logical sum*.

logical product   In Boolean logic, the result obtained when the **AND** command is used to find all the members common to two or more sets of entities. It is the search strategy used to determine which records in a library catalog or bibliographic database contain both term **A** and term **B**. Synonymous with *logical multiplication* and *conjunction*. Compare with *logical difference* and *logical sum*.

logical sum   In Boolean logic, the result obtained when the **OR** command is used to find all the members of two or more sets of entities. It is the search strategy used to determine which records in a library catalog or bibliographic database contain term **A** or term **B**, or both **A** and **B**. Synonymous with *logical addition* and *union*. Compare with *logical difference* and *logical product*.

logo   An emblem or graphic design used in publications and on promotional materials by a company, organization, agency, or institution as a trademark or symbol of its identity. Web sites often include a logo to indicate affiliation with a host organization or to suggest the nature of the site's content.

log off   The procedure by which a user closes or terminates communication with a remote computer system. The opposite of *log on*. Also spelled *log-off* or *logoff*. Compare with *exit*.

logoff   *See*: log off.

logogram   A symbol or character that stands for an entire word, for example, $ for *dollar* and # for *number*.

log on   The procedure by which a user gains access to and initiates communication with a remote computer system, usually by typing or entering an authorized username and/or password. The opposite of *log off*. Also spelled *log-on* and *logon*.

logon   *See*: log on.

logotype   In letterpress, a unit of type cast in one piece, bearing two or more characters on the body, not tied together as in a *ligature*, for example, the frequently used **Qu** letter combination.

long discount   The standard discount given by a publisher to a bookseller on trade books, usually 40 percent. Compare with *short discount*.

longitudinal study   A research methodology in which the same phenomenon is observed continuously or at intervals over an extended period of time, usually to discern temporal patterns or identify changes that occur in response to altered conditions. *See also*: *user survey*.

long page In printing, a page containing more lines of type matter than specified. In books, a typesetter may add an extra line (or lines) to avoid setting an *orphan* or *widow*. Compare with *short page*.

long-playing record (LP) A sound recording medium in which music or spoken words are recorded in a continuous spiral groove on the surface of a thin, flat vinyl disk that can be played back at 33⅓ rpm using a device called a *record player* equipped with a stylus, cartridge, and speakers to amplify the sound. Long-playing records have been superseded, first by audiocassettes and then by audio compact discs. They are purchased by collectors and retained by libraries for archival purposes. Also known as *vinyl*. *See also*: *monaural*, *quadraphonic*, and *stereophonic*.

loose Sheets of paper, parchment, etc., that are unbound, usually filed in a folder or container. The opposite of *bound*. *See also*: *loose-leaf*.

Also refers to one or more leaves, or all the sections of a book, that have become partially or completely detached from the binding through use. The term is also used to describe the binding on a well-used book that opens easily and lies flat at any page. The opposite of *tight*.

loose-back *See*: hollow back.

loose-leaf A rigid or flexible mechanical binding that can be manually opened and closed by the user to remove or insert, at any location in the sequence of pages, one or more leaves or sections with holes or slots punched along the back margin. The most common varieties are *ring binding* and *post binding*. Loose-leaf binding is used in libraries for reference serials, government documents, legal publications, instruction manuals, etc., which must be updated on a regular basis. Compare with *comb binding* and *spiral binding*.

loose-leaf service A serial publication, usually sold on subscription, designed for storage in a loose-leaf binder to permit the insertion of new and/or replacement pages and the removal of outdated material, as content is revised, cumulated, and/or indexed, a format used to disseminate information that must be updated frequently (financial, legal, scientific, etc.). Investment *advisory services* are often issued in this form. In *AACR2*, this type of integrating resource is called an *updating loose-leaf*.

lossless A conversion from one format to another that does not result in the loss of information. The opposite of *lossy*.

lossy *See*: lossless.

lost A code used in a library catalog record to indicate the circulation status of an item no longer available because it was checked out to a previous borrower and never returned. Most libraries bill the patron an amount based on the cost of replacement after a number of overdue notices have been sent without result. In some libraries, the charge may be refundable if the item is found and returned within a reasonable time. Compare with *missing*.

Also refers to a creative work whose existence is known only through allusions or quotations in the writings of contemporary authors, all manifestations having disappeared. Literary works of the classical period (poems, plays, etc.) are often known only through fragmentary quotations and references in surviving works.

lot   A regular shipment of books, periodicals, or other printed material sent by a library to a bindery for binding or rebinding. The phrase "closing the lot" refers to the point in time after which no further items are added to a shipment. Only when the lot is closed can the necessary paperwork be prepared to accompany the shipment.

low-demand   *See*: demand.

lowercase   The small letters as opposed to the capital letters of a type font. The opposite of *uppercase*. Type matter set in lowercase can be read more rapidly than the same text set in uppercase.

The words "lowercase" and "uppercase" are derived from the relative positions of the compartments within the wood or metal case designed to hold elements of type bearing small letters and capital letters at a typesetter's bench in the days when typesetting was done by hand (letterpress). Also spelled *lower case*. Compare with *minuscule*. *See also*: *ascender*, *descender*, and *x-height*.

LP   *See*: large print *and* long-playing record.

LRC   *See*: learning resources center.

LRRT   *See*: Library Research Round Table.

LSCA   *See*: *Library Services and Construction Act*.

LSO   *See*: library security officer.

LSSIRT   *See*: Library Support Staff Interests Round Table.

LSTA   *See*: *Library Services and Technology Act*.

lurk   To receive and read messages posted to an online discussion forum, or observe the exchanges in a chat room, without actively participating in the discussion. In some mailing lists, there may be more *lurkers* than active correspondents.

LVA   *See*: Literacy Volunteers of America.

lyric   In classical Greece, a song or poem performed to the accompaniment of a harp-like stringed instrument called a *lyre*. In contemporary usage, a relatively short poem in which a single speaker expresses a personal emotion or state of mind, as opposed to narrating a sequence of events. The form includes sonnets, elegies, odes, and hymns. Compare with *lyrics*.

lyricist   *See*: lyrics.

lyrics   The words of a song or musical drama, as opposed to its music. In libraries, songs and musicals are cataloged under the name of the composer, with an added entry under the name of the *lyricist* when the words are written by a person other than the composer (*examples*: **Lorenz Hart** and **Oscar Hammerstein** who wrote the words for musical works composed by Richard Rodgers). Compare with *lyric*.

M

Mac   *See*: Macintosh.

machine-aided indexing   A method of indexing in which a computer is programmed to select possible descriptors from a thesaurus of preferred terms based on an analysis of words and phrases appearing in the title and/or text of a work. Each suggestion is evaluated by a human indexer and either accepted or rejected. The indexer is also free to select additional authorized terms for indexing. Compare with *automatic indexing*.

machine-readable   Data in a form that can be recognized, accepted, and interpreted by a machine, such as a computer or other data processing device, whether created in such a form or converted from a format that a machine cannot read. Usually refers to digital information stored on hard disk, floppy disk, or magnetic tape. *See also*: *Machine-Readable Cataloging*.

Machine-Readable Cataloging (MARC)   An international standard digital format for the description of bibliographic items developed by the Library of Congress during the 1960s to facilitate the creation and dissemination of computerized cataloging from library to library within the same country and between countries. By 1971 the MARC format had become the national standard for dissemination of bibliographic data and by 1973 an international standard.

There are several versions of MARC in use in the world, the most predominant being MARC21, created in 1999 as a result of the harmonization of U.S. and Canadian MARC formats; UKMARC, used primarily in the United Kingdom; and UNIMARC, widely used in Europe. The MARC21 family of standards now includes formats for authority records, holdings records, classification schedules, and community information, in addition to the bibliographic record format.

Widespread use of the MARC standard has helped libraries acquire predictable and reliable cataloging data, make use of commercially available library automation systems, share bibliographic resources, avoid duplication of effort, and ensure that bibliographic data will be compatible when one automation system is replaced by another.

The MARC record has three components:

Record structure—an implementation of national and international standards (*Information Exchange Format* ANSI Z39.2 and *Format for Information Exchange* ISO 2709)

Content designation—codes and conventions that explicitly identify and characterize the data elements within a record to facilitate the manipulation of data, defined in the *MARC21 Format for Bibliographic Data* and other MARC21 formats maintained by the Library of Congress

Data content—defined by external standards such as *AACR2, Library of Congress Subject Headings (LCSH)*, etc.

The MARC record is divided into fields, each containing one or more related elements of bibliographic description. A field is identified by a three-digit tag designating the nature of its content. Tags are organized as follows in hundreds, indicating a group of related tags, with **XX** in the range of **00–99**:

0XX fields—Control information, numbers, codes
1XX fields—Main entry
2XX fields—Titles, edition, imprint
3XX fields—Physical description, etc.
4XX fields—Series statements (as shown in item)
5XX fields—Notes
6XX fields—Subject added entries
7XX fields—Added entries other than subject or series
8XX fields—Series added entries (other authoritative forms)

The Network Development and MARC Standards Office of the Library of Congress maintains the *MARC Standards* homepage at: lcweb.loc.gov/marc. *See also*: *Avram, Henriette D.*; *MARCese*; and *USMARC*.

machine-readable data file (MRDF)   Information stored in a form that can be used directly as computer input, without conversion from a format that is not machine-readable, for example, bibliographic records in MARC format as opposed to printed catalog cards. Storage medium varies (magnetic tape, magnetic disk, etc.). *See also*: *electronic resource.*

machine-readable records   In archives, records created and maintained in a medium that requires some kind of machine to access their content (microforms, sound recordings, videorecordings, magnetic tape and disks, optical disks, etc.). Compare with *electronic records. See also*: *machine-readable data file.*

Macintosh   The family of computers introduced by Apple in 1984 that popularized the graphical user interface (GUI), setting a precedent for the design of user-friendly graphical applications and operating systems that other software companies like Microsoft were quick to follow. Although Apple commands only 5 percent of the market for desktop computers, the company produces the largest series of non-IBM-compatible personal computers. "Macs" remain popular in desktop publishing and graphic design because of the usability of the interface. In libraries, Macs are used mainly in the children's room and curriculum room. *See also*: *UNIX* and *Windows.*

macro   In computing, a method of customizing user input in which a series of recorded keystrokes, commands, or menu options are assigned a brief name or key combination (usually **Ctrl** or **Alt** plus a specific character) to enable the user to execute a predetermined sequence of steps quickly by simply typing the name or key combination. Also called *keyboard macro.*

macroform   A general term for any storage medium bearing text and/or images large enough to be easily read without the aid of magnification. Macroforms can be transparent (*example*: **overhead transparencies**) or opaque (**photocopies**). Compare with *microform.*

made-up copy   A copy of a book assembled from parts taken from one or more defective copies of the same edition, or a copy in which imperfections are corrected by adding or substituting parts taken from other copies of the same edition. In the antiquarian book trade, the practice is not considered unethical as long as the manner in which the volume is composed is revealed rather than concealed.

magazine   A popular interest periodical usually containing articles on a variety of topics, written by various authors in a nonscholarly style. Most magazines are heavily illustrated, contain advertising, and are printed on glossy paper. Articles are usually short (less than five pages long), frequently unsigned, and do not include a bibliography or list of references for further reading. Most magazines are issued monthly or weekly for sale at newsstands, in bookstores, and by subscription. English-language magazines are listed by subject in *Magazines for Libraries* published by R.R. Bowker. Abbreviated *mag.* Compare with *journal* and *journal of commentary.* *See also*: *children's magazine, electronic magazine, general interest magazine, hybrid journal, newsmagazine, special interest magazine,* and *zine.*

Also refers to a rectangular slotted container designed to hold a sequence of slides, queued for use in a slide projector. Compare with *carousel.*

magazine pagination   Numbering the pages of a periodical, starting with one at the beginning of each issue. Magazines and trade journals are usually paginated in this way, making it more difficult to locate a specific article in a bound volume by page numbers, compared with a publication that uses *journal pagination.*

Magazines for Libraries (MFL)   Published irregularly since 1969 by R.R. Bowker, *MFL* is a subject list (with title index) of over 8,000 English-language periodicals, selected by the editors from over 170,000 possibilities as the most useful for the average public, academic, government, school, or special library. Coverage includes general interest magazines, research journals, trade journals, zines, and children's periodicals. Each entry includes a basic bibliographic description; an annotation explaining the purpose, scope, and audience of the publication; and a brief evaluation. Libraries usually place this collection development tool on standing order and shelve it in the reference section. ISSN: 0000–0914.

MAGERT   *See*: **M**ap **a**nd **Ge**ography **R**ound **T**able.

magnetic disk   A rewritable computer storage medium consisting of a revolving platter on which digital data is encoded as tiny magnetic spots arranged in tracks. Data is read by a mechanical arm designed to move a read-write head across the surface of the platter. Usually encased in a rigid, protective case, a magnetic disk can be either fixed (hard disk) or removable (floppy disk, Zip disk, etc.). Compare with *optical disk.*

magnetic strip   A thin magnetized strip of plastic firmly affixed to a book or other bibliographic item at the time it is processed, which can be set to trigger a security alarm whenever someone attempts to remove the item from the library without checking it out. Synonymous with *security strip* and *tattle-tape.* *See also*: *desensitization.*

magnetic tape   An electronic storage medium consisting of a thin strip of flexible plastic to which a metallic coating is applied that can be selectively magnetized to record information sequentially in linear or helical tracks. Magnetic tape is mounted on open reels or in cartridges. To retrieve a specific record or file on tape, all the records (or partitions) preceding it must be sequentially searched. Magnetic disk storage is faster because it allows data to be accessed randomly. For this reason, data in current use is usually stored on disk, but tape is often used for archival storage because it is more economical and has greater capacity.

magnum opus   Latin for "great work." A literary or artistic work considered by discerning critics to be of major importance, usually the crowning achievement of its author, composer, or creator (*example*: *Ulysses* by James Joyce). Not all authors and artists produce a work that is considered superior to their others (**William Shakespeare**). The opposite of *opuscule.* Compare with *masterpiece.*

mailing list   An e-mail discussion forum that allows individuals to subscribe and automatically receive messages posted to the list by other subscribers. Participants may also post their own messages and replies for distribution to the other subscribers to the list. A mailing list may be *moderated* or *unmoderated.* Synonymous with *electronic discussion list.* Compare with *bulletin board system* and *distribution list.* *See also*: *LISTSERV, lurk, Majordomo,* and *netiquette.*

A list of *Library-Oriented Lists & Electronic Serials* is maintained by the Washington Research Library Consortium (WRLC) at: www.wrlc.org/liblists. Two of the most comprehensive general directories of e-mail discussion groups are LISZT (www. liszt.com) and Tile.Net/Lists (tile.net/lists).

main class   One of the highest-level divisions of a classification system. In Library of Congress Classification, the 20 major classes are indicated by letters of the English alphabet:

A—General works	**K**—Law
B—Philosophy, psychology, religion	**L**—Education
C—Auxiliary sciences of history (archaeology, genealogy, etc.)	**M**—Music
	N—Fine arts
D—History (except America)	**P**—Language and literature
E–F—History: America and United States	**Q**—Science
G—Geography and anthropology	**R**—Medicine
H—Social sciences	**S**—Agriculture
J—Political science	**T**—Technology and engineering

U—Military science
V—Naval science

Z—History of books, library science, bibliography

In Dewey Decimal Classification, the 10 main classes are indicated by the arabic numerals 0–9 in the first digit of the notation:

000—Generalities
100—Philosophy, parapsychology and occultism, psychology
200—Religion
300—Social sciences
400—Language

500—Natural sciences and mathematics
600—Technology (Applied sciences)
700—Arts (Fine and Decorative Arts)
800—Literature (Belles-lettres) and rhetoric
900—Geography, history, and auxiliary disciplines

See also: *division* and *section*.

main entry   The entry in a library catalog that provides the fullest description of a bibliographic item, by which the work is to be uniformly identified and cited. In *AACR2*, the main entry is the primary access point. In the card catalog, it includes all the secondary headings under which the item is cataloged, called *added entries*. For most items, main entry is under the name of the author. When there is no author, main entry is under the title.

mainframe   A large computer system capable of supporting many terminals that do not have independent processing capability, used to run complex applications that require a considerable amount of computing power. Mainframes are classified by size (small, medium, and large). Compare with *microcomputer, minicomputer,* and *supercomputer.*

main heading   In pre-coordinate indexing, the first part of a composite heading divided by at least one subheading, usually separated from the first subheading by a dash or other mark of punctuation. In the Library of Congress subject heading **Information science—Research—Methodology**, the term *Information science* is the main heading and *Research* and *Methodology* are subheadings. *See also*: *subdivision.*

main library   *See*: central library.

main schedule   The list of classes used by a cataloger or indexer, individually or in combination, to classify documents by subject under the rules of a given classification system, arranged in the order of their symbolic notation. In a hierarchical classification system, the logical divisions, subdivisions, etc., of the main classes are displayed. Compare with *auxiliary schedule.*

maintenance contract   A formal agreement in which an outside company agrees to check designated equipment on a regular basis after any warranty has expired and to maintain it in good working order, including major repairs as needed, in exchange for payment of a monthly or annual fee, an arrangement common in libraries that own their own photocopiers, reader-printer machines, computer equipment, etc.

Also refers to an agreement with an outside company to clean and maintain a library facility on a regular basis in exchange for payment of a monthly or annual fee. Some libraries and library systems hire their own maintenance personnel or use the services provided by the parent organization.

major descriptor   A descriptor or identifier in an index entry or bibliographic record representing a main focus or subject of the document indexed, usually indicated by an asterisk or other symbol or distinguished typographically. *Minor descriptors* and identifiers representing less significant aspects of the content are left unmarked.

Majordomo   An Internet mailing list program designed to run on the UNIX operating system. Compare with *LISTSERV*.

Major Orchestra Librarians' Association (MOLA)   Founded in 1983 by representatives of the Philadelphia Orchestra, Boston Symphony, and Minnesota Orchestra, MOLA is an international organization devoted to improving communication among performance librarians and helping them provide better service to their orchestras. The association also presents a unified voice in relations with music publishers. Its membership includes over 170 libraries associated with orchestras, opera and ballet companies, military bands, and music conservatories. MOLA publishes the quarterly newsletter *Marcato* and hosts the *MOLAList* electronic mailing list. URL: mola-inc. org.

majuscule   A script in which the letters are of uniform height, as in modern *uppercase*. Majuscule is a *bilinear* script because all the letterforms are bounded by two imaginary horizontal lines. Examples include the square capitals and rustic capitals of Antiquity, and the uncial script used in the early Christian period for writing manuscripts in Greek and Latin, as distinct from the *minuscule* adopted as a book hand in the 8th century during the reign of Charlemagne. *See also*: *Insular majuscule*.

makeready   The process of preparing the printing press for a press run, including adjustment of the forme or plates to produce a uniform impression.

make-up   In letterpress printing, the process of removing type from the galleys and arranging it in page format, including the positioning of text, illustrations, notes, and running heads in accordance with the typographer's layout, done by a worker known as a *compositor*. Also spelled *makeup*. *See also*: *remake*.

Also refers to a list of the contents of a book in the order in which they are to be bound, provided by the publisher to the binder to ensure that any plates or other additions not printed with the text are included in correct sequence.

managed book   A book on a topic chosen by the publisher, who controls and directs every aspect of its creation. If a paid staff writer or freelancer is used for the text, the structure of the work is usually based on an outline provided by the publisher. In books with a preponderance of pictorial content, the name of the author or editor may not be given on the title page. Compare with *packaged book*.

management information system (MIS)   A computer-based information system developed and maintained by a commercial enterprise to integrate data from all its departments (product development, production and inventory, marketing and sales, personnel administration, etc.) to support managerial and supervisory decision-making with real time analysis. MIS systems are designed to track progress toward achievement of a company's goals and objectives and to aid in identifying problems or obstacles that must be resolved or removed by upper-level management. In the plural, the term refers to the study and teaching of such systems. Courses on MIS are offered as a major by some business schools in the United States.

mandatory (M)   In OCLC documentation, a field or subfield of the MARC record in which data must be entered to meet OCLC input standards for a given encoding level. Compare with *optional* and *required if applicable and readily available*.

mandorla   A decorative motif in the shape of a pointed oval, used in bookbinding, usually as a centerpiece. In medieval manuscript illumination, an almond-shaped aureole painted around the head or body of a deity or holy person (or group of holy figures), often ornamented with gilding.

manicula   *See*: fist.

manifestation   As defined in *FRBR* (*Functional Requirements for Bibliographic Records*), the result of a single act of physical embodiment/production of a specific expression of a creative work, for example, an edition of one of the variant texts of a literary work (1993 Yale University Press edition of ***Hamlet***) or a recording of a specific performance of a musical work (1998 recording of ***West Side Story*** released by Sony/Columbia on compact disc). A manifestation consists of all the physical objects (items) possessing the same characteristics with respect to intellectual/artistic content and physical form, in most instances a set of multiple copies produced for commercial distribution. However, for some expressions there may be only a single exemplar, as in the case of an archival oral history recording, an author's manuscript, or a one-of-a-kind *artist's book*.

manifesto   A public declaration, in writing or in speech, of beliefs, motives, plans, and/ or intentions, made by an individual, group, or government (*example*: ***Mein Kampf*** by Adolf Hitler).

manila   A thick, durable buff-colored paper, originally manufactured from Manila hemp fiber, used mainly for file folders, mailing envelopes, and cards. Also spelled *manilla*.

manual   A book of compact size, especially one describing in considerable detail the government of a state or the structure and functions of a government agency (*example*: ***The United States Government Manual*** published annually by the U.S. GPO).

Also refers to a book or pamphlet containing practical instructions, rules, or steps for performing a task or operation, assembling a manufactured object, or using a system or piece of equipment (*example*: ***Manual of Archival Description*** published by Gower). Used synonymously with *handbook*. *See also*: *style manual*.

Also, any operation or procedure done by hand rather than by machine.

manufacturer   In library cataloging, the agency responsible for actually making a bibliographic item. In the case of books and other printed publications, the printer is the manufacturer. Compare with *producer*.

manuscript   From the Latin phrase *codex manu scriptus*. Strictly speaking, a work of any kind (text, inscription, music score, map, etc.) written entirely by hand. A *medieval manuscript* is one written in Europe prior to the invention of printing from movable type (about 1450). Also refers to the handwritten or typescript copy of an author's work as submitted for publication, before printing. In the United States, bibliographic control of manuscript collections is provided by the National Union Catalog of Manuscript Collections (NUCMC), a cooperative cataloging program of the Library of Congress. In *AACR2*, manuscripts are cataloged under the rules for printed books. Abbreviated *ms.* and *mss.* in the plural. *See also*: *illuminated*, *manuscript book*, and *Manuscript Society, The*.

manuscript book   A book written entirely by hand, particularly one produced prior to the invention of printing from movable type, usually copied by medieval monks or scribes on leaves of parchment or vellum, bound in leather-covered wooden boards. Medieval manuscript books were often rubricated, illuminated, and/or embellished with miniatures. *See also*: *Book of Hours*.

Manuscript Society, The   Founded in 1948 as the National Society of Autograph Collectors, The Manuscript Society has since grown to a membership of over 1,800 scholars, authors, dealers, private collectors, librarians, archivists, and curators. Its membership also includes historical societies, museums, special libraries, and academic libraries with manuscript collections. The Society publishes the quarterly journal *Manuscripts* and the quarterly newsletter *Manuscript Society News*. URL: www.manuscript.org.

Manutius, Aldus (1450–1515)   The latinized name of Teobaldo Manucci (also known as Aldo Manuzio), the humanist scholar of the Italian Renaissance who established the Adline Press in Venice to print editions of the Greek and Latin classics. During his 20 years at Aldine, he also published grammars, religious works, contemporary secular texts, popular works, political and scientific treatises, history, and geography. He also commissioned the sloping type now known as *italic* and a roman typeface that influenced Garamont and its successors.

map   Any two-dimensional representation of all or a portion of the earth's surface, the heavens, another celestial body, or an imaginary geographical area, normally done to scale on a flat medium but increasingly in digital form. Early maps were drawn on parchment stored in rolls. In modern libraries, maps are usually stored flat or folded in a specially designed metal map case with wide, shallow drawers. Maps are also included as inserts or pocket parts in books and periodicals. As illustrations, they may be printed as plates with the text or on the endpapers. An *atlas* is a book consisting almost entirely of maps, with the content usually indexed in a gazetteer at the end. The largest mapping agency in the United States is the U.S. Geological Survey. The *American Memory* project at the Library of Congress provides online access to a historical map collection at: memory.loc.gov/ammem/gmdhtml/gmdhome.html. Compare with *globe*. *See also*: *cartography*, *cartouche*, *legend*, *map series*, and *projection*.

Maps are categorized by the type of content and method of presentation. *See also*: *aerial map*, *astronomical map*, *bathymetric map*, *cadastral map*, *cartogram*, *chart*, *choropleth map, city map, contour map, dynamic map, geologic map, hydrologic map, index map, inset map, interactive map, mental map, multimedia map, photomap, planimetric map, political map, rare map, relief map, road map, thematic map,* and *topographic map.*

Map and Geography Round Table (MAGERT)   A round table of the American Library Association established in 1980, MAGERT is the world's largest organization devoted to map and geography librarianship. Membership is open to ALA members who work with or have an interest in map and geography collections and information related to maps and mapping. MAGERT publishes the semiannual journal *Meridian* and the bimonthly newsletter *Base Line.* URL: magert.whoi.edu:8000.

map case   A library furnishing, usually made of wood or metal, containing a number of wide, shallow drawers in which large sheet maps can be stored flat, with a large smooth top on which they can be spread for examination.

map index   An alphabetical list of the place names written or printed on a map or series of maps, giving the location of each feature, usually as grid coordinates. Compare with *index map.*

map library   A library or unit within a library that has collections consisting primarily of cartographic materials that are of current or historic interest, including maps, atlases, gazetteers, charts, globes, relief models, digital data, remotely sensed images, etc., for example, the Perry-Castaneda Library Map Collection at the University of Texas (URL: www.lib.utexas.edu/maps/index.html). *Map librarians* are organized in the Map and Geography Round Table (MAGERT) of the American Library Association.

mappa mundi   Latin for "map of the world." Maps made by medieval scholars to show the geography of the world as it was then understood, often drawn to illustrate religious texts. Michelle Brown notes in *Understanding Illuminated Manuscripts* (Getty Museum/British Library, 1994) that although world maps existed in Antiquity, the earliest surviving example appears in an Anglo-Saxon book produced in the 11th century. Also made as altarpieces, *mappae mundi* served as visual compendia of human knowledge, incorporating biblical history and material from other works. Drawn on a single large sheet of parchment, the Hereford Mappa Mundi, on public exhibit in Hereford Cathedral, is the largest and most elaborate surviving pre-15th-century world map. As the art of making navigational charts developed, world maps became more detailed and accurate.

mapping   *See*: vocabulary mapping.

mapping agency   An organization that produces and publishes maps and other cartographic information, usually under the sponsorship of a national government or its armed forces. The largest mapping agency in the United States is the U.S. Geological Survey. In *AACR2*, name of mapping agency is given in the statement of responsibility area of the bibliographic description of a cartographic item.

map series   A series of sheet maps, all drawn to the same scale and specifications, encompassing a clearly defined geographic area when complete, identified collectively by the mapping agency that produced them.

MARBI   Machine-Readable Bibliographic Information Committee, the body within the American Library Association responsible for developing official ALA positions on standards for representing bibliographic information in machine-readable formats. Its membership includes nine voting members from ALCTS, LITA, and RUSA and three interns. MARBI's primary responsibility is to participate in deliberations of the MARC Advisory Committee, which advises the Library of Congress on changes to the MARC21 family of formats. Other members of the MARC Advisory Committee include ex-officio representatives of the U.S. national libraries, the National Library of Canada, the National Library of Australia, the bibliographic utilities, and several dozen nonvoting liaisons from other units within the ALA and from non-ALA organizations with an interest in issues related to library automation standards.

marbled paper   *See*: marbling.

marbling   A technique for producing decorated paper in which a unique design is transferred to each sheet by contact with watercolors floated on a bath of size or gum. The liquid pigments are swirled with a special implement, such as a comb, to create a pattern resembling the surface of cut stone. Marbled paper is used for doublures and endpapers in hand-bound books and as a covering material. The technique is also used to decorate the edges of the sections of books and on leather by the application of acid or inks (see *Spanish calf*). Originally developed in the East (Japanese examples survive from the 9th century), the technique was used in Persian book production as early as the 16th century. Introduced into Europe in the late 16th century, marbling was particularly popular during the Victorian period in deluxe editions. As a less expensive alternative, endpapers are sometimes printed in a pattern resembling hand-marbled paper.

MARC   *See*: Machine-Readable Cataloging.

MARC21   The version of **M**achine **R**eadable **C**ataloging that superseded USMARC in 1999 with the harmonization of U.S. and Canadian MARC formats. MARC21 is supported by OCLC and is the current official MARC standard in the United States, Canada, Australia, and numerous other countries. *See also*: *MARCXML*.

MARCese   The jargon used by librarians who work extensively with MARC records and fall into the habit of using content designators (tags, indicators, and subfield codes) instead of words and phrases to refer to areas and elements of bibliographic description.

MARC record   *See*: Machine-Readable Cataloging.

MARCXML   A flexible and extensible framework for working with **M**achine **R**eadable **C**ataloging (MARC) in the XML markup language. Developed by the Library of Congress, MARCXML allows the content of MARC21 records to be represented in XML. It is designed to support "round-trip" conversion from MARC21 to MARCXML and back to MARC21, with all field tagging, subfield coding, and indicator values preserved and with no loss of data. Compare with *Metadata Object Description Schema*.

margin   Any one of the four blank borders around the matter written or printed on a page or sheet, known as the *top* or *head* margin; the *bottom*, *foot*, or *tail* margin; the *outer*, *outside*, or *fore-edge* margin; and the *inner*, *inside*, *back*, or *binding* margin. The combined inner margins of facing pages form the *gutter*. Relative width of the margin is important in the design of a legible, aesthetically pleasing page. Standard proportions are: bottom margin double the top and inside margin one-half or two-thirds of the outside, with the height of the written or printed area roughly equal to the width of the page. Rebinding may require trimming the inner margin of a book. In medieval manuscripts, the margins were often used for glosses and corrections in the text. They also provided space for decorative extensions on initial letters and for ornamental borders. *See also*: *marginalia*.

marginalia   Latin for "things in the margin." Headings or notes printed in the margins of a page, usually in type of a size or style distinct from that of the text. Marginalia include footnotes, side notes, and shoulder notes. Also included are glosses, annotations, diagrams, doodles, etc., added by a commentator or reader. In manuscripts, corrections are sometimes made in the margins. The term does not include the ornamental borders and marginal decoration often found in medieval manuscripts and incunabula.

marginal note   *See*: side note.

mark up   In publishing, to prepare copy for printing by specifying details of typeface, fonts, layout, etc., in a code comprehensible to the compositor or typesetter.

markup   In computing, the encoding of a textual document with information external to the document, for example, to indicate the structure of the document, the type or grammatical function of words and phrases within the document, or the way in which portions of the document are displayed on screen or page, usually accomplished by inserting tags and format codes in the text. To see the markup tags used in a Web page, log on to the URL and select "View—Source" or its equivalent in the toolbar of the Web browser. Also spelled *mark-up*. *See also*: *markup language*.

markup language   In computing, a predefined set of descriptors (symbols and tags) or a method of defining descriptors that are used to embed external information in an electronic text document, usually to specify formatting or facilitate analysis. Markup languages were originally designed for use with a specific program, but in 1986 the Standard Generalized Markup Language (SGML) was adopted as an international standard. The Hypertext Markup Language (HTML) used in creating Web pages is derived from SGML (to see the markup tags in a hypertext document, log on to the URL, then select "View—Source" or its equivalent in the toolbar of the Web browser). In 1998, the World Wide Web Consortium (W3C) recommended the use of a simplified version of SGML known as Extensible Markup Language (XML). Most markup languages differ from databases in identifying elements within a stream of text, rather than discrete, structured data elements, but XML is capable of turning text into the equivalent of a database. Also spelled *mark-up language*. *See also*: *Encoded Archival Description*, *MARCXML*, and *Text Encoding Initiative*.

martyrology   A liturgical book containing narratives of the lives of Christian saints and their martyrdoms, from the earliest period of Church history, arranged in the order of their feast days, for reading in the Divine Office at the canonical hour of prime. As saints continued to be canonized, the martyrology was limited to major saints.

masque   A lavish form of court entertainment that originated in Renaissance Italy and was particularly popular during the reigns of Elizabeth I, James I, and Charles I of England. Masques combined music, song, dance, and poetic drama in a spectacular display of costume and elaborate staging held together by a loose allegorical plot, usually based on a mythological theme (*example*: *Masque of Blacknesse* by Ben Jonson). The name is derived from the face *masques* worn by the members of court who played the main characters. This costly form of royal amusement ended with the Puritan revolution of 1642.

mass deacidification   *See*: deacidification.

mass-market paperback   A new work or reprint of a title previously published in hardcover or trade paperback, produced and distributed in paperback for sale at news-stands and in supermarkets, drugstores, chain stores, etc., rather than trade bookstores. Copies are usually of standard rack size (4 $\times$ 7 inches), printed on poor-quality paper, bound with hot-melt adhesive in covers designed for sales appeal, and priced to sell to the widest possible audience. The format is used extensively for popular fiction and genre fiction. Libraries prefer them for books-by-mail programs to keep mailing costs down. In some public libraries, mass-market paperbacks received as gifts are circulated on the honor system. *See also*: *pulp fiction*.

mass media   *See*: media.

master   In reprography, the plate, stencil, negative, or document from which copies are made, usually more than once. The quality of a master copy usually deteriorates with extended use. *See also*: *generation*, *master negative*, and *print master*.

    Also refers to an artist, writer, composer, or craftsman who consistently creates works of the highest quality (*example*: **Mozart**). In medieval manuscript illustration, an artist whose work was so exceptional that it became widely known and appreciated in Europe and influenced the direction of illumination, for example, the Boucicaut Master whose Paris workshop produced highly innovative miniatures in the early 15th century. *See also*: *masterpiece*.

master negative   In microfilm, the first-generation negative, developed from the film used to shoot the image, from which at least one print master is made, usually stored in a separate location under controlled conditions and used as little as possible. *See also*: *service copy*.

masterpiece   A work of art, craftsmanship, or writing universally recognized as em-bodying the highest skill of a great master or group of masters. An artist, composer, or writer may produce a single masterpiece (*examples*: **Charlotte** and **Emily Brontë**) or more than one masterpiece in a lifetime (**Jane Austen**). Synonymous with *chef-d'oeuvre*. Compare with *magnum opus*.

masthead   A box or column printed in each issue of a newspaper or periodical stating the title of the publication, its publisher, ownership, editors, frequency, ISSN, subscription rates, and giving notice of copyright, usually with contact information. In most newspapers, the masthead is found on the editorial page or on page one. In magazines and journals, it is usually printed on or near the contents page. Compare with *flag*. *See also*: *date line*.

mat   Two pieces of board hinged along one edge for mounting a print, photograph, etc., the bottom piece providing support (backing) and the top piece cut in the shape of a window through which the image is viewed. In quality framing, prints are often *double-* or *triple-matted* in boards of contrasting color.

matching grant   A grant made by a foundation, government agency, or individual, contingent on the recipient raising sufficient funds to match the donor's contribution. Although the ratio of grant funds to contributions may vary, most are dollar-for-dollar up to a fixed amount, with a time limit imposed on fund-raising activities. Some federal LSTA grants-in-aid are structured in this way.

materials budget   The portion of a library's operating budget allocated for the purchase of books, media, serials, and other information resources for the use of its clientele and staff, as opposed to expenditures for salaries and wages, equipment, supplies, and services. Some libraries include *electronic resources* in the materials budget; others make a separate allocation.

material specific details (MSD)   A generic term for the area of a bibliographic record reserved for elements of bibliographic description specific to certain types of material (musical presentation, mathematical data, and numeric and/or alphabetic, chronological, or other designation) recorded in field 254 of the MARC record for music, field 255 for cartographic materials, and field 362 for serials.

material type   An option available to users of some online catalogs and bibliographic databases that allows search results to be limited to materials of a specific physical format (book, periodical, videocassette, sound recording, map, music score, etc.). In cataloging, material type is assigned to the item from a list established by the local library (or library system) and is not necessarily the same as the *item type* used for circulation purposes. *See also*: *general material designation*.

mathematical data   The field within the materials specific details area of a bibliographic record in which mathematical elements in the bibliographic description of cartographic materials are entered (scale, projection, coordinates, etc.).

matte   Paper that has a dull unreflective finish, easier on the eye of the reader than glossy finish but not as visually appealing for printed graphics. Also spelled *matt*.

matter   In printing, copy in the process of being set in type or already set (standing). *Live matter* has yet to be used in printing; *dead matter* has been used and is ready to be *broken up*. The terms *fat matter* and *lean matter* refer to the proportion of white space or broken lines on a page. Printers also differentiate between *body matter* and *display matter*. Also refers to copy that is to be printed, in manuscript or typescript form.

maximize   A feature of a graphical user interface that allows the user to enlarge a window to its fullest size by clicking on a small button in the upper-right-hand corner of the window. The opposite of *minimize*. *See also*: *multitasking*.

Mazarin Bible   *See*: *Gutenberg Bible*.

McLuhan, (Herbert) Marshall (1911–1980)   The University of Toronto professor of literature and culture who became famous for his innovative theories about how methods of communication influence society. In 1963, his analysis of the effect of movable type on the culture of 15th-century Europe (*The Gutenberg Galaxy: The Making of Typographic Man*) won the Governor-General's award for critical writing. In 1964, McLuhan gained considerable attention in the popular press for *Understanding Media: The Extensions of Man* in which he argued that the communication media used by humans are extensions of the physical senses that, by their very nature, introduce changes in the way societies function and in human consciousness, apart from the content they convey. His assertion that "the medium is the message" eventually became "the medium is the massage." For more about his life and work, see *Marshall McLuhan: The Medium and the Messenger* (Ticknor & Fields, 1989) by Philip Marchand.

McNaughton Plan   *See*: book lease plan.

mean line   In typography, the imaginary horizontal line running along the tops of the x-height lowercase letters of a type font that lacks ascenders. Synonymous with *x-line*. Compare with *cap line*. *See also*: *base line*.

measure   In printing, the width over which a line of type is set. A *full measure* extends across the entire width of a line in a column or on a page, without indention.

mechanical binding   A form of binding in which the leaves of a publication are held together by some type of mechanism, usually metal or plastic wire or rings threaded or inserted through holes or slots punched along the back margin parallel to the binding edge, to allow the volume to open flat. The category includes *loose-leaf binding*, *comb binding*, and *spiral binding*.

medallion   In books, a decorative element in the form of a panel or tablet, circular or oval in shape, containing a design, inscription, portrait, figure, or group of figures, sometimes made to appear in relief. Commemorative medallions almost always include an inscription, often incorporated into the curved border. Compare in this sense with *roundel*.

Also refers to the round sticker affixed to the front cover of an award-winning book or incorporated into the cover design, sometimes a representation, in metallic ink or paper, of the actual medal received.

media   A generic term for nonprint library materials (films, filmstrips, slides, videorecordings, audiorecordings, CD-ROMs, machine-readable data files, computer software, etc.). Microforms are not considered media because they are reproductions of print documents. The person responsible for managing a media collection and associated equipment is a *media specialist*. Reviews of newly published media titles are indexed annually by type of medium in *Media Review Digest*. Synonymous with *audiovisuals*.

In a more general sense, material in *any* format that carries and communicates information content.

Also refers collectively to all the channels through which information is broadcast, including radio, television, cable, and the Internet. The *mass media* disseminate public information to the widest possible audience (and some would argue to the lowest common denominator) with a close eye on the profits to be made from advertising, as in the case of major commercial television networks. Although the producers of this one-way flow of information may use polling to reveal the characteristics of their listeners or viewers, the individuals who receive their message remain largely anonymous. The *news media* (newspapers, newsmagazines, news broadcasts, news Web sites, etc.) specialize in providing the latest information about current events, with or without commentary, usually without intending to entertain. Directory information on print and broadcast media is available in the *Gale Directory of Publications and Broadcast Media*, an annual reference serial available in most academic and large public libraries. Singular: *medium*. *See also*: *public television*.

media center A facility within an educational institution responsible for providing a full-range of media resources, equipment, and services, staffed to assist students and instructors in utilizing its collections, usually supervised by a *media specialist*. A media center can be a separate facility, a separately administered unit located in the same building as a library, or an integral part of the library. Synonymous with *learning resources center*. *See also*: *listening room* and *viewing room*.

media mail A special rate available from the U.S. Postal Service to businesses and the public for mailing books of at least eight pages, film (16 mm or narrower), printed music, printed test materials, sound recordings, play scripts, printed educational charts, loose-leaf pages and binders containing medical information, and computer-readable media, lower than the rate charged for parcels of comparable weight that do not contain such items. Advertising restrictions apply. Synonymous with *book post* and *book rate*. Compare with *library rate*.

media specialist A librarian or other individual with specialized training in the creation, selection, organization, maintenance, and provision of access to media of all kinds, who may also be responsible for supervising a *media center* or the *media department* of a library, including collections, equipment, and facilities for listening and/or viewing.

mediated search A systematic search in which a trained intermediary, such as an online services librarian or information broker, assists the end-user in locating desired information, by helping to formulate and execute appropriate strategies for searching online catalogs and databases and by using more traditional bibliographic finding tools. Compare with *end-user search*.

medical book A book published in print or on CD-ROM for the use of medical practitioners, researchers, and/or students (*example*: ***Physician's Desk Reference***) or for laypersons with an interest in health care (***Harvard Medical School Family Health Guide***). The category includes textbooks, reference works, and consumer guides, often published in successive editions. Currency is essential in maintaining medical collections. *See also*: *medical library*.

medical library   A type of special library maintained by a university medical school, hospital, medical research institute, public health agency, or medical association to serve the information needs of students, researchers, and practitioners in the health sciences (medicine, nursing, dentistry, pharmacy, etc.), with collections that include print and online resources related to medicine and allied health. The largest medical library in the United States is the National Library of Medicine, located in Washington, D.C. Medical librarians are organized in the Medical Library Association. Synonymous with *health science library*. *See also*: *hospital library*.

Medical Library Association (MLA)   Founded in 1898, MLA has a membership of librarians and other individuals engaged in professional library or bibliographic work in medical libraries and allied scientific libraries. An affiliate of the American Library Association, MLA publishes the quarterly *Bulletin of the Medical Library Association (BMLA)*. URL: www.mlanet.org.

Medical Subject Headings (MeSH)   The controlled vocabulary thesaurus used by the National Library of Medicine. *MeSH* subject headings are used in the NLM's *MEDLINE* database (available on the Web as *PubMed*), in *Index Medicus*, and in bibliographic cataloging records. The *MeSH* headings are published in print by the NLM in an alphabetically arranged annotated list and in tree structures. The online *MeSH Browser* is available at: www.nlm.nih.gov/mesh/MBrowser.html.

medium   In information storage and retrieval, the physical substance or material on which data is recorded (parchment, paper, film, magnetic tape or disk, optical disk, etc.) or through which data is transmitted (optical fiber, coaxial cable, twisted pair, etc.). In a more general sense, the material or technical means by which any creative work is expressed or communicated, in print or nonprint format. Plural: *media*. *See also*: *McLuhan, Marshall*.

In printing, a typeface of intermediate weight, as distinct from *lightface* or *boldface*. Medium type is standard for printed text. *See also*: *mediumistic writing*.

mediumistic writing   A written work transmitted through a psychic medium who claims to have received it as a communication from the spirit of a dead person or entity. In libraries, such works are cataloged under the name of the medium with an added entry under the name of the purported author(s).

medium of performance   The voice(s) and/or instrument(s) for which a musical work is composed, recorded in the note area of the bibliographic description in the order given on the actual item (*example*: **soprano and piano**).

MEDLARS   An acronym for *Medical Literature Analysis and Retrieval Service*, a collection of databases maintained and leased to libraries and research institutions by the National Library of Medicine (NLM), including *MEDLINE, AIDSLINE, TOXLINE*, etc. A comprehensive list of NLM databases and electronic resources is available online at: www.nlm.nih.gov/databases/databases.html.

medley   A musical composition consisting of a string of well-known melodies or passages from various pieces that share a common characteristic (composed by the same person, during the same period, in the same genre, etc.), arranged so that the end of one coincides with the beginning of the next, with no break in continuity.

MEDLINE   Created and maintained by the National Library of Medicine, *MEDLINE* is the largest bibliographic database in the world, indexing the literature of the biomedical sciences. It includes *Index Medicus, Index to Dental Literature,* and *International Nursing.* It also covers allied health, biological and physical sciences, humanities, and information science as they relate to medicine and health care, communication disorders, population biology, and reproductive biology. *MEDLINE* contains over 11 million bibliographic records representing articles indexed since 1966 from over 3,900 journals, as well as monographs published as the result of biomedical congresses and symposia. Approximately 67 percent of the records in *MEDLINE* include abstracts. The free online version of *MEDLINE* is called *PubMed.* Sponsored by the National Center for Biotechnology Information, *PubMed* is available at: www.ncbi.nlm.nih.gov/PubMed.

megabook   *See*: blockbuster.

megabyte (MB)   *See*: byte.

MegaHertz (MHz)   A measurement of the transmission speed of electronic devices, named after the German physicist Heinrich R. Hertz. One MHz equals 1 million cycles per second. In computing, a MegaHertz is usually equal to 1 million bps (bits per second). When used in reference to a computer's clock, the number of MHz indicates the speed of the central processing unit (CPU).

melodrama   From the Greek word *melos,* meaning "music." The term originally referred to all dramatic works that included music, but in 19th-century England it was applied to a play in which the characters are stereotyped (good or bad), the action exaggerated and emotional, and the plot improbable and/or sensational, interspersed with catchy songs and orchestral accompaniment, with an invariably happy ending (*example*: **Sweeney Todd, the Demon Barber of Fleet Street**). Melodrama bears the same relationship to tragedy as farce to comedy. In contemporary usage, the adjective *melodramatic* is applied to any performance or literary work in which the characters are overdrawn and the action taxes the credulity of audience or reader.

member rate   The price paid by a member of a society or association for a subscription to one of its serial publications, usually lower than the rate charged of nonmembers.

memo   *See*: memorandum.

memoir   The record or report of a person's investigations in a specialized field, especially one prepared for presentation to members of a scholarly society. Also, a record of research or observation issued by a scholarly society or institution. Synonymous, in the plural, with *proceedings* and *transactions.*

memoirs   A narrative of events or reminiscences based on the author's own observations or personal knowledge of the world in which he (or she) lived, including events witnessed, people known or observed, places visited, etc. The life need not have been historically significant but one that placed the writer in a position to observe firsthand significant events as they unfolded. Unlike a private diary or journal, memoirs are usually written for publication long after the occurrence of the events described and do not necessarily provide a day-to-day account. Compare with *autobiography*.

memorabilia   Materials of sentimental or historical value to the person who created or collected them, including personal books and papers, clippings, photographs, sketches, correspondence, diaries, journals, notes, invitations, etc. Memorabilia are usually added to special collections, in accordance with a library's collection development policy.

memorandum   A formal note distributed internally to one or more persons in a company, agency, organization, or institution, with a header indicating the date it was sent and stating to whom it is addressed (To:), from whom it is sent (From:), and the subject of the text (Re:). Unlike a letter, a *memo* does not require a full salutation or signature at the end of the text—the sender may simply initial his or her name in the header. Plural: *memoranda*.

memory   The space available for holding or storing data on a computer. *External memory* consists of permanent storage space on hard disks and floppy disks. *Main memory* (RAM) stores data only during a single work session, which is why files must be saved before ending a session. Because main memory also allocates space to the operating system, the amount of *usable memory* is usually less than total RAM, which may limit the size of application programs that can be run on a given computer and the maximum speed at which it can process data.

mending   Minor restoration of a book's condition not requiring replacement of material or removal of the bound sections from the cover. When mending of library materials is done in-house, the job should be given to a person who is properly trained, to avoid permanent damage to items in need of attention. As a general rule, mending should be done only to the extent necessary, using reversible procedures whenever possible. Compare with *rebinding* and *repairing*.

mending tape   A generic term for various kinds of adhesive tape designed specifically for making minor repairs on books and other printed materials, available by the roll from library suppliers, either single- or double-sided, with pressure-sensitive or water-based adhesive. For mending tears in paper, acid-free tape is preferred. In conservation, reversibility may require the use of a tape that can be easily removed without damaging the item.

mental map   A map depicting a geographic area of any extent according to the subjective perceptions of a particular person or group of people, rather than in relation to physical reality, for example, a New Yorker's view of the United States west of New York City. This category also includes maps in which an area is sized according to the quantity of the subject involved, for example, human population per square mile, which would, in a map of the United States, make Texas considerably smaller and New York much larger than is actually the case.

mentor An experienced, trustworthy person who willingly provides useful advice to a new member of a community, profession, or organization to assist the person in achieving success in his or her new position and environment. Mentoring relationships can be established informally by the participants or under the formal sponsorship of the organization. Mentoring of recent library school graduates can be arranged through the New Members Round Table (NMRT) of the American Library Association.

menu In computer systems, a display of two or more options from which the user may select by typing letters or numbers (or some other combination of keys) or by clicking on a link, icon, text label, etc., with a mouse or other pointing device. *Main menu* options often lead to lower-level *submenus* in a hierarchical display. *See also*: *Gopher*.

menu bar A list of menu names, usually displayed horizontally below the title bar in a graphical user interface, with corresponding menu options hidden from view. When the user selects one of the menu names, the appropriate list of options is displayed in a drop-down, pop-up, or sidebar menu.

menu-driven A computer interface that provides a hierarchical sequence of lists of possible choices (options) from which the user must make the appropriate selections to accomplish the desired result. Menu-driven interfaces are easier for novices to negotiate but slower and less sophisticated than *command-driven* systems and consequently less attractive to experienced users. *See also*: *graphical user interface*.

merge To combine in logical sequence two or more separate files of information into one, either manually or by an automated process. When such a combination includes the recognition and removal of duplicate files, the process is known as *merge/purge*. *See also*: *deduping*.

merger The combination of two or more serials into one. A note is included in the bibliographic record for the new serial (*Merger of:*) indicating the titles of the publications that merged, and a companion note is added to the record for each of the serials that merged (*Merged with: to become:*) indicating the title(s) with which it merged and the title of the publication created as the result of the merger. The opposite of *split*. Compare with *absorption*.

MeSH *See*: *Medical Subject Headings*.

metadata Structured information used to describe information resources/objects for a variety of purposes. Although *AACR2/MARC* cataloging is formally metadata, the term is generally used in the library community for nontraditional schemes such as the Dublin Core Metadata Element Set, the VRA Core Categories, or the Encoded Archival Description (EAD). Metadata can be categorized as descriptive, structural, and administrative. *Descriptive metadata* facilitates discovery, identification, and selection. *Structural metadata* describes the internal structure of complex objects. *Administrative metadata* aids in the management of resources and may include rights management metadata, preservation metadata, and technical metadata describing the physical characteristics of a resource. For an introduction to metadata, please see Priscilla Caplan's *Metadata Fundamentals for All Librarians* (ALA, 2003). Also spelled *meta-data*. *See also*: *Metadata Encoding and Transmission Standard* and *Metadata Object Description Schema*.

metadatabase   A database of databases, usually formed by aggregating two or more smaller databases to allow the user to search their contents *as a whole*, instead of repeating the same search in each separately (*example*: *OneFile* from Gale Group, which consolidates the *InfoTrac* bibliographic databases into a single, very large finding tool). The pace of aggregation has accelerated as very large vendors have dominated the market for access to periodical databases, but however helpful "one-stop searching" may be in interdisciplinary research (and to users who lack the skill to select the optimum databases for a specialized topic), segmentation still offers significant advantages for the experienced researcher.

Metadata Encoding and Transmission Standard (METS)   An XML schema for encoding descriptive, structural, and administrative metadata for digital objects. METS can be used to facilitate the standardized exchange of digital objects between repositories, the development of common presentation utilities, and the archiving of digital objects. METS was developed by the Digital Library Federation and is maintained by the Library of Congress with the advice of the METS Editorial Board. URL: www. loc.gov/standards/mets.

Metadata Object Description Schema (MODS)   An XML schema developed by the Library of Congress for representing MARC-like semantics in the XML markup language. MODS can be used to carry selected data from MARC21 records or for creating original resource description records according to a specification richer than Dublin Core but less complex than full MARC. MODS cannot be used for the conversion of MARC to XML without loss of data (MARCXML was designed for that purpose). URL: www.loc.gov/standards/mods.

metadictionary   A search engine that allows the user to search for the definition(s) of a word or phrase in multiple online dictionaries simultaneously. *OneLook* (www. onelook.com) is an example that indexes English words and phrases in over 900 dictionary Web sites, with translation into other languages.

meta-index   An index of indexes. For a meta-index of indexes to Web sites, see the WWW Virtual Library (URL: www.vlib.org).

metal binding   A bookbinding made of one or more metallic substances (gold, silver, brass, etc.), usually by a jeweler or skilled metalworker, often in the form of surface decoration mounted on the boards.

metallic ink   Printing ink to which finely ground particles of metal (aluminum, bronze, copper, etc.) have been added to produce a decorative metallic effect. During the Middle Ages, powdered gold was added to the ink used in chrysography and gilding.

metal point   A pointed implement made of metal used from the 11th century on for ruling and writing annotations in manuscripts, and for underdrawing. It leaves a trace more discreet than pen-and-ink but more visible than *hard point*. The color of the mark left on the writing surface varies with the type of metal used: a brownish mark from a ferrous point, a gray line from silver or lead, and a grayish-green trace from copper. Instructions to illuminators and binders' notes written in metal point are sometimes detectable in early manuscripts. *See also*: *plummet*.

metaphor   From the Greek word *metapherein*, meaning to "to carry across." A figure of speech in which a word or phrase denoting a specific object, person, idea, etc., is applied to something with which it is not normally associated, to attribute one or more of its qualities to the other without using "like" or "as" to make an explicit comparison. The identification or substitution can be direct ("Oaths are straws, men's faiths are wafer-cakes" from *Henry V* 2.3.51) or merely suggested ("Upon the heat and flame of thy distemper sprinkle cool patience" from *Hamlet* 3.4.123).

Metaphor has been used as a literary device since the earliest works of recorded literature ("rosy-fingered dawn") to enable imaginative writers to expand the literal meaning(s) of a word or phrase. When the elements compared are so dissimilar as to be incongruous, the resulting *mixed metaphor* ("mixaphor") can be amusing ("rusty lips"). A *dead metaphor* has become so commonplace as to have lost its impact ("time marches on"). The history and grammar of metaphor is studied in the discipline of linguistics. Metaphors are sometimes collected and indexed, usually thematically (see the *Metaphors Dictionary* edited by Elyse Sommer and Dorrie Weiss).

metapublisher   A third-party electronic service provider in the business of enabling primary publishers to outsource some or all of the text conversion, reference linking, hosting, and gateway services that traditional publishers do not have the resources to provide in-house. Examples include HighWire (www.highwire.org), Ingenta (www.catchword.co.uk), and MetaPress (www.metapress.com).

metasearch   A search for information using software designed to optimize retrieval by querying multiple Web search engines and combining the results. *Dogpile* (www.dogpile.com), *Monster Crawler* (www.monstercrawler.com), and *ProFusion* (www.profusion.com) are commonly used *metasearch engines*.

methods journal   A scholarly periodical devoted to disseminating information about the development of new techniques in scientific research and the refinement of existing methods (*example*: the biweekly *Journal of Immunological Methods*).

metonymy   A figure of speech in which the name of one thing is used for another to which it is related, of which it is an attribute, with which it is associated, or which it suggests (*example*: "White House" for presidency or "Crown" for king). *Reverse metonymy* is the use of the name of a thing to refer to one or more of its attributes.

METS   *See*: Metadata Encoding and Transmission Standard.

MHz   *See*: MegaHertz.

microchip   *See*: chip.

microclimate   The isolated environment (ambient light, temperature, relative humidity, dust, etc.) within a small confined space such as a display case, enclosed bookcase, drawer, box, or other storage container, easier to control than a large storage area when conservation is a high priority.

microcomputer   A generic term for a programmable computer designed to handle relatively small operations, usually a desktop machine containing a single-chip microprocessor on a printed circuit board, which may be part of a larger computer system or connected to a network. The term may have been coined to distinguish personal computers from more powerful *minicomputers*. *See also*: *mainframe*.

microfiche   A small card-shaped sheet of film designed for storing miniaturized text and/or microimages arranged sequentially in a two-dimensional grid. Microfiche is available in color or black and white (negative or positive). Various formats exist, but ISO recommends 75 × 125 mm (48 frames in four rows of 12) or 105 × 148 mm (60 frames in five rows of 12). Although each sheet usually includes a title and/or index number in a heading across the top that can be read without magnification, the text itself can be read and copied only with the aid of a microform reader-printer machine. User resistance can be mitigated by keeping equipment in good repair and providing point-of-use assistance.

In most academic libraries, the ERIC document collection is available on microfiche, filed by the six-digit ED number assigned to each document. Newspaper and periodical back files and government documents may also be available on microfiche, usually stored in specially designed metal filing cabinets. The sheets of film may be enclosed in microfiche envelopes to prevent abrasion. Abbreviated *fiche*. Compare with *microfilm*. *See also*: *superfiche* and *ultrafiche*.

microfiche envelope   A small paper envelope, open at the top and right end, or at the top only, with a high throat for storing one or more sheets of microfiche so that only the title strip on the first sheet is visible. Archival quality microfiche envelopes are made of acid- and lignin-free paper.

microfilm   A continuous roll of 16 mm photographic film used for storing miniaturized text and/or microimages in a linear array consisting of a single row (cine format) or double row of frames that can be magnified and copied only with the aid of specially designed equipment. Microfilm is available in color or black and white (negative or positive). Stored under appropriate environmental conditions, its life expectancy can be measured in centuries. For this reason, it is used to preserve the content of paper documents at risk of deterioration.

In many libraries, newspaper and periodical back files are routinely converted to microfilm to save space. Microform reader-printer machines are available in libraries with microfilm holdings for viewing and making hard copies. User resistance can be mitigated by keeping equipment in good repair and by providing point-of-use assistance. Compare with *microfiche*. *See also*: *master negative*, *print master*, and *service copy*.

microfilm exchange   The replacement by a library of issues or bound volumes of a serial publication with microfilm, usually to conserve space or preserve titles that are very heavily used (*example*: **national newsmagazines**), printed on acid paper (**newspapers**), or subject to a high rate of mutilation or loss.

microform A generic term for a highly reduced photographic copy of text and/or images stored on a translucent medium (microfiche or microfilm) or on an opaque medium such as card stock (microopaque or aperture card). Microforms can be original editions or reproductions. Reader-printer machines are required to view and make hard copies. Digital storage media such as magnetic tape and disk, CD-ROM, etc., are superseding microforms in information storage and retrieval, but the transformation is far from complete. Microforms currently available for purchase are listed by author/ title and subject in the serial publication *Guide to Microforms in Print*. Compare with *macroform*. *See also*: *computer output microform*.

micrographics A general term for the techniques used to photographically reduce text and/or graphic images to a size too small to be read by the human eye without magnification, usually for the purpose of preservation or compact storage, as in the conversion of newspaper and periodical back files from print to microfilm or microfiche. Micrographic formats also include microopaque and aperture card. Compare with *micrography*.

micrography The art and practice of writing in microscopically small characters. Compare with *micrographics*.

microopaque A sheet of opaque material, such as paper or card stock, bearing miniaturized text and/or microimages arranged in a two-dimensional grid, which can be magnified and copied only with the aid of special equipment. Reader-printer machines for viewing and making hard copies are usually provided in libraries with microopaque holdings. Compare with *microfiche*.

microprocessor A central processing unit (CPU) etched or printed on a single silicon microchip. To function as a computer, a microprocessor requires a power supply, a clock, and memory. Microprocessors are used in most digital devices (PCs, personal digital assistants, clock radios, etc.).

micropublisher A commercial company or agency that specializes in publishing documents on microform, for example, the Photoduplication Service (PDS) at the Library of Congress. A list of micropublishers is provided in the front matter of the reference serial *Magazines for Libraries*.

microscope slide A small transparent mount, usually made of glass, designed for holding a minute object, such as a biological specimen or geological sample, for viewing through the lens of a microscope or microprojector. In *AACR2*, microscope slides are cataloged according to the rules for three-dimensional *artifacts* and *realia*. Compare with *microslide*.

microscopic printing Printing done in a very small type size. Although the first works printed in Europe were in large type, early printers soon realized that with smaller typefaces more matter fitted on a page. By 1825, the French type-founder Henri Didot had cast type that produced 25 lines to the inch. Because the casting of extremely small type has physical limitations, most microscopic reduction is now done photographically. *See also*: *miniature book*.

microslide   A slide consisting of a single mounted frame of microfilm, not to be confused with a *microscope slide*.

midlist   The titles on a publisher's frontlist, usually literary fiction and serious nonfiction written by new and emerging writers, not expected to become bestsellers or even leaders. Recent studies suggest that although publishers continue to issue as many new midlist titles as ever, the failure of bookstore chains to market them competitively has resulted in a decline in their percentage of total book sales.

migration   A move from one hardware platform or software system to another, usually because the purchaser or lessee believes the new system to be superior. In libraries, the most common example is from the catalog or database software of one vendor to that of another. Such a change may or may not require the conversion of data from one format to another. Compare with *upgrade*.

mildew   The growth of microorganisms whose spores remain dormant under cool, dry conditions inside libraries and other facilities but are stimulated by warm, moist air to feed on the leaves and bindings of books and other printed materials. The growth of mildew produces an acid harmful to paper and materials used in binding. It also produces a characteristic musty odor that can be prevented in libraries by maintaining good air circulation, low relative humidity, and adequate lighting. Once started, an infestation of mildew can be difficult to eradicate. ***See also***: *fumigation* and *preservation*.

military library   A library maintained by a unit of government responsible for national defense, maintaining collections for the use of military staff, but that may have a broader mandate, including accessibility to the general public (*example*: **Nimitz Library** at the U.S. Naval Academy). *Military librarians* are organized in the Federal and Armed Forces Libraries Round Table of the American Library Association.

millboard   *See*: binder's board.

milling   Cutting away a small portion of the binding edge of a book (usually less than one-eighth inch) to prepare the sections for adhesive binding or oversewing, an operation done in a bindery by moving the inner edge of the clamped text block over the rotating blades of a *milling machine*. In first-time binding, the back folds are cut away, producing loose leaves. In rebinding, the old adhesive, thread, staples, etc., are cut away along with the folds to prepare the leaves for reattachment.

MIME   An acronym that stands for **M**ultipurpose **I**nternet **M**ail **E**xtensions, a specification that allows non-ASCII files to be formatted so that they can be transmitted over the Internet via e-mail. Supported by many e-mail clients, MIME extends the SMTP protocol to allow the exchange of graphics, audio, and video files, and messages in character sets other than ASCII.

MIME media type   A designation used in Web browsers and other application software to determine file characteristics, consisting of two parts, a type and subtype, separated by a slash (*examples*: **image/tiff**, **application/pdf**, **application/msword**, etc.). The official list of MIME media types is maintained by the Internet Assigned Numbers Authority (IANA). Synonymous with *MIME type*.

miniature   A colorful hand-painted stand-alone illustration in a medieval manuscript or early printed book, often illuminated in gold or silver. The term does not refer to the size of the image (a miniature may fill an entire page); it is derived from the Latin *minium*, meaning "red lead," a substance used in painting to produce the color vermilion. Miniatures are also an integral part of the Persian manuscript tradition. *See also*: *picture cycle* and *presentation miniature*.

Also refers to a small, separate, minutely detailed drawing, painting, or portrait, usually done on ivory or vellum.

In printing and typography, a document conceived on a very small scale or a greatly reduced copy of a document, designed to be read or reproduced with the aid of special optical equipment. *See also*: *miniature book* and *miniature edition*.

miniature book   A book conceived on a very small scale, measuring no more than three inches along its greatest dimension (height or width), usually printed in 6-point type or smaller and illustrated on the same scale. Not uncommon, miniature books include Bibles, almanacs, poetry, classics, juvenile literature, tokens, etc. Very tiny books, such as those used in doll houses, are usually produced photographically. Of interest to collectors, miniature books have an enthusiastic following in the United States. For more information, see the Web site maintained by the Miniature Book Society at: www.mbs.org. *See also*: *miniature edition*.

miniature edition   An edition of very small size (three inches or less in height and width), usually printed in 6-point type or smaller and illustrated on the same scale. Synonymous with *lilliput edition* and *microscopic edition*. *See also*: *miniature book*.

miniature score   A music score printed in small type to allow the pages to be reduced to pocket size. Miniature scores are designed to be used by music lovers for study and enjoyment, not for performance.

minicomputer   A medium-sized computer introduced in the 1960s capable of serving up to several hundred users. A dedicated minicomputer is used to run the online catalog in many libraries. Synonymous with *midrange computer*. Compare with *mainframe*, *microcomputer*, and *supercomputer*.

minimal level cataloging (MLC)   An encoding level that allows more severe limitations on the description and classification of an item (and on the amount of authority control) than in *core level cataloging*, resulting in a less than complete bibliographic record. MLC was designed to provide access to materials unavailable due to cataloging arrears, as well as items worthy of retention but not considered worth the expense of full level cataloging.

minimize   A feature of a graphical user interface that allows the user to reduce a window to a tab in the taskbar, or to an icon on the desktop, by clicking on a small button in the upper-right-hand corner of the window. The opposite of *maximize*. *See also*: *multitasking*.

minor descriptor   A descriptor or identifier assigned in a bibliographic record to represent one of the *less* significant aspects of the content of the document (form, methodology, etc.). A minor descriptor or identifier is *not* marked with an asterisk or distinguished typographically in the list of preferred indexing terms, as is a *major descriptor* or identifier representing a primary focus or subject of the document. Some indexing systems do not provide minor descriptors and identifiers.

mint   In the antiquarian book trade, a copy in the same immaculate, unaltered condition as when it was first published, new and unused—the highest possible grade in any assessment of condition. Used books in mint condition command a higher price than copies showing signs of wear. Synonymous with *as new* and *pristine*. Compare with *fine copy*. **See also**: *bright copy*.

minuscule   A script written in unconnected letters, some of which have ascenders and descenders (b, d, f, g, h, j, k, l, p, q, t, y), as opposed to *majuscule* in which all the letters are the same height. When connections are made between letters, the hand is *cursive*. Minuscule is a *quadrilinear* (or *quattrolinear*) script because the letters are bounded by four imaginary horizontal lines (at the top and bottom of the *minim* stroke used to write letters like "m" and "n" and at the top of the ascenders and bottom of the descenders). The lowercase letters of the modern roman alphabet evolved from *Carolingian minuscule*, a script adopted in Europe during the reign of Charlemagne (8th century). **See also**: *Anglo-Saxon minuscule*.

minutes   Under parliamentary procedure, a written chronological account of the business conducted at a formal assembly, such as a library faculty or staff meeting, usually written from notes taken by an elected or appointed secretary, or other designated member, for distribution to all the other participants in advance of the next meeting for their correction and approval. The minutes of important meetings may be archived as a matter of record. In some libraries, minutes are ordered, received, and cataloged as serial publications.

miracle play   A form of medieval religious drama performed on a movable wagon from a script giving an account of a divine miracle, usually one believed to have occurred in the life of a Christian saint or character from the Bible. Compare with *morality play*. **See also**: *mystery play*.

mirror site   An exact copy of a Web site, installed on a server other than the one maintained by the official host, usually to handle demand for the site's content in another country or region. When the main server goes offline, the Web site it normally hosts may still be available at one or more mirror sites.

MIS   *See*: **m**anagement **i**nformation **s**ystem.

misbound   A book in which a map or illustration, a number of leaves, or a complete section has been folded incorrectly, gathered in incorrect sequence, bound in upside down, or omitted. The publisher will normally send a replacement if such a copy is returned by a bookseller or retail customer.

miscellany   A collection consisting of an assortment of writings on diverse subjects. The term also appears in the titles of books containing literary works of various forms, usually related to a specific subject (***A Miscellany of Women's Wisdom***), person (***A James Joyce Miscellany***), place (***A Handful of Spice: A Miscellany of Maine Literature and History***), etc. Compare with *anthology*.

mis-en-page   The overall arrangement of elements on a page in an early manuscript, including the number and width of columns and the placement of miniatures, initial letters, decorative borders, line fillers, bas-de-page scenes, etc. The four-column layout of early codices (presumably inherited from rolls) was reduced to two in the early Christian period, with variations depending on type of text. Books of Hours and Italian Renaissance manuscripts were usually written in a single column. *Mis-en-page* was laid down when the clean parchment or vellum sheets were ruled for copying. The designer sometimes added instructions in metal point to guide the copyist and/or illuminator. Developments in *mis-en-page* can be helpful to codicologists in dating medieval manuscripts.

misinformation   Information that is erroneous or inaccurate. Also refers to the act of *misinforming* someone, inadvertently or by intention. Compare with *disinformation*.

misprint   *See*: typographical error.

misquote   To repeat incorrectly words that another person has spoken or written, inadvertently or by intention. A quotation made out of context may be misleading, but it is not necessarily a misquote. Quotations included in written works should be properly cited and double-checked for accuracy before publication.

missal   A liturgical book containing all the texts (chants, prayers, and readings) used by the priest in the celebration of Mass, arranged according to the liturgical year. From the 10th century on, the readings formerly contained in the sacramentary were combined with the gradual, evangelary, and epistolary to form a single volume, to facilitate private masses. The earliest medieval examples were copied by hand on parchment or vellum and beautifully illuminated, especially the canon page and the *Vere dignum* monogram. In a more general sense, any book of prayers or daily devotions. Also spelled *missale*. Compare with *breviary*.

misshelved   An item in a library collection placed on the shelf out of correct sequence, usually accidentally in reshelving or by a well-intentioned patron, making it as inaccessible to users of the catalog as if it had disappeared. Sometimes an item is intentionally misshelved by a patron to assure future access or prevent others from using it. Regular, thorough shelf reading is the most effective way to control misshelving.

missing   A code used in a library catalog to indicate the circulation status of an item not checked out that cannot be found anywhere in the library. If a thorough search by library staff fails to locate the item within a reasonable time, a replacement copy may be ordered, provided demand persists and an edition of the work is still in print. Compare with *lost*.

missing copy   Parts of a book, such as the index or appendices, that may not be ready when a publisher sends the typescript and specifications to the printer. If additional copy is to follow, allowance must be made in estimating the cost of printing.

missing issue   An issue of a newspaper or periodical not received by a library subscriber within a specified period of time or after a designated number of claims, as distinct from an issue lost or stolen following receipt and check-in. The publisher or vendor may offer an extended subscription in compensation. The library may eventually fill the gap by purchasing a replacement from a back issues dealer.

mission   The basic purpose or role of an organization expressed succinctly in abstract terms. A clearly written mission statement is the basis for formulating achievable goals and objectives in strategic planning and serves as a constant reminder of the organization's primary reason for existing.

missionary book   Publisher's slang for the first book published on a subject. To catalog such a work, a new class number and subject heading may be required.

missive   A formal or official message, especially a detailed and lengthy one, such as a letter sent by a superior authority conveying a mandate, recommendation, permission, or invitation to a specific individual or group of persons concerning an action (or actions) to be undertaken. Also refers to a legal document in the form of a letter, exchanged by parties to a contractual agreement.

miter   In hand bookbinding, to bring materials together at an angle (usually 45 degrees) along an angle without overlap, as in folding the leather or cloth covering material over the edges of the boards at the corners toward the inside and pasting it down before the endpapers are applied. Also refers to the joint formed by fitting together two pieces beveled at an angle along a straight line. Also spelled *mitre*.

mixed authorship   *See*: mixed responsibility.

mixed notation   A classification notation in which two or more kinds of symbols are used, for example, the letters of the English alphabet used to indicate the main classes and first-level subdivisions in Library of Congress classification and the arabic numerals used for further subdivisions (*example*: **ND2893.A78**). Compare with *pure notation*.

mixed responsibility   In *AACR2*, a collaboration in which two or more persons or corporate bodies contribute to the intellectual or artistic content of a work, each performing a different function, for example, the author of the text of a children's picture book and the artist responsible for creating the illustrations. Synonymous with *mixed authorship*. Compare with *shared responsibility*.

MLA   *See*: Medical Library Association *and* Music Library Association.

MLA style   A format for typing research papers and citing sources in the humanities developed by the Modern Language Association of America and published in the *MLA Handbook for Writers of Research Papers*, available in the reference section of most academic libraries. *See also*: APA style and electronic style.

MLC   *See*: minimal level cataloging.

M.L.I.S.   In the United States, the postbaccalaureate degree of Master of Library and Information Science, granted by a library school upon completion of a required course of study. To be considered for a professional position in most public and academic libraries in the United States, a candidate must have earned either an M.L.I.S. or M.L.S. degree. *See also*: accredited library school and approved library school.

M.L.S.   In the United States, the postbaccalaureate degree of Master of Library Science, granted by a library school upon completion of a required course of study. To be considered for a professional position in most public and academic libraries in the United States, a candidate must have earned either an M.L.S. or M.L.I.S. degree. *See also*: *accredited library school* and *approved library school*.

mnemonic   From the Greek *mnemon*, meaning "mindful." A code in which the abbreviation(s), symbol(s), or formula(s) are easy to remember (*examples*: **DEL** for "delete" or **REF** for "reference"). Also, a word or rhyme composed by a person to be used as a mental aid in recalling something. *See also*: *mnemonic notation*.

mnemonic notation   A classification notation in which the characters representing the classes are directly linked to the name of the class, making it easier for the user to learn and recall the way the classification system is organized. Most notations used in library cataloging and indexing are *not* mnemonic.

mobile library   *See*: bookmobile.

mock-up   A rough but accurate physical representation in wood, cardboard, papier-mâché, plastic, canvas, etc., of a device, apparatus, structure, or process, usually on the same scale, with movable parts that can be manipulated or modified for the purpose of analysis, testing, demonstration, or instruction. Compare with *model* and *reproduction*.

model   An accurate three-dimensional representation of the physical appearance of a real object. A model can be the same size as the original object but is usually done to scale. Particularly useful in depicting very large objects (*example*: the **solar system**). Some models are used as toys. Compare with *mock-up* and *realia*. *See also*: *relief model*.

model book   A book in which a medieval artist recorded a repertoire of designs for decorated initials and other ornamental motifs (birds, animals, imaginary creatures, etc.) of the artist's own invention or collected from other sources, sometimes with notes concerning execution, for use in underdrawing. By the late Middle Ages, engravings were circulated for this purpose. Also refers to a book created by a master scribe and/or illuminator to instruct pupils wishing to learn the art of fine handwriting and manuscript painting. Also spelled *modelbook*. Synonymous with *pattern book*.

modem   A contraction of *modulator-demodulator*, originally a peripheral device capable of converting digital pulses into analog frequencies for transmission over telecommunication lines and data received in analog frequencies into digital pulses for display on, or processing by, a digital computer. A modem also dials the telephone line, answers calls, and controls transmission speed. Modem speed is measured in *baud*. Although external modems are still available, most new microcomputers come equipped with a built-in modem. *See also*: *dial-up access* and *WebTV*.

MODS   *See*: Metadata Object Description Schema.

module   One of several parts of an online tutorial designed in separate units to be completed in a certain sequence. Each unit is sufficiently self-contained that advanced students may skip it if they are already familiar with its content, or complete it out of sequence, although continuity may be lost in doing so. Some tutorials include a self-quiz at the end of each module.

Also, a library furnishing designed to be used alone or in combination with other units to create a customized workspace, for example, worktables of various shapes that can be pushed together to form different configurations, depending on the needs of a particular work group. Modern furnishings for office spaces and computer workstations are often *modular* in design.

moisture exchange   The migration of moisture from one component of a book (or other publication) to another, for example, from a newly adhered bookplate to the adjacent flyleaf, causing it to cockle. In some cases, such exchange can be prevented by placing a piece of waxed paper or polyester film between the moist element and the adjacent leaf or board while drying occurs.

MOLA   *See*: Major Orchestra Librarians' Association.

mold   A group of microscopic lower plants whose reproductive spores are abundant in most environments but require certain conditions of temperature and humidity to germinate and grow. In libraries and archives, the best way to prevent molds from infecting materials is to provide good air circulation and keep the temperature below 70 degrees Fahrenheit and the relative humidity below 60 percent (preferably around 50 percent). Once established, molds can be eliminated by using a fungicide or by fumigation. Also spelled *mould*.

monaural   Sound reproduced from a single channel by an audio playback device with one amplifier or speaker. The result is less realistic than stereophonic or quadraphonic sound recording. Synonymous with *monophonic*.

monetary value   *See*: archival value.

monitor   An output device consisting of an electronic display screen that, when attached to a computer, enables the user to view text and/or images. Computer monitors vary in size, shape, and resolution. A *recessed monitor* is mounted below the surface of a desk or table, usually beneath a glass panel at an angle to allow the user's line of sight to remain unobstructed in a classroom equipped with a wall screen and LCD projector. Laptop computers have a flat panel monitor that folds down to cover the keyboard. A *television monitor* is an analog device designed to display signals from a television receiver or signals prerecorded on videocassette or DVD using the appropriate playback equipment. *See also*: *LCD* and *pixel*.

Also, to check on a person or process periodically to make sure work is progressing smoothly.

monochrome plate   An illustration printed separately from the text in a *single* color, usually listed by number with any other plates in the front matter of a book. Compare with *color plate* and *duotone*.

monogram   A single character or design artfully composed of two or more letters (often a person's initials), used to ornament custom-printed stationery and other items of personal use. Monograms are sometimes found on the bindings of fine books or incorporated into the decoration and/or illustration of medieval manuscripts and early printed books. Compare with *cipher*.

monograph   A relatively short book or treatise on a single subject, complete in one physical piece, usually written by a specialist in the field. Monographic treatment is detailed and scholarly but not extensive in scope. The importance of monographs in scholarly communication depends on the discipline. In the humanities, monographs remain the format of choice for serious scholars, but in the sciences and social sciences where currency is essential, journals are usually the preferred means of publication.

For the purpose of library cataloging, any nonserial publication, complete in one volume or intended to be completed in a finite number of parts issued at regular or irregular intervals, containing a single work or collection of works. Monographs are sometimes published in *monographic series* and *subseries*. Compare with *book*.

monographic series   A series of monographs, usually issued under a collective title by a university press or scholarly society. Each volume in the series may contain more than one monograph, each with its own title in addition to the series title.

monoline   A typeface in which the strokes of which the characters are composed, whether straight or curvilinear, are all of the same thickness, including any serifs. Compare with *block letter*.

monologue   From the Greek *monologos*, meaning "speaking alone." A play, skit, or recitation in which all the lines are spoken by a single actor or a long sequence of lines within a play is spoken by one of the characters alone on the stage. In drama and narrative fiction, an *interior monologue* reveals a character's private thoughts and feelings. Compare with *soliloquy*. *See also*: *dialogue*.

Also refers to the remarks of a person who continues to speak without interruption for an extended period of time despite cues from listeners that the conversation is being monopolized.

montage   A composite image made by juxtaposing two or more images, or parts of images (drawings, photographs, pictures, etc.), without separation lines, in a composition that gives new meaning to the whole but preserves the distinctiveness of the individual elements, a technique originally developed as an art form but now used extensively in advertising and graphic design. *See also*: *photomontage*.

monthly   Issued once a month (12 times per year) with the possible exception of one or two months, usually during the summer. Many magazines and some journals are published monthly (*example*: ***Monthly Labor Review***). Also refers to a serial issued once a month.

morality play   A form of drama popular during the Middle Ages and Renaissance in which the characters are engaged in an allegorical struggle over the condition of the human soul. Unlike mystery plays and miracle plays, which were presented on mobile wagons, morality plays were usually performed on a stationary platform.

moralized bible   *See*: *Bible moralisée*.

Morgan Library, The   Assembled by the wealthy financier Pierpont Morgan and expanded by his son J. P. Morgan, who in 1924 appointed six trustees to administer it as a reference library for scholars, The Morgan Library includes approximately 55,000 rare books and manuscripts as well as a priceless collection of cuneiform clay tablets, old master drawings and prints, coins, and medals. The Library was subsequently incorporated by the State of New York and dedicated to the use of "learned men of all countries."

Between 1902 and 1906, the elder Morgan had an Italian Renaissance-style building constructed adjacent to his residence in New York City to house the collection. In 1928, an Annex was added, and in 1991 the facility doubled in size with the acquisition of the Morgan townhouse and construction of a garden court to connect the various parts. Items from its collections are selectively exhibited in a small museum associated with the Library. URL: www.morganlibrary.org.

morgue   A library maintained by the publisher of a newspaper, usually consisting of back issues, reference materials, indexes and databases, clippings, notes, photographs, illustrations, and other resources needed by reporters and staff to research, write, and edit articles for publication. The term originally referred to the repository of biographical materials collected on persons of interest, for the purpose of writing obituaries. The first newspaper library in the United States was established at the office of the *Boston Pilot* in 1831.

morocco   A fine-grained leather made from goatskin tanned with sumac, believed to have been introduced into Europe via the Italian trade with the East. According to *The Bookman's Glossary* (R.R. Bowker, 1983), the earliest European bindings in morocco with gilt ornamentation occur on books produced by the great Venetian printer Aldus Manutius in the late 15th and early 16th centuries. They are known as *Aldine bindings*. One of the most durable leathers used in bookbinding, morocco is strong yet flexible. Older books bound in morocco are often rare and valuable. Compare with *calf* and *pigskin*. *See also*: *levant*.

Morris, William (1834–1896)   Born into a fairly wealthy family, William Morris developed a passion for medieval art and culture at an early age. At Oxford University, he met Edward Burne-Jones, who would become one of the most important Pre-Raphaelite artists and a lifelong friend. Morris began his career in architecture but soon turned to art and graphic design. In 1861 he joined Burne-Jones, artist Dante Gabriel Rossetti, and two other friends in founding a company devoted to the decorative arts and at the same time began writing poetry. In the 1870s he became interested in socialism and moved from London to Kelmscott Manor in Oxfordshire. Still juggling his artistic endeavors with writing and political activism, Morris founded the Kelmscott Press in 1891 and launched a serious revival of the book arts. Unfortunately, he died in 1896 after having published only 53 books under the Kelmscott imprint, but his influence on the graphic arts and the aesthetics of book production was considerable. The Kelmscott edition of *The Works of Geoffrey Chaucer* is considered one of the finest books ever issued, and his work inspired a generation of fine presses in Britain and the United States.

motif   A term borrowed from art and music (*leitmotif*) to refer to a textual element that symbolically represents a specific theme in a literary work by virtue of repetition, usually presented in the opening verse, chapter, or paragraphs and subsequently elaborated.

motion picture   A length of film from which an unbroken sequence of still photographs can be projected at speeds of 16 to 24 frames per second, producing the illusion of continuous motion. Motion pictures are made in color or black and white, with or without recorded sound, on film 8, 16, 35, or 70 mm wide. They include documentaries, feature films, and short films. Synonymous with *cinefilm*, *flick*, *movie*, *moving image*, *pic*, and *picture show*. Compare with *cinema*. **See also**: *film clip*, *film library*, *filmography*, *International Federation of Film Archives*, *still*, and *trailer*.

mottled calf   Calfskin used in bookbinding, dabbed or sprinkled with colored dye or tanning acid to give it a decorative spotty appearance. **See also**: *tree calf*.

motto   A word, phrase, or sentence accompanying an emblem, usually drawing attention to its symbolic significance. In heraldry, the motto typically appears in Latin on a scroll or ribbon beneath a coat of arms or above a crest. It may refer directly to the name or achievements of the person or family or to the symbolic elements of the arms or be merely a pious expression of loyalty, duty, devotion, etc., adopted as a principle of behavior.

mounted   An illustration or photograph tipped onto a blank page in a book or album. Also, a fragile or damaged leaf, illustration, map, etc., strengthened with backing made of paper, card, or thin cloth.

Also refers to an artifact or specimen placed on a pedestal or inside a case and to a print, photographic image, or document protected by framing, usually against a backing material. Loose specimens and unframed prints and pictures are *unmounted*. **See also**: *mat*.

mouse   A small handheld input device that, when rolled across a hard, flat surface, allows the user to direct the motion of a cursor or pointer on a computer screen and initiate an operation or select an option displayed in a graphical user interface by pressing down on one of its buttons. Because the button makes a clicking sound when pressed, such programs are called *point-and-click* applications. In graphics programs, the mouse can be used like a pen, pencil, or paintbrush. Most mouse operations can be executed more slowly using the keyboard. Basic models are designed to be used by a right- or left-handed person. Contoured models are available for either the right or left hand. In laptops, the mouse is usually built-in.

mouse type   Very tiny, barely readable type used for the fine print in sales contracts, coupons, contest entry forms, etc., to notify the reader of legal restrictions, expiration dates, and other information that the seller is required to display but wishes to downplay.

movable book   A type of novelty children's book containing parts that move, usually through the use of tabs and/or levers, rotating wheels, ingenious folding, etc., usually designed by a paper engineer. *Pop-up books* are included in this category. Most libraries do not, as a matter of policy, purchase movable books for circulation because the mechanisms that operate them are often not designed to withstand heavy use.

movable type   Metal type cast as individual units, each bearing a single character, assembled by a typesetter into words, lines, and pages of text, then disassembled for reuse once a print job is completed. Although there is evidence that printing from wood blocks originated in China, probably during the 11th century, Johann Gutenberg is credited with the invention of modern movable type in Germany in the mid-15th century. *See also*: *printing press*.

movie   From "moving picture." *See*: motion picture.

moving   The transfer of all or a portion of the contents of a library (collections, equipment, furnishings, and personnel) from one facility to another, temporarily or permanently. Most libraries hire a professional moving company with library experience to do the actual work, but advance planning is required for a move to be executed smoothly. Library literature is available on the moving process to assist planners in avoiding common pitfalls.

moving company   A professional mover hired to transfer the contents of a library from one location to another, usually selected in a competitive process in which the company is given the opportunity to inspect the sites before submitting a bid. Unless stated otherwise in the bid specifications, the contractor determines the methods used and provides both personnel and equipment. Professional movers with experience moving libraries work very methodically and quickly because as the move slows or stops, their costs increase.

moving image   *See*: motion picture.

MPEG   Moving Picture Experts Group, a standard for compressing full-motion video in digital format. More efficient than JPEG (the standard for compressing still images), MPEG is used to transmit a wide range of audio-video formats including DVD motion pictures. MPEG-2 requires bandwidth of 4–15 MB per second and an MPEG board for playback in most computers. Pronounced "em-peg."

MRDF   *See*: machine-readable data file.

mull   *See*: crash.

multicast   In telecommunication, to transmit data simultaneously to more than one individual or site connected to the same network, for example, to all who subscribe to an e-mail mailing list, as opposed to *broadcasting* messages to all who own the appropriate receiving equipment (radio and television).

multidisciplinary journal   A scholarly periodical that publishes articles of interest to researchers in a wide range of academic disciplines (*examples*: **Nature** and **Science** in the sciences). Compare with *interdisciplinary journal*.

multimedia   A combination of two or more digital media (text, graphics, audio, animation, video, etc.) used in a computer application, such as an online encyclopedia, computer game, or Web site. Multimedia applications are often interactive. Synonymous in this sense with *digital media*.

In a more general sense, any program, presentation, or computer application in which two or more communication media are used simultaneously or in close association, for example, slides with recorded sound. Still images accompanying text are considered illustration.

multimedia item   A bibliographic item containing two or more categories of material in which no single medium predominates (*AACR2*). The general material designation **[kit]** or **[multimedia]** may be used in the bibliographic description if the item has a collective title. *See also*: *kit*.

multimedia map   A map available electronically that includes audio, video, and/or animation, in addition to graphic images and text, for example, the National Geographic Society's *WildWorld* Web site available at: www.nationalgeographic.com/wildworld.

multipart item   A monograph complete, or intended to be complete, in a finite number of physically separate parts that may or may not be numbered (*AACR2*). A library may decide to bind the parts together.

multipart volume   A work published in two or more physically separate parts that together constitute a single bibliographic volume. Reference works too large to be bound as a single volume are published in this manner, for example, some volumes of *Dictionary of Literary Biography*. Compare with *multivolume work*.

multiple access   More than one point of access to a file of data, for example, a library catalog or bibliographic database searchable by author, title, subject, keywords, etc., as opposed to a resource that has only one point of access, for example, a printed dictionary arranged alphabetically by headword. Compare with *multiple user access*.

multiple editions   In publishing, a book available in more than one edition at the same time, for example, the original trade edition, a movie or television tie-in (usually in mass market or trade paperback), and a special anniversary edition. When two editions of the same title are available at the same time, they are known as *dual editions*.

multiple user access   A file of data that can be used independently by more than one person at the same time, for example, a multivolume print encyclopedia as opposed to a single-volume dictionary. Access to online catalogs, bibliographic databases, and full-text electronic resources by more than one simultaneous user may be governed by licensing agreement. Compare with *multiple access*.

multiple year rate   The discounted price of a periodical subscription purchased for a period of two or more years, usually less than the rate charged for successive one-year subscriptions. This type of discount is normally offered on popular magazines and trade journals.

multitasking   An operating system that permits more than one application program to remain open at the same time, allowing the user to perform multiple operations through shared use of the central processor (CPU), exchanging information between applications if necessary, for example, copying a URL from a Web page to a text document.

multivolume work   A work published in two or more numbered or unnumbered volumes under a single title (*example*: **Oxford English Dictionary**), sometimes over an extended period (**Dictionary of American Regional English**). A multivolume work is cataloged as a single entity, with the volumes owned by the library listed in the holdings statement. Compare with *multipart volume* and *series*.

museum   A publicly or privately funded nonprofit institution whose primary function is the preservation and display of collections of physical artifacts and specimens for the purposes of education, scholarship, and enjoyment. Since books and bindings are physical artifacts, some museums include them in their collections, for example, the illuminated manuscripts and treasure bindings exhibited by the Metropolitan Museum in New York City. Other items found in museums and of interest to librarians include inscriptions, clay tablets, papyrus scrolls, rare maps, letters, diaries, etc. Many museums maintain a library on the premises containing books and other reference materials pertinent to their collections and activities. The concept of "museum" is often broadly interpreted to include archaeological and historical monuments, aquariums, arboreta, botanical gardens, nature centers, etc. Federal grant support is provided to museums through the Institute of Museum and Library Services (IMLS).

museum library   A type of special library maintained by a museum or gallery, usually within its walls but sometimes in a separate location, containing a collection of books, periodicals, reproductions, and other materials related to its exhibits and fields of specialization. Access may be by appointment only. Borrowing privileges may be restricted to museum staff and members. Museum librarians are organized in the Museums, Arts and Humanities Division (MAHD) of the Special Libraries Association (www.sla.org/division/dmah).

museum publisher   A museum or historical society that issues books, exhibit catalogs, and other publications under its own imprint or in cooperation with other publishers, for example, the Metropolitan Museum of Art in New York City. Museum publications are usually of fine quality, often issued in both hardcover and softcover editions to appeal to collectors and casual buyers. *See also*: *exhibit catalog*.

musical presentation statement   In *AACR2*, a term or phrase found in the chief source of information of a printed music publication or music manuscript, entered in an optional area of the bibliographic record to describe the physical form of presentation (full score, miniature score, piano score, etc.), not to be confused with a statement indicating an arrangement or edition of the musical work. If such a statement is an integral part of another area of bibliographic description, and recorded as such, it is not repeated.

musical work   Three definitions are recognized in *AACR2*: (1) a musical composition created as a single unit intended by its composer to be performed as a whole; (2) a set of musical compositions with a collective title, not necessarily intended for performance as a whole; and (3) a group of musical compositions assigned a single opus number. In cataloging musical works, main entry is under the name of the composer, with added entries for arranger, librettist, major performer(s), etc.

music library   A library containing a collection of materials on music and musicians, including printed and manuscript music scores, music periodicals, recorded music (CDs, audiocassettes, phonograph records, etc.), books about music and musicians, program notes, discographies, and music reference materials.

Music collections in public libraries are selected and maintained for lifelong learning and leisure pursuits. Academic and conservatory libraries provide resources for music study and research, including original source material. National libraries offer unique and often rare musical heritage collections. *Music librarian*s are organized in the Music Library Association.

Music Library Association (MLA)   Founded in 1931, MLA promotes the establishment, growth, and use of music libraries and collections of music, musical instruments, music literature, music recordings, and related materials in both print and nonprint format. An affiliate of the American Library Association, the organization also seeks to advance music librarianship, scholarship, and publishing. MLA publishes the monthly *Music Cataloging Bulletin*. URL: www.musiclibraryassoc.org.

music score   *See*: score.

mutilation   Damage, defacement, or destruction of library materials inflicted intentionally, rather than accidentally, including tearing covers and pages; cutting out illustrations or passages of text; marking or writing on margins or text; and removing labels, bookplates, protective covers, date due slips, etc.—all actions that drain library resources. The motives for such acts range from an attitude of entitlement, to monetary concerns (libraries generally charge for photocopying), to disapproval of the library's collection development decisions, to outright malice. *See also*: biblioclast.

mystery   A popular novel, short story, or drama about an unusual event or occurrence, such as a murder or disappearance, that remains so secret or unexplained as to excite popular curiosity and interest. An early example is *The Woman in White* (1860) by Wilkie Collins. The plot in a mystery often hinges on the efforts of a professional or amateur sleuth to uncover the truth, usually narrated by a third-party who witnessed or participated in the action. Clues are often provided by the author as the story unfolds. Subgenres include *detective fiction* and *suspense*. Historical mysteries are set in the 19th century or earlier. English-language mysteries are reviewed in *The Mystery Review* and *The Drood Review of Mystery*. For a Web site devoted to mystery fiction, see *The Mystery Reader* at: www.themysteryreader.com. Compare with *crime fiction*. *See also*: bibliomystery and gothic novel.

mystery play   A form of medieval religious drama, popular from the 14th to the 16th century, usually performed on a mobile wagon from a script based on a story from the Scriptures or a sequence of episodes from biblical history. In England, the performance of mystery plays was often financed by the local trade guilds in connection with important feast days, such as Corpus Christi. Compare with *morality play*. *See also*: miracle play.

Mystery Review, The   Published quarterly since 1992, *The Mystery Review* provides reviews, thematic articles, author interviews, out of print features, and information about new books published in the mystery/detective fiction genre in the United States, Britain, and Canada, as well as profiles of mystery bookstores. ISSN: 1192–8700. *See also*: Drood Review of Mystery, The.

myth   From the classical Greek word *mythos*, meaning "story." A narrative rooted in the traditions of a specific culture, capable of being understood and appreciated in its own right but at the same time part of a system of stories (*mythology*) transmitted orally from one generation to the next to illustrate man's relationship to the cosmos. In traditional societies, myths often serve as the basis for social customs and observances.

Many of the archetypes of classical Greek mythology recur in the literature of Western culture, and some have been appropriated by disciplines outside the arts and humanities (*example*: **Oedipus complex** in psychology). Some scholars have argued that mythic thinking is integral to human consciousness and that myths are simply a manifestation of the way culture is created by the human mind. Dictionaries of mythology are available in the reference section of public and academic libraries. Compare with *folktale* and *legend*.

N

NACO *See*: Program for Cooperative Cataloging.

NAGARA *See*: National Association of Government Archives and Records Administrators.

NAICS *See*: North American Industry Classification System.

NAL *See*: National Agricultural Library.

name authority file An authorized list giving the preferred form of entry for names (personal, corporate, and geographic) used as headings in a library catalog and any cross-references from variant forms.

name index A list of the personal names appearing in a work, arranged alphabetically by surname, with reference to the page number(s) on which each name is found in the text. Not all books have a separate name index—personal names may be included in a general index or in the subject index. When present in a single-volume work, the name index is part of the back matter. In a multivolume work, it is usually found at the end of the last volume. Compare with *author index*.

nameplate *See*: flag.

name-title added entry In *AACR2*, an added entry in a library catalog giving the name of a person (or corporate body) and the title of a work, for the purpose of identifying: (1) a work that is included in or the subject of the work being cataloged; (2) a larger work of which the work being cataloged is part; or (3) another work to which the work being cataloged is in some way related. Synonymous with *author-title added entry*.

NAMTC *See*: National Association of Media & Technology Centers.

nap In the context of manuscript production, the slight texture on writing material that causes the nib of the pen to grip the surface and allows the ink to sink in. Because the parchment and vellum sheets used by medieval scribes tended to be greasy, the surface had to be prepared by rubbing it with an abrasive substance called *pounce* to raise the nap before the work of copying commenced. Synonymous with *tooth*.

NAP   *See*: normal administrative practice.

NARA   *See*: National Archives and Records Administration.

narration   The telling of a story or an account of events, in speech or writing, usually in the first or third person. Most documentary films and television programs include a scripted narration, with the name of the *narrator* given in the credits. Celebrity narrators may be employed to enhance the appeal of a work.

narrative   A written or spoken work in the form of a story or account (real or imagined) told by one or more *narrators* as a continuous, episodic, or broken series of related events, usually in the first or third person. Narratives can be short, as in a brief anecdote, or as long as a full-length novel. A *narrative poem* is one that relates a story (ballad, epic, etc.). The *narrative structure* of a work is the sequence and voice in which the author unfolds events, for example, in a series of flashbacks.

narrow   The shape of a book in which the width of the cover is less than two-thirds its height, a format commonly used in the design of field guides and travel guides. Compare with *square*. *See also*: *oblong* and *portrait*.

narrowcast   Selective use of communication media to target a highly specialized audience, in contrast to a mass media *broadcast* intended to reach as many listeners or viewers as possible.

narrower term (NT)   In a hierarchical classification system, a subject heading or descriptor representing a subclass of a class indicated by another term, for example, "Music librarianship" under "Librarianship." A subject heading or descriptor may have more than one narrower term (also "Comparative librarianship" under "Librarianship"). Also abbreviated *N*. Compare with *broader term* and *related term*. *See also*: *hyponym*.

NASIG   *See*: North American Serials Interest Group.

NASLIN   *See*: North American Sport Library Network.

National Agricultural Library (NAL)   Established as a federal library in 1862 under legislation signed by President Abraham Lincoln, NAL is part of the Agricultural Research Service (ARS) of the U.S. Department of Agriculture (USDA). With a collection of over 3.3 million items, NAL is the primary source of agricultural information in the United States and the largest agricultural library in the world. Located in Beltsville, Maryland, NAL works closely with libraries at land-grant universities to improve access to, and utilization of, agricultural information by researchers, policymakers, educators, farmers, consumers of agricultural products, and the general public. URL: www.nal.usda.gov.

national archives   The central archives of a nation, charged with collecting, preserving, and managing documents and records of historical significance to its citizens and government. The first national archives was established in France in 1790. In democratic nations, the operation of national archives is governed by legislation. In the United States, the National Archives and Records Administration (NARA) has statutory responsibility for the preservation of archival information of national importance. Compare with *national library.*

National Archives and Records Administration (NARA)   The national archives of the United States, a federal agency established by Congress in 1934 to oversee the management of all federal records, including the public's right of access to documents and information not specifically exempted under the *Freedom of Information Act.* NARA's 33 facilities house approximately 21.5 million cubic feet of original textual materials collected from the executive, legislative, and judicial branches. It also includes nonprint materials, such as motion pictures, sound and videorecordings, maps and charts, aerial photographs, architectural drawings, computer data sets, posters, etc. NARA is administered by an Archivist of the United States appointed by the president with the approval of Congress and advised by a National Archives Council. URL: www.archives.gov/index.html. *See also*: *National Association of Government Archives and Records Administrators.*

National Association of Government Archives and Records Administrators (NAGARA)   Founded in 1984, NAGARA is a nationwide association of local, state, and federal archivists and records administrators and individuals with an interest in improving the management of government records. Its members are local, state, and federal archival and records management agencies. NAGARA publishes the quarterly newsletter *NAGARA Clearinghouse.* URL: www.nagara.org. *See also*: *National Archives and Records Administration.*

National Association of Media & Technology Centers (NAMTC)   A nonprofit association devoted to assisting specialists responsible for managing media and technology centers, through networking, advocacy, and support activities intended to enhance equitable access to nonprint media, technology, and information services to educational communities. Membership in NAMTC is open to regional, K–12, and higher education media and technology centers, as well as commercial media vendors. URL: www.namtc.org.

national bibliography   An ongoing list of the books and other materials published or distributed in a specific country, especially works written about the country and its inhabitants or in its national language, for example, *Canadiana* or the *British National Bibliography (BNB)*, which since 1950 has provided a weekly list of new titles published in Great Britain. The focus of national bibliography has traditionally been print materials (books, serials, pamphlets, maps, printed music, government documents, etc.), but nonprint media including works created in digital formats are also listed in some countries.

As noted in the *International Encyclopedia of Information and Library Science* (Routledge, 2003), current national bibliography was originally undertaken by the book trade to facilitate commerce (as exemplified by the *Cumulative Book Index* in the United States) but since the early 1950s, the regular listing of new publications has been regarded as the proper function of a national agency, usually operating within the national library. Retrospective national bibliography has been accomplished in part by publication of the catalogs of the national library, based on collections established by copyright deposit. Projects such as the *English Short title Catalogue* have extended retrospective bibliography beyond the holdings of national libraries.

national biography   A publication containing biographical information about people of noteworthy accomplishments living in or associated with a particular country. Most national biographies are multivolume reference works.

Example:

American National Biography in 24 volumes, edited by John A. Garraty. New York: Oxford University Press, 1999.

Also refers to the branch of biography devoted to describing and analyzing the lives of important people living in or associated with a country.

National Book Award   An honor awarded since 1950 by the National Book Foundation, a consortium of book publishing groups, to enhance public awareness of exceptional books written by Americans. Awards are given in four categories: fiction, nonfiction, poetry, and children's literature. Decisions are made by an independent panel of five judges. The prize in each category is $10,000 and a crystal sculpture. An annotated list of prizewinners past and present is available online from Powells Books at: www.powells.com/prizes/national.html. *See also*: *Pulitzer Prize*.

National Circulation Interchange Protocol (NCIP)   Information standard Z39.83, developed by the National Information Standards Organization (NISO) to support circulation activities among independent library systems, including patron and item inquiry, and to update transactions in circulation and interlibrary loan (hold, reserve, checkout, renew, and check-in), self-service applications, online payment, direct consortial borrowing, and controlled access to electronic resources. The NISO Standards Committee based its work on the Standard Interchange Protocol (SIP) developed by the 3M company to support self-checkout systems. Implementation is expected to facilitate the development of open systems in information exchange. URL: www.niso.org/committees/committee_at.html.

National Commission on Libraries and Information Science (NCLIS)   An independent agency within the executive branch of the U.S. federal government, established in 1970 to advise the president and Congress on national library and information policy, conduct studies of library and information needs, assess the adequacy of current resources and services, promote research, develop plans for meeting the nation's information needs, and help coordinate library-related activities at the federal, state, and local levels. URL: www.nclis.gov.

National Digital Information Infrastructure and Preservation Program (NDIIPP)
A program led by the Library of Congress and partially funded in 2000 by the U.S. Congress to assess the current state of digital archiving and preservation and to develop a national strategy for the preservation of digital content. Sometimes shortened to *Digital Preservation Program*. URL: www.digitalpreservation.gov.

National Endowment for the Humanities (NEH)   An independent grant-making agency established in 1965 by the *National Foundation on the Arts and the Humanities Act*, NEH supports research, education, and public programs in the humanities, with attention to the diverse heritage, traditions, and history of the United States and the relevance of the humanities to current conditions and events affecting American society. Each state has a Humanities Council that establishes its own guidelines and application deadlines. The state councils support a variety of projects, including library reading programs, lectures, conferences, seminars and institutes, media presentations, and museum and library traveling exhibitions. The national office is located in Washington, D.C. URL: www.neh.gov.

National Federation of Abstracting and Information Services (NFAIS)   Founded in 1958 at the instigation of the director of *BIOSIS*, NFAIS has a membership of 55 leading nonprofit, commercial, government, and academic producers and distributors of online bibliographic databases and other digital information services for research and professional use, as well as organizations that provide access to electronic databases in a wide range of disciplines. NFAIS publishes the monthly *NFAIS Newsletter*. URL: www.nfais.org.

National Film Preservation Board (NFPB)   Established by the *National Film Preservation Act* of 1988, NFPB is an advisory board authorized to assist the Librarian of Congress in preserving archival materials related to 25 films selected each year for the National Film Registry as culturally, historically, and aesthetically significant. URL: lcweb.loc.gov/film. *See also*: *International Federation of Film Archives*.

National Film Preservation Foundation (NFPF)   A nonprofit organization created by Congress to support nationwide efforts to preserve the film heritage of the United States and improve access to film for study, research, education, and exhibition, NFPF began in 1997 with the support of grants from the Academy of Motion Picture Arts and Sciences and the Film Foundation. In 2000, the organization began distributing federal matching grants to film archives to preserve endangered films and collections. URL: www.filmpreservation.org.

National Film Registry (NFR)   A list of up to 25 films selected each year by the Librarian of Congress, with the assistance of the National Film Preservation Board, for preservation in the archives of the Library of Congress. The films must be at least 10 years old but need not be feature-length or have been released to a theater audience to be eligible for selection. The *National Film Preservation Act* of 1988 authorizes the Board to consider the broadest possible range of films in its deliberations. The NFR homepage includes a list of Registry films for the current year (lcweb.loc.gov/film/filmnfr.html).

National Genealogical Society (NGS)   Founded in 1903 with headquarters in Arlington, Virginia, NGS is a service organization devoted to collecting, preserving, and disseminating genealogical information, encouraging interest in genealogical research, fostering careful documentation of genealogical data, and promoting education and training in the field of genealogy. NGS publishes the *NGS Newsmagazine* and the journal *NGS Quarterly*. URL: www.ngsgenealogy.org.

National Information Standards Organization (NISO)   A nonprofit association accredited by the American National Standards Institute (ANSI) to develop voluntary standards in library science, information science, publishing, and other information services, NISO is designated by ANSI to represent U.S. interests to the Technical Committee on Information and Documentation of the International Organization for Standardization (ISO). NISO standards are listed in the reference section at the end of *The Bowker Annual Library and Book Trade Almanac*. URL: www.niso.org. *See also*: *Z39.50*.

national library   A library designated and funded by a national government to serve the nation by maintaining a comprehensive collection of the published and unpublished literary output of the nation as a whole, including publications of the government itself. Most national libraries are also responsible for compiling a national bibliography, and some also serve as the legal depository for works protected by copyright in their country. The national library of the United States is the Library of Congress, located in Washington, D.C. Three other libraries—the National Agricultural Library, the National Library of Education, and the National Library of Medicine—contain national collections in specific subject areas. *Yahoo!* provides a list of national libraries of the world at: dir.yahoo.com/Reference/Libraries/National_Libraries. The national libraries of Europe are accessible via the *Gabriel* gateway at: www.bl.uk/gabriel. Compare with *national archives*.

National Library of Australia (NLA)   Established in 1901, the NLA moved from Melbourne to Canberra in 1927, following the opening of the Federal Parliament building, and in 1968 to its new and permanent home on the shore of Lake Burley Griffin, uniting collections formerly dispersed around Canberra. In addition to its Main Reading Room, the NLA has separate reading rooms for collections of Asian materials, manuscripts, maps, pictorial works, rare books, newspapers, oral history, music, and ephemera. The national library also has an active publishing program and is a member of the MARC Advisory Committee. URL: www.nla.gov.au.

National Library of Canada/Bibliothèque Nationale du Canada (NLC/BNC)   The national library of Canada, established by act of Parliament in 1953. Located in Ottawa, NLC/BNC is charged with acquiring, preserving, and promoting the published heritage of Canada for all Canadians. Its collections are focused mainly on Canadiana (works written by, about, or of interest to Canadians, published in Canada or abroad). In October 2002, the Minister of Canadian Heritage announced the merger of the National Library of Canada with the National Archives of Canada. URL: www.nlc-bnc.ca.

National Library of Education (NLE)   The largest library in the world devoted solely to the collection, preservation, and effective use of research and other information in the field of education. Located in Washington, D.C., NLE is funded by the U.S. federal government. It serves the U.S. Department of Education, Congress, and the Office of the President, as well as the general public, and is the center of a national network of libraries, archives, and other information providers in education. URL: www.ed.gov/NLE.

National Library of Medicine (NLM)   The largest medical library in the United States, administered by the National Institutes of Health (NIH). Located in Bethesda, Maryland, NLM provides public access to an online version of its *MEDLINE* bibliographic database at no charge under the title *PubMed*. URL: www.nlm.nih.gov.

National Library Service for the Blind and Physically Handicapped (NLS)   A national library program administered by the Library of Congress that produces and distributes Braille and recorded library materials at no charge to eligible borrowers through a national network of cooperating regional and local libraries. Established by Congress in 1931 to serve blind adults, NLS was expanded in 1952 to serve visually impaired children, in 1962 to provide music materials, and in 1966 to serve individuals with other physical impairments that prevent them from reading print of standard size. URL: lcweb.loc.gov/nls.

National Library Week   Sponsored for the first time in 1958 by the National Book Committee and the American Library Association, National Library Week is an officially recognized seven-day period in the spring of each year during which special attention is given to promoting libraries of all types in the United States. Most public libraries celebrate the event by displaying posters and exhibits, issuing press releases, and sponsoring book talks and other promotional activities. In the United Kingdom, a similar event known as National Libraries Week is celebrated in the fall of each year.

National Science Digital Library (NSDL)   A digital library of collections and services funded by the National Science Foundation and intended to become a comprehensive, online source of digital resources for use in science, technology, engineering, and mathematics education. URL: nsdl.org.

National Storytelling Network (NSN)   Formed in 1998 when the National Storytelling Association split into the National Storytelling Network and Storytelling Foundation International, NSN is an organization dedicated to improving the quality of storytelling wherever it can contribute to the quality of life. An affiliate of the American Library Association, NSN sponsors the annual National Storytelling Conference in cooperation with its local and regional members. NSN also publishes *Storytelling Magazine* and hosts the *StoryNet* Web site (www.storynet.org).

national survey   A government agency that specializes in mapping, surveying, and providing scientific information about the topography and natural resources of a country. In the United States, the national surveys are the U.S. Geological Survey (USGS) and the National Geodetic Survey (NGS).

National Technical Information Service (NTIS)   Located on the outskirts of Washington, D.C., NTIS is an agency within the Technology Administration of the U.S. Department of Commerce that is the largest centralized source of scientific, technical, engineering, and business information produced or sponsored by U.S. and international government agencies. Its collection of over 3 million items includes technical reports, statistics, business information, publications of the U.S. military, multimedia training programs, computer software, and electronic databases. URL: www.ntis.gov.

National Union Catalog (NUC)   A series of printed catalogs issued by the Library of Congress that began in 1948 as an author list of printed cards and titles reported as held by other libraries in North America—a heroic pre-digital attempt to create a union catalog of national scope to facilitate resource sharing. With the development of machine-readable records, the NUCs have been largely superseded by the availability of holdings information in the large bibliographic databases maintained by utilities such as OCLC. *See also*: *National Union Catalog of Manuscript Collections*.

National Union Catalog of Manuscript Collections (NUCMC)   A cooperative cataloging program sponsored by the Library of Congress since 1959, NUCMC provides cataloging of archival and manuscript materials at no charge to repositories in the United States that meet its eligibility guidelines. MARC records are created by NUCMC catalogers in the *RLIN* national-level database, based on cataloging data supplied by eligible repositories. URL: lcweb.loc.gov/coll/nucmc.

natural language   A human language in which the structure and rules have evolved from usage, usually over an extended period time, as opposed to an artificial language based on rules prescribed prior to its development and use, as in a computer language. In search software designed to handle input expressed in natural language, the user may enter the query in the form in which it would be spoken or written ("Where can I find information about Frederick Douglass?" as opposed to the search statement "frederick douglass" or "su:douglass"). An example of a natural language Internet search engine is *Ask Jeeves* (www.ask.com). Compare with *controlled vocabulary*.

navigation   The use of hypertext links, icons, menu options, and search engines displayed on a Web page to move to other resources available on the Internet or to other pages within the same Web site. When the user proceeds in a casual way, the activity is called *surfing*; when the approach is purposeful, it is a *search*. *See also*: *navigation bar* and *search history*.

navigation bar   A series of options, usually in the form of clickable buttons, icons, or text links arranged in a row across the top or bottom of the screen or window, or along the right- or left-hand side, indicating the main categories under which the information contained in the subpages of a Web site is organized. In a well-designed site, the navigation bar is repeated on each subpage to enable the user to select from the list of main options without having to return to the initial page. Compare with *toolbar*.

NCIP   *See*: National Circulation Interchange Protocol.

NCLIS   *See*: National Commission on Libraries and Information Science.

n.d.   *See*: no date.

NDIIPP   *See*: National Digital Information Infrastructure and Preservation Program.

NDLTD   *See*: electronic theses and dissertations.

NE   *See*: new edition pending.

neatline   The line that marks the edges of a map, separating it from the margin (if there is a margin), usually a thin rule in black or dark-colored ink.

need to know   In information security systems, the underlying principle restricting access to sensitive or classified materials to persons who have an essential and justifiable need to be informed. Under conditions of extreme secrecy, such a need may be substantiated by various levels of security clearance and the issuance of identification (badges, passwords, etc.).

negative   The image that results when negative photographic film is developed, producing tonal values (black and white) that are the reverse of the original subject and of any positive print of the same image. Negative color film not only reverses tonal values but also the colors of the subject, making them appear as complementary colors (red as green, blue as yellow, etc.). *See also*: *master negative* and *print master*.

NEH   *See*: National Endowment for the Humanities.

Nemeth code   *See*: Braille.

neologism   A new word coined from an existing term or terms (*example*: **netiquette** from "network" and "etiquette"), or a new meaning given to an existing word (*example*: **quark** from *Finnegans Wake* used in physics as the name of a subatomic particle). Acronyms are neologisms. Also refers to the use of this form of new word or meaning.

NEP   *See*: new edition pending.

nesting   In Boolean searching, the use of parentheses to embed a logical operation within another logical operation as a means of indicating the sequence (syntax) in which the logical commands are to be executed by the computer. In the following example, the Boolean "or" command will be executed first, followed by "not" and then "and."

Search statement: **children and violence and ((television or media) not cartoon*)**

net   Terms of sale in which a publisher specifies that a book must be offered at *no* retail discount or reduction in price. Synonymous with *net published price*. Compare with *non-net*.

Net   A shortened form of *Internet*.

net borrower   A library that borrows more items via interlibrary loan than it lends to other libraries over a designated period of time. The opposite of *net lender*.

netcast   *See*: Webcast.

netiquette   A neologism formed by shortening the phrase *network etiquette*. The rules of civility and good manners that apply to communication via the Internet, an environment in which the visual cues available in face-to-face communication and the auditory cues perceptible in voice communication are lacking. Virginia Shea maintains the *Netiquette Home Page* at: www.albion.com/netiquette. *See also*: *e-mail*, *flame*, *shouting*, and *smiley*.

net lender   A library that lends more items via interlibrary loan than it borrows from other libraries during a designated period of time. Net lenders are more likely than net borrowers to charge a fee for interlibrary loan service. In the OCLC ILL system, each time the status of an item requested is updated to "shipped," a small credit is given per transaction to the lender, providing some compensation to libraries that are net lenders.

net price   A bookseller's cost for a book or other publication, usually the publisher's list price or suggested price, less any discounts or allowances. Cost of shipping is usually added to net price.

net pricing   In bookselling, a method of price setting in which no cover price is printed on the item or on the dust jacket. Instead, the publisher sets the wholesale price without reference to a suggested retail price, and each bookseller or jobber is free to establish its own resale price, which may vary from one seller to another. According to *The Bookman's Glossary* (R.R. Bowker, 1983), this controversial practice began in 1979 and is used most often in the college textbook market.

Netscape Navigator   A popular software program designed to facilitate browsing for information available at sites on the World Wide Web. *Netscape Navigator* allows the user to bookmark Web sites for future reference, and to print and download search results, and includes many other user-friendly features. Its primary competitor in the Web browser market is *Internet Explorer* from Microsoft. Before AOL purchased Netscape Communications in 1998, the company formed a nonprofit arm, The Mozilla Organization, to convert *Netscape Navigator* to an open source Web browser known as *Mozilla*. URL: www.netscape.com.

netspeak   The argot of Internet enthusiasts. *Yahoo!* provides a list of links to Internet glossaries at: dir.yahoo.com/Computers_and_Internet/Dictionaries.

network   A group of physically discrete computers interconnected to allow resources to be shared and data exchanged, usually by means of telecommunication links and client/server architecture. Most networks are administered by an operations center that provides assistance to users. The largest "network of networks" in the world is the Internet, allowing users of computers of all types and sizes to communicate in real time. *See also*: *CD-ROM network, extranet, intranet, local area network,* and *wide area network.*

Also, two or more organizations engaged in the exchange of information through common communication channels, usually for the purpose of accomplishing shared objectives. When the organizations are libraries, the arrangement is a *library network,* for example, the National Network of Libraries of Medicine (URL: www.nnlm.nlm.nih.gov). Compare with *consortium.*

In communications media, a chain of television or radio broadcasting stations that share a significant portion of their programming, either because they are owned by the producer of the programming (the network) or because they are independent affiliates compensated by the network for broadcasting its programming. At one time, the major television networks (ABC, CBS, and NBC) had a virtual monopoly of television programming in the United States, but they have lost market share to the cable networks.

networking The art of developing contacts within a profession and using them to advance one's work and career. Librarians do this by meeting colleagues at library conferences, participating in colloquia and round tables, volunteering to serve on committees, running for elective office, etc.

neume From the Greek word *pneuma*, meaning "breath." One of a set of graphic signs used from the 7th to 14th centuries as musical notation in liturgical works (antiphonals, graduals, hymnals, missals, etc.) to denote movement of melody in the early chant and plainsong incorporated into medieval Church services. Originally written above the text without staves, neumes indicated neither precise pitch nor length of note, serving as a reminder of melody already familiar to the singers.

Because the form of neumes was not standardized, considerable regional variation existed in Europe. Beginning in the mid-11th century, they were written on a four-line staff. In the late 12th century, square notation replaced the earlier pointed and curved signs in France and Italy. For more information about the history of neumes, see the entry under the term in *The New Grove Dictionary of Music and Musicians* (Grove, 2001).

new adult reader A person of mature years who has recently learned to read, usually by enrolling in an adult literacy program. Public libraries try to meet the needs of new adult readers by selecting materials appropriate to their reading level and by developing services to acquaint them with available information resources.

new age book A generic term used in publishing to refer to contemporary titles written on subjects outside mainstream American culture, such as holistic health and alternative medicine, nontraditional exercise and fitness techniques, natural foods and alternative diets, self-help psychology, astrology and numerology, and non-Western spiritual practices (yoga, meditation, tai chi, etc.). New age books are selected mainly by public libraries.

Newberry Library Located in Chicago, the Newberry Library is a privately funded independent research library devoted primarily to the humanities. Free and open to the public, it contains an extensive noncirculating collection of rare books, maps, manuscripts, and other materials related to the civilizations of western Europe and the Americas. The Library was established in the late 19th century at the bequest of the wealthy Chicago businessman and philanthropist Walter Loomis Newberry. URL: www.newberry.org.

Newbery, John (1713–1767) The English writer, publisher, printer, and bookseller who first recognized the potential commercial market for books written specifically for children. Newbery began publishing works for children in 1744 with *A Little Pretty Pocket-Book*, containing rhyming fables and rules of conduct, followed by the didactic favorite *The History of Little Goody Two-Shoes* (1765), which may have been written by his friend Oliver Goldsmith. Illustrated in color, the titles in his inexpensive *Juvenile Library* series were very popular in England. He also published the first children's encyclopedia, *The Circle of the Sciences* in seven volumes (1745–1748), and the first children's periodical, *The Lilliputian Magazine* (1751). Newbery's contribution to children's literature is commemorated in the Newbery Medal, awarded annually since 1922 to the most distinguished children's book by an American author published in the United States during the preceding year.

Newbery Medal   A literary award given annually since 1922 under the auspices of the American Library Association to the author of the most distinguished children's book published in the United States during the preceding year. Sponsored by the family of Frederic G. Melcher, the medal is named after John Newbery (1713–1767), the British publisher who first published books written specifically for children. Compare with *Caldecott Medal*. *See also*: *Carnegie Medal* and *CLA Book of the Year for Children*.

newbie   A slang term for a person who is a newcomer to e-mail, electronic mailing lists, newsgroups, the World Wide Web, or the Internet in general or to any computer application or system. *See also*: *novice*.

new book   A new title issued for the first time, usually in hardcover, announced by the publisher in book trade journals and review publications and promoted through book signings, author interviews, etc. Recently published titles make up a publisher's *frontlist*. Some new books make the *bestseller list*. Compare with *backlist*. *See also*: *missionary book*.

   Also refers to a title recently added to a library collection. Public libraries often display the dust jackets of new books on a bulletin board or kiosk, or shelve them in a special location for a few weeks, to allow patrons to browse them separately before they are integrated into the general collection.

new construction   A completely new library facility, designed from scratch and constructed from the ground up, as opposed to the renovation or expansion of an existing structure. New construction allows the architect to use state-of-the-art design concepts and the latest materials, furnishings, and equipment, within the constraints imposed by the project budget. The old facility is usually converted to some other purpose once the library has moved to its new location. New library construction is reported annually in *Library Journal* and *The Bowker Annual Library and Book Trade Almanac*.

new edition   *See*: revised edition.

new edition pending (NE or NEP)   A code used on a publisher's invoice to indicate that a new edition of the title ordered is in preparation but has not yet been issued.

New Members Round Table (NMRT)   Established in 1931 as a round table of the American Library Association, NMRT assists persons who have been ALA members for under 10 years to become active in the Association and in the library profession at the national, state, and local levels. In addition to providing a resume review service and a mentoring program, NMRT sponsors the electronic mailing list *NMRT-L*. URL: www.ala.org.

new release   A media item (motion picture, videorecording, audiorecording, etc.) that has just been issued, shown, or offered for sale to the general public for the first time. *See also*: *release date*.

new series In *AACR2*, a term used in the *numeric and/or alphabetical, chronological, or other designation* area of the bibliographic record to indicate that a serial publication has been given a new numbering sequence without a change in its title proper.

newsgroup An Internet message board, usually devoted to a specific topic, to which a participant may post comments or queries, then view the replies of other participants, responses to the replies, and so on. A sequence of related postings is called a *discussion thread*. The most common types are *Usenet* and *NetNews*, which use the Network News Transfer Protocol (NNTP). Unlike e-mail mailing lists, most newsgroups are unmoderated, so postings are not filtered on the basis of content, nor are they limited to a list of registered subscribers. The *CyberFiber Newsgroups Directory* (www. cyberfiber.com/index.html) or the *Google Groups* search engine (groups.google.com) can be used to locate newsgroups on a specific topic.

newsletter A serial publication consisting of no more than a few pages, devoted to news, announcements, and current information of interest primarily to a specialized group of subscribers or members of an association or organization who receive it as part of their membership, for example, *The National Teaching & Learning Forum*, available in print and online at: www.ntlf.com. Newsletters are listed in the *Oxbridge Directory of Newsletters*, a reference serial published by Oxbridge Communications. Most periodical indexes and bibliographic databases do not cover newsletter content. *See also*: *electronic newsletter*.

news library A type of special library maintained in the offices of a newspaper publisher, or other news agency, that includes in its collection newspaper and magazine clippings, photo files (sometimes with negatives), maps, pamphlet files, microforms, reference materials, and online databases related to news and current events. Most are open to subscribers and librarians at the discretion of the *news librarian*, usually by appointment. News libraries are listed in *The International Directory of News Libraries*, a serial published in cooperation with the News Division of the Special Libraries Association.

newsmagazine A general interest magazine devoted to the publication of news and editorial comment, usually on a wide range of subjects, from politics to entertainment (*examples*: *U.S. News & World Report* and *Maclean's* in Canada). Most newsmagazines are published weekly and sold at newsstands, in bookstores, and by subscription. Some are available in an online version (*examples*: *BusinessWeek Online* at www.businessweek.com and *Time Online Edition* at www.time.com). *See also*: *newspaper*.

newspaper A serial publication, usually printed on newsprint and issued daily, on certain days of the week, or weekly, containing news, editorial comment, regular columns, letters to the editor, cartoons, advertising, and other items of current and often local interest to a general readership. Some national newspapers are issued *twice* daily in early and late editions or in different editions for different regions of the country.

According to Warren Chappell, writing in *A Short History of the Printed Word*

(Knopf, 1970), the first modern newspaper of regular publication was *Avisa Relation oder Zeitung* published by Johan Carolus of Strasbourg beginning in 1609. Because they can be used to influence public opinion, newspapers are subject to censorship in some countries. In the United States, newspapers once fiercely independent are increasingly owned by mass media conglomerates. Under such conditions, editorial decisions may be may subject to pressure from commercial interests.

In libraries, current issues of newspapers are normally available in print, but the back files are usually converted to microfilm or microfiche (or digitized) to conserve space. Most national and regional newspapers offer at least a portion of their content online (*example*: **New York Times** at www.nytimes.com). Information on local, regional, and national newspapers can be found in the annual *Gale Directory of Publications and Broadcast Media*, available in the reference section of most academic and large public libraries.

In the United States, some dailies publish their own printed indexes (*New York Times*, *Wall Street Journal*, *Washington Post*, etc.). The editorial content of a few major dailies is also indexed in general periodical databases. National and regional newspapers are indexed in specialized newspaper databases (*examples*: **DataTimes** and **NewsBank**). Compare with *newsmagazine*. **See also**: Acta Diurna, *headline*, *masthead*, *news library*, and *newspaper index*.

newspaper index   A list of the editorial content (news stories, articles, editorials, and columns) published in one or more newspapers, usually arranged alphabetically by subject (including names). Indexes to major U.S. dailies are available in print (*example*: **New York Times Index**). Newspaper indexes are also available online (*examples*: **DataTimes** and **Newspaper Abstracts** in OCLC *FirstSearch*).

newspaper library   *See*: morgue.

newspaper rod   *See*: stick.

newspeak   A neologism coined by the journalist and writer George Orwell in his anti-utopian novel *1984* (published in1949) to refer to the artificial language of government slogans, especially authoritarian propaganda. The term is also applied to euphemisms used by politicians, bureaucrats, and military personnel in public pronouncements to evade public scrutiny and deflect criticism of their actions (*example*: **incursion** instead of "invasion") and by broadcasters to lull audiences into complacency.

newsprint   A grade of coarse, absorbent, unsized paper made primarily from groundwood pulp, used in printing newspapers and newsletters to keep costs down. Because it is bulky, yellows quickly, and becomes brittle with the passage of time, libraries convert newspaper back files to microfilm or microfiche and provide reader-printer machines for enlarging and making hard copies.

newsreel   A short film, 10 to 20 minutes in length, providing documentary-style coverage of a series of news events or topics of general interest. Newsreels preceded the feature film in commercial movie theaters until the 1950s when television broadcast news replaced them. In the United States and Europe, the newsreel was an important propaganda tool during World Wars I and II. They are preserved in archival film collections.

news service   A method of pooling news-gathering resources, first developed in the mid-19th century when six highly competitive New York City newspaper publishers decided to cooperate to lower the expense of collecting and transmitting international news via telegraph to the United States. Most wire services operate through overseas bureaus to which news reporters submit their copy and photographs. A brief history of the Associated Press (AP) news service is available online at: www.ap.org/ anniversary/nhistory/index.html. Directory information for news services is available in *Literary Market Place*.

New York Public Library (NYPL)   The largest public library system in the United States, NYPL is composed of Research Libraries supported largely by private funds and Branch Libraries serving the boroughs of Manhattan, the Bronx, and Staten Island operated mainly from public funds allocated by the city and state of New York. The jewel in the crown of the NYPL is the landmark building located at 5th Avenue and 42nd Street in Manhattan. URL: www.nypl.org.

New York Review of Books (NYRB)   Published since 1963 in 20 issues per year by NYREV, Inc., *NYRB* provides in-depth commentary on literature, culture, politics, and science in the form of lengthy book reviews written for the educated reader by well-known authors and scholars. *NYRB* also includes announcements of new books published by trade and university presses. ISSN: 0028–7504. The online version of *NYRB* is available at: www.nybooks.com. *See also*: New York Times Book Review *and* Times Literary Supplement.

New York Times Book Review (NYTBR)   One of the most influential review publications in the United States, *NYTBR* is published weekly as part of the Sunday edition of the *New York Times*. It is also available by subscription as a separate section. Reviews are long and scholarly, written for the educated reader by well-known writers and scholars. Some publishers consider it the most important medium in the country for advertising new trade books. ISSN: 0028–7806. The online version of *NYTBR* is available at: www.nytimes.com/pages/books/index.html. *See also*: New York Review of Books *and* Times Literary Supplement.

New York Times Co. v. Tasini   *See*: *Tasini* decision.

NFAIS   *See*: National Federation of Abstracting and Information Services.

NFPB   *See*: National Film Preservation Board.

NFPF   *See*: National Film Preservation Foundation.

NFR   *See*: National Film Registry.

NGS   *See*: National Genealogical Society.

niche publishing   The activities of small presses and divisions within large publishing companies that limit their scope to a relatively narrow subject area (*example*: **auto repair manuals** or **travel guides**) or type of literature (**genre fiction**), producing publications intended to meet the needs of a specific market segment. Some niches are broader than others.

nickname   A familiar name of a person, usually a diminutive form of the full given name (*example*: **Bill** for William). Also, a popular name sometimes given in derision or to highlight a special attribute of the person (**Wild Bill**). Corporate entities can have nicknames (**Big Apple** for New York City). Information on nicknames can be found in the latest edition of the *Pseudonyms and Nicknames Dictionary* published by the Gale Group. Compare with *conventional name*.

nihil obstat   A Latin phrase meaning "nothing hinders" appearing on the verso of the title page of works that have been examined by officials of the Roman Catholic Church and found to contain no offense that merits censorship, still used in books that present official Catholic doctrine (*example*: *New Catholic Encyclopedia*). *See also*: *imprimatur* and Index Librorum Prohibitorum.

nipping   In bookbinding, the step in which the text block and case (or covers) are firmly pressed together to expel air from between the leaves, giving the volume its desired shape. When done after sewing to reduce swell before the covers are applied, the process is called *smashing*.

NISO   *See*: National Information Standards Organization.

nitrate film   A flexible base made of cellulose nitrate, produced by Eastman Kodak from about 1890 until 1950 for use in film negatives and motion picture film. Because it is chemically unstable and highly flammable, organizations such as the National Film Preservation Foundation provide grant assistance to film archives to facilitate the copying of moving image collections from nitrate film to a more permanent base, such as acetate or polyester.

NLA   *See*: National Library of Australia.

NLE   *See*: National Library of Education.

NLM   *See*: National Library of Medicine.

NLS   *See*: National Library Service for the Blind and Physically Handicapped.

NMRT   *See*: New Members Round Table.

NNTP   *See*: newsgroup.

Nobel Prize in Literature   A highly prestigious literary award established and funded in 1900 by Alfred B. Nobel, who made his fortune from the invention of dynamite. The Nobel Prize in Literature is given annually by the Swedish Academy in Stockholm to "the person who shall have produced in the field of literature the most distinguished work of an idealistic tendency." A list of past prizewinners is available online at: www.nobel.se/literature/laureates. *See also*: *National Book Award* and *Pulitzer Prize*.

no date   A phrase abbreviated *n.d.*, used in library cataloging to indicate that the publication date is unknown because no date can be found in or on the item. If the correct date is ascertainable from other sources, it is indicated as a bracketed interpolation in the edition area of the bibliographic record (*example*: **[1965]**). Under *AACR2*, if dates of publication and distribution are unknown, the cataloger may use date of copyright or manufacture (*example*: **c1966**). If no date of publication, distribution, copyright, or manufacture can be ascertained, the cataloger may supply an approximate date of publication, as in: [1965?], [ca. 1960], [196-?], [1965 or 1966], [18--?], etc.

node   From the Latin *nodus*, meaning "knot" or "knob." In botany, the point on the stem of a plant from which a leaf or twig grows. In communications, a junction point in a network, such as a personal computer connected to a LAN or a terminal connected to a mainframe. Each node has its own unique network address and the capacity to send, receive, and store messages. In an indexing language, the point in a tree structure at which two or more lines meet.

noise   In physics, any unwanted or unmodulated energy (audible or inaudible) accompanying a signal, especially random and persistent disturbance that obscures or interferes with transmission. Intensity is expressed as the *signal-to-noise ratio*. In communication, any distortions, distractions, irrelevancies, etc., that interfere with the transfer of desired information.

nom de plume   French for *pen name*, a name assumed by a writer, usually to disguise identity. Synonymous with *pseudonym*. According to *The Bookman's Glossary* (R.R. Bowker, 1983), the term is also used in reference to a fabricated byline adopted by one or more writers.

nomenclature   *See*: terminology.

non-adhesive binding   A method of binding used mainly in conservation in which no adhesive is used in direct contact with the book block. Some forms of non-adhesive binding use no adhesives at all (see the various volumes of *Non-Adhesive Binding* by Keith A. Smith).

nonaffiliated user   A person who uses the facilities and resources of an academic library but is not a registered student or member of the institution's faculty or staff. Most college and university libraries in the United States permit individuals lacking affiliation to use certain resources on-site, but each library determines its own policy with regard to borrowing privileges and other services for nonaffiliated users. The term also applies to users of a special library who are not affiliated with the host organization. The corresponding term in public libraries is *nonresident user*.

nonbook   A collective term for library materials that have physical form but are not bound in codex form like a book, including, but not limited to, maps and other cartographic materials (except atlases), prints, photographs, slides, filmstrips, motion pictures, videorecordings, sound recordings, kits, models, etc. Compare with *nonprint*.

noncancellable   A serial title for which the publisher or vendor will not accept a cancellation or grant a refund once the subscription has been purchased or renewed.

noncirculating   Materials that may not be charged to a borrower account except by special arrangement but are usually available for library use only, including reference books, periodical indexes, and sometimes the periodicals themselves. Whether materials in special collections are designated circulating or noncirculating depends on the policy of the individual library or library system, but their use is nearly always restricted to library premises.

noncurrent Recurring information, materials, or records that are no longer up-to-date, for example, corporate annual reports from previous years or earlier editions of a reference serial, often retained in libraries and archives for their archival value. Noncurrent holdings of print newspapers and periodicals, called *back files*, are often converted to microfilm or microfiche to conserve space. The opposite of *current*. Compare with *outdated*.

nonfiction Prose literary works describing events that actually occurred and characters or phenomena that actually exist or existed in the past. In a more general sense, any piece of prose writing in which the content is not imagined by the author. In libraries that use Library of Congress Classification or Dewey Decimal Classification, nonfiction is shelved by call number. Compare with *fiction*. *See also*: *documentary* and *faction*.

nonfiction novel A narrative of an actual historical event, or sequence of events, that closely follows established facts but also includes fictional elements, such as conjectural dialogue or one or more characters not known to have participated in the action. The event is usually contemporary or from the recent past. The author may give the reader the task of distinguishing the real from the imaginary. Truman Capote's *In Cold Blood: A True Account of a Multiple Murder and its Consequences* (1965) is an early example. *See also*: *faction*.

nonfiling character A character, such as the apostrophe, ignored in arrangement when it appears in a word, phrase, heading, or descriptor. For example, under most filing rules, the letters of the initial articles "a," "an," and "the" are ignored at the beginning of a title. In the MARC record, the number of nonfiling characters at the beginning of a title or heading is specified in the indicator at the beginning of the field. Synonymous with *nonsorting character*.

nongap break A hiatus in the publication or numbering of a serial title despite the fact that no items issued are missing. This may occur when publication ceases temporarily and later resumes under the same or a different title, sometimes with a change of numbering. Compare with *gap*.

non-net Copies of a work (usually a textbook) that a bookseller is permitted by the publisher to sell in bulk quantities to schools for educational use at a discretionary discount. Compare with *net*.

nonprint Materials published in a format other than writing or print on paper, including microfiche and microfilm, slides, filmstrips, films, videorecordings, audiorecordings, and information in digital formats such as machine-readable data files. Most nonprint library materials require special equipment for listening and/or viewing. Compare with *nonbook*.

nonrepeatable (NR) A MARC field that may appear only once in the same bibliographic record, for example, the **250** field reserved for the edition statement and other information pertaining to edition. A nonrepeatable subfield may occur only once in a field. The opposite of *repeatable*.

nonresident's card   A borrower's card issued to a person who does not reside within the legal boundaries of the district or geographic area served by the library or library system, usually upon payment of a modest fee, renewable at regular intervals.

nonresident user   A person who uses the facilities and resources of a public library without residing within the legal boundaries of the district or geographic area it serves. In the United States, nonresidents are usually allowed to use most resources on-site, but each library or library system determines its own policy with regard to borrowing privileges and other services for nonresidents. Some public libraries will issue a nonresident's card upon presentation of valid identification and payment of a modest fee. The corresponding term in academic and special libraries is *nonaffiliated user*.

nonreturnable   *See*: returns.

nonsorting character   *See*: nonfiling character.

nonsubscription serial   A serial publication not available on subscription or standing order because the publisher requires that each part or volume be ordered individually.

nonsupplier   A library or other participant in the OCLC Interlibrary Loan network that does *not* respond to requests from other libraries to borrow returnable materials. In the OCLC *WorldCat* database, the three-letter OCLC symbols of nonsuppliers appear in lowercase in the holdings display attached to the bibliographic record for an item, in contrast to the symbols of suppliers, which appear in uppercase.

nontrad   *See*: nontraditional student.

nontraditional student   A student who enrolls at an institution of higher education after several years of little or no contact with the system of formal education. *Nontrads* are usually older than *traditional students* who enter college out of high school and complete their undergraduate degree without a break. Because nontrads often lack the library skills of their younger classmates, they may require instruction and reference assistance at a more basic level, but once they gain self-confidence, they can be highly motivated. Compare with *adult learner*.

NOP   *See*: not our publication.

normal administrative practice (NAP)   The concept in archives that records such as draft documents, duplicates, and multiple copies of publications may be routinely destroyed when no longer needed, provided no information of enduring value to the organization is lost in the process.

North American Industry Classification System (NAICS)   Adopted in 1997 by the Office of Management and Budget as the industry classification system used by statistical agencies of the U.S. federal government, NAICS (pronounced *nakes*) was developed by the Economic Classification Policy Committee of the OMB, in cooperation with Statistics Canada and the Instituto Nacional de Estadística Geografía e Informática (INEGI) of Mexico to replace the Standard Industrial Classification (SIC) used since the 1930s.

Based on a new concept that classifies businesses by the processes they use to produce goods and services, NAICS is designed to reflect expansion of the service and technology sectors, provide comparable statistics across the three countries covered by the North American Free Trade Agreement (NAFTA), and be compatible with the International Industrial Classification System (ISIC) developed by the United Nations. URL: www.census.gov/epcd/www/naics.html.

North American Serials Interest Group (NASIG)   Established in 1985, NASIG is an independent organization that facilitates the sharing of information and ideas among individuals involved with serial publications, including serials publishers, librarians, subscription agents, producers and vendors of catalog software and periodical indexes/databases, representatives of bibliographic utilities, educators, and binders, mainly in the United States, Canada, and Mexico. NASIG sponsors an annual conference, hosts the electronic mailing list *NASIG-L*, and publishes the *NASIG Newsletter*. URL: www.nasig.org.

North American Sport Library Network (NASLIN)   Founded in 1989, NASLIN is dedicated to facilitating communication and resource sharing among sports libraries, archives, and information services through conferences, educational programs, and other cooperative projects. Its members are librarians, archivists, and information specialists involved in the publication, acquisition, organization, retrieval, and dissemination of information related to all aspects of sports, physical education, and recreation. NASLIN publishes the semiannual newsletter *NASLINE*. URL: www.sportquest.com/naslin.

north pointer   A standard graphic device in the form of a small cross or wheel with an arrow pointing north, printed on maps, charts, blueprints, plans, etc., usually in or near the legend to indicate compass orientation.

nos   *See*: not on shelf.

NOT   *See*: logical difference.

notation   The set of characters (numerals, letters of the alphabet, and/or symbols) used to represent the main classes and subdivisions of a classification system. In library cataloging, the class notation assigned to a bibliographic item represents its subject and is the first element of the call number, determining its position on the shelf relative to items on other subjects. For example, the class notation assigned to the title *Censorship: Opposing Viewpoints* (edited by Tamara Roleff) is **363.31** in Dewey Decimal Classification and **Z658.U5** in Library of Congress Classification. *See also*: *base of notation*, *expressive notation*, *faceted notation*, *mixed notation*, *mnemonic notation*, and *pure notation*.

Also refers to the symbols used to write music, as in a music score, and to express mathematical concepts.

notched binding   In some adhesive bindings, shallow parallel grooves are cut into the binding edge of the sections perpendicular to the spine to enlarge the surface area exposed to the adhesive. Although *notching* strengthens the binding of a book, the additional adhesive has the disadvantage of restricting openability.

note   In writing and printing, a statement explaining a point in the text of a work or giving the source of a quotation or idea that does not originate with the author. Notes are usually numbered consecutively and may be listed as *footnotes* at the bottom of the same page as the text to which they refer or as *endnotes* at the conclusion of an article, chapter, or book. *See also*: *shoulder note* and *side note*.

Also refers to a statement in the note area of a bibliographic record giving the contents of the work, its relationship to other works, and any physical characteristics not included elsewhere in the bibliographic description. If there is more than one note, each is given in a separate paragraph.

In Dewey Decimal Classification, an instruction, definition, or reference in the schedules explaining the scope and use of a class or its relationship to other classes. DDC includes over 20 different types of notes. *See also*: *add note* and *footnote*.

note area   The area following the physical description in a bibliographic record giving the contents of the work, its relationship to other works, and any physical characteristics not included in preceding areas of bibliographic description. Each note is given a separate paragraph in fields 5XX of the MARC record.

notebook   In modern usage, a loose-leaf or spiral binder with flexible or inflexible board or plastic covers, usually filled with blank leaves (ruled or unruled) for making notes. Some notebooks have a pocket folded across the lower edge inside the front and/or back cover for holding loose papers.

Historically, blankbooks or loose sheets were often used for making notes. In ancient Rome, small parchment notebooks, probably developed from wooden tablets, were extensively used in keeping accounts. In some cases, a notebook published as the work of an important historical figure is actually a collection of papers assembled after the person's death, for example, the *Leonardo Da Vinci Notebook* owned by The British Library.

In computing, the term is used synonymously with *laptop*.

notification slip   A printed form sent to the acquisitions department of a library by an approval plan vendor to announce a new book that meets the needs profile established by the library. Under most plans, rejection of the title by the library within a designated period of time will prevent shipment. *See also*: *slip plan*.

not on shelf (nos)   An item listed as available in a library catalog that cannot be located in correct call number sequence in the stacks. When this occurs, the patron may request that the library staff conduct a search for the item. If it is not found, the circulation status is changed to "missing" in the item record, and a replacement copy may be ordered or the bibliographic record removed from the catalog. *See also*: *misshelved*.

not our publication (NOP)   A term used on a publisher's invoice to indicate that the title ordered cannot be supplied because the library or bookseller apparently ordered it from the wrong publisher.

not returnable (NR)   A term used on a publisher's invoice to indicate that a book or other item cannot be returned once it has been received by the library or bookseller placing the order.

not yet published (NYP) A term used on a publisher's invoice to indicate that the title ordered cannot be immediately supplied because it is in the process of being published and will be issued at some time in the future.

novel From the Italian *novella*, meaning "a new little thing." In most European languages, the word for novel is *roman*, derived from the literary tradition of medieval romance. The origins of the modern novel can also be traced to the picaresque narratives of 16th-century Spain, of which Cervantes' *Don Quixote* is a well-known example.

As a literary form, the novel of incident began in 1719 with the publication of Daniel Defoe's *Robinson Crusoe*, followed shortly by *Moll Flanders*. The novel of character originated in 1740 with *Pamela* by Samuel Richardson. Since then, the form has evolved into many styles and genres (see *Bildungsroman*, *epistolary novel*, *gothic novel*, *Kunstlerroman*, *psychological novel*, *roman à clef*, and *sentimental novel*).

Strictly speaking, a novel is a fictional prose narrative involving people and events that exist in the imagination of the *novelist*. This is true even of historical fiction that is an imaginative attempt to reconstruct events known to have occurred in the past. There is no upper limit on the length of a novel, but a fictional narrative of *less* than 30,000 to 40,000 words is considered either a *novelette* or *short story*. Greater length gives the novelist a freer hand in developing character, plot, and setting. Most novels are divided into chapters, usually reflecting major divisions in the narrative. Long novels may be divided into "books," each containing two or more chapters. Compare with *novella*. *See also*: *archetypal novel*.

novelette A novel of 30,000 to 50,000 words (*example*: ***Sweet Smell of Success*** by Ernest Lehman). Synonymous with *short novel*. Compare with *novella*. *See also*: *short story*.

novelization A novel based on a literary work originally created in another form, often as a dramatic work, for example, *The Wave* by Morton Rhue, based on a teleplay by Johnny Dawkins, originally based on a short story by Ron Jones. Novelizations are often published as paperback originals to help merchandise a specific production. In *AACR2*, a novelization is cataloged under the name of the *novelist*, with added entries for the author and title of the work on which it is based. *See also*: *dramatization*.

novella An Italian word meaning "short story" or "tale." A short prose narrative comparable in length to a novelette or long short story, which often relates a surprising fictional event (*example*: ***Old Man and the Sea*** by Ernest Hemingway). A novella often has a moral (***Billy Budd*** by Herman Melville) and may be written in satirical style (***Goodbye, Columbus*** by Philip Roth). Although it is not unusual for novellas to be published separately in slim volumes, they are often included in collections with one or more works of similar length and/or short stories. Compare with *novel*.

novelty binding A bookbinding of unconventional shape and/or covering material (carved ivory, papier-mâché, mother-of-pearl, fur, snakeskin, etc.), fashionable during the 19th and early 20th centuries.

novice   A person who uses an unfamiliar computer system for the first time, as opposed to an experienced user. In the design of Web sites and graphical user interfaces, libraries and computer software companies may employ usability assessment techniques to judge the user-friendliness of the new system. In a more general sense, any patron for whom the procedures of a library are new and often confusing. Special consideration must be shown at the reference desk.

NR   *See*: not returnable.

NSDL   *See*: National Science Digital Library.

NSN   *See*: National Storytelling Network.

NT (or N)   *See*: narrower term.

NTIS   *See*: National Technical Information Service.

NUC   *See*: National Union Catalog.

NUCMC   *See*: National Union Catalog of Manuscript Collections.

number   A quantity that can be counted, represented by a word, numeral, or combination of numerals—*cardinal* numbers indicate how many (1, 2, 3, 14, 154); *ordinal* numbers indicate relative position in sequence (1st, 2nd, 3rd, 14th, 154th). In text, the numbers zero to nine are usually spelled out, but numbers greater than nine are given in numerals. Also, to assign a number to each item in a series, for reference and to indicate sequence. Abbreviated *no*.

   Also refers to a uniquely numbered and dated issue or part of a serial, series, or other work issued in installments (fascicles). *See also*: *back issue*, *current issue*, and *number book*.

number book   A form of book, common in the 18th and 19th centuries, published in numbered parts or installments, usually at regular intervals. *See also*: *serialized*.

number building   In Dewey Decimal Classification, when no existing class in the schedules precisely represents the subject of a work, the cataloger must construct a class number, in accordance with established rules, by adding to a base number further notation found in the tables or in another part of the main schedules. For example, the addition of the decimal fraction **.5** from the table of standard subdivisions to the base number **020** for "Library and information sciences" to construct the class number **020.5** representing "Periodicals" in the discipline. *See also*: *built number*.

numbered copy   A copy of a book published in a consecutively numbered limited edition, bearing a copy number assigned by hand by the publisher, as well as an indication of the total number of copies printed, usually in the colophon or in a certificate of issue on the verso of the leaf preceding title page. *See also*: *overrun*.

numbering   The identification of each of the successive items of a publication (issues, parts, volumes, etc.) by the assignment of a numeral, letter, or other character, or combination of characters, with or without an accompanying word ("volume," "number," etc.) and/or chronological designation (*AACR2*). Not all serial publications are numbered. *See also*: *issue number* and *volume number*.

numeral   In writing and printing, a character or set of characters used to represent a number (*example*: the arabic numeral **9** or roman numeral **IX**). General rules for the use of numerals in library cataloging are given in *Appendix C* of *AACR2*.

numeric and/or alphabetic, chronological, or other designation   In library cataloging, the material specific details area of the bibliographic description in which the publication history of a serial is given, usually in the form of an open or closed entry, as distinct from the holdings statement indicating the issues owned by a specific library or library system.

nursery rhyme   A short metrical verse or ditty originating in the oral tradition of a specific culture, taught to very young children to help them learn to speak or count. Some nursery rhymes are derived from adult sayings that had a double meaning in the cultural context in which they originated. Nursery rhymes are usually published in collections shelved in the juvenile section of a public library or in the curriculum room of an academic library. *See also*: *limerick*.

NYP   *See*: **n**ot **y**et **p**ublished.

NYPL   *See*: **N**ew **Y**ork **P**ublic **L**ibrary.

NYRB   *See*: *New York Review of Books*.

NYTBR   *See*: *New York Times Book Review*.

O

OAI   *See*: **O**pen **A**rchives **I**nitiative.

OAIS   *See*: **O**pen **A**rchival **I**nformation **S**ystem.

Oak Knoll   A company located in New Castle, Delaware, that publishes, distributes, and sells books on bibliography, book collecting, book history, bookplates, the book trade, libraries, publishing, bookbinding, book design, book illustration, papermaking, typography, fine printing, forgery, and censorship. Its inventory includes over 12,500 antiquarian titles.URL: www.oakknoll.com.

obiit   Latin for "died," usually abbreviated *ob.* before a date to indicate the year of a person's decease (*ob. 1922*).

obit   A brief note in a medieval manuscript recording the date of a person's decease, with or without comment, sometimes as a reminder to perform a Mass on the anniversary of the death. Found most frequently in liturgical calendars, obits can be helpful to codicologists in establishing provenance. Also used as an abbreviation of *obituary*.

obituary   A notice of a person's death, usually published in a newspaper or magazine, which may include a brief biographical sketch of the main events in the life of the deceased. The obituaries of well-known public figures may be researched and written long before the person's death, to be ready for printing on short notice. Obituaries are indexed under the last name of the deceased in *Biography Index*, a reference serial available in most large libraries in the United States. Abbreviated *obit*.

object   In *AACR2*, a three-dimensional artifact, replica of an artifact, or naturally occurring entity. In the British list of general material designations, the term also includes dioramas, games, microscope slides, models, and realia. *See also*: *digital object*.

objective   A specific achievable outcome of actions taken to achieve a stated goal, usually expressed in measurable terms and subject to a time limit. Although an objective does not address the specific means by which the outcome is to be achieved, it should be based upon a realistic assessment of available resources. A good set of achievable objectives can serve as an inspiration and guide for an organization in planning for the future, allocating resources, evaluating progress, adjusting strategy, and persevering until the desired result is achieved.

oblong A book wider than it is high. Children's picture books are often oblong in shape to allow the illustrator a wider canvas. In a more general sense, any publication bound on its shorter dimension. Synonymous in the printing trade with *landscape*. Compare with *portrait*. *See also*: *narrow* and *square*.

obscenity Speech, writing, or artistic expression considered indecent by conventional standards of behavior because it offends the modesty and delicacy of feeling of ordinary people. In *Miller v. California* (1973), the U.S. Supreme Court ruled that obscenity, as a judicially recognized exception to First Amendment protection, is to be defined within the context of local community standards. Synonymous with *smut*. Compare with *pornography*. *See also*: *bowdlerize*, *censorship*, *expurgated*, and *unprintable*.

OC *See*: order canceled.

occasional A document or publication issued on an irregular basis, sometimes numbered sequentially by the publisher (*example*: ***Occasional Publications in Archaeology and History*** of the Massachusetts Historical Commission).

OCLC *See*: Online Computer Library Center.

OCLC control number Whenever the bibliographic utility OCLC enters a new record into its online union catalog (*WorldCat*), a unique number is assigned to the record for the purpose of bibliographic control. The number appears in the 001 field of the MARC record and is system-supplied. Compare with *Library of Congress Control Number*. *See also*: *accession number*.

OCLC Four-Figure Cutter Tables *See*: Cutter Table.

OCLC holding library code A four-character code, unique within an OCLC symbol, identifying one location or collection within an institution. A library may choose any combination of codes, but each code must begin with an alphabetic character **A–Z**, and the last three characters must be **A–Z** or **2–9**. The holding library code determines some OCLC profile options and is exported in local OCLC field 049.

OCLC ILL *See*: OCLC Interlibrary Loan.

OCLC Interlibrary Loan (ILL) The interlibrary loan service of OCLC, a network that facilitates the borrowing and lending of materials between libraries and other institutions that are OCLC members and participants in *WorldCat*, the largest online union catalog in the world. URL: www.oclc.org/ill.

OCLC OnLine Union Catalog (OLUC) The former name of *WorldCat*, an online union catalog containing over 50 million bibliographic records representing items held by over 6,700 libraries and other institutions that are members and participants in OCLC, the largest bibliographic utility in the world.

OCLC symbol A unique code assigned by OCLC to identify a library or other institution that is a member of or participant in its cataloging, interlibrary loan, or reference systems (*example*: **DLC** for Library of Congress). OCLC symbols consisted of three characters until 2001 when five-character symbols began to be assigned to new institutions. Members with more than one library may have a different symbol for each library.

OCLC symbols are used in bibliographic records to indicate cataloging source (MARC field 040) and in holdings displays in the OCLC *WorldCat* database to identify libraries that have used a record for cataloging purposes. Symbols of interlibrary loan suppliers are displayed in uppercase, those of nonsuppliers in lowercase. OCLC publishes two alphabetically arranged print directories under the title *OCLC Participating Institutions*, one arranged by OCLC symbol and the other by name of institution. The list is also available on the World Wide Web in searchable format, updated weekly at: www.oclc.org/contacts/libraries. *See also*: *OCLC holding library code*.

OCR   *See*: optical character recognition.

Octateuch   The first eight books of the Old Testament of the Bible (the Pentateuch plus the books of Joshua, Judges, and Ruth), sometimes produced as a separate manuscript by medieval scribes. *See also*: *Hexateuch*.

octavo (8vo)   A book approximately 6 × 9 inches in size, made by folding a full sheet of book paper in three right-angle folds, producing signatures of eight leaves (16 pages). If a 32-page section is desired, as in most children's picture books, double-size sheets are folded four times. The precise size of each leaf in an octavo edition depends on the size of the original sheet. In modern printing, octavo is the most commonly used size for books published in hardcover. Compare with *folio*, *quarto*, *duodecimo*, and *sextodecimo*.

ode   A relatively long lyric poem of elaborate structure derived from songs performed by the *chorus* in ancient Greek dramatic performances, written to eulogize a hero (or heroes). In English literature, the object of praise may be a person or category of person (*example*: *Ode to the Confederate Dead* by Allen Tate), an abstraction (*example*: *Ode to Beauty* by Ralph Waldo Emerson), or an inner state expressed symbolically (*example*: *Ode on a Grecian Urn* by John Keats).

OED   *See*: *Oxford English Dictionary*.

off-duty   Time when an employee is (1) scheduled but not working (usually on a break or lunch hour), (2) not scheduled on a shift, or (3) not working if employed part-time. Off-duty public services librarians are sometimes recognized as staff when passing through a public area of the library and approached by patrons in need of assistance. The opposite of *on-duty*.

office of record   The unit within an organization responsible for systematically documenting an activity and preserving the resulting records for the normal period for which they are needed to conduct business or affairs, for example, a personnel office in the case current employment records. Synonymous with *agency of record*.

official name   The legal name of a company, agency, organization, institution, etc., which may differ from the form of name used in its publications or in cataloging them for a library collection. Compare with *corporate name*.

official publication   A document issued in multiple copies by an official body, such as a government agency or intergovernmental organization, under its legal name, often retained by libraries for reference purposes (*example*: **Budget of the United States Government** issued annually by the Office of Management and Budget). U.S. federal government documents fall into this category.

official records   The formal written documents in which the ongoing activities of a company, government, organization, or institution are recorded, usually retained in archives for their evidential, legal, informational, or historical value, in accordance with instructions contained in a disposition schedule (*example*: **Congressional Record**). *See also*: *office of record*.

official title   The full title appearing on the title page of a book or other printed publication, used by librarians in cataloging the item. *See also*: *title proper* and *uniform title*.

offline   An automated service not connected to a network, for example, a stand-alone PC running bibliographic databases on CD-ROM or an intranet not connected to the Internet. Also refers to computer accessories or devices not connected to or installed on the central processing unit (CPU) or physically connected but not turned on or standing ready for use, for example, a printer or scanner that is turned off.

Also used as a slang expression for a person who is uninformed about something of which those around him are aware. Synonymous in this sense with *out of the loop*.

offprint   A copy of an article, chapter, or portion of a publication reprinted from the same plates, usually at the same time as the original but issued separately, with or without a cover, usually for the author's personal use. Contributors to scholarly journals often receive a limited number of copies of their articles from the publisher, sometimes as a form of compensation. An offprint may or may not include a title page but retains the original pagination. The sale of offprints provides an important source of revenue for some journal publishers. Also spelled *off-print*. Synonymous with *overprint*, *run-on*, and *separate*. Compare with *reprint*.

offset   A rotary printing process in which ink is applied to a thin plate wrapped around a rotating cylinder, which transfers the image to a second rubber-coated cylinder from which an impression is made on a sheet or roll of printing paper. Offset is faster, less expensive, and capable of printing much finer detail than letterpress.

Also refers to faint traces of ink unintentionally transferred from a freshly printed text page or illustration to the facing page, usually when a publication is bound before the ink has dried, a problem averted in some editions by inserting sheets of tissue between the leaves, a procedure called *interleaving*. Also refers to the image transferred. Synonymous with *set-off*.

off-site storage   Temporary or permanent storage of archival or library materials at a location outside the walls of the main facility, usually necessitated by a shortage of space. Stored materials may be temporarily unavailable or retrievable by courier upon request during certain hours. The most common criterion used in selecting items for off-site storage is low usage. Items may be shelved by a method that maximizes storage capacity, instead of in a classified arrangement. *See also*: *annex*.

off the record   A statement or comment that the speaker does not wish recorded or made publicly known. At meetings, such remarks are not included in the minutes and may not be expressed if the proceedings are tape-recorded.

oiling   Because leather bindings dry out unless stored in a controlled environment, oil should be applied periodically to prevent deterioration. Former Yale University conservator Jane Greenfield recommends a dressing of 40 percent anhydrous lanolin and 60 percent neat's-foot oil (two natural animal oils), developed by the New York Public Library and tested by the U.S. Department of Agriculture (*The Care of Fine Books*, Nick Lyons Books, 1988). Oiling is done by grasping the book at the fore-edge and holding the boards away from the book block with the fingers while a thin coat of oil is rubbed by hand over the outside of the binding (not the turn-ins). Oil darkens leather and should not be used on fine bindings when color is an important design element. Vellum, tawed skin, and suede-type leathers should never be oiled. Over-oiling can damage the paper of a book and causes some leathers to become sticky. Oiling is not a remedy for the process of deterioration known as *red rot*.

older adult   An elderly person who may require special assistance in accessing and using the facilities, services, and collections of a library. Because the proportion of older adults is increasing in many communities across the United States, public libraries must focus more attention on providing outreach to seniors. The Reference and User Services Association (RUSA) of the American Library Association has developed guidelines on *Library Services to Older Adults*, available at: www.ala.org. *See also*: Americans with Disabilities Act.

olla   A type of writing material made in southern India and Sri Lanka from young leaves, especially of the palmyra palm, soaked in water and pressed flat, then cut into strips approximately three inches wide and one to three feet in length. Holes are made in one end of each strip through which they can be attached by a cord to wooden boards to form a book. The mixture of charcoal and oil rubbed into writing incised on the surface with a metal stylus may have helped preserve the earliest pre-Christian examples. According to *Harrod's Librarians' Glossary* (Gower, 1990), this type of book is still made by Buddhist monks in Sri Lanka. The term also applies to documents of this form and material. Also spelled *ola*.

OLUC   See: *OCLC OnLine Union Catalog*.

omnibus book   A large single-volume reprint of two or more separately published novels or other literary works, usually by the same author (*example*: *A Jeeves Omnibus* by P.G. Wodehouse). According to *The Bookman's Glossary* (R.R. Bowker, 1983), the term also applies to a single-volume collection of books or stories on the same subject, written by various authors (*example*: *One Step in the Clouds: An Omnibus of Mountaineering Novels and Stories* edited by Audrey Salkeld and Rosie Smith). In a more general sense, a volume of which the content is large and varied but usually related to a particular subject or subjects (*The Management and Ethics Omnibus* by S.K. Chakraborty).

omnibus reference   A cross-reference directing the user from a single heading to multiple headings in an index, as in the following example from the *Library of Congress Subject Headings* list:

Example:

Bibliographical cooperation *see* Bibliography, International; Cataloging, Cooperative; International cooperation; Union catalogs

omnibus review   An evaluative article in which a reviewer discusses and in some cases compares two or more books or other publications of a certain type, on a specific subject, in a particular field of study, or that have some other characteristic in common.

on approval   An arrangement with a publisher or jobber that allows a prospective buyer, such as a library, to examine newly published items before deciding to purchase. Materials sent for inspection must be returned within a designated period of time if the recipient does not intend to purchase. *See also*: *approval plan*.

on-demand publishing   The production of single copies or small quantities of printed publications in response to orders from customers, as opposed to supply from inventory. An example of such a service is *Dissertation Express*, which provides single copies of Ph.D. dissertations on order for a fee. First used to produce copies of scholarly publications from microfilm master files, on-demand publishing is expected to grow, especially to meet sci-tech and business needs, as digital archives expand.

on-duty   Time when an employee is expected to be at work, particularly the hours of a scheduled shift at a public service point, such as the circulation desk or reference desk. The opposite of *off-duty*.

one-act play   A form of modern drama in which all the action occurs in a single act (*example*: *Aria da Capo* by Edna St. Vincent Millay). Established as a literary form by the experimental theater movement that began in the late 19th century, the one-act play is usually short (20–50 minutes performed), with a limited number of characters, no breaks in the action, and little, if any, change of scene, analogous to the short story in narrative fiction.

one-of-a-kind book   A book created in a single copy, as opposed to a production book issued in multiple copies. Artist's books created for display are usually of this type. Compare with *limited edition*.

one-on-one   Services provided by a librarian or other library staff member working alone with a single patron, usually involving a high degree of interaction, as in most transactions at the reference desk. One-on-one service. Synonymous with *one-to-one*.

one-person library (OPL)   A library or information service operated and managed by a single individual, usually with minimal assistance, more common in special libraries than in other types of libraries. In public library systems, small branch libraries are often run by a solo librarian or paraprofessional, sometimes with the help of volunteers from the community. Bookmobiles are nearly always operated by a single person.

one-shot A periodical for which only a single issue was published. Also refers to a reprint of the entire text of a book or of an abridgment, published in a single issue of a periodical, as distinct from a serialized reprint.

In perfect binding, the hot-melt adhesive used to bind a book in a single application. Also, a slang term used by bibliographic instruction librarians to refer to formal instruction given in a *single* session, as opposed to instruction extended over two or more sessions.

onionskin A very thin, tough, lightweight, translucent paper with a smooth glazed or cockle finish, used for airmail stationery, tracing paper, etc. Also spelled *onion skin*.

ONIX *See*: Online Information Exchange.

onlay One or more decorative panels or thin pieces of leather or paper, often of more than one color, mounted on the cover of a book in relief, usually tooled around the edges to secure them to the surface and for decorative effect. Compare with *inlay*.

online A computer connected to the Internet, an intranet, or some other network via telecommunication links, as opposed to a stand-alone system. Also refers to computer accessories or devices physically separate from, but directly connected to and under the control of, a central processing unit (CPU) and ready for interactive use in real time. Sometimes used synonymously in libraries with *automated*, *computerized*, and *electronic*. Compare with *offline*. *See also*: *online bookstore*, *online catalog*, *online services*, and *online tutorial*.

ONLINE A magazine providing feature articles, product reviews, case studies, and informed opinion to assist information professionals in selecting, using, and managing electronic information products, including online databases, CD-ROMs, and Internet resources, published bimonthly since 1977 by Information Today, Inc. ISSN: 0146–5422.

online bookstore A commercial enterprise that electronically markets and sells books and nonprint media (videos, CDs, DVDs, CD-ROMs, etc.) mail order over the Internet. Some online booksellers have retail outlets (*example*: **Barnesandnoble.com**); others do not (**Amazon.com**). A list of links to online bookstores is maintained by Peter Scott of the University of Saskatchewan Library at: www.lights.com/publisher/bookstores.html.

online catalog A library catalog consisting of a collection of bibliographic records in machine-readable format, maintained on a dedicated computer that provides uninterrupted interactive access via terminals or workstations in direct, continuous communication with the central computer. Most online catalogs are searchable by author, title, subject heading, and keywords. The software used in online catalogs is proprietary and not standardized. Synonymous with *OPAC*.

Online Computer Library Center (OCLC) The largest bibliographic utility in the world, providing cataloging and acquisitions services, serials and circulation control, interlibrary loan support, and access to online databases. OCLC began as the Ohio College Library Center in 1967, changed its name in 1981 to reflect wider membership, and has since become a major source of cooperative cataloging data for libraries around the world. OCLC maintains *WorldCat*, the largest online bibliographic database in the world, containing over 46 million MARC records. URL: www.oclc.org.

Online Information Exchange (ONIX)   A family of XML-based metadata schemes developed by publishers to communicate book trade information such as bibliographic data, pricing, and marketing and promotional information. Some library systems are developing the capacity to use ONIX data to enrich catalog records with tables of contents, author bios, dust jacket blurbs, and similar information. The standard is maintained by EDItEUR jointly with Book Industry Communication (BIC) and the Book Industry Study Group (BISG). ONIX for Serials is under development. URL: www.editeur.org.

online public access catalog   *See*: OPAC.

online reference   *See*: digital reference.

online services   In libraries, the branch of public services concerned with selecting and providing access to electronic resources, such as online catalogs and bibliographic databases, including mediated searching, usually done by an *online services librarian*. Compare with *systems librarian*.

online tutorial   An instructional tool in electronic format, usually available via the Internet, designed to teach library users, in a step-by-step and sometimes interactive process, how to use a specific resource (usually an online catalog or bibliographic database), or all the services and resources needed to research topics in a specific discipline or subject area. Particularly helpful to students enrolled in distance education courses who may be unable to come to the library for bibliographic instruction, online tutorials are often modular in design, with a self-quiz at the end of each unit to give users the opportunity to assess their mastery of the content. For an example, please see *TILT* (tilt.lib.utsystem.edu) provided by the University of Texas System Digital Library. Synonymous with *Web-based tutorial*. Compare with *pathfinder*.

OnLine Union Catalog (OLUC)   *See*: OCLC OnLine Union Catalog.

on order   A term used in library acquisitions to describe an item ordered but not yet received from the vendor. Once the item is received and processed, the *order record* created by the library at the time the order was placed can be purged. In some online catalogs, the status of an item on order is indicated in a temporary catalog record. *See also*: *back order* and *canceled*.

on reserve   *See*: reserves.

on sale or return   Terms given by a publisher to a bookseller allowing the return for credit of copies that remain unsold. The bookseller's account is normally charged for the sale, but payment is not expected until the items have sold or a designated time limit has expired. *See also*: *overstock* and *remainders*.

on-the-job   Occurring in the course of one's employment, for example, *on-the-job training* as opposed to instruction that takes place outside the normal work routine.

ooze leather   Calf or split sheepskin given a soft velvet or suede finish on the flesh side, used mainly in binding volumes of poetry, belles lettres, etc.

OP *See*: out of print.

OPAC An acronym for *online public access catalog*, a database composed of bibliographic records describing the books and other materials owned by a library or library system, accessible via public terminals or workstations usually concentrated near the reference desk to make it easy for users to request the assistance of a trained reference librarian. Most online catalogs are searchable by author, title, subject, and keywords and allow users to print, download, or export records to an e-mail account. Compare with *WebPac*. *See also*: *Machine-Readable Cataloging*.

opacity The quality of nontransparency in printing papers, determined by the amount of air space between the fibers, apparent from the extent to which light passes through a sheet or page. If too thin a paper is used in printing, text and/or illustrations may show through on the opposite side of the sheet. As a general rule, bright white papers are less *opaque* than off-white or creamy papers, and matte finish has greater opacity than glazed finish.

Also refers to the degree to which ink obscures the color of the surface on which it is printed.

op. cit. Latin for *opere citato*, meaning "in the work previously cited." An abbreviation used in notes and bibliographic citations that allows a quotation or idea from the work previously cited to be referenced simply by giving the new page number(s).

op-ed page The page of a newspaper, usually opposite the *editorial page*, on which a variety of opinions are expressed concerning issues of the day, often written by syndicated columnists whose viewpoints may differ from the editorial position of the paper. Political cartoons are also printed on the op-ed page.

openability A binder's term for the ease with which the binding on a book can be opened at any page. In hardcover bindings, a volume with a hollow back can be opened more easily than one with a tight back. In adhesive bindings, an Otabind binding opens flat more easily than a perfect binding. In perfect bindings, an unnotched binding is easier to open than a notched binding. Most mechanical bindings are designed to open flat.

open access Information content made freely and universally available via the Internet in easily read format, usually because the publisher maintains online archives to which access is free or has deposited the information in a widely known *open access repository*. Open access is a new model of scholarly publishing developed to free researchers and libraries from the limitations imposed by excessive subscription price increases for peer-reviewed journals, particularly in the sciences and medicine. By breaking the monopoly of publishers over the distribution of scientific research, open access makes access to scientific information more equitable and has the added advantage of allowing the author to retain copyright. *See also*: *open access journal*, *Open Archives Initiative*, and *Scholarly Publishing and Academic Resources Coalition*.

open access journal A scholarly periodical that makes the full text of the articles it publishes universally and freely available via the Internet in easily read format, in some cases by depositing them immediately upon publication without embargo in at least one widely recognized *open access repository*. In this new model of scholarly communication, the costs of publication are recovered not from subscription fees, but from publication fees paid by authors out of their grant funds and from other sources. The first open access peer-reviewed journal, the monthly *PLoS Biology* (biology. plosjournals.org), was first issued online in October 2003 by the Public Library of Science (www.plos.org), a nonprofit organization of scientists and physicians.

BioMed Central (www.biomedcentral.com) is an example of an independent commercial publisher committed to providing immediate open access to peer-reviewed research. Its charter states that,

> The author(s) or copyright owner(s) irrevocably grant(s) to any third party, in advance and in perpetuity, the right to use, reproduce or disseminate the research article in its entirety or in part, in any format or medium, provided that no substantive errors are introduced in the process, proper attribution of authorship and correct citation details are given, and that the bibliographic details are not changed.

For new developments on open access e-journals, see the *SPARC Open Access Newsletter* at: www.arl.org/sparc/soa/index.html. *See also*: *Open Archives Initiative*.

open access repository   A digital archive created and maintained to provide universal and free access to information content in easily read electronic format as a means of facilitating research and scholarship. A prime example is PubMed Central (www. pubmedcentral.nih.gov), a project of National Center for Biotechnology Information at the U.S. National Library of Medicine, designed to provide open access to the journal literature of the life sciences. *See also*: *open access journal* and *Open Archives Initiative*.

Open Archival Information System (OAIS)   A reference model for digital archiving systems initially developed by the Consultative Committee for Space Data Systems and adopted by ISO as International Standard ISO 14721:2002. The OAIS model is widely used by libraries as a framework for the development of preservation archives for digital materials.

Open Archives Initiative (OAI)   An organization funded by the Digital Library Federation, the Coalition for Networked Information, and the National Science Foundation to develop and promote interoperability standards as a means of facilitating the exchange of digital information content. Its program originated in the desire to advance scholarly communication by improving access to distributed repositories of e-prints, known as "archives." The main product of the OAI is a framework for harvesting and aggregating metadata from multiple repositories and a harvesting protocol known as the OAI Protocol for Metadata Harvesting (OAI-PMH). URL: www. openarchives.org. *See also*: *open access* and *Scholarly Publishing and Academic Resources Coalition*.

open back   *See*: hollow back.

open catalog A library catalog in which there are no restrictions on the addition of new bibliographic records, and existing records are revised and corrected as the need arises. Compare with *closed catalog* and *frozen catalog*.

opened Said of a book left uncut in binding whose pages have been slit by hand with a paper-knife, usually by the person who purchases the volume or receives it as a gift. Compare with *unopened*.

open-end index An ongoing index covering a single publication (*example*: *New York Times Index*), works of a particular form (*Biography Index*), or the published literature of a specific discipline (*Art Index*) or group of related disciplines (*MEDLINE*), updated continuously or at fixed intervals. Compare with *closed-end index*.

open entry A bibliographic record, holdings statement, or entry in an index or bibliography that allows further information concerning the item to be added, used in the library catalog to describe serials for which the library does not own all the issues or parts. Open entries are indicated by a hyphen and a space following the first volume number and/or year owned (*example*: **v. 1–** , **1936–**). Compare with *closed entry*.

opening Any two facing pages in an open book or other printed publication. The right-hand page is called the *recto*; the left-hand page, the *verso*. Compare with *conjoint leaves*. *See also*: *double spread*.

Also refers to the proper preparation of a new book for reading, accomplished by holding the book block perpendicular to a flat surface with the boards open flat, then using both hands to gently press down on the leaves along the gutters, starting with the outer leaves and working toward the center.

Also, the process of slicing open the uncut bolts of a book in order to read it, done by hand with a dull blade held parallel with the plane of the paper. A *folio* edition has no folds and therefore needs no opening; a *quarto* has folds at the head only; an *octavo* has folds at the head and fore-edge. To avoid damage, the motion of cutting should be away from the book.

In library operations, the procedures followed by staff at the beginning of each workday to ready the facility for use by its patrons, such as deactivating the security system, turning on lights and equipment, checking the paper supply in printers and photocopiers, checking the book drop for materials returned after the previous day's closing, unlocking the entrance door(s), etc.

open order In acquisitions, an order for library materials that remains active because it could not be completely filled by the seller at the time it was placed, usually because one or more items are temporarily out of stock. Synonymous with *outstanding order*. *See also*: *back order*.

open reserve A reserve collection shelved in an open stack to afford library users unrestricted access. Compare with *closed reserve*.

open source A computer program for which the source code is made available without charge by the owner or licenser, usually via the Internet, to encourage the rapid development of a more useful and bug-free product through open peer review. The practice also allows the product to be customized by its users to suit local needs (*example*: **Linux** operating system). To be certified "open source" under the Open Source Initiative (OSI), software must meet certain established criteria that include no restrictions on access.

open stacks Shelving in a library to which users have unrestricted access. Synonymous with *open access*. The opposite of *closed stacks*.

Open Systems Interconnection (OSI) An ISO standard for network telecommunication developed in the 1980s to allow direct communication between computers of all types and sizes by defining a general framework for implementing communication protocols in seven layers. Apart from the X.400 e-mail and X.500 directory standards, OSI was never widely implemented and is now useful mainly as a framework or teaching model for other protocols. *See also*: *Z39.50*.

open systems Computer systems (hardware and/or software) designed to operate using standards available publicly, allowing competition among vendors based on the features and performance of their products, as opposed to systems that use *proprietary* standards developed and controlled by a single company. One important advantage of open systems is that anyone can design add-ons; however, by making specifications public, a manufacturer allows others to copy its product. Because UNIX was designed to run on more types of computers than any other operating system, it was synonymous with open systems for many years. Since the mid-1990s, Linux and Java have been the leading models for open systems/open standards.

OpenURL A framework and format for communicating bibliographic information between applications over the Internet. The information provider assigns an OpenURL to an Internet resource, instead of a traditional URL. When the user clicks on a link to the resource, the OpenURL is sent to a context-sensitive link resolution system that resolves the OpenURL to an electronic copy of the resource appropriate for the user (and potentially to a set of services associated with the resource). The OpenURL shows promise of becoming an important tool in the interoperation of distributed digital library systems and has the potential to change the nature of linking on the Web.

The OpenURL was conceived at the University of Ghent by Herbert Van de Sompel and Patrick Hochstenbach, and by Oren Beit-Arie of the ExLibris library automation company, who built a resolution system called *SFX*, now licensed to Ex Libris. *SFX* is being used by NISO to draft a U.S. national standard for OpenURL that will be compatible with other standards such as MARC21, Dublin Core, Online Information Exchange (ONIX), and the Open Archives Initiative (OAI). URL: library.caltech.edu/openurl.

operating budget Funds allocated, usually on an annual or biennial basis, to cover the ongoing expenses incurred in running a library or library system, including the payment of wages and salaries and the purchase of materials, equipment, supplies, and services. Compare with *capital expenditure*.

operating system (OS) Software designed to control the basic operation of a computer and the exchange of data between the central processing unit and any peripheral equipment, mainly input and output devices. Loaded whenever the computer is started, the OS controls the running of all other programs, including any security systems designed to prevent unauthorized use. Commonly used PC operating systems include DOS, Windows, Macintosh, and UNIX.

operational   Said of equipment and/or systems that are running in good working order.

operations   A management term encompassing all the activities and details involved in running a library or library system on a day-to-day basis, as opposed to functions requiring a long-range view of the institution's direction and priorities, such as planning and budgeting, policymaking, fund-raising, and public relations.

opisthograph   A papyrus or parchment manuscript in the form of a roll, bearing writing on both sides. Normally only the inside of a papyrus roll, the side with fibers running horizontally, was used as a writing surface. In some cases a second text may have been added when the primary text was no longer of interest to the owner or user. Also refers to a stone slab inscribed on both sides.

OPL   *See*: one-person library.

OPP   *See*: out of print at present.

OPS   *See*: out of print, searching.

optical center   In printing, the point slightly above the mathematical center of a page that the human eye perceives as the center. In page layout, the typographer fools the eye by designing around the optical center, rather than the mathematical center. The same rule applies in Web page design for computer screens.

optical character recognition (OCR)   A process by which characters typed or printed on a page are electronically scanned, analyzed, and if found recognizable on the basis of appearance, converted into a digital character code capable of being processed by a computer.

OCR eliminates the time-consuming process of re-keying information available in print, but results can be unpredictable if the scanned copy is imperfect or contains diacritical marks or unrecognizable characters.

optical disk   A high-density direct access storage medium consisting of a specially coated disk on which data is encoded in a pattern of tiny pits burned into the surface by a laser, to be read by a device that reflects a laser beam off the pitted surface, then decoded by a microprocessor into digital signals. Optical disks can be read-only (audio CDs, CD-ROMs, DVDs, photo CDs, videodiscs), write once (WORM disks), or re-writable. They have far greater storage capacity than *magnetic disks* and are more robust. Also spelled *optical disc*. Synonymous with *laser disk*.

optical fiber   A thin, flexible cable containing a bundle of very fine, highly transparent, tubular glass fibers made of pure silicon dioxide, designed to transmit information encoded in pulses of laser light at very high speed (billions of bits per second) by means of internal reflection. Telephone companies are rapidly upgrading their transmission infrastructure from copper wire to fiber-optic cable. The advantages of optical fiber over coaxial and twisted-pair cable are high bandwidths, less attenuation of signal, and lighter weight, making it possible to transmit data in digital format at very high speed from one computer to another over a network such as the Internet.

optical scanner   *See*: scanner.

optical spacing   In typesetting, the technique of adjusting the distance between the individual letters in a line of capitals to create the optical illusion of even spacing, which requires placing some letter combinations closer together than others.

option   The privilege of purchasing the rights in a book or manuscript from the copyright holder for a specific purpose (*example*: the right to adapt a novel or short story for performance on stage or screen), usually granted for a fixed period of time designated in a legally binding agreement, in exchange for some form of compensation. *See also*: *subsidiary rights*.

In computing, a choice available to the user in the form of a menu item, button, or icon appearing in the toolbar or window of a graphical user interface or as a link embedded in a Web page.

In Dewey Decimal Classification, an alternative to the standard notation provided in the schedules and tables that places special emphasis on an aspect in a library's collection not given preferred treatment in the standard notation and in some cases providing a shorter notation for the aspect (adapted from DDC).

optional   A field or subfield of the MARC record in which data may be entered at the discretion of the cataloger but is not required to meet OCLC input standards for a given cataloging level. Compare with *mandatory* and *required if applicable and readily available*.

In *AACR2*, a unit of data that may be added at the cataloger's discretion to the bibliographic description of an item but is not required, for example, the name of the releasing agent in the publication, distribution, etc., area of the bibliographic record for a motion picture.

optional number   In Dewey Decimal Classification, a class number listed in parentheses in the schedules or tables that is an alternative to the standard notation for the class. Also, a class number created by following an option in the schedules or tables.

opus   Latin for "a work." In the most general sense, any creative work or composition. In music, the term is usually followed by an opus number assigned by the composer or publisher to one of several works, or a collection of works related in form or medium, to indicate its place in the sequence in which they were composed or issued. Abbreviated *op*. Plural: *opera* or *opuses*. *See also*: *magnum opus* and *opuscule*.

opuscule   A book or treatise of small size. Also refers to a musical work or literary composition of little significance. Compare in this sense with *magnum opus*. *See also*: *opus*.

opus number   A number assigned by the composer or publisher to one of several musical works, or a set of works related in form or medium, to indicate its place in the sequence in which they were composed or issued, usually included in the title following the abbreviation *op*. (*example*: Beethoven's ***Concerto for Violin, op. 61, D major***). Special numbering exists for certain composers whose works were unnumbered when first published, for example, the universally accepted *Köchel numbers* devised by the 19th-century Austrian botanist Ludwig von Köchel in his chronological thematic catalog of the works of Wolfgang Amadeus Mozart.

OR *See*: logical sum.

oral history A sound recording or transcription of a planned interview with a person whose memories and perceptions of historical events are to be preserved as an aural record for future generations. Also refers to a historical work (published or unpublished) based on data collected orally, often retained in the archives and special collections of large libraries (*example*: ***Hard Times: An Oral History of the Great Depression*** by Studs Terkel).

orchestral score The full score of a musical work composed for orchestra, giving the parts for all the instruments.

order canceled (OC) A term used on an invoice to indicate that the order for a book or other item has been canceled by the seller, usually because copies are no longer available. Compare with *back order*. *See also*: *out of print*.

order form A preprinted card or sheet sent by a publisher or vendor with a promotional mailing, as an insert in a periodical, or as part of a trade catalog, providing blank spaces for the customer to fill in the names or titles of items to be ordered. In online sales (*e-commerce*), the order form is often called a "shopping cart."

order of precedence *See*: preference order.

order of preference *See*: preference order.

order record In acquisitions, a record created and associated with the bibliographic record for an item at the time it is ordered, containing information needed to process the order (name of selector, budgetary fund, vendor, order date, estimated price, purchase order number, date received, special handling notes, date cataloged, and pertinent characteristics of the item). After the item is received and processed, the order record is eventually purged. Compare with *item record*.

ordinal A term that applies to two types of liturgical books used in services of the Catholic Church: (1) a guide setting forth the order in which the liturgy is to be celebrated, including instructions for the clergy concerning the performance of liturgical actions, and (2) a book giving the rules and form of service to be followed in the ordination of a deacon or priest, the consecration of a bishop, or the coronation of a king. Medieval ordinals were often beautifully illuminated.

organizational culture The prevailing values, expectations, and conventions within an organization or institution, often unspoken and persistent. Advancement may depend on sensitivity to such norms.

original In literature, a work as written by the author or in the author's own words. In art, a finished work as completed by the artist and ready for reproduction. In science, a study that produces results never before reported, in some cases through the use of a new methodology or research design. In reprography, the source document from which the first copy is made or in some cases the first copy itself. In a more general sense, something new and fresh, not copied or based on a pre-existing model. Abbreviated *orig*. Compare with *copy*.

original binding   A term used in the antiquarian book trade to indicate that a book retains the binding in which it was first issued, which may show definite signs of wear if the volume is an old one. Synonymous with *primary binding*. *See also*: *rebinding*.

original cataloging   Preparation of a bibliographic record from scratch, without the aid of a pre-existing catalog record for the same edition, more time-consuming for the cataloger than *copy cataloging*.

original format   The physical form in which an item is originally issued or created, as opposed to a form produced by a process of conversion (reformatting). The following considerations in the retention of items in original format are recommended by the Preservation Committee of the Research Libraries Group: evidential value, age, scarcity, association value, aesthetic value, importance in printing history, exhibit value, monetary value, and physical features of interest.

original language   The language in which a work is first written or produced, as distinct from a language in which it is translated. In library cataloging, the original language of a translation is entered in the 765 field of the MARC record. In the bibliographic display, the note *Translation of*: appears, followed by the title in the original language or a transliteration of it.

original order   The principle in archives that records should remain in the sequence in which they were maintained when in active use, unless the method of accumulation is determined upon inspection to have been so unsystematic as to render retrieval difficult, if not impossible. Existing relationships are preserved when documents remain as originally arranged, making it easier to prepare finding aids. Original order also has evidential value. *See also*: respect des fonds.

original parts   A descriptive term used in library cataloging to indicate that a copy of a work first issued in installments has survived in its original form without having been rebound.

orihon   A manuscript or printed document in the form of a continuous length of papyrus, vellum, or paper, folded backwards and forwards accordion-style between the columns of text to divide the work into pages, which are usually fastened with a cord threaded through holes pierced in the back fold, with or without laced-on covers. Compare with *zig-zag book*.

ornament   *See*: printer's ornament *and* tooling.

orphan   In printing, an incomplete line of type, such as a heading or the first line of a paragraph, when it appears at the foot of a page or column of text. Skilled typographers consider such lines awkward and avoid setting them if possible, just as they avoid setting *widows*. Compare with *club line*.

 In indexing, a descriptor or subject heading that has no relation, hierarchic or associative, to any other term in the indexing language (*example*: **Chank**, the Library of Congress subject heading for a type of seashell used in Indian folklore and religion). Orphans are rare in indexing. *See also*: *sibling*.

orphan film Narrowly defined, a motion picture abandoned by its creator, owner, or caretaker. Broadly speaking, a film outside the commercial mainstream, including public domain materials, industrial and educational films, independent documentaries, ethnographic films, home movies, and films of small or unusual gauge. The National Film Preservation Foundation (NFPF), a charitable affiliate of the National Film Preservation Board of the Library of Congress, awards federally funded grants to archives for the preservation of historically, culturally, or aesthetically significant orphan films.

orthography Correct spelling of a written language, usually given in a standard dictionary. British spelling differs slightly from American spelling of certain words (*cataloguing/cataloging*, *grey/gray*, *theatre/theater*, etc.). Also refers to any style or method of spelling and to the study of spelling and its conventions.

OS *See*: operating system *and* out of stock.

OSI *See*: Open Systems Interconnection.

OSS An abbreviation of *open source software*. *See*: open source.

Otabind The trade name for a relatively new type of softcover adhesive binding that opens flat without any resistance and has the internal characteristics of a hardcover binding sewn through the fold. Two different cold emulsion polyvinyl acetate (PVA) adhesives are applied separately to the binding edge, providing maximum strength and flexibility when allowed to dry naturally. The cover is attached with hot-melt adhesive, not to the spine but to the sides of the text block, leaving a hollow back.

The hot-melt adhesives used in perfect binding have a clamping effect that hampers openability. They also have low cold-crack resistance, which makes them unsuitable for use in countries that experience extreme winter temperatures. The impetus for the development of an enhanced softcover binding came from the Finnish publisher Otava. Otabind International was founded in 1986 by the Dutch binder Gerard Hexspoor in cooperation with Muller Martini, a Swiss manufacturer of binding equipment. The method was introduced in the United States and Canada in 1988 and is especially suitable for volumes that must open flat (instruction manuals, music books, textbooks, travel guides, cookbooks, etc.). Its durability is several times that of conventional perfect binding.

other title information In *AACR2*, a title found on a bibliographic item, other than the title proper or parallel or series title(s). Also, any phrase appearing in conjunction with the title proper, usually indicating the contents or character of the item or explaining the motives for or occasion of its production or publication. The term includes subtitles, alternative titles, etc., but not variations on the title proper (half titles, spine titles, etc.). In the bibliographic record, other title information is transcribed following the whole or part of the title proper or parallel title to which it pertains. If the information is lengthy, it may be given in a note or abridged.

out   In printing, copy accidentally omitted in typesetting. When a bookseller or retail purchaser discovers a defect of this kind, the publisher will normally send a replacement copy at no charge. *See also*: *imperfections*.

outdated   Information that is no longer current. Publications containing such information may be misleading, as in the case of a superseded edition of a manual of medical diagnosis or prescription drugs. Books are usually updated in supplements and revised editions.

outlay   A sum of money spent, especially in the initial phase of a project, on the expectation that the investment will eventually produce a tangible or intangible return or some other desired result. Public relations expenditures usually fall into this category.

outline   A popular treatment of an extensive subject (*example*: *The Outline of History* by H.G. Wells). Also refers to a summary of the main aspects of a topic or a systematic list of the most important points of a speech or written work, often using indention to indicate logical subordination.

Also refers to a line or thin edge drawn around a picture or image, as a form of decoration or to establish its visual limits. Compare with *neatline*. *See also*: *outline letter*.

outline drawing   A style of medieval manuscript illumination in which the outlines of a figure or scene are drawn in detail in black and/or colored ink. The technique was sometimes combined with tinted or fully painted design elements.

outline letter   A letter printed from a unit of type from which the inside of each stroke has been removed, leaving a black line around the edges enclosing white space in the interior. Synonymous with *open letter*. Compare with *inline*. *See also*: *shaded letter*.

out of circulation   Not available to be checked out or used for reference, for example, library materials in the process of being mended, repaired, rebound, recataloged, etc. The opposite of *in circulation*. Compare with *noncirculating*.

out of print (OP)   A publication no longer obtainable through regular market channels because the publisher's inventory is exhausted, and there is no prospect of another printing in the foreseeable future. A book goes out of print when the publisher decides sales no longer justify the expense of maintaining inventory, when it is superseded by a later edition, or when the rights are relinquished by the publisher.

An OP title can sometimes be located in a used bookstore. Search services, antiquarian booksellers, and book scouts specialize in tracking down out of print editions (*examples*: **Abebooks** and **Alibris**). An out of print book may eventually be reissued (the review publication *Library Journal* includes a special "Classic Returns" section devoted to recent reprints). Books that have gone out of print since 1979 are indexed in *Books Out-of-Print* published by R.R. Bowker, which includes information on remainder dealers and on-demand publishers. Also abbreviated *o.p.* Compare with *out of print at present*, *out of stock*, and *temporarily out of print*.

out of print at present (OPP)   A term used on a publisher's invoice to indicate that a publication cannot be supplied because current inventory is exhausted but additional copies may be printed at some unspecified time in the future. Compare with *out of print* and *temporarily out of print.*

out of print, searching (OPS) A term used on an invoice to indicate that a publication is no longer available from the publisher but the seller is attempting to fulfill the order through other channels.

out of series The unnumbered copies of a book, printed in excess of the number specified by the publisher for a limited edition, usually bound as *overs*, for use in promotion and for distribution as review copies. Out of series copies are usually not signed by the author unless they are used as complimentary copies.

out of stock (OS) A term used on a publisher's invoice to indicate that a publication cannot be supplied at the time the order is received because it is not in inventory. Also abbreviated *o.s.* The opposite of *in stock.* Compare with *out of print.* **See also**: *temporarily out of stock.*

output The end result of processing by a computer, as opposed to data entered into or transferred to a computer system for processing (input). Output may be sent to a peripheral device for storage or display. Also refers to the signal that emanates from a video or audio player, as opposed to the signal fed into it.

Also, the total amount of work produced by a person, team, organization, machine, etc., usually during a fixed period of time (hour, day, week, or month), for example, the number of items cataloged by a technical services department in a given amount of time.

outreach Library programs and services designed to meet the information needs of users who are unserved or underserved, for example, those who are visually impaired, homebound, institutionalized, not fluent in the national language, illiterate, or marginalized in some other way. Large public libraries often have an *outreach librarian* who is responsible for providing such services. Compare with *library extension.* **See also**: Americans with Disabilities Act.

outsourcing The contracting of library services formerly performed in-house to an outside service provider, usually a for-profit enterprise. Part of a recent trend in the United States in the direction of privatizing government services, outsourcing has affected technical services to a greater extent than public services in libraries. Cost-effectiveness is the justification most often heard for this controversial management practice. One disadvantage is that in decisions requiring judgment an outside contractor may lack familiarity with local conditions and practices.

Outsourcing has generated the *least* amount of controversy in conservation and preservation (particularly binding and reformatting), purchasing catalog records in machine-readable form, acquisitions plans (approval plans, blanket order plans, subscription services, etc.), physical processing, retrospective conversion, and library automation systems. However, proposals to outsource cataloging and selection and to privatize federal and public libraries have met greater resistance.

overdue Refers to a circulating item checked out by a borrower and kept past its due date. Most circulation systems are designed to automatically generate an *overdue no-*

tice requesting prompt return of the item. Most libraries charge fines for overdue materials. A borrower account may be blocked if fines accumulate beyond a maximum amount determined by the library. Accounts long overdue may be sent to a collection agency. Overdue charges can be avoided by renewing an item on or before its due date. *See also*: *grace period*.

overdue notice   A printed or handwritten notice sent to a borrower's street address requesting the prompt return of items kept past their due date. The first notice may be followed by a second notice, then a final notice, depending on the policy of the individual library or library system. *See also*: *fines* and *renew*.

overhang   In bookbinding, the portion of covering material that extends beyond the edges of the boards before it is turned in and the endpapers pasted down.

overhead projector   A tabletop platform device used in presentations and bibliographic instruction to project clear transparencies onto a wall screen or other light-colored surface. Document cameras are superseding overhead projectors in well-equipped library instruction classrooms and labs.

overhead transparency   *See*: transparency.

overlay   A sheet of transparent material bearing text and/or images aligned in such a way that the appearance of any matter on which it is superimposed is altered, for example, the transparent sheets used in some medical textbooks and encyclopedias to illustrate the various components of human anatomy (skeleton, internal organs, circulatory system, etc.). Compare with *transparency*.

overleaf   On the other side of the leaf, a term used in captions to refer to full-page illustration on the reverse side of the same leaf.

overpainting   In manuscript painting, the application of pigment over the surface of a preliminary drawing or underpainting. In medieval manuscripts, illuminators typically sketched a design in metal point, then reworked the underdrawing in greater detail in ink before applying metallic leaf and then pigment.

overprint   To print over matter that has already been printed, sometimes in a space or box left blank for the purpose. Also refers to the printing of more copies of a work than are ordered or needed by the publisher. Unsold copies may be *remaindered*. In multicolor printing, the technique of applying ink to the same image in successive layers, each of a different color, to achieve color combinations. *See also*: *full-color printing*.

overrun   Sheets or copies of a publication printed in excess of the quantity ordered by the publisher to allow for normal spoilage in printing and binding and for distribution as presentation and review copies. Synonymous with *overs*. The opposite of *underrun*. *See also*: *out of series*.

overs   *See*: overrun.

oversewing   A method of extra-strength binding in which the back folds are removed from the sections by milling and the resulting leaves sewn through the back margin in thin groups, one to another in succession, with the needle held perpendicular to the paper surface in hand sewing or positioned at an oblique angle in machine sewing. Oversewing is also used in some fold sewn bindings to reinforce the first and last sections. The swell added by oversewing may limit a volume's openability.

oversize   A book or other item too tall or too wide to be shelved with volumes of smaller size in normal call number sequence, for example, large art books and atlases. Libraries often shelve oversize materials in a separate location, indicated by a special code or location symbol displayed in the catalog record and on the spine label.

overstaffed   Having more than enough employees to accomplish the necessary work, a situation that is usually remedied by reassigning staff to other duties and responsibilities or in extreme cases by laying off personnel. The opposite of *understaffed*.

overstock   Excess quantities of a book or other item held in stock for which demand has dropped to a low level or ceased, usually the result of overestimating the sales potential of the work or a returns policy that encourages booksellers to overorder to secure a more favorable discount. To avoid paying tax on inventory, the publisher may dispose of overstock by remaindering. Compare with *out of stock*. *See also*: *on sale or return*.

Also refers to materials held in excess of what is needed to serve the information needs of a library's clientele.

over the transom   An unsolicited manuscript or book proposal received by a publisher without prior notification, usually directly from the author without the assistance of a literary agent. Publishers generally consign such submissions to a *slushpile*, very few receiving more than a rejection slip, but occasionally a work of exceptional quality is submitted in this way, launching a successful writing career.

overtime   Time worked in excess of the maximum number of regular hours per day, week, or month specified under the terms of employment, for which an employee is normally compensated at a higher rate. Libraries pay their staff overtime only under very exceptional circumstances. Compare with *flextime*.

ownership mark   A mark in a book or other item indicating the name of the library that owns it, usually in the form of a label, bookplate, embossment, perforation, or stamp (usually in permanent ink). An ownership mark is normally placed where it can be easily located but usually not in a position of prominence or where it might cause confusion or disfigure the item. Some libraries and archives use a secret ownership mark, for example, a dot or group of dots positioned according to a system known only to the technical processing staff. *See also*: *ex-library copy*.

In a more general sense, any mark, label, or other indication in or on a book of the identity of its past or present owner(s), including signatures, inscriptions, bookplates, etc. Ownership marks can be important in establishing provenance and value in the market for antiquarian books. They are sometimes forged or altered to make a book appear older or more valuable. *See also*: *proof of ownership*.

Oxford corners   A binding decorated with plain, straight border lines that cross at the corners, popular from the 16th to the 18th century.

Oxford English Dictionary (OED)   The most complete collection of words and their definitions in the English language as spoken throughout the world, the *Oxford English Dictionary* is also the leading authority on word origins and the evolution of the English language over the past 1,000 years. Published in 20 volumes by Oxford University Press, the *OED* is currently in its second edition, with a third edition in preparation. It is available in print, on CD-ROM, and online, updated quarterly. URL: dictionary.oed.com.

P

P2P   *See*: peer-to-peer.

packaged book   A book produced wholly or in part by a freelancer or agency in the business of assembling books for publication. The extent of the *packager*'s role is determined by the agreement with the publisher, which may include writing, editing, designing, illustrating, printing, and even binding the final product. Portions of the production process may be subcontracted out to specialists. Compare with *managed book*.

packet switching   Network technology that breaks a message in digital format into tiny parcels of no more than 128 characters, each with the same destination address, then routes them separately as transmission circuits become available. When the packets reach their destination, they are checked to ensure that no data was lost in transmission, then reassembled in original sequence. Packet switching enables the transmission capability of a computer network to be used with maximum speed and efficiency, reducing costs and enhancing productivity.

packing list   A printed form sent by a vendor or supplier with a shipment of goods, listing its contents to allow the customer to compare items shipped against those that were ordered, not to be confused with an invoice. Synonymous with *packing slip* and *shipping list*.

padded binding   A book with one or more layers of compressible material, such as cotton batting, added to the surface of the boards before the outer covering is applied, to make the binding soft to the touch. The style was used in the late 19th and 20th centuries on albums, diaries, volumes of poetry, etc.

padded envelope   A flexible wrapper made of heavy-duty kraft paper and lined with soft fiber or air bubbles to protect items in shipment. Used extensively in interlibrary loan, padded envelopes are available from library suppliers in various sizes and are reusable if opened carefully. Synonymous with *padded mailer*.

page   One side of a leaf in a manuscript, book, periodical, or other printed publication, numbered or unnumbered. The right-hand page in an opening is the *recto*, the left-hand page the *verso*. Abbreviated *p.* and *pp.* (plural). ***See also***: *folio* and *jump page*. Also, a shortened form of the term *Web page*.

Also refers to a library staff member responsible for delivering materials from closed stacks and assigned the routine task of general stack maintenance (reshelving, shelf reading, etc.). Also, to call a person by name over a public address system in a large facility, a practice libraries avoid to minimize distraction.

page break   The point in a text at which one page ends and the next page begins, indicated in most word processing software by a horizontal broken line across the screen. ***See also***: *orphan* and *widow*.

page head   *See*: headline.

page number   A number assigned in sequence to a page in a manuscript, book, pamphlet, periodical, etc., to facilitate reference. Page numbers are written or printed in the head or tail margin, usually centered or in the outer corner. Front matter is usually paginated in lowercase roman numerals, text and back matter in consecutive arabic numerals. Compare with *foliation*. ***See also***: *blind page*.

page preview   A feature of most word processing software that allows the format of a page of text to be viewed on the screen exactly as it will appear when printed. ***See also***: *WYSIWYG*.

page proof   In printing, an impression made from type that has been made up into pages after the galley proofs have been inspected and any errors corrected, ready for final checking before the publication goes to press.

pagination   The practice of marking the pages of a written or printed document with consecutive numbers to indicate their sequence. Front matter is usually numbered in lowercase roman numerals, text and back matter in arabic numerals. Rare in manuscripts and documents printed prior to A.D. 1500, pagination did not become common practice until about 1550 when it replaced *foliation*. The recto traditionally bears an odd page number and the verso an even number. ***See also***: *blind page, continuous pagination, duplicate paging, journal pagination, magazine pagination, repaginated, separately paginated*, and *unpaginated*.

In library cataloging, the portion of the physical description area (MARC field 300) of the bibliographic record that indicates the number of pages and/or leaves in a bibliographic item.

paging system   *See*: public address system.

painted binding   A style of binding in which a design or picture is painted directly on one or both covers of a book. Because of its light color and smooth surface, vellum was the best covering material for this type of decoration before paper came into widespread use.

paleography   From the Greek *palaios* ("ancient") and *graphien* ("writing"). The study of early forms of writing, such as the ancient inscriptions carved on monuments and the various scripts used in classical and medieval manuscripts. A discipline that began with the 15th-century humanists, paleography includes the decipherment of ancient texts and the determination from external characteristics of date and place of origin. Also refers to the study of the origins of the alphabets and letterforms used in writing the world's languages, including the Latin alphabet. British spelling is *palaeography*. Synonymous with *diplomatic*. *See also*: *Rosetta Stone*.

palimpsest   From the Greek *palimpsestos*, meaning "scraped again." A manuscript written on papyrus, parchment, or vellum on which earlier writings, only partially or imperfectly erased, are still faintly visible. Prior to the introduction of paper, writing material was often reused because it was expensive to produce and usually in short supply. Papyrus could be washed (*lavage*), but parchment and vellum had to be scraped with pumice or some other abrasive substance. A *double palimpsest* is one that has been erased twice. The new text was often written perpendicular to the former, to reduce, if not eliminate, visual confusion. The study of palimpsests has enabled codicologists to recover portions of texts and, in some cases, entire works that would otherwise have been lost.

palm-leaf book   Leaves of a palm-like tree, trimmed to uniform size, flattened, and polished for use as a writing surface in India, Tibet, and Southeast Asia. The text was scratched in the surface, then rubbed with dark pigment to make the characters more visible. A "book" was assembled as a series of leaves strung on a rod or cord through holes in the center and/or ends of the leaves, with a slat of wood or bamboo at each end serving as a cover. *See also*: *bark cloth* and *olla*.

palmtop   *See*: personal digital assistant.

pamphlet   A nonserial publication consisting of at least 5 but no more than 48 pages exclusive of covers, stapled or sewn but not bound, usually enclosed in covers of the same paper as the text (or a slightly heavier grade). Pamphlets were first published in England to disseminate the polemical writings of 16th-century reformers but are now used mainly for material too ephemeral or too brief (500 to 10,000 words) to be printed in book form. Synonymous with *booklet*. Compare with *brochure*. *See also*: *pamphlet binding* and *pamphlet file*.

pamphlet binding   A self-cover or paper publisher's binding in which the leaves of a periodical or pamphlet are wire-stitched or stapled, rather than sewn or glued.

pamphlet file   A cardboard, plastic, or metal box or frame designed for storing, in an upright position, items such as brochures, reports, loose issues of periodicals, and other materials (unbound or bound in paper covers), usually with a blank space on the front for a label listing the contents.

panel   In binding, a square or rectangular compartment on the side of a book cover impressed in the dampened surface and/or enclosed in a border or frame, often stamped with the title or displaying a picture or design. *Panel stamps* were large tools (cast not engraved) incorporating an entire design rather than a repeatable motif. On a large book, several panels might be used to cover the entire area. According to P.J.M. Marks, panels were used in Antwerp as early as the 13th century, sometimes based on woodcuts (*The British Library Guide to Bookbinding*, University of Toronto

Press, 1998). Also refers to a similar design stamped on the spine of a book, often between raised bands on the spine of a hand-bound volume.

In printing, a "list of works by the same author" appearing in some books on the verso of the leaf immediately preceding the title page, which may include titles out of print or even issued by other publishers.

Also, one of a series of drawings in a cartoon or comic strip created as a sequence of related images to be viewed from left to right.

panel back   The spine of a hand-bound book on which the space between two or more of the bands has been enclosed in decorative tooling or panel-stamped with a similar design, in blind or gilt.

panel stamp   *See*: panel.

panorama   A map in which the angle of view is oblique, rather than from a position directly above, creating a visible horizon, used to depict towns, cities, and popular recreational areas (mountain ranges, canyon lands, etc.). Important geographic features are sometimes labeled across the top or bottom margin. Panoramas have characteristics of both maps and pictures.

paper   A flat fibrous writing or printing surface made by breaking down vegetable fiber, such as wood or rag, into pulp to which a filler is added in water suspension. As the water is drained away on a wire screen, the moist fibers bond with each other at points of contact, forming a dense mat that stiffens as it dries. Paper is graded by content and intended use and by such properties as color, brightness, opacity, finish, strength, density, weight, and chemical stability. It can be coated or uncoated, sized or unsized, handmade or machine-made. The acid content of the paper used in library materials is an issue in preservation. For more information about paper, please see the entry by Derek Priest in the *International Encyclopedia of Information and Library Science* (Routledge, 2003). Compare with *papyrus* and *parchment*. *See also*: *bible paper*, *book paper*, *buffered paper*, *cover paper*, *esparto*, *foolscap*, *kraft paper*, *laid paper*, *manila*, *newsprint*, *onionskin*, *papermaking*, *permanent paper*, and *wove paper*.

Also refers to a brief composition, especially one prepared for presentation by the author at a conference or other professional meeting. Conference papers may be published in proceedings or transactions. They are indexed in *PapersFirst*, an online database available in OCLC *FirstSearch*. Compare with *article*.

paperback   A book published in paper covers, rather than in hardcover, usually adhesive bound. The modern paperback first appeared in the 1930s when Sir Allen Lane, founder of Penguin books, published *Ariel* by Andre Maurois in paper covers. Paperback editions are normally published *after* the hardcover edition of the same title and sold at a lower price, which has made them a staple of the retail market for fiction and nonfiction. Synonymous with *paperbound* and *softcover*. Abbreviated *pb*, *pbk*, and *ppr*. Compare with *paper boards*. *See also*: *mass-market paperback* and *trade paperback*.

Also refers to a form of bookbinding in which hot-melt adhesive is applied to the flat binding edge of the unsewn sections, securing them directly to a heavy paper cover cut flush. Durability depends on the capacity of the adhesive to remain flexible over time. *See also*: *Otabind*.

paperback grading   In the used book trade, the following letter system is used by some booksellers to indicate the condition of paperback books:

A—in new, unread condition, with no marking or stamps on the front cover, edges, etc.

B—slightly creased along the spine; may be marked with a name, initials, or bookstore stamp

C—reading copy with creases on the spine and signs of wear at the corners but the text intact

paperback original   A work of fiction or nonfiction published for the first time in mass-market or trade paperback edition, not previously issued in hardcover.

paperboard   Fairly rigid sheets of matted fiber manufactured in the same manner as paper but .3 millimeter (.012 of an inch) or more in thickness. Various grades are used in the manufacture of cases for publisher's bindings. Compare with *paper boards*.

paper boards   An edition bound in boards made of pasteboard covered in heavy paper, usually not as durable as cloth binding. Compare with *paperback*.

paperbound   *See*: paperback.

paper knife   A dull blade made of metal, wood, plastic, or ivory that has the appearance of a knife but is made for slicing paper by hand along a fold, as in opening a sealed envelope or separating the leaves of an uncut book.

paperless   An automated office or system that relies primarily on electronic media rather than paper for information transmission and recordkeeping.

papermaking   According to Chinese tradition, the process of making paper from native vegetable fibers was invented in about A.D. 105 by Ts'ai Lun, an official employed in one of the workshops of the Emperor Ho-ti. The technique reached Samarkand via trade routes by A.D. 750 and was introduced into Spain by the Moors in about 1150. Papermills were in operation in Europe at least 250 years before the invention of printing from movable type, but the use of parchment as a writing and printing surface persisted well after the printing press became established. The papermaking industry became firmly established in Europe only in the mid-16th century in response to the spread of printing. The first paper mill in America was established in 1690 by William Rittenhouse near Philadelphia.

Prior to the mid-19th century, nearly all paper was made from cotton and linen rags reduced to pulp and placed in a vat containing a solution of water and size. Each sheet was produced by hand-dipping into the vat a wooden frame strung with a bed of metal wires, then agitating it to distribute the fibers evenly. The resulting mat of fiber was then dried between sheets of blotting paper and pressed flat. Manufacturers used frames with a metal device embedded in the cross-wires to produce a distinctive watermark in each sheet.

In 1798, a Frenchman named Nicolas Louis Robert invented a machine that manufactured a continuous roll of paper, subsequently developed and perfected in England in the *Fourdrinier machine*. Forty years later, a technique for making paper from wood pulp was developed in Nova Scotia. Despite these advances, the four basic steps of papermaking remain the same: (1) preparation of the fiber, (2) distribution of the resulting "stock" in a thin layer across a part of the machine called the "web," (3) removal of moisture by various means, and (4) finishing the surface to give it the desired qualities. The American Museum of Papermaking at Georgia Tech maintains a Web site devoted to the history of papermaking at: www.ipst.gatech.edu/amp/collection/index.htm *See also*: *calender, coated, dandy roll,* and *deckle edges*.

papermark   *See*: watermark.

paper mill   A site on the Internet that provides prewritten essays and term papers for students, free of charge or for a fee. Some sites charge a subscription fee and may offer custom services, usually on a per-page basis. Customers may even be provided with advice about how to avoid being caught cheating. Instructors have devised ways of detecting this form of plagiarism.

paper preferred   In acquisitions, an approval plan option specifying that the library is to receive the paperback edition in place of the cloth (hardcover) edition whenever the two are published simultaneously. The cost of rebinding a paperback is often less than the price difference between the two editions.

papers   A collection of more than one type of handwritten or typewritten document. Also refers to a group of compositions, especially those written for presentation by the author (or authors) at a conference, sometimes published as proceedings or transactions by the society or association sponsoring the meeting.

In archives and special collections, a collection of personal and family documents, as distinct from formal records, which may include correspondence, diaries, notes, etc. Personal papers are often donated to a library by the author or a member of the family after the author's death. In the United States, the trend has been for presidential papers to be archived in a special presidential library located in or near place of birth or residence prior to election.

Also refers to an individual's official documents (birth certificate, identity card, passport, etc.).

paperwork   Routine tasks having to do with matters that must be committed to paper (reports, letters, memoranda, etc.), as opposed to work that is more creative or involves other forms of communication. *See also*: *procrastination*.

papier-mâché binding   A 19th-century molded binding made from a mixture of paper fiber, plaster of Paris, and possibly antimony, formed in a rigid frame usually made of metal. The designs, mainly in black heavy-relief, sometimes in latticework over a red or metallic underlay, reflected the Victorian revival of gothic style in the decorative arts. Patented by the British firm Jackson & Sons, the method required a leather spine. *See also*: *relievo binding*.

papyrus   A tall marsh sedge (*Cyperus papyrus*) once abundant in North Africa from which the ancient Egyptians made a material used as a writing and painting surface throughout the Mediterranean basin from the 3rd millennium B.C. to the 4th century A.D. (and as late as the 11th century for some documents in the Vatican).

Although the word "paper" is derived from *papyrus*, the latter is technically not a paper since it is not made from pulped and processed fiber but from thin strips of the fibrous pith laid in layers at right angles to each other, pressed into sheets, dried under pressure, and polished to a cream or white color. For long documents, the sheets were pasted edge to edge in rolls, often wound around a stick called an *umbilicus* by the ancient Romans. Papyrus was less suitable for codices because it tends to delaminate when folded.

Writing was usually done with a reed pen called a *calamus* on the inner side of a roll (with the fibers running horizontally). Trade embargoes in late Antiquity may have led to the development of parchment as a writing surface. Papyrus was abandoned with the collapse of the Roman Empire in the West. Because papyrus is fragile and does not withstand damp conditions, very little survives of the magnificent libraries of Antiquity. The term also refers to manuscripts written on papyrus, mainly in the form of scrolls. *Papyrology* is the study of ancient papyrus texts. Plural: *papyri*.

parable   A short, simple story, usually written in the form of an allegory, intended to convey an explicit moral lesson (the Prodigal Son) or religious principle (the parables of Jesus). *See also*: *fable*.

paradigm   A model, pattern, or example, especially one that revolutionizes the standard approach to a subject or conventional modes of thinking in a profession or field of study. In library and information science, paradigm shifts are increasingly driven by technological innovation.

parallel content   In the MARC record, the same digits are assigned across fields in the second and third character positions of the tag to indicate data of the same type, for example, the digits **10** for corporate names, making **110** the main entry corporate name field, **410** the series statement corporate name field, **610** the subject heading corporate name field, **710** the added entry corporate name field, and so on. Parallel content designation can be summarized as follows, with **X** in the range of **1–9**:

X00—personal names
X10—corporate names
X11—meeting names
X30—uniform titles
X40—bibliographic titles
X50—topical terms
X51—geographic names

parallel edition   *See*: parallel texts.

parallel publishing   The publication of a work at the same time in both print and electronic format. Compare with *simultaneous publication*.

parallel texts   Different texts of the same work printed side-by-side on the same page or on facing pages of a book, for example, two versions of the Bible or a text in translation and in the original language. Such works are published in *parallel edition*. *See also*: *duplicate paging*.

parallel title   The title proper of an edition in a language or script other than that of the original title. In *AACR2*, parallel titles are entered in the title and statement of responsibility area of the bibliographic record (MARC field 245) in the order found in the chief source of information, separated by an equal sign preceded and followed by a space. The Library of Congress records all parallel titles for items issued in the United States.

parameter   An established limit whose value affects the execution or result of a process or operation, for example, a publication date range specified by the user to limit the results of a search in an online catalog or bibliographic database.

paraph   An elaborate ornamental flourish at the end of an autograph signature, added, especially by notaries, to protect official documents from forgery.

paraphrase   From the Greek *para* ("beyond") and phrasis ("to tell"). A *re*wording of the thought expressed in a previously spoken statement or written work, usually to make the meaning clearer by substituting shorter, simpler words for difficult vocabulary. Also, the use of rewording as a literary device or educational technique. Compare with *quotation*. *See also*: *plagiarism*.

paraprofessional   A member of the library support staff, usually someone who holds at least a baccalaureate degree, trained to understand specific procedures and apply them according to pre-established rules under normal circumstances without exercising professional judgment. Library paraprofessionals are usually assigned high-level technical support duties, for example, in copy cataloging and serials control. In smaller public library systems in the United States, branch librarians are sometimes paraprofessionals. A directory of U.S. *State and Regional Library Paraprofessional Associations* is available online at: flightline.highline.edu/lssrc/orgs/indexmap.htm. Synonymous with *library technician*. *See also*: *Library Support Staff Interests Round Table*.

parchment   The split skin of an animal (sheep, goat, or calf) after it has been depilated and defleshed in a bath of lime, scraped to the desired thickness while still damp using a curved instrument called a *lunellum*, then dried under tension (not tanned), and polished by a tradesman known as a *parchmenter*, for use in bookbinding and as a writing or painting surface. Parchment was used in Europe from about the 2nd century A.D. until well after the invention of printing from movable type, although it declined in importance from the 12th century on as paper gained favor. The word is derived from *Charta pergamena*, Pergamum being the name of the ancient city on the west coast of Asia Minor where King Eumenes II founded a library to rival the great center of scholarship at Alexandria in Egypt. Its adoption as a writing surface in the 2nd century B.C. may have been spurred by a trade embargo on papyrus.

Although costly to produce, parchment was more durable than papyrus, which it eventually replaced. During the Middle Ages it was used to make the leaves of manuscript books, one of the reasons books of that period are so thick. Because parchment is naturally oily, it had to be rubbed with an abrasive substance called *pounce* to prepare it for writing. It is also darker and smoother on the hair side than on the flesh side, so the quires of medieval manuscripts were assembled with hair side facing hair side and flesh side facing flesh side to make the openings in a book uniform in color and texture. Tiny specks on the hair side are traces of hair follicles. The tendency of parchment to cockle with changes in temperature and humidity, and of the grain side to curl in upon itself (the outer side of animal skin being less elastic than the flesh side), was addressed by binding the text block in heavy wooden boards fitted with straps, ties, or clasps to keep the volume firmly closed when not in use. The term also refers to a document written or printed on parchment, such as a map or diploma. Compare with *vellum*.

parchmenter *See*: parchment.

parental mediation Interaction between parent and child concerning the content of a book, videotape, or television program, usually intended to mitigate or prevent negative effects, particularly in the case of works depicting explicit violence and/or sexual behavior. Parental involvement can be active (discussion of content with child) or restrictive (imposition of rules and regulations). Reading aloud together and coviewing can also be forms of parental mediation. In public libraries, monitoring a child's choice of reading or viewing material is the responsibility of the parent. In the absence of parental guidance, it is not incumbent on the librarian to act in loco parentis, although suggestions may be offered to the child, based on age, interests, and reading level.

parentheses In writing, a word, phrase, or sentence is enclosed in a pair of curved brackets ( ) to indicate that it has been added for the sake of explanation or clarification but is not essential to the overall meaning of the text. The use of parentheses has declined since the 19th century, replaced by commas in modern writing style. Also used in the singular (*parenthesis*) to refer to the *parenthetical expression* enclosed in brackets.

Parentheses are also used in Library of Congress subject headings and in indexing to add *parenthetical qualifiers*, and in Boolean search statements to indicate syntax, a technique called *nesting*. Compare with *square bracket*.

parenthetical qualifier In indexing, a word or phrase added in parentheses at the end of a subject heading or descriptor to:

- distinguish homographs, as in **Bowls (Game)** and **Bowls (Tableware)**
- indicate a specific meaning of the term, as in **Mice (Computers)**
- eliminate ambiguity, as in **AIDS (Disease)**
- indicate a specific use of the term, as in **Nutcracker (Ballet)**
- give the context of an obscure word or phrase, as in **Obatala (Yoruba deity)**
- give the location of a geographic name that is not well known, as in **Kymi River (Finland)**
- specify the academic discipline in which a subject is studied, as in **Extinction (Psychology)**
- indicate language, as in **Sudanese fiction (English)**

- indicate that a proper name is imaginary, as in **Ophelia (Fictitious character)**
- indicate instrumentation in music, as in **Suites (Bassoon and flute)**

Compare with *scope note*.

Paris Principles   The *Statement of Principles* adopted in 1961 at the International Conference of Cataloging Principles (ICCP), which laid the foundation for the *Anglo-American Cataloguing Rules* and cataloging codes used in countries other than the United States, Great Britain, and Canada. Organized by IFLA to address international standardization in library cataloging, the conference was held in Paris, France. The *Statement* lists 12 basic principles that remain the foundation of author/title entry.

parity bit   In computing, a bit included in a unit of digital data to detect errors in transmission, for example, the eighth bit in a byte representing an ASCII character.

parody   A form of satirical imitation in which the style of a serious artistic or literary work is ridiculed by applying the same style to an inappropriate or trivial subject or by treating the original subject in a nonsensical or irreverent manner. One of the earliest examples is *The Frogs*, a play by Aristophanes believed to parody works by Aeschylus and Euripides. In a more recent example, Jane Austen parodied the gothic novels popular in early-19th-century England in *Northanger Abbey*. Parody can also be used as a form of political or social criticism (*example*: *The Wind Done Gone*, Alice Randall's African American perspective on the novel *Gone With the Wind* by Margaret Mitchell). *See also*: *burlesque*.

part   One portion of a work divided by the author, publisher, or manufacturer into two or more subordinate units, usually issued at intervals as the work is completed. The intervals may be regular or irregular, depending on the nature of the work. In printed monographs, a part is usually the equivalent of a *volume*. A part is distinguished from a *fascicle* by being a permanent component, rather than a temporary division of the work. As used in the physical description area of a bibliographic record, the term refers to one of two or more bibliographic units intended to be bound together, more than one to a volume (*AACR2*). Abbreviated *pt*. Compare with *piece*. *See also*: *multipart item*, *multipart volume*, *original parts*, and *serialized*.

In music, one of the voices or instruments for which an ensemble work is composed. Also, a written or printed copy of the notation in which the music for a voice or instrument is recorded for use in performance, indicated as *part* in the physical description area of the bibliographic record (*AACR2*). In the full score of an ensemble work, each part appears on a separate stave. *See also*: *condensed score*.

partial remainders   A quantity of books offered by the publisher at lower than list price to selected booksellers who are permitted to sell copies retail at less than the published price, even though the books are still considered net. This practice is condemned by publishers' and booksellers' associations because it gives some booksellers an unfair competitive advantage over others in the same market.

partial title   A catch title consisting of part of the title as it appears on the title page. It may be a secondary part (subtitle or alternative title) or the title with the less significant words omitted.

partitive relation   *See*: semantic relation.

parts of a book   Although the order varies slightly from one publisher to the next, the parts of a book in order of gathering are normally the half title, series title or frontispiece, title page, printer's imprint and notice of copyright, dedication or epigraph, table of contents, other front matter (list of contributors, list of illustrations, list of tables or abbreviations, chronology, etc.), preface or foreword, acknowledgments, introduction, errata, half title, text, appendices, author's notes, glossary, bibliography, index(es), colophon, and CIP if not on the verso of the title page. Contributors may be listed in the back matter, and a translator's note is sometimes included in the front matter.

part-time   Employment limited to a portion of normal working hours. Part-time employees who work less than a certain number of hours per week or month may not be entitled to full benefits. In academic institutions, the ratio of full-time to part-time (adjunct) faculty, including librarians, may be governed by a collective bargaining agreement.

pass-along   The likelihood that a copy of an issue of a newspaper or periodical will be read by more individuals than the person who actually purchases it at a newsstand or by subscription. Some publishers use this as a justification for charging libraries a substantially higher subscription price than the rate paid by individual subscribers, a practice known as *differential pricing*. Although pass-along is difficult to quantify, when combined with circulation it gives an approximate indication of total readership.

passim   Latin for "here and there" or "in various places," printed after a subject heading in an index, or in a footnote or endnote following the title of a work or the author's name, to indicate that a phrase or reference to a concept or idea is scattered throughout the chapter or entire work, too briefly or too abundantly for individual page references to be given. Abbreviated *pass*.

passive relation   *See*: semantic relation.

password   An authorized word or sequence of characters that a user must enter as input in order to log on to a computer system and gain access to desired resources. Passwords are usually managed by the operating system or a database management system (DBMS). Because system software is only capable of verifying the legitimacy of a password, not the identity of the person using it, passwords should remain confidential. In a well-designed system, passwords must be changed periodically by the user to maintain security. By contrast, the *username* is usually permanent.

paste   A type of adhesive used to stick together lightweight materials such as paper and gold leaf, made from the starch contained in a cereal grain such as wheat, corn, or rice, combined over heat with water (and sometimes alum or resin) until smooth, then allowed to cool. Paste is used to affix labels and bookplates because it is water soluble, making them easy to remove if necessary. However, water solubility also makes it susceptible to mold. Compare with *glue*. *See also*: *cut-and-paste*.

pasteboard   A rigid, relatively lightweight binding material made from layer upon layer of paper pasted together, or from thin layers of pulp bonded together, introduced in the 15th century to replace wooden boards in small- to medium-sized books. In modern bookbinding, a heavy grade of pasteboard called *binder's board* is used extensively in hardcover editions.

paste-down   In bookbinding, the half of a double-leaf endpaper firmly affixed to the inside of one of the boards of the case or cover, over the edges of the turn-in. In medieval manuscript books, the paste-down concealed grooves called *channels* cut into the inside surface of the boards to recess the cords. The parchment or vellum leaves used for the purpose were often fragments of disused manuscripts. Also spelled *pastedown*. Compare with *doublure*.

paste-in   A correction or addition supplied after the text of a work has been printed, to be tipped in opposite to or on the page containing the line or passage to which it refers. Compare with *errata*.

paste-up   In printing, the arrangement on a large sheet of paper of the page proofs of several pages, to enable the typographer to position the text, illustrations, headings, captions, and other elements of the finished publication in a design that meets the publisher's specifications. Compare with *layout*.

pasting down   In bookbinding, the process of securely affixing one half of a double-leaf endpaper to the inside of each of the boards of the cover, over the *turn-in*. In hand-binding, this step is a finishing touch, the body of the book having been laced to the cover, but in case binding, the endleaves attach the body to the case. Compare with *gluing off*.

patched   A leaf in a medieval manuscript that has been repaired by sewing a piece of parchment or vellum over a hole or tear in the original membrane.

patent   A legal document issued by the U.S. government, or the government of another country, in response to a formal application process in which the inventor or originator of a new product or process is granted the exclusive right to manufacture, use, and sell it for a designated period of time. The document is assigned a *patent number* by the patent office for future reference. Most large engineering libraries provide patent search databases and services. Compare with *trademark*. **See also**: *patent and trademark depository library*.

patent and trademark depository library (PTDL)   A library designated by the U.S. Patent and Trademark Office (PTO) to receive and store copies of U.S. patents and patent/trademark materials, make them freely available to the public, and disseminate general information about patents and trademarks. Created by federal statute in 1871, the Patent and Trademark Depository Library Program (PTDLP) has grown to include more than 80 libraries, half of which are academic libraries, with nearly as many public libraries, one state library, and a special library devoted to research. **See also**: *Patent and Trademark Depository Library Association*.

Patent and Trademark Depository Library Association (PTDLA)   An affiliate of the American Library Association, PTDLA is dedicated to advising the U.S. Patent and Trademark Office (PTO) on the interests, needs, opinions, and goals of patent and trademark depository libraries (PTDLs) and their users and to assisting the PTO in planning and implementing appropriate services. URL: www.ptdla.org.

patent file   A collection of drawings and specifications for patents, indexed by country and patent number, name of *patentee*, or subject, usually maintained in a patent and trademark depository library.

patent number   *See*: patent.

pathfinder   A subject bibliography designed to lead the user through the process of researching a specific topic, or any topic in a given field or discipline, usually in a systematic, step-by-step way, making use of the best finding tools the library has to offer. Pathfinders may be printed or available online. *See also*: *topical guide*.

Patriot Act   *See*: *USA Patriot Act*.

patron   Any person who uses the resources and services of a library, not necessarily a registered borrower. Synonymous with *user*. Compare with *client*. *See also*: *patron ID*, *patron record*, *patron type*, and *problem patron*.

Also, a person who helps sponsor the creation, copying, or printing of an original work. In medieval Europe, the patron who commissioned a manuscript was sometimes depicted in a *presentation miniature* or other illustration in the work. During the 16th and 17th centuries, when returns from the fees paid by printer/publishers were meager, many writers could not have flourished without the patronage of wealthy individuals and institutions. It was not unusual for a sponsored work to be formally dedicated to the benefactor, in gratitude and hope of further financial assistance.

In a more general sense, any person or group that encourages or supports an activity or project, especially by providing necessary funds.

patron ID   The means by which staff at the circulation desk of a library ascertain that a patron is a registered borrower, usually the person's library card, student ID card, security badge, or a substitute. Also refers to the number used in most library circulation systems to identify the borrower. Sometimes it is the library card number, but in academic libraries it may be the student ID number or the social security number. In special libraries, patron ID may be linked to the employee identification system used by the parent organization. Each library or library system adopts its own method of patron identification. *See also*: *patron record*.

patron record   A confidential record in a library circulation system containing data pertaining to a borrower account (full name, street address, telephone number, patron ID, patron type, items on loan, holds, unpaid fines, etc.). In electronic circulation systems, an authorized member of the library staff is permitted to access the patron record by scanning the barcode on the library card or by using a keyboard to enter the patron's name or library card number as input. Some online catalogs allow registered borrowers to view their own patron records with proper authorization. Synonymous with *circulation record*. *See also*: *blocked*.

patron type   In library circulation systems, a code entered in the patron record to indicate a specific category of borrower, which in conjunction with *item type* determines the loan rule applied when an item is checked out. Academic libraries usually differentiate faculty, student, alumni, and staff by patron type. Most public libraries distinguish between nonresidents and patrons who reside in the service area and between adult and juvenile users. In special libraries, patron type may reflect hierarchical rank within the parent organization, levels of security clearance, etc.

patronymic   A personal name derived from the given name of the father, or of a more distant paternal ancestor, usually by the addition of a prefix (*examples*: **ben Jacob**, **MacArthur**, **O'Brien**) or suffix (**Donaldson**, **Petrovich**).

pattern book   *See*: model book.

pattern heading   The principle incorporated into Library of Congress subject headings in 1974 that allows a full set of free-floating subdivisions to be established for one or a few representatives of a particular category of subject headings or name headings, which are appropriate for use under other main headings belonging to the same category. For example, the subdivision **—Biopsy** under the pattern heading **Heart** can be used under the heading **Breast** even though no specific authority record exists for the combination **Breast—Biopsy**. The rule does not apply when there is a conflict with a heading established in the subject authority file in another form. For example, the subdivision **—Dislocation** under the pattern heading **Foot** may not be applied to the heading **Joints** because the combination **Joints—Dislocation** is a UF (used for) reference under the general heading **Dislocations** in the subject authority file.

payment date   The date by which an outstanding bill for goods and/or services must be paid, usually printed on the seller's invoice, after which the account is delinquent. A penalty may be charged for late payment.

pay-out   In marketing, an expenditure of funds that produces a return greater than the investment. When return equals investment, the result is known as *break-even*.

pay period   The interval at which an employee is paid, usually weekly, biweekly, or monthly, depending on the payroll system of the employer. Hours worked are usually reported to the payroll department on a timesheet signed by the employee.

pay-per-view   A service enabling libraries and individual library users to purchase a copy of an article without subscribing to the newspaper or periodical in which it was published. In most cases, the library has the option of limiting service to specific categories of users, for example, faculty members or researchers. High-priced and/or low-use journals are ideal candidates for this type of access, which allows libraries to expand serials access to include titles not previously affordable.

   Current awareness service is usually available with pay-per-view access. Fees vary, with most services charging $12 to $20 per article regardless of length. Electronic delivery is often priced lower than fax. Periodic reports detailing number of purchases per title and publisher enable librarians to compare per-view costs with the price of adding a subscription.

payphone   A telephone located in a public area from which anyone may make calls in exchange for payment in cash or by calling card. Most libraries that open their doors to the public provide at least one payphone as a courtesy to their users.

payroll   The list of employees who are paid salaries and wages by an employer, usually by check or direct deposit on a weekly, biweekly, or monthly basis. Library employees may be required to sign a *timesheet* for each pay period, stating the hours they worked.

PBS   *See*: public television.

PC   *See*: personal computer *and* political correctness.

PCC   *See*: Program for Cooperatrive Cataloging.

PCD   *See*: Photo CD.

PDA   *See*: personal digital assistant.

PDF   *See*: Portable Document Format.

peak use   The period(s) in a day, week, month, and year during which the services and resources of a library or computer system are most heavily used. Transaction logs, circulation statistics, and gate counts can be compiled and analyzed to reveal recurrent periods of peak use, useful in establishing library hours, anticipating staffing needs, scheduling maintenance, etc.

peasant binding   A parchment bookbinding decorated with painted designs, made for sale to the common people during the 17th and 18th centuries, now more rare than leather bindings of the same period, which were more expensive.

pecia system   Latin for "piece." A system of book production used in Europe from the 13th century on, in which exemplars approved by university authorities were divided by stationers into portions of one or more gatherings that they hired out to scribes and students for hand-copying, a method that speeded manuscript production considerably. Prior to about 1200, books were copied mainly by monastic scribes working in scriptoria. Once book production became a commercial enterprise, stationers in university towns (Paris, Bologna, Oxford, etc.) published lists of texts available for piecemeal copying, stating the price per part for each title. Plural: *peciae*.

peer evaluation   The process in which the job performance of a librarian or other library staff member is assessed by the individual's colleagues and a recommendation made concerning contract renewal or promotion. In academic libraries at institutions that grant librarians faculty status, tenure decisions may also be based on peer evaluation. In libraries in which employment is governed by a collective bargaining agreement, the method of peer evaluation may be determined by contract.

peer review   The process in which the author of a book, article, software program, etc., submits his or her work to experts in the field for critical evaluation, usually prior to publication, a standard procedure in scholarly publishing. In computer programming, source code may be certified by its owner or licenser as *open source* to encourage development through peer review. Synonymous with *juried review*.

peer-reviewed   Said of a scholarly journal that requires an article to be subjected to a process of critical evaluation by one or more experts on the subject, known as *referees*, responsible for determining if the subject of the article falls within the scope of the publication and for evaluating originality, quality of research, clarity of presentation, etc. Changes may be suggested to the author(s) before an article is finally accepted for publication. In evaluation for tenure and promotion, academic librarians may be given publishing credit only for articles accepted by peer-reviewed journals. Some bibliographic databases allow search results to be limited to peer-reviewed journals. Synonymous with *juried* and *refereed*.

peer-to-peer (P2P)   File sharing between Internet users whose computers have been assigned IP addresses and can function as servers (as opposed to downloading files from a centralized source), a method of information exchange that became possible after 1996 when IP addresses were made available to PCs intermittently connected to the Internet, making files stored on them directly accessible to other users. Unlike client-server networks in which certain computers are dedicated to serving others, workstations in a peer-to-peer network have equivalent capabilities.

Peer-to-peer file sharing became the focus of litigation in December 1999, when the Recording Industry Association of America (RIAA) filed suit against Napster Inc. on behalf of five major record labels for facilitating the exchange of music protected by copyright. In September 2003, the American Library Association joined four other library associations in an amicus brief on behalf of peer-to-peer file-sharing companies Grokster and Morpheus in their defense against an infringement suit brought by MGM Studios and 27 other entertainment companies to ensure that file-sharing technology, which can be used to benefit society without infringing intellectual property rights, is not unduly restricted. Joining the five library associations are the Internet Archive (www.archive.org) and Project Gutenberg (www.gutenberg.net/index.shtml). For more information, see the O'Reilly Network's P2P site at: www.openp2p.com.

pen   A handheld implement used in Western cultures to write in ink on papyrus, parchment, vellum, paper, or some other prepared writing surface, as opposed to the brush used for writing in Asian and other cultures. The reed pen (*calamus*) was used in Antiquity and the early Christian period for writing on papyrus. Because of its flexibility, the quill pen was adopted in the 6th century for writing on parchment and vellum. The first five flight feathers of the goose or swan were preferred (the word is derived from the Latin *penna* for "feather"). After removing or trimming the barbs and curing the barrel, the nib of the quill was cut up the center and squared off with a knife. The nib had to be trimmed fairly often because the slit tended to spread open with extended use.

Because ink flows best from a quill pen when it is held perpendicular to the page, medieval scribes propped up their writing material at an angle and controlled the pen with the whole hand, rather than the fingers. Quills are dip pens, so the inkpot or inkhorn had to be kept close at hand. *Pen trials* to test a newly trimmed nib were made on a discarded scrap of vellum before work commenced. Illustrations in medieval manuscripts of scribes at work reveal that copying was a two-handed activity. The pen was held in one hand and a knife in the other to hold down the springy surface of the parchment and erase mistakes quickly. Dip fountain pens consisting of a steel nib mounted in a wooden holder came into use in the late 18th century. Although models with reservoirs appeared in the 1830s, the modern fountain pen did not become widespread until the late 19th century. *See also*: *penwork initial*.

pendant   An additional narrative, statement, or composition that completes or complements another work but is independent of it, for example, an essay illuminating the historical basis of a satirical work.

pending file   A paper or electronic file in which documents pertaining to matters that cannot be immediately resolved are allowed to accumulate until circumstances are more favorable for their disposition. A rapidly growing pending file may be a sign of overwork or a bottleneck in workflow.

pending request   In the OCLC Interlibrary Loan system, a loan request sent by a borrowing library that appears in the message file of a potential lending library.

pen-flourished initial   An initial letter in a medieval manuscript to which the scribe had added fine linear embellishment in the same color ink as the text or a different color (usually red, blue, and/or green). Pen flourishes were also added to other decorative elements such as borders. Compare with *penwork initial*.

pen name   A name used by an author other than his or her real name, usually adopted to conceal identity. A pen name can be an *allonym* (name of an actual person other than the author), a fictitious pseudonym (example: **Avi** for Edward Irving Wortis), a pseudonym based on the author's real name (**Dr. Seuss** for Theodor Seuss Geisel), or a word or phrase that is not a personal name (**Spy** for Sir Leslie Ward).

Pen names were used more commonly during the 19th century when writing was not as respectable as it is today and therefore considered an unsuitable occupation for women (**George Eliot** for Mary Ann Evans Cross). Some authors write under more than one pen name, adopting a different name when writing in a new genre or introducing a new lead character (or set of characters) in a series. An online dictionary of pseudonyms and pen names, titled *a.k.a.*, is available at: www.trussel.com/books/pseudo.htm. Synonymous with *nom de plume*. Compare with *autonym*. *See also*: *eponym* and *pseudandry*.

penny dreadful   A sensational melodrama in the form of a novel or novelette of mystery, crime, or adventure, printed in cheap paperback edition, the equivalent in England of the *dime novel*.

Pentateuch   The first five books of the Old Testament of the Bible, sometimes produced as a separate manuscript by medieval scribes. *See also*: *Hexateuch* and *Octateuch*.

pen trailing   Linear decoration added by the penman to an initial letter in a medieval manuscript, in ink of the same or contrasting color, common particularly in 12th- and 13th-century French manuscripts.

penwork initial   A decorated initial letter in a medieval manuscript or early printed book, done entirely in pen-and-ink, without the application of paint. Medieval scribes used black, brown, red, blue, and green ink. Some examples are very elaborate.

per diem   The rate at which a product or service is billed on a daily basis. Also refers to the maximum amount allowed by an employer for travel expenses (meals, lodging, etc.), usually calculated on the basis of average cost for a given geographic area.

perfect binding   A quick and comparatively inexpensive method of adhesive binding in which the binding edge of the text block is milled to produce a block of leaves and then roughened. Fast-drying adhesive is applied to the uneven surface and the case or cover attached without sewing and backing. Nearly all books published in paperback are bound by this method, which is also used for some hardcover special editions, for example, book club editions. Durability depends on the strength of the adhesive and its capacity to remain flexible over time, usually not as long-lasting as a sewn or stitched binding. Compare with *Otabind*. *See also*: *double-fan adhesive binding*, *hot-melt*, and *notched binding*.

perfecting   The process of printing the second side of a sheet. On a *perfecting press*, both sides are printed in a single pass. Synonymous with *backing up*. *See also*: *register*.

perforating stamp   A mechanical device designed to produce a permanent mark on a sheet of paper or page in a book by punching a pattern of tiny holes in the fibers, once used by libraries to mark ownership but now largely replaced by the rubber stamp. Notaries still use this tool to validate their signatures.

perforation   Cutting or punching a line of small, closely spaced holes or slits along the inner margin of a page, or around matter printed on a sheet, to make a page or portion of a page easier to tear out or off. Also refers to the line of holes produced for that purpose. *See also*: *perforating stamp*.

performance evaluation   The process of judging the competence with which an employee has performed the duties and responsibilities associated with the position for which the person was hired by a company or organization, usually for the purpose of contract renewal or promotion. In libraries, job performance may be evaluated entirely by management or in a process of *peer evaluation*. Synonymous with *performance measurement*. *See also*: *accountability*.

performance indicator   A measure of how well an employee, department, organization, or institution is meeting its goals and objectives, for example, the percentage of borrowing requests received by the interlibrary loan department of a library that are successfully filled within a given period of time.

performance measurement   *See*: performance evaluation.

performer   An individual who plays a visible part in a work created for a medium of performance (play, motion picture, musical composition, dance, etc.). In library cataloging, the names of leading performers may be included as added entries (MARC field 700) in the bibliographic description of a recorded performance (film, videocassette, audiocassette, CD, etc.). *See also*: *composer* and *director*.

Pergamum   An ancient city on the west coast of Asia Minor near the modern town of Bergama, Turkey, the location of a magnificent royal library and museum built during the Hellenistic period by Eumenes II of the Attalid dynasty to rival the great center of learning at Alexandria in Egypt. The use of parchment as a writing surface is believed to have originated at Pergamum.

period   The punctuation mark that indicates the end of an ordinary sentence, also used as a mark of abbreviation. Synonymous with *full point* and *full stop*. *See also*: *dot*.

In history and literature, an interval of time, usually of indefinite beginning and/or ending date(s), characterized by certain events, conditions, or characteristics of style, such as the Romantic period (early 19th century in Europe) or the Victorian period (late 19th century in Britain).

period bibliography   A bibliography limited to works covering a specific period of time, for example, American history of the *colonial period* or the *progressive era*.

periodical   A serial publication with its own distinctive title, containing a mix of articles, editorials, reviews, columns, short stories, poems, and other short works written by more than one contributor, issued in softcover more than once, generally at regular stated intervals of less than a year, without prior decision as to when the final issue will appear. Although each issue is complete in itself, its relationship to preceding issues is indicated by enumeration, usually issue number and volume number printed on the front cover. Content is controlled by an editor or editorial board.

The category includes *magazines*, sold on subscription and at newsstands; *journals*, sold on subscription and/or distributed to members of scholarly societies and professional associations; and *newsletters*, but not proceedings or the other regular publications of corporate bodies as they relate primarily to meetings. Nor are newspapers formally classified as periodicals—although many libraries store newspapers with magazines and journals, separate values are assigned for periodicals and newspapers in the 008 code of the MARC record to indicate type of serial, and the statement in *AACR2* that serials include periodicals, newspapers, annuals, proceedings, and numbered monographic series implies that newspapers are not considered periodicals.

Periodicals are published by scholarly societies, university presses, trade and professional associations, government agencies, commercial publishers, and nonprofit organizations. The most comprehensive directory of periodicals is *Ulrich's International Periodicals Directory* published annually by R.R. Bowker, available in the reference section of libraries in the United States. Content is indexed in finding tools called *periodical indexes* and *abstracting services*, usually by subject and author.

Most academic libraries bind all the issues for a given publication year in one or more physical volumes. The bibliographic volumes are numbered consecutively, starting with number one for the first year the title was issued. Periodicals are usually shelved alphabetically by title in a separate section of the library stacks. In some libraries, current issues are shelved separately from the back files, which may be converted to microfiche or microfilm to conserve space. Microform reader-printer machines are provided for viewing and making copies. Periodicals published by the U.S. federal government may be shelved by SuDocs number in a separate section reserved for government documents. For many print periodicals, content is also available electronically in full-text bibliographic databases or via the publisher's Web site. Some periodicals are born digital and never issued in print (*example*: *Slate* published by Microsoft and available at: slate.msn.com). *See also*: *frequency*, *holdings statement*, and *one shot*.

periodical index   A cumulative list of periodical articles in which the citations are entered by subject (or in classified arrangement) and sometimes under the author's last name, separately or in a single alphabetic sequence. Periodical indexes may be general (*example*: ***Reader's Guide to Periodical Literature***), devoted to a specific academic discipline (***Education Index***) or group of disciplines (***Humanities Index***), or limited to a particular type of publication (***Alternative Press Index***). In libraries, periodical indexes are available in print and as bibliographic databases, online or on CD-ROM. Compare with *abstracting service*. *See also*: *H.W. Wilson*.

periodical stand   A piece of display furniture with sloping shelves used in libraries to display current issues of periodicals face out, not as compact as conventional shelving but more accessible to browsers. The sloping shelf may be hinged to allow a limited number of back issues to be stored on a flat shelf behind it.

period printing   The production of books or other printed publications in a style appropriate to the period of time in which the material was originally issued. Compare with *facsimile*.

Also, the production of a book in a style resembling that of an earlier period, although the text may have been written by a contemporary author, usually conceived by the publisher as a promotional device.

period subdivision   *See*: chronological subdivision.

period table   In Dewey Decimal Classification, a table giving chronological time periods with their notation. For the literatures of many cultures, period tables are included in the main schedules. They vary in length, depending on the literary history of the culture.

Example:

895.8 Burmese literature
PERIOD TABLE
　　1 Early period to 1800
　　2 1800–1900
　　3 1900–2000
　　4 2000–

For works not limited to a specific language, period notation is taken from Table 1— 0901–0905 of the auxiliary schedules.

peripheral   A device used in conjunction with a computer that is not an indispensable or inseparable part of it. Microcomputer peripherals are used for input (keyboard, mouse, scanner), output (printer, monitor, audio speakers), storage (floppy disk, CD-

ROM), and communication (modem). The trend has been to build peripherals into PCs, especially laptops. Synonymous with *auxiliary equipment*. *See also*: *central processing unit*.

periphrasis   Saying something in a less direct, more roundabout way. Synonymous in this sense with *circumlocution*. Also refers to speech or writing that uses an excess of words to convey an idea or concept that could be expressed more succinctly. Compare with *paraphrase*.

perk   An advantage enjoyed by an employee over and above the normal benefits to which the position is entitled, for example, exemption from overdue fines for the staff of some libraries.

permanence   The quality of library materials designed to last indefinitely without significant deterioration, defined by preservation librarians as a change of 1 percent or less in 100 years. *See also*: *permanent paper*.

permanent ink   A type of visible ink used in applying ownership marks to library materials because it cannot be easily removed.

permanent paper   Paper manufactured to resist chemical deterioration that occurs as a result of aging. The most important factor in permanence is a minimum pH of 7.0 (neutral). Acid-free paper is preferred in library and archival materials because it contains low levels of lignin, an acidic substance that causes paper documents to yellow and become brittle over time. The acid paper used for printing books and other publications during the 19th and early 20th centuries has created a major preservation imperative for research libraries and special collections. Some permanent papers are buffered with an alkaline substance to counteract acids that develop after manufacture or are introduced from an outside source.

ANSI/NISO has established a standard (Z39.48) for the permanence of paper used in materials for libraries and archives, based on specifications for acidity, tear resistance, alkaline reserve, fiber content, and residual amounts of certain substances used in manufacture (rosin, chlorine, etc.). Under normal use and storage conditions, paper meeting the ANSI standard should last for several hundred years without significant deterioration. In books, compliance is indicated by the mathematical symbol for infinity ∞ printed inside a circle on the copyright page or in the colophon. Synonymous with *acid-free paper*, *durable paper*, and *non-acidic paper*.

permission   Authorization, usually granted in writing by the copyright holder, to quote or excerpt passages of text or reproduce illustrations from a work protected by copyright law. Failure to obtain permission may constitute *infringement*. *See also*: *Copyright Clearance Center, Inc.*

permissions copy   A copy of a book containing quoted or excerpted material sent to the copyright holder at first publication to confirm that passages were used in accordance with the permissions granted.

permuted index   A type of subject index in which a string of significant words or phrases, usually extracted from the title of a work or assigned as content descriptors by an indexer, are rotated to bring each word or phrase into first-word position in the alphabetical sequence of entries. For example, in the subject index to *America: History and Life*, the string of descriptors assigned to the article titled "Library Services and the African-American Intelligentsia Before 1960" (*Libraries & Culture* 33: 91–97) is rotated to produce the following index entries:

Blacks. Higher education. Intellectuals. Libraries. 1900–1960.
Higher education. Intellectuals. Libraries. Blacks. 1900–1960.
Intellectuals. Libraries. Blacks. Higher education. 1900–1960.
Libraries. Blacks. Higher education. Intellectuals. 1900–1960.

per search   A database for which access is billed by the search, rather than by subscription. The charge may be a fixed amount per search, as in OCLC *FirstSearch*, or based on connect time.

Persistent URL (PURL)   A type of URL (Uniform **R**esource **L**ocator) that does not point directly to the location of an Internet resource, but rather to an intermediate resolution service (*PURL server*) that associates the stable **PURL** with the actual URL, and returns the URL to the client, which then processes the request in the usual manner. PURLs were developed through OCLC participation in the Internet Engineering Task Force (IETF) Uniform Resource Identifier working groups as an interim solution to the problem posed by URL changes (lack of persistence) in the MARC description of Internet resources. They are an intermediate step on the path to URNs (Universal Resource Names) in Internet information architecture. URL: purl.oclc.org.

personal archives   A category of collecting archives devoted to preserving the private papers and memorabilia of one or more persons or of a family or group of families. In the United States, the presidential libraries function as archives for the personal papers of the presidents.

personal author   The person primarily responsible for the literary, musical, artistic, or intellectual content of a creative work, whose full name is entered in the statement of responsibility area of the bibliographic description when the item is cataloged. Compare with *corporate author*. *See also*: *joint author* and *pseudonym*.

personal computer (PC)   Any microcomputer designed for individual use, usually in a personal workspace or in travel, consisting of a CPU and associated peripheral devices. The term is often restricted to IBM-compatible microcomputers in which the hardware is controlled by Intel and the operating system by Microsoft. A PC may function as a stand-alone workstation or be connected to a network. In a LAN, PCs may function as client workstations or as file servers. *See also*: *laptop*.

personal data   Information about an individual person, such as name, social security number, occupation, martial status, etc. Most public and academic libraries maintain records of the names, addresses, and phone numbers of registered patrons. Although personal information in the library patron record is confidential, the federal government can gain access to it under the provisions of the *USA Patriot Act*.

personal digital assistant (PDA)   A computer small enough to fit in the palm of the hand or in a small pocket. Some models accept handwritten input; others are equipped with a small keyboard. Because of their small size, most PDAs do not include a disk drive. Their capabilities are therefore limited to scheduling, note-taking, simple calculations, and storing addresses and phone numbers, but some models include slots into which modems and other peripheral devices can be inserted to allow users to exchange e-mail, access the Web, and upload/download information. Synonymous with *handheld computer*, *palmtop*, and *pocket computer*.

personal identification number *See*: PIN.

personal name The name given to an animate being, real or imaginary. In the case of a human being, usually a forename and surname or family name, but sometimes a single name (*examples*: **Moses, Socrates**, etc.), used as the main entry when works by the person are listed in the library catalog. In a subject heading, the name may be followed by a parenthetical qualifier for clarification, as in **Tarzan (Fictitious character)**. A qualifier is also added to the personal name of a nonhuman being to indicate species, as in **Dolly (Sheep)**. Compare with *corporate name* and *geographic name*. *See also*: *nickname* and *pseudonym*.

personal papers In archives, the private documents and related materials accumulated by an individual in the course of a lifetime (letters, diaries, legal documents, etc.). Personal papers are subject to the owner's disposition, in contrast to official papers, which may be subject to the disposition of an employer or government. *See also*: *papers*.

personal Web page A Web page maintained by or for an individual for the purpose of acquainting other Internet users with the views, activities, or works of the person whose name is identified with it, sometimes installed at the author's expense on a server maintained by a commercial Internet service provider (ISP). Synonymous with *personal homepage*.

personnel *See*: human resources.

pertinence In information retrieval, the extent to which a document retrieved in response to a query actually satisfies the information need, depending on the user's current state of knowledge—a narrower concept than *relevance*. Although a document may be relevant to the subject of the inquiry, it may already be known to the searcher, written in a language the user does not read, or available in a format the researcher is unable or unwilling to use.

pest management Physical and chemical methods employed by a library or archive to control or eliminate living organisms that infest collections (mildew, mould, insects, rodents, etc.), for example, freezing or fumigation. *Integrated pest management* (IPM) strategies begin with careful identification of the nature and habits of the offender(s), then rely on nonchemical preventive methods as the first line of defense (control of climate, entry points, food sources, etc.). Chemical treatments are usually reserved for infestations of crisis proportions and pests that do not succumb to less toxic alternatives. *Conservation OnLine (CoOL)* provides information about pest management at: palimpsest.stanford.edu/bytopic/pest.

pH A chemical symbol representing the concentration of hydrogen ions in a given substance in aqueous solution, a standard measure of its acidity or alkalinity (basicity) on a scale of 0–14, with 0 = strongly acidic and 14 = strongly alkaline, used in preservation to detect acid paper, board, etc. Since pH is a logarithmic measure, each unit on the scale represents a factor of 10, with 7.0 (the pH of pure water) the neutral point. In papermaking, a product with a pH of 6.0 or higher is considered acid-free, but a pH of 7.0+ is often preferred to neutralize residual acidity that may develop over time.

pharmacopoeia   A book or online resource that lists drugs, chemical compounds, and biological substances, providing information on molecular structure and properties, therapeutic uses, derivatives, and sometimes formulas for manufacture, with tests for establishing identity, purity, strength, etc. (*example*: ***The Merck Index*** or ***PDR: Physicians' Desk Reference***). Most libraries keep the current edition of at least one modern pharmacopoeia in the reference section.

philatelic library   A library devoted to the history of postage stamps and stamp collecting, with a collection consisting of books and periodicals on philately, auction catalogs, government documents, maps, clippings, etc., for example, the American Philatelic Research Library in State College, Pennsylvania (www.stamplibrary.org).

philately   The collection and study of postage stamps and related materials, usually as a hobby. *See also*: *philatelic library*.

phoenix   A complete revision of a class in Dewey Decimal Classification. Synonymous with *phoenix schedule* (see *revision*).

phone book   *See*: telephone directory.

phonogram   A written sign, symbol, or character that represents a sound, syllable, or word spoken in a language, as opposed to an ideogram that represents an object, idea, or concept without phonetically expressing the sound of its name. The Latin alphabet is a set of phonograms.

phonograph record   A thin, flat disk, usually made of vinyl, impressed on one or both sides with a continuous spiral groove in which audible sounds are recorded. As the disk revolves on a playback machine called a *record player*, the groove causes a stylus to vibrate, producing electrical impulses in a cartridge that can be amplified as sound. The most common playing speed is 33⅓ rpm (long-playing), but 78 and 45 rpm disks were also manufactured. Audio compact discs have superseded phonograph records in the retail market for sound recordings, but there is still a market for secondhand records, some of which have become collectible. In libraries, "vinyl" is preserved primarily for its archival value. In *AACR2*, the term "sound disc" is used in the physical description area of the bibliographic record for a phonograph record, with "analog" given as type of recording. Synonymous with *audiodisc* and *gramophone record*. *See also*: *record album*.

photo CD (PCD)   A digital imaging system developed by Kodak that enables a photofinisher to record, organize, and store large numbers of high-resolution photographs (negatives, slides, or prints) on compact disc. Some film processors offer the medium as an add-on to conventional film processing. Various graphics software packages have been designed to support the PCD file format. A similar system, called *Picture*

CD, has been developed for consumer use. It allows images to be preformatted for commercial printing and for digital transmission and display. The term *photo CD* is also used for a compact disc produced by such an imaging system.

photocopier   A machine available in most libraries for making xerographic copies of documents, usually in black and white. Some photocopiers are capable of enlarging or reducing the size of the original. Most copiers are coin-operated, with payment by the page in cash or by debit card (fee varies). Sophisticated photocopy machines available in commercial copy shops are capable of color copying and handling large jobs that require collating and stapling. Compare with *reader-printer*. *See also*: *copy card*.

photocopy   A macroform photographic reproduction of printed or graphic material, produced directly on a sheet of paper or other opaque surface, in black and white or color, usually by radiant energy through contact or projection, a process known as *xerography*. Photocopy machines are available in most libraries for making hard copies of materials that may not be removed from the premises (reference books, closed reserves, periodicals, etc.). Photocopying is subject to the fair use provisions of U.S. copyright law. *See also*: *preservation photocopy*.

Also refers to a photographic copy of an existing photograph, as opposed to a duplicate print made from the same negative.

photograph   The unique negative image produced on chemically sensitized film when it is exposed to light through a focusing lens. Also, the repeatable positive image printed in any size on light-sensitive paper after exposed film has been developed. *Photography* is the science, technology, and art of producing photographic images. Photographs were originally produced in black and white, with or without subsequent tinting, but color film is used in modern photography. Synonymous with *still*. Compare with *motion picture*. *See also*: *aerial photograph*, *photomap*, *photomontage*, and *photomosaic*.

In libraries, photographs are collected as original prints and reproductions. They are also published as illustrations in books and periodicals. Still photographs are also digitized for use as illustrations in documents available online and on CD-ROM. *See also*: *stock photograph*.

photogravure   An illustration or print made from an image etched or engraved on a metal plate or cylinder by any one of several photographic processes. Also refers to the intaglio technique used to print such images. Synonymous with *gravure*.

photomap   An aerial photograph on which cartographic information is superimposed, for example, an aerial photograph of a major city with lines of various colors superimposed to indicate subway routes.

photomontage   A creative work in which several photographs, or portions of photographs, are combined to form a single composite image (montage). The effect can be achieved by cutting and pasting together the component parts, by exposing the same negative several times, or by combining several negatives in the developing process to produce a single composite print. Compare with *photomosaic*.

In motion pictures, a similar effect is achieved in time, rather than space, by showing a selection of images in such rapid succession that in the mind of the viewer they are associated in a way that gives them meaning not apparent when viewed separately or at a slower pace.

photomosaic   An aerial map made by combining several aerial photographs, or portions of them, in a way that covers a specific area of the surface of the earth or another celestial body. Compare with *photomontage*.

Photostat   A copy of a document made by photographic process, using a Photostat machine. The first copy is a negative image. If a positive image is desired, a positive Photostat must be made from the negative. A photostatic copy can be a reduction, an enlargement, or the same size as the original. The term is also used in a more general sense to mean a *photocopy* made by any means.

phrase   Grammatically speaking, two or more words that convey a single concept or thought or that constitute a part of a sentence that does not contain a subject or predicate. An *adjectival phrase* is a noun modified by one or more adjectives (*examples*: **digital archives** and **small press**). In a *prepositional phrase*, two words are joined by a preposition (**gone to press** and **out of print**).

phylactery   A narrow banner or ribbon extending from the mouth or held in the hand of a human figure drawn in a medieval manuscript, inscribed with the individual's name or words spoken by the person depicted. This technique for combining text with graphics survives in contemporary cartoons in the balloons used to convey speech or thought.

physical carrier   The physical medium in or on which data, sound, images, etc., are stored, for example, magnetic tape or disk. For some categories of material, the medium may be permanently encased in a protective housing made of another material (plastic, metal, etc.) that is integral to the item, as in a floppy disk or Zip disk (*AACR2*). The same work may be stored in or on more than one type of physical carrier, for example, on film, videocassette, and DVD. Compare with *container*.

physical description   In library cataloging, the area of the bibliographic record (MARC field 300) in which the extent of an item is recorded. For books, extent of item includes the number of volumes, leaves or pages, columns, plates, and the presence of illustrations, maps, and/or accompanying material. The physical description also gives the dimensions and format of the item. In most cases, the physical description of a book (*example*: **xiv, 508 p. : ill. ; 22 cm.**) is shorter than that of a nonprint item (*example*: **3 filmstrips : col. ; 35 mm. + 3 sound cassettes + 3 guides**). Synonymous with *collation*.

physical processing   The activities carried out by the technical processing department of a library to prepare items for use by patrons. The specific techniques used in physical processing depend on the format of the item. A book is usually stamped with at least one ownership mark, labeled, jacketed, and barcoded. A magnetic strip may also be applied to prevent theft. Physical processing also includes mending, repairing, and rebinding in libraries that have an in-house bindery. ***See also***: *preprocessing*.

piano score   An arrangement for solo piano of a vocal, instrumental, or orchestral work, written or printed on two staves.

piano [violin, etc.] conductor part   A performance part for a specific instrument in an ensemble work, to which cues have been added for the other instruments, to enable the performer to conduct while performing (*AACR2*).

pica   In typography, a standard measurement based on a unit of type 12 points in size (about 4.2 mm or ⅙ inch wide), used to indicate line length and spacing. On the hand typewriter, pica is the larger of the two most common type sizes, having 10 characters per linear inch, as opposed to *elite* with 12 characters per linear inch.

pick-up location   The place to which an item requested on interlibrary, intercampus, or intracampus loan is delivered and stored until the borrower responds to notification of its arrival, usually the circulation desk or interlibrary loan office of the library from which it was requested. Online catalogs that provide an electronic request option may permit the borrower to specify pick-up location in the initial request.

PICS   *See*: **P**latform for **I**nternet **C**ontent **S**election.

pictogram   *See*: pictograph.

pictograph   A sign in the form of a picture representing or suggesting the thing signified, for example, a street sign bearing a symbol of a person reading a book to indicate that a library is located in the vicinity. Also refers to a prehistoric drawing made on a rock surface, such as the side of a cliff or the wall of a cave, one of the earliest forms of "written" communication. Synonymous with *pictogram*.

pictorial   A term used in the book trade to refer to a book with a picture on the cover, exclusive of the dust jacket. The image may be limited to the front or back cover or extend across the spine to occupy both covers.

pictorial dictionary   *See*: visual dictionary.

pictorial map   A map on which small drawings or pictographs are used to indicate the geographic distribution and/or concentration of physical features, economic resources, demographic characteristics, etc. The meaning of the symbols representing the variables is given in the legend.

picture   A two-dimensional visual representation or image large enough to be easily viewed without magnification, usually rendered in black and white or color on a flat, opaque surface. The term includes paintings, drawings, art prints, photographs, reproductions, illustrations, clippings of pictorial matter, etc., and is often used in a generic sense when a more specific word is inappropriate. *See also*: *picture book*, *picture file*, and *picture library*.

Also used synonymously with *motion picture*.

picture bible   A medieval Bible in which the text, renarrated in abridged form, is accompanied by brief commentaries and extensively illustrated. Included in this category are the *Bible historiale*, *Bible moralisée*, and *Biblia Pauperum*.

picture book   A book consisting mainly of visual content, with little or no text, intended mainly for children of preschool age but sometimes of interest to adults because of the artistic quality of the illustrations and/or the originality of the text, often used by children's librarians in storytelling. Published in large format, picture books are frequently oblong in shape to give the artist a broader canvas. Compare with *picture storybook*. *See also*: *Amelia Frances Howard-Gibbon Illustrator's Award*, *big book*, *Caldecott Medal*, and *Greenaway Medal*.

picture collection   *See*: picture library.

picture cycle   A series of illustrations in a medieval manuscript, usually appearing on the same page, on successive pages, or at major divisions in the text, forming a set because they are related in subject and often similar in treatment, for example, scenes of events in the life of the Virgin traditionally associated with the canonical hours in a Book of Hours, or seasonal labors traditionally associated with the months of the year in calendars. When it introduces the main text, such a series is a *prefatory cycle*.

picture dictionary   *See*: visual dictionary.

picture file   A collection of mounted or unmounted photographs, illustrations, art prints, clippings, and other images, usually small enough to be filed in folders and stored in a filing cabinet. In libraries, the files may be arranged by subject, theme, name of artist, or other characteristic. *See also*: *jumbo file* and *vertical file*.

picture library   A library collection consisting primarily of visual documents (prints, photographs, illustrations, posters, postcards, clippings, etc.), mounted or unmounted. The largest collections are maintained by national libraries and museums. Indexing is usually limited to a specific collection. Digitization has made picture collections more accessible. The Library of Congress maintains an online Prints & Photographs Reading Room at: lcweb.loc.gov/rr/print. For more information on picture libraries, please see the entry by Hilary Evans in the *International Encyclopedia of Information and Library Science* (Routledge, 2003).

picture storybook   A short book containing one or more simple narratives accompanied by illustrations coordinated with the text, intended for children of at least third-grade reading level. Compare with *picture book* and *storybook*.

piece   A fragment or portion of a document in any format that has become detached from the whole by cutting, tearing, breaking, or some other physical means, accidental or intentional, or as a result of normal wear and tear. Compare with *part*.

In archives, the most basic unit of description and arrangement that can be retrieved from a repository as a separate and distinct entity under its own reference, regardless of format. If a file of documents is described as a single unit, a document within that file would not be considered a piece; however, a single document once part of a file, such as a letter or memorandum, might be a piece, provided the file as a whole is not made a unit of description.

Synonymous in music with a *single composition*.

pie chart   A graphical representation of statistical data in the form of a circle divided into pie-shaped slices, the relative size of each piece indicating percentage of the whole, a technique used to show the relative proportions of budget allocations, funding by source, etc.

Pierpont Morgan Library *See*: Morgan Library, The.

pigment The coloring matter in paint, usually an insoluble powder mixed with water or oil. The pigments used in medieval manuscript painting were mineral, vegetable, and animal extracts, usually pulverized or soaked out, then mixed with a binding medium such as glair (clarified egg white). Other ingredients (gum arabic, honey, chalk or eggshell) might be added to alter color, texture, and opacity. Some pigments were obtained locally (turnsole); others like *lapis lazuli* had to be imported from distant locations. During the early Middle Ages, monastic scribes and illuminators prepared their own pigments, but as manuscript production became more commercial, prepared ingredients could be purchased from an apothecary or stationer.

pigskin A tough covering material made from the skin of a pig, used for its strength and durability, especially in binding large, heavy books. The grain of pigskin can be distinguished from morocco by small punctures in groups of three where the bristles were once attached, interconnected by a distinctive crisscross pattern. Popular in Germany from the mid-16th to mid-17th century, pigskin was usually alum-tawed, a process that turned it a whitish color.

pilot A small-scale experimental study conducted in advance of a full-scale research project to test an initial hypothesis, research design, or methodology or to determine whether a large-scale study is necessary. Also, a preliminary test or prototype of a system, program, or solution, designed to determine the feasibility of implementation on a wider scale.

PIN An acronym for *personal identification number*, a code used in automated systems to identify authorized users. Whether the PIN is created by or issued to the user depends on the policy governing access to the system. The practice originated in the banking industry and is used in some libraries and library systems to verify that a patron is registered to use electronic resources restricted by licensing agreement.

pinyin (PY) A system of writing the Chinese language in the roman alphabet, used by the news media, by the U.S. government, and throughout the world. In 1997, the Library of Congress announced its intention to begin converting bibliographic records created in the older Wade-Giles (WG) system to the new pinyin standard for romanizing Chinese, a decision that will affect millions of authority records and is expected to facilitate the international exchange of bibliographic data. The Library of Congress maintains a Web page on its *Pinyin Conversion Project* at: www.loc.gov/catdir/pinyin.

pipe roll A roll of parchment used to record the annual audit at exchequer of the king's revenues and expenses. Of interest primarily to historians, the pipe rolls are the oldest and longest series of public records in England, continuing without significant interruption from 1156 to 1832.

piracy *See*: copyright piracy *and* pirated edition.

pirated edition An edition issued in violation of existing copyright law, without permission of the author or copyright holder, usually outside the country in which it was originally published to avoid the legal consequences of infringement. Compare with *authorized edition* and *unauthorized edition*.

pixel   A neologism coined from the term "picture element," any one of the tiny dots of uniform illumination that in the aggregate comprise the image on a television screen or computer monitor. Pixels may be binary (black and white) or multivalued to display colors or gradations of a gray scale. A pixel on a color screen is a combination of three dots—blue, green, and red. To see the pixels on a computer monitor, try wiping the surface of the screen with a clean, damp cloth or tissue. Synonymous with *pel*. *See also*: *bitmap*.

PLA   *See*: Public Library Association.

placard   *See*: poster.

place index   *See*: geographic index.

place name   *See*: geographic name.

place of publication   The geographic location in which an edition of a work is issued, usually given on the title page of a book as the city (or city and state) and sometimes more completely on the verso. In library cataloging, place of publication is one of the elements recorded in the publication, distribution, etc., area of the bibliographic description.

place subdivision   *See*: geographic subdivision.

plagiarism   From the Latin *plagiarius*, meaning "kidnapper." Copying or closely imitating the work of another writer, composer, etc., without permission and with the intention of passing the results off as original work. In publishing, copyright law makes literary theft a criminal offense. At most colleges and universities, plagiarism is considered a moral and ethical issue, and instructors impose penalties on students who engage in it. Plagiarism can be avoided by expressing a thought, idea, or concept in one's own words. When it is necessary to paraphrase closely, the source should be documented in a footnote or endnote, in the same manner as a direct quotation.

The use of the Internet to appropriate the ideas or expressions of another has been dubbed *cyberplagiarism*. The cut-and-paste capability of most word processing and Web browser software has facilitated plagiarism. Submission of an essay or term paper purchased prewritten from an online paper mill is one of the most flagrant forms of plagiarism. Astute instructors keep abreast of the latest techniques for detecting this and other forms of cheating. Compare with *forgery*.

plagiary   Work offered as original that has, in fact, been copied (plagiarized) from another source, usually without permission.

plain text   Text that can be read by most text editors and word processing software because it has not been encrypted and does not include formatting for page layout or content definition, for example, files in ASCII code. Also spelled *plaintext*. Synonymous with *vanilla text*. Compare with *rich text*.

plan   A large-scale (1:5,000 or greater) map of a relatively small area, such as a university campus, small park, garden, battlefield, or site on which a building or complex of buildings stands, showing relative position on a horizontal plane. An *architectural plan* shows the internal arrangement of a building, or room in a building, rather than its site. *See also*: *floor plan*.

planimetric map   A map showing locations and distances on a horizontal plane, with no indication of elevation, as distinct from a relief map showing height and/or depth of surface (relative to sea level if the subject is a portion of the surface of the earth).

plaquette   From the French word for a small, thin plate or slab. A small circular or oval tablet with a design in relief cast in bronze or lead from a wax mold, originally used during the Renaissance to decorate boxes and other personal items. According to Geoffrey Glaister, writing in the *Encyclopedia of the Book* (Oak Knoll/British Library, 1996), metal dies for casting plaquettes were sometimes used in Italian book-binding of the 16th century to stamp designs in relief on leather bindings, which were subsequently hand-painted. *See also*: *cameo binding*.

plat   A diagram or map drawn to scale, showing boundaries, subdivisions, and other important data for a relatively small piece of land, established by survey, usually for legal purposes.

plate   Illustrative matter in a book or other publication usually printed on a leaf of different quality paper than the text, with the reverse side often blank or bearing a descriptive legend. Plates are usually inserted in the sections after gathering, either distributed throughout the text or in one or more groups. A *tissued plate* is separated from the facing page by a loose sheet of interleaved tissue paper, usually to prevent offset or rubbing.

Because they are not integral to the gathering, plates are excluded from the pagination; however, they are usually numbered in roman or arabic numerals and listed in order of appearance in a separate part of the front matter. In the bibliographic record created to represent an item in the library catalog, the number of leaves or pages of plates is indicated in the physical description area, following extent of text. Compare with *cut*. *See also*: *color plate*, *double plate*, *monochrome plate*, and *plate number*.

Originally, a flat piece of wood or sheet of metal used to print, emboss, or engrave a design, illustration, or image on paper, vellum, or some other printing surface. In modern printing, photomechanical plates are used to print both text and illustrations.

plate number   One of the numbers assigned sequentially to illustrations printed separately from the text in a book, pamphlet, periodical, or other publication, appearing on the same page as the plate, sometimes followed by a caption. In a book, the plates are often listed by number in the front matter to facilitate reference.

Also, a designation assigned to an item of music by the publisher, consisting of an abbreviation, initials, or words identifying the publisher, sometimes followed by a number corresponding to the number of pages or plates, usually printed at the foot of each page and sometimes on the title page (*AACR2*). In music cataloging, a plate number is recorded in the note area of the bibliographic description (*example*: **Pl. no.: B. & H. 8797-8806**). Compare with *publisher's number*.

platform   Originally referred to a specific type of computer hardware architecture, but the term now includes both the hardware and operating system installed on the CPU, usually for a model or entire family of computers (*examples*: **Windows**, **Macintosh**, **UNIX**). The term *cross-platform* is used in reference to devices, application programs, and data formats designed to function on more than one type of computer system.

Platform for Internet Content Selection (PICS)   A specification for associating metadata with Internet content, designed to support content rating and filtering services. PICS was developed in the mid-1990s by the Recreational Software Advisory Council and the World Wide Web Consortium (W3C) to give parents and teachers, concerned about explicit violence and sex, a degree of voluntary control over what children can access on the Internet, but it can also be used for other types of labeling, for example, code signing and privacy. URL: www.w3.org/PICS.

play   A literary work in prose or verse that presents a narrative in words and action, intended for live performance on a stage by a cast of players. In the earliest known dramas, performed at religious festivals in ancient Greece, a clear distinction was maintained between comedy and tragedy. Plays are written for adults or children by a *playwright*, usually in one or more major divisions called *acts*. When published in collections, they are indexed by author, title, subject, and dramatic style in *Play Index*, published by H.W. Wilson. Compare with *screenplay*. *See also*: *acting edition*, *closet drama*, *masque*, *melodrama*, *miracle play*, *morality play*, *mystery play*, *one-act play*, *script*, *teleplay*, and *thesis play*.

In publishing, the emphasis or attention given a news story or article by virtue of its position in the publication (front or back), placement on the page (top or bottom), or typographical treatment (*played up* or *played down*). Also, to operate any device designed to receive broadcast signals (radio or television) or reproduce sound recorded on any medium (phonograph record, audiotape, compact disc, videotape, etc.). *See also*: *playback*.

playback   Any recording heard or viewed as soon as it is produced, usually to enable the performers, producers, etc., to evaluate its quality and select the version to be used for manufacture and distribution. In a more general sense, the reproduction of sounds and/or images from the medium on which they are recorded (phonograph record, audiotape, compact disc, videotape, DVD, etc.). A *playback device* is capable of reproducing audio and/or video but is not designed for recording.

playbill   A printed poster or circular advertising the performance of a play, usually indicating the names of the actors and actresses cast in the leading roles. Also, the performance program for a play.

playing speed   In sound recording, the speed at which the carrier of a message recorded in a specific medium must be operated to reproduce the sound intended by the manufacturer, for example, $33\frac{1}{3}$ rpm (revolutions per minute) for a long-playing phonograph record, or $1\frac{7}{8}$ ips (inches per second) for an analog audiocassette. Compare with *projection speed*.

playing time   The duration of a nonprint media item that requires equipment for play-back (sound recording, motion picture, videorecording, DVD, etc.). In library cataloging, playing time is given under extent of item in the physical description area of the bibliographic record, as stated on the item. If not readily ascertainable, an approximate length is given.

playwright   The author of a dramatic work written to be read (closet drama) or performed live on a stage, whose name is entered in the statement of responsibility area of the bibliographic description of an edition of the work. The best-known example is William Shakespeare, whose plays are still performed and adapted around the world, more than 400 years after he wrote them. Synonymous with *dramatist*. Compare with *screenwriter*. **See also**: *director* and *performer*.

plot   The organization of incidents or episodes in a narrative work (novel, short story, play, motion picture) in a sequence that unfolds to the reader or viewer the relationship between character and events. Most literary plots present a struggle between opposing forces leading to a conclusion, or *denouement*, in which the author employs an element of suspense to heighten dramatic effect. Complicated plots may include one or more subplots. To encourage patrons to read the original work, libraries do not as a rule purchase resources that provide synopses or plot summaries of literary works. **See also**: *character* and *setting*.

plot summary   A concise account of the sequence of events or incidents in a fairly long narrative work (novel, play, epic poem, etc.). Most libraries do not, as a matter of policy, select series such as *Cliff Notes* and *Masterplots*, which provide plot summaries of literary works, because they are too easily used by students to avoid reading assignments. Synonymous with *synopsis*.

PLR   *See*: **P**ublic **L**ending **R**ight.

plug   To attempt to boost sales and readership of a book by praising its strengths and ignoring or downplaying its weaknesses. Such an endorsement may be unsolicited by the author or publisher. **See also**: *puff*.

In the book trade, a disused slang term for a new book that does not sell.

plug-in   An easy-to-install supplementary program or module designed to extend the capability of a major software package, usually by adding a new feature, for example, an application added to a Web browser that enables it to support nontextual content (graphics, animation, audio, video, etc.). *Netscape* provides a list of browser plug-ins at: wp.netscape.com/plugins/index.html.

plummet   Precursor to the graphite pencil, plummet was a piece of lead alloy, sometimes mounted in a holder, used from the 11th and 12th century for ruling and writing annotations in manuscripts and for underdrawing. Before plummet, medieval scribes and illuminators used hard point and metal point. Synonymous with *lead point*.

ply   A single thickness or layer of paper or fiber laminated or pressed together to build up heavier sheets, as in certain types of board. Thickness is normally indicated by the number of layers (2-ply, 3-ply, etc.). Also refers to one of the twisted strands that make up the sewing thread used in bookbinding.

PMEST   The five main facets in S.R. Ranganathan's *Colon Classification*: personality, matter, energy, space, and time (see *faceted classification*).

pochoir   From the French word meaning "stencil." A method of hand illustration used primarily in deluxe editions in which color is applied by dabbing watercolor ink or paint through a sheet of paper, metal, or celluloid into which a design has been cut, producing an uneven hand-crafted effect not obtainable when color printing is done under pressure or when ink is drawn across a stencil, as in screen printing. The same technique can be used to add color to a preprinted design.

pocket   A receptacle for loose parts (supplements, maps, music parts, etc.) made from a piece of stiff paper or fabric pasted inside the front or back cover of a book. *See also*: *book pocket*.

pocket bible   A portable bible of small size, written in condensed script or printed in small type, used mainly for home study.

pocket computer   *See*: personal digital assistant.

pocket dictionary   A dictionary of the words of a language published in inexpensive paperback edition. Most contain no more than 30,000 to 55,000 words and are small enough to be carried conveniently in a pocket. Some include a thesaurus (*example*: *The Pocket Oxford Dictionary and Thesaurus*). Foreign language dictionaries are often published in small format for the convenience of students and travelers. Compare with *desk dictionary*.

pocket edition   A small, inexpensive portable octavo edition, usually no larger than $6\frac{3}{4} \times 4\frac{1}{4}$ inches in size, called a *paperback* when bound in paper covers.

pocket part   A separately published supplement bound in limp or paper covers and inserted in a pocket inside the front or back cover of a previously published book. Pocket parts are used mainly to update law books and other reference works. Also refers to separately printed material, such as a map or music score, or to nonprint material (usually a floppy disk or CD-ROM), inserted in a pocket inside the cover of a book by the publisher. In library cataloging, the presence of a pocket part is indicated in the physical description area of the bibliographic record.

pocket volume   A binder's term for a book that has a cover made with an inside pocket to hold one or more unbound pocket parts, such as a printed supplement, map, CD-ROM, etc.

poetic license   In poetry, the liberty granted a writer to manipulate conventional word order, rhyme, diction, etc., within the limits of poetic form, to achieve a desired effect. In fiction, the freedom of a writer to alter historical fact or logic in the interest of producing a more interesting or compelling narrative, for example, Shakespeare's use of the Holinshed account of the murder by Donwald of an earlier King Duff as source material for the murder of Duncan in the play *Macbeth*.

poet laureate   Literally, a poet "crowned with laurel." An honorific title and stipend, usually bestowed by a university or head of state on an eminent poet who is expected to compose poems commemorating dates and occasions of national importance and is called upon to read or recite from his or her own works, and from the works of other poets, on special occasions. Poet laureates were originally appointed for life as officers of the royal household in England, where they were expected to compose poems for state occasions, but the post is now conferred mainly as a mark of distinction. In the United States, the Poet Laureate Consultant in Poetry is appointed annually by the Librarian of Congress and receives a stipend.

poetry   A spoken or written work consciously created in metrical form by a speaker or writer who has a gift for imaginative and symbolic use of language. Also, the art of metrical composition, intended to express sublime thought and emotion and give aesthetic pleasure through the ingenious combination of well-chosen words and rhythmic phrases (sound and sense). Poetry is classified by form (ballad, eclogue, elegy, epic, idyl, idyll, lai, limerick, lyric, ode, sonnet, etc.) and often published in anthology. Poems in collections are indexed by first line, last line, and title in *The Columbia Granger's Index to Poetry in Anthologies*. Compare with *prose*. *See also*: *poet laureate*.

point   In printing, a unit of measurement created in 1737 by the French typographer Pierre Fournier, revised by Firmin-Didot in 1770, and formalized in the United States in the 1870s for indicating the body size (height and width) of type and other elements used in typography (rules, borders, etc.). One point equals approximately $\frac{1}{72}$ or 0.013837 of an inch and 1 inch equals 72.25433 points. Before the point system was developed, descriptive terms were used for the various type sizes: nonpareil (6-point), brevier (8-point), pica (12-point), etc. Also, a unit for measuring the thickness of paper and board, one point equal to one-thousandth ($\frac{1}{1000}$) of an inch.

In historical bibliography and the antiquarian book trade, a specific characteristic or peculiarity of printing or binding (usually a minor defect or error) by which copies of a first edition can be distinguished or priority of issue established within an edition that has undergone multiple printings. *See also*: *fingerprint*.

pointillé   From the French verb *pointiller*, meaning "to mark with dots." In hand bookbinding, a style of tooling used in leather-bound deluxe editions, characterized by delicate scrollwork in which the lines are not solid but composed of tiny, closely spaced dots, usually highlighted in gold.

point of access   *See*: access point.

point of service   *See*: service point.

point-of-use instruction   An explanation of how to use a specific resource or research tool (catalog, printed index, abstracting service, bibliographic database, etc.), provided to a library user orally, online, or in print at the time and place assistance is needed, usually by a public services librarian or other trained expert. *See also*: *help screen*.

polaire   The sturdily made leather satchel or case used by monks, scribes, and other literate persons of the medieval period for transporting manuscript books. Most were plain, but examples custom-made for persons of wealth or prominence sometimes bore an insignia or other distinctive design stamped in relief. *See also*: *girdle book*.

polarity   The relationship of the colors or tones of a photographic image to those of the actual object or scene captured on film—*positive* if the image reflects the original, *negative* if the colors/tones are reversed. A bibliographic item composed of more than one photographic image may have *mixed polarity*. The term is also used in reprography to describe the reversal of tones from positive to negative, or vice versa.

polemic   An argument or debate on a controversial subject. Also refers to a person inclined to argument or debate. A skilled debater or writer of polemical works is a *polemicist*. The art or practice of disputation is called *polemics*.

political correctness (PC)   A term that came into widespread use during the early 1990s to describe the influence of liberal political views on American culture, particularly speech and other forms of social behavior, for example, the replacement of the title "chairman" with "chairperson" to avoid the appearance of gender discrimination (this particular problem has not arisen in the library profession because the term "librarian" is gender-neutral). In literary studies, the debate centered around whether to abolish the traditional canon, dominated by works written primarily by males of European descent. Some universities have sidestepped this dilemma by making the debate over political correctness part of the curriculum.

political map   A map showing the political boundaries of nations and states, the political affiliations (formal or informal) of people living within a given geographic area, official names of capital cities, voting districts, etc.

political name   The legally designated name of a geographic feature, location, area, or public entity, which may change as governments change (*example*: **St. Petersburg** to **Petrograd** to **Leningrad** to **St. Petersburg**). Compare with *geographic name*.

poll   Statistical data produced by surveying selected individuals on their opinions concerning an issue or event, usually reported by the institution that conducted or commissioned the survey, for example, the annual *Gallup Poll* of American public opinion, available in the reference section of large public and academic libraries. Sampling methods can influence results.

polyester   A clear, flexible plastic used as a base in photographic film, for encapsulation, and to protect book covers. Polyester is chemically stable, has high tensile strength, and is very resistant to moisture and other chemicals. Trade names are Mylar and Melinex.

polyethylene   A chemically stable, somewhat flexible, translucent waxy plastic with a low melting point, used in conservation to protect brittle paper because it is resistant to acid. Also used as a coating in papermaking to provide finish and add strength. Less expensive than polyester. Nonbiodegradable.

polyglot   A book or series of books containing the same text in several languages, sometimes arranged in parallel columns across facing pages, for example, the polyglot Bibles first published in the 16th century, with the text in Greek, Latin, and Hebrew. *See also*: *parallel title* and *polyglot dictionary*.

polyglot dictionary   A list of the words of a language with a translation of each word into two or more other languages (*example*: *The Multilingual Dictionary of Printing and Publishing* edited by Alan Isaacs). Polyglot dictionaries are usually shelved in the reference section of a library. Compare with *language dictionary*.

polypropylene   A stiff, hard, heat-resistant, chemically stable plastic that can be extruded and cast. It has better clarity than polyethylene and less static charge than polyester. Polypropylene self-adhesive protective book covers can be ordered from library suppliers, preshaped, with peel-off paper backing. Also used as an additive in papermaking. Nonbiodegradable.

polysemy   Having multiple meanings, some of which may overlap. By way of example, the *Oxford English Dictionary* gives 14 definitions of the word "power." In cataloging and indexing, a parenthetical qualifier is usually added to a polysemic subject heading or descriptor for semantic clarification, as in the Library of Congress subject headings **Power (Electronics)** and **Power (Social sciences)**. *See also*: *homograph*.

polyvinyl acetate (PVA)   A transparent, water-based chemical adhesive used in bookbinding to produce a very strong bond. Applied cold, it is allowed to dry naturally for maximum strength and flexibility. PVA is not as strong as hot-melt adhesive, but it is more flexible, longer lasting, and more resistant to cold-crack. For these reasons, it is used in Otabind binding.

polyvinyl chloride (PVC)   A form of plastic that has high chemical resistance but is not chemically stable. Because it emits hydrochloric acid as it ages, it has very limited application in the preservation of documents made of paper. The volatile plasticizers that make it flexible are hazardous to humans. Nonbiodegradable. Abbreviated *vinyl*. Compare with *polyester*.

pontifical   A liturgical book containing the order of service for episcopal offices, the sacraments administered only by popes and bishops (ordination, confirmation, dedication of churches and altars, consecration of liturgical objects, etc.). Pontificals sometimes include illustrations of the equipment used in performing the ceremonies. Medieval examples are often beautifully illuminated.

popular edition   An edition of a book printed on poorer-quality paper than the trade edition, sometimes without illustrations and in a less sturdy cloth or softcover binding, usually sold at a lower price. Some book club editions fall into this category.

popular fiction   Serious works of narrative fiction widely read when first published and superior in quality to pulp fiction but not as enduring as literary fiction (*example*: the novels of **Jeffrey Archer**). *See also*: *bestseller*.

popular name   A shortened or simplified form of the official name by which a company, government agency, or other corporate entity is known (*example*: "The Fed" for Federal Reserve Board).

popular press   A publishing house that issues publications for the mass market, sold at newsstands and in supermarkets and chain stores. Compare with *trade publisher*. *See also*: *mass-market paperback*.

popular reference book   A reference work intended primarily for the general reader, as opposed to one published mainly for use in libraries and related institutions. Unlike specialized reference works that must be ordered from the publisher, popular reference titles are sold retail in trade bookstores. The category includes almanacs, desk dictionaries and thesauri, foreign language dictionaries, world atlases, road atlases, medical encyclopedias, field guides, etc.

pop-up book   A type of novelty children's book, manufactured as early as the 19th century, containing cut-out illustrations ingeniously designed to spring up in three dimensions from the surface of the page when the book is opened or a tab is pulled and fold back down when the page is turned or the tab is pushed in. Because they require special assembly, pop-up books are usually more expensive than standard children's picture books. Most libraries do not, as a matter of policy, select them for circulation because the movable parts are easily damaged. Synonymous with *stand-up book.*

pornography   From the ancient Greek *porne* and *graphos*, meaning "writing about prostitutes." Works of no artistic value, depicting sexuality with the conscious intent to arouse sexual desire. The qualifiers *soft core* and *hard core* are often added to indicate degree of licentiousness. Ownership of print collections is generally limited to private individuals and the special collections of large libraries. Proliferation of pornographic Web sites has been a major impetus for advocates of Internet filtering. In the antiquarian and used book trade, pornographic works are often listed in catalogs under *curiosa, erotica,* or *facetiae.* Compare with *obscenity.* **See also**: *banned book, censorship, cyberporn,* and *expurgated.*

port   A physical connection on a computer or network device, usually in the form of a socket, that allows data to be received from and transmitted to an external device. The number of available ports may determine the number of simultaneous users who may access a system such as an online catalog or bibliographic database. Most libraries reserve a fixed number of ports for local use. Any remaining ports are made available for remote access.

portability   The capacity of an operating system, programming language, or application program to operate independently of a specific hardware platform, usually achieved by designing a different version for each platform or by building in mechanisms for switching between platforms or converting from one type of machine to another.

Portable Document Format (PDF)   The format used for page description in the *Adobe Acrobat* document exchange program. In *Acrobat*, the *PDF Writer* converts most DOS, Windows, UNIX, and Macintosh data files into PDF format. Since the original fonts are embedded in the PDF file, there is no need to install them on the receiving machine. With *Adobe Acrobat Reader* installed at the receiving end, PDF files can be displayed and printed in original format.

In full-text bibliographic databases, a "native PDF" file is received in digital format from the publisher, reproducing the appearance of the original text and images with a high degree of clarity. A "scanned PDF" file is created by running a print copy of the text through a high-quality scanner. The result is then examined closely for legibility.

portal Originally, a general purpose Web site offering a wide variety of resources and services, such as news, weather, directory information, Web searching, free e-mail accounts, chat groups, mailing lists, online shopping, and links to other Web sites (*example*: **America Online**). However, the term is increasingly applied to Web sites that offer such services only within a particular industry, occupation, or field (*example*: *AcqWeb* at: acqweb.library.vanderbilt.edu). *See also*: *library portal*.

portfolio A container designed to hold loose materials (papers, drawings, paintings, prints, photographs, manuscripts, unbound sections of a book, etc.), consisting of two rigid boards joined at the spine by a wide band of cloth, with ties attached to the fore-edge and sometimes to the other edges to prevent sheets from sliding out. Also refers to the contents of such a case.

In publishing, a single- or multivolume work containing plates with little or no text, usually executed by an artist and devoted to a central theme, for example, George Catlin's North American *Indian Portfolio*, a collection of 25 color plates first published in 1844, an artistic success but financial failure for the artist.

In art, a collection of the original works of an artist, usually selected to illustrate range of talent. The term is also used in reference to the entire body of an artist's work.

In business, a comprehensive list of all the securities (stocks, bonds, etc.) owned by an investor or financial institution. Publicly held corporations are required by law to disclose such holdings.

portrait The representational likeness of a person (especially the face), photographed or drawn, painted, or sculpted from life. Most full-length biographies and some biographical reference works include at least one portrait of the *biographee*, often as the frontispiece. A *self-portrait* is a representational likeness of a person made by its subject, who is usually an artist or photographer. Author/illustrator self-portraits are rare in books and manuscripts. Abbreviated *port*. Compare with *caricature*. *See also*: *author portrait* and *portrait miniature*.

In publishing, an illustration, leaf, or book of a height approximately 25 percent greater than its width, the norm in printed publications. Synonymous in this sense with *long way*. Compare with *oblong*. *See also*: *narrow* and *square*.

portrait miniature A painting in a book intended by the artist to be the likeness of an individual who actually lived (sometimes drawn from life), as distinct from a picture of a fictional character or mythological person. The image may be full-figure or from the shoulders up, in some cases occupying an entire page. Portrait miniatures are common in the "book of friends" (*album amicorum*) popular during the 16th and 17th centuries.

position The duties for which an employee is responsible in an organization, usually described in detail in the *position description* used in the hiring process, along with the minimum qualifications considered necessary for satisfactory performance. In libraries, a position usually corresponds to a specific function or closely related group of functions (*cataloger, instruction librarian, interlibrary loan assistant*, etc.) and is associated with a specific rate or range of compensation. As functional needs change, so do the duties and responsibilities required of a specific position. *Digital services librarian* is an example of a comparatively new position. Compare with *rank*.

position description   A written statement providing a general description of the duties and responsibilities associated with a specific position in an organization, the minimum qualifications considered necessary for satisfactory performance, and the rank, compensation, and benefits that the prospective employer is prepared to offer, for use in hiring. Compare with *job description*.

position title   The official name associated with a set of duties and responsibilities within an organization, assigned to an employee at the time of hiring. Each library or library system develops its own set of titles for professional positions, which typically include: access services or circulation librarian, acquisitions librarian, archivist, bibliographer, cataloger, children's librarian, collection management specialist, digital or online services librarian, instruction librarian, media specialist, outreach services librarian, reference librarian, serials librarian, systems librarian, young adult services librarian, library director, etc. As functions are added and dropped, a position title may be changed to reflect current conditions, usually at the time a new person is hired to fill the position.

post binding   A form of expandable loose-leaf binder in which screw posts, usually made of metal or plastic, are inserted through holes prepunched in the leaves to allow them to be individually added or removed. Often used for materials that require regular updating. Post bindings do not open flat, as do ring bindings.

postcard   A picture, photograph, or collage of images, with or without accompanying text or caption, printed on card stock and intended for delivery by post, usually with space on the back for the sender to fill in the name and street address of the recipient and add a brief message. Postcards are usually of standard size (4 × 6 inches in the United States and most other countries), but panoramic landscapes may require a larger format. Considered ephemera, postcards are sometimes archived with the memorabilia of important individuals. Very old or rare postcards, and those commemorating important historical events, may be of value to collectors. Libraries catalog postcards as graphic materials.

post-coordinate indexing   A method of indexing in which the subject headings or descriptors assigned to documents represent simple concepts that the user must combine at the time of searching to retrieve information on a complex subject (*example*: Annotation + Bibliography for "Annotated bibliography"). Synonymous with *coordinate indexing* and *post-coordination*. Compare with *pre-coordinate indexing*. *See also*: *syntax*.

post-coordination   *See*: post-coordinate indexing.

postdated   An item bearing a publication date *later* than the actual date of publication. In *AACR*, the date given on the item is used in cataloging even if it is known to be incorrect, and the correct date is added as an interpolation in square brackets (*example*: **1959 [1958]**), with an explanatory note if necessary. The opposite of *antedated*. Also spelled *post-dated*.

poster A large single sheet of heavy paper or cardboard, usually printed on one side only, with or without illustration, to advertise a product/service or publicize a forthcoming event (meeting, concert, dramatic performance, etc.), intended for display on a bulletin board, kiosk, wall, or other suitable surface. Poster design is a branch of the graphic arts made famous by the 19th-century French artist Henri de Toulouse-Lautrec and his contemporaries. Synonymous with *placard*. Compare with *handbill*. *See also*: *ephemera*.

poster session A conference event at which one or more attendees visually exhibit the salient points of their research, practice, or experimentation on a series of poster-sized sheets mounted on a large upright board behind a table. The presenters make themselves available at the table during the display to answer questions, distribute handouts, and clarify the exhibit to other attendees on a walk-through basis. At large library conferences, poster sessions are usually conducted in the exhibits area during periods that do not conflict with more formal presentations, providing attendees the opportunity to spend as much time as they wish viewing topics of interest. A juried review process is often used to select proposals from abstracts submitted in advance. Because many academic institutions view such sessions as a form of publishing or creative work, they can be helpful to librarians in meeting promotion and tenure requirements.

posthumous A work published for the first time after the death of the author. Works left unfinished at the time of an author's death may be continued by another writer, for example, the completion of Dorothy L. Sayers' unfinished detective novel *Thrones, Dominations* by Jill Paton Walsh (St. Martin's, 1998). *See also*: *redaction*.

posting The assignment in cataloging of a heading to an item in a library collection, or a descriptor to a document in indexing, based on its content, form, or other distinguishing feature. In some subject thesauri, the number of times an authorized term has been assigned is indicated in a *postings note* included in the entry for the term.

postings note A note added in the entry for a descriptor in a thesaurus of indexing terms, indicating the number of times the term has been assigned as a major or minor descriptor to documents indexed, usually since its addition to the authorized list. The note gives the user some idea of the number of entries a search for the term is likely to retrieve. A small number of postings might suggest a search strategy that includes related terms or even broader terms; a large number might suggest the substitution of one or more narrower terms.

postliminary matter *See*: back matter.

postscript A sentence or paragraph following the signature at the end of a letter, or a note written or printed at the close of a composition, conveying a further thought or additional information. In a letter, the postscript usually follows the abbreviation "PS." In a more general sense, any comment or remark appended as an afterthought in speech or writing.

posttest   A quiz or test administered to students following instruction in a specific library skill to assess the effectiveness of pedagogical methods. Ideally, it is administered in conjunction with a pretest for purposes of comparison.

potboiler   A literary work written primarily to earn money for the author and publisher ("to keep the pot boiling"). Such works are usually of little or no artistic merit, but financial pressures are rarely absent from the consideration of writers who have no other source of income, particularly in the early stages of a literary career. The problem with publishing such works at the beginning of a career is that once the author earns a reputation for producing popular works, any future attempt at serious writing is likely to be met with skepticism by reviewers, unless a pseudonym is used.

pounce   *See*: pouncing.

pouncing   Rubbing an abrasive substance such as chalk, wood ash, ground pumice, or pulverized bone (called *pounce*) into the surface of a sheet of parchment or vellum to prepare it for writing and/or painting. The process removes grease, whitens the surface, and raises the nap to provide good "tooth" for the quill pen.

Also refers to the transfer of an image by piercing the edges of an exemplar with tiny holes to enable it to be used as a stencil, more common in bestiaries than in other medieval texts because the animal motifs used by illuminators to decorate initial letters and borders were not easy to copy freehand.

powdered   A leather binding that appears to be covered in a golden cloud, an effect achieved by sprinkling the outer surface with minute flecks of gold or rubbing it with gold leaf in finishing, a form of decoration popular in French binding of the mid-16th century.

power down   To turn a computer off at the power switch. Because RAM chips require electrical power, data will be lost when a computer is powered down unless it is saved to a storage medium (hard disk, floppy disk, etc.).

practicum   A limited period of hands-on work in a library or other information service agency structured to provide an opportunity for a novice to relate theory to practical experience, usually within the student's field(s) of specialization. Compare with *internship*.

praeses   The faculty moderator of a formal academic disputation, responsible for proposing the thesis that the degree candidate (respondent) must defend or oppose. The praeses is expected to participate with a panel of other faculty members in the ensuing debate.

prayer book   A collection of prayers for private devotion, usually organized around a central theme (or themes), used as early as the 8th century as a supplement to the Book of Hours and psalter. The prayer book became especially popular during the late Middle Ages when some very fine illuminated examples were commissioned by wealthy patrons.

preamble   From the Latin *prae* ("before") and *ambulare* ("to go"). An introductory statement or preface to a written document, especially a statute or constitution, stating its purpose. One of the best-known examples is the *Preamble to the United States Constitution*, which establishes the basic principles on which American government is based.

prebinding   *See*: prelibrary binding.

precedence order   *See*: preference order.

precensorship   The restriction of materials from a library collection during the selection process by a collection development librarian or other person authorized to select, based on conscious or unconscious bias. Although the *Library Bill of Rights* of the American Library Association charges librarians to "provide materials and information presenting all points of view on current and historical issues," some studies have found that librarians tend to avoid selecting potentially controversial books and media. The prefix "pre" added to the term "censorship" indicates that restriction occurs *before* library materials are made available to patrons. Compare with *censorship*.

precis   A concise abridgment or summary that captures the essential thought(s) or idea(s) expressed in a longer work and retains something of the original tone and spirit.

PRECIS   *See*: Preserved Context Indexing System.

precision   In information retrieval, a measure of search effectiveness, expressed as the ratio of relevant records or documents retrieved in a search of a database to the total number retrieved in response to the query; for example, in a database containing 100 records relevant to the topic "book history," a search retrieving 50 records, 25 of which are relevant to the topic, would have 50 percent precision (25/50). Synonymous with *relevance ratio*. Compare with *recall*. *See also*: *fallout*.

preconference   A mini-conference scheduled in advance of a longer conference, usually on the preceding day (or days) for attendees who wish to spend additional time meeting with colleagues. Most preconferences are organized around a central theme that may or may not be related to that of the main conference. The theme is usually addressed by a panel, rather than a keynote speaker, with break-out sessions on related topics. *Preconferees* are normally charged an additional fee at registration.

pre-coordinate indexing   A method of indexing in which multiple concepts are combined by the indexer to form subject headings or descriptors assigned to documents to facilitate the retrieval of information on complex subjects (*example*: "Libraries and the blind—United States—Directories" instead of Libraries + Blind + United States + Directories). Synonymous with *pre-coordination*. Compare with *post-coordinate indexing*.

predominant name   In authority work, when a person or corporate body is known by more than one name, entry is made under the most commonly known name, whether it is the real name or a nickname, pseudonym, shortened name, or other form. Under this rule, the works of Samuel Langhorne Clemens are cataloged under **Twain, Mark**. In *AACR2*, the predominant name is that which occurs most frequently in (1) the works of a person or works issued by a corporate body or (2) in reference sources, in that order of preference. If no predominance is found, the latest form is used.

preface   A preliminary statement at the beginning of a book, usually written by the author, stating the origin, scope, purpose, plan, and intended audience of the work and including any afterthoughts and acknowledgments of assistance, usually in the final paragraphs. When written by a person *other* than the author, the preliminary statement is called a *foreword*. Abbreviated *pref.*

The preface or foreword is distinct from the *introduction*, which addresses the subject of the work and prepares the reader for the treatment to follow. When a new edition is published, the preface may be rewritten to alert the reader to the extent of additions or changes in the text, but the introduction usually remains unchanged. The preface or foreword normally follows the dedication and precedes the introduction in the front matter of a book.

The term is sometimes used in the title of a book-length treatment of a subject to indicate that the author's comments are introductory or preliminary (*example*: ***A Preface to Eighteenth Century Poetry*** [1963] by James Sutherland).

prefatory cycle   A series of miniatures in an illuminated manuscript serving as an introduction to the following text, usually arranged in square frames or medallions in a design covering the entire page, leaving little or no room for text. Psalter cycles usually depict the life of King David, to whom many of the *Psalms* are attributed, and/or the life of Christ.

preference order   In Dewey Decimal Classification, the order in which one of two or more numbers is to be chosen when different characteristics of a subject cannot be shown in full by number building, indicated in a note, sometimes containing a table of preference (*DDC*). When the class notation can be synthesized to show two or more characteristics, the decision is governed by *citation order*. Synonymous with *order of preference* and *precedence order*.

preferred term   In an indexing language, a descriptive word or phrase selected as an authorized subject heading or descriptor to represent a discrete subject or concept. For the convenience of the user, cross-references to the preferred form are made from synonyms and closely related terms, making materials on the same subject accessible at a single point in the catalog, index, or bibliographic database. Preferred terms and cross-references are usually listed in a printed or online thesaurus to assist users in planning search strategy. ***See also***: *controlled vocabulary*.

prelibrary binding   The binding of new books to meet a higher standard of durability than the normal hardcover publisher's binding. A graphic design similar to that of the original binding is usually preserved on the front cover. In public libraries, *prebinding* is used extensively for children's books, which must withstand heavy wear. Standards for prebinding, issued by the Library Binding Institute, include oversewn sections, a rounded and backed spine, and hinges made of cloth instead of paper. Directory information on prebinders is available in the annual reference serial *Literary Market Place*. Compare with *library edition*. ***See also***: *Bound to Stay Bound*.

preliminaries   Shortened form of *preliminary matter*. In *AACR2*, the title page(s) of a bibliographic item, the verso of the title page(s), any pages preceding the title page(s), and the cover. The term is also used synonymously with *front matter*. Abbreviated *prelims*.

preliminary edition   An edition issued by the publisher prior to the final edition, sometimes to allow time for criticism of the text before the final version is published. In *AACR2*, the title and publication date of a preliminary edition are given in the note area of the bibliographic description of the final edition. Synonymous with *provisional edition*.

preliminary matter   *See*: preliminaries.

prelims   *See*: preliminaries.

premium book   A book given as a reward for action taken by the recipient, such as becoming a member of a book club. Also refers to a book or other item offered as an inducement, for example, to order a certain volume of materials. Librarians apply the same selection criteria used in evaluating materials for purchase.

pre-order searching   In acquisitions, work done by a bibliographic searcher prior to ordering an item, including a search of the library catalog for duplicate and related titles; verifying the name of the publisher and/or distributor, price, availability, and standard number; and locating other pertinent information (terms of licensing agreement, restrictions on use, etc.).

prepaid   *See*: prepayment.

prepayment   In purchasing, an order for which full payment must be made in advance of shipment, usually with the purchase order rather than in response to an invoice. If the order is canceled or the merchandise is returned in compliance with the seller's return policy, a credit may be issued. Small independent vendors and electronic retailers are more likely to require prepayment than large publishers and book jobbers. Most journal publishers require prepayment before beginning a new subscription. Abbreviated *prepay*.

prepayment discount   *See*: discount.

preprint   A portion of a work printed and distributed for a special purpose in advance of the publication date announced for the whole, for example, an article to be published in a periodical or a work selected for inclusion in an anthology or collection. Also, a paper prepared for presentation at a conference, printed in multiple copies in advance of the conference date, usually for distribution to participants and other interested persons. In some academic disciplines, preprints are an important medium of scholarly communication. Also refers to a few copies of an author's manuscript produced by a method such as xerography for circulation within the office of the publisher, usually to facilitate reading, evaluation, and editing. *See also*: *e-print*.

Also refers to an advertising insert printed by a manufacturer to be included in a periodical, sometimes designed to accommodate local copy, such as the names and addresses of sales outlets located in the area of circulation.

preprocessing   One or more steps in physical processing, completed before a new bibliographic item is shipped by the seller to the ordering library.

prepub   An abbreviation of *prepublication*.

prepublication   An adjective referring to activities that occur *before* a work is published, for example, an offer by the publisher of a prepublication price on advance orders of a book or other item. Abbreviated *prepub*.

prepublication discount   A discount or reduction in the list price of a new book or other publication, offered by the publisher on orders placed before the publication date to encourage advance orders. Compare with *prepublication price*.

prepublication price   The price at which a book or other publication is sold if ordered before a specified date in advance of the publication date, after which it is sold at the higher *list price*. Expensive multivolume reference sets may be offered to libraries by the publisher at a substantially lower price several months before the publication date as an inducement to order. Compare with *introductory price* and *prepublication discount*. **See also**: *expiration date*.

prequel   A work of fiction (usually a novel) complete in itself, which extends the narrative back in time from the beginning of a previously published work, retaining at least some of the same characters, although the action may occur in a different setting (*example*: *Mossflower*, prequel to *Redwall* by Brian Jacques). A prequel may be written by a person other than the author of the work on which it is based (*Gertrude and Claudius* by John Updike). In a more general sense, anything that precedes, especially a preceding sequence of events. The opposite of *sequel*.

prerecorded message   A telephone message recorded in advance for automatic playback when no one is present or able to answer a call. Libraries often use a prerecorded message when the facility is closed to inform callers of library hours and sometimes when open to direct calls to the appropriate service desk.

presentation binding   The distinctive binding on a book designed to be bestowed, usually as a token of respect, on a specific individual or on a special occasion, often bearing an inscription or the initials or arms of the recipient on the front cover.

presentation copy   A copy of a book bearing a *presentation inscription*, usually written spontaneously by the author or illustrator on the flyleaf at the time the gift was made, often to commemorate the occasion. When dated, the inscription usually indicates that the item was presented on or near date of publication. If a signature or inscription is requested by the book's owner, the volume is considered an *inscribed copy*.

presentation miniature   A small stand-alone painting in an illuminated manuscript, representing the formal presentation of a book to the patron or donor who commissioned it, usually a wealthy aristocrat or ecclesiastic. Michelle Brown notes in *Understanding Illuminated Manuscripts* (Getty Museum/British Library, 1994) that this type of image was sometimes incorporated into subsequent copies where it is more appropriately termed a *dedication miniature*. The popularity of presentation miniatures reached its highest point in the 15th century.

presentation software   Application software designed to assist a presenter in preparing text and/or graphics for visual display via a computer attached to a projector (*example*: *PowerPoint*). The graphic quality of such presentations is usually superior to overhead transparencies, but a well-prepared speaker brings backup to use in the event of machine or network failure. Presentation software is becoming more common in bibliographic instruction, particularly in academic libraries as instruction librarians become proficient users.

preservation   Prolonging the existence of library and archival materials by maintaining them in condition suitable for use, either in their original format or in a form more durable, through retention under proper environmental conditions or actions taken after a book or collection has been damaged to prevent further deterioration. Former Yale University conservator Jane Greenfield lists the factors affecting the condition of books as light, temperature, relative humidity, pollution, inherent vice, biological attack, human error (including improper storage and handling), deliberate mutilation, and disasters (*The Care of Fine Books*, Nick Lyons Books, 1988).

Single sheets may be encapsulated or laminated for protection. Materials printed on acid paper may be deacidified if their value warrants the expense; however, when the original has deteriorated beyond the point of salvation, reformatting may be necessary. Publications with soiled or foxed leaves are sometimes washed in rebinding. Materials infected with mildew or mold require fumigation. Insects can be eliminated by freezing the infested item. Rare books and manuscripts are usually stored in a darkened room, with temperature and humidity strictly controlled. The Library of Congress maintains a Web page on preservation at: lcweb.loc.gov/preserv. Sherelyn Ogden's *Preservation of Library & Archival Materials: A Manual* (1999) is available online from the Northeast Document Conservation Center at: www.nedcc.org/plam3/manhome.htm. Compare with *conservation*. *See also*: *digital preservation* and *environmental control*.

preservation metadata   In digital preservation, a component of administrative metadata supporting resource management within a digital collection. Preservation metadata may record the technical specifications of the archived digital object, including resource type, file format, encoding and storage size; important characteristics of the object's access environment, such as the name, version, and configuration of required rendering applications, operating systems, and hardware; evolution of the archived object as it is migrated to new formats to keep pace with changing access technologies; a check sum or digital signature verifying authenticity of content; and the chain of custody documenting provenance (adapted from "Metadata for Digital Preservation" by Brian F. Lavoie, *OCLC Newsletter*, September–October 2001).

preservation photocopy   A facsimile of a written or printed document, reproduced on a high-end photocopy machine according to strict criteria, usually when the condition of the original has deteriorated and the content is worth preserving in the same form. The paper on which such a copy is made must meet ANSI standards for permanence and durability (Z39.48). If the document is a book, the leaves should be bound according to ANSI standards for library binding (Z39.78). The facsimile should bear a statement clearly identifying the item as a copy. If the original is of "poor quality," its condition may also be noted. The Library of Congress maintains a Web page adapted from the *ALA Guidelines for Preservation Photocopying of Replacement Pages* at: lcweb.loc.gov/preserv/care/photocpy.html.

Preserved Context Indexing System (PRECIS)   A computer-assisted string indexing system developed and used since 1971 in the *British National Bibliography*, PRECIS is also used by library services in Canada and in the *Australian National Bibliography*. In contrast to the Library of Congress subject headings used by libraries in the United States, PRECIS attempts coextensive entry.

presidential library   A special library housing the papers of a former president of the United States (since Herbert Hoover) and documents pertaining to his term of office, usually located in or near the president's place of birth or residence prior to election. Although funds for the construction of presidential library facilities are provided by private donors, the National Archives and Records Administration operates and maintains them as research libraries. NARA provides a list of links to presidential libraries at: www.archives.gov/presidential_libraries/addresses/addresses.html.

press   A general term for the news media that traditionally included only print sources (newspapers and newsmagazines) but has expanded to include news services and radio and television broadcasting. A *press corps* is a body of reporters who cover breaking news, usually from a particular location, such as the White House. *See also*: *press release*.

Also used in the same sense as "publisher" (*example*: **Oxford University Press**), to refer to the publishing industry in general (as in *popular press*), and as a shortened form of the term *printing press*.

Also refers to the initial response of reviewers to a new book or creative work, which may have an effect on public demand in bookstores, libraries, theaters, etc. Press can be "bad" (panned), "good" (well-received), or "excellent" (laudatory).

Historically, the term was also used for a large wooden cupboard containing shelves for storing books and manuscripts, clothing and linens, etc., especially one recessed in a wall. Early books were placed flat on the shelves, often with the title handwritten on the tail or fore-edge.

pressboard   A highly glazed form of paperboard used when strength and rigidity are required of comparatively thin board because it is very dense and tough. Made from rag or chemical wood pulp, it is less acidic than board made from mechanical wood pulp.

press clipping service   An organization in the business of collecting copies of reviews, articles, columns, photographs, etc., published in newspapers and magazines about authors, prominent people, news events, or other topics of interest to clients who pay a fee to receive them on a regular basis.

press conference   A formal meeting to which members of the press are invited to hear an announcement or statement concerning an important event, project, topic, or development that the sponsors of the meeting wish to see publicized in the media. The attendees are usually given the opportunity to question the spokesperson(s) closely.

Library associations and large libraries sometimes schedule press conferences to publicize major initiatives. Compare with *press release*.

press release   An official or authoritative statement of news or other information intended for publication in a newspaper or news broadcast or for dissemination via some other news medium, usually written and issued by a press secretary or public relations office, giving the point of view of a person, company, or organization on a current event or situation. Synonymous with *news release*. *See also*: *press conference*.

press run   The number of copies of a publication to be printed at any one time, usually more than the binding order calls for, to allow for a reasonable amount of spoilage during the printing process. Also spelled *pressrun*. *See also*: *overrun* and *underrun*.

pressure group   An organized group that attempts to influence a library's policies or practices, usually to secure the removal of items considered objectionable by its members or the addition to the collection of materials that advocate or substantiate its point of view on a controversial political or social issue. Public libraries in the United States are frequent targets because they are supported by public funds and serve a diverse clientele. A carefully worded collection development policy is a library's best defense against threats to intellectual freedom.

pressure-sensitive   An adhesive designed to work by means of gentle compression, which may or may not allow the material to be easily removed from a surface once it has adhered. Pressure-sensitive labels are used extensively by libraries in technical processing.

pretest   A quiz or test administered to students prior to receiving instruction in the use of the library to assess their entry-level knowledge and identify deficiencies that need to be addressed. Ideally, a pretest is administered in conjunction with a posttest, for the purpose of comparison.

preventive maintenance   The cost-effective practice of regularly checking equipment and making minor repairs as needed to prevent more serious problems from developing.

preview   A private showing of a motion picture or exhibition to a limited audience in advance of the official public release or opening date. Also refers to a brief sequence of scenes taken from a motion picture, to be shown in a movie theater, on television, or on videotape, DVD, etc., to advertise the work as a coming attraction. Also spelled *prevue*. *See also*: *trailer*.

price   The amount actually paid by a library for a specific item after any discount is deducted, as stated on the invoice, not including the cost of shipping. Price is entered in the order record and also in the item record to facilitate billing if the item is lost or damaged beyond repair after the order record has been purged. *See also*: *average price*.

price clipped   The condition of a hardcover book from which the list price printed on the front flap of the dust jacket has been snipped off.

price guide   A publication that gives current prices of rare books and manuscripts, as well as books that are comparatively scarce, usually because they are out of print. The information is usually based on prices paid at book auctions (*example*: *American Book Prices Current*) or asked in dealer catalogs (*Bookman's Price Index*).

price index   A statistical method of showing the relative change in the average price of products, such as library materials, sold in the market place over a given period of time (usually one or more years), for use in materials cost analysis and budgeting. The average list price of a product in the base year is assigned the index value 100. Average prices for the same product in succeeding years are divided by the base period average price and multiplied by 100 to yield the price index for each year.

As a standard economic indicator of the market dynamics of a particular type of publication, independent of context (library, publisher, method of sale, etc.), price index is particularly useful in measuring inflation. The ANSI/NISO Z39.20 standard establishes criteria for compiling price indexes for printed library materials (hardcover trade and technical books, paperback books, and periodicals). *Library Journal* publishes an annual periodical price survey in its April 15 issue. Price indexes for library materials are also available in *The Bowker Annual Library and Book Trade Almanac*.

price resistance   The point at which the value of a book or other item is perceived by prospective buyers to be lower than the stated price. Under normal conditions, the customer will decide not to purchase or postpone purchase until the price comes down. Library continuation orders and approval plans may state a maximum price not to be exceeded for a specific category of item.

pricking   To prepare parchment or vellum for writing or illumination, tiny guide holes were made along the edges of a sheet (bifolium) with the point of a knife or awl to guide the scribe in drawing vertical and horizontal lines framing the area to bear text, illustration, and/or decoration. The punctures were often removed as the edges of the leaves were trimmed in binding. Christopher de Hamel suggests in *The British Library Guide to Manuscript Illumination* (University of Toronto Press, 2001) that once lines were drawn on the first sheet, holes were pricked through the entire gathering to ensure that all the leaves were identically ruled. Small spiked wheels or metal combs with widely space teeth may also have been used for this purpose.

The term is also used for small holes made around the outline of a design in an exemplar to allow it to be transferred to another surface by a stencil technique called *pouncing*.

primary author   The author whose name appears first on the chief source of information in the case of a work by two or more joint authors, in whose name the main entry is made in a library catalog. Added entries are made under the names of each of the other authors.

primary journal   A scholarly journal devoted to disseminating the results of original research in the field(s) or discipline(s) it covers (*example*: *Journal of Experimental Psychology*).

primary letter   A letter of the roman alphabet that does not have an ascender or descender (**a, c, e, m, n, o, r, s, u, v, w, x,** and **z**). *See also*: *x-height*.

primary source   In scholarship, a document or record containing firsthand information or original data on a topic, used in preparing a derivative work. Primary sources include original manuscripts, articles reporting original research or thought, diaries, memoirs, letters, journals, photographs, drawings, posters, film footage, sheet music, songs, interviews, government documents, public records, eyewitness accounts, newspaper clippings, etc. Compare with *secondary source* and *tertiary source*.

primary values   In archives, the values of records for the purpose(s) and activities for which they were created. Compare with *secondary values*.

primer   Originally a Book of Hours. Later, a book written for young children to teach them how to read and spell. Synonymous in this sense with *Dick and Jane book*. *See also*: *abecedary*, *battledore*, and *horn book*.

In a more general sense, any book that gives the first principles of a subject or basic instruction for beginners.

princeps edition   *See*: first edition.

print   To transfer an inked image or text from blocks, type, or plates onto a sheet or roll of paper, or onto some other printing surface, by the application of pressure. Also refers to the result of such a process, whether it be a string of characters on a page or an entire page of text and/or illustration. Also used as a generic term for the medium of print, as opposed to *nonprint* media. *See also*: *offprint* and *preprint*.

Also refers to a copy of a picture (mounted or unmounted) made by any printing process. An *art print* is an original drawing, woodcut, etching, engraving, lithograph, or photograph transferred to the medium of print from a plate cut by the artist. Prints made from the same plate may vary in quality. *See also*: ukiyo-e.

In photography, a copy of a photograph made on paper from a negative. In cinematography, a copy on film of a motion picture.

printer   The person or firm that prints a book, pamphlet, periodical, or other document, as distinct from the publisher who issues the item and the bookseller who offers it for sale. In early printed books, the printer and publisher were often the same, but in modern book production, the two functions are almost always performed by separate establishments. *See also*: *Gutenberg, Johann* and *Manutius, Aldus*.

Also refers to a mechanical or electronic device that produces printed copies of a document, including computer peripherals designed to produce hard copy output. The most common types are laser printers, dot-matrix printers, and ink-jet printers.

printer's copy   The manuscript version of a work used as the model for setting the type used in a printed edition. Survival of such copies is rare, but when properly authenticated, they can be of considerable interest to scholars engaged in textual bibliography and criticism.

printer's flower   A small graphic printer's ornament in the form of a flower or piece of foliage cast as a single unit in letterpress, which can be repeated to form a decorative border. Synonymous with *fleuron* and *floret*.

printer's ornament   Type matter used by a printer to add touches of embellishment to a text, including arabesques, borders (plain and fancy), flowers, headpieces, rules, etc.

printing   The production of identical copies of written or graphic material by means of a printing press or other mechanical device. Printing began in Germany in the mid-15th century with the invention by Johann Gutenberg of movable type and spread rapidly throughout Europe, replacing manuscript books as the primary medium of written communication. Compare with *reprography* and *xerography*. **See also**: *American Printing History Association, letterpress, offset*, and *typography*.

Also refers to all the copies of a book or other publication printed at one time in the same press run. A copy of the first printing of the first edition of a work is usually of greater value to book collectors than a copy of a subsequent printing in comparable condition. Also refers to the art of hand-lettering made to look like printed letters.

printing press   A machine designed to make impressions from an inked plate or block, or from type, on paper or some other printing surface. The modern printing press was invented at Mainz, Germany, in about 1456 by Johann Gutenberg, whose first publication was a 42-line Bible known as the *Gutenberg Bible*. The invention spread rapidly throughout continental Europe and to the British Isles, becoming well established by the 1480s. It put ownership of books within the reach of people who had previously been unable to afford hand-copied reading material. **See also**: *chase, forme, letterpress*, and *offset*.

print master   In microfilm, a second-generation negative made directly from the master negative, used to make service copies. The print master is usually stored under controlled conditions in a separate location.

printout   Text, images, or other data from a computer file printed as output on paper or some other printing surface by a peripheral device called a *printer*. Compare with *hard copy*.

prior publication   A work submitted to a publisher after it has already been published, usually in a different form, for example, an article initially published in a journal, later submitted by the author as a chapter in a book. Whether electronic theses and dissertations constitute prior publication is an issue currently in debate. The policy of a publishing company with regard to prior publication is usually stated in its guidelines for contributors.

prison library   *See*: correctional library.

privacy   The right of an individual (or group) to keep information about personal and professional life from disclosure, especially to government and commercial enterprises, and to remain free from surveillance except as authorized under provisions of law. In the *ALA Code of Ethics*, librarians and library staff are encouraged to "protect each library user's right to privacy and confidentiality with respect to information sought or received and resources consulted, borrowed, acquired, or transmitted." Many libraries in the United States have decided as a matter of policy not to retain circulation records for materials returned by the user to prevent misuse of such information. *See also*: USA Patriot Act.

private library   A library of any size that is not supported by public funds, especially one owned by an individual or family for personal enjoyment or by a private club, corporation, or foundation. Historically, large private collections have been the nucleus of many academic, research, and national libraries. Examples include the private collection of Thomas Jefferson acquired by the Library of Congress and the personal library of financier Pierpont Morgan, founder of The Morgan Library in New York City.

privately printed   In the antiquarian book trade, works printed but not offered for sale to the general public, usually intended solely for private distribution. The term is also applied to publications issued by a private press. Such works normally come to public attention when they are offered for sale in a book auction.

private press   A small printing establishment, often operated by a single person, offering limited editions at the discretion of the owner. The results are usually of fine quality and, when offered for sale, may not be distributed through regular market channels. A prime example is the Kelmscott Press founded in England in 1891 by William Morris, leader of the 19th-century English revival of the art and craft of bookmaking. Compare with *vanity publisher*.

privatization   The contracting out of library services under an agreement that transfers control over policy decisions and management of collections and services from the public to the private sector, usually to an external agency that operates on a for-profit basis. Compare with *outsourcing*.

probation volunteer   *See*: community service volunteer.

problem patron   A user whose behavior disrupts the normal functioning of a library, for example, one whose actions annoy others (staring, harassment, talking on cell phones), who exhibits aberrant behavior (mental and/or emotional disturbances, influence of drugs or alcohol, etc.), who engages in illegal activities (vandalism, theft, sex offenses), or who uses the library for purposes other than reading and study (socializing, soliciting, sleeping, bathing). Most larger libraries in the United States have installed security systems to prevent theft. Public libraries plagued with chronic problem behavior may hire a security guard to monitor the premises during hours when the library is open. Academic libraries can rely upon campus police when necessary. Synonymous with *difficult patron*. Euphemism: *atypical patron*. *See also*: *latchkey child* and *pyro-patron*.

procedure manual   A systematic list documenting the tasks involved in a specific job, sometimes including a description of the manner in which they are to be performed, given in sufficient detail that after careful reading, someone unfamiliar with the job is able to perform basic functions with a minimal amount of assistance. Procedure manuals are often maintained in loose-leaf format to facilitate revision. Compare with *employee handbook*.

proceedings   The published record of a conference, congress, symposium, or other meeting sponsored by a society or association, usually but not necessarily including abstracts or reports of papers presented by the participants. When the entire text of the papers presented is included, the result is called *transactions*. Conference proceedings are indexed worldwide in *ProceedingsFirst*, an online database available in OCLC *FirstSearch*. Abbreviated *proc.*

The term is also used in the titles of journals published by long-established scholarly societies (*example*: ***Proceedings of the National Academy of Sciences of the United States of America***), and also for the records of certain courts of law (***The Proceedings of the Old Bailey***).

processing   Everything done to a bibliographic item after it is acquired by a library, before it is placed on the shelf, including accessioning, cataloging, stamping, labeling, numbering, jacketing, etc. In some libraries, items *in process* are identified as such in the online catalog. The user may request that processing be expedited if an item is urgently needed. Compare with *technical processing*.

processing center   *See*: centralized processing.

processional   A liturgical book of portable size containing the chants and prayers used in ceremonial processions in certain services of the Catholic Church. Medieval processionals are often beautifully illuminated.

proclamation   An official announcement, especially one made by a governing authority to the general public. Also refers to the thing proclaimed. In the United States, presidential proclamations are published in the *Federal Register* but do not have the force of law.

procrastination   Putting off until tomorrow work that can and should be done today, sometimes with serious or vexing consequences for oneself and others. Persons overloaded with paperwork are particularly prone to this affliction. Training in time management is sometimes helpful.

producer   The person(s), company, or agency primarily responsible for determining the artistic form and intellectual content of a media item, such as a motion picture or television program, usually listed in the credits at the beginning or end of the work. The producer is also responsible for financing and making arrangements for the technical production and manufacture of the final product and for promoting it in the market place. Synonymous in this sense with *production company*. Abbreviated *prod.* Compare with *distributor*.

Also, the organization responsible for creating the content of a machine-readable data file such as a bibliographic database, usually indicated on the welcome screen, not necessarily the same as the vendor that markets and provides access to the product.

production company   *See*: producer.

professional book   A book intended to be used by members of a profession in the course of their work or in continuing education (*example*: ***Countdown to a New Library: Managing the Building Project*** by Jeannette A. Woodward). Books for the library profession are reviewed in a separate section of *Library Journal* and *Booklist*.

Because professional books appeal to a limited audience, press runs tend to be small, and they are sold at a short discount.

professional development   Further study undertaken during employment by a person trained and educated in a profession, sometimes at the initiative of the employer but also through voluntary attendance at conferences, workshops, seminars, or enrollment in postgraduate courses, particularly important in professions that have a rapidly changing knowledge base. Compare with *in-service training*.

professionalism   Exercise of a high standard of trained judgment in meeting the needs of the clients or users of a service. In most countries, professional qualifications are awarded by the leading professional association, on the expectation that competencies will be maintained through the continuing development of knowledge and skills. In most professions, standards are reinforced by government licensing and by a professional code of ethics. The American Library Association established its *Code of Ethics* in 1939. Adherence has brought some librarians into conflict with members of the local community and with persons of power and influence, particularly over issues of censorship and privacy.

profile   A demographic study of the community served by a library or library system, or of its registered users or user group, for the purpose of measuring economic, social, and educational variables pertinent to the development of collections, services, and programs and to the design of new facilities. A profile is usually conducted with the aid of a survey instrument but may also include data compiled from other sources.

Also refers to the list of needs established by a library with a publisher or wholesaler that supplies materials on approval or blanket order, usually including subject areas, levels of specialization and/or difficulty, languages, series, formats, maximum prices, etc.

Also, the degree to which the activities of an individual, organization, or institution are known in its community. Libraries typically emerge from their *low-profile* role in society when faced with the necessity of persuading their constituency to approve a funding measure. Library policy can also become *high-profile* when a challenge sparks a conflict over censorship or privacy.

In cartography, a scale representation of the intersection of a vertical surface (not necessarily a plane) with the surface of the ground, or of the intersection of such a vertical surface with that of a conceptual three-dimensional model representing phenomena having the characteristic of continuous distribution (*AACR2*).

Program for Cooperative Cataloging (PCC)   An international program coordinated by the Library of Congress and participants from other countries, aimed at expanding access to library collections by providing useful, timely, and cost-effective cooperative cataloging that meets the mutually accepted standards of libraries around the world. PCC has four components: NACO (name authority program), SACO (subject authority program), BIBCO (monographic bibliographic record program), and CONSER (cooperative online serials program), guided by a policy committee that includes as permanent representatives The British Library, Library of Congress, National Library of Canada, OCLC, and Research Libraries Group. URL: www.loc.gov/catdir/pcc.

programmed text   An instructional book presented as a sequence of self-paced units that require the student to demonstrate an understanding of the content by responding appropriately at various steps along the way. If the correct answer is given, the lesson continues; if the student answers incorrectly, additional instruction and practice are provided until the unit is mastered. Programmed instruction is suitable only for material that can be learned in a step-by-step process.

programming language   A set of symbols with its own vocabulary, grammar, and syntax in which a person called a *programmer* writes statements instructing a computer to accomplish a specific task by executing a sequence of logical operations (*examples*: **BASIC, C, C++, COBOL, FORTRAN**, etc.). The instructions, known as *source code*, are translated into the machine language specific to each type of CPU by special programs called *assemblers*, *compilers*, and *interpreters*. Standards for programming languages are set by the American National Standards Institute (ANSI).

program notes   Explanatory notes accompanying a printed list of the works performed in a concert or theater, usually distributed by an usher to attendees upon entering the hall. Intended to be read before the curtain rises and during intermission, program notes contain information about the compositions to be performed and the people involved (composer or playwright, conductor or director, performers, etc.), usually written by a knowledgeable person. Of particular interest to music historians, program notes are classified by librarians as ephemera and can therefore be difficult to locate, with the exception of performances given in major venues that maintain their own archives.

projection   In cartography, the result produced when the spherical surface of a globe is placed in a position relative to a light source from which an image of its surface can be projected onto a plane or onto a curved surface such as a cone or cylinder that can be cut and laid flat. The normal orientation for a *planar projection* is polar; for a *conical projection*, oblique; and for a *cylindrical projection*, equatorial. All projections involve some degree of distortion. The type of projection used in making a map of the earth or another celestial body is usually indicated in the legend, with the *Mercator projection* being the most common. When a map is cataloged by a library, the *statement of projection* is given in the mathematical data area of the bibliographic description.

Also refers to a future need or condition that can be forecast from a known set of data, for example, the amount of expansion space needed in the stacks of a library, based on average annual collection growth.

projection speed   The rate at which images on film are made to appear on a screen, using a machine called a *film projector*, the standard being 24 fps (frames per second) for sound film and 16 fps for silent film. In *AACR2*, projection speed is given in the physical description area of the bibliographic description only if it is not standard for the item. Compare with *playing speed*.

Project MUSE   A grant-funded joint project of Johns Hopkins University Press (JHUP) and the Milton S. Eisenhower Library at Johns Hopkins University, *Project MUSE* began in 1995 by offering online access by subscription to the full-text of its own journals. In 2000, the *Project* added 60 journals from other scholarly publishers, bringing the total coverage of the database to over 100 titles, mostly in the arts, humanities, and social sciences. URL: muse.jhu.edu. *See also*: JSTOR.

prolegomenon   A prologue or preliminary essay, especially one that is long and scholarly. The term is often seen in the titles of theses and dissertations (*example*: *A Prolegomenon on Moderation in Plato's Republic* by Stephen John Lange). Plural: *prolegomena*.

prologue   An introduction to a play, novel, poem, or other literary work placed by the author at the opening of the text, rather than in the front matter (*example*: *The Wife of Bath's Prologue* in Chaucer's *The Canterbury Tales*). Also refers to introductory lines spoken by a member of the cast before the beginning of the first act of a dramatic performance to prepare the audience for the theme to be developed or state the moral embodied in the action that follows. Compare with *epilogue*. In a broader sense, preliminary events leading to more weighty consequences.

promotion   Advancement of a librarian or other library staff member to a higher rank within the same library or library system, usually on the basis of favorable performance evaluation and accompanied by an increase in salary or wages. A change of position can be a promotion if it involves more responsibility and authority. In libraries in which employment is governed by a collective bargaining agreement, eligibility for promotion and method of evaluation may be determined by contract. Compare with *tenure*. *See also*: *peer evaluation*.

Also refers to the activity of marketing a product, service, or institution to people in a position to buy, use, or support it. National Children's Book Week is an example of an activity intended to promote the use of libraries in the United States.

promotional book   A profusely illustrated book on a popular subject, usually an out of print trade title reprinted in a less expensive edition specifically for sale as a bargain item in trade bookstores. Art, travel, cooking, gardening, and natural history are favorite subjects. In public libraries, a promotional book received in good condition as a gift may be added to the collection if demand exists for the subject. Abbreviated *promo book*.

prompt   A message at a point on a computer screen, usually in the form of a small blinking cursor (with or without explanatory text), indicating that data is to be entered or an operation initiated by the user.

promptbook   The version of the script of a play used during a performance by the person responsible for jogging the memory of the actors and stage hands when they forget their lines or miss their cues. A promptbook indicates the lines, action, cues, props, costumes, lighting, etc., at each point in the production. Synonymous with *prompt copy*.

proof   In printing, a trial impression made from metal type, plates, photographic film, or magnetic tape or disk, for inspection and correction at the various stages of composition. Proofs of textual matter are known as *proof sheets*. In book production, a different kind of proof is made at each stage of the printing process. Designated by form, purpose, or destination, proofs are taken in the following sequence:

first proof—a preliminary galley proof, corrected by the printer's reader for return to the typesetter

galley or *slip proof*—taken before matter is made up into pages, checked by the printer's reader and sent to publisher for author corrections

page proof—taken after the author's corrections are made and the type is made up into pages, sent to the author for final corrections

marked proof—includes the author's corrections, checked by the printer's reader for conformity with house style

show revise—the reader requires a further proof

clean proof—a statement by the reader that the copy is completely corrected

press—final instruction from the publisher that the work is ready to go to press

See also: *proof print* and *proofreading*.

proof impression   *See*: proof print.

proof of ownership   The means by which right of possession of a book, manuscript, or other item is conclusively established, important in the identification and recovery of materials stolen from libraries and archives and difficult to establish in some cases. Ownership marks are helpful, as are photographs of the binding, title page, or a page with physical peculiarities (typographical irregularities, identifiable discolorations, etc.) or bibliographic idiosyncrasies (inscriptions, marginal notes, etc.).

proof of payment   Verification, usually in the form of a canceled check, that an amount due has been paid, usually provided at the request of a vendor or supplier, but the customer may also make such a request.

proof print   In printing, an impression of an illustration made from the final plate before the regular impression is published, usually prior to the addition of title or caption. Synonymous with *proof impression*.

proofreading   The step in the publishing process in which the printer's proof is meticulously read and compared with the original manuscript or typescript copy to detect errors in typesetting. Corrections are noted on the proof by the *proofreader* and sent back to the printer. *See also*: *typographical error*.

propaganda   Originally referred to the activities of a committee of cardinals called the *congregatio de propaganda fide* (Congregation for the Propagation of the Faith), established in the 17th century by the Roman Catholic Church to oversee the training of priests for foreign missions.

In modern usage, the organized dissemination of information, doctrines, or practices by a person, group, organization, or government with intent to manipulate or control public opinion in support of a specific political, social, economic, or religious agenda. In democratic societies, the term has acquired a pejorative connotation. *See also*: *intellectual freedom*.

proper name   An appellation identifying a specific person, corporate body, place, event, period of history, or entity, as opposed to the common name. In the English language, each noun and adjective in a proper name is capitalized, as in: Johann Gutenberg, Library of Congress, New York City, American Revolution, Renaissance, Statue of Liberty, etc. When a proper name is used as a heading in indexing or library cataloging, the order of words may be inverted to bring the most significant word into filing position ("Gutenberg, Johann" and "Revolution, American," but not "Liberty, Statue of").

property stamp   A rubber stamp used to mark ownership of library materials in ink, usually on the inside of the cover of a book, on one of the endpaper(s), on one or more of the leaves, or across the top, bottom, or fore-edge of the sections.

proposal   A plan for a project involving research, scholarship, or creative endeavor, usually written as part of an application for grant funding by the person or group who conceived the idea with the intention of pursuing it to fruition. A proposal typically includes a brief abstract, a detailed narrative description, a statement of goals and objectives, a realistic timetable, a list of resources (human and material), an itemized budget, criteria for evaluating success, a commitment to specific reporting procedures, and letters of support affirming the value of the project. Manuals on proposal writing are available in most academic libraries.

proprietary   Something that is privately owned and controlled, usually by a person or commercial company. The term implies that the specifications or authority needed to reproduce the thing are withheld from public knowledge or protected by law (copyright or patent). In computing, a system, interface, program, or file available only by permission of the owner or author, as opposed to one available for use without restrictions. Compare with *open systems*. *See also*: *licensing agreement*.

proprietary library   An early form of library in which the capital (property) was held in a common fund as joint stock owned by the members in shares that could be sold or transferred independently. Proprietors were required to pay an annual assessment on their shares, and nonproprietors were allowed use of the library only upon payment of an annual fee. Compare with *subscription library*.

ProQuest   An information service that provides online indexing of articles published in thousands of current periodicals, including the full-text of a significant number of titles. One of the three leading aggregators of journals available in electronic format, ProQuest relies on the extensive UMI microfilm collection to expand its digital back files. URL: www.proquest.com. *See also*: *EBSCO* and *Gale Group*.

prose   Spoken and written language in its ordinary everyday form, as distinct from poetic language consciously given metric structure. Samuel Taylor Coleridge defined prose as "words in their best order" and poetry as "the best words in the best order." *See also*: *purple prose*.

prospectus   A separately printed advertisement, usually in the form of a leaflet distributed by a publisher to prospective purchasers, describing or sketching the plan of a forthcoming publication for the purpose of soliciting advance orders, sometimes with the added inducement of a prepublication price or discount. Usually includes a sample page and illustration, table of contents, list of contributors, and information about price and estimated date of publication. Used for major works, such as serials and expensive multivolume reference sets, to provide more detailed information than a selector can normally obtain from reading reviews and book announcements.

protocol   A set of formal conventions for the exchange of data between workstations connected to a computer network, including the rules governing data format and control of input, transmission, and output. Data transmission over the Internet is governed by the TCP/IP protocol implemented in 1982, which allows users of different types of computers to communicate seamlessly. The six main protocols used in Internet addresses (URLs) are:

ftp://—FTP directory of downloadable data or program files
gopher://—Gopher server
http://—World Wide Web page
mailto:—Electronic mail (e-mail)
news:—Usenet newsgroup
telnet://—Application program running on a remote host

Also refers to a signed diplomatic document recording points of agreement reached at a conference between two or more nations, preliminary to negotiating a formal treaty.

provenance   A record of the origin and history of ownership or custodianship of a book, manuscript, or other object of value. In medieval manuscripts, evidence of who commissioned the work can sometimes be found in emblems, mottos, heraldic devices, and miniatures that include an image of the patron or donor. References in catalogs, correspondence, and other historical records can also provide clues. In later works, bookplates, ownership marks, inscriptions, inserted matter, a special binding, and notes written in or on the item often provide evidence of provenance, often important in establishing value. *See also*: *ex-library copy*.

In archives, the succession of custodians responsible for creating, receiving, or accumulating a collection of records or personal papers. Authentication of archival materials requires that provenance be determined with certainty. The related principle of *respect des fonds* requires that records known to have originated from a given source be documented and retained separately from those of other agencies or persons and in their original order and organizational context, whenever possible.

proverb   A short, memorable saying of unknown origin, but in common use, expressing in simple yet vivid language an obvious truth, familiar experience, or piece of sage advice, often metaphorical or alliterative (*example*: **look before you leap**). Proverbs are collected and published in dictionaries, usually shelved in the reference section of a library.

provisional edition   *See*: preliminary edition.

provisional serial   A publication cataloged as a serial while in the process of being published but as a nonserial when complete, usually because the period of publication is lengthy and/or the numbering of issues complicated. Compare with *pseudo-serial*.

provisional term   A descriptor or subject heading added temporarily to an indexing language, subject to future evaluation, often representing a new concept in a field whose terminology is still growing. Compare with *identifier*.

proximity   The search software of some bibliographic databases allows a *proximity operator* to be used in search statements to specify that a record will be retrieved only if the keywords typed as search terms appear within a designated number of words of each other or within the same sentence or paragraph. The proximity operator is not standardized (in some databases it is "adj," for *adjacent to*; in others it is "w," for *with*).

Example:

publication adj1 date or **publication w1 date**

In the example given above, the query will retrieve records in which the word "publication" appears within one word of "date," for example, record containing the phrase *date of publication* or *publication date* (or both) and also *date for publication, publication and date, publication to date*, etc.

If proximity searching is available in a specific database, instructions concerning its use can usually be found in the help screen(s). Synonymous with *adjacency*.

proxy server   An application program that operates *between* a client and server on a computer network, usually installed as a firewall to provide security or to increase speed of access by performing some of the housekeeping tasks that would normally be handled by the server itself, such as checking authentication or validating user requests. Also called a *proxy*. *See also*: daemon.

psalter   A liturgical book containing the 150 Psalms of the Bible, usually combined with the calendar of Church feasts, Old Testament canticles, creeds, litany of saints, and additional prayers. Prior to the emergence of the Book of Hours in the 13th century, the psalter was also the most important book used in private devotion. Medieval psalters were often beautifully illuminated, especially the initial letter "B" of the first word (*Beatus*) of the first Psalm. The life of King David, to whom most of the Psalms are attributed, is often the subject of historiated initials and miniatures in psalters.

pseudandry   A female author writing under a masculine pseudonym, a common literary practice during the 18th and 19th centuries when writing was considered an unsuitable occupation for a woman (*example*: **George Eliot**, whose real name was Mary Ann Evans Cross).

pseudepigrapha   Literally, writings that bear a false title, especially texts ascribed to characters appearing in the Old Testament, subsequently found to have been written by Jews and Christians between 300 B.C. and A.D. 200. In a general sense, any text falsely attributed to a major author. Some scholars have argued that all the works of William Shakespeare fall into this category.

pseudonym   A fictitious name, especially one assumed by an author to conceal or obscure identity. The classic example in American literature is **Mark Twain** whose real name was Samuel Langhorne Clemens. The writer François-Marie Arouet (**Voltaire**) probably holds the record for the most pseudonyms, with Daniel Foe (**Defoe**) a close second. Prior to the mid-19th century, women writers often used male pseudonyms (pseudandry) to get their works published and to attract readership (*example*: **George Sand** whose real name was Amandine-Aurore-Lucile Dupin Dudevant), although there were notable exceptions (**Jane Austen** and the **Brontë sisters**). A *joint pseudonym* is one shared by two or more collaborators in a work (**Rosetta Stone** used by Dr. Seuss and the illustrator Michael K. Frith). Information on pseudonyms can be found in the latest edition of the *Pseudonyms and Nicknames Dictionary* published by the Gale Group. An online dictionary of pseudonyms titled *a.k.a.* is available at: www.trussel.com/books/pseudo.htm. Abbreviated *pseud*. Compare with *allonym*. *See also*: *pen name*.

pseudo-serial   A publication treated by a library cataloger as a monographic work when first published but subsequently as a serial, usually after having been repeatedly revised and reissued (*example*: *Guide to Reference Books* published by the American Library Association). Compare with *provisional serial*.

PSP   The **P**rofessional/**S**cholarly **P**ublishing Division of the Association of American Publishers (AAP), including in its membership publishers of books, journals, looseleaf materials, computer software, databases, and CD-ROMs in science, medicine, technology, law, business, the social and behavioral sciences, and the humanities. A title published by such a company is known in the book trade as a *PSP book*. URL: www.pspcentral.org. *See also*: *professional book* and *STM*.

psychological novel   A type of novel in which the plot and setting are secondary to the author's exploration of the mind and emotions of the principal characters in the narrative (*example*: *Crime and Punishment* by Fyodor Dostoyevsky).

PTDL   *See*: **p**atent and **t**rademark **d**epository **l**ibrary.

PTDLA   *See*: **P**atent and **T**rademark **D**epository **L**ibrary **A**ssociation.

public address system   A voice amplification system installed in a large facility, used for paging staff when their presence is required and for informing patrons of closing time, emergencies, etc. In libraries, the microphone is usually installed behind the circulation desk and used only when necessary, to minimize distraction.

publication   Under U.S. copyright law, the act of distributing copies of a creative work to the public by sale, lease, rental, or lending. Also refers to a work capable of being read or otherwise perceived (book, audiorecording, videorecording, CD-ROM, etc.), issued by a publisher for sale to the general public, usually in multiple copies and sometimes in multiple editions. Compare with *privately printed*. *See also*: *electronic publication*, *library publication*, *publication date*, and *publication history*.

publication date   The date on which copies of a creative work are officially offered for sale to the public. For trade books, the date is announced by the publisher in advance and promotional activities are orchestrated to coincide with it. In printed books, the publication date is given as the year, usually on the verso of the title page. When date of first publication differs from date of current edition, first and subsequent dates are indicated. In older books, publication date may be given in the colophon. In periodicals, it is the day and month, or just the month or period of issue (spring, summer, fall, winter), usually printed on the front cover. For motion pictures, release date is used. For a Web page, it is usually the date of last update. In library cataloging, publication date is recorded as one of the elements in the publication, distribution, etc., area of the bibliographic description. Abbreviated *pub date*. Synonymous with *imprint date*. Compare with *copyright date*. *See also*: *date range*, *false date*, *no date*, and *postdated*.

publication, distribution, etc.   The area of description in a bibliographic record reserved for information about the act of publishing, distributing, releasing, or issuing a specific bibliographic item (MARC field 260), including place of publication, name of publisher, and date of publication or release.

publication history   For books published in one or more volumes, the sequence of printings and editions of a work and especially any changes in the title or publisher. For serials, the sequence of volumes, parts, or numbers issued, including any breaks, title changes, or changes in publisher. In library cataloging, details of publication are given for a serial in the numeric and/or alphabetic, chronological, or other designation area of the bibliographic description, in an open or closed entry.

publication schedule   In publishing, a timetable established by the managing editor for the process of editing, printing, and binding a new publication (or new edition of an existing one) to ensure that it will be ready for distribution by the projected publication date. Also refers to the sequence or frequency with which works are issued by the publisher, especially serial publications. In the case of periodicals, the schedule is announced in advance of subscription. *See also*: *additional volume* and *delayed publication*.

publication type   *See*: material type.

publication year   The 12-month period during which all the issues or parts of a volume of a serial publication are issued, which may not coincide with the calendar year, for example, some of the periodical indexes published by H.W. Wilson (*Art Index*, *Education Index*, *Social Sciences Index*, etc.).

public domain   Works *not* protected by copyright, or for which copyright has expired, which may be printed for distribution and sale, quoted, excerpted, reproduced, and made available online to the public without infringement, for example, a government document over which an agency decides not to exercise copyright in order to make its content widely known. The term also applies to computer software (freeware and shareware) that the designers make available at no charge as a public service.

publicity   Information publicly distributed in a variety of forms (announcements, advertisements, press releases, fliers, posters, etc.) with the intention of making something widely known. Libraries sponsor special events, especially during National Library Week, to *publicize* their services and programs. *See also*: *public relations*.

Public Lending Right (PLR)   Under programs funded by the national governments of Britain, Denmark, Finland, Norway, and Sweden, authors of works circulated by public libraries are entitled to receive a subsidy based on the number of times a book is borrowed. In Britain, living authors and illustrators named on the title page may register to receive compensation, provided they are UK residents. Periodicals, reference books, and conference proceedings are excluded, as are works of less than 32 pages (24 pages for poetry and drama). For a more detailed discussion of PLR, please see the entry by Jim Parker in the *International Encyclopedia of Information and Library Science* (Routledge, 2003).

public library   A library or library system that provides unrestricted access to library resources and services free of charge to *all* the residents of a given community, district, or geographic region, supported wholly or in part by public funds. Because public libraries have a broader mandate than academic libraries and most special libraries, they must develop their collections to reflect diversity. The largest public library system in the United States is the New York Public Library. The UC Berkeley Libraries maintain an online directory of U.S. public libraries as part of *Libweb* (sunsite. berkeley.edu/Libweb/Public_main.html). *See also*: *Public Library Association.*

Public Library Association (PLA)   A division of the American Library Association since 1944, PLA has a membership consisting of librarians, library trustees, and friends interested in the general improvement and expansion of public library services for readers of all ages. PLA publishes the bimonthly magazine *Public Libraries*. URL: www.pla.org.

public relations   Publicity designed to create favorable public opinion and boost awareness of the benefits of library services, resources, and programs and promote the interests of libraries in society. Large public library systems usually employ at least one librarian or library staff member specializing in public relations. The American Library Association actively promotes libraries, especially during National Library Week, through its *Celebrating America's Libraries* Web page (www.ala.org). *See also*: *Friends of the Library* and *fund-raising*.

public services   Activities and operations of a library that bring the staff into regular direct contact with its users, including circulation, reference, online services, bibliographic instruction, serials assistance, government documents, and interlibrary loan/document delivery, as opposed to *technical services*, which are performed behind the scenes, out of contact with library users.

public television   Television broadcast stations supported by foundation grants, government subsidies, and contributions from viewers, commercial companies, and other benefactors, providing cultural, educational, and recreational programming for adults and children. Public television stations do not rely on ratings, so the quality of their programming is not dictated by the need to cater to the widest possible viewing audience. In the United States, the public broadcasting system is PBS (www.pbs.org). In Great Britain, it is the BBC (www.bbc.co.uk), and in Canada, CBC (www.cbc.ca). Compare with *commercial television*. *See also*: Reading Rainbow.

published price   The retail price at which a publisher offers a book for sale at the time of publication, usually printed on the inside flap of the dust jacket in hardcover editions and on the back cover in softcover editions. Under certain conditions, a discount may be given on specific titles. Synonymous with *list price*. *See also*: *prepublication price*.

publisher   A person or corporate entity that prepares and issues printed materials for public sale or distribution, normally on the basis of a legal contract in which the publisher is granted certain exclusive rights in exchange for assuming the financial risk of publication and agreeing to compensate the author, usually with a share of the profits. In older books, the publisher and printer are often the same, but since the mid-19th century, the two functions have been performed by separate entities. The name of the publisher is usually printed at the foot of the title page and on the verso. In library cataloging, name of publisher is entered in the publication, distribution, etc., area of the bibliographic description. Compare with *distributor*. *See also*: *device*.

In the United States, the trade association of the publishing industry is the Association of American Publishers (AAP). An international Directory of Publishers and Vendors is available online from *AcqWeb* (acqweb.library.vanderbilt.edu), a Website created and maintained especially for acquisitions and collection development librarians. One of the volumes of *Books in Print* (*BIP*) is a print directory of U.S. publishers, available in the reference section of most libraries. *See also*: *commercial publisher*, *foreign subsidiary*, *metapublisher*, *micropublisher*, *museum publisher*, *popular press*, *private press*, *small press*, *trade publisher*, *university press*, and *vanity publisher*.

publisher's agreement   A contract between a writer and publisher stating the terms under which the author's work(s) will be published and sold. The publisher is granted certain exclusive rights in exchange for assuming the financial risk of publication. Under most agreements, the author is compensated in one of four ways: royalties based on a percentage of sales, profit sharing, commission, or outright sale of copyright. Synonymous with *book contract*.

publisher's binding   The binding on a trade book as originally issued in multiple copies by the publisher (usually a cloth case binding), as distinct from a binding made to special order. Not all copies of an edition are cased at the same time, or even by the same bindery, which may lead to slight variations in state within the same edition. Synonymous with *edition binding*. Compare with *popular edition* and *prelibrary binding*.

publisher's catalog   A free advertising brochure sent by a publisher to libraries, booksellers, and other prospective customers, describing new books (frontlist) and listing titles on the backlist, usually indexed by author and title, with an order form in the back. Publisher's catalogs are issued seasonally, usually in the spring and fall of each year. Librarians select on the basis of reviews but may use publisher's catalogs to verify information prior to ordering. A searchable database of *Publishers' Catalogues* is maintained by Peter Scott of the University of Saskatchewan Library at: www.lights.com/publisher. *See also*: *blurb*.

publisher's number   A numbering designation assigned to an item of music by the publisher, which may include abbreviations, initials, or words identifying the publisher, normally appearing only on the title page, cover, and/or first page of music (*AACR2*). In music cataloging, a publisher's number is recorded in the note area of the bibliographic description (*example*: **Publisher's no.: 6201/9935**). Compare with *plate number*.

publisher's reader   *See*: reader.

Publishers Weekly (PW)   The weekly trade journal of the American publishing industry. Founded in 1872, *Publishers Weekly* provides news and announcements; feature articles; author interviews; advance reviews of fiction, nonfiction, and children's books; lists of hardcover and paperback bestsellers; and analysis of trends of interest to publishers, librarians, booksellers, and others involved in the book trade. *PW* is published by Reed Business Information. ISSN: 0000–0019. The online version is available at: www.publishersweekly.com/index.asp.

publishing   The business of issuing books, music, photographs, maps, and other printed materials for sale to the public, which includes negotiating contracts with authors and their literary agents, editing the author's manuscript, designing the physical item (typography, layout, etc.), producing the finished product (printing, binding etc.), marketing the work, and making arrangements for its distribution through regular market channels. In the United States, the trade association of the publishing industry is the American Association of Publishers (AAP). The industry's trade journal is *Publishers Weekly*. *See also*: co-publishing, desktop publishing, electronic publishing, and *niche publishing*.

publishing season   *See*: season.

PubMed   *See*: *MEDLINE*.

puff   A pejorative term used since the 17th century to refer to immoderate praise of a book or other creative work, usually in the form of a review or advertisement written by the publisher, author, or a copy writer, intended to influence opinion and promote sales. In book publishing, a puff is usually printed on the dust jacket or included in an advertisement published in a review publication. A *preliminary puff* is written prior to publication for the use of traveling sales representatives. *See also*: blurb.

puffery   Biased literary criticism emanating from a small clique or coterie, usually individuals who have a vested interest in promoting the work, either because they stand to gain financially from its success, are indebted to the publisher for some reason, or are personal friends of the author or illustrator.

pugillaria   In ancient Rome, a book small enough to be held in the hand, consisting of two to eight leaves made of wood, ivory, or metal, covered on one side with wax on which characters were incised with a sharp writing implement called a *stylus*. Covered in parchment or leather, the tablets were held together by leather cords or rings. Synonymous with *tablet book*. Compare with *diptych*. *See also*: codex.

Pulitzer Prize   Named after the Hungarian American journalist and philanthropist Joseph Pulitzer who initially endowed them, the Pulitzer Prizes have been awarded annually by Columbia University since 1917 for exemplary achievements in American journalism, letters, drama, and music. Fourteen prizes are given in journalism, including a gold medal for public service. The prizes in letters are for fiction, history, poetry, biography or autobiography, and general nonfiction. Each prize includes $5,000 paid by the Pulitzer endowments. A list of Pulitzer Prize winners is available online at: www.pulitzer.org/index.html. *See also*: *National Book Award* and *Nobel Prize in Literature*.

pull   A small ribbon or tab attached to the binding of a book, usually at the side of the spine, to facilitate removal from a slipcase or other close-fitting container. The term is also used in letterpress to mean an impression of type.

pull-case   A telescoping box in two separable parts, upper fitting over lower, designed as a container for one or more books, pamphlets, or other printed material. A pull-case differs from a *slipcase* in leaving no portion of the contents exposed, providing virtually airtight protection. *See also*: *solander*.

pulling   Disassembling a book to prepare it for rebinding, a process that requires the removal of case or cover, boards, endpapers, tapes, and lining. The sections are then freed by stripping the adhesive from the binding edge and cutting the sewing threads. Pulling sometimes damages the back folds, requiring repair, usually by the use of guards. Synonymous with *take down*.

pull-out   *See*: throw-out.

pulp   Vegetable material reduced to a liquid fibrous mass by mechanical and/or chemical means for use in papermaking. Most pulp is manufactured from wood, but permanent paper usually contains a percentage of cotton and/or linen rag. *Chemical wood pulp* is treated in manufacture to remove lignin, an acidic substance that causes the leaves and bindings of books to deteriorate over time. Untreated *mechanical wood paper* is used for low-grade papers such as newsprint when permanence is not essential. *See also*: *fiber content*.

According to *The Bookman's Glossary* (R.R. Bowker, 1983), the term is also used in publishing to refer to a magazine printed on inexpensive, poor-quality paper manufactured from groundwood pulp (newsprint).

pulp fiction   Sensational fiction of no enduring literary value, popular from the 1920s through the 1940s. Written for the mass market, usually according to formula, pulp fiction was printed on poor-quality paper, bound in softcover, and easily recognized by the lurid design on the front cover. Popular genres include romance, adventure, westerns, etc. Compare with *popular fiction*. *See also*: *mass-market paperback*.

pulp magazine   An inexpensive popular magazine of the early 20th century devoted to sensational stories of love, adventure, mystery, or intrigue, usually printed on newsprint. *See also*: *ephemera*.

pumice   Lightweight, porous, highly abrasive volcanic glass, used in powdered form as *pounce* to prepare the surface of a new sheet of parchment or vellum for writing.

In solid form, pumice is used to polish new skins in the making of parchment and to scrape writing from an existing manuscript to prepare it for reuse (see *palimpsest*).

punctuation   The use of standard characters in writing and printing to separate words, clauses, parenthetical phrases, sentences, etc., and to indicate meaning or tone. In the English language, the most frequently used *punctuation marks* are the period (.), comma (,), colon (:), semicolon (;), question mark(?), exclamation point (!), apostrophe ('), quotation marks (" "), parentheses ( ), hyphen (-), dash (—), and square brackets [ ]. In *AACR2*, precise rules for the use of punctuation in library catalog records are given in the instructions for each area of bibliographic description. ***See also***: spacing.

puppetry   A technique used in storytelling in which each character in the narrative is represented by a doll with movable parts operated with wire, strings, and/or sticks or in the form of a cloth mitten or glove designed to fit over the hand of the *puppeteer*, who synchronizes the movements of the doll with dialogue and action in the text. A small portable stage may be used as a backdrop. Some public libraries include circulating *puppets* in the juvenile collection.

purchase order (PO)   In acquisitions, the official record of an order placed by a library, authorizing a publisher, jobber, dealer, or vendor to deliver materials or services at a set price. A PO becomes a contract once it is accepted by the seller. Most purchase orders include the purchase order number, name and address of seller, name and address of ordering agency, description and quantity of items ordered, price per item, discount or credit terms, fund to be charged, time for completion, shipping terms, and delivery address and instructions. Compare with *invoice*.

pure notation   A classification notation in which only one kind of symbol is used, usually numerals *or* letters of the alphabet but not both, for example, the arabic numerals used to indicate class numbers in Dewey Decimal Classification. Compare with *mixed notation*.

PURL   *See*: Persistent **URL**.

purple prose   A pejorative term for a passage or entire literary work written in a prose style so extravagantly overdone as to tax the reader with its incongruity. Synonymous with *purple patch*.

purple vellum   Sheets of fine parchment dyed or painted dark purple to create a high-contrast background for script or illumination in gold, silver, or white. Introduced in late Antiquity and the early Christian period, the technique was reserved for the finest books as a mark of luxury and status. *Purple pages* were also used in Anglo-Saxon, Carolingian, and Ottonian manuscripts and enjoyed a revival during the Renaissance.

putto   The image of a nude infant boy (often depicted with wings) tucked into a decorated border or initial letter in a medieval illuminated manuscript or early printed book. *Putti* were also used in other decorative contexts.

PVA   *See*: polyvinyl acetate.

PVC   *See*: polyvinyl chloride.

PW   *See*: *Publishers Weekly*.

pyro-patron   A library patron who is (1) showing signs of combustability, (2) in imminent danger of igniting, or (3) already on fire, usually a test of civility and self-control for the reference librarian. For possible responses, please see: John Herbert, "Pyro-Patron Policy" in *The Unabashed Librarian* (1998). Synonymous with *flaming patron* and *conflagrated patron*. *See also*: *problem patron*.

pyroxylin   A chemical substance (partially nitrated cellulose) used in the manufacture of lacquers, plastics, and artificial leathers. In bookbinding, it is used to coat or impregnate book cloth to enhance durability.

Q

_____

quad   *See*: quadrangle.

quadrangle   A four-sided area of the earth's surface bounded by parallels of latitude and meridians of longitude, used as a unit in mapping. The dimensions of a *quad* are not necessarily the same in both directions. The 1:24,000 7.5-minute topographic quadrangle is the base map used by the U.S. Geological Survey, the largest mapping agency in the United States.

quadraphonic   Sound reproduced by an audio device simultaneously from four separate channels with four amplifiers or speakers. Quadraphonic sound separation produces a more realistic result than monaural or stereophonic sound recording.

quadrennial   Issued every four years. Also refers to a serial publication issued every four years. *See also*: *annual, biennial, triennial, quinquennial, sexennial, septennial*, and *decennial*.

quadrilinear script   *See*: minuscule.

qualification   Evidence that a person applying for employment has passed the requisite examinations or acquired the education, experience, and skills necessary to meet the requirements stated in the position description. Usually used in the plural: *qualifications*.

In Dublin Core and some other metadata schemes, the process of using qualifiers to provide additional information about a metadata element.

qualifier   In Dublin Core and some other metadata schemes, a term added to provide information about the value of a metadata element. In Dublin Core, qualifiers may refine the meaning of an element or identify encoding schemes that aid in interpreting the element value. In subject indexing, see *parenthetical qualifier*.

quality of service   The degree to which the services provided by a library or library system meet the needs of its users and the standards established by the profession, usually assessed statistically and on the basis of qualitative feedback (user surveys, suggestion box, etc.). Quality of service is affected by budgetary constraints, management policies, design and condition of facilities, personnel decisions, and employee morale. Abbreviated *QoS*.

quality paperback   *See*: trade paperback.

quantity discount   A discount offered by a publisher or jobber to booksellers and libraries on orders for a minimum number of copies of the same item or a minimum number of assorted titles. Large libraries are usually in a better position than small libraries to take advantage of such offers.

quarter binding   A style of bookbinding in which the spine is bound in a different material than the sides, usually a more durable covering such as leather, often in a contrasting color, extending no more than one-eighth of the width of the boards. Compare with *full binding*, *half-binding*, and *three-quarter binding*. ***See also***: *quarter leather*.

quarter leather   A book in which the spine is bound in leather and the rest covered in some other material, such as cloth, often in a contrasting color. Compare with *half leather*.

quarterly   Issued four times a year. Also refers to a serial issued every three months, usually in spring, summer, fall, and winter. Most scholarly journals are published quarterly (*example*: ***Shakespeare Quarterly***).

quarto (4to)   A book, approximately 13 inches in height, made by folding a full sheet of book paper in two right-angle folds, producing signatures of four leaves (eight pages). The precise size of each leaf in a quarto edition depends on the size of the original sheet. Some early editions are known by the number of leaves in their sections, for example, the *Quarto Edition* of Shakespeare's plays. Compare with *folio*, *octavo*, *duodecimo*, and *sextodecimo*.

quasi-synonym   A word or phrase not precisely the same in meaning as another term, which is nevertheless treated as synonymous in a given indexing language, for example, the term "Library science" used for (UF) "Librarianship" in the *Library of Congress Subject Headings* list. Synonymous with *near-synonym*.

quatern book   In hand-binding, the binder traditionally bound the thirteenth book at no charge, presumably as an incentive to place larger binding orders, but by the early 19th century, this custom was restricted in England to all the copies of a single title delivered to the bindery at the same time and was not carried over into machine binding.

quaternion   In bookbinding, a gathering consisting of four sheets of paper, parchment, or vellum folded once to create eight leaves, used in assembling some manuscript books and early printed books. ***See also***: *quinternion*, *sextern*, and *ternion*.

quatrefoil   An ornament or illustration resembling a four-lobed leaf or flower, commonly used in medieval architecture and manuscript illumination.

query   A request submitted as input in a search of an online catalog or bibliographic database to retrieve records or documents relevant to the user's information need(s). Some information storage and retrieval systems allow queries to be submitted in natural language, but most systems require the user to formulate search statements in the artificial language used for indexing and in syntax acceptable to the search software. The query is an approximation of the information need that gives rise to the search.

Also refers to the symbol **?** used by the copy editor or by the printer's reader in the margins of a proof to indicate to the author the need for clarification of a detail in the text.

questionnaire   A list of written questions carefully formulated to be administered to a selected group of people for the purpose of gathering information (feedback) in survey research. In libraries, patrons may be asked to fill out questionnaires designed to assess the perceived quality and usefulness of services and resources. The results are then compiled and analyzed for use in planning.

queue   A temporary storage location in a computer, reserved for data awaiting processing, usually organized chronologically (first-in-first-out) or according to some other pre-established priority. Also refers to a line of people waiting to be served or a series of tasks waiting to be executed, usually in the order in which they arrived or were received.

Quill & Quire   A monthly magazine published in Toronto since 1935, providing news and reviews of books published in Canada. The June and December issues include the *Canadian Publishers Directory* as a free supplement. ISSN: 0033–6491. The on-line version of *Q&Q* is available at: www.quillandquire.com.

quinquennial   Issued very five years. Also refers to a serial publication issued every five years (*example*: ***Biography and Genealogy Master Index***). ***See also***: *annual, biennial, triennial, quadrennial, sexennial, septennial*, and *decennial*.

quinternion   In bookbinding, a gathering consisting of five sheets of paper, parchment, or vellum folded once to create 10 leaves, used in assembling some manuscript books and early printed books. ***See also***: *quaternion, sextern*, and *ternion*.

quire   Originally, a gathering consisting of two or more (usually four) parchment or vellum *bifolia* nested one inside another to form eight leaves (16 pages), convenient for hand-sewn books. Michelle Brown notes in *Understanding Illuminated Manuscripts* (Getty Museum/British Library, 1994) that *quire numeration* (numbers written on the final verso to facilitate collation in binding) began in late Antiquity, and *quire signatures* (numbers and/or letters written within a quire to facilitate internal arrangement) began around 1400. When paper came into widespread use after the invention of printing from movable type, its thinness enabled more sheets to be included in a gathering. In modern usage, the term is synonymous with *gathering, section*, and *signature*. Also refers to one-twentieth of a ream, equal to 24 sheets of handmade paper or 25 sheets of machine-made paper.

quorum   The minimum number of members who must be present for business to be conducted at a meeting governed by the rules of parliamentary procedure. When a quorum is not present, a meeting may proceed without formally transacting business.

quotation   Words or passages reproduced from a written work or repeated verbatim from an oral statement. Because words and phrases taken out of context may give a misleading impression of the whole, care must be taken in selecting quotations. A passage quoted incorrectly is a *misquotation*. In publishing, the accuracy of quotations is checked by the editor. Collections of literary quotations are available in the reference section of most libraries.

In printing, brief quotations are set in the text, enclosed in "quotation marks." Long quotations, called *block quotations*, are set apart from the main text by indention and are printed in a smaller type size without quotation marks, preceded and followed by a blank line. A very long quotation is called an *excerpt*. To avoid copyright infringement, quotations in a written work should be documented in footnotes or endnotes. In an oral statement, the source should be verbally acknowledged as a courtesy to the original author. Synonymous with *quote*. Compare with *excerpt*. ***See also***: *permission*.

In acquisitions, a general term for a library's request that a publisher or vendor state the price of an item, and for the seller's response.

R

---

radio frequency identification (RFID)   The use of microchips to tag library materials and the library card, enabling patrons to check out items by walking through a self-service station equipped with an antenna that emits low-frequency radio waves. When an RF tag (transponder) passes through the electromagnetic zone, a reader (antenna + transceiver) decodes the data encoded in the tag's integrated circuit, passing it to a computer that automatically links data from the physical item(s) to the patron record that corresponds to the library card. Line-of-sight is not required for this noncontact system. RFID technology may eventually replace the barcode and optical technology in library circulation systems. Tags are available in various shapes and sizes for use in a wide range of applications, with read/write capability for interactive applications. The fact that high-frequency radio waves can be used to track moving objects at a distance has raised concerns about privacy.

radiograph   An image produced by exposing a photosensitive surface (film or plate) to radiation other than visible light (X-rays, gamma rays, neutrons) through an opaque object. Collected mainly by medical libraries, radiographs are cataloged in *AACR2* as graphic materials. They are also used in the study of watermarks.

rag book   *See*: cloth book.

ragged   Refers to a page of type with lines of variable length, usually *ragged right*, set flush (aligned) with the left-hand margin but unjustified on the right, as in the lines of a poem.

rag paper   Paper made from cotton and/or linen rags, stronger and more permanent than paper made from wood or most other fibers but also more expensive. Rag content is usually indicated as a percentage. Paper made from 100 percent rag fiber is called *all-rag*. *See also*: *bible paper*.

raised bands   Narrow, slightly elevated ridges visible at intervals across the spine of a hand-bound book, produced by the hidden sewing supports to which the sections are attached. On some bindings, raised bands were made more prominent by *nipping up* the leather on either side, as the covering material was applied. When faked on a decorative binding, raised ridges are called *false bands*. Compare with *sunk bands*. *See also*: *smooth spine*.

raised capital   In printing, an initial letter, usually at the beginning of the first paragraph of a chapter, projecting above the line of type on which it appears. Synonymous with *cocked-up initial*. Compare with *drop initial*.

RAM   *See*: random access memory.

ramie   Fiber of the Asiatic plant species *Baehmeria nivea*, in the nettle family, one of the most durable materials for weaving and papermaking, used in printing bank notes. *See also*: *rag paper*.

random access memory (RAM)   A group of high-speed memory chips that perform most of the processing in a computer, allowing users to access bytes of data in any order, rather than sequentially. At startup, the operating system and any application programs are routinely loaded from the hard disk into RAM to allow processing to begin. Any data in current use is also stored in RAM. To retain their content, RAM chips must have electric power, which is why users must save data to a slower storage medium (hard disk, floppy disk, Zip disk, etc.) before powering down. *See also*: *buffer*.

Ranganathan, S(hiyali) R(amamrita) (1892–1972)   A former mathematics professor who, after receiving an honors certificate in library science from the University of London in 1925, served as first librarian of the University of Madras until 1944, where he developed *Colon Classification* (1933), a classification system used in research libraries worldwide.

Ranganathan's pioneering work in library education established him as the "father" of librarianship in India. He helped found the Indian Library Association in 1933 and served as its president from 1944 to 1953. From 1948 to 1958 he served on the Indian national committee for cooperation with UNESCO, focusing his attention on issues of concern to libraries, and from 1951 to 1962 he was *rapporteur-general* for the documentation classification section of the International Federation for Documentation.

In 1956, Ranganathan gave his life savings to endow a professorship in library science at the University of Madras, the first such chair outside the United States. In 1962, he used the royalties from his books to establish an endowment for annual lectures given in India by eminent contributors to library science from around the world. He is famous for his *Five Laws of Library Science* (1931):

1. Books are for use.
2. Every reader his book.
3. Every book its reader.
4. Save the time of the reader.
5. A library is a growing organism.

range   A component of a library stack, consisting of a row of two or more sections of single- or double-faced fixed or adjustable shelving, with common uprights or shelf supports between each section. The row may be free-standing or assembled against a wall.

Also refers to the difference between the largest value and the smallest in a given set of numerical data, for example, a publication date range specified by the user in a search of an online catalog or bibliographic database to limit retrieval to items published within a certain period.

range aisle   The narrow corridor or passageway between two ranges of shelves in the stacks of a library. In the United States, the standard minimum aisle width in new and renovated facilities is 36 inches. Some kinds of compact shelving allow the distance between ranges to be adjusted as needed. Synonymous with *stack aisle*. Compare with *cross aisle*.

rank   Any one of a number of grades of employment within a library or library system, reflecting the qualifications, experience, skill, and length of tenure of the person occupying the position to which the rank applies, usually associated with a given rate or range of compensation. In academic libraries at institutions that grant faculty status to librarians, the ranks are usually *Instructor*, *Assistant Librarian*, *Associate Librarian*, and *Librarian*. The ranks for library staff who do not hold the M.L.S. or M.L.I.S. degree are based on technical skill and experience. *See also*: *promotion*.

Also, to arrange a series of items, records, citations, applicants, etc., in sequence based on one or more evaluative criteria, such as relevance, usefulness, merit, etc. The presence of an option allowing users to rank search results by relevance is a mark of sophistication in database search software. Compare with *sorting*.

ranking   In information retrieval, the presentation of search results in a sequence based on one or more criteria that, in some systems, the user may specify in advance. The most common are currency (publication date) and relevance, usually determined by the number of occurrences of the search terms typed as input and their location in the record (in title, descriptors, abstract, or text). Compare with *sorting*. *See also*: *weighting*.

rare book   A valuable book so difficult to find that only a few copies are known to antiquarian booksellers. Those that do exist seldom appear on the market and are consequently coveted. Most libraries keep their rare books in a secure location to which access is restricted (usually in special collections). Very rare books are sold at book auctions and by dealers serving collectors. For a detailed discussion of the history of rare book libraries, please see the entry by Daniel Traister in the *International Encyclopedia of Information and Library Science* (Routledge, 2003). *See also*: *first edition*, *incunabula*, *price guide*, and *Rare Books and Manuscripts Section*.

Rare Books and Manuscripts Section (RBMS)   Created in 1948 as a special committee of the Association of College and Research Libraries, RBMS exercises leadership in local, national, and international special collections communities to represent and promote the interests of librarians, curators, and other specialists concerned with the acquisition, organization, security, preservation, administration, and use of special collections, including rare books and manuscripts, archives, graphic materials, music, ephemera, etc. RBMS publishes the semiannual *RBM: A Journal of Rare Books, Man-*

uscripts, and Cultural Heritage and the semiannual *RBMS Newsletter*. URL: www. rbms.nd.edu.

rare map Rarity in maps depends on the history of the country or region depicted. As a general rule, any map of the United States published before 1900 is considered rare, especially if it depicts an area west of the Rocky Mountains. In Great Britain, a map is considered rare if published prior to 1825. As historical documents, rare maps are often of considerable interest to scholars and collectors. They can also be aesthetically pleasing.

rarity The degree to which a book or other item is scarce or uncommon, which, in combination with its age, condition, and aesthetic qualities, helps determine its value in the market place. In the antiquarian book trade, degrees of rarity are generally classified as follows:

Scarce—comes to the attention of an expert in rare books no more than once in a year
Rare—comes to the attention of an expert once in a decade
Very rare—comes to the attention of an expert once in a lifetime
Unique—one-of-a-kind, no other copies known to exist

See also: *Rare Books and Manuscripts Section* and *rare map*.

rate adjustment A change in the price of a serial subscription that occurs after the publisher or vendor has billed the library, usually handled with either a supplemental invoice or credit memo.

ratings *See*: content rating *and* library rating.

RBB *See*: *Reference Books Bulletin*.

RBMS *See*: **R**are **B**ooks and **M**anuscripts **S**ection.

readability In typography, the characteristics of a typeface that make it easy for the human eye to read large blocks of printed matter, in contrast to *legibility*, which allows the eye to comprehend a few words or phrases on a page rapidly and accurately. As a general rule, roman typefaces have the highest readability and sans-serifs the highest legibility. Most italics are too light to be readable en masse. Typefaces lose readability in condensation.

In literary composition, prose written in a style that makes the content easy to comprehend. Some publishers use a *fog index* to measure readability.

readable Capable of being read. Also refers to reading material that is interesting and written in a style that makes the content easy for most readers to comprehend. Sometimes used synonymously with *legible*. *See also*: *fog index*.

read-a-thon A contraction of *reading marathon*, a school or library event in which young readers are given an incentive to read a certain number of pages or books within a designated period of time. The event may be tied to fund-raising, with sponsors pledging to contribute a certain amount to a worthy cause when the reading goal is met.

reader   A person who reads silently to himself (or herself) or aloud to others, from a book or other written or printed source, or from an electronic medium displaying text. One of the primary goals of libraries is to encourage reading and literacy. Reading preferences are of particular interest to publishers who use survey techniques to measure them. *See also*: *new adult reader* and *reluctant reader*.

In publishing, a person asked to read and evaluate for potential publication manuscripts submitted by authors and their agents. Large publishing houses often employ a *first reader* to screen incoming manuscripts and select those deemed worthy of further consideration, usually by specialists. In printing, a person responsible for reading proofs and comparing them with the original copy to detect typographical errors, a process called *proofreading*. Also, a person who volunteers or is paid to read a book onto audiotape for distribution as an audiobook, sometimes a professionally trained actor or actress.

In special libraries, a staff member responsible for scanning current materials to select items to be routed to persons within the organization who have requested current awareness service, based on their interest profiles.

Also refers to a textbook containing reading exercises, especially one intended for young schoolchildren. Synonymous in this sense with *primer*.

reader-printer   A machine designed for enlarging, viewing, and making printed copies of microforms (microfiche, microfilm, microopaque), usually coin-operated (fee varies). Libraries with microform holdings usually provide at least one reader-printer for patron use. Compare with *photocopier*. *See also*: *copy card*.

readers' advisory   Services provided by an experienced public services librarian who specializes in the reading needs of the adult patrons of a public library. A readers' advisor recommends specific titles and/or authors, based on knowledge of the patron's past reading preferences, and may also compile lists of recommended titles and serve as liaison to other adult education agencies in the community. The same type of information is provided by reference books such as *Reader's Adviser: A Layman's Guide to Reading* published by R.R. Bowker. Compare with *bibliographic instruction*.

readership   The total number of people who read, or are estimated to read, a given publication, not necessarily equal to the number who purchase or subscribe to it. In periodical publishing, total readership equals base circulation plus pass-along. The term is also used to refer to a particular class of reader, for example, *educated readership* as opposed to *general readership*.

reading copy   A complimentary copy of a forthcoming book sent at no charge by the publisher to selected booksellers in advance of the publication date to promote sales. Reading copies may be printed as part of the regular edition and distributed in the same binding as the trade edition. Compare with *advance copy*.

Also refers to a used book so worn that it is not considered collectible in the antiquarian book trade unless rebound but is suitable for reading because no portion of the text is missing.

reading group   An organized group, usually sponsored by a library, school, church, or bookstore, whose members meet to talk about books they have read. Most groups coordinate their reading so that everyone has read the same book, or a work by the same author, in advance of meeting. In some groups, a facilitator is selected, sometimes on a rotating basis, who begins the session with a brief talk about the author or the book, then opens the floor for discussion. *See also*: *Great Books*.

reading habits   *See*: reading preference.

reading lamp   A man-made light source specifically designed to provide the optimum amount of illumination for a person sitting and reading in a chair or at a desk, usually shaded to direct the light downward onto the page without glare. Very small models designed to clip onto the cover of a book can be purchased for reading in bed.

reading level   One of several degrees of proficiency in reading, usually defined in reference to a specific academic grade level (*example*: **third-grade level**) or stage of reading development, applicable to both reader and reading material. Factors determining reading level include vocabulary, sentence structure, length of text, and difficulty of content.

reading list   A list of recommended resources (books, articles, Web sites, etc.) on a topic, usually compiled by a teacher or librarian with an interest or expertise on the subject, for distribution to students enrolled in a course of study or available to readers on a library display rack, kiosk, or bulletin board, not as comprehensive or scholarly as a research bibliography. Compare with *pathfinder* and *research guide*.

reading matter   Anything that can be read, from the back of a cereal box to a philosophical treatise. Reading material need not be written or printed on paper, merely text-based, for example, a news article published at a Web site. Choice of reading material reflects a person's interests, tastes, education, and experience. *See also*: *readers' advisory* and *reading preference*.

reading preference   A reader's taste in reading matter as to format (books, magazines, comic books, etc.), genre (fiction or nonfiction), subject (biography, crime, travel, etc.), and author. Although reading preferences often change with age, studies have shown that in some individuals they remain remarkably constant. Gender and age are important factors in fiction preferences (adventure and westerns for men, mystery and romance for women, science fiction and fantasy for adolescents). Psychological factors such as mood may also influence reader choice. Publishers rely on survey research to examine consumer choice. Niche publishing appeals to consumers who have developed specific interests. User surveys enable librarians to develop typologies of borrowers, based on habitual preferences. In public libraries, experienced public services librarians often make an effort to learn the reading habits of regular patrons, and may select materials with the preferences of specific individuals in mind. *See also*: *readers' advisory*.

Reading Rainbow   A television series designed to interest children 4–8 years of age in the pleasures of reading outstanding books for children, *Reading Rainbow* is broadcast daily (M–F) for one-half hour by 95 percent of the public television (PBS) stations in the United States. Its fast-paced magazine-style format has garnered over 150 awards since its inception, including 13 Emmy Awards. URL: gpn.unl.edu/rainbow.

reading room   A specially designated room in a library, usually furnished with comfortable chairs, study tables, and reading lamps, where a person can study or read quietly without being disturbed. Reading rooms may also contain library materials such as reference books. Some libraries have wired their reading rooms to accommodate patrons using laptops, who require Internet access. Reading rooms in very large libraries, such as the New York Public Library at 5th Avenue and 42nd Street, are often beautifully designed and furnished.

Also applies to a community facility administered independently of a library, equipped with tables, chairs, and illumination but containing little or no reading matter, to which a person in need of a quiet retreat may bring his or her own materials for study, more common in less developed countries where comfortable space for individual study is at a premium.

readme   A small text file containing important instructions on how to use a computer program, or information about new developments affecting the user of a software system, which may not be included in the printed documentation. To avoid computer viruses, caution should be exercised when opening a readme file sent as an e-mail attachment.

read-only   A digital storage medium capable of being read but not modified or erased, used for data that is to be retained permanently, for example, ROM (read-only memory) and CD-ROM. The opposite of *rewritable*. *See also*: *WORM*.

read-only memory (ROM)   A memory chip containing instructions and/or data that cannot be changed or erased because the manufacturer created it in unalterable form. Usually contains the programs required to start the computer. Compare with *CD-ROM*.

ready reference   A reference question that can be answered by a reference librarian in one or two minutes by providing a fact or piece of information found in a single source, a type of question that sometimes turns out to be an opening gambit that develops into a more comprehensive search.

Also refers to the reference materials used most often in answering such questions, shelved for convenience in a separate location near the reference desk rather than in the reference stacks (*Books in Print*, *Encyclopedia of Associations*, *Statistical Abstract of the U.S.*, world almanacs, city directories, *Ulrich's Periodicals Directory*, etc.). Shelf dummies are used in the reference stacks to direct users to the correct location. Some libraries also provide online ready reference resources via their Web pages. Selection decisions are usually made by the public services librarians who work at the reference desk, based on consensus developed over time.

realia   Three-dimensional objects from real life, whether man-made (artifacts, tools, utensils, etc.) or naturally occurring (specimens, samples, etc.), usually borrowed, purchased, or received as gifts by a library for use in classroom instruction or in exhibits. In *AACR2*, the term is added inside square brackets **[realia]** as a general material designation following the title proper in the bibliographic description. Compare with *replica*.

real time   Happening immediately, in the present moment, for example, a report on or record of events made simultaneously with their occurrence. In computing, an electronic process, operation, or routine that occurs quickly enough to affect or respond to a related process taking place simultaneously in actual time, for example, *chat reference*. The opposite of *asynchronous*.

ream   As originally used in papermaking, the term referred to a unit of measurement consisting of 20 quires or 480 sheets of handmade paper, but the number of sheets in a ream eventually became standardized at 500 sheets of machine-made paper. More recently, European papermakers have adopted 1,000 sheets as the standard number.

rebacked   A book given a new spine and mended hinges, usually because the spine was cracked or the hinges weakened. Rebacking is not as extensive as *rebinding* since some of the original binding materials (usually the boards) are retained. *See also*: *backstrip*.

rebinding   The complete rehabilitation of a book too worn to be mended or repaired, a process that usually entails removing the cover or case, resewing the sections, and applying a new cover or case. In some instances, parts of an old binding can be incorporated into a new one. When this is impossible and the old binding is important, it should be kept as part of the book's history. The steps involved in preparing a book for rebinding are collectively known as *pulling*. Very large libraries are often equipped to perform rebinding in-house, but smaller libraries must rely on the services of a commercial bindery. Compare with *recased* and *recover*. *See also*: *covers bound in*.

reboot   To cause the files in the operating system of a computer to be re-executed, usually by selecting the option to "Restart" or "Reset" or by pressing **Ctrl+Alt+Del** on the keyboard. This procedure is sometimes helpful in getting a computer "unstuck" after it locks up unexpectedly during processing. If it fails, the user can cold boot the system, but powering down will result in the loss of unsaved data. Synonymous with *warm boot*. *See also*: *boot*.

rebus   A type of puzzle in which certain words in a sentence are replaced by pictures of objects whose names suggest the meaning or sound of the words they are intended to represent, for example, a picture of a bed to suggest "sleep" or of an eye to represent the pronoun "I." According to James Bettley (*The Art of the Book*, V&A Publications, 2001), the earliest known example appears in a treatise on penmanship by Giovambattista Palatino printed in 1540.

recall   A request by a library to one of its borrowers to return a borrowed item before its due date. In academic libraries, this occasionally happens when an instructor wishes to place the item on reserve.

   In information retrieval, a measure of the effectiveness of a search, expressed as the ratio of the number of relevant records or documents retrieved in response to the query to the total number of relevant records or documents in the database; for example, in a database containing 100 records relevant to the topic "book history," a search retrieving 50 records, 25 of which are relevant to the topic, would have 25 percent recall (25/100). One of the main difficulties in using recall as a measure of search effectiveness is that it can be nearly impossible to determine the total number of relevant entries in all but very small databases. Compare with *precision*. ***See also***: *fallout*.

recased   A text block that has come loose in, or fallen out of, its case or cover and been reglued into it, a process that usually requires new endpapers but not resewing. The term is also used for a book rebound in a case taken from another copy of the same title or in an entirely new case. Compare with *rebinding* and *recover*.

recataloging   The process of making substantial revisions in bibliographic records for items that have already been cataloged, usually in response to changes in the needs or policies of a library, for example, the addition of contents notes in records representing anthologies and other collected works. Compare with *reclassification*.

receiving   In acquisitions, the initial processing of an item shipped to the library by a publisher, jobber, or vendor, including verification that the correct item was shipped with all parts included, routing the invoice to the appropriate accounting office for payment, and updating the order record, usually with date received, number of parts received, and an indication of where the item was sent for the next step in processing.

recension   A revision of the text of a work, often a literary classic, based on a critical examination of earlier texts and authoritative sources, usually undertaken only after a consensus has developed among scholars concerning the weight of evidence. Compare with *redaction*. ***See also***: textus receptus.

recently returned   A code used in online catalogs and circulation systems to indicate the circulation status of an item returned by a borrower and checked in by library staff so recently that it may still be on a holding shelf or in the process of being reshelved. The temporary designation assists staff in tracing the item if it cannot be located by call number in the stacks.

recessed monitor   *See*: monitor.

reciprocal agreement   A mutual understanding between libraries, usually concerning fees for lending via interlibrary loan, typically "We will not charge you if you do not charge us."

reciprocal borrowing privileges   Loan privileges granted by independent cooperating libraries to members of each other's user groups, sometimes for a modest fee.

reclassification   Revision of the call numbers assigned to selected items to make their relationship to other items in the collection more consistent, for example, to reflect the merger of two classes very similar in subject. Also refers to the conversion of a collection (or part of a collection) originally cataloged under one classification system to another, for example, from Dewey Decimal Classification to Library of Congress Classification, or vice versa.

recon   *See*: **re**trospective **con**version.

reconfigure   To change the way data is structured in a computer system.

record   An account of something, put down in writing, usually as a means of documenting facts for legal or historical purposes. Also, to make such an account. In a narrower sense, a formal document in which the content is presented in a named set of standardized data elements treated as a single unit, for example, a certificate, deed, lease, etc. In archives, a document created or received, and subsequently maintained, by an institution, organization, or individual in the transaction of official or personal business or in the fulfillment of a legal obligation. *See also*: *bibliographic record* and *catalog record*.

In computing, a collection of related data fields organized and accessible as a single entity. A *machine-readable data file* is a collection of such records.

Also, to use an audiorecording device to capture and store audio signals for playback. Also refers to any sound recording made on a vinyl disk, for example, a *phonograph record*.

record album   One or more paper sleeves designed to hold phonograph records, usually enclosed in a colorful pasteboard cover, often with a list of the contents and descriptive notes printed on the back or on the inside. The sleeves may have wide circles cut from the center, sometimes replaced with transparent material to allow the record labels to remain visible.

recorded book   *See*: audiobook.

record group   In archives, an aggregation of all the records of a particular agency or person, or a body of records known to be related on the basis of provenance, usually stored together in their original order (see *respect des fonds*). A *record subgroup* consists of records within a record group, related in some way (functionally, chronologically, geographically, etc.) or produced by a subordinate unit of the agency responsible for creating, receiving, or accumulating the group. Subgroups may be further subdivided.

record item   In archives, the smallest separate and distinct unit of recorded material that, when accumulated, constitutes a record series, for example, a file in a group of related files. Compare with *bibliographic item*.

recordkeeping system   The methods and procedures used in creating, arranging, and maintaining records of the activities of an agency or individual, usually in some kind of systematic order (alphabetical, chronological, topical, functional, etc.), which may appear idiosyncratic to outsiders unfamiliar with the system. *See also*: *original order*.

records   Documents in any form, created or received by an agency or person, accumulated in the normal conduct of business or affairs, and retained as evidence of such activity, usually arranged according to a discernible system of recordkeeping. *See also*: *active records, electronic records, inactive records, intermediate records, machine-readable records, official records, records management, temporary records, time-expired records*, and *vital records*.

record series   In archives, records of the same provenance, determined upon inspection to belong together because they (1) are part of a recognizable filing system, (2) have been stored together because they were produced by the same activity, (3) are related to the same function or activity and are similar in format, or (4) comprise a set logically grouped in some other way. A record series is usually identified by a unique *series number* and may in some cases consist of a single record item.

records management   The field of management devoted to achieving accuracy, efficiency, and economy in the systematic creation, retention, conservation, dissemination, use, and disposition of the official records of a company, government agency, organization, or institution, whether in physical or electronic form, usually undertaken by a professionally trained *records manager* on the basis of a thorough *records survey*. Security and disaster preparedness are essential elements of a good records management program.

records survey   The systematic process of examining archival records in their administrative context to determine their content, format, provenance, original order, physical quantities and condition, rates of accumulation, and other characteristics, before beginning the work of describing and arranging them. The information gained in such a survey is also of use in developing disposition schedules, planning conservation, determining access policy, and estimating the amount of space required to store them.

record structure   The pre-established sequence of fields and subfields used to describe a single item in a library catalog or bibliographic database, each field containing one or more related elements of description. For example, the journal title, volume number, date of issue, and page numbers in the source field of a record representing a journal article in a periodical database. Most catalogs and databases include textual field labels in the record display to help users distinguish the various categories of description.

recover   To apply a new cover to a volume, without resewing the sections. The process of making the new cover and attaching it to the sections is called *recovering*. Compare with *rebinding* and *recased*.

Also, to get back something that was lost, for example, library materials known to have been stolen or checked out and lost by the borrower. Fees may be refunded, depending on the circumstances. *See also*: *replevin*.

recruitment   The process of attracting qualified personnel to work in a library or library system by posting a notice and position description in library journals and to library-related electronic mailing lists and by publicizing the vacancy at job fairs and word-of-mouth. Also refers to the efforts of library schools and professional library associations to attract promising students to careers in library and information science.

recto   The upper side of a leaf of parchment, vellum, or paper, or the right-hand page in a bound volume when opened, usually assigned an odd page number. The opposite of *verso*. The title page and dedication, and the first page of the preface, introduction, table of contents, chapters, appendices, indexes, and other major parts of a book are printed on the recto. Also, the side of a single printed sheet intended to be read first, unless both sides are identically printed. Also known as the *obverse*.

recycled paper   Paper manufactured from reclaimed wastepaper that has been reduced to pulp and processed to remove ink and other impurities. Recycled paper is used in printing and as writing paper to conserve natural resources and reduce the volume of refuse in sanitary landfills. Book publishers consider the highest grades suitable for printing fiction.

redaction The process of editing, revising, and/or arranging to publish a work left incomplete or in a condition not suitable for publication, usually at the death of the author, done by a *redactor*. Also refers to the result of such an endeavor. Compare with *continuation* and *recension*.

red book The popular name given to a manual containing official lists of state employees or other eminent people, for example, members of the British peerage, known by the color of its cover. Compare with *blue book*.

redirect Forwarding by a Web server that changes an incoming URL to another URL, usually when the Internet address of a Web page has changed. The simplest method is a dummy page at the old address displaying a link to the new address, or the Webmaster may insert an HTML "meta refresh" statement that automatically transfers the user to the new address, usually after an interval of a few seconds. Some Web servers are capable of handling *redirection* with look-up tables that pair the old URL with the new URL. Redirection based on the IP address of the incoming user is accomplished by writing a CGI script.

reduction A reproduction or copy produced on a smaller scale than the original, usually indicated as a percentage of the initial size (a 50 percent reduction of an 8 × 10 inch original produces a copy measuring 4 × 5 inches). Most photocopiers available in libraries have reduction capability for the convenience of users. The opposite of *enlargement*. *See also*: *micrographics* and *reduction ratio*.

reduction ratio In microphotography, an indication of the number of times the size of a document or other object is reduced to form a microimage. For example, 25× means that the image is 25 times smaller than the linear dimensions of the original. Reduction ratios are classified as follows:

Low—up to 15×
Medium—15× to 30×
High—30× to 60×
Very high—60× to 90×
Ultrahigh—above 90×

redundancy In communication, the use of repetition to reinforce a message and prevent misunderstanding, as in a sign that reads, "This Way to the Library" instead of simply "Library" or "To the Library." In a more general sense, any words or symbols not essential to the meaning of a message.

In computer systems, devices that stand ready to handle transmission or processing if and when the units normally used for the purpose fail or have to be taken offline.

reel A flanged circular holder with a hole running from end to end onto which a roll of processed film is wound, usually designed to be inserted in a projector, reader, reader-printer, or other display device. Open reels were once used for magnetic tape but have been largely replaced by cartridges. Compare with *spool*.

referee   In scholarly publishing, an expert whose areas of specialization include the subject of a journal article or book, usually a professional peer of the author, to whom the editor or publisher sends the manuscript for critical evaluation before accepting it for publication. *See also*: *peer-reviewed*.

refereed   *See*: peer-reviewed.

reference   A conventional word or phrase used in a work to refer the reader to another part of the text (*see above* or *see below*) or a similar word or phrase used in an index, catalog, or reference work to direct the user from one heading or entry to another (*see* or *see also*). Also refers to any Latin phrase used in footnotes, endnotes, and bibliographies to refer the reader to works previously quoted or cited, for example, *ibid.* and *op. cit.* Sometimes used synonymously with *citation*.

Also refers to a letter written in support of a person's application for employment or housing, usually by someone familiar with the applicant's qualifications or reputation, or to a person who agrees to be contacted for such a recommendation, usually by telephone.

Reference and User Services Association (RUSA)   Established as a division of the American Library Association in 1972, RUSA has a membership consisting of librarians and other individuals committed to promoting the delivery of reference and information services to all persons, regardless of age, in libraries of all kinds. RUSA publishes the journal *Reference and User Services Quarterly (RUSQ)*. URL: www.ala.org.

reference book   A book designed to be consulted when authoritative information is needed, rather than read cover to cover. Reference books often consist of a series of signed or unsigned "entries" listed alphabetically under headwords or headings, or in some other arrangement (classified, numeric, etc.). The category includes almanacs, atlases, bibliographies, biographical sources, catalogs, concordances, dictionaries, directories, discographies and filmographies, encyclopedias, glossaries, handbooks, indexes, manuals, research guides, union lists, and yearbooks, whether published commercially or as government documents. Long reference works may be issued in multivolume sets, with any indexes in the last volume. Reference works that require continuous updating may be published serially, sometimes as loose-leaf services.

In libraries, reference books are shelved in a separate section called the *reference stacks* and are not allowed to circulate because they are needed to answer questions at the reference desk. Reference books are reviewed in *American Reference Books Annual, CHOICE, Library Journal*, the *Reference Books Bulletin* section of *Booklist, Reference Services Review*, and *Reference and User Services Quarterly* published by RUSA. The two leading bibliographies of English-language reference materials are *Guide to Reference Books* published by the American Library Association and *Walford's Guide to Reference Materials* published by the Library Association (UK). Compare with *circulating book*. *See also*: *popular reference book*.

Reference Books Bulletin (RBB)   A separate section at the end of the review publication *Booklist*, providing reviews of approximately 500 reference books and electronic reference materials annually. General encyclopedias and certain types of dictionaries are often reviewed together to facilitate comparison. *RBB* has its own editorial board and, unlike *Booklist*, publishes reviews of items *not* recommended for purchase. ISSN: 0006–7385.

reference collection   Books not meant to be read cover to cover, such as dictionaries, handbooks, and encyclopedias, shelved together by call number in a special section of the library called the *reference stacks*. Reference books may not be checked out because they are needed by librarians to answer questions at the reference desk. Their location and circulation status is usually indicated by the symbol "R" or "Ref" preceding the call number in the catalog record and on the spine label. *See also*: *ready reference*.

reference desk   When a person has a question about how to find specific information or how to use library services and resources, assistance can be obtained by contacting the public service point located near the reference collection of the library (in person, by telephone, or in some libraries via e-mail). A professionally trained reference librarian scheduled to work at the reference desk will try to provide an answer or refer the inquirer to a knowledgeable source. In large public and academic libraries, the reference desk may be staffed by two librarians, especially during periods of peak use. Compare with *information desk*. *See also*: *reference interview* and *roving*.

reference interview   The interpersonal communication that occurs between a reference librarian and a library user to determine the person's specific information need(s), which may turn out to be different than the reference question as initially posed. Because patrons are often reticent, especially in face-to-face interaction, patience and tact may be required on the part of the librarian. A reference interview may occur in person, by telephone, or electronically (usually via e-mail) at the request of the user, but a well-trained reference librarian will sometimes initiate communication if a hesitant user appears to need assistance. For more information, please see *The Reference Interview as a Creative Art* by Elaine and Edward Jennerich (Libraries Unlimited, 1997). *See also*: *digital reference* and *roving*.

reference librarian   A librarian who works in public services, answering questions posed by library patrons at a reference desk, by telephone, or via e-mail. A reference librarian may also be called upon to provide point-of-use instruction on the use of library resources and information technology. Most reference librarians also assist in the selection of a balanced collection of reference materials to meet the information needs of the library's clientele.

reference mark   A printer's symbol used in text to refer to material printed in a different place, for example, in a footnote or in another passage on the same page. When more than one reference is given on a page, the order of symbols is the asterisk (*), dagger (†), double dagger (‡), section mark (§), parallel mark (‖), and paragraph mark (¶). When necessary the sequence can be repeated, but most publishers prefer to indicate multiple references by the use of numerals in superscript.

reference matter   *See*: back matter.

reference question   A request from a library user for assistance in locating specific information or in using library resources in general, made in person, by telephone, or electronically. In most libraries, reference questions are answered by a professionally trained *reference librarian* during a regularly scheduled shift at the reference desk, but in small libraries this function may be performed by a paraprofessional. A *reference interview* may be required to determine the precise nature of the information need. Questions are usually recorded in a transaction log by category (directional, informational, instructional, referral) for statistical purposes.

reference serial   A publication used by reference librarians to find authoritative information, which is issued successively at regular or irregular intervals with no indication of an ending date. The category includes dictionaries and encyclopedias (*example*: ***Contemporary Authors***), directories (***AV Market Place***), annuals (***Europa World Year Book***), loose-leaf services (***Facts on File***), etc. Reference serials are normally placed on continuation order and shelved with other reference materials in the reference stacks.

reference services   All the functions performed by a trained librarian employed in the reference section of a library to meet the information needs of patrons (in person, by telephone, or electronically), including but not limited to answering substantive questions, instructing users in the selection and use of appropriate tools and techniques for finding information, conducting searches on behalf of the patron, directing users to the location of library resources, assisting in the evaluation of information, referring patrons to resources outside the library when appropriate, keeping reference statistics, and participating in the development of the reference collection. *See also*: *collaborative reference*, *cooperative reference*, and *digital reference*.

reference source   Any publication from which authoritative information may be obtained, including but not limited to reference books, catalog records, printed indexes and abstracting services, and bibliographic databases. Individuals and services outside the library that can be relied upon to provide authoritative information are considered *resources* for referral.

reference stacks   The area of a library in which the reference collection is shelved in call number order, usually located near the reference desk, open to the public in most public and academic libraries in the United States. Printed periodical indexes may be shelved separately from the reference book collection, usually alphabetically by title or in a classified arrangement. *See also*: *ready reference*.

reference statistics   In most libraries, the librarians who work at the reference desk keep a daily transaction log in which they record reference questions, usually by hour and type of question (informational, directional, instructional, referral, etc.). Compiled by week, month, and year, the results are analyzed to reveal patterns and trends helpful in anticipating staffing needs, scheduling the reference desk, developing the reference collection, and planning new services. The librarian responsible for supervising reference services may also cite them in reports submitted to the library administration.

referral   A type of reference transaction in which a patron with an information need is directed to a reputable person or agency outside the library, better qualified to provide assistance. In some public libraries, a list or index of referral agencies and resources, with contact information, is maintained at the reference desk for this purpose. *See also*: *information and referral*.

Reforma   Established in 1971 as an affiliate of the American Library Association, Reforma actively promotes the development of Spanish-language and Latino-oriented library collections, recruitment of bilingual and multicultural librarians and support staff, development of library programs and services for the Latino community, public awareness of library services among Latinos, lobbying on behalf of the information needs of Latinos, and liaison with other professional organizations. URL: www. reforma.org.

reformat   To convert a document from one format to another without changing its content, for example, a journal article published in print to microform for compact storage or from print to ASCII text for inclusion in a full-text bibliographic database. In preservation, reformatting is usually undertaken when the long-term survival of a document in its current format is unlikely, for example, a work published electronically in a medium rapidly becoming obsolete or a document printed on acid paper that is in an advanced state of deterioration. *See also*: *original format*.

Also, to prepare a floppy disk for a new use by completely erasing any data stored on it. Normally when a disk is reinitialized, it is also tested to make sure it is still reliable.

refresh   *See*: reload.

regional book   A term used in the publishing industry for a book written to appeal to readers who live in, or have an interest in, a specific geographic area. Regional books are often published by small presses for sale in local bookstores or by mail order. They include local histories, biographies, genealogies, directories, cookbooks, travel guides, field guides, etc. Some public libraries shelve them in a separate section to make them more accessible.

regional library   A public library serving the information needs of a group of communities or counties in the United States, supported by public funds provided by the units of government within its service area, for example, the Fort Vancouver Regional Library serving southwest Washington State.

register   The alignment of pages back-to-back during the printing of the second side of a sheet to make the text blocks coincide exactly. In multicolor printing, the precise alignment of the impression for each color with the one(s) preceding it to produce an image that is *in register* (sharp), rather than *out of register* (blurred). Also refers to the list of symbols by which the signatures of a book are marked to indicate their sequence in binding.

In bookbinding, a length of thin ribbon glued to the top of the spine of a book before lining, for use as a bookmark. Books used in the services of the Roman Catholic Church sometimes have several ribbons in different colors for marking more than one page in the text. In French bookbinding of the 16th century, a precious stone or other ornament was sometimes attached to the ribbon. Synonymous in this sense with *signet*.

Also refers to a list of names, addresses, events, dates, etc., usually compiled in a single chronological or numerical sequence and maintained as an official log or record. The term is also used for the act of recording information in such a list. *See also*: *registry*.

registry   The office responsible for maintaining one or more official lists or registers of names, addresses, events, dates, or other information, usually for legal purposes. For example, in the United States the official registry for copyrights is the U.S. Copyright Office of the Library of Congress. The term is sometimes used for the list or record itself. *See also*: *International Serials Data System* and *National Film Registry*.

A *metadata registry* is an application that records the authoritative definitions of terms and shows relationships between terms from the same metadata scheme or from multiple schemes.

regular   The frequency of a serial publication issued at intervals governed by an established rule, usually of uniform length, expressed in days, weeks, months, quarters, years, etc., for example, monthly with the exception of August and December. The opposite of *irregular*. The term also describes a contribution to a newspaper or periodical, appearing in every issue or at stated intervals, for example, "The Back Page" column in the review publication *Booklist*.

Also refers to a person who attends a certain type of event or uses the same service(s) at fairly predictable intervals. Libraries often have regular patrons whose habits and reading preferences become familiar to the public services librarians who serve them.

reimburse   To pay back money spent by another person or compensate someone for damages or expenses incurred, usually upon presentation of a receipt verifying the amount. In libraries, employees may be reimbursed for travel expenses, office supplies purchased out of pocket, etc.

reinforced binding   A publisher's binding that has been strengthened, usually by adding a strip of cloth to each hinge and using stronger thread to sew the sections, but that does not meet the standards for *prelibrary binding*.

reinstate   To return something to a former condition, or a person to a position from which he or she has been removed, sometimes in compliance with the outcome of a grievance procedure or lawsuit.

reissue   A second or subsequent impression of a previously published edition in which the text remains substantially the same, but the title page may be redesigned and the front matter and back matter altered. When a mass-market paperback is reissued, the cover design of the earlier edition is often changed.

rejection rate   In journal publishing, the percentage of the total number of articles submitted for publication during a given period of time that are rejected or returned to the author (or authors) for revision as a condition of acceptance, usually as the result of a peer-review process.

rejection slip   A printed slip sent by a publisher with a returned manuscript informing the author (or authors) that the work has *not* been accepted for publication. *See also*: *over the transom*.

related body   A corporate body associated with another corporate body but not functioning under its direct authority, for example, a Friends group that supports a library through volunteer work, fund-raising, advocacy, and other activities but is not a unit of its organizational structure. *AACR2* includes in this category a corporate body founded but not controlled by another body, one receiving support from or providing financial and/or other assistance to another body, and one whose members also have membership in, or an association with, another body. Compare with *subordinate body*.

related term (RT)   In a hierarchical classification system, a descriptor or subject heading closely related to another term conceptually but not hierarchically, for example, "Media specialists" listed as a related term under "School libraries." A descriptor or subject heading may have more than one related term (also "Children's libraries" under "School libraries"). Also abbreviated *R*. Compare with *broader term* and *narrower term*.

related work   *See*: dependent work.

relationship   As defined in *FRBR* (*Functional Requirements for Bibliographic Records*), the nature of the link between entities, for example, between one work and another (a **prequel** to the play *Hamlet* by William Shakespeare), between a work and one of its expressions (the **film version** of *Hamlet* adapted and directed by Kenneth Branagh), between an expression and one of its manifestations (Branagh's adaptation of *Hamlet*, as embodied in the **videorecording** released in 1996 by Columbia TriStar Home Video), or between a manifestation and one of its items (a **set of videocassettes** exemplifying the 1996 videorecording of Branagh's interpretation of *Hamlet*).

relative humidity   *See*: humidity.

relative index   A subject index to a classification system indicating the classes under which subjects are listed, with their notations. In the Dewey Decimal Classification schedules, subjects are arranged by discipline. At the end of the schedules, an alphabetical index of subjects is provided (the Relative Index). Indented under each subject heading is an alphabetical list of the disciplines in which the subject is found, with corresponding class numbers. For example, the entry in the index for the subject "Books" directs the cataloger to the discipline "Bibliographies" with the notation **011** and also to "Publishing" (**070.5**), "Sociology" (**302.232**), and "Technology" (**686**).

release   To allow copies of a recorded work to be issued, shown, or sold to the general public for the first time. In the case of motion pictures and videorecordings, to permit copies to be distributed for public viewing. In exceptional cases, a motion picture may be *rereleased* in significantly altered form. In library cataloging, the release date is used as the publication date in the bibliographic description. *See also*: *releasing agent*.

release date   The date on which a motion picture or videorecording is officially made available for distribution to theaters for public viewing or to wholesale and retail outlets for sale. In library cataloging, year of release is entered in the publication distribution, etc., area of the bibliographic record representing the item. Compare with *publication date*.

release print   The final version of a motion picture, intended for distribution to public audiences, in some cases shorter than the director intended. In some cases, an initial print found to be too long is *rereleased* after having been cut (*example*: Disney's **Fantasia**). On very rare occasions, a motion picture from which important scenes were cut is rereleased after having been restored to its original length (Frank Capra's **Lost Horizon**). When such an item is cataloged by a library, the phrase "original restored version" is added as a note in the bibliographic description. Synonymous with *showprint*.

releasing agent   A person or agency responsible for the initial distribution (release) of a motion picture. In *AACR2*, the name is recorded optionally in the publication, distribution, etc., area of the bibliographic description following the name of the publisher.

relevance   The extent to which information retrieved in a search of a library collection or other resource, such as an online catalog or bibliographic database, is judged by the user to be applicable to ("about") the subject of the query. Relevance depends on the searcher's subjective perception of the degree to which the document fulfills the information need, which may or may not have been expressed fully or with precision in the search statement. Measures of the effectiveness of information retrieval, such as *precision* and *recall*, depend on the relevance of search results. Compare with *pertinence*. *See also*: *false drop* and *relevance ranking*.

relevance ranking   A feature of some search software that weights the documents or records retrieved in a search according to the degree to which they meet the requirements of the query. Ranked results are normally presented in decreasing order of relevance, computed on the basis of the number of occurrences of each search term in the document or record, and the weight assigned to the field(s) in which each term appears (title, subject headings, abstract, or full-text).

relevance ratio   *See*: precision.

relief map   A topographic map showing the elevation of an area of the surface of the earth by means of standard graphic techniques, such as linear contour lines, hachures, shading, or tint. The U.S. Geological Survey (USGS) issues relief maps of the 50 states, available in the government documents collections of larger depository libraries. Compare with *planimetric map*. *See also*: *bathymetric map* and *relief model*.

relief model   In cartography, a three-dimensional relief map constructed of papier mâché, plaster, or plastic on which elevation is indicated by the relative height of the surface. Tactile raised-relief maps are manufactured for the use of persons who are visually impaired.

relievo binding   In Italian *relievo* means "relief." A binding made from leather that is softened, then molded and deeply embossed, a technique used in 19th-century England to introduce designs reflecting the Victorian revival of gothic style. *See also*: *papier mâché binding*.

religious book   A work of fiction or nonfiction in which the main theme is based on a particular religious faith. Included in the category are sacred texts, devotional works, materials for religious professionals, textbooks for religious education, and inspirational titles intended for laypersons. Some publishers specialize in religious works (*examples*: **Zondervan**, **Judaica Press**, **Kazi Publications**, etc.). Large publishers may have a division devoted to religious publishing (**Schocken Books** within Random House). New Christian fiction is reviewed regularly in a separate section of *Booklist*. Religious books are sold in religious bookstores, through religious book clubs, and increasingly in trade bookstores. Public libraries select judiciously with an eye toward maintaining a balanced collection.

reload   An option in the toolbar of a Web browser that causes the currently displayed Web page to be retrieved from its original remote address, rather than from the browser cache of the computer used to retrieve it, necessary if the data available from the site is time-sensitive (news, stock quotes, weather reports, current statistics, etc.). Some Web pages are designed to automatically *refresh* at regular intervals.

relocation   In Dewey Decimal Classification, the editorial decision to shift a subject from one class number to another in a new edition of the schedules, the two numbers differing in more than length of notation (*example*: "sociolinguistics" relocated in the 20th edition from **401.9** to **306.44**). Reciprocal notes are added in the schedules to inform the user of the new and former numbers.

reluctant reader   A person who, for whatever reason, chooses not to read, doing so only when necessary, usually a sign of poor reading skills or fear of being stereotyped. Young adult librarians often coax adolescent boys into reading by providing them with easy-to-read materials on subjects that appeal to their interests. The Young Adult Library Services Association publishes "Quick Picks for Reluctant Young Adult Readers" in *Booklist*, *The Bowker Annual Library and Book Trade Almanac*, and *School Library Journal*.

remainder binding   *See*: remainders.

remainder mark   A mark made by the publisher on the bottom edge of a book, usually with a stamp, permanent marking pen, or spray paint to indicate that it has been remaindered, as a means of distinguishing it from copies sold at list price or regular discount.

remainders   A publisher's overstock (unsold copies of a book or other item) purchased by lot by a *remainder dealer* on the understanding that the items may be offered for sale at a substantially reduced price. Bound remainders may be marked to distinguish them from copies sold at list price. Unbound overstock may be bound in an inexpensive *remainder binding* or reduced to pulp if there is no market for the title. The author receives no royalty on remaindered copies. The fact that a book is *remaindered* does not necessarily reflect the quality of the work—the edition may have been too large, the published price too high, the subject matter esoteric or ephemeral, or the content revised and issued in a new edition. Abbreviated *rem*. Compare with *job lot*.

remake   In printing, to rearrange the typographic elements that make up a printed page or an entire publication. Also, to repaginate a publication from beginning to end or just a portion of it. *See also*: *make-up*.

remboîté   From the French word *remboîter*, meaning "to fit back into." A book that has been rebound, sometimes with fraudulent intent, in covers removed from another volume, usually a binding that is in better condition or more valuable or attractive. There is no equivalent in the English language for the term *remboîtage*.

remote access   Communication with a geographically distant computer system or network as if one were a local user. To log on to a network server, the user may be required to enter an authorized username and/or password. Special communications software and/or hardware, such as a modem or dedicated line, may also be required. Wireless, cable modem, and DSL (Digital Subscriber Line) technologies provide alternative methods of accessing computer systems remotely. In most online library catalogs, a certain number of ports are reserved for remote access to accommodate off-site users. Compare with *direct access*. *See also*: *authentication*.

remote sensing image   A visual representation of the surface of the earth, or of another celestial body, obtained at a distance by means of a recording device designed to extend the reach of the human eye. Most remote sensing techniques use the electromagnetic spectrum. Examples include aerial photographs, thermal (infrared) images, microwave images, sound traces (seismic, sonar, etc.), gamma ray images, etc. Examples can be seen in the online exhibit *Earth as Art: A Landsat Perspective*, sponsored by the Library of Congress at: www.loc.gov/exhibits/earthasart. *See also*: *aerial map*.

removes   A printing term for notes or quotations set in smaller type at the foot of a page of text, for cxample, a book set in 12-poinl might have footnotes or endnotes set in 10-point or smaller type.

renaissance librarian   A librarian who cultivates a broad and deep understanding and appreciation of, and lively interest in, all aspects of librarianship, despite having developed at least one area of specialization.

renew   To extend the period of time for which a book or other item is loaned by a library, usually by the length of the normal loan period. Renewal policies vary, but most libraries allow at least one renewal for most types of materials. To avoid fines, items checked out must be renewed by the borrower on or before the due date. *See also*: *overdue notice*.

Also, to extend the period for which a periodical subscription is to be delivered, usually by an additional year or period of years, in exchange for payment of a renewal fee by the subscriber. A price break may be given to subscribers who renew for more than one year. *See also*: *automatic renewal* and *renewal notice*.

renewal   An extension of the loan period for a book or other item, usually for the length of the normal borrowing period. Also, the reregistration of a borrower at the end of an established period of library membership. *See also*: *overdue notice*.

Also refers to an extension of the period during which a periodical subscription is to be delivered following payment of a renewal fee by the subscriber. *See also*: *automatic renewal* and *renewal notice*.

renewal invoice   An annual invoice authorizing the publisher or vendor to continue, upon payment, a library's subscriptions to one or more serial publications for an additional subscription period.

renewal list   An annual list of a library's subscriptions, provided by the publisher or vendor to enable the library to select the titles it wishes to continue receiving. The vendor uses the returned list to prepare a *renewal invoice*.

renewal notice   A notice sent by the publisher of a periodical to inform a subscriber or subscription agent that unless a renewal fee is paid before a designated expiration date, the subscription will end.

renovation   A major refurbishing of existing facilities to make them appear new or like new. In a library, this can mean anything from repainting, recarpeting, and installing new ADA-compliant furnishings and equipment to the complete gutting of an old building and reconstruction to meet current needs and contemporary design standards. Extensive renovation may require moving the library to a temporary location until alterations are completed. Major renovations are reported annually in *Library Journal* and in *The Bowker Annual Library and Book Trade Almanac*. Compare with *expansion* and *new construction*. *See also*: *retrofit*.

rental collection   Books in high demand, circulated by a public library or bookstore for a small fee, often fiction bestsellers. Not all public libraries provide rental collections; some use a waiting list or allow holds to be placed on high-demand items. Also refers to a nonbook collection such as a videocassette or film library for which a rental fee is charged when an item is borrowed, usually to help meet the costs of acquisitions and maintenance (*example*: **Facets** at www.facets.org).

reorder   In library acquisitions and bookselling, any order for a stock item placed after an initial order has been received. Reordering is necessary when the original order was lost or canceled (usually because the item was unavailable when the order was first placed).

repackaging   Reissuing a previously published book in a different format to enhance its appeal to readers outside its primary market, sometimes by making it more affordable, as in a paperback edition, or easier to read, as in a large print edition.

repaginated   A book or other publication in which the numbers originally assigned to successive pages have been changed. Synonymous with *repaged*. *See also*: *remake*.

repairing   The partial rehabilitation of a worn book or other item, including restoration of the cover and reinforcement of the hinges or joints, more extensive than mending but less extensive than recasing or rebinding. In most libraries, repairs are done in-house. The Preservation Services department of the Dartmouth College Library provides *A Simple Book Repair Manual* online at: www.dartmouth.edu/~preserve/repair/repairindex.htm.

repeatable (R)   A MARC field that may occur more than once in the same bibliographic record, for example, the **600** field, reserved for personal names used as subject added entries. A repeatable subfield may occur more than once in the same field. The opposite of *nonrepeatable (NR)*.

replacement   A book or other item purchased by a library to take the place of a lost, damaged, or worn-out copy of the same title, not necessarily of the same edition if the original edition is out of print. Also, a copy sent by a publisher or jobber as a substitute for one found by a library or other purchaser to contain imperfections.

replevin   The recovery of archived property (records, manuscripts, documents, etc.) by an organization or institution claiming ownership. Also refers to the writ or legal action by which such property is recovered.

replica   A reproduction or copy of a work of art, especially one made by the artist who created the original or produced under the artist's supervision. In a more general sense, any very close reproduction or copy of an object, especially one made on a smaller scale than the original. Synonymous with *doublette*. Compare with *facsimile* and *realia*.

report   A separately published record of research findings, research still in progress, or other technical findings, usually bearing a *report number* and sometimes a *grant number* assigned by the funding agency. *See also*: ERIC document.

   Also, an official record of the activities of a committee or corporate entity, the proceedings of a government body, or an investigation by an agency, whether published or private, usually archived or submitted to a higher authority, voluntarily or under mandate. In a more general sense, any formal account of facts or information related to a specific event or phenomenon, sometimes given at regular intervals. Abbreviated *rept*. *See also*: annual report.

repository   The physical space (building, room, area) reserved for the permanent or intermediate storage of archival materials (manuscripts, rare books, government documents, papers, photographs, etc.). To preserve and protect archival collections, modern repositories are equipped to meet current standards of environmental control and security. Whether a repository is open or closed to the public depends on the policy of the parent institution. Sometimes used synonymously with *depository*.

representative fraction (RF)   In cartography, the relationship of scale between distance on a map or chart and the actual distance on the surface of land or sea represented by the map, given in the legend as a ratio understood to be in standard units of measurement (*example*: **1:1,000,000** or **1/1,000,000**).

reprint   A new impression of an existing edition, often made by photographic means, or a new edition made from a new setting of type that is a copy of a previous impression, with no alterations in the text except perhaps the correction of typographical errors. The work may also be given a redesigned title page and cover. Date of reprinting is usually included in the details of publication on the verso of the title page. The review publication *Library Journal* includes a "Classic Returns" section in each issue, highlighting recent reprints. *The Bookman's Glossary* (R.R. Bowker, 1983) specifically recommends that the term be avoided in bibliographic description because it fails to distinguish *edition*, *impression*, *issue*, and *state*. Abbreviated *repr*. Compare with *reissue*. *See also*: *reprint book* and *reprint publisher*.

Also refers to a separately issued article, essay, chapter, or other portion of a previously published work, whether printed from a new setting of type or reproduced by other means. A directory listing of reprint services can be found at the beginning of the reference serial *Magazines for Libraries*. Compare with *offprint*.

reprint book   A collection consisting of articles previously published in one or more magazines or journals. The articles are used in their original format as camera-ready copy, rather than reset by the printer in uniform typographic style.

reprint publisher   A publishing company that specializes in new impressions of previously published titles that the original publisher has allowed to go out of print, despite continuing demand. Reprint rights must be negotiated with the copyright holder. The number of copies in a reprint edition is usually less than in the original edition.

reproduction   A close copy of a two- or three-dimensional work of art, made by mechanical means or by hand, generally for the commercial market, for example, a printed poster of a painting or drawing. Reproductions of large works are usually done on a smaller scale than the original. Price usually depends on quality and fidelity to the original. Also refers to an exact copy of a written or printed document made by mechanical or electronic means, for example, a photocopy. *See also*: *reprography*.

reprography   A general term encompassing quick-service document reproduction or copying by any means except large-scale professional printing, including photography, microphotography, xerography, and photoduplication. For a more detailed overview of the various methods, please see the entry by J.E. Davies in the *International Encyclopedia of Information and Library Science* (Routledge, 2003). Information on reprographics is available on the Web from *Conservation OnLine (CoOL)* at: palimpsest.stanford.edu/bytopic/repro.

republication   The process by which a previously published work is reissued by a *different* publisher, without alteration of the text. Sometimes refers to the reprinting of such a work in another country. Also refers to any publication reissued in this manner.

Request for Comments (RFC)   A technical or organizational specification about the Internet published by the Internet Engineering Task Force (IETF). RFCs are either informational or standards track. A standards track RFC may eventually become an Internet Standard. URL: www.ietf.org/rfc.html.

Request for Proposal (RFP)   A document prepared by a prospective purchaser, such as a library or library system, inviting a vendor or supplier to submit a bid for the acquisition of materials, equipment, and/or services, usually based on a statement detailing specifications. Most public agencies use an RFP process in awarding contracts.

required if applicable and readily available (R)   Under OCLC input standards, a field or subfield of the MARC record in which data must be entered if (1) appropriate in *AACR2* or essential for efficient access or effective processing, and (2) it is available in or on the item at hand, from other bibliographic records in the OCLC online union catalog, or from OCLC authority file records. Compare with *mandatory* and *optional*.

requisition   A written request, usually submitted to the acquisitions department of a library on a standardized form, for the order of materials, equipment, supplies, or services. Compare with *purchase order*.

rerun   In printing, a job redone because the quality of the first press run was not acceptable. Also refers to the rebroadcast of previously released television programming, more common during the summer months than at other times of the year.

research   Systematic, painstaking investigation of a topic, or in a field of study, often employing techniques of hypothesis and experimentation, undertaken by a person intent on revealing new facts, theories, or principles, or determining the current state of knowledge of the subject. The results are usually reported in a primary journal, in conference proceedings, or in a monograph by the researcher(s) who conducted the study. In the sciences, methodology is also reported to allow the results to be verified. *See also*: *heuristic* and *library research*.

research collection   A library collection sufficiently comprehensive to support specialized research in an academic discipline or field. A good research collection includes primary sources, secondary sources, and the bibliographic tools needed to conduct an exhaustive search of the literature. Development of such a collection requires considerable time and the knowledge and experience of one or more subject specialists. *See also*: *research library*.

researcher   A person who undertakes a careful, systematic investigation of a subject, or inquiry in a field of study, to establish facts, reveal underlying principles, or determine the current state of knowledge. *See also*: *research library*.

research guide   A printed or online resource that provides detailed information, instructions, and advice concerning the best strategies, techniques, and resources for research in a subject or field of study. Book-length research guides are usually shelved in the reference section of a library (*example*: ***Shakespeare: A Study and Research Guide*** by David M. Bergeron and Geraldo U. de Sousa). Most academic libraries provide one- or two-page handouts on a display rack near the reference desk, explaining research techniques and listing finding tools appropriate to each discipline.

Research Libraries Group (RLG)   Founded in 1974, RLG is a consortium of over 160 universities, national libraries, archives, historical societies, museums, and related institutions with substantial collections for research and learning. Devoted to improving access to information through collaboration, RLG maintains the *RLIN* online bibliographic database of nearly 88 million items and publishes *Research Libraries Group News* in three issues per year. URL: www.rlg.org. *See also*: *conspectus*.

Research Libraries Information Network (RLIN)   An information management and retrieval system consisting of an online union catalog of the holdings of members of the Research Libraries Group (RLG) combined with the *English Short Title Catalog (ESTC)* and authority files. *RLIN* contains over 88 million records and is used by hundreds of libraries, archives, and museums for cataloging, interlibrary loan, and control of manuscript and archival collections. URL: www.rlg.org/rlin.html.

research library   A library containing a comprehensive collection of materials in a specific field, academic discipline, or group of disciplines, including primary and secondary sources, selected to meet the information needs of serious researchers (*example*: **Folger Shakespeare Library** in Washington, D.C.). The primary emphasis in research libraries is on the *accumulation* of materials and the provision of access services to scholars qualified to make use of them. In most large research libraries, access to collections containing rare books and manuscripts is restricted. *See also*: *Association of Research Libraries*, *Center for Research Libraries*, and *Research Libraries Group*.

research paper   A written composition, usually five or more pages in length, assigned as an exercise in a formal course of study. The writer is expected to state a thesis and advance a logical argument based on supporting information found in a systematic investigation of the topic. The source of quotations, facts, and ideas not those of the author must be documented in footnotes or endnotes and a bibliography.

reserves   In academic libraries, materials given a shorter loan period (one-hour, three-hour, overnight, three-day, etc.) for a limited period of time (usually one term or semester) at the request of the instructor, to ensure that all the students enrolled in a course have an opportunity to use them. Items on *closed reserve* must be used on library premises. Instructors sometimes put personal copies on reserve, usually at their own risk.

Fines charged for overdue reserve items are higher than for materials not on reserve to encourage prompt return. In some academic libraries, reserves are available electronically, usually as an option in the online catalog or through software accessible via the library's Web site. Synonymous with *reserve collection* and *short loan collection*. *See also*: *open reserve*.

reshelving   The job of returning books and other items to the shelves of a library in correct call number sequence after they have been used, usually performed by a student assistant in an academic library or by a staff member called a *page* in a public library. *See also*: *reshelving cart* and *shelf reading*.

reshelving cart   A double-sided wheeled cart equipped with two to three shelves to hold recently returned items until they are ready to be transported to the stacks and placed back on the shelf. If a book or periodical volume is listed as available in the catalog but is "not on the shelf" (nos), it may be on a cart waiting to be reshelved. Some online catalogs indicate in the catalog record the circulation status of items recently returned. Synonymous with *book truck*.

reshipment   A two-step delivery method in which a publication ordered from a vendor is first shipped by the publisher to the vendor, then sent by the vendor to the library accompanied by an invoice. Total shipping cost is usually higher than in *drop shipment*.

residual rights   Legal rights in a creative work that remain with the copyright holder subsequent to signing a contract with the publisher. Also, any rights that eventually revert to the copyright holder when the time period or purpose stated in the contract has elapsed or been discharged. Compare with *subsidiary rights*.

residuum   The portion of an author's total body of work considered by scholars and critics to be of lasting value. *See also*: *classic*.

resignation   Formal notice of an employee's intention to terminate employment, usually given to the employer in writing, effective on a specific date. Most employment contracts require 30–60 days notice to allow the employer sufficient time to reallocate workload while a search for a replacement is conducted. Compare with *retirement*.

resized   A printed sheet or leaf in a book that has been washed, usually to remove writing, stains, or acid from the paper, and then recoated with a sizing compound to add stiffness and provide a protective finish.

resolution   A measure of the amount of fine detail in an image rendered or retained on a computer or television screen, in a photograph, or on a printed page, expressed as the number of pixels or dots per inch, line, or centimeter. The more units, the higher the resolution and the sharper the image. In remote sensing, the rate or intensity of data sampling, significant in four measurement dimensions: radiometric, spectral, spatial, and temporal (USGS Landsat Project). *See also*: *SVGA* and *VGA*.

Also refers to a formal statement of opinion or intention, issued by an assembly, organization, or group. In the United States, the text of congressional resolutions can be found in the federal government documents section of depository libraries and online via *GPO Access* at: www.gpoaccess.gov/index.html.

In literature, the term is used synonymously with *denouement*, the final phase of a work of narrative fiction or drama in which unanswered questions are resolved and the action brought to a logical conclusion.

resource sharing   The activities that result from an agreement, formal or informal, among a group of libraries (usually a consortium or network) to share collections, data, facilities, personnel, etc., for the benefit of their users and to reduce the expense of collection development.

respect des fonds   The principle of provenance first developed by French archivists in the early 19th century under which the organic nature of the archival records of an individual or agency dictates that they be maintained separately with respect to source and in their original physical order, rather than combined or intermingled with those of different origin.

respondent   A candidate for an academic degree who must defend, against one or more opponents, a thesis proposed by a faculty moderator acting as the praeses in a formal disputation.

response time   In computing, the amount of time that elapses between the submission of input (a query, command, data, etc.) and the return of results (output) by the system. On the Internet, response time depends on speed of connection and amount of traffic on the network, which varies with time of day, day of week, etc. When a server goes offline, response time may be delayed indefinitely. Compare with *turnaround time*.

restoration   In conservation, the physical process of returning a damaged, worn, or otherwise altered document to its original condition or as close an approximation of the original condition as possible. Before restoration can begin, deterioration must be stabilized by whatever method is most appropriate. To preserve the evidential value of an item in its altered condition, care is taken to make repairs both visible and reversible, if possible.

restricted access   The privilege of using a library collection under specific conditions established as a matter of library policy. In archives and special collections, the use of rare books, manuscripts, and other unique and valuable materials may be limited to a particular room or a certain method or by appointment only. In the United States, large private university libraries may limit access to the stacks to registered students, faculty, and staff and to outside researchers granted special permission to use specific collections. The opposite of *unrestricted*. Compare with *controlled access*. **See also**: *closed stacks* and *open stacks*.

   Also refers to the policy of limiting access to an online resource or service to members of a particular community, such as the students, faculty, and staff of a university or walk-in patrons of a public library. The most common method is for the vendor to check the network address of the user's computer. Passwords or certificates may also be used.

resume   A summing up. In hiring, a statement of the experience and qualifications an applicant brings to the position. Handbooks on resume preparation are available in the reference section of most public and academic libraries. The New Members Round Table (NMRT) of the American Library Association provides a resume review service for recent library school graduates (www.ala.org). Tips on resume writing are also available online (try a search on the keyword "resumes" in *Yahoo!* at: www.yahoo. com). **See also**: *curriculum vitae*.

resumed   A serial for which publication has started up again following a temporary suspension. *Resumed numbering* means the same sequence is used for numbering successive issues/parts as was in place when publication halted.

retail price   *See*: list price.

retention   Holding or keeping materials in possession, usually in a desired state or condition, as opposed to disposing of them. In archives, the retention period for documents is usually indicated in the disposition schedule. Academic and research libraries generally purchase materials with the intention of keeping them indefinitely; public libraries weed on the basis of usage. Long-term retention of library materials may require preservation measures, such as reformatting.

   Also refers to the extent to which a company, organization, or institution is able to keep its personnel from accepting employment elsewhere and to the capacity of an academic institution to keep students enrolled through graduation.

retention period   In archives, the length of time that records of a specific category or origin must be retained before they are transferred to intermediate storage or given some other disposition. In the absence of statutory or regulatory stipulations, the period is usually determined by current usage and projected need.

retention schedule   *See*: disposition schedule.

retirement   Resignation from a position of employment with the intention of ending a career, a step usually taken at an age when the *retiree* is in a position to live on other income (pension, retirement savings, social security, etc.). *Early retirement* is resignation before the age at which most employees cease working, sometimes in response to a special offer of eligibility or compensation made by management ("golden handshake"). Under a policy of *mandatory retirement*, employees are not allowed to continue working beyond a certain age.

retitled edition   All the copies of a book reissued under a title that is not the same as the title of the original edition (*example*: **Profiles of American Labor Unions** [1998], a retitled second edition of *American Directory of Organized Labor*, first published in 1992). In *AACR2*, the original title is entered as a note in the bibliographic description when the item is cataloged.

retrofit   To adapt an older library facility to accommodate improvements in information technology, a process that often not only involves the installation of new equipment and furnishings but may also require structural alterations, reallocation of space, changes in lighting and HVAC, additional electrical and telecom wiring, and attention to noise control, traffic patterns, etc.

retrospective   Including works created or published in the past, rather than current or recently issued materials, as in a *retrospective bibliography*. In a more general sense, anything pertaining to events or activities that occurred in the past, rather than the present, as in the *retrospective conversion* of previously cataloged bibliographic records to another format.

retrospective bibliography   A bibliography restricted to materials published in the past, usually limited to a specific period of time (*example*: **Agriculture and the GATT: A Retrospective Bibliography, 1948–1980** by Wayne K. Olson). The opposite of *current bibliography*.

retrospective binding   A binding done in conscious imitation of an earlier style (not necessarily of the period in which the work was originally published), fashionable during the 19th century. Synonymous with *antique* and *period binding*. Compare with *facsimile binding*.

retrospective conversion   The process of converting existing bibliographic records from manual, human-readable form, such as a cards in a card catalog, into machine-readable format, usually by matching the old records one at a time to those contained in an authoritative database of machine-readable records. Once a match is made, the cataloger downloads as much of the machine-readable record as the library needs, usually for a modest fee. In the United States, OCLC provides most of the MARC records used in retrospective conversion. Abbreviated *recon*. Compare with *recataloging*.

In a more general sense, the process of converting nondigital source material to digital form.

retrospective search A search for information that is no longer current. Bibliographic databases that support this type of searching usually index information in repositories and archival collections in which documents may be added but are rarely modified or removed. Some search software allows the user to specify a publication date range, to exclude current materials.

returnable In interlibrary loan, materials that the lending library expects the borrowing library to return, usually within a designated period of time unless renewed, as opposed to materials, such as photocopied articles, provided without expectation of return.

Also refers to an item that may be returned by a library to the seller for credit, usually under specific conditions explicitly stated in the seller's return policy.

return policy The conditions established by a publisher under which items ordered, shipped, and delivered may be returned for credit by a library or bookseller. Items received in damaged condition not the fault of the receiver are understood to be returnable. The return policy for undamaged items is normally stated on the publisher's invoice, usually in code, **NR** or **XR** indicating *no returns* or *nonreturnable*. Items that have been processed or specially bound at the purchaser's request are not returnable unless a major defect is found within a reasonable time. When an item is returned for a valid reason, a replacement copy is usually sent by the publisher. *See also*: *returns*.

returns Books or other items sent back to the publisher by a bookseller who purchased them under terms allowing unsold stock to be returned for credit. Also, items returned to a publisher or jobber by a library under an approval plan or book lease plan or because they were found upon delivery to be damaged or defective. The conditions under which items may be returned for credit are stated in the publisher's *return policy*. On the invoice, the symbol **NR** or **XR** indicates that returns are *not* allowed.

reused number In Dewey Decimal Classification, a class number assigned to a different subject than the one it represented in a previous edition. As a general rule, numbers are reused only in complete revisions or when the reused number has been vacant for at least two consecutive editions.

reverse chronological The arrangement of data, records, items, headings, entries, etc., according to their relation in time, from the most recent to the earliest. In online catalogs and bibliographic databases, the default display of records retrieved in a keywords search is often reverse chronological order. The opposite of *chronological*.

reversibility In document conservation, the degree to which a procedure can be *undone* without adversely affecting the condition of the item. As a general rule, reversibility is preferred because future research or legal developments may require that an item be restored to its original condition. However, since complete reversibility may be difficult, if not impossible, to achieve, it must be balanced against other priorities.

review   An evaluative account of a recent artistic performance or exhibit, or of newly published literary or scholarly work, usually written and signed by a qualified person, for publication in a current newspaper, magazine, or journal. The account can be descriptive, reportorial, comparative, or critical or serve as a vehicle for a lengthy essay in which the *reviewer* discusses several recently published works (omnibus review) or a broader topic for which the works reviewed serve as a springboard. In libraries, selection decisions are based primarily on reviews. Synonymous with *critique*. Compare with *puff*. *See also*: *review lag*.

   Book reviews are indexed by the year in which they were published and by author of title reviewed in *Book Review Digest* and *Book Review Index*, available in the reference section of most academic and large public libraries. Film reviews are indexed by title of film under the heading "Motion picture reviews—Single works" in the volume of *Reader's Guide to Periodical Literature* corresponding to date of release. Reviews can also be located online in general periodical databases by entering keywords from the title of the work reviewed as search terms. For a list of online review sources, please see the *AcqWeb Directory of Book Reviews on the Web* at: www.library.vanderbilt.edu/acqweb/bookrev.html.

   Also refers to a periodical devoted primarily to publishing articles of criticism and appraisal (*example*: **Romantic Review**).

review copy   A complimentary copy of a new book or other work in its final form sent by the publisher at no charge to a person who writes reviews, to the editor of a publication that includes reviews or book announcements, to an opinion leader in the field, or to a bookseller in the hope of attracting favorable comment, often with a review slip laid in. Academic libraries sometimes receive review copies as gifts from faculty members who write reviews. Synonymous with *press copy*. Compare with *advance copy*. *See also*: *review publication*.

reviewer   A person who writes a brief or extended evaluation of a new book or other creative work, usually at the request of the editor of a publication that includes reviews. Scholarly works are usually reviewed by the author's peers. Reviews published in library review publications such as *CHOICE*, *Library Journal*, and *Booklist* are written by librarians and academic professionals actively engaged in collection development. In the performing arts, reviews are written by critics whose response can determine the success or failure of a production.

review journal   A scholarly journal devoted to the publication of articles providing analysis of trends in an academic field or summaries of the current state of research on topics of particular interest within the field (*example*: **Statistical Science: A Review Journal of the Institute of Mathematical Statistics**). Articles may be submitted at the editor's invitation. *See also*: *annual review*.

review lag   The interval of time between the publication of a new book, or the release or first performance of a creative work, and the appearance of reviews. For popular fiction and nonfiction written by well-known authors, the delay may be a matter of days or weeks, especially if galleys or review copies are distributed by the publisher to prospective reviewers in advance of the publication date, but for scholarly titles, the lag may exceed a year.

review of the literature   *See*: literature review.

review publication   A newspaper, magazine, or journal devoted primarily to publishing reviews of new books and other publications (serials, nonprint media, etc.). Some also provide feature articles, regular columns, author interviews, literature reviews, etc., and most include book announcements and other advertising. Directory information for review publications is available in *Literary Market Place*.

General review publications:
Booklist
CHOICE: Current Reviews for Academic Libraries
Kirkus Reviews
Library Journal (LJ)
Publisher's Weekly (PW)
Quill & Quire
New York Review of Books (NYRB)
New York Times Book Review (NYTBR)
Times Literary Supplement (TLS)

Children's and young adult literature:
Bulletin of the Center for Children's Books (BCCB)
Children's Literature Review (CLR)
The Horn Book Magazine
KLIATT
The Lion and the Unicorn
School Library Journal (SLJ)

Specialized review publications:
American Reference Books Annual (ARBA)
AudioFile Magazine
CRÍTICAS: An English Speaker's Guide to the Latest Spanish Language Titles
The Drood Review of Mystery
Lambda Book Report
The Mystery Review
Video Librarian

review slip   A brief notice or form letter sent by the publisher of a new book to a book reviewer or bookseller with a free copy of the work, informing the recipient that the item is a review copy and requesting its consideration.

Reviews on Cards (ROC)   *See*: *CHOICE*.

revised edition   An edition in which a previously published work is substantially altered by correction, deletion, or the addition of supplementary material, either by the original author/editor or another writer, usually to expand the content or bring it up-to-date. Some revised editions are not as "revised" as they claim to be (*caveat emptor*). The extent of revision may be indicated in a new foreword or preface. Frequency of revision usually depends on the amount of new material available but may also be linked to a decline in sales of the preceding edition. In library cataloging, the abbreviation *Rev. ed.* is given in the edition statement of the bibliographic record to indicate that an edition has been revised. Usually synonymous with *second edition*. Compare with *expanded edition*.

revision   Text that has been altered by the original author, or by another writer, usually to correct, amend, update, or otherwise improve it. In books, the result may be published as a *revised edition*. Compare with *rewrite*.

In Dewey Decimal Classification, the published result of editorial work that changes the text of any class of the schedules. Three degrees of revision are recognized:

Routine revision—Updates terminology, clarifies notes, provides modest expansions of existing notation

Extensive revision—Major reworking of subdivisions, but basic outline of the schedule is left intact

Complete revision (formerly called a *phoenix*)—Base numbers remain the same as in previous edition, but virtually all subdivisions are altered

In an extensive or complete revision, changes are indicated in comparative and equivalence tables, rather than by the addition of relocation notes in the affected schedule or table.

rewritable   A digital storage medium capable of being written, erased, and rewritten repeatedly, for example, magnetic tape or disk, as opposed to a medium that is *read-only* or *write once, read many* (WORM).

rewrite   To put text already written into different words or form, making more extensive changes than in a revision. In journalism, to convert news copy submitted in rough form by one or more reporters into a version suitable for publication.

RF   *See*: representative fraction.

RFC   *See*: Request for Comments.

RFID   *See*: radio frequency identification.

RFP   *See*: Request for Proposal.

RH   An abbreviation of *relative humidity*. *See*: humidity.

rhyming dictionary   A dictionary in which the words of a language are listed alphabetically by phonetic ending to assist writers of verse. In libraries, rhyming dictionaries are usually shelved in the language section of the reference collection. They are also available online (see *RhymeZone* from *Lycos* at: rhyme.lycos.com).

RI   *See*: rule interpretation.

rich text   Machine-readable text that includes formatting for page layout (boldface, underlining, italic, fonts, etc.). The term is also used for a text document that includes multimedia (graphics, audio, and video). Compare with *plain text*.

riddle   A puzzle or problem in the form of a misleading statement or question containing clues expressed in a manner requiring ingenuity and a sense of humor to arrive at the correct answer or solution (in the parlor game "Charades" the clues are visual). Exceedingly popular with young readers, collections of riddles are available in the juvenile section of most public libraries. Synonymous with *conundrum*.

In a more general sense, any puzzling or enigmatic person, phenomenon, or saying.

rights   The exclusive privilege of receiving the benefits associated with ownership of a literary property, the most important of which is the right of first publication, protected under *copyright* law in most countries. In the case of books, *volume rights* give the publisher the exclusive right to publish a work in volume form within a specific geographic territory, including the right to reprint in paperback, book club, or textbook edition and to reprint the work in its entirety in a single issue of a periodical or in an anthology. *Subsidiary rights* include serialization, abridgment, translation, foreign publication, excerpt, quotation, reproduction, commercial exploitation, and adaptation for performance on stage, as a motion picture, or on radio or television. Rights may be transferred or sold by the owner to another person or entity. Under U.S. copyright law, rights are subject to limitation (see *fair use* and *first sale*). *See also*: *infringement* and *residual rights*.

rinceaux   A style of border decoration used in 14th- and 15th-century illuminated manuscripts, composed of an intricately branching pattern of thin foliage, more spiky in appearance and usually less colorful than acanthus but very beautiful when highlighted in gold.

ring binding   A form of loose-leaf binder consisting of a number of metal rings (usually three) fixed in a metal or hard plastic spine. The rings are designed to open, usually at the center, by means of pressure tabs at the top and bottom of the spine, allowing prepunched leaves to be individually added or removed, used in libraries for materials such as loose-leaf services that require frequent updating. Unlike post bindings, ring bindings open flat.

RLG   *See*: **Research Libraries Group**.

RLIN   *See*: *Research Libraries Information Network*.

road atlas   A book of maps showing the roads, highways, towns, and cities in a specific state, province, region, or country, often with mileage between major destinations (*example*: *Rand McNally Road Atlas and Vacation Guide*). Updated annually for retail sale to motorists and travelers, most include an index of place names (gazetteer) at the end, giving the location of cities, towns, and other geographic features by means of grid coordinates on the road maps. For an interactive online road atlas, see *MapQuest* at: www.mapquest.com.

road map   A map showing the location of the roads and highways passable to motorized vehicles within a given area (county, state, province, country), for the use of motorists and travelers. Smaller in scale than a city map, a road map usually includes a table of distances between major towns and cities, a gazetteer, one or more larger-scale inset maps of major metropolitan areas, and symbols indicating service and rest areas, scenic routes, toll roads, major parks and museums, campgrounds, airports, etc. A *road atlas* is a collection of road maps covering a larger area, usually bound in the form of a book or pamphlet.

roan   A thin, soft, flexible sheepskin, usually dyed a dark color, used in bookbinding from the late 18th century as a substitute for morocco, which was more elegant but also more expensive.

ROC   *See*: *CHOICE Reviews on Cards*.

role indicator   In indexing, a code used to indicate the syntactic relationship between two or more index terms (subject headings or descriptors) assigned to a document to facilitate retrieval by subject (adapted from the *ASIS Thesaurus of Information Science and Librarianship*, Information Today, 1998).

roll   Latin: *rotulus*. A manuscript written on a length of papyrus, parchment, or vellum, assembled from sheets (*kollemata*) pasted edge-to-edge with the overlapped sheet to the left to prevent the pen from catching on the join (*kollesis*). The oldest surviving examples are from ancient Egypt on papyrus. Writing was usually on the inside surface only—the side with the fibers running horizontally—with details of author, title, and production given in the *colophon*, *incipit*, and *explicit*. The reader unrolled the manuscript from left to right, exposing about four columns of text at a time. A sheet of reverse fiber direction, called the *protokollon*, began the roll, and a long wooden rod (the *umbilicus*) was sometimes attached to the opposite end to facilitate rerolling. In Antiquity, rolls were stored horizontally on a shelf or vertically in a box or cylindrical receptacle called a *capsa*, often with the title of the work written on a small label called a *syllabus* attached to one edge.

As a format, the roll had the advantage of not requiring binding to keep the text in order, but it had to be rewound by the reader, made reference to a specific portion of text cumbersome, and could become tangled if dropped. It was superseded by the *codex* in about the 3rd century A.D. but continued to be used during the Middle Ages for specialized purposes (genealogies, chronicles, Exchequer Rolls, etc.), read from top to bottom. Synonymous with *volumen*. Compare with *scroll*. *See also*: *opisthograph*.

Also refers to a list of names, especially the members of an organization, assembly, or official body, used to "call the roll" in a roll-call vote.

ROM   *See*: **r**ead-**o**nly **m**emory.

roman   The formal Latin alphabet consisting of minuscule (lowercase) and majuscule (uppercase) letters, as distinct from gothic or *black letter*. Minuscules were adapted from the noncursive book hand used in medieval Europe; majuscules evolved from the capitals used in the inscriptions carved on tombs and other stone monuments by the ancient Romans. *See also*: *Cyrillic*.

In typography, a typeface in which the characters are not slanted, as in italic, but stand straight up. Also used as a generic term for all typefaces with serifs, as opposed to those that are sans-serif.

roman à clef   French for "novel with a key." A form of novel in which real people or institutions are given fictitious names but depicted in such a way that well-informed readers can penetrate the disguise. Such works are often satirical, as in Robert Penn Warren's thinly veiled characterization of the Louisiana demagogue Huey Long in *All the King's Men*. Compare with *historical fiction*.

roman à these   French for "novel with a thesis." A form of novel in which the author presents a moral dilemma or social problem in order to advance a specific point of view or programmatic solution, instead of leaving the resolution to the reader (*example*: ***The Grapes of Wrath*** by John Steinbeck). Synonymous with *problem novel* and *protest novel*. ***See also***: *thesis play*.

romance   A narrative in which the primary themes are passionate love and adventure, usually depicted in an exotic rather than realistic setting, involving characters that are larger-than-life stereotypes. The origins of romance as a literary form can be traced to the gothic novel of the 18th century and to the earlier tradition of medieval chivalry. In English literature, Samuel Richardson's *Pamela, or, Virtue Rewarded* (1740) is considered a seminal work. Nineteenth-century *romanticism* revived the romance in verse form and also in the visual arts. Most contemporary romance is written to appeal to female readers. In *Genreflecting: A Guide to Reading Interests in Genre Fiction* (Libraries Unlimited, 2000), Diana Tixier Herald notes that, "In these novels, emotional experiences might be tinged with religious spirituality or aimed at sexual fulfillment, but the desired conclusion is always marriage." Subgenres include *historical romance*, *romantic suspense*, and *supernatural romance*. Pulp romance is often published in series. For a Web site devoted to romance fiction, see *The Romance Reader* at: www.theromancereader.com.

Also refers to a genre of vernacular literature that developed in France during the 12th and 13th centuries, consisting of narrative tales describing the chivalric adventures of noble men and women, composed in verse and later in prose. Although often based on historical themes (***Morte D'Arthur***, ***Havelock the Dane***, etc.), the stories were fictional, often combining allegory and satire with moral tales of courtly love. Compare with *chanson de geste*.

roman-fleuve   A French term for a form of novel in which the narrative covers the fortunes of an entire family, sometimes over several generations (*example*: ***One Hundred Years of Solitude*** by Gabriel Garcia Márquez).

romanization   Conversion of words, names, titles, or text from nonroman script into the letters of the roman alphabet. The Cataloging Distribution Service of the Library of Congress publishes *ALA-LC Romanization Tables; Transliteration Schemes for Non-Roman Scripts*, containing 54 transliteration tables for over 150 languages and dialects written in nonroman scripts (lcweb.loc.gov/catdir/cpso/roman.html). ***See also***: *pinyin*.

roman numeral   A system of numerals developed by the ancient Romans, used throughout Europe prior to the introduction of arabic numerals in the 11th century. Capital letters of the Latin alphabet are used to indicate number, either alone ($I = 1$, $V = 5$, $X = 10$, $L = 50$, $C = 100$, $D = 500$, and $M = 1,000$) or in combination, according to established conventions ($IV = 4$, $VI = 6$, $IX = 9$, $XI = 11$, etc.). In printing, roman numerals are used for chapter headings, lists, dates, and in lowercase, to paginate the front matter of books.

root   *See*: stem.

Rosetta Stone   A smooth slab of dark granite, approximately 2.5 feet wide and 3.75 feet high, bearing the same inscription, a decree honoring Ptolemy V Epiphanes, written in 196 B.C. in two languages: Greek and Egyptian. The Egyptian version of the text is carved in hieroglyphs and in the demotic cursive script. Discovered in Egypt in 1799 by a party of French soldiers under the command of Napoleon Bonaparte, the stone was subsequently used by the British physicist Thomas Young and the French Egyptologist Jean-François Champollion to decipher the meaning of Egyptian hieroglyphic writing.

rotated display   An alphabetically arranged display of all the significant words contained in the descriptors listed in a thesaurus of indexing terms, in which each word is treated as a filing unit. Descriptors are repeated in the alphabetic sequence under each of their significant words, single-word descriptors appearing only once. Word order within terms is not altered. The following example is from the "Rotated Descriptor Display" in the *Thesaurus of ERIC Descriptors*. ***See also***: *permuted index*.

Example:

```
                    Literacy
             Adult  Litcracy
      Child Parent  Literacy Use Family Literacy
                    Literacy Classes (1966 1980) Use Literacy Education
          Computer  Literacy
          Cultural  Literacy
             Early  Literacy Use Emergent Literacy
                    Literacy Education
          Emergent  Literacy
                    Family Literacy
```

rotated index   *See*: permuted index.

rotating display   A highly compact bookcase with shelves on four faces, mounted on a cylindrical spindle that allows it to be turned by the person browsing its contents, used in libraries for displaying paperbacks and media items (videocassettes, CDs, etc.). Synonymous with *rotor display* and *revolving case*.

rotation   A method of scheduling shifts at a library service point in which a group of librarians or other staff members take turns, usually in predetermined sequence. Evening and weekend reference desk hours are often scheduled in this manner to distribute workload equitably.

rotulus   *See*: roll.

rotunda   A type of gothic script developed in Italy and Spain during the 15th century. Its broad, round letterforms retain some of the features of the earlier Carolingian minuscule. Widely used by scribes for copying theological, legal, and scholastic texts, its use eventually spread north of the Alps. After the invention of printing from movable type in the mid-15th century, it was adapted for use in typefaces.

rough   Calfskin given a suede-like nap, instead of the usual polished surface, used in binding from the 17th century on. Synonymous with *reversed calf*.

rough edges   A generic term used in bookbinding to refer to the irregular deckle edges of paper, left uncut by the binder in some editions, more difficult to clean than *cut edges* on books exposed to dust.

roundel   A decorative panel or plate of circular or oval shape. The decorative borders of medieval manuscripts sometimes contain figures, scenes, or ornamentation enclosed in a plain or embellished circular or oval frame. In foliate borders, roundels may be framed by vines and leaves. Compare with *medallion*.

rounding   In bookbinding, a procedure performed after first gluing, before the lining is applied to the back, in which the binding edge of the sewn sections is hammered or otherwise physically manipulated to give the spine a convex shape in preparation for *backing*. Used in hand-binding since the 16th century, the procedure gives the book a concave fore-edge, diminishes swell, and prevents the binding edge from falling forward with extended use or from the force of gravity as the volume stands upright on the shelf. Compare with *flat back*.

round table   In modern usage, a group established to discuss on an ongoing basis a range of topics and/or issues of concern to its members, usually within the context of a larger organization. The original "Round Table" preserved at Winchester, England, is believed to have been the center around which the King Arthur of medieval legend met with his knights, its shape intended to prevent quarrels over pre-eminence.

Within the American Library Association, each of the following permanent round tables has its own membership:

Exhibits Round Table (ERT)
Federal and Armed Forces Libraries Round Table (FAFLRT)
Gay, Lesbian, Bisexual, and Transgendered Round Table (GLBTRT)
Government Documents Round Table (GODORT)
Intellectual Freedom Round Table (IFRT)
International Relations Round Table (IRRT)
Library History Round Table (LHRT
Library Instruction Round Table (LIRT)
Library Research Round Table (LRRT)
Library Support Staff Interests Round Table (LSSIRT)
Map and Geography Round Table (MAGERT)
New Members Round Table (NMRT)

Social Responsibilities Round Table (SRRT)

Video Round Table (VRT)

router   A hardware device designed to direct the tiny packets of digital data comprising an electronic message from one node on a computer network to another by the most efficient pathway. Routers also perform other functions in the control of network traffic.

routine   A component of a computer program written to execute a given operation or function under specific conditions, for example, an *error routine*. Also refers to an operation or procedure that, if performed regularly in the same manner, increases efficiency.

routing   The routine circulation of new publications, such as the current issues of library journals, to a list of library staff in accordance with their preferences, to allow them to keep abreast of recent developments in their field(s) of interest and specialization.

In special libraries, new publications may be circulated to a list of personnel within the host organization based on their interests, usually by means of a routing slip listing the names of the individuals who wish to see each issue of a title. When finished, each person crosses his or her name off the list and sends the item to another person on the list. When all the names have been crossed off, the item is usually returned to the serials desk or acquisitions librarian to be processed for general circulation. Also spelled *routeing*.

routing slip   A list attached to the front cover of a new document or periodical issue, giving the names of the people within a department or organization who would like to receive it. Each person crosses his or her name off the list when finished, then sends the item to another on the list. After the last person has seen the item, it is returned to the person responsible for processing, filing, or disposing of it.

roving   In the delivery of reference services, the practice of discreetly walking about the reference area of a library in search of users who need assistance, as opposed to remaining seated at the reference desk, waiting for patrons to approach with their questions. Experienced reference librarians learn to tell by body language and other nonverbal cues when a user is experiencing difficulty. They may initiate a reference interview by politely asking if the person is finding the information needed. In large libraries, when two librarians are scheduled on reference duty at the same time, one may rove while the other remains at the desk.

royal binding   A binding with the coat of arms of a sovereign, or some other symbol of royal lineage, tooled or stamped on one or both sides of the cover, a form of decoration popular in Europe through the end of the 19th century, not necessarily signifying ownership. Compare with *armorial binding*.

royalties   A term used in the book trade for the regular payments made by a publisher to the author or creator of a work for copies sold, usually a percentage of the published price (10-15 percent) but sometimes a percentage of the wholesale price or of the publisher's total receipts (*The Bookman's Glossary*, R.R. Bowker, 1983). The royalty paid on reprints, book club editions, scholarly publications, and copies exported or sold by mail order is normally lower, and no royalty is paid on review copies or remainders. Negotiated in advance by the parties or their agents, royalty and advance on royalty are stipulated in the book contract. Most publishers have an established policy regarding royalty percentage, but in the case of books with very high sales potential, a higher percentage may be offered as an inducement to sign. In the case of electronic resources, royalty has been extended to include any portion of the fee paid under a license to use the product.

rpm   An abbreviation of *revolutions per minute*, a unit of measurement indicating the playing speed of a phonograph record. The most common speed is 33⅓ rpm (long-playing).

R.R. Bowker   Founded in New York City in 1872, the publisher R.R. Bowker specializes in reference works on publishing, libraries, and the book trade. The company is known for its long-standing reference serials (*Books in Print, American Library Directory, The Bowker Annual Library and Book Trade Almanac, Literary Market Place, Magazines for Libraries, Ulrich's International Periodicals Directory*, etc.). R.R. Bowker has also served as the official ISBN agency for the United States since 1968. URL: www.bowker.com. *See also*: *Bowker, Richard Rogers*.

RT (or R)   *See*: related term *and* running title.

rubbed   The condition of a book that has a visibly chafed binding but is otherwise undamaged. Synonymous with *barked*. Compare with *scuffed*.

rubber stamp   A small block of wood or metal covered on one side with a thin layer of rubber into which letters, numbers, and/or a design have been cut in relief. When inked and pressed against a smooth, clean surface, the block leaves a mark, used in libraries to stamp ownership marks on books and other materials and to stamp the due date on items at the time they are checked out. Some models are self-inking.

rubric   From the Latin *rubrica*, meaning "red." An initial letter, word, phrase, title, or instruction written in red ink, in contrast to the text written or printed in black. Used in medieval manuscripts and early printed books for descriptive headings and to mark divisions in the text, the practice has been traced to late Antiquity and was common from the 5th century on. Distinctive headings served an important function in books produced before the 9th century when the text was written in *scriptio continuo* without word division or punctuation.

The phrase "red letter day" refers to the practice of recording major feast days in red in the calendar sections of liturgical books and Books of Hours. The ink was made from red lead or vermilion, substances readily available in Europe during the Middle Ages. Eventually the term included headings written in other colors (blue, green, etc.). *Rubrication* was normally done by a scribe known as a *rubrisher* or *rubricator*, in spaces left blank during the writing of the text. Compare with *illuminated initial*.

rubrication   From the Latin *rubrica*, meaning "red." In medieval manuscripts and early printed books, the writing of letters, headings, and instructions in red ink to distinguish them from the text. Rubrics were inserted by the *rubrisher* in spaces left blank by the scribe when the text was written. Eventually the term was applied to letters, words, and headings written in any color (blue, green, purple, etc.) other than the blue or dark brown ink used for the text.

The term also refers to a style of Celtic manuscript decoration in which initial letters and other motifs are surrounded by a multitude of tiny, evenly spaced red dots, arranged in rows and other patterns. Also called *dotting*.

rule   A thin metal strip of type-height used to print continuous lines, or lines of dots or pattern, as in a plain or decorative border around a title page. Rule-borders on bindings can be in blind or gilt. Thickness of rule (measured in points) determines thickness of line. A rule may be thicker at the center with tapered ends. *See also*: *dash* and *hyphen*.

Also refers to a regulation or principle governing acceptable conduct, usually within a specific social, cultural, or organizational context. Most libraries have written rules concerning computer use and unacceptable behavior, usually posted near the circulation desk or reference desk and sometimes on the library's Web site.

In library cataloging, a standard procedure, usually governed by a catalog code, such as the *Anglo-American Cataloguing Rules (AACR2)* or the *ALA Filing Rules*. *See also*: *rule interpretation*.

rule interpretation (RI)   A formal explanation, clarification, or expansion of existing cataloging rules, usually resulting from a case that raises questions concerning the applicability of established policy and/or procedure. In the United States, the Library of Congress issues a series of rule interpretations (*LCRI*) for *AACR2*, formulated by the Cataloging Policy and Support Office, which reflect internal LC policy decisions. Distributed by the Cataloging Distribution Service, *LCRI* are followed by other libraries for the sake of consistency.

rule of application   The instruction in Dewey Decimal Classification to classify works about the application of one subject to a second subject, or the influence of one subject on another, under the second of the two, for example, the classification of a monograph on the literary influence of Ovid on Chaucer with works about Chaucer.

rule of three   The instruction in Dewey Decimal Classification to classify works in which equal treatment is given to three or more subjects (all subdivisions of a broader subject) under the first higher class number encompassing them all. *See also*: *first-of-two rule*.

Also, in the days when most libraries used the card catalog, an effort was made by catalogers to assign no more than three subject headings per item to limit growth of the catalog. When libraries began converting catalog cards to machine-readable records, the number of access points per item ceased to be an issue because the online catalog occupies no physical space.

rule of zero   In Dewey Decimal Classification, when two or more class numbers are found to be equally suitable for a work, the cataloger is instructed to avoid subdivisions beginning with zero if there is a choice between 0 and 1–9 in the same position in the notation and to avoid subdivisions beginning with 00 when there is a choice between 00 and 0.

ruling   Vertical and horizontal lines carefully drawn on the blank sheets of a medieval manuscript to aid the scribe and illuminator in copying and decorating the text. A rectangular frame was first drawn on the page to delimit the text area, with two vertical lines down the center in manuscripts written in two columns, establishing the margin between them. Tiny holes pricked through the entire thickness of a gathering along the edges of the *bifolia* ensured that the horizontal lines ruled within the frames were identical on every page.

Prior to the 11th century, ruling was usually done by scoring the surface of the parchment with a stylus or metal implement. However, scoring creates a small furrow that tends to collect ink or paint, so writing was between the lines, not on them. During the 11th and 12th centuries, plummet was widely used to rule manuscripts, and from the late 13th century on, the lines were often drawn in pale red or brown ink. Ruling was so much a part of the overall design that in early printed books they were sometimes hand-drawn around the text and between the lines of type to duplicate the appearance of a manuscript. *See also*: mis-en-page.

rums   A slang expression used by London booksellers of the 18th century for a miscellaneous assortment of unsalable books, probably derived from the telltale odor imparted by the previous contents of the wooden barrels used for storing them.

run   In printing, the number of impressions taken from a plate or setting of type at one time. A completed job is said to have been *run-off*.

run-around   In printing, a reduction in the line width of a column of type, on either the left- or right-hand side, to accommodate an illustration or note set into the text. Synonymous with *set-around*.

rune   From the Anglo-Saxon *run*, meaning "secret" or "mystery." A letter of the earliest Scandinavian and Anglo-Saxon alphabet (called *Futhark*) consisting of 24 letters in three families of eight, used from about A.D. 200 to 750. The angular letterforms were probably derived from characters carved on metal, wood, or stone by the ancient Teutonic peoples of northern Europe. Michelle Brown notes in *The British Library Guide to Writing and Scripts* (University of Toronto Press, 1998) that in Old English several runic characters were added to the Roman alphabet. The use of runes died out after the 13th century.

In a more general sense, an aphorism, riddle, or saying believed to have mystical meaning or magical powers.

runners   A sequence of numbers or letters printed at regular intervals down one or both side margins in a book to indicate the position of any line on a page. Used in long poems, plays, and text in a foreign language to enable the reader to reference a specific line (or lines) by page number.

running foot   The line of type printed below the text at the bottom of a page in a book or periodical, uniform in style and content, usually giving the same information as a *running head*. Synonymous with *footline*. *See also*: *footer*.

running head   The line of type printed above the text at the top of a page. In a book, it usually gives the title of the work on the verso and the chapter title on the recto. In periodicals, the running head gives the name of the publication, issue date, and page number and may also include the volume number and issue number. Some books and periodicals are printed without running heads. Synonymous with *headline* and *page head*.

running time   The duration of a motion picture, including the credits but not any trailer(s) or supplemental material. In library cataloging, running time is given under extent of item in the physical description area of the bibliographic record. Compare with *playing time*.

running title   The title or abbreviated title of a book, or section of a book, repeated in uniform style at the head or foot of each page or verso, usually the same as the drop-down title. Also known as a *running head*.

run-on chapter   A chapter that does not begin on a new page but is set immediately following the end of the text of the preceding chapter, usually to minimize the amount of paper required to print the work. In quality printing, it is standard practice to begin a new chapter on the recto of the leaf following the last page of the preceding chapter.

rural library   A library or library system that serves a population living primarily on farms and ranches, and in remote communities, rather than in a town or city. Rural libraries typically provide outreach services such as bookmobiles and books-by-mail to bring library resources and services to users.

RUSA   *See*: Reference and User Services Association.

rush order   A request made by a library to a publisher, jobber, or dealer that a specific title be supplied as quickly as possible, usually because it is needed by a professor for course reserves, to meet heavy demand, or to satisfy a patron who has requested it. Compare with *special order*. *See also*: *rush processing*.

rush processing   In acquisitions, an item sent to cataloging to be processed as soon as it is received, usually a rush order or an item for which a patron is waiting.

russia   Calfskin tanned and treated with birch bark oil to give it a pleasant aroma that supposedly acts as an insect repellent. Popular in England as a binding material from about 1780 to 1830, russia calf was often dyed red with brazilwood and scored in a crisscross pattern of diagonal lines called *dicing*. The process was abandoned because it had a drying effect that caused the covers to eventually disintegrate.

rustic capital   Calligraphic capital letters used as a book hand by scribes from the 1st to the 6th century, in contrast to the wide, heavy square capitals adapted from Roman inscriptions for use in formal documents. Vertical strokes were thinned by holding the pen at an oblique angle and previously rounded letterforms condensed to one-half the width of square capitals, allowing more text to fit on a page, a distinct advantage when writing material (parchment and vellum) was costly and in limited supply. Latin: *capitalis rustica*. Compare with *uncial*.

Also refers to a capital letter with a design painted or engraved on its face in the form of vines and leaves, or the textured bark of a tree. Compare with *foliate initial*.

S

SA   An abbreviation of *see also*.

SAA   *See*: Society of American Archivists.

sabbatical   A paid leave of absence granted to an academic professional for the purpose of research or scholarly endeavor, usually for one semester or a full academic year, following six or seven years of full-time service, sometimes involving travel. At many colleges and universities, applications are evaluated on a competitive basis by a faculty committee or in some other manner determined by institutional governance. Librarians employed in academic libraries may be eligible for sabbatic leave, depending on the provisions of the contract governing terms of employment.

SACO   *See*: Program for Cooperative Cataloging.

sacramentary   A liturgical book containing prayers recited by the celebrant during the consecration of the Eucharist at high Mass (other parts were contained in the evangelary, gradual, and epistolary). Michelle Brown notes in *Understanding Illuminated Manuscripts* (Getty Museum/British Library, 1994) that by the end of the 13th century the sacramentary had been superseded by the *missal*, a new book combining the various texts in a single volume, introduced during the Carolingian period to standardize Church ritual.

sacred text   A written work revered by people who believe in one of the world's organized religions. In library cataloging, such works are entered under a uniform title (***Bible***, ***Torah***, ***Koran***, ***Vedas***, etc.). Most libraries in the United States keep at least one English translation of the Bible in the reference collection, usually with commentaries, concordances, etc. The sacred books of the other major world religions may be available in the circulating collection of academic libraries, especially at universities offering a major or graduate degree in comparative religion. Compare with *liturgical work*. *See also*: *scripture*.

saddle-stitching   A method used to bind magazines and pamphlets in which the leaves are secured by round wire staples driven completely through the back fold at two or more places, usually by machine. Metal staples were introduced in about 1875. Unlike *side-stitching*, this method allows the leaves to open flat, but its strength is not sufficient to bind publications of more than 100 pages. Synonymous with *stapling* and *saddle-wire stitching*. Compare with *fold sewn*.

saga   From the Old Norse word for "thing said," a lengthy narrative in prose or verse, telling of adventure and heroic events, usually involving the history of a legendary Norse lineage. In modern usage, any long, complicated tale in which the plot has many unexpected twists and turns, particularly one recounting the fortunes of an extended family (*example*: *The Forsyte Saga* by John Galsworthy).

salary   A sum of money paid to an employee on a regular basis (weekly, biweekly, monthly) for performing a specific job. In the United States, most full-time librarians and technical support staff are salaried. Statistical information on salaries for librarians employed in the United States and Canada is reported annually in *Library Journal* (usually in the October 15 issue) and in *The Bowker Annual Library and Book Trade Almanac*. Compare with *wages*.

SALIS   *See*: **S**ubstance **A**buse **L**ibrarians & **I**nformation **S**pecialists.

salvage   Measures taken to recover materials, equipment, and furnishings damaged outside of normal use, for example, by water as a result of a major leak or flood. Salvaged materials may require special conservation procedures such as vacuum drying or fumigation. Items not *salvageable* are usually discarded. Also refers collectively to the materials recovered.

same size   Instructions from the publisher to the printer to reproduce an illustration submitted as copy without enlargement or reduction in size.

sample issue   An issue of a periodical, usually the first of an entirely new publication, sent at no charge by the publisher to a potential subscriber for inspection. In libraries, such copies are usually received and evaluated for selection by the serials department. In academic libraries, they may be routed to the appropriate department of the teaching faculty for evaluation.

sans-serif   A style of typeface, often used for headlines, that lacks short finishing projections, called *serifs*, at the end of each main stroke. Also spelled *sanserif*. *See also*: *block letter*.

satire   The use of sarcasm, irony, and wit to expose to ridicule the weaknesses or foibles of a person, group, or institution, often used to call public attention to a moral lapse or abuse of public trust, to damage the reputation of the victim for political or personal reasons, or as entertainment (*example*: *An Ideal Husband*, a comic drama by Oscar Wilde). *See also*: *caricature*, *cartoon*, *lampoon*, and *libel*.

save   To preserve a data file by copying it from main memory (RAM) to a permanent storage medium, such as a hard disk or floppy disk, at the end of a session on a computer. Unsaved data may be lost when the application is closed or the computer powered down.

scale   In cartography, the ratio of distance shown on a map, photograph, or other graphic representation of a given geographic phenomenon to its corresponding dimension on the ground or to another graphic representation. On maps, the scale is usually printed beneath the title in the legend, in the form of a bar scale or as a representative fraction (*example*: **1:24,000**). When a map is cataloged by a library, the *statement of scale* is given in the mathematical data area of the bibliographic description.

Also, the ratio of the size of a model or reproduction to the size of the original object. Also refers to the size of an item relative to others of its class. Compare with *reduction ratio*.

scanner   In data processing, a peripheral device that reads and converts handwritten or printed text, graphics, or barcodes into digital format (a *bitmap*) for processing or display on a computer screen, without actually recognizing the content. In libraries, optical scanners are used to create digital images of materials for interlibrary loan, document delivery, and electronic reserves and in circulation to read the barcode on the patron's library card and on items in the collection. Some barcode scanners require an external decoder.

scatter   The separation of entries on the same subject in a catalog or index, a condition that occurs when entries are made under (1) both the singular and plural forms of a heading, (2) variant forms of a name or title, or (3) a broad heading in one instance and a more specific heading in another. Scatter may also occur when there is inadequate control of synonyms or lack of precision in the assignment of subject headings or descriptors. Scatter is reduced by *authority control* and *vocabulary control*.

scattered   *See*: completeness.

scatter note   A note in a classification schedule instructing the cataloger to classify works in multiple locations. In Dewey Decimal Classification, the instruction is given in a class-elsewhere, see-reference, or relocation note, for example, the instruction under **023.7** (Title and job descriptions) to class titles and job descriptions for specific types of library positions in **023.2–023.4** (Types of positions).

In a list of pre-coordinate indexing terms, a note indicating that a term is used as a subheading under one or more categories of headings, for example, the note in the Library of Congress Subject Headings list under the heading "Catalogs, Union" indicating that "Union lists" is used as a subdivision under *"types of printed or nonbook materials, e.g.* Italian imprints—Union lists."

scenario   An outline or sketch of the plot of a dramatic work (play, opera, ballet, etc.) indicating the order of scenes and the characters involved in the action. Compare with *treatment*.

schedule   *See*: classification schedule.

schedule reduction   The elimination of some of the provisions made in a previous edition of a classification schedule, resulting in the discontinuation of certain class numbers, usually because the literature on the subject has dwindled significantly or because the class represents a distinction no longer recognized in the discipline or field.

schematic   A clear, simple line drawing or diagram used in textbooks and technical books to illustrate an operating principle or mechanism (or one of its parts).

scholarly book   A publishing term for a book that is: (1) written in scholarly style (2) about a specialized subject, (3) aimed at a relatively narrow, clearly defined market segment, (4) sold primarily within that market, (5) often purchased on the basis of imprint, (6) not price-sensitive, (7) not highly profitable for the publisher, (8) usually published by a university press or the publishing arm of a scholarly society, (9) reviewed mainly in scholarly journals, and (10) indexed, with a bibliography or list of references for further reading at the end. Scholarly books normally generate little income from the sale of subsidiary rights but attract a more sustained readership than most trade titles (adapted from *Bodian's Publishing Desk Reference*, Oryx Press, 1988). *See also*: *monograph*.

scholarly communication   The means by which individuals engaged in academic research and creative endeavor inform their peers, formally or informally, of the work they are engaged in or have accomplished. Following a tradition that began with the Academy in ancient Athens, scholars communicate by writing monographs and journal articles for publication, presenting conference papers that may subsequently be published in proceedings and transactions, submitting reports in fulfillment of grant requirements, creating and maintaining Web sites for the academic community, and corresponding with peers via e-mail and electronic mailing lists. Broadly defined, the process includes not only the creation and dissemination of scholarly works but also evaluation for quality (peer review) and preservation for future use. One of the goals of academic libraries is to facilitate scholarly communication in all its forms. In 2003, the Association of College and Research Libraries (ACRL) issued a formal statement on *Principles and Strategies for the Reform of Scholarly Communication* (see *C&RL News*, September 2003).

scholarly journal   *See*: journal.

Scholarly Publishing and Academic Resources Coalition (SPARC)   An international alliance of approximately 200 universities, research libraries, and library associations, SPARC was created in 1998 by several Association of Research Libraries (ARL) directors to address the pricing practices and policies of scientific, technical, and medical (STM) journal publishers. The coalition seeks to educate faculty on academic serials issues, fosters competition in the scholarly communication market, and advocates fundamental changes in the system and culture of scholarly communication. URL: www.arl.org/sparc/home. *See also*: *Open Archives Initiative*.

scholium   A marginal note explaining, interpreting, or commenting on a text, especially an annotation added by a classical grammarian on a passage from a work by a Greek or Latin author of Antiquity. Plural: *scholia*. *See also*: *exegesis*.

schoolbook   In the context of medieval manuscripts, a book made for the purpose of teaching and learning, mainly in an ecclesiastical or academic setting, often containing marginal notes made by the reader. From the 12th century on, the production of textbooks increased with the growth of European universities. Copied from authorized exemplars available for hire from stationers under the *pecia system*, schoolbooks included biblical texts and commentaries, grammars, legal and medical texts, scientific treatises, and classical works in Greek and Latin. *Abecedarii* designed for juvenile instruction are also included in this category.

school library   A library in a public or private elementary or secondary school that serves the information needs of its students and the curriculum needs of its teachers and staff, usually managed by a *school librarian* or *media specialist*. A school library collection usually contains books, periodicals, and educational media suitable for the grade levels served. A worldwide directory of *School Libraries on the Web* is available online at: www.sldirectory.com/index.html. Synonymous with *learning resources center* and *school library media center*. *See also*: *American Association of School Librarians* and School Library Journal.

School Library Journal (SLJ)   Published by R.R. Bowker since 1961, *SLJ* is a monthly trade journal and review publication for school, children's, and young adult librarians. In addition to regular columns, feature articles, and news of interest to the profession, *SLJ* reviews approximately 4,000 general trade books for children and young adult readers each year and over 1,000 educational media titles, including CD-ROMs. The reviews are short but evaluative, written by and for librarians. ISSN: 0362–8930. Previous title: *Junior Libraries*.

school library media center   *See*: school library.

science fiction (SF)   A highly imaginative form of fiction or motion picture based on scientific speculation, usually depicting life and adventure in the future or on other worlds, not outside the realm of possibility, sometimes prophetically (*example*: ***1984*** by George Orwell) or as a commentary on existing conditions (***Brave New World*** by Aldous Huxley). Science fiction is so popular that most large cities in the United States have at least one bookstore specializing in the genre. Science fiction readers communicate through fanzines and at conventions. Serious enthusiasts prefer the abbreviation *SF*, rather than *sci fi*. Compare with *fantasy*.

scope   The area or field within which a specific activity occurs. Also, the range or extent of action, observation, meaning, inquiry, etc. In libraries, the range of subjects or fields covered in a catalog, index, abstracting service, bibliographic database, reference work, etc. Compare with *coverage*. *See also*: *scope note*.

scope note (SN)   A brief statement included in an entry in a list of subject headings or thesaurus of indexing terms to indicate the intended use or meaning of the term in the indexing language and any special rules for assigning it in indexing. Scope notes are usually added for clarification or to restrict the use of a term to one of several possible meanings. Not all terms require a scope note, but if one is given, it normally precedes any synonyms (UF), broader terms (BT), narrower terms (NT), or related terms (RT). Compare with *parenthetical qualifier*.

In Dewey Decimal Classification, a note in the schedules indicating that the subject represented by a class number is broader or narrower than the heading implies.

score   A record of a musical work in which the parts to be played or sung are written or printed in musical notation on separate staves, vertically aligned to enable them to be read at the same time. *See also*: *chorus score*, *close score*, *condensed score*, *full score*, *miniature score*, *part*, *piano score*, *short score*, and *vocal score*.

scoring   To make a linear indentation on a piece of paper or card to allow it to turn or fold more easily without damaging the fibers. When done with a dull rule or disk, the process is called *creasing*. When a sharp rule is used, the fibers are partially broken, producing an effect similar to perforation, which allows the paper to tear more cleanly along the fold. In binding, to compress the fibers of a leaf in a line along the inner edge to allow the volume to open more easily.

scout   A person with experience in the book trade, employed by a publisher to seek out new writers and illustrators whose early works show promise and to explore with them possibilities for new books. In the motion picture industry, producers also employ such persons to locate books, manuscripts, etc., with potential for film adaptation. Compare with *book scout*.

scrapbook   A blankbook, usually of large size, containing unprinted leaves for mounting or inserting photographs, pictures, clippings, letters, invitations, and other memorabilia, usually to preserve them for sentimental reasons. Compare with *album*.

screen capture   *See*: screen dump.

screen dump   The process of saving as a file, or sending to a printer, a copy of the image displayed on the monitor of a computer, usually to create a record that can be used to document and/or diagnose a malfunction. Synonymous with *screen capture*.

screenplay   A story written in a form suitable for motion picture or television production or adapted for that purpose from an existing novel, short story, or stage play by a *screenwriter* whose name is given in the credits. *See also*: *script* and *treatment*.

screen printing   A method of stencil printing in which the areas of a design to be left unprinted are masked on the underside of a screen made of fabric, plastic, or woven metal stretched tightly across a frame. Ink or paint is forced through the holes in the unmasked areas onto the printing surface by hand using a squeegie or by machine. Each color must be applied separately using a different stencil. Screen printing is often used for signs and posters when vivid colors are desired and for printing on surfaces such as glass, metal, plastic, wood, etc. Synonymous with *serigraphy* and *silk screen*.

screen saver   A utility program that blanks out the image displayed on the monitor of a computer, or replaces it with a continuously changing pattern, to prevent *ghosting*, the permanent etching of a still image on the monitor. Most screen savers can be set to commence after a designated period of inactivity and remain on the screen until the mouse is moved or a key is depressed, restoring the original image.

screenwriter   The person responsible for writing the screenplay for a motion picture, videorecording, or television program or the scripted narration for a documentary, whose name is usually given in the credits. In library cataloging, the name of the screenwriter is entered in the note area of the bibliographic record representing the item.

scribal copy   A written work produced by hand by an experienced copyist who usually works from an exemplar, as distinct from the original manuscript produced by the author or at the author's dictation. Before the invention of the printing press in the mid-15th century, production of multiple copies was done entirely by scribes.

scribe   A professional penman who copied manuscripts by hand before the invention of printing from movable type. Throughout Antiquity, scribes and notaries were members of a profession. During the Middle Ages, most copyists were attached to a court or chancery (official record office) or were monks working in the *scriptoria* of Catholic religious establishments, often as part of a team that included parchmenters, illuminators, and binders.

With the rise of universities in the 12th century, scribes and illuminators of both sexes began to function independently in urban centers, often in association with stationers. Christopher de Hamel notes in *Scribes and Illuminators* (University of Toronto Press, 1992) that a medieval scribe could be an author, student, notary, moonlighting royal clerk, parish priest unable to live on his stipend, book collector making a copy for personal use, or even an inmate working toward release from debtor's prison. *See also*: *calligraphy*.

scrinium   A container in the shape of a cylinder with a removable top, used by the ancient Romans for storing manuscripts in the form of scrolls. *See also*: *capsa*.

script   The text of a play, motion picture, videorecording, or television or radio program indicating the lines to be spoken by each character, with directions for staging the work. Compare with *acting edition* and *promptbook*.

Also refers to a set of alphabetic, syllabic, or ideographic characters used in writing one or more languages. In the early majuscule scripts, the letters are of uniform height (uppercase). Majuscule is *bilinear*, its letterforms bounded by two horizontal lines. In the minuscule scripts adopted in the 8th century, the letters are of unequal height (lowercase), some having ascenders and descenders. Minuscule is *quadralinear*, bounded by four horizontal lines. As Michelle Brown notes in *Understanding Illuminated Manuscripts* (Getty Museum/British Library, 1994), the form and function of a medieval manuscript book determined the general appearance of the script (its aspect), the speed and care with which it was written (ductus), and the devices employed to conserve space (abbreviations, etc.).

Classified by time period, the scripts used in Europe were subject to far stricter conventions than personal handwriting because they were used for book production. With considerable overlap, the following succession of scripts occurred from Antiquity through the medieval period, ending with the spread of printing from movable type: square capitals, rustic capitals, uncial, half uncial, Insular majuscule, Carolingian minuscule, Anglo-Saxon minuscule, gothic, and humanistic. Less formal hands, written with greater speed and less lifting of the pen, are *cursive*. Bastard scripts, a fusion of formal and cursive, exhibit greater variability. In the early 15th century, efforts by the

Italian humanists to reform medieval scripts inspired many early typefaces. Compare with *hand*. **See also**: *chancery script*.

In printing, a typeface or font that has the appearance of continuously flowing handwriting or calligraphy.

In computer programming, a program or set of instructions associated with a particular event or condition, interpreted or carried out by another program, rather than by the processor. Programming languages conceived as script languages include Perl and JavaScript, often used by Web servers to handle forms input. Also refers to the set of rules used by a filter to eliminate unwanted content sent to an Internet user, for example, the rules governing a filter designed to reject spam e-mail messages.

scriptio continuo   Latin for "continuous writing." In Antiquity and the early Christian period, writing was in capital letters with no word or sentence division and no punctuation. In *scriptio continuo*, the preceding sentence would look like this:

INANTIQUITYANDTHEEARLYCHRISTIANPERIOD
WRITINGWASINCAPITALLETTERSWITHNOWORD
ORSENTENCEDIVISIONANDNOPUNCTUATION

In some manuscripts, raised points or full stops were used between words to make the text easier to read. Use of a space to separate words did not become standard practice until the late 8th century. Synonymous with *scriptura continua*.

scriptorium   The room or area of a medieval monastery reserved for the preparation of manuscripts, in some establishments a single large room, in others partitioned into individual cells. Standard equipment included a sloping writing desk for each copyist, equipped with chalk, pumice, inkhorns (one for each color), plummet, pens and brushes, and a sharp knife, straight edge, pointed stylus, and ruling stick. A scribe might work independently until a book was completed or as part of a team that included illuminators, correctors, and binders. After the parchment or vellum sheets were ruled, the text was written, then rubricated, illuminated, corrected and cleaned, and bound. To minimize distraction, silence was maintained while work was in progress. Plural: *scriptoria*. **See also**: *armarian*.

scriptura continua   **See**: *scriptio continuo*.

scripture   Originally, any written composition, but the term is now used mainly for the Old and New Testaments of the Christian Bible, sometimes in the plural (*Holy Scriptures*). In a more general sense, any religious or sacred text or record.

scroll   Originally, a manuscript in the form of a length of papyrus, usually rolled around a sturdy wooden rod (*umbilicus*) with knobbed ends, sometimes with a vellum tag attached to one end for identification. In Antiquity, texts were written in columns on sheets of papyrus glued together in a continuous roll called a *volumen* by the Romans (papyrus tends to delaminate when folded).

The *codex* or book with pages replaced the scroll after animal skin (parchment and vellum) came into widespread use as a writing surface. Centuries later, the Chinese made scrolls from paper (see *Diamond Sutra*). Scrolls are still used in Jewish synagogues to preserve the *Torah*. **See also**: *capsa*, *Dead Sea Scrolls*, and *scrinium*.

Also, to cause the text or images on a computer screen to move vertically or horizontally, by typing strokes on a keyboard or by using a pointing device such as a mouse to manipulate a scroll bar along one side, or across the top or bottom, of a window or frame in a graphical user interface.

scuffed   The condition of a book with a binding so badly scraped that it has become frayed or roughened in places. Compare with *rubbed*.

SDI   An abbreviation of *selective dissemination of information*. *See*: current awareness service.

seal   A stamp, carved cylinder, signet ring, etc., used to make an impression in molten wax to secure a letter or other document, confirming the identity of the sender and/ or the authenticity of the contents. Also refers to the design or mark itself, a broken seal indicating that the document has been opened. The use of gummed envelopes has replaced the seal.

Also, a soft but coarse-grained leather made from the skin of a seal. According to *The Bookman's Glossary* (R.R. Bowker, 1983), leather made from the skin of a very young or baby seal, called *pin seal*, is finer-grained and has a lustrous finish. Synonymous with *sealskin*.

sealskin   *See*: seal.

search   A systematic effort on the part of a library user or librarian to locate desired information by manual or electronic means, whether successful or not, as opposed to browsing a library collection with no clear intention in mind. *See also*: *mediated search*, *search statement*, *search strategy*, and *serendipity*.

Also refers to an attempt by a member of the circulation staff of a library to find an item listed as available in the catalog but not in its correct location on the shelf. *See also*: *missing*.

In employment, the formal process of seeking qualified candidates to fill a vacant position, usually undertaken by a search committee composed of staff members and/ or supervisors who will work closely with the new employee. In libraries, national searches are usually announced in professional publications, such as *American Libraries*, *College & Research Libraries News*, and the *Chronicle of Higher Education*.

searchable   An electronic resource running on software designed to allow the user to type a word, phrase, or string of words or phrases as input to find all the records, entries, or text containing the search term(s). Most online catalogs and bibliographic databases can be searched by author, title, subject heading (descriptor), and keywords. Boolean logic and truncation are permitted in a keywords search in most library catalogs and databases; wildcard and proximity searching in some.

search committee   A group of people, usually three or more library staff members, elected or appointed to assist in the process of selecting a candidate (or list of candidates) to fill a vacant position in the library. Their responsibilities may include drafting the position description, posting the vacancy, evaluating applications, selecting candidates for interviewing, drafting interview questions, conducting interviews, and selecting and recommending finalist(s) to library administration.

search engine   Originally, a hardware device designed to search a text-based database for specific character strings (queries) typed as input by the user. More recently, computer software designed to help the user locate information available at sites on the World Wide Web by selecting categories from a hierarchical directory of subjects (*example*: *Yahoo!*) or by entering appropriate keywords or phrases (*Google*, *Hotbot*, etc.). Most Web search engines allow the searcher to use Boolean logic and truncation in search statements. Results may be ranked according to relevance or some other criterion. Functionality varies, but many search engines provide both basic and advanced search modes. For more information about search engines, please see the entry by Mark Hepworth and Ian Murray in the *International Encyclopedia of Information and Library Science* (Routledge, 2003) or log on to *Search Engine Watch* (searchenginewatch.com) or *Search Engine Guide* (www.searchengineguide.com.) *See also*: *crawler* and *metasearch*.

search history   A feature of some search software systems and Web browsers that allows the user to view a consecutive list of all the searches executed during the current search session or all the sites visited in a browsing session. Some systems allow the user to select a previous search from the list and re-execute it or print or save the search history, if desired.

search mode   Most bibliographic databases provide a basic approach for novices and more advanced methods for experienced users. In *basic mode*, keywords typed as input are located by default in predetermined fields of the bibliographic record (usually in the title, abstract, and full-text). In some databases, the user may also limit search results within certain parameters and decide whether the system will search for *all words*, *any words*, or the *exact phrase* as entered. In *advanced mode*, most search software allows the user to specify the fields to be searched and provides a wider range of limit options. Some Web search engines are also designed to allow the user to select advanced search, rather than the default, usually basic mode.

search service   A business that specializes in locating out of print books at the request of libraries and private collectors, often a dealer in used, old, or rare books. Acquisitions librarians sometimes rely on such services when a replacement copy is needed for an item still in demand but no longer in print. *See also*: *Abebooks* and *Alibris*.

search software   A computer program designed to execute a search for information when queried by a user. User-friendly search software provides both a menu-driven interface for novices and a command-driven interface for experienced searchers. Sophisticated search software permits the use of Boolean logic, nesting, truncation, wildcard, and proximity operators in search statements and allows the user to limit search results by various parameters. Compare with *search engine*. *See also*: *functionality*.

search statement   In information retrieval, an information need or query entered as input in a form acceptable to the search software used by the retrieval system. Most online catalogs, bibliographic databases, and search engines allow Boolean logic, nesting, truncation, wildcard, and proximity operators to be used in keyword(s) search statements and permit the user to limit search results. *See also*: *controlled vocabulary* and *natural language*.

search strategy   In information retrieval, a systematic *plan* for conducting a search. In most cases, the first step is to formulate a clear and concise *topic statement*. The next step is to identify the main concepts in the topic. Then the most appropriate finding tools for the subject must be identified and located. Lists of authorized subject heading(s) and descriptors in the appropriate indexing systems can then be consulted to find preferred terms to represent the main concepts.

In computer-based information retrieval, keywords can be combined using Boolean logic to form one or more queries expressed in syntax acceptable to the catalogs, bibliographic databases, and search engines most likely to contain information on the subject. If the initial results of a search are unsatisfactory, the user can modify the search statement by adding related terms or substituting broader terms to expand retrieval or by substituting narrower terms to restrict retrieval. In most systems, limiting can be employed to restrict retrieval to entries that meet specific parameters. *See also*: *heuristic*, *proximity*, and *truncation*.

search term   A word or phrase representing one of the main concepts in a research topic, used alone or in combination with other terms in a *search statement*, to query an online catalog, bibliographic database, or search engine and retrieve relevant information. A search term can be a keyword or phrase supplied by the user, an authorized subject heading or descriptor selected from a prescribed list, or a word or phrase found in a thesaurus, for example, *The Contemporary Thesaurus of Search Terms and Synonyms* by Sara Knapp (Oryx, 2000).

Sears subject heading   A subject heading from a list created by Minnie E. Sears, first published in 1923 for use in school libraries and small public libraries. Although it is based on Library of Congress subject headings, the *Sears List of Subject Headings* published by H.W. Wilson is narrower in scope and its headings are more general. Small libraries supplement it with LC headings as needed.

season   One of the annual cycles in the publishing industry. When publishers introduce their frontlist in the spring and fall of each year, the previous year's frontlist titles move to the backlist. New and backlisted titles are described in the seasonal publisher's catalog distributed by mail to libraries and booksellers.

seasonal catalog   *See*: season.

secondary binding   When potential sales of a new book are difficult to predict, the publisher may decide to bind an edition in batches over a period of years. The color or quality of the binding material and the lettering on the spine may differ slightly from one batch to another. To distinguish the *primary binding* from subsequent bindings, the order in which the batches were bound must be determined, if possible.

secondary entry   *See*: added entry.

secondary source   Any published or unpublished work that is one step removed from the original source, usually describing, summarizing, analyzing, evaluating, derived from, or based on *primary source* materials, for example, a review, critical analysis, second-person account, or biographical or historical study. Also refers to material other than primary sources used in the preparation of a written work. Compare with *tertiary source*.

secondary values   In archives, the values of records for the activities of users other than the office of record or its successors. Compare with *primary values*.

secondhand book   *See*: used book.

secondhand bookstore   *See*: used bookstore.

section   In library cataloging, a separately published part of a bibliographic resource usually representing a subject category within the whole and indicated by a topical heading or an alphabetical or numeric designation or both (*AACR2*). Also, a similar division within a law book. Also refers to one of the separately folded parts of a newspaper, for example, the *Entertainment Section*.

In printing, a unit of paper that when folded, gathered, and sewn or glued together with similar units constitutes the *book block*, usually a single folded sheet but in some cases one-and-a-half or two sheets or one sheet with an extra leaf added. Strictly speaking, a section is a signature to which any plates and/or inserts have been added.

In Dewey Decimal Classification, the third level of subdivision, represented by a three-digit notation not ending in zero (*example*: **947** for works on the history of Russia). There are 1,000 sections in DDC (10 × 10 × 10). Further subdivision is indicated by the addition of a decimal fraction (**947.084** for history of the Russian Revolution). *See also*: *division* and *main class*.

In cartography, a scale representation of a vertical plane of intersection, showing both the surface profile of the ground (and any large bodies of water) and underlying geological features along the plane of intersection, for example, rock formations and sedimentary strata. Also, a unit of subdivision of a township, usually a quadrangle one mile square.

In library shelving, the vertical unit between two uprights in a single- or double-faced range. In the United States, a standard section is 7.5 feet high and 3 feet wide. Synonymous in Britain with *tier*.

Also refers to one of the main divisions of the Association of College and Research Libraries (ACRL), many of which have their own newsletters, electronic discussion lists, specialized programming, preconferences, etc. A complete alphabetic list of ACRL sections is available at: www.ala.org.

section title   *See*: divisional title.

security   In computing, the technology developed to prevent unauthorized persons, particularly hackers and crackers, from gaining entry to protected systems and files, including data encryption, virus detection, firewalls, and the authentication of authorization codes (usernames, passwords, PINs, etc.). In a more general sense, all the measures taken to prevent unauthorized persons from accessing confidential information.

In the operation of libraries and archives, a general term encompassing all the equipment, personnel, practices, and procedures used to prevent the theft or destruction of materials and equipment and to protect patrons and employees from the harmful actions of persons intent on mischief. Large libraries and library systems often appoint a library security officer (LSO) to develop and implement a *security plan*. *See also*: *key control*, *security audit*, *security guard*, and *security system*.

security audit A thorough on-site inspection in which a person (or persons) trained and experienced in library security critically examines and analyzes all the existing security systems and procedures used in a library to ascertain current status, identify deficiencies or excesses, and make recommendations based on findings. A professional security audit may include the analysis of crime statistics, an assessment of insurance needs, and discussion of sensitive topics, such as internal theft and personal security issues.

security gate A device installed near the entrance and/or exit of a library, usually in the form of a swing-arm or pair of uprights positioned in such a way that persons entering or leaving the premises must pass through a magnetic detection system designed to trigger an alarm if an attempt is made to remove library materials without checking them out. Less obtrusive laser systems are also available. Some security gates include a counter that provides traffic statistics.

security guard An employee responsible for patrolling the premises of a library to discourage disruptive behavior and illegal activities, such as vandalism and the unauthorized removal of materials (theft), and to deal with individuals who do not comply with library policies and rules. Most security guards wear uniforms and are trained to handle problem patrons and various types of emergency situations. Synonymous with *security officer*.

security strip *See*: magnetic strip.

security system An electronic alarm system installed at the entrance and exit of a library facility to detect the unauthorized removal of library materials (theft). Most security systems use a swing-arm or pair of uprights called a security gate, activated by a magnetic strip affixed to each item, which must be desensitized by circulation staff at the time an item is checked out to avoid triggering the alarm. Some security systems include a counting device for gathering statistics on traffic patterns.

see A cross-reference in a library catalog, index, or reference work directing the user from a synonym (or other equivalent term) to the preferred heading or descriptor for a given name, place, or subject (*example*: **Beyle, Marie Henri** *see* **Stendahl, 1783– 1842**). Synonymous with *search under*. Compare with *USE*.

see also A cross-reference in a library catalog, index, or reference work directing the user to a heading under which related information can be found on a given subject (*example*: **Treaty of Versailles, 1919** *see also* **Paris Peace Conference, 1919**). Abbreviated *SA*. Synonymous with *search also under*.

segmentation In Dewey Decimal Classification, the indication of logical breaks in a number by means of a typographical device, such as a slash or a prime mark used to indicate the end of an abridged class number or the beginning of a standard subdivision (*DDC*).

selection   The process of deciding which materials should be added to a library collection. Selection decisions are usually made on the basis of reviews and standard collection development tools by librarians designated as *selectors* in specific subject areas, based on their interests and fields of specialization. In academic libraries, selection may also be done by members of the teaching faculty in their disciplines. Very large academic and public libraries may use an approval plan or blanket order plan to assist selectors. Library patrons also recommend titles for purchase, especially in libraries that provide a suggestion box. The opposite of *deselection*. **See also**: *selection aid* and *selection criteria*.

selection aid   A publication used by librarians to develop a balanced collection that meets the information needs of library users. The category includes bestseller lists, best books lists, core lists, national bibliographies, etc.

selection criteria   The set of standards used by librarians to decide whether an item should be added to the collection, which normally include a list of subjects or fields to be covered, levels of specialization, editions, currency, languages, and formats (large print, nonprint, abridgments, etc.). Selection criteria usually reflect the library's mission and the information needs of its clientele, but selection decisions are also influenced by budgetary constraints and qualitative evaluation in the form of reviews, recommended core lists, and other selection tools. **See also**: *collection development policy*.

selective   Chosen in preference to another or others on the basis of a special characteristic or quality. In library research, a finding tool such as an index or bibliography that includes only a portion of the available literature, usually limited to sources that meet certain pre-established criteria (quality, currency, reading level, degree of specialization, etc.). Compare with *comprehensive*.

selective bibliography   A bibliography that includes only a portion of the relevant literature, usually based on predetermined selection criteria, such as the needs of a particular group of users, desire for current versus retrospective material, or an evaluation of quality.

selective dissemination of information (SDI)   *See*: current awareness service.

self-checkout   An automated circulation system that allows registered patrons to check out circulating materials on their own without the assistance of library staff, usually by means of barcodes attached to the item and appearing on the patron's library card. Self-checkout is part of a trend toward self-service in library operations. **See also**: *radio frequency identification*.

self-citation   Reference made in a written work to one or more of the author's previous publications, an accepted practice in scholarly communication, provided important works written on the subject by other authors are not neglected or ignored.

self-cover   A pamphlet or periodical covered in the same paper stock used to print the text, rather than a heavier grade of paper.

self end   In bookbinding, an endpaper that is not separate from the text but rather part of the first or last section and therefore of the same paper stock as the text.

self-help publication   A book, audiotape, or videotape intended to assist the reader, listener, or viewer in solving a personal problem, for example, finding the best treatment for a physical illness or condition or the answer to a legal question without having to pay for professional services. Some publishers specialize in self-help publications (*example*: **Nolo Press**, providing legal books for laypersons). Compare with *how-to publication*.

self-publishing   The editing, design, printing, and marketing of a work at the author's own expense, without the assistance of a commercial publisher, often undertaken out of devotion to the subject. Sophisticated desktop publishing software and high-quality photocopiers have made this option easier and less expensive than it once was. Also refers to the electronic publication of a work by its author, usually installed on a server publicly accessible over the Internet.

It can be difficult to get a self-published work reviewed. Because libraries select largely on the basis of reviews and order materials through regular market channels, this type of work is rarely added to library collections. Compare with *vanity publisher*. *See also*: *zine*.

self-service   Library functions that can be initiated, controlled, and/or executed by the patron without the assistance of library staff, including self-checkout, patron-initiated interlibrary loan service, and online catalogs that allow users to view their own patron records, place holds, renew items on loan, etc. Synonymous with *disintermediated service*.

self-wrapper   *See*: wrapper.

semantic factoring   An indexing technique in which a compound heading or descriptor is divided into its constituent parts (*example*: "Annotated bibliography" → Annotation + Bibliography). In some cases, semantic factoring yields false drops (Library + Research → "Library research" and "Research library").

semantic relation   The connection in meaning between two or more concepts and between the terms (subject headings or descriptors) used to represent them in an indexing language. Semantic relations can be classified as follows:

Relation	Description	Example
Active	Action, process, or operation directly performed by one on the other	Scanner / Barcode
Associative	Linked conceptually but not hierarchically	Library statistics / Bibliometrics
Causal	One responsible for the occurrence of the other	Acquisitions / Collection growth
Generic	Genus to species	Library / Academic library
Hierarchic	One a logical subclass of the other	Bookbinding / Binding

Locative	One located at, in, or on a place specified by the other	Mainz Psalter
Partitive	Part to whole	Chapter / Book
Passive	One influenced by or subjected to the action of the other with no reciprocal influence	Library collection / Selection criteria
Autonymous	Opposite in meaning	Selection / Deselection
Synonymous	Having the same or nearly the same meaning	Booklet / Pamphlet

semantics   The branch of linguistics concerned with the *meaning* of the words, signs, and symbols that constitute the elements of change and evolution in a spoken or written language. Also, the branch of semiotics that deals with relationships of meaning between signs, and between signs and their referents, within a system of communication. *See also*: *semantic relation*.

semé   The past tense of the French verb *semer*, meaning "to sow." Used to describe a bookbinding on which the surface of one or both covers is decorated in a pattern created by the regular repetition of one or more small ornamental motifs against an open ground. A *fleuron* is often used for this purpose. The noun is *semis*.

semiannual   Issued at intervals of six months. Also refers to a serial issued every six months. Compare with *biennial*. Synonymous with *half yearly* and *twice yearly*.

semicurrent   Archival materials too old to be considered current but still useful and therefore retained for a certain period, usually in a location reserved for intermediate storage, pending final disposition.

semi-limp   A binding in boards made of thin, flexible card or some other material that bends easily. Compare with *limp binding*.

semimonthly   Issued twice each month or every two weeks. Also refers to a serial issued twice a month, with the possible exception of certain issues (*example*: **Library Journal**). Synonymous with *biweekly*. Compare with *bimonthly*.

seminal   From the Latin word for "seed." An idea or work so original when first expressed, composed, created, released, or published that it has considerable influence on the thought and work of contemporaries and on succeeding generations of writers, scholars, or artists who may give it further development in their own works.

semiotics   The systematic study of the linguistic and nonlinguistic signs and symbols used in both natural and artificially constructed languages. The three branches of semiotics are: (1) pragmatics (how signs are used by those who make use of them), (2) semantics (relationships of meaning between signs and their referents), and (3) syntax (how signs are combined). Each of the branches has theoretical, descriptive, and applied aspects.

semipublished   Works such as reports, internal documents, theses, etc., that are difficult, if not impossible, to obtain through regular market channels because they were never intended for publication but that may be obtainable via interlibrary loan, document delivery service, or some other method of retrieval. Compare with *unpublished*. *See also*: *gray literature*.

semiweekly   Issued twice each week. Also refers to a serial publication issued twice a week. Synonymous with *twice weekly*. Compare with *biweekly*.

send   To transmit data from one node to another on a computer network, as in the exchange of e-mail messages or the export of bibliographic data from an online catalog or bibliographic database to an e-mail account. Also refers to the command in a computer program that initiates such a transmission. The opposite of *receive*.

seniority   The numerical position of an individual with respect to longevity of employment, which may be a factor in certain personnel decisions (assignment of duties and responsibilities, promotion, layoff, etc.).

sentencing   The application of the appropriate disposition schedule to a group or collection of archival records.

sentimental novel   A work of serious fiction, popular in 18th-century England and 19th-century America, in which the author portrays the afflictions of one or more heroes and/or heroines of unblemished character to demonstrate the rewards of virtuous conduct (*example*: ***Uncle Tom's Cabin*** by Harriet Beecher Stowe). Synonymous with *domestic novel*.

separately paginated   Numbering the pages of each volume or part of a set, or of each issue of a single volume of a periodical, in a separate sequence, starting with number one. Compare with *continuous pagination*. *See also*: *magazine pagination*.

separately published   An item issued by a publisher or distributor as an independent entity, usually under its own title and copyright, as opposed to a work published in a collection or as a serial, for example, the individual works in a monographic series, each published under a separate title.

septennial   Issued every seven years. Also refers to a serial publication issued every seven years. *See also*: *annual*, *biennial*, *triennial*, *quadrennial*, *quinquennial*, *sexennial*, and *decennial*.

sequel   A work of narrative fiction, in most instances a novel, that is complete in itself but continues a previous work in plot, setting, and characters. A sequel usually (but not always) begins where the action in the previous work left off and is usually (but not always) written by the author of the work it continues (*example*: ***Let the Circle Be Unbroken*** by Mildred D. Taylor, a sequel to ***Roll of Thunder, Hear My Cry***). A literary work may have more than one sequel. The opposite of *prequel*. Compare with *continuation*. *See also*: *trilogy*.

   In a more general sense, anything that follows; a subsequent series of events or course of affairs.

sequential   The arrangement of a series of entries or items in prescribed order based on a predetermined system of priority, for example, reverse chronological order. In computing, *sequential access* refers to data stored in a manner that allows pieces of it to be accessed only in a certain order, as in the medium of magnetic tape. Compare with *random access memory*.

sequential locator   *See*: locator.

serendipity   A word first coined by the English writer Horace Walpole in *The Three Princes of Serendip* to refer to the knack of making fortunate discoveries unexpectedly, by accident or coincidence. In information retrieval, this usually depends on the ability of the browser to recognize the relevance or utility of data not actively sought at the time it is encountered. Flexibility is one of the qualities of a good researcher. *See also*: *heuristic*.

serial   A publication in any medium issued under the same title in a succession of discrete parts usually numbered (or dated) and appearing at regular or irregular intervals with no predetermined conclusion. In *AACR2 2002*, serials are considered a type of *continuing resource*. *See also*: *seriality*.

Serial publications include print periodicals and newspapers, electronic magazines and journals, annuals (reports, yearbooks, etc.), continuing directories, proceedings and transactions, and numbered monographic series cataloged separately. When serials split, merge, or are absorbed, a title change may occur. Most libraries purchase serials on subscription or continuation order. *See also*: *nonsubscription serial*, *provisional serial*, *pseudo-serial*, *reference serial*, *serial bibliography*, and *serial index*.

A specific serial title is identified by a unique International Standard Serials Number (ISSN) and key title, assigned and maintained by the International Serials Data System (ISDS), a network of national serials data centers. Serials and annuals are listed in *Ulrich's International Periodicals Directory* published annually by R.R. Bowker and in *The Serials Directory* published by EBSCO. A library's holdings of a serial title are indicated in an open or closed entry in the *serial record* representing the item in the catalog. The librarian responsible for managing a serials collection is a *serials librarian*. *See also*: *CONSER*, *North American Serials Interest Group*, and *serials control*.

serial bibliography   A bibliography published in successive parts, at fairly regular intervals, usually limited to a specialized field of study (*example*: ***Bibliography of Asian Studies*** published every one or two years).

serial cancellation   Notice given to a publisher or subscription agent that a library no longer wishes to subscribe to a specific serial publication. In recent years, the relentless increase in subscription prices and the inability of acquisitions budgets to keep pace with inflation have forced academic and research libraries to cancel periodical subscriptions to maintain balance in the purchase of serials and monographs. The scientific disciplines are most affected by such cuts because they are more serial-dependent than the arts and humanities and because average subscription price is highest for scientific journals. Some serials are *noncancellable*. *See also*: *serials review*.

serial index   An index to the content of a publication issued in successively numbered parts, usually a cumulative author and/or title index compiled by the publisher, appearing at the end of the last issue of the publication year. Most magazines (and some journals) do not provide such an index.

Serial Item and Contribution Identifier (SICI)   A variable length code assigned to identify serial items (*example*: **individual issues**) and contributions (*example*: **articles**) contained in a serial publication, independent of distribution medium (print, microform, digital). Defined in ANSI/NISO standard Z39.56–199X, the SICI consists of three parts (item segment, contribution segment, and control segment), all of which are required. Because the SICI employs the International Standard Serial Number (ISSN) to identify serial title, assignment of ISSN is prerequisite. Implementation of the SICI standard by serial publishers provides unique identifiers for serial items and contributions to libraries and other members of the bibliographic community engaged in serials control and use. URL: sunsite.berkeley.edu/SICI.

seriality   When library collections consisted primarily of materials printed on paper, a fundamental distinction was made in cataloging between monographic and serial publications, but certain types of print publications, such as loose-leaf services and monographs with serial supplementation, were not easy to classify by this simple dichotomy. Problems of definition were further complicated with the advent of regularly updated bibliographic databases and Web sites modified or updated on a regular or irregular basis. In 1997 Jean Hirons, CONSER Coordinator at the Library of Congress, and Crystal Graham, serials librarian at the University of California, San Diego, presented a paper on "Issues Related to Seriality" at the International Conference on the Principles and Future Development of *AACR* in Toronto, proposing a new model of the bibliographic universe in which resources in any medium are classified as either "finite" or "continuing," a distinction adopted in *AACR2 2002*. *See also*: *bibliographic hermaphrodite*.

NEW MODEL OF BIBLIOGRAPHIC RESOURCES*

Finite resources (complete as first issued or intended to be complete in a finite number of parts or revisions)
  Complete
    Monographs
    Multivolume sets
    Electronic texts
    Maps, sound recordings, software, etc.
  Incomplete
    Successively issued (in discrete parts)
      Multi-parts
      Supplemented monographs
    Integrating (updated over time, updates incorporated into the resource without remaining discrete)
      Revised e-texts
      Some loose-leaf services

Continuing resources (not complete as first issued and intended to be ongoing, though not necessarily indefinitely)
> *Successively issued*
>> Serials (including electronic magazines and journals)
>> Series
> *Integrating*
>> Most loose-leaf services
>> Databases
>> Web sites

*Adapted from "Teaching Seriality: A Major Educational Challenge" by Arlene G. Taylor in *The Serials Librarian* 41 (2002): 78.

serialized   A work published in installments, usually at regular intervals. During the 18th and early 19th centuries, books were often published in numbered parts or fascicles, but by the late 19th century most serialized works appeared in consecutive issues of newspapers and magazines. In modern publishing, *serialization* is the publication of a work in installments, before or after its appearance in book form. *See also*: *number book* and *serial rights*.

serial number   A number identifying the place in sequence of a publication issued as part of a series. Also refers to a unique identification number assigned to a serial title for identification purposes, such as the International Standard Serial Number (ISSN).

serial record   A bibliographic record created to represent a serial publication in a library catalog, including as elements of bibliographic description the title, place of publication, name of publisher, publication history, physical description, frequency, indexing, subject headings, and ISSN. Library holdings, subscription source, payment record, and binding history are usually indicated in a separate *item record*. The CONSER program is a major source of high-quality serial records. *See also*: *serials list*.

serial rights   Under copyright law, the subsidiary rights of an author or publisher to control the publication of a work in installments, usually in a magazine or newspaper. Serial rights can be sold or transferred by the owner.

serials control   A general term encompassing all the activities involved in managing a serials collection, including but not limited to receiving, claiming, invoice processing, binding, circulation, and record maintenance (bibliographic, check-in, bindery, etc.), usually accomplished by the serials department of a library, manually or with the aid of an automated serials control system.

serials desk   A service point, usually located near the periodicals section in a library, staffed by a person trained to assist patrons in locating serials and in using equipment available for making copies of articles (photocopiers, microform reader-printers, etc.).

Serials Directory, The   A directory issued annually by EBSCO in print, online, and on CD-ROM, providing bibliographic information and pricing for a classified list of over 140,000 serials currently published in the United States and internationally. Indexed alphabetically by serial title, ceased title, ISSN, and peer-reviewed title, *The Serials*

Directory is usually shelved in the reference section of large libraries. ISSN: 0886–4179. *See also*: Ulrich's International Periodicals Directory.

serials list   A list of all the serials held by a library, including any titles that have ceased publication or been canceled for which the library retains back files, usually arranged in alphabetical order by title, with holdings indicated in open and closed entries and cross-references to and from changed titles. *See also*: *serial record*.

serials review   A systematic examination of a library's serials list to identify titles to be retained and subscriptions to be canceled, usually conducted by a serials librarian or serials department, ideally with input solicited from persons likely to be affected by the decisions. Titles suggested for addition or substitution may also be considered, depending on the amount budgeted for serials expenditures. In some libraries, serials reviews are scheduled on a regular basis (usually every one to three years), but in others, the process occurs irregularly. Decisions are based on usage, subscription price, importance to the discipline, and availability of full-text in online databases.

serial title   The name of a publication issued in successive parts, usually printed on the front cover and in the masthead of each issue or on the title page of a monographic serial. In electronic serials, the title appears on the welcome screen. Serial title is uniquely identified by the International Standard Serial Number (ISSN). Title changes are more frequent in serials than in other types of publications. In most libraries in the United States, periodicals are shelved alphabetically by title.

series   A group of separately published works related in subject and/or form, issued in succession (numbered or unnumbered) by a single publisher or distributor, usually in uniform style, each bearing, in addition to its own title, a collective or *series title* applied by the publisher to the group as a whole. The individual volumes or parts may not share the same author or editor, nor is it necessary for them to be published at regular intervals. The series title is given on a separate *series title page*, usually the verso of the leaf bearing the half title. It also appears at the top of the title page or on a page following the title page. Some reference books are published in open-ended series (*example*: **Contemporary World Issues** from ABC-CLIO). In library cataloging, information describing series (title proper, statements of responsibility, ISSN, number, etc.) is given in the series area of the bibliographic record. Abbreviated *ser.* Compare with *serial*. *See also*: *continuation order*, *map series*, *monographic series*, *record series*, and *subseries*.

The term is also applied to each of two or more volumes of essays, articles, lectures, or other writings, similar in character and issued in sequence, for example, *Among My Books*, second series, by James Russell Lowell (*AACR2*).

Also, a separately numbered sequence of volumes *within* a serial publication (*example*: **Contemporary Authors**, *New Revision Series*).

In typography, all the type fonts available in a given typeface, usually ranging in size from 5 points to 80 points. Compare with *type family*.

series area   The area of bibliographic description reserved in library cataloging for information about a work separately published as one of a group of items, including the title proper of the series, statements of responsibility concerning the series, ISSN, and the number within the series (if the individual items are numbered). In the MARC record, series statements are entered in the fields tagged 4XX.

series author   A writer of works published in series (*example*: **J.K. Rowling**, author of the Harry Potter books for children).

series statement   The portion of a bibliographic record reserved for description of the group of which the publication is a member (if applicable), including the title proper of the series, statements of responsibility concerning the series, ISSN, and number within the series (if the items are numbered). In the MARC record, series statements are entered in fields tagged 4XX.

series title   A collective title applied to a group of separately published materials issued in succession in uniform style by a single publisher or distributor. In books, the series title is usually printed on the verso of the leaf bearing the half title, often with a list of previously published works in the same series. In the bibliographic record, the title proper is given in the series statements (MARC fields 4XX).

series title page   An added title page appearing before the main title page in a work issued as part of a group of publications, giving the title proper of the series and, in some cases, additional information, such as a list of previously published titles in the series, names of authors, dates of publication, numeric designations, etc. The series title page is usually the verso of the page bearing the half title.

serif   A term used by the English since 1825, probably derived from the Dutch *Schreef*, meaning "flick of the pen." A fine, short line crossing or projecting as a finishing touch from the end of one of the main strokes of a letter of the Latin alphabet in a typeface that includes such extensions. Warren Chappell describes the serif as "a terminal device, functionally employed to strengthen lines which otherwise would tend to fall away optically" (*A Short History of the Printed Word*, Knopf, 1970).

   Marc Drogin notes in *Medieval Calligraphy: Its History and Technique* (Allanheld & Schram, 1980) that serifs evolved from the brief perpendicular line used by the ancient Greeks to end most straight or curved strokes, adopted by the Romans in the mid-1st century B.C. The practice continued in the form of a small foot at the ending of, or the lead into, letters of the scripts used in writing medieval manuscripts. Serifs enhance the legibility of printed and handwritten text matter. The opposite of *sans-serif* and *block letter*. *See also*: *wedge-serif*.

serigraphy   *See*: screen printing.

server   A host computer on a network, programmed to answer requests to download data or program files, received from client computers connected to the same network. Also refers to the software that makes serving clients possible over a network. Servers are classified by the functions they perform (*application server, database server, fax server, file server, intranet server, mail server, proxy server, terminal server, Web server*, etc.).

service area   The geographic area served by a public library or library system, from which it derives a major portion, if not all, of its funding, usually through taxation. *See also*: *library district*.

service book   *See*: liturgical work.

service charge   A fee added by some jobbers to orders placed by libraries for materials sold by the publisher at little or no discount or for special services provided by the jobber in filling the order, usually on an item-by-item basis. Also refers to a fee charged by a subscription agent for filling orders for periodical subscriptions, usually 5 to 10 percent of the total annual amount paid by the library for subscriptions.

service contract   An arrangement in which the supplier (or some other service provider) agrees to regularly maintain and repair one or more pieces of equipment after any warranties have expired, usually in exchange for payment of an annual or monthly fee. Libraries enter into such agreements to keep photocopiers, microform reader-printer machines, security devices, automation equipment, etc., in working order. Synonymous with *service agreement*.

service copy   A third-generation microfilm copy, produced from a print master to be cataloged, stored, and used as an information source in a library. *See also*: *master negative*.

service point   A fixed location within a library or information center staffed to provide a specific service or services to users, for example, the circulation desk, reference desk, serials desk, interlibrary loan office, etc.

set   Two or more related bibliographic items in any format, published or issued as a single entity in uniform style and cataloged as a unit, for example, a multivolume dictionary or encyclopedia. Normally, all the volumes in a set are published at the same time, but there are notable exceptions (*example*: **Dictionary of American Regional English**). Compare with *series*. *See also*: *set discount* and *volume number*.

In a more general sense, any group of entities that together constitute a whole. In information retrieval, the group of entries or records retrieved in response to a query, containing the keywords or indexing terms specified in the search statement. In most bibliographic databases, retrieval sets can be combined in a keywords search using Boolean logic to produce a logical product, logical sum, or logical difference. *See also*: *subset*.

set discount   The price charged by the publisher when all the volumes in a multivolume set are ordered at the same time, as opposed to the higher price charged per volume when one or more volumes are purchased separately. The price difference is usually 5 to 20 percent.

set-off   *See*: offset.

setting   The overall locale and historical period in which the action in a narrative work occurs. In a specific scene or episode, the setting consists of the actual physical surroundings (indoors or out), an element of the *atmosphere*. For example, the general setting of the play *Hamlet* by William Shakespeare is medieval Denmark, with the duel scene at the end of the play set inside the castle at Elsinore. In a theater production, the setting is the scenery and properties, synonymous with the French term *mise-en-scene*. *See also*: *character* and *plot*.

Also refers to the position of an indicator that controls the operation of a machine, for example, the option on a photocopier allowing the user to enlarge or reduce the size of an original.

sewing   A method of binding in which the sections of a publication are held together with thread, usually machine-stitched through the back fold before the lining is glued to the back. In quality binding, the sewn sections are stitched to two or more sewing supports (usually narrow cloth tapes) spaced at intervals across the binding edge of the text block. Sewing allows the leaves to open without pulling loose, as they often do in adhesive bindings. For an illustrated description of the modern process, see the entry on "Machine sewing" in Geoffrey Glaister's *Encyclopedia of the Book* (Oak Knoll/British Library, 1996). Hand-sewing is used today only in custom binding. Compare with *stitching*. *See also*: *all along*, *chain stitch*, *kettle stitch*, *oversewing*, *side sewing*, and *two on*.

sewing supports   In hand bookbinding, narrow strips of material to which the sewn sections are attached, spaced at regular intervals perpendicular to the binding edge. In older bindings, the collated quires were sewn to cords of flax or hemp, producing a series of raised bands at right angles to the spine in the covering material, unless sunk by the binder into grooves sawn across the back of the sections. Cords replaced the leather thongs used to attach boards to book block in the earliest codex volumes.

In medieval manuscript books, the cords were often thin strips of leather, sometimes split to allow sewing in a figure-eight for maximum strength. The ends of the cords were recessed in *channels* cut into the wooden boards and secured with pegs or nails, firmly attaching the text block to the boards. The channels were concealed by a leaf of parchment or vellum glued to the inside of each board. In modern bookbinding, cords have been replaced by cloth tapes in quality bindings or omitted entirely in trade editions in which the case is attached to the sections by the paste-downs.

sexennial   Issued every six years. Also refers to a serial publication issued every six years. *See also*: *annual*, *biennial*, *triennial*, *quadrennial*, *quinquennial*, *septennial*, and *decennial*.

sextern   In bookbinding, a gathering consisting of six sheets of paper, parchment, or vellum folded once to create 12 leaves, used in some manuscript books and early printed books. *See also*: *quaternion*, *quinternion*, and *ternion*.

sextodecimo (16mo)   A small book, approximately six inches in height, made by folding each sheet of book paper to form signatures of 16 leaves (32 pages). *See also*: *folio*, *quarto*, *octavo*, and *duodecimo*.

sexual harassment   Any unwelcome sexual advance, request for sexual favors (explicit or implicit), or other verbal or physical conduct of a sexual nature, when submission to such conduct is made a condition of employment or used as the basis for employment decisions affecting the recipient, or when such conduct interferes with an employee's work performance or creates an intimidating, hostile, or offensive work environment. Libraries deal with sexual harassment by formulating and disseminating clear policies, screening applicants carefully, providing in-service training, keeping complete and accurate personnel records, and taking appropriate disciplinary action. *See also*: *hostile work environment*.

SF   *See*: science fiction.

SGML   *See*: Standard Generalized Markup Language.

sgraffito   A design or writing produced on a surface, such as parchment or plaster, by scratching through an upper coat of pigment to reveal an underlying layer of contrasting color or the natural color of the surface.

shaded letter   In printing, an outline letter made to appear three-dimensional by the presence of a dark shadow along the same side of each stroke, used mainly in display work.

shagreen   The untanned skin of a shark or ray used as a covering material in bookbinding, usually green in color and covered with small hard bumps. Jane Greenfield notes in *ABC of Bookbinding* (Oak Knoll/Lyons Press, 1998) that the word may be derived from "chagrin," the French term for goatskin with a hard pimpled grain.

shaken   A book in which the leaves are beginning to come loose but are still attached to the binding, usually caused by loosening of the sewing threads or wear on the hinges, a condition more advanced than *started* but not yet *sprung*. *See also*: *tight*.

shaped binding   A binding that is not rectangular or square in shape, rare in the history of book production. In modern publishing, shaped bindings are a novelty, used mainly for children's books.

shared authorship   *See*: shared responsibility.

shared cataloging   *See*: cooperative cataloging.

shared responsibility   In *AACR2*, a work in which two or more persons or corporate bodies collaborate in creating the content, each performing the same type of activity, with the contribution of each participant either distinct or indistinguishable from that of the others. Synonymous with *shared authorship*. Compare with *mixed responsibility*. *See also*: *joint author*.

shareware   Software available over the Internet that the user may download and try on the "honor system" before deciding to purchase. Payment of a nominal registration fee is expected following a reasonable trial period, entitling the user to receive documentation, technical support, and updated versions as they become available. CNet provides access to shareware at: www.shareware.com. Compare with *freeware*.

sharing violation   An attempt by a computer user to open a data or program file currently in use in another application, an action that generates a message on the screen saying the file must be "closed" before it can be used in another application.

SHARP   *See*: Society for the History of Authorship, Reading and Publishing.

shaved   Said of a book in which the pages have been trimmed so closely in binding that the text is touched but not cut into. Compare with *cropped*.

sheepskin   The skin of a sheep, used in medieval book production to make parchment and vellum and in bookbinding. When converted to leather, it is comparatively soft and loose-fibered, easily separated into layers. Jane Greenfield notes in *ABC of Bookbinding* (Oak Knoll/Lyons Press, 1998) that it can be prepared to resemble goatskin and makes a durable covering material for books when properly processed. *See also*: *roan* and *skiver*.

sheet   As used to describe an item cataloged in *AACR2*, a single whole piece of thin, flat opaque or transparent material other than a broadside, bearing printed and/or handwritten matter on one or both sides. In printing, a unit of paper as manufactured, whether printed or blank. In hand papermaking, a unit of paper the same size as the physical mold used to make it. In microforms, a single piece of fiche (microfiche, superfiche, ultrafiche), usually 4 × 6 inches in size. *See also*: *sheet map* and *sheet music*.

sheet map   A map printed on one side of a single sheet of paper, with or without explanatory matter printed on the reverse side. In libraries, sheet maps are usually stored flat or folded in a map case with wide shallow drawers.

sheet music   A musical work written or printed on one or more unbound sheets of paper. Libraries usually place sheet music inside a protective folder or binder in physical processing. *See also*: *score*.

shelf back   *See*: spine.

shelf capacity   The average number of volumes that will fit on a bookshelf, depending on the width of the shelf from upright to upright, the average depth (thickness) per volume, and the portion of each shelf left empty to facilitate reshelving. *Total stack capacity* can be computed by multiplying shelf capacity by the number of available shelves in the library stacks. *See also*: *cubook*.

shelf-cocked   A permanent deformation in the binding of a book that develops when it is allowed to lean at an angle against a shelf upright or nearby volume over a prolonged period of time. The condition is caused by the force of gravity and can be prevented by using a sturdy bookend at the end of each row on shelves that are not full. Also known as *spine lean*. Compare with *cocked*.

shelf dummy   A piece of wood, cardboard, or plastic in the shape of a book, placed on a shelf in a library, with a spine label directing the user to the location of a title shelved out of normal sequence. Shelf dummies are often used in reference stacks to indicate the location of items shelved in ready reference and in periodical stacks to indicate that back files are located elsewhere, for example, in microfilm or microfiche cabinets. Compare with *dummy*.

shelf guide   A sign or label attached to the end or edge of a shelf in a library indicating its contents, usually by call number, or alphabetically by title (periodicals) or last name of author (fiction). Synonymous with *shelf label*.

shelf height   The vertical distance between two shelves. Adjustable shelving allows the distance to be altered to accommodate items of varying height. Average shelf height is one of the factors determining stack capacity. *See also*: *oversize*.

shelf life   The average length of time an item owned by a library, such as a book, audiocassette, videocassette, or CD, is likely to remain in usable condition before it must be replaced due to normal wear. *See also*: *library binding*.

shelflist   A nonpublic catalog of a library collection containing a single bibliographic record for each item, filed in the order in which the items are arranged on the shelf (usually by call number), used for inventory because it contains the most current information on copy and volume holdings. Card shelflists are being phased out by libraries that have converted their public catalogs to machine-readable records.

shelf mark   Historically, a mark or code written on or affixed to a manuscript or printed book, indicating its proper physical location in a specific library, precursor of the call number. Shelf marks are helpful to bibliographers and antiquarians in identifying individual manuscripts.

shelf reading   Periodic examination of the arrangement of books and other materials in the stacks of a library to ensure that items are in correct call number sequence on the shelf, usually performed by a student assistant or staff member called a *page*, during slack periods. An item shelved out of order may be lost to users until the shelves are read. Synonymous with *shelf checking*. Compare with *inventory*.

shelf-sitter   A slang term used by librarians for an item in the circulating collection that is seldom, if ever, checked out or a reference book that is rarely used. In public libraries with limited shelf space, items with low circulation are eventually weeded, but in the collections of academic and research libraries, where *accumulation* is a priority, they may be retained indefinitely.

shelf-time   The length of time an item remains on the shelf of a library between uses. *First shelf-time* is the period that elapses before its first use, determined by recording the date on which it was first shelved. *Closed-end shelf-time* is the length of time between the last two uses. *Open-end shelf-time* is the period since the last use of the item and the date on which the collection is examined, usually for the purpose of weeding (adapted from *Weeding Library Collections: Library Weeding Methods* by Stanley J. Slote, Libraries Unlimited, 1997).

shelf-worn   The condition of a book that shows visible signs of having been repeatedly removed from and replaced on the shelf, usually along the lower edges of the binding, on the sides of the dust jacket or covers, and/or at the head of the spine. In libraries, the most shelf-worn volumes are often well-loved children's books, standard dictionaries, general encyclopedias, and other heavily used reference books. Library binding can lengthen the *shelf life* of a book.

shelving   *See*: bookshelves.

shelving by size   Storing books by height rather than by subject classification, usually in four or more groups ranging from the smallest to the largest. This method increases shelf capacity by up to 25 percent, but when subject access is sacrificed, browsing capability is diminished. For this reason, shelving by size is used mainly in storage locations inaccessible to the public. *See also*: *double shelving*, *flat shelving*, and *fore-edge shelving*.

Shibboleth   An Internet2 project to develop open source, standards-based software and procedures to support inter-institutional sharing of Web resources, subject to access controls. A hallmark of the Shibboleth architecture is that no more information about the user is revealed to the target Web site than it needs to know, and the user retains control over the information released. URL: shibboleth.internet2.edu/shib-intro.html.

shift   The length of time spent working at one job in any 24-hour period, no more than 8 hours for full-time employment in most workplaces. Also refers to the length of time a person performs a particular task before being relieved by the next person scheduled to do the same work. Librarians scheduled at a service point such as the reference desk may rotate shifts, especially in the evening and on weekends.

shifting   The laborious process of moving an entire collection, or sections of a collection, from one location to another in the stacks of a library, usually to create shelf space in classifications that have become overcrowded.

shipping   The delivery of materials, equipment, or supplies ordered from a publisher, jobber, dealer, or supplier to a library by post or some other method. Also refers to the charge for delivery, usually included as a separate amount on the invoice. Directory information on shipping services is available in the annual reference serial *Literary Market Place*. *See also*: *consolidated shipment*, *drop shipment*, and *reshipment*.

shipping list   *See*: packing list.

shoe   One of a set of four metal sheaths custom-fitted to the corners of a large hand-bound book to protect the leather binding, usually made of brass or silver, plain or decorated.

short   *See*: short film.

shortcut   Some operating systems allow the user to create an icon or pointer on the desktop that can be double-clicked to directly access a program or document, without having to click the **Start** button and select the application or filename from a menu or directory system.

short discount   In the book trade, a discount less than the one normally allowed by the publisher, jobber, or bookseller, usually 5–35 percent. Professional books, text-books, and reference books are normally sold at short discount, as are items on special order. Compare with *long discount*.

short film   Any motion picture with a running time of less than 30 minutes (three reels or less). The category includes cartoons, newsreels, documentaries, and experimental films. The once common practice of showing one or more *shorts* before a feature film has ceased in commercial movie theaters. Short films are now shown mainly at film festivals. Synonymous with *short subject*.

short list   A small group of candidates chosen from a larger group, from which the final selection is made when filling a vacant position, awarding a prize, or determining the winner of a competition.

short loan   *See*: reserves.

short novel   *See*: novelette.

short page   In printing, a page with fewer lines of type matter than the specified number, as at the end of a chapter. In contemporary books, the unfilled space is usually left blank, but in older editions it was sometimes adorned with a printer's ornament. Compare with *long page*.

shorts   *See*: short shipment.

short score   A sketch of an ensemble work in which the composer sets forth the main elements on a few staves, with the intention of elaborating the themes at some time in the future. Compare with *close score* and *condensed score*.

short shipment   An order shipped with one or more items lacking, usually because they were out of stock at the time the order was filled. The absent titles, known as *shorts*, are usually placed on *back order* to be shipped as soon as they become available.

short short story   A fictional prose narrative of 500 to 1,500 words, containing all the elements of a short story in very concise form (*example*: "The Mad Woman" by Guy de Maupassant). *See also*: conte.

short story   A work of short fiction, usually 2,000 to 10,000 words in length, in which the author limits the narrative to a single character (or group of characters) acting in a limited setting, usually at a single point in time, to achieve a unified effect (*example*: "The Yellow Wallpaper" by Charlotte Perkins Gilman). Short fiction is published in literary magazines and collections. Stories considered outstanding by editors and critics may be anthologized following initial publication. Short stories published in collections are indexed in *Short Story Index* published annually by H.W. Wilson. Compare with *novelette* and *short short story*. *See also*: conte, fable, and tale.

short subject   *See*: short film.

short title   An abbreviated title of a book or other publication, usually enough of the full title to enable the item to be identified in a catalog or bibliography or on a price list or order form. Also spelled *short-title*. *See also*: English Short Title Catalogue *and* Short-Title Catalogue.

Short-Title Catalogue (STC)   Compiled by A.W. Pollard and G.R. Redgrave, *Short-Title Catalogue of Books Printed in England, Scotland, and Ireland, and of English Books Printed Abroad, 1475–1640* was published in 1926 by the Bibliographical Society, London. Revision and enlargement of the first edition, begun by W.A. Jackson and F.S. Ferguson, was completed by Katherine F. Pantzer from 1976 to 1986. *Short-Title Catalogue of Books Printed in England, Scotland, Ireland, Wales, and British America, and of English Books Printed in Other Countries, 1641–1700*, compiled by Donald G. Wing of the Yale University Library as a continuation of Pollard and

Redgrave's work, was published in three volumes by the Index Society, New York from 1945 to 1951. *See also*: English Short Title Catalogue.

shoulder   In bookbinding, the ridge along the binding edge of the text block, made to accommodate the boards of the cover by bending the backs of the sewn sections from the center toward the front and back, a process called *backing*, done with a hammer in hand-binding, or by machine in commercial binding, after the back has been rounded and before the lining is applied. Also called an *abutment, flange, groove,* or *ledge*.

shoulder note   A note written or printed on the outer corner of the head margin of a page, usually in handwriting or a type size (or style) that distinguishes it from the text.

shouting   When specific words within an e-mail message (or its entire text) are typed in uppercase, THE TONE MAY BE INTERPRETED AS RUDE by its recipient(s). *See also*: *flame* and *netiquette*.

show through   A printing defect in which text or illustration printed on one side of a leaf is visible through the paper from the other side, usually the result of a mismatch between paper stock and ink on the part of the typographer. *See also*: *opacity*.

shrink-wrap license   Licensing terms stated in a notice printed on or in the package containing a new software product, which the manufacturer considers the purchaser to have accepted by the act of removing the plastic wrapper from the container ("breaking the seal") and keeping the product. Such agreements often include provisions and restrictions that have not been uniformly enforced in the courts, because they give software publishers more rights than are permitted under federal copyright or patent law. The controversial *Uniform Computer Information Transactions Act (UCITA)* would allow software publishers to embed non-negotiable, enforceable contract terms in this type of mass-market license. Also spelled *shrinkwrap*. *See also*: *click-on license*.

sibling   In indexing, a descriptor or subject heading that shares a broader term (one level up in hierarchy) with one or more other descriptors in the same indexing language. The meanings of sibling terms may overlap (*example*: "Children's librarians" and "School librarians" under the broader term "Librarians"). Compare with *orphan*.

sic   The Latin word for "thus" written inside square brackets [*sic*] or parentheses (*sic*) after a quotation to indicate that a misspelled word or grammatical error has been reproduced verbatim. In continental Europe, the exclamation mark (!) is used for the same purpose.

SIC   *See*: Standard Industrial Classification.

SICI   *See*: Serial Item and Contribution Identifier.

sidebar   Information printed alongside a text and set apart visually, usually inside a box or by shading. Sidebars are used in magazines, textbooks, popular reference books, how-to books, etc., to present related or supplementary material that the author does not wish to include in the text. Compare with *side note*.

side note A note written or printed on one of the side margins of a page, opposite the passage of text to which it refers, usually in writing or type that distinguishes it from the text. A *cut-in side note* is set in from the left- or right-hand margin, with text surrounding it on three sides. Synonymous with *marginal note*. Compare with *gloss*. *See also*: *scholium*.

side sewing In binding, to fasten sections or loose leaves together by sewing the entire text block through the side along the binding margin in a single pass, a method that considerably restricts openability. The ANSI standard for library binding specifies that a lock-stitch be used in side sewing and does not recommend the method for text blocks over one-half-inch thick or when the binding margin is less than three-quarter-inch wide. Synonymous with *stab sewing*. Compare with *fold sewn*.

side-stitching A method of binding in which flat wire staples are driven by machine through the entire thickness of the sections of a publication, parallel with the back fold, close to the binding edge. Used primarily for textbooks and periodical issues of more than one section, the method is stronger than *saddle-stitching* but does not allow the leaves to open easily. For this reason, side-stitched publications must have a wide gutter margin. Synonymous with *side-wire stitching*. Compare with *side sewing*.

side title The title impressed on the outside of the front cover of a book, or written or printed on a pasted label, sometimes a shortened version of the *title proper* printed on the title page. Jane Greenfield notes in *ABC of Bookbinding* (Oak Knoll/Lyons Press, 1998) that a vellum label in a small brass plate was popular during the 16th century in northern Europe. *See also*: *binder's title* and *cover title*.

signage A collective term for all the static visual symbols and devices posted in a library to direct patrons to specific resources, services, and facilities and to inform them of library hours, policies, programs, and events, including their size, design, and placement. Signs that are clear, concise, consistent, courteous, and appropriately placed can significantly reduce the number of directional questions received at the reference desk and make using the library less stressful, especially for inexperienced patrons.

To comply with ADA requirements, many libraries in the United States have added Braille to signs posted within reach of patrons. In libraries that serve a significant number of non-English-speaking users, signs may be provided in more than one language. An effort is made in new construction and major renovations to avoid a piecemeal approach by incorporating the style and placement of signs into the overall interior design.

signatory A government or agency that has the legal right to sign an official document, such as a treaty or trade agreement. Also refers to a person whose signature appears on such a document.

signature In printing, a single sheet of paper folded one or more times to become, with the addition of any plates or other inserts, one section in a bound publication. In modern book production, signatures are usually in multiples of 8 pages, with 32 pages the norm. According to *The Bookman's Glossary* (R.R. Bowker, 1983), the term originated when signatures, folded by hand, were initialed by the person doing the folding, to facilitate error tracing. In modern printing, a signature mark called a *register* is applied by the printer to alert the binder to the order in which the folded sheets are to be gathered.

Also refers to a person's name, written in his or her own hand, usually appearing at the end of an original document, such as a letter or legal instrument. Verification of a signature's authenticity may require expert analysis. *See also*: *forgery* and *signatory*.

In e-mail messages, a standard ending that usually includes the sender's full name, position, affiliation, contact information, and sometimes a brief quotation or favorite saying. Synonymous in this sense with *footer*.

In written music, a symbol or symbols appearing at the beginning of a staff to indicate key and/or time.

signed   An entry in a reference work or an article in a periodical that includes the name of the author (or authors), usually given at the beginning or end of the text. Also refers to a copy of a limited edition bearing the signature of the author or illustrator in the statement of limitation. In a more general sense, any written document, such as a letter or legal instrument, that indicates the identity of the person who wrote it, usually by the presence of a signature. The opposite of *unsigned*. *See also*: *byline*.

signed binding   A binding that bears the name, initials, or cipher of the binder, usually tooled in blind or gilt at the foot of the spine, on the upper cover, or on one of the turn-ins; stamped in ink on one of the endpapers; printed on a trade label pasted inside the cover; or incorporated (less frequently) in the edge painting.

signe-de-renvoi   French for "mark of return." A graphic symbol used in the margin of a manuscript and in the text to associate a location in the text with material provided in the margin, especially a correction adding a sentence or passage omitted by the scribe.

signet   *See*: register.

silent film   Any motion picture produced without sound, usually from the period before "talkies" were introduced (1895 until about 1927). Also refers to the entire body of motion pictures produced during this early period. Classic American examples include the early films of comedians Charlie Chaplin and Buster Keaton and the works of D.W. Griffith. When early silent films were shown to live audiences, the movie theater usually hired an orchestra or pianist to provide musical accompaniment. Projection speed for silent films is usually 16 fps (frames per second). In library cataloging, lack of sound track is indicated by the abbreviation *si.* in the physical description area of the bibliographic record for a film.

silica gel   Silicon dioxide in hard granular or beaded form, used as a desiccant because of its hygroscopic properties. Highly porous, its crystalline structure adsorbs and holds moisture by physical rather than chemical means, without swelling or changing shape. Capable of adsorbing up to one-third its weight in water, silica gel can reduce the relative humidity in a closed container to about 40 percent. Conservators use it to control moisture in small enclosed spaces (exhibition cases, storage boxes, etc.). Non-indicating silica gel is white and remains white as it adsorbs moisture. Indicating silica gel impregnated with moisture-sensitive cobalt chloride turns from blue to pink when saturated. Packaged in oven-safe containers, the gel can be dried for reuse by heating above 300 degrees Fahrenheit. The substance is inert, nontoxic, and nonflammable and has a very high melting point.

silking The process of affixing chiffon silk, or some other gossamer material, to one or both sides of a sheet of paper, or to a leaf in a book, to repair or preserve it. The result is said to have been *silked*.

silk screen *See*: screen printing.

simplex In communications, a channel that has the capacity to transmit signals in one direction but not in the other. Compare with *duplex*.

simplified edition An adaptation that makes the text of a previously published work easier to read, usually for a specific age group or category of reader, by substituting less difficult words, shortening the narrative, and adding a glossary, commonly used in ESL (English as a second language) instruction. Compare with *abridgment*.

simultaneous publication Publication of the hardcover and paperback editions of a new book at the same time. Normally, the softcover edition is published months or even years after the cloth edition. Compare with *parallel publishing*.

simultaneous submission Submission of a completed manuscript by the author or the author's agent to more than one publisher at the same time. A journal publisher's policy concerning simultaneous submission is usually stated in its guidelines for contributors.

simultaneous user A person who accesses a bibliographic database or other online resource at the same time as other users. Licensing agreements usually specify the maximum number of users who may log on simultaneously at a given subscription rate. Most vendors have designed their proprietary search software to deny access when the limit is exceeded.

sine loco A Latin phrase meaning "without place." In library cataloging, the abbreviation *s.l.* is used inside square brackets [s.l.] in the publication, distribution, etc., area of the bibliographic description to indicate that the place of publication is unknown. Compare with sine nomine.

sine nomine A Latin phrase meaning "without name." In library cataloging, the abbreviation *s.n.* is used inside square brackets [s.n.] in the publication, distribution, etc., area of the bibliographic description to indicate that the name of the publisher or distributor is unknown. Compare with sine loco.

single index An index compiled all at one time to facilitate access to the content of a single publication, for example, an index at the back of a book or at the end of the last volume of a multivolume reference work. Compare with *cumulative index* and *open-end index*.

singleton   In the bibliographic sense, a single leaf (folio) bound into a book where one would expect to find conjoint leaves. A singleton is usually one-half of a bifolium, severed to allow one of the pair to be interleaved out of normal sequence in the collation, but it can also be an additional leaf hand-copied or printed separately from the gathering for insertion in it.

sinkage   In printing, the amount of space left blank above the first line of type at the top of a page of text, for example, at the beginning of a chapter or other major division of a book. *See also*: *headpiece*.

site license   Official permission granted to a company, agency, organization, or institution by a software producer or vendor to use a software product under specified conditions on all the computers at a designated IP address, or range of IP addresses, usually in exchange for payment by the *licensee* of an annual fee. Pricing may be based on number of users in the community, number of simultaneous users, potential number of users of specific content, or a combination of factors. Compare with *software license*.

sized   Paper treated in manufacture with a substance that makes its surface less porous, reducing its capacity to absorb moisture. Blotting paper is left *unsized*. Also refers to book cloth treated with a stiffener. *See also*: *resized*.

sizing   Substances such as resin, gelatin, glue, or starch added to paper stock in manufacture to promote the bonding of cellulose fibers or as a coating to fill pores in the surface after sheets have been formed. Sizing makes paper less permeable to water, preventing the ink used in printing from bleeding. Sizing also gives definition to the printed image. Some sizings are acidic and contribute to the deterioration of paper.

Also refers to the process of sorting a number of books into batches of similar size in preparation for some kind of treatment or processing, such as the application of clear plastic jacket covers.

skeleton staff   The minimum number of employees required to operate a library, usually those necessary to staff essential service points and maintain security. Libraries chronically understaffed may be forced to operate with minimal staff in the evening and on weekends or remain closed.

sketch   A brief essay, story, or play developed in less detail than a more complete work of the same literary form. A *character sketch* captures the essence of one or more individuals, with little or no plot. Also refers to a drawing that provides a rough outline of its subject without adding much detail, usually done rapidly, in a single sitting, sometimes as a study for a more elaborate treatment of the same subject.

skiver   A binder's term for a thin, dressed leather made from the hair side of an animal skin (usually sheepskin) split with a sharp-bladed implement, used on less expensive bookbindings in England after 1768 when the technique was first introduced (Geoffrey Glaister, *Encyclopedia of the Book*, Oak Knoll/British Library, 1996).

skyline   In newspaper publishing, any headline printed across the top of the first page above the flag. Compare with *banner*.

s.l.   *See*: *sine loco*.

SLA   *See*: Special Libraries Association.

slander   *See*: libel.

slang   An informal or colloquial expression peculiar to a specific group, often unintelligible to outsiders but sometimes decipherable from its context, for example, the term "mimbo" used (in some circles) to refer to an unintelligent male person. Slang expressions are subject to linguistic fashion. Most serious authors use slang terms only in dialogue or when writing informally. In libraries, dictionaries of slang are available in the reference section (*example*: ***A Dictionary of Slang and Unconventional English*** by Eric Partridge). Compare with *argot*, *idiom*, and *jargon*.

slash   In writing, printing, and computing, a character in the form of a line slanting diagonally from upper right to lower left, used to indicate division, fractions, and ratios (**miles/hour**); to combine dates (**1905/06**); to indicate alternatives (**and/or**); and to separate the parts of an Internet address (**http://www.myuniversity.edu/library**). Synonymous with *forward slash*, *solidus*, and *virgule*. Compare with *backslash*.

sleeper   In the retail book trade, a trade book that sells slowly when first published but develops a strong, steady market over a period of months or even years. In libraries, a new book that circulates slowly when first added to the collection but in time attracts a strong, steady readership. In the antiquarian book trade, a valuable item priced well below its market value in a dealer's catalog or on the shelf because the seller is unaware of its actual worth.

sleeve   A transparent plastic covering designed to fit snugly over the paper dust jacket of a hardcover book. Applied by a library staff member during physical processing, plastic sleeves are used in public libraries to a greater extent than in other types of libraries to protect book covers and enhance their visual appeal.

Also, the paper envelope provided by the manufacturer of a phonograph record to protect the disc from dust and abrasion as it is removed from and replaced in the jacket or album, sometimes with a wide circle cut from the center or replaced with transparent material, to allow the record label to remain visible. In a more general sense, a protective envelope for any bibliographic resource (*AACR2*).

slick   A term used in publishing to describe a heavily illustrated consumer magazine of high circulation, printed in color on glossy paper, for sale at newsstands, in bookstores and supermarkets, and by subscription (*example*: ***Cosmopolitan***).

slide   A small transparent, positive still image in color or black and white, produced on film or glass, usually mounted in a rigid cardboard or plastic frame of standard size (2 × 2 inches), for projection one at a time on a screen using a *slide projector*, with or without recorded sound (modern stereographs, such as Viewmaster reels, are also included in this category). Slide projectors designed to take carousels in which dozens of slides are queued often have an automatic advance that can be activated remotely by the presenter. Models intended for professional use may include a microprocessor enabling individual slides to be accessed randomly. Slides may also be viewed using a *slide viewer*, a smaller device with built-in rear-screen projection.

Some models have audio and automatic advance capability similar to slide projectors. Compare with *filmstrip*. *See also*: *microscope slide* and *microslide*.

In computing, one of a numbered sequence of screens created using presentation software, such as *PowerPoint*, for display with the aid of a projector, as part of an oral presentation.

slide mount   A rigid cardboard or plastic frame, usually of standard size (2 × 2 inches), designed to hold a single slide to protect it from damage and make it easier to label, store, and handle.

slide projector   *See*: slide.

slide viewer   *See*: slide.

slipcase   A sturdy cardboard box covered in paper, cloth, or leather, designed to snugly contain a book or set of books, with the front open to expose the spines, leaving the spine title(s) visible. Provided to keep volumes together and protect them from damage, slipcases are more common in deluxe editions and videocassette sets than in trade book editions. A single book may be given a semi-limp wrapper inside the slipcase to protect the sides of its cover from abrasion. A *double slipcase* is divided by a partition, allowing two volumes to be encased without contact. Also spelled *slip-case*. Compare with *pull-case* and *solander*.

slip plan   In acquisitions, a type of approval plan in which a printed or electronic form called a *notification slip* is sent by the vendor, describing each new book that meets the library's profile, as opposed to automatic shipment of the item itself. Some vendors provide a multipart form with a tear strip, for use as order slip, file copy, etc. Electronic slips may include table of contents, digital image of front cover, and review information.

slip proof   *See*: galley proof.

SLJ   *See*: *School Library Journal*.

small capital   A capital letter of x-height, about two-thirds as large as the full-size capital of the same type size, used for emphasis in printed text. Abbreviated *small cap*. Abbreviated *s.c*. *See also*: *lowercase* and *uppercase*.

small press   A small publisher of comparatively limited resources, functioning independently of the publishing "establishment" and consequently more likely to issue works outside the cultural mainstream. Most small presses employ fewer than a dozen people and publish no more than 20 to 30 new titles per year. Synonymous with *little press*.

Small Press, the trade publication of small publishers, provides approximately 100 reviews of small press books in each bimonthly issue. Directory information on small presses is available in *Literary Market Place* and *Writer's Market*. The Small Press Center is a nonprofit cultural and educational institution dedicated to promoting awareness of small independent publishers and their contributions to society (URL: www.smallpress.org/index.htm). *See also*: *niche publishing*.

smartboard   A general term for several types of electronic whiteboard, the most sophisticated of which can be synchronized with a computer to function like an oversize touch screen, allowing users to interact directly with the display, instead of using a keyboard, mouse, or other input device. Smartboards are used for bibliographic instruction in very well equipped academic libraries. Also spelled *smart board*.

smashing   *See*: nipping.

smiley   A whimsical sequence of punctuation marks and special characters arranged to suggest the expression on a human face, used in e-mail and on message boards to symbolically communicate emotion or humor. Frequently used examples include:

:-)	Smiling
;-)	Ironic smile
:-(	Not amused
>:(	Very angry
:O	Yelling
:D	Laughing

For more smileys, please see the *Unofficial Smiley Dictionary* at: paul.merton.ox.ac. uk/ascii/smileys.html. Synonymous with *emoticon*.

smooth spine   The spine of a book that lacks the raised bands produced by unrecessed sewing supports, not to be confused with the flat back of a book not rounded in the process of binding.

SMTP   **S**imple **M**ail **T**ransfer **P**rotocol, the standard TCP/IP e-mail protocol used on the Internet, originally designed for ASCII text but subsequently enhanced to permit the attachment of other file types. *See also*: *MIME*.

s.n.   *See*: *sine nomine*.

SN   *See*: scope note.

sobriquet   A nickname, assumed name, or other imaginative appellation applied to a person (*example*: **Sachmo**), group (**Copperheads**), place (**Dixie**), thing (**Old Ironsides**), or institution (**Uncle Sam**). An author is occasionally known by such a name (**The Bard**). Compare with *pseudonym*.

Social Responsibilities Round Table (SRRT)   Established over 25 years ago as a permanent round table of the American Library Association to make the organization more democratic and to establish progressive priorities for the library profession, SRRT has been particularly active on issues involving civil and economic rights. SRRT publishes the quarterly *SRRT Newsletter* and is affiliated with the Alternative Press Center (APC), which publishes the *Alternative Press Index*. URL: libr.org/ SRRT.

social science data set   A file of structured data, usually statistical in nature, for use in social science research. The most common types contain census and survey data.

Archives of social science data sets are available online, often by subscription. For the benefit of social science students, the American Sociological Association provides a list of *Available Data Resources* for students at: www.asanet.org/student/data.html. Also spelled *social science dataset*. *See also*: *codebook*.

society   A corporate entity consisting of a group of people who meet periodically to share a common interest, especially one that is academic or professional. The most comprehensive directory of such organizations is the *Encyclopedia of Associations*, available in the reference section of most libraries in the United States. The University of Waterloo Library maintains an online directory of scholarly societies in North America at: www.lib.uwaterloo.ca/society/subjects_soc.html. Abbreviated *soc*. Synonymous with *association*. *See also*: *dues*, *proceedings*, and *transactions*.

Society for Scholarly Publishing (SSP)   An organization that grew out of the Association of Scientific Journals (ASJ) and the Innovation Guide project of the National Science Foundation during the 1970s, SSP is devoted to advancing scholarly communication and publishing and the professional development of its members through education, collaboration, and networking. Its members include scholarly book and journal publishers, librarians, manufacturers, booksellers, and Web editors. URL: www.sspnet.org.

Society for the History of Authorship, Reading and Publishing (SHARP)   Created in 1991, SHARP provides a global network for book historians. Its membership includes literature professors, historians, librarians, publishing professionals, sociologists, bibliophiles, classicists, booksellers, art historians, reading instructors, and independent scholars from over 20 countries. SHARP sponsors an annual conference, maintains an online discussion forum, and publishes the quarterly newsletter *SHARP News*. URL: www.sharpweb.org.

Society of American Archivists (SAA)   Founded in 1934, SAA is the oldest professional organization of archivists in North America, dedicated to promoting the identification, preservation, and use of records of historical value. SAA publishes the newsletter *Archival Outlook* and the semiannual journal *American Archivist*. URL: www.archivists.org.

softcover   A publication bound in covers that are not rigid, usually a paperback, but the term also includes limp and flexible bindings. Most periodicals are issued in softcover. For trade books that sell well in hardcover, a lower-priced softcover edition is usually issued at a later date. Pulp fiction and some trade titles are published initially in softcover without a hardcover edition. Used synonymously with *paperback* and *paperbound*.

software   A generic term for computer programs and their associated documentation, as opposed to *data* used as input and generated as output. In computing, data is "processed"—software "runs." A software product is a set of instructions written by a programmer, distinct from the manufactured *hardware* used to run it. The term includes systems programs such as operating systems (OS), database management systems (DBMS), utilities that control the operation of the computer itself, and application programs designed to process data and accomplish specific tasks for the user. *See also*: *search software* and *Web browser*.

software license   A formal agreement between the producer and purchaser of a software product concerning permissible use, especially with regard to sharing and making copies. *Software piracy* is the unauthorized copying of licensed software, usually for sale in a country other than the one in which it is copyrighted. Compare with *site license*.

solander   A box in the shape of a book, wide enough to stand upright, hinged to fold open at the front or side, with a clasp or spring catch, used for storing books, pamphlets, maps, plates, papers, and other documents. Named after Daniel C. Solander, the 18th-century Swedish botanist who designed it for storing specimens at The British Museum, this type of container is virtually dustproof and waterproof. Compare with *pull-case* and *slipcase*.

solidus   *See*: slash.

soliloquy   A long sequence of lines addressed by an actor or actress, not to the other players on stage but directly to the audience, revealing private thoughts, feelings, or intentions. Perhaps the best known example is the "To Be or Not to Be" speech in Shakespeare's *Hamlet* in which the protagonist expresses the personal dilemma posed by the unexpected allegation of murder made by his father's ghost. A shorter speech intended to be inaudible to the other characters in a scene is an *aside*. Compare with *monologue*.

solo librarian   A librarian solely responsible for managing a small library, without the assistance of other paid staff. Solo public librarians often rely on the assistance of volunteers from the community served. Running even a small library single-handedly requires energy, initiative, versatility, and self-sufficiency. Judith Siess reports in the February 1999 issue of *American Libraries* that nearly 80 percent of public libraries serving populations under 25,000 are staffed by only one professional librarian, according to statistics compiled by the U.S. Department of Education. Solo librarians are organized in the Solo Librarians Division of the Special Libraries Association and in the Independent Librarian's Exchange (ILEX), a section of the Association of Specialized and Cooperative Library Agencies (ASCLA) of the American Library Association. Compare with *independent librarian*. *See also*: *one-person library*.

sombre   A style of hand-binding, used mainly for Christian devotional books, characterized by blind tooling on black or dark-colored leather.

songster   An inexpensive collection of ballads and verse published during the 18th and 19th centuries in the form of a broadside or chapbook. Songsters did not necessarily include musical notation because the lyrics were often intended to be sung to melodies familiar to the general public.

sonnet   A lyric poem of 14 lines, written in iambic pentameter. A *sonnet sequence* is a group of sonnets written by a single poet, usually on a common theme. The form originated in Italy in the 13th century. The most common rhyme schemes were developed by Petrarch and Shakespeare.

sorting   In a search of a online catalog or bibliographic database, the default display is normally alphabetical order by author or title, or reverse chronological order by publication date. However, in some online catalogs and databases, the user may select the sequence in which results will be displayed, usually from a list of options, either before or after the search is executed. Compare with *ranking*. *See also*: *arrangement*.

sound archives   A permanent collection of sound recordings preserved for research purposes, for example, the Stanford Archive of Recorded Sound, which maintains a Web site at: www-sul.stanford.edu/depts/ars/ars.html. Materials collected include wax cylinders, shellac and vinyl phonograph records, audiotape, digital compact discs, etc. One of the earliest comprehensive archives of sound recordings was established in the early 20th century by the British Broadcasting Corporation (BBC).

sound disc   *See*: compact disc *and* phonograph record.

sound recording   A generic term for sound vibrations that have been mechanically, electromagnetically, or digitally recorded onto a medium designed for playback with the aid of audio equipment. The category includes phonograph records, audiotapes, compact discs, and the sound track on motion pictures, videorecordings, DVDs, etc. Libraries collect sound recordings of music and human speech (poetry, drama, speeches, interviews, broadcasts, audiobooks, etc.). The proceedings of meetings and conferences are sometimes recorded for archival purposes. The Library of Congress provides online access to its Recorded Sound Reference Center at: lcweb.loc.gov/rr/record. Synonymous with *audiorecording*. *See also*: *Alpha-Numeric System for Classification of Recordings*, *sound archives*, and *type of recording*.

sound track   The sound component of a motion picture or video usually recorded along one or both edges of the film or tape, on a magnetically coated stripe, synchronizing sound with image. Also refers to the music score of a motion picture, released separately on audiocassette or compact disc, sometimes under a slightly different title. Silent films have no sound track.

source   Any document that provides information sought by a writer, researcher, library user, or person searching an online catalog or bibliographic database. Also refers to a document that provides information copied or reproduced in another document, for example, a quotation or excerpt. In literature, the story, legend, or work that inspires or provides elements of plot or characterization for another literary work, for example, the chronicles of English history on which Shakespeare based some of his history plays. *See also*: *primary source*, *secondary source*, and *tertiary source*.

    In acquisitions, the seller or donor from whom an item is obtained, usually indicated in the accession record.

    In Web browsers, a menu option in the toolbar that allows the user to view the HTML code in which the document on the screen is written.

source code   A computer program as written by the programmer in a high-level programming language. Source code is human-readable ASCII text. Before it can be executed by a computer, it must be translated into machine language by a utility called a *compiler* (sometimes with an *assembler*) or by a utility called an *interpreter*. Software sold retail to computer users cannot be read or modified because it is in machine language.

source document   In reprography, the original document from which copies are made, usually containing text and/or graphic material that can be read by the human eye without magnification. Compare with *master. See also*: *camera microfilm.*

source field   In the record structure of most bibliographic databases, the data field containing the journal title, volume number, date of issue, and page numbers of a periodical article; the book title, publisher, publication date, and page numbers for an essay in a collection; or the title, publisher, and publication date of a book or book chapter. In the record display, the field label may be abbreviated *SO.*

source language   The original language of a text that has been translated into one or more other languages. In library cataloging, the language of the original work is indicated in a parallel title or *Translation of*: note in the bibliographic description.

spacing   The use of one or more blank characters to separate words in printing and typing. Also refers to one or more lines left blank at the beginning of type matter, or between lines of type, for example, the three lines left blank at the top of a typed or printed catalog card or the double space before the first note and before the tracings. In *AACR2*, the use of spacing in catalog records is governed by the general rules for punctuation and by the specific rules for punctuation in each area of bibliographic description. *See also*: *white line.*

spam   Unsolicited e-mail messages, usually containing advertising or solicitations, mass-mailed to large numbers of newsgroups, mailing lists, and/or individuals with little concern for the burden such activity places on the recipients. *Spamming* is considered one of the worst violations of netiquette because it compels Internet users to waste precious time scanning and deleting unwanted messages that may contain images, links, or attachments bearing viruses. The development of e-mail address harvesting software has contributed to a sharp rise in the proportion of e-mail messages that are unsolicited. Of the various defenses against spam (address disguises, host and personal filters, white and black lists, add-on programs), none is completely effective and some risk blocking legitimate e-mail. Legislative and regulatory measures are under consideration to discourage *spammers*. For more information on this nuisance, see spam.abuse.net. Synonymous with *unsolicited commercial e-mail (UCE).*

Spanish calf   A bookbinding in calfskin, acid-stained in large blotches of boldly contrasting color, such as red and black.

SPARC   *See*: Scholarly Publishing and Academic Resources Coalition.

spatial data   Information about the physical properties of all or a portion of the surface of the earth or another celestial body, or of the heavens, in any form. The category includes two- and three-dimensional maps, charts, profiles, sections, views, globes, atlases, remote sensing images, and especially data in digital form (spatial data sets, databases, associated software, etc.). As map libraries have expanded their scope to include spatial data in a wide range of formats, the librarians responsible for managing such collections have been renamed *spatial-data librarians*. For the most part, libraries catalog spatial data as either *cartographic materials* or *electronic resources*.

spatial information system   A computer-based system that links data to spatial coordinates, for example, architectural software that records the spatial relationship of beams to foundation in the design of a building. A *geographic information system (GIS)* is a particular type of spatial information system that links data to geographic location, usually by geographic coordinates.

special collections   Some libraries segregate from the general collection rare books, manuscripts, papers, and other items that are (1) of a certain form, (2) on a certain subject, (3) of a certain time period or geographic area, (4) in fragile or poor condition, or (5) especially valuable. Such materials are usually not allowed to circulate and access to them may be restricted. An illustrated online guide to the special collections of the Library of Congress is available at: lcweb.loc.gov/rr/rarebook/guide. Compare with *archives*. *See also*: *Rare Books and Manuscripts Section*.

special edition   An edition or issue of a work (or works) produced in a format that differs from previous editions, usually for a special purpose and sometimes under a distinctive title, with a new introduction and sometimes additional notes, appendices, or illustrations. The term is also used synonymously with *library edition*. *See also*: *anniversary edition*.

Also, a special issue of a newspaper, usually devoted wholly or in large part to a specific subject or occasion, for example, in commemoration of a national event. Synonymous with *special number*.

special interest magazine   A magazine devoted to a specific topic of interest to a fairly narrow, well-defined audience, for example, golfing enthusiasts (***Golf Digest***) or yoga teachers and practitioners (***Yoga Journal***). Public libraries usually subscribe to special interest titles on the basis of demand, as indicated by patron requests and usage statistics for related items. Compare with *general interest magazine*.

special issue   An issue of a periodical devoted wholly or substantially to a specific subject or occasion, often the proceedings of a conference in the case of trade journals. A special issue may have its own editor and title and be promoted separately by the publisher. When published more than once on the same topic, a special issue usually appears at the same time in consecutive years, for example, the annual swimsuit issue of *Sports Illustrated*, a high-demand item in public libraries. *See also*: *convention issue*.

specialization   Concentration on a limited aspect of a subject or discipline, often to the exclusion of related areas of study or inquiry. The breadth of librarianship is so great that most librarians decide to focus on one or two aspects of the profession. In library school, students usually select a functional specialization (public services, technical services, automated systems, etc.). Each of these tracks is divided into narrower branches, for example, subject analysis within technical services, or bibliographic instruction within public services. In public libraries, librarians specialize in services for adults, young adults, or children. Librarians employed in special libraries focus on a particular subject or field (art, business, engineering, law, medicine), type of material (government documents, film and video), type of institution (correctional, military, museum), or type of collection (archives, special collections). The professional organizations and journal literature of librarianship reflect these divisions.

Also refers to the level of detail or difficulty of the materials in a library collection, which depends on the library's mission and the clientele served; for example, a public library may provide a selection of the novels of Thomas Hardy in at least one edition but not his poetry or the literary criticism and multiple editions one would expect to find in the holdings of an academic library at a university offering advanced degrees in English language and literature.

Special Libraries Association (SLA)   Founded in 1909, SLA has an international membership of librarians and information specialists employed in special libraries serving the information needs of business, research, governments, universities, museums, newspapers, and other organizations and institutions (public and private) that use or produce specialized information. SLA publishes the monthly magazine *Information Outlook*. URL: www.sla.org. *See also*: *Dana, John Cotton*.

special library   A library established and funded by a commercial firm, private association, government agency, nonprofit organization, or special interest group to meet the information needs of its employees, members, or staff in accordance with the organization's mission and goals. The scope of the collection is usually limited to the interests of its host organization. Special librarians are organized in the Special Libraries Association. Information on special libraries in the United States and Canada is available in the *Directory of Special Libraries and Information Centers* published by the Gale Group. *See also*: *church library*, *corporation library*, *correctional library*, *medical library*, *museum library*, and *news library*.

special offer   An offer by a vendor or supplier to sell goods and/or services at a lower price, usually for a limited period of time, or to provide a trial period, premium, or other inducement to purchase or subscribe. Other restrictions, such as minimum purchase amount, may apply.

special order   In acquisitions, a request to purchase a single copy of a publication, requiring special handling by the publisher or bookseller, usually because the item is not in stock. Special orders are generally sold at no discount or a short discount, and a modest service charge may be added to compensate the seller for extra effort.

specifications   The instructions sent by a publisher to a printer with the typescript of a work regarding its characteristics as a prospective publication, including its dimensions, paper stock, typeface, quantity of illustration, extent of front and back matter, etc., from which the printer creates a *specimen page* to indicate the proposed style of typesetting. Cost of production is determined by *specs* and size of edition.

In computing, a formal description containing details of the components built into a hardware device or software system. In a more general sense, detailed instructions concerning work to be done, products or services to be supplied, etc., especially when a contract is to be signed. Abbreviated *specs*.

specific entry   In subject analysis, the principle that a work is listed in a library catalog, index, or bibliographic database under the most specific subject heading(s) or descriptor(s) that fully describe its content. For example, a book about poets would be entered under "Poets" not "Writers" and a work about French poets under "French poets" or "Poets, French" rather than "Poets." Compare with *coextensive entry*.

specificity   In indexing, the degree to which the meaning of a subject heading or descriptor matches in breadth one of the major subjects of the document to which it is assigned. For example, although the Library of Congress subject heading "Gardening" applies to a book about gardening inside the house, the heading "Indoor gardening" describes the content more specifically. In this sense, specificity is relative to the work described, independent of the breadth of the indexing term itself. An assigned term can be specific, whether broad or narrow, as long as it closely matches a main subject of the work.

In an indexing language, the specificity of a descriptor or subject heading depends on its relationship to other authorized terms broader or narrower in meaning, usually indicated in a thesaurus or headings list by indention or by the codes **BT** (broader term) or **NT** (narrower term). *See also*: *top term*.

specific material designation (SMD)   The most specific designation of the type of material to which an item belongs (usually the class of physical object), given under *extent of item* in the physical description area of the bibliographic description, for example, "videodisc" under the general material designation [videorecording].

specimen   A single individual or member of a group or class selected as an example or sample of the whole, for example, an item of a specific type selected to represent a group of items, or an entire collection, in a library display or exhibit. Compare with *artifact*. *See also*: *specimen case*.

specimen case   A wide flat storage container, usually with a transparent top, divided into compartments usually backed with soft material, used for mounting and storing specimens in rows to facilitate comparison. Some models are lockable. In museums, specimen cases may be built to specific dimensions to allow them to be stored, one atop another inside a specially designed cabinet.

Also refers to a sample book cover, submitted by an edition binder to the publisher for approval, showing the proposed size, boards, covering, lettering, and squares of a case binding.

specimen page   One of several sample pages submitted by the printer to the publisher to show the proposed typographic style for a prospective publication, usually *four* in number, including the first page of a chapter and at least one subhead to show display type. Also refers to a copy of a page from a book or other publication reproduced on any scale for use by the publisher in marketing.

specs   *See*: specifications.

speech recognition   *See*: voice recognition.

spell checker   A feature of most word processing software that automatically checks the spelling of words typed in a document against a built-in dictionary, alerting the user to any misspelled words and even correcting typos on the fly. Spell checkers are not infallible. A misspelling will not be flagged if it is itself a word ("their" for "there"). The option can usually be turned "off" by the user if not desired. Also spelled *spellchecker*.

spider *See*: crawler.

spine The part of the binding on a book, between the front and back covers, that conceals and protects the binding edge of the sections, the only part of the cover visible when the volume is placed alongside others on the shelf. In modern book-binding, the spine is usually stamped with the *spine title* (or an abbreviated title) and the volume number (if applicable) and sometimes with the last name or full name of the author and the publisher. Because medieval manuscript books were generally stored flat with one edge facing out, the title was often written in ink on the edge of the sections, instead of on the spine.

In libraries, a label bearing the location symbol and call number is affixed to the lower spine of each item to facilitate retrieval and reshelving. In older bindings, the spine is sometimes covered in a different material than the boards (see *half-binding*, *quarter binding*, and *three-quarter binding*). Spines hammered into convex shape (rounding) prior to backing were introduced in the early 16th century, replacing spines that were flat except for the raised bands over the sewing supports. On fine leather bindings, the spine may be heavily decorated. Synonymous with *backbone* and *shelf back*. Compare with *back*. **See also**: *cocked*.

spine label A small typed or printed label affixed to the lower spine of a book or other bibliographic item at the time it is processed, displaying its location symbol and call number, for use in reshelving and to assist the user in retrieving the item from the shelf once the call number has been found in the library catalog.

spine-out Books displayed on a shelf with their spines facing the front, usually one alongside the other with a bookend at the end of the row to keep them upright—the shelving method used in the stacks of most libraries because it allows the spine title and call number on each volume to be seen at a glance. Compare with *face out*.

spine title The title written or impressed on the spine of a volume, sometimes a short-ened form of the title appearing on the cover or of the title proper given on the title page. Synonymous with *back title*. Compare with *binder's title*. **See also**: *side title*.

spin-off An independently published book or set of books containing material extracted from a longer work published by the same company, for example, the three-volume **New Grove Dictionary of Musical Instruments** containing entries that are nearly identical to those in the much longer *New Grove Dictionary of Music and Musicians*. Compare with *abridgment*.

Also refers to a journal that became a separate periodical after having been part of a more comprehensive publication, for example, **School Library Journal**, once part of *Library Journal*. The proliferation of scholarly publications into increasingly spe-cialized fields and subfields has been called *twigging*.

In a more general sense, any publication that is a by-product of an earlier publication, for example, a bibliographic database of limited focus, created from a larger database.

spiral binding   A form of mechanical binding in which a continuous coil of wire or hard plastic is drawn through small holes or slots punched in the binding edge of the covers and leaves of a publication to hold them together, used mainly for reports, manuals, workbooks, and notebooks containing blank or ruled pages. Spiral bindings open flat. Synonymous with *coil binding*. Compare with *comb binding*. *See also*: *loose-leaf*.

split   The permanent division of a serial into two or more separate parts, based on the editorial decision that some aspect of the original publication deserves independent treatment. The note *Continues in part:* is included in the bibliographic record for each of the parts to indicate the title of the publication that split, and the corresponding note *Split into:* is added in the record for the serial that split to indicate the titles of the publications created by the division. The opposite of *merger*.

Also, to divide an animal hide into two or more layers for use in book production. The term is also used for one of the layers produced by such a division (or the leather made from it), usually an underlayer rather than the grain layer. In modern book-binding, to cut a signature thicker than three-fourths inch through the back fold in preparation for fan gluing or oversewing.

split catalog   *See*: divided catalog.

spoilage   In book production, printed sheets or entire copies discarded because they contain imperfections or were damaged in printing or binding. Allowance for spoilage is included in the size of printing and binding orders.

sponsor   A person or corporate entity that subsidizes or provides encouragement, funding, or some other kind of practical assistance in the production of a radio or television program, Web site, or other work, usually in exchange for some form of publicity. Compare with *patron*.

sponsored book   A book issued by an established commercial publisher for which the cost of publication is subsidized by an organization or company with an interest in seeing it published. The subsidy may be a direct payment to the publisher to cover losses in the event of disappointing sales or an agreement to purchase enough copies at an established price to make the publication profitable. Compare with *vanity publisher*.

spoof site   A slang term for a Web site created as a good-natured hoax, joke, or deception, for example, *The White House* at: www.whitehouse.org.

spool   A cylindrical flanged wheel with a hole running from end to end onto which a roll of unprocessed film is wound, designed to be inserted in a camera or processing machine. Compare with *reel*.

spread   The full expanse of facing pages in an opening in a book or other bound publication. The page on the right-hand side is the *recto*; the one on the left is the *verso*. *See also*: *double spread*.

spreadsheet   In computing, an application program designed to assist the user in creating and maintaining two-dimensional tables of numerical data and textual information, widely used in budgeting, financial and statistical analysis, and reports. Spreadsheet software allows the user to create mathematical formulas to compute row and column totals, variances, etc., automatically whenever new values are supplied. Most programs allow two or more spreadsheets to be linked by formulas, so that a change in one is automatically reflected in the others. Sophisticated spreadsheet applications support graphics features, enabling the user to manipulate data and display the results in charts and graphs. *Excel* and *Lotus 1-2-3* are the two most widely used spreadsheet packages. Also refers to the result of using such a program, in print or electronic format.

sprinkled   In binding, a book decorated by irregularly spraying or spattering the cut edges of the sections with tiny flecks of color, a technique used mainly on large dictionaries and expensive reference sets. Sometimes just the top edge is sprinkled, making dust and any natural discoloration less noticeable. Leather bindings are sometimes decorated by sprinkling the surface with acid.

sprung   The condition of a book in which the text block has separated from its cover, either in the process of rebinding or through wear on the hinges. Mending may require new endpapers. Compare with *shaken*.

spurious work   A written work known to be counterfeit (not genuine), usually one uncritically ascribed to a known author and subsequently discovered to be of unknown or uncertain authorship. *See also*: *apocryphal*.

square   A book in which the width of the cover is more than three-quarters (but not greater than) its height, a shape often used in art books and children's picture books. Compare with *narrow* and *oblong*. *See also*: *portrait*.

square bracket   One of a pair of angled lines [ ] enclosing a word, phrase, or numeric figure in text, usually to indicate insertion. In library cataloging, square brackets are used to indicate an interpolation made by the cataloger (*example*: **[48] p**.) and to enclose the general material designation that follows the title in a bibliographic record representing a nonbook item (*example*: **[sound recording]**). Compare with *parentheses*.

square capital   A letter of the Latin alphabet derived from the lapidary capitals used in Antiquity for monumental inscriptions, most notably on the base of Trajan's column erected in Rome in A.D. 113. When square capitals were adapted for use as a book hand (3rd to 5th century), the pointed serifs incised in stone were replaced by wider square serifs, easier to execute with a reed or quill pen. Contrast between thick and thin strokes was also enhanced in square capitals. However, the difficulty and amount of space required to write them led to the development of more compressed *rustic capitals* during the same period. Marc Drogin notes in *Medieval Calligraphy: Its History and Technique* (Allanheld & Schram, 1980) that square capitals were used throughout the Middle Ages as a script for writing titles and headings. Revived during the Renaissance, they became the basis of modern capital letters. Latin: *capitalis quadrata*.

squares   In bookbinding, the edges of the boards of a cover, extending beyond the text block at the head, fore-edge, and tail to protect the bound sections from damage. Cased books have equal margins of cover around the edges, usually one-eighth to three-sixteenths of an inch. The term is also used for the part of the cover that is turned in on the inside but not covered by the endpapers after they have been pasted down. Compare with *cut flush*.

SRRT   *See*: **S**ocial **R**esponsibilities **R**ound **T**able.

SSP ·   *See*: **S**ociety for **S**cholarly **P**ublishing.

stabilization   Chemical or physical methods applied in conservation to maintain the integrity of a document by arresting deterioration already in progress, for example, the neutralization of acid in the paper used for printing books and other publications. The *stability* of a document is its ability to resist changes of physical state when exposed to normal use and storage conditions. Compare with *restoration*. *See also*: *permanence*.

stab sewing   *See*: side sewing.

stack aisle   *See*: range aisle.

stack capacity   The amount of material that can be contained in the stack area of a library, expressed as the total linear or square feet of available shelving, or the maximum number of volumes or other physical units that can be accommodated, sometimes computed by means of a formula. *See also*: *cubook* and *shelf height*.

stacked advertising   Advertising that appears only in the front or back, or in the front *and* back, of a periodical and nowhere else in the issue (*example*: **National Geographic**). In custom binding of periodicals, unpaginated advertisements appearing in the front and/or back of each issue may be removed to reduce bulk.

stack maintenance   All the duties involved in keeping the books and other materials stored in the stacks of a library in good order, including reshelving, shelf reading, shifting the collection when certain classifications become overcrowded, and relabeling shelf ranges to indicate their contents.

stacks   The area of a library where the main body of the collection (usually books and periodicals) is stored when not in use, usually on rows of free-standing double-faced shelving. In some libraries, the stacks are closed to the public, but most libraries in the United States allow patrons to browse all or part of their primary collections in *open stacks*. *See also*: *stack capacity* and *stack maintenance*.

staff   The set of parallel horizontal lines on which musical notation is written or printed. The four-line staff was used for plainchant beginning in the 12th century. The five-line staff came into use for polyphonic music in the 13th century. In the full score of an ensemble work, each part is written on a separate staff. Plural: *staves*. *See also*: *library staff*.

staff retreat   An opportunity provided by the administration of a library for the professional, technical, and administrative staff to meet in a comfortable location away from the workplace, usually once or twice a year for at least a full or half day, to discuss issues affecting the library and the clientele it serves. To avoid distraction, strategic planning is often conducted in such a setting.

staff room   A room in a library usually equipped with comfortable furniture and a kitchenette, where staff members can go when they are not on-duty to eat, relax on a break, or meet informally. Synonymous with *staff lounge*.

stamping   *See*: blocking.

stand-alone   A computer *not* connected to a network, which functions independently of other computers and systems. In libraries, bibliographic databases on CD-ROM may be installed on a stand-alone PC workstation, especially when licensing agreements restrict usage to one simultaneous user.

stand-alone library   A library containing no nonlibrary component within the building, as opposed to a library occupying a multipurpose facility. More common in recently constructed/renovated libraries than in older buildings, nonlibrary facilities typically include a separately administered conference room, technology center, multimedia center, art gallery, and/or snack bar or cybercafe.

standard   An acceptable level or criterion according to which something is compared, measured, or judged. Also refers to an amount, extent, quality, pattern, criterion, etc., fixed by usage or convention or established as the norm by prevailing authority, as in the standard size of a catalog card used by libraries prior to the development of machine-readable cataloging. A standard may also be a specification that identifies model methods, materials, or practices. A standard may be approved by a formal ANSI-accredited standards body, such as NISO. A *de facto standard* is one that becomes generally accepted without the formal endorsement of a standard-setting organization. A *community standard* is a de facto standard developed and used within a particular user group. Compare with *benchmark*, *best practices*, and *guidelines*. *See also*: *standards*.

Also, any object, such as a flag or banner, used to symbolize a nation, people, military unit, etc.

standard author   An author whose literary works have earned such a respected place in the national literature of a country that they are frequently taught in literature courses and included in anthologies, for example, William Faulkner, Jane Austen, Gustave Flaubert, Henrik Ibsen, Anton Chekhov, etc.

standard deviation   In statistical analysis, a quantitative measure of how far a variable differs from the norm, calculated as the square root of the variance.

standard format   The most common form of a specific type of document, for example, the sequence in which the parts of a journal article reporting the results of original scientific research are presented (review of existing literature, research methodology, results or findings, discussion or analysis of results, conclusions, suggestions for further research, and list of works cited).

Standard Generalized Markup Language (SGML)   Established in 1986, SGML is an ISO standard governing the rules for defining tag sets that determine how machine-readable text documents are formatted. Not dependent on a specific computer system or type of software, SGML is widely used in preparing machine-readable text archives. The HTML code used to create Web pages is an SGML markup language that uses a fixed set of predefined tags. XML is a subset of SGML in which the tags are unlimited and not predefined.

Standard Industrial Classification (SIC)   A system of four-digit product codes developed in the 1930s by the Statistical Policy Division of the U.S. Office of Management and Budget to represent categories of products and services sold by commercial companies, for the purpose of compiling economic statistics. In 1997, the OMB adopted the North American Industry Classification System (NAICS) to replace the SIC, a change that has affected some business reference books.

standardization   The process of establishing uniform procedures and standards in a specific field of endeavor, usually to facilitate exchange and cooperation and to assure quality and enhance productivity. In librarianship, standards are established by professional associations, accrediting bodies, and government agencies. *See also*: *National Information Standards Organization*.

standard list   A list of titles recommended for any library collection of a particular type and size, usually published under the auspices of a library association (*example*: *Books for College Libraries*). Standard lists are difficult to keep current. Synonymous with *selection guide*. *See also*: *core collection*.

standard number   The unique identification number assigned to an edition at the time of first publication, in accordance with an internationally standardized identification system, usually appearing somewhere on the item. In books published in hardcover, the International Standard Book Number (ISBN) is printed on the verso of the title page and usually on the front flap of the dust jacket. In paperback editions, it appears on the verso of the title page and on the back cover (usually in the lower-right-hand corner). In serials, the International Standard Serial Number (ISSN) appears in the masthead or with the table of contents of each issue or on the copyright page of each volume or part of a series. In printed music, the International Standard Music Number (ISMN) appears on the copyright page. In *AACR2*, the standard number is entered in the standard number and terms of availability area of the bibliographic description.

standard number and terms of availability   In *AACR2*, the area of bibliographic description in which the standard number (ISBN, ISMN, ISSN, etc.), list price, and any other terms under which the item is available are entered (field 020 or 022 of the MARC record).

standards   Criteria established by professional associations, accrediting bodies, or agencies of government for measuring and evaluating library services, collections, and programs. For example, *Standards for College Libraries* and *Information Literacy Competency Standards for Higher Education*, published by the Association of College and Research Libraries. Also refers to any code of rules or procedures established by national and international library organizations to govern bibliographic control, such as the MARC record format, CIP, and the ISBN/ISSN adopted by the publishing industry. The Library of Congress maintains a Web page on standards at: lcweb.loc. gov/standards. Compare with *best practices* and *guidelines*.

In a more general sense, any criteria established by law, agreement, or custom, according to which values, quantities, procedures, performance, etc., are measured or evaluated, and to which manufacturers, practitioners, researchers, etc., seek to conform in order to ensure quality and/or uniformity of results. *See also*: *American National Standards Institute* and *National Information Standards Organization*.

standard subdivision   In Dewey Decimal Classification, a subdivision applicable to any subject or discipline, which may be added to a class in the main schedules to represent bibliographic form (dictionaries, periodicals, etc.), approach or method (management, education, research, etc.), geographic area, historical period, or category of person, indicated in the notation by the addition of a decimal fraction to the class number. Standard subdivisions are never used alone and, as a general rule, should not be used in doubtful cases because they tend to segregate specialized material from works of general interest. They are given in Table 1 of DDC. *See also*: *free-floating subdivision*.

standard title   *See*: uniform title.

standard work   A work widely recognized as a model of excellence in its field, which libraries may order in multiple copies or editions (*example*: ***The Elements of Style*** by William Strunk, Jr.). A standard reference work is usually published in successive editions (*example*: ***The Columbia Granger's Index to Poetry in Anthologies***). Compare with *classic*.

standing committee   A permanent committee appointed by management or selected according to established procedures to handle specific ongoing responsibilities, usually in support of an organization's mission and goals, as opposed to an *ad hoc committee* established to address a particular issue or accomplish a specific task, then dissolved once its goals and objectives have been met.

standing order   An order placed by a library with a publisher, jobber, or dealer to supply each volume or part of a specific title or type of publication as published, until further notice. Unlike subscriptions that must be paid in advance, standing orders are billed as each volume is shipped. Sometimes used synonymously with *continuation order*.

standing room   In Dewey Decimal Classification, topics considerably narrower in scope than the subject represented by a class, usually given in the schedules immediately following the notation and heading in a note that begins with "Including," "Contains," "Example(s)," or "Common names." Standing room provides a location for topics for which the amount of published literature is limited but expected to grow, possibly to the point of warranting a separate class number. Catalogers are not permitted to add standard subdivisions to such topics, nor are other number building techniques allowed (*DDC*). Compare with *approximate the whole*.

stapling *See*: saddle-stitching.

star map *See*: astronomical map.

start A binding defect in which one of the sections of a book projects beyond the others at the fore-edge because it has not been properly secured at the binding edge. Also refers to a crack between sections at the binding edge, usually the result of forcing the leaves open while they are held down, instead of pressing gently along the inner margin to form a slight fold at the binding edge.

started A book in which a portion of the body is so loose in the binding that it protrudes beyond the fore-edge but remains attached, a condition not as advanced as *shaken*.

state Part of an edition that differs from other copies of the same printing by virtue of minor changes in make-up or typesetting made during the process of printing or binding, usually additions, deletions, corrections, and transpositions. During the 16th and 17th centuries, such variations were often the result of allowing the author to visit the pressroom while printing was in progress. In historical bibliography and the antiquarian book trade, variations in state may provide clues to priority of issue. Used in this sense, state has no relation to *condition*. Compare with *variant*. *See also*: *ideal copy*.

Also refers to a preliminary impression taken of a print by the artist as a test prior to completion of the plate or perfection of inking.

state library In the United States, a library supported by state funds for the use of state employees and citizens, usually located in the state capital, containing a comprehensive collection of the state's official documents, books written by authors living in the state, and newspapers published in the state. A state library typically sponsors programs in support of the public libraries in its state and manages grant programs such as the *LSTA*. The first state library was established in Pennsylvania in 1816. *See also*: *Association of Specialized and Cooperative Library Agencies* and *Chief Officers of State Library Agencies*.

state manual A publication issued annually or semiannually by a state government, usually containing the text of the state charter and/or constitution, election statistics, and information about government structure, elected and appointed officials, voting districts, and the towns or boroughs, cities, and counties within the state. Also known as a *blue book*.

statement A financial report sent by a vendor or supplier giving the current status of a library's account, including any orders shipped for which payment is outstanding.

statement of responsibility In *AACR2*, the portion of the bibliographic description indicating by name the person(s) responsible for creating the intellectual or artistic content of the item (author, editor, compiler, composer, arranger, etc.), the corporate body from which the content emanates, or the person(s) or corporate body responsible for performing the content. In most cases, the statement of responsibility is transcribed from the chief source of information for the item. When more than one kind of responsibility is indicated (multiple statements of responsibility), the names are transcribed in the order in which they appear on the chief source of information.

state-of-the-art   A product, system, or design that represents the most advanced degree of technical achievement in its field at the present time. In the construction of new facilities, libraries typically strive for state-of-the-art design and technology but must often settle for what is financially feasible.

stationer   In Europe, the earliest nonmonastic producer and lender of manuscript books for profit. From the 12th century on, *stationarii* (Latin) were licensed by medieval universities to oversee the copying, binding, distribution, and repair of officially approved texts. They also received commissions from wealthy patrons and subcontracted the work out to independent scribes and illuminators. In England, the earliest commercial booksellers, who sold their wares from market stalls, were known as stationers. French: *libraire*. *See also*: *exemplar* and *pecia system*.

stationery binding   A general term for the binding of books designed to be written in (blankbooks, ledgers, etc.), as opposed to the binding of printed books meant for reading, typically more sturdy than the usual publisher's binding.

statistical bibliography   *See*: bibliometrics.

status   *See*: borrower status, circulation status, *and* loan status.

statutory copy   *See*: deposit copy.

stave   *See*: staff.

STC   *See*: *Short-Title Catalogue*.

steady state   A library collection in which the number of items weeded equals the number acquired over time. Libraries with a limited amount of shelf space and no prospect of expansion must maintain a constant collection size. Synonymous with *no growth* or *zero growth*.

steering committee   A group of people appointed or elected to take charge of a complex project, for example, the task of planning the renovation of an existing library or organizing a move into a new library facility. Their responsibilities include setting priorities and establishing the sequence in which various stages of the work are to proceed.

stem   The root of a word used as a search term in a query entered as input in information retrieval, to which one or more truncation symbols are added to retrieve variant forms (*example*: ***witch*** to retrieve *bewitch*, *bewitched*, *bewitching*, *witch*, *witches*, *witchery*, *witchcraft*, etc.).

stemma codicum   A diagram in the form of an inverted "tree" showing all the steps in the transmission of a specific text or program of illumination, reconstructed by establishing relationships with other manuscripts through possible exemplars (witness for the text).

stemming   *See*: truncation.

stencil   A thin sheet of parchment, metal, cardboard, or plastic perforated with a design or lettering that can be reproduced on paper, fabric, wood, plaster, etc., when color is laid on with a brush through the openings. The stencil is then removed for reuse. When this technique is used in book illustration, it is called *pochoir*. Also refers to a sheet, usually of paper, with lettering or a design cut out, to which a colored backing sheet is attached to bring out the design—a technique sometimes used in contemporary greeting cards. Stencil technique is also the basis of *screen printing*.

step index   A series of shallow indentations resembling a staircase, cut into the fore-edge of a book, bearing a sequence of characters or headings, sometimes printed against a dark ground to facilitate reference. Synonymous with *cut-in index*. Compare with *tab index* and *thumb index*.

stereogram   *See*: stereograph.

stereograph   A visual medium in which a transparent or opaque image, or two slightly different images of the same scene arranged side-by-side, appear three-dimensional when seen through the lenses of a binocular instrument called a *stereoscope*. In *AACR2*, stereographs are cataloged as graphic materials. Synonymous with *stereogram*. *See also*: *anaglyph*.

stereophonic   Sound reproduced by an audio device simultaneously from two separate channels with two amplifiers or speakers. Stereophonic sound separation produces a more realistic effect than earlier monaural recording but not as realistic as quadraphonic sound.

stereotype   A fixed impression that may have little basis in fact but is nevertheless perpetuated by persons unwilling to look more deeply into the matter. Librarians are often typecast in the mass media because few people outside the library profession understand what librarians do when they are not shushing people. Library humor often makes light of the absurdities inherent in the notion of the "typical librarian." ***See also***: *image*.

stick   A sturdy hardwood rod about three feet long, divided lengthwise down the center, usually into four thin shafts, with a handle on one end and a rubber ring at the other to hold the most recent issue of a newspaper securely along the fold. When not in use, the rods are designed to rest horizontally in a rack high enough to allow the leaves to hang freely without touching the floor. Synonymous with *newspaper rod*.

Also refers to a handheld adjustable wood or metal frame used to hold in sequence the individual units of type as they are composed in letterpress, each unit bearing a single character, arranged in reverse order from right to left and upside down. The frame is usually calibrated to allow line-length to be fixed. After several lines of type have been assembled, the typesetter transfers them to a holding tray called a *galley* to await make-up into page form.

sticker   A small preprinted adhesive label placed inside a book imported from another country, usually on the title page to indicate the name of the domestic distributor. Stickers are also used by publishers and booksellers to indicate price changes.

still A term used in the movie industry for a single frame taken from a motion picture or videotape, often used for promotional purposes. Also refers to a single photograph taken with a conventional camera, especially one in which the subject is a performer, for use in publicity. Compare with *still image*.

still image A two-dimensional image produced on film (often by photographic process) that does not produce the optical effect of motion when viewed by the human eye, for example, a transparency, slide, or single frame from a filmstrip, motion picture, or videotape. In a more general sense, an image in any medium that does not give the impression of movement. Compare with *still*.

stilted A book given wider squares to bring the height of its binding up to that of other volumes in the same set, or on the same shelf, when the book block is slightly shorter.

stipple A pattern of small dots of varying color and/or density used in drawing, painting, or printing to create the impression of gradations of light and shadow in an image. *See also*: *stipple engraving*.

  Also refers to an uneven, pebble-grained finish on certain grades of paper.

stipple engraving A graphic technique that combines etching and engraving to produce designs in which outlines are etched by hand and shading is produced by a pattern of small dots of varying size and density, cut into the same plate with a graver. Also refers to a print made by this technique.

stitching Binding by means of wire staples driven through the leaves or signatures of a publication. Compare with *sewing*. *See also*: *saddle-stitching* and *side-stitching*.

STM An abbreviation used in the publishing trade for the scientific, technical, and medical segment of the market for journals, books, and other forms of scholarly communication. Leading STM publishers include Elsevier Science and Springer-Verlag. *See also*: *PSP*.

stock photograph A photograph taken in the past, kept on file for use when no current picture is available, in contrast to one taken specifically for the purpose at hand. Newspapers usually maintain a file of stock photographs, especially portraits of well-known individuals, pictures of landmarks, etc., for use as the occasion arises. Directory information for stock photo agencies is available in *Literary Market Place*. Copyright law applies.

stolen book A book taken from its owner without permission. Theft of rare and valuable books from libraries and archives has increased dramatically over the last two decades. When a book received by a library is found to belong to someone else, there is a moral and legal obligation to return it to the owner and absorb as a loss any cost incurred in acquiring it. When ownership of a book is suspect, the library can check with the national headquarters of the Antiquarian Booksellers Association of America (ABAA) to see if it has been reported as stolen. *See also*: *ownership mark*.

stop list *See*: stopword.

stop word *See*: stopword.

stopword   A frequently used word—usually an article, conjunction, or preposition with little semantic content—ignored when a keywords search is executed because it adds little value to the search statement and is not helpful for retrieval (*examples*: **a, an, as, at, by, for, from, of, on, the, to**). Some systems have a predetermined list of stopwords, which may be given in the help screen(s). In some systems, a stopword may be context-dependent, for example, the word "education" in a bibliographic database providing access to materials on education but not in a database indexing articles published in newspapers or general interest periodicals. Also spelled *stop word*.

storage   In computing, *external* memory used to store data for an indefinite period of time (usually on hard disk or floppy disk), as opposed to *main* memory or RAM used to store data only during a work session. Storage capacity is measured in bytes. *See also*: *save*.

storage area   A location within a library building or outside its walls where infrequently used materials and equipment are housed until needed. In some libraries, items in storage may be retrieved by courier at the user's request. The status of items in a *storage collection* may be indicated in the catalog record.

Former Yale University conservator Jane Greenfield recommends that books be stored in an area that is weatherproof, insect and animal proof, secure from theft and vandalism, and easy to clean, with proper environmental controls, a floor strong enough to support 350 pounds per square foot, and sufficient space for processing. She also recommends that books never be stored in an attic, cellar, or barn (*The Care of Fine Books*, Nick Lyons Books, 1988).

storyboard   A series of pictures or rough sketches with accompanying text, used in the production of an audiovisual or multimedia work to help the creators visualize the sequence of its parts. Also spelled *story board*.

storybook   A book of stories for children, often an illustrated collection of well-known fables, fairy tales, nursery rhymes, and poems, sometimes devoted to a specific topic or theme (*example*: ***The Japanese Children's Storybook on the Bombing of Hiroshima*** by Toshi and Iri Maruki). The term is also seen in the titles of collections of Bible stories written for children. Compare with *picture storybook*.

story hour   A period of time set aside for reading and telling stories to the youngest members of a library's clientele, a regularly scheduled event in some public libraries. The *storyteller* is usually a trained children's librarian, but *storytelling* may also be done by a particularly talented or experienced assistant or volunteer. In some public libraries the children's room includes a special room or corner with soft furniture, designed to put young listeners at ease. Also spelled *storyhour*. Synonymous with *storytime*.

storytelling   The art of telling and reading stories to young children, for pleasure and to interest them in books and reading. The practice was first introduced in libraries by Caroline Hewins at the Hartford Public Library in Connecticut in 1882. Storytelling is sometimes done with the aid of a flannel board or puppets. In audiobooks for children, the story is sometimes told by a celebrity narrator whose voice is easily recognized. *See also*: *National Storytelling Network* and *story hour*.

storytime   *See*: story hour.

strap   A type of fastening used on medieval manuscript books consisting of a length of plain or braided leather with one end permanently attached to the outside surface of one of the boards of a binding, with a hole or slit in the free end designed to fit over a pin or peg on the other board. Straps were used singly or in pairs usually on the fore-edge to keep the covers firmly closed, preventing the parchment or vellum leaves from cockling with changes in temperature and humidity. Michelle Brown notes in *Understanding Illuminated Manuscripts* (Getty Museum/British Library, 1994) that in English bindings the pin or catch was attached to the lower board and in most continental bindings to the upper board. *See also*: *clasp*.

strapwork   An open pattern of interlaced ribbons used as a decorative motif in book-binding. Strapwork is one of the distinguishing characteristics of bindings done in *Grolier style*. Synonymous in 16th-century French binding with *entrelac*.

strategic alliance   A collaborative partnership between a library and one or more external departments, agencies, organizations, etc., for the mutual benefit of all the participants. Examples include mentoring relationships between undergraduate libraries and athletics programs; digitization projects involving libraries, archives, museums, and historical societies; and library events involving authors, sponsored in conjunction with local booksellers.

strategic planning   The systematic process by which a company, organization, or institution (or one of its units) formulates achievable policy objectives for future growth and development over a period of years, based on its mission and goals and on a realistic assessment of the resources, human and material, available to implement the plan. The process may require the collection and analysis of data on current operations and user preferences to evaluate competing options. A well-developed *strategic plan* is the basis for effective performance evaluation.

strawboard   A coarse board sometimes used in case binding, made from unbleached straw and repulped waste fiber. *Binder's board* is preferred in trade editions because it is stronger.

streaming video   A method of sending a sequence of compressed moving images one way over a data network, at the user's request or broadcast at a fixed time, which allows viewing to begin before the entire file has been transmitted. To counteract any delays caused by packet switching and maintain the impression of continuous motion, a buffer is used on the client computer to store a few seconds of video before it is displayed on the screen. Unlike video that is downloaded for subsequent playback, streaming video is stored as a *temporary* file and deleted when the application used to view it is closed. Videoconferencing differs from streaming video in providing two-way transmission in real time.

string indexing   A method of indexing in which a set of indexing terms is assigned to a document by a human indexer according to the set of rules governing the system, to describe its content. The terms are then manipulated by computer to create an index in which each term is listed in correct alphabetical sequence, providing access to the document under each of the terms. PRECIS is an example of a highly developed string indexing system.

stripe   A narrow band of magnetic material applied as a coating along one or both edges of a length of motion picture film on which the sound track is recorded.

stub   The narrow strip of paper remaining along the inner edge when a leaf is sliced cleanly out of a book, used to tip in another leaf when a replacement is required. Also refers to a narrow strip of cloth or paper sewn between the sections of a book to attach a folded map or illustration, or bound into the front or back to secure a pocket. In binding, the process of adding such strips to a text block is called *stubbing*.

student assistant   A part-time employee in an academic library, school library, or media center, enrolled as a student at the institution served by the library. Student assistants are usually paid an hourly wage for performing routine tasks such as stack maintenance and checking items in and out at the circulation desk.

student publication   A newspaper or magazine published in print or online by students enrolled at a high school, college, or university, usually funded by student fees and edited by journalism majors or members of an interest group or club. Most student newspapers are issued daily or weekly. Links to U.S. college and university newspapers available online are listed by state in *Yahoo!* (www.yahoo.com). *See also*: *yearbook*.

style manual   A guide to a prescribed set of rules for typing research papers and theses, usually written for a specific academic discipline or group of related disciplines, covering the mechanics of writing (punctuation, capitalization, quotations, plagiarism, etc.), format (spacing, headings, tables and illustrations, etc.), and correct form of documentation (footnotes, endnotes, and bibliographies), usually including pertinent examples. In academic libraries, the latest editions of leading style manuals are available on reserve or in the reference section. Compare with *style sheet*.

Examples:
Chicago Manual of Style
Complete Guide to Citing Government Documents (American Library Association)
A Manual for Writers of Term Papers, Theses, and Dissertations (Kate Turabian)
MLA Handbook for Writers of Research Papers
Publication Manual of the American Psychological Association

style sheet   A list of the rules of spelling, punctuation, usage, and citation employed by the publisher of a periodical to which an author who submits a manuscript for publication is expected to conform. In book publishing, adherence to house style is usually checked by the copy editor in the process of marking up a manuscript for the printer. Compare with *style manual*.

Also, a file containing rules for adding style (fonts, colors, spacing, etc.) to Web documents. The two main style sheet languages are cascading style sheets (CSS) and Extensible Stylesheet Language (XSL). CSS can be used on HTML and XML, while XSL can be used only on XML. Also spelled *stylesheet*.

stylus   The earliest known writing implement, consisting of a sharp, pointed stick made of wood, bone, metal, or reed, usually with a small flat spatula on the nonwriting end for making erasures, used in ancient Mesopotamia to cut or impress straight, wedge-shaped pictographic characters into the surface of clay tablets and later by the ancient Greeks and Romans to write on wax tablets. When clay was superseded by papyrus, then parchment, and finally paper as a writing surface, brush and pen replaced the stylus. *See also*: *cuneiform*.

Also, a small electronic pen-shaped device used on touch screens and in computer graphics applications to direct the cursor. Also refers to the needle of a record player, which transmits mechanical vibrations from the surface of a phonograph record to the cartridge where they are converted into electrical impulses amplified as audible sound.

subclass   In classification, a class of which each and every member is a member of another, usually more encompassing class (*example*: Periodical / Publication). In close classification systems, subclasses are subdivided into sub-subclasses (Magazine / Periodical), and so on (Newsmagazine / Magazine). *See also*: *cross-classification*.

subcommittee   Two or more members of a larger committee, elected or appointed to address one or more specific issues or needs on behalf of the larger group and report back in a timely manner. A subcommittee that begins ad hoc may eventually become permanent or develop into an independent committee.

subdirectory   *See*: directory.

subdivision   In library cataloging, the division of a class or subject heading into aspects by the addition of notation or a subheading following a dash or other mark of punctuation, for example, **—History** in the heading **Libraries—History**. In Library of Congress subject headings, there are four types of subdivisions: topical (*example*: **Library—Automation**), geographic (**Libraries—United States**), chronological (**Libraries—United States—History—19th century**), and form (**Libraries—Directories**). *See also*: *divide-like note* and *free-floating subdivision*.

In Dewey Decimal Classification, a subordinate member of a class. For example, 028 *Reading and use of other information media*, a subdivision of the class 020 *Library and information sciences*, and more specifically 028.9 *Reading interests and habits*, a subdivision of the class 028. Also refers to the notation added to other numbers to make a class number specific to the work being classified (*DDC*).

subfield   Because most variable fields in the MARC record contain two or more related pieces of information, they are subdivided to allow each element of bibliographic description to be recorded separately. A subfield contains the smallest logical unit of descriptive data pertaining to a bibliographic item. Within a field, each subfield is preceded by a two-character *delimiter*. The Library of Congress uses the dollar sign ($) and OCLC the double dagger (‡) as the first character. The second character, the *subfield code*, is usually a lowercase alphabetic character, although arabic numerals are permitted. For example, subfield **$c** of the physical description (field 300) is reserved for the dimensions of an item.

subfield code   A one-character code used in the MARC record to indicate the portion of a variable field reserved for a single data element, usually a lowercase alphabetic character (although arabic numerals are permitted) preceded by a delimiter code, for example, **$c** to indicate date of publication in the publication, distribution, etc. area (field 260) of a Library of Congress record. Because the subfield **$a** is *implicit* at the beginning of most fields, the subfield code **$a** is often not displayed.

subfield delimiter   A one-character code used in the MARC record to indicate that the following character is to be understood as a subfield code. The subfield delimiter is defined as ASCII "1F"—an unprintable value often displayed as the dollar sign ($), double dagger (‡), or vertical bar (|).

subgenre   A subcategory of an existing class of literature or art that has its own distinguishing characteristics, for example, detective fiction within the mystery genre.

subgroup   *See*: record group.

subhead   Any secondary heading or title in a written work, intended to subdivide the text of a chapter or other major division, usually printed in a smaller size of the typeface used for the main heading. In textbooks and long entries in reference books, subheads may be further subdivided into *sub-subheads* indicated by an even smaller type size. Also spelled *sub-head*. Compare with *subheading*.

subheading   A secondary heading added to a main subject heading or descriptor in a pre-coordinate indexing system, usually following a dash or other mark of punctuation, to allow documents to be indexed more specifically. Subheadings may be further subdivided; for example, in the Library of Congress subject heading **United States— History—Civil War 1861–1864**, *United States* is the main heading, and *History* and *Civil War 1861–1864* are subheadings. In a printed list of indexing terms, subheadings are indented to provide visual representation of the hierarchic relations between terms. Compare with *subhead*. *See also*: *subdivision*.

subject   Any one of the topics or themes of a work, stated explicitly in the text or title or implicit in its message. In library cataloging, a book or other item is assigned one or more *subject heading*s as access points, to assist users in locating its content by subject. In abstracting and indexing services, the headings assigned to represent the content of a document are called *descriptors*. Abbreviated *subj*. *See also*: *aboutness* and *subject analysis*.

In a more general sense, any topic of study or discussion, or theme expressed in writing, painting, etc. In Dewey Decimal Classification, subjects are arranged by discipline. Because a subject can be studied in more than one discipline (*example*: **marriage** in law, psychology, religion, sociology, etc.), the choices made in classification are governed by rules.

Also refers to the line in the header of an e-mail message consisting of a word or phrase provided by the sender to inform the addressee of its content. The subject line appears, with the name of the sender, in the recipient's list of incoming mail.

subject analysis   Examination of a bibliographic item by a trained subject specialist to determine the most specific subject heading(s) or descriptor(s) that fully describe its content, to serve in the bibliographic record as access points in a subject search of a library catalog, index, abstracting service, or bibliographic database. When no applicable subject heading can be found in the existing headings list or thesaurus of indexing terms, a new one must be created.

subject bibliography   A list of resources (books, articles, reports, etc.) on a specific topic, usually compiled by a librarian or researcher with specialized knowledge of the subject to acquaint other researchers with the existing literature. A *retrospective* subject bibliography may be selective or comprehensive within a designated publication period. A *current* subject bibliography quickly becomes outdated unless updated, usually in supplements. Book-length subject bibliographies may be shelved in the reference section of the library. Compare with *reading list*. **See also**: *webliography*.

subject collection   An extensive collection of library materials related to a particular subject or group of closely related subjects, for example, the South Asia collection at the UC Berkeley Library or the collection on printing history at the Newberry Library in Chicago. Special security precautions may be taken to protect subject collections if they contain rare and/or valuable items. For a list of subject emphases, as reported by university, college, public, and special libraries and museums in the United States and Canada, please see *Subject Collections*, a directory published by R.R. Bowker. Compare with *special collections*.

subject encyclopedia   An encyclopedia in one or more volumes devoted to a specific subject, field of study, or academic discipline, as opposed to a *general encyclopedia* containing information on a broad range of subjects. Entries in a subject encyclopedia are usually written and signed by an expert on the topic and may include a brief bibliography.

Examples:
Encyclopedia of Psychology
Encyclopedia of the Holocaust
International Encyclopedia of Linguistics

subject heading   The most specific word or phrase that describes the subject, or one of the subjects, of a work, selected from a list of preferred terms (controlled vocabulary) and assigned as an added entry in the bibliographic record to serve as an access point in the library catalog. A subject heading may be subdivided by the addition of subheadings (*example*: **Libraries—History—20th century**) or include a parenthetical qualifier for semantic clarification as in **Mice (Computers)**. The use of cross-references to indicate semantic relations between subject headings is called *syndetic structure*. The process of examining the content of new publications and assigning appropriate subject headings is *subject analysis*. In the United States, most libraries use Library of Congress subject headings (*LCSH*), but small libraries may use *Sears subject headings*. Compare with *descriptor*. **See also**: *aboutness* and *summarization*.

subject index   An alphabetically arranged list of headings selected by an indexer to represent the subject content of one or more works, with locators (usually page numbers) to direct the user to the appropriate point in the text. Names are usually included in the subject index, but in some publications there is a separate name index and possibly even a separate geographic index of place names. The subject index is sometimes combined with the author index, in a single alphabetic sequence. *See also*: *title index*.

Also refers to an alphabetically arranged index to the schedules of a classification system, also called a *relative index*.

subject specialist   A librarian qualified by virtue of specialized knowledge and experience to select materials and provide bibliographic instruction and reference services to users in a specific subject area or academic discipline (or subdiscipline). In academic libraries, subject specialists often hold a second master's degree in their field of specialization. Also refers to a librarian trained in *subject analysis*.

submenu   *See*: menu.

subordinate body   A corporate body integrally related to a larger corporate entity on which it depends for its existence and identity, occupying an inferior hierarchical rank, for example, a subsidiary of a large commercial corporation or a round table of the American Library Association. Compare with *related body*.

subpage   A Web page designed as part of a Web site, linked to the site's homepage directly or through one or more layers of pages linked to the main page. In the Internet address (URL) **www.myuniversity.edu/library/hours.html**, the subdirectory **/library** is added to the address of the main page (**www.myuniversity.edu**) to direct users to the subpage for the university library, and the filename **/hours.html** takes the user to the sub-subpage displaying library hours. For convenience, a well-designed subpage should include a direct link back to the main page.

subplot   In literature, a second complete story within the main action of a narrative work, sometimes involving the same or a related set of characters (*example*: the **Laertes subplot** in Shakespeare's play *Hamlet*). More common in comedy than in tragedy, a subplot may be used to reinforce the main plot or as a counterpoint to it. Complex literary works may have more than one subplot, intertwined for dramatic effect.

subscriber   A person entitled to receive successive issues of a newspaper or periodical for a prescribed period of time in exchange for payment of a subscription fee, payable in advance. Also refers to a paying member of a book club or rental library and to a person who receives Internet access from an Internet service provider (ISP). Libraries that pay for access to licensed bibliographic databases and individuals who sign on to receive e-mail messages from an electronic mailing list are also subscribers. *See also*: *subscriber's edition*.

subscriber's edition   An edition of uncertain sales potential issued only after a sufficient number of customers agree to purchase a copy, usually in response to an announcement by the publisher. The work may be printed on a better grade of paper and bound more attractively than the trade edition, with a list of subscribers included. Synonymous with *subscription work*. Compare with *limited edition*.

subscript   A character written or printed slightly below the line, usually a numeral or figure, as in a chemical formula (*example*: CO_2). Also refers to anything written or printed at the bottom of a document, such as a signature. Compare with *superscript*.

subscription   The right to receive a newspaper or periodical for a designated period of time (or prescribed number of successive issues), upon payment of a subscription fee, payable in advance to the publisher or *subscription agent*. For journals, the period is usually one calendar year (January 1 through December 31); for newspapers and magazines, one year from the date of the first issue received. First-time subscribers may be offered a heavily discounted *subscription price* as an inducement to subscribe. Most subscriptions are delivered by post and renewed annually. *See also*: *bulk subscription*, *expiration date*, and *fulfillment year*.

Also refers to the right of a library or library system to provide access to a bibliographic database, or other online resource, to its patrons under licensing agreement with a vendor, upon payment of an annual subscription price, subject to renewal.

subscription agent   A company in the business of providing centralized serial subscription services, to relieve libraries of the time-consuming task of dealing with publishers individually. Customers are required to pay a service charge, usually 5–10 percent of total annual subscription cost. Some subscription agents also provide access to bibliographic and full-text databases. *See also*: *EBSCO*.

subscription cycle   *See*: subscription period.

subscription library   An early type of private library first conceived by London booksellers in the early 18th century whose members paid annual dues or a subscription fee in exchange for the privilege of using library materials and services. Ownership was by the members acting as a single corporate entity, not individually in shares. For a brief history of subscription libraries, please see the entry by Peter Hoare in the *International Encyclopedia of Information and Library Science* (Routledge, 2003). Compare with *proprietary library*.

subscription period   The interval of time for which a periodical subscription is sold, for journals usually one calendar year beginning January 1 and ending December 31. For newspapers and magazines, the period is usually one year from the date of the first issue received. Subscribers who renew for multiple years may received a price break. Synonymous with *subscription cycle*. *See also*: *fulfillment year*.

subscription price   The amount charged by the publisher of a newspaper or periodical, or by a subscription agent, for the right to receive successive issues for a prescribed period of time, usually one year. A financial incentive may be offered to subscribe for two or more years. Some journal publishers charge libraries a substantially higher price than the rate paid by individual subscribers (see *differential pricing*). In recent years, relentless price increases for journal subscriptions have forced cancellations on most academic libraries and spurred the development of new models of scholarly publishing (see *open access*). Also refers to the annual amount charged by a vendor for access to an electronic database, usually based on size of library, FTE, and/or number of simultaneous users. Synonymous with *subscription rate*. *See also*: *combination rate* and *multiple year rate*.

subscription rate   *See*: subscription price.

subscription terms   Terms under which a publisher offers a discount of up to 35 percent on the published price of general interest titles ordered prior to first publication to compensate for the risk taken by the bookseller in purchasing stock before sales potential has been adequately tested in the market place.

subscription work   *See*: subscriber's edition.

subseries   A series published in conjunction with another (usually more encompassing) series of which it is a section. The title of a subseries may or may not be independent of the title of the main series (*example*: **History of Japanese Business and Industry**, a subseries of **Harvard East Asian Monographs**).

subset   In logic, a set in which each and every entity is also an entity of another, usually more encompassing, set (*examples*: Journal / Periodical *and* Magazine / Periodical).

subsidiaries   *See*: back matter.

subsidiary rights   Under copyright law, the rights to publish a work in a form other than the original publication, for example, in installments in a periodical; as a work included in a collection or anthology; as an adaptation for performance as a play, motion picture, or television program; or as an abridgment, digest, translation, excerpt, or quotation. Subsidiary rights also include control over commercial exploitation and reproduction not covered under fair use. Subject to formal agreement between author and publisher, they can be sold or transferred by the person or corporate entity owning them. Compare with *volume rights*.

subsidy publishing   Publication of works too limited in appeal to turn a profit for which the publisher receives funds from the author or a grant from a foundation, corporation, or other organization to cover costs. The result is considered a *sponsored book*, especially when the person or entity providing the subsidy agrees in advance to purchase a significant number of copies. The term is also used synonymously with *vanity publishing*.

Substance Abuse Librarians & Information Specialists (SALIS)   Created in 1978 with assistance from the U.S. National Institute on Drug Abuse (NIDA) and the National Institute on Alcohol Abuse and Alcoholism (NIAAA), SALIS is an international association of individuals and organizations interested in the exchange and dissemination of objective, accurate information about the abuse of alcohol, tobacco, and other drugs. In 1986, SALIS merged with its Canadian counterpart, Librarians and Information Specialists in Addictions (LISA), and in 1989 the organization became an affiliate of the International Council on Alcohol and Addictions (ICAA). URL: www.salis.org.

subtext   In a work of literature, an implicit meaning or significance, usually on another level of understanding than the explicit meaning of the text. In contemporary dramatic performance, an actor's interpretation of the inner motives and emotional state of a character, evident from the implied meaning of the lines spoken.

subtitle   A secondary portion of the title proper of a work, consisting of an explanatory or limiting phrase following a colon or semicolon, often beginning with "a" or "an." In the title *New York: A Documentary Film*, the phrase *A Documentary Film* is the subtitle. On the title page of a book, the subtitle is usually set in smaller type than the first part of the title. The subtitle is often omitted from the spine title. Compare with *alternative title*. *See also*: *partial title*.

Also refers to a line of text along the bottom of a motion picture or television screen giving the dialogue or narration in a language other than that of the sound track.

successive entry   A method of cataloging serials that have undergone title changes in which a new bibliographic record (main entry) is created for each title or major change, with explanatory notes indicating the publication's relationships to earlier and later titles. This convention is prescribed in *AACR2*. Compare with *earliest entry* and *latest entry*.

SuDocs   An acronym for the **Su**perintendent of **Doc**uments classification system. Publications of the U.S. federal government are assigned call numbers based on a unique classification system developed between 1893 and 1903 by GPO librarian Adeliade Hasse, currently maintained by the Superintendent of Documents at the U.S. Government Printing Office. SuDocs call numbers begin with letters of the roman alphabet.

Example:

J 29.9/6:998 assigned to the 1998 edition of the *Sourcebook of Criminal Justice Statistics*

Libraries that use SuDocs numbers shelve government documents in a separate location. Those that use Library of Congress Classification or Dewey Decimal Classification for govdocs shelve them in reference or with the general collection.

suede binding   A bookbinding in kidskin or calf, dyed or undyed, with the flesh side facing out, buffed to a velvety nap. Used from the 17th century on, suede is not as easily scratched or scuffed as a smooth leather binding, but it is difficult to clean.

suggestion box   Some libraries in the United States provide a means for patrons to suggest improvements in services, request the purchase of a specific item, or comment on library policies and practices in writing on a slip of paper deposited in a small box provided for the purpose near the circulation desk, reference desk, or main entrance. Some online catalogs and library Web pages allow users to post suggestions and comments electronically. The responses of library staff and administration may be posted on a public bulletin board or kiosk or in a special section of the library homepage.

summarization   In library cataloging, a brief statement of the overall subject of a work that serves as the basis for assigning one or more subject headings as access points in the bibliographic record to facilitate retrieval by subject. *See also*: *aboutness*.

summary   A brief statement expressing the general substance or overall idea of a work (or a portion of it), recapitulating its main points, findings, and conclusions, usually given at the end. Compare with *abstract*. *See also*: *synopsis*.

Also refers to a brief statement added as a note in the bibliographic record to describe the content of a nonbook item produced in a format difficult to browse.

In Dewey Decimal Classification, a list of the main subdivisions of a class, providing an overview of its structure, printed in the schedules immediately following the entry for the class. Summaries for the entire Classification (main classes, divisions, and sections) are given at the beginning of the schedules.

summer reading program   A program offered during the summer months by the staff of the children's room of most public libraries in the United States to keep children reading during the long vacation. Usually organized around a theme, summer reading programs sometimes include special events such as contests and read-a-thons to encourage young readers to practice their reading skills. *See also*: Reading Rainbow.

Sunday supplement   A magazine of tabloid size published regularly as part of a Sunday newspaper, usually in color (*example*: **Parade**).

sunk bands   In hand bookbinding, sewing supports recessed by the binder in shallow grooves cut across the binding edge of the sections to eliminate ridges (*raised bands*) in the material covering the spine.

sunned   A book or other publication that has a cover, dust jacket, or pages faded or discolored from prolonged exposure to direct sunlight or some other strong light source, a condition that affects its value in the antiquarian and used book market.

super   *See*: crash.

supercomputer   A very large, fast computer capable of executing millions of instructions per second, used mainly by government agencies, such as the U.S. Department of Defense, and major research centers at large universities that process large quantities of data. Compare with *mainframe*, *microcomputer*, and *minicomputer*.

superfiche   A type of transparent microform in the shape of a card, with a reduction ratio greater than standard *microfiche* (up to 400 images per 4 × 6 inch sheet, instead of the usual 48–60 images) but less than *ultrafiche*.

superimposition   The principle in library cataloging that when new rules are introduced, only entries made *after* the rules take effect need conform to the changes, making it unnecessary to recatalog materials processed under the old rules. New entries are interfiled with the old. The principle was adopted in 1967 by libraries throughout the United States, following Library of Congress practice, when the *Anglo-American Cataloguing Rules* were adopted as the national catalog code.

Superintendent of Documents   The official at the U.S. Government Printing Office responsible for the distribution of federal government information to the American public, in both print and digital format. *See also*: *Federal Depository Library Program* and GPO Access.

Superintendent of Documents classification   *See*: SuDocs.

superior numeral   *See*: superscript.

supers   In motion picture and television production, any lettering or graphics super-imposed on existing footage (credits, subtitles, etc.).

superscript   A character written or printed slightly above the line, for example, a su-perior numeral used to indicate a footnote or endnote, or in a mathematical expression (*example*: x^2). Compare with *subscript*. *See also*: *reference mark*.

superscription   Something written, printed, or engraved at the top or on the outside surface of an object, especially a name and/or address on the outside of an envelope or parcel.

superseded   Something old or outdated replaced by something more modern or current. In library collections, superseded items may be retained if they have historical value, for example, older editions of almanacs and statistical publications.

supervision   Responsibility for overseeing the performance of one or more persons or machines to ensure that work assignments are properly and efficiently completed. A person with the authority to *supervise* is called a *supervisor*.

supplement   Additional matter, more extensive than an addendum, issued under sep-arate cover and title page, in serial or monographic form, for the stated purpose of complementing a previously published work, usually to clarify, continue, expand, or update it or to add a special feature (maps, statistics, directory information, etc.). Supplements are usually written by the original author and published under the same title or subtitle. When available as part of the original purchase price, they are nor-mally sent automatically. In a subsequent edition, supplementary material may be included immediately following the original text or as an appendix. Most printed periodical indexes are updated in monthly or quarterly paperbound supplements, cu-mulated annually. Abbreviated *suppl.* Compare with *continuation* and *sequel*.

In newspapers, an extra sheet, section, or entire issue in addition to the regular issue, usually containing items of special interest to subscribers. *See also*: *color sup-plement* and *Sunday supplement*.

supplemental invoice   In acquisitions, an invoice sent by a publisher or vendor of books or serials for added charges not covered by prepayments, usually an unexpected price increase by the publisher, publication of additional volumes, or fluctuations in currency exchange rates.

supplied title   The title provided by the cataloger as an interpolation in the title and statement of responsibility area of the bibliographic description of an item lacking a title proper on the chief source of information (the title page or a substitute). A supplied title may be (1) a word or phrase found elsewhere in or on the item, (2) taken from a reference to the work found in another source, or (3) composed by the cataloger based on an assessment of the scope and content of the work.

supplier   A library or other participant in the OCLC Interlibrary Loan network that responds to OCLC requests from other libraries to borrow returnable materials. In the OCLC *WorldCat* database, the three-letter OCLC symbols of suppliers appear in uppercase in the holdings display attached to the bibliographic record representing the item. If the symbol is preceded by a $, the institution may charge for the loan of certain types of materials. Compare with *nonsupplier*.

Also refers to a commercial enterprise in the business of selling equipment, furnishings, and/or supplies to libraries and related institutions. Some supply companies provide other services in support of technical processing. Compare with *vendor*. The UC Berkeley Libraries provide an online list of links to library-related companies in *Libweb* at: sunsite.berkeley.edu/Libweb/comp.html.

support staff   Library staff members not trained as librarians who have acquired a technical understanding of library practices and procedures and contribute on a daily basis to the smooth operation of a library but are not qualified to make policy decisions or participate in other activities of a professional nature. *Library Mosaics* is a bimonthly magazine for library support staff published by Yenor, Inc. *See also*: *Library Support Staff Interests Round Table* and *paraprofessional*.

supposed author   *See*: attributed author.

suppositious author   A person whose name is substituted for that of the real author, with intent to deceive others concerning responsibility for the work. Compare with *attributed author*.

suppressed   A work or part of a work withheld or withdrawn from publication or circulation by the author or publisher, by an ecclesiastic or government authority, or by court action, usually because it contains material considered objectionable by those with the authority to prevent public distribution. *See also*: *banned book* and *censorship*.

Also, a leaf canceled from a book or other publication due to an error or for some other technical reason.

Also refers to a catalog record available to staff but hidden from public view, perhaps because the record is incomplete or the volume it represents is unavailable.

surf   To navigate the World Wide Web in an exploratory manner, moving from one document to another, using search engines, Web indexes, hypertext links, navigation bars, icons, etc., with no definite purpose in mind. A person who navigates in such a way is called a *surfer*. Compare with *browse*.

surname   A shared name that identifies members of the same family (*example*: **Patterson**), as distinct from a given name (*example*: **Samantha**) that may be the same as that of a close or distant relative but is also likely to be shared with persons outside the family. In library cataloging, personal name entries begin with the surname, and form of name is subject to authority control. Synonymous with *last name*. *See also*: *compound surname* and *patronymic*.

surrogate   A substitute used in place of an original item, for example, a facsimile or photocopy of a document too rare or fragile to be handled by library users or an abstract or summary that provides desired information without requiring the reader to examine the entire document. In preservation, a surrogate is usually made in a more durable medium. In a library catalog, the description provided in the bibliographic record serves as a surrogate for the actual physical item.

survey   A scientifically conducted study, or account of a study, in which data is systematically collected from a selected group of sources or informants, usually concerning general conditions, practices, habits, preferences, etc. (*example*: *The Survey of Academic Libraries* published by the Primary Research Group in 2002). The statistical results of survey research are usually presented in graphic, tabular, or summary form. Also refers to a brief overview of the main aspects of a subject or field of study (*The Death Penalty: A Historical and Theological Survey* by James Megivern). Compare with *questionnaire*. *See also*: *user survey*.

suspense   In literature and film, a narrative that keeps its reader, viewer, or listener in a state of heightened mental and emotional uncertainty about the outcome (*example*: the French film *Diabolique*) or about how one or more characters will respond to the discovery of a fact known only to the reader or audience. Compare with *thriller*. *See also*: *espionage* and *mystery*.

SVGA   Super Video Graphics Array, an enhancement of the standard 640 × 480 VGA graphics display system, capable of producing screen resolutions of 800 × 600 pixels with up to 16 million colors. A further enhancement called XVGA increases resolution to 1024 × 768 pixels.

swash letter   An ornamental capital letter written or printed in italic with at least one long tail or flourish added for dramatic effect, used mainly in display work.

swell   In bookbinding, unwanted bulk at the binding edge produced by the back folds, the accumulation of sewing thread, and/or guarding. Although some swell is desirable to facilitate rounding and backing, in books composed of numerous thin sections, additional thickness may hinder subsequent binding procedures. If the paper used to print the text is soft, the spine can normally be compacted by smashing, an operation that embeds the sewing threads in the paper, but with hard papers, excessive pressure on the threads may cut through the paper. Swell can be reduced in hand-binding by sewing the sections two-on.

syllabary   A system of writing a language in which each character or symbol represents a spoken syllable, rather than a single sound (*phoneme*). The number of characters in a syllabary is usually greater than in a phonetic alphabet, but words can be written in fewer characters. Also refers to a list or table of syllables in a language. A *monosyllabary* is a list of words of one syllable (*example*: the word **book**).

syllabication   The division of a word into units of pronunciation (syllables), indicated in standard dictionaries by a centered period or a hyphen to help writers, editors, and secretaries divide words at the end of a line. Most word processing software has a feature that accomplishes this automatically.

syllabus   An outline of the topics to be covered in a formal course of study, given in the order in which they are to be discussed in class, with any assignments and related readings also indicated. Some college and university faculty make their *syllabi* available online, usually on the World Wide Web, or place printed copies on reserve at the library.

Also, the Latin term for a small label attached to one edge of a manuscript in the form of a roll, usually bearing the title of the work.

symbol   A character, image, mark, shape, or thing used to represent or denote something else by association, convention, or unintended resemblance, especially an intangible quality or abstraction, for example, a heart or rose to represent "love" or the skull-and-crossbones for "death." When words are used to create such an image, the result is *symbolic language*.

symposium   A group of specialists or experts gathered to deliver brief addresses or remarks on a topic (or topics) of mutual interest, often of a theoretical or philosophical nature, followed by a formal discussion, as in Plato's *Symposium*. In ancient Greece, music and drinking were traditional accompaniments at such gatherings, with participation restricted to males. Plural: *symposia*.

synchronous   The occurrence of two or more separate events or actions at the same moment in time. The events or actions may occur at regular or irregular intervals. The opposite of *asynchronous*. *See also*: *real time*.

syndetic index   *See*: syndetic structure.

syndetic structure   The web of interconnected and reciprocal *see* and *see also* cross-references indicating the semantic relations between headings used in a catalog, index, or reference work, or between descriptors used in an abstracting service or bibliographic database. The opposite of *asyndetic*.

syndicate   A company in the business of distributing columns, cartoons, feature articles, or radio and television programs to a number of newspapers, magazines, trade journals, news services, or broadcast media. A columnist whose work is marketed in this way is known as a *syndicated columnist*. Often time-sensitive, a syndicated work is usually intended for more or less simultaneous publication. Directory information for syndicates is available in the reference serials *Literary Market Place* and *Writer's Market*, available in most large libraries.

synonym   A word or phrase that has the same (or very nearly the same) meaning as another term in the same language, for example, the terms "book jacket" and "dust jacket." Synonyms in a language are collected in a thesaurus, available in the reference section of most libraries. In the indexing languages used in library catalogs, periodical indexes, abstracting services, and bibliographic databases, synonyms are controlled by establishing an authorized list of preferred indexing terms (*subject headings* or *descriptors*). In information retrieval, the Boolean **OR** command is used to expand the results of a keywords search by including synonyms and closely related terms. Abbreviated *syn*. The opposite of *antonym*. Compare with *quasi-synonym*. *See also*: *homonym*.

synopsis   A concise written description of the plot of a long narrative work (novel, play, opera, epic poem, etc.) giving a quick, orderly overview of the whole, usually prepared by a person other than the author. As a general rule, academic libraries do not purchase reference works that specialize in providing *synopses* (*example*: **Master-plots**) because they are too easily used by students to avoid reading assignments. Synonymous with *plot summary*. Compare with *abstract* and *summary*.

synoptic journal A journal that publishes brief reports of research findings and abstracts of articles for which the entire text is available on request, usually from a data bank or in a microform edition of the publication.

syntax The *order* in which search terms and Boolean operators in a keywords search statement are typed, determining the sequence in which a computer-based information retrieval system executes the search. In most bibliographic databases, commands are executed from left to right unless parentheses are used to indicate otherwise (a technique called *nesting*). *See also*: *proximity* and *truncation*.

Example:

children and television and (violence or aggression)

In this search statement, the Boolean "or" operator will be performed before the "and."

In indexing, the rules that determine how headings are constructed and how semantic relations among terms are indicated in an indexing language, for example, the conditions under which a parenthetical qualifier is added to a heading, or an inverted heading is used instead of conventional word order.

Also, the order in which the components of a URL (Web address) must appear and the punctuation marks used to separate the various parts (*example*: **http://www.census.gov/main/www/popclock.html**).

Also refers to the grammar and sentence structure of a language and to the branch of linguistics devoted to its study.

synthetic classification A classification system in which the classes are formed by combining characteristics or facets of subjects according to a pre-established set of rules (*example*: **Colon Classification** developed by S.R. Ranganathan). Compare with *enumerative classification*. *See also*: *hierarchical classification*.

systems All the computer hardware, software, and electronic resources on which a library or library system depends in its daily operations, including the online catalog and circulation system, bibliographic databases, networked and stand-alone PCs, Web server(s), application programs, etc. It is the responsibility of the *systems librarian* to keep the various components running smoothly, including any connections to outside networks.

systems librarian A librarian whose primary responsibility is the development and maintenance of the hardware and software systems used in a library or library system, especially the online catalog and access to any bibliographic databases and other electronic resources. In some libraries, the systems librarian may also serve as Webmaster and be responsible for training staff members in the use of library systems. Systems librarians are organized in the Library and Information Technology Association (LITA), a division of the American Library Association.

system-supplied (SS)   Under OCLC input standards, cataloging data generated by the cataloging system itself, which cannot be altered by the cataloger, for example, the OCLC control number and the date a record is entered into the system, elements of the leader in the MARC record.

T

T1 A term introduced by AT&T to refer to a dedicated digital circuit provided by the telephone companies capable of transmitting data point-to-point at the rate of 1.544 Mbps (megabits per second), containing 24 individual channels, each capable of transmitting voice or data at the rate of 64 Kbps (kilobits per second). Individuals may purchase one of these channels in an arrangement known as *fractional T1* access. Businesses and academic institutions lease T1 lines to connect to the Internet and may also use them for local area networks. The monthly charge is usually determined by distance. T1 lines are also used by Internet service providers to provide Internet access to individuals and small businesses. The Internet backbone is constructed of higher-speed T3 lines. Synonymous with *DS1*. *See also*: *bandwidth*.

T3 A term introduced by AT&T to refer to a dedicated digital circuit provided by the telephone companies capable of transmitting data point-to-point at the rate of 44.736 Mbps (megabits per second), used mainly by Internet service providers to connect to the Internet backbone and for the backbone itself. A T3 line contains 672 individual channels, each capable of transmitting 64 Kbps (kilobits per second). Synonymous with *DS3*. Compare with *T1*. *See also*: *bandwidth*.

tab A short leather tongue, usually rounded at the corners, projecting from the head and/or tail of the spine on some bindings of the 7th to 12th century, to facilitate removal of the volume from a storage chest. *See also*: *finger tab*.

tab index A set of small projections called finger tabs extending from the fore-edge of a book like a series of steps, bearing a sequence of letters, numbers, or other characters, sometimes printed against a dark background, to show the alphabetic, subject, numeric, or other arrangement of the text for rapid reference. Compare with *step index* and *thumb index*.

table A compact, systematic list of data, as in a table of contents listing the chapters or major divisions of a book. Also refers to the compact arrangement of facts, figures, or other data in vertical rows and columns to facilitate comparison, usually with a title across the top or an explanatory caption or note written or printed underneath. In books containing information in tabular format, a list of tables is usually provided in the front matter with page numbers as locators. Some statistical reference works consist entirely of tables (*example*: ***Statistical Abstract of the United States***).

In Dewey Decimal Classification, lists of notation that may be added in number building to other numbers in the schedules to form a class number appropriate to the content of a work. There are two kinds of tables in DDC: (1) six numbered auxiliary schedules containing numbers representing standard subdivisions, geographic areas, literary forms, languages, ethnic and other groups, etc., and (2) lists of special notation found in add notes under specific numbers in the main schedules and in Tables 1–6 (called *add tables*). In DDC, numbers from the tables are never used alone.

table book   A luxurious edition, usually covered in silk or velvet, intended for display in the private drawing rooms of wealthy people of the 19th century. Its modern counterpart is the *coffee table book*.

table of contents (TOC)   A list of the contents of a printed publication in the order of their appearance, usually with page numbers as locators. In a book, the TOC lists the front matter, chapters or other major divisions of the work, and the back matter. In an anthology or collection, the TOC lists the titles of the works included by the editor(s) (stories, poems, plays, essays, etc.), in order of appearance. In books, the TOC is printed in the front matter on the first recto following the dedication or title page. In periodicals, the TOC appears near the front of each issue or on the back cover, listing the editorial content (articles, columns, reviews, etc.) but not any advertising. *See also*: *current contents*.

tablet   A flat piece of wood or ivory hollowed out on one side and filled with beeswax to allow a scribe to write on the surface with a stylus. Throughout Antiquity and the Middle Ages, wax tablets were used for teaching, taking dictation, drafting texts, writing letters, computation, and other informal purposes. A text could easily be erased by warming and smoothing the wax with the blunt end of the stylus. Some were designed with handles. A *diptych* consisted of two tablets hinged along one side to close like a book. A thong was sometimes used to hold several tablets together, suspended from a belt or girdle. Latin: *tabula*. *See also*: *pugillaria*.

tabloid   A newspaper printed in a format half the size of an ordinary broadsheet newspaper, containing short news stories of a highly sensational and improbable nature, abundantly illustrated (usually with photographs), sold mainly at newsstands and in supermarkets. *See also*: *yellow press*.

Also refers to an advertising preprint of four or more pages, normally one-half the size of the newspaper into which it is inserted.

tactile materials   Reading materials in which the text is converted into a series of raised symbols, as in braille, or is presented in surfaces of contrasting texture, for the manual use of visually impaired persons. *See also*: *National Library Service for the Blind and Physically Handicapped*.

tag   A three-character numeric code in the range of 0XX–9XX with XX = 01–99, used in the MARC record to identify the kind of data contained in a field. The numbering system allows fields to be grouped by function in hundreds. In fields requiring authority control, the second and third character positions in the tag indicate parallel content. According to Betty Furrie, approximately 10 percent of all MARC tags are used in most bibliographic records; the other 90 percent are used infrequently (*Understanding MARC Bibliographic Machine-Readable Cataloging* available online at: www.loc.gov/marc/umb). For books, the most frequently used tags are:

010 tag—Library of Congress Control Number (LCCN)
020 tag—International Standard Book Number (ISBN) and terms of availability
040 tag—cataloging source
050 tag—Library of Congress call number
100 tag—personal name main entry (primary author)
130 tag—uniform title main entry
240 tag—uniform title
245 tag—title and statement of responsibility (title proper, name of part/section of work, remainder of title, etc.)
246 tag—varying form of title (cover title, parallel title, spine title, etc.)
250 tag—edition (edition statement, other information about edition)
260 tag—publication, distribution, etc. (imprint)
300 tag—physical description (collation)
440 tag—scries statcmcnt addcd entry (title)
500 tag—general note
504 tag—bibliography note
505 tag—formatted contents note
520 tag—annotation or summary note
600 tag—personal name subject added entry
610 tag—corporate name subject added entry
650 tag—topical subject heading
651 tag—geographic name subject added entry
700 tag—personal name added entry (joint author, editor, illustrator)
710 tag—corporate name added entry (other than subject or series)
800 tag—series personal name added entry
830 tag—series uniform title added entry

Also refers to a character string attached to a portion of text in an HTML, SGML, or XML document, usually at the beginning and end, to identify elements of the file, specify formatting, or establish a link. To see the tags in a hypertext document, click on "View" or its equivalent in the Web browser and then select the option "Page Source" or "View Source."

tag group   The three-digit content designators (called tags), used to identify fields in the MARC record, are grouped by function in hundreds as follows, with XX in the range of 00–99:

0XX tags—Bibliographic control numbers and coded information
1XX tags—Main entries
2XX tags—Titles, edition, imprint
3XX tags—Physical description, etc.

4XX tags—Series statements

5XX tags—Notes

6XX tags—Subject added entries

7XX tags—Added entries other than subject or series; linking fields

8XX tags—Series added entries and holdings

9XX tags—Fields for local use

See also: *parallel content*.

tail   The bottom edge of a book, on which it rests when shelved in an upright position. Also refers to the margin at the foot of a page, as opposed to the margin at the *head*. In typography, the lower loop of the letters *g*, *q*, and *y* of the roman alphabet.

tailband   **See**: headband.

tailcap   *See*: headcap.

tailpiece   A decoration printed in the blank space at the end of a chapter or other division of a book, usually a printer's ornament or a small illustration done by a professional illustrator. In medieval manuscripts, the tailpiece sometimes included a colophon that was in some cases rubricated. Also spelled *tail-piece*. Synonymous with *tail ornament*. Compare with *headpiece*. *See also*: *frontispiece*.

take down   The process of preparing a book for rebinding by removing its cover, boards, endpapers, sewing threads, and lining, including any cleaning or repair. When a volume has been reduced to its original sections, it is said to have been *taken down*. Synonymous with *pulling*.

take-over   The acquisition of exclusive rights in a book or other work by a new publisher, following initial publication by another company, sometimes the result of a legal custody fight, as in the case of the long battle between HarperCollins and Macmillan over the U.S. rights to publish *The Chronicles of Narnia* by C.S. Lewis.

tale   A narrative account of a real, imaginary, or legendary incident, usually told in the first person in a rambling style, with more attention to plot and setting than to character development. Most tales are works of short fiction (*example*: "The Legend of Sleepy Hollow" by Washington Irving), but the term has also been applied to novels (*Tale of Two Cities* by Charles Dickens). In a *tall tale*, the plot is deliberately far-fetched, usually for comic effect ("Cannibalism in the Cars" by Mark Twain). *See also*: *short story*.

talkie   From "talking picture" (as *movie* is derived from "moving picture"). A popular term for a motion picture produced with synchronized sound, used during the period immediately following the introduction of sound in 1927 to distinguish sound films from earlier silent films. The most successful of the early talkies was *The Jazz Singer* with Al Jolson, released in 1927. Producers that did not immediately embrace the new technology went out of business, abandoning many of the silent films made in 1926 and 1927, now lost forever.

talking book   *See*: audiobook.

tanning The process of converting an animal skin or hide into leather by soaking it in lime to remove the hair and then steeping it in liquid containing *tannic acid*, an astringent derived from vegetable materials such as oak bark, oak gall, acacia, or sumach. Used in ancient Egypt as early as 5000 B.C., tanning turns a skin brown in color and renders it more durable. Tanned goatskin was used on Coptic bindings as early as the 7th century A.D. The covers of books bound in tanned leather should be oiled periodically to prevent drying. Compare with *tawing*.

tape recording *See*: audiotape.

tapes Narrow strips of tightly woven cotton or linen fabric to which the sections of a book are sewn in quality binding. Two half-inch-wide strips are the norm, but in larger volumes as many as five may be used, spaced at regular intervals across the binding edge. Sewing supports are no longer used in most trade bindings. In older bindings, vellum tapes were used, or *cords* made from vegetable fiber.

target audience The group or category of persons for whom a literary or artistic work is written or produced or for whom a library collection is developed (students, professionals, recreational readers, a particular age or interest group, grade or reading level, etc.). In library cataloging, target audience is indicated in the 521 field of the MARC record.

***Tasini* decision** On June 25, 2001, the U.S. Supreme Court ruled 7–2 in *New York Times Co. v. Tasini* that publishers of newspapers and periodicals infringed the copyrights of freelance writers by making the full-text of their articles publicly available in computer databases without prior consent. The suit was filed in 1993 against the New York Times Co., Inc. and four database providers by Jonathan Tasini, president of the 7,200-member National Writers Union. The American Library Association filed an amicus curiae brief on the side of the freelancers.

Upholding the 1999 decision of the Federal Appeals Court in favor of Tasini and five other freelance writers, the high court rejected the contention that reproduction in an electronic database is a "revision" of a collective work and therefore permissible under existing copyright law, instead ruling that because articles distributed in a database are taken out of the context of the original print publication, the author retains online rights unless a prior agreement was made with the publisher. The case was sent back to the lower court for determination of appropriate remedies.

The New York Times Co. reacted to the decision by announcing its intention to withdraw up to 115,000 articles from its full-text electronic archives, mostly published between January 1, 1978 (the date the *Copyright Act of 1976* went into effect) and 1995 when most periodical publishers began including electronic rights clauses in contracts with freelance writers. The effect of the decision on academic authors who publish in scholarly journals remains unclear. Most database vendors have been less than forthright in revealing to libraries the extent of removal of full-text from their products in compliance with the *Tasini* decision.

taskbar A row of tabs in a graphical user interface, usually located across the bottom of the screen, with text labels indicating the applications and files currently open. In multitasking, a tab can be clicked by the user to bring the corresponding window to the foreground or to restore it to its original size after it has been minimized. In the Windows operating system, the **Start** button is also located in the taskbar, which may contain other information such as date and time.

task force   A group of individuals drawn from various units within an organization charged with accomplishing a specific objective or set of objectives. Once the task is completed, the group is disbanded and its members return to their former units.

tattle-tape   *See*: magnetic strip.

tawing   Preparation of an animal skin by treating it with alum and salts of iron or chromium, rendering it flexible and whitish in color. Tawed skins are very durable and more resistant to deterioration caused by atmospheric pollution than tanned leather. Geoffrey Glaister notes in *Encyclopedia of the Book* (Oak Knoll/British Library, 1996) that alum-tawed skins were used for bookbinding in England from the mid-12th to the mid-15th century and in Germany for panel-stamped bindings during the 16th century, sometimes dyed bright pink with *kermes*, a substance derived from the dried bodies of a scale insect that feeds on oak trees. Synonymous with *whittawed*.

taxonomy   The science of classification, including the general principles by which objects and phenomena are divided into classes, which are subdivided into subclasses, then into sub-subclasses, and so on. Taxonomies have traditionally been used in the life sciences to classify living organisms, but the term has been applied more recently within the information sector to the classification of resources available via the World Wide Web. For a discussion of taxonomies in the information science context, see the entry by Alan Gilchrist in the *International Encyclopedia of Information and Library Science* (Routledge, 2003).

TCP/IP   An initialism for **T**ransmission **C**ontrol **P**rotocol/**I**nternet **P**rotocol, a set of communications protocols developed by the U.S. Department of Defense and implemented in 1982 to allow the users of host computers of different types and sizes to communicate with each other and exchange data via the Internet and other networks (intranets and extranets). Supported on most platforms, TCP/IP has become *the* protocol of the Internet. TCP ensures that the total amount of data (bytes) sent is received correctly, and IP provides the mechanism for routing the packets of data comprising a message to the destination address as efficiently as possible.

TEACH   *See*: *Technology, Education and Copyright Harmonization Act.*

teacher's manual   A booklet or softcover book issued in conjunction with a textbook to assist instructors in using the text to teach their classes. In library cataloging, the presence of a teacher's manual is indicated as accompanying material in the physical description area of the bibliographic record representing the textbook.

tear sheet   A page of editorial content or advertising torn from a periodical or other printed publication for use as a press clipping or file copy.

tear test   *See*: grain.

teaser   Advertising copy supplied by the marketing department of a publishing company, usually printed on the dust jacket of a new book to entice the reader to open the cover and sample the text.

techie *See*: technician.

technical drawing   A drawing made specifically for use in engineering or some other technical context (diagram, cross section, detail, elevation, perspective, plan, working plan, etc.). Architectural drawings are included in this category.

technical journal   A journal devoted to a particular branch of engineering or technology, providing information for technicians in the field (*example*: **Computing in Science and Engineering**). Articles published in technical journals are indexed in *Applied Science and Technology Index, Compendex, INSPEC*, etc.

technical library   A library that supports one or more of the applied sciences, such as engineering or computer science. A technical library can be a branch library in a large university, a major collection within a large academic or public library, or a special library maintained by a private corporation or government agency. *See also*: *National Technical Information Service*.

technical processing   All the activities and processes concerned with acquiring, organizing, preparing, and maintaining library collections, including cataloging and physical processing, usually accomplished "behind the scenes" by the technical services department of a library. *See also*: *centralized processing*.

technical report   A scientific paper or article describing research or other significant developments in a field of the applied sciences. When submitted to a military agency, such a report may be "classified" or subject to other access restrictions. *See also*: *National Technical Information Service*.

technical services (TS)   Library operations concerned with the acquisition, organization (bibliographic control), physical processing, and maintenance of library collections, as opposed to the delivery of public services. Technical processing is performed "behind the scenes," usually in a *technical services department*. When the department is understaffed, arrears may accumulate. *See also*: *Association for Library Collections and Technical Services*.

technician   A person who has special expertise in the maintenance of high-tech machines, particularly computer and scientific equipment. Libraries with automated systems require the services of a "techie" to keep hardware and software running smoothly. Compare with *systems librarian*.

Technology, Education and Copyright Harmonization Act (TEACH)   When the *Digital Millennium Copyright Act* of 1998 was debated, lobbyists and educators reached an impasse on new exemptions for digital distance education. Enacted in 2002 following five years of negotiations between educators and the publishing and entertainment industries, *TEACH* amends the *DMCA* to permit nonprofit, accredited educational institutions certain exemptions in the use of copyrighted materials. Under *Section 110*, educators and enrolled students are allowed to display or perform the entire text of a nondramatic literary work in the digital classroom without obtaining prior permission from the copyright holder and without paying fees, provided proper notice is given of copyright protection. Reasonable and limited portions of dramatic literary works, such as narrative motion pictures, operas, plays, etc., may also be used in the digital classroom.

Under *Section 112*, eligible institutions are permitted to copy an analog version of a copyrighted work to a digitized format for use in the digital classroom, only if a digital version is not available or the available digital version is subject to technological protections that prevent its use. *TEACH* exemptions apply only to mediated instruction in which the learning process is initiated and supervised by course instructor(s) responsible for determining that the use of copyrighted materials is essential to meeting specific learning objectives. Instructors are required to make a "reasonable" effort to prevent students from disseminating copyrighted materials to others. Many institutions have interpreted password protection of digital course materials as meeting this requirement.

technology plan   A carefully developed strategy for identifying, evaluating, acquiring, and implementing technological systems and services to fulfill a library's mission and optimally serve the needs of its users, usually over a multiyear period. In addition to determining the hardware, software, telecommunication, technical support, and training the library will need, a technology plan addresses how objectives will be accomplished with reference to the goals of the library's overall service program and the environment in which it operates, particularly institutional priorities and funding. Basic components of a technology plan include:

- A summary providing a synopsis of the plan's primary recommendations and conclusions
- Background information, including an overview of the library, its mission, the community or user group served, and the process used to develop the plan
- A description of the existing technological resources
- A complete description of the technology plan, including goals and objectives, needs, action plan, and proposed budget
- An evaluation process for monitoring progress toward the achievement of goals and objectives, including a timetable and specific measures of success

Under the *Telecommunications Act of 1996 (TCA)*, public libraries are required to provide a technology plan when applying for E-rate discounts on telephone, telecommunication, and Internet services and for funding to purchase equipment and wiring. Applications for *LSTA* technology grants must also include a technology plan.

TEI   *See*: Text Encoding Initiative.

TEI Header   A section of metadata that can be attached to a document encoded under the Text Encoding Initiative standard to describe the original source file and indicate who converted it to machine-readable form, the encoding and markup principles used, etc. The TEI Header is defined in Chapter 5 of the *TEI Guidelines*.

telecommunication   The process of sending and receiving signals or messages at a distance via telegraph, telephone, radio, television, cable, microwave, or any other electromagnetic method on which modern information technology depends. Also, any transmission, emission, or reception of signals by such means. Compare with *telecommunications*.

telecommunications   The individual messages transmitted and/or received via telegraph, telephone, radio, television, cable, microwave, or other electromagnetic means. Sometimes used synonymously with *telecommunication*.

telecommute   To work from home using a computer and telecommunication links, instead of traveling to an office to conduct business. Some library functions, such as the design and maintenance of Web sites, can be accomplished at a distance, but most library personnel work on-site.

teleconference   A live, two-way conference of two or more people using audio and video transmission technology that enables the participants to see and hear each other in real time without having to meet in the same physical location.

telephone directory   A large format paperback publication distributed annually by a telephone company at no charge to its customers, containing an alphabetic list of the names, telephone numbers, and street addresses of people served in a given city, town, or geographic area in a section called the *white pages*, and an alphabetic list of businesses with phone numbers and addresses in the *yellow pages* at the back. For very large cities, the white pages and yellow pages may be published in separate volumes.

Library collections of print phone books have been largely replaced by directories available online at no charge via the Internet (*example*: **Switchboard.com**). Most libraries continue to provide print phone books only for the major towns and cities in their state.

teleplay   A drama written to be recorded in a studio and broadcast on television, rather than for live performance on stage or to be filmed as a motion picture. Synonymous with *television drama*. Compare with *screenplay*.

teletext   A type of one-way broadcasting service that allows digital information provided by a television station, such as closed captions or continuously updated news, to be displayed on a television receiver specially adapted to allow text and graphics to be superimposed over regular programming, usually in frames. Teletext is not interactive. Compare with *videotex*.

Telnet   Terminal emulation software governed by the TCP/IP protocol, which allows the user to log on to a remote computer or terminal and use its systems as if on-site. Designed to transmit ASCII text, Telnet was once widely used in libraries to provide remote access to online catalogs but has been largely superseded by graphical Web-based access to electronic resources.

temperature   An important environmental factor affecting the condition of library collections. Paper and other materials used in the production of books expand and contract with changes in temperature, sometimes at unequal rates, creating stresses that contribute to deterioration. Conservators consider 60–70 degrees Fahrenheit best for storing books and other printed materials. The simplest instrument for monitoring temperature is the *thermometer*. A high-low thermometer, checked at the same time each day, is useful for recording temperature over an extended period. Small *thermo-hygrometers* are used to monitor temperature and relative humidity in small enclosed spaces, such as exhibit cases, and *hygrothermographs* are available for charting temperature and relative humidity, usually on a seven-day cycle.

temporarily out of print (TOP)   A term used on a publisher's invoice to indicate that the title ordered cannot be supplied because the last printing is sold out and to inform prospective purchasers that additional copies are expected from the printer in the near future. Compare with *out of print at present*. *See also*: *out of print*.

temporarily out of stock (TOS)   A term used on a publisher's invoice to indicate that the title ordered cannot be supplied because current inventory is exhausted, but additional copies are expected, usually from the binder or manufacturer. Compare with *out of stock*. *See also*: *in stock*.

temporary records   Documents intended by their creator to remain useful for a short time only, which have no archival value and can be discarded or destroyed when no longer needed without loss to the individual or organization, for example, draft versions not required to document a process.

temporary storage   A space within an archive or library facility, or located off-site, where materials, equipment, or supplies are kept for a short time until they can be processed, installed, distributed, transferred to a permanent location, or disposed of in some other way, for example, a large gift collection awaiting examination by selectors.

tenure   The guarantee of permanent employment, granted by an academic institution to a faculty member for satisfactory performance upon completion of a specified number of years of service. A position for which tenure is granted is classified as *tenure-track*. Academic librarians who have *faculty status* are eligible for tenure; those with *academic status* usually are not. In a more general sense, the length of time a person has been employed, or may be expected to be employed, by a company, agency, organization, or institution. Compare with *promotion*.

term   A word, phrase, or symbol, especially one used to represent, in a dictionary, catalog, index, or database, a subject or other feature of a work. *See also*: *search term*.

term frequency (TF)   The number of times a search term occurs in a record or document included in a database, one of the variables used in assigning a weight to the record or document in relation to others retrieved in the same search.

terminal   An electronic device consisting of a computer keyboard and screen or optical scanner, which can be used to enter data (input) and display output from a central computer (usually a minicomputer or mainframe) but is not capable of independent processing. Synonymous with *dumb terminal* and *visual display terminal (VDT)*. Compare with *personal computer* and *thin client*. *See also*: *dedicated*, *emulation*, and *VT100*.

terminal emulation *See*: emulation.

terminology Words, phrases, and symbols representing the concepts and subjects used in a specific field of research, study, or activity, for which the meaning (established by convention or explicit agreement among its practitioners) is clearly defined, sometimes in a published glossary or lexicon. Synonymous with *nomenclature*.

terms of availability The conditions under which a bibliographic item is available for sale in the market place, usually the list price, entered in field 020 or 022 of the MARC record.

ternion In bookbinding, a gathering consisting of three sheets of paper, parchment, or vellum folded once to create six leaves, used in some manuscript books and early printed books. *See also*: *quaternion*, *quinternion*, and *sextern*.

tertiary source A written work, such as a chapter in a textbook or entry in a reference book, based entirely on secondary sources, rather than on original research involving primary documents. Whether a source is secondary or tertiary can be determined by examining the bibliography (if one is provided). Another clue is that secondary sources are almost always written by experts, but tertiary sources may be written by staff writers who have an interest in the topic but are not scholars on the subject.

test collection A library collection consisting of assessment instruments used by researchers and practitioners in education, psychology, counseling, and allied fields. Information on test collections is available in the *Directory of Test Collections in Academic, Professional, and Research Libraries* (2002) published by the Association of College & Research Libraries. Tests are reviewed in the *Mental Measurements Yearbook* published by the Buros Institute of Mental Measurements.

tête-bêche A form of binding in which the text of one work begins at the "front" of the book and the text of a second work at the "back," inverted (upside down) with respect to the other so that their last pages meet somewhere in the middle of the sections. Also, a volume bound in the same manner, which contains different versions of the same text. Compare with *dos-à-dos*.

tetrology *See*: trilogy.

text In a written, printed, or digital work, the words or (in the absence of words) signs or symbols used to express the author's thoughts, feelings, and ideas. Compare with *wordless*. *See also*: *electronic text*, *subtext*, and *textual criticism*.

Also refers to the body of a book, excluding the front matter, back matter, and any notes, illustrations, captions, headings, or other display matter. Also used as a shortened form of *textbook*. *See also*: *text block*.

In library cataloging, the general material designation for printed material that can be read by the human eye without the aid of magnification, for example, a book, pamphlet, periodical, broadside, etc. Also, the words of a song, cycle of songs, or (in the plural) a collection of songs (*AACR2*).

In computing, a machine-readable data file containing elements (letters, characters, ideographs) that can be read as words and sentences, as opposed to a file consisting of nontextual symbols, graphics, audio, and/or video. *See also*: *plain text* and *rich text*. In e-mail, the body of a message, as distinct from its *header* and *footer*.

text block   The gathered signatures of a written or printed book sewn or adhered in a single unit and usually trimmed before attachment to the case or cover, not including any paper added by the binder, such as endpapers or doublures. Compare in this sense with *book block*.

Also used in a narrower sense to refer to the leaves of a book that bear the actual text of the work, as opposed to the front matter, back matter, and any plates printed separately (usually on a different paper stock) to be added in binding.

textbook   An edition of a book specifically intended for the use of students enrolled in a course of study or preparing for an examination on a subject or in an academic discipline, as distinct from the trade edition of the same title, sometimes published in conjunction with a workbook, lab manual, and/or teacher's manual. Also refers to the standard work used for a specific course of study, whether published in special edition or not.

Textbooks are usually ordered by college bookstores in quantity, based on projected course enrollment. The standard publisher's discount on textbook orders is 20 percent. Used copies in good condition may be sold back to the bookstore for resale at a lower price than new copies. *See also*: El-Hi Textbooks & Serials in Print and *textbook edition*.

textbook edition   A trade book issued in a separate edition specifically for the use of students enrolled in a course of study. The format may be altered to make it more useful, for example, by the addition of study questions and bibliographies at the end of each section or chapter. Textbook editions are sold at short discount, usually 20 percent when ordered in quantity. Synonymous with *text edition*.

Text Encoding Initiative (TEI)   Introduced in 1987, TEI is an international interdisciplinary standard intended to assist libraries, museums, publishers, and scholars in representing literary and linguistic texts in digital form to facilitate research and teaching. The encoding scheme is designed to maximize expressivity and minimize obsolescence. TEI began as a research project organized cooperatively by the Association for Computers and the Humanities, the Association for Computational Linguistics, and the Association for Literary and Linguistic Computing, funded by research grants from the National Endowment for the Humanities, the European Union, the Canadian Social Science Research Council, the Mellon Foundation, and others. URL: www. tei-c.org. *See also*: *TEI Header*.

textile binding   A style of bookbinding popular in Europe from the 12th to 15th century in which the boards were covered in velvet and/or silk brocade, usually adorned with gold or silver clasps. From the 16th to 18th century, velvet and satin bindings sumptuously embroidered by skilled needle workers were popular with women of means. Generally fragile, luxury fabrics are easily abraded or torn. Fabric can also be damaged by mold if it becomes wet or damp. For these reasons, few examples of fine textile bindings survive in good condition.

Canvas came into limited use as a binding material in England during the late 18th century, and cotton book cloth was commonly used on book covers in the 19th century, often with embossed grains. Since then, the quality of book cloth has declined, except in library binding where it is governed by strict standards.

text type   Type used to print reading material, for example, the body of a book or other publication, as opposed to the *display type* used to print headings, running titles, etc., or the *extract type* used to print notes and long quotations. Synonymous with *body type*. *See also*: *type size*.

textual criticism   Close study and comparison of the various texts of a literary work to determine the version that reflects most faithfully the writer's intentions, particularly important in the case of older works for which the original manuscript is missing or incomplete or for which multiple versions exist. *See also*: *recension* and textus receptus.

textura   Latin for "weaving" or "woven." In printing, the most formal of the gothic or black letter type fonts, used for early editions of the Bible. Textura is based on the gothic minuscule script widely used in Europe as a book hand during the late Middle Ages. It is characterized by extreme contrast between wide and hairline strokes, narrow letterforms often conjoined at the vertical stroke, short ascenders and descenders, forked ends on ascenders, and a dark, heavy, monotonous aspect to the page caused by compression (the space between vertical strokes reduced to the width of the vertical stroke, and the space between words twice the width of the vertical). Versals were used for important initial letters.

textus receptus   Latin for "received text." The version of a work that, in the absence of indisputable proof to the contrary, is considered by scholars to represent the author's intentions to a greater degree than other versions known to exist. Consensus is reached through the process of textual criticism, as in the case of *The Canterbury Tales* by Geoffrey Chaucer. *See also*: *recension*.

TF   *See*: **t**erm **f**requency.

TGN   *See*: *Getty Thesaurus of Geographic Names*.

Theatre Library Association (TLA)   Established in 1937, TLA has an international membership consisting of curators, librarians, archivists, writers, historians, stage designers, actors, booksellers, collectors, and other individuals with an interest in research in the performing arts and in the collection, preservation, and use of performing arts materials. Based in New York City, TLA is an affiliate of the American Library Association. Its publications include the annual journal *Performing Arts Resources* and the quarterly newsletter *Broadside*. URL: tla.library.unt.edu.

theft   The unauthorized removal of materials or equipment from library premises. Theft and vandalism of library materials is punishable as a misdemeanor in most states in the United States. This persistent problem is controlled by restricting access to the technical processing area and by installing security gates at public exits, equipped with an alarm system automatically activated by a magnetic strip affixed to the item unless the strip is desensitized at checkout. Unfortunately, determined thieves learn to locate and remove the strips to avoid detection. Closed circuit television surveillance systems have been installed in the rare books reading rooms of some large libraries to deter theft. The Association of College and Research Libraries (ACRL) has issued *Guidelines Regarding Thefts in Libraries*. *See also*: *crime* and *stolen book*.

thematic atlas   A book of maps devoted to a specific topic, subject, or theme, usually including text, illustrations, and other graphic material explaining their meaning and significance (*example*: *The Atlas of Endangered Species*).

thematic catalog   A list of the works of a composer, arranged chronologically or by category, in which the major theme is given for each composition, or section of a long composition, usually in a few bars. Some thematic catalogs are devoted to musical works of a particular form and period, usually arranged alphabetically by name of composer. Compare with *thematic index*.

thematic index   A list of the major themes in a musical composition, or group of compositions, usually printed in the front or back of the score, with references to the work(s) in which they appear. For short pieces, the theme is usually given as the first few bars. Compare with *thematic catalog*.

thematic map   A map showing one or more features or aspects of a given area of the surface of the earth or of another celestial body. Thematic maps can be *quantitative*, illustrating statistical data, such as average annual precipitation, or *qualitative*, indicating the distribution of characteristics such as predominant language, ethnic group, religious affiliation, etc.

thesaurus   A book of synonyms and near-synonyms in a written language, usually arranged conceptually, although dictionary arrangement is not uncommon. The first thesaurus of the English language, published in 1852, was compiled by Peter Mark Roget. For an online thesaurus of the English language, please see *Merriam-Webster Online* at: www.merriam-webster.com.

Also refers to an alphabetically arranged lexicon of terms comprising the specialized vocabulary of an academic discipline or field of study, showing the logical and semantic relations among terms, particularly a list of subject headings or descriptors used as preferred terms in indexing the literature of the field. In information retrieval, a thesaurus can be used to locate broader terms and related terms if the user wishes to expand retrieval or narrower terms to make a search statement more specific. A well-designed thesaurus also enables the indexer to maintain consistency in the assignment of indexing terms to documents. Plural: *thesauri*. *See also*: *controlled vocabulary* and *lead-in vocabulary*.

Examples:
  Art & Architecture Thesaurus (AAT)
  GeoRef Thesaurus
  Thesaurus of ERIC Descriptors
  Thesaurus of Psychological Index Terms
  Thesaurus of Sociological Indexing Terms

Thesaurus of Geographic Names   *See*: *Getty Thesaurus of Geographic Names*.

thesis   A proposition advanced and defended in a formal disputation, especially by a candidate in partial fulfillment of university requirements for a master's degree. Master's theses are indexed annually by discipline, subject, and author in *Master's Theses Directories* and in *Disseration Abstracts International*. They can also be located in the *WorldCat* database in OCLC *FirstSearch*. Compare with *dissertation*. *See also*: *praeses* and *respondent*.

In a more general sense, any proposition advanced and defended in expository speech or writing, usually given in the opening lines or paragraph(s).

thesis play   A dramatic work in which the playwright consciously attempts to illustrate a social problem and suggests to the reader or audience a possible solution (*example*: *Mrs. Warren's Profession* by George Bernard Shaw). *See also*: *roman à these*.

thin client   A computer connected to a client-server network that does very little independent processing, all or most of the application processing being done on the server. Also, a client computer capable of downloading a program from a server and processing data like a PC without storing data locally. Compare with *terminal*.

THOMAS   Named in honor of Thomas Jefferson, *THOMAS* is a database designed and maintained since 1995 by the Library of Congress to make legislative information, such as the *Congressional Record*, more accessible to the public. Available on the Internet 24 hours a day free of charge, *THOMAS* also provides answers to FAQs, links to the full-text of historical documents such as the *Declaration of Independence* and the *Constitution of the United States*, and a section on bills recently in the news. URL: thomas.loc.gov.

thong   A sturdy strip of tawed skin or leather used as a wrap-around fastening or as a sewing support in early bookbinding. Thongs were replaced by *cords* made of vegetable fiber as sewing supports in the binding of medieval manuscript books.

thread   A theme or topic that generates an ongoing e-mail discussion among participants in an Internet newsgroup or mailing list, usually repeated in the header of each message posted on the subject. Excerpts from the text of preceding messages may be included in the body of a threaded message. In literature, an idea or theme that connects the various parts of a narrative.

Also refers to the strand (or strands) of spun fiber used in bookbinding to sew the sections of a book together, usually made of cotton or linen in machine-sewn bindings. Silk or linen thread may be used in hand-sewing. Thread is also differentiated by gauge (thickness), the binder's choice depending on whether the paper is hard or soft, thickness of sections, and amount of swell anticipated from the accumulation of sewing thread, which can be reduced in binding by a procedure called *smashing*.

three-decker   A novel published in three octavo volumes. First issued in paper-covered boards without illustration and later in cloth-covered boards, three-deckers became the standard format for Victorian novels published in England between about 1850 and 1870. The discount offered to circulating libraries kept this form of publication going until the 1890s, when inexpensive reprint editions became widely available (*Encyclopedia of the Book*, Oak Knoll/British Library, 1996).

three on   *See*: two on.

three-quarter binding   A style of bookbinding in which the spine and corners are bound in a different material than the sides, usually a more durable covering such as leather. Similar to half-binding except that the corners are larger and the material covering the spine extends up to half the width of the boards. Compare with *full binding* and *quarter binding*.

three-quarter border   *See*: full border.

thriller   A novel, play, or motion picture that produces feelings of intense excitement in the reader or audience by depicting dangerous action (crime, espionage, etc.), usually culminating in a narrow escape in which a high level of suspense is maintained up to the final denouement (*example*: Alfred Hitchcock's film **North by Northwest**). In the *techno-thriller*, the plot often turns on the inner workings of technology, approaching science fiction when the technology is speculative. Tom Clancy's **The Hunt for Red October** is considered the first techno-thriller.

throw-out   A leaf larger than the book block, usually bearing a map, table, diagram, wide-angle photograph, or other illustration, sewn or tipped in and folded so that it can be opened out for reference while the corresponding text is read. Also spelled *throwout*. Synonymous with *fold-out* and *pull-out*. *See also*: gatefold.

thumb book   *See*: bibelot.

thumbed   The condition of a book soiled from heavy use, usually on the edges of the sections and/or binding.

thumb index   A series of semicircular thumb-sized notches cut into the fore-edge of a book, bearing a sequence of letters, words, numbers, or symbols, usually printed against a dark background to show the alphabetic, subject, numeric, or other arrangement of the text and facilitate reference, seen most often in hardcover editions of language dictionaries and handbooks. Compare with *step index* and *tab index*.

thumbnail   A very small image of a page of text or graphic element used in a Web page as a link to the same image in larger format. Since thumbnail graphics take less time to load than a full-size image, they are often used in Web pages to provide the option of enlarging an image without significantly increasing the time required to transmit the document.

In the context of medieval manuscript production, a small rough sketch of *mis-en-page*, made before copying begins, to indicate to scribe and illuminator the arrangement of text, illustration, and decoration on the page.

tie-in   In publishing, a magazine or book issued in conjunction with a motion picture, dramatic performance, or television program for promotional reasons. Book tie-ins are usually published in paperback edition, with cover art derived from the production. A tie-in is often a novelization, but if the production is based on a published work of fiction or nonfiction, the tie-in may replace the original edition, at least until interest in the film or television version wanes. However, if backlist sales remain strong, the original edition may be retained to attract a more literary audience. Libraries prefer to purchase the regular edition because the association of movie tie-ins with Hollywood repels some readers. Compare with *companion book*.

tier   One of two or more distinct levels, as of shelves in a section of library shelving, priorities for resource allocation or acquisition, payment or benefit options in a health care plan, etc.

ties   Narrow strips of leather, cloth, ribbon, or other material attached in pairs to the boards of a book, usually along the fore-edge but sometimes also at head and foot, enabling the binding to be tied shut when not in use. Some older bindings have clasps or straps for the same purpose. Ties are also commonly used on modern portfolios.

TIFF   An acronym for **T**agged **I**mage **F**ile **F**ormat, a widely supported data format developed by Aldus and Microsoft for storing black and white, gray scale, or color bitmapped images. Files in TIFF format may be uncompressed or compressed using LZW or a variety of other compression schemes. They usually have the extension *.tif* or *.tiff* added to the filename. *See also*: *GIF* and *JPEG*.

tight   The condition of a book so tightly bound that the spine is inflexible, preventing the leaves from opening and staying open at a particular page. As new books are used, their bindings gradually loosen, allowing them to open flat at any page. Library bindings are usually tighter than trade bindings. Compare with *tight back*.

tight back   A method of binding in which the back of a volume is glued to the cover, leaving no hollow to allow the binding to flex as it is opened. Books bound by this method do not open flat. Another disadvantage is that the lettering printed on the spine tends to crack with extended use. For these reasons, hardcover editions are nearly always bound with a *hollow back*. Synonymous with *fast back*.

tilde   A mark in the form of a horizontal inverted "s" (~) used as a diacritical mark over certain letters in the Spanish and Portuguese languages to indicate pronunciation, as a symbol indicating negation in logic and the geometric relation "is similar to" in mathematics, and in URLs, usually followed by the name of the person responsible for creating and/or maintaining the Web page.

'til forbid   An instruction, usually given by the purchaser of a subscription, to treat the title as a continuation order until further notification. Synonymous with *till-forbid order*.

time-expired records   In archives, temporary records assigned a specific date for destruction that has passed without the occurrence of appropriate action, usually due to a backlog in processing.

timeout   In computing, a routine that automatically terminates a period of waiting when a screen requiring user input receives no response within a designated time, for example, an interface that logs off whenever a predetermined period of inactivity occurs during an online session. The term is also used in communications to refer to the automatic termination of a waiting period when no response is received. Also spelled *time out*.

timesheet   *See*: payroll.

Times Literary Supplement (TLS)   First published in 1902, *TLS* is one of the most influential book review publications in the United Kingdom. Published weekly in newspaper format, it provides in-depth reviews of current fiction and nonfiction on a wide range of subjects, as well as reviews of contemporary theater, opera, and film. Like its American counterparts, the *New York Review of Books* and the *New York Times Book Review*, *TLS* is noted for its coverage of literary works. It also carries announcements of new books published by scholarly and university presses. ISSN: 0307–661X. URL: www.the-tls.co.uk.

tinted drawing   A style of medieval manuscript illumination in which the subject is first outlined in black or colored ink and a lightly tinted color wash added to some or all of the drawing to give the impression of modeling. Michelle Brown notes in *Understanding Illuminated Manuscripts* (Getty Museum/British Library, 1994) that this technique, sometimes combined with fully painted design elements, was first popularized in Anglo-Saxon England, then revived in 13th-century England in the work of Matthew Paris and the Court School of Henry III. Synonymous with *pen and wash*.

tintype   A positive photographic image made with a wet collodion emulsion on a thin iron plate darkened with black lacquer. As in a *daguerreotype*, the image is reversed laterally. Inexpensive and fast, the process was widely used for portraiture from the 1850s to the end of the 19th century, bringing photographic images within reach of the masses. In the 1880s, the wet emulsion was replaced by a dry gelatin. Synonymous with *ferrotype*.

tip in   *See*: tipped in.

tipped in   A single leaf, errata slip, or separately printed map or illustration trimmed to page size and pasted into a book against the following page after the text has been printed and bound, by applying a thin line of adhesive to one of its edges, usually the one closest to the binding edge. A tipped in leaf ("paste-in") may be somewhat restricted in its openability. *See also*: *guard*.

tissue   A sheet of very thin paper inserted loose between the leaves of a book or affixed to the inner margin, usually to protect the surface of a plate or prevent the offset of fresh ink onto the facing page.

title   A word, phrase, sentence, single character, or sequence of characters usually appearing on or in an item, naming the work(s) contained in it, for purposes of identification and reference. Choice of title usually reflects the content of the work, distinguishing it from others of similar subject. A *subtitle* may be included following a colon or semicolon. Translations may have a *parallel title* in the original language. The full title is usually printed on the *title page* of a book or at the beginning of an article or essay published in a book or periodical. The title given on the title page may differ from the one printed or impressed on the spine or cover. In a film or videorecording, the title is usually given in the first few frames.

In library cataloging, the *title proper* is entered in the title and statement of responsibility area of the bibliographic description as it appears on the chief source of information. A work published under more than one title is cataloged under a *uniform title* (*example*: **Bible**). The term is also used in a less precise way to refer to any bibliographic item known by its title, as in the phrase "list of titles ordered." *See also*: *alternative title, binder's title, catchword title, chapter title, cover title, divisional title, edge title, half title, partial title, running title, series title, short title, side title, spine title, supplied title, title change,* and *working title.*

Also refers to a formal name or appellation given to an individual or family in recognition of privilege, distinction, office, or profession, for example, baron, saint, president, doctor, etc. In *AACR2*, titles of nobility are included in the personal name heading when used to refer to the individual, titles indicating high office are given in English whenever possible, and titles of address (Miss, Mr., Mrs., etc.) are omitted from the heading, as are minor ecclesiastical titles, military titles, academic and professional titles, and government titles below the highest rank.

In employment, the official name assigned to a specific position within the organization, for example, *Instruction Librarian*. Usually based on function, library position titles vary from one institution to another (*Instructional Services Librarian*).

title and statement of responsibility   In library cataloging, the area of bibliographic description in which the title proper of a work and information concerning authorship (statement of responsibility) are recorded (field 245 of the MARC record).

title change   The title proper of a publication bearing a title different from the one under which it was previously published. In *AACR2*, a title proper is considered to have changed if any word (other than an article, preposition, or conjunction) is added, deleted, or changed, or if the order of the first five words is altered, necessitating the creation of a new bibliographic record. *AACR2 2002* adopts the ISBD terminology "major" and "minor" to describe title changes and recognizes five additional categories of minor change that can be simply noted in the existing record. *See also*: *retitled edition.*

Title changes occur most often in serial publications, compounding the work of librarians and complicating access for users. A new bibliographic record must be created for each successive serial title, with a *Continues*: note given in the record representing the new title and a *Continued by*: note in the record for the earlier title. Latest entry cataloging is used for integrating resources. *See also*: *earliest entry* and *title varies.*

title frame   One or more frames usually found at the beginning of a work produced on film (motion picture, filmstrip, etc.), containing textual information distinct from the subject content, used as the chief source of information in creating the bibliographic record that describes the item in the library catalog. Compare with *title screen.*

title index   An alphabetically arranged list of the titles of the works covered in a serial or nonserial publication (*example*: the *Film Title Index* in **America: History and Life**). Title and author indexes are sometimes combined. *See also*: *subject index.*

title leaf   The leaf of a book bearing the title page on the recto and the publisher's imprint, notice of copyright, cataloging-in-publication (CIP), ISBN, and printing history on the verso. In the front matter of a book, the title leaf follows the half title and precedes the dedication.

title page   The page at the beginning of a manuscript, book, or other printed publication, often of special design, bearing the title proper of the work and usually, but not necessarily, the name of the author(s), editor(s), translator(s), and publisher or printer and in some cases the volume number (if applicable) and date and place of publication. The title page is the chief source of information used by librarians in cataloging a book. In most books, the title page is the recto of the leaf following the half title. The verso of the title leaf bears the notice of copyright, publication date, publisher's imprint, CIP, ISBN, and in some cases, the printer's imprint.

According to Geoffrey Glaister, the first complete title pages appeared in early printed books around 1500, and by the late 16th century the decorative possibilities of the title page had been fully realized (*Encyclopedia of the Book*, Oak Knoll/British Library, 1996). For a scholarly treatment of the early history of the title page, see *The Title-Page: Its Early Development, 1460–1510* (British Library/Oak Knoll, 2000) by Margaret M. Smith. Abbreviated *tp*. Also spelled *title-page*. Compare with *title piece*. *See also*: *added title page* and *series title page*.

title piece   Before it was customary to include title pages in books, some manuscripts bore the title on a decorative panel or page or on a label attached to the binding. The style of presentation and location of the title piece may suggest the methods used in storing a book and provide clues to its provenance.

title proper   The primary name of a bibliographic item, usually found on the chief source of information, including any alternative title but not parallel titles or other title information. In *AACR2*, the title proper is entered in the title and statement of responsibility area of the bibliographic description (field 245 of the MARC record). *See also*: *uniform title*.

title screen   In an electronic resource, such as a bibliographic database or Web page, a display of text giving the title proper of the work and, in most cases, the name of the author(s), editor(s), or compiler (statement of responsibility) and details of publication, used in library cataloging as the chief source of information in creating the bibliographic description of the resource. Compare with *title frame*.

title statement   The title proper of a work, plus the optional general material designation and remainder of the title (if applicable), given in the title and statement of responsibility area of the bibliographic description (field 245 of the MARC record). In *AACR2*, the wording, order, and spelling of the title proper is followed exactly as it appears in or on the item, but punctuation and capitalization may be changed by the cataloger.

title varies   A phrase used as a note in the bibliographic record of a serial publication to indicate that the title appears in slightly different form from one issue or volume to another, when it is clear that the publisher did not intend a change of title, or when nearly all the issues or volumes bear one title, discrepancies occurring in only a few random issues or volumes.

titulus   Introductory words added in capital letters by a rubrisher in red or blue ink in a space left blank at the beginning of a chapter when the text of a medieval manuscript was hand-copied, often filling several lines. Gold leaf was used instead of ink in more important works. *See also*: *illuminated*.

TLA   *See*: Theatre Library Association.

TLD   *See*: top level domain.

TLS   *See*: *Times Literary Supplement*.

TOC   *See*: table of contents.

tome   Originally, any volume of a work published in more than one volume. In modern usage, a book of very large size, also weighty in subject or treatment. Pronounced like "Rome."

toolbar   A narrow band along one side or across the top or bottom of a window or frame in the graphical user interface of a microcomputer application, displaying a row of buttons or icons that can be clicked with a pointing device such as a mouse to access menus and open other windows, allowing the user to select options, set parameters, and perform functions. Compare with *navigation bar*.

tooling   A finishing technique in which decorative designs are hand-stamped with a heated brass tool on the outer surface of a book covered in leather or cloth. A *fillet* produces a straight line, a *roll* or *wheel* makes a continuous ornamental strip, and individual *tools* create small motifs that can be repeated to form patterns. *Blind tooling* usually darkens the surface slightly. In *gold tooling*, the brass die is pressed through gold leaf or foil onto a surface prepared with an adhesive such as glair. Tooling can also be done in ink. Compare in this sense with *blocking*. In medieval illuminated manuscripts, gilded surfaces in miniatures, initial letters, and ornamental borders were sometimes tooled for decorative effect. *See also*: *gauffered edges*.

toolkit   A printed or online guide that brings together in one place practical information for accomplishing a goal or beginning a project, including but not limited to case studies, action plans, policies, learning modules, resource lists, useful terminology, important contacts, etc. (*example*: ***The Ethnographer's Toolkit***, edited by Jean Schensul and Margaret LeCompte). Also spelled *tool kit*.

In computing, a set of programs, scripts, macros, documentation, and other aids to help a developer build applications faster.

tooth   *See*: nap.

TOP   *See*: temporarily out of print.

topic   A subject for research or discussion. The first step in a library research project is the formulation of a workable *topic statement*. As a literature search progresses, the topic may require refinement (change of specificity or focus), depending on the amount of published information available and the time constraints of the researcher. *See also*: *search strategy*.

topical guide   A printed or online list or description of the best bibliographic tools and resources available to a researcher for conducting a literature search on a specific topic, presented in the sequence in which they would optimally be used. Also known as a *pathfinder*. *See also*: *search strategy*.

topical subdivision   In library cataloging, the division of a class or subject heading to limit the concept to a specific subtopic (action, attribute, aspect, etc.) by the addition of notation or a subheading following a dash or other mark of punctuation, as in the addition of the subheading **—Security measures** to the Library of Congress subject heading **Libraries** to form the heading **Libraries—Security measures**. A topical subdivision can itself be subdivided topically, as in the addition of **—Planning** to create the more specific heading **Libraries—Security measures—Planning**.

top level domain (TLD)   The last portion of an IP address, indicating the type of entity serving as network host; for example, in the URL: **www.xyzuniversity.edu**, the top level domain **.edu** indicates that the host is an educational institution. In the United States, seven generic Top Level Domains (gTLDs) were established in the 1980s (.com, .edu, .gov, .int, .mil, .net, and .org). Domain names may be registered without restriction in three of these (.com, .net, and .org); the other four have limited uses. In November 2000, the Internet Corporation for Assigned Names and Numbers (ICANN) authorized seven new TLDs (.aero, .biz, .coop, .info, .museum, .name, and .pro) and is considering proposals to activate additional TLDs. There are also over 240 two-character country code Top Level Domains (ccTLDs) representing countries (*example*: **.uk** for the United Kingdom) and external territories (**.vg** for the British Virgin Islands), many with subdomains (**.co.uk** for commercial enterprises in the UK).

topo   *See*: topographic map.

topographic map   A map on any scale showing in relief the geographic features of a given area of the surface of the earth (or another celestial body), usually by means of contour lines. When unbound, such a map is called a *topographic sheet*. Abbreviated *topo*.

topographic series   A group of topographic sheet maps showing the geographic features of the surface of a country at scales of 1:10,000 to 1:250,000, usually issued by an agency of civilian or military government, such as a national survey or mapping division of a defense department. Topographic series are also issued internationally at scales of 1:1,000,000 to 1:5,000,000. *See also*: *base map*.

top-stain   A solid color applied as decoration to the trimmed upper edge of the sections of a book.

top term (TT)   The most general term in a hierarchical classification system, indicated by the abbreviation TT in the thesaurus of indexing terms (*example*: *INSPEC Thesaurus*) or by the narrowest indention under the heading to which it applies. *See also*: *broader term*, *narrower term*, and *related term*.

tortoise-shell binding   A style of 17th-century luxury bookbinding with boards and spine covered in thin pieces of polished tortoise shell, often embellished with silver fittings.

TOS   *See*: temporarily out of stock.

total circulation   In publishing, the entire distribution of any issue of a newspaper or periodical, including copies sent to paid subscribers, single-copy retail sales, in-house use, and complimentary copies distributed for promotional purposes.

total publication   An agreement between an author and publisher in which a work is issued in hardcover and also in a mass-market paperback edition under the publisher's separate paperback imprint, as opposed to leasing the paperback rights to an independent publisher for which the author is usually paid a higher royalty. The term does *not* apply to simultaneous publication under a single imprint of hardcover and softcover trade editions or to the subsequent issuance of a trade paperback edition in which the text and illustrations remain the same as in the hardcover edition.

touchpad   An electronic pointing device consisting of a small flat surface connected to a computer, which the user can activate with the touch of a finger, instead of depressing the keys on a keyboard or moving a mouse. Synonymous with *touch panel*. Compare with *touch screen*.

touch screen   A computer screen covered with a clear touch-sensitive panel that enables the user to make selections from a menu of options or initiate specific operations by touching the part of the screen that displays the appropriate word, phrase, symbol, icon, or button. Pressure-sensitive cells in the panel transmit data to the screen software, activating the selection. Also spelled *touchscreen*. Compare with *touchpad*. *See also*: *mouse*.

toy   A three-dimensional object designed for imaginative play or to provide amusement to children or adults. In a more general sense, a *plaything* contrived for amusement rather than for practical use. Some public libraries maintain toy collections (puppets, games, etc.), sometimes available for loan, helpful in serving families, especially in low-income communities. *See also*: *game*.

toy book   A small, illustrated book for young children, published in 19th-century England and America, usually consisting of eight leaves of vivid, hand-colored pictures with very little text (alphabets and simple tales were popular). Originally issued in paper covers, later variations included cloth books printed on sturdy fabric, pop-up books, and flicker books. Toy books were often published in series to encourage gift buying and collecting.

tracing   A record of the additional headings under which a bibliographic item is listed in a library catalog, usually associated with the main entry, enabling the cataloger to "trace" all the entries referring to the item whenever a change or correction is made or when the item is withdrawn from the collection. In an authority file, a record of all the references made to and from the headings to be used in a given file of bibliographic records (adapted from *The ALA Glossary of Library and Information Science*, ALA, 1983). Often used in the plural: *tracings*.

track   In information storage and retrieval, one of the concentric rings or spirals on the surface of a magnetic disk on which data is recorded. A standard floppy disk has either 80 tracks (double-density) or 160 tracks (high-density). In sound recording, one or more optical or magnetic bands running parallel with the long dimension of an audiotape, videotape, or film on which signals are recorded for playback as synchronized sound. In a general sense, the portion of a moving storage medium accessible to a single reading device (*The Bookman's Glossary*, R.R. Bowker, 1983).

tract   A book or pamphlet containing a treatise or discourse on a political, social, or religious topic, usually issued as propaganda or for doctrinal purposes. Also refers to a pamphlet made from a single sheet of printing paper folded one or more times to create leaves.

trade association   An organization dedicated to promoting a specific line of business, such as the book trade, for example, the Association of American Publishers or the American Booksellers Association. Most trade associations publish a trade journal to keep members informed of new products and developments affecting their interests. Directory information on book trade associations is available in the annual reference serial *Literary Market Place*.

trade binding   The plain, unlettered calf or sheepskin binding used by booksellers of the 15th to 18th centuries on books bound in advance of sale, as opposed to *craft binding* executed per the customer's instructions. Also used synonymously with *publisher's binding*.

trade book   A general term encompassing quality fiction and nonfiction for adults, trade paperbacks, and children's books issued by a commercial publisher for sale to the general public, as distinct from mass-market paperbacks, reference books, scholarly books, textbooks, and other books intended for a limited market segment. The standard publisher's discount on trade books is 40 percent. *See also*: *trade bookstore* and *trade publisher*.

trade bookstore   A bookstore that sells books of good quality, published for the general public rather than for a narrow segment of the market. Large chains may also sell newspapers, general interest magazines, videorecordings, DVDs, music CDs, road maps, calendars, greeting cards, etc. (*examples*: **Barnes and Noble** and **Borders Books & Music**). Trade bookstores normally do not stock expensive reference books, scholarly and technical books, and textbooks. Mass-market paperbacks are stocked selectively, based on reputation of author.

trade catalog   A list of all the books (currently in print) published in a specific country or in other countries for which domestic publishers act as agents (*example*: *Books in Print*). Also, any publication that lists and describes the products manufactured and sold by a commercial company, with prices, illustrations, and information on how to order, for use in sales. The publisher's catalogs sent by post to booksellers and libraries are a prime example. Some booksellers also publish their own trade catalogs for distribution to potential retail customers or make catalog information available on the Web.

trade directory   A serial publication, usually issued annually, listing the companies and organizations engaged in buying, selling, or exchanging a specific category of goods and services. Entries include the official name, mailing address, phone/fax numbers, key personnel, and other important information (*example*: ***American Book Trade Directory*** published by R.R. Bowker).

trade edition   An edition produced by a trade publisher in hardcover and/or paperback publisher's binding for sale to quality booksellers and libraries. Trade editions are published for the general reader, rather than a specific segment of the market. Compare with *mass-market paperback*, *scholarly book*, and *textbook*.

trade journal   A periodical devoted to disseminating news and information of interest to a specific category of business or industry, often published by a trade association. Some trade journals are available in an online version, as well as in print (*example*: ***Publishers Weekly*** at: www.publishersweekly.com/index.asp).

trade list   *See*: trade catalog.

trademark   A letter, numeral, word, phrase, logo, device, design, sound, or symbol (or combination of these) used in connection with a product or service to signify, directly or by association, the identity of the owner, usually a commercial enterprise that has reserved to itself the use of the distinctive mark by registering it with the U.S. Patent and Trademark Office. Trademarks of successful products and services are jealously guarded by their owners to prevent competitors from imitating them. Registration, indicated by a small "R" inside a circle ® following the name ("TM" if registration is pending), gives the owner the right to legal redress in case of infringement. Also spelled *trade mark*. ***See also***: *infringement* and *patent and trademark depository library*.

trade name   The name used to designate a specific business enterprise and the reputation it has acquired in the market place (*example*: **Microsoft**), as distinct from any trademark associated with the firm's products (*Windows*). ***See also***: *brand name*.

trade paperback   A softcover edition published by a university press or trade publisher in larger format and better-quality binding than a mass-market paperback, for retail sale in college and trade bookstores. Most trade editions are published first in hardcover, then reprinted in paperback from the same plates after sales potential in hardcover has been realized. In some instances, paperback rights are sold by the original publisher to a trade paperback publisher. Synonymous with *quality paperback*. Compare with *mass-market paperback*.

trade publisher   A publishing house that issues books of interest to the educated reader, for sale in college and quality retail bookstores, for example, Farrar, Straus and Giroux or St. Martin's Press. Few large trade publishers remain independent. A case in point is Alfred A. Knopf, now owned by Random House, which is in turn owned by the international publishing and entertainment conglomerate Bertelsmann AG. Compare with *popular press* and *university press*. ***See also***: *trade book* and *trade edition*.

tragedy   A literary work in prose or verse in which a catastrophe or sudden reversal of fortune befalls the protagonist, usually due to uncontrollable circumstances (*example*: Arthur Miller's ***Death of a Salesman***) or as a result of an error of judgment or serious flaw in character (***Macbeth***). In classical Greek drama, the weakness that brings about the downfall of the tragic hero (or heroine) is typically *hubris* (pride). Compare with *comedy* and *tragicomedy*.

tragicomedy   A form of drama that originated in Elizabethan and Jacobean England, combining the forms and conventions of tragedy *and* comedy, usually by including characters of both high and low social position and by unfolding unfortunate events that unexpectedly result in a happy ending (*example*: Shakespeare's play **Cymbeline**).

trailer   A very short film used primarily for advertising purposes, consisting of carefully selected extracts from a longer motion picture to be shown at a later date. In library cataloging, the term is added inside square brackets [trailer] following the title proper in the bibliographic description to indicate material type. Compare with *film clip*. **See also**: *preview*.

Also refers to the short strip of film without images at the end of a filmstrip, motion picture, or unexposed roll of film added to allow the item to be handled without damage. Compare with *leader*.

training   Instruction designed to teach a person or group of people (*trainees*) a specific skill or set of skills, for example, how to check books and other materials in and out at the circulation desk of a library or how to reshelve items in correct call number sequence. *In-service training* occurs in the workplace during normal working hours, sometimes in the context in which the skill(s) will be used.

transaction log   A continuous record of the operations initiated by users of an automated system during a designated period of time (week, month, year). In online catalogs and bibliographic databases, the "transactions" are usually searches recorded by type (author, title, subject, keywords, etc.) that can be analyzed to reveal usage patterns and longitudinal changes in search behavior. **See also**: *peak use*.

Also refers to a record kept for statistical purposes of the number of library patrons who receive assistance from staff at a service point, or the number of questions answered by librarians at the reference desk, usually broken down by type of question (directional, informational, instructional, referral).

transactions   The published papers or abstracts of papers presented at a conference or meeting of a society or association, usually including a record of what transpired. Compare with *proceedings*.

transcribe   To make a written or typewritten copy, usually of a speech, broadcast, sound recording, or other oral presentation, or a copy of notes taken on the content of such a presentation. **See also**: *transcript*.

Also, to adapt or arrange a piece of music for a voice, instrument, or ensemble different from that for which the work was originally intended. In computing, to copy a data or program file from one external storage medium to another without altering its content.

transcript   A copy of an original, usually made by hand or typewritten, particularly a legal document or official record. Also refers to the written record of words spoken in court proceedings or in a speech, interview, broadcast, or sound recording. **See also**: *transcribe*.

transfer   A change in the physical custody of archival materials from one location or agency to another, usually without a corresponding change of legal ownership and responsibility, for example, the relocation of records no longer current to temporary storage to await final disposition.

translation   A passage from a speech or written work, or an entire speech or work, put into the words of another language (English into Spanish) or into a more modern form of the same language (Old English or Middle English into contemporary English), usually to make the text more accessible to individuals who are unable to read it in the original language. Translations differ in the degree to which they follow the original. The name of the *translator* usually appears on the title page of a book, following the name of the author. A translation may have a parallel title in the source language. In library cataloging, the note *Translation of:* is added in the bibliographic description, giving the title in the original language. Abbreviated *trans.*

translator   A person who renders speech or text from one language into another or from an older form of a language into a more modern form. Translations of a work may differ in fidelity to the original. Name of translator usually appears on the title page of a book, following the name of the author. In *AACR2*, name of translator is recorded in the statement of responsibility area of the bibliographic description, following name of author, and an added entry may be made in the name under prescribed conditions.

transliteration   Rendering the characters of one alphabet in characters representing the same sound (or sounds) in another alphabet (*example*: **Greek** or **Cyrillic** into **Roman**). Each character is treated independently of the others. *See also*: *romanization*.

transparency   A sheet of transparent material bearing text and/or image in color or black and white, sometimes mounted in a frame, for projection on a large screen using an overhead projector or document camera. Standard size for film transparencies is $8\frac{1}{2} \times 11$ inches. Presentation software has replaced overhead transparencies, but a well-prepared presenter brings them as backup in case of equipment or network failure. Compare with *overlay*.

travel book   A work of nonfiction in which the author describes, for the enjoyment and consideration of the reader, his or her travel experiences, usually in a specific region or country (a modern example: *Travels with Charley: In Search of America* by John Steinbeck). Travel books became popular during the 19th century when railroads and steamships made long-distance travel more accessible to writers. Compare with *travel guide*.

travel guide   A handbook designed for persons interested in touring a foreign country or an unfamiliar city, state, province, or region of their own country. In addition to describing major attractions, most travel guides include maps and directions, information about dining and overnight accommodations, and advice about currency exchange, immunizations, personal safety, and communication with the local inhabitants. Some guides specialize in a particular type of travel, such as bicycle touring or ecotourism.

In public libraries, travel guides are usually shelved by call number in the nonfiction section. Some academic libraries keep current editions in reference. Because currency is important, travel guides may be placed on standing order. Synonymous with *tour guide*. Compare with *guidebook* and *travel book*.

treasure   An item that is extremely rare and very valuable, in some cases unique and priceless, usually stored under controlled conditions in a library's special collections. Some libraries exhibit their treasures (see *Book of Kells*); others make them accessible through digitization.

treasure binding   A luxurious cover made from precious metals, usually by a jeweler or metalworker, often ornamented with gems, carved ivory, or enamelwork, in the form of a separate case into which a book was inserted or as removable plaques that could be transferred from the boards of one binding to another. During the Middle Ages, treasure bindings were reserved for the most highly prized liturgical books used on the altar on important feast days. When not in use, they were stored in the *treasury*, rather than in the monastery library. Compare with *jeweled binding*.

treasure hunt   An exercise in which students are required by their instructor to use the resources of the library to find answers to a list of very specific and often unrelated questions, sometimes as a contest. This type of assignment usually puts a temporary strain on the reference desk, especially when a large number of students converge on the library, all needing the same information at the same time. For this reason, it is one of the "pet peeves" of reference librarians who believe library skills are best learned in the context of a more meaningful research assignment.

treatise   A book or long formal essay, usually on an abstruse or complex subject, especially a systematic well-documented presentation of facts or evidence and the principles or conclusions drawn from them. The term is sometimes used in a pejorative sense to refer to a written work in which the treatment is dry and scholarly or unnecessarily thorough or detailed.

treatment   A narrative account of the screenplay for a motion picture or television broadcast, including a detailed description of characters, scenes, sets, camerawork, etc., but without the dialogue. Compare with *scenario*.

In a more general sense, the manner in which a subject or theme is handled stylistically in a literary or artistic work (comically, tragically, satirically, etc.).

In conservation, use of a specific technique or set of procedures to deliberately alter the chemical or physical condition of a document or other object for the purpose of prolonging its existence, including stabilization and possible restoration. *See also*: *treatment history*.

treatment history   A record of the conservation procedures applied to an item (deacidification, fumigation, rebinding, restoration, etc.), usually including date of application and any details concerning the treatment process that might be of future use to conservators, particularly in cases requiring reversal.

treaty   A formal written agreement between two or more governments concerning peace, military alliance, trade relations, economic assistance, etc., often the result of protracted negotiations. Also refers to the signed document serving as the official record of such an agreement. The texts of important treaties are available in the government documents or reference section of large libraries. The originals are usually housed in national archives or in the special collections of national libraries.

tree calf   A decorative design in the form of a gnarled tree on the leather binding of a book, produced by pouring streams of water down the inclined surface of the tanned skin in the direction of a central point at the foot of the board. The area is then sprinkled with *copperas* (copper or iron sulfate) and salts of tartar, which react with the calfskin in the presence of moisture, leaving a permanent dark pattern resembling a tree trunk and branches. Geoffrey Glaister notes in *Encyclopedia of the Book* (Oak Knoll/British Library, 1996) that the chemical reaction may continue long after the book is bound, causing the covers to eventually disintegrate. The style was popular from the 1770s until the late 1920s. Synonymous with *tree-marbled calf*. *See also*: *mottled calf*.

tree structure   A classified display in a thesaurus of indexing terms showing the complete hierarchy of descriptors, from the broadest to the most specific, usually by indention, sometimes with a tree number indicating the location of the heading in the tree, as in the *Medical Subject Headings*. *Tree Structures* developed and maintained by the National Library of Medicine:

Example:

Diagnosis	E1
Diagnosis, Cardiovascular	E1.145
Angiography	E1.145.77
Angiocardiography	E1.145.102
Angiography, Digital subtraction	E1.145.141
Aortography	E1.145.181
Cerebral angiography	E1.145.300
Cineangiography	E1.145.385
Angioscopy	E1.145.90

See also: *explode*.

trend   Movement in the development of a phenomenon, usually in a certain direction, sometimes measured statistically. Organizations use *trend analysis* to anticipate future developments that might affect their interests. The term is also used in the more general sense of "current fashion." In large public libraries, a recent trend has been to include, in plans for renovation and new construction, a gift shop operated by the Friends of the Library. Academic libraries are more likely to provide a cybercafe on the premises.

trial   A test conducted for a limited period of time to determine the suitability of a new person in a position or the quality or feasibility of a new system, product, or service. Database vendors usually offer a free 30-day trial to libraries as an inducement to subscribe.

trial user   A person or organization asked to use a new service or computer system, usually for a limited period of time, to test its usefulness and effectiveness and to help identify problems that need to be corrected before the final version is released for general use.

triennial   Issued every three years. Also refers to a serial publication issued every three years. *See also*: *annual*, *biennial*, *quadrennial*, *quinquennial*, *sexennial*, *septennial*, and *decennial*.

trilogy   A set of three narrative works related in theme or plot, which together form a larger work (*example*: the **Oresteia** of Aeschylus). Four similarly related works are called a *tetrology* (**The Alexandria Quartet** by Lawrence Durrell). *See also*: *prequel* and *sequel*.

trimmed   A term used in the book trade to indicate that the leaves of a book have been cut down to a size smaller than the publication as originally issued. *See also*: *trimming*.

trimming   In bookbinding, the process of slicing approximately one-eighth of an inch from the head, tail, and fore-edge of the body of a book to remove the folds of its signatures, done on a machine called a *guillotine*. In paperback books, the cover is usually cut flush or even with the sections. Compare with *uncut*. *See also*: *shaved*.

trim size   The finished dimensions of a printed sheet or publication after waste has been trimmed away to prepare it for binding, usually indicated in the specifications for the print job.

triptych   *See*: diptych.

triquarterly   Issued three times a year. Also refers to a serial publication issued three times a year.

trompe l'oeil   A French phrase meaning "deceives the eye." In illuminated manuscripts, painting that creates the illusion of three-dimensional reality, sometimes with startling effect. By controlling light and shadow, the illuminator represents objects as if resting on or projecting from the painted surface. In 15th-century Flemish manuscripts, the technique was used extensively in decorative borders.

true crime story   A nonfiction narrative in which the subject is an actual crime (murder, abduction, theft, etc.) so serious, bizarre, or inexplicable that it excites popular interest and curiosity (*example*: **Small Sacrifices: A True Story of Passion and Murder** by Ann Rule). Unusual serial murders and murderers often receive book-length treatment. Compare with *crime fiction*.

truncation   The dropping of characters and the addition of a symbol at the end, beginning, or within a word in a keywords search to retrieve variant forms. Truncation is particularly useful in retrieving the *singular* and *plural* forms of a word in the same search.

Example:
  librar to retrieve records containing "interlibrary," "intralibrary," "librarian," "librariana," "librarianship," "libraries," "library," etc.

In most online catalogs and bibliographic databases, the end truncation symbol is the * (asterisk), but since the truncation symbol is not standardized, other symbols may be used (?, $, #, +). In some databases, the user may add a number after the symbol to specify how many characters the symbol may represent (*example*: **facet?1** to retrieve "facets" but not "faceted" or "facetiae").

As a general rule, it is unwise to truncate fewer than four characters (*example*: **art*** retrieves "artist," "artistic," "artistry," and "artwork" but also "artichoke," "artillery," etc.). Some databases are designed to truncate automatically. Users are advised to read carefully any help screens before truncating in an unfamiliar database. Synonymous with *character masking*. *See also*: *wildcard*.

trustee   *See*: library trustee.

TT   *See*: top term.

turnaround time   In data processing, the amount of time that elapses between the initiation of a process or operation and its completion. Compare with *response time*.

turn-in   In bookbinding, the portion of the covering of a book folded over the head, tail, and fore-edge of the boards, from outside to inside, mitered at the corners, and covered to within one-eighth to three-sixteenths inch of the edge by the paste-down. On *library corners*, the turn-in is folded; on *Dutch corners*, it is cut. On fine leather bindings, the turn-ins may be decorated.

turnover   The rate at which employees leave a company, organization, or institution and are replaced. A high *turnover rate* may be a sign of difficult working conditions, inadequate compensation, poor management, burnout, etc.

Also, a measure of library use computed by dividing circulation by number of items owned, usually for a specific category of resource. Turnover for media items (videocassettes, DVDs, CDs, etc.) is usually measured in days; for books, in weeks. Turnover is influenced by shelf arrangement and point-of-use marketing (displays, themes, tie-ins, etc.).

tutorial   A printed or online instructional tool designed to teach novices how to use a computer system or electronic resource, usually in a self-paced step-by-step manner, often with questions at the end for testing proficiency. *Online tutorials* have been developed by instruction librarians to accommodate distance learners and students who prefer online library instruction. Compare with *help screen*.

twice weekly   *See*: semiweekly.

twice yearly   *See*: semiannual.

twisted pair   A cable of relatively low bandwidth used in older telephone networks and less costly LANs, consisting of two separately insulated thin-diameter wires twisted around each other, one to carry the signal and the other grounded to absorb interference. Most computer networks use coaxial cable and/or optical fiber, which provide the higher bandwidth required for high-speed data transmission. Telephone companies in the United States are upgrading their infrastructure to coax and fiber-optic cable.

two-double fold test   A simple trial used by conservators to detect brittle paper. One corner of a leaf is gently folded diagonally forward and back twice about one-half inch in from the point where the edges meet. Paper is found to be brittle if the corner breaks off or detaches with a slight pull after the fourth fold.

two on   A sewing method used in hand-binding in which two sections are sewn along the fold with a single length of thread, alternating between the sections from kettle stitch to kettle stitch. Today, the technique is used mainly in fine binding to minimize swell (most trade bindings are sewn *all along*). Hand sewing three sections together in similar fashion is known as *three on*.

type   Small, separately cast rectangular metal units, each bearing on its face a single character cut in relief. In letterpress printing, the units are assembled by a typesetter into pages of text, locked in a chase and transferred to the bed of a printing press, where they are inked and an impression of the type matter made under pressure on a printing surface such as paper. After the print job is completed, the units are disassembled for reuse. Johann Gutenberg is credited with inventing movable type in Germany in or around the year 1456. *See also*: *display type*, *extract type*, *mouse type*, *text type*, *typeface*, *type family*, and *type size*.

Also, to manually key input into a computer system via a keyboard, for example, a search statement to retrieve information from an online catalog or bibliographic database.

typeface   The upper surface of a unit of type, bearing in relief the character to be printed. Also refers to the general design or style of the characters of a font of type, including all the sizes and weights in which the font is made. Designing a new typeface is a major undertaking, even for an experienced typographer. It is therefore not unusual for a typeface to be named after the person who designed it (*example*: **Garamond**). There does not appear to be universal agreement on the classification of typefaces. Also spelled *type face*. Sometimes abbreviated *face*. *See also*: *cameo*, *condensed*, *expanded*, *fat face*, *glyphic*, *gothic*, *graphic*, *inline*, *italic*, *monoline*, *online*, *roman*, and *script*.

type facsimile   A reprint of a work made from a new setting of type in which every detail of the appearance of printed matter in the original edition is copied as precisely as possible. Synonymous with *facsimile reprint*. Compare with *facsimile edition*.

type family   In printing, all the variants of the same basic type design, including uppercase, lowercase, and small capitals in both roman and italic in all sizes and weights (lightface, medium, semi-bold, boldface, condensed, expanded). Compare with *font*.

type of recording   In *AACR2*, the method used to encode sound on a sound disc or tape (analog, digital, magnetic, or optical) is given in the physical description area of the bibliographic record created to represent the item in the library catalog, as in the following examples:

5 sound discs : analog, 33⅓ rpm, stereo. ; 12 min
1 sound disc (59 min.) : digital, stereo. ; 4¾ in
2 sound cassettes (129 min.) : analog, 1⅞ ips., stereo

1 sound cassette (60 min.) : digital
1 sound track film reel (10 min.) : magnetic, 24 fps

type page The area or part of a printed page that is printed upon, excluding the margins, headlines, footlines, and page numbers.

typescript An author's original typewritten copy of a work in the form in which it is submitted for publication, or a typewritten copy of the original commissioned by the author or publisher, as opposed to a manuscript written by hand. Abbreviated *ts.* and *tss.* (plural).

typesetting In printing, the setting of type from copy, either by hand or by machine, done by a person called a *typesetter*. *See also*: *typography*.

type size The dimensions (height and width) of the body size of a type font, usually given in points. Most books are printed in type sizes ranging from 5-point to 22-point. Larger types sizes are used mainly for display matter. On the old-fashioned typewriter, pica was the most common type size. *See also*: *extract type* and *text type*.

typical librarian *See*: stereotype.

typo *See*: typographical error.

typographical error A mistake in a printed work made by the typesetter. Also refers to a similar error made by a person using a keyboard to type a text. Most word processing software includes an automatic spell checker to alert writers to such errors. Abbreviated *typo*. Synonymous with *misprint*. *See also*: *proofreading*.

typography The art and craft of setting and arranging type and making impressions from the result, which began with the invention of movable type by Johann Gutenberg in Germany in the mid-15th century Also refers to the general style, arrangement, and appearance of a work printed from type and to the skill involved in selecting a suitable ink and grade of paper, choosing an appropriate typeface and type size, determining page layout, etc. The person responsible for the final appearance of a printed publication is the *typographer*.

typology A system of biblical interpretation in which New Testament themes are juxtaposed with people and events described in the Old Testament, to suggest prefiguration. In medieval manuscripts, such events are illustrated in a series of miniatures arranged in a horizontal row or in parallel columns or in a single miniature surrounded by a historiated border. Typology was the basis of the *Bible moralisée* and the *Biblia Pauperum*.

U

UBCIM   An initialism for Universal **B**ibliographic **C**ontrol and **I**nternational **MARC** Core **A**ctivity. *See*: *Universal Machine-Readable Cataloging.*

UCC   *See*: *Universal Copyright Convention.*

UCE   An abbreviation of *unsolicited commercial e-mail*, known unaffectionately as *spam.*

UCITA   *See*: *Uniform Computer Information Transactions Act.*

UDC   *See*: Universal **D**ecimal Classification.

UF   *See*: **u**sed **f**or.

ukiyo-e   The Japanese word meaning "pictures of the floating or sorrowful world." Single-sheet prints and picture books (*ehon*) produced from woodblocks in Edo (Tokyo) during the Tokugawa period (1615–1868), reflecting the combined efforts of the artist who created the design drawn in ink on paper; the wood carver who transferred the image to the block (or series of blocks); the printer who applied pigment to the blocks and printed copies on hand-made paper; and the publisher who coordinated their efforts and marketed the final product to members of the merchant class at relatively low cost. In its earliest manifestations, *ukiyo-e* reflected classical, literary, and historical themes, but as the medium developed, scenes from contemporary life became popular.

UKMARC   A MARC record format originally developed to facilitate the production of the print *British National Bibliography (BNB)*, UKMARC closely reflects the cataloging practice of The British Library in its interpretation of *AACR2* and other standards. However, a distinction can be drawn between UKMARC as a national bibliographic format and its use by the national library in preparing records for the *BNB*. UKMARC is maintained by the National Bibliographic Service of The British Library. URL: www.bl.uk/services/bibliographic/marc/marcman.html.

ULC   *See*: Urban Libraries Council.

Ulrich's International Periodicals Directory   An annual reference serial published since 1932 by R.R. Bowker, *Ulrich's International Periodicals Directory* provides bibliographic information and pricing for a classified list of over 164,000 regularly and irregularly issued periodicals currently published in the United States and internationally, including titles available electronically. The directory is indexed by title and ISSN, with separate sections for cessations, title changes, refereed journals, and titles available in various digital formats. *Ulrich's* is also available on CD-ROM and online by licensing agreement. ISSN: 0000–2100. *See also*: Serials Directory, The.

ultrafiche   A card-shaped transparent microform with a reduction ratio considerably greater than that of standard *microfiche* or *superfiche* (up to 3,000 frames per 4 × 6 inch sheet). A special ultrafiche reader-printer machine is required to view and make hard copies of documents stored in this medium.

ultraviolet (UV)   Electromagnetic radiation beyond the spectrum visible to humans as light, shorter in wavelength than violet light but longer than X-rays. The sun is the chief source of natural ultraviolet radiation. Because UV radiation can damage photographs and accelerate the deterioration of certain grades of paper, prolonged exposure of library and archival materials to direct sunlight should be avoided and incandescent lighting installed in storage areas where preservation is a high priority. Monitors can be used to measure UV exposure and filters installed to keep levels below the recommended 75 lux. Control is important because UV damage to books continues to a lesser extent even after the source is removed.

umbilicus   In Antiquity, a knobbed wooden rod attached to one end of a papyrus scroll around which the manuscript was rolled when not in use. A vellum tag was usually attached to one end, noting the title and/or contents.

unabridged   A version of a written work that has not been shortened and is therefore considered to be complete. The fact that an edition is unabridged is sometimes indicated on the title page of long works issued in paperback, but unless otherwise stated, a published work is assumed to be unabridged. An unabridged dictionary is the version containing the most words (*example*: **Webster's Third New International Dictionary**). Compare with *abridgment*.

unabridged dictionary   A dictionary that attempts to include *all* the words of a language. For the English language, there are only three, *Webster's Third New International Dictionary* (1961), *Random House Unabridged Dictionary* (1993), and the *Oxford English Dictionary* (1989). The latter is concerned more with etymology than with definition. First published in 1909, *Webster's Third* has about 450,000 entries (down from 600,000 in the second edition). The *Random House Unabridged Dictionary* has fewer words but more illustrations. Compare with *desk dictionary*.

unauthorized biography   A biographical work written without the consent of its subject or the subject's family if the *biographee* is deceased, sometimes more objective in its analysis than an *authorized biography* because the biographer does not have to make concessions to gain access to confidential sources. However, an unauthorized biography may be less detailed or complete if the author was denied important information.

unauthorized edition   An edition printed without the consent of the author, the author's legal representative, or the original publisher but not in violation of existing copyright law. Compare with *authorized edition*. *See also*: *pirated edition*.

unbacked   Printed on only one side of a blank sheet of paper, as in a poster.

unbound   A printed publication issued without a binding or cover or with its cover removed. Prior to the 19th century, books were sold in the form of printed sections to be bound to the purchaser's specifications. Also refers to an issue of a periodical or part of a serial that will eventually be bound, usually with others, to form a volume. Compare with *disbound* and *loose*.

uncial   From Latin *uncialis*, meaning "of an inch" or "inch-high." A large, full majuscule script probably developed in the Christian monasteries of Egypt and North Africa during the late 2nd or early 3rd century, used in the earliest biblical codices and as a book hand in manuscripts written from the 4th to 8th century, reaching its fullest expression in the 5th century. The calligraphic capital letters of uncial were broad and rounded, probably to enhance speed, with the beginnings of ascenders and descenders suggestive of later lowercase letters. *Half uncial* gradually replaced uncial as a book hand after the 6th century. The term also refers to manuscripts written in the script. *See also*: *rustic capital*.

uncut   A volume in which the bolts were not trimmed to uniform size in binding, leaving the leaves to be separated by hand by the owner of the book, using a paper knife or similar instrument. Synonymous with *untrimmed*. Compare with *unopened*.

underdrawing   In medieval manuscript painting, the preliminary design laid down before paint or ink was applied. Drawings done in metal point are revealed beneath the painted surface by infrared spectroscopy or by shining a bright light through the leaf or examining the reverse side if it happens to be blank. In unfinished manuscripts, underdrawing sometimes survives in miniatures that were never painted.

Christopher de Hamel notes in *The British Library Guide to Manuscript Illumination* (University of Toronto Press, 2001) that underdrawing was done in two stages. First the overall composition was sketched in hard point, plummet, or charcoal, then the sketch was reworked by the artist in greater detail using pale ink. If the design involved geometric shapes, small holes in the parchment often reveal that a compass was used. *See also*: *overpainting*.

underfunded   An organization, institution, or project allocated insufficient monies to accomplish its goals and objectives. Chronic underfunding can lead to a decline in quality of service and is demoralizing for staff and management.

undergraduate library   A separate library established, supported, and maintained by a university to serve the information and research needs of its undergraduate students and the instructional requirements of the undergraduate curriculum. Sometimes administered as a branch library. Compare with *graduate library*. *See also*: *college library*.

underground press   A publisher that issues printed publications unofficially or clandestinely, usually to members of a group or organization that opposes the policies of an established government or other authority, more common during periods of civil unrest than in times of peace and prosperity. Eventually, most underground presses either disband or become "above ground" publishing houses.

underlining   Words, phrases, or passages of text underscored in pencil or ink by a previous reader, usually for future reference. As a general rule, libraries do not add heavily underlined gift books to the collection. Also refers to a formatting option available in word processing software that can be used to place a line beneath a single character, word, phrase, line, or entire passage of text. Compare with *highlighting*.

underrun   A press run that produces fewer copies than the number ordered, sometimes causing a shortage of publisher's inventory. The opposite of *overrun*.

underserved   Persons within the geographic area or clientele served by a library or library system who use its services infrequently for a variety of reasons, including limited awareness of available resources and services, lack of familiarity with the national language, illiteracy, poor health, lack of transportation, etc. *Outreach programs* help bridge these gaps.

understaffed   Having an insufficient number of employees to do the work required. Signs of overwork (fatigue, absenteeism, arrears, etc.) can be the result of understaffing. Synonymous with *short-staffed* and *short-handed*. The opposite of *overstaffed*. *See also*: *skeleton staff* and *underfunded*.

underutilized   A library service, resource, or item used less often than it ought to be, usually because its usefulness is not widely appreciated or because it is not as accessible as other alternatives, for example, collections of theses and dissertations in some academic libraries.

undocumented   Lacking official papers or other tangible evidence in support of existence, identity, validity, authenticity, provenance, etc. *See also: documentation*.

unexpurgated   A text or edition that includes passages omitted from other versions or editions, usually because they were considered offensive to some readers. Compare with *expurgated*. *See also*: *bowdlerize* and *censorship*.

unfinished   A work left incomplete at the death of the author, composer, or creator. Unfinished literary works are sometimes published posthumously (*example*: *The Last Tycoon* by F. Scott Fitzgerald). *See also*: *continuation* and *redaction*.

Unicode   A universal 16-bit (two-byte) standard character set for representing plain text in computer processing, which includes the major modern scripts; classical forms of Greek, Sanskrit, and Pali; the symbols used in Braille; mathematical and technical symbols; and over 21,000 East Asian ideographs—7,000 more than the East Asian Character Code (EACC) used in USMARC. Many more scripts have been proposed for inclusion and are under consideration.

Development of Unicode began in 1987 when Joe Becker and Lee Collins of Xerox and Mark Davis of Apple sought to devise a character set as simple as ASCII to meet the needs of the entire computing world. Joe Becker is credited with coining the term, which stands for "unique, universal, and uniform character encoding." The Research Libraries Group (RLG), developer of EACC, joined the project in its early stages, and in 1991 the Unicode Consortium was established to develop and promote the new standard. At the same time, the Joint Technical Committee 1 (JTC 1) of the International Organization for Standardization (ISO) and the International Electrotechnical Commission (IEC) were also working on a global character set. In 1992, the two initiatives merged. Since then, Unicode has been synchronized with ISO/IEC 10646.

The current version of Unicode can define approximately 65,000 characters, with extensions accommodating an additional 1 million characters. Duplication is avoided by assigning a single code when a character is common to more than one language. The standard also provides guidelines for sorting and searching, compression and transmission, transcoding to other standards, and truncation. Library issues center on the use of Unicode data in machine-readable bibliographic records, since large numbers of existing records are encoded in 7- and 8-bit character sets. The MARBI Committee of the American Library Association, responsible for advising the Library of Congress on the USMARC formats, has delegated work on the use of Unicode to its Subcommittee on Character Sets and to special task forces. Unicode is currently used in Java from Sun, *Windows NT* and *Internet Explorer* from Microsoft, *Netscape Navigator*, the Macintosh operating system from Apple, database applications from Oracle, Sybase, etc. Many vendors of integrated library systems are moving toward implementing Unicode in their systems. URL: www.unicode.org. *See also*: *UTF-8*.

Uniform Computer Information Transactions Act (UCITA)   A proposed state contract law intended to standardize and provide default rules for the licensing of software and other digital information products accessed over the Internet and by other electronic means. *UCITA* began as a proposed amendment to Article 2B of the U.S. *Uniform Commercial Code (UCC)*, a body of laws written by the National Conference of Commissioners on Uniform State Laws (NCCUSL) with the approval of the American Law Institute (ALI), to make commerce uniform across the 50 states. Finding no consensus among its membership on the scope and wording of the proposed *UCC2B* amendments, ALI withdrew from the drafting process in 1999, leaving NCCUSL to sponsor the legislation as a stand-alone bill. Congress passed *UCITA* later in 1999 as a "uniform law" requiring legislative approval in each of the 50 states. It was adopted in Virginia and Maryland but met opposition in other state legislatures.

Supported by the largest vendors of software and electronic information (Microsoft, AOL, Reed Elsevier, LexisNexis, Business Software Alliance, Information Technology Association of America, Software and Information Industry Association, etc.), *UCITA* was designed to make shrink-wrap and click-on licenses more enforceable; prohibit the transfer of licenses (pass-alongs) from one party to another without vendor permission; give vendors the right to repossess software by disabling it remotely if the vendor finds the customer in violation of the license; allow vendors to disclaim warranties for defective, bug-laden, or virus-infested software; and protect vendors from liability for defective products.

In response to criticisms voiced at hearings held in 2001 and recommendations made by the American Bar Association, NCCUSL approved 38 amendments to *UCITA* in August 2002, but the law continued to be opposed by Americans for Fair Electronic Commerce Transactions (AFFECT), formerly known as 4CITE, a broad-based coalition of retailers and manufacturers, consumers, financial services institutions, technology professionals, and libraries, and by a large number of state attorneys general, and even by the two leading associations of computing professionals, the ACM and IEEE.

The American Library Association, Association of Research Libraries, American Association of Law Libraries, Special Libraries Association, Medical Library Association, and Art Libraries Society joined AFFECT in actively opposing *UCITA*, citing its potentially negative impact on the fair use provisions of U.S. copyright law, the freedom to negotiate licensing agreements, and preservation of electronic resources. In September 2003, *Library Journal* announced that NCCUSL officially abandoned *UCITA* at its 112th annual meeting in August 2003, but because *UCITA* was enacted in Virginia and Maryland, contracts can name either state as the law governing a software license, even if the vendor has no presence in the state.

uniform edition   Two or more books printed, bound, and jacketed in the same style to show that they constitute a single entity, such as a multivolume encyclopedia, or that they are related to each other in some other way, for example, the individual titles in a monographic series or the collected works of an author.

Uniform Resource Locator (URL)   The unique address identifying a resource accessible at a particular location on the Internet for routing purposes (the same resource, or different versions of it, may be available simultaneously at other Internet addresses).

Example:

http://www.myuniversity.edu/library/hours.html

The first part of the URL designates the TCP/IP protocol used to access the resource. In the example given above, **http://** indicates that the resource is accessible through the Hypertext Transfer Protocol. In most Web browsers, the default setting in the "Open" or "Location" field is http:// so there is no need to include the protocol when opening a Web document. The remaining parts of a URL are separated by either a full stop (dot) or a slash. URLs are case sensitive. The six main protocols used in URLs are:

ftp://—FTP directory of downloadable data or program files
gopher://—Gopher server
http://—Document on the World Wide Web
mailto:—Electronic mail (e-mail)
news:—Usenet newsgroup
telnet://—Application program running on a remote host

See also: *IP address*, *OpenURL*, and *Persistent URL (PURL)*.

uniform style   The appearance of publications printed in the same typographical style on the same grade of paper, issued in a binding of the same size and design. Volumes published as a set or series are usually produced in this fashion. *See also*: *uniform edition*.

Also refers to the appearance of any element of a printed work that is repeated in the same style throughout the text, such as the chapter headings, running titles, headpieces or tailpieces, etc.

uniform title   In authority control, the distinctive title selected for cataloging purposes to represent a work issued under more than one title, usually in more than one expression or manifestation. Uniform titles are commonly used to catalog sacred texts (*example*: **Bible**) and liturgical and musical works.

Also refers to the collective title used by convention to collocate publications of an author, composer, or corporate body in a single volume or set of volumes containing two or more complete works, or extracts from several works, usually of a particular literary or musical form (*AACR2*). Synonymous with *filing title* and *standard title*.

In serials cataloging, a heading created to distinguish between two serial publications of the same title, consisting of the title proper followed in parentheses by a unique qualifier, usually place of publication, corporate body, date, or a combination of two of these descriptive elements. For example, the heading **The Bankers Magazine (Boston)**.

UNIMARC   *See*: **Uni**versal **M**achine-**R**eadable **C**ataloging.

union catalog   A list of the holdings of all the libraries in a library system, or of all or a portion of the collections of a group of independent libraries, indicating by name and/or location symbol which libraries own at least one copy of each item. When the main purpose of a union catalog is to indicate location, the bibliographic description provided in each entry may be reduced to a minimum, but when it also serves other purposes, description is more complete. The arrangement of a union catalog is normally alphabetical by author or title. *See also*: *National Union Catalog*, *virtual union catalog*, and WorldCat.

union list   A complete list of the holdings of a group of libraries of materials (1) of a specific type, (2) on a certain subject, or (3) in a particular field, usually compiled for the purpose of resource sharing (*example*: ***Union List of Serials in the Libraries of the United States and Canada*** and its continuation ***New Serial Titles***, issued by the Library of Congress). The entry for each bibliographic item includes a list of codes representing the libraries owning at least one copy. Union lists are usually printed, but some have been converted into online databases.

unitary term   A heading or indexing term composed of two or more nouns joined by the conjunction "and," treated as a single subject because their meanings overlap to such an extent that the literature about them is not clearly separated. Each part is seen as approximating the whole, as in the Library of Congress subject heading **Forests and forestry**. Not all headings of this form are unitary (*example*: **Forestry and community**).

United States Book Exchange (USBE)   A 60-year-old nonprofit membership organization devoted to supplying back issues of scholarly periodicals, trade journals, popular magazines, and other serials to libraries worldwide. Also known as the *Universal Serials and Book Exchange*. URL: www.usbe.com.

Universal Copyright Convention (UCC)   An international copyright convention drafted in 1952 under the auspices of UNESCO, revised in 1971 and ratified by over 65 countries, including the United States. Under its terms, each signatory nation extends to foreign works the same copyright protection it gives to works published within its territory by one of its own citizens. URL: www.unesco.org/culture/laws/copyright/html_eng/page1.shtml. *See also*: Berne Convention.

Universal Decimal Classification (UDC)   An elaborate expansion of Dewey Decimal Classification in which symbols are used, in addition to arabic numerals, to create longer notations, making it more flexible and precise than DDC and particularly suitable for the classification of specialized collections. Structured in such a way that new developments and new fields of knowledge can be easily incorporated, UDC is used to catalog reports, patents, and periodical articles, as well as books and media items.

Developed by Henri La Fontaine and Paul Otlet of the Institut Internationale de Bibliographie, UDC was first published in a French edition in 1905. Adopted by the International Organization for Standardization (ISO), it has been translated into many languages, is revised regularly by an international group, and has become the most widely used classification system in the world. The UDC Consortium maintains a Web site at: www.udcc.org.

Universal Machine-Readable Cataloging (UNIMARC)   The most comprehensive version of the MARC format for cataloging bibliographic items, UNIMARC was first published in 1977 and is currently developed under the sponsorship of the IFLA Universal Bibliographic Control and International MARC Core Activity (UBCIM) program to facilitate the international exchange of bibliographic records between national bibliographic agencies. URL: www.ifla.org/VI/3/ubcim.htm.

Universal Serials and Book Exchange   *See*: United States Book Exchange.

university library   A library or library system established, administered, and funded by a university to meet the information, research, and curriculum needs of its students, faculty, and staff. Some large universities maintain separate undergraduate and graduate libraries. Compare with *college library*. *See also*: *Association of College and Research Libraries* and *departmental library*.

university press   A publishing house associated with a university or other scholarly institution, specializing in the publication of scholarly books and journals, particularly works written by its faculty (*example*: **Johns Hopkins University Press**). Most university presses operate on a nonprofit basis, relying on a committee of senior faculty members to select manuscripts for publication. The trade association of university presses in North America is the Association of American University Presses (AAUP). Compare with *popular press* and *trade publisher*.

UNIX   An operating system developed at Bell Labs in 1969, UNIX supports multiple users and multitasking and has gone through many versions. It runs on a variety of hardware platforms and remains popular at academic and scientific institutions, particularly those that received it free of charge from AT&T in the early stages of its development. *See also*: *Windows*.

unknown authorship   A work for which the author (or authors) is unknown or cannot be identified with certainty, including works emanating from a corporate body that is unknown or lacks a name. Libraries catalog such works under the title (*example*: ***Chanson de Roland***). In *AACR2*, if the work is attributed to one or more persons or corporate bodies, added entries are made under their names. Synonymous with *anonymous*. Compare with *diffuse authorship*.

unlettered   A binding with neither the title nor the author's name displayed on the spine (or sides), making its content difficult to identify when placed upright alongside other volumes on the shelf. Prior to the 17th century, books were often marked by the owner with the title in ink on at least one edge of the sections to facilitate identification during a period when books were usually stored flat with one edge facing out. Compare with *lettered*.

unmounted   *See*: mounted.

unopened   A book in which the bolts are left untrimmed in binding. Once the leaves have been slit by hand with a paper knife or other thin-edged implement, the volume is said to have been *opened*. Compare with *uncut*.

unpaged   Pages of a book or other publication not assigned individual page numbers, usually found in the front matter. The cataloger records the number of such pages in the physical description area of the bibliographic record, as an interpolation inside square brackets (*example*: **[15] p**.). Compare with *unpaginated*.

unpaginated   A book or other publication in which the pages of the text are not numbered or sequentially marked. The total number of pages in an unpaginated work is noted by the cataloger as an interpolation inside square brackets in the physical description area of the bibliographic record (*example*: **[118] p**.). The opposite of *paginated*. Compare with *unpaged*.

unprintable   A word or phrase considered unfit to be printed, usually for reasons of obscenity, sometimes indicated in text by the first letter followed by an asterisk substituted for each of the remaining letters (**h*****).

unprotected   Data accessible to modification or deletion by unauthorized persons because it is stored in a file or on a disk that is not secured.

unpublished   A work in the process of publication that has yet to be issued. Also, a manuscript or typescript never published, either because it was not intended for publication or because the author was unable to find a publisher. Compare with *semipublished*.

unrecorded   A descriptive term used in the antiquarian book trade for a rare book or manuscript unnoticed by collectors and bibliographers (usually for centuries), whose discovery is of sufficient importance to merit recording an account of its existence.

unsigned   A written work, such as an entry in a reference book or article in a magazine, that does not include the name of the author, usually an indication that the piece was written by a paid staff writer. In a more general sense, any written document that does not indicate the identity of the author, especially a letter or legal instrument lacking a signature. The opposite of *signed*. Compare with *anonymous*.

unsophisticated   A term used in the antiquarian book trade to describe a book that has not undergone restoration or been altered with intent to deceive. Such a volume may, however, show definite signs of ownership and use.

untitled   A literary or other work that lacks a title, usually because it was given no name by its creator or publisher, a common occurrence in medieval manuscripts and books printed before it became standard practice to include a title page. Also refers to a person of noble birth who has no title and hence no right to rule.

untouched   A term describing early printed books (incunabula) that have been neither rubricated nor illuminated.

untrimmed   *See*: uncut.

unzip   *See*: zip.

update   To make a news story, data file, reference work, or other information source current, usually by revising existing content or substituting new material. Bibliographic databases are updated on a regular basis by adding records representing newly published items. Frequency of update is usually given in the database description. Printed indexes and abstracting services are updated monthly or quarterly in paperbound supplements, usually cumulated annually. Legal publications (statutes, case law, etc.) may also be updated in supplements, but most reference works are revised and republished in a new edition.

updated   A work from which outdated information has been removed and current information substituted or to which more recent information has been added. Printed publications may be updated in supplements (*examples*: **legal statutes** and **case law**) or revised and republished in a new edition. The currency of information provided on a Web site is indicated in the note "Last updated on [date]" usually found near the bottom of the welcome screen. *See also*: *expanded edition* and *revised edition*.

updating loose-leaf   *See*: loose-leaf service.

upgrade   To improve existing hardware or software by replacing it with a model or version that has new features and/or additional capabilities. Software upgrades are usually indicated sequentially by a decimal number added to the name of the application. Compare with *migration*.

In employment, to reclassify a job at a higher grade, usually moving it to a higher pay scale.

upload   To transmit a copy of one or more files from a local computer to the hard disk of another (usually more remote) computer, such as a mainframe or network server, a process that may require terminal emulation software. The opposite of *download*.

uppercase   Capital letters, as opposed to the small or lowercase letters of a type font. The terms *uppercase* and *lowercase* are derived from the relative positions of the compartments in the wood or metal case containing elements of type bearing capital letters and small letters at a typesetter's bench in the days when type was set by hand (letterpress). Also spelled *upper case*. *See also*: *majuscule*.

Urban Libraries Council (ULC) Founded in 1971, ULC is an association of approximately 150 public libraries located in metropolitan areas of the United States with 50,000 or more inhabitants, and the corporations that serve them, organized to solve common problems, take advantage of new opportunities, and foster applied research to improve professional practice. ULC is an affiliate of the American Library Association. URL: www.urbanlibraries.org.

URL *See*: Uniform Resource Locator.

usability The ease with which a computer interface can be efficiently and effectively used, especially by a novice. The first priority in designing for usability is to provide clear, consistent navigation of content. Some libraries employ *usability assessment* techniques to evaluate the user-friendliness of their Web pages. *See also*: *help screen*.

usability assessment A variety of techniques for measuring or comparing the ease with which a computer system or interface, such as an online catalog or Web site, meets the needs of its users, including focus groups, surveys, direct observation of actual search behavior, exploratory activities in which volunteers are asked to organize categories of information or work with a prototype, comparison with existing guidelines and benchmarks, and formal or informal testing. Without this process, librarians and technicians tend to design systems from a trained perspective, based on assumptions about information-seeking that may not reflect the behavior of actual users. A long-term *usability assessment plan* can become an ongoing component of library systems design. Used synonymously with *usability testing*.

usability testing *See*: usability assessment.

usage The number of times a bibliographic item is used by library patrons during a given period of time, including the number of times it is checked out and any in-house use measured by the number of times it is picked up from a desk or table in a public area for reshelving. In academic libraries, *high-use* materials may be given a shorter loan period or placed on reserve or in the reference section. In some libraries, *low-use* items may be candidates for weeding. Usage statistics are also helpful in collection development. *See also*: *e-usage*.

Also refers to the generally accepted way in which a word, phrase, or language is used to express an idea in speech or writing, which may or may not be grammatically correct. Handbooks of English usage are available in the reference section of most academic libraries (*example*: *The New Fowler's Modern English Usage*).

USA Patriot Act Signed on October 26, 2001, by President George W. Bush, the *USA Patriot Act* (full title: *United and Strengthening America by Providing Appropriate Tools Required to Intercept and Obstruct Terrorism Act*) passed the Senate by a vote of 98 to 1 and the House by 356 to 66, six weeks after the September 11 attacks on the World Trade Center and the Pentagon. It is not a stand-alone law but an extensive, complex omnibus act amending 15 existing federal statutes to significantly expand federal investigatory powers. For example, it broadens the *Federal Intelligence Sur-*

veillance Act of 1978 to allow roving wiretaps, and the *Electronic Communications Privacy Act* of 1986 to permit nationwide search warrants for e-mail and voice mail. Introduced at the height of the anthrax scare when many legislators did not have access to their offices, the bill passed with little debate because the normal process of inter-agency review and committee hearings was suspended. Concerned about free speech issues, Russell Feingold (D–Wisconsin), the lone dissenter in the Senate, proposed several amendments from the Senate floor, all tabled.

Library issues concerning the *USA Patriot Act* (PL 107-56) can be divided into two main categories: (1) civil liberties, especially the privacy and confidentiality of patron records, and (2) denial of access to information, such as the removal of information resources from publicly accessible government Web sites and from the Federal Depository Library Program. The *Patriot Act* redefines "business records" to include medical, library, and educational records. Under Section 215, law enforcement agencies can compel libraries to produce circulation records, patron registration information, Internet usage records, etc., stored in or on any medium, by presenting a search warrant obtained in a nonadversarial hearing before a Federal Intelligence Surveillance Court closed to public scrutiny. The law also includes a "gag order" prohibiting any library or librarian from disclosing the existence of such a warrant, even to the person whose records have been inspected and/or seized. Although the *Patriot Act* supersedes state laws protecting the confidentiality of library records, it includes a "sunset clause" under which many of its provisions will expire on December 31, 2005, unless extended by Congress.

On June 13, 2002, James Sensenbrenner (R–Wisconsin), conservative chair of the House Judiciary Committee, and ranking Democrat John Conyers (Michigan) sent a 12-page letter to Attorney General John Ashcroft requesting answers to 50 questions concerning the implementation of the *Patriot Act*. The following month, Assistant Attorney General Daniel Bryant replied in a letter that the requested information was confidential and would be turned over only to the House Intelligence Committee, which has no statutory responsibility for overseeing the *Patriot Act*. On August 21, 2002, the American Civil Liberties Union (ACLU), the American Booksellers Foundation for Free Expression (ABFFE), and the Electronic Privacy Information Center (EPIC) filed a formal request under the *Freedom of Information Act* (*FOIA*) to learn how many court orders have been issued to libraries, bookstores, and newspapers under the *Patriot Act*. Receiving no response, the Freedom to Read Foundation (FTRF) joined the ACLU, ABFFE, and EPIC in filing a suit on October 24, 2002 against the Department of Justice to obtain information about how the government has used its expanded surveillance powers.

On March 6, 2003, Representative Bernard Sanders (I–Vermont) introduced the *Freedom to Read Protection Act* (H.R. 1157), which would exempt libraries and book-stores from provisions of the *Patriot Act* that expand law enforcement authority to seize information on terrorist suspects. The Sanders bill has the bipartisan support of 129 cosponsors, including Ron Paul (R–Texas) and John Conyers. In July 2003, the American Civil Liberties Union filed suit in U.S. District Court in Michigan, on behalf of six mostly Arab and Muslim groups, claiming that Section 215 of the *Patriot Act* violates the U.S. Constitution by expanding the power of the Federal Bureau of Investigation (FBI) to obtain records of people not suspected of criminal activity, and naming Attorney General Ashcroft and FBI Director Robert Mueller as codefendants in the case. On July 21, 2003, Senator Feingold introduced the *Library, Bookseller, and Personal Records Privacy Act* (S. 1507), which would amend Section 215 of the *Patriot Act* to require the FBI to provide facts that any person whose records are sought is a suspected terrorist or spy, and add a similar requirement to National Security Letters issued under Section 505. On July 31, 2003, Senators Lisa Murkowski (R–Alaska) and Ron Wyden (D–Oregon) introduced the bipartisan *Protecting the Rights of Individuals Act* (S. 1552) to restore the requirement that the FBI show "probable cause" that any individual whose medical or library records are sought under the *Patriot Act* is an agent of a foreign power, and to amend the definition of "Internet service provider" to exclude libraries.

Faced with growing resistance, Attorney General Ashcroft embarked on a speaking tour in defense of the *Patriot Act*, using an appearance before the National Restaurant Association on September 15, 2003 to slam the American Library Association and other critics for creating "baseless hysteria" over the law's impact on libraries. In the November 2003 issue of *American Libraries*, Justice Department spokesman Mark Corallo is reported to have informed the *New York Times* that the speech was not intended as an attack on libraries, but on groups like the American Civil Liberties Union and political ideologues whom Ashcroft regarded as having duped librarians into mistrusting the government. ALA president Carla Hayden responded on September 17, "We are deeply concerned that the Attorney General should be so openly contemptuous of those who seek to defend our Constitution. Rather than ask . . . librarians and Americans nationwide to 'just trust him,' Ashcroft could allay concerns by releasing aggregate information about the number of libraries visited using the expanded powers created by the *USA Patriot Act*." In a subsequent telephone call to Hayden, Ashcroft promised to release classified information concerning the use of Section 215 to obtain records from libraries, and in a follow-up memo to FBI Director Robert Mueller, he wrote, "The number of times Section 215 has been used to date is zero." However, the Justice Department had already acknowledged on May 20, 2003 that the FBI had contacted about 50 libraries in its investigations of terrorists, and a survey conducted by the Library Research Center (LRC) at the University of Illinois, Urbana-Champaign, showed that in the year following the attacks on the World Trade Center and the Pentagon, law enforcement officials visited 545 libraries in the United States, with about one-third of the visits made by the FBI.

At the 69th annual World Library and Information Congress of the International Federation of Library Associations and Institutions (IFLA) in August 2003, the membership issued a resolution calling for the repeal or amendment of the *USA Patriot Act* and similar laws in other nations. On September 24, 2003, Dennis Kucinich (D–Ohio) and Ron Paul introduced the *Benjamin Franklin True Patriot Act* (H.R. 3171) to repeal eleven sections of the *Patriot Act* that expand government surveillance powers, including Section 213 (sneak and peek searches), Section 215 (records), Section 216 (pen register/wiretap), and the provision granting the FBI authority to issue National Security Letters. Further legal challenges are likely, but the sunset provision may go into effect before such suits make their way through the U.S. judicial system. The ALA Office of Intellectual Freedom maintains a Web site on the *Patriot Act* at: www.ala.org/alaorg/oif/usapatriotact.html. The text of the *Patriot Act* is provided online by the Electronic Privacy Information Center at: www.epic.org/privacy/terrorism/hr3162.html. A chart created by Mary Minow of Law Library Resource Xchange (LLRX.com) showing how the *Patriot Act* changed the way the federal government can request library records is available at: www.llrx.com/features/libraryrecords.htm. *See also*: *Library Awareness Program*.

USBE *See*: United States Book Exchange.

USCO *See*: U.S. Copyright Office.

U.S. Copyright Office (USCO) The agency of the U.S. federal government responsible for administering copyright law, a unit of the Library of Congress. Although the first federal copyright law was passed in 1790, copyright functions were not centralized under the Library of Congress until 1870, and the Copyright Office did not become a separate department of the Library of Congress until 1897. In addition to administering federal law protecting the intellectual property rights of American citizens, the Copyright Office also provides expertise to Congress on matters related to intellectual property, advises and assists Congress in drafting proposed changes in U.S. copyright law, advises Congress on compliance with international copyright agreements, serves as a depository for works registered under U.S. copyright law, and furnishes information to the general public on copyright law and registration. URL: www.copyright.gov.

USE An instruction used in an entry in a subject headings list or thesaurus of controlled vocabulary to direct the user from a synonym or quasi-synonym to the preferred term under which items on the topic are cataloged or indexed (*example*: **Reading Therapy** USE **Bibliotherapy** in the *Thesaurus of ERIC Descriptors*). Compare with "see."

used book A book that has had at least one previous owner. The condition of the cover and leaves is an indication of the amount of use a volume has received. Sometimes used books are found upon appraisal to be rare and valuable, especially copies of a first edition. Synonymous with *secondhand book*. *See also*: *ex-library copy* and *used bookstore*.

used bookstore A bookstore that specializes in books that have had at least one previous owner, sometimes limited to a particular genre, such as mystery or science fiction. Unless a used book is rare or out of print, it is usually priced on the basis of condition, lower than the list price of a new copy. Some bookstores sell both new *and* used books. Synonymous with *secondhand bookstore*.

used for (UF) A phrase indicating a term (or terms) synonymous with an authorized subject heading or descriptor, *not* used in cataloging or indexing to avoid scatter. In a subject headings list or thesaurus of controlled vocabulary, synonyms are given immediately following the official heading. In the alphabetical list of indexing terms, they are included as lead-in vocabulary, followed by a *see* or USE cross-reference directing the user to the correct heading. *See also*: *syndetic structure*.

Examples:

Library of Congress Subject Headings (LCSH):

Domestic violence

USE Family violence

Family violence

UF Domestic violence

Thesaurus of ERIC Descriptors:

Physical Disabilities

UF Physical Handicaps

Physical Handicaps

USE Physical Disabilities

use life   The length of time or number of times an item can be used before it becomes so worn that it is no longer fit for use and has to be discarded. For books, use life depends on quality of paper, strength of binding, and actions taken to protect the cover, such as enclosing the dust jacket in a washable plastic sleeve.

user   *See*: patron.

user area   The amount of floor space in a library that can be assigned for the use of patrons, as opposed to the area required for the use of staff, closed stacks, automation and HVAC equipment, maintenance, storage, etc.

user education   All the activities involved in teaching users how to make the best possible use of library resources, services, and facilities, including formal and informal instruction delivered by a librarian or other staff member one-on-one or in a group. Also includes online tutorials, audiovisual materials, and printed guides and pathfinders. A broader term than *bibliographic instruction*.

user-friendly   Computer software or hardware designed to be easy to use or operate, even by a complete novice. Most user-friendly systems include point-of-use instruction and readily accessible help screens, written in language that is clear and easy to comprehend. User-friendliness was a prime consideration in the design of the graphical user interface (GUI) that made the Windows and Macintosh operating systems a commercial success. *See also*: *usability assessment*.

user group   The individuals within the population served by a library who actually make use of its services and collections on a fairly regular basis. Synonymous with *clientele*. Compare with *constituency*.

Also refers to a group of users of a service or software/hardware product (or brand of products) who meet periodically and keep in contact, usually via e-mail, to enhance their understanding of the product(s), discuss problems they experience, and suggest improvements to the vendor. Systems librarians often participate in the user group for their library's catalog software.

user ID   *See*: username.

username A permanent code that an authorized user must enter into a computer system to log on and gain access to its resources, usually consisting of the full name (**johnwilson**) or the surname plus the initial(s) of the given name(s) (**wilsonj**) or plus one or more arabic numerals (**wilson001**). Synonymous with *user ID*. *See also*: *password* and *PIN*.

user profile *See*: interest profile.

user survey A questionnaire administered to users of a library or library system to find out what brings them to the library, how they normally use the resources and services it provides, their subjective evaluation of the quality of their library experiences, and any suggestions for improvement (feedback). In a *longitudinal study*, the same or a similar survey instrument is administered more than once, after a suitable interval of time has elapsed, to measure changes in patterns of usage, perceptions, attitudes, etc.

user warrant The addition of a term to an indexing language, or the assignment of an existing descriptor to documents by an indexer, based on the frequency with which it is requested or included in the search statements entered as input by the users of an information retrieval system. Compare with *literary warrant*.

U.S. Government Printing Office *See*: GPO.

USMARC A set of standards for the representation and communication of bibliographic data and related information in machine-readable format, originally developed and maintained for use in the United States and superseded in 1999 by MARC21 with the harmonization of U.S. and Canadian MARC formats. USMARC governed three aspects of bibliographic description: (1) record structure, (2) content designation, and (3) the actual data content of the record. The Library of Congress is advised in the maintenance and development of MARC standards by the U.S. MARC Advisory Committee, representing various user communities in North America. *See also*: *UKMARC* and *Universal Machine-Readable Cataloging (UNIMARC)*.

uterine vellum A thin, smooth writing material made from the processed skin of an unborn, stillborn, or newborn calf, used sparingly because of its cost when medieval and Renaissance scribes required an especially fine, white unblemished surface. *See also*: *vellum*.

UTF-8 A scheme for encoding Unicode values in sets of 8 bits, facilitating Unicode implementation on UNIX systems.

utility A small program that expands the capability of a computer's operating system by enabling it to perform an additional task, usually something as routine as managing a disk drive, printer, scanner, or other peripheral device. Unlike the basic operating system, utilities can be added and removed as needed. A utility differs from an application program in being less complex, usually limited to a single function.

utopia A term coined by Thomas More from the Greek *ou* ("no" or "not") and *topos* ("place"). A literary or artistic work in which the setting is an ideal society, usually one existing in a future time or imaginary place (*example*: ***Looking Backward*** by

Edward Bellamy). Utopias are created by authors who feel nostalgia for an idealized past or who wish to call attention to the need to reform existing social, political, or economic institutions. The opposite of *dystopia*. *See also*: *fantasy*.

UV   *See*: ultraviolet.

V

vacuum drying   A conservation procedure in which water-saturated books are frozen, then placed in a chamber from which the air is extracted, causing the water (in the form of ice) to vaporize. Wet materials must be sent to a treatment facility equipped with a vacuum sealer. According to former Yale University conservator Jane Greenfield, this method minimizes swelling and distortion of the book's structure (*The Care of Fine books*, Nick Lyons Books, 1988). Because vacuum drying is labor-intensive, it is not practical for large quantities of water-damaged items. *See also*: *fan drying*.

vade mecum   A Latin phrase meaning "goes with me." A small book such as a guidebook, handbook, or manual meant to be carried about, used during the Middle Ages by physicians, astrologers, and tradesmen for quick reference and computation. Often suspended from a girdle or belt, some were designed so that the pages folded out like a map or accordion-style. In a more general sense, any item regularly carried by a person. Also spelled *vade-mecum*. Plural: *vade mecums*.

vandalism   Damage to library collections, furnishings, or facilities that is intentional rather than accidental, usually motivated by anger or malice on the part of the perpetrator. Vandalism detracts from the physical appearance of a library and its resources. The cost of repair or replacement puts an unwelcome burden on the budget. To avoid detection, most acts of vandalism are committed in unstaffed locations or after hours. Some libraries employ a security guard to keep an eye on areas not visible from at least one public service point when the library is open.

vanilla text   Text written on a computer, usually with the aid of a text editor or word processing software, in a standard font with no formatting (boldface, italics, etc.), usually with a filename ending in **.txt**. Synonymous with *plaintext*. *See also*: *ASCII*.

vanity press   *See*: vanity publisher.

vanity publisher   A type of publisher, more common in the United States than in other countries, that specializes in producing books at the author's expense, used mainly by writers whose works have been rejected by commercial publishers and by individuals of private means who are convinced they have an important message to impart to the world. In England, vanity publishing is used primarily for poetry. Books published by vanity publishers are avoided by reviewers and rarely purchased by retail booksellers and libraries. Synonymous with *vanity press*. Compare with *private press* and *self-publishing*. ***See also***: *sponsored book*.

variable control field   *See*: control field.

variable data field   A variable field of the MARC record (tagged 1XX–9XX with XX in the range of 00–99) that has two indicator positions following the tag and usually contains textual rather than coded information, consisting of one or more elements of bibliographic description, each recorded in a separate subfield preceded by a two-character subfield code. Compare with *control field*.

variable field   A field of the MARC record that varies in length, containing either coded data or text, subdivided into logical elements recorded in separate subfields. All the fields in the MARC record are variable except the 24-character leader (field 001) and the 005, 006, 007, and 008 fields, which are also of fixed length. Variable fields are of two types: *control fields* (tagged 00X), which include neither indicators nor subfield codes, and *variable data fields* (tagged 1XX–9XX with XX in the range of 00–99), which include two indicator positions following the tag and a subfield code at the beginning of each data element.

variant   A copy of a book that differs slightly in one or more points from others of the same impression or from a previous printing of the same edition. The differences may occur in the sections, binding, or both. More than one variant may exist within a single impression. Once priority of publication has been conclusively established, such variations are referred to as *issues* and *states*. Also refers to one of two or more slightly different early texts of a literary work, for example, the plays of Shakespeare that survive in multiple versions. Abbreviated *var.*

Also, one of several forms of a word retrieved when the truncated stem of a word is used as a search term in a keywords search, for example, the terms *videocassette, videodisc, videorecording,* and *videotape* retrieved by truncating the root "video" with **video*** or **video$**.

variant edition   An edition that includes changes made in the work by the author, sometimes ranging from first composition all the way to publication in a definitive edition, allowing the reader to see the evolution of the text. Compare with *variorum edition*.

variorum edition   From the Latin phrase *cum notis variorum*, meaning "with notes from various persons." An edition based on scholarly comparison and interpretation of several previously published versions of the text, which also includes commentary written by various editors. Compare with *variant edition*. ***See also***: *definitive edition*.

various dates (v.d.)   A phrase used to indicate that a set or series of volumes contains works that have different publication dates.

varnish   The glossy coating applied to the printed surface of the paper cover or dust jacket on a new book for protection and to enhance its visual appeal. Varnish can be expensive when applied in a separate press run. A second pass is not required when varnish is added to gloss ink.

Vatican Library Although the Catholic popes always had private libraries, in the 15th century Pope Nicholas V created a library specifically for the clerics and scholars who lived and worked in and around the papal palace. A suite of rooms was set aside, and he began collecting the most beautiful manuscript books of the time. Pope Sixtus IV continued the work, and the library's holdings grew rapidly from about 1,200 books in 1455 to 3,500 in 1481 when the first handwritten catalog was made by the librarian Platina.

From the beginning, the library included not only Bibles and works on theology and canon law but also secular works, particularly the Greek and Latin classics, which the popes collected in texts as close to the original as they could find. During the Renaissance, the Vatican Library became a center of classical culture in Europe, and its librarians were often distinguished scholars. It continues to be one of the great libraries of the Western world, attracting scholars of all nationalities to its collections of important historical documents and rare and fine books. The Library of Congress sponsors the online exhibit *Rome Reborn: The Vatican Library & Renaissance Culture* at: lcweb.loc.gov/exhibits/vatican/toc.html.

V-chip A microchip installed in a television set, designed to allow parents to block access to programs containing content considered unsuitable for children (violence, explicit sex, adult language, etc.). In 1996, Congress passed legislation requiring manufacturers of television receivers to install the V-chip in sets sold in the United States (13-inch or larger). However, according to the *Christian Science Monitor*, a survey released in July 2001 found that only 7 percent of parents with children 2–17 years old use the V-chip in their television set, either because they own an older set, do not know if their set has a V-chip, or find it difficult to use. Some 56 percent said they use the rating displayed on the screen before a program begins to make decisions about their children's viewing. *See also*: *censorship*.

VCR An abbreviation of *videocassette recorder*, an electronic device designed to record onto videotape (in VHS format) signals received by a standard television receiver for playback on a television monitor. VCRs are also used to play prerecorded videocassettes (feature films, documentaries, etc.). Although VCRs are analog machines, adapters are available that enable digital data to be stored on videotape as computer backup.

v.d. *See*: various dates.

VDT *See*: terminal.

vellum A thin, fine writing material made from the unsplit skin of a newborn animal (usually a calf, but lamb, kid, and deerskin were also used), dressed and polished with alum for use as a writing surface during the Middle Ages, before paper came into widespread use in Europe and for a few copies of various editions (including the *Gutenberg Bible*) during the first 75 years of printing. Also used in early bookbinding as a covering material and for paste-downs. At one time the term was used interchangeably with *parchment*, but vellum is of finer quality. According to *The Book-man's Glossary* (R.R. Bowker, 1983), the finest vellum, known as *uterine vellum*, was made during the 13th and 14th centuries from the skins of stillborn or unborn animals and reserved for the most costly manuscripts. Because vellum is made from the entire unsplit skin, tiny marks of hair follicles are visible on one side. Highly durable, vellum has a tendency to curl toward the grain side under conditions of low humidity. *See also*: *purple vellum*.

Also refers to a manuscript written on the material and to a fine-quality off-white paper made to resemble the membrane.

velvet   Silk or cotton cloth with a thick soft pile (plush), popular as a covering material in *textile binding* of the 16th and 17th centuries when it was often embroidered in silk and/or metallic thread.

vending machine   A machine designed to automatically dispense goods when the correct amount of money, or a credit or debit card, is inserted and a selection made. In libraries, copy cards are often dispensed in this way.

vendor   A company in the business of providing access to a selection of bibliographic databases, online or on CD-ROM, by subscription (*examples*: **EBSCO**, **ProQuest**, **Gale Group**, etc.) or on a per search basis (**OCLC** *FirstSearch* and **DIALOG**), usually under licensing agreement. Providers of nonprint media are also commonly referred to as vendors.

In a more general sense, any individual, company, or agency, other than a publisher, that provides products and/or services to a library or library system for a fee. A distinction is normally made between book vendors (booksellers, dealers, jobbers, etc.) and serials vendors (subscription agents, continuation dealers, etc.). A vendor may also provide automated customer services such as management reports and electronic transmission of bibliographic or invoice data. The term is also used for businesses that specialize in developing and marketing library systems, such as online catalog software. The *Libweb* directory, maintained by the Berkeley Digital Library, provides a list of links to library-related companies at: sunsite.berkeley.edu/Libweb/comp.html.

Venn diagram   A graphical device in which closed circles (or ovals) are used to illustrate the logical relationship between sets of data: nonintersecting circles for sets with *no* elements in common; overlapping circles for sets with *some* but not all elements in common; and a circle within a circle for a set that is a subset of another. Invented by Johann Sturm in 1661 and named after the English logician John Venn (1834–1923) who used them from 1880 on, Venn diagrams are used in bibliographic instruction to help students visualize the results of Boolean logic in keyword searching.

verbatim   In exactly the same words as the original source or text, word for word, as in a direct quotation. It is *plagiarism* to quote verbatim without acknowledging the source.

verbatim et literatim   A Latin phrase meaning "word for word and letter for letter," precisely as written or printed. More loosely, a quotation, transcription, or translation that is faithful to the original. Also refers to a literal translation.

verification   The process of using bibliographic sources to ascertain that an author actually exists, or to determine the proper form of a name or the correct title of a work, usually prior to ordering or cataloging the item for a library collection. Compare with *pre-order searching*. In a more general sense, checking the truth or accuracy of any fact or statement, usually by consulting a source of authoritative information.

vernacular   From the Latin *vernaculus*, meaning "native." In literature, works written in the daily language of a group of people, particularly the inhabitants of a specific geographic region, as distinct from the literary or official language of the same population or area, for example, the language of the novels of Thomas Hardy, in which English country folk speak and act in a manner appropriate to their rural origins. In the context of the Middle Ages, a vernacular language was one spoken in a particular region, as distinct from Latin and Greek, the international literary languages of the time. The slow growth of vernacular literature in Europe was enhanced by the expansion of secular literacy following the development of universities in the 12th century. *See also*: *vernacular name*.

vernacular name   The form of a person's name used in reference sources published in his or her country of birth or permanent residence. In *AACR2*, the cataloger is instructed to use the form of the name that has become well established in English-language reference sources and to make appropriate references from other forms (*example*: **'Umar Khayyam** *see* **Omar Khayyam**).

versal   A large ornamental capital letter written at the left-hand margin or in the text of a manuscript to indicate the beginning of a paragraph, verse, or other division. Using square capitals, rustic capitals, or uncials as models, medieval scribes exaggerated the round or vertical strokes or serifs for decorative effect. Early examples were sometimes outlined in small dots. Versals were usually written in ink of a different color than the text (most commonly red and/or blue). The larger size meant that a versal occupied more than one line, its top usually aligned with the minuscules of the word to which it belonged. Compare with *initial letter*.

verse   A sequence of words arranged in accordance with established rules of metrical composition, rhyme, etc. Also, a set of lines comprising one unit in the overall pattern of a metrical composition (song, ballad, etc.) written in several sections of similar form, aside from any refrain. Synonymous in this sense with *stanza*. Also used as a general term for light poetry. *See also*: *doggerel* and *limerick*.

In a sacred text, such as the Bible, one or more sentences forming a division of a chapter, usually numbered for reference.

versification   The transformation of a prose work into poetic or metrical language. Also, the overall structure or style in which a poetic work is composed.

version   One of several variations of an intellectual work, possibly created for a purpose or use other than the one originally intended. Also, a variant form of a work of unknown or uncertain authorship, such as a fairy tale or legend. Also refers to a specific translation of the Bible or any of its parts (*example*: **King James Version**). Abbreviated *vers*. Compare with *adaptation* and *edition*.

In computer software, a specific upgrade of an operating system or application program, usually indicated by a decimal number following the title, for example, **5.0** to indicate a significant upgrade, **5.1** a modification containing routine enhancements, and **5.11** a follow-up, perhaps to correct a minor bug in the previous version. As a general rule, there is greater risk in purchasing version 1.0 of a software program than in purchasing subsequent versions.

verso   From the Latin phrase *verso folio*, meaning "with the page turned." The back side of a book or the left-hand page of an opening in a book or other publication, usually assigned an even page number. Publisher's imprint, publication date, notice of copyright, ISBN, and CIP are usually given on the verso of the title page of a book. Also refers to the reverse side of a single printed sheet, the side intended by the printer to be read second. The opposite of *recto*.

vertical file   A collection of loose clippings, pictures, illustrations, pamphlets, or other materials of an ephemeral nature that, because of size and format, are filed on edge in drawers or in a box, usually organized in folders by subject or some other classification system to facilitate retrieval. Also refers to the filing cabinet in which such materials are stored.

VGA   An initialism for **V**ideo **G**raphics **A**rray, a standard video adapter in an IBM PC, capable of producing resolutions of 640 × 480 pixels in up to 256 colors. VGA circuits convert the digital signals generated by the computer into analog used by CRTs and most flat-backed monitors. Superseded by *SVGA*.

VHS   An initialism for **V**ideo **H**ome **S**ystem, a video recording and playback format consisting of hard plastic cassettes containing half-inch videotape. Introduced by JVC in 1976 to compete with Sony's Beta format, VHS has since become the industry standard for both home and commercial use. SVHS (Super VHS) was developed to improve resolution. The DVD format is gaining on VHS in library collections, particularly in public libraries. *See also*: *VCR*.

vide   The imperative form of the Latin verb *videre*, "to see." Used in the sense of "refer to" in footnotes to direct the reader's attention to a specific passage, page, chapter, or work. Abbreviated *v*. or *vid*.

videocassette   A blank or prerecorded videotape permanently enclosed in a hard plastic case containing two take-up reels to which the ends of the tape are permanently attached for playback and rewinding. In the United States, the standard format for videotapes is VHS. Most libraries shelve videocassettes in a separate section, but in some libraries they are integrated into the circulating collection by call number. To satisfy demand, the loan period for videocassettes may be shorter and the overdue fine higher than for books. Compare with *videorecording*.

video clip   A short section of a longer work produced on videotape, used in a broadcast or incorporated into another work such as a Web page, usually for promotional purposes or to give the viewer a brief impression of the whole. Compare with *film clip*.

videoconference   A meeting of two or more participants conducted in real time at a distance using a video camera, microphone, and large television monitor or computer screen installed at each location, linked by satellite or digital network. *Videoconferencing* can save time and travel expense, especially in distance learning and in organizations with geographically separate units. Also spelled *video conference*.

videodisc   A large read-only optical disk usually made of plastic with a reflective metal coating on which visual images and associated audio signals are recorded for subsequent playback on a *videodisc player* attached to a television receiver and monitor. Compare with *videorecording*. Synonymous with *optical digital disk*. *See also*: DVD.

Video Librarian   Published bimonthly since 1986, *Video Librarian* provides over 200 reviews per issue of videorecordings in over 20 subject areas and current motion pictures available on videotape and DVD. A subscription to *Video Librarian PLUS* includes access to archives of previously published reviews, a new release calendar with links to prepublication reviews, a biweekly collection development column, and a searchable database of distributors. ISSN: 0887–6851. URL: www.videolibrarian. com.

videorecording   A generic term for an electronic medium in which visual images, usually in motion and accompanied by sound, are recorded for playback by means of a television receiver or monitor. The category includes *videotape* and *videodisc*. Videorecordings are listed by title and indexed by subject, credits, awards, and special formats in *The Video Source Book*, an annual reference serial published by the National Video Clearinghouse. *See also*: *full-motion video*, Video Librarian, and *Video Round Table*.

Video Round Table (VRT)   A round table of the American Library Association, VRT provides leadership on issues related to video collections, programs, and services in all types of libraries, including copyright, pricing, censorship, and preservation. VRT also forms alliances with the film and video production and distribution industry to promote diverse, high-quality video production. URL: www.ala.org.

videotape   Magnetic tape on which visual images and accompanying sound are recorded for subsequent playback via a television receiver and monitor, usually sold in the form of a *videocassette*. The industry standard is one-half-inch-wide tape (VHS). Compare with *videorecording*. *See also*: *educational videotape* and *streaming video*.

videotex   An interactive (two-way) telecommunication system in which a television receiver is adapted to enable computer databases to be searched over a telephone line or cable, using a menu-system or keyboard for input. Search results are displayed on the television screen. Synonymous in Britain with *viewdata*. Compare with *teletext*.

view   In cartography, a representation of a landscape from a perspective that makes details appear as if projected on an oblique plane, for example, a *panorama* or *bird's-eye view*. Sometimes used for comic effect, as in a *worm's-eye view*.

viewing room   A special room in a library equipped with projection equipment for viewing motion pictures, videorecordings, or DVDs, individually or in a group. Viewing equipment may include a film projector and screen and a VCR and/or DVD player attached to a large-screen television monitor or projector. Use of the equipment is usually limited to registered borrowers and may be by appointment only. *See also*: *listening room*.

vignette   A small illustration or decoration appearing on or before a title page or at the beginning or end of a chapter in a book. In illuminated manuscripts, a small image or design, usually circular or oval in shape, often framed by vine leaves and tendrils, used to decorate an initial letter, border, or miniature. Vignettes were also used to decorate bookbindings, especially in the 19th and early 20th centuries.

Also refers to a circular or oval image without a border, the edges of the background gradually shading into the blank space of the page, a technique widely used in portraits, photographs, and engravings of the 18th and 19th centuries.

In literature, a sketch characterized by conciseness of style and delicacy of feeling, which gives a brief but poignant impression of a scene, character, or situation, without elements of plot. A vignette can be part of a longer work.

vinyl   *See*: phonograph record.

virgule   *See*: slash.

virtual   An adjective referring to activities, objects, beings, and places that have no actual physical reality because they exist only in digital form (in cyberspace), for example, an e-mail "box" or an electronic "shopping cart."

virtual library   A "library without walls" in which the collections do not exist on paper, microform, or other tangible form at a physical location but are electronically accessible in digital format via computer networks. Such libraries exist only on a very limited scale, but in most traditional print-based libraries in the United States, catalogs and periodical indexes are available online, and some periodicals and reference works are often available in electronic full-text. Some libraries and library systems call themselves "virtual" because they offer online services (see the *Colorado Virtual Library* at: www.aclin.org).

The term *digital library* is more appropriate because the term *virtual* (borrowed from "virtual reality") suggests that the experience of using such a library is not the same as the "real" thing when in fact the experience of reading or viewing a document on a computer screen may be qualitatively different from reading the same publication in print, but the information content is the same regardless of format.

virtual reality   An electronic environment created especially for computer users through the use of software that simulates the visual appearance of three-dimensional reality but lacks physical substance, used mainly for training purposes and popular entertainment.

virtual reference   *See*: digital reference.

virtual tour   An online tour of a library's facilities, usually available over the Internet. Formats vary but some include clickable floor plans linked to photographs with accompanying text describing the collections and services available at each location.

virtual union catalog   An automated system for searching the holdings of two or more discrete library catalogs together, using Z39.50 and/or other mechanisms for broadcast search and retrieval, in contrast to a centralized union catalog in which catalog records are gathered in a single database or physical location.

virus   Software intended to harm the computers connected to a network, usually disseminated with malicious or hostile intent by persons who try to conceal their identity to avoid detection and prosecution. Most viruses are designed to attach to programs or parts of the operating system, where they replicate with destructive effect. To prevent this type of damage, LAN administrators install anti-virus software that automatically checks for viruses and eliminates them whenever possible. Anti-virus software can also be purchased by individual computer users who wish to protect their PCs. *See also*: *security* and *worm*.

visual aid   An item, such as a motion picture, videocassette, slide, photograph, map, chart, model, specimen, etc., used by an instructor or presenter to allow the audience to view an example or representation of what is being taught. Instruction librarians sometimes bring to the classroom reference books containing information pertinent to course content to enable students to recognize them by sight.

visual dictionary   A dictionary in which words and phrases (grouped by subject, theme, or activity) are illustrated, usually in a line drawing on the same or the opposite page, with each term keyed to the corresponding feature in the diagram by a thin line or small reference number printed on the illustration. The format is also used in language dictionaries in which the terms corresponding to the illustrations are given in two languages. Synonymous with *pictorial dictionary* and *picture dictionary*.

visual display terminal (VDT)   *See*: terminal.

visually impaired   A person whose sight makes using library materials in conventional formats difficult, if not impossible. Library services designed to meet the needs of persons with visual impairments include Braille, large print, audiobooks, and other recorded media and radio reading service. In the United States, these services are available through the federally funded National Library Service for the Blind and Physically Handicapped (NLS).

Visual Resources Association (VRA)   An international organization established in 1982 to advance knowledge, research, and education in the field of visual information resources, VRA has a membership consisting of information media professionals, including digital image specialists; art, architecture, film, and video librarians and museum curators; slide, photograph, microfilm, and digital archivists; architectural firms; museums and galleries; publishers and image system vendors; rights and reproduction officials; photographers and artists; art historians; and scientists. VRA sponsors an annual conference and publishes the quarterly *VRA Bulletin*. URL: www.vraweb.org. *See also*: *VRA Core Categories*.

vital records   Records essential to an agency in the ongoing conduct of its business or affairs, without which it would cease to function effectively, for example, the file of patron records used by a library in circulation transactions. For archivists, identifying and protecting vital records under every conceivable circumstance is a primary concern in records management and disaster planning.

Also refers to the official records of births, deaths, and marriages maintained by an agency of local, state, or national government. *Ancestry.com* provides a Web page on *Vital Records Information: United States* at: www.vitalrec.com. Synonymous with *vital statistics*.

viz.   An abbreviation of the Latin *videlicet*, meaning "namely," "that is to say," or "to wit," used in text and footnotes to introduce a word or phrase added to explain more completely or precisely a previous word, phrase, or statement.

vocabulary   All the words used in a language. Also, all the words and phrases used by a particular person, group, or profession. Also refers to a list of words in a textbook for students learning a foreign language, usually printed at the end of the text containing them or at the end of each chapter. Compare with *glossary* and *lexicon*. Sometimes used synonymously with *controlled vocabulary*.

vocabulary control   In indexing, the process of creating and maintaining a list of preferred terms to indicate (1) which of two or more equivalent terms will represent a concept as the authorized subject heading or descriptor in the classification system and (2) the relations of hierarchy (broader and narrower terms) and association (related terms) among headings once they have been selected. *Controlled vocabulary* is recorded in a subject headings list or thesaurus updated as new concepts emerge and older terminology becomes obsolete. Compare with *authority control*.

vocabulary mapping   A function built into the search software of some bibliographic databases that allows the user to relate a specific search term to the appropriate subject heading(s) or descriptor(s), read a scope note explaining how the heading is used, view the hierarchical tree of headings to which it belongs, and select broader headings or narrower terms or subheadings to include in the search. Vocabulary mapping is available in large databases, such as *MEDLINE* and *PsycINFO*, which have a well-developed *controlled vocabulary*.

vocal score   The score of a musical work composed for voice (opera, oratorio, cantata, etc.) in which all the parts are shown in normal size on separate staves, with any accompaniment (ordinarily written for orchestra) reduced to two staves for performance on a keyboard instrument. Compare with *chorus score*.

voice mail   A messaging system that allows a person to send, receive, and store audio messages using a standard telephone receiver. Also spelled *voicemail*. *See also*: *e-mail* and *facsimile transmission (fax)*.

voice-over   In motion pictures, video, and television, a narration, commentary, or prepared text spoken by a person who is not seen on the screen, a technique widely used in advertising. In documentaries, the name of the narrator is usually given in the credits.

voice recognition   Technology capable of recognizing the sounds of human speech and converting them into digital signals for processing as input by a computer, used mainly in communications. In computing, command systems capable of recognizing a few hundred words eliminate the need for a mouse or keyboard in repetitive operations. Discrete systems, used in dictation, require the speaker to pause between words. Continuous recognition handles natural language at normal speed but requires considerably more processing capability. Systems capable of understanding large vocabularies spoken at any speed are anticipated in the foreseeable future. *See also*: *artificial intelligence*.

volume   In the bibliographic sense, a major division of a work, distinguished from other major divisions of the same work by having its own chief source of information and, in most cases, independent pagination, foliation, or signatures, even when not bound under separate cover and regardless of the publisher's designation. In a set, the individual volumes are usually numbered, with any indexes at the end of the last volume. For a periodical, all the issues published during a given publishing period (usually a calendar year), bound or unbound. The *volume number* is usually printed on the front cover of each issue and on the same page as the table of contents. In bound periodicals, it is impressed on the spine. Abbreviated *v.* or *vol.*

In the physical sense, all the written or printed matter contained in a single binding, portfolio, etc., as originally issued or bound subsequent to issue (*AACR2*). Often used synonymously, in this sense, with *book*. Volume as material entity does not necessarily coincide with volume as bibliographic entity (see *multipart volume*).

Also refers to the loudness of the sound(s) produced by a receiver (radio or television) or an electronic playback machine (phonograph, audiocassette or CD player, VCR, etc.), usually regulated by a *volume control* device that can be manipulated by the listener.

volumen   Latin for "a thing rolled up." A writing surface used in Antiquity, consisting of papyrus or vellum sheets attached end-to-end, with text handwritten in columns on one side only, in lines running parallel with the edges of the roll. The last sheet was attached to a straight stick with knobbed ends called an *umbilicus*, around which the manuscript was rolled. The rolls were stored in a box called a *capsa* or on deep shelves with a vellum label or ticket attached to one end for identification by title or contents. Synonymous with *scroll*. *See also*: *scrinium*.

volume number   The number assigned to all the issues of a periodical published during a given publication period (usually a calendar year), beginning with number one for the period (year) in which the title was first issued. If the issues are bound in one or more physical volumes, the number is printed or impressed on the spine(s). In a multivolume reference work, such as an encyclopedia, the volume number appears on the spine and on the title page.

volume rights   The rights, usually negotiated with a publisher by the author or author's agent, to publish a work in volume form, including hardcover, paperback, book club, and textbook editions. Volume rights also include publication of the work in its entirety in a single issue of a periodical and reprinting, in full or in part, in an anthology. Compare with *subsidiary rights*.

volunteer   A person who works for a library or other organization without material recompense. Library volunteers are often retirees who wish to make a contribution by remaining actively engaged in their community. They perform a variety of tasks, depending on their skills and talents, including reshelving, physical processing, mending, storytelling, landscape maintenance, etc. Compare with *internship*. ***See also***: *community service volunteer* and *Friends of the Library*.

volvelle   A diagram written or printed on a parchment or paper wheel, or series of superimposed wheels (or segments of wheels), placed within a book or fastened to a bookmarker in a manner that allows them to be rotated manually on a central axis, used during the Middle Ages for computation and in astronomy and astrology to show the positions of celestial bodies.

v.p.   An abbreviation of *various publishers* and *various places*.

VRA   *See*: Visual Resources Association.

VRA Core Categories   A metadata element scheme developed by the Visual Resources Association for describing works of visual culture and images that document them, to facilitate the sharing of information among visual resources collections. URL: www. vraweb.org.

VRT   *See*: Video Round Table.

VT100   A type of mainframe terminal developed by Digital Equipment Corporation (DEC) that became the de facto industry standard, creating an environment in which other types of computers are required to use software that emulates VT100 in order to log on via Telnet to a mainframe.

Vulgate   From the Latin *vulgata*, meaning "popular." A Latin translation of the Bible prepared in the 4th century by St. Jerome, which remained for centuries the version authorized by the Roman Catholic Church. In 1546, the Council of Trent, after considering all extant Latin translations, reaffirmed the Vulgate as the official version. The first book printed in Europe, the *Gutenberg Bible*, was an edition of the Vulgate.

v.y.   An abbreviation of *various years*.

W

W3C   *See*: World Wide Web Consortium.

w.a.f.   *See*: with all faults.

wages   Money paid to an employee for the total number of hours worked in a given period (weekly, biweekly, monthly), computed at an hourly rate. Library staff employed part-time are usually paid by the hour. Compare with *salary*.

wallet   A style of limp leather binding in which the lower cover of the book extends beyond the sections in a flap as wide as the fore-edge that folds over and is fastened by a clasp or a tongue designed to fit into a slot in the upper cover. *See also*: *flap binding*.

wallpaper   The decorative background pattern or image against which windows, menus, icons, and other visual elements are displayed and manipulated in a graphical user interface (GUI), usually created in JPEG or GIF file format. Some systems allow the user to select a wallpaper from a variety of different designs. Files of wallpaper designs are also available online from third parties. Wallpapers can be custom-designed to display a distinctive element, such as a logo, trademark, or other symbol of institutional identity. Compare with *screen saver*.

wall shelving   Single-sided shelving placed against a wall and sometimes attached to it, as opposed to free-standing shelving (usually double-sided) designed to stand on its own away from a wall or other support. Shelving of both types is manufactured in sections to allow libraries to assemble ranges of varying length.

WAN   *See*: wide area network.

wand   *See*: light pen.

warm boot   *See*: reboot.

warping   A twist or bend in a book cover that occurs after binding or casing, severe enough to prevent the volume from lying flat, usually caused by dampness. In newly bound books, the condition may be caused by differences in the expansion and/or contraction of the materials used in the case or cover. Warping can be minimized in binding by using well-dried boards, endpapers with the grain running from head to foot, and adhesives of low water content and by proper pressing. In libraries, it is controlled by storing books in a dry, well-ventilated place. *See also*: *bowed*.

warranty   A fixed period of time, specified in the sales agreement, during which the seller is required to repair or replace a piece of equipment that does not function properly. Once the warranty period has expired, the purchaser must pay for repairs unless a maintenance contract has been signed. As a general rule, length of warranty is an indication of the manufacturer's confidence in the product.

washing   A labor-intensive preservation technique in which an item printed on paper, such as a map or print, is treated with a mild chemical solution to remove stains, writing, foxing, or acid, then pressed and resized. For bound publications, the process usually requires pulling and rebinding.

In photography, immersion of a print in clean running water during the developing process to remove fixatives. Improperly washed photographic prints eventually discolor and deteriorate.

water-damaged   Library materials that have been exposed to wet or damp conditions, usually as a result of leakage, flooding, or accident. Exposure of print materials to moisture can cause swelling, warping, staining, and subsequent contamination with mildew and mold, damage that is very difficult to repair. The leaves of publications printed on coated paper often fuse when wet, a problem that can be prevented by freezing and vacuum drying the damaged item.

watermark   A faintly translucent papermaker's mark, consisting of lettering and/or a design that can be seen faintly in a sheet of quality paper when it is held up to a light source. In hand papermaking, the design is made by sewing or soldering twisted wire to the mold, causing the layer of moist fiber to be thinner over the wire. In mechanized papermaking, the wire is impressed on the moist fiber by a cylinder called the *dandy roll* before the sheet is sent through a sequence of drying rolls.

Watermarks were originally intended to identify and date the source of production but in time came to designate paper size. Modern watermarks are sometimes used to provide security against forgery. The paper used in a deluxe edition may be watermarked to indicate that it was made especially for the edition. Synonymous with *papermark*. *See also*: *countermark*.

In word processing, a design or lettering printed in a shade of gray across a page, over which the text appears to be superimposed, for example, the word "Draft" to indicate that the text is not the final version. A *digital watermark* is a sequence of bits skillfully embedded in a data file, such as an audio CD or motion picture on DVD, to help identify the source of copies manufactured or distributed in violation of copyright.

waterstained   The condition of a book or other printed publication that has leaves or binding discolored by contact with water. *See also*: *water-damaged*.

water tear   Paper separated along a moistened line to give the tear a soft, uneven, feathered edge as the fibers gently pull apart without breaking, a technique used in making delicate paste repairs in books and other print materials.

wax tablet   *See*: tablet.

Web   *See*: World Wide Web (WWW).

Web address   *See*: Uniform Resource Locator.

Web browser   Client software that interprets the hypertext (HTML) code in which Web pages are written and allows documents and other data files available over the Internet to be viewed in graphical, as opposed to text-only, format. The appearance of a Web page may vary slightly depending on the type and version of browser used to view it. In the United States, the most widely used Web browsers are *Netscape Navigator* and Microsoft *Internet Explorer*. Netscape Communications is developing an open source Web browser called *Mozilla* (www.mozilla.org).

Webcast   Simultaneous transmission of live or delayed audio or video programming over the World Wide Web to all who own the equipment needed to receive it, the Internet counterpart of broadcasting via radio or television. In a narrower sense, to send the same Web-based content (audio, video, graphics, text) to a group of Internet users, based on their individual needs or interests. The receiver must install special software known as *plug-ins* (*RealPlayer*, Apple *QuickTime*, *Windows Media Player*, etc.). Synonymous with *netcast*.

Web credibility   *See*: credibility.

WebDewey   An enhanced version of the full Dewey Decimal Classification database available to full members and partial users of OCLC in conjunction with the CORC online cataloging project, *WebDewey* can be used to generate proposed Dewey class numbers for Web pages and other electronic resources. The system is also available in an abridged version. URL: www.oclc.org/dewey/versions/webdewey.

Web index   A search engine that organizes Web sites by subject content in a hierarchy of subject categories, from the most general to the most specific. For example, links to Web sites for "library and information science organizations" are listed in *Yahoo!* under:

Reference
  Libraries
    Library and Information Science
      Organizations

The URL in a Web index may reflect the hierarchical arrangement, as in dir.yahoo.com/Reference/Libraries/Library_and_Information_Science/Organizations.

webliography   An enumerative list of digital resources on a specific topic or subject, available in print or on the Web, for example, *Ralph Ellison Webliography* by Claude H. Potts (www.centerx.gseis.ucla.edu/weblio/ellison.html). Typically, the URLs of any Web sites included in the resource list are embedded in the HTML document, enabling users to connect to the site by clicking on its hypertext link. The OCLC CORC project is creating a database of electronic pathfinders to assist librarians in integrating and organizing their print and digital topic-specific resource guides. Also known as a *subject gateway*.

Weblog   A Web page that provides frequent, continuing publication of Web links and/ or comments on a specific topic or subject (broad or narrow in scope), often in the form of short entries arranged in reverse chronological order, the most recently added piece of information appearing first. An example in the field of library and information science is *LISNews.com* (www.lisnews.com), which accepts postings from its readers. A list of library Weblog sites is maintained by Peter Scott on *LibDex* (www.libdex. com/weblogs.html). Scott also manages the Weblog *Library News Daily* (www. lights.com/scott). Also spelled *Web log*. Synonymous with *blog*. The process of maintaining a Weblog is known as *blogging*.

Webmaster   The individual responsible for managing and maintaining a Web site, often the person who designed it, whose name usually appears near the bottom of the main page or welcome screen, usually with a contact link. In libraries, the Webmaster may be the systems librarian, a "techie," or someone who has acquired a knowledge of HTML and Web servers. Synonymous with *Web manager*.

WebPac   An online public access catalog (OPAC) that uses a graphical user interface (GUI) accessible via the World Wide Web, as opposed to a text-based interface accessible via Telnet.

Web page   An electronic document written in HTML script, stored on a *Web server* and accessible using *Web browser* software at a unique Internet address called a URL, usually one of a group of related, interlinked files that together comprise a *Web site*. A Web page may include formatted text, graphic material, audio and/or video elements, and links to other files on the Internet. *See also*: *personal Web page*.

Web server   A system capable of providing Internet access to Web-based resources and services in response to requests from client computers on which Web browser software is installed. A Web server includes the necessary hardware and also the operating system, TCP/IP protocols, server software, and information content of the Web sites installed on it. Web server software is designed to accept requests from users to download HTML text, image, and audio files. *See also*: *client-server*.

Web site   A group of related, interlinked Web pages installed on a Web server and accessible 24 hours a day to Internet users equipped with browser software. Most Web sites are created to represent the online presence of a company, organization, or institution or are the work of a group or individual. The main page or welcome screen, called the *homepage*, usually displays the title of the site, the name of the person (or persons) responsible for creating and maintaining it, and date of last update. Also spelled *Website* and *website*. *See also*: *mirror site* and *spoof site*.

WebTV   A Microsoft trademark applied to technology that enables the user to search the Web via television, rather than a PC. A set-top box is installed containing an analog modem designed to make the connection to the Internet via a telephone line and convert data to a format that can be displayed on the television monitor, with navigation by handheld remote control device or optional keyboard. To gain access, the user must establish an account with an Internet service provider. Synonymous with *Internet TV*.

Webzine   *See*: electronic magazine.

wedge-serif   A typeface with serifs that are triangular in shape, also known as *latin*. Wedge-shaped serifs are also found in medieval manuscripts written in Insular majuscule script from about A.D. 550 to 900.

weeding   The process of examining items in a library collection title by title to identify for permanent withdrawal those that meet pre-established *weeding criteria*, especially when space in the stacks is limited. Public libraries usually weed routinely on the basis of circulation. In academic libraries, weeding is done less frequently, usually only when the shelves become overcrowded, in anticipation of a move, or when a significant change occurs in curriculum, such as the elimination of a major. Weeding should be undertaken judiciously because out of print titles can be difficult to replace. Compare with *deselection*. *See also*: *exchange*.

weeding criteria   Factors considered by one or more librarians when deciding whether an item should be permanently removed from a library collection or retained, usually in the context of a structured weeding project. The most universally accepted criteria are based on the condition or physical appearance of the item. Most librarians also find it easy to agree on weeding duplicate copies no longer needed. Weeding based on age usually depends on the importance of currency for a particular category of material (*examples*: **textbooks** and **curriculum materials**), type of collection (**reference** or **circulating**), or subject area (**medical encyclopedias** or **travel guides**). Weeding based on content is more problematic because it involves subjective judgment. Public libraries are most likely to weed on the basis of usage. In academic libraries, faculty members in the teaching departments are often asked to assist in establishing appropriate weeding criteria for research collections. For detailed lists of weeding criteria, see *Weeding Library Collections: Library Weeding Methods* by Stanley J. Slote (Libraries Unlimited, 1997). *See also*: *shelf-time*.

weekly   Issued once a week. Also refers to a serial issued once a week (*example*: *Publishers Weekly*). Most newsmagazines and some newspapers are published weekly (*Newsweek* and *Barron's*).

weight   The relative thickness of a typeface, which determines how dark it will appear on a printed page, indicated in typography by gradation (extra-light, light, semi-light, medium, semi-bold, bold, extra-bold, and ultra-bold). In selecting an appropriate weight of type for a proposed publication, the typographer must consider grade of paper, type of ink, and method of printing. Most books are printed in medium type, with bold or semi-bold used for headings and emphasis.

Also refers to the basis on which a unit of paper, such as a ream, is sold in the market place. The *M-weight* of a given size of paper is the weight of 1,000 sheets, measured in pounds.

weighting   Use of an algorithm to predict the relevance of documents retrieved in a search, usually based on the frequency of search terms and their location in the bibliographic record (in title, descriptors, abstract, or text). Often expressed as a percentage, weighting allows scored records to be presented to the user in ranked order.

welcome screen   The first screen a user encounters upon logging on to a database, Web site, or application program. A well-designed welcome screen gives the title, scope and coverage, name of author and/or producer, host, and a basic set of options, with instructions for using the system and a link to a more detailed help screen if needed. A well-designed interface includes a direct link back to the welcome screen on all the subordinate screens.

western   A work of fiction (novel, short story, etc.), motion picture, or television program or series in which adventure is the primary theme; the narrative is secondary to the setting (the 19th-century American West); and the characters are typically cowboys, frontiersmen, outlaws, ranchers, miners, settlers, indigenous peoples, etc. In series westerns, the hero is often a lawman. In movie westerns, the hero usually wears a light-colored Stetson and the villain a black hat. As Diana Tixier Herald notes in *Genreflecting: A Guide to Reading Interests in Genre Fiction* (Libraries Unlimited, 2000), "The appeal of this genre is worldwide, based on a dream of freedom in a world of unspoiled nature, a world independent of the trammels of restraining society." The audience for western fiction is predominantly male. Compare, in this respect, with *romance*.

wheel binding   A style of leather binding developed during the 18th century by Scottish binders in which the center of the cover is embellished with a circular design in the shape of a wheel, with spokes radiating from a central point. The style may have evolved from fan binding, popular throughout Europe during the 17th century.

whiteboard   A modern version of the erasable chalkboard, with a surface that is white, rather than the traditional black or green, made of a smooth material that can be written upon with *dry-erase* marking pens in various colors, easy to erase and not as messy as chalk. However, the plastic pens cannot be refilled and become nonbiodegradable waste. Whiteboards are available from library suppliers in reversible free-standing and single-sided wall-mountable models. Porcelain steel models are available for use with magnets. Synonymous with *markerboard*. *See also*: *smartboard*.

white letter   A term used in early printing for roman type, as opposed to gothic or *black letter*.

white line   In printing, a line of spacing equal in depth to a line of printed matter, used before and after headings, long quotations, etc., to set them apart from the text.

white pages   The portion of a telephone directory in which the names, phone numbers, and street addresses of individuals residing in a specific city, town, or geographic area are listed alphabetically by surname, usually preceding the classified section (yellow pages) listing similar information for businesses and other organizations. White pages available on the Internet sometimes include e-mail addresses (*example*: *WhoWhere?* at: www.whowhere.lycos.com).

white paper   An official government report on any subject, especially one summarizing the results of an investigation or important policy decision of the British Parliament. Compare in this sense with *green paper*. The term is also used to refer to an authoritative report on a topic in technology, such as a new line of product development, sometimes available online, usually written by a person employed by a research company or vendor or by an independent consultant.

white space In printing, any area of a page (other than the margins) not occupied by type matter or illustration, for example, the unfilled space at the end of each line of a poem or at the end of a chapter. Compare with *blank*. *See also*: *fat matter* and *lean matter*.

white vine In medieval manuscripts, a border motif developed in the 15th century by the Italian humanists, composed of an interlace pattern of vine stems made to appear light in color by applying paint to the surrounding background and leaving the vine unpainted, to allow the bare surface of the parchment or paper to show through. Michelle Brown notes in *Understanding Illuminated Manuscripts* (Getty Museum/ British Library, 1994) that the technique was a conscious imitation of 12th-century Italian manuscripts mistaken for works of Antiquity. Italian: *bianchi girari*. Synonymous with *whitevine interlace*.

wholesaler *See*: jobber.

Who's Who A reference book or reference serial providing brief biographical information about well-known people who are still living. *Who Was Who* covers the lives of *deceased* persons of prominence. Titles beginning *Who's Who in . . .* cover the lives of important persons in a given field or profession. Those beginning *Who's Who of . . .* are usually devoted to notable individuals of a specific gender, nationality, or ethnic origin.

wide area network (WAN) A communication network covering an extensive geographic area, such as a country, region, province, or state. Compare with *local area network*.

widow A dangling word or phrase or line shorter than one-third the specified line length, at the end of a paragraph, especially when it falls at the head of a column or page of text matter, considered awkward by typographers and eliminated in typesetting whenever possible. *See also*: *orphan*.

width The dimension of a book or other bound item from spine to fore-edge, usually less than its height, the exception being volumes square or oblong in shape. In library cataloging, the height of a book is given in the physical description area of the bibliographic record in centimeters but not the width. Also refers to the horizontal dimension of a section of single- or double-sided shelving. Most library shelving is sold in sections 36 inches wide. *See also*: *depth*.

wildcard The search software used in some bibliographic databases and search engines allows the user to insert a special character in the middle of a search term in a keyword(s) search, to retrieve records or sites containing words with *any* character or *no* character in the position, useful for retrieving irregular plurals and variant spellings of a word. The wildcard symbol is *not* standardized. Users are advised to read the help screen(s) in an unfamiliar interface to see if wildcard is available and, if so, what symbol is used. *See also*: *truncation*.

Examples:

wom#n or **wom?n** to retrieve records containing *woman* or *women*

colo#r or **colo?r** to retrieve records containing *color* or *colour*

In computing, a symbol available in most operating systems and application programs (usually the asterisk), which can be used in a filename to identify multiple files and directories, for example, *letter*.doc* to retrieve all the "doc" files with names beginning with "letter." Most word processing applications also allow the user to employ wildcard in text searches.

Wilson   *See*: H.W. Wilson.

WIMPS   An acronym for "**w**indows, **i**cons, **m**ouse, **p**ull-down menus." Synonymous with *graphical user interface*.

window   A rectangular, scrollable viewing area in the graphical user interface of a microcomputer application that can be opened by the user, overwriting the entire screen or a portion of it. Windows can be resized, minimized to an icon when not in use, selected for editing and reference, or closed by the user at any time to facilitate multitasking (the use of two or more programs at the same time). Compare with *frame*.

Also refers to the opening cut out of the center of a mat through which a mounted print is viewed or out of the center of a card through which a mounted slide or frame of microfilm is viewed.

Windows   A user-friendly operating system developed in 1985 by Microsoft for PCs running on DOS, progressively upgraded to its current version. Windows got its start by emulating the graphical user interface (GUI) developed by Apple and has since become the industry standard for desktop microcomputers. *See also*: *Macintosh* and *UNIX*.

WIPO   *See*: **W**orld **I**ntellectual **P**roperty **O**rganization.

wire coil   A continuous length of metal wire threaded through holes punched along the binding edge of the leaves of a book or notebook in spiral binding. Flexible hard plastic is also used for this purpose.

wireless   A method of connecting to the Internet via electromagnetic airwaves, rather than wire or cable. Telecommunication charges are eliminated, but an Internet service provider is still required to gain access to the Internet. Wireless technology enables the ISP to offer greater bandwidth without the expense of adding cable to its own connection. However, in most wireless systems "line of sight" is required, which means that the radio antenna installed at a library must have an unobstructed path to the antenna maintained by the ISP. Each client antenna can serve 50-100 workstations at T1 speed. Wireless technology is also be used *internally* by libraries with a direct connection to the Internet, for example, to network an instruction lab equipped with PCs or laptops. Newer PCs are being marketed with wireless keyboard and wireless mouse.

wire service   *See*: news service.

with all faults (w.a.f.)   A term used by booksellers, book dealers, and auctioneers to inform prospective buyers that an item is offered for sale *as is* and may not be returned if found to be in defective condition.

withdrawal   The process of deleting all references in a library catalog to an item that has been permanently removed from the collection without being replaced by another copy of the same edition. The item is usually stamped "withdrawn" to avoid confusion in the disposition process. Also refers to the item *withdrawn*. ***See also***: *tracing* and *weeding*.

witness   In the context of bibliography and textual criticism, a manuscript or incunabulum regarded by scholars as evidence of authority for a text. A *codex unicus* is a text for which only one witness exists. ***See also***: stemma codicum.

In binding, a book with the fore-edge so lightly trimmed that some leaves are left rough.

wizard   An interactive utility available in some computer applications, usually in the form of a context-sensitive dialog box that provides step-by-step assistance in completing a complex task, as distinct from a general help menu accessible via the toolbar, from which the user may select as needed. Wizards can usually be turned "off" if found intrusive.

woodcut   A method of printing from an inked block of medium-soft wood (usually pear or cherry) from which an artist has excised all but an illustration, working by hand with knife and gouge in the same direction as the grain of a plank cut lengthwise from the tree. The design may be drawn directly on the plank (usually in pencil) or transferred by rubbing a tracing made on paper. Also refers to the block itself and to the print made from it. By contrast, *wood engraving* is done with a tool called a *burin* or *graver* across the grain of a block of hardwood cut in cross section.

The earliest known example of a woodcut is a copy of the *Diamond Sutra* printed in China in the 9th century A.D. In early printing in Europe, woodblocks were locked with movable type to allow text and illustration to be inked together. To produce colored prints, separate blocks were cut for each color and successive impressions made on the same sheet. ***See also***: *xylography*.

word-by-word   A method of alphabetization in which headings that begin with the same word are arranged in alphabetical order by the next word, and so on, with alphabetizing continued across spaces, commas, hyphens, slashes, and apostrophes ("New Testament" filed before "New, William" before "newt"). Also known as *nothing before something*. Compare with *letter-by-letter*.

wordless   A book or other publication without words, in which the story is told in a sequence of illustrations, a format used mainly in children's picture books (*example*: *Clown* [1995] by Quentin Blake). Without text, the "reader" must interpret the meaning of the story from the visual images. Each reader may perceive a slightly different meaning in the pictures.

word processing   A method of converting information into readable text in which personnel, procedures, and equipment are organized for maximum efficiency and effectiveness. Word processing systems usually include a microcomputer with a keyboard for typing input, a monitor for the display of text, and a laser printer for producing high-quality output. An interface with a photosetting machine allows offset plates to be produced for printing.

work   A distinct expression of human thought or emotion in language, signs, symbols, numerals, images, or some other medium, for purposes of communication and record. When such an expression is issued to the public, it is considered a *published work*. If the original author or creator is unknown, the work is *anonymous*. **See also**: *literary work*, *musical work*, *work for hire*, and *work in progress*.

As defined in *FRBR* (*Functional Requirements for Bibliographic Records*), a distinct intellectual or artistic creation, independent of any concrete realization or expression of its content (*example*: **Beowulf** as opposed to a specific text of the epic). The concept is abstract in specifying only the content that the various expressions of a work have in common. Under this definition, the boundaries of a work may be culturally determined. When modification of a work entails considerable independent intellectual or artistic endeavor, the result is treated as a *new work* (*example*: an **adaptation** of *Beowulf* intended for juvenile readers).

workaholic   A person who fails to balance work with activities that provide rest and relaxation. When chronic, this condition can eventually lead to *burnout*.

workbook   A separately published learning resource containing exercises, sample problems, worksheets, review questions, and other practice materials, usually with blank space for recording answers. When published in conjunction with a textbook, a workbook is usually bound in softcover, sometimes in a spiral or comb binding to allow it to open flat.

workflow   The manner in which work is passed from one member of a department to another, or from one department to another within a company, organization, or institution, to allow the steps necessary for completion to be executed in proper sequence. Efficiencies can sometimes be achieved by systematic analysis of workflow.

work for hire   A category of creative activity, recognized under U.S. copyright law, for which the employer, or the person or entity responsible for commissioning the work, becomes the initial copyright holder, rather than the creator who is generally paid a salary or fixed fee, instead of the royalty on sales customary for an independently produced work.

work form   In technical processing, a card or paper form that accompanies a newly acquired item from the beginning of cataloging to the point at which it is ready to be placed on the shelf, with space for library staff to note any special instructions and data necessary to prepare catalog records, add cross-references, and physically prepare the item for use. Synonymous with *worksheet*.

working conditions   The surroundings in which work is accomplished, including factors affecting health and safety (lighting, sanitation, heating/cooling, noise, air quality, etc.) and comfort (parking, break time, child care, etc.). Companies, organizations, and institutions that employ large numbers of people often have a formal procedure or standing committee for handling complaints and suggestions concerning working conditions.

working paper   A preliminary paper, usually based on research, not intended for publication but rather for circulation by the author (or authors) to professional peers for comment. Working papers are usually not covered in periodical indexes and abstracting services, but online archives of working papers are available in some academic disciplines (*example*: ***EconWPA*** maintained by the Economics Department of Washington University at: econwpa.wustl.edu). Synonymous with *discussion paper*.

working title   The title provided by the author at the time a manuscript is submitted to the publisher, used during the editorial process but sometimes altered slightly or changed completely before final publication to reflect the content more accurately or make the work more marketable.

work in progress   A written or artistic work published or exhibited in incomplete form, sometimes in parts, to be continued or completed by the author or creator at a later date. Large reference works requiring many years of painstaking research are sometimes published as the work progresses (*example*: ***Dictionary of American Regional English***).

workload   The amount of work to be completed in a given time by an employee or group of employees. How much is actually accomplished depends on speed, skill, motivation, working conditions, etc.

work mark   The part of a book number added by the cataloger to the author (or biographee) designation at the end of a call number, consisting of the first letter or two of the first word of the title (or the first letter or two of the surname of the biographer), to distinguish works by the same writer that have the same classification (*example*: **d** in the book number **D548d**, added to identify *David Copperfield* by Charles Dickens) or to subarrange editions of the same work. Synonymous with *work number*.

work number   *See*: work mark.

workroom   A room closed to the public where technical processes and routine tasks are carried out in the library, for example, the receiving area of the serials department, where current issues of periodicals are checked in and prepared for use and back issues are boxed to be shipped to the bindery or discarded.

worksheet   *See*: work form.

workshop   A meeting of people interested in learning more about a subject or who wish to gain practical experience in the use of a technique, system, or resource, usually for the purpose of training or professional development. A workshop differs from a conference in being task-oriented and of shorter duration (usually one day or less) and may be open to attendees who do not necessarily share membership in a voluntary organization.

workstation   An area within a workplace equipped with a personal computer and high-resolution monitor for accomplishing tasks that require the use of information in digital format (especially graphics), usually furnished with a desk, chair, and specially designed table to accommodate the PC and any peripheral equipment. If the microcomputer is networked, special wiring may be required. Also refers to a PC functioning as a client in a network. In this sense, compare with *server*.

world atlas   A reference book, usually of large size, containing maps of all the countries and regions of the world, printed in color, sometimes accompanied by explanatory text and statistical information, with an index of place names (gazetteer) in the back (*example*: **The Times Atlas of the World**). The *Atlapedia* world atlas is available online at: www.atlapedia.com.

WorldCat   Formerly known as *OLUC*, *WorldCat* is the online union catalog of materials cataloged by OCLC member libraries and institutions, a rapidly growing bibliographic database containing over 52 million records representing materials published since 1000 B.C. in over 400 languages in a variety of formats (books, manuscripts, maps, music scores, newspapers, magazines, journals, theses and dissertations, sound recordings, films, videorecordings, computer programs, machine-readable data files, etc.). Updated daily, *WorldCat* is used by OCLC members and participants for cataloging and interlibrary loan and is available for general use by licensing agreement through OCLC *FirstSearch*. URL: www.oclc.org/worldcat.

World Intellectual Property Organization (WIPO)   A specialized agency of the United Nations with headquarters in Geneva, WIPO is responsible for administering 21 international treaties concerning the protection of intellectual property under copyright, patent, and trademark law for the benefit of its 177 member nations. URL: www.wipo.org.

World Library and Information Congress   The annual conference of the International Federation of Library Associations and Institutions (IFLA), the world summit of libraries and librarians, held in a different member country each year, with the host country responsible for local arrangements (exhibits, receptions, tours, plenary program, etc.) in close cooperation with the international headquarters of IFLA. The 69th congress held in Berlin in August 2003 was attended by 4,500 people. URL: www.ifla.org/IV/index.htm.

World Wide Web (WWW)   A global network of Internet servers providing access to documents written in a script called Hypertext Markup Language (HTML) that allows content to be interlinked, locally and remotely. The "Web" was designed in 1989 by Tim Berners-Lee, working at the CERN high-energy physics lab in Geneva. Mark Andreeson, a student a the University of Illinois, later devised a simple point-and-click system called *Mosaic* that subsequently evolved into the *Netscape* Web browser. *See also*: *deep Web*, *Web page*, and *Web site*.

World Wide Web Consortium (W3C)   A nonprofit organization whose mission is to lead the Web to its full potential by developing technologies (standards, specifications, guidelines, software, and tools) that will create a forum for information, commerce, inspiration, independent thought, and collective understanding. Its members include corporations, research institutions, government agencies, universities, libraries, and nonprofit organizations. Libraries in the United States are represented by the Library of Congress, the National Library of Medicine, and OCLC. URL: www.w3c.org.

worm   A type of computer virus that incapacitates a system by replicating itself through hard disk and memory, consuming space and resources without attaching itself to other programs. Security from worms and other viruses is greater in the Apple Macintosh operating system than in Windows. Anti-virus software is available to detect and eliminate known computer viruses before damage occurs. *See also*: *bookworm*.

WORM   An initialism for *write once, read many*. Digital storage technology that allows data to be written once and read an unlimited number of times but not erased, used mainly to prevent archival data from being accidentally lost. WORM devices use double-sided optical disks that range in size from 5.25 to 14 inches wide, capable of storing 140MB to 3GB on each side. Acceptance in the market place has been hampered by the fact that WORM disks are not standardized, making them readable only on the type of drive used to write them. *See also*: *read-only* and *rewritable*.

worming   The condition of a book in which small insects called *bookworms* have bored holes through the text block or binding or left other visible traces of their unwelcome presence.

wove paper   Handmade paper that reveals a faintly translucent, fine mesh pattern when held up to a light source, the result of wires woven evenly like cloth in the paper mold. The same effect is achieved in machine-made paper by the pressure of the *dandy roll*. Compare with *laid paper*.

wrap-around   A publishing term for a cover design extending all the way from the front edge of a book over the spine and across the back board, usually seen in volumes containing a large proportion of pictorial content. *See also*: *pictorial*.

wrapper   The printed or unprinted cover of a paperbound book or pamphlet applied in binding, usually of a heavier grade of paper than the text, not part of the printing that produced the publication. A *self-wrapper* is made from the same paper as the text and integral to the sheets comprising the body of the publication, not a binder's addition. Also refers to the outer covering on a magazine, usually made of kraft paper, added to protect the glossy cover from damage in the post. Compare with *dust jacket*.

In the context of medieval manuscripts, the term refers to the limp covers of a book bound without boards, usually in parchment or vellum, a method reserved for music scores and less important texts. *See also*: *in quaternis*.

writ   Historically, a command written in epistolary form, addressed to one or more officials under the seal of an English king, indicating that a specific action is to be performed or is prohibited. In a more general sense, any formal written document issued by a court or other judicial authority in the name of a sovereign or state, forbidding or ordering the person(s) to whom it is directed to perform a specific action (*example*: **Writ of Habeas Corpus**, known as the "Great Writ" in English common law).

write-off   A bibliographic item or other piece of library property so badly damaged that it cannot be repaired, for which the cost of replacement cannot be recovered.

Also refers to a debt that cannot be recovered, for example, an overdue fine that remains unpaid for so long that the library must clear it from the circulation record.

write once *See*: WORM.

Writer's Market An annual reference publication that provides directory listings for literary agents, book publishers, small presses, book producers, consumer magazines, trade journals, scriptwriting, newspaper syndicates, writing contests and literary awards, and other resources for professional writers. ISSN: 0084–2729. URL: www.writersmarket.com. *See also*: Literary Market Place.

WWW *See*: World Wide Web.

WYSIWYG What You See Is What You Get (pronounced "wizzy-wig"), an exact correspondence between text and/or graphics as displayed on a computer screen and its appearance when printed, difficult to achieve in reality because the resolution of monitor and printer rarely match. *See also*: *page preview*.

X

xerography From the Greek *xeros* and *graphos*, meaning "dry writing." A method of reproducing text and/or images in which dry resinous toner transferred from an electrostatically charged plate is thermally adhered to a sheet of paper or some other copying surface inside a photocopier (originally called a *xerox machine*). The result is a *photocopy* or *xerox copy*. Xerography is a form of reprography.

x-height The mean height of the lowercase letters of a typeface that have neither ascenders nor descenders, sometimes used instead of point size as an indication of type size. The x-height letters of the roman alphabet are: **a**, **c**, **e**, **m**, **n**, **o**, **r**, **s**, **u**, **v**, **w**, **x**, and **z**. The tops and bottoms of some letters such as the "c" and "o" may extend slightly above the mean line and below the base line. Also spelled *ex-height*. *See also*: *primary letter*.

XML *See*: Extensible Markup Language.

XR *See*: returns.

x-rated A motion picture or videorecording containing material considered suitable for adults only, usually because it contains material considered pornographic. The term is also applied to print publications containing adult material (magazines, photographs, etc.). *See also*: *unexpurgated*.

x-ref *See*: cross-reference.

XSL *See*: Extensible Stylesheet Language.

XVGA *See*: SVGA.

xylograph Text and/or image printed from a woodblock. The blockbooks of the 15th and 16th centuries are a prime example. Xylographic illustration was also used in manuscripts and press-printed books of the same period, sometimes hand-tinted. *See also*: *chiro-xylographic*.

xylography Printing done from blocks of wood, especially by the early process of wood engraving, concurrent with the early development of printing from movable type. The results, known as *xylographica*, often contain more illustration than text. *See also*: *blockbook* and *woodcut*.

Y

YA An abbreviation of *young adult*, an adolescent aged 12-18, usually in the ninth to twelfth grade. *See also*: *young adult book* and *young adult services*.

YA book *See*: young adult book.

Yahoo! An acronym for *yet another hierarchically officious oracle*, a worldwide directory of Web sites developed in 1994 by two Stanford University engineering students to organize Web content in a hierarchical system of subject categories. *Yahoo!* also provides other Web-based services (news, weather, travel service, e-mail, shopping, games, etc.). It uses a smaller database than most other Web search engines, but searches in *Yahoo!* usually have high precision because the Web sites it lists are selected by human beings rather than robot software. Jonathan Swift coined the term "yahoo" in *Gulliver's Travels* (1726) to refer to an imaginary race of coarse, brutish creatures in human form. Mark Twain later applied it to any boorish person. URL: www.yahoo.com.

YALSA *See*: Young Adult Library Services Association.

Yapp binding A form of limp or semi-limp leather binding with rounded corners and bent-in edges that overlap the sections, sometimes by as much as half the thickness of the text block, named after William Yapp, the 19th-century bookseller who designed the style for pocket bibles sold in England. Geoffrey A. Glaister notes in *Encyclopedia of the Book* (Oak Knoll/British Library, 1996) that a similar style of binding with tooled edges was used in the mid-16th century. Synonymous with *Yapp edges*. Compare with *circuit edges*.

yearbook An annual documentary, historical, or memorial compendium of facts, photographs, statistics, etc., about the events of the preceding year, often limited to a specific country, institution, discipline, or subject (*example*: **Supreme Court Yearbook** published by Congressional Quarterly). Optional yearbooks are offered by some publishers of general encyclopedias. Most libraries place yearbooks on continuation order and shelve them in the reference collection. Yearbooks of historical significance may be stored in archives or special collections. Also spelled *year book*. Compare with *annual*.

Also refers to an annual high school or college publication commemorating a particular school year or graduating class in photographs, usually sold in hardcover to seniors by advance special order at the end of the school year.

yellowback   An inexpensive popular novel bound in a shiny yellow paper or board cover with a picture printed on the front, usually a woodcut in three colors, a type of publication that originated in England in the 1850s and was used until the end of the century for inexpensive reprint editions. Also spelled *yellow back*. Compare with *dime novel*.

yellowing   A color change that occurs in the condition of certain grades of paper with age, particularly those made from unbleached or groundwood pulp, one of the reasons most libraries convert newspaper back files to microfilm or microfiche. The problem can be averted in libraries by purchasing materials printed on acid-free permanent paper. *See also*: *brittle*.

yellow pages   The portion of a telephone directory or trade directory following the white pages in which the names, phone numbers, and mailing addresses of commercial enterprises are listed, usually alphabetically by subject or in a classified arrangement, so named because the section is printed on yellow paper. Yellow pages are also available online (*SuperPages.com* from Verizon at: www.superpages.com) and for specific professions (*Librarian's Yellow Pages* at: www.librariansyellowpages.com).

yellow press   A popular name for newspapers and periodicals of the early 20th century that published news stories of a vulgarly sensational nature, comparable to the modern *tabloid*. Synonymous with *gutter press*.

young adult book   A book intended to be read and enjoyed by adolescents 12 to 18 years of age. Also refers to a book intended for adults but considered suitable by reviewers and librarians for mature ninth- to twelfth-grade readers. Public libraries usually maintain a separate section of *young adult literature* managed by a librarian who specializes in YA services, including collection development. Compare with *children's book*. *See also*: KLIATT and *Young Adult Library Services Association*.

Young Adult Library Services Association (YALSA)   A division of the American Library Association founded in 1930, YALSA has a membership of librarians responsible for evaluating and selecting books and nonprint materials for young adults (age 12 to 18) and for promoting and strengthening library services for young adult readers. YALSA publishes the journal *Young Adult Library Services*. URL: www.ala.org.

young adult services   Library services intended specifically for adolescent patrons (ninth through twelfth graders), including collection development, programming, and readers' advisory. Public libraries usually have a room or section devoted specifically to young adult materials, managed by a librarian who specializes in providing services for this age group. Compare with *adult services* and *children's services*. *See also*: *Young Adult Library Services Association*.

Z

Z39.50 A client-server protocol established as a NISO standard that allows a computer user to query a remote information retrieval system using the software of the local system and receive results in the format of the local system, often used in portal and gateway products to search several sources simultaneously and integrate the results. The Network Development and MARC Standards Office of the Library of Congress maintains a Web page devoted to Z39.50 at: lcweb.loc.gov/z3950/agency. *See also*: *Z39.50 International: Next Generation*.

Z39.50 International: Next Generation (ZING) An umbrella term for a number of initiatives by Z39.50 implementers to make Z39.50 more usable in the Web environment. The intent is to make the protocol more attractive to information providers, developers, vendors, and users by lowering the barriers to implementation while preserving existing intellectual contributions accumulated over nearly 20 years of development. URL: www.loc.gov/z3950/agency/zing/zing-home.html.

zero-base budgeting (ZBB) Financial planning that starts from zero at the beginning of each new budget cycle, with no assumptions carried over from previous experience, a method used in both the public and private sectors. In ZBB, every expense must be justified in each new cycle.

zero growth *See*: steady state.

z-fold *See*: accordion fold.

zig-zag book A book made by folding a continuous strip of paper backward and forward accordion-style. When the pages are sewn at the back fold, the strip is printed on one side only. When both sides are printed, the folds are left unsewn to allow the volume to be opened to its full length. This form of book is called an *orihon* when made from a manuscript or printed document originally produced as a roll. Compare with *concertina*.

zine Derived from "fanzine" (a contraction of "fan magazine"), pronounced "zeen." The term came into use during the 1980s to refer to a small, low-circulation magazine or newspaper, self-published out of passion for the subject rather than for personal gain, usually produced with the aid of desktop publishing software and high-quality photocopy machines.

Zines represent the convergence of amateur publishing hobbyists, high school underground newspapers, the literary small press, political radicalism, and do-it-yourself popular culture. They are usually not available by subscription, often appear irregularly or infrequently, and may have a lifetime of only one or two issues. Some are available online via the World Wide Web. Selected zines are evaluated in the reference serial *Magazines for Libraries*. To learn more, see *The Book of Zines* at: www.zinebook.com.

ZING   *See*: Z39.50 International: Next Generation.

zip   To compress a data file using PKZIP software or some other utility capable of compressing data into PKZIP format. When such a file is restored to an uncompressed format, it is said to have been *unzipped*.

Zip disk   A 3.5-inch removable disk cartridge developed by Iomega, capable of storing 100MB or more of data (much more than a standard floppy disk) at relatively low cost. A special Zip drive must be installed on a microcomputer to allow a Zip disk to be used.

Zip drive   A disk drive developed by Iomega that uses a 3.5-inch removable *Zip disk* capable of storing 100MB or more of data at relatively low cost, used for storing very large files and collections of files. The drive usually comes with software that catalogs the contents of the disk and provides file security.

zoo-anthropomorphic initial   A figure initial in a medieval manuscript or early printed book composed wholly or in part of one or more animal/human hybrids, often a human head on an animal body, or vice versa. Zoo-anthropomorphic motifs also appear in inhabited initials, line fillers, and ornamental borders. Compare with *anthropomorphic initial* and *zoomorphic initial*.

zoom   In photography, to alter the size of an image from a stationary camera position without changing perspective by using a *zoom lens* to increase or decrease the focal length. In cinematography, this type of lens appears to make the camera advance toward the subject when *zooming in*, or retreat from it when *zooming out*.

In word processing software, a feature that allows the user to enlarge or reduce the size of a page displayed on the screen, usually by a fixed percentage or in small increments. In Web browsers, a feature that allows the viewer to enlarge all or a portion of the image, sometimes in increments. Also, a feature on some photocopy machines that allows the user to specify the extent to which an original will be enlarged or reduced in size.

zoomorphic initial   A figure initial in a medieval manuscript or early printed book composed wholly or in part of forms recognizable as animals or imaginary beasts. Zoomorphic motifs are also used in decorative borders and line fillers. Compare with *anthropomorphic initial* and *zoo-anthropomorphic initial*.

Bibliography

In expanding the dictionary from a brief printed handout to its present form, the author relied on her own understanding of library terminology, on her routine reading of the library literature, and on research that included, but was not limited to, the following print and online sources. Credit is given at the end of definitions closely adapted.

ABC for Book Collectors
   By John Carter. New Castle, DE: Oak Knoll Press, 1995.
ABC of Bookbinding
   By Jane Greenfield. New Castle, DE: Oak Knoll Press; New York: Lyons Press, 1998.
Advances in Librarianship
   New York: Academic Press, 1970–.
The ALA Glossary of Library and Information Science
   Edited by Heartsill Young. Chicago: American Library Association, 1983.
American Libraries
   Chicago: American Library Association, 1970–.
Anglo-American Cataloguing Rules
   Second edition. 2002 Revision. Chicago: American Library Association, 2002.
Annual Review of Information Science and Technology
   American Society for Information Science. 1966–.
The Art of the Book: From Medieval Manuscript to Graphic Novel
   Edited by James Bettley. London: V&A Publications, 2001.
ASIS Thesaurus of Information Science and Librarianship
   Second edition. Edited by Jessica L. Milstead. Medford, NJ: Information Today, Inc., 1998.
The Bloomsbury Review Booklover's Guide
   By Patricia Jean Wagner. Denver, CO: Bloomsbury Review, 1996.
Bodian's Publishing Desk Reference
   By Nat G. Bodian. New York: Oryx Press, 1988.
The Book. A History of the Bible
   By Christopher de Hamel. London; New York: Phaidon, 2001.
Bookbinding and the Conservation of Books: A Dictionary of Descriptive Terminology
   By Matt T. Roberts and Don Etherington (palimpsest.stanford.edu/don/don.html).

Bookbinding as a Handcraft
    By Manly Banister. New York: Sterling Publishing Co., 1975.
The Bookman's Glossary
    Sixth edition. Edited by Jean Peters. New York: R.R. Bowker, 1983.
Book Publishing: A Basic Introduction
    New expanded edition. By John P. Dessauer. New York: Continuum, 1989.
The Bowker Annual Library and Book Trade Almanac
    Edited by Dave Bogart. New York: R.R. Bowker, 1962–.
The British Library Guide to Bookbinding: History and Techniques
    By P.J.M. Marks. Toronto: University of Toronto Press, 1998.
The British Library Guide to Manuscript Illumination: History and Techniques
    By Christopher de Hamel. Toronto: University of Toronto Press, 2001.
The British Library Guide to Printing: History and Techniques
    By Michael Twyman. Toronto: University of Toronto Press, 1999.
The British Library Guide to Writing and Scripts: History and Techniques
    By Michelle P. Brown. Toronto: University of Toronto Press, 1998.
The Care of Fine Books
    By Jane Greenfield. New York: Nick Lyons Books, 1988.
Cleaning and Preserving Bindings and Related Materials
    By Carolyn Horton. Chicago: American Library Association, 1967.
The Collection Building Reader
    Edited by Betty-Carol Sellen and Arthur Curley. New York: Neal-Schuman, 1992.
The Complete Film Dictionary
    Second edition. By Ira Konigsberg. New York: Penguin, 1997.
Concise Dictionary of Library and Information Science
    By Stella Keenan. London: Bowker-Saur, 1996.
Descriptive Cataloging for the AACR2R and the Integrated MARC Format: A How-to-Do-It Workbook
    Revised edition. By Larry Millsap and Terry Ellen Ferl. New York: Neal-Schuman, 1997.
Developing and Maintaining Practical Archives: A How-to-Do-It Manual
    By Gregory S. Hunter. New York: Neal-Schuman, 1997.
Dewey Decimal Classification and Relative Index
    Twenty-second edition. Dublin, OH: OCLC, 2003.
A Dictionary of Book History
    By John Feather. New York: Oxford University Press, 1986.
Dictionary of Information Science and Technology
    By Carolyn Watters. New York: Academic Press, 1992.
Dictionary of Library and Information Management
    By Janet Stevenson. Teddington, Middlesex: Peter Collin Publishing, 1997.
A Dictionary of Literary and Thematic Terms
    By Edward Quinn. New York: Facts on File, 1999.
Dictionary of Publishing and Printing
    Second edition. By Peter Hodgson Collin. Teddington, Middlesex: Peter Collin Publishing, 1997.
A Dictionary of the Internet
    By Darrel Ince. New York: Oxford University Press, 2001.
Encyclopedia of Communication and Information
    Edited by Jorge Reina Schement. New York: Macmillan Library Reference, 2002.

Encyclopedia of Librarianship
  Edited by Thomas Landau. London: Bowes & Bowes, 1958.
Encyclopedia of the Book
  Second edition. By Geoffrey Ashall Glaister. New Castle, DE: Oak Knoll Press; London:
  The British Library, 1996.
Free Expression and Censorship in America: An Encyclopedia
  By Herbet N. Foerstel. Westport, CT: Greenwood Press, 1997.
Functional Requirements for Bibliographic Records: Final Report
  By the IFLA Study Group on the Functional Requirements for Bibliographic Records. The
  Hague, Netherlands: IFLA/K.G. Saur Verlag, 1998.
Genreflecting: A Guide to Reading Interests in Genre Fiction
  Fifth edition. By Diana Tixier Herald. Westport, CT: Libraries Unlimited, 2000.
A Glossary of Literary Terms
  Third edition. By M.H. Abrams. New York: Holt, Rinehart and Winston, 1971.
Graphics, Design and Printing Terms: An International Dictionary
  By Ken Garland. New York: Design Press, 1989.
The Great Libraries: From Antiquity to the Renaissance (3000 B.C. to A.D. 1600)
  By Konstantinos Sp. Staikos. New Castle, DE: Oak Knoll Press; London: The British Li-
  brary, 2000.
Harrod's Librarians' Glossary and Reference Book
  Seventh edition. Compiled by Ray Prytherch. Brookfield, VT: Gower Publishing Company,
  1990.
A History of Illuminated Manuscripts
  By Christopher de Hamel. London; New York: Phaidon Press, 1997.
History of the Internet: A Chronology, 1843 to the Present
  By Christos J.P. Moschovitis. Santa Barbara, CA: ABC-CLIO, 1999.
Indexing from A to Z
  Second edition. By Hans H. Wellisch. New York: H.W. Wilson, 1995.
Ink on Paper: A Handbook of the Graphic Arts
  By Edmund C. Arnold. New York: Harper & Row, 1963.
International Encyclopedia of Information and Library Science
  Edited by John Feather and Paul Sturges. New York: Routledge, 2003.
The Internet Glossary and Quick Reference Guide
  By Alan Freedman and Alfred and Emily Glossbrenner. New York: AMACOM, 1998.
Introduction to Cataloging and Classification
  By Bohdan S. Wynar. Eighth edition by Arlene G. Taylor. Littleton, CO: Libraries Unlim-
  ited, 1992.
Introduction to Reference Work
  Eighth edition. By William A. Katz. Boston: McGraw-Hill, 2002.
The Librarian's Thesaurus
  By Mary Ellen Soper, Larry N. Osborne, and Douglas L. Zweizig. Chicago: American
  Library Association, 1990.
Library Journal
  New York: Cahners Business Information, 1976–.
Library Literature & Information Science
  Edited by Cathy Rentschler. New York: H.W. Wilson Co., 1961–.
*Library Safety and Security: A Comprehensive Manual for Library Administrators and Police and
Security Officers*
  Goshen, KY: Campus Crime Prevention Programs, 1992.

Library Security and Safety Handbook: Prevention, Policies, and Procedures
    By Bruce A. Shuman. Chicago: American Library Association, 1999.
Map Librarianship
    Third edition. By Mary Lynette Larsgaard. Englewood, CO: Libraries Unlimited, 1998.
Medieval Calligraphy: Its History and Technique
    By Marc Drogin. Montclair, NJ: Allanheld & Schram, 1980.
Medieval Illuminators and Their Methods of Work
    By Jonathan G. Alexander. New Haven, CT: Yale University Press, 1992.
Merriam-Webster Online
    Merriam-Webster, Inc. (www.merriam-webster.com).
NTC's Mass Media Dictionary
    By R. Terry Ellmore. Lincolnwood, IL: National Textbook Co., 1991.
Online
    Weston, CT: Online, Inc., 1977–.
The Organization of Information
    By Arlene G. Taylor. Englewood, CO: Libraries Unlimited, 1999.
The Oxford English Dictionary
    Second edition. Edited by J.A. Simpson and E.S.C. Weiner. Oxford: Clarendon Press, 1989.
The Oxford Thesaurus
    American edition. Edited by Laurence Urdang. New York: Oxford University Press, 1992.
Preservation and Management of Library Collections
    Second edition. By John Feather. London: Library Association, 1996.
Scribes and Illuminators
    By Christopher de Hamel. Toronto: University of Toronto Press, 1992.
Serials Acquisitions Glossary
    Prepared by the Serials Section, Acquisitions Committee, Association for Library Collections
    & Technical Services. Chicago: American Library Association, 1993.
A Short History of the Printed Word
    By Warren Chappell. New York: Knopf, 1970.
TechEncyclopedia
    CMPnet and The Computer Language Company, Inc. (www.techweb.com/encyclopedia).
Textual Scholarship: An Introduction
    By David C. Greetham. New York: Garland, 1992.
Understanding Illuminated Manuscripts: A Guide to Technical Terms
    By Michelle P. Brown. Malibu, CA; London: J. Paul Getty Museum/The British Library,
    1994.
Understanding MARC Bibliographic Machine-Readable Cataloging
    Fifth edition. By Betty Furrie. Washington, DC: Cataloging Distribution Service, Library of
    Congress in collaboration with Follett Software Company, 2000 (lcweb.loc.gov/marc/umb).
Weeding Library Collections: Library Weeding Methods
    Fourth edition. By Stanley J. Slote. Englewood, CO: Libraries Unlimited, 1997.
The Whole Library Handbook 3
    Compiled by George M. Eberhart. Chicago: American Library Association, 2000.

About the Author

JOAN M. REITZ is Associate Librarian, Instructional Services, Ruth A. Haas Library, Western Connecticut State University, Danbury.